A Critical Bibliography of French Literature

PART 1

General Subjects and Principally the Novel before 1940
(Nos. 1–6789)

PART 3

All Genres since 1940, Index
(Nos. 12804–17939)

A Critical Bibliography of French Literature

RICHARD A. BROOKS

General Editor

VOLUME VI

THE TWENTIETH CENTURY
IN THREE PARTS

Edited by
DOUGLAS W. ALDEN
University of Virginia
and
RICHARD A. BROOKS
The College of Staten Island and The Graduate School of
The City University of New York

PART 2

Principally Poetry, Theater, and Criticism before 1940, and Essay
(Nos. 6790–12803)

SYRACUSE UNIVERSITY PRESS
1980

Copyright © 1979 by Syracuse University Press,
Syracuse, New York 13210

ALL RIGHTS RESERVED
First Edition

Publication of this book was assisted by a grant from
the Publications Program of the National Endowment for
the Humanities, an independent federal agency.

Library of Congress Cataloging in Publication Data (Revised)

Cabeen, David Clark, 1886–1965, ed.
A critical bibliography of French literature.

CONTENTS: v. 1. The mediaeval period, edited by
U. T. Holmes, jr.—v. 2. The sixteenth century,
edited by A. H. Schutz.—[etc.]—v. 6. The
twentieth century, edited by D. W. Alden and
R. A. Brooks.
Z2171.C3 [PQ103] 016.84 47–3282
ISBN 0-8156-2204-X (The set)
ISBN 0-8156-2205-8 (Part 1)
ISBN 0-8156-2206-8 (Part 2)
ISBN 0-8156-2207-4 (Part 3)

Manufactured in the United States of America

TABLE OF CONTENTS
VOLUME VI

PART 2

Principally Poetry, Theater, and Criticism before 1940, and Essay

v

CHAPTER XV

POETRY IN GENERAL AND POETRY BEFORE 1940 (PART ONE)

(Nos. 6790–7869)

WALTER ALBERT, GLORIA BIEN, CAROL J. BREAM, BIRUTA CAP, JEAN-PIERRE CAP,
E. BRUCE CARPENTER, CARROL F. COATES, JACQUES COTNAM, URS EGLI,
LAWRENCE D. JOINER, PAULINE JONES, REINHARD KUHN, PHILIPPE LEROUX,
SIDNEY LÉVY, WILL L. MCLENDON, MARIE NAUDIN, DAVID J. NIEDERAUER,
CLAUDE PICHOIS, LESTER J. PRONGER, BENJAMIN C. ROUNTREE, JUDITH M. SCHNEIDER,
LOUISE RYPKO SCHUB, CLAUDE SENNINGER, GENEVIÈVE SUTTON,
PIERRE-OLIVIER WALZER, SEYMOUR S. WEINER, AND ALISTAIR WHYTE

Poetry in General
(Exclusive of Surrealism)
(Nos. 6790–6901)

MARIE NAUDIN

Alyn, Marc. La nouvelle poésie française.
Mane, R. Morel, 1968. 251 p.   **6790**

This work, conscious of the difficulty
of judging contemporaries, presents the
metamorphoses undergone by poetry
from the end of romanticism to surrealism. A brief study of nine leaders
and forty contemporary poets. Scattered
but valid.

Reviews: J. Breton in MagL 26:44–
45, 1969; H. Gershman in BA 43:552,
1969; R. Kanters in FL 1179:17–18,
Dec. 9–15, 1968; A. Marissel in RdP
76:20, 1969.

Apollinaire, Guillaume. L'antitradition futuriste: manifeste-synthèse. Milan, Direction du mouvement futuriste, 1913. 4 p.
Also in his: Œuvres complètes, V. 3. Balland et Lecat, 1966. p. 877–80.   **6791**

Pagesetting and summary of major
guidelines of futurism. French, Italian,
Spanish, and Russian disciples of the
movement given due mention.

————. L'esprit nouveau et les poètes.
Haumont, 1946. 40 p. *Also in his:* Œuvres
complètes. Balland et Lecat, 1966. p.
900–10.   **6792**

Manifesto favoring the renewal of
poetry by use of techniques and materials furnished by the great modern
discoveries. Paradoxically, addressing
himself to all the poets of the world,
Apollinaire advocates nationalistic poetry. However, this text was written in
1917.

Aragon, Louis. Chroniques du bel canto.
Geneva, Skira, 1947. 274 p.   **6793**

Collection of twelve reviews written
for *La revue européenne* in 1946. Fine
analysis of the poetry collections and
of the principal works of criticism
published or republished that year. Extremely interesting for Aragon's conception of poetry on the morrow of the
Second World War. Panoramic view of
the poetry of the first half of the 20th
century with emphasis on Reverdy,
Apollinaire, Jacob, Eluard, Supervielle,
La Tour du Pin, etc.

————. Journal d'une poésie nationale.
Lyon, Les écrivains réunis, 1954. 164 p.
      6794

A discontinuous notebook, taken
from *Les lettres françaises,* in which
Aragon joyfully underscores the return
to classical verse form and to the sonnet
in particular. The cause for this is
attributed to the renunciation of individualism which the war provoked.
Places of prominence are accorded to
Eluard and Guillevic. Numerous poems
of secondary authors are cited. Good
work for a study of the period.

Aspel, Alexander, and Donald Justice. Contemporary French poetry. Fourteen witnesses of man's fate. Ann Arbor, Univ. of
Michigan press, 1965. 208 p.   **6795**

In the perspective of the 60's, a
selection of poets born during or even
before the 20's, along with their masters: Reverdy, Ponge, Audiberti, Michaux, Follain, Char and Frénaud.
Good introduction. Bilingual presentation of poems chosen. List of principal
collections of each poet and major
critical works dealing with each one.
Biographies. Very valuable work for
anyone wanting to know the important

names and schools of post Second World War poetry.
Reviews: R. Federman in RR 57: 154–55, 1966; R. Magowan in EspCr 5:246–47, 1965.

Aury, Dominique, and Jean Paulhan. Poètes d'aujourd'hui. Lausanne, La guilde du livre, 1947. 440 p. *Also:* Paris-Lausanne, Clairefontaine, 1947. 435 p.   **6796**
With a provocative preface by Paulhan who takes exception to the intentional obscurity of modern poetry, this anthology has the advantage of presenting accessible poems by reputedly difficult poets. Translations of foreign poets, a selection devoted to Belgian poets and another to Swiss and amateur poets are included. Very pleasant to skim through.

Bachelard, Gaston. La poétique de l'espace. Presses univ. de France, 1957. 219 p. (Bibliothèque de philosophie contemporaine) *Trans.:* The poetics of space. Trans. by Maria Jolas. New York, Orion press, 1964. 240 p.   **6797**
Refutation of the study of a work by means of psychoanalysis or even psychology. Establishment of a fundamental distinction between a metaphor and an image. Emphasis on the poetic image through examples taken from poets and writers of prose. Series of phenomenological observations on the level of estranged images.
Review: E. Noulet in SynB 134: 254–65, 1957.

———. La poétique de la rêverie. Presses univ. de France, 1960. 189 p. (Bibliothèque de philosophie contemporaine. Logique et philosophie des sciences) *Trans.:* The poetics of reverie. Trans. by Daniel Russell. Orion press, 1969. 219 p. **6798**
With phenomenological philosophy as a basis, a study of the imagining and creating conscience of the poet. One of the foundation books of modern criticsm which refuses to judge the work by the man.

Barrat, Denise. Espoir et parole. Seghers, 1963. 252 p.   **6799**
Very good thematic anthology of the Algerian resistance and liberation. Bio-biblographic notes. The names of Kréa, Amrouche and Sénac dominate.

Beaunier, André. La poésie nouvelle. Mercure de France, 1902. 401 p.   **6800**
A monographic work on well-known poets at beginning of 20th century. Profound introduction dealing with symbolism. No bibliography.

Belaval, Yvon. Poèmes d'aujourd'hui. Gallimard, 1964. 223 p.   **6801**
Series of essays covering the period from 1947 to 1963, analyzing, in particular, the works of "les amis de Rochefort," Michaux, Jarry and Tardieu. Highly pertinent chapter on the theme of poetry and knowledge.
Review: R. Jean in Monde 6151: 12, Oct. 10, 1964.

Bernard, Suzanne. Le poème en prose dans la tourmente contemporaine. *In her:* Le poème en prose de Baudelaire jusqu'à nos jours. Nizet, 1959. p. 573–762. **6802**
Less detailed, less profound than her study dealing with the works of the 19th century, this work covering the 20th nevertheless remains valuable. Serious bibliography.
Reviews: M. Décaudin in RHL 61: 623–26, 1961; J. Gaugeard in LetF 8, June 11, 1959.

Bertelé, René. Panorama de la jeune poésie française. Marseille, Laffont, 1942. 345 p.   **6803**
After a good introduction treating poetry from Baudelaire to the Second World War, Bertelé presents and gives a summary of ten years of French poetry, from 1930 to 1940, from Audiberti to Emmanuel. A résumé of their poetic theories and a bibliography. Work valid for the study of a poetry affected by surrealism but not surrealistic properly speaking.

Bessette, Gérard. Les tropes en poésie canadienne française. *In his:* Les images en poésie canadienne française. Montreal, Beauchemin, 1960. p. 93–213.   **6804**
Summary of poetic works of Crémazie, Fréchette, Beauchemin, Gill, Desaulniers, Choquette, Morin, Desrochers. The author describes and comments upon established diagrams using style of each author as a base. Similes, metaphors and symbols are fully discussed. Dry yet interesting criticism.
Reviews: E. Chartier in Lect 7:108, 1960–61; D. Hayne in CanL 7:80–81,

1961; P. Wyczynski in RUO 31:301–04, 1961.

Bonnefoy, Yves. La poésie française et le principe d'identité. *In his:* Un rêve fait à Mantoue. Mercure de France, 1967. p. 91–125.   **6805**
Valuable essay dealing with the poetic search for interiorization of reality and of presence in the world which govern the particular use of words. Provocative remarks on the qualities and faults of the French language in the poetic domain. Substantially coincides with Jaccottet's work.

Bosquet, Alain. La poésie canadienne. Paris-Montreal, Seghers, 1962. 218 p. *Also (rev.):* La poésie canadienne contemporaine de langue française. Paris, Seghers, 1966. 272 p. *Also (rev.):* Poésie du Québec. Paris, Seghers; Montreal, HMH, 1968. 272 p.   **6806**
Anthology of 25 poets (7 added in revisions) based on the love poetry rather than on the history of its development in Canada. From 1830 to 1937, for Bosquet, nothing happens. The introduction brings out the essential traits of this poetry, devoid of cerebralism, not aiming for an excessively formal perfection and maintaining contact with the earth. List of principal works and notation of characteristics of each poet. Valuable work of popularization.
Reviews: R. Dionne in Rel 268:69–70, 1963; R. Garneau in NL 4, Nov. 15, 1962; R. Lacôte in LetF 1181:8, May 4, 1967.

———. Verbe et vertige. Situations de la poésie. Hachette, 1961. 373 p.   **6807**
Pertinent study of the evolution of French poetry from its origins to the present day. Emphasis on the decisive turning point marked by Nerval, Baudelaire, Rimbaud and Mallarmé. Accurate outline of the diverse currents of the 20th century. Analysis of works of Perse, Michaux and Bonnefoy. Choice of manifestoes and texts on poetry since 1916.
Reviews: Anon. in RFB 2:10–11, 1962; R. Albérès in TR 172:101–03, 1962; M. Goffin in RUB 14:420–22, 1961–62; A. Guibert in Preu 132:78–81, 1962; R. Kanters in FL 818:2, Dec. 23, 1961; H. Prigogine in SynB

190:494–98, 1962; A. Viatte in RUL 6:612–17, 1961–62.

———, **and Pierre Seghers.** Les poèmes de l'année. Seghers, 1955. 318 p.   **6808**
Anthology of seventy poets of the French language whose works appeared in 1954. The choice is drawn from 600 collections and 150 issues of reviews. No biographical notices but references are given to sources of the poems. Series continued from 1956 through 1959.

———. Les poèmes de l'année. Seghers, 1967. 274 p.   **6809**
Anthology of 74 poets of the French language whose works appeared in 1966. In a foreword, the editors excuse themselves for the seven-year interruption in this publication and summarize the predominant traits of French poetry in 1966. Continued in 1968 and 1969.

Bremond, Henri. La poésie pure avec un débat sur la poésie par Robert de Souza. Grasset, 1926. 321 p.   **6810**
Speech made before the five academies of Paris on Oct. 24, 1925 concerning the inexpressible in poetry, followed by a summary of explanations published in NL in 1925–26 and excerpts from Bremond's letters to admirers and critics. Part two: Souza gives a fine analysis of differences between the concept of pure poetry in Bremond and Valéry.

———. Prière et poésie. Grasset, 1926. 240 p.   **6811**
Supplement to his work on pure poetry. Bremond admits that in contrast to the mystic, the poet speaks. Material which cannot be reduced to speech is the catharsis, a kind of flow of spiritual reflections of divine origin. Bremond concedes to God that which surrealism concedes to the unconscious. Neoromanticism. Delicate critique of methods used in evaluating poetry from Plato to a particularly English romanticism.

Breton, Jean. La poésie féminine contemporaine. V. 1. Librairie Saint-Germain-des-Prés, 1969. 123 p. (Poésie 1)   **6812**
Anthology including nine women (de Burine, Caroutch, Curtil, Jallais, Mail-

lard, Miège, Plantier, Prager, Salager) whose first publications appeared around 1960. Bibliography of their work and extracts of critical opinions from the press. Themes parallel to those expressed by men with the addition of theme of the womb.

Brincourt, André. Satan et la poésie. Grasset, 1946. 196 p.   6813
Felicitous criticism and synthesis of the ideas formulated from Baudelaire to the surrealists. Excellent analysis of the constituents of the artist's satanism. In the poetic domain, pertinent study of the priority which is given to form, words or rhythm in relation to thought. Final pages devoted to Baudelaire, Rimbaud and Mallarmé are superfluous.

Cabiac, Pierre. Feuilles d'érables et fleurs de lys. Anthologie de la poésie canadienne française. Diaspora française, 1965–66. 2 v. (Les essais)   6814
55 poets classified in four periods: the precursors, the patriotic Quebec school, the early 20th century, and contemporary poetry. Cabiac's choice is willfully traditionalist but the presentation of each of the poets is praiseworthy. Completes and counterbalances Bosquet's admirable anthology.
Review: A. Viatte in Cul 15, 1:37, 1966.

Caillois, Roger. Art poétique, commentaires, préface aux poésies, l'énigme et l'image. Gallimard, 1958. 202 p. (Coll. blanche)   6815
Development of the ideas set forth in *Les impostures de la poésie*. The essential goal of poetry would be to fix certain states of the soul. Very fine observations on the importance of the image to support this thesis. Brutal and elementary condemnation, in the name of harmony and clarity, of metaphysics, of innovations which shatter versification and, with only two exceptions, of the poets of the 20th century.
Reviews: J. Lepage in Bay 24:418–23, 1961; E. Noulet in SynB May 1959.

————. Les impostures de la poésie. Buenos-Aires, Les lettres françaises, 1944. 69 p. (La porte étroite, 5) *Also:* Gallimard, 1945. 87 p. (Métamorphoses, 26)   6816
Acerbic criticism of lyricism, symbolism, surrealism and pure poetry. Slightly too much insistence on bringing poetry and prose closer together. Oversimplified relegation of mystery to apologue and to interior landscapes. Intelligent pages on the self-generation of the work of art.
Review: E. Noulet in Orbe March 1, 1946.

Caminade, Pierre. Image et métaphore. Bordas, 1970. 160 p. (Coll. études supérieures)   6817
Interesting comparison of the ideas expressed by Valéry, Reverdy, Breton, "le groupe de Rochefort," Robbe-Grillet, Deguy, Garelli, Bachelard, Belaval, Paz, Cohen, Ricardou, Genette. In spite of the ambiguity of the question raised, Caminade detects a current trend giving more importance to the metaphor present at the level of the structure of the text and in the composition of the poetic language.

Chapelan, Maurice. Le foisonnement contemporain. *In his:* Anthologie du poème en prose. Julliard, 1946. p. 130–372. 6818
From Tailhade to Follain and Béalu, 45 poets in all. First anthology of this type. Incomplete and superficially presented, but useful since, aside from the work of S. Bernard, this area has not been extensively explored. Bibliography of principal collections.
Review: H. Fluchère in FS 2:187–88, 1948.

Chiari, Joseph. Contemporary French poetry. Manchester, Manchester univ. press, 1952. 196 p. *Also:* New York, Philosophical library, 1952. xvi, 180 p. *Also:* Freeport, N.Y., Books for libraries press, 1968. xvi, 180 p.   6819
A solid book. Intelligent study analyzing the work of the principal poets of the first half of the 20th century: Valéry, Supervielle, Claudel, Emmanuel, Éluard, Perse, Michaux. The analytic section is followed by a list of each poet's principal works.
Reviews: V. Daniel in Eras 8:154, 1955; M. Hamburger in NSN 110:710, June 4, 1952.

Clancier, Georges-Emmanuel. Panorama critique de Rimbaud au surréalisme. Seghers, 1953. 499 p. *Also:* Seghers, 1970. 437 p.   6820

Anthology designed to examine the period preceding that established by Rousselot. Consequently neither Artaud, Char, Desnos, nor Michaux is mentioned. After two sections given over to *phares* and the symbolists, begins the section dealing with the modern period, covering 227 pages with classification according to school, presentation of authors, bibliography of principal works. This book complements usefully by illustration the theoretical volume of M. Raymond.

Reviews: A. Alter in MerF 339:702–05, 1960; G. Né in Conv 31:103–04, 1963.

Claudel, Paul. Art poétique. Mercure de France, 1907. 206 p.   6821

Three essays dated 1900, 1903, 1904 (*Connaissance du temps, Traité de la co-naissance au monde et de soi-même, Développement de l'église*). Metaphysical foundation of a new poetic art of the universe and of metaphor. Difficult style, ideas comprehensible: man, in the center of the world, sets down the principle according to which everything falls into place.

————. Réflexions sur la poésie. Presses univ. de France, 1963. 187 p. (Idées, 29) 6822

Six essays appearing between 1921 and 1928 which make more explicit than the *Art poétique* the ideas of Claudel on poetry. They also justify, in the name of his entire period (40 years), the repudiation of classical verse and rhyme.

Cohen, Jean. Structure du langage poétique. Flammarion, 1966. 235 p. (Nouvelle bibliothèque scientifique)   6823

One of the first systematic studies undertaken to detect to what degree poetic syntax and vocabulary are alienated from the denotative language of scientific prose. Presentation of frequency tables enumerating language deviations found in the works of certain representatives of the classical, romantic and symbolist schools. Frequency of language deviation shown to rise steadily. Partiality in the choice of poets

and periods studied. However, fundamental idea and overall process are interesting.

Reviews: A. Benzimra in TM 247: 1084–93, 1966; M. Décaudin in RHL 70:1096–99, 1970; G. Mead in FR 42:630–31, 1969; M. Naudin in FR 40:423–24, 1966; D. Perret in QL 7:19–20, June 15, 1966.

Cooper, Clarissa Burnham. Women poets of the twentieth century in France; a critical bibliography. King's crown press, 1943. 327 p.   6824

Reference work concerning feminine poetry from 1900–1939. Introduction, quite superficial, is a condensation of critical works, not an in-depth study of the texts themselves.

Cornell, Kenneth. The post-symbolist period. French poetic currents, 1900–1920. New Haven, Yale univ. press; Paris, Presses univ. de France, 1958. 190 p. (Yale romanic studies, 2nd series) *Also:* Hamden, Conn., Archon, 1970.   6825

Valuable work. Critical and chronological reviews of magazines, theoretical works and collections of poetry. Shows well the confusion and mediocrity which reigned in 1914, but also the landmarks leading to the blossoming of a poetic renewal beginning in 1917. The last two chapters which summarize the period are excellent. The bibliography at the end of the book is regrettably not more extensive.

Reviews: L. Breunig in FR 33:88–89, 1959–60; B. Morrissette in Sym 13: 328–33, 1959; R. Pouilliart in LR 17: 103–05, 1963; R. Taupin in RR 50: 154–56, 1959; P. Wadsworth in MLJ 43:407, 1959.

Corzani, Jack. Littérature antillaise (poésie). Fort de France, E. Gros Desormeaux, 1971. 318 p. (Encyclopédie antillaise) 6826

Work by a white who, in this anthology, brings together white and black poets in an intelligent manner. Solid introduction which clearly divides the evolution of the poetry of the Antilles into periods. Biography and bibliography for each poet. Good choice of texts. The anthology begins with the poets of the 18th century. But the relatively few poets of the 18th and 19th centuries serve as points of reference for the state of 20th century poetry.

Damas, Léon-G. Poètes d'expression française 1900–1945. Seuil, 1947. 324 p. (Pierres vives)   **6827**

First anthology of overseas poets including those from Indochina who figure alongside the European poets. Poems of conventional exoticism, poems claiming the colonized patrimony. Foreword a bit virulent paying homage to Etienne Léon and to *Légitime défense* denouncing in 1932 the failure of three centuries of French colonization of the West Indies.

Décaudin, Michel. La crise des valeurs symbolistes. Vingt ans de poésie française 1895–1914. Toulouse, Privat, 1960. 530 p. (Universitas)   **6828**

Serious, basic work for study of the period. Completes and develops M. Raymond's and K. Cornell's studies. Select bibliography. Numerous, careful reference notes.

Reviews: A. Billy in FL 4:164, 1960; MerF 338:248–58, 1960; IL 12: 199–203, 1960; L. Breunig in RR 51: 302–04, 1960; A. Fongaro in SFr 15: 508–09, 1961; E. Mora in RDM 21: 156–60, 1958; H. Sckommodau in Archiv 116:236–38, 1964; A. Vandegans in RBPH 41:533–54, 1963.

Decker, Henry Wallace. Pure poetry, 1925–1930; theory and debate in France. Berkeley, Univ. of California press, 1962. 137 p. (Univ. of California publications in modern philology, 64)   **6829**

Very fine critical analysis of Bremond's theories. Interesting parallel with the conceptions formulated by Claudel and Valéry. Thematic synthesis of the reactions produced in Paris and in English speaking countries. Extremely useful bibliography for further research on this debate and on this period.

Reviews: J. Bellemin-Noël in RHL 66:538–39, 1966; C. G. Whittingin in RR 58:309–10, 1967.

Dubacq, Jean. L'école de Rochefort. Librairie Saint-Germain-des-Prés, 1970. 124 p. (Poésie 1)   **6830**

Foundation tool. Rather summary but valid for the study of some friends who, in 1940, met again at Rochefort-

sur-Loire at Jean Bouhier's. Anthology and listing of works by Béalu, Bérimont, Cadou, Chaulot, Follain, Guillaume, Manoll, Rousselot. Visual poets expressing the whole physique of life.

Dufrenne, Mikel. Le poétique. Presses univ. de France, 1963. 200 p. (Bibliothèque de philosophie contemporaine)   **6831**

Significant work. Interesting considerations on language, on the ontological character of poetry which reveals the world, and on the fundamental inspirational role of nature. Dufrenne carries on his study with the works of Saussure, Spire, Kant, Hegel, Heidegger, Sartre and Bachelard as his point of departure.

Reviews: N. Mouloud in RE 17: 319–22, 1964; J. C. Piguet in RTP 97:61–62, 1964.

Eluard, Paul. Poésie involontaire et poésie intentionnelle. Villeneuve-lès-Avignon, Poésie 42, 1942. 67 p. *Also:* Seghers, 1963. 71 p. *Also in his:* Œuvres complètes. V. 1. Gallimard, 1968. p. 1129–79. (Pléiade)   **6832**

In the foreword, Eluard stresses the simplicity and the universally understood nature of the poem. There follows a sort of anthology where famous and not-so-famous names are closely mixed, poetry for specialists and popular poetry, to show the equality of values. Representative of the change undergone by Eluard and his contemporaries of the Second World War.

———. Les sentiers et les routes de la poésie. Gallimard, 1954. 173 p. *Also in his:* Œuvres complètes. V. 2. Gallimard, 1968. p. 525–76. (Pléiade)   **6833**

In favor of heartfelt, simple and sincere poetry. For the use of all popular verbal forms and expressions. Numerous quotations in every possible domain. Certain of the author's poems figure with those of the greatest poets as well as those of anonymous poets.

Emmanuel, Pierre. La face humaine. Seuil, 1965. 283 p.   **6834**

Refutation of poetic monachism (La Tour du Pin) and of passive submission to the film of the psyche (surrealism). In favor of poetry beginning with the real, where language is not privileged in relation with life. In favor of a poetry of relevancy and of brotherhood under myth or symbol. In favor of poetry expressing the tension which exists between the spirit and its nothingness.

Etiemble, [René]. Poètes ou faiseurs? (1936–1966). Gallimard, 1966. 400 p. (Hygiène des lettres, 4) **6835**

Series of humorous and lively essays, notably on Perse, Char, Ponge, Valéry, Claudel, Aragon, Supervielle, Audiberti. In the tradition of Caillois and Paulhan for a genuine poetry, syntactically correct.

Reviews: L. Gaspar in Monde 6932: 8, April 26, 1967; R. Georgin in VL 187:577–83, 1967.

Faÿ, Bernard. Panorama de la littérature contemporaine. Kra, 1929. 265 p. *Orig. ed.:* Kra, 1925. **6836**

Perspective of period from 1880 to 1928 — prose as well as poetry. Well done section covering 1900–1923. A correct historical presentation where great writers are studied. More a testimonial than a reference work.

Garnier, Pierre. Manifeste pour une poésie nouvelle, visuelle et phonique. André Silvaire, 1963. 16 p. (Les lettres, 29, 8e série) **6837**

An attempt at rejuvenating poetry in the direction of lettrism. Juxtaposition of words to be read by one or several voices, capable of lending itself to additions and improvisations, transforming, in turn, the reader's role from passive to active. In fact, the texts presented following the manifesto are highly comprehensible and employ the unified rhythm of repetition.

———. Spatialisme et poésie concrète. Gallimard, 1968. 202 p. **6838**

Illustrated by graphic examples followed by a bibliography, this work presents a historical account, an explanation and a few manifestoes of spatialism. In the wake of futurism, dadaism and lettrism, return to the letter, to the word, to the breath, to the sound. The setting up of the poem is done thanks to a typewriter or a tape recorder. It is structured not taking into account the meaning but mainly the sensation and esthetics. Debatable but real and with international poets.

Reviews: Anon. in BCLF 23:492, 1968; M. Deguy in QL 54:13–14, July 16, 1968.

Garret, Naomi. The renaissance of Haitian poetry. Présence africaine, 1963. 257 p. **6839**

Both an historic study and an anthology of the principal Haitian poets from the beginning of the 19th century to 1950. Certainly a basic work for complementary studies. Bibliography.

Review: L. Hoffmann in FR 38: 277–78, 1964–65.

Gavronsky, Serge. Poems and texts. October house, 1969. 223 p. **6840**

Bilingual anthology including six poets (Ponge, Frénaud, Bonnefoy, du Bouchet, Roche, Pleynet). Excellent introduction laying stress on the post-surrealist and post-existentialist generation which is interested in the function of the language and which, on the formalistic point of view, denies the separateness of poetry from the other literary genres. Each poet is presented by his principal books and an interview with the editor.

Review: A. Hartley in ChiTBW 43: 8, Oct. 26, 1969.

Genette, Gérard. Langage poétique, poétique du langage. *In his:* Figures 2. Seuil, 1969. p. 123–53. (Tel quel) **6841**

Beginning with a very pertinent critique of the work of J. Cohen, emphasizes that the study of poetic language must depend upon poetic nature of language, that is upon the innumerable forms of linguistic imagination.

Godel, Vahé. La poésie française de Suisse. Librairie Saint-Germain-des-Prés, 1973. 120 p. (Poésie 1) **6842**

Aside from Rousseau, Amiel, Duchosal, eight 20th century poets are treated. Bibliography, press reviews and choice of poems for each poet. Not lengthy but valuable.

Gros, Léon-Gabriel. Poètes contemporains. Marseille, Cahiers du sud, 1944. 308 p. **6843**

Gathering of a series of articles devoted to collections of poems which appeared between 1933 and 1943 and which are representative of the period.

Penetrating analyses are to be found of the poetry of Eluard, Jouve, La Tour du Pin, Emmanuel and Guillevic. Initially relying on Raymond's *De Baudelaire au surréalisme,* Gros completes and surpasses it. Importance given to 1933 as the pivotal point of a new generation transcending surrealism.

————. Poètes contemporains. Cahiers du sud, 1951. 250 p.   **6844**

Starting with the Breton of the 1940's, and then studying Bousquet, Ponge, Char, Michaux, Audiberti, Ganzo, Thomas, Tardieu, Lacôte, Follain, Fombeure and Prévert, the author attempts to define the new trend which appears in the years following the war. This poetry of consciousness attempts to be objective, dispenses with lyric exaltation, and is interested in the problems of language. Serious work. The author is well acquainted with the works and the criticism they provoked. The author's preferences are easily discernible.

Hugues, Langston, and Christiane Reygnault. Poèmes. *In their:* Anthologie africaine et malgache. Seghers, 1962. p. 151–227.   **6845**

The French texts of about 20 poets of both the French and English language are presented. The Egyptians, Maghrebins and Antilleans are excluded. This very valuable section is the central portion of a work devoted also to prose fiction, documents and articles.

Hytier, Jean. Le plaisir poétique. Etude de psychologie. Presses univ. de France, 1923. 139 p.   **6846**

From the esthetic works of Brunschvig and Souriau, Hytier clearly differentiates between esthetic pleasure (rhythm, tone, versification) and poetic pleasure (imagery, play on images). The role of the affective imagination is well defined.

Isou, Isidore. Introduction à une nouvelle poésie et à une nouvelle musique. Gallimard, 1947. 416 p.   **6847**

Curious book. Sagacious analysis of the evolution of poetry from Baudelaire to Valéry, Breton and Tzara. The literary currents of dadaism and pure poetry engender the destruction of words and meaning. Taking into consideration these circumstances, Isou advocates a new form of poetry: lettrism. With the alphabet as his starting point, the poet will compose while declaiming in irregular phonetic succession. Poetry and music will combine in a common return to voice.

Jaccottet, Philippe. L'entretien des muses. Chroniques de poésie. Gallimard, 1968. 313 p.   **6848**

Monographic studies of 29 French and Swiss poets all written between 1955 and 1966. Counterattacks work of Etiemble by criticism based not on a single book but on the ensemble of the work produced, not on the prosody but on the use, more or less well done, of analogy, of metaphor, or of any other means of comparison. Jaccottet comes as close as possible to the center around which each production pivots. Very valuable for understanding the essentially visual and attentive nature of post-surrealist, that is contemporary, poetry.

Jacob, Max. Art poétique. Emile-Paul, 1922. 75 p.   **6849**

Series of aphorisms. An exact notation on modern poetry refusing all purpose and avoiding explanation and on the poems executed in prose by the author, in which neither the subject nor the graphics are important.

Jouffroy, Alain. La fin des alternances. Gallimard, 1970. 308 p.   **6850**

Series of essays covering a friendship with Breton, a retrospective of the poetry of the years 1947–68, a subtle analysis of the works of Artaud, Michaux, Mandiargues, Aragon and of the beat generation in the U.S., complemented by an exchange of ideas with Faye on the revolutionary import of speech. Unbalanced critical work which is, however, highly representative of the French direction of searching and aspiration in the year 1970.

Review: Anon. in TLS 3578:1085, Sept. 25, 1970.

Jouve, Pierre-Jean. Apologie du poète; suivie de textes commentés de Nerval, Baudelaire, Rimbaud, Mallarmé, Claudel, Saint-John Perse, Aragon, Emmanuel. G.L.M., 1948. 61 p.   **6851**

In the lineage of Claudel, Perse and Emmanuel, Jouve is opposed to the absolute esthetics of surrealism and pure poetry and also to the utilitarianism of committed poetry. Poetry agglutinates all conscious and subconscious facts but transcends them by spirituality in search of irrational invisible order.

Kanters, Robert, and Maurice Nadeau. Anthologie de la, poésie française. Le 20e siècle. V. 1. Rencontre, 1967. 438 p.
6852
Very good foreword giving the great names and features that, in the perspective of the 60's, have marked the poetry of the beginning of the century at the dawn of surrealism. This anthology could serve as an illustration for the book of M. Raymond.
Review: S. de Sacy in QL 27:15, May 1–15, 1967.

Kesteloot, Lilyan. Anthologie négro-africaine: panorama critique des prosateurs, poètes et dramaturges noirs du 20e siècle. Verviers, Gérard, 1967. 430 p. (Marabout université, 129)
6853
Anthologies written in French or translated into French covering American, Haitian, West Indian and African authors. Divided into three large parts with analysis of each of the stages of black literature: 1. 1918–47, awakening consciousness of the intellectuals; 2. 1948–60, militant blackness; 3. after 1960 since the independence of the African countries. A very important place has been given to poetry written in French.
Review: A. Laude in Monde 7062: 1–2, Sept. 27, 1967.

Loisy, Jean. Un certain choix de poèmes 1935–1965. Points et contrepoints, 1968. 333 p.
6854
Anthology grouping 52 poets who collaborated in the magazine *Points et contrepoints*. Only one fifth of these achieved fame. All are characterized by their respect for syntax, for prosody and for the public's comprehension. Valuable if not invaluable as proof of a countercurrent against difficulty. Bibliography of collected works.
Reviews: R. Georgin in DLF 45:7–9, 1968; R. Kanters in FL 1179:17–18, Dec. 9–15, 1968; J. Morvan in PoCp 88:45–49, 1968.

Marinetti, Filippo Tommaso. L'imagination sans fils et les mots en liberté. Manifeste futuriste. Milan, Direction du mouvement futuriste, 1913. 4 p.
6855
Definition of the futurist sensitivity. Emphasis on a certain liberty to be carried out in the arrangement of words, images and spelling. Desire for a typographical revolution and for an animalization of the style.

————. Manifeste du futurisme. Milan, Direction du mouvement futuriste, 1909. 4 p. *Also in:* Fig Feb. 20, 1909.
6856
First manifesto of modernism in the 20th century. Emphasis on action, movement, speed, victory over time and space, beauty of the automobile, etc.

————. Manifeste technique de la littérature futuriste. Milan, Direction du mouvement futuriste, 1912. 4 p.
6857
Destruction and abolition of all syntax. Use of a compact chain of images and analogies whose relationships become so farfetched that they lose touch with one another. Devaluation of ego and psychology replaced by importance of material and objects. Justification of chaos and the ugly.

————. Supplément au manifeste technique de la littérature futuriste. Milan, Direction du mouvement futuriste, 1912. 4 p.
6858
Intuition reigns over intelligence. Stylistic harmony replaced by abstract dryness of mathematical signs. Example of a futurist text.

Maritain, Jacques. L'intuition créatrice dans l'art et dans la poésie. Desclée De Brouwer, 1966. 433 p. *Trans.:* Creative intuition in art and poetry. New York, Pantheon books, 1953. 453 p. (Bollingen series 35. 1)
6859
A slightly conservative yet valuable analysis, based on St. Thomas and Aristotle as well as Baudelaire and Eliot, of the poetic phenomenon and of art in the 20th century. Synthesis and enlargement of author's previous works.
Review: V. Turner in Month 12: 270–80, 1954.

Maritain, Jacques and Raïssa. Situation de la poésie. Desclée De Brouwer, 1938. 159 p. *Also:* Paris-Bruges, Desclée De Brouwer, 1964. 139 p. *Trans.:* The situa-

tion of poetry. Four essays on the relation between poetry, mysticism, magic and knowledge. Trans. by Marshall Suther. Philosophical library, 1955. 85 p.
6860

Excellent work. Insistence on the revolutionary role of Baudelaire who founded poetry on awareness and, in so doing, initiated modern poetry. Very clear demarcation between poetry and speculative knowledge. Emphasis on poetry's ontological, existential character which in fact creates a new object, a new world.

Review: P.-H. Simon in MondeH 849:10, Jan. 27, 1965.

Maugey, Axel. Poésie et société au Québec (1937–1970). Quebec, Presses de l'univ. Laval, 1972. 304 p.   **6861**

Work especially valid for its presentation of the principal poetic journals of Quebec, and the comparative analysis of the main ideas contained, between 1947 and 1967, in the works of ten poets: Paul-Marie Lapointe, Giguère, Pilon, Miron, Préfontaine, Gatien Lapointe, Chamberland, Brault, Ouellette, Godin.

Review: J. Bonenfant in PFr 5:162–63, 1972.

Mauron, Charles. Introduction. *In his:* Des métaphores obsédantes au mythe personnel. Introduction à la psychocritique. Corti, 1963. p. 9–34.   **6862**

Mauron takes a stand in relation to Baudoin, Fry and the representatives of thematic criticism, Bachelard, Poulet, Richard, Starobinski. Search for associations of involuntary ideas under the deliberate structures of a given text. By superimposition of texts, discovery of a personal myth verified by comparison with the writer's life. Debatable but valuable.

Reviews: Anon. in RFB 1:11, 1964; A. Blanchet in Et 11:277–78, 1963; M. Milner in RHL 66:353–55, 1966.

Ménard, René. La condition poétique. Gallimard, 1959. 165 p. (Espoir)   **6863**

Solid work made up of different essays, five of which deal with René Char's poetry. Intelligently preaches in favor of the liberation of form and the abolition of the genres corresponding to the abolition of the mental categories which justified them.

Miguel, André. La nouvelle poésie française de Belgique. Librairie Saint-Germain-des-Prés, 1972. 121 p. (Poésie 1)
6864

Twelve poets aged 17 to 42 (Bauwens, Beni, Crickillon, Doms, Hubin, Izoard, Meurant, Puttemans, Rombaut, Verheggen, Vernal, Volpe). Bibliography of their principal works, references to articles of criticism concerning them, and press commentaries on the value and the meaning of their creations. Brief preface groups these poets by trends and influences (surrealist, African, American, French). Poems selected are lively and of high quality.

Moore, Gerald, and Ulli Beier. Modern poetry from Africa. Harmondsworth, Middlesex, Penguin books, 1963. 192 p.
6865

Thirty-two black poets writing in one or another of the European languages spoken in Africa. All texts are presented in English. The introduction drawn up from the works of Senghor, Sartre, and Jahn (Muntu) affirms the preeminence of the production from West Africa, that of Nigeria over Senegal since the end of the 50's, and everyday problems over *négritude*. Bio-bibliographies.

Review: H. Marsden-Smedley in PoetryR 54:256–57, 259, 1963.

Moulin, Jeanine. La poésie féminine. Seghers, 1963. 338 p. (Melior)   **6866**

Certainly valid anthology with introductory notes, list of works and principal bibliography of each of the forty poets studied. Nevertheless it corresponds mostly to the first half of the 20th century. The choice is determined by a search for a psychological and formal evolution.

Mounin, Georges. Poésie et société. Presses univ. de France, 1962. 112 p. *Also:* 1968. 113 p.   **6867**

Delicate analysis of the crisis of French poetry during the 50's and 60's. Pertinent chapter on the education of poets and on publishing and broadcasting of poetry. Exposure of the esthetic of Hegel and socio-historical criticism announcing the devaluation of the art. Rather good panorama of evolution of French poetry from its beginnings.

Review: J. Rousselot in NL 2058:6, Feb. 9, 1967.

Nola, Jean-Paul de. Les poètes de la rue des Sols. Eds. universitaires, 1963. 397 p. **6868**
Anthology including biography and bibliography of twenty poets who took courses at the free university of Brussels between 1920 and 1930. Three significant names: Michaux, Plisnier and Goffin. Not an essential work, yet one which still sheds some light on Belgian poetry.

Onimus, Jean. La connaissance poétique. Introduction à la lecture des poèmes modernes. Desclée De Brouwer, 1966. 255 p. **6869**
Excellent work emphasizing the existential side of poetry. Large number of quotations from Heidegger, Merleau-Ponty, Bonnefoy, Emmanuel, Jouve, Perse, Supervielle, Valéry, etc.
Reviews: Anon. in TLS 3412:648, July 20, 1967; M. Beaujour in FR 42:459, 1969; R. Boirel in EP 22:344, 1967; A. Fongaro in SFr 12:117–18, 1968; S. Givone in RdE 14:125–28, 1969; H. Seidler in DLit 88:291–98, 1967.

Paris, Jean. Anthologie de la poésie nouvelle. Monaco, Eds. du rocher, 1956. 251 p. **6870**
Good introduction tending to justify present interest in the collections of thirteen poets, products of the Second World War and colonialism. Their work asserts itself around the 50's. Brief biographies centered on their intellectual formation. Bibliographies. Wise choice of poets (Bonnefoy, du Bouchet, Charpier, Dupin, Giroux, Glissant, Grosjean, Kateb, Laude, Oster, Pichette, Tarpignan, Weingarten).
Reviews: L.-G. Gros in CahS 341:126–32, 1957; J. Legrand in WZ 4, no. 5:38–41, 1958; O. de Magny in LetN 56:115–18, 1958.

Porché, François. Poètes français depuis Verlaine. La nouvelle revue critique, 1929. 238 p. **6871**
Intelligent and valuable work. Fairly exact analysis principally dealing with symbolism, pure poetry, Valéry, and certain other poets never recognized

before the war of 1914: Moréas, Jammes, Fort, Romains, Noailles, Claudel, Péguy. Less stress on the innovators of cubism, dadaism, and surrealism. But the leading writers and essential trends are mentioned. No bibliography.

Prampolini, Enrico, Ivo Pannagi and Vinicio Paladini. L'art mécanique. Milan, Direction du mouvement futuriste, 1923. 4 p. **6872**
Balance-sheet of literary and artistic activities of futurism. The machine is in the forefront.

Raymond, Marcel. De Baudelaire au surréalisme. Corrêa, 1933. 413 p. *Also:* Corti, 1940, 1947. 367 p. *Also:* Corti, 1952, 1960, 1966. 369 p. *Trans.:* From Baudelaire to surrealism. New York, Wittenborn, Schultz, 1949. 428 p. (Documents of modern art series, 10) *Also:* London, Peter Owen, 1957. 428 p. *Also:* London, Methuen, 1970. 356 p. (University paperbacks, UP 355) **6873**
Extremely important work for the period Baudelaire-1940. Particularly remarkable are: the introduction, the first book which treats the diverse currents present at the beginning of the century, the third book which traces the line from Apollinaire to the surrealist and non-surrealist poets, and the conclusion. The critical considerations on the various concepts enunciated about poetry are especially pertinent. It lacks a bibliography however.
Review: R. Cohn in PR 17:627–30, 1950.

Reed, John, and Clive Wake. French African verse. London, Ibadan, Nairobi, Heinemann, 1972. 229 p. **6874**
Bilingual anthology intended to renew and extend that of Senghor. Twenty-two poets divided into three generations from 1945–1970: negritude, protest against colonialism, and emphasis on the value of African life and imagery. Short but substantial introduction, bibliography and glossary. Solid work.

Reverdy, Pierre. Le gant de crin. Plon, 1926. 256 p. (Le roseau d'or) *Also:* Flammarion, 1968. 217 p. **6875**
In the midst of aphorisms and varying thoughts on dreams, poetry, morals and God, statement of the theory ac-

cording to which the strength of the image depends on the remoteness of two realities it has brought together. Reprinting of the famous text, published in *Nord-Sud* in 1917, which was to have a great influence.

Reviews: R. Kanters in FL 1188: 19–20, Feb. 10–16, 1969; J. Mambrino in Et 330:464–65, 1969; R. Terdjan in TR 253:159–61, 1969.

Richard, Jean-Pierre. Onze études sur la poésie moderne. Seuil, 1964. 299 p. (Pierres vives)   **6876**

Very valuable thematic criticism of the works of Reverdy, Perse, Char, Eluard, Schehadé, Ponge, Guillevic, Bonnefoy, du Bouchet, Jaccottet, Dupin. The reveries of each of these poets deal with the problem of death and the limitations of the human condition.

Reviews: J. Bellemin-Noël in RHL 66:542–43, 1966; C. Ernoult in LetN 13:166–70, 1965; G. Mermier in BA 40:47, 1966; G. Raillard in FMonde 32:41–42, 1965; R. Riese-Hubert in MLN 81:345–48, 1966; P.-H. Simon in MondeH 849:10, Jan. 27, 1965; C. Van Roes in FrB 35:83–86, 1965.

Rolland, Roger. Poésie et versification; essai sur la liberté du vers. Montreal, Fides, 1949. 189 p.   **6877**

Using the flowering of free verse Canadian poetry in the twentieth century as his point of departure, the author becomes the self-proclaimed defender of metric liberty. Commendable work, much more finely nuanced than those of Caillois or Maulnier. One only regrets that the author did not deal with the prose poem. One could also object to too many references to the works of Jousse and Servien which cause certain chapters to border on periphrasis.

Rolland de Renéville, André. L'expérience poétique. Gallimard, 1938. 195 p. *Also:* Neuchâtel, La Baconnière, 1948. 174 p.   **6878**

In the same style as the studies of Bremond and Maritain, an essay on the function of knowledge and the approaches to the absolute attempted by poets from romanticism up to and including surrealism. Interesting ideas concerning the common consciousness

shared by primitive man, the child and the poet.

Rousselot, Jean. Panorama critique des nouveaux poètes français. Seghers, 1952. 388 p. *Also:* 1953.   **6879**

Valuable and accurate panorama grouping significant poets and works of the years 1935–1950. Refusal of a systematic classification. Rather friendly commentaries. Summary bibliography for the poets cited. This is, however, no more than a panorama.

Reviews: A. Alter in MerF 339: 705–06, 1960; A. Viatte in Cul 9: 32–33, June 1960.

Saint-John Perse. Poésie. Gallimard, 1961. 9 p. *Also in his:* Œuvres complètes. Gallimard, 1972. p. 443–47. (Pléiade) *Also in his:* Œuvres poétiques. Presses du compagnonnage, 1965. p. 21–26. *Trans.:* On poetry. Trans. by W. H. Auden. New York, Bollingen foundation, 1961. 21 p. (Bollingen series)   **6880**

Short speech delivered at the banquet for the Nobel prize he had just been awarded. Very representative of the poetic concept of the 60's with its approach to absolute reality, its language communicating the being's movements, its ambiguity of expression.

Sauvage, Marcel. Poésie du temps. Marseille, Cahiers du sud, 1927. 161 p.   **6881**

Conference report especially valuable concerning pioneer thoughts during first quarter of the century. Better known poets of this period mentioned. High degree of scholarship revealed on a light note. Abundance of footnotes. Reliable judgment.

Séguin, Jean-Paul. La nouvelle poésie française de Suisse. Librairie Saint-Germain-des-Prés, 1973. 110 p. (Poésie 1)   **6882**

Seven poets (Brachetto, Godel, Jaccottet, Pache, Perrier, Tache, Schlunegger) treated with biography, bibliography, selected poems and press reviews for each. General overview of the meaning of each poet's creations. Good, short collection.

Sénac, Jean. Anthologie de la nouvelle poésie algérienne. Librairie Saint-Germain-des-Prés, 1971. 126 p. (Poésie 1)   **6883**

Anthology of nine poets below 35 years of age who had not yet published

(Sebti, Laghouati, Bey, Imaziten, Abdoun, Kharchi, Skif, Benkamla, Nacer-Khodja). Poems in free verse, direct tone, of good quality. Excellent introduction analyzing the work of the previous generation.

Senghor, Léopold-Sédar. Anthologie de la nouvelle poésie nègre et malgache. Presses univ. de France, 1948. 267 p. *Also:* Presses univ. de France, 1972. 272 p. (Colonies et empires, 5ᵉ série. Art et littérature, 1)   **6884**

On the occasion of the 100th anniversary of the revolution of 1848, Senghor presents sixteen poets from Guiana, Martinique, Guadeloupe, Haiti, Black Africa and Madagascar. A bibliography of their works is included. Very important foreword by Sartre entitled *Orphée noir* in which he defines the theme of blackness and the carnal and erotic character of the images created by these poets. Sartre shows how blackness responds to the essence of poetry and constitutes the true revolutionary poetry of our time.

Review: J. Decock in FR 45:215–16, 1971.

————. Comme les lamantins vont boire à la source. *In his:* Ethiopiques. Seuil, 1956. p. 103–23.   **6885**

Attempt to explain the originality of black poetry in relation to French poetry. Examples taken from Césaire, Camara, B. Diop, Damas, Senghor. Analysis bearing principally on image and rhythm.

Review: J. Grosjean in NRF 7: 1093–95, 1956.

Shapiro, Norman R. Négritude. Black poetry from Africa and the Caribbean. October house, 1970. 247 p.   **6886**

Good bilingual anthology of the principal black French language poets of Guiana, Guadeloupe, Martinique, Haiti, Senegal, Ivory Coast, Congo, Central African Republic, Cameroon, Guinea, Mali, Dahomey, French Somaliland, Mauritius and Malagasy Republic. 44 poets in all. Preface indicates the similitudes of the whole of the poetry of each region. Bio-bibliography with each poet's publisher's name. A solid work.

Soupault, Philippe. Essai sur la poésie. Rolle. Eynard, 1950. 27 p.   **6887**

Introduction to the presentation in French of the *Song of prince Igor*. Relating to this, a poetic reflection. Generative role of the image, the flow of which is determined by a natural rhythm. If one accepts this concept, primitive poetry and surrealist poetry are brought together. Brief but pertinent essay.

Sylvestre, Guy. Anthologie de la poésie canadienne française. Montreal, Bernard Valiquette, 1942. 139 p. *Also (rev.):* Montreal, Beauchemin, 1961. 320 p. *Also (rev.):* 1963. 398 p.   **6888**

Excluding three poets, 72 are from the 20th century. Division in six groups from romanticism to the young poetry. Very good historical and analytical introduction of the new tendencies initiated by Grandbois, Hertel, Garneau, Lasnier, Hébert. Bibliography of each poet and general works on each of them. Lack the publishers' names.

Review: R. Légaré in Cul 25:291–92, 1964.

————. Poètes catholiques de la France contemporaine. Montreal, Fides, 1943. 161 p.   **6889**

After one chapter devoted to Verlaine there follow seven others devoted successively to Claudel, Péguy, Jammes, Vielé-Griffin, Ghéon, Raïssa Maritain, Marie Noël. The analyses of the works of these poets are nuanced and clear.

Taylor, Simon, and Edward Lucie-Smith. French poetry to-day. Schocken, 1971. 408 p.   **6890**

Extremely interesting anthology presenting an intelligent selection of the poetry written between 1955 and 1970. A solid introduction clearly establishes the French currents: both Anglo-American and French from Nerval and Baudelaire. Biographical and bibliographical notice for each poet included. Bilingual edition.

Thomas, Henri. La chasse aux trésors. Gallimard, 1961. 266 p.   **6891**

Collection of book reviews and short essays. Informs us as to the genesis of Henri Thomas' poetic formation as well as of modern French poetry. Brief but subtle observations on poetry itself and more especially on the work of Aragon, Eluard, Char, Michaux, Reverdy, Bosschère, Schehadé, Saint-John Perse, Valéry, Fargue, Supervielle, Bousquet. Approximately half of the collection is devoted to the novel and in particular the German and Anglo-Saxon.

Thomas, Lucien-Paul. Le vers moderne. Ses moyens d'expression, son esthétique. Brussels, Palais des académies; Liège, Vaillant-Carmanne, 1943. 251 p. (Académie royale de langue et de littérature françaises de Belgique)   **6892**

Interesting considerations on the structure of free verse considered to be the best means of expression of modern sensitivity. Several details are arguable, but the aggregate is rather good.

Review: A Fontainas in MerF 304: 509–13, 1948.

Valéry, Paul. The art of poetry. Trans. by Denise Folliot. Pantheon, 1958. 369 p. (Bollingen series 45, no. 7)   **6893**

Twenty-seven essays taken from *Variétés* presented intelligently by T. S. Eliot. Especially interesting in view of the theories expressed by Breton on the priority given to reflection and form in the elaboration of the poem. Insistence after Poe and Baudelaire that poetry has no goal other than itself.

Reviews: N. Frye in HudR 12:124–29, 1959; J. O'Brien in Repo 19, no. 1:38–39, July 10, 1958.

Verhesen, Fernand. Voies et voix de la poésie française contemporaine. Brussels, Eds. des artistes, 1960. 104 p.   **6894**

Brief but extremely clear essay. The author establishes a panorama of 20th-century French poetry which has as its starting point the dominant current of the 1950's: the provisional definition of man. Verhesen emphasizes 1912 as the year announcing modern times. Importance is placed on the lesser known poets of the Belgian pleiad of the years 1935 to 1960.

Le vers français au 20ᵉ siècle. Ed. by Monique Parent. Klincksieck, 1967. 323 p.   **6895**

Transcription of sixteen lectures from a symposium held at the University of Strasbourg, May 3–6, 1966. Collection of great documentary value due to concrete examples of various poets of the 20th century which constitute a veritable overview of the evolution of French verse. Research presenting the unifying elements of the poetry of many languages.

Reviews: W. Albert in FR 42:459–50, 1968–69; A. Fierro-Domenech in BBF 14, 1969; G. Giorgi in SFr 13: 183, 1969; C. Scott in MLR 65:430–34, 1970; T. Van Dijk in FrB 38: 205–08, 1968.

Villard, Emile. Guerre et poésie; la poésie patriotique française de 1914 à 1918. Neuchâtel, La Baconnière, 1949. 324 p.   **6896**

Interesting and well documented work. A study of the poets who, in general, were too old to go to war. The author shows that, with the exception of Claudel, none of the poets seriously pondered the phenomenon of the war. Rather, their poetry is stereotyped, conventional and pharisaical.

Visan, Tancrède de. L'attitude du lyrisme contemporain. Mercure de France, 1911. 475 p.   **6897**

Monographs of Régnier, Vielé-Griffin, Fort, Maeterlinck, Mockel seen according to Bergson's *Les données immédiates de la conscience.* Symbolism tinged with naturism and representing the perplexity of the period. Two well-done chapters on the masters of thought of the time, Barrès and Gide. No bibliography.

Wahl, Jean. Essence et phénomène: la poésie comme source de philosophie. Centre de documentation universitaire, 1958. 161 p. (Les cours de Sorbonne)   **6898**

A rather interesting panorama of the treatment of essence and phenomenon from the pre-Socratics to Heidegger serves as an introduction. There follows an analysis of the philosophical elements contained in the *Four quartets* of Eliot and in the *Elegies of Duino* by Rilke.

Walzer, Pierre Olivier. Poètes. *In his:* Anthologie jurassienne. V. 2. Le 20ᵉ siècle. Porrentruy, Société jurassienne d'émulation, 1965. p. 17–188.   **6899**

Eighteen poets beginning with Werner Renfer. Good introduction, biography and critical bibliography for each.

Review: A. Viatte in Cul 14:46, 1965.

Weber, Jean-Paul. Genèse de l'œuvre poétique. Gallimard, 1960. 564 p. (Bibliothèque des idées) **6900**

Interesting work emphasizing the personal theme peculiar to different poets (in the 20th century: Claudel, Valéry, Apollinaire) by a study of the recurring motifs in the whole of their work. Although rather similar to the proposition supported by Mauron, Weber's work differs from it by the essential uniqueness of the theme and by the refusal of classical psychoanalysis. The theme is seen to be a particularly gripping event occurring during the poet's infancy.

Reviews: M. Chapelan in FL 775:2, Feb. 25, 1961; C. Cuénot in TR 162: 118–22, 1961; E. Mora in RDM 13: 163–66, 1961; J. Piatier in Monde 8, Jan. 21, 1961; G. Rosolato in TM 186:593–602, 1961; A. Treisman and N. Moray in BJA 2:280–83, 1962; A. Zatloukal in BRP 3:123–24, 1964.

Wilder, Amos N. Modern poetry and the Christian tradition: a study in the relation of Christianity to culture. Scribner, 1952. 307 p. **6901**

Although the French poets studied are limited to Péguy and Perse, this work constitutes a very good study of the difficulties offered to orthodox Christian poetry. Also considers the rich possibilities offered to the poets who deviate from their period without, however, totally repudiating their culture. The work is centered on Anglo-Saxon, American and French literature.

Nérée Beauchemin
(Nos. 6902–6903)

JACQUES COTNAM

Beauchemin, Nérée. Nérée Beauchemin, son œuvre. Ed. critique préparée par Armand Guilmette. Montreal, Presses de l'univ. du Québec, 1973–74. 3 v. **6902**

Richly annotated, including variants. First volume is devoted to *Floraisons matutinales* and to *La patrie intime,* second contains posthumous poetry, and third contains correspondence, critical articles, "notes intimes," and a

bibliography. Introduction to first volume explains Guilmette's method and provides a detailed chronology.

Paul-Crouzet, Jeanne. Nérée Beauchemin. *In her:* Poésie au Canada. Didier, 1946. p. 91–106. **6903**

After some generalities and biographical information, most of the article is devoted to a detailed analysis of "La cloche de Louisbourg." In fact, this analysis still stands up to scrutiny. The critic notes that, in this poem, Beauchemin reveals himself to be more of a musician than a painter, and she stresses his painstaking choice of words and phrases.

Jean-Marc Bernard
(Nos. 6904–6924)

SEYMOUR S. WEINER

Edition

Bernard, Jean Marc. Œuvres, suivies des Reliquiae de Raoul Monier. Le divan, 1923. 2 v. **6904**

Compiled and edited by Henri Clouard and Henri Martineau. V. I. includes *Sub tegmine fagi, Premiers poèmes, Vers inédits, La vallée du Rhône* [prose], and Monier's *Reliquiae.* Does not include certain early verse as well as *Vers de jeunesse* (Div 251:200–09, 1939) except for *Phaéton* (Œuvres, I, 137–38); *Savinien de Cyrano et Edmond Rostand* (Valence, Impr. Céas, 1903); *Feuillets de journal* (RU 76, no. 19:43–61, 1939). V. II includes *Petits sentiers de la poésie française, Symbolisme et classicisme, Etudes et portraits.* Includes the introduction to *Rondeaux choisis de Charles d'Orléans* (Sansot, 1913).

Biography

Bellet, Charles, monseigneur. Marc Bernard, Raoul Monier. BSASD 50, 197:404–28, Oct. 1916. *Also:* Notes sur Jean-Marc Bernard et Raoul Monier. Valence, Impr. Céas, 1916. **6905**

Includes excerpts from B.'s correspondence. Emphasizes B.'s religious faith and his conservatism.

Boncompain, Claude. Eloge du poète dauphinois Jean-Marc Bernard. BMAD 1:11–36, 1967. **6906**

Apparently a *reprise* of 1942 study published in *Journal de Valence*. Attempts to show relationship between B. and his generation. In a psychological portrait, stresses paternal as well as literary and intellectual influences.

Cheyre, Jean. Mon amitié avec Jean-Marc Bernard. Valence, Eds. du Centre départemental d'études de la Drôme, 1944. 63 p.   **6907**

Cheyre knew B. at Saint-Rambert d'Albon during publication of *Les guêpes*, 1909–12. Includes text of letters from Paris in 1911 and a facsimile. Furnishes details on publication in periodicals and the influence of poets. *Les guêpes* was a satirical periodical allied to *Revue critique des idées et des livres*, supportive of Maurras and the Action française. Founded by B., Louis du Charmeil, René Dumaine, Raoul Monier. Edited by B. Maurice de Noisay shared the responsibility from Paris; Henri Clouard became *secrétaire*.

Derème, Tristan. La bride et le cheval, ou Le souvenir de Jean-Marc Bernard. Tarbes, [Presses de Lesbordes], 1925. 30 p.   **6908**

Discusses reason versus sentiment: "un homme sincère et remué jusqu'au fond de l'âme, peut-il rester maître de soi?" Includes correspondence with B.

Fromentoux, Michel. Le pigeonnier; quarante années de décentralisation littéraire et artistique en Vivarais. Annonay, chez l'auteur, 1969. passim.   **6909**

Shows intellectual sympathies between B. and Charles Forot, who published an edition of B.'s *Haut-Vivarais d'hiver*.

Richard, Noël. Louis Le Cardonnel. Paris, Didier; Toulouse, Privat, 1946. passim, esp. p. 322–27.   **6910**

Discusses the profound influence Le Cardonnel exerted on B. as a priest and as a poet.

General Studies

Beaunier, André. Un de nos morts: Jean-Marc Bernard. RDM ser. 7:697–708, 1923.   **6911**

Reviewing *Œuvres,* finds "les commencements d'un grand poète." Iden-

tifies sources "de discipline et de méthode." Criticizes B.'s notions on classicism. Finds the adaptations from Omar Khayyam truly a "poème français."

Carco, Francis. A voix basse. A. Michel, 1938. p. 138–55.   **6912**

Reveals the personal experiences which account for the Berthe of B.'s poetry. The poetry has an "accent dont la sourde gravité déconcerte." Discusses B. again in *Francis Carco vous parle...* Denoël, 1953. p. 227–28, 233.

Fernandat, René (pseud. of Louis Genet). Un poète mort au champ d'honneur: Jean-Marc Bernard, dauphinois. RHeb 29, no. 5:92–109, May 1, 1920.   **6913**

Considers B. "un cœur impressionnable à l'excès." Compares B. to Desportes, M. Régnier, Parny; but Ronsard his real affinity. Analyzes *La mort de Narcisse*. Believes the *Rubaiyat* foreign to B.'s temperament.

———. Les premiers vers de Jean-Marc Bernard. Div 223:261–66, 1938.   **6914**

Sees in verses of Sept. 1899 and 1901 the influence of Musset and of Albert Giraud. B. tried writing German verse. B. partial to Van Lerberghe. Discusses B.'s temporary loss of religious faith.

Hommage à Jean-Marc Bernard. RevFéd 4:105–99, 1921.   **6915**

Special number. Poems, brief essays, reminiscences by Jacques Bainville, Charles Maurras, Louis Aguettant, Tristan Derème, René Fernandat, Charles Forot, Paul Garcin, Louis Pize, etc.

Marsan, Eugène. Jean-Marc Bernard. *In:* Anthologie des écrivains morts à la guerre 1914–1918, publiée par l'Association des écrivains combattants. V. IV. Amiens, Malfère, 1926. p. 80–83, 84–101.   **6916**

Praises the Attic quality of B.'s prose as well as his poetry. Offers a sketch of B. on holiday in Paris, but the country is really B.'s domain. Supplies a bibliography and a *florilège* of verse and prose.

———. Jean-Marc Bernard. *In his:* Instances. Prométhée, 1930. p. 262–74.   **6917**

Articles written in 1923 and 1925. Gives a physical description of B. Points up affinity between B. and Pierre Gilbert. His poems "cadencés de bout en bout d'une seule et pure coulée." The second half of the article is a sketch of B.'s life.

Martineau, Henri. Jean-Marc Bernard. EcrN 3, no. 23–24:33–53, 1919. **6918**

Two parts: I. *Son âme et sa vie;* II. *Son œuvre.* Reviews and criticizes B.'s poetic evolution. Toulet was right to see in him an Epicurean. The *Odelettes printanières* are "aussi belles que du Ronsard, aussi parfaites que du Banville." The second part emphasizes B. as a critic.

———. Jean-Marc Bernard et Paul Léautaud. Div 282:384–89, 1952. **6919**

On poem of admiration by B. to Léautaud regarding the latter's *Petit ami.*

Maurras, Charles. Jean-Marc Bernard. *In his:* Poètes. Le divan, 1924. p. 79–88. **6920**

Reprint of *Le poète savant,* RevFéd April 1921. "Ce poète écrit et discourt en vers comme dans sa langue naturelle et familière." Relates B. to poets of the Pléiade and to André Chénier.

Rambaud, Henri. Jean-Marc Bernard critique. RevFéd 20:57–68, 1920. **6921**

Praises B., "âme d'intelligent flâneur," for stating the "lois éternelles de l'art." Agrees with him that "le lyrisme inconsidéré s'oppose à l'œuvre d'art." Sees an affinity between "some" of Desportes and B.

Richard, Pierre. Jean-Marc Bernard, dauphinois. Valence, Galerie drômoise, 1926. 48 p. **6922**

Contains B.'s wartime correspondence and a section of "Opinions:" excerpts from critics. *See* 6923.

———. Une terre inspirée: La Drôme et ses poètes. Valence, Galerie drômoise, 1929. p. 75–119. **6923**

New version of 6922, but deletes paragraphs on the Camelots du roi, "admirable phalange nationale et école de discipline et de courage." Suppresses comments in 1926 publication on B.'s *Quelques essais.*

Toulet, Paul Jean. Jean-Marc Bernard. *In his:* Notes de littérature. Le Divan, 1926. p. 25–29. **6924**

Written in 1915. Discusses affinities between B. and Greek poets, Moréas, Ronsard. Finds that B. neglected the rhythm of Khayyam.

Jean de Boschère
(called Jean de Bosschère
before World War II)
(Nos. 6925–6948)

BENJAMIN COX ROUNTREE

Correspondence

Boschère, Jean de. Lettres de La Châtre (1939–1953) à André Lebois. Blainville-sur-Mer, L'amitié par le livre, 1969. 181 p. *Also:* Denoël, 1969. 176 p. **6925**

Lebois makes largest single publication of B.'s letters.

Reviews: M. Chapelan in FL 1223: 25, Oct. 27–Nov. 2, 1969; R. De Smedt in LR 25:85–86, 1971; E. Vandercammen in Marg 130:78–79, 1970.

Elskamp, Max, and Jean de Boschère. Correspondance: Max Elskamp & Jean de Boschère. Introd. et notes de Robert Guiette. Brussels, Palais des académies, 1963. 70 p. (Académie royale de langue et de littérature françaises) **6926**

Witness of B.'s most significant friendship before World War I.

Rountree, Benjamin. Joë Bousquet à Jean de Boschère: Correspondance 1933–49. RHL 71:281–89, 1971. **6927**

Witness of a fervent literary friendship.

Review: C. Berg in RBPH 52:231–32, 1974.

———. Lettres inédites d'Edmund Dulac à Jean de Boschère. AnT 9, fasc, 2:141–49, 1973. **6928**

Correspondence (1934–5) recalls B.'s continued contact with the Anglo-Saxon world.

———. Quelques lettres inédites à Jean de Boschère: Alain Borne, Alain Bosquet, André Gide, Franz Hellens, Max Jacob et Paul Valéry. RSH 144:617–26, 1971. **6929**

Some of the most significant unpublished correspondence in B.'s possession at his death.
Review: C. Berg in RBPH 52:231–32, 1974.

Rountree, Mary. Lettres inédites d'Audiberti à Jean de Boschère. AnT 9, fasc, 2:151–67, 1973.   **6930**
Lively collection of letters where Audiberti's harried life as a journalist contrasts with B.'s relative retirement.

Collected Articles

Hommage à Jean de Boschère. FrA 87:680–714, 1953.   **6931**
Special issue in commemoration of B.'s death.

Hommage à Jean de Boschère. JdP 3–4:1–32, 1946.   **6932**
Special issue for B.'s 65th birthday.

Jean de Boschère l'admirable. Essais par Luc Estang, Hélène Frémont, Charles-André Grouas, André Lebois. Au parchemin d'antan, Intercontinentale du livre, 1952. 207 p.   **6933**
Four essays of varying length on B. plus two unpublished poems by B. Estang stresses the Christian elements in *Héritiers de l'abîme*. Frémont's lucid study of the *Derniers "poèmes" de l'obscur* and the *Héritiers de l'abîme* is welcome in such cryptic poetry. Grouas does little to ease the task of entering into B.'s metaphysics. Lebois gives first-hand biographical details, copious quotations, especially from his prose, and B.'s spiritual relationships with other poets.
Reviews: P. Bay in QV 5:47–49, 1952; F. Hellens in DH Aug. 7, 1952; G. Lavaud in Renc July–Aug. 1952; J. Rousselot in Sex 9–10, 1952.

General

Berg, Christian. L'attente de Jean de Boschère. RBPH 49:842–55, 1971.   **6934**
Valuable study of B.'s religious quest, of B. the *révolté*, of his stance before the Absolute, and his attempt to make poetry the voice of mysticism.

Bousquet, Joë. Jean de Boschère ou la liberté d'une âme. *In:* Hommage à Jean de Boschère. *See* 6932. p. 7–10.   **6935**
Bousquet's introspective, seminal study on B.'s esthetics and metaphysics is, though difficult, one of the most significant of the 20 contributions included in this issue.

Desbruyères, Michel-François. L'évolution spirituelle de Jean de Boschère. FrA 76:638–45, 1952.   **6936**
Skilful summary of problem.

Eliot, T. S. Reflexions on contemporary poetry (Jean de Bosschère and Henry Monro). Eg 4:133–34, 1917.   **6937**
Brief, incisive comment on strength and weakness of B.'s poetry up until 1917.

Ennetières, Elisabeth d'. Nous, et les autres. Souvenirs d'un tiers de siècle avec Jean de Boschère. Aurillac, Eds. du centre, 1967. 103 p.   **6938**
The subtitle suggests the book's chief value.

Gros, Léon-Gabriel. Jean de Boschère. Une grande œuvre enfin accessible. CahS 301:486–91, 1950.   **6939**
Intelligent, stalwart defense of B.'s unique position as poet-prophet, prompted by recent publication of *Derniers "poèmes" de l'obscur* and *Héritiers de l'abîme*.

Guiette, Robert. Jean de Boschère l'enragé d'espoir. Cr 85:508–17, 1954.   **6940**
Useful general view of personality, life and poetry of B.

———. La voix de Jean de Boschère. *In:* Hommage à Jean de Boschère. *See* 6932. p. 16–17.   **6941**
Good essay, seeks to define B.'s poetry by linking it to Bosch and Anglo-Saxons.

Lannes, Roger. La poésie de Jean de Boschère. *In:* Hommage à Jean de Boschère. *See* 6932. p. 18–21.   **6942**
Judicious article on evolution of B.'s poetry.

Lanza del Vasto [Giuseppe Giovanni]. La conversion du révolté. *In:* Hommage à Jean de Boschère. *See* 6932. p. 10–12. 3–4:10–12, 1946.   **6943**
Illuminating essay on the *révolté*

generally and his proximity to religious faith.

Lebois, André. La rencontre au-dessus du Cloaque. *In:* Hommage à Jean de Boschère. *See* 6932. p. 29–32. **6944**
Emphasis on novels *Marthe et l'enragé* and *Satan l'obscur.*

———. T. S. Eliot, les imagistes et Jean de Boschère. RLC 26: 365–79, 1952. *Also in:* Lettres de la Châtre. *See* 6925. p. 159–78. **6945**
Author maintains B. had significant influence on Eliot and Imagists.

Putnam, Samuel. The world of Jean de Bosschère. London, Fortune press, 1932. 160 p. **6946**
Only single full-length book by professional critic on B.'s life and work. Publication date limits value since a very large number of B.'s significant writings were produced in the following twenty years.

Ridler, William. Jean de Boschère: A brief appraisal and a check-list of books in English with his illustrations. PrLib 4: 103–12, 1971. **6947**
Books illustrated by B. in England and U.S.

Vandercammen, Edmond. Jean de Boschère l'obscur et le Paria couronné. BARLLF 46:87–96, 1968. **6948**
Valuable on B.'s last volume of poetry. Stresses similarities to Blake, his exploration of the grotesque and the hallucinatory (the "baroque"), which link him with both the medieval world and 20th-century surrealism. B.'s blasphemy appears as a means of encountering the supernatural.

René-Guy Cadou
(Nos. 6949–6962)

E. BRUCE CARPENTER

Bouhier, Jean. Position poétique de l'école de Rochefort. Cahiers de l'école de Rochefort, hors série. Debresse, 1941. p. 1–7. **6949**
Valuable observations on the group of which C. was the leading member.

Brindeau, Serge. Le beau village de René-Guy Cadou. *In his:* Affinités, la matière et

l'esprit du poème: Pierre Reverdy, René-Guy Cadou, André Marissel. Les paragraphes littéraires de Paris, 1962. 29–42. **6950**
Brings out the significance for C.'s poetry of the basic, well-known themes: childhood, countryside, wife, feeling for eternity, religious feeling, importance of words. C.'s search for permanence and identity. The naturalness of C.'s art, deriving from his distrust of artifice and rhetoric.

Cadou, René-Guy. Mon enfance est à tout le monde. Jean Munier, 1969. 199 p. **6951**
Noteworthy reminiscences, especially for stylistic and thematic reasons. Valuable insights into the poet's sensitivity, which responded early to the major themes of his adult work.

———. Œuvres poétiques complètes. Ed. by Michel Manoll. Seghers, 1973. 2 v. **6952**
Extremely useful collected ed. Unscholarly bibliography. No notes. Definitely not a critical ed.

Dubacq, Jean. L'école de Rochefort. PoéI 2:51–64, 1970. **6953**
In his introduction to poems by the group the author evokes the spirit of Rochefort: liberty and independence of the "refugees" from Paris. Refutes the notion that the poets constituted a "school."

Gaucheron, Jacques. La poésie institutrice: le mythe du cancre. Eur 372:163–76, 1960. **6954**
Attacks myth of the poet-rebel, the perpetual troublemaker. Pleads for more serious treatment of C. than the common "témoignages." Considers C.'s work to be less escapist than a search for the essential.

Le Bras, Yvon. Notes d'esthétique en marge de Cadou. AnBret 72:421–36, 1965. **6955**
Attacks those commentators who merely paraphrase C.'s poetry without revealing its true significance. Claims that psychological interpretations misrepresent C. Important article.

Luzi, Mario. René-Guy Cadou. *In his:* Aspetti della generazione napoleonica ed altri saggi di letteratura francese. Parma, Guanda, 1956. p. 231–34.   **6956**

Places the Rochefort group in its contemporary position in French poetry, contrasting it in sentiment and experience with the surrealists. Despite his debt to Baudelaire and Apollinaire C. is an original and authentic voice.

Manoll, Michel. René-Guy Cadou. Une étude par Michel Manoll. Inédits, poèmes et textes choisis, bibliographie, portraits et documents. Pierre Seghers, 1954. 229 p. (Poètes d'aujourd'hui, 41) *Also (rev.):* René-Guy Cadou. Une étude de Michel Manoll. Avec un choix de textes... une chronologie bibliographique; René Cadou et son temps. Seghers, 1969. 191 p. (Poètes d'aujourd'hui, 41)   **6957**

Bibliography contains eds. of C.'s poetry as well as articles on the poet. Bibliographical information tantalizingly incomplete.

———. René-Guy Cadou ou le monde enchanté. Preu 38:33–35, 1954.   **6958**

Links C.'s use of the visible world and humble things to his consciousness of the universal. Good, pertinent article.

Maublanc, Jean-Daniel. René-Guy Cadou ou le surréalisme fantaisiste. AlmP 7:17–25, 1942.   **6959**

Inherent surrealism of the young C. Sees the poet pulled in two contradictory directions: the descriptive and the emotional. Advises him to go his own way. An early and perceptive appreciation of C.'s gifts.

René-Guy Cadou. L'herne, 1961. 96 p. (Les cahiers de l'herne, 1)   **6960**

Articles, poems and reminiscences in an issue marking tenth anniversary of C.'s death. Most contributions effusive and anecdotal. Those of Lorho, Toulouse, Manoll and Lacotte have most substance.

Rousselot, Jean. René-Guy Cadou et l'école de Rochefort. *In his:* Présences contemporaines, rencontres sur le chemin de la poésie. Debresse, 1958. p. 311–25.   **6961**

Important account of crucial relationship.

* With a contribution by Phyllis Zatlin Boring.

Thomas, Charles. René-Guy Cadou poète des pays de l'ouest. RBPoi 73:357–75, 1962.   **6962**

Studies the importance of C.'s fidelity to the countryside of his birth for the development of the major themes of his poetry. Good discussion of the poetry, not simply the poet.

Blaise Cendrars
(Nos. 6963–6994)

WALTER ALBERT*

General Studies: Books

Amaral, Aracy A. Blaise Cendrars no Brasil e os modernistas. São Paulo, Martins, 1970. 197 p.   **6963**

Detailed discussion of C.'s early influence on the Brazilian modernists, of his acquaintance with Brazilians in Paris in 1923, and of his trip to Brazil in 1924. Numerous photographs, drawings and other illustrations. Quotes frequently from the works of C. and the Brazilians to support statements on C.'s importance in Brazil. Particular emphasis on C.'s friendship with Tarsilia, Oswald de Andrade and Paulo Prado. Includes collection of C.'s poetry written in Brazil and four important articles by João Alves das Neves on aspects of Brazil in specific works of C. Useful bibliography. [PZB]

Blaise Cendrars vous parle... Ed. by Michel Manoll. Denoël, 1952. 268 p. (Entretiens de la radiodiffusion française)   **6964**

An afternote by C. describes how the thirteen original interviews were reduced to ten with whole sections recast by him for the published text. The informality of the format, the lack of dates, the absence of an index, and the willing suspension of disbelief by the interviewer make of this an exercise in C.'s self-promoting. Very entertaining.

Bozon-Scalzitti, Yvette. Blaise Cendrars et le symbolisme: de Moganni Nameh au Transsibérien. [Lettres modernes, 1972] 60 p. (ALM 137, 1972)   **6965**

A first-rate study of an important prose text of 1911. A comparative analysis of *Moganni Nameh* and Remy de

Gourmont's *Sixtine* is followed by an illuminating reading of *M.N.* in which the author finds the source of much of the imagery of *Pâques* and *Prose du transsibérien*. The discussion of the theme of *l'écriture* is particularly fine.

Buhler, Jean. Blaise Cendrars homme libre poète au cœur du monde. Bienne (Switzerland), Eds. du panorama, 1960. 156 p. (Célébrités suisses)   6966

Undocumented biography of C.'s life and work. Extravagantly overwritten. Interesting photographs from C.'s wife's collection suggest that Buhler had access to material that should have been presented in a more reliable form.

Dites-nous, monsieur Blaise Cendrars... réponses aux enquêtes littéraires de 1919 à 1957. Ed. by Hughes Richard. Lausanne, Eds. rencontre, 1969. 208 p.   6967

Includes the majority of C.'s playful, often ironic answers to literary questionnaires. Factual notes clarifying allusions in the text, and an uninformative introduction. List of sources and index of persons cited.

Lepage, Albert. Blaise Cendrars — étude critique, lettre préface de Georges Charles. Les écrivains réunis, 1926. 66 p.   6968

An early harbinger of things to come in writings on C. Discusses C.'s cosmopolitanism, the emotional coloration of his poetry, and his dynamism. Rails against the professional man of letters while idealizing and canonizing C. in the cosmic language so often used in talking about him.

Lévesque, Jacques-Henri. Blaise Cendrars, avec une anthologie des plus belles pages de Blaise Cendrars, une bibliographie et 6 planches hors texte. Nouvelle revue critique 1947. 286 p.   6969

Strikes a pose of unreserved approval of "la vie extraordinaire et déjà légendaire." This inflated panegyric is, unfortunately, the source for much of the subsequent writing on C. The bibliography is useful but incomplete.

Lovey, Jean-Claude. Situation de Blaise Cendrars. Neuchâtel, A la Baconnière, 1965. 358 p.   6970

This study is divided into three sections: biography, philosophy ("conscience") and style. The biographical

material uses no sources that have not been sufficiently — and tediously — exploited by other critics. The attempt to make of C. a proto-Existentialist and and archetypal Dadaist is based on vaguely supported generalizations by Lovey and sparse quotes from C.'s work. The stylistic discussion consists of a random series of topics like C. and simultaneity and C. and the cinema in which no solid theoretical or factual thesis is presented. No index. Incomplete bibliography of primary and secondary sources.

Reviews: E. Bastiaenen in LR 22: 294–96, 1968; R. Carrier in EF 3:115–21, 1967; P. Pettiaux in LetN 139–51, Oct.-Nov. 1966.

Parrot, Louis. Blaise Cendrars. Une étude par Louis Parrot, un choix de poèmes et de textes, une bibliographie établie par J.-H. Lévesque. Seghers, 1948. 238 p. (Poètes d'aujourd'hui, 11)   6971

The most sober of the early studies of the life and work, but flawed by the usual tendency to see the life through the unverified prism of the poetry and prose. The comments on the prose works are less oriented toward a hagiographic reading and the conclusion makes some sketchy but sensible points about C.'s use of language.

Poupon, Marc. Apollinaire et Cendrars. [Lettres nouvelles, 1969] 66 p. (ALM 103)   6972

Focuses on 1912 and, on the basis of the "known" evidence, tries to set the date of the first meeting in May. The context is fuzzy and Poupon brings no new insights to points that have been extensively discussed elsewhere. In an appendix, added after the publication of *Inédits secrets*, he finds this position no longer tenable, situates the "véritable premier contact" at the end of the summer and concludes that Apollinaire's poetic evolution in 1912 could only have been precipitated by C., not initiated by him. As Poupon says, an exhaustive study of the relationship remains to be done.

Rousselot, Jean. Blaise Cendrars. Eds. universitaires, 1955. 124 p. (Témoins du XXᵉ siècle)   6973

Rousselot describes C. as a rhapsodist and this is also an apt description of Rousselot's approach to his subject. Sees the life as C.'s work, the work as not literature but something more dynamic and vital. Mixture of biography and quotes — often quite long ones — from C.'s poetry and prose. C. as fabulist, mystic, adventurer and sensualist. Brief, schematic chronology of C.'s life and a modest bibliography of primary works.

t'Serstevens, A. L'homme que fut Blaise Cendrars. Denoël, 1972. 234 p.   6974

In this "histoire d'une amitié," it is t'Serstevens who comes through the more vividly. He attempts to correct some of the factual errors in published biographies of C., but the style is largely, and affectionately, impressionistic. The most provocative pages are those on C.'s relationship with Raymone and there are tantalizing selections from a correspondence with C. which dates back to 1913.

Review: H. Richard in QL 147:15–16, Sept. 1–15, 1972.

General Studies: Articles

Albert, Walter. Blaise Cendrars: a temporal perspective. TSLL 4:321–29, 1962.   6975

Discusses C. and the poetry of romanticism and surrealism, insisting upon the ways in which his poetics both relates to, and is distinct from, those two movements. Conclusion is unjust in its limiting of C.'s richness and variety of invention to a single "success" in *Prose du transsibérien.* Most of material is included in his *Blaise Cendrars: selected writings.*

————. Introduction. *In:* Blaise Cendrars: selected writings. New directions, 1966. p. 1–44.   6976

Situates C.'s life and writings for the non-specialist reader but also studies the poetry and prose in some detail. The editor examines verse techniques in *Prose du transsibérien* and in *Le Panama,* and treats the novels and chronicles as extensions and elaborations of principles and techniques developed in the poetry "years" (1910–1924).

Reviews: J. Houston in SoR 6:561–65, 1970; F. Busi in FR 40:850–51, 1967.

Barret, Andrée. Blaise Cendrars et l'esprit nouveau. Eur 421–22:137–46, 1964. 6977

C. celebrated the humanitarian impulses of the Russian revolution in its early stages but eventually, according to Barret, lost himself in an individualism which had nothing to do with "le commun de l'humanité." A welcome—but limited—examination of C.'s political sympathies.

Blaise Cendrars. MerF 345, no. 1185, May 1962. 208 p.   6978

Special issue devoted to C. Composed, for the most part, of commentaries on C.'s life by people who know him more or less well. Makes little effort to separate the life from the legend and presents a mass of raw, often casual material as artless as C. is artful.

Carrier, Roch. Blaise Cendrars: un début dans la vie. EF 2:163–89, 1966.   6979

A biography of C. through World War I, based on his own "testimony" in his works and on a few exterior, but sparse sources. The presentation is not unreasonable but adds nothing to readily accessible material.

Caws, Mary Ann. Blaise Cendrars: a cinema of poetry. KRQ 17:345–55, 1970. *Also in her:* The inner theatre of recent French poetry. Princeton univ. press, 1972. p. 26–51.   6980

A chaotic discussion of C. as adventurer/traveler and the ways in which he transcribes in his work the material of his real and imaginary wanderings. C.'s language is described as "words in motion" and the subjects of simultaneity and cinematic language are briefly touched on.

Cendrars, Blaise. Panama ou la véritable histoire de mes sept oncles. Dialogue de Raymone et de Blaise Cendrars. MerF 345:11–22, 1962.   6981

Transcript of a radio broadcast. Raymone questions the reality of the seven uncles while C. appears to affirm their historical fact. Important record of a mythomaniac at bay.

Dumay, Raymond. Blaise Cendrars à Port-Enfance. RDM n.s. 6:633–44, 1970. 6982

More properly, "Raymond Dumay à

Port-Enfance." Oblique consideration of writer as child and fabulist.

————. De Sauser à Cendrars. RDM n.s. 3:523–37, 1969.   6983

Under the provocative title lurks another assessment of the Apollinaire-Cendrars relationship which attempts to establish a probable first meeting of the two poets quite late in 1912. Finds little reliable evidence that Apollinaire had read *Pâques* at the time of the composition of *Zone*.

Eulalio, Alexandre. L'aventure brésilienne de Blaise Cendrars. EPB 5:19–55, 1969.   6984

Largely biographical, this essay also suggests ways in which C.'s acquaintance with contemporary Brazilian writers may have influenced his poetry and prose. Very rich in accurate factual information with occasional brief stylistic comments.

Fouchet, Max-Pol. Un brahmane imprévu. *In his:* Les appels. Mercure de France, 1967. p. 45–49.   6985

A brief and moving statement of the writer as fabulist and composer of "documents imaginaires, où l'image l'emporte sur le réel sans le détruire." The best of the concise, personal summations of C.'s work.

Goffin, Robert. Blaise Cendrars et son influence. *In his:* Entrer en poésie. Gand, A l'enseigne du chat qui pêche, 1948. p. 159–70.   6986

Draws on meeting with C. in Brussels to capture some of the flavor of the writer's presence. Substantial comparison of *Zone* and *Pâques* to show striking similarities in tone and image. Earliest extensive treatment of a relationship about which there are still many unresolved questions.

Goldenstein, Jean-Pierre. Blaise Cendrars, Indédits secrets. Présentation de Miriam Cendrars. RLM 276–79:149–60, 1972.   6987

A judicious examination of the references in *Inédits secrets* which concern the Cendrars-Apollinaire relationship. Notes that the choice of documents here is selective and expresses the hope that Miriam C. may someday publish the material in her possession in a more complete form.

Manoll, Michel. Blaise Cendrars. Trans. by William Brandon. *In:* Writers at work. The Paris review interviews, third series. Ed. by George Plimpton. The Viking press, 1967. p. 31–56.   6988

An effective condensation and translation of the Manoll-conducted interviews. The condensation makes of C. a less garrulous and leaner figure. One can understand how Alfred Kazin, in his introduction to this series, can speak of the "extraordinary impression [this makes] on us who are saturated in literature...." This comment also underscores the difficulty C. continues to have to be defined as a writer rather than as a legend.

Miller, Henry. Blaise Cendrars. *In his:* The books in my life. London, Peter Owen, 1952. p. 58–80.   6989

A lyrical, loving tribute to C. by a writer who knew him in the Paris of the 30's. The tribute, however, is a reading of the books rather than of the life. Soft where C. is tough, the panegyric is, finally, cloying.

Pettiaux, Paul. Cendrars défiguré. LetN 133–51, Oct.-Nov. 1966.   6990

Essay-review of Lovey's *Situation de Blaise Cendrars*. Pettiaux is devastating in his detailed recounting of Lovey's unattributed borrowings from other critics, inaccurate bibliographical and biographical references, and biased, prejudicial attitudes.

Richard, Hughes. Cendrars ou la volonté du mythe. LetN 105–14, Dec. 1969–Jan. 1970.   6991

Referring to documents which he claims to have in his possession, Richard corrects a number of inaccuracies in *Vol à voile* which he attributes to C.'s faulty memory. Suggests that C. operated on the principle of an evolving rather than a static biographical past.

Tosi, Guy. En relisant quelques lettres de Blaise Cendrars. Let 25:16–25, 1961.   6992

Selected, edited letters from a correspondence Tosi maintained with C. from 1945–52 as "directeur littéraire des Editions Denoël." Of particular interest is a long letter in which C. talks about his lengthy fascination with the Eiffel Tower and its designer.

Vigneras, L. A. Blaise Cendrars. FR 14:311–18, 1941.   **6993**
Cendrars and the "new Romanticism of travel, adventure and action." Cursory overview of the work.

Warnier, Raymond. A propos de Blaise Cendrars. ArcR 74:617–59, 1965. **6994**
Reviews problems of establishing a valid and credible biography of C. Much of the succeeding discussion is concerned with C. and Apollinaire. Warnier relies heavily on shaky evidence to claim a relationship beginning as early as 1910. A *Note d'orientation bibliographique* is the most accurate and useful part of the study. Warnier corrects some errors in the Lévesque bibliography of 1947 and updates it to 1965.

René Chopin
(Nos. 6995–6997)

JACQUES COTNAM

Dugas, Marcel. René Chopin. *In his: Apologies.* Montreal, Paradis-Vincent, 1919. p. 89–110.   **6995**
Dugas writes that the author of *Le cœur en exil* is "a consummate artist, for whom beauty is a religion." He is not a poet for the masses, and Dugas praises him for it. Chopin exults in life. He points the way; keeping an individual accent, he knows how to use the riches of the great poetic traditions of the past. Article highly recommended.

Marcotte, Gilles. Poètes artistes: Paul Morin et René Chopin. *In his: Une littérature qui se fait.* Montreal, HMH, 1962. p. 107–16.   **6996**
First half of article devoted to Morin. Marcotte thinks that C. can be distinguished from Paul Morin by the force, the violence, the severity, and the coldness of his verse, which is also characterized by a sense of impending doom. Though both Morin and C. are poets of alienation and exile, these dimensions are transformed into a love of the exotic with Morin, whereas with

C. they are internalized and become part of the poet's *vie intérieure.*

Paul-Crouzet, Jeanne. René Chopin. *In her: Poésie au Canada.* Didier, 1946. p. 232–48.   **6997**
Along with Paul Morin, C. belongs to the group known in Canada as "artists of form." Whereas Morin finds themes for his poetry in faraway places, C., being of a more sedentary character, seeks his inspiration in Canadian sources. C. is "a voice crying out in revolt against the uncomprehending masses," a trait which would tend to put him into the same league as Nelligan, Gill, Ferland and, "in an ironical sense," as Morin himself.

Charles-Albert Cingria
(Nos. 6998–7009)

PIERRE-OLIVIER WALZER

Edition & Correspondence

Cingria, Charles-Albert. Correspondance générale. Préf. de P. O. Walzer. Lausanne, Eds. de l'âge d'homme, 1975–   **6998**
Two volumes published so far; will make ultimately five volumes. A remarkable conversationalist, C. displays verve and wit in the written conversation of these letters (to his Swiss friends, Ramuz, Bovy, Auberjonois, Budry, or to his French friends, Claudel, Cocteau, Jacob, Paulhan) assembled here for the first time. Only the *Vingt-cinq lettres à Adrien Bovy* (Lausanne, Eds. de l'âge d'homme, 1967) have appeared previously.

———. Œuvres complètes. Préf. de Jean Paulhan. Lausanne, Eds. de l'âge d'homme, 1967–69. 10 v.   **6999**
This edition brings together for the first time a work previously dispersed in various limited eds. and in a large number of periodicals.
Reviews: G. Anex in JdG Jan. 24–25, 1970; M. Bernard in MagL 27:30–31, 1969; C.-M. Cluny in LetF 1299:9, Sept. 10–22, 1969; A. Desponds in FALau Dec. 14, 1967; E. Dune in QL 45:14–15, Feb. 15–19, 1968; J.-F. Revel in Exp 865:47, Jan. 15–21, 1968.

Special Numbers

Charles-Albert Cingria 1883–1954. RdBL
91, no. 37–73, 1966.   **7000**
Studies by J. Chessex, P.-A. Tâche,
Bernard Christoff. Personal attestations
and reminiscences by A. Pieyre de
Mandiargues, Jean Follain, Georges
Borgeaud, Dick Aeschlimann, P. O.
Walzer, Roger Nordmann, Isabelle and
Robert Melley-Cingria, Gilbert Guisan.
Interesting collection of personal testi-
monies emanating for the most part
from the writer's personal friends.

Couronne de Charles-Albert Cingria. NRF
27:427–84, 1955.   **7001**
Special section devoted to C. Tributes
by P. Claudel, Igor Stravinsky, Jean
Cocteau, Marcel Jouhandeau, Jean
Follain; studies and personal testimony
by André Pieyre de Mandiargues, François Michel, Etiemble, Jean Starobinski, Georges Borgeaud, F. Auberjonois,
Constant Rey-Millet, Pierre Guéguen,
A.-J. Bataillard, Henri Noverraz. Important collection if only because of
the significance of the contributors.

General Studies

Berchtold, Alfred. C.-A. Cingria. *In his:*
La Suisse romande au cap du XXᵉ siècle,
portrait littéraire et moral. Lausanne,
Payot, 1963. p. 867–81.   **7002**
Emphasizes the Swiss-ness of the
writer, the originality of his concept
of musical evolution, and his concept
of history which leads the author to
emphasize the perenniality of phenomena and to prefer fabulous heroes.
Above all, a constantly marveling observer. A mystic as well as a jokester
prone to laugh.

Chessex, Jacques. Charles-Albert Cingria.
Etude, choix de textes et bibliographie
par Jacques Chessex. Dessins, portraits,
fac-similés. Seghers, 1967. 191 p. (Poètes
d'aujourd'hui, 170)   **7003**
General study of a little known Swiss
writer, a kind of wandering velocipedist
passionate about musicology and medieval history, influenced by Maurras and
Chesterton who accentuated his taste
for Roman and Christian Latinity. A
rapid study but which opens up es-

sential perspectives (the scholarly contribution is reduced to one note).
Reviews: G. Anex in JdG Nov. 25–
26, 1967; M. Bernard in MagL 27:
March 30–31, 1969.

Christoff, Bernard. La révolte de Cingria.
RdBL 91, no. 3:28–38, 1966.   **7004**
The fragmentation and the dispersal
of C.'s work prove nothing with respect
to its unity. On the contrary they are
what expresses the intention of the
text to devote itself to a single purpose:
the impossible "représentation totale et
exhaustive du monde." This work is
not gratuitous; it fosters a deep revolt.

Gilliard, Edmond. Présentation des lau-
réats—C.-A. Cingria et P. Beausire—du
Prix Rambert 1935. FCdZ 577–80, July–
Aug. 1935.   **7005**
If he did not exist, C. should be
invented in the interests of liberty. In
this country, "où il y a tant de ti-
midités, de gêne d'expression, de super-
stition universitaire," the C. brothers
have lavished treasures of generous
imprudence, they have carved out
"trous d'air" and authorized the voluptuousness of escape.

Magny, Olivier de. Charles-Albert Cingria
et le style. MNP 99:88–93, 1956.   **7006**
His golden rule can be defined as an
authoritarian spontaneity. He writes
through desire and for the pleasure of
writing, to communicate to us his
pleasure and his joy of feeling, seeing
and knowing. The style galvanizes itself
into a tension which reminds one, in
the plastic domain, of baroque mannerism.

Pieyre de Mandiargues, André. D'écureuils
et de foudre. *In:* Couronne de C.-A.
Cingria. *See* 7001. p. 433–39. *Also in his:*
Le belvédère. Grasset, 1958. p. 69–80.
                7007
Article presenting an unknown writer.
Includes a bibliography of all the unavailable *plaquettes.* Emphasizes the
qualities of the conversationalist, but
who must have had to "causer pour
vivre, misérablement par ailleurs," and
especially of the stylist whose art par-
takes of the romanesque and of the
baroque, of the primitive as well as of
the precious. His devices—original
constructions, inversions, ruptures, pho-

netic discoveries, accumulation of adjectives, etc.—should be the subject of detailed study. Relates him to Chirico, Raymond Roussel, Max Jacob, Apollinaire, Aragon.

Stelling-Michaud, Sven. Préface. *In:* Cingria, Charles-Albert. La civilisation de Saint-Gall. Lausanne, Payot, 1929. p. 9–14.   **7008**

C. is not what one would call an "auteur gai," for he is too emotional. He knows that nothing lasts, and he consoles himself by a mad abandonment to life. C. lives for music, which was so to speak his only nourishment.

Thée, Pierre. Hommage à Charles-Albert Cingria. TrG Feb. 15–16, 1958.   **7009**

In C. one finds an irresistible talker, a modern *trouvère,* an old scholiast somewhat monk-like and very childish, making entirely of life "un plain-chant de routes, de blé, de chevaux et de rivières." The pages of this author wearing as a halo an "air de vaudrouille" conceal a miracle of poetry in which each word stands out as an image and in which are joined science, wisdom, drollery, fraternity and religion.

Louis Dantin
(Nos. 7010–7015)

JACQUES COTNAM

Bastien, Hermas. Louis Dantin. *In his:* Ces écrivains qui nous habitent. Montreal, Beauchemin, 1969. p. 111–23.   **7010**

Useful for information on "unhappy" life of this poet.

Garon, Yves. Louis Dantin. CahACF 7:105–16, 1963.   **7011**

Overview of D.'s life and works. Characterizes the salient traits of D.'s poetry and stresses his role as a literary critic.

———. Louis Dantin et la critique intime. RUL 16:421–32, 521–35, 1962.   **7012**

Important biographical article emphasizing D.'s dominant role when consulted by other writers. First article treats relations with Emile Nelligan, Germain Beaulieu, Alphonse Beauregard and Robert Choquette. Second article

treats Rosaire Dion, who benefited the most from his "critique préventive," and Alfred Desrochers with whom D. exchanged an important correspondence.

Marion, Séraphin. Le coffret de Crusoe. *In his:* Sur les pas de nos littérateurs. Montreal, Albert Lévesque, 1933. p. 23–41.   **7013**

Although the variety of artifacts in *Le coffret de Crusoe* does not hold much appeal for this critic, he recognizes that D. is a skilled versifier, apt to borrow techniques from various literary schools. He is at his best when he cultivates symbolism.

———. La vie en rêve. *In his:* Sur les pas de nos littérateurs. Montreal, Albert Lévesque, 1933. p. 9–22.   **7014**

Considers D. to be a master of style and esthetics, a writer whose life was wholly devoted to the cult of beauty. Nevertheless, such immoderate praise does not blind Marion to a certain number of flaws which, in his opinion, seriously mar *La vie en rêve.* Though the critic affirms that this collection of short stories is one of the best French Canada has produced, he finds them far-fetched at times and draws the reader's attention to a few cases of faulty usage. Interesting for remarks on literary realism and use of French-Canadian language.

Pelletier, Albert. Poètes de l'Amérique française. *In his:* Carquois. Montreal, Librairie d'action canadienne-française, 1931. p. 75–93. *And:* Gloses critiques. *In his:* Egrappages. Montreal, Albert Lévesque, 1933. p. 82–93.   **7015**

Although he recognizes D. as one of the finest Canadian poets of the period, Pelletier, in these two separate articles, emphasizes the shortcomings of D.'s poetry.

Lucie Delarue-Mardrus
(Nos. 7016–7033)

CLAUDE SENNINGER

Bonnefon, Jean de. Lucie Delarue-Mardrus. *In his:* La corbeille de roses ou les dames de lettres. De Bouville, 1909. p. 91–97.   **7016**

Charming evocation of the poet and her work.

Clifford-Barney, Natalie. Les Mardrus. *In her:* Souvenirs indiscrets. Flammarion, 1960. p. 146–85.   **7017**
Book of biographical interest.

———. Lucie Delarue-Mardrus, présidente. *In her:* Aventures de l'esprit. Emile-Paul, 1929. p. 186–90.   **7018**
Additional details about Lucie's life.

Delarue-Mardrus, Lucie. Mes mémoires. Gallimard, 1938. 328 p.   **7019**
There is a bit of everything in this book which could be called "Histoire d'une âme."

Descaves, Pierre. Lucie Delarue-Mardrus. *In his:* Visites à mes fantômes. Denoël, 1949. p. 111–29.   **7020**
Vivid sketches of Lucie's life.

Ernest-Charles, J. Lucie Delarue-Mardrus. *In his:* Les samedis littéraires. 4ᵉ série. E. Sansot, 1905. p. 227–40.   **7021**
Claims that the woman writer does nothing but imitate and in this respect Lucie is very much a woman!

Flat, Paul. Nos femmes de lettres. Madame Lucie Delarue-Mardrus. RBPL 393–400, Sept. 26, 1908.   **7022**
Enormous article, not too well constructed. The author examines the interaction woman/poet within D.-M.'s work.

———. Madame Lucie Delarue-Mardrus. *In his:* Nos femmes de lettres. Perrin, 1909. p. 57–97.   **7023**
Excellent account of Lucie's talent which is "precise but limited."

Harry, Myriam. Mon amie Lucie Delarue-Mardrus. Ariane, 1946. 210 p.   **7024**
Enlightening account of Lucie's life and works. Jules Lemaître, according to the author, held in great respect *Le roman comme tout le monde* which he finds "a less well written *Madame Bovary*."

Leroy, Paul. Lucie Delarue-Mardrus. *In his:* Muses de France. Rouen, Maugard, 1943. p. 15–39.   **7025**

Insists on the multiplicity of Lucie's talent: "She switched from poetry to novel, from the song to the lecture, from diary to sculpture."

———. Lucie Delarue-Mardrus. *In his:* Femmes d'aujourd'hui. Rouen, Maugard, 1936. p. 111–80.   **7026**
Vivid study of Lucie's life, personality and works.

Maurras, Charles. Madame Lucie Delarue-Mardrus. *In his:* L'avenir de l'intelligence. Fontemoing, 1905. p. 202–19.   **7027**
Excellent study of the writers who have influenced Lucie's works. Maurras compares her state of mind to that of a rebellious Petrus Borel at the dawn of romanticism.

Maury, Lucien. Lucie Delarue-Mardrus. *In his:* Figures littéraires. Ecrivains français et étrangers. Perrin, 1911. p. 297–308.   **7028**
Insists on Lucie's healthy animality, her accuracy and her frankness.

Montesquiou, Robert de. Madame Delarue-Mardrus. *In his:* Professionnelles beautés. F. Juven, 1905. p. 51–67.   **7029**
Lucie is the bard of the sea, of the storms and of the calm. Montesquiou discusses her realism and delicacy.

Savigny-Vesco, Marguerite. Une voix d'outre-tombe; les messages secrets de Lucie Delarue-Mardrus. Rol 539–43:April 28, May 5, May 19, May 26, 1955.   **7030**
Biobibliography of D. M. in 4 short articles.

Sirieyx de Villers. Lucie Delarue-Mardrus. *In his:* Biographie-critique. V. 3. R. Chiberre, 1923. p. 458–63.   **7031**
Good critical biography. Bird's-eye view of Lucie's work as a poet and as a novelist.

Souday, Paul. Six poèmes d'Edgar Allan Poë. Temps. Dec. 8, 1922.   **7032**
D.-M.'s translation is excellent. It is in fact a transposition more than a translation.

van Bever, Ad. Lucie Delarue-Mardrus. *In his:* Les poètes du terroir. V. 2. Delagrave, 1923. p. 541–44.   **7033**
Brief biography and analysis of Lucie's original talent.

Tristan Derème
(pseud. of Philippe Huc)
(Nos. 7034–7059)

SEYMOUR S. WEINER

Special Numbers

Hommage à François de Curel et Tristan Derème. Cap spec. no., March 1924.   **7034**

Eulogizes D.'s wit and grace, his participation in public lectures and inclusion in the *matinées poétiques* of the Comédie-Française. Philippe Chabaneix writes on D. and *La verdure dorée.*

Hommage à Tristan Derème. Cerf 32:3–14, 1960.   **7035**

Whole number on D. Contributions by Dussane, Maurice Rat, Tristan Klingsor (Leclère), Philippe Chabaneix. See individual entries.

Le souvenir de Tristan Derème. Div. 244:265–312, 1942.   **7036**

Number devoted to D. a year after his death.

Biography

Catala, Jules André. Le bibliophile et le poète: trente-cinq lettres de Louis Barthou à Tristan Derème (1926–1934). BSBG 35, no. 83:1–52, 1966.   **7037**

Barthou, born at Oloron, collected mss. and eds. of D. Facsimiles of texts. Catala explains circumstances— e.g., literary prizes and honors. Appendix includes *Dédicaces* and other texts.

———. Onze lettres de Francis Jammes à Tristan Derème. BSBG 31, no. 75–76:9–30, 1962.   **7038**

These letters written between 1921 and 1935. Introduction and notes by Catala.

Fidus. Silhouettes contemporaines. Tristan Derème. RDM ser. 8, no. 46:467–70, 1938.   **7039**

A physical and social portrait of D. when he was awarded the Grand Prize for Literature of the French Academy.

Martin du Gard, Maurice. Pages de journal. EPar 90:61–71 [65–66], 1952.   **7040**

Text, "Derème, en passant," dated Oct. 1921. Useful for perspective on their relations, since D. wrote in *Les nouvelles littéraires.*

Mieille, Paul. Les débuts provinciaux de Tristan Derème, 1911–1912. GraR 34:420–34, 1930. *Also:* Tristan Derème à vingt ans (Tarbes, 1911–1912). Tarbes, Impr. Lesbordes, 1930. 11 p.   **7041**

On D. at Pyrénées-Océan, where he published poetry and "silhouettes pyrénéennes." Gives excerpts from D.'s articles on Laforgue, Gautier, de Mun.

Planes, Louis Georges. Tristan Derème, poète élégiaque. AAB ser. 4, no. 17:152–72, 1961. *Also in:* BouF 42, n.s. 38:40–45, 1962.   **7042**

Met D. at Oloron in 1928. Sketches D.'s career.

Rat, Maurice. En rêvant à Tristan Derème. *In:* Hommage à Tristan Derème. *See* 7035. p. 5–9.   **7043**

Friendship with D., "le prince débonnaire de l'élégie souriante et de la plus authentique et divine fantaisie," dates from 1924. D. a master of the resources and mechanics of verse.

General Studies

Beaunier, André. Les poètes fantaisistes. M. Tristan Derème et ses amis. RDM ser. 7, no. 23:218–29, 1924.   **7044**

The *fantaisistes* have a common understanding of life, similar tastes in poetry. D., who is unjust to romanticism, has abundance and variety. D. influenced by Laforgue. *Contre-assonance* not a license, but rather an additional restraint.

Carco, Francis. Tristan Derème. DouB 5:283–95, 1914.   **7045**

Praises D. for the use of precise detail and for the "authenticity" of his poetry.

———. Ombres vivantes. Ferenczi, 1948. p. 129–52.   **7046**

Discusses portraits of D.: "au fond, c'était un tendre et qui se défendit de l'être." Prefers *La verdure dorée* to the greater perfection of his later verse.

Mentions trial of Alice (girl friend of D.) for murder, and D.'s relations with Mme de Noailles. See also Carco's *A voix basse* (A. Michel, 1938), p. 131–37.

Décaudin, Michel. Etudes sur la poésie française contemporaine. IL 14:197–203, 1962.   **7047**

D. mentioned briefly among *fantaisistes,* "aux confins de la tradition néoclassique et d'une certaine poésie moderne." D.'s work assumed form of "réflexions paradoxales sur la poésie."

Dubech, Lucien. Les chefs de file de la jeune génération. Plon, 1925. p. 99–110.
                                                     7048
There is no "école fantaisiste." But the *fantaisistes* respect the laws of versification; they also have *pudeur.* D. born at Tarbes [sic]; one of the best poets of his day, but "s'abaisse trop souvent à n'être qu'un poète facétieux."

Duclos, Henri. Tristan Derème. FaV 8:71–79, 1925.   **7049**
Whole number (128 p.) on the *poètes fantaisistes.* "On ne comprendrait rien à sa poésie si l'on ne connaissait pas la mentalité et le cœur du Gascon." Prince of the imaginative, D. excels in awakening in us "le désir des évasions."

Gauchez, Maurice. Romantiques d'aujourd'hui. Essais consacrés à René Arcos... Tristan Derème... Brussels, Eds. de la renaissance d'Occident, 1924. p. 121–30.
                                                     7050
Gauchez analyzes aspects of *La verdure dorée.* D. likes "apostrophes, hypotyposes et prosopopées," and reminds him of Musset. Gauchez criticizes D.'s verbal subtleties.

Georlette, René. Tristan Derème, prince de la fantaisie. FO 13:27–33, 1950. **7051**
Popular survey of D.'s wit and versatility.

Giron, Robert. Tristan Derème. RDM ser. 8, no. 68:92–98. 1942.   **7052**
Discusses D.'s bitterness and pessimism during World War II. His usual philosophy "douce-amère." Relates D. to Horace, Ovid, Catullus, La Fontaine. Extraordinarily erudite, and had drafted 300 pages of a "Traité de l'harmonie des vers français."

Martineau, Henri. Tristan Derème. Avec une préface de Pol Neveux, un portrait et un essai de bibliographie. Le divan, 1927. 84 p.   **7053**
Neveux notes: "Notre poète béarnais est arrivé à posséder l'intuition parfaite de l'esprit et du génie champenois [i.e., La Fontaine]." Martineau discusses irony in D., an Epicurean. D. has "le don inné de la mesure," but Martineau objects to his "rimes méridionales."

———. Tristan Derème et la poésie. Div 258:313–17, 1946.   **7054**
Introduction to the posthumously published *De l'harmonie des vers français* (nos. 258–260, p. 318–23, 343–50, 445–50).

Parvillez, Alphonse de. Avec Tristan Derème au pays des merveilles. Et 236:92–99, 1938.   **7055**
Supplies bibliographical details on D.'s early writings. Emphasizes D.'s "arc-en-ciel" (ensemble of writings), in which fantasy complements reality.

Rat, Maurice. De Philippe Huc à Tristan Derème. Div 157:97–109, 1930.   **7056**
Philippe Huc is D.'s civil name. Rat traces the development of D.'s themes and technical skill.

———. Grammairiens et amateurs de beau langage: Tristan Derème. VL 131:62–66, 1963.   **7057**
D. a fine stylist, with a keen sensitivity to niceties of expression. A classicist, he was a philologist (in the broad sense).

Rousseaux, André. M. Tristan Derème et ses élégies. RU 31:747–52, 1927. **7058**
D. uses pseudonyms to protect his *pudeur.* His irony is an excessive reaction to the excesses of romanticism. D. a virtuoso, with a profound knowledge of rhythm and rhyme. Praises *Le livre de Clymène.*

Weiner, Seymour S. A round Derème. PCP 4:65–69, 1969.   **7059**
Concerns primarily D.'s early years with *Pyrénées-et-Océan,* and contributions to *Le cri de Toulouse* and to *Burdigala.* Discusses his political writings in *Les Pyrénées* and associates him with *Action française* and conservatism.

Alfred Desrochers
(Nos. 7060–7063)

JACQUES COTNAM

Paul-Crouzet, Jeanne. Alfred Desrochers. *In her:* Poésie au Canada. Didier, 1946. p. 313–37.   **7060**

After characterizing the high points of D.'s literary career, the critic mentions the works most likely to have influenced his development and outlook and then proceeds to a detailed analysis of the poem "Je suis un fils déchu," a study well worth reading.

Pelletier, Albert. L'offrande aux vierges folles et A l'ombre de l'Orford. *In his:* Carquois. Montreal, Librairie d'action canadienne-française, 1931. p. 135–54.   **7061**

A highly flattering critique of the poet's two published volumes in which Pelletier recognizes D. for an authentically French-Canadian poet. He emphasizes the "lively, original and essentially personal nature" of this poet's inspiration. In any anthology, he concludes, D. could easily take his place alongside the best of contemporary French poets.

————. Paragraphes. *In his:* Egrappages. Montreal, Albert Lévesque, 1933. p. 114–22.   **7062**

Far from being a work of impressionistic criticism, as its author claims, *Paragraphes* is, in Pelletier's opinion, nothing less than the exposé of an unconsciously dogmatic style of literary criticism. Here and there, Pelletier cannot resist taking swipes at Quebec's educational system.

Pelletier, Jacques. Alfred Desrochers, critique. VIP 7:121–36, 1973.   **7063**

Although he has published but one critical work, D. should occupy an important place, according to Pelletier, in the history of Quebec's ideological development. What distinguishes D. from his contemporaries, the author suggests, is the originality of his critical reflections, whether they bear on the concept of literary criticism itself, on the socio-historical conditioning of art, or on the situation of French-Canadian literature in 1930.

Léon-Paul Fargue
(Nos. 7064–7159)

LOUISE RYPKO SCHUB

Bibliography

Schub, Louise Rypko. Bibliographie. *In her:* Léon-Paul Fargue. *See* 7139. p. 203–59.   **7064**

An exhaustive bibliography listing all of F.'s published works in books and periodicals. Books and articles on F., other references to F., and other works and articles cited.

Talvart, Hector, and Joseph Place. Léon-Paul Fargue. *In their:* Bibliographie des auteurs modernes de langue française (1801–1934). V. 5. Horizons de France, 1935. p. 314–15.   **7065**

The "notice biographique" which summarily situates F. among major poets of his time, is followed by an adequate bibliography of F.'s own works (with a few misprints), and an incomplete listing of critical writings on him, up to 1934.

Edition and Correspondence

Fargue, Léon-Paul. Correspondance avec Valery Larbaud, 1910–1946. Ed. by Th. Alajouanine. Gallimard, 1971. 365 p.   **7066**

An extremely important source of information concerning the life of F., his character, his relationship with Larbaud and the rest of the literary world, mainly between 1910 and 1924, when their friendship came to an end. 274 letters written by the two poets to each other during these 14 years appear here, and are followed by 3 more letters from F.: one written in 1935 or 1936 (when Larbaud became paralyzed) and 2 in 1946. Also an excellent picture of the fireworks of F.'s conversation: images, puns, "contrepetteries," picturesque neologisms and nicknames, imaginative spelling, etc. F. being a negligent correspondent, unfortunately only about one fourth of the letters are from him. Alajouanine's comments and annotations constitute a very rich research instrument for studying the two poets and the literary scene in 1910–1924. Weaknesses of the study: a few minor factual errors; lack of bibliographically precise references; lack of an index, which would have infinitely multiplied the usefulness of this study; lack of one vital letter of Larbaud to F. dated Dec. 5, 1924, quoted by Schub, p. 166–67 (*see* 7139)—and which explains Larbaud's reasons for the break between the two friends.

Reviews: Anon. in TLS 3618:758, July 2, 1971; J. Charpentier in CahAVL 8:13–49, 1971; A. Clerval in QL 115:10–12, 1971; B. Delvaille in Comb Jan. 28, 1971 and in MagL 51: 40–41, 1971; M. Dessert in CahBC 59:322–23, 1971; Y. Florenne in Monde March 5, 1971; E. Lerch in SchR 72:81–83, 1973; C. Mauriac in Fig. Feb. 15, 1971; P. Pia in CarI March 3, 1971; J.-P. Segonds in CahBC 58:289–91, 1971, and in NRF 227:84–86, 1971.

———. Poésies. Gallimard, 1963. 355 p.
7067

This new ed. includes a number of out-of-print works. All these poetic and prose-poetic writings can be considered autobiographical to varying degrees since they find their origin in F.'s own life, his memories of his family and friends. The preface (p. 7–31) is by Saint-John Perse, and is analyzed separately, *infra*. *Epaisseurs* (p. 167–210 and *Vulturne* (p. 211–49) were also republished in 1971 by Gallimard (Coll. Poésie) with a preface by Jacques Borel also analyzed separately, *infra*.

Biographical Texts

Fargue, Léon-Paul. Bengoechea ou l'âme d'un poète. Amiot-Dumont, 1948. 321 p.
7068

F.'s presentation (p. 7–100) of this Bogota poet, who wrote in French, includes autobiographical souvenirs of F.'s first contacts with *Mercure de France,* Lugné Poe's *L'œuvre,* Henri de Régnier, etc. and is F.'s last writing, being dated Nov. 1947.

———. D'après Paris, lithographies de J. L. Boussingault. Librairie de France (pour les amis de l'amour de l'Art), 1931 ("tirage limité à 170 exemplaires"). *Also* (*rev.*): Gallimard, 1932. 143 p. *Also in*

his: Le piéton de Paris, suivi de D'après Paris. Gallimard, 1964. p. 191–246. **7069**

This is a collection of prose-poetic articles which had appeared in *Commerce* and/or NL, and/or NRF. They have an autobiographical origin, and show F. with the image that he wanted to project.

———. Haute solitude. Emile-Paul, 1941. 271 p. *Also:* Gallimard, 1966. **7070**

Poetic, partly oneiric, partly autobiographical prose-poems defined by F. himself: "Je ne sais si j'ai vécu, je ne sais si j'ai rêvé" (p. 233). If some of the facts are definitely "rêvés," the feelings and atmosphere are of course "vécus."

———. Jeunesse de poète — rectificatif sur l'article de mon vieil et excellent ami Saint-Georges de Bouhélier. FL 3, Jan. 4, 1947. **7071**

An outraged answer to Saint-Georges de Bouhélier's article (FL Feb. 21, 1942) two weeks earlier. F. insists on some of the myths of his legend: "je n'en [des artisans] vois pas dans ma famille...et je suis bachelier," etc.

———. Maurice Ravel. Domat, 1949. p. 51–57 (Au voilier). **7072**

Memories of Ravel include autobiographical remarks (which appear also in his *Refuges,* see *infra.*), mainly about F.'s relations with those intimate friends of his who died young.

———. Méandres. Geneva, Eds. du milieu du monde, 1946. 270 p. **7073**

Poetically autobiographical — including of course all the myths that F. was eager to perpetuate — but also giving F.'s own view of his life, some remembrances being typically Proustian, others being completely invented, sometimes with the help of a secretary's research at the Bibliothèque Nationale [cf. Schub, *infra*]. The chapter "En rampant au chevet de ma vie" (p. 170–222) is a poetic and pathetic description of his illness after his stroke.

———. Le piéton de Paris. Gallimard, 1939. 253 p. *Also:* Le piéton de Paris, suivi de D'après Paris. Gallimard, 1950. 250 p. **7074**

This collection of articles, which first appeared in *Voilà,* gives poetic characterizations of the various neighborhoods and customs of Paris, as seen by a poet whose own background and tastes are an integral part of each piece; in this sense, *Le piéton de Paris* may be considered autobiographical. It inspired beautiful sets of illustrations.

————. Portraits de famille, avec un portrait de l'auteur par Denise Lannes, et des photographies. J. B. Janin, 1947. 231 p.   **7075**

Collection of 17 essays (which had appeared in a variety of periodicals) on F.'s colleagues and friends. All these portraits, drawn from F.'s personal recollections, include a wealth of autobiographical material—not always accurate as far as dates are concerned, but otherwise very important as far as F.'s own life and his relations with contemporary literature are concerned.

————. Refuges. Emile-Paul, 1942. 306 p. *Also:* Gallimard, 1966.   **7076**

A collection of 37 short chapters, some reprints of articles published in various papers (*Marianne, Aujourd'hui, Le Figaro, Mercure de France,* etc.) more or less modified, and almost all autobiographical.

————. Rue de Villejust. Jacques Haumont, 1946. 59 p.   **7077**

This "plaquette" contains several articles which had previously appeared in newspapers and periodicals. These very touching tributes, recalling the lives of members of the Valéry-Rouart family, residing on the rue de Villejust, include important autobiographical elements, since F. worked very closely with Valéry on many occasions, in A. Monnier's "boutique," as co-editors of *Commerce,* etc.

Special Numbers

Hommage à Fargue. CahS 286:881–932, 1947.   **7078**

The regular issue of this periodical contains a special section devoted to F. shortly after his death. Includes several "Poèmes inédits de Léon-Paul Fargue." The significant articles have been analyzed separately.

Hommage à Léon-Paul Fargue. FLib 45–46:1–207, 1927.   **7079**

Whole issue, edited by Marcel Raval. Includes photographs; music by Maurice Ravel, Frédéric Mompou, and Ricardo Vinès; illustrations by Daragnès, Picasso, Ernest La Jeunesse, F. himself, Chirico, Henry Michaux, Marie Laurencin, Marie Monnier, a "hors-texte" by Paul Klee; a "texte inédit" by F.; a bibliography of F.'s writings, with some inaccuracies as far as dates are concerned. Also prose poems and poems by P. Drieu la Rochelle, L. Durtain, B. Groethuysen, R. Güiraldes, A. MacLeish. Also a large number of short articles by various hands.

Biography

Arbour, Roméo. Henri Bergson et les lettres françaises. José Corti, 1955. 460 p., passim.   **7080**

Several references to F., particularly on p. 377, where Arbour follows the myth of placing F. in Bergson's "Khâgne."

Beach, Sylvia. *In her:* Shakespeare and company. Harcourt Brace, 1959. p. 149–53. *Trans. into French:* Shakespeare and company. Trans. by George Adam. Mercure de France, 1962. p. 163–69.   **7081**

Anecdotes about F., and Sylvia Beach, Adrienne Monnier, James Joyce, Marguerite Caetani (Princesse di Bassiano), Guili-Guili, Valery Larbaud, Raymonde Linossier, Erik Satie, and others. F.'s taxis, his ceramics and stained glass factory.

Beucler, André. Chez Léon-Paul Fargue, boulevard Montparnasse. FL Aug. 3, 1946.   **7082**

Typical portrait of F. paralyzed. Anecdotes emphasizing his extraordinary memory, his cat, his telephone, his visitors, his wife Chériane.

————. Dimanche avec Léon-Paul Fargue. Eds. du point du jour, 1947. 109 p.   **7083**

Excellent picture of everyday life with F. by a much younger colleague and great admirer. Very important for knowing F., the man.

————. Léon-Paul Fargue. LarM 403:40–41, 1948.   **7084**

Dictionary article by F.'s deeply admiring young friend, based on F.'s own tales to Beucler, in which he carefully preserves many of his favorite myths. Beucler considers F. as a forerunner of surrealism, and his journalism (since 1935) as that of a great poet.

————. Vingt ans avec Léon-Paul Fargue, avec un frontispice de Chériane. Geneva, Eds. du milieu du monde, 1952. 282 p. *Trans.:* The last of the Bohemians; twenty years with Léon-Paul Fargue. Trans. by Geoffrey Sainsbury with introd. by Archibald MacLeish. New York, W. Sloane, 1954. xii, 237 p. *Also:* Poet of Paris; twenty years with Léon-Paul Fargue. Trans. by Geoffrey Sainsbury. London, Chatto & Windus, 1955. 249 p.   **7085**

In 1945, F. wrote, in collaboration with Beucler, *Composite*, a collection of souvenirs, anecdotes, amusing dialogs on a variety of important and unimportant subjects — and for some twenty years, this younger colleague, friend and devoted admirer of F., took notes on the daily conversations he had with the poet, with the intention of publishing them, and thus preserving F.'s incredibly rich oral style which otherwise would have been lost to posterity. The suitcase containing this day-by-day transcription as well as the first draft of the book was stolen in a train, and Beucler had to rewrite it from memory. Even with this limitation, the book is absolutely unique in its importance. A great many episodes are described, those shared with Beucler as well as those told to Beucler (F.'s childhood, his family, friends, including the usual myths that F. kept up all along); and F.'s oral style is preserved.
Review of original: M. Thiébaut, *see* 7140. Review of trans.: Anon. in TLS 2786:410, July 22, 1955; R. Mayne in NSN 1254:409–10, March 19, 1955.

Bour, Louis. Les nôtres. Impr. Paul Dupont, 1945. 206 p.   **7086**

Thorough and well-documented description of the solid "bourgeoisie française chrétienne" background of some of the families to which Léon Fargue (F.'s father) was related. Reading this book helps to explain why Léon Fargue did not marry F.'s mother, a peasant seamstress, until after his own mother's death, when F. was 31 years old, and what this meant for F.'s psychological make-up as well as his constant need for protection of the aristocracy.

Brassaï, Gyula Halasz. Conversations avec Picasso. Gallimard, 1964. 340 p., passim. *Trans.:* Picasso & Co. Trans. by Francis Price. Pref. by Henry Miller. Garden City, N.Y., Doubleday, 1966. p. 13–14, 44, 78.   **7087**

Circumstances of F.'s collaboration on the surrealist review *Minotaure,* with the prose poem "Pigeondre" (p. 13–14). F. at Brasserie Lipp (p. 44). Description of F.'s stroke, during lunch with Picasso, and his attitude toward his illness (p. 78). References are to translation.

Cassou, Jean. A vingt ans. *In:* Hommage à Fargue. *See* 7078. p. 882–86.   **7088**

Beautiful portrait of F., the "noctambule... cocasse," as well as the great poet and the human being — written at his death.

Charensol, G. Comment ils écrivent... Aubanel, 1932. p. 94–98.   **7089**

Long quotation of F. describing his own way of writing, mainly through the night; preferably dictation, then reworking the text in great detail, up to, and including, on the printer's galleys. This description is authentic.

Colette, [Sidonie Gabrielle.] Œuvres complètes. V. 14. Flammarion, 1950. p. 40–42, 198–200.   **7090**

Description of the way the two writers communicated with each other, when they were both paralyzed. Also reminiscences of a walk through Paris at night with a young F.

Dufrène, Elysée Maurice. Oiseaux, mes petits frères. Presses d'Ile-de-France, 1946. [unpaginated]   **7091**

Memories from early childhood, Dufrène and F. having met in nursery school.

Fort, Paul. Mes mémoires — toute la vie d'un poète, 1872–1943. Flammarion, 1944. p. 47–52, 80–84.   **7092**

F. introduced Fort to the writings of Jammes and Claudel, in the early

1890's. Fort also describes how *Le livre d'art* was founded.

Harper, Allanah. Recollections of Léon-Paul Fargue. Hor 19:354–67, 1949. *Also in her:* All trivial fond records. New York, Harper, 1968. p. 192–96.   **7093**

Emphasis on the consubstantiality of F.'s poetry and his life; his sensitivity, his oneness with Paris; his constant lateness.

Henriot, Emile. La soirée avec Léon-Paul. *In his:* Maîtres d'hier et contemporains. V. 2. Albin Michel, 1956. p. 202–08.   **7094**

Personal memories about F. added to a combined review of *Méandres, Portraits de famille,* and Beucler's *Vingt ans avec Léon-Paul Fargue.* All three books are very highly praised.

Hugo, Valentine. Et pour finir... mangeur de roses. CRB 29:81–85, 1960.   **7095**

F.'s extraordinary gift with the spoken word and his background in natural history allowed him to recreate for his night-walking companions prehistoric animals as if he had lived among them. He had planned to write a book on this subject to be illustrated by Valentine Hugo.

Ils ont perdu la face: des poètes que nous ne pouvons plus aimer. LetF 2, Aug. 1944. (Last clandestine number)   **7096**

Article violently attacking Salmon, Fort and F. for participating in the jury of *Les nouveaux temps,* a collaborationist periodical. LetF published a retraction, Sept. 16, 1944, and a final "mise au point" after F.'s death, Dec. 4, 1947.

Jourdain, Francis. Né en 76. Eds. du Pavillon, 1951. p. 132–44 and passim.   **7097**

Reminiscences by the painter, art critic and politically active leftist writer who was F.'s closest friend (both born in '76) at the turn of the century and who remained constantly faithful to that friendship until he died. The very numerous references to F. throughout the book give an excellent portrait of F. This portrait is loving, understanding, and absolutely authentic, explaining F.'s need to lie and thus create a legend, and also telling many true anecdotes about his biography and of

his creative manner. Essential for understanding F., the man, and the poet.

Labracherie, Pierre. Ombres fantasques et personnages singuliers. NRDM 74–78, April 1973.   **7098**

Memories of F. at St.-Germain-des-Prés, and anecdotes, particularly concerning trips through Paris in Philippe Dumaine's taxi, when F. was already paralyzed. Reproduction of a beautiful picture of F. painted by Raymond Wood.

Larbaud, Valery. Œuvres complètes. V. 9. Journal inédit. Gallimard, 1954. 541 p.   **7099**

With the help of the good index, a dozen references to F. are easily found in the *Journal* covering the years of friendship. The references are mainly of two natures: mention of F.'s letters announcing visits; praise of some of F.'s poetry, recently rediscovered by Larbaud.

————, and G. Jean-Aubry. Correspondance, 1920–1935. Introduction et notes de Frida Weissman. Gallimard, 1971. 264 p., passim.   **7100**

Numerous references to F. especially in the period 1920–1924.

Lefèvre, Frédéric. Léon-Paul Fargue. *In his:* Une heure avec... 5ᵉ série. Gallimard, 1929. p. 263–82.   **7101**

Interview with F. A mixture of true facts and legends encouraged by F. himself. Does give an idea of F.'s brilliant conversation, but is of course full of inaccuracies as far as its biographical value is concerned.

Levet, Henry J.-M. Conversation entre Léon-Paul Fargue et Valery Larbaud. *In his:* Poèmes, précédés d'une conversation de Léon-Paul Fargue et Valery Larbaud. La maison des amis des livres, 1921. p. 9–42. *Also:* Gallimard, 1943. p. 9–33. (Métamorphoses, 18)   **7102**

The "conversation," which is transcribed as having taken place in 1911, right after Levet's death, between his two friends Larbaud and F., gives a presentation of Levet, but is particularly interesting insofar as it is autobiographical for the two interlocutors. F. evokes the founding of *Le centaure* in 1895 with Gide, Valéry, etc., his night strolls through Paris with F. Jourdain, and their mutual friends, his discovery of *Le Mercure de France,* the episode with Marie Pamelart.

Lhoste, Pierre. Une matinée avec Léon-Paul Fargue. MariM 14:41–43, June 27, 1939. **7103**

Series of good photographs accompanied by an interview where F. obviously was pulling Lhoste's leg by accumulating lies about himself and his family that go well beyond his usual "legend."

Monnier, Adrienne. Rue de l'Odéon. Albin Michel, 1960. passim. **7104**

Book of reminiscences by the owner-directress of "La maison des amis des livres," about the outstanding figures who regularly came to her store located on the Rue de l'Odéon, and gave it its very special "chapelle littéraire" character. Many references to F. Very important for the portrait of F. as a man and a poet, his relationships with his friends, Larbaud, Valéry, Joyce, Adrienne Monnier, and their collaboration on the review *Commerce.*

Nattier-Natanson, Evelyn. Les amitiés de la Revue Blanche et quelques autres. Vincennes, Eds. du donjon, 1959. p. 199–205. **7105**

Excellent portrait of F. The dual character of his poetry is well explained: grave tenderness as well as "fulgurante cocasserie."

Porel, Jacques. Au bras d'un vieil ami... *In:* Hommage à Léon-Paul Fargue. *See* 7079. p. 145–51. **7106**

Recollections of strolls through Paris at night with F. Evocation of F.'s favorites: Alfred Jarry, Charles-Louis Philippe, Debussy, Adrienne Monnier, the Saint-Martin canal.

————. Fils de Réjane, souvenirs (1895–1920). Plon, 1951. p. 338–47, passim. **7107**

Loving portrait of F. whom Réjane's son, Jacques Porel, knew well. Personal anecdotes illustrating his legendary characteristics, his typical poet-like behavior. Excellent portrayal of the literary and "mondain" milieu in which F. moved.

Segonds, Jean-Philippe. Sur la correspondance Fargue-Larbaud: précisions, énigmes, controverses. CahBC 59:324–30, 1971. **7108**

Careful and intelligent study of the "mystérieux complot" surrounding the first publication of *Tancrède* by Larbaud. Using the recently published Alajouanine's F.-Larbaud correspondence, Segonds destroys F.'s official myth on the subject, but overlooks some additional arguments and details found in Schub's *Léon-Paul Fargue* (p. 51–53), *infra.*

Troulay, Marcel. Valery Larbaud et Les cahiers d'aujourd'hui. CahAVL 7:1–12, 1971. **7109**

A good description of the group of friends who, at the beginning of the century, surrounded Charles-Louis Philippe, and included among others Marguerite Audoux, Valery Larbaud, Léon Werth and F.

General Studies

Blanchet, André. Léon-Paul Fargue et ses fantômes. *In his:* La littérature et le spirituel. V. 1. Aubier, 1959. p. 85–101. **7110**

Study of F.'s extraordinary usage of words — compared to his father's minute work with ceramics — changing his descriptions into visions. His philosophy, however, is inadequate, therefore "sa représentation du monde n'a pas l'admirable équilibre de la construction dantesque affermie sur le dogme catholique."

Blanchot, Maurice. Léon-Paul Fargue et la création poétique. *In his:* Faux-pas. Gallimard, 1943. p. 178–82. **7111**

Short but good evaluation of F.'s later prose-poetic writings: dream-like quality and tremendously rich vocabulary, much of it invented by F. But Blanchot reproaches F. for his lack of discrimination, especially in newspaper articles; he also deplores the fact that F.'s own personality is too often apparent in his later writings, which diminishes their value.

Borel, Jacques. Passé et solitude dans l'œuvre de Léon-Paul Fargue. Cr 218: 604–14, 1965. *Also in:* Fargue, Léon-Paul. Epaisseurs suivi de Vulturne. Gallimard, 1971. p. 7–22. (Poésie) **7112**

A very good study of the role of memory in F.'s writings, especially as opposed to that of Proust. For F. the remembrances of things past are always painful because of his constant solitude.

Bounoure, Gabriel. Enfances de Fargue. NRF 190:26–38, 1929.   **7113**

Good study of F.'s writings to date of article, including their content and form. For Bounoure, "c'est un enfant terrible doué d'un sens extraordinaire de l'intimité des êtres." His poetry is based on his memories and reveries (compared to Proust) as well as on his emotions and on his verbal invention: "vocabulaire farguien, pour ses leçons de choses lyriques."

Brisson, Pierre. Le vrai surréaliste. FL 1, 5, July 26, 1958. *Also in his:* Vingt ans de Figaro (1938–1958). Gallimard, 1959. p. 246–50.   **7114**

According to Brisson, even though F. was not officially a member of any school or coterie, "le vrai surréaliste, pourtant, le seul qui justifiât le nom, c'est lui. Certaines de ses pages se situent aux frontières du cauchemar."

Cassou, Jean. Pour la poésie. Corrêa, 1935. p. 215–25.   **7115**

Study of the "vraie poésie philosophique" of *Vulturne,* where F. is compared to Rimbaud for his "merveilleuse fusion de la vie et de la parole" — followed by a study of *D'après Paris* where F.'s re-creation of Paris is compared to that of *Le temps retrouvé,* of Villon, and of Baudelaire.

Chonez, Claudine. Léon-Paul Fargue. Une étude... œuvres choisies... Seghers, 1950. 209 p. (Poètes d'aujourd'hui, 19). *Another ed.:* 1959.   **7116**

Very good study (p. 9–75) of F., his poetry, his style and his themes. This is the first book devoted to F. and his writings. Unfortunately, Chonez' study of F.'s life was superficial and she accepted all the myths without question. This study is followed by a selection of texts (p. 77–196) and a very incomplete and sometimes incorrect bibliography (p. 198–202), and includes many illustrations.

Review: P. Macaigne in Fig May 10, 1950.

Clancier, Georges-Emmanuel. Léon-Paul Fargue. *In his:* De Rimbaud au surréalisme. Seghers, 1959. p. 241–80.   **7117**

Excellent study of F.'s poetry, his various themes, his ultimate solitude, his rapport with Paris, his succulent language. His independence and individuality as far as literary schools are concerned, although many of his poems are naturally surrealistic.

Clouard, Henri. L.-P. Fargue. *In his:* Histoire de la littérature française du symbolisme à nos jours. V. 1. Albin Michel, 1947. p. 576–77.   **7118**

Shows F.'s influence in his poetic youth, but also his lack of importance in 1947. Emphasizes picturesque style, his beautiful images. Gives wrong birth date (1878, instead of the true one, 1876).

Crémieux, Benjamin. Note pour une étude critique. *In:* Hommage à Léon-Paul Fargue. *See* 7079. p. 106–12.   **7119**

Excellent outline for a possible detailed study of F.'s poetry, with many quotations as samples of themes, feelings, classified sensations, style, images, choice of words, presentation of memories.

Criticus (pseud. of Marcel Berger). Léon-Paul Fargue. *In his:* Le style au microscope. Calmann-Lévy, 1949. p. 45–61.   **7120**

A very detailed *explication de texte* of two paragraphs of F.'s posthumous *Les grandes heures du Louvre* (Les deux Sirènes, 1948, p. 109–10). This interesting study of each metaphor, of each word, is done tongue in cheek, even sarcastically at times, in order to show how F. is using his "pure poetry" in this chronicle which is fundamentally journalism rather than poetry. The biographical introduction is also sarcastic and not really truthful: "F. vient de disparaître, après une longue maladie sans grandes souffrances" [!]

Georgesco, Valentin-Al. Visages de Paris: Verlaine, Léon-Paul Fargue. Corymbe, 1939. p. 9–15.   **7121**

Sensitive study of F.'s dreams of his

childhood and pre-1914 Paris in his poetry.

Ghéon, Henri. Le poème en prose — forme naturelle de l'illumination (à propos des Poèmes de M. Léon-Paul Fargue [et al.]). NRF 44:345–54, 1912.   **7122**

Excellent study of the history of the "poème en prose." Includes a very sensitive study of F.'s *Poëmes* in which Ghéon prefers those pieces which are more "dépouillés," F.'s style being too rich in images.

Guilleré, René. Fargue dans Fargue. *In:* Hommage à Léon-Paul Fargue. *See* 7079. p. 61–74.   **7123**

A very sensitive and sensible, as well as authentic description of the man, the poet, and his writings. Emphasis on the absence of pretentiousness in a poet who developed his art at the height of the symbolist period; even his neologisms are always "le mot juste." F. is compared here to Picasso, La Fontaine, Cézanne.

Jaloux, Edmond. Visite à Léon-Paul Fargue. *In his:* D'Eschyle à Giraudoux. Fribourg, Egloff, 1946. p. 289–96.   **7124**

References to F.'s legend, to his *Tancrède.* F. compared to Rimbaud and to the surrealists because of his visions and style.

————. M. Léon-Paul Fargue. *In his:* Perspectives et personnages. Plon, 1931, p. 191–99.   **7125**

Intelligent study of F.'s sensitivity, his rich and picturesque vocabulary, comparing F. to Loti, Proust, Rabelais, Rimbaud, Villon, Cyrano de Bergerac, Aloysius Bertrand, Lautréamont.

Kemp, Robert. Les Méandres de Léon-Paul Fargue. *In his:* La vie des livres. Albin Michel, 1955. p. 266–73.   **7126**

Review of *Méandres* and *Portraits de famille,* giving an excellent characterization of F.'s style. Compares him to Proust because he is "un trésor de sensations, un coffre de souvenirs," and his images — "'illuminations' rimbaldiennes" — make of him another Joyce, but a spontaneous one. For Kemp, F. will survive because of his sincerity.

Larbaud, Valery. Farguiana. *In:* Hommage à Léon-Paul Fargue. *See* 7079. p. 27–32.

Also in his: Ce vice impuni, la lecture. Domaine français. Gallimard, 1941. 283 p. *Also in his:* Œuvres complètes. V. 7. Gallimard, 1953. p. 359–65.   **7127**

Larbaud, who was no longer F.'s best friend, describes how F.'s typically French beautiful poems were born out of F.'s endless strolls about Paris. This text is extracted from his "Les poèmes de Léon-Paul Fargue," *infra.*

————. Les poèmes de Léon-Paul Fargue. MerF 1196:252–66, 1963.   **7128**

Article written at the height of the Larbaud-F. friendship in 1912 for Jean Royère's *La phalange.* Royère rejected it then because Larbaud was speaking too much about himself and was praising his personal friend.

La Rochefoucauld, Edmée de. Léon-Paul Fargue. Eds universitaires, 1958. 121 p. (Classiques du XXᵉ siècle, 32)   **7129**

Very good short monograph by a sensitive poet and "femme de lettres" who was a friend of F. Her own reminiscences are enriched and authenticated by serious sources, not all of which, however, are scholarly and reliable: Beucler, Larbaud, Monnier, Chonez and Schub. In spite of some superficial errors, this is a very readable biographical portrait, punctuated with quotations from F.'s writings and citations of the above-mentioned sources. The text is followed by a practical chronology, an incomplete bibliography of F.'s works, and a very sketchy bibliography on F.

Reviews: R. Dardenne in TR 139–40:150–51, 1959; V.-H. Debidour in BdL 212:406–07, Nov. 15, 1959; E. Henriot in Monde 8–9, Nov. 11, 1959.

Monnier, Adrienne. Les poèmes de Commerce. *In:* Hommage à Léon-Paul Fargue. *See* 7079. p. 83–87. *Also (rev.) in her:* Les gazettes d'Adrienne Monnier, 1925–1945. Julliard, 1953. p. 58–62.   **7130**

Even though this is a highly laudatory description of F.'s poetry, first and second manner, for the homage issue, it is a very intelligent study of his writings.

Pelmont, Raoul. Léon-Paul Fargue et la poésie. FR 31:469–78, 1958.   **7131**

An interesting study of what poetry meant for F. or rather what F. wrote it meant for him — with a tremendous number of well-identified quotations to prove each point, quotations taken directly from F.'s various writings, or, on occasion, from Beucler's *Vingt ans avec Léon-Paul Fargue,* where innumerable statements are attributed to F. by his admiring younger colleague and friend.

Primauld, Max, Henry Lhong, and Jean Malrieu. Terres de l'enfance; le mythe de l'enfance dans la littérature contemporaine. Presses univ. de France, 1961. p. 133, 136–39.   **7132**

How F.'s highly musical poetry in *Ludions* has its roots in his own childhood.

Raymond, Marcel. De Baudelaire au surréalisme. Corti, 1940. p. 315–20.   **7133**

Considers F. "en marge du surréalisme," but certainly worthy of Jarry's "Pataphysique," especially in *Espaces.* Mentions F.'s various themes, and the music of his prose poetry. Some of the facts he gives, however, are incorrect (e.g., *Poèmes* 1902, should be 1907 or 1912, and *Tancrède* was not published by the NRF in 1911, but privately by Valery Larbaud).

Roche, Juliette. La mission poétique de Léon-Paul Fargue. Témoi 366–70, July, 1947.   **7134**

Attempts to determine F.'s exact place in French literature. Unlike some of his elders who either died too young (Apollinaire, Rimbaud, Laforgue) or did not live up to their full potential, F. does not evade anything, and no young writers — particularly those of "la très jeune équipe du Grand Jeu" — could have escaped his influence.

Rolland de Renéville, A. Léon-Paul Fargue et l'art des vers. Nef 42:101–03, 1948.   **7135**

Discussion of F.'s choice of prose or verse in his various pieces, all of them being highly poetic, and all of them being made up of verses, even in prose form.

————. La poésie de Léon-Paul Fargue. *In his:* Univers de la parole. Gallimard, 1944. p. 86–101, 172–74.   **7136**

Gives a short biography of F. (with the usual mistake regarding his date of

birth: 1878, instead of 1876), followed by a lovingly admiring analysis of most of F.'s poetic writings. Traces his origins to Rimbaud (and his "voyance") and even to *Aurélia,* as far as *Vulturne* is concerned; and shows his influence upon Morand, Giraudoux, Michaux, and Audiberti. A review of *Refuges* (1942) appears on p. 172–74 with emphasis on verbal associations, metaphors and images.

Roy, Claude. Léon-Paul Fargue. *In his:* Descriptions critiques. Gallimard, 1949. p. 304–07.   **7137**

F. is compared to H. Bosch for his metaphors; his descriptions are medieval, epic, and full of music at the same time.

Saint-John Perse (pseud. of Alexis St. Léger Léger). Léon-Paul Fargue, poète. NRF 128:197–210, 1963; 129:406–22, 1963. *Also in his:* Œuvres complètes. Gallimard, 1972. p. 507–32. *Also:* Préface. *In:* Fargue, Léon-Paul. Poésies. Gallimard, 1963. p. 7–31.   **7138**

Very important article. Saint-John Perse places F. between Claudel and Valéry, but insists that "il ne fut point d'école ni de secte, étant de cette communauté française où s'assemble vivante, la somme toujours accrue d'un héritage en cours d'évolution." However, Baudelaire rather than Hugo, Nerval rather than Verlaine, Rimbaud rather than Mallarmé and Corbière rather than Laforgue influenced him. Since F.'s style did not follow fads, his poetry, or rather his musical, harmonious prose-poetry, will survive and will not date. Aside from the importance of images and words, Saint-John Perse sees in F.'s writings a happy mixture of the abstract and the concrete, of the imaginary and the real, but they are mainly French in their essence: "son cynisme est courtois, son sarcasme, français..."

Schub, Louise Rypko. Léon-Paul Fargue. Geneva, Droz, 1973. 278 p. (Histoire des idées et critique littéraire, 132)   **7139**

This book was originally presented as a Sorbonne doctoral thesis, and reviewed by: M. Abraham in Arts 393:1, 6, Jan. 9–15, 1953; A. B. in NL 6, June 12, 1952; P. Mazars in FL June 14, 1952. Rewritten after additional research and entirely brought up to date, this is the first — and so far only — important scholarly work on F. In 1949 F.'s widow put all his remaining papers at Schub's disposal. Between 1949 and 1972, she interviewed and corresponded with some 60 friends of F. regarding the various periods of his life and the various aspects of his literary production. The many myths surrounding F., mostly originated and propagated by him, are thoroughly investigated. Includes 57 pages of exhaustive bibliographies of F.'s writings bringing out interrelationships among various appearances of each text. Includes many "inédits" and also letters from a variety of significant contemporary writers. Reviews: Anon. in BCLF Aug.-Sept. 1973; P. Brodin in FrAm no. 76:13, Nov. 8–15, 1973; F. Caradec in Tonus 12, spring 1973; J. Charpentier in RHL 75:149–51, 1975; A. G. in SoirB Nov. 14, 1973; E. Morot-Sir in FR 48:438–39, 1974; R. Pouilliart in LR 28:293–95, 1974; R. Rancœur in BBF 20:242–43, 1975.

Thiébaut, Marcel. Léon-Paul Fargue. RdP 60:156–61, April 1953. *Also in his:* Entre les lignes. Hachette, 1962. p. 130–39.
7140
A review of Beucler's *Vingt ans avec Léon-Paul Fargue* is the starting point of this study of F.'s style. Inaccuracies: all the myths about F. are repeated here.

Valéry, Paul. Notules sur Léon-Paul Fargue. *In:* Hommage à Léon-Paul Fargue. *See* 7079. p. 24–26.
7141
Very perceptive analysis of F.'s style, which Valéry calls "la caricature phonétique:" play on words with very unexpected and richly fascinating results. Also description of his even richer style.

Vitrac, Roger. Léon-Paul Fargue, seul. *In:* Hommage à Léon-Paul Fargue. *See* 7079. p. 123–32.
7142
Emphasis on the delicate emotions expressed in *Tancrède,* with a mention of F.'s *Poèmes* as well as his more recent poems.

Walter, Jean-Claude. Léon-Paul Fargue ou l'homme en proie à la ville. Gallimard, 1973. 155 p. (Les essais, 178) 7143

The author, a young novelist and poet himself, tries to understand and explain F.'s poetry as it is inspired and defined by Paris, the city which in turn helped F. find himself when he identified with it. Many well-chosen quotations which serve as points of departure for detailed *explications de textes.* Extremely interesting book where one poet's writings are poetically explained by another poet, who understands him with his feelings as well as with his reason. The text is followed by a very short and incomplete bibliography. Reviews: H. Juin in MagL no. 81: 44–46, 1973; C. Mauriac in FL 1397:15, Feb. 24, 1973; A. Miguel in Marg 155–56:73–74, 1973; P. Pia in Car 16–17, March 15, 1973.

Individual Works

Apollinaire, Guillaume. La poésie symboliste. L'édition, 1908. p. 176–78. 7144
Introduction to the reading, by Mlle Maud Sterny, of F.'s "Un jour au crépuscule," from his *Pour la musique,* at the Salon des artistes indépendants (l'après-midi des poètes), on April 25, 1908. F. obtained the most enthusiastic comments by Apollinaire.

————. Revue de la quinzaine. MerF 42: 442, July 16, 1911. *Also in his:* Anecdotiques. Stock, 1926. p. 34–35. 7145
Review of F.'s *Tancrède,* with background information (some of it erroneous) regarding the 1911 ed.

Audiberti, Jacques. L'air du mois: Le piéton de Paris. NRF 32:521–23, 1939. 7146
Review of F.'s book. Emphasis on his mastery of words, his love for Paris.

————. Chronique des temps présents: la Haute solitude du poète Léon-Paul Fargue. Auj 1–2, July 11, 1941. 7147
Review of the book. Study of F.'s rich vocabulary which reflects the universe and which makes him comparable to Mallarmé, Rimbaud, Baudelaire, in that he, as a poet, exists and functions for us all.

Bidou, Henry. Parmi les livres. RdP 23: 687–91, 1928. 7148

Review of *Vulturne* and *Banalité*.
For Bidou, *Vulturne* is the description
of a dream, showing F.'s extreme sensitivity and his "tentative d'évasion hors
de ce monde qui lui fait horreur;"
Banalité is a book of memories whose
themes are classified and described as
pathetic and tender. Good study of F.'s
style.

Fernandez, Ramon. Notes: Haute solitude.
NRF 330:230–32, 1941.   **7149**
   For his images and his vocabulary,
F. is comparable to Mallarmé, and for
his remembrance of the past, to Proust.

Ghéon, Henri. Notes: Tancrède. NRF 32:
237–39, 1911.   **7150**
   Review of *Tancrède,* praising F. for
his real sensitivity and "délicatesse la
plus rare," in spite of the surface affectation due to the symbolistic atmosphere
where *Tancrède* was written, some 15
years before its publication. Influences:
Rimbaud, Laforgue, Barrès.

Gide, André. A propos du Tancrède de
Léon-Paul Fargue. Bib 16, no. 4:3, 1948.
                               7151
   Gide attempts to explain the origin
of the "épigraphe" for *Tancrède:* "Les
capitaines vainqueurs ont une odeur
forte," attributed by F. to Gide. The
latter only confuses the issue, as explained in great detail by Schub (p.
44–47), *infra*.

Rolland de Renéville, A. Deux grands poètes de Paris. Nef 32:127–30, 1947. **7152**
   F.'s *Méandres* is compared to Villon's
nostalgic "neiges d'antan." Words are
living beings for F.

Tinan, Jean de. La poésie du sentiment:
Henry Bataille, Francis Jammes, Léon-
Paul Fargue [p. 128–31]. *In his:* Chronique du règne de Félix Faure. Cent 2:
119–56, 1896. *Also in:* MerF 273–88,
June 1965. .   **7153**
   Praises *Tancrède* for its "ironie tendre," compares it to Marcel Schwob's
description of mysterious and pitiful
prostitutes. Even though F.'s simple and
direct poetry is more "habile et... tru-
quée" than Bataille's and Jammes',
Tinan is sure that this very young poet
has a brilliant future.

Reputation

Claudel, Paul. Léon-Paul Fargue. FL 1,
Nov. 29, 1947,   **7154**
   Obituary article giving an excellent
appraisal of F.'s style, his poetic genius.

Colette, [Sidonie Gabrielle]. La dernière
soirée. Fig. 1, Nov. 26, 1947. **7155**
   Obituary article evoking F.'s voice,
his walks through Paris streets.

Kemp, Robert. Adieu à Léon-Paul Fargue.
NL 1, Nov. 27, 1947.   **7156**
   Presents F. as an heir to Villon,
Rabelais, Scève, Rimbaud, Lautréamont,
Laforgue, Huysmans, and also as having
influenced Morand, Delteil, Crevel,
Breton, Giraudoux; but considers him
mainly as a musician, whose language
sings like the music of Debussy and
Ravel. Very serious and rich obituary
article.

Vuillermoz, Emile. Un grand musicien.
Spect Dec. 9, 1947.   **7157**
   A beautifully moving long obituary,
emphasizing F.'s "influence spirituelle"
upon Ravel and therefore upon music
history of the period. F. himself is considered as a musician, "créateur d'harmonies" whose poems read aloud are
compared to Debussy's pieces.

Comparison and Influence

Blasi, Alberto Oscar. Güiraldes y Larbaud,
una amistad creadora. Buenos Aires, Nova,
1970. 119 p.   **7158**
   Interesting because of the references
to the F.-Larbaud friendship as seen
from the Argentinian vantage point:
Ricardo Güiraldes' introduction to F.,
the man and his poetry, through Larbaud, and also the introduction of F.
to South American audiences and his
influence upon Güiraldes.

Delange, René. Anniversaires: Ravel et
Fargue. Car Dec. 31, 1947.   **7159**
   Influence of F. on Ravel who wrote
two pieces, one for piano, one for voice,
inspired by F.'s poems, and who accompanied F. at night through the
streets of Paris.

Fernand Gregh
(Nos. 7160–7162)

Lawrence D. Joiner

Druon, Maurice S. Fernand Gregh et son œuvre. Alépée, 1937. 29 p.   **7160**
Lecture given at the Lycée Michelet on April 29, 1937. Limited but is an effort to deal with the total work of G. at that time.

Figueras, André. Fernand Gregh, poète moderne. Jouve, 1946. 31 p.   **7161**
An effort to relate G. to the various developments in modern poetry.

Messières, René de. Un document probable sur le premier état de la pensée de Proust: Mystères par Fernand Gregh. RR 32:113–31, 1942.   **7162**
Most valuable of several articles which suggest the same possibility.

Max Jacob
(Nos. 7163–7262)

Judith Morganroth Schneider
and Sydney Lévy*

Editions

Jacob, Max. Le cornet à dés. Préf. de Michel Leiris. Gallimard, 1967. 257 p. (Poésie/Gallimard)   **7163**
The most popular and available of J.'s work. Included are "Petite historique du Cornet à dés" (p. 15–17) written in 1943 by J. and the famous "Préface de 1916" (p. 19–24) where J. defines his concept of the *poème en prose*. Leiris' "Préface" (p. 9–13) is an exquisite short essay which attempts to situate J. between the classic and romantic traditions with the help of J.'s own esthetic pronouncements. [SL]

———. La défense de Tartufe; extases, remords, visions, prières, poèmes et méditations d'un Juif converti. Ed. by André Blanchet. Gallimard, 1964. 299 p.   **7164**
Blanchet's authoritative introduction explains, in the light of J.'s conversion, changes made in his representation of his mystical vision between *Saint Matorel* (1911), *Les œuvres burlesques et*

mystiques de Frère Matorel (1912), and *La défense* (1919). Extensive notes on ms. and appendix including "Récit de ma conversion" and "Défense de Tartufe ou portrait de l'auteur en martyr." [JMS]
Reviews: R. Abirached in NRF 24: 141–43, 1964; P.-H. Simon in MondeH April 2–8, 1964.

———. Méditations. Ed. by René Plantier. Gallimard, 1972. 225 p.   **7165**
Plantier's presentation discloses the origins of these 62 meditations written by J. at St.-Benoît in the *Introduction à la vie dévote* by St. François de Sales, *The Imitation of Christ* and the Gospels, with special emphasis on the influence of Saint Paul's *Epistles*. Also points out Jacobean literary traits and biographical confidences within his devotional prose. [JMS]
Review: J.-M. Dunoyer in Monde March 22, 1973.

Correspondence

Jacob, Max. Correspondance. Ed. by François Garnier. Eds. de Paris, 1953–55. 2 v. (Collection correspondance)   **7166**
Spanning the Quimper-Paris (1876–1921) and the Saint-Benoît-sur-Loire (1921–24) periods respectively, these two volumes are the only collections to offer a composite portrait of J. as a correspondent. The diversity of responses to various addresses, subjects, and circumstances makes these letters an abundant source of biography, poetic theory, and history of artistic movements. [JMS]
Reviews: Anon. in TLS May 28, 1954; A. Billy in FL Feb. 20, 1954; G. Visenti in Id 8, no. 5:3, 4, 1956.

———. Lettres (1920–1941). Ed. by S. J. Collier. Oxford, Basil Blackwell, 1966. 159 p.   **7167**
Correspondence sent to Théophile Briant, painter, poet, art-dealer, and Conrad Moricand (pseud. Claude Valence), co-author with J. of the *Miroir d'astrologie*, with a short, biographical introduction by Collier. Most letters postdate 1936 return to St.-Benoît and are concerned with religion, personal relationships, astrology, art, and ulti-

* With assistance from Kurt Weinberg.

mately, with J.'s reaction to the holocaust. [JMS]
Reviews: Anon. in TLS Dec. 1, 1966; A. Blanchet in Et 325:607, 1966; J. Duncan in MLR 63:485–86, 1968; P. Thody in FS 21:374–75, 1967.

————. Lettres à Bernard Esdras-Gosse. Pierre Seghers, 1953. 47 p. (Poésie 53, Cahiers bi-mensuels, 248)   **7168**
Twenty-nine letters salvaged from a prolific correspondence continued for twenty years (1924–44). J. appears preoccupied with material problems, reveals paternal, emotive side of his temperament, and offers advice for ethical living. [JMS]

————. Lettres à Marcel Béalu. *In:* Béalu, Marcel. Dernier visage de Max Jacob suivi de Lettres à Marcel Béalu. Lyon, Emmanuel Vitte, 1959. 334 p. (Singuliers et mal connus, 1) *See* 7175.   **7169**
An extraordinarily rich collection of 212 letters dating from April 1937 to February 1944 reveals J.'s enduring passion for literature and for spiritual and human communion in spite of deepening feelings of despair. The correspondence addressed to Béalu reformulates the most fundamental and consistent of J.'s reflections concerning poetry. [JMS]
Reviews: F. Conem in RSH 100: 529–33, 1960; A. Loranquin in BdL 209:271, 1959.

————. Lettres à Michel Levanti, suivies des Poèmes de Michel Levanti. Ed. by Lawrence A. Joseph. Limoges, Rougerie, 1975. 155 p.   **7170**
In these 24 fervent letters and 3 postcards (1936–1941) to a young Catholic poet/disciple, J. expresses views on religion which demonstrate the renewed intensity of his mysticism and cabbalism. On poetry, several new reflections, including judgment on Rimbaud's style, are interesting and revealing. The editor's notes and introduction provide adequate background information. [JMS]

————. Lettres à un ami, correspondance 1922–1937 avec Jean Grenier. Lausanne, Eds. Vineta, 99 p.   **7171**
Information on first productive years at St.-Benoît and on obscure rue Nollet

epoch, but not a particularly brilliant sample of letters. [JMS]

————. Lettres aux Salacrou (août 1923–janvier 1926). Gallimard, 1957. 146 p.   **7172**
Sixty-one letters to well-loved, artistic friends reflect exuberance of highly productive period for J. Illustrative of his manner of encouraging and advising young writers with specific criticism as well as general esthetic recommendations. [JMS]

————, and Jean Cocteau. Choix de lettres de Max Jacob à Jean Cocteau 1919–1944. Paul Morihien, 1949. 158 p. *Also:* O.C.O., 1963. 164 p.   **7173**
Of these 55 precious letters (selected from hundreds written by J. to Cocteau) all but 11 date from 1926–27. Rich in studiously playful accounts of provincial life, literary gossip, specific and general comments on writers and writing. [JMS]

Biography

Andreu, Pierre. Max Jacob. Wesmael-Charlier, 1962. 147 p. (Conversions célèbres)   **7174**
Useful biographical sketch with emphasis on rue Nollet period and on religious faith. Disputes Rousselot's hypothesis that J.'s Catholicism conflicted with his poetic creativity. Contains seven letters (1930–43) and three meditations received from J. [JMS]
Review: R. Calmel in Itin 68:156–58, 1962.

Béalu, Marcel. Dernier visage de Max Jacob, 1937–1944. Périgueux, Pierre Fanlac, 1946. 103 p. *Also in his:* Dernier visage de Max Jacob suivi de Lettres à Marcel Béalu. *See* 7169. p. 9–92.   **7175**
Best source of information on J.'s day-to-day existence and state of mind during last seven years at St.-Benoît. Béalu, unlike most of J.'s biographers, avoids idolatry. [JMS]

Billy, André. Max Jacob, une étude, avec des lettres inédites du poète à Guillaume Apollinaire, un choix de poèmes, une bibliographie. Seghers, 1945, 211 p. (Poètes d'aujourd'hui, 3) *Also:* Max Jacob, une étude, avec des lettres du poète à

Guillaume Apollinaire et à Jean Cocteau, un choix de poèmes, des inédits, des manuscrits, des dessins, des portraits, une bibliographie. Seghers, 1963. 223 p. (Poètes d'aujourd'hui, 3) *Also (in part):* Max Jacob. *In his:* Huysmans & Cie. Brussels, La renaissance du livre, 1963. p. 195–227. (La lettre et l'esprit)   **7176**

Condensed biographical introduction, focusing on Bohemian life (1902–1920) in Montmartre, mystical visions, and religious conversion, constitutes J. legend of elusive "être exceptionnel," part devil, part saint. Bibliography of second ed. lists J.'s works to 1960. [JMS]

Blanchet, André, S. J. La conversion de Max Jacob. *In his:* La mêlée littéraire. Eds. Montaigne, 1959. p. 15–83. (La littérature et le spirituel, v. 1)   **7177**

Carefully reconstitutes stages of J.'s spiritual evolution through reference to correspondence and biographical fiction. Believes a common impulse toward the marvelous and the supernatural motivated religious faith, eccentricity in life, poetic experimentation. [JMS]

Breunig, Leroy C. Max Jacob et Picasso. MerF 1312:581–96, 1957.   **7178**

Traces friendship and artistic collaboration of poet and painter until 1920. Through scrutiny of J.'s responses to Picasso, Breunig arrives at convincing psychological conclusions about the poet. [JMS]

Collier, S. J. The correspondence of Max Jacob. FS 7:235–56, 1953.   **7179**

Deals chiefly with two problems: the circumstances surrounding J.'s retreat to St.-Benoît in 1921 and his return there in 1936. Portrays the state of his mind and his finances implied by both Briant and Valence correspondence as well as testimony of other contemporaries. [JMS]

Emié, Louis. Dialogues avec Max Jacob. Corrêa, Buchet, Chastel, 1954. 263 p. (Mises au point)   **7180**

Cultish, sentimental memoirs describing J.'s artistic and spiritual influence on aspiring poets during the 20's and 30's. Contains letters, meditations, photo portraits from wide-spanned periods. Letters of 1941 are frequently cited in debate on J.'s attitude toward poetry and religion. [JMS]

Review: A. Loranquin in BdL 164: 9–10, 1955.

Guiette, Robert. Vie de Max Jacob. NRF 42:5–20, 248–59, 1934.   **7181**

Biographical and transcribed autobiographical narration alternate in this account based on an interview with J. From his childhood in Quimper to 1921 retreat to St.-Benoît, his life is represented as "un merveilleux poème" in which J. appears as epic hero rather than existent subject. [JMS]

Henry, Hélène. Bio-bibliographie de Max Jacob. *In:* Max Jacob. *See* 7198. p. 110–20.   **7182**

Most substantial, accurate chronology of J.'s life available. Notation style enlivened by allusions to contemporary artistic milieu, literary gossip, J.'s letters and fiction. [JMS]

————. Guillaume et Max. Eur 451–52: 124–32, 1966.   **7183**

Collection of J.'s diverse comments on Apollinaire. Although many have been cited in previous criticism, Henry's compilation is useful as a starting point for biographical research. [JMS]

————. Max Jacob et Picasso: jalons chronologiques pour une amitié: 1901–1944. Eur 492–93:191–210, 1970.   **7184**

From an impressive variety of sources including letters, biographical accounts, literary works, and graphics, Henry depicts the collaboration of Picasso and J. essentially until 1923. A concise, chronological summary of texts and dates marking their personal and artistic relations. [JMS]

Hertz, Henry. Sur une vie, sur un art. *In:* Max Jacob. *See* 7198. p. 18–25.   **7185**

A recollection of the years spent on rue Ravignan with Picasso, Apollinaire and the author. [SL]

Jouhandeau, Marcel. Max Jacob et Supervielle à Guéret. *In his:* Bon an, mal an, 1908–1928, Mémorial VII. Gallimard, 1972. p. 185–92.   **7186**

Unfortunately curt account of Jouhandeau's first meeting with J. and of their literary affinity. One of the rare biographical sources to describe the effect of J.'s homosexuality on his social relations. [JMS]

Lagarde, Pierre. Max Jacob, mystique et martyr, avec trente-deux méditations inédites, cinq poèmes, deux autographes, un dessin, par Max Jacob, et un profil du poète par Serge. Eds. Baudinière, 1944. 191 p.   **7187**

Interesting documentation on J.'s last years at St.-Benoît, relating especially to his views on cosmology and salvation. [JMS]

Parturier, Maurice. Max Jacob: notes biographiques. Le divan, 1944. 12 p. **7188**

Rare but exceedingly skimpy recollections of J.'s youth in Quimper. [JMS]

Psichari, Henriette. Entre le vice et la vertu. *In her:* Les convertis de la belle époque. Eds. rationalistes, 1971. p. 93–102.   **7189**

In this book devoted to the various controversies surrounding the church and its relationship to the main literary and philosophical figures, Psichari describes J.'s torment between vice and virtue, and criticizes the church for not accepting him more readily. [SL]

Romains, Jules. Max Jacob. RDM, no. 10: 13–18, 1970. *Also in his:* Amitiés et rencontres. Flammarion, 1970. p. 80–87. **7190**

The interest of these anecdotes of the rue Ravignan period lies in the fact that Romains' recollections contradict generally accepted views about J.'s opinion of Picasso, the sincerity of his conversion, the composition of *La côte.* [JMS]

Rousselot, Jean. Max Jacob, l'homme qui faisait penser à Dieu. Laffont, 1946. 183 p. *Also in his:* Max Jacob au sérieux. *See* 7222. p. 13–128.   **7191**

Lyrical evocation of J.'s final St.-Benoît days: relationships with local residents, proselytizing of young poets, persecution by the Gestapo, persistent religious faith. Contains 15 letters (1937–43). [JMS]

Salmon, André. Max Jacob: poète, peintre, mystique et homme de qualité. René Girard, 1927. 59 p.   **7192**

Moving tribute by a friend and writer, including biographical material on Montmartre period. [JMS]

Collected Articles

Les cahiers du nord [special section on Max Jacob]. 22:178–215, 1950. **7193**

Contents: René Guy Cadou, *L'œuvre de Max Jacob;* Marcel Béalu, *Max Jacob poète;* Jean Rousselot, *Max Jacob, épistolier* (also *in his:* Max Jacob au sérieux. Rodez, Subervie, 1958. p. 175–80); Paul Dewalhens, *Tombeau de Max Jacob.* Articles of appreciation rather than interpretation which attempt to introduce the works of J., showing the variety and originality of his writings. [SL]

Le diable et Max Jacob. RdF 69:1–22, 1969.   **7194**

Contents: René Plantier, *Max Jacob et le Prince des ténèbres,* p. 1–11; Stanislas Fumet, *Drôle de frère Matorel, pénitent et martyr,* p. 12–16; Michel Ozenne, *Max Jacob: le joueur mystique,* p. 17–20. Also texts by J. [SL]

Le disque vert. 2, no. 2:1–67, 1923. **7195**

Noteworthy, among the numerous, short contributions to this first periodical dedicated to J., are those of André Salmon, *L'homme,* p. 11–12; Benjamin Crémieux, *Max Jacob et le poème en prose,* p. 13–15; Pierre MacOrlan, *Max Jacob et l'art littéraire entre 1914 et...,* p. 17–18; Jean Cocteau, *Max Jacob,* p. 30–31; Philippe Soupault, *Max Jacob,* p. 42; Jules Supervielle, *Lettre à Max Jacob,* p. 43–44; *Apparition de Max Jacob,* p. 54–55; Marcel Arland, *Le charmant exemple de Max Jacob;* Marcel Jouhandeau, *Le mage,* p. 60. [JMS]

Hommage à Max Jacob. Agu 4, no. 2, 1939. *Also:* Tombeau de Max Jacob. Agu no. 1–2:1–110, 1944.   **7196**

In the augmented second ed. of this tribute appear testimonials by André Gide, Paul Claudel, Francis Carco, Charles-Albert Cingria, Alain Messiaen, Gertrude Stein, Saint-Pol Roux, René Villard, etc. [JMS]

Hommage à Max Jacob. BoiCl 10:1–31, 1951.   **7197**

Texts by J. and short articles by Jean Cassou, Yanette Delétang-Tardif, Henri Sauguet, Louis Emié, and Jean Rousselot. [SL]

Max Jacob. Eur 348–49:3–122, 1958. **7198**
Contains primarily biographical commentary by various hands. Also *Lettres* of J., p. 102–09. Significant articles have been analyzed separately. [JMS]

Max Jacob. Hommages d'A. Salmon, L. Guilloux, L. Guillaume, avec des lettres inédites du poète. FrA no. 24:353–68, 1948. **7199**
Salmon's "Cinq mars (1944–48)," p. 353–56, is a personal tribute to J. which ends with a poem. Guilloux's "Max Jacob," p. 357–63, is a reminiscence of J. and Guillaume's "Max nous parle," p. 364–68, is a short introduction to three letters that J. sent to him. [SL]

Max Jacob, 1944. C'était il y a trente ans. Association des Amis de Max Jacob, 1974. 75 p. **7200**
Statements in commemoration of J.'s death. These moving tributes by friends and admirers furnish a few biographical details. [JMS]

Max Jacob 1; autour du poème en prose. RLM 336–39:1–207, 1973. **7201**
Edited by Jean de Palacio, whose *Bibliographie sélective des origines à 1970,* p. 194–205, lists re-editions and correspondence along with criticism in the form of articles, chapters, periodicals devoted to J. Significant articles have been analyzed separately.

Max Jacob centennial (1876–1976). Folio no. 9:1–54, 1976. **7202**
Comprises significant criticism of J.'s texts, including articles on his poetry by Mary Ann Caws, Sydney Lévy, Marilyn Gaddis Rose, and Judith Morganroth Schneider. Analysis of his prose by Renée Riese Hubert. Also, discussion of literary relations by Gerald Kamber and Annette Thau. Includes previously unpublished letters by J. to his mother (1927) and to Gertrude Stein (1929–39). [JMS]

Max Jacob et la Bretagne suivi de La couronne de Vulcain, conte breton de Max Jacob. Les amis de Max Jacob, 1960–61. 79 p. (Les cahiers Max Jacob, 5) **7203**
Short articles by Georges Desse, Florian LeRoy, Louis Guillause, Pierre Guéguen, Marcel Béalu. None of these articles qualifies as a literary study, but

taken together they give a good impression of the role Brittany played in J.'s life and writings. [SL]

Max Jacob et la croix. RdF 54:1–17, 1965. **7204**
Short articles by Henri Bosco, Henri Dion, and Père Grégoire, with texts by J. [SL]

Max Jacob, le poète pénitent de Saint-Benoît-sur-Loire. DocVdO 31:1–62, 1945. **7205**
Short articles by Georges Durand, Yanette Delétang-Tardif, F. Weill, François Garnier, Maurice Gouchault, J. Perrodon, L. Hatton, Henri Dion, and Albert Fleureau. [SL]

Max Jacob magicien et martyr. Monde March 22, 1969. **7206**
Contents: Jean-Marie Dunoyer, *Etude;* Jean Cassou, *Un poète habité par la grâce;* Louis Guilloux, *Témoignage;* Jean Grenier, *Cet homme était Protée;* Gabriel Bounoure, *Une complainte mystique;* Jean Follain, *Entre le badinage comique et la gravité douloureuse.* [SL]

Max Jacob ou le poète de Saint-Benoît-sur Loire. Mail 5:1–67, 1928. **7207**
Short articles by Roger Secrétain, Jacques De Voragine, Paul Florens, Pierre Guéguen, Georges Hugnet, Marcel Jouhandeau, Jean Cassou, Jean Cocteau, Florent Fels, Marcel Abraham, Julien Lanoë, Y. G. Le Dantec, and Saint-Pol-Roux. [SL]

La Pâque de Max Jacob. RdF 65:1–19, 1968. **7208**
Principal article: René Plantier, *Max Jacob et le plus grand amour de Dieu,* p. 1–13. Brief articles by Alain Messiaen and Michel Ozenne. [SL]

Passage de Max Jacob. CahS 273:561–96, 1945. **7209**
Contents: Jean Cassou, *Adieu à Max Jacob,* p. 561–64; Maurice Morel, *Max Jacob, l'ombre et la proie,* p. 565–73; Léon-Gabriel Gros, *Tartuffe a dit vrai,* p. 574–80; Roger Lannes, *Max Jacob après lui,* p. 581–89. Also unpublished texts by J. [SL]

Pour en revenir à Max Jacob. Iô Numéro spécial:1–112, 1969. **7210**

Succinct, commemorative pieces by various hands, presented by Serge Brindeau and Jean Dubacq, extoll multiple facets of J.'s talent. Of special value are Claude Dinant's bibliography of J.'s works complete to 1968, and previously unpublished letter in which J. recalls Apollinaire. [JMS]

Speciaal Max Jacob nummer. Roep 30:1–144, 1954.   **7211**

Articles in Dutch by various hands. Includes texts by J. [SL]

Tombeau de Max Jacob. Sim n.s. 17–18: 1–104, n.d. [1955]   **7212**

Elegiac evocations by Jean Cocteau, Louis Emié, René-Guy Cadou, André Salmon, Franz Hellens, Marcel Béalu, Maurice Fombeure, François Garnier. Four articles explore the Breton inspiration in J.'s writing. Bibliography contains valuable list of collective works on which J. collaborated. [JMS]

General Studies: Books

Belaval, Yvon. La rencontre avec Max Jacob. Charlot, 1946. 176 p. *Also:* Vrin, 1974. 180 p.   **7213**

Three essays. Biographical account of J.'s meetings with Belaval in 1928–29, followed by correspondence of 1930, 1941–43. Perceptive, impressionistic commentary on *Cornet à dés* is first to underscore oneirism, metamorphosis, play, hidden anguish. Essay on J.'s Christianity includes abundant citation of his religious meditations. [JMS]

Cadou, René Guy. Esthétique de Max Jacob. Seghers, 1956. 95 p.   **7214**

In a short preface Cadou pays homage to J.'s continual eagerness to help young poets. The text is a collage from several sources, including letters to the author, esthetic meditations, aphorisms, notes on art, judgments and advice. [SL]

Fabureau, Hubert. Max Jacob: son œuvre. Eds. de la Nouvelle revue critique, 1935. 95 p. (Célébrités contemporaines, sér. 3, 3)   **7215**

Mainly anecdotal. First book-length study devoted to J. Criticism of *Cornet à dés* prejudiced by Fabureau's distaste

for parody, irony, verbal play in poetry. [JMS]

Jannini, Pasquale Aniel. L'esprit nouveau e le poetiche di Max Jacob. Milan, Editrice Viscontea, 1966. *Also:* L'angelo funambolo; Le poetiche di Max Jacob. Milan, Istituto editoriale Cisalpino-La Goliardica, 1973. 245 p.   **7216**

Views J.'s poetics, based on free play and order, as quintessence of "l'esprit nouveau" animating early twentieth-century artistic movements. Delineates evolution of J.'s poetry, while insisting on constancy of themes (angelism, funambulism, theater) and language. [JMS]

Kamber, Gerald. Max Jacob and the poetics of cubism. Baltimore and London, Johns Hopkins press, 1971. xxviii, 182 p.   **7217**

First detailed analysis of J.'s poetry in perspective of cubism. By comparing poems with techniques and theories of cubist painting, Kamber ascertains structural analogies. Interpretations of recurrent imagery are fascinating; claims of J.'s influence on modern writers rather broad. A significant, lively, controversial study. Bibliography of works by J. [JMS, SL]

Reviews: L. Breunig in RR 63:162–64, 1972; S. Collier in FS 28:224–25, 1974; B. Dijkstron in JML 3:658–60, 1973; J. McClelland in QQ 79:554–55, 1972.

[Oxenhandler, Neal] Max Jacob and Les feux de Paris. Letters and texts presented by Neal Oxenhandler. Berkeley and Los Angeles, Univ. of California press, 1964. 221–307 p. [Univ. of California publications in modern philology, vol. 35, no. 4]   **7218**

Outlines the metaphysical quest that brought about evolution in J.'s writing. Close readings by Oxenhandler reveal poet's obsession with multiplicity and transformation as both theme and basis of poetic rhythm. Presents and annotates twenty-five letters of J. to Jean Fraysse dating from 1934–37. [JMS, SL]

Reviews: J. Bellemin-Noël in RHL 66:748–49, 1966; L. Breuning in RR 57:314–15, 1966; G. Kamber in MLN 81:348–54, 1966; G. Trembley in FR 39:177–78, 1966.

Pérard, Joseph. Max Jacob l'universel. Colmar, Éds. Alsatia, 1974. 191 p. **7219**

A critique of one hundred pages followed by previously unpublished religious meditations sent to Pérard, an intimate friend, from 1927–37. Compendious survey of J.'s works with extensive quotes but lacking original judgments or interpretation. [JMS]

Pfau, Una. Zur Antinomie der bürgerlichen Satire; Untersuchungen über Leben und Werk Max Jacobs. Bern, Herbert Lang; Frankfurt, Peter Lang, 1975. 352 p. (Europäische Hochschulschriften, Reihe xiii, Französische Sprache und Literatur) **7220**

Investigates J.'s ironic critique of the bourgeoisie. It is based on a rejection of positivism and of a type of rationalism which had its origins in the spirit of the Enlightenment—a bourgeois movement. Pfau adds a biography, p. 162–233; a lengthy bibliography of primary and secondary literature; and reproduces mss. (*Annales*, 1923–24; *Carnet de voyage*, 1925: *Italie; Voyage en Espagne* 1926, *Carnet de Voyage de M. J.*). Of these only the *Carnet de voyage en Italie* was previously published (TR 66:121–45, 1953). [KW]

Plantier, René. Max Jacob. Desclée De Brouwer, 1972, 173 p. (Les écrivains devant Dieu) **7221**

Sensitive, thorough analysis of religious themes in J.'s works. Basically psychoanalytic approach, which refutes Rousselot's claim of conflict between poetry and religion by demonstrating ethical function of literary creation. According to Plantier, writing transposed and resolved J.'s spiritual and psychological divisions. [JMS]

Review: J. Dunoyer in Monde March 22, 1973; J. Schneider in FR 48:439–40, 1974.

Rousselot, Jean. Max Jacob au sérieux. Rodez, Eds. Subervie, 1958. 225 p. **7222**

In addition to previously published essay, "L'homme qui faisait penser à Dieu," includes seminal discussion of J.'s poetics, in theory and practice (previously published as "Contribution à une esthétique de Max Jacob," RE 10:296–318, 1957). Rousselot believes ethical opposition of Catholicism to occult tradition produced esthetic contradiction between emotion and invention. J.'s poetic vision, argues Rousselot, derives from occult not Christian (anti-poetic) mysticism. [JMS, SL]

Reviews: J. Adrien in RGB 95:67–76, 1959; A. Bernier in Thy 61:63–65, 1961.

Thau, Annette. Poetry and antipoetry; a study of selected aspects of Max Jacob's poetic style. Chapel Hill, Univ. of North Carolina department of Romance languages, 1976. 128 p. (North Carolina Studies in the Romance languages and literatures, Essays, number 5) **7223**

Throughout this rigorous, comprehensive survey of Jacobean stylistic structures, Thau defends hypothesis that J. used traditionally antipoetic aspects of language to extend the meaning of words. Abundant explications of devices within poetic contexts elucidate effects on reader. In addition to primary and critical sources, bibliography (p. 114–25) includes general reference works on stylistics. [JMS]

Wyss, Tobias. Dialog und Stille; Max Jacob, Giuseppe Ungaretti, Fernando Pessoa. Zurich, Juris Druck, 1969. 301 p. **7224**

Wyss defends his thesis that dialog exists only in privileged moments of openness, love, self-effacement: "Si tu regardes en toi, que tout soit blanc" (in Marcel Schwob's words). The essence of dialog is seen in a climate of quietude, not in the spoken word. To make his point, he looks at three authors whose productivity roughly spans the years between 1914 and 1934 (Ungaretti, Pessoa and J.) [KW]

General Studies: Articles

Antoine, Gérald. Max Jacob; une doctrine littéraire. FMonde 53:16–21, 1967. **7225**

An attempt to explicate the ambiguous Jacobean terms "style" and "situation" which represent, in Antoine's judgment, stylistic concepts basic to the modern literary text. Style would refer to a sense of unity, of a closed system; situation, to a margin or Brechtian "distanciation" analogous to the classical notion of genre. [JMS]

Attal, J.-P. La vocation de Max Jacob. MerF 1212:320–28, 1964. *Also in his:* L'image métaphysique et autres essais. Gallimard, 1969. p. 191–98.   **7226**

In this concise and stimulating article, Attal sees in J. two incompatible vocations: the mystic who calls for a "vie intérieure" and the artist who calls for "style," "situation" and distance. *La défense de Tartufe* could be read then as a typical spiritual experience or as a long modern poem. But Attal argues that the true reading is the one which will make these two perspectives coincide since J.'s biggest torment has been to find a point where art and faith unite without destroying each other. [SL]

Béguin, Albert. Destin de Max Jacob. *In his:* Poésie de la présence. Neuchâtel, La Baconnière, 1957. p. 275–83.   **7227**

Impressionistic appreciation of J.'s work and personality. [SL]

Belaval, Yvon. Le laboratoire central. NRF 15:295–305; 735–44, 1960. *Also:* Préface. *In:* Jacob, Max. Le laboratoire central, poèmes. Gallimard, 1960. p. 9–41.   **7228**

Study of versification in *Le laboratoire central* emphasizing variety in meter, rhyme, theme, image, and tone. Brief comparison of techniques with J.'s theories of style and situation and with methods of *Le cornet à dés.* [JMS, SL]

Bernard, Suzanne. Les précurseurs de l'Esprit nouveau: Max Jacob et Pierre Reverdy. *In her:* Le poème en prose de Baudelaire jusqu'à nos jours. Nizet, 1959. p. 627–37.   **7229**

Bernard sees in J. a fundamental step in the development of dada and surrealism. She rightly insists that with his *Cornet à dés* J. opened the door to a liberating language consisting of puns, parodies and fantasies which became for the surrealists a way of liberating the mind. J., however, had a concern also for construction and unity in his poems which the surrealists disregarded according to Bernard. These opposed tendencies, which correspond to "situation" and "style" respectively, are also fundamental to the prose poems as a genre. Interesting chapter in generally excellent book. [SL]

Bounoure, Gabriel. Les pénitents en maillots roses; Visions infernales; Fond de l'eau; Rivage, par Max Jacob. NRF 43: 109–18, 1934.   **7230**

Certain judgments made here by Bounoure have had prolonged resonance among critics. Notably, his characterization of J. as the malific Breton spirit, Korrigan, as a Jewish mystic whose poetry is based on the Kabbalistic cosmogony, and especially, his suggestion that J. was neither an artist nor a poet but rather "un grand inventeur de poésie." [JMS]

Cassou, Jean. Max Jacob et la liberté. NRF 30:455–63, 1928.   **7231**

In this essay on language in J., Cassou demonstrates the characteristics of his wit and shows its relevance. Argues that his use of non-utilitarian language destroys reality and makes a sharp social critique. [SL]

Collier, S. J. Max Jacob and the poème en prose. MLR 51:522–35, 1956.   **7232**

Values *Le cornet à dés,* above all, for its determination of the form and direction of the prose poem. J.'s conception of the genre is compared in some detail to that of Baudelaire, Bertrand, Rimbaud, Mallarmé, the Imagists, Renard, and Schwob. [JMS]

———. Max Jacob's Le cornet à dés; a critical analysis. FS 11:149–67, 1957.   **7233**

Fundamental investigation identifying features that give J.'s prose poems "their finished quality, their compact unity, and their internal tension." Cubist construction, automatic writing, verbal chain-composition, extension of literal meaning through "juggling" with words are devices exemplified. [JMS]

Fowlie, Wallace. Homage to Max Jacob. Poetry 75:352–56, 1950.   **7234**

An introduction to J.'s life and works. Fowlie insists on the contradictory (clown and mystic) and shows some resemblances to Rouault, Satie and others. [SL]

———. Max Jacob; violence of the supernatural. *In his:* Climate of violence. Macmillan, 1967. p. 188–202.   **7235**

An astute appraisal of J.'s poetic method, which followed principles identical to the precepts of surrealism before they were officially proclaimed by André Breton. Through verbal experimentation—in poems devoid of any visible relationship with the real world —J. transposes the violence of emotion dictated by the subconscious. [JMS]

Greene, Tatiana. Max Jacob et le surréalisme. FrFo 1:251–67, 1976.   **7236**

Greene's precise, well-documented examination, from several perspectives, of J.'s situation with respect to the surrealists clarifies a thorny question. By identifying surrealist traits in a wide range of J.'s texts preceding Breton's *Manifeste du surréalisme,* she proves that the poet proscribed by the founder of surrealism merits the often-claimed title of precursor. The information compiled here concerning literary relations and the publication of small reviews around 1920 is equally valuable. [JMS]

Henry, Hélène. Max Jacob et la Bretagne. *In:* Max Jacob. *See* 7198. p. 7–18. **7237**

Argues for the authentic regional inspiration of the themes, syntax, and vocabulary of *La côte* as well as the *Poèmes de Morven le Gaëlique* and *Le terrain Bouchaballe.* Also provides biographical facts relating to J.'s adolescence and his family's situation in Quimper. [JMS]

Hubert, Renée Riese. Max Jacob: the poetics of Le cornet à dés. *In:* About French poetry from dada to Tel Quel: text and theory. Ed. by Mary Ann Caws. Detroit, Wayne State univ. press, 1974. p. 99–111.   **7238**

A reading of texts as metapoems substantiating theoretical principles of J.'s preface: the undefinable subject matter of poetry and the demand for relinquishment by the reader of usual critical responses. Hubert's subtle interpretations point toward the coherence and esthetic significance of J.'s parodies of genres and artistic traditions. [JMS]

Kamber, Gerald. Max Jacob et Charles Baudelaire: une étude de sources. MLN 78:252–60, 1963.   **7239**

Refuting critical assumption that J.'s works resist exegesis, Kamber explicates passages from *Saint Matorel* and poems with reference to Baudelairian themes. J.'s recurrent "marionnette-vieille-paria" image-complex is considered a sign of his attachment to nineteenth-century romanticism. [JMS]

Le Bot, Marc. Max Jacob esthéticien? *In:* Max Jacob. *See* 7198. p. 46–56.   **7240**

Rather than forming a closed system, J.'s reflections on art represent to Le Bot a part of the poet's effort to develop his inner spiritual existence, to live the "esthetic life," in order eventually to reach divine perfection. Interprets J.'s conception of poetry as a means of fusing spirit with matter, of humanizing (i.e., spiritualizing) the objects of the universe. [JMS]

Leiris, Michel. Saint Matorel martyr. *In his:* Brisées. Mercure de France, 1966. p. 82–90.   **7241**

General observations on meaning and value of J.'s poetry and prose. Of interest because of Leiris' exceptional perspicacity as a reader. [JMS]

Lévy, Sydney. Jeu et poésie: une lecture du Cornet à dés de Max Jacob. SubS no. 4: 27–44, 1972.   **7242**

Considering prose poems in a theoretical framework of writing as play, Lévy keenly explicates texts as masks invented by the poet in order to overcome an obstacle that prevents communication and self-discovery. The tension between J.'s search for an idealist "moi" and his precontrived failure marks the transitional situation of his writing between two esthetics: romantic/surrealist; prosaic/structural; linear/profound. [JMS]

———. Que faire de Max Jacob? SubS no. zéro:31–37, 1971.   **7243**

An emphatic enunciation of the focus of new Jacobean criticism. Instead of superimposing myths, the critic should disclose J.'s textual processes, as illustrated by Lévy's paradigmatic reading of the poem "Intérimes." [JMS]

Lockerbie, S. I. Realism and fantasy in the work of Max Jacob; some verse poems. *In:* Order and adventure in post-romantic

French poetry. Essays presented to C. A. Hackett. Ed. by E. M. Beaumont, J. M. Cocking and J. Cruickshank. Oxford, Basil Blackwell, 1973. p. 149–61.   **7244**

In addition to exhibiting J.'s focus on details of ordinary life in his lesser known texts of 1910–20 period, Lockerbie proposes an original approach to the question of poetic evolution. [JMS]

Malraux, André. Art poétique par Max Jacob. NRF 19:227–28, 1922.   **7245**

Calling J.'s *Art poétique* a "critique du beau," Malraux claims that psychology is at the base of his system. He disputes, however, J.'s characterization of passion in Christian art. [SL]

Oxenhandler, Neal. Concealed emotions in the poetry of Max Jacob. DadaS no. 5: 53–57, 1975.   **7246**

Oxenhandler's examination of *L'homme de cristal* uncovers emotional zones of alienation and fears of erotic temptation and sentimentality. But within the poems, he believes, J. transcends his schizoid tendency through mystical incorporation in the body of Christ. [JMS]

———. Jacob's struggle with the angel. YFS 12:41–66, 1953.   **7247**

In a comparison of J. with Verlaine, Oxenhandler underscores the difficulty of using the *esprit nouveau* style to write religious lyrics. Evasions and parodies of emotion indicate J.'s consciousness of his post-romantic historical situation. [JMS]

Palacio, Jean de. Max Jacob et Apollinaire: documents inédits. SF 42:467–74, 1970.   **7248**

With much care Palacio shows some ambiguity in J.'s judgment of Apollinaire and his poetry. The study is based on a series of documents dating mostly from the end of J.'s life. [SL]

———. La postérité du Gaspard de la nuit: de Baudelaire à Max Jacob. *In:* Max Jacob 1. *See* 7201. p. 157–89.   **7249**

Elucidates the dialectics of theme and form in the prose poem as originated by Bertrand, transformed by Baudelaire, reinvented by J. The latter accomplished alliance of tradition and modernity by eliminating picturesque

and romantic elements, while retaining syntactic and incantatory devices of his predecessors, as well as their tendency to construct an imaginary reality with concrete, realistic objects. [JMS]

———. Un précurseur inattendu de Max Jacob: Lord Byron. RLC 45:187–207, 1971.   **7250**

Shows influence of Byron's *Don Juan* on J.'s preface to *La côte, Phanérogame, Cinématoma.* Comparison infers a Byronic inspiration (humor and parody) at the core of J.'s vision. [JMS]

———. Le sang et la crucifixion; Max Jacob d'après ses variantes, ou la passion de l'écrivain. RSH 35:593–601, 1970.   **7251**

Rejecting the myth of J. as perpetual improvisor, this perusal of published and unpublished texts reveals the meticulousness of the poet's revisions. Exegesis of Jacobean analogy between writing and Christian suffering confirms hypothesis of J.'s view of creation as labor. [JMS]

Pelletier, Christian. Le manuscrit du Cornet à dés de Max Jacob. IL no. 5:226–28, 1974.   **7252**

Scrutiny of *Cornet* manuscript results in the following conclusions: texts are not direct oneiric transcriptions; strong, anti-militarist satire was censored; biographical and religious confidences were repressed. [JMS]

Pinguet, Maurice. L'écriture du rêve dans Le cornet à dés. *In:* Max Jacob 1. *See* 7201. p. 13–52.   **7253**

Penetrating analysis of *Cornet*'s style as a representation of the dream process previously unknown to literature and comparable to the principles elaborated by Freud. Interpretation of J.'s preface as an exposition of the theory of dream writing is original but questionable. [JMS]

Plantier, René. La mythologie dans l'œuvre poétique de Max Jacob. *In:* Max Jacob 1. *See* 7201. p. 53–123.   **7254**

Plantier's comprehensive, systematic study classifies J.'s allusions to mythology according to origin and analyzes both their rhetorical function and thematic significance. An index (p.

101–23) lists more than 100 mythological references drawn from over 200
citations of J.'s poetry. [JMS]

Raymond, Marcel. Les jeux de l'esprit
libre. *In his:* De Baudelaire au surréalisme. Corrêa, 1933. p. 252–62. *Also:*
José Corti, 1952.   **7255**
   In retrospect, these few pages in
Raymond's classic study seem to contain most of the future serious criticism
on J. He emphasizes the role of word
play, the reader's estrangement at the
contact of the poem and the irrational
realism. Most interesting is his thesis
that J. makes an effort not to be identified, or rather to empty himself of any
identity. [SL]

Rousselot, Jean. Max Jacob ou le sel dans
la plaie. *In his:* Présences contemporaines.: rencontres sur le chemin de la
poésie. Debresse, 1958. p. 127–39.   **7256**
   Short biography with an attempt to
correct J.'s image of the mystifier.
Rousselot claims that his work is an
alliance of "prosaïsme et musique,
familiarité et illusionnisme, humour et
abandon." [SL]

Schneider, Judith Morganroth. Max Jacob
on poetry. MLR 69:290–96, 1974.   **7257**
   An exposition of contradictions informing J.'s statements on traditional
topics of poetics. Sets forth oppositions
among theories reflecting cubist, Kabbalistic, orthodox and mystical Christian, romantic, classical, and surrealist
conceptions of poetry. [JMS]

Thau, Annette. The esthetic reflections of
Max Jacob. FR 45:800–12, 1972.   **7258**
   Within heterogeneous texts concerning poetry, Thau finds a coherence deriving from recurrent reflections on a
core of problems. This summary delineation of J.'s basic ideas insists upon
his anti-romantic view of the artist as
autonomous technician and of poetry
as gratuitous form. [JMS]

————. Play with words and sounds in the
poetry of Max Jacob. *In:* Max Jacob
1. *See* 7201. p. 125–56.   **7259**
   J.'s "verbal acrobatics" are divided
into clearly defined rhetorical categories: puns with a single reference,
paronomasia based on the repetition of
homonyms or homophones, sound links

emphasizing patterns of sound before
associations of sense. In individual
poems, verbal play may produce comic,
lyrical, fantastical, or analytical effects
or create ambiguity demanding (or
blocking) interpretation by the reader.
[JMS]

Whiteman, H. G. The poetics of Max
Jacob. Nonp no. 1:92–100, 1959.   **7260**
   A good description of J.'s poetics in
context of the avant-garde and Rimbaud's influence and in context of his
religious beliefs. [SL]

Drama

Garnier, François. Max Jacob et le théâtre.
In: Max Jacob. *See* 7198. p. 37–46. **7261**
   Catalogs J.'s little-known dramatic
works, comprising mystical and satirical
plays, sketches for improvisation, musical comedies, one-act plays. Especially
valuable for data on circumstances
surrounding composition, performance,
and publication. [JMS]

Jacob, Max. Théâtre. Un amour du Titien.
La police napolitaine. Les Amis de Max
Jacob, 1953. 100 p. (Cahiers Max Jacob,
3)   **7262**
   Contains a chronology of J.'s writing
for the theater, a short biographical
essay by Henri Sauguet entitled
"Quand j'écrivais une opérette avec
Max Jacob" as well as the two previously unpublished "comédies musi-
cales." [SL]

Francis Jammes
(Nos. 7263–7291)

REINHARD KUHN

Correspondence & Memoirs

**Colette, [Sidonie Gabrielle] and Francis
Jammes.** Une amitié inattendue. Introduction et notes de Robert Mallet. Emile-
Paul, 1945. 77 p.   **7263**
   A well edited collection of letters
which go far toward elucidating the
sensibilities of both writers. The introduction is particularly valuable as a
source of biographical information.

Jammes, Francis. Mémoires. Mercure de
France, 1971. 299 p.   **7264**

Sheds considerable light on the early life of J. (1868–1906). Especially interesting for the extensive discussion and documentation of "naturisme." Review: T. Shealy in FR 46:659–60, 1973.

———, and André Gide. Correspondance 1893–1938. Préface et notes par Robert Mallet. Gallimard, 1948. 388 p.   **7265**

A classic confrontation between a cynic and a sentimentalist through which the foibles of both writers come to the fore in exaggerated fashion.

———, and Arthur Fontaine. Correspondance 1898–1930. Introduction et notes de Jean Labbé. Gallimard, 1959. 322 p.   **7266**

Contains important biographical data concerning both writers.

———, and Francis Vielé-Griffin. Correspondance de Francis Jammes et de Francis Vielé-Griffin (1893–1937). Introduction et notes par Reinhard Kuhn. Geneva, Droz, 1966. 93 p. (Textes littéraires français, 122)   **7267**

Contains important biographical material and some unpublished poems. Useful for the understanding of "jammisme."
Reviews: P. Béarn in RevRP 68:282–83, 1966; S. Braun in FR 40:849–50, 1967; M. Caws in EspCr 9:58–59, 1969; M. Décaudin in IL 19:30, 1967.

———, and Paul Claudel. Correspondance de Francis Jammes avec Paul Claudel et Gabriel Frizeau. Introduction et notes du Père Blanchet. Gallimard, 1952. 465 p.   **7268**

An important elucidation of very different types of Catholicism which goes far toward explaining the impact of faith on the poetics of both Jammes and Claudel. Of special interest are some letters of Rivière.

———, and Thomas Braun. Correspondance 1898–1937. Texte établi et présenté par Daniel Laroche. Introduction de Benoît Braun. Brussels, Palais des académies, 1972. 239 p. (Académie royale de langue et de littératures françaises)   **7269**

Carelessly edited letters devoid of literary value. No discussion of esthetic questions. Provides some information

useful for the reconstitution of the period 1889–1937.
Review: R. Kuhn in FR 47:998–99, 1974.

———, and Valery Larbaud. Correspondance inédite. Introduction et notes de G. Jean-Aubry. The Hague, Stols, 1947. 88 p.   **7270**

A carefully annotated edition of the sporadic exchange of letters between two writers who were not very close. A good illustration of J.'s sensibility.

Samain, Albert, and Francis Jammes. Une amitié lyrique: Albert Samain et Francis Jammes, correspondance inédite. Introduction et notes de Jules Mouquet. Emile-Paul, 1946. 198 p.   **7271**

Contains interesting documents concerning the relationship of J. to the Symbolists. Useful for the understanding of the esthetics of both poets and of the social milieu in which they moved.

General Studies: Books

Bersancourt, Albert de. Francis Jammes, poète chrétien. H. Falque, 1910. 85 p.   **7272**

A minor treatise which illustrates the variety of Christian themes in the poetry of J.

Burkhardt, Heinz. Natur und Heimat bei Francis Jammes. Würzburg, K. Triltsch, 1937. 113 p.   **7273**

A superficial discussion of J. as a regionalist.

Dyson, Rose M. Les sensations et la sensibilité chez Francis Jammes. Geneva, Droz, 1954. 147 p.   **7274**

An undistinguished essay which places the emphasis on the clichés which have grown up around the work of J. Invaluable because it contains the only fairly extensive bibliography of the works of J. which appeared in periodicals and of critical essays devoted to his work.

Flory, Albert. Francis Jammes. Maison de la bonne presse, 1941. 109 p.   **7275**

A minor essay in which the transition of J. from a pagan to a religious poet is delineated.

Inda, Jean-Pierre. Francis Jammes, du faune au patriarque. Lyon, Presses académiques, 1952. 403 p. **7276**

A dissertation which traces in schematic form the development of J. from sensualist to Christian apologist.

———. Francis Jammes et le pays basque. Lyon, Presses académiques, 1952. 120 p. **7277**

A standard analysis of the regionalist themes in J.'s writings.

Mallet, Robert. Francis Jammes. Une étude par Robert Mallet; inédits, œuvres choisies... Seghers, 1950. 223 p. (Poètes d'aujourd'hui, 20) **7278**

A well-written brief biography and a concise resumé of the development of J.'s poetics. Contains a rudimentary bibliography.

———. Francis Jammes, sa vie, son œuvre (1868–1938). Mercure de France, 1961. 323 p. **7279**

The definitive biography of J. and a detailed description of his entire work. Well documented and meticulously accurate. Very useful index. The only flaw is the lack of a bibliography.

Reviews: H. Charasson in EdP 202: 110–16, 1962; S. Fumet in TR 166: 9–18, 1961; M. d'Hartoy in RBPH 42: 145–46, 1964; C. Le Quintrec in Thy 55:54–56, 1962; A. Loranquin in BdL 231:341–43, 1961; H, Perrau in BouF 41:185–90, 1961; G. Piroué in MerF 342:363–65, 1961.

———. Le jammisme. Mercure de France, 1961. 252 p. **7280**

The definitive exposition of the esthetics of Jammes. An introductory depiction of the ideas which influenced the formulation of "jammisme," followed by an analytic essay in which it is defined. A concluding section outlines the impact of "jammisme" on the poet's contemporaries.

Reviews: M. d'Hartoy in RBPH 42: 145–46, 1964; A. Loranquin in BdL 231:341–43, 1961.

Marie-Margarita, S.N.D., Soeur (i.e. Mildred Mary McDevitt). La métrique de Francis Jammes vue dans le cadre de celles de ses contemporains et de ses prédécesseurs immédiats. Boston, Spaulding-Moss Cie., 1959. 226 p. **7281**

An inaccurate stylistic analysis of some verses of J. seemingly chosen at random followed by an unconvincing essay on the originality of J.

Parent, Monique. Francis Jammes. Etude de langue et de style. Les belles lettres, 1957. 535 p. **7282**

A traditional and meticulous analysis of all of J.'s major poems. The closely reasoned individual explications help towards an understanding of J.'s esthetics.

Reviews: A. Gill in MLR 54:282–85, 1959; J. Ireson in ArL 10:160–63, 1958; Y. Le Hir in FM 26:151–53, 1958; H. Mitterand in FM 26:223–29, 1959; R. Sodergard in SN 31:306–09, 1959; R. Wagner in BSLP 54: 158–61, 1959.

———. Rythme et versification dans la poésie de Francis Jammes. Les belles lettres, 1957. 254 p. **7283**

A technical analysis of most of J.'s major poems which elucidates his poetic techniques.

Perticucci Bernardini, Ada. Jammes e la poesia crepuscolare. Rome, Palombi, 1940. 187 p. **7284**

A discussion of J.'s place in the tradition of romantic nature poets.

Soulairol, Jean. Francis Jammes. P. Lethielleux, 1941. 40 p. (Collection publicistes chrétiens) **7285**

An unoriginal defense of J. as a Christian poet.

Van der Burght, Raymond and Laure. Francis Jammes, le faune chrétien. Brussels, Brépols, 1961. 240 p. (Le cheval insolite) **7286**

Another statement of the ambiguity of J.'s verse as both sensual and Christian.

Review: J. Vanham in RNa 340: 91–92, 1962.

General Studies: Articles

Lasserre, Pierre. Les chapelles littéraires: Claudel, Jammes, Péguy. Garnier, 1920. 252 p. **7287**

A statement of the obvious thesis that J.'s early work is that of a nature poet and his later work that of a religious poet.

Lowell, Amy. Francis Jammes. *In her:* Six French poets; studies in contemporary literature. Macmillan, 1915. p. 213–68.
7288

A good introductory essay to J. in which his work is studied within the same context as that of Verhaeren, Samain, Rémy de Gourmont, Régnier and Fort.

Revue régionaliste des Pyrénées. Organe périodique de l'Association régionaliste du Béarn et du Pays Basque. Pau, Nov. 1917–
7289

A good source for otherwise unpublished works of J. and for secondary essays.

Riffaterre, Michel. Problèmes d'analyse du style littéraire. RPh 14:216–27, 1961.
7290

A demonstration of how the structuralist approach, as opposed to the traditional stylistic analysis of Parent, can add a new dimension to the interpretation of the poetry of J.

Valeri, Diego. Poeti francesi del nostro tempo. Jammes, Gide, Guérin, Fort, Philippe. Piacenza, Società tipografica editoriale, 1924. 118 p.
7291

A general introductory essay to the work of J.

Pierre Jean Jouve
(Nos. 7292–7387)

Claude Pichois*

Biography

Boisdeffre, Pierre de. Pierre Jean Jouve. NL 4 Oct. 16, 1958. *Also:* MerF 334: 724–26, 1958.
7292

Interview with the poet revealing his elective affinities with other artists and the catharsis he was able to achieve through the war.

Chalon, Jean. Pierre Jean Jouve par lui-même et par Jean Chalon. FL 30, Dec. 10, 1964.
7293

* With assistance from Gabrielle Jung Sayn.

Revealing statement about J.'s personality as he freely admits to giving out press communiqués rather than interviews. Explains why so many articles about his life and work are repetitious. Notes an interesting comment of Claudel about the novel *Paulina 1880*.

Donnadieu, Jean-Léon. Pierre Jean Jouve. FrA 2:140–46, 1947.
7294

Homage to J. as a writer and a person with special emphasis on his role in the Second World War.

Jouve, Pierre Jean. En miroir: journal sans date. Mercure de France, 1954. 215 p. *Also (rev.):* Mercure de France, 1970. 211 p.
7295

J.'s masterly manifesto about his work. Invaluable document ranking among his finest prose because of its style and the important biographical revelations it contains. The genesis of the Helen figure as well as the swan motif in *Langue* are elucidated through several women the poet encountered. J. also incorporates such texts as the *avant-propos* to *Vegadu* (1931), the *Considérations sur le sujet* of *Histoires sanglantes* (1932), the all important essay *Inconscient, spiritualité et catastrophe* of *Sueur de sang* (1933) and *La faute,* an explanation of his concept of original sin serving as a preface for the republication of *Le paradis perdu* (1938). *En miroir* is probably the best single work on J. in existence.

Reviews: A. Béguin in Esp 22:288–93, 1954; Y. Bonnefoy in LetN 2:93–97, 1954; M.-P. Fouchet *in his: Les appels.* Mercure de France, 1967. p. 65–73; R. Lacôte in LetF 2, June 14–20, 1956; R. Lalou in NL 3, June 24, 1954; G. Piroué in TR 128–29, Sept. 1954; J. Rousselot in NL 4, Dec. 30, 1954; P. Toynbee in TLS 607, Sept. 24, 1954.

———. Six lectures de radio. TR 48–60, Nov. 1950.
7296

J. considers modern poetry a meditation on the human condition and since Baudelaire a way of deciphering the struggles in the unconscious of man. This brief analysis is followed by remarks on Baudelaire, Rimbaud, Mallarmé, Claudel and Saint-John Perse.

Raymond, Marcel. Pierre Jean Jouve quand il était à Genève. GazLit 31, Dec. 10–11, 1966.   **7297**
Personal recollections of J.'s exile in Geneva during the Second World War.

Rhodes, S. A. A disciple of William Blake: Pierre Jean Jouve. *In his:* Candles for Isis. SR 41:287–90, 1933.   **7298**
Interview with the poet about his work and his relation to Freudian psychoanalysis. Also revelatory about J.'s feelings towards Paul Valéry.

Vadja, Peter. Stefan Zweig und Pierre Jean Jouve. LJGG 7:229–32, 1966.   **7299**
Concise article about Stefan Zweig's relationship with J. including a letter of Zweig expressing his opinion about the novel *Vagadu.* Essentially very similar to certain passages on J. in Robert Dumont's *Zweig et la France. Un dialogue franco-allemand.* Didier, 1967. p. 156–61. (Coll. des Etudes de littérature étrangère et comparée)

Iconography

Catalogue de l'exposition Pierre Jean Jouve. Ed. by François Chapon. Bibliothèque littéraire Jacques Doucet, 1959. 24 p. **7300**
Catalog of the J. exhibit in 1959 listing valuable information on mss., first eds., iconography and correspondence of the author.

General Studies: Books

Callander, Margaret. The poetry of Pierre Jean Jouve. Manchester, University press, 1965. 308 p.   **7301**
Useful, clear, well documented. Probably the most detailed and competent study of J.'s poetry, summed up as a remarkable combination of Christian meditation and Rimbaldian magic. Callander, besides giving a rigorous stylistic analysis of the major themes evolving in the work, also furnishes valuable biographical and bibliographical material.
Reviews: Anon. in TLS 45, Jan. 20, 1966; J.-P. Forster in EdL 10:61–63, 1967; S. I. Lockerbie in FMLS 368–76, Oct. 1966.

Micha, René. L'œuvre de Pierre Jean Jouve. Brussels, Cahiers du journal des poètes, 1940. 37 p. (Les cahiers du journal des poètes)   **7302**
J.'s novels and poetry seen as poetic and mystical narratives. Micha, a journalist friend of J., tries to define the poet's conception of God and sin. Very close interpretation to the one given by the author himself in the preface to *Sueur de sang* and the 1938 ed. of *Le paradis perdu.*

————. Pierre Jean Jouve. Présentation par René Micha, choix de textes... Seghers, 1956. 219 p. (Poètes d'aujourd'hui, 48) **7303**
Introduction to J.'s work and personality mainly derived from the poet's own work. Micha endeavors to sum up the essential elements found therein. Divides J.'s novels and related poetry into four cycles.
Review: G. Picon in MerF 328: 296–301, 1956.

Special Number

Pierre Jean Jouve. Ed. by Robert Kopp and Dominique de Roux. Eds. de l'herne, 1972. 423 p. (Cahiers de l'herne, 19) **7304**
Vast amalgam of texts on J. and by him. Contains valuable little known correspondence with such literary figures as Jean Paulhan, Rainer Maria Rilke, André Gide, Gabriel Bounoure, Gaston Bachelard, etc. Introduces new articles by such important authors and critics as Yves Bonnefoy, Jean Cassou, Marc Eigeldinger, Marcel Raymond and Jean Starobinski, as well as reprints of excellent texts by Pierre Emmanuel and Giuseppe Ungaretti. Also to be noted are several revealing commentaries on J.'s life by people who have known him intimately (Jean R. de Salis, Jules Roy, Henry Bauchau, S. Corinna Bille) and the most extensive iconography in print. Good introduction to the life and work of J; one could however question its overall objectivity, as all the texts were submitted to the author, and also deplore the lack of an article on J.'s second wife, Blanche Reverchon-Jouve, whose considerable influence on the poet is only indirectly acknowledged. At the

end, one finds a bibliography containing many errors. Complying with a desire of J., all entries prior to 1925 are eliminated.

Reviews: A. Flory in Croix, June 17–18, 1973; F. Kemp in NZZ 49, Jan. 14, 1973.

General Studies: Articles

Arland, Marcel. Pierre Jean Jouve. *In his:* Anthologie de la poésie française. New revised ed. Stock, 1960. p. 798–801. **7305**

Notes the resemblance of J.'s poetry to that of Baudelaire, Mallarmé and Rimbaud, but also to that of Sponde and La Ceppède.

Berger, Yves. Pierre Jean Jouve: l'homme qui ne croit pas à la liberté. Exp 28–29, March 7, 1963. **7306**

Considers J. the greatest baroque novelist of the twentieth century. The spirit of the Middle Ages is however apparent in all his work as the poet does not believe in personal liberty.

Carmody, Francis, J. Jouve the architect. BA 32:248–53, 1958. **7307**

Emphasizes J.'s interpretation of dreams as a way of reading the meaning of existence.

Cassou, Jean. Etapes de l'œuvre de Pierre Jean Jouve. *In his:* Pour la poésie. Corrêa, 1935. **7308**

Sensitive appraisal of J.'s poetry between 1925–1933 and its reflection in the author's novels and translations. Cassou, a personal friend as well as a constant reviewer of J.'s work, gives remarkable insight into the concepts and style of *Noces* in which he also notes certain similarities with the poetry of William Blake. Cassou stresses the dramatic quality of J.'s work as well as its purity and inherent cruelty.

Chessex, Jacques. Pierre Jean Jouve. La rose et le crachat. GazLit 32, Dec. 10–11, 1962. **7309**

Elucidation of carnal desire and sin in J.'s work.

Clancier, Georges-Emmanuel. Pierre Jean Jouve. *In his:* De Rimbaud au surré-alisme: panorama critique. Seghers, 1953. p. 357–63. **7310**

Good evaluation of the overall aspects of J.'s poetry. Clancier acknowledges the poet's feeling for the tragic and the civic-mindedness apparent in most of his work.

Du Bois, Pierre. Une heure avec Pierre Jean Jouve. GazL Sept. 13–14, 1969. **7311**

Interview with J. about his life and his work. Interesting as the poet discloses certain biographical elements prior to 1925.

Dumur, Guy. Poétique de Pierre Jean Jouve. MerF 336:392–419, 1959. **7312**

Good summary of the major trends in J.'s work. Discusses his relationship with certain other artists, his *engagement* during the Second World War, the myths evolving in his poetry and the author's personal obsessions.

El Kayem, Henri. Rencontre avec trois poètes: Shehadé, Jouve, Bonnefoy. RduC 18:87–110, 1955. **7313**

Contains certain interesting biographical revelations about J.'s life, as well as a discussion of his work which the author considers based on observation and prophetic vision.

Emmanuel, Pierre. Pierre Jean Jouve architecte de l'âme. FL 2, Nov. 24, 1962. **7314**

Emphasizes the architectural quality of J.'s work as well as that of his life. Notes the avant-garde quality of his literary production, strongly defending his use of psychoanalysis.

———. Pierre Jean Jouve ou la poésie à plusieurs hauteurs. Font 45:736–41, 1945. **7315**

Examines how J. came to consider time as the essential element of human solidarity. Accountable for this development are psychoanalysis, the Second World War and art.

———. Qui est cet homme ou le singulier universel. Egloff, 1947. p. 145–353. *Also in his:* Autobiographies. Seuil, [1970]. p. 122–271. *Also:* Ma fidélité continue. *In:* Pierre Jean Jouve. *See* 7304. p. 43–59. **7316**

Excellent narrative taken from Emmanuel's autobiography relating his discovery of *Sueur de sang* and the immense influence this book of verse was going to exercise upon him. Interesting demonstration of J.'s influence on young minds.

Fouchet, Max-Pol. L'éros et la mort. NL 40:6–7, 1962. *Also in:* Exp 31–32, Nov. 29, 1962. **7317**

The importance of psychoanalysis in J.'s work is explained through his interpretation of eros and death.

Groethuysen, B. Sueur de sang, Matière céleste, Le paradis perdu, Kyrie. NRF 26:140–42, 1938. **7318**

Explanation of J.'s metaphysics.

Gros, Léon-Gabriel. Morale et poésie. CahS 25:866–78, 1938. **7319**

Elucidates the poetry of Eluard, Supervielle and J. Considers J. as a conscientious artist, essentially a Parnassian, who claims as his ancestors the German Romantics. Gros also studies the formation of the landscapes in his poetry and the juxtaposition of obscene and formal vocabulary.

Israël, Madeleine. Pierre Jean Jouve ou la métamorphose du poète. CahS 19:682–94, 1932. **7320**

Brief but interesting review of the poet's early work. Israël shows fine psychological insight as well as biographical knowledge. However one should be careful not to attach too much value to the influence accorded to Hölderlin as early as 1915.

Jaccottet, Philippe. Jouve (1925–1947). *In his:* L'entretien des muses. Gallimard, 1968. p. 45–54. **7321**

Personal objective evalution of the poet's work commenting on its baroque elements as well as its characteristic juxtaposition of sensuality and mysticism.

Juin, Hubert. Commentaire à Pierre Jean Jouve. Comb 11, March 31, 1960. **7322**

Good summary of J.'s work. Juin notes that the author converted to a more interior form of poetry in order to express his spiritual values.

Kemp, Friedhelm. Nachwort. *In his:* Jouve, Pierre-Jean. Gedichte. Heidelberg, Drei Brücken Verlag, 1957. p. 97–104. **7323**

Short biographical sketch and an outline of the main influences on his work considered as a mixture of passion and asceticism.

Reviews: K. Krolow in NDH 357–58, July 1958; B. Titec in FH 14:443–47, 1959.

Kushner, Eva. Le mythe d'Orphée dans l'œuvre de Pierre Jean Jouve. *In her:* Le mythe d'Orphée dans la littérature française contemporaine. Nizet, 1961. p. 264–97. **7324**

Analysis of the myth of Orpheus in J.'s poetry and prose works which, according to Kushner, could be entitled the myth of Hélène. A correlation is drawn between the poet's biography and his interpretation of the myth.

Lorent, Laure. La culpabilité de l'amour charnel chez Pierre Jean Jouve. RevN 20:467–79. 1964. **7325**

Investigates J.'s dilemma, torn on the one hand between a sincere longing for purity, and on the other carnal desires.

Micha, René. Univers de Jouve. CahS 28:563–70, 1941. **7326**

Explanation of J.'s metaphysics in a Christian and Freudian perspective.

Miomandre, Francis de. La scène capitale. Jour 2, Feb. 7, 1936. **7327**

Interesting development of J.'s relationship to music.

Pieyre de Mandiargues, André. Le philtre noir de Pierre Jean Jouve. NouvO 163:30–31, 1968. **7328**

Defines J. as an Elizabethan as he does not fear excess and as he shows a marked predilection for sublime or terrible stories.

Raymond, Marcel. Pierre Jean Jouve. *In his:* De Baudelaire au surréalisme. Corrêa, 1933. p. 376–80. *Also (rev.):* Corti, 1940. *Also:* From Baudelaire to surrealism. London, Methuen 1970. (University paperbacks, UP 355) *Trans.:* From Baudelaire to surrealism. New York, Wittenborn, Schultz, 1949. **7329**

Brief but excellent synthesis of the writer. Particular attention is granted to J. as a mystical poet.

Risi, Nelo. Settant'anni di Pierre Jean Jouve: una terrestre fanfara. FLe 3, March 1957.   **7330**
Probably one of the only articles to draw a parallel between J. and D. H. Lawrence.

Rousselot, Jean. Pierre Jean Jouve ou le rôle sanctificateur de l'œuvre d'art. EspL 6:10–24, 1955. *Also in his:* Présences contemporaines. Debresse, 1958. p. 183–96.   **7331**
Study of the role J. imparts to his poetry.

Sacy, Samuel S. de. En hommage à Pierre Jean Jouve. LetN 7:5–7, 1959.   **7332**
Sees J. as a pure poet whose whole work is based on solitude and isolation. This article also serves as a foreword to the catalog of the J. exhibit held at the Bibliothèque littéraire Jacques Doucet May 25–June 6, 1959.

Starobinski, Jean. Pierre Jean Jouve. Poé 47:90–109, 1947.   **7333**
Scholarly, lively and interesting. Although an admirer of J., Starobinski analyzes with detachment the qualities and shortcomings of J.'s poetry and prose. He particularly stresses the interrelationship of these two genres, noting the dramatic quality of the poems and the necessity for J. to express his tragic feeling of life in his novels. He also explains J.'s relationship to other literary figures with whom he identifies and from whom he draws inspiration. An excellent study of the themes, style and characterization, this study is probably the best single article on J.

———. Pierre Jean Jouve un paysage s'élève. GazLit 33, Dec. 10–11, 1966.   **7334**
The landscapes in J.'s work are not to be regarded as simple decors, but as visual manifestations of sin, anguish, hope and intimations of liberation.

Ungaretti, Giuseppe. Sous le signe de Niobé. NRF 16:385–86, 1968. *Also in:* Pierre Jean Jouve. *See* 7304. p. 41–42.   **7335**
Ungaretti's very personal homage to a fellow poet.

Vivier, Robert. Pierre Jean Jouve. JdP 16, June 10, 1933.   **7336**

J.'s evolution from mysticism to psychoanalysis in his poetry.

Wahl, Jean. La pierre et le feu: la poésie de Pierre Jean Jouve. Cr 7:291–303, 1952.   **7337**
J. essentially places himself in the poetic tradition of Baudelaire, Rimbaud, Mallarmé and Nerval.

Individual Poems and Collections

Bastide, Roger. Sueur de sang et l'unité de la pensée de Pierre Jean Jouve. CahS 23: 293–99, 1936.   **7338**
Sueur de sang contains all the myths inherent in J.'s poetry since *Tragiques.* Special emphasis is placed on the myth of birth with all the different kinds of symbols it evokes.

Béguin, Albert. Quatre de nos poètes. Font 141–68, June 1942.   **7339**
Excellent comparison between *Porche à la nuit des saints* and *Gloire.* Study of their rhythmic structures and themes in comparison with earlier works profoundly marked by Freudian psychoanalysis.

Bosquet, Alain. Ténèbre de Pierre Jean Jouve. Monde 13, April 3, 1965.   **7340**
Review of *Ténèbre* noting the enlargement of themes in the work compared to prior volumes of poetry. Bosquet considers J. a true twentieth century poet as he deals with the problem of the absurd.

Bounoure, Gabriel. Récents poèmes de Pierre Jean Jouve. MerF 287–95, Feb. 1953.   **7341**
Notes the "baudelairisme taoïste" in *Langue* and *Ode.* Finds some of these poems akin to the orphic poems of Rilke.

Cassou, Jean. Pierre Jean Jouve. Comb 7, March 27, 1952.   **7342**
Review of *Génie, Diadème* and *Ode.* Cassou notes that the author only identifies with the purest poets: Nerval, Baudelaire, Rimbaud, Mallarmé and Hölderlin.

Clancier, G. E. Inventions. MerF 335:290–95, 1959.   **7343**
Review of the work of which many

poems are to be regarded as a spiritual testament of the author.

Couffignal, Robert. Pierre Jean Jouve 1929. Le paradis perdu. *In his:* Aux premiers jours du monde... la paraphrase poétique de la Genèse de Hugo à Supervielle. Minard, 1970. p. 278–308. (Bibliothèque des lettres modernes)   **7344**

Sensitive, documented analysis of the concept of original sin in J.'s *Le paradis perdu* as compared with the text of Genesis. Milton is cited among some of J.'s possible sources.

Emmanuel, Pierre. Pierre Jean Jouve. RduC 14:47–50, 1951.   **7345**

Review of *Ode*. Emmanuel considers the work a poetic meditation on the human condition and not as a spontaneous outbreak of emotion.

————. Pierre Jean Jouve poète sacré. RduC 16:376–80, 1954.   **7346**

Review of *Langue*. Emmanuel notes the possible influence of Saint-John Perse and sets forth J.'s interpretation of Eros and original sin.

————. Porche à la nuit des saints. Poé 59–63, Feb.-March, 1942.   **7347**

In this review of *Porche à la nuit des saints,* Emmanuel explores the relationship between mysticism and poetry.

Fierens, Paul. Tragiques par Pierre Jean Jouve. NRF 11:827–28, 1923.   **7348**

Synopsis of J.'s poetic work up to *Tragiques.* Fierens notes the weakness of the propaganda poems inspired by the First World War.

Gascoyne, David. A new poem by Pierre Jean Jouve: Language. LonM 49–52, Feb. 1955.   **7349**

Notes a certain essential similarity to T. S. Eliot's *Four quartets* and the difficulties involved in translating J.'s poetry into English.

Gros, Léon-Gabriel. Architecture de Pierre Jean Jouve. CahS 246:391–97, 1942.   **7350**

Review of *Porche à la nuit des saints* and *Gloire* with emphasis on J.'s constant quest for purity. Indicates the progression of his poetry from such works as *Sueur de sang* and *Matière céleste.*

————. Pierre Jean Jouve et l'événement. CahS 26:121–25, 1947.   **7351**

J. envisages war as a punishment for mankind's sins or as a participation in the redemption of humanity. In his entire work the poet seeks transcendence through sublimation.

Hackett, C. A. Quatre suites. FS 14:276–77, 1960.   **7352**

Review of *Quatre suites.* Notes the development toward less metaphysical and more musical modes of expression.

Hell, Henri. Poètes de ce temps. Font 803–16, Dec.-Jan. 1946–47.   **7353**

Assesses that J. has finally attained maturity in his war poems. Develops the theme of night in these.

Jaccottet, Philippe. Pierre Jean Jouve: Inventions. NRF 7:712–13, 1959.   **7354**

Review of *Inventions* which Jaccottet considers to be solitary and aristocratic poetry.

Noulet, Emilie. Inventions. SynB 14:137–39, 1960.   **7355**

Review of *Inventions* noting the influence of Mallarmé on J.

Parrot, Louis. Paradis perdus. LetG 51–63, July 1943. *Also in:* Paradis retrouvés. CahS 260:736–48, 1943.   **7356**

Retrospective of J.'s work in the light of the war poems *Kyrie* and *Gloria.* A comparison with the *Carmen de Deo* of Dracontius in drawn.

Pichois, Claude. Tombeau de Baudelaire. MerF 334:664–68, 1958.   **7357**

Presents J. as the true representative of Baudelairianism in the middle of the twentieth century; underlines the pertinence of his analyses of Baudelaire, Delacroix, Courbet and Meryon.

Picon, Gaëtan. L'œuvre de Pierre Jean Jouve. MerF 324:679–84, 1955.   **7358**

Convinced that there is nothing fortuitous in J.'s work, Picon relates the intrinsic relationship between J.'s translation of Shakespeare's *Sonnets* and *Sueur de sang.*

Schwab, Raymond. Sueur de sang. NRF 41:627–30, 1933.   **7359**

Review of *Sueur de sang* in which Schwab draws attention to the fragmentary aspect of J.'s vision and his obsession with certain sexual images, notably the *cerf*. Judges J.'s explanation of original sin through psychoanalysis excessive. This article then gave rise to a polemic with Joë Bousquet defending J.'s position in CahS 713–18, Nov. 1933 and a confrontation between the two critics in CahS 790–97, Dec. 1933.

Starobinski, Jean. La mélancolie d'une belle journée. NRF 16:381–402, 1968.   **7360**

Textual analysis of *Le monde désert* and a poem in *Noces*. Structuralist approach stressing the essentially dramatic quality of all of J.'s poetry.

Novels

Amer, Henry. Pierre Jean Jouve: Paulina 1880. NRF 7:325–28, 1959. *Also:* MerF (gazette) 362, Oct. 1, 1959.   **7361**

Review of the republication of *Paulina 1880* taking into consideration biographical elements never before emphasized in earlier accounts of the work.

Arban, Dominique. Pierre Jean Jouve explore les abîmes. Bat 4, March 24, 1948.   **7362**

Emphasis on the relationship of poetry and psychoanalysis in the novels *Hécate* and *Vagadu*.

Betz, Maurice. Paulina 1880. JourE 6, Jan. 6, 1926.   **7363**

Notes the influence of Stendhal on this novel.

Blot, Christiane. Relation de la faute de l'Éros et de la mort dans l'œuvre romanesque de Pierre Jean Jouve. Aix-en-Provence, La Pensée Universitaire, 1962. 129 p. multigraphié. (Publication des Annales de la Faculté des Lettres d'Aix. Travaux et Mémoires, 18)   **7364**

Somewhat of a paraphrase of J.'s work. It does not contribute any new elements furthering a better understanding.

Blot-Labarrère, Christiane. Le bleu et le noir dans Paulina 1880 de Jouve. AFLSHN 2:131–38, 1967.   **7365**

Investigation of the use of colors in *Paulina 1880*.

Charpentier, John. Paulina 1880. MerF 37: 399–400, 1926.   **7366**

Emphasizes passion, mysticism and the cinematographical technique of the novel. However, deplores the lack of adequate transitions between the chapters.

Chéronnet, Louis. Paulina 1880. REur 567–68, April 1926.   **7367**

Review of the novel commenting on the possible influence of Stendhal and Barbey d'Aurevilly, besides providing a short analysis of its style and the character of Paulina.

Duhamel, Georges. La rencontre dans le carrefour. BandO 126–27, Jan. 1912.   **7368**

Although J. is trying his hand at unanimism, Duhamel feels that he has not yet properly integrated it into his writing. Also reproaches J. for some of the scabrous elements in the novel.

Grössel, Hans. Verklärung der Verzweiflung zum Werk Pierre Jean Jouve. Monat 72–77, April 1967.   **7369**

Introduction to the novels of J. considered as a sublimation of despair.

Groethuysen, Bernard. Hécate. NRF 17: 401–04, 1929.   **7370**

Interesting article about J.'s novelistic technique. Groethuysen notes the fragmentary aspects of the characters and their very particular kind of involvement with their creator, thus becoming one of the first to recognize him as one of the precursors of the *nouveau roman*.

Jouve, Pierre Jean. Lettre de Pierre Jean Jouve contre Jean Chambon. NouvO 44, Feb. 23, 1970.   **7371**

J.'s criticism of Chambon plagiarizing the novel *Les aventures de Catherine Crachat* in his own novel *La sentinelle*.

Klossowski, Pierre. Pierre Jean Jouve romancier: Catherine Crachat. Cr 3:675–88, 1948.   **7372**

According to Klossowski, J. is one of the few contemporary authors whose entire prose work deals with the "itinéraire de l'âme sous le signe du péché." In this light he examines the novels *Hécate* and *Vagadu* emphasizing that his work is constantly torn between theology and psychoanalysis. Essential article to an understanding of the evolution of the personality of Catherine Crachat, the heroine of these two rather difficult novels.

Micha, René. A partir des proses de Jouve. CahS 48:428–35, 1960–61.   **7373**
  The republication of J.'s novels gave rise to numerous articles about his work, if not mass recognition. Micha asserts that his novels are the novels of a poet, and not to be mistaken for the poetical novel.

————. La scène capitale. Brussels, La maison du poète, 1942. 68 p.   **7374**
  Exegesis of *La scène capitale,* important novel of J., essential to an understanding of the author's metaphysics.

Rousselot, Jean. Paulina 1880. Marg 71–73, Dec. 1959.   **7375**
  Review of the novel revealing affinities with *Aurélia* and *Les lettres de la religieuse portugaise.*

Sanzenbach, Simonne Cholin. Les romans de Pierre Jean Jouve: le romancier en son miroir. Vrin, 1972. 141 p.   **7376**
  Sanzenbach's knowledge of J.'s life is insufficient for the type of study she proposes. Excessive emphasis is thus placed on statements from the author himself in *En miroir* to be an objective analysis of the novels.

Simon, Pierre-Henri. Les romans de Pierre Jean Jouve. Monde 8–9, July 5, 1961.   **7377**
  Clear, well-written article dealing with the republication of J.'s novels in the sixties. Dwells on the author's concept of sin and sex resulting in death. Ranks him among the romantics due to the importance he attaches to the uncontrolled demonic forces governing mankind.

Thérive, André. Le monde désert. Op 12–14, Feb. 19, 1927.   **7378**
  Enlightening review of the novel. Draws attention to the fact that, contrary to the cries of originality with which latter critics greeted the work, it was very much a reflection of its time in so far as setting, characterization and novelistic technique were concerned.

Theater

G[héon], H[enri]. Les deux forces par Pierre Jean Jouve. NRF 5:985–87, 1913.   **7379**
  Review of this play influenced by J.'s association with the unanimists.

Jouve, Pierre Jean. Lulu et la censure. MerF 346:321–32, 1962.   **7380**
  Fascinating text about J.'s adaptation of Wedekind's *Der Erdgeist* and *Die Büsche der Pandora* revealing his affinities with the German playwright. Also includes the preface to *Lulu* which will only appear in 1969 after Wedekind's work had fallen in the public domain.

Marrey, Jean-Claude. Une tragédie lyrique: Wozzeck. MerF 352:561–62, 1964. **7381**
  Review of *Wozzeck ou le nouvel opéra* considered as an enlightened lay introduction to the work.

Piroué, Georges. Jouve et Shakespeare. MerF 344:753–57, 1962.   **7382**
  Very conclusive interview with the author about his translations of Shakespeare. Discusses why and how he attempted to translate *Romeo and Juliet,* the *Sonnets* and *Othello.* Essentially summarizes the 1937 preface to *Roméo et Juliette* and the 1955 introduction to the *Sonnets.*

Miscellaneous

Paseyro, Ricardo. Jouve, chirurgien de sainte Thérèse. CahSa 20:612–13, 1959.   **7383**
  A good example of J.'s method of translating and his desire to mystify the reader, already demonstrated by his translation of Blake and of Hölderlin in *Noces.*

Reuter, Evelyn. Pierre Jean Jouve et le Don Juan de Mozart. RMus 210:181–92, 1952.   **7384**
  Review of J.'s study on *Don Juan.* According to Reuter the author emphasizes the tragic aspects of the work and gives a very personal interpretation of the psychology of the characters.

Sackville-West, Edward. Mozart in purple. Obs 17, May 26, 1957.   **7385**

Review of the English translation of *Don Juan* by Eric Earnshaw Smith, disapproving the romantic overtones of J.'s interpretation.

Schlœzer, Boris de. Wozzeck ou le nouvel opéra. NRF 2:333–35, 1954.   **7386**
Criticism of J.'s interpretation of *Wozzeck*. According to Schlœzer, too great an emphasis is laid on the poetical, psychological, metaphysical and mystical aspects of the work. J. also shows, according to the critic, a severe lack of critical judgment as well as a thorough knowledge of music.

Viollier, Renée. Don Juan. SuiC 4:367–71, 1943.   **7387**
Reveals the influence of romanticism and psychoanalysis in J.'s interpretation of Don Juan.

Tristan Klingsor
(pseud. of Arthur Justin Léon Leclère)
(Nos. 7388–7391)

LESTER J. PRONGER

Menanteau, Pierre. Tristan Klingsor, une étude et un choix de poèmes par Pierre Mentaneau. Seghers, 1965. 192 p. (Poètes d'aujourd'hui, 130)   **7388**
Useful introduction to K. by a friend of the poet. Complements Pronger's book on some points.
Reviews: B. Bolsée in CahJT 37–43, Autumn 1966; J. Morvan in PoCp 79:49–51, 1966.

———. Preface. *In:* Klingsor, Tristan. Jean de Rodan. Blainville-sur-Mer, L'amitié par le livre, 1970. p. 9–10.   **7389**
Presents a work printed after publication of the books on K. by Pronger and Menanteau.

———. Preface. *In:* Klingsor, Tristan. Poèmes de la Princesse Chou. Eds. Saint Germain des Prés, 1974. p. 7–17.   **7390**
Presents a work printed after publication of the books on K. by Pronger and Menanteau.

Pronger, Lester J. La poésie de Tristan Klingsor (1890–1960). Minard, 1965. 299 p. (Bibliothèque des lettres modernes, 6)   **7391**

The most comprehensive book on K., using various approaches. As literary history it relates the development of his poetry to the evolution of the ambient literary sensibility and shifts in taste, including only essential biographical information. Psychocritical analysis of themes, symbols, imagery and style. Technical study of metrical structure and prosody. Based in part on conversations and correspondence with K.
Reviews: F. Conem in RSH 120:609–16, 1965; C. Grivel in FrB 36:37–39, 1966; W. Ince in FS 20:318–19, 1966; R. Jasinski in Cerf 55:9–16, 1966; B. Jourdan in Liv 841, Nov. 8, 1966; L. Lachgar in LivF May 1966; Pascal Pia in Car 1313:18, Nov. 26, 1969; R. Pouilliart in LR 22:381–82, 1968.

Patrice de La Tour du Pin
(pseud. of Patrice de Champhy de la Charce)
(Nos. 7392–7438)

PAULINE JONES

General Studies

Biéville-Noyant, Anne. Patrice de La Tour du Pin. Eds. de la nouvelle critique, 1948. 274 p.   **7392**
Fine account of parallel development of life, personality, and poetry of L. written by close friend of poet. Enriched by excerpts from L.'s letters and notes on reading. Admittedly incomplete and deliberately uncommitted to one specific methodology, but extremely illuminating, particularly as mirror of L.'s understanding of his own poetry. Essential tool for study of L.
Reviews: T. Maulnier in RevHM 32:498–503, 1949; A. Rousseaux in FL 147:2, Feb. 12, 1949.

Bosquet, Alain. Patrice de La Tour du Pin. RdP 67:167–68, 1960.   **7393**
Concise summary of L.'s career to 1960, emphasizing patient construction of vast work.

Champagne, Maurice. Préface. *In:* La Tour du Pin, Patrice de. La quête de joie, suivi de Petite somme de poésie. Gallimard, 1967. p. 9–21. (Coll. poésie) **7394**

Complex, highly-informative analysis of *Quête de joie* as expression of ambivalent mental structure on which all L.'s poetry depends. Detailed commentary on relation between *Quête* and other books of *Une somme de poésie*, symbolism of four Patrician races of living creatures, enigmatic role of Ullin, themes of genesis, death, and damnation. Defines L.'s concept of poetry as attempt to expiate sin by sacrifice of instinct to intelligence and to confer order on chaotic inner life through reason infused by faith.

Daniel-Rops, Henri (pseud. of Henry-Jules Petiot). L'œuvre grandissante de Patrice de La Tour du Pin. *In:* La Tour du Pin, Patrice de. La vie recluse en poésie, suivi de Présence de poésie, par Daniel-Rops. Plon, 1938. p. 201–37. (Présences, 2e série). *Also:* L'œuvre grandissante de Patrice de La Tour du Pin, suivi d'un poème de Patrice de La Tour du Pin, Les anges. Desclée De Brouwer, 1942; Brussels, Édition universelle, 1942. 61 p. (Cahiers des poètes catholiques, 41) **7395**

Study of L.'s first six volumes of poetry in context of vast plan of projected *Somme de poésie*. Emphasizes paradisiac and apocalyptic poles of L.'s work and combination of mystery with concrete elements and characters. L.'s hermeticism partially explained in terms of Catholic symbolism. Favorable judgments somewhat general and overstated.

Jans, Adrien. Où en est Patrice de La Tour du Pin? RGB 96:95–103, 1960. **7396**

Judicious appraisal of L.'s poetic development from 1933 to 1960, centered on *Le second jeu*. Well-informed commentary on L.'s opposition to poetry as means of knowledge, continual appeal to poetry as tool for expressing experience of invisible, and "bodily grasp." Believes poet's essential theme of Redemption not clearly expressed. Deplores increasing austerity of L.'s language, loss of spontaneity and "baroque obscurity," but considers poet capable of better reconciliation of prayer and poetry.

Kushner, Eva. Patrice de La Tour du Pin. Seghers, 1961. 224 p. (Poètes d'aujourd'hui, 79) **7397**

Concise study of L.'s life, influences on work, and each stage of multi-layered quests in *Une somme de poésie* and *Le second jeu*. Traces clearly three-part evolution of poet's work: solitary search within self in *Somme* and reconciliation with earth and mankind through Eucharist in *Second jeu* prepare poetry yet to be written on man's revolution around divine center. Excellent pages on proteism of characters, symbolism of night, water, desert, father-son double, and reflection of contemporary preoccupations in L.'s work. Astute but not exhaustive remarks on spatial-time imagery and poetic technique.

Review: Anon. in RFB 4:3, 1961.

Rousseaux, André. La vie littéraire. FL 6, May 7, 1938. *Also:* La légende mystique de Patrice de La Tour du Pin, Partie 1. *In his:* Littérature du XXe siècle. Albin Michel, 1948. 2:148–57. **7398**

Discusses L.'s mysticism, talent for creating legends, dangers of obscurity and limited appeal to those who do not share poet's beliefs. Calls L.'s symbolic but antisymbolist poetry challenge to supremacy of demiurgic poetics since Baudelaire. Admires ambitious plan for vast poem, but suspends judgment on poet's greatness until completion of *Somme*.

Stanford, Derek. First thoughts on Patrice de La Tour du Pin. PoetryQ 9:225–31, 1947–48. **7399**

Stresses poet's identification of imagination with grace, combination of pantheistic instinct with Christian mysticism, and paradox of classical form and romantic content and images. Claims women and landscapes poles of Patrician ecstasy. Astute analysis of individuality of characters representing fissions of single mind. Notes stylistic parallels with Rembrandt, Rouault, El Greco. Well organized and lively introduction of L. to English-speaking public.

Poetics and Themes

Deschamps, Nicole. Le bestiaire retrouvé. EF 10:283–307, 1974. **7400**

Treats various aspects of bestiary of Apollinaire, Eluard, Claudel, L. Links meaning of L.'s "Petite faune" to hermetic world of *Une somme de poésie.* Quotes description of "Les idris à manteau" as example of invented mystery surrounding name, legends, and habitat of each animal. Fascinating idea, but not explored in depth. Comparison with other poets lacking.

Favre, Yves-Alain. Notes sur le symbolisme mystique de La Tour du Pin. *In:* Missions et démarches de la critique. Mélanges offerts au Professeur J. Vier. Klincksieck, 1873. p. 247–50. (Publications de l'Université de Haute-Bretagne, 2)   **7401**

Believes originality of L.'s polyvalent symbolism lies in links established between spiritual reality and entirely imaginary creations. Emphasizes its fundamental justification in Christian faith. Contrasts man as closed Trinitarian symbol in *Une somme de poésie* and as living sign of divine Presence and Word in *Le jeu de l'homme devant Dieu.* Very brief, but valuable. Gives specific examples and is one of few articles to refer both to *Une somme* and published volumes of unfinished *Le troisième jeu.*

La Tour du Pin, Patrice de. Préface. *In:* Renard, Jean-Claude. Cantiques pour des pays perdus. Laffont, 1947. p. 9–15. **7402**

Important statement by L. Reveals doubts he must surmount, suggests future trajectory of his poetry from particular to universal, and justifies digressions in own work as abortive but necessary efforts to pursue a personal quest that is also mankind's.
Review: A. Rolland de Renéville in Nef 40:119–22, 1948.

————. Témoignage d'un poète. *In:* Chercher Dieu. Eds. du cerf, 1943. p. 131–49. *Also:* Lyon, Eds. de l'abeille, 1943.   **7403**

Text of speech delivered by L. when prisoner of war. Supplements 1938 version of *La vie recluse en poésie.* Emphasizes role of words—particularly "parole animée"—as elements of spiritual inner life and universe of expression. Believes criticism useless in explaining poetry: understanding of a poem requires act of creation by reader capable of effacing self and replacing own inner life by that of poet. Interesting echoes of Mallarmé, Rimbaud, Claudel, Valéry. Important as courageous attempt at clarifying concepts of *La vie recluse,* but shows L. can justify obscurity of work only by claiming to write for a limited group of readers who already share his views or are willing to accept them on faith.

————. La vie recluse en poésie, suivi de Présence de poésie, par Daniel-Rops. Plon, 1938. p. 5–133. (Présences, 2ᵉ série) *Also (rev.) in his:* Une somme de poésie. Gallimard, 1946. p. 217–36. *Trans.:* The dedicated life in poetry and The correspondence of Laurent de Cayeux, trans. by G. S. Fraser. Introduction by Stephen Spender. London, Harvill press, 1948. 63 p. (Changing world series)   **7404**

L.'s lyrical treatise on own concept of poetry. Defines chief elements as poetic virginity, bodily grasp, and equilibrium of solitude and communion. Attempts to reconcile conflict between spiritual life and poetry by Christian humanism: places poetry at service of each man in search of God. Emphasizes liberty of every poet and respect for individual experience. Profound but diffuse expression of states of mind rather than closely structured system of esthetics. Text in *Somme* warmer and more natural than 1938 version. Valuable key to understanding of L.'s intentions and later development.
Reviews: Anon. in TLS 2406:150, March 13, 1948; J. Baudry in CahS 220:61–67, 1940; R. Church in NSN 35, no. 880:56, Jan. 17, 1948; P. Donnelly in NewER 16:378–79, 1948; R. Speaight in T&T 49:515–16, 1948; D. Stanford in PoetryQ 10:122–26, 1948; J. Waller in PoetryR 39:349–52, 1947; Y.L. in DM 23, no. 4:39–47, 1948.

L., Y. The poet's virginity. DM 23, no. 4: 39–47, 1948.   **7405**

Comparison of L.'s, Valéry's and Ponge's ideas of poetic virginity and bodily grasp. Terms represent for Valéry poet's attitude toward material; for Ponge, means of exploring external world; for L., spiritual states essential for poetic communion with man and search for God. Emphasizes Patrician concept of virginity as perpetual exploration of world and soul and condition preceding bodily grasp—incarnation of poetic potentiality by Word made flesh. Abstract but useful. One of few systematic comparisons of L. with other poets.

Onimus, Jean. La poétique du fauve. RSH 94:195–206, 1959. **7406**

Rich study of archetypal savage animal in works of wide range of authors. Interprets beast in L.'s poetry as instrument for reaching untamed depths of soul and symbol of wild romantic impatience, tragic vocation and alienation. Perceptive treatment of ambiguity of L.'s winged-animal angels, dream and reality in bestiary, hunter's instinctive search for soul, slaughter of wild beast as act of communion with mystery of life. Illuminating comparisons with symbolism of beast in Chateaubriand, Maurice de Guérin, Rilke, Melville. Probing and thoroughly absorbing invitation to further investigation.

Rolland de Renéville, A. Diversité de la poésie contemporaine. Nef 40:119–22, 1948. **7407**

Review of Jean-Claude Renard's *Cantiques pour des pays perdus* and L.'s preface to volume. Very valuable. Few critics see so clearly ambiguity in L.'s concept of poetry and conflict between his religious faith and poetic vocation.

Spender, Stephen. Introduction. *In:* La Tour du Pin, Patrice de. The dedicated life in poetry and The correspondence of Laurent de Cayeux, trans. by G. S. Fraser. London, Harvill press, 1948. p. vii–xix. (Changing world series) **7408**

Close analysis of L.'s attitude toward poetry. Distinguishes between "objective" poets primarily concerned with perfection of form and "subjective" poets like L. whose chief preoccupation is content—poetic and religious experience of inner life. Believes L. dominated by "egotistical sublime" vision which defies complete expression. Thoughtful comparison of L. and Whitman. Emphasizes L.'s affinity with younger Yeats and modern English poets.

Individual Works Before 1940

Barjon, Louis. Quête de joie! (Patrice de La Tour du Pin). *In his:* Le silence de Dieu dans la littérature contemporaine. Eds. du centurion, 1955. p. 151–76. (Le poids du jour) **7409**

Short but rich study of *Quête de joie* in light of doctrine of "La vie recluse." Sees heroes torn between temptations of flesh and intelligence and discovery of sole salvation in Christ. Gives particular attention to desolate landscapes, characters, and role of natural creatures. Frequently mentions powerful spell of L.'s poetry, but more interested in volume's spiritual message than in close analysis of literary qualities.

Baudry, Jean. L'enfer. RHeb 44, no. 7:476–78, July 27, 1935. **7410**

Useful as example of generally enthusiastic and somewhat overstated reception of L.'s early work, and interesting reply to critics who reproach L. with awkwardness of versification.

————. La quête de joie. RHeb 43, no. 44: 112–15, Nov. 3, 1934. **7411**

Interesting remarks on stylization of meaning by use of proper names, denunciation of death by instinct of pleasure, physical sense of life and natural world in volume. Sometimes over-enthusiastic, but most judgments well-founded. One of few critics to make precise and intelligent remarks on versification.

Fontainas, André. L'enfer. D'un aventurier. MerF 263:362–64, Oct. 15, 1935. **7412**

Brief statements on profound thoughts in *L'enfer* and suggestions for improvement of L.'s technique, which needs variety, lighter touch, expansion.

Gros, Léon-Gabriel. Patrice de La Tour du Pin: un paysage mental. *In his:* Poètes contemporains. Ire série. Cahiers du sud, 1944. p. 111–33. **7413**

Believes *Quête de joie* unified by instinctive but systematic imagery and central myth of pursuit of angel. Astute remarks on L.'s combination of the precise and fantastic in invention of landscape and wild creatures, intellectual sensuality and voluntary asceticism of poet, and "prise de chair" in *Quête*. Some contradictions; overemphasis on lifelike qualities of invented characters and coherence of L.'s vision. Characterization of *Quête* as poem that provokes anxiety to which it provides response neglects ambiguity of response. Valuable as one of few early critical studies to admit serious flaws in L.'s religious imagery, to recognize poet's fervent faith without transforming him into mystic, and to place him in tradition of both symbolists of 1890's and great poets of nature.

Guibert, Armand. La quête de joie. CahS 161:309–14, 1934.   **7414**

Defines originality of *Quête de joie* as "merveilleux chrétien" tinged with magic reflection of man's division between angelism and sensuality. Believes secret of *Quête* is Ullin-Roi, incarnation of demon of knowledge and prophet of Lorenquin. Does not deny existence of technical imperfections, but stresses poet's mastery of form and melodious orphism. Interesting choice of authors and works with which L.'s is compared: Milton, Claudel, Milosz, Keats, Psalms, Revelations.

Patrice de La Tour du Pin. Par Armand Guibert, Camille Bégué, A. Denis-Dagieu, Jean Amrouche, avec un poème inédit de Patrice de La Tour du Pin [D'un aventurier]. Tunis, Eds. de mirages, 1934. 136 p.   **7415**

Six articles on *Quête de joie* intended to arouse interest in L. Excellent pages by Guibert and Bégué on Patrician asceticism, mingling of idealism and sensuality, imagery of night. Short but enlightening comparisons by Guibert between L. and mystics such as Böhme, Saint John of the Cross, Henry Vaughan, Francis Thompson. Amrouche's thoughtful discussion of coherent doctrine of *Quête* emphasizes pessimism of conclusion. Denis-Dagieu's references to parallels between *Quête* and Egyptian, Greek, Biblical and medieval mysteries particularly valuable. Overly optimistic predictions of poet's place in literary history redeemed by judicious treatment of enduring qualities of L.'s talent.

Schwab, Raymond. La quête de joie. NRF 42:552–54, 1934.   **7416**

Discussion of spatial and spiritual geography of *Quête* and quite remarkable recreation of dream-like climate of work. Ascribes flaws in imagery and prosody to poet's inexperience. Stresses appeal of new poetic voice. Enlightening and fair: criticisms inserted in framework of generous admiration.

Individual Works After 1940

Aragon, Louis. Chronique du bel canto. Eur 24, no. 12:93–102, 1946.   **7417**

Briefly notes beauties of *Une somme de poésie*, but accuses L. of contempt for masses and lack of social commitment in work. Most serious charge calls into question value of L.'s message: claims poet not truly Catholic but uses heretical mechanism to create personal and individual poetry, truth and religion.

Bancal, Jean. La quête de Patrice de La Tour du Pin. TR 213:40–54, 1965. **7418**

Short but very useful discussion of evolution of L.'s poetry from *Somme de poésie* ("jeu de l'homme devant lui-même") through *Second jeu* ("jeu de l'homme devant les autres") to a third and last part of *Somme* ("jeu de l'homme devant Dieu"), of which *Le petit théâtre crépusculaire* is first part. Very careful study of *Petit théâtre* as log of first stage of mystic voyage around liturgical orbit (Christian ceremonies during year) from Advent to Epiphany. Clear definition of significance of title of volume and meaning of space-age vocabulary employed by L. Close analysis of key elements and symbols of alternating prose reflections and poetry. Especially lucid commentary on Patrician concepts of time and supra-reality of language, and on symbolic themes of tree and gifts of Magi. Very complex, but rewarding introduction to *Petit théâtre*.

Barjon, Louis. Le monde du recueillement. Patrice de La Tour du Pin. *In his:* De Baudelaire à Mauriac. L'inquiétude contemporaine. Tournai, Casterman, 1962. p. 199–207.   **7419**

Study of ascending curve of L.'s spiritual life in *Une somme de poésie* as example of poetic doctrine rooted in childhood's imaginative games and religious faith. Emphasizes central symbolism of School and Tess; short but illuminating contrast with Rabelais' Thélème. Inventory of flora, fauna, landscapes, nomenclature, and characters suggests fruitful avenues of exploration. Thinks barren style of *Le second jeu* reveals paralyzing interiorization and produces non-literature. Sound introduction to *Somme.* Discussion of *Second jeu* limited in scope.

———. Une somme de poésie. Genèse d'un monde intérieur. Et 252:58–75, 1947. **7420**

Well-synthesized discussion of L.'s phenomenology in *Une somme de poésie.* Emphasizes intense spirituality of fictitious universe, progressive enrichment of meaning of "jeu," poet's reorientation from private to public world through experience of war and love. Thoughtful treatment of importance of "La vie recluse en poésie" and L.'s adoption of rule of School of Tess—reconciliation of spontaneity and discipline. Excellent pages on meaning of *L'enfer,* poet's sacrifice of partial images of self in favor of totality incarnated in Christ.

Béguin, Albert. Approches de l'incommunicable. Esp 128:881–88, 1946. **7421**

Sound, sympathetic judgment of *Une somme de poésie.* Stresses hermeticism and ambiguity of volume: believes object of quest not clear and claims poet uses Christian symbolism to express not global vision of universe but personal mythology and nostalgia. Finds progressive constriction of L.'s verbal facility in works after *Quête de joie* both disappointing and moving. Singles out for praise fragments of musical verse and passages evoking conflict of spirit and flesh and simple human aspirations and failures. Béguin's assessment of *Somme* not meant to be definitive, but is fair and important: sees behind ambitious plan essential pathos of work.

———. Un poète cherche à s'insérer dans le monde. Cr 32:83–86, 1949. **7422**

Short assessment of *La contemplation errante* as L.'s *Vita nuova*—farewell to solitude of "La vie recluse" and childhood dreams, accession to maturity, and beginning of search for instrument of communication with others. Close examination of multiple symbolism of father-son dualism; believes drama has psychological overtones, but L. goes beyond Freudian interpretations by making dualism analogy of relations between Father and Son in Trinity and using metaphysical symbolism in tradition of medieval works.

Bosquet, Alain. Patrice de La Tour du Pin ou La poésie recluse. NRF 135:504–08, 1964. **7423**

Commentary on *Le petit théâtre crépusculaire,* preceded by short statement on L.'s originality. Believes object of *Petit théâtre* is to illuminate relation between poet and thinker. Finds volume most successful when L.'s attempt to separate song from thought fails. Defines L.'s major preoccupation as theoretical incompatibility between pure religion and poetry.

Daniel-Rops, Henri (pseud. of Henry-Jules Petiot). Poésie et adoration. Patrice de La Tour du Pin. NRel 5:677–92, 849–58, 1947. *Also:* Patrice de La Tour du Pin. Poésie et adoration. *In his:* Où passent des anges. 2d ed. Plon, 1947. p. 175–200. *Also (rev.):* Plon, 1957. p. 186–208. *Trans.:* Patrice de La Tour du Pin. Poetry and adoration. *In his:* Where angels pass. Trans. by Emma Craufurd. London, Cassell, 1950. p. 137–60. **7424**

Previous doubts about plan of *Une somme de poésie* retracted. Believes completed volume proof of L.'s ability to fuse lyricism with lucid analysis of poetry as means of knowledge and transfiguration of man. Attributes power of work to symphonic composition, analogical language, mysterious veracity of geography and nomenclature, and pervasive religious fervor equal to mysticism of greatest Christian poets. Persuasive but not always analytical. Section on L. does not appear in first ed. of *Où passent des anges.*

Estang, Luc. Une somme de poésie. CahMN 4, no. 3:72–81, 1948. **7425**

Discerning overall study of *Une somme de poésie* emphasizing evocative quality of L.'s symbolism rather than obscurity. Thoughtful definition of "jeu" as Claudelian recreation of total universe by power of word. Sees parallel with Biblical Genesis: poet reverses demiurgic/Satanic drama of Garden of Eden by relating man's creation to God's. Perceptive analysis of Patrician angelism: ascribes failure of quest and damnation of disciples of Tess to identification of poetry with mysticism and lack of Christian charity. Stresses importance of promise of salvation by love in volumes's conclusion. Intelligent and well-organized treatment of *Somme* by one of few critics who seems able to handle L.'s concepts with ease.

Guibert, Armand. Poètes et poésie. TwC 6:81–84, 1966.   **7426**

Calls *Le second jeu* monument of the apologetic, impossible to judge definitively before completion of entire *Somme* but tentatively situated somewhere between Maurice Scève's *Microcosme* and Bunyan's *Pilgrim's progress.* Thoughtful remarks on heterogeneous character of volume and uneven quality of L.'s art, flawed by repetitions, exegetic tone, didacticism. Sees relationship between L.'s isolation from all major literary currents of his time and creation of increasingly impenetrable subterranean world. Telling criticisms by "discoverer" of L. and fervent admirer of *Quête de joie* and other works emphasize L.'s evolution from lyric to homiletic poet.

Harcourt, Bernard d'. Patrice de La Tour du Pin et La poésie inhumaine. Témoi 14:308–33, 1947.   **7427**

Quotes L.'s answer to those who question humanity of *Somme:* "Ça dépend de l'homme." Believes human note occurs often in volume, but poet's keen transparent glance gives *Somme* inhuman character. Excellent pages on images of hunter and prey and sterility resulting from poet's deliberate effort to divert gifts from esthetic to moral aim. Interesting comparisons with Vigny, Maurice de Guérin, Baudelaire, Racine.

LeDantec, Y.-G. Une somme de poésie de Patrice de La Tour du Pin. AeLet 10: 97–102, 1948.   **7428**

Brief allusions to L.'s courage in launching ambitious project of *Somme* and to importance of monumental volume in article devoted to its weaknesses: obscure title, architecture *a posteriori,* artificiality of legends, forced quality and irrelevance of fabulous characters and background. Lengthy inventory of examples of L.'s infractions of laws of meter and prosody. Concludes dissonant and barbaric verse of *Somme* inferior to instinctive melodies of *Quête.* Many criticisms valid, but neglects essential religious elements of *Somme* and shows no understanding of relations of part to whole or of poet's intentions.

Lobet, Marcel. Patrice de La Tour du Pin. La poésie à la rencontre de la foi. RG 107, no. 10:53–62, 1971.   **7429**

Résumé of *Une lutte pour la vie.* Useful comments on key symbols of volume: city, solid and liquid elements, liturgical cycle. Stresses L.'s concern with problems of modern man. Considers his theopoetics renewal of neo-Thomist concept of poetry as vehicle of true faith. Informative but fragmented. Avoids literary judgments.

Loranquin, Albert. Une somme de poésie II. Le second jeu. BdL 213:436–38, Dec. 15, 1959.   **7430**

Summary assessment of serious weaknesses of *Le second jeu.* Stresses pathos of L.'s awareness of diminished creative powers and labored attempt to make poetic impoverishment serve God.

Mambrino, Jean. L'anneau d'alliance. Et 307:78–91, 1961.   **7431**

Résumé of story of André Vincentenaire in *Le second jeu.* Clear explanation of stages of hero's quest in terms of Biblical symbolism of desert, Exodus, Passion, Covenant with God, Incarnation, Baptism. Considers prosaic dryness of language reflection of poet's Night of the soul. Sees volume as preparation of Patrician movement in liturgical orbit of Paschal sun in *Le troisième jeu,* yet to be written.

Marissel, André. Patrice de La Tour du Pin. Une lutte pour la vie. NRF 218:63–64, 1971.   **7432**

Calls *Une lutte pour la vie* series of admirable meditations on faith, poetic art, modern world. Praises poet's courageous attempt to take place in center of human community and defend his idea of poetry against detractors. Finds volume simplistic, despite quasi Bergsonian and near Freudian language, and unlikely to convince readers without same religious orientation as L. Well-balanced assessment of strengths and weaknesses of *Une lutte.*

Maulnier, Thierry. A propos de Patrice de La Tour du Pin. RevHM 32:498–503, 1949.   **7433**

Emphasizes uniqueness of L.'s creation of purely poetic world, combination of logic and mystery, necessity for reader's acceptance of Patrician mythology on faith. Insists on importance of L.'s word as example of serious play of poetic genius. Does not consider *Somme* hermetic, but admits keys needed to penetrate closed universe. Valuable as discreet but convincing defense of L. against charge of lack of social commitment.

Onimus, Jean. Patrice de La Tour du Pin. Son message spirituel. Et 288:201–18, 1956.   **7434**

Interpretation of *Une somme de poésie* as creation of paradisiac universe and heroic destruction of this creation in search of unity with universe and God. Thoughtful discussion of ambiguous spiritual purity and savage fervor in symbol of hunt and L.'s zoology. Believes poet surmounts temptation of narcissism and death-like lucidity by bodily grasp—i.e., movement toward external world. Important remarks on role of Trinity, Incarnation, Genesis, and Last Judgment in L.'s poetry. Main emphasis on depth of spiritual commitment revealed in L.'s work.

Reid, J. C. Poetry and Patrice de La Tour du Pin. Ren 7:17–29, 1954.   **7435**

Sees in *Une somme de poésie* steady movement from self-preoccupations of youth to mature acceptance of responsibilities and consecration of human condition. Mentions wide range of influences and parallels—from Dante and Milton to Dame Edith Sitwell. Aware of uneven quality of *Somme* (mentions overabundance of characters, repetition, complication), but believes volume should be judged, albeit tentatively, as unique in modern literature. One of the more illuminating studies of *Somme*.

Rousseaux, André. La somme de poésie de Patrice de La Tour du Pin. FL 2, Nov. 28, 1959.   **7436**

Concise study of evolution of L.'s poetry since 1933, with particular emphasis on *Le second jeu*. Valuable remarks on Patrician concept of poetry and important distinction between Christian literature and great religious poetry. Finds realization of idea of *Somme* increasingly labored and more worthy of esteem than enthusiasm.

———. Une somme de poésie de Patrice de La Tour du Pin. FL 37:2, Nov. 30,

1946. *Also:* La légende mystique de Patrice de la Tour du Pin, Partie 2. *In his:* Littérature du XXᵉ siècle. V. 2. Albin Michel, 1948. p. 157–64.   **7437**

Believes *Une somme de poésie* failure as ensemble but contains fragments of remarkable lyric intensity. Thoughtful treatment of L.'s angelism and obscurity of mythology. Interprets work as record of dramatic conflict between poetic and religious life. Predicts victory of commonplace will prevent completion of plans for additional volumes of *Somme*. Perceptive but somewhat discursive.

———. Vers l'an deux mille avec Patrice de La Tour du Pin. FL 147:2, Feb. 12, 1949.   **7438**

Study of *La contemplation errante* as transitional work leading to second volume of uncompleted *Somme*. Analyzes dual father-son hero, movement from solitary to secular life, extension of Patrician "nuptial order" to universe of second millenium. Lauds L.'s Christian humanism. Criticizes flat expository prose, complicated symbolism, and absence of lyricism, which he hopes poet can recapture. Enlightening quotations from L.'s letters.

Pamphile Le May
(Nos. 7439–7441)

Jacques Cotnam

Roy, Camille. Les goutellettes. *In his:* Essais sur la littérature canadienne. Montreal, Beauchemin, 1925. p. 105–23. *Also in his:* Poètes de chez nous. Montreal, Beauchemin, 1934. p. 75–100.   **7439**

With considerable gusto, Roy studies principal themes of L.'s sonnets, commenting briefly on his talent for the poetic craft.

———. Pamphile Le May. *In his:* A l'ombre des érables. Quebec, Imprimerie de l'Action sociale, 1924. p. 9–62.   **7440**

A traditional critical analysis of L.'s life and poetry. Draws attention to the romantic inspiration. The researcher may still glean some useful information from these pages.

————. Pamphile Le May. *In his:* Poètes de chez nous. Montreal, Beauchemin, 1934. p. 75–100.   **7441**

Although L. is hardly the equal of the poetic geniuses who have used the sonnet, he is the first in Canada to have composed an entire volume of sonnets and to have raised "ce genre de poésie à un haut degré de perfection." Discusses major themes, images and versification.

Pierre Louÿs
(i.e. Pierre Louis)
(Nos. 7442–7497)

David J. Niederauer

Bibliography

Perceau, Louis. Bibliographie du roman érotique au XIXe siècle, donnant une description complète de tous les romans, nouvelles, et autres ouvrages en prose, publiés sous le manteau en français, de 1800 à nos jours, et de toutes leurs réimpressions. V. 2. Georges Fourdrinier, 1930. 401 p.   **7442**

Useful for indicating the authenticity of some of L.'s prose erotica. In his second and final volume, this authoritative bibliographer attributes four erotic works to L. Listed chronologically, these are: *Manuel de civilité pour les petites filles,* 1926 (p. 166–67); *Trois filles de leur mère,* 1926 (p. 168); *Histoire du roi Gonzalve et des douze princesses,* 1927 (p. 171); *Aphrodite, édition intégrale,* 1928 (p. 175–77).

Talvart, Hector, and Joseph Place. Bibliographie des auteurs modernes de langue française (1801–1953). V. 12. Chronique des lettres françaises, 1954. p. 317–56.   **7443**

Extensive bibliographical study devoted to L. Small section (p. 341–42), devoted to L.'s erotic works, gives an indication of those titles which may be considered to have been written by L. although even among these some are of doubtful authenticity.

Editions

Louÿs, Pierre. Journal intime. 1882–1891. Eds. Montaigne, 1929. 377 p.   **7444**

Slightly more complete version of L.'s *Journal* than that found in v. 9 of the *Œuvres complètes.* This volume contains approximately 8 pages of text which do not appear in the *Œuvres complètes* version. These pages (p. 279–83; 291–94) cover entries for April and May 1890.

————. Œuvres complètes. Eds. Montaigne, 1929–31. 13 v. and a supplement to v. 12.   **7445**

Most complete ed. available of L.'s works. Included are his diary, his principal translations, novels, tales and some articles on literary history and criticism. Some material was previously unpublished. His poetry is sparsely represented but this is now extremely well covered in Le Dantec, *Les poèmes de Pierre Louÿs.* None of the texts is accompanied by any critical apparatus.

————. Les poèmes de Pierre Louÿs. Edition définitive établie par Yves-Gérard Le Dantec. Albin Michel, 1945. 2 v., xxiv, 913 p.   **7446**

Indispensable work for the full appreciation of L. as a poet. The two v. contain 326 p. of Le Dantec's exhaustive notes which elucidate almost every poem. Long an admirer of L. as a poet and well acquainted with his life and his literary productions, Le Dantec brought to his editorial task an excellent blend of knowledge, fervor and critical acumen. The notes contain considerable unpublished material, especially in connection with variants, and they often include material which reveals much about L. the man as well as L. the poet. However, since Mme Henri de Régnier was still alive at the time of publication, Le Dantec was unwilling to identify her clearly as the woman who inspired L.'s lyric masterpiece, the *Pervigilium mortis.* V. 1 contains Le Dantec's very clear Introduction, followed by *Poétique, Isthi, Astarté, Iris, Aquarelles passionnées, Hivernales, La forêt des nymphes, Stances, Pervigilium mortis, Autres stances, Derniers vers, Poèmes divers, Appendice à Poétique.* V. 2. contains *Inscriptions et belles lettres, Fantaisies, Poèmes inachevés, Premiers vers.* V. 1 also contains a brief bibliography concerned chiefly with the appearance of L.'s poetry in periodicals.

Review: R. Kemp in NL May 2, 1946.

Correspondence

Debussy, Claude, and Pierre Louÿs. Correspondance...(1893–1904). Ed. by Henri Borgeaud with an introduction by G. Jean-Aubry. Corti, 1945. 207 p. **7447**

Good introduction traces the history of this interesting friendship. Dispels the notion that L. was Debussy's literary mentor. Details the extent of their collaboration on various works. The carefully annotated letters and elements of the appendix give considerable information on joint projects which never fully materialized. The level of humor in the letters is noteworthy.

Iseler, Paul. Les débuts d'André Gide vus par Pierre Louÿs avec une lettre d'André Gide à l'auteur et de nombreuses lettres inédites de Pierre Louÿs à André Gide. Sagittaire, 1937. 137 p. **7448**

Gide's letter to Iseler reveals Gide's ambiguous attitude toward L. Throughout the volume the stimulating effect on Gide of L.'s divergent attitudes toward life and literature can be felt. Author generally sympathetic to Gide while remaining open to L.'s positions. Work studies, mainly in excerpts, some 60 letters of L. to Gide written from 1889 to 1896. Important letters of L. to Gide are omitted and Iseler did not have access to Gide's letters to L. Dating of letters is often approximate. Little background material given. Good brief analysis of the opposing doctrines of Gide and L. ·

Lachèvre, Frédéric. Poésies de Héliette de Vivonne attribuées à tort à Madeleine de Laubespine...précédées d'une introduction par Frédéric Lachèvre et suivies de douze lettres inédites de Pierre Louÿs non envoyées à leurs destinataires. Librairie historique Alph. Margraff, 1932. 96 p. **7449**

Good introduction by Lachèvre includes excerpts from a number of letters of L. to Lachèvre. These letters reveal his expertise in early seventeenth-century collections of *poésies libres et satiriques*. The dozen letters Lachèvre appended to this volume are of interest to the biographer and to the critic

concerned with such matters as L.'s methods of composition and his inability to finish his novel *Psyché*.

Louÿs, Pierre. Quelques lettres de Pierre Louÿs à André Gide. NRF 33:640–49; 782–99, 1929. **7450**

Six remarkable letters selected by André Gide. Written between 1899 (L. was 18) and 1894, they reveal the fervor of L.'s precocious preoccupation with literature. All are full of advice and offer pronouncements and judgments on contemporary literature. One contains an outline for an exuberant iconoclastic novel which prefigures Jarry's *Ubu roi* and L.'s own *Aventures du roi Pausole*.

Valéry, Paul. Lettres à quelques-uns. Gallimard, 1952. 253 p. **7451**

Of this collection of 130 letters, sixteen are addressed to L. Especially revealing of the nature of L.'s early influence on Valéry are the ten letters written in 1890. The three letters of 1916–1917 indicate the similarity of poetic feeling these two outwardly different poets shared at the time they both resumed writing poetry in 1916 after an interval of many years.

Catalogs

Catalogue de livres anciens et modernes, rares et précieux. L. Giraud-Badin, 1930. 243 p. **7452**

As the *Avertissement* of this catalog intimates, the 666 volumes critically described in this work all came from L.'s private library. The catalog therefore offers a fairly comprehensive view of L.'s activities as a bibliophile and bibliographer. The collection is especially rich in items by Latin authors and by French authors of the 16th and 17th centuries. Apparent also is L.'s interest in *curiosa* of all types, not exclusively the erotic sort.

Livres anciens et modernes. Lettres et manuscrits de Pierre Louÿs. C. Coulet et A. Faure, 1974. 96 p. (Coulet and Faure catalog 138, spring 1974) **7453**

One-third of this catalog (p. 60–96) covering 152 items is devoted principally to letters and mss. of L. Some of these items are volumes by or concerning L. All items are well described with significant extracts from the letters and good descriptions and résumés of the important mss. Many items (e.g., a file on L.'s marriage; his sporadic diary for the period 1898–1911) are of considerable interest for the biography of L. Other mss., often abandoned literary projects, give clear indication of L.'s interests and erudition.

Livres anciens, romantiques et modernes d'occasion. Importante correspondance autographe inédite de Pierre Louÿs à son frère (1890–1915). Librairie Biblis [Jean Porson] Nᵒ 14, 1936. 56 p.   **7454**

This is catalog number 14 of the Librairie Biblis, 20 rue du Vieux Colombier, Paris. This rare catalog and similar subsequent listings by the same publisher (*see* H. Talvart and J. Place, *Bibliographie...*, V. 12, p. 349–50) are invaluable for understanding L.'s life and times and for the full appreciation of his writings. These various catalogs list L.'s letters, each of which is analyzed in a condensed form which usually includes abundant quotations from the letter itself. The letters thus presented shed considerable light on 25 years of L.'s private life. They also contain much information concerning L.'s literary tastes, sources and aims and they reveal the circumstances surrounding the composition of many of L.'s works. The letters were written to Georges Louis (1847–1917), L.'s older half-brother and a senior French diplomat. Catalog number 14 contains 262 letters from L. to this half-brother (dated from 1890 to 1914) and one 1917 letter to Madame Georges Louis.

Manuscrits de Pierre Louÿs et de divers auteurs contemporains: Claude Farrère, André Gide, Jean de Tinan, Oscar Wilde. Poésies et lettres autographes d'auteurs modernes et contemporains. L. Carteret, 1926. 107 p.   **7455**

Catalog of 178 items for the sale, held May 14, 1926, of a part of L.'s estate. Extremely valuable for the information contained regarding the mss. of many of L.'s own works. Also very useful for determining L.'s relations with the authors who gave him mss. of their works and who wrote him letters. All items are carefully described and many are accompanied by photographic reproductions of key pages. (There are 19 reproductions of portions of L.'s manuscripts, 15 of portions of works by L.'s contemporaries.) The entire text of many of the letters is given.

Vente volontaire pour cause de départ au château d'Ecrouves près Toul, Monsieur et Madame Serrière — P. Louÿs, propriétaires. Mᵉˢ Henri Martin et Robert Menoux, huissiers, Mᵉ René Larchet, Commissaire-Priseur, Toul, chez lesquels se distribue le présent catalogue... [No place, No publisher] 1934. 36 p.   **7456**

Interesting catalog for auction sale held by widow of L. at Toul June 30–July 8, 1934. The 202 lots offered in the catalog are composed principally of correspondence sent to L., mostly from writers and artists of secondary importance. While most lots are merely briefly described, 14 letters are photographically reproduced, and excerpts are given for over 50 letters. Catalog thus contains numerous indications of L.'s dealings with such figures as N. C. Barney, Colette, Curnonsky, Farrère, Frondaie, Marie de Heredia, Hérold, Loviot, Mauclair, Sherard, Leoncavallo and Puccini. More important figures in L.'s life (Debussy, Gide, Régnier, Valéry, etc.) are also well represented.

Collected Articles

Pierre Louÿs, l'écrivain, le poète, l'homme. Cap 1–65, 1925.   **7457**

Commemorative issue of irregularly appearing serial. Article by Armandie analyzed separately.

Le tombeau de Pierre Louÿs: tel que l'édifièrent A. de Monzie, Paul Valéry, Claude Farrère, André Lebey, Fernand Gregh, Jacques-Emile Blanche, Franz Toussaint, Thierry Sandre, Emile Henriot, Maurice Martin du Gard, K. Nizam el Moulk, Andrée Sikorska. Monde moderne, 1925. 158 p.   **7458**

Good collection of 12 articles paying homage to L. Most deal with various aspects of L.'s life while some offer assessments of L.'s works and of his influence. Particularly interesting are the contributions by Lebey (p. 49–63), Gregh (p. 61–79), Henriot (p. 131–39), and by Valéry (p. 23–39) who presents a touching reminiscence of the young L.'s fervent devotion to literature and avers that L. felt despair and bitterness because the public failed to recognize the high artistic inspiration which motivated his writings.

Biography

Barney, Natalie Clifford. Aventures de l'esprit. Emile-Paul, 1929. 278 p.   **7459**

In one section (p. 21–40) of this collection of literary reminiscences, Barney evokes her friendship with L. Since she considered L. a champion of moral freedom in general and of Lesbianism in particular, she first turned to him to enlist his aid in getting her first novel published. The first of the five letters from L. which Barney publishes here reveals L.'s opposition to novels which are too obviously autobiographical.

Cardinne-Petit, Robert. Pierre Louÿs inconnu. L'élan, 1948. 256 p.   **7460**

Very anecdotal account of major episodes in L.'s life and literary career. Useful mainly because no complete and scholarly biography of L. exists. States that L.'s erotic works were composed in his later years and were never intended for publication. Contends other more pornographic works attributed to L. are in reality the work of a secretary of L. who imitated L.'s handwriting.

————. Pierre Louÿs intime. Jean-Renard, 1942. 182 p.   **7461**

First biographical treatment of L. to appear after his death. Cardinne-Petit was L.'s secretary in 1917 and 1918. Biographical material is sketchy, romanticized and always sympathetic to L. Allusions to L.'s liaison with Mme Henri de Régnier (Gérard d'Houville) are veiled in anonymity as are later episodes in L.'s life. His second marriage is not mentioned. Also relates with occasional inaccuracies a number of anecdotes concerning the composition of some of L.'s works.

Cassou, Jean. La querelle Corneille-Molière. MerFl 73–74, March 1928.   **7462**

Some background notes by this former secretary of L. concerning L.'s thesis that Corneille was responsible for

certain of Molière's works. This is one of 23 brief articles devoted to L. by various authors in this special number of the *Mercure de Flandre.*

Clive, H. P. Notes on La conque and on the early friendship of Pierre Louÿs and Paul Valéry. SFr 52:94–103, 1974. **7463**

Careful study of L.'s relations with Valéry at the time of L.'s editorship of *La conque* (1890–1892).

————. Pierre Louÿs and Oscar Wilde; a chronicle of their friendship. RLC 43: 353–84, 1969.   **7464**

Long, carefully researched article demonstrating complete familiarity with all the literature available on L.'s relationship with Wilde. Presents clearly for the first time the principal events in this 1891–1893 friendship. Particularly well treated are L.'s part in revising the French ms. of Wilde's play *Salomé* and L.'s role in Wilde's trials. Shows the admiration L. and Wilde felt for each other's talents. Argues convincingly that L.'s decision to break with Wilde was not prompted by any deep abhorrence of Wilde's sexual mores. Rather it was chiefly due to his fear for his own reputation and a desire not to be mistaken for a homosexual because of his acquaintance with Wilde and Douglas.

Farrère, Claude. Mon ami Pierre Louÿs avec des lettres inédites de Pierre Louÿs à Claude Farrère et des fac-similés. Domat, 1953. 190 p.   **7465**

Gives a brief and rather romanticized version of L.'s life. Includes some interesting details and some personal recollections of L. and of the composition of some of L.'s works. Refrains from identifying Marie de Heredia as the principal love in L.'s life. Particularly sketchy and reticent discussion of precisely those later years of L.'s life which Farrère knew most intimately. Some of L.'s letters do reveal the level of L.'s culture and the general soundness of his advice in literary matters. Others are anecdotal or merely puzzling; none is accompanied by proper explanatory notes.

Fleury, R[obert]. Junot, Duc d'Abrantès, et Pierre Louÿs. BBB 2:86–92, 1962. **7466**

Traces the exact relationship between L. and his great-granduncle Andoche Junot. Based on L.'s own painstaking research and documentation carried out from 1903 to 1909. Illustrates how L.'s growing interest in such matters as research in genealogy and in the minor mysteries of literary history came to divert his attention from writing any works of imagination during his final years.

Fleury, Robert. Pierre Louÿs et Gilbert de Voisins: une curieuse amitié. Tête de feuilles, 1973. 255 p. (Archives et documents)   **7467**

Only authoritative work on L.'s life. Indispensable for any serious study of L. Based extensively on rare or hitherto unpublished documents. Well-written text concentrates on L. between 1897 and 1915. Chronicles in accurate detail L.'s relations with Marie de Heredia (later Mme Henri de Régnier), with her sister Louise (whom he married in 1899), with Germaine Dethomas and with Zohra ben Brahim. Signals parallels between these relations and L.'s posthumous novel *Psyché,* his poem *Pervigilium mortis* and other works, though in general refrains from any literary appraisals. Relates Voisins' role in aiding L. and his wife through their many financial problems caused by L.'s impractical nature. Covers the circumstances of the L. divorce and the subsequent marriage of Louise and Voisins. Gives an authentic picture of the life and manners of the literary *haute bourgeoisie* during the *belle époque.* Concludes with an excellent 36-page Chronology which outlines L.'s entire life.

Gaubert, Ernest. Pierre Louÿs. Sansot, 1904. 41 p. (Les célébrités d'aujourd'hui)   **7468**

Interesting as an early and rare biographical study of L. Extremely sketchy and at times incorrect. For example, gives Paris as L.'s birthplace; inaccurately reports that L.'s attempt to pass off his *Chansons de Bilitis* as a translation from the Greek was completely successful. Absolutely silent on L.'s private life. Notes L.'s early tendency to flee publicity; foreshadows his subsequent hermit-like existence. Brief remarks on L.'s literary productions are generally valid and are representative of contemporary appraisals of L. Almost reduces L.'s role as a moral philosopher to that of a latter-day Epicurean. See L.'s campaign for moral freedom as stemming from Nietzsche's call for individual liberty. Concludes with a brief selection of contemporary assessments of L. (by Coppée, Léautaud, Wyzéva, Gourmont, Mauclair, Voisins) and a serious bibliography established by A. B. [Ad. van Bever].

Gide, André. Journal 1889–1939 avec un index des noms et des œuvres cités. Gallimard, 1954. 1378 p. (La Pléiade)   **7469**

L.'s is the first name mentioned in this famous literary diary. In all Gide speaks of L. about a score of times in this volume. A few passages are quite revealing. For example, on p. 882 Gide gives his assessment of those elements in L. which made him a friend and those which led to the inevitable end of their friendship.

———. Journal 1939–1949. Souvenirs. Avec un index des noms et des œuvres cités. Gallimard, 1954. 1280 p. (La Pléiade)   **7470**

Because of its useful general index, this is the handiest volume in which to read what Gide had to say about his friendship with L. in his book of memoirs, *Si le grain ne meurt.* In these reminiscences (p. 349–613) there are some thirty pages concerning L.

———, **and Paul Valéry.** Correspondance 1890–1942. Préface et notes de Robert Mallet. Gallimard, 1955. 559 p.   **7471**

L.'s is the name most often mentioned in this voluminous correspondence. Excellent notes and a good index allow the careful reader to acquire a fairly accurate idea of L.'s attitudes toward literature and toward these two friends whom he brought together.

Gregh, Fernand. L'âge d'arain (souvenirs 1905–1925). Grasset, 1951. 272 p.   **7472**

Literary memories by a poet and close friend of L.'s. Gives details on the publication by Gregh of L.'s poem L'*apogée* (p. 83–84).

———. L'âge de fer (souvenirs 1925–1955). Grasset, 1956. 293 p.   **7473**

Gregh includes in these memories his final tribute to his friend L. (p. 34–41).

These pages are taken from Gregh's article on L. in *Le tombeau de Pierre Louÿs*.

――. L'âge d'or. Souvenirs d'enfance et de jeunesse. Grasset, 1947. 334 p.   **7474**
Literary memories valuable for understanding L.'s period. Gregh describes L. courting the Heredia girls and touches on the drama of his marriage (p. 227–33). No index.

Jaloux, Edmond. Les saisons littéraires. V. 1. 1896–1903. Fribourg, Eds. de la Librairie de l'université, 1942. 342 p. *And:* Les saisons littéraires. V. 2. 1904–1914. Plon, 1950. 325 p.   **7475**
Index at end of V. 2 indicates the dozen brief passages concerned with L. in Jaloux's literary memoirs. Chiefly valuable for Jaloux's treatment of many of L.'s contemporaries. Jaloux knew well Régnier and Gide and many others close to L., including Gilbert de Voisins. V. 2 contains two short chapters devoted to L. One studies his character (p. 149–53); the second (p. 213–21) is a critical appreciation of some of his works.

Léautaud, Paul. Journal littéraire. Mercure de France, 1954–64. 16 v.   **7476**
Léautaud makes frequent allusions to L. and his contemporaries, usually on level of social and professional gossip with little literary evaluation of L.'s works. Unfortunately, index of names begins only with v. 6 (July, 1927).

Mirandola, Giorgio. André Gide e Pierre Louÿs: fasti e miserie di un'amicizia sbagliata. SFr 45:443–63, 1971.   **7477**
Generally accurate account based on a careful reading of much of the literature available concerning this famous 8-year friendship. Argues that L.'s cocksure nature and imperious manner in conflict with Gide's possessive attitude toward friends and his inability to accept values dictated by others led to the end of their friendship in 1896. Adopts a point of view more sympathetic to L. than to Gide, unusual for authors dealing with this subject. Some elements broached are very conjectural, e.g., the "mystery" of L.'s birth; the reasons for L.'s break with Wilde. Gives incorrect family name of

Gide's and L.'s companion Méryem (bent Ali or ben Atala, not ben Sala). Repeats Le Dantec's error of considering Méryem as the model for the character Aracoeli in L.'s posthumous novel *Psyché.* (L.'s 1897 mistress Zohra ben Brahim was the principal model for Aracoeli.)

Mondor, Henri. Les premiers temps d'une amitié. André Gide et Paul Valéry. Monaco, Eds. du rocher, 1947. 161 p.   **7478**
Early study based on then largely unpublished correspondence between Gide, Valéry and L. Traces accurately the role L. played in bringing Gide and Valéry together and in guiding their first steps into Parisian literary circles. There are no notes and only rarely are the precise dates indicated for the letters excerpted.

General Studies

Armandie, Anne. L'œuvre de Pierre Louÿs. *In:* Pierre Louÿs. *See* 7457. p. 12–15.   **7479**
One of the least superficial articles in this special number.

Clerc, Charly. Le règne d'Eros et d'Aphrodite. *In his:* Le génie du paganisme: essais sur l'inspiration antique dans la littérature française contemporaine. Payot, 1926. p. 131–47.   **7480**
Briefly discusses L.'s *Chansons de Bilitis, Aphrodite,* and his collection of symbolist tales, *Le crépuscule des nymphes.* Attempts to demonstrate that L. was chiefly an apologist for the sensual elements in life that are exemplified by the ancient civilization of Alexandria.

Criton (pseud. of Charles Maurras). Pierre Louÿs. ActF 3, Jan. 4, 1910.   **7481**
Maurras is still critical of L.'s *Aphrodite* and his *Chansons de Bilitis* as examples of Alexandrian art. However, he now considers *La femme et le pantin* and *Les aventures du roi Pausole* to be worthy works written by a fellow conservative whose classical culture and taste were formed before the onset of the decadence which Maurras sees all around him in early twentieth-century France.

Croce, Benedetto. La frase indimenticabile dello Chateaubriand e il commento di P. Louÿs. QdC 6:210–13, 1950. *Also in his:* Aneddoti di varia letteratura. Bari, G. Laterza, 1954.   **7482**

Translates into Italian L.'s 1913 article in *La phrase inoubliable.* Confesses astonishment at finding that L. produced this article, a rather fanciful attempt at historical criticism but done with great sensitivity; the other works of L. which Croce had read in past (*Aphrodite, Bilitis, La femme et le pantin*) Croce considers almost libidinous in their exalting of physical love to the level of a religion. Opposes L.'s theory that a return to the Greek concept of physical love is necessary for the moral elevation of humanity.

Farrère, Claude. Sillages. Flammarion, 1936. 247 p.   **7483**

In the first chapters of this book of memoirs Farrère occasionally evokes his good friend and mentor, L. Chapter IV, *Souvenirs de Pierre Louÿs* (p. 123–85) is Farrère's first long tribute to L. the writer. He briefly analyzes L.'s principal works and comments favorably on L.'s theory that Corneille often collaborated with Molière and that Molière's *Amphitryon* is a work by Corneille. This chapter includes 17 pages of excerpts from L.'s works and Farrère's own 17-page version of the end of *Psyché,* L.'s unfinished novel.

Gide, André. Lettre à Angèle, V. *In his:* Prétextes: réflexions sur quelques points de littérature et de morale. Mercure de France, 1947. p. 90–94. (First ed.: 1903)   **7484**

Essentially a harsh review of L.'s 1899 tale *Une volupté nouvelle.* Accuses L. of confusing the idea of perfection with that of progress. Adopts a rather puritanical note and deprecates L.'s admiration for antiquity and his insistence on the importance of pleasure.

Gourmont, Remy de. Pierre Louÿs. *In his:* Le livre des masques. Mercure de France, 1896. p. 181–86.   **7485**

Brief, 4-page assessment of L.'s novel *Aphrodite* written during period of the startling success of this novel. See it as signaling a possible return to a more permissive morality.

Henriot, Emile. Pierre Louÿs. Quand Pierre Louÿs parlait de ses livres. Les manuscrits de Pierre Louÿs. *In his:* Livres et portraits. V. 3. Plon, 1927. p. 262–86. (Courrier littéraire)   **7486**

Group of three brief articles written shortly after L.'s death. The first gives a sympathetic but valid recapitulation of L.'s contributions to French literature. The last two give interesting details on L.'s activities as an erudite bibliophile and on his collection of mss. offered for sale in 1926 as described in the Carteret catalog (*see* 7455).

Highet, Gilbert. The classical tradition. Greek and Roman influences on western literature. Oxford univ. press, 1957. 763 p.   **7487**

This ed. has corrections added to the first 1949 ed. In his chapter 20 ("Parnassus and Antichrist"), Highet studies many of the authors who shared a common philosophy with L. The *Chansons de Bilitis* and *Aphrodite* are criticized in the sub-section entitled "Christianity means repression, paganism means liberty" (p. 457–59). In these works L. is accused of having given a false interpretation of Greek morality. In his criticism Highet follows closely the assessment of *Bilitis* made by Wilamowitz in 1896. (*See* 7497).

Lebey, André. Disques et pellicules. Librairie Valois, 1929. 256 p.   **7488**

Lebey was a close and early friend of L.'s. In this volume of literary memoirs and judgments, Lebey devotes a number of chapters to various friends and contemporaries that he and L. knew (Heredia, J.-E. Blanche, Tinan, Valéry). A substantial portion of the volume (p. 193–235) concerns L. In these pages Lebey does manage to establish his admiration for L. and to evaluate certain elements of L.'s work. However, Lebey's general style is too impressionistic to be of much value for the serious biographer or critic seeking clear and precise statements.

Martin-Mamy, M. Pierre Louÿs, moraliste. *In his:* Les nouveaux païens. Sansot, n.d. [1914]. p. 233–55.   **7489**

Briefly reviews the principal works in which L. presents his pleas for a new morality. Useful as a starting point for any new study of L.'s social theories.

Maurras, Charles. Pierre Louÿs. *In his:* Pages littéraires choisies. Champion, 1922. p. 168–76.   **7490**

Written from Maurras' conservative point of view. Maurras, as champion of an austere interpretation of Athenian culture, attacks L.'s *Aphrodite* for presenting a distorted picture of antiquity.

Mirandola, Giorgio. Pierre Louÿs. Milan, Mursia, 1974. 333 p.   **7491**

Competently updated life and works treatment of L. by young Italian scholar. Short 60-page biographical section relies chiefly on Fleury for new, accurate data. Perpetuates some minor errors, especially regarding L.'s early schooling. The remainder of the study presents in chronological order brief critical essays on L.'s major works. These essays and the biography suffer because the author apparently did not have access to the invaluable Biblis catalogs (*see* 7454). No new unpublished material is presented. The 23-page bibliography (some entries are briefly annotated) is fairly complete but only includes works by L. Has index of names only, making it difficult to locate specific works.

Praz, Mario. The romantic agony. Trans. from the Italian by Angus Davidson. Second edition. London, New York, Oxford univ. press, 1970. 479 p.   **7492**

This revised ed. is valuable for its study of a considerable body of decadent literature dealing with *homo sensualis*. Many of the literary influences which affected L.'s works can be detected principally in Praz's Chapter IV, *"La belle dame sans merci."* Praz deals briefly with L.'s heroine Conchita (*La femme et le pantin*), seeing parallels between her and Merimée's Carmen and Eugène Sue's Cécily (*Les mystères de Paris*). A good index guides the reader towards his specific interests.

Segard, Achille. Pierre Louÿs. *In his:* Les voluptueux et les hommes d'action. Société d'éds. littéraires et artistiques [P. Ollendorf], 1900. p. 37–72.   **7493**

Interesting contemporary assessment of L. naturally ranks L. among the *voluptueux.* Criticizes L.'s *Aphrodite*

for presenting only the sensual side of love, ignoring all sentiment. Avers the novel's characters lack any psychological depth. *Aphrodite* contrasted unfavorably with *Thaïs* and *Salammbô*, novels which Segard considers more accurate historical reconstitutions. L.'s *Chansons de Bilitis* are criticized for their insistence on tribadism. Correctly equates the moral lesson of *La femme et le pantin* to that of *Aphrodite*.

Thompson, Vance. The paganism of Pierre Louÿs. *In his:* French portraits, being appreciations of the writers of young France. Boston, Richard G. Badger & Co., 1900. p. 130–36.   **7494**

Early evaluation in English of L.'s influence and moral preachments. Avers that L.'s anti-Protestant neopaganism, as found in *Aphrodite* and the *Chansons de Bilitis,* is based on a misinterpretation of Greek moral life which, according to Thompson, was probably as puritanical and intolerant as the contemporary standards of French morality which L. was criticizing.

Van Bever, Adolphe, and Paul Léautaud. Pierre Louÿs. *In their:* Poètes d'aujourd'hui. Morceaux choisis accompagnés de notices biographiques et d'un essai de bibliographie. V. 2. 53rd ed. Mercure de France, 1929. p. 175–85.   **7495**

In this 53rd ed. of this famous anthology, Léautaud presents a revised and slightly expanded biographical sketch of L. The bibliography by Van Bever, though now outdated, is quite complete and characteristically accurate.

Walch, G[érard]. Pierre Louÿs. *In his:* Anthologie des poètes français contemporains. V. 3. Nouvelle éd. Delagrave, 1930. p. 55–63.   **7496**

Brief biographical introduction and bibliography. Both outdated and at times incorrect. Even repeats the error of the first ed. (1903) in giving Paris as L.'s birthplace.

Wilamowitz-Moellendorff, Ulrich von. Les chansons de Bilitis. *In his:* Sappho und Simonides. Second ed. Berlin, Zurich, Dublin, Weidmann, 1966. p. 63–78. **7497**

This is a reprint of the young Wilamowitz's famous review of L.'s *Les chansons de Bilitis traduites du grec pour la première fois*. This review first appeared in the *Göttinger Gelehrte Anzeigen,* 1896, p. 623 f. Wilamowitz's avowed purpose in the review is to defend the purity of a great woman (Sappho). By pointing out anachronisms and by using various philological proofs, Wilamowitz easily shows that the *Chansons* could not be authentic translations from the Greek. He condemns L.'s heroine Bilitis for being psychologically unthinkable; according to Wilamowitz, such a woman, living only a life of the senses, could not possibly translate her feelings into poetry. Recognizes L. as a particular type of classicist, much in the same vein as Goethe and Wieland, all sincere admirers of the Greek ideal. The last half of the review is directed against any homosexual interpretation of Sappho's poetry.

Albert Lozeau
(Nos. 7498–7502)

JACQUES COTNAM

Dugas, Marcel. Albert Lozeau. *In his:* Apologies. Montreal, Paradis-Vincent, 1919. p. 13–35.   **7498**
States that L. introduces a new element of emotion into French-Canadian poetry and stresses the sincerity of this poet of interior spaces. Finds that technically *Miroir des jours* is superior to *L'âme solitaire.* Finally he detects in this poetry traces of Rodenbach.

Marcotte, Gilles. Poètes de la solitude: Alfred Garneau et Albert Lozeau. *In his:* Une littérature qui se fait. Montreal, HMH, 1962, p. 84–97.   **7499**
Summary of theme of solitude in works of these two poets. He concludes regarding L.: "His Christian voice is amongst the purest, most sincere and also most humble that our poetry has to offer."

Margerie, Yves de. Albert Lozeau. Montreal and Paris, Fides, 1958. 95 p.   **7500**
Selected texts preceded by an introduction emphasizing themes of suffering and isolation in L.'s poetry. Includes chronological biography and short bibliography.

Paul-Crouzet, Jeanne. Albert Lozeau. *In her:* Poésie au Canada. Didier, 1946. p. 139–55.   **7501**
In the biographical part of her essay, Paul-Crouzet stresses the influence of physical pain on this poet, a disciple of Musset, who also reminds her at times of Sully-Prudhomme. She also notes the extent to which daydream and fantasy were the very stuff of L.'s life. In the second part, she presents a detailed analysis of "Effets de neige et de givre," a poem she ranks as one of L.'s most important. The critic concludes her analysis with a brief comparison of L. and Nelligan, stressing the features which most effectively differentiate one from the other.

Roy, Camille. Albert Lozeau. *In his:* A l'ombre des érables. Quebec, L'action sociale, 1924. p. 179–200.   **7502**
Roy first compares L.'s main themes with those of such French-Canadian poets as Fréchette, Crémazie, Chapman, Nelligan and Lemay. L.'s poetry, which reminds him of Wordsworth's, is a "poetry of the soul" and an authentic "poetry of nature." Although he is clearly favorable to L., he stresses that some of the poet's work is not sufficiently Christian, an obvious shortcoming in the critic's eyes.

Alphonse Métérié
(Nos. 7503–7507)

URS EGLI

Gros, Léon-Gabriel. Cophetuesques. CahS 21:734–36, 1934. *Also in:* Atlas 14: Nov. 25, 1934.   **7503**
There exists a "cas Métérié" because of the discrepancy between the elegiac sincerity of M.'s poetry and the cynical attitude of the era M. has to live with. Admires the undeniable qualities of M.'s poems and shares M.'s conviction that happiness does not exist in this world. Claims that it is not sufficient to state this fact, but that a poet, as anybody else, has to contribute to the general effort of those who want to make happiness possible. For M.'s answer, *see* his *Lettre sur la poésie* in RHeb 43:614–20, Dec. 29, 1934.

————. Vacances de l'idéalisme. CahS 22: 139–44, 1935. **7504**

Answers M.'s reply, *supra*. Accepts M.'s arguments in general, but not for the time being. Poetry like M.'s will only have a right to exist once the material conditions of mankind have been improved.

Pichois, Claude. Alphonse Métérié ou des paradoxes de la gloire poétique. EcCSC 43:223–24, Dec. 22, 1951. **7505**

Short study of M.'s life and literary career, followed by a subtle appreciation of M.'s poetry. Emphasizes the importance of time and memory in M.'s transmutation of everyday events into highly immaterial poetry. Opens parallels to Proust, Chateaubriand, Nerval and Laforgue. Particular references to *Proella* (Geneva, Cailler, 1951).

Orion (pseud. of Eugène Marsan). Le carnet des lettres, des sciences et des arts. ActF 17:Sept. 30, 1924. **7506**

Good presentation of M.'s second volume of poetry, *Le cahier noir* (Amiens, Malfère, 1923). Compares this work to the former, *Le livre des sœurs* (Amiens, Malfère, 1922). Refers to some of the major themes of M.'s poetry.

————. Carnet des lettres, des sciences et des arts. ActF 17: Oct. 2, 1924. **7507**

Excellent and close analysis of M.'s prosody. Shows how M. succeeds in finding his own original art of versification by developing and refining the elements of classical prosody.

Oscar Vladislas de L. Milosz
(Nos. 7508–7533)

BIRUTA CAP

Bibliography

Place, Georges G. O. V. de L. Milosz. Précédé de Milosz à Fontainebleau et de Une prière dans la nuit. Eds. de la Chronique des lettres françaises, 1971. 63 p. (Coll. Georges Place) **7508**

A bibliography of works by and on M. Includes school eds. and popular magazines alluding to M. Essential for any thorough study on M.

Editions

Milosz, Oscar Vladislas de L. Œuvres complètes. Introd. Edmond Jaloux. Fribourg, Egloff, 1944–63. 10 v. **7509**

M.'s own prefaces to many works are invaluable. Jaloux stresses the importance of M.'s autobiographical and only novel, *L'amoureuse initiation,* as the key to his entire work. The unsold vols. IV, V and VIII of the Egloff ed. were bought by André Silvaire and integrated into his ed. with new covers. Vols. IV and VIII retain identical numbering, while Egloff V becomes Silvaire VI, incorporating the projected Egloff VI.

————. Œuvres complètes. A Silvaire, 1945–1970. 11 v. **7510**

Contrary to what was announced in previous volumes, v. 11 contains the drama *Saül de Tarse* (1913), third part of M.'s dramatic trilogy. The other two plays, *Miguel Manara* (1911) and *Méphiboseth* (1912) are included in vols. III and IV, respectively. Silvaire did not take possession of *Saül de Tarse* until 1970, which explains its inclusion in v. 11, also containing *Daïnos* and translations of poetry. Notes by the editor in v. 11.

Inédits and Correspondence

Bellemin-Noël, Jean. Douze lettres inédites de Milosz à Roland Boris (1897–1923). RHL 67:617–21, 1967. **7511**

These brief letters to his schoolday friend, spanning 26 years, outline M.'s spiritual evolution of that period. Several dwell heavily on *Epître à Storge.* Presentation by Bellemin-Noël.

Milosz, O. V. de L. Le cahier déchiré. A. Silvaire, 1969. 64 p. **7512**

Limited ed. of thirteen poems written by M. at about age seventeen, torn up in a moment of discouragement, but reconstituted and preciously preserved by a friend who submitted them to M.'s editor in 1957. Rhymed alexandrine verse and verse dialogs on themes of death and suffering. Preface and notes by the editor.

————. Milosz. Choix de textes présentés par Jacques Buge. André Silvaire, 1965. 126 p. (Connaissez-vous?)   **7513**

Introduction and excerpts from what most critics consider M.'s most representative works. Statements and opinions of contemporaries. Photographs. Reviews: M. Alyn in FL Dec. 2, 1965; J. Groffier in SynB 242–43:97, 1966; J.-B. Morvan in PoCp 76–77: 93–94, 1966; B. Robert in RUO 39:426–28, 1969.

————. Dix-sept lettres de Milosz [à Armand Guibert]. Guy-Lévi Mano, 1958. 17 p. 4 p. notes.   **7514**

M.'s letters to one of his editors. Some information on the composition of his works.

————. Soixante-quinze lettres inédites et sept documents originaux. A. Silvaire, 1969. 164 p. Plates.   **7515**

Twenty letters to his friend the sculptor Léon Vogt, from 1906 to 1924; followed by 55 to his widow (1924–1931). Illustrations (inconography). Important commentary by M. on his works and activities, his sources of inspiration. Notes.

————. Textes inédits de O. V. de L. Milosz. A. Silvaire, 1959. 111 p.   **7516**

Five short texts by M., letters from M. to six correspondents, letters from Valéry, Suarès, Bourdelle and Supervielle to M. Also M. on poetry. Critical and perceptive comments by Bourdelle and Suarès on M.'s work.

General Studies: Books

Bellemin-Noël, Jean. Poèmes d'adolescence de Milosz; le Cahier déchiré. Lettres modernes, 1972. 135 p. (Avant-siècle, 13)   **7517**

Detailed thematic study and critical ed. of M.'s earliest poetry.

————. Le texte et l'avant-texte; les brouillons d'un poème de Milosz. Larousse, 1972. 143 p. (Coll. L)   **7518**

M.'s poem of 65 verses, La charrette, is compared to its early version of 75 p. to illustrate Bellemin-Noël's method which seeks to apply literary analysis to all stages of a work, culminating in a complementary confrontation of successive drafts with the "final" text.

Buge, Jacques. Milosz en quête du divin. Nizet, 1963. 319 p.   **7519**

Demonstrates the unity of M.'s work in its diverse forms of poetry, drama, fiction, philosophy, ethnography and biblical exegesis. Compares M. to Teilhard de Chardin and Einstein as precursors of a new humanism which reconciles faith and science. Appendices of unpublished letters and documents. Chronology. Valuable in situating M. in 20th century thought. Reviews: M. D[écaudin] in IL 5: 211–12, 1965; A. Lebois in RHL 64:502–03, 1964.

————. Milosz et la notion sainte du rien. In: Le vide. Expérience spirituelle en occident et en orient. Minard, 1969. p. 227–40. (Hermes)   **7520**

A masterful explanation of M.'s metaphysics based on his concept of Rien and his new logic. A key to the comprehension of M.'s philosophical works.

Godoy, Armand. Milosz, le poète de l'amour. Fribourg, Egloff, 1944. 265 p. Also: A. Silvaire, 1960. 282 p.   **7521**

A general, yet thorough introduction to M.: short biography, description of his work with résumés and numerous quotations, analysis of his technique, his faith as a constant throughout his life and works.

Lebois, André. L'œuvre de Milosz. Essai. Denoël, 1960. 198 p.   **7522**

A chronological appraisal of M.'s literary works only. Spiritual affinities.

Richter, Anne. Milosz. Eds. universitaires, 1965. 127 p. (Classiques du XXᵉ siècle)   **7523**

A brief introduction of M. through his major poetic and dramatic works. Bio-bibliography.

Rousselot, Jean. O. V. de L. Milosz; une étude. Œuvres choisies, bibliographie. Seghers, 1949. 219 p. (Poètes d'aujourd'hui). Also: Seghers, 1972. 200 p. (Poètes d'aujourd'hui, 205)   **7524**

The first book on M. to be published for a general audience. 95 p. of introductory remarks. M.'s poems, scenes from *Miguel Manara* and *Méphiboseth* and a few prose passages.

Zidonis, Geneviève-Irène. O. V. de L. Milosz. Sa vie, son œuvre, son rayonnement. Olivier Perrin, 1951. 293 p. **7525**

Chronological study of M.'s life and works, with emphasis on psychological factors (the major key to the understanding of his poetry), particularly the impact of his childhood experiences in his native Lithuania. Last chapter a stylistic study.

Collected Articles

Où en sont les recherches et travaux sur Milosz? A. Silvaire, 1972. 48 p. (CahAAM, 7)   **7526**

Useful summary of research.

O. V. de L. Milosz (1877–1939). Inédits—Hors-texte et fac-similés—Etudes et notes. A. Silvaire, 1959. 222 p. (Les lettres)   **7527**

Two poems, ten letters and numerous short articles by M.'s friends and critics. Particularly noteworthy is the article by S. Backis on M.'s diplomatic activities and political thought. Bibliographies of the original eds. of M.'s works.

General Studies: Articles

Bellemin-Noël, Jean. Milosz et Dante: La divina commedia et les noms des personnages de l'Amoureuse initiation. SFr 3:496–501, 1962.   **7528**

Thorough and well-documented comparison of characters in Dante's and M.'s works. Traces M.'s spiritual development and influences which led him to Dante.

————. Milosz lecteur de Swedenborg. RSH 116:521–62, 1964.   **7529**

A grouping and analysis of the equivalent of 40 typewritten pages of marginal notes M. made when reading Swedenborg's *Conjugial love* and *True Christian religion* as well as R. L. Tafel's study of Swedenborg, all in English translations. Sheds light on M.'s spirituality and reveals his own idea of his relationship to Swedenborg. Establishes M.'s preoccupations during 1914–

15 and at later moments, and his debt to Swedenborg. Gives sources of M.'s use of poetic words, M.'s value judgments of poetry and the creative act. Well written and well organized article on a difficult subject. *See also:* Guise, Stanley. Milosz et Swedenborg. *In:* O. V. de L. Milosz (1877–1939). *See* 7527. p. 178–86.

Blanchet, André. Le destin bizarre du grand Milosz. Et 296–97:289–308, 1958. *Also:* La nuit de feu (Le destin bizarre du grand Milosz). *In his:* La littérature et le spirituel, t. II. Aubier-Eds. Montaigne, 1960. p. 265–86.   **7530**

Claims M. was not religious until his night of illumination in 1914. Compares M. to Léon Bloy and Pascal. A capital study on M.'s religiosity.

Cassou, Jean. Milosz. *In his:* Trois poètes—Rilke, Milosz, Machado. Plon, 1954. p. 44–84.   **7531**

Praises M. as the greatest poet of the French language in the 20th century. Highlights his moral qualities of simplicity and serenity and gives reasons for M.'s relative obscurity.

Garnier, Pierre. Milosz au cœur de notre temps. Cr 143:305–18, 1959.   **7532**

Emphasizes the prophetic qualities of M.'s work.

Lebois, André. Milosz et Hölderlin. EG 4:345–60, 1949.   **7533**

Traces the two poets' parallel characters and destinies and analyzes common themes (childhood, conflict of dream-action, love and the role of woman, divinity). While this comparison highlights some of their respective traits, it may lead the reader to make false inferences about M.'s silent years (1927–1939).

Robert de Montesquiou
(Nos. 7534–7552)

WILL L. McLENDON

Barbier, Carl Paul. Correspondance de Mallarmé avec Robert de Montesquiou. *In his:* Documents Stéphane Mallarmé. V. 2. Nizet, 1970. p. 43–74.   **7534**

Reproduction, without commentary, of calling cards, notes, and letters of varying length exchanged between M. and Mallarmé. Principal sources are Fonds Montesquiou at Bibliothèque Nationale and ms. copies of letters made by Pinard, secretary and executor of M.'s estate, just prior to auction sale.

Bibliothèque de Robert de Montesquiou. Librairie M. Escoffier, 1923. 252 p.   **7535**

Sumptuous catalog of books and documents sold at auction in the Hôtel Drouot, April 23–26, 1923. Contains detailed descriptions of articles, numerous facsimile mss. of Leconte de Lisle, Verlaine, Montesquiou, Desbordes-Valmore, Heredia. Excellent repertory of M.'s tastes in literature.

Carassus, Emilien. Le snobisme et les lettres françaises de Paul Bourget à Marcel Proust, 1884–1914. A. Colin, 1966. 645 p., passim.   **7536**

Contains references to M., too numerous to list, and several extended sections within various chapters devoted primarily to a study of M.'s role in literary snobbism.

Clermont-Tonnerre, Elisabeth de. Robert de Montesquiou et Marcel Proust. Flammarion, 1925. 248 p.   **7537**

Important source book of many modern studies of Proust and M. Wealth of personal reminiscences and anecdotic material on both men in social and literary contexts.

Daudet, Léon. Robert de Montesquiou. *In his:* Fantômes et vivants. Nouvelle librairie nationale, 1914. p. 283–87.   **7538**

Incisive portrait of M. the artist in his all-encompassing egoism.

De Montera, Pierre, and Guy Tosi. D'Annunzio, Montesquiou, Matilde Serao. Rome, Ed. di storia e letteratura, 1972. 200 p.   **7539**

M. is the common denominator in this two-part study of two Italian novelists whose friendship M. sought and cultivated for several years. Text, footnotes and appendix are rich in hitherto unpublished letters, poems, *dédicaces,* etc. of M. now in the Bibliothèque Nationale or the Vittoriale archives. New insights into character not only of M. and his two correspondents but also of Romaine Brooks.

Juin, Hubert. Robert de Montesquiou, poète. *In his:* Ecrivains de l'avant-siècle. Seghers, 1972. p. 179–88.   **7540**

Interesting sampling of M.'s epigrams and other verse, both light and serious. Much quotation and little critical effort.

Jullian, Philippe. Un prince 1900: Robert de Montesquiou. Perrin, 1965. 395 p. *Trans.:* Robert de Montesquiou, a fin de siècle prince. Trans. by John Haylock and Francis King. London, Secker & Warburg, 1967. 288 p. *Also:* Prince of aesthetes. Count Robert de Montesquiou, 1855–1921. Trans. by John Haylock and Francis King. New York, Viking press, 1968. 288 p.   **7541**

Highly significant contribution toward understanding of the man M. as well as his social and artistic milieux. Superficial study of some of M.'s poetry. Excellent photographic documentation. The definitive biography.

Reviews: A. Brookmer in NewS 74: 881–82, 1967; J. Calmann in SunTM 24–25, 27, Aug. 1, 1965; M. Décaudin in IL 18:164, 1966; J. Grenier in NouvO 35:19–20, 1965.

Kessedjian, François. La décadence de Robert de Montesquiou. BMP 17:616–26, 1967.   **7542**

Retraces romantic origins of *décadentisme* in French poetry via Gautier, Baudelaire, and Mallarmé. Presents young M. as incarnation of decadent or "Byzantine" ideal circa 1885. Redefines M.'s *dandysme* as based more on esthetic attitudes than on sartorial refinements.

Larcher, P.-L. Les œuvres poétiques de Montesquiou. BMP 11:440–44, 1961.   **7543**

Account of Proust's article on M. rediscovered by Prof. A. Artinian. Brief commentary on M.'s plan and intentions for *Les hortensias bleus.*

LeSage, Laurent. Proust's professor of beauty: Count Robert de Montesquiou. ASLHM 27:65–76, 1956.   **7544**

Succinct and interesting résumé of M.'s social position, talents, and career as related to Proust. Does not study in detail M.'s great influence on young Proust's esthetic concepts, as title would seem to suggest.

Lethève, Jacques. Un personnage typique de la fin du XIXe siècle: l'esthète. GazBA 65:181–92, 1965.   **7545**

Reexamines definitions of the esthete and concludes he is one for whom art is the supreme value. Cites M. as one of foremost examples along with Huysmans, Lorrain, Goncourt, Louÿs, G. Moreau, et al. Studies the esthete's debt to, and influence on, decorative arts with particular attention to M.'s residences. Includes several photographs of M.'s furnishings.

Murray, Jack. Proust, Montesquiou, and Balzac. TSLL 15:177–87, 1973.   **7546**

Considers factors conditioning unintentional self-revelation in writings of M. and Balzac. This penchant, as seen through Proust's eyes, is basis for his perception of similarities in two men and writers of outwardly different types.

Porter, Agnes R. Proust's final Montesquiou pastiche. *In:* Marcel Proust, a critical panorama. Ed. by Larkin B. Price. Urbana, Univ. of Illinois press, 1973. p. 124–46.   **7547**

A significant, detailed study of M.'s role in the direct inspiration of specific episodes of *A la recherche du temps perdu.* Analyzes striking parallels of language and attitudes between M. and Baron de Charlus, Proust's admirable monument of malice and kindness to a man whom he considered the epitome of his class and generation.

Proust, Marcel. Correspondance générale: lettres à Robert de Montesquiou, 1893 à 1921. Plon, 1930. 291 p.   **7548**

Rich source of information on M.'s moods and character as seen through the eyes of the person most responsible for whatever degree of immortality M. may have attained.

————. Un professeur de beauté. ArtV 20: 67–79, 1905. *Also:* RHL 49:161–75, 1949. *Also in:* Marcel Proust. Textes retrouvés. Ed. by Philip Kolb and Larkin B. Price. Urbana, Univ. of Illinois press, 1968. p. 155–66. *Also (rev.):* Gallimard, 1971. p. 208–22. (Cahiers Marcel Proust, 3)   **7549**

Proust, searching for a definition of his own esthetic principles, and under the influence of Ruskin and the pre-

Raphaelites, engages in some obvious flattery of M.

Ricaumont, Jacques de. Lettres inédites de Robert de Montesquiou au prince Sévastos. RdP 54:128–42, 1947.   **7550**

Equates M. and Proust's Charlus. Insists on irony of fate in M.'s realization that Proust's carciature was his only chance for enduring fame. Series of letters to adolescent boy reveals aging M.'s mellowed attitudes at very end of his life.

Thomas, Louis. L'esprit de Montesquiou. Mercure de France, 1943. 117 p.   **7551**

A fine example of the anti-Semitic propaganda which many French writers produced under the Nazi occupation. A slim 13-page preface praises M.'s qualities as individual and writer and explains his failure to achieve literary fame through a conspiracy of the Jewish press. The remaining 104 pages are lists of M.'s witticisms, snide remarks about his contemporaries and assorted rhymes called "Papillotes mondaines."

Vigneron, Robert. Marcel Proust et Robert de Montesquiou. Autour de Professionnelles beautés. MP 39:159–95, 1941. **7552**

Trials and tribulations of Proust as torchbearer of M. Basic early study of M.'s profound influence on young Proust. Wealth of details and notes on their correspondence.

Paul Morin
(Nos. 7553–7561)

JACQUES COTNAM

Barbeau, Victor. Paul Morin. CahACF 13: 45–119, 1970.   **7553**

From certain of the poet's letters, from personal recollections and confidences, and finally from M.'s own works, Barbeau has put together an excellent portrait of the artist. He stresses the originality and the foppish aspect of the author of *Le paon d'émail,* who never made a secret of his admiration for Robert de Montesquiou or of his debt to Henri de Régnier, "who taught him about verbal elegance." Barbeau takes issue with those critics who see in

M. a "déraciné." Well written and interesting.

Dantin, Louis. Paul Morin. *In his:* Poètes de l'Amérique française. Montreal, New York and London, Louis Carrier et Cie., 1928. p. 55–65.   **7554**

In this study of *Poèmes de cendre et d'or,* Dantin praises M.'s artistry and pays homage to his poetic craftmanship but criticizes him for frequenting too many artistic schools and for putting his erudition on display. Despite his reservations, he concludes that M. stands comparison with "the most highly regarded poets of postwar France."

Dugas, Marcel. Paul Morin. *In his:* Apologies. Montreal, Paradis-Vincent, 1919. p. 39–60.   **7555**

After bringing to mind the controversy surrounding the appearance of *Le paon d'émail,* Dugas insists on the book's indebtedness to exoticism and pagan thinking. He underlines also the poet's passion for the unusual word and his technical abilities.

Harvey, Jean-Charles. Poèmes de cendre et d'or. *In his:* Pages de critique. Quebec, Le soleil, 1926. p. 124–36.   **7556**

According to Harvey, no other Canadian poet "has written both so well and so badly." These words set the tone of this article in which Harvey explains that, in attempting to combat the cult of rustic life which then dominated the French-Canadian literary scene, M. goes too far when he exalts restlessness and cultivates the exotic. A valuable piece of literary criticism.

Major, André. Les poètes artistes: l'école de l'exil. *In:* La poésie canadienne-française. V. IV. Montreal, Fides, 1969. p. 135–42.   **7557**

Although primarily concerned with M., the article also deals with Marcel Dugas, Guy Delahaye, and René Chopin, poets who had much in common since they substituted for "the nationalistic commitment of their predecessors" a theory of "l'art pour l'art."

Marcotte, Gilles. Poètes artistes: Paul Morin et René Chopin. *In his:* Une littérature qui se fait. Montreal, HMH, 1962. p. 107–16.   **7558**

Undeniably, Paul Morin is the outstanding antiregionalist of French-Canadian literature. Conceivably, thinks Marcotte, *Le paon d'émail* "may have been a kind of *Nourritures terrestres* for the young people of the day." Marcotte characterizes the main themes of *Le paon d'émail* and the *Poèmes de cendre et d'or.* Second half of article devoted to Chopin.

Paul-Crouzet, Jeanne. Paul Morin. *In her:* Poésie au Canada. Didier, 1946. p. 207–31.   **7559**

Discusses the exotic aspects of M.'s work, stressing the preponderance of Oriental influence. This disciple of Heredia, she declares, launches a quest for the unusual, but sometimes finds the *précieux.* Second part of this article is a detailed analysis of the poem "Le plus aimé de mes jardins arabes." Excellent article, the best in Paul-Crouzet's collection.

Plante, Jean-Paul. Paul Morin. Montreal and Paris, Fides, 1958. 96 p. (Classiques canadiens)   **7560**

A selection of M.'s writings, a brief introduction to the author and his works. Chronological biography and brief bibliographical notes.

Roy, Camille. Paul Morin. *In his:* Poètes de chez nous. Montreal, Beauchemin, 1945. p. 157–71.   **7561**

Observing that there is nothing in this poetry to betray its French-Canadian origins, Roy defines M. as a visual poet with highly developed esthetic sensitivities. He singles out a number of qualities for praise in *Le paon d'émail,* in particular, intensity of color, sharpness of definition and sobriety of artistic conception. On the other hand, he finds M. much too preoccupied with his search for the unusual.

Emile Nelligan
(Nos. 7562–7570)

Jacques Cotnam

Bessette, Gérard. Le complexe parental chez Nelligan. *In his:* Une littérature en ébullition. Montreal, Eds. du jour, 1968. p. 63–85.   **7562**

A very interesting psychoanalytical study of the work of N. stressing poems developing the theme of death.

Nelligan, Emile. Poésies complètes, 1896–1899. Texte établi et annoté par Luc Lacourcière. Montreal and Paris, Fides, 1966. 331 p. **7563**

An admirable critical ed. faultlessly compiled. The introduction by Luc Lacourcière is a rich source of information, demonstrating his sound judgment.

Nelligan: poésie rêvée, poésie vécue. Montreal, Cercle du livre de France, 1969. 192 p. **7564**

Eight papers given at the N. colloquium, organized by McGill university, in Nov. 1966. Although these papers differ greatly in quality, they are certainly worth consulting.

Smith, Donald. Nelligan et le feu. VIP 7: 113–19, 1973. **7565**

Declaring that N.'s work "has not yet been examined in depth, in a synchronic perspective," Smith highlights the symbolic meanings of fire in N.'s poetry, seeking to prove that "through the medium of mythological representations," N. expresses "with considerable originality the condition of the Quebec collectivity," without allowing any of its universality to be lost. It is noteworthy that, in the context of this article, the author restricts himself to a detailed analysis of two poems: "Devant le feu" and "Rondel à ma pipe."

Wyczynski, Paul. Bibliographie descriptive et critique d'Emile Nelligan. Ottawa, Eds. de l'univ. d'Ottawa, 1973. 319 p. **7566**

This bibliography of exceptional quality will prove to be indispensable to those undertaking research on the work of N. The author demonstrates great objectivity in his descriptions and critical judgments.

———. Emile Nelligan, poète de l'inquiétude. CanL 10:40–50, 1961. *Also* (*rev.*) *in his:* Poésie et symbole. Montreal, Déom, 1965. p. 83–108. **7567**

A thematic analysis in which the author attempts to deal with N.'s anxiety as it becomes deeper and deeper.

———. Emile Nelligan, sources et originalité de son œuvre. Ottawa, Eds. de l'univ. d'Ottawa, 1960. 349 p. **7568**

This study is certainly the best available on N. The author has chosen a comparatist point of view which enables him to demonstrate interesting similarities between N. and several French poets, at the same time clearly showing N.'s authentic originality.

———. L'influence de Verlaine sur Nelligan. RHL 69:778–94, 1969. **7569**

Demonstrates that Verlaine's influenced is revealed, above all, in the structure and tone of many of N.'s poems.

———. Nelligan et la musique. Ottawa, Eds. de l'univ. d'Ottawa, 1971. 149 p. **7570**

Study of the relationship between music and the poetry of N. The author attempts to "grasp in the rhythmic lines, words, pulsations and forms, this verbal melody, which is infinitely more authentic in the imaginative realm than in traditional semantics."

Anna de Noailles
(i.e. Anna Elisabeth de Brancovan, comtesse Matthieu de Noailles)
(Nos. 7571–7631)

CLAUDE SENNINGER

Iconography

Anna de Noailles. Exposition de manuscrits, livres et documents donnés ou prêtés à la Bibliothèque Nationale. Impr. Tournon, 1953. 21 p. **7571**

The catalog of the Anna de Noailles exhibit at the BN in 1953 is perhaps a little smaller than usual, but is nevertheless invaluable for the study of her mss. Many documents of importance, quotations of letters from famous people, Valéry, Proust, Gide, Mauriac.

Autobiographical Texts

Noailles, Anna de. De la rive d'Europe à la rive d'Asie. Dorbon aîné, 1913. 130 p. **7572**

Series of remembrances of Anna's childhood, some of which are reproduced in *Exactitudes*. Anna evokes a vacation she took in Turkey, a trip to Spain; she meditates on Buddha and on pain.

———. Derniers vers et Poèmes d'enfances. Grasset, 1934. 203 p., 2l.   **7573**

Constantin Photiadès collected the last verses dictated by the poetess before her death and her childhood poems. Useful book for information on N.'s life and especially for the introduction to *Poèmes d'enfances.*

———. Exactitudes. Grasset, 1930. 231 p.   **7574**

This book, partly published under the title of *De la rive d'Europe à la rive d'Asie,* contains reminiscences and meditations with autobiographical overtones.

———. Le livre de ma vie. Hachette, 1932. 256 p.   **7575**

N. recalls her youth in a whimsical manner, insisting not so much on the facts but on her impressions of those facts. She sketches out small portraits of those people who had influenced or molded her mind.

———. (Anna de Brancovan). Poèmes d'enfances. Grasset, 1928. 96 p.   **7576**

Very enlightening autobiography which relates Anna's childhood, her readings and her pastimes and her first encounter with poetry.

Biography

Benjamin, René. Au soleil de la poésie: sous l'œil en fleur de la comtesse de Noailles. Librairie des Champs Elysées, 1928. 254 p.   **7577**

Lively portrait of N. after the First World War, between 1918 and 1925. Series of sketches relating imaginary visits with journalists, publishers, authors, etc.

Bonmariage, Sylvain. Anna de Noailles. *In his:* Catherine et ses amis. Gap, Ophrys, 1949. p. 119–49.   **7578**

Bonmariage writes a few vivid pages about his friendship with N. without studding it with anecdotes like many other commentators.

Boylesve, René. Visages. MerF 1009:5–16, 1947.   **7579**

These notes, written in the form of a diary, are quite frank and consequently very amusing. "Anna is a woman who has nothing to say, except that she feels like moving about, stomping her feet, smashing something."

Cocteau, Jean. La Comtesse de Noailles. *In:* Cahiers Jean Cocteau, 3. Gallimard, 1972. p. 43–50.   **7580**

Cocteau expresses his admiration for Anna. She understands, he says, "the dangerous error of supposing that one cannot be intellectual among intimates." *See also* Cocteau's "Anna de Noailles" in his *Reines de France* (Grasset, 1952), p. 115–50.

Corpechot, Lucien. Anna de Noailles. *In his:* Souvenirs d'un journaliste. V. 3. Plon, 1936. p. 105–86.   **7581**

Important study by an intelligent man who knew both N. and her poetry well.

Fargue, Léon-Paul. Noailles. *In his:* Portraits de famille. J. B. Janin, 1947. P. 7–16.   **7582**

Charming evocation of N.'s personality and talent.

Gillouin, René. Souvenirs sur Madame de Noailles. RDM 9:74–87, 1956.   **7583**

Probably the best collection of reminiscences about Anna. Collection of witticisms. The tone is neither too flattering nor too deprecatory. Letters.

Gourmont, Jean de. Anna de Noailles. *In his:* Muses d'aujourd'hui. Essai de physiologie poétique. Mercure de France, 1910. p. 35–45.   **7584**

Two great ideas haunt N.'s poetry: a fear of death and night and a search for happiness. Her writings are for her an assurance that she will not die in her entirety. Her oriental soul feels exiled in France and she still sings of the orient in poems like *Constantinople.*

Martin du Gard, Maurice. Les mémorables. RDM 13:9–25, 1967.   **7585**

Dialog between M. Martin du Gard and Cocteau after Anna's death.

———. Noailles. *In his:* Les mémorables. Tome I. (1918–1923). Flammarion, 1957. 361 p.   **7586**

The best social tidbits one can read on Anna.

Montesquiou, Robert de. Anna de Noailles. *In his:* Mémoires. V. 3. Emile-Paul, 1923. p. 90–104. **7587**

This account of Anna's talent and personality is frank and unbiased, not always very laudatory. Letter from Anna to Montesquiou.

Pourtalès, Guy de. Le jardin de Madame de Noailles. RdP 5:601–11, 1935. **7588**

Short biography of N. stressing the influence of music and of the dreams of childhood on her poetry.

Proust, Marcel. Lettres à la Comtesse de Noailles. Plon, 1931. 241 p. (Correspondance générale, 2) **7589**

A faithful friendship: fifty letters from Proust to N. from May 1901 to Dec. 1920.

Rostand, Jean. Anna de Noailles. *In his:* Le droit d'être naturaliste. Stock, 1963. p. 100–07. **7590**

Interesting account of a scientist's friendship for a poetess who had, according to Jean Rostand, the "psychological sagacity of a Marcel Proust, the sharpness of a Mirbeau, the cruel neatness of a Jules Renard."

Tharaud, Jérôme and Jean. Le roman d'Aïssé. Self, 1946. 189 p. **7591**

Extremely enlightening physical and psychological description of N. as seen through her liaison with Maurice Barrès.

Tosi, G. Anna de Noailles et Gabriel d'Annunzio (d'après une correspondance inédite). QuD 12–13:199–206, 1958. **7592**

Enlightening article on the friendship between N. and Gabriel D'Annunzio. A few unpublished letters are printed.

General Studies: Books

Borély, Marthe. L'émouvante destinée d'Anna de Noailles. Albert, 1939. 220 p. **7593**

Introduces us into the intimacy of N. from childhood to death. A biography which can be read like a novel. N.'s work is not studied in and for itself but as an outgrowth of her sensibility. Extremely useful. Intelligent, human and warm.

Brodlova, Vlasta. La poésie d'Anna de Noailles. Dijon, Jobard, 1931. 152 p. **7594**

A rather superficial dissertation on Anna's poetry. Seven pages of bibliography. A chapter on the influences that Anna has undergone.

Cocteau, Jean. La comtesse de Noailles, oui et non. Perrin, 1963. 294 p. (Coll. Littérature) **7595**

A *portrait-souvenir,* some notes, and critical opinions by E. Berl, R. Aron, and M. Barrès who loved Anna, and by Gide who despised her talent. Very interesting book forming a fresco in which Anna's texts, both prose and poetry, are interspersed among the others. A portfolio of iconography is followed by a paradoxical article by Cocteau about "Order considered as anarchy."

Du Bos, Charles. La comtesse de Noailles et le climat du génie, précédé de la Rencontre avec Charles Du Bos, par Daniel-Rops. La table ronde, 1949. 240 p. **7596**

Very useful, intelligent and perceptive study of N.'s temperament and poetry. Du Bos, in this short book, attempts to render homage to N. and analyze the climate in which her genius blossomed forth. The poetess belongs to the French tradition of those poets who "tell" and do not suggest. A human being without any interior contradiction, she is primarily lyric like Shelley, Hölderlin and Swinburne. Her talent is not of a contemplative type.

Fournet, Charles. Un grand poète français moderne: La comtesse de Noailles. Geneva, Roulet, 1950. 86 p. **7597**

Very clear and precise little book, summarizing admirably the life and career of N. After a more detailed than usual evocation of N.'s childhood in Savoy, Fournet draws different portraits of the poetess: Anna, adolescent, religious, passionate, thoughtful; then, married and living in Paris, sensitive, brilliant though not modest, her poetry reflecting the pantheistic ardor of the Renaissance. The later Anna withdraws from society and like Vigny takes refuge in the "majesty of human suffering."

Her conception of poetry, "une chance," a stroke of luck, as she says, is dangerous. Her lyrical exuberance was the cause of her success but also of her failures. She is not fashionable any more, and her poetry has been replaced by a more hermetic one. She will be appreciated by posterity nevertheless.

Gillouin, René. La comtesse de Noailles. Biographie critique..., suivie d'opinions et d'une bibliographie. E. Sansot, 1908. 72 p. **7598**

This biography, in which Gillouin analyzes N.'s life and talent, scrutinizes her novels as a complement of her lyrical work and criticizes her lax poetic style. Followed by opinions of M. Barrès, L. Blum, L. Daudet, M. Proust and others. The bibliography is very short.

Larnac, Jean. Comtesse de Noailles, sa vie, son œuvre. Eds. du sagittaire, 1931. 259 p. **7599**

Excellent study (dedicated to Maurice Martin du Gard). The tone is not scholarly, yet Larnac has read most of the articles written on Anna. The ample bibliography is replete with errors.

La Rochefoucauld, Edmée de. Anna de Noailles. Eds. universitaires, 1956. 136 p. (Classiques du XXe siècle) **7600**

Excellent book which contains the synopsis of *Octave,* Anna's last unfinished novel. After a concise and accurate summary of Anna's life, Edmée de La Rochefoucauld analyzes the author's books of poetry and prose, and ends with a few pages on Anna's place among contemporary authors. Succinct bibliography.

Masson, Georges-Armand. La comtesse de Noailles, son œuvre; portrait, autographe, document pour l'histoire de la littérature française. Eds. du Carnet critique, 1922. 52 p. **7601**

Excellent book which analyzes pertinently the duality of N.'s personality: "Deux êtres qui luttent dans mon cœur/c'est la bacchante avec la nonne..." According to Masson, this duality explains N.'s attitude toward love, death, and war.

Perche, Louis. Anna de Noailles. Présentation par Louis Perche. Choix de textes... Seghers, 1964. 192 p. (Poètes d'aujour-d'hui, 116) *Also:* Anna de Noailles. Une étude de Louis Perche, avec un choix de poèmes... Seghers, 1969. 188 p. (Poètes d'aujourd'hui, 116) **7602**

Louis Perche's 100-page study, abundantly illustrated and followed by a chronology of N.'s life and a bibliography, is the best pedagogical tool to get to know N.'s poetry accurately and quickly.

Pittion-Rossillon, L. La poésie de Madame de Noailles. Grenoble, 1927. 32 p. **7603**

Sharp criticism of N.'s success which is accounted for by her money and her acquaintances. Then Pittion-Rossillon quotes a series of poetic blunders in N.'s poetry. Furthermore the poetess understands nothing about war, sufferings, the spirit of sacrifice. She has no moral principles.

General Studies: Articles

Allard, Roger. Anna de Noailles. NRF 17: 301–14, 1921. **7604**

Very intelligent article which contains a vivid analysis, perhaps a little too severe, of this "descriptive hypertrophy" which renders the face of poetry a little bizarre and monstrous.

Arbour, Roméo. Anna de Noailles. *In his:* Henri Bergson et les lettres françaises. Corti, 1955. p. 261–67. **7605**

Although N. was not directly influenced by Bergson, whom she admired very much, she appears Bergsonian at times. If indeed her gift for pure perception and her participation in the universal rhythm of life lack Bergson's sensitive and spiritual emotion, the multiplicity of the poetic images and the importance of music in her inspiration are Bergsonian.

Barral, Louis. Anna de Noailles devant l'horizontale Porte. RdCE 1:29–41, 1951. **7606**

Eighteen years before the writing of this article N. died as a Christian, reconciled with God. Barral gives the cycle of N.'s poetry to point out the way she came back to God.

Brasillach, Robert. Anna de Noailles. *In his:* Portraits. Plon, 1952. p. 165–73. **7607**

After the poetry of Parnassus and that of symbolism, N.'s poetry is as simple as sunshine.

Chaigne, Louis. Noailles. *In his:* Vies et œuvres d'écrivains. F. Lanore, 1940. p. 9–34. **7608**

Excellent chronological summary of the life and works of N. Chaigne thinks that her poetry is at times weak because she does not work enough on her poems and her adjectives are often fuzzy. But she has a greater feeling for nature than any of the poets that have preceded her. She has an innate pantheism which makes her descriptions of landscapes especially beautiful, those of the Ile-de-France in particular.

Clouard, Henri. Anna de Noailles. *In his:* La poésie française moderne des romantiques à nos jours. Gauthier-Villars, 1924. p. 254–61. **7609**

For H. Clouard, the best collection of N.'s poetry has been gathered under the title of *Les vivants et les morts.*

Colette, Sidonie Gabrielle. Discours de réception à l'Académie royale belge de langue et de littérature françaises, 4 avril 1936. Grasset, 1936. 55 p. *Also:* Discours de réception de madame Colette, successeur de la comtesse de Noailles à l'Académie royale de Belgique. *In:* Cocteau, Jean. La comtesse de Noailles, oui et non. *See* 7595. p. 197–209. **7610**

Beautifully written evocation of the personality of N. and of their friendship which was more formal than close, being built on mutual respect. Compares also their literary style. [DWA]

Du Bos, Charles. Anna de Noailles. *In his:* Approximations. Fayard, 1965. p. 55–66. **7611**

The most immediate aspects of the poetry of N. are sudden bursts of energy and sudden leaps of insight. Her masterpieces all derive from inspiration rather than mere calculation.

Duclaux, Agnès Mary Frances. Anna de Noailles. *In her:* Twentieth century French writers: reviews and reminiscences. Freeport, N.Y., Books for libraries, 1966. p. 178–94. **7612**

"Anna's inspiration rings out intoxicated with the wonder of the universe." Intelligent summary of her talent and work.

Flat, Paul. Anna de Noailles. *In his:* Nos femmes de lettres. Perrin, 1908. p. 19–53. **7613**

Emphasizes N.'s gift for plasticity. As heir to romanticism, she has borrowed the best cadences from Chateaubriand, Byron and Berlioz.

Gillouin, René. Anna de Noailles. *In his:* Essais de critique littéraire et philosophique. Grasset, 1913. p. 9–86. **7614**

Thorough study of N.'s poetry and novels, and of the themes which are at the center of her work.

Jammes, Francis. L'évolution spirituelle de Madame la Comtesse de Noailles. RHeb 433–49, Sept. 27, 1913. **7615**

In his article on *Les vivants et les morts,* Jammes emphasizes the spiritual evolution of N. whom he would like to convert to Christianity.

Lacher, W. Anna de Noailles. *In his:* L'amour et le divan. Geneva, Perret-Gentil, 1961. p. 39–61. **7616**

N.'s preoccupation with death makes her look for a solution in the universe which she finds empty. She does not recognize the ethics of the big pantheistic systems.

La Rochefoucauld, Edmée de. Noailles et le goût de l'éternel. RdP 90–102, Jan. 1956. **7617**

Studies N.'s penchant for eternity and her sense of the annihilation of death.

Lasserre, Pierre. Anna de Noailles. *In his:* Portraits et discussions. Mercure de France, 1914. p. 266–78. **7618**

Intelligent account of N.'s talent which is abundant if disorderly and which lacks a feeling for hierarchy in its rich impressionism.

Le Dantec, Yves-Gérard. La place d'Anna de Noailles dans la poésie française. MerF 244:276–98, 1933. **7619**

Enlightening overall study of N.'s poetry. Written just after her death, it attempts to situate the poet within the evolution of modern lyricism.

————. Le souvenir d'Anna de Noailles. RDM 11:523–26, 1953. **7620**

Twenty years after N.'s death, Le Dantec tries to establish the nature of her talent. "Her work contains unsuspected riches, but it is perhaps outmoded in the eyes of the new generation."

Lièvre, Pierre. Esquisses critiques. Deuxième série. Le divan, 1924. p. 50–67. (Les quatorze, no. 6)   **7621**
Appreciates the "poetic substance" of Anna's work and quotes her masters: Chénier, Lamartine, Hugo, Musset, Baudelaire, Verlaine, Rimbaud. She seems to have inherited the essence of the great romantics.

Mauriac, François. Anna de Noailles. *In his:* Second thoughts. Reflexions on literature and life. Cleveland and New York, The world publishing Co., 1961 p. 89–104.   **7622**
Unlike Baudelaire and Verlaine, there is a cleavage between N.'s life and work, between her wit in life and her voluntary lack of it in her poetry. N., who had everything in life, still knew despair. It was the Bergsonian theme of duration which supplied her with a source of inspiration. Mauriac evokes N.'s unhappiness when she saw her poetry pushed aside for that of Valéry.

Maurras, Charles. Anna de Noailles. *In his:* L'avenir de l'intelligence. Deuxième éd. revue et corrigée. Fontemoing, 1917. p. 220–69.   **7623**
"Feminine romanticism: an allegory of disorderly feelings" is the title of the chapter written mainly on Anna by Charles Maurras. Excellent study.

Murciaux, Christian. Anna de Noailles, poète héroïque. RdM 32:436–49; 34:696–707, 1949; 35:37–51, 1950.   **7624**
Essays putting N.'s poetry into focus fifteen years after her death. Murciaux recalls her childhood, her first poetry falsely naive, the Dionysian breath that blew on the next poems and her "Promethean ambition."

Proust, Marcel. Les éblouissements. Fig June 15, 1907. *Also in his:* Contre Sainte-Beuve, précédé de Pastiches et mélanges et suivi de Essais et articles. Gallimard, 1971. p. 533–45. (Bibliothèque de la Pléiade)   **7625**

Extremely beautiful article in which Proust emphasizes Anna's renewal of poetry by being poet and heroine, Racine and the princess. *Les éblouissements* is perhaps the masterpiece of literary impressionism.

Rageot, Gaston. Madame de Noailles et la sensualité mystique. *In his:* Le succès, auteurs et publics. Essai de critique sociologique. Alcan, 1906. p. 103–12.   **7626**
A "chaotic genius" which forces one to pay attention to it. Rageot reports on *La nouvelle espérance, Le visage émerveillé, La domination.*

Romain, Yvonne de. Madame de Noailles. *In her:* Semeurs d'idées. E. Sansot, 1909. p. 31–43.   **7627**
Compares N.'s talent to that of Gérard d'Houville.

Sabourdin, Angel. La poésie de la comtesse de Noailles. GraR 141:529–37, 1933.   **7628**
Intelligent article which synthesizes quite aptly N.'s poetry: her sensitivity which springs forth from the depths of her being reveals her subconscious.

Séché, A. Anna de Noailles. *In his:* Les caractères de la poésie contemporaine. E. Sansot, 1913. p. 94–95, 222–28, 233–38.   **7629**
The book contains an excessively biased account of feminine literature. What counts for Anna is "a delirium above all remorse" but "no objectivity, no attentive effort to penetrate the intimate and obscure life of things."

Novels

Maurras, Charles. Le romantisme féminin. Min 5–26, May 1, 1903.   **7630**
Finds in Anna's novels "more sensitivity than art," "more emotions than description" and "no real structure."

Régnier, Henri de. Les innocents ou la sagesse des femmes. Fig Aug. 14, 1923.   **7631**
In this review, Régnier expands on N.'s talent as a novelist, at the same time incomplete and bewitching. He prefers her poetry.

Marie Noël
(pseud. of Marie Mélanie Rouget)
(Nos. 7632–7674)

GENEVIÈVE SUTTON

General Studies: Books

Blanchet, André. Marie Noël. Présentation par André Blanchet. Choix de textes, bibliographie, portraits, fac-similés. Seghers, 1962. 223 p. (Poètes d'aujourd'hui, 89) *Also (rev.):* Marie Noël. Une étude de André Blanchet, avec un choix de poèmes, quarante-cinq illustrations, une chronologie bibliographique: Marie Noël et son temps. Seghers, 1970. 187 p. (Poètes d'aujourd'hui, 89)   **7632**

Basic and penetrating study. Believing at first that N.'s work was only vapid feminine poetry, B.'s mind was changed by *Chants et psaumes d'automne.* Shows N. as possessing a sense of rhythm, as hiding in her early verse a sort of somber gaiety under the lightheartedness of the tone. Emphasizes the sentiment of revolt, of isolation, of metaphysical fear which the poetess will continue to feel throughout her life. Also stresses her fascination with the *néant,* her taste for the absolute, her profound need for love wherein her sensuality reveals itself. N. presents in literature the exceptional case of a Christian whose faith has not flagged in spite of difficulties.

Escholier, Raymond. La neige qui brûle: Marie Noël. Fayard, 1957. 430 p.   **7633**

Authoritative study. Escholier has written a poetic life of N. whose character and work are mutually illuminating. Biography, abundant correspondence (often previously unpublished), numerous quotations from poems both well-known and unpublished, and critical opinions combine to shed light on the life, heretofore unknown, of N., her character and her art of poetry. It should be noted that this work was composed before the publication of *Notes intimes,* from which he nevertheless made extensive borrowings.

Gouhier, Henri. Le combat de Marie Noël. Stock, 1971. 168 p.   **7634**

Indispensable for understanding N. whose religious experience is inseparable from her work. The conflict between the poetic vocation and ethical and spiritual requirements; the excruciating pain, experienced in real life and violently expressed before the mystery of death and of a God responsible for evil, whose perfect unity includes nevertheless a duality. Major themes of the work of N.: love, solitude, death, annihilation, which owe their dramatic profundity to a faith lived in the theological, mystical and liturgical universe of the Church.

Reviews: R. Denux in EcL 23:1095, 1972; L. Guissard in Croix 26:856, 1971; R. Kanters in Fig Sept. 3, 1971; H. Juin in Comb 8331:7, 1971; N. Lambillot in SynB 298:9–12, 1971.

Manoll, Michel. Marie Noël. Eds. universitaires, 1962. 124 p. (Classiques du XXe siècle)   **7635**

Includes a letter-preface by N. This work comprises two parts: a biography illuminating the work and a study of the work which illuminates N.'s life. Brief picture of the family and childhood of the poet, her taste for affabulation, for the gracefulness of words, and for spiritual searching. Analysis of *Heures,* written at Vézelay, and of the correspondences between the plastic melodies of the stone and the immaterial structures of the poetic language. Criticizes Abbé Bremond who, as a fervent exponent of pure poetry, effaced the carnal contour and human content of poetry, and stresses the influence of Abbé Mugnier on N. Study of rhythm and vocabulary. A few pages devoted to prose writings with a short analysis of the *contes.*

Marie-Tharsicius, Sœur. L'expérience poétique de Marie Noël d'après Petit jour et Les chansons et les heures. Montreal-Paris, Fides, 1962. 160 p.   **7636**

In a long introduction, the author emphasizes the spirit of childhood in N.: fantasy, amazement, meditation before the "whys" of life. Two chapters devoted to the poetic experience in *Petit jour* and *Les chansons et les heures,* with stress on the subjective elements, an inner world based on the real one, and on the objective elements, the real world itself. Author studies by way of myth of Cinderella the anxiety of N., her inability to capture love, her expectation, then her appeasement in the love of God. Study rich in insights which N. herself appreciated.

Special Numbers

Cahiers Marie Noël. No. 1– . Association Marie Noël, 1969–   **7637**
An occasional publication by the Association Marie Noël, 19 rue Casimir-Périer, Paris.

Hommage à Marie Noël. PoCp 27–28:3–50, 1954.   **7638**
Homage to N. on her seventy-first birthday. Contributions by Daniel-Rops, Escholier, Montherlant, Paul Fort, Georges Duhamel, Maria Gevers, Vincent Muselli, Henry Dalby, Jean Soulairol.

Littérature [Marie Noël]. *In:* Association bourguignonne des sociétés savantes. Auxerre, Société des sciences historiques et naturelles de l'Yonne, 1971. p. 7–87.   **7639**
Papers on N. presented in meeting at Auxerre in May 1970.

General Studies: Articles

Bindel, Victor. Le génie féminin de Marie Noël. AmSF 30:1–23, 1941.   **7640**
Particularly penetrating study emphasizing Greco-Latin, Judeo-Christian and medieval traditions. Main themes of metaphysical anxiety, sorrow, love and death culminating in joy of religion. Comparisons with Maeterlinck and Vigny.

Blanchet, André. Un génie nocturne: Marie Noël. Et 293:169–85, 1957. *Also in his:* La littérature et le spirituel. V. 2. Aubier, 1960. p. 227–45.   **7641**
Presenting her *Œuvre poétique,* cautions against error of considering N. as a devout shepherdess. In-depth study of that which is somber, tormented, anxious and savage in certain poems revealing a sublimation of the ego and a contradiction which caused great anguish in the poetess. Comparisons with Michaux, Artaud, Kafka, Green and Bernanos.

———. Marie Noël entre deux mondes. Et 304:145–58, 1960. *Also in his:* La littéra-

ture et le spirituel. V. 2. Aubier, 1960. p. 247–61.   **7642**
Using *Notes intimes,* a psychological and religious study of the struggle in N. refusing both revolt and cowardly submission, and aspiring to liberty.

Bosquet, Alain. Poésie: Marie Noël. RdP 2:150–53, 1968.   **7643**
N., discreet and characterized by the pious clientele which knows only her least original verses, is one of the most truly tragic poets, the equal of d'Aubigné, superior to Louise Labé and Marceline Desbordes-Valmore.

Bremond, Henri. Marie Noël. VieC March 14, 1925. *Also:* CahMNo 2:11–15, 1970.   **7644**
One of the earliest articles concerning N., in which one finds the famous qualifier "gaminerie angélique." Compares *Vision* with Cardinal John H. Newman's *Dream of Gerontius.*

———. Introduction. *In his:* Manuel illustré de la littérature catholique en France de 1870 à nos jours. Spes, 1925. p. 76–80.   **7645**
In this introduction, B. makes amends for his failure to recognize N. in the body of his text.

———. La vision et le rêve. Marie Noël et Newman, poètes du purgatoire. Et 227: 590–605, 1936.   **7646**
Apropros of the new edition of *Les chansons et les heures,* takes up again the parallel between N. and Newman, she, the unliterary artist, he, the intellectual, but, dominating literature, both poets in the profound unity and naïveté of their faith. Compares her *Vision* with Cardinal John H. Newman's *Dream of Gerontius.*

Charasson, Henriette. La poésie chrétienne, Marie Noël. Et 195:317–30, 1928.   **7647**
Contribution to the study of N., still relatively unknown to the general public at this time. Points out the originality of the poetess; realism and mysticism, gravity of the inspiration, subtlety and personality.

Davignon, Henri. La vie et les idées: la poésie féminine en Belgique et en France. RGB 377–82, Sept. 15, 1935.   **7648**

Includes a brief comparison between Anna de Noailles, the oriental full of pathos and ardor, and N., the occidental of the harmonious and disciplined strength. Sees N.'s work as inspired poetry in the mystical sense of the word, in which H. Bremond finds the total justification of his theory: *poésie-prière,* and which evolves, from the pleasing and naive *Chansons* to the more poignant lines of *Heures.*

Dejaifve, G. Marie Noël ou la grâce de l'incarnation. ECl 20:22–51, 1952. **7649**

Very interesting study. After a brief biography accompanied by a portrait of the poetess, the author demonstrates, with long quotations (*Chants de la merci, Jugement*), the medieval lyricism, the sensitivity of the poetess, so distant from "poésie pure." Studies the great themes of human love, solitariness, anxiety, and death, sung by a Christian for whom poetry is contemplation and prayer, rhythm and incantation. Utilization of all of the resources of metrics.

Estaunié, Raymond. Une lyrique de province. In his: Roman et province. Laffont, 1943. p. 136–77. **7650**

Lecture given in Switzerland in 1933. Basing his remarks on *Les chansons de Cendrillon, Les chansons et les heures* and *Le rosaire des joies,* Estaunié defines the work as naive and audacious, familiar and refined (beauty of the verbal sonorities, of the rhythm), evolving from the dreams of a young girl to deep religious inspiration. Interesting text although somewhat verbose.

Giraud, Victor. Un poète. RdJ 4:433–41, 1921. **7651**

One of the earliest studies on N. *Les chansons et les heures,* poetry with origins more musical than literary, is related to both Villon and Pascal.

Gouhier, Henri. L'expérience religieuse de Marie Noël. CahMNo 2:22–31, 1970. **7652**

Personality of N. from the point of view of the conflict between faith and reason, religion and science, belief and doubt, taking place within faith. Refers to *Notes intimes* in which the Platonic theme of the opposition between being and becoming and the sovereignty of the One is found.

————. Lutter pour la divinité de son âme. CahMNo 3:13–20, 1971. **7653**

Studies from an existential point of view the position of N. regarding the notions of individuality and eternity which seem to be mutually exclusive.

Lacôte, Henri. Marie Noël. LetF 1214:1, 7–8, 19, Dec. 27, 1967. **7654**

Article written both on the occasion of the death of N. and the appearance of *Cru d'Auxerre.* Insists on the error of cataloging the poetess in the category of "bien pensants" because she was launched by Abbé Bremond and Abbé Mugnier. Situates N. in the first rank of the poets of this century, worthy of the appreciation of agnostics, of which he is one.

Larcena, Jean. Marie Noël. RGB 43:65–71, 1949. **7655**

Shows the course of the poet from the anguish of solitude and exile to the full light and peace. Points to the revolt expressed by her verse, finally subsiding into a Franciscan renunciation.

Mauriac, François. Les Notes intimes de Marie Noël. In his: Nouveaux mémoires intérieurs. Flammarion, 1965. p. 53–57. **7656**

Admits being prejudiced against the destiny, which he knows well, of saintly girls crushed by ungrateful lives. He observes the strength of N. She has knocked herself against a bruising religion and has submitted to its law.

Mavel, Léna. Marie Noël, ma marraine; témoignage. PoéV 25–26:72–82, 1967. **7657**

A poetess and a convert, Mavel had N. as *marraine.* Discusses N.'s influence on her.

Monadon, Louis de. Mademoiselle Marie Noël. Et 209:200–16, 1931. **7658**

Study of *Chants de la merci* and *Rosaire des joies.* Praises them but does not see in them a personal drama. A few remarks on versification.

Petit, Henri. Notes intimes de Marie Noël. NL 1686:2–3, 1959. **7659**

Penetrating analysis.

Peyrade, Jean. Marie Noël, poète et mystique. PenF 10:38–45, 1959.   **7660**

Behind the angelic roguishness of N. one finds a profound anguish regarding human destiny. A poetic monument of magnificent amplitude.

Sutton, Howard. Afterword. *In:* Noël, Marie. Notes for myself (Notes intimes). Trans. by Howard Sutton, with a foreword by François Mauriac. Ithaca, N.Y., Cornell univ. press, 1968. p. 257–72. **7661**

Afterword offers a general presentation of N.'s life, character and works, followed by a brief but perceptive study of *Notes.* Foreword by Mauriac translated from his *Nouveaux mémoires intérieurs* (*see* 7656). Text is an abridged and annotated translation, omitting about one-fifth of the original. Translator, a friend of N., worked closely with the poetess. While the translation reads smoothly like an original it has preserved to the utmost the flavor of N.'s prose style, with its mingling of gravity and playfulness, pathos and humor, its frequent ellipses, poetic metaphors, and syntactical audacities.

———. Marie Noël: A life in songs. ASLHM 37:153–63, 1966.   **7662**

Probably the first article on N. published in the United States. A general introduction to the poet's life and works, with reference to the early and late tributes paid to her by various French critics and authors.

———. Two poets of childhood: Marcel Proust and Marie Noël. BA 261–66, summer 1967. *Trans.:* Deux poètes de l'enfance: Marcel Proust et Marie Noël. BMP 19:853–63, 1969. *Also in:* CahMNo 5:37–42, 1973.   **7663**

Referring to Proust's *Temps perdu* and N.'s *Petit-jour,* Sutton points out that, while there can be no question of literary influence, one can find striking affinities with corresponding emotional experiences reported in their childhood memories by these two extremely sensitive writers. Through entirely different means, both express a comparable feeling of the inexorable flow of time with a tragic sense of the transitory nature of all things and seek in literature a revelation of truth and in art a rediscovery of the inner reality of life.

Review: Y. Florenne in Monde April 29, 1973.

Woodruff, Sara. Introduction. *In:* Noël, Marie. Reflected light. Poems of Marie Noël. Trans. by Sara Woodruff. New York, Pageant press, 1964. 193 p.   **7664**

Eighteen-page biographical introduction.

Style and Themes

Blanchet, André. Le thème de l'eau dans la poésie et le drame intime de Marie Noël. CahMNo 6:17–31, 1974.   **7665**

Inspired by Bachelard. Without claiming to make an exhaustive study, notes numerous allusions to water, the privileged element of N.'s poetry and the key to its most profound meaning. Demonstrates, with quotations, the various symbolic functions of water in N.'s poetry; purification, song, gift, flight towards the infinite and death. Also terrifying water of the deep abyss, symbol of the tragic drama of existence intensely felt by N.

Bonnardot, J. and G. Marie Noël et le Cantique des cantiques. CahMNo 6:32–44, 1974.   **7666**

Interesting parallel of some poems from *Les chansons et les heures* with passages in *The song of songs.* Evocation of themes common to the two poetic works: "inclosed garden," "shuttered lodging," anguished expectations, mystical love. Tends to bring N. out of the pious iconography built up by some early critics.

Camproux, Charles. La langue et le style des écrivains. Chants d'arrière-saison. LetF 930:4, June 7–13, 1962.   **7667**

Important study of *Chants d'arrière-saison* which are characterized by the absence of revolutionary and glittering devices but which take their strength from a technique that is perfect in its simplicity. Definition of the linguistic devices used.

Doucet, J. A propos d'Enterrement. ECl 33:54–58, 1966.   **7668**

Interesting and short grammatical analysis of the story *Enterrement de première classe,* which Doucet calls a "poème en prose."

Fabre, Marie-Thérèse. Métamorphoses de l'eau chez Marie Noël. Et 330:104–14, 1969.   **7669**

Interesting study, in the context of Bachelard, of the theme of water, which suggests the psychic unity of N.'s work. Around these images evoking the inner adventure of N. is organized the poetic expression of her innermost being: the river, multi-formed element; the pond, threatening through its immobility, image of death; the spring, fluid and pure water, personifying song and love.

Lechanteur, Jean. Un poème de Marie Noël. CahAT 8:40–47, 1966.   **7670**

Analytical study of *Chanson*, line by line: construction, style, rhythm, syntax, means of expression. Interesting from a philological point of view.

Le Hir, Yves. Structures rythmiques dans l'œuvre poétique de Marie Noël avec une lettre inédite de Marie Noël. *In:* Studi in onore di Vittorio Lugli & Diego Valeri. Parte 2. Venice, Nera Pozzo, 1961. p. 589–602.   **7671**

Interesting study bringing out the constant elements of a subtle art, in conjunction with a will to personal expression. Extracts from *Notes sur le rythme,* published in *Points et contrepoints* in 1950, in which N. speaks of the "ondulations psychiques" of the verse. The *vers impair,* with free accents, is the instinctive form of the crepuscular states of being, whereas the measured verse, in traditional form, provides a solid and serene progression for the feelings. According to N. poetic rhythm is tied to vital rhythm and certain words are the key to the subconscious of the poet. Le Hir concludes with a technical study of meters and strophic forms used by N.

Parent, Monique. Une poésie habillée en pauvre. TLL 4, vol. 1:381–98, 1966. **7672**

Very technical study of the images and rhythms of the *Chant au bord de la rivière.* Emphasizes N.'s amazing instinctive mastery of the rhythmic resources of the French language. Notes the musicality, the gracefulness and the harmony, the subtle connection between the rhythmic impetus and the harmony, anxiety and anguish finding an image in the running of the water.

Petit, Françoise. Marie Noël et la musique. CahMNo 4:16–28, 1972.   **7673**

Interesting study, partly technical, devoted to the musical inclinations of N. (a musician and an inspirer of musicians and interpreters), who conceives, in one inspiration, both the poem and the music, like the troubadours. The great diversity of the poetic rhythm expresses the most intense intimate expression. Refers to the problems of putting a literary text to music.

Drama

Davignon, Henri. Marie Noël dramaturge. BARLLF 36:117–24, 1958.   **7674**

Critical study of the *Jugement de Don Juan,* a work which is linked to the tradition of the Middle Ages by its absence of conformism, by the intervention of the supernatural, and which, on a threadbare theme, offers an expression which is feminine, Christian and universal, opposing dramatic realism to the sublime of Christianity. Alludes to the interest shown in this drama by Montherlant and J. Hébertot.

Hector de Saint-Denys Garneau (Nos. 7675–7723)

CARROL F. COATES

Bibliography

Blais, Jacques. Bibliographie. *In his:* De Saint-Denys Garneau. Montreal, Fides, 1971. p. 53–65.   **7675**

Annotated. Most extensive bibliography to date: G.'s writings (including poems set to music), studies on G. (including theses), and various "témoignages" (creative evocations as well as film, television and radio documentaries).

——. Documents pour servir à la bibliographie critique de l'œuvre de Saint-Denys Garneau. RUL 18:424–38, 1964. **7676**

Superseded by the "Bibliographie" in his *De Saint-Denys Garneau,* supra.

Cartier, Georges. Bio-bibliographie de Saint-Denys Garneau. Montreal, Ecole des bibliothécaires, 1952. 85 p.   **7677**

Bibliography (p. 36–68) superseded by Blais (1971).

Editions and Correspondence

Saint-Denys Garneau, Hector de. Journal. Préface de Gilles Marcotte. Avertissement de Robert Elie et Jean Le Moyne. Montreal, Beauchemin, 1964. 270 p. *Original ed.:* 1954. *Trans.:* The journal of Saint-Denys Garneau. Trans. by John Glassco. Introd. by Gilles Marcotte. Toronto, McClelland & Stewart, 1962. 140 p. **7678**

Extensively edited to judge by the "Avertissement": some working notes, "confused" or repeated passages, poems, letters, and "indiscreet" passages are eliminated; spelling, punctuation, and other textual corrections. Present ed. goes from Jan. 1935 to Jan 22, 1939 (certain early *cahiers* not included; others lost). Important reflections on G.'s thought in the Preface.

Reviews: G. Cartier in Lect 10:344–47, 1954; P. Emmanuel in JMC June 1954, p. 3; D. Hayne in CanL 67–68, summer 1963; B. Lacroix in RevD 60: 130–36, 1954; F. Lairgue in AmF 12: 206–08, 1954.

———. Lettres à ses amis. Ed. by Robert Elie, Claude Hurtubise, and Jean Le Moyne. Montreal, Eds. HMH, 1967. 489 p. (Constantes, 8) **7679**

Letters dated July 6, 1930 to August 21, 1943, most of them written to the three editors. Minimum of explanatory notes.

Reviews: J. Blais in RechS 8:405–07, 1967; R. Duhamel in RDM 241–44, Jan. 15, 1968; J.-P. Vanasse in Liberté 9:16–22, 1967.

———. Œuvres. Ed. by Jacques Brault and Benoît Lacroix. Montreal, Presses de l'Univ. de Montréal, 1971. xxvii, 1320 p. **7680**

The most complete compilation of G.'s writing to date, carefully edited, with variant readings. Contains: *Regards et jeux dans l'espace, Juvenilia, Poèmes retrouvés, Prose (Œuvres publiées par l'auteur),* and, among the *Œuvres posthumes,* the *Journal, Nouvelles et essais, Correspondance,* etc. The critical apparatus includes a chronology with extensive bibliographical informa-tion and indices of titles, themes, and names of persons.

Reviews: P. Gathercole in FR 45: 506–07, 1971; R. Vigneault in EF 7:389–97, 1971.

———. Saint-Denys Garneau. Choix de textes groupés et annotés par Benoît Lacroix. Montreal, Fides, 1956. 96 p. (Classiques canadiens, 4) *Also:* Textes choisis et présentés par Benoît Lacroix. 3e édition revue et corrigée. Montreal & Paris, Fides, 1967. 96 p. (Classiques canadiens, 4) **7621**

Brief introduction, chronology, and bibliography.

Biography

Dugas, Marcel. Saint-Denys Garneau. *In his:* Approches. Quebec, Eds. du chien d'or, 1942. p. 79–98. **7682**

Blais (1971) finds that allusions to schizophrenia are "digressions de dilettante."

Falardeau, Jean-Charles. La génération de La relève. RechS 6:123–33, 1965. *Also in:* QuéS 3:37–49, 1966. *Also in his:* Notre société et son roman. Montreal, Eds. HMH, 1967. p. 101–13. **7683**

"Importante étude bien documentée" (Blais, 1971).

Gagnon, Jean-Louis. En ce temps-là. EF 5:457–65, 1969. **7684**

Reminiscences by a friend of G.

Hébert, Anne. Saint-Denys Garneau. *In:* Lacôte, René. Anne Hébert. Seghers, 1969. p. 126–33. **7685**

Biographical commentary for a documentary film on G. (1960).

General Studies

Béguin, Albert. Saint-Denys Garneau: solitude canadienne. GazL Oct. 17, 1954. *Also (first part of article):* Le Canada en question. CiL 40:5–7, 1960. *Also (second part of article):* Réduit en sequelette. Esp 22:640–49, 1954. **7686**

"Béguin affirme que le débat solitaire de G. correspond au drame national de solitude et à l'angoisse de sa généra-tion . . ." (Blais, 1971). Important analysis of G.'s relationship to his time.

Belleau, André. Le nœud éclaté. Liberté 60:74–78, 1960. **7687**
Contra Le Moyne (1960): the answer to alienation lies in a deepening of religious faith.

Blais, Jacques. De Saint-Denys Garneau. Montreal, Fides, 1971. 65 p. (Dossiers de documentation sur la littérature canadienne-française, 7). **7688**
Extremely useful collection of commentaries on aspects of G.'s life, works, relationship to his milieu; most extensive annotated bibliography to date. Review: R. Vigneault in EF 9:166–67, 1973.

———. Un nouvel Icare. Le thème de l'eau. RUL 18:210–35, 1963. **7689**
Important study of the related symbolisms of bird and water in G.'s writing.

Bourneuf, Roland. La culture européenne de Saint-Denys Garneau d'après les inédits. EF 5:473–79, 1969. **7690**
Believes that G. had the makings of a first-rate critic of art. Treats primarily his literary preferences.

———. Saint-Denys Garneau et l'avenir de la littérature canadienne-française. ESec 45:209–12, 1966. **7691**
Reservations of G. on French-Canadian literature.

———. Saint-Denys Garneau et ses lectures européennes. Quebec, Presses de l'univ. Laval, 1969. 333 p. (Vie des lettres canadiennes, 6) **7692**
Careful view of the extent and importance of G.'s European culture, especially French. Studies effects on his critical views, style, poetics, and spiritual thought. Chapter on Baudelaire published as "Saint-Denys Garneau lecteur de Baudelaire" in ELit 1:83–112, 1968.
Reviews: R. Gathercole in FR 44:475–76, 1970; D. Hayne in FS 26:108, 1972; J.-L. Major in Livres et auteurs québécois. Montreal, Eds. Jumonville, 1970. p. 128–30; G. Poulin in ELit 3:433–36, 1970.

Brault, Jacques. Saint-Denys Garneau, réduit au silence. In: La poésie canadienne-française. Perspectives historiques et thématiques—profils de poètes—témoi-

gnages—bibliographie. Ed. by Paul Wyczynski et al. Montreal, Fides, 1969. p. 323–31. (Archives des lettres canadiennes, 4) **7693**
Intelligent effort to view poetry as "la vérité de Saint-Denys Garneau," rather than as documentation on his biographies. Finds his thematics tending to "dépasser la parole vers le silence."

Cartier, Georges. Le tombeau d'un poète: paysage de Saint-Denys Garneau. ActU 20:26–34, 1953. **7694**
G.'s love of nature.

Debien, Léon. Saint-Denys Garneau et François Mauriac. Liberté 10:20–28, 1968. Also: QuéS 5:67–75, 1968. **7695**
G. found a spiritual brother in Mauriac.

Elie, Robert. La poésie de Saint-Denys Garneau. ActU 16:36–47, 1949. Also: Introduction. In: Saint-Denys-Garneau [sic]. Poésies complètes: Regards et jeux dans l'espace, Les solitudes. Montreal & Paris, Fides, 1949. 226 p. Also: 1968. **7696**
An essay on the poet's two spiritual crises: the confrontation with himself and with death. Evolution of poetic themes and forms under the influence of the poet's experience. Substantially reprinted in Elie's introduction to the Poésies complètes.

———. Saint-Denys Garneau. In: Our living tradition. Ed. by Robert L. McDougall. 4th Ser. Toronto, Univ. of Toronto press, 1962. p. 77–92. **7697**
G.'s four years of creative work, "l'expérience de maturité la plus intense qu'ait connue le Canada français jusqu'alors" (Blais, 1971).

Ellis, M. B. De Saint-Denys Garneau. Art et réalisme, suivi d'Un petit dictionnaire poétique. Montreal, Eds. Chantecler, 1949. 197 p. **7698**
In spite of some erroneous suggestions, Blais (1971) finds Ellis to the point on the "rapport étroit qui relie l'œuvre et la vie, sur l'art spiritualiste, sur le vœu de libération de l'univers sensible."
Review: H.-M. Robillard in RevD 56:308–11, 1950 (see also reply by R. Elie in RevD 56:302–05, 1950).

Fortier, Lévis, frère. Le message poétique de Saint-Denys Garneau. Préface de Guy Sylvestre. Ottawa, Eds. de l'univ., 1954. 231 p.   **7699**

Sees G.'s work as "l'expression pathétique et ouverte d'un drame spirituel..." Examines G.'s poetics (nature of the word, themes, the poetic act), his experience of existence and world, his literary technique, and literary influences on his work. Blais (1971) says that "le parallèle avec Supervielle manque de précision." Reviews: E. Chartier in Lect 43, Nov. 20, 1954; G. Marcotte in Dev 6, Nov. 6, 1954; A. Vachon in ColeF 12:42, 1955.

Gathercole, Patricia M. Two contemporary French-Canadian Poets. FR 28:309–17, 1955.   **7700**

In spite of "heavy" prosaic rhythms, G.'s poetry displays "skilful depiction of a mood" and "originality" in his imagery. Compares the work to that of his younger cousin, Anne Hébert, as "poetry of self-analysis." "Their verse is no longer regional in character; it seeks to portray the human soul in its most universal aspects."

Hénault, Gilles. Saint-Denys Garneau ou la vie impossible. EF 5:480–88, 1969.   **7701**

Sees G.'s poetry as a kind of mythical journey, "un Voyage au bout du monde."

Huot, Giselle. A propos du Saint-Denys Garneau d'Eva Kushner. Cul 29:133–41, 1968.   **7702**

A detailed examination of Kushner's essay (1967), pointing out where reservations or corrections are in order. Concludes: "Nous y avons rencontré le poète mais non l'homme tout court..."

Kushner, Eva. La poétique de l'espace chez Saint-Denys Garneau. RUO 43:540–56, 1973.   **7703**

For G., difficulty of creating deeply linked to that of living, both frequently expressed "au moyen de variations sur le thème de l'espace." Intelligent analysis.

——. Saint-Denys Garneau. Choix de textes, inédits. Bibliographie, portraits,

fac-similé. Seghers, 1967. 191 p. (Poètes d'aujourd'hui, 158)   **7704**

Sensitive evocation of G.'s poetry and thought as an effort at "la possession compensatrice" of a world which threatens to destroy his frail being. Blais finds that she reduces "l'aventure poétique de G. à la simple expression d'un malaise ontologique" and is reluctant to admit any other critical approach (1971).

Reviews: J. Blais in ELit 1:153–55, 1968; F. Gallays in Livres et auteurs canadiens 1967. Montreal, Eds. Jumonville, 1968. p. 111; G. Huot in Cul 29:133–41, 1968; G. Marcotte in Liberté 9:82 f., 1967; E. Mora in Liberté 9:23–29, 1967.

Légaré, Romain. L'aventure spirituelle de Saint-Denys Garneau. Montreal and Paris, Fides, 1957. 190 p. Chap. I publ. as: Un aventurier solitaire: Saint-Denys Garneau. Cul 16:241–51, 1955. Chap. II publ. as: L'expérience poétique de Saint-Denys Garneau. Cul 16:393–403, 1955.   **7705**

Heavily documented from the Journal, G.'s poetry, and previous studies. Blais finds it an "essai de bonne volonté mais de valeur inégale" (1971).

Reviews: R.-M. Charland in Lect 37–39, Oct. 1, 1957; B. Lacroix in RevD 64, 60 f., 1958.

Le Moyne, Jean. De Saint-Denys Garneau. NRel 3:514–21, 1944.   **7706**

"Les attitudes fondamentales qui ont commandé la vie et l'œuvre de G." (Blais, 1971).

——. Saint-Denys Garneau, témoin de son temps. SemRC 15–19, March 19–25, 1960. Also: ECF 7:11–34, 1960. Also in his: Convergences. Montreal, Eds. HMH, 1961. p. 219–41. Trans.: Saint-Denys Garneau's testimony to his times. Trans. by Philip Stratford. CanL 28:31–46, 1966.   **7707**

A radio talk which attributed G.'s alienation to his moral and religious education. An indictment of the educational system which elicited articles listed by Anjou, Beaudin, Belleau, Dionne (1964), A. Major, and Robillard (June, Sept. 1960).

Lussier, Gabriel-M. Deux poètes de chez nous. RevD 244–51, May 1937.   **7708**

Spiritualist aspect of G.'s poetry (Blais, 1971).

Major, Jean-Louis. Petit exercice à propos du mythe de Saint-Denys Garneau. RUO 42:528–49, 1972. **7709**
An enlightening critique of the tendency to "mythify" a poet instead of dealing directly with his poetry.

——. Saint-Denys Garneau et la poésie. EF 8:176–94, 1972. **7710**
Concludes that, by a sort of interiorized exile, G.'s poetry "ne pouvait qu'être une activité utopique, mais destructrice."

Marcotte, Gilles. La poésie de Saint-Denys Garneau. ECF 3:137–231, 1957. *Also in his:* Une littérature qui se fait. Essais critiques sur la littérature canadienne-française. Montreal, Eds. HMH, 1962. p. 140–218. **7711**
Bachelardian study of themes of air and water. Blais finds a rigorous examination of the "exacte convenance de la forme et du sens," constituting a sketch of G.'s poetics (1971).

Ménard, Jean. Saint-Denys Garneau et le drame de la jeune poésie canadienne. RevD 60:74–80, 1954. **7712**
G. guilty of "une anarchie morale et intellectuelle." His failure "symbolise en quelque sorte celui de la poésie canadienne actuelle. . . ." (cited by Blais, 1971). See reply by Pilon.

Pilon, Jean-Guy. Réflexions sur un jugement hâtif. RevD 60:245–47, 1954. **7713**
Reply to Ménard (1954).

Robillard, Hyacinthe-Marie. De Saint-Denys Garneau: destinée inachevée. RevD 66:282–89, 1960. **7714**
Argues against Le Moyne's (1960) "interprétation presque uniquement pathologique du drame de G." (Blais, 1971).

——. De Saint-Denys Garneau: la mort pour la vie. RevD 66:85–91, 1960. **7715**
"Le drame de G. est le drame de l'espérance chrétienne." (Blais, 1971).

Turcotte, Lucie. Inédits de Saint-Denys Garneau. EF 8:398–407, 1972. **7716**
Additions to the Brault-Lacroix ed. of G.'s *Œuvres:* new version of "La

vieille roue du moulin"; unpublished response to a questionnaire ("Mes confidences"), and two poems ("Mes très chères amies..."; "Navigation").

Wilson, Edmund. O Canada. An American's notes on Canadian culture. Farrar, Straus and Giroux, 1965. p. 127–31. **7717**
Brief comments on the effect of the stifling atmosphere of Montreal in the thirties on G.

Wyczynski, Paul. Saint-Denys Garneau ou les métamorphoses du regard. *In his:* Poésie et symbole. Perspectives du symbolisme, Emile Nelligan, Saint-Denys Garneau, Anne Hébert, le langage des arbres. Montreal, Deom, 1965. p. 109–46. **7718**
Phenomenologically oriented analysis of motifs: house, road, water; hands, bird, bones. Some errors (G. listed as "Henri" instead of "Hector").

Individual Works

Haeck, Philippe. Naissance de la poésie moderne au Québec. EF 9:95–113, 1973. **7719**
Analysis of G.'s "Accompagnement" (p. 97–101), along with poems by Hébert, Grandbois, and Lapointe. Severe judgment of G.'s work: "sa valeur poétique est presque nulle."

Hébert, Maurice. Regards et jeux dans l'espace. CanF 26:464–77, 1939. **7720**
Sees G. preoccupied with the looks and games of the child. Finds his poetry characterized by a minor key at times, by perceptions of grace, and occasionally by over-subtlety.

Marcotte, Gilles. Le Journal de Saint-Denys Garneau. *In his:* Une littérature qui se fait. Essais critiques sur la littérature canadienne-française. Montreal, Eds. HMH, 1962. p. 219–42. **7721**
Reprinted from his preface to G.'s *Journal* (q.v.). Examines G.'s "prise de conscience." Finds a tendency to seek confirmation of his own ideas in other writers. Sources of the "pression de déterminismes psychiques." Testimony of progress from solitude to "la forme la plus haute de la fraternité spirituelle."

Ménard, Jean. Réflexions sur le Journal de Saint-Denys Garneau. RUL 11:885–64, 1957. *Also in his:* De Corneille à Saint-Denys Garneau. Montreal, Eds. Beauchemin, 1957. p. 203–14.   **7722**

Blais says that this negative criticism of the *Journal* is erudite, but that it is "trop facile de prouver que G. n'est pas cartésien" (1971).

Vigneault, Robert. Saint-Denys Garneau à travers Regards et jeux dans l'espace. Montreal, Presses de l'univ. de Montréal, 1973. 70 p. (Coll. Lignes québécoises)   **7723**

Lucid poem by poem commentary on *Regards et jeux....* Brief chapters of synthesis on the *recueil* and on G.

Saint-Georges de Bouhélier
(pseud. of Stéphane Georges de Bouhélier)
(Nos. 7724–7743)

JEAN-PIERRE CAP

Bardel, Pierre. Naturisme et populisme. Saint-Georges de Bouhélier et Léon Lemonnier. AFLT 12:79–89, 1965.   **7724**

A rare study focusing on the important populist aspect of *naturisme*.

Blanchart, Paul. Saint-Georges de Bouhélier. Son œuvre. Eds. du carnet critique, 1920. 64 p.   **7725**

Very concise but useful study of B.'s life and his works. Also a good definition of *naturisme*. Passages from B.'s most significant works of criticism quoted p. 49–58.

Christie, John. An interview with Emile Zola: an unpublished manuscript by Saint-Georges de Bouhélier. NFS 2:45–52, 1972.   **7726**

This article shows that the *naturistes* were very favorable to Zola. It is followed by a reprint of "L'opinion de M. Emile Zola" on *naturisme* which had appeared earlier in *La plume* 205: Nov. 1, 1897.

———. Naturalisme et naturisme: les relations d'Emile Zola avec Saint-Georges de Bouhélier et Maurice Leblond. NFS 2:11–24, 1963. [With unpublished letters by B., Mme Vve Alexandrine Zola and Maurice Leblond.]   **7727**

Very useful in establishing a distinc-

tion between naturalism and *naturisme*. Also shows that Zola, whom B. knew well and about whom he wrote extensively, would have preferred *naturisme* to be a school recognizing him as its master. Excellent.

———. Saint-Georges de Bouhélier (1876–1947), poet, playwright and novelist, I. NFS 2:73–81, 1964.   **7728**

This biographical article deals with B.'s earlier years and supplements B.'s autobiography, *Le printemps d'une génération*. The second part has not yet appeared.

———. Zola and Bouhélier: their times and relationship, based on the unpublished correspondence of Saint-Georges de Bouhélier. NFS 2:83–100, 1969. **7729**

Zola craved for support from young writers. B., whose esthetic theories were derived from Z.'s, had a very close relationship with him during the last eight years of the naturalist writer's life. This article shows not only the extent to which B. consulted Z., but Z.'s support of *naturisme*.

Coindreau, Maurice. La farce est jouée. New York, Eds. de la maison française, 1942. p. 173–76.   **7730**

Sketchy but judicious criticism of B.'s *naturisme* and of his attempt at its implementation on the stage.

Gide, André. Prétextes. Suivi de Nouveaux prétextes. Réflexions sur quelques points de littérature et de morale. Mercure de France, 1963. p. 51–52, 106–14.   **7731**

Gide was most critical of *naturisme* and contributed much to causing its failure.

Leblond, Maurice. Essai sur le naturisme, études sur la littérature artificielle et Stéphane Mallarmé, Maurice Barrès, la littérature allégorique, quelques poètes et le naturisme de Saint-Georges de Bouhélier. Eds. du Mercure de France, 1896. 151 p.   **7732**

This essay helps place *naturisme* within the contemporary literary context and shows its opposition to both symbolism and egotistic literature.

———. Saint-Georges de Bouhélier. Biographie critique. Sansot, 1909. 47 p.   **7733**

A useful biographical sketch by B.'s best friend and disciple in *naturisme*.

Lerner, Michael G. Edouard Rod and the Naturistes. NFS 2:67–73, 1971. **7734**
Attests to Rod's interest and support of *naturisme*.

Lombard, Paul. Le théâtre de St.-Georges de Bouhélier et l'avenir de l'art dramatique. Messein, 1912. 143 p. **7735**
Still useful though impressionistic essay by someone who knew B. personally and had a high opinion of his esthetic theories. He saw a relationship between B. and Ibsen.

Mitchell, Bonner. Manifeste naturiste de Saint-Georges de Bouhélier. *In his:* Les manifestes littéraires de la belle époque, 1886–1914. Anthologie critique. Seghers, 1966. p. 51–61. **7736**
A reprint of B.'s manifesto which had appeared in *Le Figaro* (Jan. 12, 1897), preceded by an excellent concise introduction by Mitchell.

Morawski, Kalikst. Les drames historiques de Saint-Georges de Bouhélier. Fil 5:97–138, 1964. **7737**
A detailed and useful definition of *naturisme;* an explanation of how B. came to choose historical subjects for his drama. Morawski explains that after his initial fascination with heroism found in daily life, B. attempted to create a national art in which social and revolutionary ideals were to inspire modern man. Morawski shows how B., through his choices and treatment of historical subjects, expresses the tragedy of a group. Demonstrates that for B. tragedy was a popular art in which he modernizes the psychology of his heroes.

La plume. 205:Nov. 1, 1897. **7738**
The entire issue is dedicated to *naturisme*. Contains articles defending naturalism, including "L'opinion de M. Emile Zola."

Saint-Georges de Bouhélier. Les éléments d'une renaissance française. Bibliothèque artistique et littéraire, 1899. 222 p. **7739**
In addition to a restatement of many of his literary theories, B. stresses the patriotic aspect of *naturisme*.

———. L'hiver en méditation; ou le passe-temps de Clarisse. Suivi d'un opuscule sur

Hugo, Richard Wagner, Zola et poésie nationale. Mercure de France, 1896. 283 p. **7740**
Very useful for the understanding of B.'s theories at the time he was elaborating them.

———. Le printemps d'une génération. Nagel, 1946. 360 p. **7741**
These candid memoirs condense information found in numerous articles published by B. in *Comœdia, Le Figaro, Paris-Soir* and *L'écho de Paris*. This volume covers B.'s life and career to the end of the Dreyfus Affair. B. planned to publish a continuation based on articles he published in *Le temps* during World War II. Indispensable for the study of B., this volume is also an excellent source of information on the 1890–1914 generation, the genesis and essence of *naturisme* and such figures as Gide, Verlaine and Zola.

———. Voyage dans la Suisse d'autrefois. 2ᵉ éd. Avignon, Aubanel, 1940. 125 p. **7742**
Partly autobiographical. B. elaborated many of his literary theories in Switzerland.

Torre, Michel della. Essai sur la dramaturgie de St.-Georges de Bouhélier. Bruges, The St. Catherine press ltd., 1910. 47 p. **7743**
Impressionistic analysis of B.'s works. B. is presented as an impressive theoretician and playwright. This opinion was contested then and is generally not held today. (Cf. Bloch, Jean-Richard. *Carnaval est mort. Premiers essais pour mieux comprendre mon temps.* N.R.F., 1920. p. 152–58).

Saint-Pol-Roux
(Pseud. of Paul Roux)
(Nos. 7744–7776)

ALISTAIR WHYTE

Editions

Briant, Théophile. Saint-Pol-Roux. Un essai par Théophile Briant, œuvres choisies, facsimilés, inédits, portraits, documents, bibliographie. Seghers, 1952. 221 p. (Poètes d'aujourd'hui, 28) *Also:* Saint-Pol-Roux. Une étude de Théophile Briant avec un choix de textes, des illustrations, une chronologie bibliographique: Saint-Paul-Roux et son temps. Troisième édition. Seghers, 1971. 220 p. (Poètes d'aujourd'hui, 28)   **7744**

Briant's essay has been undeniably influential but it should not be taken as authoritative. It contains several factual errors and adopts a lyrical rather than scholarly approach, promoting the image of S. as an "initié" and a "poète maudit." Nevertheless still a good general introduction to his life and works. The third ed. is more lavishly illustrated, adds a further *inédit* to the choice of texts, and includes a revised but still incomplete bio-bibliography. The index and a number of letters have been omitted. No critical apparatus.

Jouffroy, Alain. [Les plus belles pages de] Saint-Pol-Roux. Introd. et choix de textes par Alain Jouffroy. Mercure de France, 1966. ix–xxv, 296 p. (Les plus belles pages)   **7745**

The widest selection of texts at present available. Also includes letters from Jammes, Debussy, Honegger, Valéry, et al. and the 1925 "Hommage des surréalistes." No critical apparatus. The bibliography omits the dramatic monologs of 1883 and 1884. While not without interest in its presentation of S. as the "premier baroque moderne," Jouffroy's introduction (p. ix–xxv) is yet another "poetic" rather than scholarly essay.

Reviews: Anon. in BCLF 22:290, 1967; Anon. in RDM no. 1:637, 1967; Anon. in TLS March 14, 1968; M. Schneider in NRF 29:1105–06, 1967; A. Whyte in FS 25:107–08, 1971.

Saint-Pol-Roux (pseud. of Paul Roux). Anciennetés. Suivi d'un choix des Reposoirs de la procession. Avant-dire de Paul Eluard, introd. de A. Rolland de Renéville. Seuil, 1946. 153 p. (Coll. poétique)   **7746**

At one time the only selection of S.'s work in print. No critical apparatus. Eluard's preface (p. 9–10) is his 1925 homage. The introduction (p. 13–26) repeats the basic ideas of the article in *Univers de la parole,* but here the author gives a more exact definition of "idéoréalisme." Reproduces Peladan's *Acta rosae crucis,* but the publication of the poet's correspondence with

Segalen has cast some doubt on the authenticity of S.'s signature.

————. Cinéma vivant. Précédé de: L'empire du soleil, par Gérard Macé. Limoges, Rougerie, 1972. 119 p.   **7747**

Various fragments, *brouillons,* and the contents of two notebooks. Apart from an explanatory note about the form of the mss. and their dates of composition, no critical apparatus. A short but interesting introduction by Macé presents S.'s prophetic vision of a cinema genuinely capable of reconstructing the world as part of his whole concern with the union of science and poetry.

Reviews: Anon. in BCLF 27:520, 1973; J.-L. Bourget in Cr 329:891–97, 1974.

————. La répoétique. Préface de Raymond Datheil. Suivie de: Le Poème du monde nouveau, par Gérard Macé. Limoges, Rougerie, 1971. 116 p.   **7748**

A 1932 version of the "Liminare" and various fragments from the main body of the "Répoétique." Macé describes how he classified the mss. and gives dates of composition. Datheil gives background details to the publication of the "Liminaire" in the *Mercure de France* in 1932 and makes a few lyrical comments about the work itself. Like his contribution to "Poésie vivante" this essay is of little academic interest.

Reviews: Anon. in BCLF 27:308, 1972; J.-L. Bourget in Cr 329:891–97, 1974; R. Pouilliart in LR 27:208–09, 1973.

————. Les traditions de l'avenir. Ed. by Gerard Macé. Limoges, Rougerie, 1974. 115 p.   **7749**

A collection of published and unpublished articles from the 1930's. There are a few bibliographical notes but as with all the posthumous volumes there is no real critical apparatus.

————. Le trésor de l'homme. Préf. de André Pieyre de Mandiargues. Suivi de: L'œuvre en miettes de Saint-Pol-Roux, par Gérard Macé. Limoges, Rougerie, 1970. 173 p.   **7750**

The text of two lectures given by S. in 1925, the contents of three contemporary notebooks and an article published in the same year. Macé, who painstakingly classified the mass of surviving documents, gives variants but no critical notes. In his documentary essay, he argues that the form of writing employed in all the "inédits" reveals a change in the poet—"à partir de 1905 environ, une difficulté à construire un discours à longue haleine." Despite Macé's assertions, however, S. did complete after 1905 several dramas (which were destroyed in the looting of his home), would have liked to continue publishing volumes of poetry, and had already written, in the 1890's, "Tablettes" not unlike these texts in both form and content. It is nevertheless true that the often lacunary style and prophetic nature of these "inédits" convey the impression of an unleashed imagination and a feverish attempt to put on paper an explosion of ideas.

Reviews: Anon. in BCLF 26:354, 1971; J.-L. Bourget in Cr 329:891–97, 1974; M. Petit in NRF 225:89–90, 1975.

————. Vitesse. Précédée de: Une définition sans fin, par Gérard Macé. Limoges, Rougerie, 1973. 99 p.   **7751**

The most fragmentary of the *inédits*. In his prefatory essay (p. 7–18), Macé explains the plan he adopted in classifying these texts, gives the date of composition and coins the useful term "métaphorisme" to describe S.'s form of axioms. He relates the poet's interest in speed to his concern with mankind's progression towards perfection. A provocative conclusion suggests that the open-ended, incomplete nature of all the "inédits" reflects S.'s unceasing search for a definition of God.

Review: J.-L. Bourget in Cr 329: 891–97, 1974.

Correspondence

Saint-Pol-Roux (pseud. of Paul Roux) and Victor Segalen. Correspondance. Ed. by Annie Joly-Segalen and Gérard Macé. Limoges, Rougerie, 1975. 115 p.   **7752**

What survives of the correspondence, running from 1901–1916, is extremely interesting, e.g. the letter of April 25, 1902 in which S. states that he does not know Peladan. Unfortunately there is a serious error on p. 56 where the letter of April 29, 1906 is wrongly accredited and the notes are disappointingly inadequate. Nevertheless an important publication.

Biography

Pelleau, Paul T. Saint-Pol-Roux le crucifié. Nantes, Eds. du fleuve, 1946. 207 p.   **7753**

Inaccurate and disappointingly brief on the Parisian years, but a moving firsthand account of S.'s last months and death. Still the only attempt at a full-length biography and worth a cursory glance despite its limitations.

Tarquis, Alexis. Sur quelques amis de Saint-Pol-Roux: un écrivain, un peintre, un musicien. *In:* En Bretagne avec André Gide et Saint-Pol-Roux. *See* 7755. p. 201–12.   **7754**

Eye-witness accounts of the poet's meetings with Georges d'Esparbès, Filiger, and Vincent d'Indy during his Breton years. Inevitably anecdotal but also touches on wider issues, such as S.'s contacts, when he lived in Paris, with various painters including Gauguin, and his views on the relationship between poetry and music.

Collected Articles

En Bretagne avec André Gide et Saint-Pol-Roux. CahI 17:200–24, 1970.   **7755**

The title of this special issue is not intended to signify any link between the two writers other than their separate contacts with Brittany. The significant article by Tarquis analyzed *supra*.

Hommage à Saint-Pol-Roux. Ess 32:1–15, 1965.   **7756**

This special issue contains no significant articles but is worth consulting for the text of a radio broadcast given by S. towards the end of his life, *Quelques remarques sur la poésie contemporaine*, p. 4–5.

Hommage à Saint-Pol-Roux. PoéV 15:1–32, 1965.   **7757**

A brief bio-bibliography, several *inédits* and various short articles. An untidily presented but interesting special issue. The significant article by André Lebois analyzed *infra*.

Saint-Pol-Roux. CahI 8:126–54, 1961. **7758**

Homages by Jean Cocteau (very brief) and Jean Bars, a few *inédits*, and a series of laudatory articles, mainly concerned with the poet's Breton period. Of little academic significance, but includes a number of interesting illustrations, and S.'s impressions of his first flight in an aircraft in 1913, p. 137–39.

Tombeau de Saint-Pol-Roux (1861–1940). Brest, Imprimerie commerciale et administrative, 1941. 224 p. **7759**

The prime mover of this volume and its main contributor was Auguste Bergot. In his "Souvenirs" (p. 7–112), he recalls conversations, recounts numerous anecdotes, and reproduces several letters from S. Unfortunately his lyrical style, his lack of organization and his self-praise are constant irritants. Of great interest, however, are the obituaries by Jacob (p. 115) and Cocteau (p. 221), the preface by Valéry (p. 1–2), and the various "témoignages." The significant article by Charles Chassé analyzed *infra.*

General Studies

Amiot, Anne-Marie. Les fondements mystiques de la poétique de Saint-Pol-Roux. AFLSHN 15:89–111, 1971. **7760**

Covers much the same ground as Rolland de Renéville (*see* 7770), but this is a far more scholarly piece of writing. Making abundant use of A. Koyré's *La philosophie de J. Boehme* (published 1920), the author draws parallels between S. and the German mystic. Little or no reference to more recent or contemporary occultists apart from Peladan whom, it now appears, the poet may not have known. Nevertheless an interesting survey of S.'s cosmogony and his resultant conceptions of beauty, language and the creative artist.

Balakian, Anna. Saint-Pol-Roux and the apocalypse. *In her:* Surrealism: The road to the absolute. Rev. and enl. ed. Dutton, 1970. p. 67–78. **7761**

A summary of S.'s connections with Breton and his colleagues, followed by an analysis of those features of his thought and poetic practice which appear to herald surrealism. Emphasizes his "simultaneous acceptance and re-fusal of reality," his faith in the power of language to transform the world, his interest in the madman's view of life, and his kaleidoscopic imagery. Despite one or two factual errors a good critical appraisal.

Bernard, Suzanne. Saint-Pol-Roux, maître de l'image. *In her:* Le poème en prose de Baudelaire jusqu'à nos jours. Nizet, 1954. p. 564–71. **7762**

One of the first important pieces of scholarly writing on S. Discusses the wide range, both stylistic and thematic, of his prose poetry, showing that his imagery and linguistic experiments are a direct consequence of his "idéo-réalisme." Points out the constant features of his work, traces his development, and assesses his importance as a link between symbolism and surrealism. A short but excellent critical assessment.

Besnier, Patrick. Le secret de Saint-Pol-Roux. AnBret 79:763–70, 1972. **7763**

Mainly a discussion of "Le trésor de l'homme" and "La répoétique." Outlines S.'s belief that the divine perfection which existed in the past can only be regained by looking to the future, and stresses his prophetic vision of a world transformed by poetry allied to science. Like Macé, the author plays down the importance of S.'s published volumes and makes the debatable assertion that he lost interest in producing "completed" works of literature.

Chassé, Charles. Le romantisme de Saint-Pol-Roux. *In:* Tombeau de Saint-Pol-Roux. *See* 7759. p. 175–90. **7764**

Devotes considerable space to a general discussion of romanticism and its relationship to symbolism. Considers that the mystical idealism which typifies the later movement is present in the English romantics but little in evidence in their French counterparts. Argues that the main features which distinguish S. from his symbolist contemporaries — his love of nature, his eloquence, his increasing desire to become an "aède populaire" — reveal his kinship with French romantic writers. A stimulating article which raises a number of interesting, if often debatable, issues.

Juin, Hubert. Saint-Pol-Roux le magnifique. MagL 63:40–42, 1972. *Also in his:* Écri-

vains de l'avant-siècle. Seghers, 1972. p.
275–82. (L'archipel) **7765**

A wide-ranging but unoriginal and
extremely disjointed assessment of S.
Of little or no interest apart from its
emphasis on the poet's humanism.

Lavaud, Guy. Mallarmé et Saint-Pol-Roux.
Arts Nov. 15, 1946. **7766**

Contains the text of an interesting
letter in which S. confesses that, although he greatly admired Mallarmé's
poetry, he never dared attend the
"Mardis" and only met him once in
person. Surprising that so many subsequent commentators are unaware of this
fact.

Lebois, André. Notes sur Saint-Pol-Roux.
Prés 5:23–27, 1966. **7767**

The author makes revealing comments about the S. "legend," the poet's
kinship with Villiers de l'Isle-Adam, his
humor, his links with occultism, etc.
and argues in favor of the verse poems
but more cogently than in his contribution to *Poésie vivante*. Again criticizes
commentators who concentrate on S.'s
esthetic doctrine and also warns against
the image of the poet promoted by the
surrealists. Despite its unambitious title
and format, a stimulating article which
raises important issues and challenges
certain conventional approaches to S.

———. Saint-Pol-Roux le magnifique était
aussi prince des sonnets. *In:* Hommage
à Saint-Pol-Roux. *See* 7757. p. 17–20.
7768

Questions Rolland de Renéville's assertion that a poet's "greatness" depends upon whether or not he has
evolved a supporting esthetic philosophy.
Declares that a writer's poetic practice
is more important than his poetic theory
and stresses S.'s mastery of conventional
verse. Does not, unfortunately, analyze
the four sonnets quoted in support of
his argument. Nevertheless an interesting attempt to shift critical emphasis.

Mercier, Alain. Les sources ésotériques et
occultes de la poésie symboliste (1870–
1914). I. Le symbolisme français. Nizet,
1969. p. 265–68. **7769**

Makes the surprising claim that S.
became involved in occultist circles as a
schoolboy in Lyons. There is, however,
nothing to support this assertion any-

where in Théophile Briant's "Poètes
d'aujourd'hui" monograph, which M.
Mercier gives as his source. He undeniably shows that there are strong
echoes of esoteric thought in the poet's
works but his view of S. as an "adepte
des sciences traditionnelles," shared by
many commentators, and the whole
question of Peladan's "Rose-Croix
esthétique" need to be examined in
greater depth.

Rolland de Renéville, André. L'idéoréalisme
de Saint-Pol-Roux. NRF 342:174–80,
1942. *Also in his:* Univers de la parole.
Gallimard, 1944. p. 50–60. **7770**

A fairly influential but somewhat misleading essay. The author tends to over-
look the "réalisme" of "idéoréalisme"
and emphasizes the poet's "idéalisme"
or "mysticisme," the extreme forms of
which S. himself condemned in the
very documents on which this article is
based.

Steinmetz, Jean-Luc. Saint-Pol-Roux ou les
dangers de l'écriture. AnBret 73:463–82,
1966. **7771**

An extensive appraisal of the poet's
stylistic devices, their implications, and
the major themes of his work. Argues
that, despite his sincerity and the success of certain verbal experiments, S.
fails to realize his intentions because of
his own weakness for excessive elaboration and because of the very nature of
language itself. An important article.
One of the best pieces of critical writing
on S. to date.

Whyte, Alistair. Saint-Pol-Roux et la
Bretagne. CahI 22:218–22, 1975. **7772**

Attempts to dispel certain myths
about S.'s knowledge of Brittany when
he settled in the Presqu'île de Crozon
in 1898. Shows that not only had he
spent some time there in 1890 and
1892, composing a number of poems on
both occasions, but that he first visited
the region as early as 1883, when he
wrote the play, "La ferme," which has
a Breton setting.

Drama

Edwards, John O. Une mystification littéraire de Saint-Pol-Roux. RSH 32, fasc.
128:633–43, 1967. **7773**

Gives a detailed background on the hoax of "Les personnages de l'individu," for which S. invented an American pseudonym, Daniel Harcoland. Surprisingly there is no mention of the poet's unsuccessful attempt to gain the directorship of the Odéon in 1892, and unfortunately the date of Sarah Bernhardt's death is mistakenly given as 1930. Little analysis in depth of the play itself, of the concept of the "monodrame," or of S.'s dramatic theories in general, but interesting for the many unpublished documents and letters quoted by the author.

Knowles, Dorothy. Saint-Pol-Roux, le magnifique. *In her:* La réaction idéaliste au théâtre depuis 1890. Droz, 1934. p. 343–54. **7774**

The approach is thematic rather than stylistic. The author gives an analysis of each dramatic work and briefly discusses such concepts as the "monodrame" and "idéoréalisme." A lucid, well-documented survey which is still the best introduction to S.'s theater.

Marie, Gisèle. Saint-Pol-Roux, le magnifique. *In her:* Le théâtre symboliste. Nizet, 1973. p. 141–47. **7775**

In view of its date, a surprisingly inaccurate article. The author mistakenly claims that S. arrived in Paris around 1885 and wrongly presents "La Dame à la faulx" as his only drama. Of little academic interest but does convey something of the poet's unbridled flow of images.

Monférier, Jacques. Symbolisme et anarchie. RHL 65:233–38, 1965. **7776**

Does not deal solely with S. but comments on his play, "Le fumier," relating it to the concerns of contemporary anarchists, many of whom were fellow contributors to *La revue blanche* and *Entretiens politiques et littéraires.* Short but interesting.

André Salmon
(Nos. 7777–7783)

CAROL J. BREAM

Apollinaire, Guillaume. André Salmon. VPr 14:118–24, 1908. **7777**

First study of S.'s poetry that is a bit longer than a simple review. Traces sources of *Poèmes* and *Les féeries* to Banville and early symbolists in general. Praise somewhat overdone, but understandable if one takes into account the source and the place where it appeared. Perhaps most interesting feature is typically rich style of Apollinaire.

Berger, Pierre. André Salmon. Essai par Pierre Berger. Inédits, poèmes choisis... Seghers, 1956. 219 p. (Poètes d'aujourd'hui, 53) **7778**

Medium-length essay. Somewhat rambling, but mentions major poetry of S., if only briefly. Underlines role of S. in early twentieth century avant-garde movement, and attempts to define principal traits of the man and his work. Worthwhile survey, but lacking footnotes, and thus difficult to follow for one who does not know S.'s poetry well.

Chassé, Charles. André Salmon et le douanier savant. *In his:* Dans les coulisses de la gloire. D'Ubu-roi au douanier Rousseau. Nouvelle revue critique, 1947. p. 126–33. **7779**

Brief study of S.'s role in the evolution of the "mythe Rousseau." Interesting particularly for those studying S.'s art criticism.

Décaudin, Michel. Etudes sur la poésie contemporaine VI: trois poètes des années vingt: André Salmon, Blaise Cendrars, Max Jacob. IL 22:219–29, 1970. **7780**

Brief overview of principal traits of S.'s poetry from 1905 to 1936.

Salmon, André. Montparnasse. A. Bonne, 1950. 287 p. **7781**

Earlier version of material reused in *Souvenirs sans fin.*

Review: E. Richard in Rol 440:1–4, 1953.

————. Souvenirs sans fin. Gallimard, 1955–56. 2 v. **7782**

Interesting and valuable anecdotal presentation of the pre- and post-war French literary and artistic scene. Includes a great deal of autobiographical material. Especially good are sketches of life in the cubist and avant-garde circles, but other aspects of the periods covered are included as well. Fully indexed.

Reviews: A. Billy in LivF 5:17–18, 1955, in FL 2, Sept. 29, 1956, and in RDM 15:431–35, 1957; C. M. in Car 864:21, 1961.

————. Souvenirs sans fin. L'air de la butte. Eds. de la Nouvelle France, 1945. 224 p.
7783

Earlier version of material reused in *Souvenirs sans fin.*

Victor Segalen
(Nos. 7784–7824)

GLORIA BIEN

Editions

Segalen, Victor. Le Combat pour le sol. Présentation de Eugène Roberto. Ottawa, Eds. de l'univ. d'Ottawa, 1974. 165 p. (Cahiers d'inédits, 5)   **7784**

Roberto introduces his posthumous publication (not a critical edition) in the context of S.'s *Notes sur l'exotisme* rather than (as Bouillier judged it to be on ample grounds) as an antithesis to Claudel's *Le repos du septième jour.* The appendices include S.'s letters and A. Joly-Segalen's notes bearing on the composition of this drama.
Review: G. Germain in QL 212:6–8, 1975.

————. Odes suivies de Thibet. Texte établi et présenté par Annie Joly-Segalen. Mercure de France, 1963. 121 p.   **7785**

In a succinct introduction, Joly-Segalen quotes her father's own remarks on the *Odes,* first published in 1922, and on *Thibet,* for which she stresses an allegorical interpretation. The latter work was left unfinished, and Joly-Segalen does not indicate the principles she followed in choosing 18 from the first series of 21, 7 from the second part of 27, and only one from the third part originally composed of 10 sequences.
Reviews: G. Germain in CahS 377: 473–75, 1964; R. Kanters in FL Jan. 2, 1964.

————. Stèles. Edition critique, commentée et augmentée d'un inédit, établie par Henry Bouillier. Plon, 1963. 291 p.   **7786**

Each poem in the collection, headed by an epigraph in Chinese characters and enclosed in a rectangle as in the original edition, is followed by long passages giving sources, variants, and commentaries. The commentaries submit the poems to minute analysis, extending even to typographical disposition, but they too often paraphrase, and differ from the Chinese commentaries they claim to imitate by being more often objectively intellectual than lyrically enthusiastic. An additional poem published here for the first time gives precious insight into S.'s poetics.
Reviews: M. du Cheyron in RHL 65:146–47, 1965; G. Germain in MerF 1203:103–09, 1964; M. Goffin in RUB 15:329–31, 1962–63; A. Lebois in Thy 56:276–80, 1963.

————. Stèles, Peintures, Equipée. Club du meilleur livre, 1955. 638 p.   **7787**

This volume with its introduction by Pierre-Jean Jouve is still indispensable as the letters and notes in the appendices have been reprinted neither in the 1970 Plon edition nor elsewhere.
Reviews: H. Amer (pseud. of Henry Bouillier) in CahS 333:317–19, 1956; A. Billy in FL Sept. 24, 1955; E. Glissant in LetN 32:627–33, 1955; H. Juin in Esp 232:1794–1800, 1955; V. Lacôte in LetF Sept. 22–28, 1955; J. Laude in Cr 104:14–32, 1956; E. Noulet in Syn 147–60, April–May 1956, and in her *Alphabet critique* (Brussels, Presses univ. de Bruxelles, 1966) v. 4, p. 99–101; P. Oster in NRF 44:330–34, 1956; G. Picon in MerF 1106:682–89, 1955, and in his *L'usage de la lecture* (Mercure de France, 1961) v. 2, p. 139–46; M.-J. Rustan in VI 27:114–33, 1956.

Other Texts

Joly-Segalen, Annie, and André Schaeffner. Segalen et Debussy. Textes recueillis et présentés par Annie Joly-Segalen et André Schaeffner. Monaco, Eds. du rocher, 1961. 341 p.   **7788**

Collected here are the correspondence between S. and Debussy, long summaries of their conversations recorded by S., and other texts deriving from S.'s relationship with Debussy. The introductions place each artist in the context of the other's life and work.

Reviews: G. Germain in CahS 369: 313–14, 1962–63; E. Lockspeiser in M&L 43:361–63, 1962.

Segalen, Victor. Inédits de douze stèles présentés par Marie-Jeanne Durry. Créa 4:5–88, 1973.   **7789**

These facsimile reproductions of the manuscript versions of twelve *stèles* which S. did not include in his collection of 64 (number chosen to correspond to the hexagrams of the *I Ching*) reveal his careful craftsmanship; they are annotated by Mme Durry, who found as many as ten versions of one *stèle*. The Chinese references are explained by Paul Demiéville.

Review: Y. Florenne in Monde Dec. 9–10, 1973.

————. Journal des Iles (Océanie 1903–1904). MerF 1113:5–33; 1114:270–92, 1956.   **7790**

S.'s own account of his tour of duty in the South Seas after a devastating storm, his visit to Gauguin's hut shortly after the artist's death, and various observations which were to enter his novel *Les immémoriaux.*

————. Notes sur l'exotisme. MerF 1099: 385–402; 1100:594–612, 1955.   **7791**

S. attempts in these rather fragmentary notes to develop his theory of exoticism, central to much of his work, as an "esthétique du divers."

Reviews: J. Guillou in FR 41:243–49, 1967; H. Juin in Esp 232:1794–1800, 1955.

————. Premier exposé des résultats archéologiques obtenus dans la Chine occidentale par la mission Gilbert de Voisins, Jean Lartigue et Victor Segalen, 1914. JAsiat 11, no. 5:467–85; no. 6:282–306, 1915; no 7:369–424, 1916.   **7792**

S.'s archeological discoveries were important enough to be translated into Chinese in 1930 (Segalen, Victor. Chung-kuo Hsi-pu K'ao-ku Chi. Trans. by Ch'eng-chün Feng. Shanghai, Commercial press, 1930). Reprinted in 1962.

Correspondence

Saint-Pol-Roux (pseud. of Paul Roux), and Victor Segalen. Correspondance. Préfacée

par Annie Joly-Segalen. Présentée et annotée par Annie Joly-Segalen et Gérard Macé. Limoges, Rougerie, 1975. 117 p.   **7793**

Fire destroyed most of Saint-Pol-Roux's papers in 1940, and many of S.'s papers were lost in transit from China in 1914. The scant remaining letters collected here include even dinner invitations and date mainly from S.'s Oceania period. Saint-Pol-Roux showed great interest and faith in the literary career of his younger friend. S.'s "Hommage à Saint-Pol-Roux" is appended.

Segalen, Victor. Correspondance avec Paul Claudel. *In:* Départs avec Victor Segalen. *See* 7800. p. 275–94.   **7794**

Most important S. correspondence published so far.

————. Lettres à Henry Manceron. MerF 1186:241–71, 1962.   **7795**

In these letters written from China 1909–1914, S. shares reflections on Chinese society and culture, exoticism and his readings in Nietzsche, Claudel, Bergson and others.

————. Lettres de Chine. Ed. by Jean-Louis Bédouin. Plon, 1967. 278 p.   **7796**

In these delightful letters to his wife written in 1909–1910 during an equestrian journey across China with his friend Auguste Gilbert de Voisins, S. shares his many literary projects as well as intimate details of everyday life. The introduction by Bédouin and the annotated index by Mmes A. Joly-Segalen and D. Lelong make this work a valuable resource.

Reviews: Anon. in TLS Oct. 12, 1967; J. L. Bory in NouvO 130:28–29, 1967; C. Dedet in AeLo 87:38–39, 1967; R. Kanters in FL Oct 2–8, 1967; C. Malraux in QL 34:7, 1967; M. Pirazzoli-t'Serstevens in NRF 180: 1090–92, 1967.

Biography

Gilbert de Voisins, Auguste, comte. Le souvenir de Victor Segalen. *In his:* Voyages: Ecrit en Chine. Crès, 1924. p. 159–95.   **7797**

In affectionate remembrance of his friend and companion on the equestrian journey across China which was the background for S.'s *Lettres de Chine*, Gilbert de Voisins stresses S.'s generosity and points out his essential poetic talent: he revealed the beauty of things.

Lebois, André. Agonie et mort de Victor Segalen d'après les cahiers inédits de Jeanne Perdriel-Vaissière. Thy 58:551–62, 1965.   **7798**
Personal, rather romanticized account of S.'s death.

Remy, Pierre-Jean. Le sac du palais d'été. Gallimard, 1971. 591 p.   **7799**
S., his friends, and excerpts from his writings, in a strange interplay of the real and the imaginary, weave in and out of Remy's novel, set in Peking during the Cultural Revolution of the sixties. "The real China" remains as inaccessible to Remy's characters, members of the European community, as it had been to S. in *René Leys*. Gallimard published the definitive version of *René Leys* in the same year, and many of the reviews reexamine S.'s original novel. Reviews: C. Bourniquel in Esp 409: 1038–40, 1971; C.-M. Cluny in MagL 58:43–44, 1971; M. Cournot in NouvO 365: 54–55, 1971; D. Fernandez in QL 130:5–6, 1971; H. Juin in LetF Nov. 10–16, 1971; C. Mauriac in FL Nov. 26, 1971; F. C. St. Aubyn in FR 46: 451–53, 1972.

Special Numbers

Départs avec Victor Segalen. CahS 288: 178–314, 1948.   **7800**
Special issue which effectively revived interest in S. after a long period. Excerpts from his works are included, as well as his very important correspondence with Claudel and a letter to Debussy written from China. Significant articles analyzed separately. Review: R. Lalou in NL May 8, 1948.

Hommage à Victor Segalen. FrA 124:185–214, 1956.   **7801**
A group of articles devoted to S. following the publication of *Stèles, Peintures, Equipée* by the Club du meilleur livre.

General Studies: Books

Bédouin, Jean-Louis. Victor Segalen. Présentation par Jean-Louis Bédouin. Choix de textes. Bibliographie, portraits, facsimilés. Seghers, 1963. 214 p. (Poètes d'aujourd'hui, 102)   **7802**
A brief and effective introduction placing S.'s works in a biographical context is followed by selected poems, excerpts, and a bibliography calculated to stimulate further reading. Reviews: R. Kanters in FL Jan. 2, 1964.

Bol, Victor. Lecture de Stèles de Victor Segalen. Minard, 1972. 254 p. (Avant-siècle, 9)   **7803**
Revised from a 1959 Ph.D. thesis written before Bouillier's critical ed. of 1961, this work painstakingly examines the vocabulary, syntax, imagery, themes, structures, and motifs of *Stèles*. The background material is thin, and like the bibliography, has not been sufficiently updated; the study might benefit from being published together with a concordance. Reviews: J. Plottel in FR 47:645–46, 1974; J. Roudaut in RHL 74:923–24, 1974; M. Schaettel in RSH 39: 356–57, 1974.

Bouillier, Henry. Victor Segalen. Mercure de France, 1961. 421 p.   **7804**
In this comprehensive study, originally his state doctoral thesis, Bouillier studies all of S.'s published works, mss., letters, and unfinished projects within a biographical framework. In his penetrating analyses of S.'s major works, he examines the search for knowledge, the constant interplay of the real and the imaginary, diversity sought in travel, and return to the self. Excessive paraphrasing; excellent bibliography, which not only lists S.'s published works, but serves as a guide to the gradual appearance of hitherto unpublished works. Reviews: Anon. in AUP 31:547–48, 1961; J. Barrère in RSH 110:257–59, 1963; G. Bounoure in CahS 368:3–20, 1962; Y. Cosson in RdBP 56–62, 1964; G. Germain in FrA 172:225–29, 1962; A. Lebois in Thy 54:483–88, 1961; E. Mora in RDM 4:618–22, 1962; P. Moreau in RLC 36:144–50, 1962; P. Pia in Car 894:20, 1961; E. Roberto

in CahCC 4:207–11, 1966; J.-P. Weber in Monde, July 8, 1961.

Articles: Poetry and General Studies

Amer, Henry (pseud. of Henry Bouillier). Etude. *In:* Segalen, Victor. Les immémoriaux. Union générale d'éditions, 1966. 377 p. (Le monde en 10/18, 335–336)
7805

Postface by Bouillier draws largely on his own book and discusses S.'s entire work rather than this one novel. No critical apparatus in this ed.

Fombeure, Maurice. La poésie de Victor Segalen. *In:* Départs avec Victor Segalen. *See* 7800. p. 205–10. **7806**

Comments on certain passages from *Thibet, Stèles* and *Odes.*

Germain, Gabriel. Victor Segalen, poète de la Chine primordiale. CahS 368:21–38, 1962. **7807**

Proposes reading the *Stèles* "à la chinoise," with specific reference to Taoism.

Kushner, Eva. Exotisme et morale chez Victor Segalen. RUL 17:701–15, 1963. **7808**

Are exoticism and ethics contradictory terms? Reproaches S. for taking pleasure in inaccessibility.

———. Orphée et orphisme chez Victor Segalen. CAIEF 22:197–214, 303–04, 1970. **7809**

Treats *Dans un monde sonore* as well as *Orphée-Roi* in the literary and philosophical history of the Orpheus myth.

———. L'Orphée-Roi de Victor Segalen. *In her:* Le mythe d'Orphée dans la littérature française contemporaine. A.G. Nizet, 1961. p. 136–76. **7810**

In this useful compilation, Kushner points out that S., in presenting Orpheus as the creator of music and poetry, went back beyond Latin authors to one of the original meanings of the myth; that he differs from other modern writers who used the myth in effacing himself before the hero he created, and that he subordinated himself to Debussy's every wish in writing the book. For Kushner, S.'s exoticism loses its "usual literary sense" to take on an "esthetic

and moral sense" applicable to *Orphée-Roi.* Her attempt to place *Orphée-Roi* in the context of S.'s other work, contrasting its "hermetically lyrical" style to the "aristocratic simplicity" of the works inspired by China is not altogether successful, however. Although she had the use of mss., Annie Joly-Segalen and André Schaeffner's *Segalen et Debussy* did not appear until the same year.

Lebois, André. Une source chinoise des *Stèles* et du chiffre des choses. RLC 22:110–14, 1948. **7811**

Lebois' suggestion that some of the *Stèles* are translations has been disproved by later publications from S.'s notes and letters.

Messemaecker, G. (pseud. of J. d'Aulan), and Charles Guibier. Victor Segalen, l'homme, l'écrivain. RevInd 36:327–42, 1921. **7812**

S.'s life is treated by Guibier, who knew him personally. His work is dealt with by Messemaecker.

Miomandre, Francis de. Victor Segalen et l'esprit de la Chine. *In his:* Le pavillon du mandarin. Emile Paul, 1921. p. 89–111. **7813**

In one of the earliest appreciations of S., Miomandre rails against the negligence of "official criticism" in France, and offers remarkable, often still fresh, insights into S.'s *Immémoriaux, Stèles,* and *Peintures.*

Murciaux, Christian. Victor Segalen. RDM 3:460–74, 1953. *Also (rev.):* RevN 31:119–30, 1960. **7814**

Presenting S.'s work in a biographical context, Murciaux compares him to Rimbaud, Claudel, and Saint-John Perse. Particularly interesting is his exploration of the "striking community of themes and mysterious affinities of language" between *Stèles* and the works of Saint-John Perse.

Norge, Geo. (pseud. of Georges Mogin). Equipée. Voyage au pays du réel. *In:* Départs avec Victor Segalen. *See* 7800. p. 255–62. **7815**

Equipée considered in the light of *Odes, Stèles,* and *Peintures.*

———. Un grand poète méconnu. CahBl 1:19–28, 1936. **7816**

Although China inspired much of S.'s work, it would be a mistake to look to this work for knowledge about China. S.'s interest in China was sparked by a visit to the Musée Carnuschi. Much of the information for this article came from S.'s friend Adrienne de Tizac.

Paribatra, Marsi, princesse. Victor Segalen. Un exotisme sans mensonge. RLC 30: 497–506, 1956. **7817**

Observes that what sets S. apart from exotic writers of his time is that his vision of China was not a dream prefabricated in Europe, and that he was one of the first to find in Asia enrichment for his literary technique.

Roudaut, Jean. L'absence de Victor Segalen. Cr 190:203–23; 191:314–24, 1963. **7818**

For Roudaut, S.'s esthetic solution to his religious quest relates him to the Parnasse. After a vain search for documents, Roudaut could conclude on S.'s mysterious death only that, falling halfway between dream and act, it reinforces the ambiguity of his works. Review: D. R. Bienaimé in SFr 8: 289, 1964.

Rousseaux, André. Situation de Victor Segalen. *In his:* Littérature du XXᵉ siècle. 6ᵉ série. Albin Michel, 1958. p. 76–91. **7819**

Names S. one of the great poets of the century, one who has renewed our vision of the world.

Schwartz, William Leonard. Victor Segalen's interpretation of China. *In his:* The imaginative interpretation of the Far East in modern French literature. 1800–1920. Champion, 1927. p. 187–95. **7820**

In this broad survey which formed the basis for many later studies, Schwartz points out S.'s qualifications through study and travel, and names him "the most talented French writer to attempt an imaginative interpretation of China." This article is particularly interesting in the context of Schwartz's treatment of S.'s contemporaries.

Novel

Gautier, J.-M. Les immémoriaux de Segalen et leurs sources anglaises. RLC 26:106–15, 1952. **7821**

Contrary to common claims, S. relied not solely on actual experience to write *Les immémoriaux,* but carefully documented his writings through the works of Cook and William Ellis.

———. Victor Segalen: notes sur le vocabulaire des Immémoriaux. FM 4:303–08, 1948. **7822**

Lists S.'s use of rare words, neologisms, technical terms and "other peculiarities;" he finds archaisms rare and suggests future study of the style of the novel *Les immémoriaux.*

Minoret, Bernard, and Danielle Vezolles. La fuite en Chine. Inspirée librement de René Leys de Victor Segalen. Introd. de Roland Barthes. C. Bourgois, 1970. 151 p. **7823**

This dramatic adaptation of S.'s novel *René Leys* transforms S. into a rather sinister character.

Underwood, J. A. Introduction. *In:* Segalen, Victor. René Leys. Trans. by J. A. Underwood. Chicago, J. P. O'Hara, 1974. 222 p. **7824**

Introduction states briefly the circumstances under which S. composed the novel. This recent translation bears witness to the "modernity" of S.'s novel. Underwood successfully captures the ruminative, mysterious tone. Review: N. Bliven in NY 189–90, Dec. 9, 1974.

Paul-Jean Toulet
(Nos. 7825–7869)

PHILIPPE LEROUX

Correspondence and Journal

Toulet, Paul-Jean. Correspondance avec un ami pendant la guerre. Le divan, 1922. 235 p. **7825**

T.'s letters to René Philipon, a bibliophile, from 1918 to 1920, show him struggling with illness and moral solitude. Brief preface by H. Martineau. Review: P. Lièvre in Mar 26:92–93, 1923.

———. Correspondance de Claude Debussy et P.-J. Toulet. Le divan, 1929. 132 p. (Coll. Saint-Germain-des-Prés, 10) **7826**

Demonstrates their friendship and mutual esteem and tells the story of their unsuccessful collaboration on an adaptation of *As you like it*. On this question, see Schaefner's *Claude Debussy et ses projets shakespeariens* in RHT 446–53, Oct.–Dec. 1964.

————. Journal et voyages. Le divan, 1934. 183 p. *Also:* Nouvelle édition augmentée des *Lettres à soi-même* et de nombreux fragments inédits. Le divan, 1955. 299 p. **7827**

Contains T.'s journal written at intervals from 1885 on and the records of his travels. The *Lettres à soi-même* have been incorporated somewhat artificially into the revised ed. Brief introduction by the editor, H. Martineau.

————. Lettres à Madame Bulteau. Pref. by Jean-Louis Vandoyer. Le divan, 1924. 111 p. **7828**

Twenty-nine letters from 1901 to 1905 interesting for the light they shed on the personality of the virtuoso epistolarian. They also provide significant information on T.'s life and work during his Parisian period. The preface evokes Mme Bulteau's salon, frequented by Barrès, H. de Régnier, A. de Noailles, Forain and her relations with T.

————. Lettres à soi-même. Le divan, 1927. 123 p. (Les soirées du Divan, 23) *Also:* Eds. du globe, 1950. 113 p. **7829**

These letters were for T. an original way of taking notes, a literary game, and above all, a means of exposing his Self and its peculiar apperception of people and events: "Ce n'est peut-être pas, mon ami, vous faire un compliment excessif de vous accorder un cœur moins coriace que le monde ne pense." Indispensable for a study of T. The later ed. includes three previously unpublished letters.

————. Lettres de P.-J. Toulet et d'Emile Henriot. Mercure de France, 1959. 146 p. **7830**

Except for the first two, T.'s letters to Henriot were written after his definitive departure from Paris in July 1912. Estrangement from the *Café* life, illness and financial difficulties do not prevent T. from displaying his wit, stylistic brilliance and jingoism.

Review: J. Piatier in Monde Aug. 1, 1959.

Biography

Boulenger, Jacques. Toulet au bar et à la poste. Le divan, 1935. 148 p. (Coll. Saint-Germain-des-Prés, 15) **7831**

Aspects of T.'s Parisian life and insights into his art through extensive quotation of previously unpublished texts and T.'s letters to the author.

Carco, Francis. Amitié avec Toulet, suivi des lettres de Toulet à Francis Carco et d'une lettre de l'éditeur. Le divan, 1934. 57 p. **7832**

A sensitive but rather slim essay prefaces nine letters T. sent to Carco regarding mainly the publication of the *Contrerimes*.

Catala, J. A. Paul-Jean Toulet Palois. Pau, Garet-Haristoy, 1926. 62 p. *Also:* Pau, Marrimpouey jeune, 1961. 69 p. **7833**

Evokes T.'s love for his native Béarn and friendship with J. Guillemin. Second ed. includes three previously unpublished letters.

Dyssord, Jacques. L'aventure de Paul-Jean Toulet, gentilhomme des lettres. Grasset, 1928. 231 p. **7834**

Author expands a few episodes in T.'s life into a biographical novel for the general public.

Jammes, Francis. P.-J. Toulet. *In his:* Leçons poétiques. Mercure de France, 1930. p. 173–83. **7835**

Short psychological and moral portrait of T. in Pau.

Lebois, André. Douze lettres de Toulet à Pierre Labrouche. Thy 64:156–65, 1964. **7836**

Lebois provides biographical information about Pierre Labrouche, an engraver and friend of T., and annotates T.'s letters, previously unpublished.

————. Le cœur de P.-J. Toulet. RdM 21: 59–82, 1961. **7837**

A perceptive if eulogistic review of T.'s life and works.

————. Toulet, Casanova et Henri de Régnier (Documents inédits). Thy 65: 551–68, 1963. **7838**

Useful article. Besides giving the full text of T.'s letters to his friend, the novelist J. Casanova, author reproduces the thirteen letters of T. to H. de Régnier from 1902 to 1914 from the *Lettres de P.-J. Toulet à Henri de Régnier,* "livret polycopié à vingt exemplaires, en tirage privé," ed. by P. O. Walzer.

Martineau, Henri. La famille, l'enfance, les collèges de P.-J. Toulet; son voyage à l'île Maurice. Le divan, 1957. 98 p. (La vie de Paul-Jean Toulet)   **7839**
A documented examination of T.'s formative years.
Review: C. Pichois in RHL 59:563–65, 1959.

————. P.-J. Toulet collaborateur de Willy. Le divan, 1957. 90 p. (La vie de Paul-Jean Toulet)   **7840**
Thorough treatment of T.'s collaboration in the *usine de romans* of Willy superseding that of P. O. Walzer in *Paul-Jean Toulet; l'œuvre, l'écrivain.*
Review: A Billy in FL 2, Nov. 3, 1956.

————. P.-J. Toulet et Arthur Machen. Monsieur du Paur homme public et le grand dieu Pan. Le divan, 1957. 100 p. (La vie de Paul-Jean Toulet)   **7841**
First of a series of authoritative monographs by T.'s principal publisher, editor and scholar. Martineau's intent is to clarify important stages in T.'s life and literary career. Orderly study of composition and projected changes and additions of T.'s first novel. Author evaluates T.'s debt to A. Machen's novel: "Cela est aussi loin du plagiat que de la vraie filiation d'auteur à auteur." Reproduces the correspondence between the two authors.
Review: C. Pichois in RLC 32:446–47, 1958.

————. Paul-Jean Toulet et Francis Jammes. MerF 331:228–46, 1957.   **7842**
Painstaking account of relations between the two writers with full reproduction of their correspondence.

————. P.-J. Toulet, Jean de Tinan et Mme Bulteau. Le mariage de Don Quichotte. Le divan, 1958. 129 p. (La vie de Paul-Jean Toulet)   **7843**

Discusses briefly T.'s friendship with Jean de Tinan before examining in great detail his relations with Mme Bulteau. Sees parallel between his attitude toward her and the sadistic scenes in his novels. Meticulously provides all available information on *Le mariage*'s composition and publication.
Review: V. Del Litto in SC 2:364, 1960.

————. Le séjour de P.-J. Toulet à Alger. Le divan, 1959. 90 p. (La vie de Paul-Jean Toulet)   **7844**
Judicious detailed account of T.'s literary beginnings. T.'s adventures in Algiers did not influence his pessimism as much as is commonly thought.

————. La vie de P.-J. Toulet. Le divan, 1921. 125 p.   **7845**
Though superseded by author's later work on the subject, remains a valuable introduction to T.'s personality and art by a fervent admirer.
Review: E. Berl in EN 6:1083, 1923.

General Studies

Boulenger, Jacques. P.-J. Toulet. *In his:* ...Mais l'art est difficile: première série. Plon, 1921. p. 154–63.   **7846**
First part of article contains some interesting remarks on the un-novelistic qualities of T.'s novels. Second part is a brief analysis of T.'s art in *Les trois impostures.*

Buenzod, Emmanuel. P.-J. Toulet. *In his:* Une époque littéraire. 1890–1910. Neuchâtel, La Baconnière, 1941. p. 117–23.
                                  7847
Maintains that the thematic and stylistic dissonances in T.'s works are to be examined in terms of the conflict between sensibility and disillusioned knowledge.

Carrat, Simone. Paul-Jean Toulet coloriste. *In:* Approches: essais sur la poésie moderne de langue française. Les belles lettres, 1971. p. 79–85. (AFLSHN 15)
                                  7848
Relates T.'s abundant utilization of color terms in the *Contrerimes* to his personal experience and painterly vision. Suggestive but too short.

Chabaneix, Philippe. Les éditions de P.-J. Toulet. Por 6:35–54, 1947. **7849**
Intended for bibliophiles. Reproduces illustrations of T.'s works with some comments on the artists.

———. Paul-Jean Toulet. RDM 1:19–25, 1968. **7850**
Slight appreciation of T.'s poetry, intended for the general reader.

Charles, Gilbert. Toulet moraliste. Div 10: 361–68, 1922. **7851**
"C'est cette beauté du langage, matière du style qui, pour une part, confère aux *Trois impostures*, leur densité." Author finds in T.'s work evidence of *dandysme spirituel* according to Baudelaire's definition.

Collin, W. E. Clockmaker of souls; a study of Paul-Jean Toulet. Claude Kendall, 1933. 203 p. **7852**
Only full-length study available in English of T. First part is longer than, but adds nothing important to, Martineau's *Vie*, which it closely follows. In the second, shorter part, author makes extensive use of plot summaries and translated excerpts in his attempt to discuss the art of T.'s prose. Random and superficial critical comments. Ch. 4 on T. as poet offers an anthology but no analysis of his poems. No bibliography.

Derème, Tristan. En rêvant à P.-J. Toulet. Le divan, 1927. 154 p. *Also in his:* Le violon des muses. Grasset, 1935. P. 219–316. **7853**
Incidental, capricious. Starts dealing with T. on p. 81 only. Offers random comments on T.'s poetic technique and includes unpublished letters.

Du Bos, Charles. Les trois impostures, almanach, par P.-J. Toulet. NRF 19:472–76, 1922. *Also in his:* Approximations. Deuxième série. Corrêa, 1932. p. 76–80. **7854**
"Bien plus cependant que dans les maximes, c'est dans la réduction à l'unité d'impressions venues des quatre points de l'horizon, mais perçues et senties simultanément, et comme avec instantanéité, sur le seul plan de l'imagination, que Toulet est incomparable." Suggestive in spite of its shortness.

Duclos, Henri. Toulet et le grand dieu Pan. Div 15:304–15, 1923. **7855**
Perceptive, useful article. Discusses T.'s translation of A. Machen's novel. Concludes that it is ingenious and in general very faithful. Establishes that the three sentences in English in *Monsieur du Paur* are directly borrowed from *The great god Pan*. Traces influence of Machen in other works of T., but like Martineau after him, author emphasizes T.'s own taste for the supernatural.

Legros, Georges. En Arles de Paul-Jean Toulet. CahAT 10:53–67, 1968. **7856**
Sensitive close examination of the poem.

Lièvre, Pierre. P.-J. Toulet. Div 8:97–118, 1920. *Also in his:* Esquisses critiques. La renaissance du livre, 1921. p. 151–71. **7857**
Contains excellent remarks on T.'s style and a perceptive analysis of his disenchantment.

Martineau, Henri. Les vers inédits de P.-J. Toulet. Div 28:145–56, 1936. **7858**
Sketches the evolution of T.'s poetry by means of a description of the contents of *Vers inédits*.

[Paul-Jean Toulet] Div 6:233–332, 1914. **7859**
Special number. Interpretative, often chatty articles by J. Boulenger (same as in ...*Mais l'art est difficile:*, supra), J. L. Vaudoyer, E. Jaloux, H. Clouard, E. Henriot and others.

Paul-Jean Toulet. Bibliothèque nationale. Paris, 1968. xi, 81 p. **7860**
Interesting catalog of T. material (mss., books, photographs, objects) exhibited at the B.N., May–June 1968. Notes by Jean Adhémar and Marie-Christine Angebault.

Rat, Maurice. P.-J. Toulet, poète et latiniste. Div 26:140–46, 1934. **7861**
T. borrows from the Latin and Latin authors for his own special aims. Author finds in the *Contrerimes* similarities of sentence construction and rhythm with Horace's *Odes* and *Epodes*.

———. Les poésies de Toulet et l'anthologie grecque. Div 29:129–34, 1937. **7862**

A brief demonstration of T.'s creative imitation of Rufin and *Asclépiade de Samos.*

Réda, Jacques. Sur les poèmes de Toulet. CahCh 16:77–82, 1972.   **7863**

Personal, provocative article. Argues that T.'s poems, in their disconcerting limpidity, are fascinating ideograms, fulfilling the ultimate function of poetry: "mots restitués au silence et silence pris dans les mots."

Stétié, Salah. Pour Toulet. LetN 19:435–41, 1954.   **7864**

"...l'on n'a rien résolu ni justifié en faisant de l'art de Toulet un *jeu*" (p. 438). Answer to, and rebuttal of, P. O. Walzer's statements in his *Paul-Jean Toulet* (Seghers, 1954).

Toso Rodinis, Giuliana. Toulet. Florence, La nuova Italia, 1967. 182 p. (Il castoro, 12)   **7865**

A very good, sensitive study of T.'s works with detailed analysis of the *Contrerimes.* Includes an interesting, if incomplete, critical bibliography.

La vie et l'œuvre de Paul-Jean Toulet, 1867–1920. Exposition organisée pour célébrer le centenaire de la naissance du poète. Pau. Bibliothèque municipale. Pau, 1967. 40 p.   **7866**

Useful list of items associated with T.'s life and of successive eds. of his works.

Walzer, Pierre-Olivier. Paul-Jean Toulet: l'œuvre, l'écrivain. Avec de nombreux documents inédits. Préf. de Philippe Chabaneix. Eds. des portes de France, 1949. 391 p.   **7867**

The most important book on T. Part I contains well-documented discussion of T.'s development as a novelist and a poet and a study of the composition of his works. In part II, after a chapter devoted to the main themes of the work, author examines T. successively as a moralist, a poet and a stylist. Concludes with assessment of T.'s place in modern poetry. Painstaking and perceptive study which, because of its organization, suffers from some repetition. Includes interesting appendices (VI and VII reproduce four unpublished letters) and exhaustive bibliography.

Reviews: A. Billy in FL 4, Oct. 29, 1949; H. Martineau in Div 42:249–54, 1950.

———. Paul-Jean Toulet et Paul Budry. MerF 337:93–112, 1959.   **7868**

Useful, somewhat condescending account of T.'s collaboration on the *Ecrits nouveaux* with extensive quotations from T.'s letters to P. Budry, the Swiss director of the review.

———. P.-J. Toulet. Inédits, œuvres choisies, bibliographie, portraits, documents. Seghers, 1954. 222 p. (Poètes d'aujourd'hui, 42) *Also:* 1963.   **7869**

General introduction to T. with emphasis on the poet. While based largely on author's comprehensive *thèse,* the essay somehow lacks the balance of the previous work, as Walzer systematically reduces T. to a *petit précieux.*

Review: D. Parmée in FS 9:178–79, 1955.

CHAPTER XVI

GUILLAUME APOLLINAIRE

(Pseud. of Guillaume Albert Wladimir Alexandre Apollinaire Kostrowitzky)

(Nos. 7870–8047)

SCOTT BATES

Bibliography

Adéma, Marcel. Bibliographie générale de l'œuvre de Guillaume Apollinaire. Chez l'auteur, 1949. 101 p. **7870**

First major bibliography. Published works, erotic works (points out that *Le verger des amours* is probably not by A.), prefaces to books and catalogs, writings in journals. Translations and main studies of poet. Essential section to A. student is p. 89–99, a listing of more than 200 articles on A. in 136 periodicals, many of which are not found in later bibliographies. This book is quite rare, having been published in a limited edition.

Décaudin, Michel. Bibliographie. FldDR 1–3, 5–8, March 1954–Dec. 1955. **7871**

Bibliography in every issue with the exception of 4 (Dec. 1954).

———. Bibliographie. GAp 1–11, 1962–72. **7872**

In every number of this publication, continuing bibliographies of Adéma and FldDR. Also includes discography by Jacqueline Bellas (2:169–78, 1963; 5:131–37, 1966; 7:237–42, 1968); bibliography of Hungarian studies (5:128–30, 1966) and of Hungarian translations (6:167–71, 1967) established by György Rába; of English translations from 1940–70 (Peter C. Hoy, 9:183–88, 1970); of Slovakian translations (Viola Cigerova, 9:189–98, 1970); and an index of correspondence by Victor Martin-Schmets, 9:193–98, 1970; 10:129–36, 1971; 11:183–90, 1972. Other bibliographies may be found in separate works as noted *infra;* of special note are those of Warnier for Germany and Poland and Jannini for Italy.

Warnier, Raymond. Etudes apollinariennes dans trois continents. SFr 8:489–91, 1964. **7873**

Work on A. in Poland, Italy, and U.S.; history of A. translations in Japan.

———. Guillaume Apollinaire et l'Allemagne. RLC 28:168–88, 1954. **7874**

General, rather wandering study full of references to the research of Wolf, Adéma, Breunig, etc. Main value is a bibliography with brief commentary on translations and studies of A. in Germany. Continued in RLC 33:573–84, 1959, *Ouvrages français traduits et étudiés en Allemagne.*

Editions

Apollinaire, Guillaume. Alcools. Trans. and ed. by Anne Hyde Greet. Berkeley, Univ. of California press, 1965. 289 p. **7875**

By general critical consensus the most accurate and poetic English trans. of *Alcools* to date. Has original text on facing pages. Ends with 75 p. of notes which explain principal references of poems, biographical and historical contexts, and difficult words. This section, which also contains original discoveries and interpretations of the translator, constitutes a helpful summary of interpretation and guide to the common reader.

Review: L. Breunig in RLM 123–26 (GAp 4):149–50, 1965.

———. Alcools. Ed. by A. E. Pilkington. Oxford, Blackwell, 1970. 162 p. (Blackwell's French texts) **7876**

Textbook ed. of *Alcools* for undergraduates. Brief biography, long introduction on structure and imagery of work, 56 p. of notes at end summarizing main findings of scholars on individual poems. A number of omissions and questionable readings, but in general a good workmanlike introduction for the English-speaking reader.

————. Anecdotiques, Gallimard, 1955. 333 p. **7877**

Collection of A.'s chronicles in MerF 1911–18. Introduction and notes by Marcel Adéma. Best ed. of this work, as it has an index of names, p. 315–26, not included in the Œuvres complètes.

————. Apollinaire et La démocratie sociale. Ed. by Pierre Caizergues. Minard, 1969. 80 p. (Archives des lettres modernes, 101. Archives Guillaume Apollinaire, 1) **7878**

Texts of columns A. wrote for this socialist, anticlerical paper in 1909–10. With brief commentary and notes by a specialist on A.'s journalistic career. Review: C. Tournadre in RHL 71: 325–26, 1971.

————. Chroniques d'art (1902–1918). Ed. by L. C. Breunig. Gallimard, 1960. 524 p. *Trans.*: Apollinaire on art: essays and reviews 1902–1918. Trans. by Susan Suleiman. Viking, 1972. 546 p. (The documents of twentieth-century art) **7879**

Excellent critical edition of A.'s art reviews, originally published in newspapers and little magazines. Covers impressionism, fauvism, cubism, orphism, and futurism and contains some of the earliest appraisals of Picasso, Matisse, Braque, Rousseau, etc. Preface, notes, and index of names. Translation is superior in some ways to the original, as it contains an excellent introduction by Breunig on America's discovery of A. and on his role in France as an art critic, important articles from *Il y a* and a 1912 essay on Black art not included in the French ed., and a selected bibliography.

Reviews: A. Billy in *Avec Apollinaire*, p. 150–54; J. Carre in RR 53:74–75, 1962; A. Chastel in Monde, Feb. 3, 1961; J.-C. Chevalier in RLM 69–70: 102–04, 1962; M. Gauthier in NL Sept. 13, 1962; R. Pouilliart in LR 18:362–64, 1963.

Apollinaire, Guillaume. CTNXN [Poems]. Trans. by M. Koudinov. Moscow, Nauka, 1967. 336 p. **7880**

First major translation into Russian. Accurate translations, fully rhymed, of 14 poems of the *Bestiaire* (with Dufy's woodcuts); 32 poems from *Alcools,* including a remarkably lyrical trans. of *La chanson du mal-aimé;* 23 poems from *Calligrammes;* and more than 35 poems from the other works. No French. All poems punctuated; no calligrams included. Photographs, drawings, notes. Long critical article by N. Balachov on A., literary history of poetry, origins and influence. Explications of a few major poems. A. seen primarily as an innovative realist and humanist; emphasis on Slavic influences and connections (e.g., in the Cossack's letter to the Sultan, in the short story *L'otmika*, etc.). Inexpensive 115,000 copy edition obviously intended to introduce A. to Russian public.
Review: G. Bouatchidzé in RLM 249–53:213–18, 1970.

————. The cubist painters: aesthetic meditations, 1913. Trans. by Lionel Abel. [2nd rev. ed.] Wittenborn, Schultz, 1949. 66 p. (The documents of modern art) **7881**

Good idiomatic translation. Brief preface by Robert Motherwell, notes, and useful critical bibliography by Bernard Karpel of A.'s works relating to modern art and cubism. A few reproductions and photographs.
Review: J. Millquist in SR 14:317–19, 1946.

————. Les diables amoureux. Ed. by Michel Décaudin. Gallimard, 1964. 288 p. **7882**

Collection of prefaces A. wrote between 1908–18 for the series of erotic classics by Sade, Aretino, Mirabeau, Cleland, etc., published by the Bibliothèque des curieux. The essays are uneven and to a great extent cribbed from other works, particularly those of Alcide Bonneau. But as Chevalier points out in his review of the book, this ed. is at the *maquette* stage, and A. would doubtless have revised it considerably had he lived. Includes famous preface of 1917 attacking Baudelaire's decadence. Notes. No table of names.
Reviews: J.-C. Chevalier in RLM 123–26 (GAp 4):140–41, 1965; M.-P.

Fouchet in Exp Dec. 14–20, 1964; Latis in CahCP 28; R. Lacôte in LetF Nov. 23–Dec. 2, 1964; A. Pieyre de Mandiargues in NouvO Dec. 3, 1964.

————. *L'enchanteur pourrissant.* Ed. by Jean Burgos. Lettres modernes, 1972, clxii, 245 [414] p. (Paralogue 5)   **7883**

Large critical edition (official pagination figure deceptive as it does not include many lettered pages of notes; the work actually contains almost 500 pages). The long introduction describes in detail the genesis of the prose poem from 1898 to 1909, its first three editions, its structures, and its significance in A.'s total work. The final, corrected text of 1921 is then given with all variants and with facing pages of exhaustive notes—210 p. of notes to 93 p. of text. Appendices give 16th-c. source of first chapter; unused mss. now in the Fonds Jacques Doucet collection; and a chronology. Bibliography, p. 218–33; indices of *personnages, paysages, thèmes et images;* table of contents. An impressive study of the depth and range of a relatively unknown poem, commonly overlooked or belittled by literary critics; author proves conclusively that its themes and myths are basic to A.'s total ethos. Unfortunately, the work is marred by a large amount of extraneous erudition and a number of dubious sources, unfounded generalities, and especially a dangerous tendency to present conjectures as facts; the first part of the chronology, for the years 1898–1903, for example, is highly questionable. Yet for the most part a solid work of scholarship, essential as a basis for all future research on A.

————. *Méditations esthétiques: les peintres cubistes.* Ed. by L. C. Breunig and J.-Cl. Chevalier. Herman, 1965. 192 p. (Miroirs de l'art)   **7884**

Critical edition. Introduction on genesis, structure of work, and its place in art criticism. Biographical chronology. 10 p. mss. Contains A.'s 1908 essay on André Salmon. A few illustrations and portraits, but none of the reproductions of paintings included in original text. No index or table of contents, yet excellent exegesis and careful historical reconstruction of the life and times of a monument of modern art criticism.

Reviews: H. Béhar in RHL 67:650–51, 1967; P. Daix in LetF July 1, 1965; M. Décaudin in IL 18:29, Jan.-Feb. 1966; I. Lockerbie in RLM 146–49 (GAp 5):142–45, 1966; S. Zoppi in RLMC 19:63–74, 1966.

————. *Œuvres complètes.* Ed. by Michel Décaudin, iconography by Marcel Adéma. Balland et Lecat, 1966. 4 v. with 4 supplementary v. of facsimiles.   **7885**

V. 1, preface by Max-Paul Fouchet, introduction by M. Décaudin. *L'enchanteur pourrissant, L'hérésiarque et cie., Le poète assassiné, La femme assise, contes retrouvés, Les trois Don Juan, Pages d'histoire: chronique des grands siècles de France.* V. 2, *Le flâneur des deux rives, Les diables amoureux,* articles from MerF, articles and criticism from political and literary reviews. V. 3, *Le bestiaire,* with Dufy's woodcuts, *Alcools, Vitam impendere amore, Calligrammes, Il y a, Poèmes à Lou, Le guetteur mélancolique,* poems from letters and papers, *Les mamelles de Tirésias, Couleur du temps, Casanova, L'esprit nouveau et les poètes,* literary criticism from reviews. V. 4, *Les peintres cubistes, Chroniques d'art, Tendre comme le souvenir* and other correspondence (with the exception of *Lettres à Lou*). De luxe ed. with excellent, concise notes by Décaudin. Fairly complete; main omissions are a number of articles, especially those from *La démocratie sociale,* several chapters of *Que faire?, La grâce et le maintien français, Les exploits d'un jeune Don Juan, Les onze mille verges, La fin de Babylone,* and much correspondence. An index of names would have been exceedingly useful. Despite these omissions, work is an indispensable tool for the A. scholar and a fascinating collection for the general reader.

Reviews: L. Breunig in RLM 166–69 (GAp 6):175–79, 1967; P. Vialleneuve in Cr 200:41–53, 1969.

————. *Œuvres poétiques.* Ed. by Marcel Adéma and Michel Décaudin. Gallimard, 1956. 1284 p. (Bibliothèque de la Pléiade)   **7886**

Main ed. of poetic works. Contains poems and plays found in *Œuvres com-*

plètes, supra, with 150 p. of notes and variants. Excellent biographical introduction by André Billy, thorough bibliography of all articles and books dealing with poetry, chronologies of poet's life and published poetic works, alphabetic index of titles, table of contents. Reviews: A. Fongaro in Id March 17, 1957; R. Lacôte in LetF Feb. 21–27, March 7–13, 1957; P. Pia in Car March 13, 1957.

————. Les onze mille verges. L'or du temps, 1970. 223 p. (Bibliothèque privée)   **7887**

Popular ed. of A.'s principal erotic novel with 1930 anonymous preface (by Louis Aragon) which asserts book was considered A.'s masterpiece by Picasso. Critical postface by Toussaint Médecin-Molinier. According to Décaudin's review, this ed. is full of typographical and other errors. Reviews: M. Décaudin in RLM 276–79 (GAp 10):139–40, 1971; R. Jean in QL Dec. 16–31, 1970; P. Pia in MagL Nov. 1970.

————. Le poète assassiné. Ed. by Michel Décaudin. Club du meilleur livre, 1959. 293 p.   **7888**

Best ed. of work published in 1916. Introduction, mss., variants, notes, and stories cut by A. from first ed. Omits many variants, particularly corrections made on proofs, and a number of mss. in the Fonds Jacques Doucet collection of the Bibliothèque Ste-Geneviève in Paris. Review: P. Pia in Car Jan. 6, 1960.

————. Que faire? Ed. by Noëmi Onimus-Blumenkranz. La nouvelle édition, 1950. 285 p.   **7889**

Unique ed. of the *feuilleton* published in *Le Matin* from Feb. to May 1900 by Henry Esnard, for whom A. served as ghostwriter. Editor points out that chapters 12–15 were undoubtedly written by A. and are important indications of the young writer's early interests in the occult, in science fiction, and in the superman. The preface by Jean Marcenac is one of few good studies of A. as a writer of science fiction.

————. Tendre comme le souvenir. Ed. by Marcel Adéma. Gallimard, 1952. 355 p. *Rev. ed.:* Œuvres complètes, v. 4. *See* 7885.   **7890**

First ed. of A.'s letters and poems to his fiancée, Madeleine Pagès, from the Western front in 1915–16. Preface by Mlle Pagès relates her first meeting with A. Many cuts in letters of erotic passages and personal remarks on contemporaries (i.e., Delaunay, Colette). A few non-erotic passages restored in notes, *Œuvres complètes,* v. 4, p. 945–52.

Apollinaire, Guillaume, and André Billy. La Bréhatine, cinéma-drame. Avant-propos et établissement du texte par Claude Tournadre. Lettres modernes, 1971. 117 p. (Archives des lettres modernes, 126. Archives Guillaume Apollinaire, 5)   **7891**

Text of scenario written by A. and Billy in 1917 and sold to a film producer but never produced. Banal Breton love story, but with poetic and ironical touches added by A. Text introduced by studies of genesis and themes of work by Claude Tournadre and of its cinematographic import by Alain Virmaux. Fairly good introduction to the important question of A.'s relation to the cinema, but leaves out any reference to his other, more original "scenario," the story *Un beau film.* The studies also neglect A.'s satire of commercial novels in *La Bréhatine* and his use there of the "lost ring" theme. Best article to date on A. and cinema is Décaudin, *Apollinaire et le cinéma image par image, infra.*

Correspondence

Apollinaire, Guillaume. Lettres à Lou. Ed. by Michel Décaudin. Gallimard, 1969. 530 p.   **7892**

220 letters sent to Louise de Coligny from Sept. 1914 to Jan. 1916. Short introduction on history and chronology of the Lou liaison; notes, photographs. Reviews: M. Décaudin in NouvO 270:35, Jan. 12–18, 1970; R. Lacôte in LetF Jan. 14–20, 1970; J. Moulin in An 238:54, Aug. 1970; F. Nourissier in NL Jan. 1, 1970; P. Pia in QL Jan. 16–31, 1970; M. Slonim in TBR Feb. 15, 1970. F. de Towarnich in Exp Jan. 12–18, 1970.

Iconography

Adéma, Pierre-Marcel, and Michel Décaudin. Album Apollinaire. Gallimard, 1971. 320 p. (Albums de la Pléiade, 10)   **7893**

Biography with anywhere from 1 to 5 black-and-white illustrations per page, many of them unpublished. Portraits, post cards, paintings, mss., official papers, letters, etc. Popular, unscholarly presentation, yet very accurate text. Unfortunately, format is so small as to make many of the photos, especially those of handwritten material, virtually useless. Still, a good illustrated guide to poet's life and works, complementing Cailler.

Review: L. Lelan in RLM 327-30 (GAp 11):194, 1972.

Apollinaire. Bibliothèque nationale, 1969. 174 p.   **7894**

Catalog of the 573 exhibits of the 50th-anniversary Bibliothèque nationale exhibition of 1968. Preface, *Présence d'Apollinaire,* by Michel Décaudin. Chronological list of exhibits taken from libraries, museums, and private collections. Many *inédits.* Summary biography with, however, many factual errors.

Review: A. Caxton in RLM 249-53 (GAp 9):201-03, 1970.

Cailler, Pierre. Guillaume Apollinaire, documents iconographiques. Geneva, Cailler, 1965. n.p. (Visages d'hommes célèbres)   **7895**

Black-and-white photographs with minimal text of titles and brief explanations. Arranged in 6 sections: (1) family portraits; (2) A.'s residences; (3) official papers; (4) portraits of A.; (5) calligrams, mss., and a few drawings; and (6) A.'s own art collection. Last section particularly interesting, contains photos of rare Derains, Dufys, Picassos, Chiricos, Laurencins, Vlamincks, etc., some of which are referred to in writings of A.

Review: M. Poupon in RLM 166-69 GAp 6):107-24, 1967.

Biography

Adéma, Marcel. Guillaume Apollinaire le mal-aimé. Plon, 1952. 296 p. *Also (rev.):* Guillaume Apollinaire. La table ronde, 1968. 390 p. (Les vies perpendiculaires) *Trans.:* Apollinaire. Trans. by Denise Folliot. Grove, 1955. 298 p.   **7896**

First and principal biography of A. Second ed. thoroughly revised, much new material added, letters, mss., photographs. A somewhat prosaic chronological history of the man not the poet, factual, anecdotic, little psychological or literary criticism. Careful tracing of A.'s origins and his Italian father; convincing refutation of Polish thesis of Napoleonic ancestry. Bibliography, p. 349-71, in revised ed. A starting point for all A. scholarship.

Reviews: A. Billy in FL Dec. 23-29, 1968; M. Décaudin in RLM 217-22 (GAp 8):239, 1969; R. Lacôte in LetF Dec. 31, 1968-Jan. 7, 1969; M. Poupon in Monde Sept. 6, 1969.

Boisson, Madeleine. En marge des Lettres à Lou. RLM 380-84 (GAp 12): 45-65, 1973.   **7897**

Precise biographical details concerning A.'s sojourn in Nice in the fall of 1914 and his liaison there with Louise de Coligny. Many new facts gathered from an interview with Lou's cousin, the countess Edmée de Marotte de Montigny, at whose seaside villa at Saint-Jean-Cap-Ferrat she was residing.

Bouret, Jean. Une amitié esthétique au début du siècle: Apollinaire et Paul Guillaume (1911-1918) d'après une correspondance inédite. GazBA 76:373-99, 1970.   **7898**

A. and Guillaume met through A.'s interest in African sculpture in Guillaume's shop window in 1911. Very close relationship through 1914. A. introduced art dealer to Picabia and Chirico; they went to Ballets Russes together. A. dubious about Modigliani, preferred Kisling, but wrote Guillaume, "N'oubliez pas qu'ils sont juifs et tenezvous à carreau" (Sept. 7, 1915). Friendship remained close after 1916. Most letters of minor importance.

Caizergues, Pierre. Apollinaire et la politique pendant la guerre. RLM 380-84 (GAp 12): 67-101, 1973.   **7899**

A.'s journalistic political positions and fairly conventional ideas on Allied strategy and German villainy during his year of active service in the Army (1915). His growing conservatism of the 1916–18 period when he shared certain ideas with Charles Maurras and Léon Daudet. His ambivalent socialism in the prewar period. Stressed are his anglophobia and germanophobia, his admiration for Clemenceau, his initial sympathy with the Russian revolution turning to criticism of restrictions of individual freedom ·in Russia. Important *inédits* include an article of 1917 against the Russian aristocracy, and a letter urging a policy of military pillage in Germany.

Dalliouse, Joseph. [Letter on Apollinaire]. *Nice-Matin,* Nov. 26, 1966.   **7900**

Letter from school friend of A. from 1893–98, on "Wilhelm's" study habits, his temper, his care in reworking mss. of poems, his literary reunions of friends. Part of three articles by Pierre Humbourg on A. at Nice in the *Nice-Matin* Sept. 5, 15, and Nov. 26, 1966.

Diviš, Vladimir. Apollinaire, chronique de la vie du poète. Prague, Artia, 1967. 149 p.   **7901**

Chronological biography of poet, year by year, with many photographs. A few factual errors. Most original contribution is study of A.'s relations with Czechoslovakia, his visit in 1902, his later reputation there and Czech translations of his works.

Review: M. Décaudin in RLM 183–88 (GAp 7):247, 19–68.

Faure-Favier, Louise de. Guillaume · Apollinaire et la musique *In:* Guillaume Apollinaire. *See* 7926. p. 15–22.   **7902**

Anecdotes on A.'s incompetence and/ or indifference in matters of music by a friend. The music of *Les mamelles de Tirésias.* A.'s friendship with Eric Satie. An evening with Vincent d'Indy in 1918.

————. Souvenirs sur Apollinaire. Grasset, 1945. 244 p.   **7903**

Memoirs of a close friend of A. from Sept. 1912 until his death in 1918. Author, also friend of Marie Laurencin, documents her liaison with poet, their rupture. Dialogued, anecdotic, often inaccurate, delightfully written, and important source of much biographical information not found elsewhere.

Reviews: R. Kemp in NL Dec. 27, 1945; J. Lapp in FR 21:71–73, 1947.

Fettweiss, Christian. Apollinaire en Ardenne. Brussels, Henriquez, 1934. 98 p.   **7904**

History of A.'s stay with his brother Albert in Stavelot, Belgium, in Aug.– Sept. 1899 while his mother was gambling at Spa. References to Ardennes in works of A. Photographs.

Fleuret, Fernand. Guillaume Apollinaire. *In his:* De Gilles de Rais à Guillaume Apollinaire. Mercure de France, 1933. p. 283–93.   **7905**

Reminscences of rambles with A. during the period both men were collaborating on *L'enfer de la Bibliothèque nationale.* Tells of their cult for Casanova and various Renaissance and 18th-c. works. Short descriptions of A. taking Remy de Gourmont on walks and to bordellos (p. 212–14) and of Raoul Dufy cutting wood plates for *Le bestiaire* (p. 271, 276–77).

Gabory, Georges. Apollinaire ou la leçon d'écriture. KRQ 14:89–98, 1967.   **7906**

Irreverent anecdotes by a former friend of Max Jacob about A. in 1917, his pontifical attitudes, his slander of Marie Laurencin, his banishment of Radiguet. Vivid description of the first (and last) night of *Les mamelles de Tirésias.*

Gleizes, Albert. Apollinaire, la justice et moi. *In:* Guillaume Apollinaire. *See* 7926. p. 53–65.   **7907**

Significant testimony concerning A.'s arrest in Sept. 1911. Tells how his intercession with le Substitut Granier, an influential magistrate at the Palais de Justice, led to the suppression of the case. Also how Granier stopped judicial pursuit of A. for publishing erotic classics, and how he saved him from a spying charge during World War I.

Hartwig, Julia. Apollinaire. Trans. from Polish into French by Jean-Yves Erhel. Mercure de France, 1972. 417 p.   **7908**

Lyrical, anecdotic biography, yet based on historical research, interviews with A.'s friends, etc. Not completely reliable as to facts, yet often effective in establishing tone of *la belle époque,* the characters, customs, and activities of Montmartre and Montparnasse. Effusive, over-rich in psychological description. By a leading Polish translator of A.'s poetry.

Jacob, Max. Chronique des temps héroïques, illustré de dessins gravés sur bois et de lithographies et pointes sèches originales par Pablo Picasso. Paris, 1956. 126 p. **7909**

Rare work (ed. limited to 170 copies) written in 1936–37 ostensibly in memory of Paul Guillaume. Chapters 5 and 6 devoted to A., with many references to him throughout. Violent, unsympathetic portrait of his mother. Anecdotes concerning Picasso, Jarry, Marinetti. Fanciful, elegiac, satirical, confused (intentionally?) as to facts, an important testimony to the love-hate relationship of two great poets who were too idiosyncratic and close to get along well together.
Review: L. Breunig in RLM 166–69: 179–82, 1967.

————. Fox. LetF Oct. 22–28, 1964. **7910**
Memories of first meeting A. in bar, of Picasso first discovering Black art at Matisse's, of two refrains A. sang on which he built rhythms for his poetry, etc.

Luca, Toussaint. Guillaume Apollinaire, souvenirs d'un ami. Monaco, Eds. du rocher, 1954. 138 p. **7911**
Delightful reminiscences by a classmate and companion at Nice lycée, their adventures on the Riviera together. Collaboration on the review *Festin d'Esope* in 1903–04. A.'s 1908 lecture on modern poets. A. and Henri Rousseau. How Luca helped A. get out of prison. Early correspondence. Illustrated with 10 sketches by A., some of them very significant symbolically. Preface and notes by Marcel Adéma.

Mackworth, Cecily. Guillaume Apollinaire and the cubist life. London, John Murray, 1961. 244 p. *Also:* New York, Horizon, 1963. **7912**
Picturesque biography, with many translations of articles by A. Some minor misinformation. Best chapters are on painter and poet friends and on life in the ateliers of Montmartre.
Reviews: M. Décaudin in RLM 69–70:99–100, 1062; R. Shattuck in TBR

May 12, 1963; B. Wall in TC 169: 311–13, 1961.

Michaud, Guy. Comme un guetteur mélancolique, essai sur la personnalité d'Apollinaire. RLM 276–79 (GAp 10):7–34, 1971. **7913**
Attempt to combine morphopsychology (study of facial structure), graphology, and astrology in arriving at a unified portrait of A.'s personality. Finds him a mixture of the *plastique* (social, outgoing) and the *mou* (vulnerable, melancholy), with high development of the upper and lower sections of the face, i.e., the cerebral-nervous and the instinctive-digestive. Final section is good résumé of astrological data of A.'s birth and career, mainly important because he was aware of them and used them in his writings. A technical and questionable essay in the new "science" of *caractérologie,* using the latest hypotheses of Louis Corman, G. G. Granger, Le Senne, R. Mucchielli, and others.

Mollet, Jean. Les mémoires du baron Mollet. Gallimard, 1963. 200 p. **7914**
Anecdotes by a close associate and literary assistant of A. A.'s anarchism, his friendship with Bourges, Picasso, Marinetti, his writing of *Le poète assassiné,* and his editing of the two reviews *Le festin d'Esope* and *Les soirées de Paris.* Work complemented by author's brief later memoir, *Lettres à Guillaume Apollinaire* (Liège, Dynamo, 1968, 16 p.).
Review: L. Lelan in RLM 104–07 (GAp 3):153–54, 1964.

Mollet, [Jean] Baron. Soirées à Paris et ballets russes avec Guillaume Apollinaire. LetF 8:3, Nov. 11, 1948. **7915**
Reminiscences, some of them also in *Mémoires, supra.* A. with Serge Férat, Paul Guillaume, Picasso, etc. Anecdotes concerning *Le musicien de Saint-Merry, Le roi-lune, Le poète assassiné* and *Zone.* As usual, delightful.

Montfort, Eugène. La véritable histoire de Louise Lalanne ou le poète d'Alcools travesti en femme. Les marges, n.d. *Another ed.:* Apollinaire travesti. Seghers, 1948. 26 p. **7916**

Lively account of A.'s literary hoax in 1909 when he reviewed contemporary feminine works (by Colette, Jane Catulle-Mendès, etc.) for *Les marges* under the pseudonym of Louise Lalanne. By his editor and collaborator in the hoax.

Onimus, James. Souvenirs. LetF 392, Dec. 13, 1951. **7917**

Portrait of A. as an adolescent on the Riviera by a former friend and schoolmate. Collaborated together on an abortive novel, *Orindiculo*. Later wrote him from Paris (a few letters in *Œuvres complètes*, v. 4, p. 714–18).

Pia, Pascal. Les paradis artificiels, de Baudelaire à Apollinaire. MagL 34:9–12, Nov. 1969. **7918**

On use of drugs by various writers including A. Includes letter from a journalist who claims to have met A. in a *fumerie* on the Avenue Henri Martin on the night of July 31, 1914; they all left about 6:00 or 7:00 in the morning, A. with three girls.

Salmon, André. Souvenirs sans fin. Gallimard, 1955–61. 3 v. **7919**

Reminiscences of one of A.'s earliest and best friends. Many references to A. throughout. Particularly noteworthy are passages in v. 1 (p. 53–55) on A.'s recital at the *caveau* Le soleil d'or of *Schinderhannes* and *L'ermite* (elsewhere Salmon has said A. read *Le larron* instead of *L'ermite*); on A.'s "peur de manquer" (p. 86); on the first sketch of *Les mamelles de Tirésias* in 1903 (p. 109); on his scatological interests (p. 113–14); on his *grandes grues* (p. 161); and on his mother and brother (p. 311–12).

Severini, Gino. Apollinaire et le futurisme. XXs 13–17, June 1952. **7920**

One of the original futurists discusses history of his friendship with A.

Vergnes, Georges. Le substitut Granié et Guillaume Apollinaire. RevA 46–54, Jan.–June 1959. **7921**

Two letters and a telegram to Granié, from which only a part of one letter is printed in the *Œuvres complètes*. Several valuable biographical indications, including the opinion that Derain is the most important modern French painter (Nov. 8, 1915) and that he fears that he will not get the Légion d'honneur (Dec. 30, 1917).

Collected Articles

Apollinaire. Saggi di R. Warnier, M. Décaudin, P. A. Jannini, M. L. Belleli, L. Tarantino, S. Zoppi. Ed. by M. Bonfantini. Turin, Giappichelli; Paris, Nizet, 1970. 149 p. **7922**

Collection of critical essays. For articles of Décaudin, *Apollinaire et le cinéma image par image*, and Belleli, *Ricchezza di temi nel Bestiaire di G. Apollinaire*, see separate headings. R. Warnier in *Bribes pour un tombeau d'Apollinaire* (p. 1–17) gives general résumé of state of A. studies in Europe and Japan in 1968 and before. A. Jannini in *Apollinaire e Louis de Gonzague Frick* (p. 29–36) pinpoints the relationship of these two old school friends and poets. Tarantino, *Ingres e Cezanne visti da Apollinaire* (p. 109–26), finds that A.'s attitudes towards these artists anticipate modern views. S. Zoppi traces history of A.'s maternal family in Italy (*I Kostrowitzky a Roma*, p. 127–45).

Reviews: M. Streiff in CulF 18:101–02, 1971; C. Tournadre in RLM 327–30 (GAp 11):195–98, 1972.

Apollinaire et la musique, actes du colloque, Stavelot, 27–29 août 1965, réunis par Michel Décaudin. Stavelot, Eds. Les amis de G. Apollinaire, 1967. 108 p. **7923**

Arsène Soreil, *Jeu et musicalité poétiques*, p. 13–19; Philippe Renaud, *Ondes, ou les métamorphoses de la musique*, p. 21–32; Robert Guiette, *Rosemonde*, p. 33–38; Margaret Davies, *La petite musique d'Apollinaire*, p. 43–48; Jacqueline Bellas, *Apollinaire et Poulenc: peut-on mettre Alcools en musique?*, p. 49–57; Raymond Pouilliart, *Apollinaire et quelques musiciens*, p. 59–67; Robert Couffignal, *Genèse de Zone*, p. 73–80; S. I. Lockerbie, *Qu'est-ce que l'Orphisme d'Apollinaire?*, p. 81–87; Arlette Lafont, *Hommage à Serge Férat*, p. 89–93. Article by Philippe Renaud analyzed separately. Résumés of discussions following papers. In appendices list of musicians having set A. poems to music and list of the poems.

Reviews: A. Fongaro in SFr 39: 513–16, 1968; P. Pia in Car July 12, 1967.

Les critiques de notre temps et Apollinaire. Ed. by Claude Tournadre. Garnier, 1971. 191 p. (Les critiques de notre temps, 5) 7924

Collection of excerpts from leading books and articles covering biography, *Alcools, Calligrammes,* lesser works, and esthetics. More theoretical than factual. Short selections; no complete texts; primarily criticism of the 1960's. A good panorama, an *état présent,* of wide divergence of critical approaches. Brief chronology of life. Introduction by editor gives brief history of A. criticism. Work ends with excellent bibliography of principal critical works.

Reviews: M. Décaudin in RLM 327–30 (GAp 11):195, 1972; A. Grini in CulF 18:113, 1971.

Du monde européen à l'univers des mythes, actes du colloque de Stavelot, 1968, réunis par Michel Décaudin. Minard, 1970. 191 p. (Bibliothèque Guillaume Apollinaire des lettres modernes, 5) 7925

Robert Goffin, *Apollinaire et ses amis,* p. 13–19; Robert Guiette, *Le cri des Neuf de la Renommée,* p. 20–30; Mechthild Cranston, *Voyage en Rhénanie,* p. 33–47; Vladimir Brett, *Apollinaire et les Tchèques,* p. 48–64; Etienne Schoonhoven, *Apollinaire et la poésie néerlandaise,* p. 65–78; Pierre Caizergues, *Apollinaire et la politique européenne,* p. 79–90; Scott Bates, *Deux mystères apollinariens,* p. 91–102; Victor Martin-Schmets, *La correspondance de Guillaume Apollinaire,* p. 103–13; Jean Burgos, *Apollinaire et le recours au mythe,* p. 117–31; Marc Poupon, *Lul de Faltenin et l'étymologie,* p. 132–51; Lionel Follet, *Les sept épées, débat,* p. 152–63, with additional comment by P.-P. Gossiaux, p. 164–70, and a final note by Follet, p. 171. Articles by Burgos and Poupon are analyzed separately. Each article followed by discussion. Volume ends with an appendix listing mss. in Stavelot Apollinaire Museum, established by Victor Martin-Schmets.

Reviews: H. Gershman in BA 45:

658, 1971; B. Jourdan in Liv 173:63, 1971; M. Lauren in AuvL 209-10, 1971.

Guillaume Apollinaire. Souvenirs et témoignages inédits de Louis de Gonzague Frick [et al.] réunis et présentés par Marcel Adéma. Albi, Tête noire, 1946. 91 p. (Cahier spécial de Rimes et raisons) 7926

Significant articles have been analyzed separately.

Que vlo-ve? Bulletin de l'association internationale des amis de Guillaume Apollinaire. Ed. by Victor Martin-Schmets. Namur, 1973—. 7927

Michel Décaudin, *L'affaire des statuettes et la presse belge,* 1:7–11, Jan. 1973; P. M. Adéma, *Une plaque, un mémorial,* 2:5–14, 1973; François Duysinx, *La Bréhatine et nous,* 3:9–13, 1974; *Articles d'hommage pour Armand Huysmans, 1907–74,* 4:1974; Marcel Lobet, *L'amitié d'Apollinaire et de Louis de Gonzague Frick,* 5:5–24, 1975; Monique Jutrin, *Calligrames: une poésie "engagée"?,* 5:27–42, 1975. Information, documents, notes, reviews, bibliography, appreciations, and articles from the association whose headquarters are the Apollinaire museum at Stavelot, Belgium.

General Studies

Balakian, Anna. Apollinaire and the modern mind. YFS 2:79–90, 1949. *Also in her:* Surrealism, the road to the absolute. Dutton, 1970. p. 80–99. 7928

Summary of attitudes toward scientific discovery and scientism, from mistrust in *Le poète assassiné* to conciliation in *L'esprit nouveau et les poètes.* His break with symbolism and the *mal du siècle,* and the influence of his optimistic metaphysic of imaginative estheticism on the surrealists. Does not treat subject of science fiction. Slightly revised in 1970 ed. to include more on *L'enchanteur pourrissant* and *Alcools.*

Barrère, Jean-Bertrand. Apollinaire obscène et tendre. RSH 84:373–90, 1956. 7929

General, impressionistic study of A.'s eroticism. Comparison with that of Villon, Hugo, Rimbaud, Verlaine, and Mallarmé; finds little Baudelairean sense of sin, little mysticism (this article appeared before certain wartime letters to Louise de Coligny, full of erotic transcendentalism, were published). But does find need for profanation as in Huysmans. Main omission is influence of Mme de Kostrowitzky on his sado-masochistic tendencies.

Bates, Scott. Petit glossaire des mots libres d'Apollinaire. Sewanee, Tennessee, Chez l'auteur, 1975. 117 p. **7930**

Glossary of erotic terms. Comprehensive lists of metaphors for sexual actions and for parts of body, of which those for *sexe de l'homme* (169) and for *sexe de la femme* (132) are most numerous. Explanations and sources of many unusual and obscure expressions, such as *cordeau, jeu de la grande oie, libellule, merde de pape, Mony, Pata, zon*, etc. Gives as a main source for A.'s folk erotology the *Kryptádia*, from which he drew the Cosaques Zaporogues passage in *La chanson du mal-aimé*. Very limited edition.

————. Guillaume Apollinaire. Twayne, 1967. 204 p. (Twayne world authors series, 14) **7931**

Analysis of major themes and symbols in principal works, arranged chronologically, with explications of key poems (*Un soir, Le larron, La chanson du mal-aimé, Les fiançailles*, etc.). Traces particularly theme of A. as a secular Christ-Antichrist attempting to bring a New Jerusalem of art to the 20th c. Chronology of poet's life and of the poems of *Alcools*. Appendices have a glossary of 300 difficult terms and references and a list of erotic metaphors. Index of names and works.
Reviews: A. Greet in FR 42:327–28, 1968 and in RLM 183–88:245–47, 1968; F. Kalister in SHR 2:375–76, 1968; P. Pia in Car July 12, 1967.

Bellas, Jacqueline. Apollinaire devant la musique et les musiciens. RLM 217–222: 114–40, 1969. **7932**

One of the best of many articles summarizing A.'s positions on music. Demonstrates that even though he claimed to know little about it, serious music was for him a stimulator of poetic thought, and that he appreciated the best composers of his time. Does not discuss his preferences in popular music. Ends by summarizing problems of setting A.'s poems to music and analyzes a few works of Poulenc, by far his best interpreter (among many).

Bergman, Pär. Guillaume Apollinaire et les discussions sur la simultanéité de 1912 à 1914. *In his:* Modernolatria et simultaneità. Uppsala, Bonniers, 1962. p. 337–411. **7933**

A.'s relation to modern movements in Italy and France, primarily from 1909 to 1914. Influence on him of futurism, cubism, Barzun, Delaunay, Cendrars, and Marinetti. Carefully documents ambivalent, evolving relationship with Marinetti and futurism, showing that A. had definite futurist leanings—more towards *simultaneità* than *modernolatria*—and that his futurist manifesto of 1913 was more carefully prepared and less of a joke than has been thought. Documents A.'s modernism and finds it begins mainly in the summer of 1912. *Zone* his first simultaneous, cinematographic poem; *Fantômas* a major influence on his cosmic vision; the poems of *Ondes* his most simultaneous ones. Good bibliography on futurism (p. 412–40). The remainder of work before this chapter has many references to A. and is a good basic study on the influence of futurism in France.
Review: M. Décaudin in RLM 104–07 (GAp 3):181–82, 1963.

Berry, David. Apollinaire and the Tantalus complex. AJFS 9:55–79, 1972. **7934**

Rapid survey of food imagery and themes in prose and poetry with emphasis on erotic import. A. creates a sacred and profane feast of poetry but, like Tantalus, remains continually unsatisfied.

————. Apollinaire et la poétique de l'œil. RHL 70:640–652, 1970. **7935**

Theme of visual imagery in total work, from the stellar eyes of the Beloved and the solar eye of Poetry to the poet's ubiquitous Argus eyes, reflecting the universe (end of *Onirocritique*).

Billy, André. Avec Apollinaire, souvenirs inédits. Paris, Geneva, La palatine, 1966. 176 p.   **7936**

Assorted Apollinariana, much of it quite trivial, by a friend and close associate of the poet. Of special interest are chapter 5, on the review founded by Billy and other friends for A., *Les soirées de Paris,* and chapter 7, on A.'s addresses.

Reviews: F. Conem in RSH 122–23: 317–19, 1966; P. Dermée in ImP 49–50, Jan.–Feb. 1967.

———. Apollinaire vivant. La sirène, 1923. 125 p.   **7937**

The first and still one of the best book-length portraits of A., written by one of his closest friends during the years 1910–18. Anecdotic, elegiac, but also critical and humanist; it tends to underplay A.'s modernism (it is obviously anti-dadaist) and emphasize his Rabelaisian universality. Particularly valuable passages on René Dalize, A.'s terror after his 1911 arrest, the history of *Les soirées de Paris,* A.'s love of food, his war correspondence, and his character changes and activities from 1916–18. Believes he died primarily from his war wound. Final pages have Billy's letters to A. during the war.

———. Guillaume Apollinaire. Seghers, 1947. 246 p. (Poètes d'aujourd'hui, 8)   **7938**

Preface (p. 9–40) to a selection of A.'s poems. Main events of life and some psychological analysis. Less anecdotic than *Apollinaire vivant* to which it serves as supplement. A. as the last great French Romantic poet.

Boisson, Madeleine. Orphée et anti-Orphée dans l'œuvre d'Apollinaire. RLM 249–53 (GAp 9):7–43, 1970.   **7939**

The Orphic solar myth appears in imagery relating to onanism, castration, and lyrical transcendency in various works, particularly *Le roi-lune, La chanson du mal-aimé, Vendémiaire,* and *Lul de Faltenin.* For the narrative line of the latter poem a striking parallel is found in the legend of Butes, the Argonaut who threw himself into the sea after the Sirens but who was saved by Orpheus. Textual analysis of *Le roi lune,* giving valuable literary and historical sources.

Bonnet, Marguerite. Aux sources du surréalisme: place d'Apollinaire. RLM 104–07 (GAp 3):38–74, 1964.   **7940**

Influence of A. on Breton, Soupault, and Aragon from 1917–24. He introduced them to Sade (p. 68). Their changing attitudes towards him. Place of A. in *L'allure poétique* of Jacques Baron, in *Le fard des Argonautes* and *L'ode à coco* of Robert Desnos, and in *Désert de mains* of Michel Leiris. Her conclusion, refuted by Henri Meschonnic in *Illuminé au milieu d'ombres, infra,* p. 161, is that while A.'s poetry was a liberating force for the surrealists, it did not go as far as their works—or the works of Lautréamont and Rimbaud—in seeking to change life and establish a new reality.

Bowra, C. M. Order and adventure in Guillaume Apollinaire. *In his:* The creative experiment. London, Macmillan, 1949. p. 61–93.   **7941**

General, often inaccurate, but warm and intelligent appreciation of A.'s contribution to modern poetry. Many quotations. Emphasizes spontaneous, life-supporting muse, simplicity, sensuousness, guiltlessness. One of the first serious critical studies of A. in English, with the first structural analysis of *La chanson du mal-aimé* in any language.

Breton, André. Guillaume Apollinaire. *In his:* Les pas perdus. Gallimard, 1924. p. 25–45.   **7942**

Famous celebration, written with the encouragement of the poet himself, of A. as *annonciateur,* lyrical innovator, libertarian, eroticist, tale-spinner, enchanter. Admires especially *Calligrammes, L'hérésiarque et cie., Le poète assassiné.* Dated 1917. In same collection, passage from Breton's 1922 lecture in which he regards A. as "le dernier poète" with great failings—artiness, love of trivia, war poetry—but with commendable love of license (p. 203–05).

Breunig, Leroy C. Guillaume Apollinaire. Columbia univ. press, 1969. 48 p. (Columbia essays on modern writers, 46)   **7943**

A leading Apollinarian's balanced appraisal of the strengths and weaknesses of the poet. Chronological review of major poems from *L'ermite* to *La jolie rousse*. Emphasizes A.'s multi-directional, intuitive lyricism, his creative *incertitude*, the universality of his modern sensibility; deemphasizes his professional modernism, his revolutionary estheticism, his messianism. Reviews: A. Fongaro in SFr 15:188, 1971; C. Morhange-Bégué in RLM 249–53 (GAp 9):207–08, 1970.

———. The laughter of Apollinaire. YFS 31:66–73, 1964. **7944**
Examples of A.'s self-destructive laughter, his black humor, prophetic in its resemblance to the laughter of the absurd in the '50's and '60's.

Burgos, Jean. Apollinaire et le recours au mythe. *In:* Du monde européen à l'univers des mythes. *See* 7925. p. 117–27. **7945**
Principal myths in A.'s work: Prometheus, the fall, the Antichrist, erotic metamorphosis, redemptive Beauty, the eternal return, and resurrection. Psychological procedures realized by poet in his thematic and imagistic use of myth: *travestissement,* disguising of biographical self and creating of poetic self through fictional character; *justification* of poet's supremacy through the verb, his ubiquitous conquest of universe, even after Icarian fall; and *mémorisation,* refusal of oblivion and inclusion of past and present in simultaneous poetic vision. Good summing-up, based on author's exhaustive study of *L'enchanteur pourrissant, supra.*

———. Pour une approche de l'univers imaginaire d'Apollinaire. RLM 276–79 (GAp 10):35–67, 1971. **7946**
Based on Jung's definition of the image as "à la fois une expression momentanée du conscient et de l'inconscient" (p. 39). Analysis of three main groups of themes: (1) *éloignement,* the removal of external, false world and its replacement by poet's own *irréalités vraies;* (2) *séparation,* the cubist-like fragmentation of self and the self's creation (in prosody, past, parts of the body, etc.); and (3) *agrandissement,* the simultaneous filling of a *présent spatialisé* with a ubiquitous multiplication of the self and its vision in a conquest of time and space. These three themes extended by final theme of the constant confrontation of contraries, not for synthesis, but for Promethean victory over universe through dynamic change. Burgos places themes in a psychotic structure of schizophrenia to demonstrate how A. used image as a retreat from the world and a defense against time. A thoughtful, profound study. For a semiclinical approach, however, there is a noticeable absence of any discussion of the sexuality of the imagery, the castration of *séparation,* the Don Juanism of *agrandissement,* etc.

Butor, Michel. Monument de rien pour Apollinaire. NRF 147:503–14; 148:694–708, 1965. *Also in his:* Répertoire III. Eds. de minuit, 1968. p. 269–305. *Trans.:* Monument of nothing for Apollinaire. Trans. by Richard Howard. TriQ 4:23–40, 1965. **7947**
A. as precursor of modern style with his calligrams, suppression of punctuation for necessary ambiguity and surprise, cosmopolitanism, use of graffiti, puns, etc. Examples from *Calligrammes, Zone, Que vlo-ve?, La chanson du mal-aimé,* introduction to *Fanny Hill, Le roi-lune,* and *Les fenêtres.*

Cadou, René-Guy. Guillaume Apollinaire ou l'artilleur de Metz. Nantes, Chiffoleau, 1948. 150 p. **7948**
On A.'s eroticism as principal source of his lyricism (*L'artilleur de Metz* is a bawdy song). Most original chapters: 6, on underground works; 8, on affinities with Rabelais.

———. Testament d'Apollinaire. Debresse, 1945. 190 p. **7949**
Lyrical appreciation of A. at the 25th anniversary of his death, by a leading French poet. Often incorrect factually, but a well-written, moving *témoignage.* Reviews: R. Kemp in NL Dec. 27, 1945; J. Lapp in FR 21:71–73, 1947.

Caxton, Austin. Apollinaire et l'Avalon des avalés. LetN 131–45, Sept.–Oct. 1969. **7950**
Brilliant dialog between author and "Jean-Baptiste Ange Toussaint Moroni"

commemorating 50th anniversary of A.'s death. Basically on *jardin terrestre* theme, ranges far and wide, opening many new possibilities for scholarly investigation into A.'s messianism.

Chevalier, Jean-Claude. La poésie d'Apollinaire et le calembour. Eur 44:56–76, 1966.   **7951**

Touchstone article by a noted grammarian and linguist on A.'s use of language, particularly the pun. Shows how puns, including paranomasia and alliteration, involve metaphors in their relation to symbols and calligrams, expressing A.'s *profanation* of a Godless world of unrequited love and his *conception* of a new, ordered, moral world. Analysis of the creative role puns play in *La montre, Le brasier, Rosemonde, Vendémiaire,* etc. This article serves as an excellent introduction to author's admirable linguistic treatise, *Alcools d'Apollinaire, infra.*

Clancier, Anne. Ebauche d'une étude psychocritique de l'œuvre de Guillaume Apollinaire. RLM 327–30 (GAp 11):7–39, 1972.   **7952**

Brief, classical Freudian analysis of primary themes, viz. *castration, contenant-contenu, amour dangereux, stades de la libido* (sadistic anal regression found to be prevalent), *oralité, narcissisme, Imagos parentales, mythe personnel* (anal-sadistic mastery of object), *le double sombre, idéal du moi,* and *recherche d'une identité.* Basic subconscious personality is phallic-narcissistic with great castration anguish. Somewhat superficial and insufficiently researched, but with several original interpretations of individual works, e.g., *L'Infirme divinisé* as phallus (no mention of *Le musicien de Saint-Merry* or *Chantre*); and *Le brasier,* part 3, and *Les colchiques* as poems of mother lovehatred.

Couffignal, Robert. Apollinaire. Desclée De Brouwer, 1966. 144 p. (Les écrivains devant Dieu, 10)   **7953**

Short literary biography of A. from Catholic point of view. A. presented as messiah who abandoned Catholic orthodoxy for a kingdom of art. Covers same material as *L'inspiration biblique dans l'œuvre de Guillaume Apollinaire,* but

more popular presentation and fewer exegeses.

Reviews: J.-C. Chevalier in RHL 68:146–48, 1968; A. Fonteyn in RLM 166–69:182–84, 1967; C. Gothot-Mersch in RLV 35:334, 1969; J.-L. Jacques in SynB 248:128–29, 1967; B. Robert in Droit Feb. 25, 1967.

————. L'inspiration biblique dans l'œuvre de Guillaume Apollinaire. Minard, 1966. 212 p. (Bibliothèque des lettres modernes, 8)   **7954**

An examination of more than 200 biblical references in A.'s works to show how he evolved from a Catholic heretic to the prophet of a secular religion of art. Explications of key stories and poems, notably *Simon Mage, La chanson du mal-aimé, Un soir, Les collines,* and *Zone,* the last of which is considered to be a great religious poem. Excellent section on A.'s Catholic upbringing. Fairly thorough, but omission of important influences from Revelation and the Song of Solomon (for the latter, see Follet and Poupon, *Lecture de Palais d'Apollinaire*). Also slights important semi-religious poems like *Le brasier, Les fiançailles* and *Vendémiaire.* Selected bibliography and list of number of biblical borrowings in each work (without identifying them, however). Proves in general that both the Bible and the various Catholic Church services played an important role in all of A.'s work.

Reviews: S. Bates in FR 42:326–27, 1968; J.-C. Chevalier in RHL 68:146–49, 1968; B. Duchatelet in FrB 37, 1967; A. Fonteyne in RLM 166–69 (GAp 6): 182–84, 1967; Y. Le Hir in Liv 7:18, Oct. 1967; P. Pia in Car July 12, 1967: R. Pouilliart in LR 22:287–88, 1968.

Davies, Margaret. Apollinaire. Edinburgh, London, Oliver and Boyd, 1964. 312 p. (Biography and criticism, 5) *Also:* New York, St. Martin's press, 1964.   **7955**

Excellent literary biography, well-written, penetrating. Extensive commentary on important works, notably *Que vlo-ve?, La chanson du mal-aimé, Le brasier, Les fiançailles, Les collines,* and *Vitam impendere amore.* Short bibliography. Fully indexed.

Reviews: Anon. in TLS 56:17, Sept.

17, 1964; G. Brée in KR 28:125–26, 1966; A. Greet in RLM 104–07 (GAp 3):152–53, 1964; A. Hartley in Gua 36:7, Aug. 14, 1964; F. Hemmings in NewS 68:284, 286, Aug. 28. 1964; J. Houston in SoR 1:955–58, Oct. 1965; U. O'Connor in DM 4:76, 1965; R. Shattuck in TBR, Feb. 21, 1965; A. Smith in List 72:315, Aug. 27, 1964.

Décaudin, Michel. Apollinaire et le cinéma image par image. *In:* Apollinaire. *See* 7922. p. 19–28. **7956**

Résumé of attitudes towards cinema from 1907 short story, *Un beau film,* to comments on film in *L'esprit nouveau et les poètes* in 1917. His film script with André Billy, *La Bréhatine,* considered unexceptional. A. loved the cinema, saw its great potential, included it in his crusade for the art of the future, but was not inspired by it in his poetry. One brief mention of Chaplin in his writings. A devotee of *Fantômas.*

———. Le changement de front d'Apollinaire. RSH 60:255–60, 1950. **7957**

First and most important of several articles about the possibility of a radical change in A.'s poetics in 1912–13, an idea first suggested by Jules Romains. Décaudin opts for the negative, while recognizing a gradual evolution of esthetics at this time. See Poupon, *Apollinaire et Cendrars,* and Renaud, *Lecture d'Apollinaire.*

———. Guillaume Apollinaire, tradition et invention. *In his:* La crise des valeurs symbolistes, vingt ans de poésie française, 1895–1914. Toulouse, Privat, 1960. p. 484–91. **7958**

Composition of *Alcools* and its place in the avant-garde movements of 1913. Role of review *Les soirées de Paris.* An impressive panorama of French literary movements before World War I. A. is discussed as leader of the group around the review *Le festin d'Esope,* as polemicist for the unity of literary movements in 1908, and as the writer of *L'antitradition futuriste* (p. 473–74).

Fabureau, Hubert. Guillaume Apollinaire. La nouvelle revue critique, 1932. 94 p. **7959**

Critical essay and introduction to life and works. One of first attempts at thoroughness, very descriptive, and anti-analytic. Yet many keen insights, solid judgments, especially concerning A.'s Rabelaisian tendencies (cf. Cadou), his interest in bawdy songs, and his unusual erudition.

Fowlie, Wallace. Apollinaire: the poet. *In his:* Age of surrealism. Bloomington, Univ. of Indiana press, 1963. p. 83–101. **7960**

A. a lyrical clown who brought French poetry back from Rimbaud's destructiveness and Mallarmé's hermeticism to the tender heroism of the surrealist myth. Analysis of *La chanson du mal-aimé* (written before exegesis of L. C. Breunig). The poet as Petroushka.

———. Apollinaire: violence of the surreal. *In his:* Climate of violence, the French literary tradition from Baudelaire to the present. Macmillan, 1967. p. 173–87. **7961**

Introduction to the poet through brief analyses of *L'esprit nouveau et les poètes, La chanson du mal-aimé,* and the first section of *Le brasier.* Mostly descriptive. Stresses modernity.

Goffin, Robert. Entrer en poésie. Gand, A l'enseigne du chat qui pêche, 1948. p. 99–170. **7962**

Chapters on: A. at Stavelot, Belgium, in 1899; an examination of proofs of *Alcools;* A.'s collaboration with Belgian satirical review *Le passant;* author's discovery of Annie Playden, muse of *La chanson du mal-aimé,* and letters from her to author on A.; A.'s relationships with Delaunay and Cendrars. Polemic for Cendrars as major influence on A. (discussed by Poupon in *Apollinaire et Cendrars*).

Hoog, Armand. Apollinaire ou le pays sans paysage. *In his:* Littérature en Silésie. Grasset, 1944. p. 281–308. **7963**

Poetic essay partly written in a Nazi POW camp. One of the first studies of the apocalyptic nature of A.'s self-given mission, his role of *grand hérésiarque,* his Luciferian attempt to re-create the world in new innocence. Briefly follows the lines or origin of this new esthetics from Maurice Scève to Nietzsche and finds parallel evolution in painting. Also discusses the Icarus myth, the demiurgic meaning of the calligrams, and A.'s final martyrdom and canonization.

Jannini, P. A. Le avanguardie letterarie nell'idea critica di Guillaume Apollinaire. Rome, Bulzoni, 1971. 277 p. (Biblioteca di cultura, 21)   **7964**

Solidly documented overview of A.'s attitudes towards selected members of the avant-garde, from Vielé-Griffin and Rimbaud to Breton (arranged chronologically). Most important chapter is on Marinetti and futurism, with extensive bibliography in notes, p. 125–85. Other passages of special interest: p. 54 on Jouve; the *fantaisistes* and A., p. 87–89; Radiguet on A. in 1920, p. 103; attack on A. by André t'Serstevens, p. 104–05; Max Jacob, p. 113–17; reproduction of ms. of *Lettre-océan*, p. 207–08; and A. on Baudelaire, p. 247–51. Index of names.

——. La fortuna di Apollinaire in Italia. Milan, Istituto editoriale Cisalpino, 1959. 220 p. (Lingue e letterature straniere, 5) *Also (rev.)*: 1965. 294 p.   **7965**

First part: A. and futurism, relations with futurist friends, influence on Italian literature, Italian translations, and testimonies. Second part, ed. by Raymond Warnier: collection of A.'s writings that deal with Italy. A book which can be used profitably in conjunction with Pär Bergman's *Modernolatria et simultaneità*, Jannini's *Le avanguardie letterarie...*, *supra*, and Antoine Fongaro's *Un moment de célébrité en Italie pour Apollinaire, en 1911* in *Quaderni francesi, a cura di Enzo Guidici*, v. 1, p. 679–98 (Naples, Istituto Universitario Orientale, 1970). Reviews: M. Décaudin in RLC 34: 611–13, 1960; H. Meschonnic and J.-C. Chevalier in RSH 32:664–66, 1967.

Jean, Raymond. L'érotique de Guillaume Apollinaire. CahS 386:13–21, 1966.   **7966**

Rapid psychological portrait. A. feared Beauty (key poem is *1909*), had as main defenses *le gros rire* of the libertine (not the smirk or the seriousness of the pornographer), the strategic attack of the soldier, the violation and possession of the girl-woman, his favorite prey. His main weapons were the word, *le blason du corps, la prière érotique, l'énumération métaphorique.* His main search was for a sensual, Edenic innocence in the pure-impure *enfant-sorcière.* His poetry of erotic possession rises above vice or perversion by its intensity, faith in itself, and freedom, becoming "le lumineux langage de l'amour," very influential on surrealist love poetry. Profound analysis; main omissions are anal obsessions, castration fears, roles of parents; some aspects of these discussed, however, in author's *Nerval et Apollinaire, infra.*

——. Nerval et Apollinaire. CahS 347: 106–16, 1958.   **7967**

Good study of parallels between these two similar authors: their rare erudition, orientalism, obscene and tender attitudes toward haunting women, their *amour,* both *fou* and *faux,* for "l'Amante-Sœur-Mère-Déesse" who is at the same time innocent and vicious. Does not deal with textual influences of Nerval on A.

Lawler, James R. Apollinaire inédit: le séjour à Stavelot. MerF 1098:269–309, 1955.   **7968**

The first of three articles by various authors describing the famous *cahier de Stavelot,* the poetic notebook (which has since mysteriously disappeared) kept by A. in Stavelot, Belgium, in Aug.–Sept. 1899. Comments on science, Maurras, and socialism; lists of Walloon words and expressions; quotations from Maeterlinck, Moréas, Léon Daudet, etc. Other two articles, by Michel Décaudin in the MerF of June of the same year, and by Maurice Piron in SaBe 44: 2712–19, 1964, pick up omissions and a few incorrect readings made by Lawler. Piron emphasizes the *cahier*'s revelation of the major role played by the Belgian forests in the inspiration of the poet.

Meschonnic, Henri. Apollinaire illuminé au milieu d'ombres. Eur 44:141–69, 1966.   **7969**

Subtle treatise on A.'s symbolism and influence on surrealists. Considers A. leading French poet of 20th c. in the line of Nerval and Rimbaud because of his apocalyptic symbolism of light, love, knowledge (gnosis), errancy, and illuminating laughter ("le rire est le sens du sacré"). Excellent résumé of A.'s occultism, p. 153–55. Discusses his links with Desnos and Eluard, p. 162–65.

Moulin, Jeanine. Poète de l'invention. *In her:* Guillaume Apollinaire, textes inédits. Geneva, Droz; Lille, Giard, 1952. p. 92–146. **7970**

Early textual study, too general for the most part, is still useful for its comparison between Rimbaud and A., and parallels between the *Lettres du voyant* and *Les collines, Illuminations* and *Onirocritique,* etc.

Oxenhandler, Neal. Toward the new aesthetic. ConL 2:169–71, 1971. **7971**

Incisive synopsis of the new 20th c. esthetic found in the works of Sartre, Camus, Robbe-Grillet, Sarraute, and Beckett as compared to the old esthetic of Baudelaire's *correspondances* and Mallarmé's Hegelianism. "...Apollinaire ...strikes a perfect balance between continuity, sequential connections, organic form, and the juxtaposition, disjunction, and improvisation that come to characterize much of the work in the new aesthetic."

Pia, Pascal. Apollinaire aux Antilles. QV 71–73:30–33, 1954. **7972**

Antillean sources of various words and expressions in the works of A.

———. Apollinaire par lui-même. Seuil, 1954. 192 p. (Ecrivains de toujours, 20) **7973**

Critical biography with a good selection of extracts from A.'s works by a leading 20th-c. writer and critic. Profusely illustrated. 15-p. chronology of life; 10-p. bibliography. Probably the best short introduction to A. in French for the general reader.

———. La mort d'Apollinaire. MagL 23: 8–11, 1968. **7974**

On A. and Léautaud; A.'s necessary patriotism at the end of his life; Max Jacob's slanders of him; and his final novel, *La dame des Hohenzollern,* which never got written.

Piron, Maurice. Les wallonismes de Guillaume Apollinaire. *In:* Mélanges de lin-

guistique française offerts à M. Charles Bruneau. Geneva, Droz, 1954. p. 193–207. **7975**

Concise linguistic study and glossary of Walloon terms used in *Que vlo-ve?* and first chapter of *Le poète assassiné.* Proves that A. developed a very good grasp of the oral speech and folklore during his two months in the Walloon area of Belgium. In a follow-up article, *Apollinaire et le wallon,* in RLC 2: 260–62, 1956, Piron cites literary sources for some of A.'s *wallonismes* in humorous newspapers from Liège, and names a singer residing in Stavelot who was his "professeur de wallon."

Poupon, Marc. L'année allemande d'Apollinaire. RLM 183–88 (GAp 7):9–45, 1968. **7976**

Detailed reconstruction of A.'s *annus mirabilis* in the Rhineland (1901–02) which inspired at least half the poems in *Alcools.* A major addition to the research of E. M. Wolf, *infra.*

———. Apollinaire et Cendrars. Minard, 1969. 68 p. (Archives des lettres modernes, 103. Archives Guillaume Apollinaire, 2) **7977**

Thorough investigation of much-debated questions of the relationship between A. and Cendrars between 1912–18, and A.'s possible *changement de front* (phrase of Jules Romains) after meeting Cendrars. Poupon finds reciprocal influences of two poets in 1912–13 and the definite influence of *Pâques à New-York* on *Zone.* Discusses Cendrars' influence on *Arbre* and *Anecdotiques.* Brief appendix covers important *inédits* of Cendrars published, unfortunately, after body of study was written and which definitely prove that Cendrars still had not met A. by mid-September 1912. These *inédits,* edited by Miriam Cendrars (Club français du livre, 1969. 432 p.), are further analyzed from an Apollinarian's point of view by J.-P. Goldenstein in RLM 276–79 (GAp 10):146–60, 1971.

Raymond, Marcel. Les origines de la nouvelle poésie. Guillaume Apollinaire. *In his:* De Baudelaire au surréalisme. Corti, 1947. p. 217–38. (*Original ed.:* Corrêa, 1933) *Trans.:* The origins of the new poetry. Guillaume Apollinaire. *In his:* From Baudelaire to surrealism. Wittenborn, Schultz, 1950. p. 227–39.   **7978**

Introduction to poet, stressing his lyrical enchantment, his Jarry-influenced joy in profanation, and his adventurous and prophetic modernity. Finds him something of a gratuitous mystifier and asks, if he had not died so young, whether ultimately he "might have been that great poet of whom he makes us think."

Renaud, Philippe. Lecture d'Apollinaire. Lausanne, Eds. L'âge d'homme, 1969. 571 p. (Lettera, 1)   **7979**

Attempt at synthesis of main themes and myths in total body of poetry by a disciple of Bachelard and Marcel Raymond. Covers chronologically (for the most part) *Alcools* (p. 39–211), *Ondes* (p. 215–379), and "les poèmes de guerre" (p. 383–477). A summary and an appendix in which *Lul de Faltenin* is explicated complete the work. In *Alcools,* Renaud finds the leading myth to be oriented towards the past through memory and the "tradition orphéo-prométhéenne." In the *Ondes* section of *Calligrammes,* the author shows how influences of futurism, Dramatism, Delaunay, Duchamp, and Picabia help to bring about a break with the musicality of *Alcools* and to create a musicality of form in a new poetics that transfers the poet's demiurgic powers to his reader. The ideas of this section, the most profound and original of the book, are enlarged upon in the essay, *Ondes, ou les métamorphoses de la musique, infra.* The final section, on the poems of 1915–18, is more critical as A. becomes less creative and more subject to History. In all, a remarkable study, full of discerning interpretation and balanced judgment by a highly learned myth critic.

Reviews: M. Davies in MLR 66: 900–02, 1971; D. Delbreil in RLM 249–53 (GAp 9):249–53, 1970; A. Fongaro in SFr 47–48:417–24, 1972; D. Jakubec in EdL 3:165–67, 1970; L. Somville in ELit 3:142–45, April 1970; C. Tournadre in RHL 71:129–31, 1971.

Richard, J.-P. Etoiles chez Apollinaire. *In:* De Ronsard à Breton. Recueil d'essais.

Hommage à Marcel Raymond. Corti, 1967. p. 223–34.   **7980**

Chronological survey of the theme of stars from *La chanson du mal-aimé* (feminine, fluid, shivering, fleeing) to the virile, fecundating fireworks of *Les mamelles de Tirésias.*

Roudaut, Jean. La fête d'Apollinaire. Cr 199:1034–45, 1963.   **7981**

A. as demiurge ritualizing the world through the word: "La parole est un dieu." *Alcools* anticipates the poetry of the war, giving the war a sense, making it into a *fête.*

———. Le temps et l'espace sacré dans la poésie d'Apollinaire. Cr 14:690–708, 1958.   **7982**

Alcools is a poem of time and *Calligrammes* a poem of space. Woman, equivalent to poetry for A. after 1902, is used by him to fight time. His erotic struggles became his warrior instincts; he sought to overcome time in his serious desire for children (*L'enchanteur pourrissant, Tendre comme le souvenir, Les mamelles de Tirésias*). An early essay that anticipates more recent mythic and structural studies.

Rouveyre, André. Amour et poésie d'Apollinaire. Seuil, 1955. 256 p.   **7983**

Subtle, poetic, semi-Freudian meditations on a few poems and prose passages. Exegeses of *Chantre, Le pont Mirabeau, Refus de la colombe, Crépuscule,* and *Palais.* Finds phallic symbolism in *Le pont Mirabeau* and yonic symbolism in *Palais.* Chapter on *Le poète assassiné* discusses A.'s aspirations for virginity. Preliminary section contains photographs from film of A. and author in 1914. Last section, on the *amours de guerre,* is a revision of a part of author's *Apollinaire, infra.*

———. Apollinaire. Gallimard, 1945. 270 p. *Also (rev.):* Eds. Raison d'être, 1952. 268 p.   **7984**

Rouveyre met A. in the summer of 1914, went with him to Deauville on a journalistic assignment (the trip back is the subject of *La petite auto*), remained a close friend and correspondent until his death. P. 9–64, written in 1919 and subsequently published in MerF,

Sept. 1, 1920, discuss this relationship, contain important and now well-known details on A.'s mother, his wife, his job in 1918, etc. The most valuable part of work is a semi-historical, semi-psychological account of the liaison in 1914–15 between A. and Louise de Coligny whom Rouveyre had known since 1910 or 1912. P. 115–253 contain, along with the first publication of letters and poems to Lou and Madeleine, the most comprehensive discussion of A.'s wartime psychology to date. Often conjectural, it is nonetheless based on author's friendship with A. and provides many significant revelations concerning A.'s deficiencies as a lover, Lou's inability to give herself fully, and the extent of the tragedy that the affair became for A. P. 115–22 give the principal biography of Lou that we have; later facts will be added by Décaudin in his introduction to *Lettres à Lou, supra,* and by Lou's doctor at the end of her life (RLM 123–26:86–89, 1965).
Reviews: R. K. in NL Dec. 27, 1945; J. Lapp in FR 21:71–73, 1947.

Shattuck, Roger. Apollinaire, hero-poet. *In his:* Selected writings of Guillaume Apollinaire. New directions, 1950. p. 3–54. **7985**
Portrait of A. as courageous searcher, whose biography, myth, and verse combine to constitute an attempt to find his identity in all aspects of life as he "dared to live his art." The poet as heroic gambler on life and art challenging the unknown for the sake of his poetic self. Includes analysis of style, imagery and prosody of several works.
Reviews: L. Breunig in KR 13:335–42, 1951; R. Campbell in Cat 1:547–52, 1950–51 and in Nine 3:76–77, 1950; R. Humphries in Nat 171:292–93, Sept. 30, 1950; M. Turnell in PoeR 5:23–25, Nov. 1950.

———. Guillaume Apollinaire: the impresario of the avant-garde. Guillaume Apollinaire: painter-poet. *In his:* The banquet years. Harcourt, Brace, 1955. p. 195–248. *Also (rev.):* 1968. **7986**
Two chapters on A.'s place in the Promethean panorama of arts in France from 1885–1918; remainder of book deals with other radical creators, Jarry, Satie, and Henri Rousseau. Biography

of A.; relation to cubism and orphism; relations between painting and poetry. Finds primary quality of A.'s poetry to be *ambiguity* and *simultanism* uniting tradition and invention, lucid consciousness and the subconscious, light and shadow, the modern world and the past. In this union, A. seeks his identity and an esthetic future for society.
Review: M. Décaudin in RLM 104–07 (GAp 3):185–86, 1963.

Soupault, Philippe. Guillaume Apollinaire ou reflets de l'incendie. Marseille, Cahiers du sud, 1926. 71 p. **7987**
Hommage, written soon after A.'s death by noted Surrealist. Lyrical impressions by a companion and disciple of the post-1916 years. Some character study (A.'s fears, his obstinacy, his inability to stop), a few revelations on poems (*Poème lu au mariage d'André Salmon, Ombre*). P. 47–65, *Banalités* and *Quelconqueries* reprinted from reviews.

Steegmuller, Francis. Apollinaire, poet among the painters. Farrar, Straus, 1963. 365 p. **7988**
Popular biography of A., emphasizing picturesque, cosmopolitan side of his life. Documents birth in Rome. Translates poems, letters, articles in English. Good sections on relationships with painters. Notes, index. Appendix contains report of author's 1962 visit with Anne Playden Postings, A.'s first great love.
Reviews: G. Brett in Gua 36:8, Jan. 31, 1964; C. Connolly in SuT 7341:36, Jan. 26, 1964; M. Décaudin in RLM 123–26 (GAp 4):153, 1965; J. Houston in SoR 1:945–58, 1965; F. Kermode in NewS 67:258–59, Feb. 14, 1964; N. Oxenhandler in NYRB 6:7–8, Nov. 14, 1963; E. Starkie in TBR Nov. 10, 1963.

Taupin, René, and Louis Zukofsky. Le style Apollinaire. Les presses modernes, 1934. 134 p. **7989**
Impressionistic, surrealistic *flânerie* through A.'s (and others') works, juxtaposing quotations and commentary. A mixture of perspicacity and nonsense. The last chapter offers some interesting comparisons with English authors.

Turnell, Martin. The poetry of Guillaume Apollinaire. SoR 5:953–75, 1969. **7990**

Descriptive introduction to A. with some value judgments. Ultimately agrees with C. A. Hackett (and Georges Duhamel) that A. is a minor poet.

Warnier, Raymond. Apollinaire a Polska. PHum 2:53–68; 3:87–98; 4:35–66, 1961. **7991**

Long article in Polish in three parts on A.'s relations with Poland, works in which he deals with Polish matters, Polish theory of his Napoleonic ancestry, etc. Some bibliography in notes.

————. Apollinaire à Strasbourg (1904). RHL 56:251–55, 1956. **7992**

A. probably went to Strasbourg in Feb. 1904 as a journalist for the *Européen* to cover the Bilse trial, a court-martial of a German lieutenant who wrote a novel under an assumed name against the German military system. The poem *1904* (*Il y a*) undoubtedly composed at this time.

Wolf, E. M. Guillaume Apollinaire und das Rheinland. Bonn, Dortmund-Husen, 1937. 170 p. **7993**

Printed dissertation, the first university thesis on A. Close search into literary and biographical backgrounds of the prose and poetry written out of the Rhineland sojourn of 1901–02. Contains valuable list of German books in the poet's personal library.

Yurkievich, Saül. Modernidad de Apollinaire. Buenos Aires, Editorial Losada S.A., 1968. 268 p. **7994**

Long enthusiastic description, larded with many quotations in French, of techniques, subject matter, innovations, poetics, imagery, etc. of poems. No explications or treatment of style or themes; rather, almost a catalog or check list, which could serve as an introduction to A. for a Spanish-speaking public.

Review: C. Mastronardi in Sur 319: 88–91, 1969.

Alcools

Bégué, Claude, and Pierre Lartigue. Alcools Apollinaire. Hatier, 1972. 80 p. (Collection profil d'une œuvre, 25). **7995**

Structuralist description of *Alcools,* its themes and style. Remarkably comprehensive summary for so small a format, primarily designed for high-school and university use. Provides brief biography of A. and genesis of work. *Description* divides poems in two categories: *les arts poétiques,* the early symbolist narrative poems and the later demiurgic poems of 1908–10, and (2) *la poésie élégiaque,* subdivided into *cycle rhénan, cycle d'Annie, cycle de Marie,* and *A la Santé.* Necessarily introductory, this little book provides admirable point of departure, along structuralist lines, for students and general public; however, it does slight the mythology, philosophy, erotology, and psychology of *Alcools.* No index or table of contents.

Breunig, Leroy C. Apollinaire's Les fiançailles. EFL 3:1–32, Nov. 1966. **7996**

Major explication, continuing studies by Bates, Durry, and Greet, of work A. called "avec *Le brasier*...mon meilleur poème." Line by line examination, comparing ms. to published versions and relating poem to Picasso's work, particularly *Les demoiselles d'Avignon.* The poem, like the painting, is too innovative to be entirely successful, but it was the key to A.'s discovery in 1908 of the profound meaning—with all its messianic implications—of true creation.

————. The chronology of Apollinaire's Alcools. PMLA 67:907–23, 1952. **7997**

Dating of the 50 poems in *Alcools* by means of mss, biography, and internal evidence. Should be used in conjunction with later scholarship, particularly Décaudin's *Le dossier d'Alcools* and Bates' *Guillaume Apollinaire.*

————. Le roman du mal-aimé. TR 57: 117–23, 1952. **7998**

A key critical article, the basic study for the vast body of exegesis surrounding one of modern poetry's most influential and widely discussed works. Sets forth chronological, biographical, and psychological structure of poem, from the poet's experience of a Rhenish spring in 1902 (*Aubade*) to his return to Paris from London in June 1904, revealing its essential unity and profundity.

Chevalier, Jean-Claude. Alcools d'Apollinaire, essai d'analyse des formes poétiques. Minard, 1970. 282 p. (Bibliothèque des lettres modernes, 17) **7999**

Brilliant structuralist study of two main types of poetic discourse in *Alcools:* that of the early *grandes machines* (*Le larron, L'ermite,* and *Merlin et la vieille femme*) in which the unhappy poet seeks his role in Promethean and Christian dramas; and that of the poems of critical creation in the visionary period of 1907–10, *Lul de Faltenin, Le brasier, Vendémiaire,* and *Les fiançailles,* with its relation to modern art criticism, Nietzsche and Jarry, and, later, surrealism (*Parade*). Basing his study on linguistic theories of Jakobson, Chomsky, and Riffaterre which deal with the necessarily demiurgic nature of poetic language, author reveals by intricate examination of words and lines and their use and creation of myths how A.'s new esthetic rose out of the symbolism of his early works.

Reviews: M. Arrivé in RLM 276–79 (GAp 10):140–43, 1971; E. Fuzellier in Liv 174:58, 1971; P. Pia in Car Oct. 28, 1970.

Couffignal, Robert. Zone d'Apollinaire, structure et confrontations. Minard, 1970. 72 p. (Archives des lettres modernes, 118. Archives Guillaume Apollinaire, 4) **8000**

Zone seen as A.'s descent into Hell. Parallels with Dante, Nerval, Rimbaud, Péguy, Eliot, Baudelaire, and Jacob. Influence of Cendrars. Study of confessional aspects of poem, its descending and ascending movements between night and light, Hell and Heaven, spleen and ideal, the absence and presence of Christ. Main thesis: the great religious poem of A.

Review: P. Menanteau in Liv 177: 64, 1971.

Cranston, Mechthild. Guillaume Apollinaire: La blanche neige. *In her:* Enfance mon amour, la rêverie vers l'enfance dans l'œuvre de Guillaume Apollinaire, Saint-John Perse et René Char. Debresse, 1970. p. 22–83. **8001**

Thematic and psychological study of Rhenish poem as a characteristic example of the magic folktale vision in A.'s verse. Poetic, penetrating, many revealing *correspondances.*

Décaudin, Michel. Le dossier d'Alcools. Paris, Minard; Geneva, Droz, 1960. 242 p. *Also:* 1965. **8002**

Invaluable compendium of mss. and first-publications of poems of *Alcools,* with notes, variants, critical bibliography, and a 57 p. introduction establishing the history and structure of the book. A basic work of A. scholarship. A few important additional notes to the book may be found in Décaudin's *Compléments à un dossier,* RLM 69–70 (GAp 1):57–65, 1962.

Reviews: E. Mora in RDM 21:156–60, 1958; R. Pouilliart in LR 17:105–07, 1963.

Derche, Roland. Guillaume Apollinaire: Alcools, Rhénanes, La Loreley. Centre de documentation universitaire, 1957. 30 p. **8003**

Mainly an explication of *La Loreley,* based on E. Wolf's article, *Apollinaire und die Lore Lay Brentanos* (RLC 25, Oct.–Dec. 1951) but, disagreeing with Wolf's narcissistic interpretation of end of poem, believes Lore's death caused by error of love rather than suicide. Study continued in later work, *Quatre mythes poétiques, Œdipe-Narcisse-Psyché-Lorelei* (Société d'édition d'enseignement supérieur, 1962. 198 p.).

Durry, Marie-Jeanne. Guillaume Apollinaire, Alcools. Société d'édition d'enseignement supérieur, 1956–64. 3 v. **8004**

Text of tapes made from Mme Durry's courses on A. at the Sorbonne during the 1950's adapted into book form. Constitutes a careful reading of the poet's work before 1913 and is an important introduction both for the general reader and the specialist. V. 1 begins with lively biography, portrait, and character analysis based on interviews with A.'s friends and written sources. Most valuable section of volume for A. student is review of A.'s attitudes towards religion (p. 145–91). Believes with Billy that A. had none of the anguished mystic in him. Last pages contain exegesis of *L'ermite,* the first major explication of *Merlin et la vieille femme,* a discussion of *Le larron,* and a comparison of *Zone* and Cendrars' *Prose du Transsibérien.* V. 2 discusses A.'s debt to symbolism, his closeness to, and departure from, Baudelaire, Rimbaud, Verlaine, Mallarmé, Régnier, Maeterlinck, and others (p. 17–174). This section is somewhat impressionistic and misses much—particularly in Régnier—but does name several important sources. Best section is on sources and style of *Le bestiaire* (p. 128–37). A critical history of relationships with painters and discussion of cubist parallels and orphic Prometheanism in certain poems (p. 117–29). Legacy to surrealism of *Que vlo-ve?*, *Onirocritique*, *Lundi rue Christine*, *Le poète assassiné*, etc. (p. 223–50). Ends with somewhat outmoded view that A. was not a revolutionary in art or politics. V. 3 is primarily devoted to *Alcools* as a whole, but also has explications of several individual works including *L'émigrant de Landor Road*, certain Rhineland poems, and, in the last chapter, *les poèmes de feu* of 1907–10. Epilogue has two excellent thematic essays, *Ombre-lumière* and *Passe et dure sans t'arrêter*. Indices of names and poems in each v.

Reviews: R.-M. Albérès in Comb April 25, 1957 and in NL March 11, 1965; M. Décaudin in RLM 123–26 (GAp 4):138–39, 1965 (for v. 2, 3); R. Kanters in FL April 15, 1965; L. Perche in EdNa 21:24, June 3, 1965.

———. Sur La tzigane. RLM 85–89 (GAp 2):76–89, 1963. **8005**

Analysis of this poem and other writings from the Rhineland period in order to get at truth of physical relationship between A. and Annie Playden. Uses internal evidence for the most part to conclude that Annie was a *demi-vierge* who replaced with her lover *l'amour total par des ruses du corps*.

Follet, Lionel, and Marc Poupon. Lecture de Palais d'Apollinaire. Minard, 1972. 104 p. (Archives des lettres modernes, 518–24. Archives Guillaume Apollinaire, 6) **8006**

Comprehensive study of this semi-satirical poem. In the first part of book, Poupon characterizes the persona of the poem as a burlesque Christ-A. desecrating His Lady in the figure of Rosamund, Henry II's cruel courtesan, and desecrating himself in the description of the unholy Eucharist at which he is eaten. It also contains a possible source for the main theme in a nuns' drinking

song (drinking Christ-roses) from the Rhineland. In the second part (p. 15–102), Follet traces the intricate play of puns and obscure references into a major poetic cosmogony, pictured on p. 90, which summarizes A.'s early defeated ethos: a negative microcosm of the universe, a garden of the dead, in which the Christ-poet-sun (also Apollo and Eros) becomes sterile, love is lost, and the poet's agapes can only be erotic, scatological, and red with menstrual blood. Parallels are found in other works, particularly in *Merlin et la vieille femme*. An important source for the *vin de Chypre* (1.11) is found in the Song of Solomon 1:12–13 (p. 38–39). This is one of the best structural studies of A.; it only neglects to delineate his anal mystique in the poem.

Goosse, Marie-Thérèse. Une lecture du Larron d'Apollinaire. Minard, 1970. 68 p. (Archives des lettres modernes, 112. Archives Guillaume Apollinaire, 3) **8007**

Exegesis of poem enlarging upon Durry's thesis that the protagonist is basically the poet. Believes Renan's *Marc-Aurèle et la fin du monde*, with its discussion of Roman criticism of Christianity, is a major source of historical detail in background.

Review: P. Pia in Car Oct. 28, 1970.

Guiraud, Pierre. Index du vocabulaire du symbolisme. Fascicule I: index des mots d'Alcools d'Apollinaire. Klincksieck, n.d. n.p. **8008**

Concordance of *Alcools*.

Lawler, James R. Music in Apollinaire. In his: The language of symbolism. Princeton, Princeton univ. press, 1969. p. 212–62. **8009**

Summary of A.'s attitudes toward music, his use of folk song in poetry (no mention of his use of erotic songs however), and the musicality of *La chanson du mal-aimé*, of which poem thorough analysis is given. Believes that Annie slept with A. and that "les sept épées" sequence symbolically relate this liaison. Finds a source for poem in Lamartine's *Adieux à la poésie*. Includes a musical transcription of A. recording of *Le pont Mirabeau*.

Lockerbie, S. I. Alcools et le symbolisme. RLM 85–89 (GAp 2):6–40, 1963. **8010**

Important study of how A.'s youthful indoctrination in *fin-de-siècle* symbolist works affected all his later poetry, especially through his major theme of the medieval quest, *la chasse spirituelle*. Influence of similar preoccupations in Picasso and in Royère's neo-symbolism. After the transfigurating poetry of 1908 there was more inclusion of contemporary reality in the quest, modernization of the medieval knight into the wandering poet of *Le voyageur, Zone,* and *Les collines*—yet continuing the visionary aspirations of a Baudelaire, a Mallarmé and a Rimbaud.

Mazaleyrat, Jean. Problèmes de scansion du vers libre. A propos d'un poème d'Apollinaire. *In:* Philologische Studien für Joseph M. Piel zu seinem 65. Geburtstag. Heidelberg, Winter, 1969. p. 140–47. **8011**

The prosody of *Les colchiques.* An example of traditional use and complete knowledge of the alexandrine together with easy freedom, spontaneous impressionism and colloquialism in metrics. Observations apply generally to A.'s metrics.

————. Simplicité et poésie dans le style d'Apollinaire. *In:* Mélanges de linguistique et de philologie romanes dédiés à la mémoire de Pierre Fouché. Réunis par Georges Matoré avec la collaboration de Jeanne Cadiot-Cueilleron. Klincksieck, 1970. p. 233–45. (Etudes linguistiques, 11) **8012**

Intelligent, balanced structuralist analysis of *Cors de chasse.*

Morhange-Bégué, Claude. La chanson du mal-aimé d'Apollinaire, essai d'analyse structurale et stylistique. Minard, 1970. 305 p. (Bibliothèque Guillaume Apollinaire des lettres modernes, 4) **8013**

Meticulous, stanza-by-stanza stylistic analysis using methodology and terminology of Jakobson, Lévi-Strauss, Barthes, Todorov, etc. Finds four main structures: the apparent one of seven parts of poem, and three deeper ones, *une structure linéaire symétrique, une structure linéaire périodique,* and *une structure circulaire fondée sur l'existence d'un double registre.* Interpretation of poem offers new hypotheses and insights, although these are obscured by the top-heavy critical apparatus.

Reviews: L. Follet in RLM 276–79 (GAp 10):143–49, 1971; H. Gershman in BA 45:280, 1970; M. Laurent in AuvL 209–10, 1971; P. Pia in Car Oct. 28, 1970.

Orecchioni, Pierre. Le thème du Rhin dans l'inspiration de Guillaume Apollinaire. Lettres modernes, 1956. 144 p. (Thèmes et mythes, 3) **8014**

An updating of E. M. Wolf's *Guillaume Apollinaire und das Rheinland.* Primarily a separation of traditional, touristic attitudes toward the Rhine-picturesque in A.'s poems from his original, spontaneous vision. Influence of the Rhenish *Volkslied.* Major themes. Somewhat superficial and inconclusive study; author seems to be overly intimidated by critical difficulties of his task —which he spells out clearly p. 3–29.

Poupon, Marc. Le larron, essai d'exégèse. RLM 166–69 (GAp 6):35–51, 1967. **8015**

Imaginative explication of the great dramatic poem. Thesis that mysterious *larron* is both Jesus and A. caught between the wealth of pagan myth and the poverty of Christian sin in an earthly paradise of the dead. Some highly speculative interpretations—especially the opinion that the pagans are converted to Nestorianism at the end—but in general a penetrating and stimulating study.

————. Lul de Faltenin et l'étymologie. *In:* Du monde européen à l'univers des mythes. *See* 7925. p. 132–51. **8016**

Close analysis of this poem, summarizing and adding to other exegeses. Discussion of key words. Principal theme outlined: the poet-Christ's sacred and profane passion and his sunset at sea.

Renaud, Philippe. L'effraie et le rossignol ou les énigmes du tremblement. RLM 249–53 (GAp 9):45–67, 1970. **8017**

Remarkable study *à la* Bachelard of words *tremblement, trembler, trembleur,* primarily in works before 1907. Their relation to the flame and the eye-star-*alcools correspondance,* to vertical vertigo, and to death and suicide by drowning. Finds archetypal dichotomy in *Les femmes* of blind nightingale which becomes silent and trembles when owl hoots, the tensions between sight and sound. An article full of insights into the subconscious complexes reflected in the image groups of the Rhineland lyrics.

Ropars, Marie-Claire. Deux explications de texte (poésie et prose). FMonde 58:32–35, 1968.   **8018**

Structural, phonetic explication of last eleven stanzas of *La chanson du mal-aimé*. Convincing thesis of optimistic ending; reveals tight structural unity of whole passage.

Calligrammes

Bates, Scott. Les collines, dernier testament d'Apollinaire. RLM 69–70 (GAp 1):25–39, 1962.   **8019**

Attempt to show by internal evidence that this major poem, in spite of its position in *Calligrammes* among the poems written 1913–14, was actually composed after the war experience. Believes that *Ombre* and the non-calligrammatic part of *La petite auto* were also written at this time.

Centre d'étude du vocabulaire français, Faculté des lettres et sciences humaines de Besançon, ed. Guillaume Apollinaire, Calligrammes. Larousse, 1967. 179 p.   **8020**

Computerized concordance of *Calligrammes,* followed by statistical indices: parts of speech, frequencies, foreign and dialectal words, rimes, capitalized words. A useful linguistic tool, complementary to Pierre Guiraud's *Index des mots d'Alcools de Guillaume Apollinaire.* Should be used in conjunction with J.-C. Chevalier's remarks on it in RLM 69–70 (GAp 1):40–53, 1962.
Review: G. Rees in FS 25:483, 1971.

Levaillant, Jean. L'espace dans Calligrammes. RLM 217–22 (GAp 8):48–65, 1969.   **8021**

A.'s conquest of a new space for poetry shown to be a demiurgic, sexual act of possession emphasizing will (desire) and a mythology of fission and explosion. Examples of various compositional structures, the sexual juxtaposition of the circle and the line in *Saillant* and *Tour,* the porous space of

flight in *Liens,* the ubiquitous, cosmic creation and possession of another world in *La petite auto,* etc. Comparison between this new semi-cubist, 20th-c. concretization of space with Romantic revery, Baudelairean claustrophobia, and symbolist idealism.

Lockerbie, S. I. Le rôle de l'imagination dans Calligrammes. Première partie: Les fenêtres et le poème-créé. RLM 146–49 (GAp 5):6–22, 1966. Deuxième partie: les poèmes du monde intérieur. RLM 166–69 (GAp 6):85–105, 1967.   **8022**

Attempt to prove in first part of article that A. aspired after the autonomy of works of painting, similar to that of the *tableau-objet* of the cubists, in his poems of 1913–14, and that he best achieved this goal in *Les fenêtres.* Questionable thesis that he was closer to "l'acte de création absolue" in these poems than in *Alcools* where he was searching for his symbolist self. In the second part of article, *Les collines, La jolie rousse,* and *Vitam impendere amore* are shown to represent a return to the poetry of errancy and the quest of the *moi* of *Alcools.* Thus the *poème-créé* of 1913–14 is succeeded by the future-oriented *poème-méditation* of 1916–18, which is more characteristic of A.'s poetry as a whole.

Poupon, Marc. Le musicien de Saint-Merry. CAIEF 23:211–20, 1971.   **8023**

Best explication to date of this important poem, seen as inspired by the loss of Marie Laurencin in 1912–13, by the poet's interest in the old quarter of St. Merry with its prostitutes and its diabolism, and by his knowledge of the Pied Piper legend. Only omits—for reasons of propriety, no doubt—the musician's phallic symbolism. Considers poem another *Chanson du mal-aimé.*

Renaud, Philippe. Ondes, ou les métamorphoses de la musique. *In:* Apollinaire et la musique. *See* 7923. p. 21–32.   **8024**

Subtle tracing of evolution from the more traditional lyricism of *Alcools* to the denial of lyricism in *Ondes* and its replacement by the essence of music, "une musique des formes." Demonstration of this process by exegeses of *Liens, Le musicien de Saint-Merry,* and *Un fantôme de nuées.*

Schleifenbaum, Ingrid. Guillaume Apollinaire: Ondes, exemplarische Einzelinterpretationen zu Calligrammes. Bonn, Grundmann, 1972. 310 p. (Abhandlungen zur Kunst-, Musik- und Literaturwissenschaft, 132) **8025**

Close examination of four poems from the first section of *Calligrammes: Un fantôme de nuées* (p. 23–66), *Le musicien de Saint-Merry* (p. 67–117), *Arbre* (p. 119–67), and *Les collines* (p. 169–271). Emphasis on archetypal structure and psychology, but with chronological, biographical reconstruction of the history of the poems and of *Ondes* as a whole. In German, with 8 p. résumé in French. Thematic index, 9 p. bibliography.

Themerson, Stefan. Apollinaire's lyrical ideograms. London, Gaberbocchus, 1968. 40 p. **8026**

Perhaps the best presentation of calligrams to date (not complete, however), accompanied by appreciative text underlining their modernism and graphic sensitivity. Other presentations criticized, especially that of the *Œuvres poétiques* (Pléiade). Precursors discussed. Two Japanese translations shown. A *souvenir inédit* by Pierre Albert-Birot on how *Il pleut* was set up for its appearance in *Sic*.
Reviews: Anon. in TLS Jan. 23, 1969. M. Décaudin in RLM 217–22 (GAp 8):239, 1961.

Other Works

Albert-Birot, Pierre. Les mamelles de Tirésias. *In:* Guillaume Apollinaire. *See* 7926. p. 43–47. **8027**

On the chaotic genesis of the play, by A.'s main collaborator. Tells of its beginning with a conversation in Nov. 1916 and its evolution up to the historic performance of June 24, 1917. Creation of the adjective *surréaliste* to describe the play. One of several testimonies which seem to indicate that very little of the play was written before 1916—contrary to what A. claimed. For another detailed article by Albert-Birot covering the same material, see Marg Dec. 1958.

Bates, Scott. Guillaume Apollinaire et L'enchanteur pourrissant. RSH 84:425–35, 1956. **8028**

Brief analysis of prose poem, bringing out its apocalyptic character and its revelation of the state of mind of the *mal-aimé*, buried alive by love like Merlin. Underlines anti-Christian, materialistic satire. Finds that the poem is positive in heralding the powers of the poet-enchanter.

Belleli, Maria Luisa. Ricchezza di temi nel Bestiaire di G. Apollinaire. *In:* Apollinaire. *See* 7922. p. 37–107. **8029**

Orpheus and his animals in *Le bestiaire* traced through the rest of A.'s works. Somewhat unsystematic and undiscriminating, but a helpful reference tool. Compendium of findings by Poupon, Durry, Fongaro, and others. Ends with listing and brief discussion of French bestiaries after A.

Blumenkranz-Onimus, Noémi. Vers une esthétique de la raison ardente. Eur 44: 173–92, 1966. **8030**

Follows esthetics of art criticism from the mixture of naturalism and idealism of the early years towards "une esthétique de la raison ardente" which sought to be a dynamic realism incorporating all the modern arts. Article based on research carefully documented in author's outstanding but unpublished thesis, *Apollinaire témoin des peintres de son temps*. Ecole du Louvre, 1960.

Breunig, Leroy C. Apollinaire et le cubisme. RLM 69–70 (GAp 1):7–24, 1962. **8031**

Chronological history of A.'s relationship to cubism showing that, far from being the convinced apologist for the movement he is commonly considered to be, he was always uneasy with it and more in tune with the tendency toward colorful abstraction he labeled *orphisme* in 1912. Both movements, he realized, were part of an esthetic doctrine which, says Breunig, "bien qu'en poésie elle existât depuis Baudelaire, était révolutionnaire en peinture" (p. 19). His own poems are far from cubist austerity in style and intellectualism, and deserve to be called more orphist (Dionysian) than cubist (Apollonian).

Burgos, Jean. La fin de Babylone, un ouvrage signé Guillaume Apollinaire. RLM 183–88 (GAp 7) : 125–55, 1968.   **8032**

Demonstration by interior, thematic evidence that this 1914 novel, which was formerly thought to have been written partly or largely by René Dalize, was mainly by A., with himself as the hero Vietrix. Symbolism of the dance, of the color white, and of the swastika related to other works of A. Main source of book's documentation: P. Dhorme's 1907 and 1910 studies of Babylon. Biblical sources listed p. 144–45.

Cameron, John W. Apollinaire, Spuller, and l'esprit nouveau. RomN 4 : 3–7, 1962.   **8033**

Possible sources of A.'s 1917 title of movement, *l'esprit nouveau*, in Havelock Ellis, Henri de Régnier, Baudelaire, etc. Thinks most likely main source the speech made by Eugène Spuller, Minister of Public Education, to Chambre des Députés on March 3, 1894, when he used the term to reconcile all opposing factions.

Chevalier, J.-C., and L. C. Breunig. Apollinaire et les peintres cubistes. RLM 104–07 (GAp 3) : 89–112, 1964.   **8034**

Examination of original ms. and three sets of proofs of A.'s book. Clearer exposition than in authors' critical edition of 1965, *supra*. Conclusive demonstration that A. became apologist for cubism and orphism in 1912 while preparing the work for publication.

Décaudin, Michel. Sur la composition du Poète assassiné. RSH 84 : 437–54, 1956.   **8035**

Description of two mss., one in the Fonds Jacques Doucet at the Bibliothèque Ste-Geneviève at Paris, the other owned by M. Matarasso, and two sets of proofs. P. 446–56 prints extracts from ms. of ch. 12. An important first study, but unfortunately far from complete. Continued by author's critical edition of work which, like this article, omits mss. from the Fonds Jacques Doucet.

Delaunay, Robert. Du cubisme à l'art abstrait. Ed. by P. Francastel. Geneva, Droz; Paris, S.E.V.P.E.N., 1958. 415 p.   **8036**

The *cahiers* of one of the artists most frequented by A. in 1912–13 and to whom he owed many ideas on orphism. P. 106–75 precious for picture of relationship between the two men and for Delaunay's ideas on A.'s attempts to create a popular front of avant-garde movements.

Review: M. Décaudin in RLM 69–70 (GAp 1) : 100–02, 1962.

Fonteyne, André. Apollinaire prosateur, L'hérésiarque et cie. Nizet, 1964. 199 p.   **8037**

Stylistic study of A.'s first collection of stories. Describes themes, characters, tonalities and three characteristic elements: exotic erudition, eroticism, surprise. Best section is on vocabulary and style. Many insights, yet little profundity; an initiatory work.

Reviews: M. Arrivé in RHL 66 : 740–41, 1966; L. Breunig in RR 57 : 236–37, 1966; R. Couffignal in RLM 104–07 : 148–51, 1964; A. Fongaro in SFr 35 : 320–22, 1968; M. Hamburger in Spec 7102 : 188–89, Aug. 7, 1964; S. Lockerbie in FS 19 : 419–20, 1965; J. Onimus in RSH 119 : 466–67, 1965.

Garvey, Eleanor M. Cubist and Fauve illustrated books. GazBA 37–50, Jan. 1964.   **8038**

P. 38–41 on Derain's 31 woodcuts for *L'enchanteur pourrissant* which "revolutionized the medium" because of their simplicity and strongly cut line. P. 43–44 on Dufy's more decorative woodcuts for *Le bestiaire*. This section, which also discusses the genesis of that work, refers to the ms. of 13 signed drawings, 57 signed proofs, and a proof of the first imprint page designed by Dufy.

Golding, John. Guillaume Apollinaire and the art of the twentieth century. BMAN 26–27 : 3–31, 1963.   **8039**

Stimulating if controversial view of A.'s critical contribution to modern art by a leading English art critic and expert on cubism. Arranged on a biographical, chronological basis. Believes A. best as impresario, propagandist, discoverer of great unknowns (Picasso, Braque, Chirico, etc.) and as influence on Delaunay's orphism, Picabia's and Duchamp's dadaism, and Breton's surrealism. Questionable thesis that he was primarily an anti-intellectual, instinctive critic without a true understanding of art and that he never knew what cubism was all about. Important idea that *Lul de Faltenin* may commemorate *Les demoiselles d'Avignon*. Article well-illustrated with reproductions.

Guiette, Robert. Notes sur La femme assise. RSH 84:459–60, 1956.   **8040**

One of the rare critical articles on this posthumous novel about the Mormons reveals that A. was well versed in Mormon history and writings. Some possible French sources. Study continued by Scott Bates' *Apollinaire en Amérique* (SaBe 44:2675–80, 1964) where Elder John Taylor, a leading figure in the novel, is discussed; and by Robert Guiette's *Le cri des neuf de la renommé* (RLM 183–88:188–94, 1968 and *Du monde européen à l'univers des mythes*, p. 20–30, *supra*), where chapter 7 of the novel, the evocation of war heroes of the past, is analyzed.

Pia, Pascal. Apollinaire et le bon ton. QL 5:13, May 16, 1966.   **8041**

The only article to date on Molina da Silva's book *La grâce et le maintien français* (1902), most of which was probably written by A.

Pierssens, Michel. Apollinaire, Picasso, et la mort de la poésie. Eur 48:178–90, 1970.   **8042**

Considers A. a decadent critic who tried to put Picasso in 19th-c. symbolist camp and make a reactionary demiurge out of him. Art is pure plasticity and has nothing to do with poetry. Picasso modern, A. not. "Pour parler comme Breton, Apollinaire représente bien la fin de la Poésie."

Poupon, Marc. Quelques énigmes du Bestiaire. RLM 146–49 (GAp 5):85–96, 1966.   **8043**

Elucidation of a few of the hermetic references in this little work; mostly speculative, however. Parallels with *L'émigrant de Landor Road*. Finds a few sources for quatrains cut from final copy (*Le singe, L'araignée*).

Thenen, Rhéa. Apollinaire juge de Baudelaire. RSH 138:239–50, 1970.   **8044**

Continues Durry's study of this important subject (in *Alcools*, v. 2, p. 51–59). Mainly discusses A.'s article of 1917, *Baudelaire dans le domaine public*. Also lists principal references to Baudelaire in other writings.

Torre, Guillermo de. Apollinaire y las teorías del cubismo. Barcelona, Buenos Aires, E.D.H.A.S.A., 1967. 166 p. (Colección el puente)   **8045**

Thoughtful, general essay on theories and background of cubism, its messianism, constructionism, dehumanization, and creation of new reality out of the old. A. considered as the movement's most representative critic and poet. Brief chapters on his life and work; war poetry; use of surprise, tradition and invention; the genius of *Les fenêtres*, his reputation in Spain; his links to painters. A few photographs of paintings and documents.

Warnier, Raymond. Apollinaire journaliste. RHL 56:107–22, 1956.   **8046**

Valuable discussion of the beginnings of A.'s journalistic career with *La grande France* and *L'européen* (1902–04); not always accurate, however.

Zoppi, Sergio. Apollinaire teorico. Naples, Edizioni scientifiche italiane, 1970. 127 p. (Testi e saggi di letteratura francese, 3)   **8047**

Tracing of main esthetic ideas from the first writings to *l'esprit nouveau*. Finds that main lines center about the elaboration of an esthetic humanism synthesizing tradition and invention, and that these lines were present from the beginning.

Reviews: L. Beneventi in SFr 44:390–91, 1971; M. Décaudin in RLM 327–30 (GAp 11):198, 1972.

CHAPTER XVII

CHARLES PÉGUY
(Nos. 8048–8388)

Roy Jay Nelson

Bibliography and Iconography

Bilan bibliographique. Ed. by Auguste Martin. CACP 2:65–88, 1948. **8048**

Critical bibliography of books concerning P. published from 1940 to 1948.

Carnet Péguy 1965. Ed. by Auguste Martin. Minard, 1966. 200 p. (CACP 20) **8049**

Record of virtually all activity related to P. occurring in 1965, under four headings: *Ephémérides* (lectures, meetings, manuscript sales, etc.); *Généralités* (transcripts of speeches, reviews of colloquia, etc); *la Presse* (summary of press references to P.); *Bibliographie* (reviews of books on or relating to P., some from before 1965). Continued in *Carnet Péguy 1966* (Minard, 1969), 232 p.; *Carnet Péguy 1967* (Minard, 1969), 168 p.; *Carnet Péguy 1968* in ACPFM 168:5–36, 1971; 169:7–36, 1971; 170:1–38, 1971; 173:2–48, 1971; and *Carnet Péguy 1969* in ACPFM 184:19–40, 1973; 185:39–48, 1973.

Charles Péguy. Bibliothèque nationale, 1974. xvi, 185 p. **8050**

Illustrated catalog of the exhibition in commemoration of the hundredth anniversary of P.'s birth. 506 items listed, including many extant autographs by P., manuscripts, memoranda and correspondence, with descriptions and indications of present location (including call numbers for B. N. documents). Documentary proof of biographical information (e.g., P.'s marriage announcement, P.'s signature on pro-Dreyfus petitions in 1898, P.'s notes to printers, etc.). Bibliographical details on various editions of his work.

Feuillets, tables décennales. Ed. by Auguste Martin. Amitié Charles Péguy, 1968. 140 p. (ACPFM 68; numéro hors exercice). **8051**

Complete bibliography (by author, title, subject, and issue) of everything published in ACPFM, nos. 1–67 (1948–1958). The *Bilan bibliographique*, p. 94–105, includes a list of editions of P.'s works published in France and abroad, a virtually complete bibliography of works dealing, in whole or in part, with P. published 1940–1958, and references to a few earlier studies.

Hardré, Jacques. Etats-Unis: liste d'ouvrages consacrés à, ou contenant d'importantes remarques sur Péguy. ACPFM 195:19–22, 1974. **8052**

Chronological bibliography of works partially or completely devoted to P., written by U. S. critics and/or published in the United States between 1920 and 1971. 68 entries, including M.A. and Ph.D. theses, as well as references to partial translations of P.'s works.

Manuscrits de Péguy; exposition pour le centième anniversaire de sa naissance. Orléans, Centre Charles Péguy, 1973. 67 p. **8053**

Detailed description of more than forty manuscripts at the Centre Péguy in Orléans, ranging from single sonnets to the most important prose and poetic works. Description of paper used, P.'s handwriting variations, diverse cuts, additions and inserts, showing in what order P. composed various sections of his works. Photographic reproductions on unnumbered pages of eight significant manuscript pages.

Martin, Auguste. Carnet Péguy, Centenaire 1973. ACPFM 195:1–63, 1974; 196:1–80, 1974; 197:1–64, 1974; 198:1–64, 1974. **8054**

Book reviews; calendar and review of events connected with the 1973 centenary of P.'s birth; review of articles and of 1973 press references to P. and the anniversary.

Onimus, Jean. Travaux et recherches concernant Péguy: suggestions et perspectives d'avenir. *In:* Péguy, actes du colloque international d'Orléans. *See* 8179. p. 376–83. **8055**

Systematic listing of suggested studies on P.'s work. Broad yet specific program of research which, to date, remains virtually untouched.

Schmitt, Hans A. Péguy à l'étranger: essai d'une bibliographie de 1910 à 1930. ACPFM 36:23–26, 1953. **8056**

56 entries, including book reviews, with a comment on the contents of each. A most valuable reference.

Editions

Fossier, Andrée. Tables analytiques des œuvres de Péguy. A l'Orante, 1947. 431 p. **8057**

Concordance for P.'s *De Jean Coste, Zangwill, Les suppliants parallèles, Louis de Gonzague, Notre patrie,* the *Situations, Le mystère de la charité, Notre jeunesse, Victor-Marie, comte Hugo,* the *Laudet,* the *Porche,* the *Saints Innocents, L'argent* and *L'argent suite,* the *Note sur M. Bergson,* the *Note conjointe,* and *Clio* (1917 edition). Invaluable tool, adequate indeed for the works treated, but needs to be extended to the rest of P.'s production. Review: Anon. in CACP 2:88, 1948.

Péguy, Charles. Le choix de Péguy. Gallimard, 1952. 363 p. *Orig. ed.:* Œuvres choisies, 1900–1910. Grasset, 1911. **8058**

Edition of the famous 1911 selection of excerpts made by P.'s friend Charles Lucas de Pesloüan from the period 1900–1910. P. later praised both the selection, indicating thus what elements of his own work he considered most important, and the excerpting, shedding light in this way on his conception of the organization of his works.

—. Morceaux choisis des œuvres poétiques. Ollendorf, 1914. 246 p. **8059**

Selection made during P.'s lifetime and dedicated by him to Louis Boitier.

—. Le mystère de la charité de Jeanne d'Arc, avec deux actes inédits, édition établie d'après les manuscrits par Albert Béguin, avec le concours de Mme Charles Péguy et de M. Alfred Saffrey. Le club du meilleur livre, 1956. 418, 43 p. **8060**

The only true critical edition of a work by P. Uses typographical signs to indicate the various layers of the text created by successive additions and changes. Includes two acts of the play never published by P., a history of the composition of the work by A. Béguin, and photographs of selected parts of P.'s manuscript and corrected proof. Review: A. Martin in ACPFM 61: 22–23, 1957.

—. Notes politiques et sociales. Avant-propos par André Boisserie. L'amitié Charles Péguy, 1957. 93 p. (CACP 11) **8061**

Republication of P.'s articles from the *Revue blanche* (1899). Best readily available primary source for the comprehension of his early socialism. He published other notes and articles elsewhere during the period 1897–1900, but these are the major pieces. Preface provides valuable insights. Reviews: P. Guiral in ACPFM 61: 24–25, 1957; J. Onimus in LR 13: 205–07, 1959.

—. Œuvres complètes. NRF, 1916–1955. 20 v. **8062**

While presenting P.'s works in no comprehensible order, and while still incomplete (the *Quatrains,* the *Prière de déférence* and the *Suite d'Eve* are notably lacking), this collection has revealed to the public a number of posthumous works, including *Pierre* (Vol. 10), *Clio* (V. 8), and in the five most recent volumes (1952–1955) an important body of posthumous essays: "Par ce demi-clair matin" (V. 16), "L'esprit de système" (V. 17), "Un poète l'a dit..." (V. 18), "Deuxième élégie XXX" (V. 19), and "La thèse" (V. 20). For analysis and additional posthumous works, *see* 8375.

————. Œuvres en prose, 1898–1908. Introduction, chronologie, notes, bibliographie et index par Marcel Péguy. Gallimard, 1959. xxvii, 1534 p. (Bibliothèque de la Pléiade) **8063**

Contains most of P.'s important prose works for the period, but omits numerous writings published in the *Cahiers* as well as major posthumous works written before 1908. Includes *Marcel* and an edited version of *Pierre, commencement d'une vie bourgeoise*. Chronology of P.'s life 1873–1908 and notes are not quite adequate and not always accurate. Bibliography of P.'s published works, 1897–1909.

Reviews: A. Martin in ACPFM 77: 38–39, 1960; A. Rousseaux in FL 789: 2, 1960.

————. Œuvres en prose, 1909–1914. Avant-propos, chronologie, notes, bibliographie et index par Marcel Péguy. Gallimard, 1957. xxxii, 1598 p. (Bibliothèque de la Pléiade). *Also:* 1961. xxxvi, 1646 p. **8064**

Contains most of P.'s important prose works of the period (major exception: *La thèse*). Notes do not always provide identification of persons mentioned in the works or full background of events P. discusses. Bibliography of P.'s prose works published 1909–1914.

Reviews: B. Guyon in RHL 60:238–41, 1960; J. Onimus in ACPFM 61: 26–28, 1957.

————. Œuvres poétiques complètes. Introduction de François Porché; chronologie de la vie et de l'œuvre par Pierre Péguy. Gallimard, 1941. xl, 1371 p. (Bibliothèque de la Pléiade, 60) *Also (rev.):* 1948. xli, 1408 p. *Also (rev.):* 1954. xl, 1454 p. **8065**

Contains most of P.'s known poetic works. 1941 ed. is first ed. of the *Quatrains* (albeit published partly in reverse order omitting 304 verses since discovered (*see* 8367), of the *Prière de déférence* and of the so-called *Suite d'Eve*. 1948 ed. adds a new version of the continuation of the *Mystère de la charité*. 1954 ed. adds *Jeanne et Hauviette, La chanson du roi Dagobert* and *Paris double théâtre*. Each subsequent ed. makes major changes in pagination, rendering obsolete all previous scholarly references.

Review: A. Martin in ACPFM 61: 22, 1957.

————. Péguy & les Cahiers. Textes concernant la gérance des Cahiers de la quinzaine, choisis par Madame Charles Péguy. Sixième édition. Gallimard, 1947. 339 p. **8066**

Selected passages from the early *Cahiers*, some of them little known.

Correspondence

Alain-Fournier and Charles Péguy. Correspondance Péguy—Alain-Fournier. ACPFM 174:1–52, 1972. **8067**

74 letters exchanged between P. and Alain-Fournier (1910–1914), many heretofore unpublished, with a few other documents concerning their relationship. Important correspondence between two writers of surprisingly similar tastes. Introduction and notes by Yves Rey-Herme.

Allier, Raoul, and Charles Péguy. Correspondance. ACPFM 160:11–44, 1970. **8068**

The file of correspondence exchanged (1904–1914) between Allier and P., with a few other relevant letters: 45 in all. Mutual respect throughout, despite occasional differences (e.g., about Jaurès, 1904) between the editor and his Protestant contributor; Allier's financial help for P. Notes by F. Laichter.

Bellais, Georges. Lettres. ACPFM 24:27–28, 1951. **8069**

Important data on Bellais's relationship with P. and on the rough edges of P.'s personality: "C'était assez rude l'amitié de Péguy mais c'était puissant."

Bergson, Henri, and Charles Péguy. Le dossier Bergson-Péguy. EtBer 8:3–60, 1968. **8070**

The rich file of all known correspondence between P. and Bergson (1902–1914) and other letters pertaining to their relationship, with introduction and notes by A. Martin. Many of these key documents on a cooperative friendship appear here for the first time. They show P.'s continuing respect for Bergson, Bergson's understanding and approval of P.'s work, and a 1914 misunderstanding and reconciliation. Includes

Bergson's 1939 letter to D. Halévy in *hommage* to P.

Boitier, Louis, et al. Péguy, Louis Boitier et le radicalisme orléanais: correspondance, dossier présenté et commenté par Jacques Birnberg. ACPFM 192:1–71; 193:1–56, 1974. **8071**

No. 192 contains Birnberg's masterful, detailed and documented presentation of turn-of-the-century politics in Orléans, where P. received his initial political experience, and of Louis Boitier, the wise *charron* from Orléans who introduced P. to republican ideals and kept him informed, throughout his life, of the vicissitudes of their common struggle against sectarian radical-socialism. No. 193 contains 74 letters (1902–1915) by Boitier, H. Roy, F. Rabier, R. HalmaGrand, A. Vazeille, A. Bourgeois, A. Baudouin, V. Boudon and P., tracing Boitier's influential relationship with P.

Bourgeois, André, and Charles Péguy. Correspondance André Bourgeois — Charles Péguy. ACPFM 142:1–29, 1968; 143:13–24, 1968; 146:31, 1969. **8072**

Completes 8087. 45 letters exchanged between P. and his business manager at the *Cahiers*, including a few relevant ones to third parties. Letters date only from periods when P. or Bourgeois was absent from *Cahiers* office. Superior documents on relations with printers; some information on dealings with subscribers and contributors. Introduction and notes by A. Martin.

Bremond, Henri. Péguy et Bremond. ACPFM 171:1–13, 1971. **8073**

Six letters (1910–1912) from Henri Bremond to P., heretofore unpublished, with other documents concerning their relationship. Bremond's favorable judgment of P. and his efforts to help him obtain the 1911 Grand Prize for Literature of the French Academy. Introduction and notes by André Blanchet.

Casimir-Périer, Simone, Claude Casimir-Périer, and Charles Péguy. Correspondance Péguy—Simone et Claude Casimir-Périer. ACPFM 187:1–48, 1973; 188:1–55, 1973. **8074**

186 letters exchanged (1905–1914) between P. and two of his closest friends, with introduction by J. Bastaire.

Important information on P.'s relationships with Pierre Marcel, Blanche Raphaël, Daniel Halévy and others. Sheds light on evolution of P.'s literary attitudes and production; drafts of certain of his poems. Details on P.'s death and burial by Claude Casimir-Périer, who assumed P.'s command.

Challaye, Félicien, and Charles Péguy. Correspondance Challaye-Péguy. ACPFM 131:13–41, 1967. **8075**

21 letters by Challaye, nine by P. and five by André Bouregois, business manager at the *Cahiers,* make up this collection spanning the years 1904–1913. Shows friendly collaboration between the anticolonialist Challaye and P. until their 1913 quarrel, the causes of which are evident in Challaye's last letters. Introduction and notes by A. Martin.

Copeau, Jacques, and Charles Péguy. Péguy et Copeau: lettres et documents. ACPFM 44:1–11, 1955. **8076**

Georges Lerminer presents twelve letters exchanged by Péguy and Copeau, 1910 to 1914. An increasingly friendly relationship: Copeau's appreciation of P.'s *Mystère de la charité* and his efforts to console P. upon the loss of the Grand Prix de l'Académie.

Deshairs, Léon. Léon Deshairs, 1874–1967. ACPFM 131:47–55, 1967. **8077**

Four letters from Deshairs, art critic and professor at the Ecole du Louvre, to P. (1900, 1901, 1904, 1914).

Garnier, Charles-Marie, and Charles Péguy. Péguy et Charles-Marie Garnier. ACPFM 83:3–12, 1961. **8078**

Letters by P., first drafts of letters and notes by Garnier. Jacques Maritain's brother-in-law sheds some light on the relationship of P. and Maritain, and of P. and Barrès, 1909 to 1913.

Gide, André, and Charles Péguy. Correspondance André Gide—Péguy. ACPFM 65:3–28, 1958. **8079**

Twenty documents, including all correspondence known to date between the two authors. Shows Gide as a subscriber to, and enthusiastic reader of, the *Cahiers* ("j'ai lu votre dernier cahier d'une seule haleine ! ! !," p. 25). In a well-documented preface, p. 3–19, A.

Saffrey analyzes Gide's changing attitude toward P.'s work.

Lévy, Albert, and Charles Péguy. Lettres de Péguy et Albert Lévy à Théo Wœhrel. ACPFM 56:3–24, 1957. **8080**

Letters dating from 1895–1896, showing P.'s zealous efforts at proselytism for the socialist cause and his attitude toward university studies and degrees. Biographical information on the period of the composition of *Jeanne d'Arc* (1897). Explanatory preface and notes by A. Martin.

Maritain, Jacques, and Charles Péguy. Correspondance Péguy—Jacques Maritain. ACPFM 176:1–39, 1972; 177:1–28, 1972. **8081**

The history of the P.-Maritain relationship recalled in a superior introduction and notes by A. Martin; preface by J. Maritain, explaining his positions relative to P.'s work; heretofore unpublished correspondence (59 letters and documents, 1901–1911) of great importance for the understanding of P.'s relationship with the Church.

Martin, Auguste. Au Centre Péguy d'Orléans: vingt lettres inédites de Péguy. ACPFM 102:20–28, 1963. **8082**

Summaries of twenty letters from P. to Paul Bondois, 1883 to 1905. The first ones, written between P.'s tenth and fifteenth years, are among his earliest existing letters and reveal a childhood preoccupation with schoolwork and academic success. Precocious interest in history and politics is evident. Indications are present in later letters of the origins of P.'s difficulties with his mother, at the time of his marriage.

Mathiez, Albert. Correspondance [avec Péguy]. ACPFM 181:17–26, 1972. **8083**

Eight heretofore unpublished letters between P. and Mathiez, former schoolmate of P.'s at the Lycée Lakanal (1900–1912).

Millerand, Alexandre, and Charles Péguy. Correspondance Péguy—Alexandre Millerand. ACPFM 178:1–48, 1972; 179:1–32, 1972; 180:1–10, 1972. **8084**

Over one hundred letters and documents concerning P.'s relationship with his lawyer, the future President of the Republic. (23 of the letters previously published, ACPFM 79:5–23, 1960.) Covers period 1903–1914 (for earlier letters see ACPFM 78:14–28, 1960). Important details on *Cahiers'* financial difficulties, on the 1905 sale of shares in the *Cahiers*, and on P.'s legal struggle with the Société nouvelle de librairie et d'édition. Includes P.'s bellicose, anti-German outburst of 1912. Introduction and notes by A. Martin.

Moselly, Emile, and Charles Péguy. Péguy et Emile Moselly; introduction par Alfred Saffrey; correspondance échangée; souvenirs par Emile Moselly. Minard, 1966. 83 p. (CACP 18) **8085**

Text of 37 letters (1902–1913) from Emile Moselly (Chénin) to P. and André Bourgeois; two letters from P. to Moselly; four other documents. Excellent example of one of the contributors to the *Cahiers* keeping P. informed of the politics of the literary world. Review: T. Quoniam in ACPFM 138:34–35, 1968.

Péguy, Charles. Lettre à Franklin-Bouillon. Labergerie, 1948. 56 p. (L'amitié Charles Péguy) **8086**

Long letter, written in 1898 but never sent to its intended recipient, the editorial director of *La volonté*. Important expression of P.'s attitude toward journalism and its role in revolutionary political activity. Preface by Daniel Halévy. (Reprinted, without the preface, in ACPFM 60:1–6, 1957.)

————. Lettres à André Bourgeois. ACPFM 8:3–11, 1950; 9:2–3, 1950. **8087**

21 letters, from 1896 to 1914 from P. to his old high-school friend and eventual business manager at the *Cahiers*. Excellent documents on P. as a young socialist and on his feelings as he left for the front in 1914. Completed by further letters published in ACPFM 142, 143 and 146 (*see* 8072).

————. Lettres à Edouard Berth, Bernard-Lazare, Louis Bompard, et autres. ACPFM 24:1–8, 1951. **8088**

Eleven letters (1900–1906) from P. to divers persons, generally concerning the management of the *Cahiers*.

————. Lettres à Léon Deshairs. ACPFM 38:3–23, 1954. **8089**

Twelve letters from P. to an old school chum (1895–1914).

——. Lettres à Madame Godard-Decrais. ACPFM 4:2–6, 1949. **8090**
Fifteen letters (1911–1913) from P. to a prominent socialite and subscriber to *Cahiers*.

——. Lettres à Paul Crouzet. ACPFM 32:22–26, 1953. **8091**
Nineteen letters (1898, 1912–1914) from P. to his old friend from the Ecole normale supérieure.

——. Lettres à Pierre Laurens. ACPFM 87:3–10, 1961. **8092**
Letters (1908–1914) to the artist who painted P.'s most famous portrait.

——. Lettres de Péguy à divers amis. ACPFM 67:3–9, 1958. **8093**
From 1896 to 1914. A few insights into P.'s personal relationships.

——. Lettres de Péguy à Georges et Lucie Goyau. ACPFM 50:3–14, 1956. **8094**
Six letters from 1910–1911, revealing P.'s state of mind after publishing the *Mystère de la charité* and as he worked on the *Porche*.

——. Lettres de Péguy à Louis Gillet. ACPFM 21:1–7, 1951. **8095**
Ten letters (1901–1912) from P. to the critic and art historian he had known at the Ecole normale supérieure. Of lesser importance.

——. Lettres de Péguy à Lucien Herr. ACPFM 11:1–8, 1950. **8096**
Nine important letters, with historical perspective by A. Martin, from November 21, 1899 to July 3, 1900.

——. Péguy à Blanche Bernard. ACPFM 161:5–18, 1970. **8097**
37 letters from P. to the object of his affection, from the time of her marriage (1910) until P.'s death. Several of the letters previously published separately (see especially ACPFM 80:5–8, 1960). For correspondence between Blanche and P. before 1910, see ACPFM 185 and 186.

——. Péguy: lettres à des amis. ACPFM 13:1–10, 1950. **8098**

23 letters (1895–1914) mostly concerning the management of the *Cahiers*.

——. Péguy: lettres à sa mère, écrites du Lycée Lakanal, 1891–1892. ACPFM 115:3–33, 1965. **8099**
Among the best existing documents on P.'s warm relationship with his mother prior to his marriage; insights into P.'s academic strengths and weaknesses.

——. Quatre lettres de Péguy à Jean Schlumberger. ACPFM 70:3–6, 1959. **8100**
A few details on the good working relationship existing between P. and the young NRF.

——. Quelques lettres de Péguy à Pierre Marcel. ACPFM 69:3–11, 1959. **8101**
Marcel seeks to demonstrate that his friend P. was never really a Catholic, but that Catholics appropriated him after his death.

Péguy, Charles, et al. Lettres inédites: de Péguy (16), Léon Daudet (1), René Salomé (1), Charles Cuissard (1). ACPFM 95:3–14, 1962. **8102**
Letters and fragments revealing P.'s political activity in his native Orléans, 1898. Details on P.'s relationships with authors and publishers (1907–1912).

Péguy, Charles, et al. Rome et Péguy. ACPFM 167:1–28, 1971. **8103**
Collection of letters concerning the Church's attitude toward P. and his defense of Bergson in 1914. Suggestion that a group opposed to P. existed in the Church hierarchy.

Perrot, Georges, et al. Le normalien Péguy: Georges Perrot et le Ministre de l'instruction publique. ACPFM 116:7–17, 1965. **8104**
Leters concerning P. from Perrot (director of the Ecole normale supérieure, 1883–1904) to the Minister of public instruction, with other relevant documents.

Raphaël, Blanche, Gaston and Félix, and Charles Péguy. Correspondance intégrale présentée et commentée par Julie Saniani. ACPFM 185:3–38, 1973; 186:4–31, 1973. **8105**

Not quite "intégrale," this correspondence completes P.'s letters to Blanche Bernard (ACPFM 161:5–18, 1970). 99 documents covering the period 1899–1912, including letters by P., by Blanche, the object of his affection, by Gaston, her brother and a contributor to the *Cahiers,* by Félix, her father, by André Bourgeois, Mme Emile Boivin, Jacques Copeau and others. Blanche's letters show her to be an enterprising and relatively liberated woman.

Reclus, Maurice, and Charles Péguy. Correspondance. ACPFM 183:14–32, 1973.
8106

38 letters (1901–1914), for the most part previously unpublished, exchanged between P., Reclus and A. Bourgeois, P.'s business manager.

Riby, Jules. Lettres à Joseph Lotte. ACPFM 98:11–33, 1963; 99:3–38, 1963; 101:5–29, 1963; 102:3–19, 1963; 104:17–36, 1963; 105:5–31, 1964; 106:13–39, 1964; 108:5–40, 1964; 109:7–30, 1964; 112:11–35, 1965; 113:4–22, 1965.
8107

255 letters (1910–1915) from one young disciple of P. to another illustrating the influence of P. and the *Cahiers* on a young contemporary's attitudes toward Bergsonism, Jews, the Action Française, historical truth, scientism, pacifism, militarism, Catholicism and Catholic literature, etc. Introduction and notes by Théo Quoniam.

Roberty, J.-Emile, and Charles Péguy. Correspondance. CdO 29:18–33, 1969. **8108**

Twenty letters (1906–1914) from the Protestant pastor Roberty to P., with one reply from P. and relevant letters from other correspondents.

Rolland, Romain, and Charles Péguy. Pour l'honneur de l'esprit. Correspondance entre Charles Péguy et Romain Rolland (1898–1914). Albin-Michel, 1973. 384 p. (CahRR 22)
8109

Complete known correspondence. Adds over 130 letters discovered in the archives of CahQ. Introduction and notes by A. Martin.

———. Une amitié française. Correspondance présentée par Alfred Saffrey. Albin Michel, 1955. 357 p. (CACP 10) **8110**

Seriously incomplete edition of the correspondence, but it contains an impor-

tant and detailed biographical preface by Saffrey (p. 13–174), telling the story of the friendship. For a more complete edition of the correspondance, *see* 8109.

Reviews: J. Bruch in RduC 185:296–99, 1955; H. Juin in TR 101:141–42, 1956.

Sorel, Georges. Lettres à Joseph Lotte. ACPFM 33:9–17, 1953; 34:6–16, 1953.
8111

Fourteen letters (1912–1915) from Sorel, a long-time habitué of the offices of the *Cahiers,* to P.'s most faithful disciple.

Spire, André, and Charles Péguy. Péguy et André Spire: correspondance. ACPFM 132:13–36, 1967. **8112**

45 letters (1900–1910) exchanged primarily between the Jewish poet Spire and P., most of them published here for the first time.

Suarès, André, and Charles Péguy. Correspondance, présentée par Alfred Saffrey. Minard, 1961. 85 p. (CACP 14) **8113**

Nearly sixty letters exchanged between Suarès and P. (1899–1914) and numerous related documents and a biographical introduction on the two men.

Suarès, André, and Romain Rolland. Extraits de la correspondance Suarès—Romain Rolland. ACPFM 76:3–14, 1960.
8114

Suarès' letters (1900–1911) to his intimate friend reveal the nature of his difficulties with P. and how he surmounted them.

Walras, Léon, and Charles Péguy. Péguy et le socialisme scientifique: sa correspondance avec l'économiste Walras. ACPFM 121:30–39, 1966. **8115**

Six letters exchanged by Walras and P. in 1897.

Biography

Andler, Charles. Vie de Lucien Herr (1864–1926). Rieder, 1932. 336 p. **8116**

Life story of the socialist leader and librarian at the Ecole normale supérieure and his relations with P.

Andreu, Pierre. Charles Péguy, Georges Sorel et Joseph Lotte. ACPFM 31:7–17, 1953. 8117

Documented account of the relationship of these three men.

——. Notre maître M. Sorel. Grasset, 1953. 338 p. 8118

Biography of Georges Sorel, who, for years, led the Thursday-afternoon discussions in the office of the *Cahiers*. Study, without definitive conclusions, of the P.-Sorel relationship.

Review: Anon. in ACPFM 37:29, 1954.

Artadi, Vicente de. Charles Péguy, lucha y pasión de un poeta. Barcelona, Edic. del Zodiaco, 1948. 377 p. 8119

Spanish popular biography, occasionally novelistic in style. Although generally chronological in the presentation of P.'s writings, the work eschews dates, facts and anecdotal material. Strives to portray P. as a reaction to the particular social, philosophical and literary problems of his times. The numerous quotations from P.'s prose and poetry are translated into Spanish.

Reviews: B. Fortin in ACPFM 2:14, 1948; P. Vovard in ACPFM 7:19, 1949.

Bastaire, Jean. Romain Rolland et Péguy. ACPFM 119:47–57, 1966. 8120

Comparison and contrast of two personalities, based on their works. P. seen as an intellectual genius, Rolland as a lyrical genius.

Beaujard, Paul. Péguy socialiste et l'incident du mandat. ACPFM 88:38–48, 1961. 8121

Historical and biographical details helpful for full comprehension of P.'s early socialism and of the mandate incident recounted by P. in "Compte rendu du mandat."

Boivin, Emile. Mes années d'intimité avec Péguy. Notes établies par A. Martin. ACPFM 60:7–22, 1957; 62:21–28, 1958; 64:7–29, 1958. 8122

Boivin presents, excerpted from his own letters to his parents (1898–1908), all the passages concerning P. Accurate, detailed biographical information on P., particularly for the period 1898–1902,

is to be found in these letters of a close friend.

Borgal, Clément. Charles Péguy et Alain-Fournier. TR 202:68–78, 1964. 8123

Brief history of the P.-Fournier relationship. Suggests that P. freed Fournier from the idea of myth, leading him to become more realistic and more adult.

Boudon, Victor. Mon lieutenant Charles Péguy. Albin-Michel, 1964. 307 p. (Revised and expanded from orig. ed., Avec Charles Péguy de la Lorraine à la Marne. Hachette, 1916.) 8124

Well documented, day-by-day account, by an eyewitness, of P.'s last weeks, July 27 to Sept. 5, 1914. Slightly hagiographical in tone, but apparently quite accurate in historical detail.

Review: A. Martin in ACPFM 107:31–32, 1964.

Chapon, François. Péguy et André Suarès. ACPFM 147:1–16, 1969. 8125

Article, followed by seven heretofore unpublished letters by Suarès, giving fine, unbiased analysis of Suarès's opinions on P.

Chronologie de la vie et de l'œuvre de Péguy. I: De janvier 1873 au 31 décembre 1899 inclus. ACPFM 183 (supplement):1–7, 1973. 8126

Relatively detailed chronology of the first 26 years of P.'s life, accurate according to the most recent biographical research.

Delage, A. A propos de la mort de Péguy. ACPFM 116:4–6, 1965. 8127

An eyewitness account of P.'s battlefield burial.

Duchatelet, Bernard. Les Cahiers de la quinzaine. FMonde 58:17–25, 1968. 8128

Remarkably sound factual introduction for non-specialists, to the history of P.'s *Cahiers*, 1900–1914. Neglects some data, however, on P.'s relationship with the socialist party leaders and on the financing of the *Cahiers*.

Favre, Geneviève. Souvenirs sur Péguy (1903–1914). Eur 46:145–69, 319–44, 475–503, 1938. 8129

Reminiscences about P. by a most intimate confidante. An exceptionally important biographical document.

Fraisse, Simone. Deux professeurs de Péguy en rhétorique supérieure: Georges Edet et Louis Bompard. ACPFM 141:24–32, 1968. **8130**

Analysis of the influence of two professors of classical languages on P. See also "Trois professeurs de Péguy à Orléans" by Fraisse in ACPFM 129:5–47, 1967 for more on P.'s teachers and their influence on him.

Frigulietti, James. Péguy et Albert Mathiez. ACPFM 181:2–16, 1972. **8131**

Objective, documented study of P.'s friendship with Mathiez. Mathiez shown to be one of the rare revolutionary pacifists to remain on friendly terms with P. to the end. P. seen as evolving toward political conservatism in his last years.

Fritz, Gérard. Péguy et la social-démocratie allemande. ACPFM 134:15–40, 1967. **8132**

Well-documented historical article on P.'s attitude toward Germany, showing that P.'s antagonism to Germany after 1905 was essentially a criticism of German socialism.

Gillet, Jérôme. Charles Péguy et Louis Gillet à l'Ecole normale supérieure. ACPFM 94:6–28, 1962. **8133**

Well-documented, although not totally objective, historical study. Relationship of P. to Marxists in the 1890's: P. saw Marxism as systematic, rigid, nondynamic.

Guillemin, Henri. Péguy et le sixième commandement. TM 175–76:538–66, 1960. **8134**

Story of P.'s affection for Blanche Raphaël; suggestion of possible adultery; opinion that P.'s "Prières dans la cathédrale" are insincere.

Halévy, Daniel. Péguy et les Cahiers de la quinzaine. Grasset, 1941. 395 p. (Expanded and revised from orig. ed., Charles Péguy et les Cahiers de la quinzaine. Payot, 1918. 250 p.) **8135**

Important biography by a close friend and contributor to the Cahiers. Good comprehension of many of the subtle distinctions on which P.'s thought is based, but pushes P. somewhat to the political right.

Reviews: A. Guérard in Nat 17:445–46, 1948; J. Riby in CACP 2:65–67, 1948.

Isaac, Jules. Expériences de ma vie. I: Péguy. Calmann-Lévy, 1959. 378 p. **8136**

Isaac recounts the story of his relationship with P., begun in 1891 at Lakanal, through 1902. P.'s school and college friends; how his socialist beliefs were formed; P.'s personality as a young man; detailed account of P.'s break with the socialist leaders and of launching of the Cahiers. Careful attention to biographical detail. Appendices include important documents.

Reviews: B. Guyon in RHL 2:241–45, 1960; A. Martin in ACPFM 73:3–7, 1959; R. Nelson in FR 3:309–10, 1960.

Johannet, René. Vie et mort de Péguy. Flammarion, 1950. 476 p. **8137**

P.'s life as seen from the political right and used in defense of Vichy and collaborationist attitudes. P. portrayed as evolving from an erroneous (perhaps hypocritical) socialism toward a sincere nationalism. Contains factual errors. The author achieves a style that depreciates everything it touches.

Reviews: A. Béguin in ACPFM 21:12–15, 1951; A. Martin in ACPFM 21:21–22, 1951; A. Thérive in EdP 75:109–10, 1951.

Laichter, Frantisek. André Spire. ACPFM 132:49–59, 1967. **8138**

Analysis of the relationship between P. and the poet Spire, whom P. published.

———. Péguy, avec des lettres inédites de Romain Rolland. ACPFM 58:3–26, 1957. **8139**

Contains letters (1925–26) from Rolland to Laichter concerning Rolland's memories of P.; information in letters may not be totally accurate, but they reveal the nature of the P.-Rolland relationship.

———. Romain Rolland et Charles Péguy. ACPFM 119:28–40, 1966. **8140**

Commentary on Rolland's statements to others about P.

———. Une amitié protestante, Péguy-Raoul Allier. ACPFM 159:3–33, 1970. **8141**
Chronological survey of the P.-Allier relationship, based heavily on their correspondence.

Leroy, Géraldi. Notes sur la formation civique et morale de Charles Péguy à l'école primaire 1879–1884. ACPFM 149: 1–12, 1969. **8142**
Brief study of the influence on P.'s thought of such values as republicanism, the ideals of the French Revolution, and bourgeois individualism, as they were presented in the primary schools of P.'s time.

———. Notes sur la formation politique de Charles Péguy à l'école primaire 1879–1884. ACPFM 141:11–20, 1968. **8143**
Effort to recreate historically the mentality of revenge against Prussia for the 1870 invasion, which was current in the schools in which P. was raised and the militant patriotism of the period, which could have influenced P. as a child.

———. Péguy-Bellais et la Société nouvelle de librairie et d'édition. ACPFM 158:5–24, 1970. **8144**
Brilliantly clear historical presentation of P.'s break with the S. N. L. E. and with L. Herr, based in part on the Société's papers in the Archives nationales.

Mabille de Poncheville, André. Jeunesse de Péguy. Alsatia, 1943. 96 p. **8145**
Text of the author's interview with P.'s mother, concerning P.'s childhood, including the text of one of P.'s school compositions (1887); excerpts from P.'s correspondence with his mother, plus the only known letter by P.'s father (12 Sept. 1870); complete text of an essay written by P. in 1887 for his religious education class: "Du rôle de la volonté dans la croyance."
Review: Anon. in CACP 2:77, 1948.

———. Vie de Péguy. La bonne presse, 1943. 237 p. **8146**
Patriotic, popularized biography. Few revelations.
Review: Anon. in CACP 2:78, 1948.

Maritain, Raïssa. Les grandes amitiés. Les aventures de la grâce. New York, Eds. de la maison française, 1944. 326 p. **8147**
Continues Mme Maritain's *Les grandes amitiés, souvenirs;* covers approximately 1907–1917. Important chapter on the character of P.'s religious faith, p. 61–104.
Review: Criticus in RevD 51:59–60, 1945.

———. Les grandes amitiés. Souvenirs. New York, Eds. de la maison française, 1941. 289 p. **8148**
These memoirs, covering a period from the 1880's to about 1909, include information on prominent Catholic intellectuals in Paris at the turn of the century: Psichari, Bloy and Péguy.
Review: G. Lussier in RevD 48:248–49, 1942.

Marix-Spire, Thérèse. Autour d'André Spire, de Péguy et de Daniel Halévy. ACPFM 132:37–47, 1967. **8149**
Candid explanation of André Spire's true feelings for P. (mixture of annoyance and admiration), based primarily on the important Spire-Halévy correspondence, which is quoted here at some length by Madame Spire. P. had admired André Spire and published some of his poetry.

Martin, Auguste. Albert Thierry, Pierre Monatte et la Vie ouvrière. ACPFM 75: 23–31, 1960. **8150**
Brief presentation of opposing attitudes toward P. current in 1914, before his death, with reprint of letters to the editor of the *Vie ouvrière* from 1914; excellent example of an early form of the controversy over the worth of P.'s contribution to French literature.

———. Documents et témoignages sur la Librairie Bellais, la Société nouvelle et les Cahiers de la quinzaine. ACPFM 66: 15–26, 1958. **8151**
Presents historical information on P.'s creation of the Librairie Bellais (1898) and of the *Cahiers* (1900); P.'s financial problems; his break with the Société nouvelle de librairie et d'édition.

———. Péguy écolier et lycéen (1879–1891). ACPFM 117:1–91, 1965. **8152**
P.'s entire academic record is published, showing grades and professors'

comments. Valuable biographical document.

————. Péguy et Alain-Fournier. Amitié Charles Péguy, 1954. 67 p. (CACP 8) **8153**

Description and account of the P.-Fournier friendship, followed by a reply to objections raised by Isabelle Rivière to the foregoing account (which had appeared in part in FL), and by summaries of P.'s letters to Fournier and of related letters by Fournier. Stresses religious sentiments of both authors.

Reviews: A. Rousseaux in FL 482:2, 1955; B. Voyenne in RdPF 7–8:81–83, 1955.

————. Péguy et Millerand. ACPFM 78: 10–29, 1960; 79:2–23, 1960. **8154**

Sound, objective presentation of the relationship (1898–1914) between P. and his lawyer, Alexandre Millerand, future President of the Republic.

————. Péguy, pèlerin de Chartres. ACPFM 5:4–13; 7:14–15, 1949. **8155**

Best historical evidence on the nature, number and dates of P.'s pilgrimages to Chartres.

Moselly, Emile. Souvenirs sur Charles Péguy et sur les Cahiers de la quinzaine. ACPFM 122:9–30, 1966. **8156**

Memories of a man who knew P. well, who knew P.'s mother and many of his friends. Fine brief portrait of P.'s personality, seeking to resolve paradoxes arising from the fact that some saw P. as authoritarian, others as open-minded, some as joyful, others as morose. Treats relationship between P. and Jaurès and between P. and Barrès.

Mounier, Emmanuel. Entretien avec la mère de Péguy. ACPFM 12:5–7, 1950. **8157**

Brief account, dating from 1930, of a visit by Mounier to P.'s mother. Nothing factual about P.'s childhood that is not already in P.'s own accounts, but Mounier seems to have captured the flavor of Mme P.'s conversation.

Onimus, Jean. Péguy et Sorel. ACPFM 77: 3–22, 1960. **8158**

Superior presentation and analysis of the relationship of P. and Georges Sorel, theoretician of revolutionary violence

and regular discussion leader in the offices of the *Cahiers.*

Péguy, Charles. Lettres et entretiens. Eds. de Paris, 1954. 222 p. **8159**

Texts of P.'s conversations with his disciple Joseph Lotte give the best extant indication of P.'s personality and oral style. Includes numerous letters by P. to Lotte, L. Baillet and others. Texts arranged chronologically, introduced and commented upon at length by Marcel Péguy, so as to form a sort of documented biography. Essential work.

Reviews: R. Lalou in NL 1409:3, 1954; A. Martin in ACPFM 61:21, 1957.

Pesloüan, Charles Lucas de. Jeunesse de Péguy. ACPFM 8:12–16, 1950. **8160**

Notes, dating from 1919, on P.'s youth, composed by a close friend and confidant. Information concerning P.'s early attitudes toward the military, the socialist party, the bourgeoisie, the Georges Bellais bookstore founded by P., and about P.'s marriage.

Reclus, Maurice. Le Péguy que j'ai connu; avec 100 lettres de Charles Péguy, 1905–1914. Hachette, 1951. 191 p. **8161**

Memories of P. by a close friend from the Geneviève Favre group. The letters published in appendix are from P. to Mme Favre, a true confidante.

Roche, Anne. Péguy et Antonin Lavergne: la genèse de Jean Coste et ses problèmes d'édition. ACPFM 171:15–26, 1971. **8162**

Life of Lavergne and sources of his novel, *Jean Coste* which P. published in his *Cahiers.* Heavily documented from heretofore unpublished sources.

Rolland, Romain. Péguy. Albin-Michel, 1944. 2 v. (358, 334 p.) *Also (rev.)* Péguy. Avec une préf. de Hubert Juin et un essai inédit [Les deux visages de Péguy] de Henri Guillemin. Illus. originales de Madeline Grot. Evreux: Cercle du bibliophile, 1971. 2 v. (xxiv, 359, 365 p.). (Les chefs-d'œuvre de Romain Rolland) **8163**

Essential biography and analysis of P.'s personality and thought by a principal contributor to the *Cahiers.* Detailed account of P.'s relations with the political, academic and religious communities of his time. Despite occasional errors in fact and lacunae (Rolland relies partly on memory; he was unaware of the important posthumous works published 1952–55; he seems to lack detailed information on P. and Blanche Raphaël), this remains the most detailed and often the most objective general biography.

Reviews: R. Kemp in his *La vie des livres*. Albin-Michel, 1955. p. 158–64; A. Martin in ACPFM 184:3–18, 1973; J. Soulairol in CACP 2:80–81, 1948.

Roy, Henri. Péguy que j'ai connu. ACPFM 17:2–15, 1950.   **8164**

Roy's memories of conversations with P. about P.'s childhood.

Saffrey, Alfred. Barrès et Péguy: lettres et documents inédits. ACPFM 28:3–32, 1952; 29:9–20, 1952.   **8165**

P.'s warm relationship with Barrès and Barrès' success in attracting attention to P.'s work outside the circle of the *Cahiers*. Numerous complete letters from the Péguy-Barrès correspondence cited; other relevant documents.

———. Paul Milliet: une famille de républicains fouriéristes. ACPFM 166:9–26, 1971.   **8166**

Well-documented history of P.'s long, serial publication of the Milliet papers; summaries of the thirteen volumes of Milliet memoirs; why the *Cahiers* published only eleven of them.

———. Péguy et Jérôme et Jean Tharaud. ACPFM 83:13–32, 1961.   **8167**

Biographical information on P. and the Tharaud brothers. Role of P. in the development of their literary career. Based on long quotations from their correspondence.

Spire, André. Lettres de Péguy. ACPFM 40:1–20, 1954.   **8168**

Spire's comments on his relationship with P., documented with thirteen letters from P. to Spire. Spire's early enthusiasm and help for P., until P., as his publisher, altered three lines of his copy.

Tharaud, Jérôme, and Jean. Notre cher Péguy. Plon, 1926. 2 v. (273, 255 p.) **8169**

P.'s life story, told by two of his closest friends, from their days together in the rose courtyard at the Collège Sainte-Barbe until P.'s death. Detailed biographical information (including the first revelation of P.'s love for Blanche Raphaël); heavy reliance on memory; more anecdotal than studiously historical. P. comes to life here almost as does a character in a novel. Still, this is the seminal biography, known to most subsequent biographers and students of P.'s work.

Reviews: Anon. in CahNJ 7:215, 1926; P. Desjardins in SemL 1685:181–84, 1926; F. Gribble in EngRev 44:199–206, 1927.

———. Pour les fidèles de Péguy. Dumas, 1949. 214 p.   **8170**

Anecdotes about P. by men who knew him well, illuminating various facets of his personality, of his relationships with others, and of his political attitudes. Sometimes based on letters or documents not used by the authors in the preparation of their *Notre cher Péguy, supra,* but more often on the authors' memories.

Review: Anon. in ACPFM 4:16, 1949.

Van Itterbeek, Eugène. Les emprunts de Péguy à la bibliothèque de l'École normale. ACPFM 86:4–13, 1961.   **8171**

Solid historical study, suggesting that P. read less than his classmates, limiting himself to a few great philosophical authors and to research on specific projects.

Viard, Jacques, Michel Jordan, and Geneviève Dautremant. Les Cahiers de la quinzaine: deux listes d'abonnés. ACPFM 151:5–39, 1969.   **8172**

The *Cahiers'* subscriber lists for 1900 and 1905. Names of prominent literary and political figures appear on both lists.

Villiers, Marjorie. Charles Péguy, a study in integrity. London, Collins, 1965. 412 p.   **8173**

The most comprehensive biography of P. in English. Generally sound and carefully researched (posits, however, three pilgrimages to Chartres, despite evidence to the contrary; suggests P. brought J. Isaac to socialism around 1894, while Isaac says 1897). Impartial representation of the content of P.'s major works.

Reviews: E. Cahm in ACPFM 126: 184–85, 1966; J. Cameron in NYRB 1:4–5, 1966; J. Cruickshank in List 1891:947, 1965.

Zoppi, Gilbert. Péguy et la Revue bleue. ACPFM 146:1–10, 1969.   **8174**

Summary of P.'s relationship with the eclectic and reputedly bourgeois periodical.

Collected Articles

Amitié Charles Péguy: Feuillets mensuels. Ed. by Auguste Martin. 1– . 1948– .   **8175**

Periodical appearing irregularly, about seven times per year (191 issues appeared 1948 through 1973), and reviewing virtually all the books, theses and monographs concerning or related to P. as they appear.

Cahiers de la quinzaine. Ed. by Charles Péguy. 1900–1914. 15 series.   **8176**

P.'s fortnightly journal in which appeared most of his works published during his lifetime. Also contains works by numerous other authors, which P. selected for publication, generally of political, social or literary interest. Essential primary source for scholars. (Beginning with series number 16, Marcel Péguy takes over his father's publication, after P.'s death, and uses it for his own purposes.)

Les critiques de notre temps et Péguy. Présentation par Simone Fraisse. Garnier, 1973. 190 p.   **8177**

Excellent and varied choice of critical excerpts on P. and his work. Clear, objective presentation.

Péguy. RHL 73:193–544, 1973.   **8178**

Special issue for the hundredth anniversary of P.'s birth. Contains articles by: J. Bastaire, B. Guyon, R. Balibar, F. Gerbod, P. Albouy, S. Fraisse, A. Devaux, J. Marchand, Y. Rey-Herme, J. Viard, M. Péguy, G. Leroy, A. Roche, D. Bonnaud-Lamotte, R. Burac, Y. Favre, F. Desplanques, P. Duployé, J. Onimus, G. Fritz, R. Francis, and G. Antoine. Significant articles are analyzed separately.
Review: A. Martin et al. in ACPFM 196:17–24, 1974.

Péguy, actes du colloque international d'Orléans, 7, 8, 9, septembre 1964. Minard, 1966. 400 p. (CACP 19)   **8179**

Papers presented at the colloquium commemorating the fiftieth anniversary of P.'s death and treating P.'s loyalties, P.'s religion, and the state of scholarship on his work. Contains transcripts of five discussions on the papers. Contains papers by B. Guyon, R. Nelson, Y. Vadé, S. Taylor, E. Cahm, P. Barbéris, J. Bastaire, J. Viard, M. Jordan, P. Thibaud, P. Thisse, P. Duployé, S. Fraisse, H. Jenny, T. Quoniam, J. Delaporte, L. Christophe, P. Guiberteau, C. Guyot, H. Saffrey, H. Féret, J. Gaulmier, K. Kurata, A. Martin, G. Antoine, H. Giordan, A. Espiau de la Maëstre, F. Laichter and J. Onimus. Significant articles have been analyzed separately.
Reviews: A. Devaux in ACPFM 134:2–24, 1967; S. Fraisse in Esp 3:532–34, 1969; R. Nelson in FR 3:424–25, 1967.

Péguy et la vraie France. Montreal, Serge, 1944. 286 p.   **8180**

Volume of articles apparently published to keep alive love for France during the dark hours of the German occupation. Characteristic articles are treated separately under appropriate headings. Authors include Daniel-Rops, Pierre Péguy, Stanislas Fumet, Philippe Guiberteau, Paul Doncœur, Emmanuel Mounier, Marcel Péguy, L.-M. Bellerose, Louis Doucy, Guy Frégaut and Jean-Marie Parent, Henri Ghéon, Claude Franchet, and Alexandre Marc.
Review: Anon. in CACP 2:77–78, 1948.

Péguy reconnu. Esp 8–9:192–544, 1964.   **8181**

Special number for the fiftieth anniversary of P.'s death. Principal articles are analyzed separately under the appropriate headings. Contains articles by: Y. Vadé, J. Viard, P. Thibaud, P. Duployé, H. von Balthasar, S. Fraisse, Rabi, J. Birnberg, P. Emmanuel, R. Marteau, C. Blanchot, J. Bestaire, Y. Avril, E. Cahm, W. Bartenstein, F. Laichter, G. Bernanos and A. Béguin.
Review: P. Duployé in ACPFM 110:142–46, 1964.

La table ronde, numéro 202. S.E.P.A.L., 1964. 160 p. **8182**

Issue commemorating the fiftieth anniversary of P.'s death, with all complete articles (p. 7–84) devoted to P. Articles by H. Contamine, S. Fumet, J. Delaporte, B. Guyon, C. Borgal and P. Chauchard.

General Studies

Chaigne, Louis. Péguy hérault de l'espérance. Eds. des loisirs, 1944. 166 p. **8183**

Short biography of P. for the general reader, with comments on the principal works. Relatively accurate, given the data available at time of writing. Bibliography of major works on P., 1914 to 1941.

Review: Anon. in CACP 7:78, 1948.

Christophe, Lucien. Les grandes heures de Charles Péguy; du fleuve à la mer (1905–1914). Brussels, La renaissance du livre, 1964. 215 p. **8184**

Continuation of Christophe's *Le jeune homme Péguy*. Traces evolution of P.'s thought through his works. Shows more profound appreciation of P.'s religious and patriotic themes than of his socialistic thought, except insofar as socialism prefigures P.'s return to the faith. Treats the posthumous works published 1952–1955. Passes rather hastily over some biographical details, such as P.'s affection for Blanche Raphaël.

Reviews: A. Martin in ACPFM 116: 26–27, 1965; G. Sion in RGB 1:115–17, 1965.

———. Le jeune homme Péguy; de la source au fleuve (1897–1905). Brussels, La renaissance du livre, 1964. 229 p. **8185**

Biographical data based on latest information. Chronological presentation of P.'s principal early works. Excellent appreciation of P.'s humor in the early dialogs, but no serious appreciation of P.'s socialism. Sees P. as a man facing his destiny rather than as the representative of an ideology.

Reviews: A. Martin in ACPFM 104: 37–39, 1963; G. Sion in RGB 1:115–17, 1965.

Curtius, Ernst Robert. Charles Péguy. *In his:* Französischer Geist im zwanzigsten

Jahrhundert. Bern, Francke, 1952. p. 187–223. **8186**

Conventional portrait of an admirable P., based heavily on P.'s statements about himself and on early articles about P., neglecting some more recently uncovered data. Sound explanation of P.'s opposition to the intellectuals of his day and to the general contemporary conception of the historical method. Includes German translation of long, well-selected passages from P.'s essays.

Daniel-Rops (pseud. of Henri-Jules Petiot). Péguy. Flammarion, 1933. 250 p. *Also:* Plon, 1941. 239 p. *Also:* Péguy. Ed. revue et augmentée d'une préface inédite. Plon, 1951. x, 239 p. **8187**

P. portrayed as hero and model of spiritual life, as an ardent patriot and defender of spiritual values. Study of notions of evil and Christian virtue in P.'s work. Widely read general study.

David, Maurice. Initiation à Charles Péguy. La nouvelle édition, 1945. 129 p. **8188**

Brief general study: P.'s thought, style and principal themes. Generally objective approach to P. on all three levels; reaction to use of P.'s work for propaganda purposes by various factions during World War II.

Review: Anon. in CACP 2:82, 1948.

Delaporte, Jean. Connaissance de Péguy. Plon, 1944. 2 v. (333, 441 p.) *Also:* 1946, 1959. **8189**

Major non-technical exegesis of P.'s thought that treats its sources and affinities. Elucidates P.'s principal Christian themes and seeks to derive his theology therefrom; suggests P.'s doctrines are applicable to today's world. Important bibliography.

Reviews: P. Archambault in CACP 2:78–79, 1948; A. Martin in ACPFM 74:28–29, 1959.

———. Péguy dans son temps et dans le nôtre. Union générale d'édition, 1967, 512 p. (Le monde en 10/18, 353–55) **8190**

Carefully reworked to include recent biographical discoveries, cut and divested of scholarly apparatus. This work retains nonetheless the skeletal framework and many important passages of Delaporte's *Connaissance de Péguy, supra*. Valuable information on the various separate social circles in which P. moved, and a concise history of P.'s affection for Blanche Raphaël. Stresses P.'s lessons for our times. Reviews: A. Devaux in ACPFM 152: 8–11, 1969.

Dugas, Marcel. Charles Péguy. *In his:* Versions. Montréal, Maison Francq, 1917. p. 31–88.   **8191**

Text of an early lecture on P., given in Canada, praising P. as a Christian for his energetic independence from Church orthodoxy. Necessity to reconstruct the world, after the holocaust of the war, in conformity with P.'s mystique.

Fowlie, Wallace. Nuit-aube. *In his:* De Villon à Péguy. Montréal, L'arbre, 1944. p. 85–100.   **8192**

Fervent expression of love for the French spirit, composed during the German occupation. Intuited comparisons of P., as a man and a writer, to Baudelaire, Pascal, Rimbaud, St. Thomas Aquinas, *et al.* Sees P. as the very symbol of French grandeur, rising, like Joan of Arc, above venality and intellectualism, to call France to a great religious vocation.

————. Péguy, the presence of a prophet. *In his:* Jacob's night, the religious renascence in France. Sheed & Ward, 1947. 3–24.   **8193**

Sees P.'s art as "magic," involving ability to see spiritual meanings behind material phenomena and to transform physical reality into spiritual truth through use of language. Comments upon the parallelism, seen by P., between Antigone's relationship to Thebes and P.'s to France; develops comparison of P. and Cocteau on Antigone theme.

Gándara, Carmen. Prologo a Péguy. *In her:* El mundo del narrador. Buenos Aires, Editorial Sudamericana, 1968. p. 161–81.   **8194**

Brief general introduction to P. for the Spanish reader.

Gillet, Jérôme. Charles Péguy et Louis Gillet à l'Ecole normale supérieure. ACPFM 94: 6–28, 1962.   **8195**

Well-documented, although not totally objective, historical study. Relationship of P. to Marxists in the 1890's:

P. saw Marxism as systematic, rigid, non-dynamic.

Gremminger, Elsbeth. Péguy. Olten, Verlag Otto Walter, 1949. xx, 331 p.   **8196**

General study for German readers, including biographical material. Chronological evolution of P.'s thought. P.'s *Mystères* seen as resolutely antimodern in form and content; careful analysis of *Eve.* Does not stress P.'s attitude toward Germany. Bibliography. Review: A. Béguin in ACPFM 7:20, 1949.

Guyon, Bernard. Péguy. Hatier, 1960. 288 p. (Connaissance des lettres) *Also:* 1973.   **8197**

Superior general study stressing the development of P.'s thought. Well-documented biographical information gives historical perspective to the works. Sympathetic analyses of the major poems and essays, including important posthumous texts published 1952–55. Dwells at greatest length on Christian themes. Sees P.'s thought as fundamentally unified and rejects artificial divisions between poems and prose, socialism and Christianity, internationalism and nationalism in P.'s work. Reviews: P. Duployé in ACPFM 79: 25–28, 1960; R. Jean in CahS 356: 143–44, 1960; L. Roudiez in RR 1:72–76, 1961.

————. Péguy devant Dieu. Desclée De Brouwer, 1974. 196 p.   **8198**

Chronicle of the evolution of P.'s attitude toward God and toward the Church; effort to discover, on the basis of P.'s writings and other biographical data, the reasons, both philosophical and psychological, for P.'s departure from and return to the faith. A personal, non-scholarly work, but factual and convincing, by one of the foremost students of P.'s life and writings. Review: A. Devaux in ACPFM 197: 60–62, 1974.

Jussem-Wilson, N. Charles Péguy. Hillary house, 1965. 111 p.   **8199**

Very brief, objective history, in English, of P.'s artistic and intellectual development. Detailed study of a few exemplary texts. Brevity causes author, on occasion, to fail to elucidate all nuances of P.'s meaning. Explains P.'s patriotism in later years as an outburst of resentment against Germany, harbored since childhood, caused by the invasion and defeat of France in 1870.

Reviews: E. Cahm in ACPFM 126: 194–96, 1966; R. Nelson in FR 40: 150–51, 1966.

Lalou, René. Charles Péguy. *In his:* Histoire de la littérature française contemporaine. v. 1. Presses univ. de France, 1947. p. 318–33. **8200**

Accurate, balanced assessment of the place of P. and his *Cahiers* in modern French intellectual and literary history.

MacCunn, Florence A. The poetry of Charles Péguy. CorM n.s. 50:574–93, 1921. **8201**

Favorable appreciation of the relationship between the events of P.'s life and those of his poetic works published in the first five volumes of the *Œuvres complètes*. Calls the Hearth, the Altar, the Workshop and the Army the four pillars of P.'s life and of his poetics; describes a peasant's love of the French soil and love of the Republic as the twin towers flanking the "Cathedral" of his life and work.

Martin, Auguste. Courrier littéraire d'Alain Fournier. ACPFM 36:9–14, 1953. **8202**

Summaries, with comments, by A. Martin, of 42 notes on literary matters originally published by Fournier in the Paris *Journal* from 1910 to 1912. All notes summarized concern P. and the *Cahiers*.

Maurois, André. Charles Péguy. *In his:* De Gide à Sartre. Perrin, 1965. p. 83–105. **8203**

Brief and touching intuitive appreciation. P.'s life story quickly told; his affinities (ancient Greece, Bergson, etc.) and his hatreds (Lanson, Langlois, Lavisse). P.'s exceptional understanding of the French mentality; necessity to read P.'s work aloud to appreciate it.

Murray, John Middleton. Charles Péguy. QR 229:91–109, 1918. **8204**

Early British article. Indicates P. found his roots in the soil of France and became in time "the representative of ideal France." The organic unity of P.'s work and his affinity for Bergson-

ism. High praise for P.'s literary criticism.

Nostiz, Oswald von. Charles Péguy. *In:* Christliche Dichter der Gegenwart. Beiträge zur Europäischen Literatur. Herausgegeben von Hermann Friedmann und Otto Mann. Heidelberg, Wolfgang Rothe Verlag, 1955. p. 98–110. *Another ed.:* Christliche Dichter im 20. Jahrhundert. Bern, Francke, 1968. p. 116–28. **8205**

P.'s thought and major themes, especially as presented in his poetry, for German readers. Some reference to events of P.'s life and to his prose works. P.'s anti-German patriotism in 1913–1914 explained as the voice of a naive generation that had not yet experienced the World Wars.

Onimus, Jean. La route de Péguy. Plon, 1962. 205 p. **8206**

Analysis of the chronological evolution of P.'s thought, with relation to the events of his life. Suggests P. is read and remembered, not for solutions to human problems, nor for the literary artistry of his work, but for his personal life and commitments.

Reviews: J. Jehasse in RHL 63:501–02, 1963; T. Quoniam in ACPFM 94: 33–35, 1962.

Péguy, Marcel. Le destin de Charles Péguy. Perrin, 1946. 315 p. **8207**

Differs from introduction of the same title in P.'s *Lettres et entretiens, supra.* P.'s oldest son, in this biography and analysis of P.'s thought, presents his father as the author of certain "théories racistes" (p. 292). Stresses themes related to the work ethic in P. Contains anti-Semitic, anti-Marxist and anti-clerical propaganda. Bitter criticism of other members of the Péguy family, p. 24. Interesting because so blatantly tendentious.

Review: Anon. in CACP 2:70–71, 1948.

Perche, Louis. Essai sur Charles Péguy. Seghers, 1957. 223 p. (Poètes d'aujourd'hui, 60) **8208**

Popularized general study, carefully linking biographical information to commentary on the major works. Appears to follow R. Rolland and data from ACPFM. Stresses apparently pro-

phetic character of some of P.'s utterances. Bibliography.
Review: S. Storelv in ACPFM 67: 84–85, 1958.

Ramirez, Isolina. Charles Péguy, filosofo de la esperanza. Buenos Aires, Rivadavia 5061, 1949. 110 p.   **8209**
Brief general study of P.'s life and work, not limited to the theme of hope. Translation into Spanish of selected passages by P.
Review: A. Béguin in ACPFM 37: 25, 1954.

Schmitt, Hans A. Charles Péguy: autobiographer. Ren 9:68–76, 1956.   **8210**
A summary of the primary personal influences on P.'s thought as they appear in his writings.

Secrétain, Roger. Péguy soldat de la vérité. Marseille, Sagittaire, 1941. 285 p. *Also:* Perrin, 1972. 463 p.   **8211**
The biographical information given is particularly interesting for the period of P.'s childhood in Orléans, well researched by the Orléanais author. P.'s individualism stressed. His religion, as described here, may appear too Protestant to some readers. Valuable insights into the workings of P.'s literary style (Chap VIII).
Reviews: P. Dournes in CACP 2: 67–68, 1948; J. Ducange in CahS 238:407–14; A. Spire in Re 1:315–21, 1943.

Servais, Yvonne. Charles Péguy: the pursuit of salvation. Cork, Cork univ. press, 1953. 401 p.   **8212**
Superior interpretive study in English of P.'s life and work up to 1909. Valuable analyses of *Notre patrie, Clio* and other major works. Accurate presentation of P.'s political and philosophical positions; P.'s inherent contradictions are not glossed over, and his personal problems are adequately treated. Bias explicit in the title (existence of a single, inherent and upward direction in P.'s life) is not overstressed in the text. Knowledge of the five volumes of posthumous essays published 1952–1955 might well have modified some conclusions slightly, notably in chapters XIV, XV and XVI.

Stolpe, Sven. Sjalar i brand, Kristna essayer. Stockholm, Albert Bonniers förlag, 1938. 253 p.   **8213**
Essays on a number of Christian authors. Includes brief and anecdotic summary of P.'s life; sees P.'s socialism as theoretical and of little practical value; seems to prefer Jaurès' approach. Translation into Swedish of passages from *Jeanne d'Arc, Mystère de la charité* and *Porche.*
Review: S. Storelv in ACPFM 60: 23–24, 1957.

Suarès, André. Péguy. Emile-Paul frères, 1915. 102 p.   **8214**
Homage to P., but unlike others. Brusk, ultimately sincere, often unflattering. Claims P. was a heretic to all his religions except one: love of France. Finds P. repetitive; says P. wrote much good prose, few beautiful verses.
Reviews: S. Braun and J. Schlumberger in FR 39:533–35, 1966; F. Chapon in ACPFM 147:1–8, 1969.

Sylvestre, Charles. Charles Péguy. Lettre-préface de Madame Charles Péguy. Bloud et Gay, 1916. 122 p.   **8215**
Homage to the "premier soldat de la pensée française." Numerous and lengthy quotations from P.'s work. The emotional approval expressed here signals the beginning of P.'s status as a legendary national hero.

Turnell, Martin. A hero of our time. Cweal 85:251–54, 1966.   **8216**
A standard introduction to P. for the non-specialist, based heavily on Villiers, *supra.* Author remained unaware in 1966 of Blanche Raphaël's identity. Praises P.'s "courage" and "integrity," but finds P.'s work repetitive and wearisome.

Studies on His Thought

Adereth, Maxwell. Commitment in modern French literature: a brief study of littérature engagée in the works of Péguy, Aragon, and Sartre. London, V. Gollancz, 1967. 240 p. *Also:* Politics and society in Péguy, Aragon, and Sartre. New York, Schocken Books, 1968.   **8217**
25 pages on P. Interesting comparison, where P. serves, however, as some-

thing of a foil for the more communistic authors. Information on P., coming too often from secondary sources, is not always accurate. Reviews. J. Cruickshank in LonM 12:94–96, 1968; H. Mason in MLR 64:438–39, 1969; R. Nelson in ACPFM 173:10–12, 1971.

Albouy, Pierre. Péguy et Hugo. *In:* Péguy. *See* 8178. p. 254–63. **8218**
An eminent Hugo specialist studies P.'s principal pronouncements on Hugo from 1909 to 1912. Notes P.'s criticism of Hugo's romanticism and "carriérisme," and his admiration of Hugo as an enduring example of the pagan mentality, entirely outside of the Christian tradition.

Antoine, Gérald. Péguy et Claudel: deux itinéraires politiques et mystiques. ACPFM 165:23–48, 1971. **8219**
Comparative study of major importance, based heavily on documentary evidence. Claudel's letters reveal his anti-Semitic and ultraconservative attitudes, which turned him against P. (in whom he saw an anarchistic destroyer), as well as his anti-intellectualism and his sense of the vitality of Christianity, which led him to admire certain of P.'s writings; Claudel's judgments on P.'s style; comparison of thematically similar passages in both authors reveals sixteen points of resemblance and four principal areas of disagreement.

Archidec, Alain. Mystique et politique: Péguy et les socialistes du groupe Jules Guesde. ACPFM 69:12–19, 1959; 70:7–21, 1959. **8220**
Early effort to distinguish P.'s socialism from other socialist tendencies, including Marxist dialectical materialism, as all segments of socialist opinion were polarized by the Dreyfus case.

Arnauld, Michel (pseud. of Marcel Drouin). Les Cahiers de Charles Péguy. NRF 2: 258–83, 1910. **8221**
Remarkably accurate contemporary appreciation of P.'s thought. Description of the Thursday discussions in the offices of the *Cahiers*. Notes relationship of P.'s attitudes to those of Proudhon and Michelet, but distinguishes P. from Rousseau and certain romantic authors. Includes a summary, with long

quotations, of P.'s second "Situation" (Oct. 6, 1907).

Avril, Yves. Exigence et acceptation. *In:* Péguy reconnu. *See* 8181. p. 407–10. **8222**
P. seen as resolving, in the end, to accept the human condition, rather than to struggle against it.

Balthasar, Hans Urs von. Péguy. *In his:* Herrlichkeit. v. 2. Einsiedeln, Johannes Verlag, 1962. p. 767–880. **8223**
General presentation of P.'s thought, indicating unity of form and content in P.'s work. Seeks to define the place of Judaism in P.'s work; presents P.'s view of Hell; relationship of Greek thought to P.'s Christianity; P.'s view of history and historiography; P.'s conception of God.

Bancquart, Marie-Claire. Les écrivains et l'histoire. Nizet, 1966. 389 p. **8224**
Comparison of attitudes toward history in Barrès, France, Bloy and P. Finds that P. was not marked psychologically by the 1870 defeat. Superior analysis of P.'s attitude toward historiography. See conclusion (p. 273–327) for major comparison of the four authors, as well as the special section on Joan of Arc in their works (P. treated p. 345–61).

Barbéris, Pierre. La notion du peuple chez Péguy. *In:* Péguy, actes du colloque international d'Orléans. *See* 8179. p. 78–91. **8225**
Criticism, on Marxist grounds, of P.'s socialism. Sees P. as adopting a spiritualistic, reactionary and unrealistic tradition not grounded, like Marxism, on scientific, social and economic analysis.

———. Péguy: actualité et signification. NCr 144:118–30, 1963. **8226**
Introduction to P. for Marxist readers. Finds P. to be a moralist rather than a socialist; classes P. as a reactionary anticapitalist: one who seeks a return to pre-industrial society.

Barbier, Joseph. La prière chrétienne à travers l'œuvre de Charles Péguy. Eds. de l'école, 1959. viii, 201 p. **8227**
Rapid, sentimental, and often pietistic presentation of the primary religious themes in P.'s major poems, with brief

but interesting references to P.'s style, sources and symbols.

Review: G. Péguy in ACPFM 74:29, 1959.

Bastaire, Jean. Le patriotisme de Péguy avant 1905. *In:* Péguy, actes du colloque international d'Orléans. *See* 8179. p. 92–108.   **8228**

Careful analysis, distinguishing between patriotism and chauvinism. Stresses P.'s view of France as an exemplary civilization, whose pacifism and internationalism are subjects of pride.

Béguin, Albert. La prière de Péguy. Neuchâtel, La Baconnière, 1942. 135 p. *Also:* Cahiers du Rhône, La Baconnière, 1944. *Also:* 1948.   **8229**

P.'s Catholic outlook; his religious beliefs. Treats the prayers in the cathedral of the *Tapisserie de Notre Dame* and parts of the *Porche*. Develops, in a note on litany, an important psychological and religious explanation of certain of P.'s repetitions in *Eve*.

Reviews: P. Dournes in CACP 2: 72–73, 1948; R. Secrétain in CahS 30: 38–55, 1943.

Benda, Julien. La trahison des clercs. Grasset, 1948. 309 p. *Orig. ed.:* 1927.   **8230**

Well-known diatribe against those writers and intellectuals who descend into the relativism of the political fray, for their own glory. P. criticized with Barrès, Maurras and Claudel (p. 128, 130, 217, 223 *et passim*).

Bernanos, Georges. Péguy. ACPFM 3:4–8, 1949.   **8231**

Two passages from Bernanos' journal, one dating from the early 1930's and the other from 1939. Expression of admiration for P.'s thought and continuing influence.

————. Son heure sonnera.... *In:* Péguy reconnu. *See* 8181. p. 437–41.   **8232**

Written in 1943; reprinted from BuB 10:June 1952. Bernanos regretted that P.'s thought had been appropriated by the "intellectuals" and the "plotting ecclesiastics;" he foresaw the day when P.'s meaning would be truly understood.

Bespaloff, Rachel. The humanism of Péguy. RPol 9:92–106, 1947.   **8233**

The "passion of authenticity" seen as the source of P.'s humanism, patriotism and Christianity. P. presented as consistent defender of spiritual values common to Homeric Greece and Christianity and as the constant opponent of materialists. P. compared with Kierkegaard and Nietzsche.

Birnberg, Jacques. Le socialisme intégral. *In:* Péguy reconnu. *See* 8181. p. 343–57.   **8234**

Sees three competing socialist ideologies in France in P.'s time: Marxism, integral socialism and libertarian socialism. Comparison and contrast of these ideologies; P.'s relationship to each. P.'s Utopian attitudes.

Blanchot, Charles. Péguy et Ramuz. *In:* Péguy reconnu. *See* 8181. p. 379–87.   **8235**

Common love of the earth and of peasants in P. and Ramuz. In the face of the unhappy human condition, P. turns to religion, while Ramuz remains agnostic.

Bodart, Roger. Péguy et Malraux ou la dégradation nécessaire. *In his:* Dialogues européens, de Montaigne à Sartre. Brussels, Eds. des artistes, 1950. p. 97–119.   **8236**

P. and Malraux treated separately. Section on P. praises him for willingness to change freely in a changing world and for opposing permanent commitment to any "politique." Author considers P. the most powerful spokesman today for a Church he allegedly refused to enter.

Brugmans, Henri. La notion de peuple chez Michelet et chez Péguy. ACPFM 20:3–19, 1951.   **8237**

Michelet and Péguy compared with respect to their definitions of the "peuple" of France, their notions of a French "race," a French mentality, a French destiny. Michelet's influence on P. implied. Little attempt at contrast, except in the suggestion that P.'s style is itself more "populaire" than Michelet's.

Cahm, Eric. Péguy et le nationalisme français. Minard, 1972. 251 p. (CACP 25)   **8238**

146 pages of Cahm's text and notes, plus 93 pages of documents: republication of articles dating from P.'s lifetime, and up until 1916, concerning P. and his work. Valuable indication of how P.'s work was received by Barrès, Maurras, Acker, Sorel, Le Grix and others during his lifetime. Cahm's impartial study demonstrates P.'s constant love for France, which was shared by most of his compatriots: they differed primarily over the sort of government France should have.

Reviews: J. Bastaire in Esp 419:977–78, 1972; J. Delaporte in ACPFM 183: 33–35, 1973.

Cardarelli, Vicenzo. Charles Péguy. Voce 3:644–46, 1911. **8239**

Penetrating early analysis of P.'s 1910–1911 publications.

Cattaui, Georges. Péguy, témoin du temporel chrétien. Eds. du centurion, 1964. 189 p. **8240**

Brief, laudatory introduction to P.'s thought. Stresses theme of incarnation (and Incarnation). Adds little to Onimus, *Incarnation, infra.*

Review: A. Devaux in ACPFM 126: 175–76, 1966.

Chabot, Jacques. Bernanos et Péguy. *In:* Bernanos. Centre culturel de Cerisy-la-Salle. Ed. by Max Milner. Plon, 1972. p. 465–79. **8241**

Shows similar attitude of both writers toward human history under the influence of Michelet; stresses importance of P. in providing a formula which Bernanos could use to express his political thought as he evolved away from Maurras; sees both writers as seeking a libertarian revolution against the pagan totalitarian State. Transcript of discussion at Cerisy on patriotism and nationalism of both authors, p. 480–87.

Challaye, Félicien. Péguy socialiste. Amiot-Dumont, 1954. 334 p. **8242**

Portrait of P. by one of the members of the *Cahiers* "team;" paints P. as a youthful idealist, turned brutally practical in later years. Less an analysis of P.'s political philosophy than the story of the P.-Challaye relationship, a key relationship for the understanding of P.'s development.

Reviews: A. Béguin in Esp 213:

631–32, 1954; R. Kemp in NL 1380:2, 1954; A. Rousseaux in FL 415:2, 1954.

Cimon, Paul. Péguy et le temps présent. Montréal and Paris, Fides 1964. 105 p. **8243**

Philosophical analysis of the notion of present time in P.'s work.

Review: A. Devaux in ACPFM 126: 177, 1966.

Copeau, Jacques. Charles Péguy. ACPFM 44:22–24, 1955. **8244**

Text of a 1940 lecture by Copeau which captures the tone of the times: he sees P.'s writings as a source of national hope and solace in defeat.

————. Péguy et l'espérance. ACPFM 44: 12–21, 1955. **8245**

Text of a laudatory lecture by Copeau, given June 22, 1934; some reference to Copeau's personal acquaintanceship with P.

Crémieux, Fernand M. Charles Péguy et les Cahiers de la quinzaine. ACPFM 115:34–44, 1965. **8246**

First publication of an article written in 1911. Shows superior comprehension of the subtleties of the political and social position the *Cahiers* sought to defend.

Desplanques, François. Lecture-création-génie selon Clio. ACPFM 167:29–49, 1971. **8247**

Superior analysis of P.'s notion of literary creation as revealed in *Clio.*

Doubrovsky, Serge. Polyeucte ou la conquête de Dieu. *In his:* Corneille et la dialectique du héros. Gallimard, 1963. p. 222–61. **8248**

Proposes a logical refutation of P.'s famous analysis of *Polyeucte* set forth in *Victor-Marie, comte Hugo.* Sees *Polyeucte* not as a Christian play, but as a play about Christians. Suggests a single character cannot be both hero and saint as P. had claimed, for heroism is absent in a world where individual will does not make all decisions and where death is no longer an ultimate loss.

Dubois-Dumée, J. P. Solitude de Péguy. Plon, 1946. iv, 180 p. **8249**

P.'s early libertarian socialism shown to be Christian in character, while his later Catholicism is seen as tinged with libertarian ideas. P.'s individualism and integrity condemned him to solitude; while others changed, he remained constant.

Reviews: G. Cattaui in CACP 2:82–84, 1948; W. Stewart in FS 4:168–71, 1950.

Duguy, Roger. Le renouveau littéraire catholique. ACPFM 170:41–50, 1971. **8250**

Original publication in *La critique du libéralisme, religieux, politique, social* 133:3–13, 1914. A clerical reply to P.'s attacks on the clergy, and an appeal to P. as a Christian to help the Church's cause. Example of the very ecclesiastical intolerance and anti-Semitism against which P. fought.

Duployé, Pie. La religion de Péguy. Klinck-sieck, 1965. 693 p. (Bibliothèque française et romane, series C, 10)   **8251**

Most comprehensive book on P.'s religious beliefs. P.'s theology, metaphysics and "prophetic" capacity as deduced from his writings. This study, in its apparent lack of thorough organization, tends to neglect P.'s early religious training.

Reviews: J. Onimus in ACPFM 126:187–92, 1966; P. Thibaud in Esp 355:864–76, 1966.

————. La religion de Péguy. *In:* Péguy, actes du colloque international d'Orléans. *See* 8179. p. 176–87.   **8252**

Develops three central ideas: that P.'s religious attitudes were not constant; that, as a Christian genius, he was able to comprehend atheists and Jews exceptionally well; and that P. was a true Thomist, if a Thomist is a Christian capable of dialog with the best contemporary minds.

Erro, Carlos Alberto. Charles Péguy: el mensaje actual de su vida y de su obra. Sur 144:11–34, 1946.   **8253**

Traces the origins of P.'s thought in the events of his life; stresses P.'s sincerity; sees P. as being more Catholic than Protestant in his religious thought and more libertarian than fascistic in his politics. Relationship of P.'s atti-

tudes and positions to the political and social problems of 1946.

Fraisse, Simone. Péguy et le monde antique. Armand Colin, 1973. 567 p.   **8254**

Definitive study. Evolution of the humanities; gradual growth of materialistic values; P.'s polemical exaggerations in criticizing the evolution; P.'s classical education and readings; his efforts to adapt this culture to his own struggles, 1905–1914; the ambiguities of P.'s *Clio;* P.'s search for lasting fame; P.'s use of classical ideas and symbols; certain inconsistencies and errors on his part in interpreting Greek and Roman language and culture; P.'s antitheses without syntheses. Pertinent remarks on P.'s *Thèse.*

Fumet, Stanislas. Péguy. *In:* Péguy et la vraie France. *See* 8180. p. 29–59.   **8255**

Primarily a pietistic panegyric, but a few interesting memories of P.

Galli, Attilio. Charles Péguy, contestataire global. ACPFM 166:4–8, 1971.   **8256**

Summary of some of P.'s social attitudes, seen as similar to those held during the civil-protest movements of the late 1960's.

Gallie, W. B. Péguy the moralist. FS 2:68–82, 1948.   **8257**

Fruitful analysis of P.'s moral positions as evidenced in *Marcel* and in his early socialist activity. Discovers in P. a defender of selfless dedication to humanity and of reverence for life; evokes similarity between P.'s socialist ethic and traditional Christian principles.

Gerbod, Françoise. La figure de Polyeucte dans l'œuvre de Péguy. *In:* Péguy. *See* 8178. p. 237–53.   **8258**

Shows that P.'s admiration for Polyeucte precedes his return to the faith and continues until his death. Contends that Polyeucte, a Cornelian hero who rejects personal glory as a goal, becomes a mythical model for P.'s own life, in whom P. recognizes his personal struggle between hope and despair, between eagerness to act and disgust with action.

Gillet, Louis, Claudel, Péguy. Sagittaire, 1946. 248 p.   **8259**

Text of lectures given by Gillet in Lyon in 1943 in which he strives to evoke a rebirth of pride in French culture during the occupation. In the text dealing specially with P. (p. 109–241), he treats his personal relationship with P., suggesting however that he hardly noticed, at the time, P.'s evolution toward Christian faith. He has since come to feel that P.'s *Mystères* and *Tapisseries*—especially *Eve,* his crowning work—will make P. live on.
Review: G. Lerminier in CACP 2: 85–86, 1948.

Goldberger, Avriel. The will to save: Charles Péguy. *In his:* Visions of a new hero: the heroic life according to André Malraux and earlier advocates of human grandeur. Minard, 1965. p. 85–118. (Bibliothèque des lettres modernes, 7) **8260**
Cogent, brief presentation in English of P.'s political and religious commitments. Accurate comparison with Proust, Malraux, Rolland, Sorel and Suarès; P. situated in his period with some biographical detail. P. seen as "impervious to rational argument, averse to the golden mean."

Goldie, Rosemary. Vers un héroïsme intégral, dans la lignée de Péguy. Amitié Charles Péguy, 1951. 123 p. (CACP 5) **8261**
Well-written essay on the conception of the hero in 20th-century French literature. P. seen as best example of modern French heroism. Strong expression of the values of Christianity and of French patriotism; saintliness seen as the ultimate French heroism.
Reviews: A. Martin in ACPFM 21: 24, 1951.

Grasset, Bernard. L'évangile de l'édition selon Péguy. André Bonne, 1955. 363 p. **8262**
Rambling analysis of P.'s position as editor with respect to contributors to his *Cahiers.* Some excellent insights, but uses P.'s stated attitudes on the editor's role to justify his (Grasset's) position in a lawsuit with Montherlant.

Gregor, Paul. Charles Péguy und die christliche Revolution. Einsiedeln, Johannes Verlag, 1969. 132 p. **8263**
A series of very brief essays on individual works by P. (*Notre jeunesse,* for example, is treated in two pages; *Eve,*

in nine). Salient elements of P.'s thought, plus the usual clichés are presented.

Griffiths, Richard. The reactionary revolution: the Catholic revival in French literature, 1870–1914. London, Constable, 1966. 394 p. **8264**
P. treated *passim.* Impressively erudite study, seeking to show that the return of numerous writers to the faith at this time was reactionary, a flight in panic from the changes brought by scientific progress. Tends at times to force individual writers, of differing opinions, abilities and historical circumstances, into the same mold.
Reviews: D. Charleton in MLR 62: 535–37, 1967; J. Onimus in ACPFM 138:14–17, 1968.

Guiberteau, Philippe. Péguy, Guénon et les anciens mondes. *In:* Péguy, actes du colloque international d'Orléans. *See* 8179. p. 235–44. **8265**
Example of the conservative approach to P. Seeks to show that P., by his special genius, could criticize with prophetic accuracy the incursions of "modernism" into the social fabric and foresee the dangers of the increasing democratization of social and religious institutions.

———. Péguy, le clerc sans reproche (polémique avec Julien Benda). *In:* Péguy et la vraie France. *See* 8180. p. 61–81. **8266**
Points out distortions in P.'s thought promulgated by Benda in his *Trahison des clercs,* for the purpose of better attacking P.

Guillemin, Henri. Contre-expertise: un autre Péguy. Exp 480:21–23, 1960. **8267**
Seeks to destroy the "image d'Epinal" and portray the true P. Suggests it is not without cause that P. has been seen as a spiritual father of Nazism. Expresses admiration for P.'s poetry and for his religious faith, akin to that of the common folk.

———. Péguy et Jaurès. TM 194:78–108, 1962. **8268**
Energetic criticism of P.'s dealings with socialist leaders (Herr, Jaurès, etc.) from P.'s entry into the socialist movement until 1913. P. seen as egotistical, self-seeking and vengeful. Argues for

the fundamental disunity of P.'s political life (P. a turncoat), but misuses some quotations out of context, taking humor for irony and contrition for self-incrimination.

———. Pour une image vraie de Péguy. FrOb 513:22–23, 1960.   8269

Portrays P. as having a writer's vocation early on, then sacrificing it for social action, and, finally, unable to maintain the sacrifice, returning to his original literary calling; it is suggested, however, that fame escaped him because he refused to play the political games of the Action française. A refreshing theory, but hard to substantiate in its totality.

Guyon, Bernard. Fidélités ou reniements. *In:* Péguy, actes du colloque international d'Orléans. *See* 8179. p. 13–24.   8270

Seeks to demonstrate the fundamental unity of P.'s lifelong attitudes through divers political and religious vicissitudes.

———. Le patriotisme de Péguy. ACPFM 59 (supplement):2–16, 1957.   8271

Defense of P.'s nationalism as realistic in its historical context, and as socialistic in its origin.

Guyot, Charly. Péguy et la critique protestante. *In:* Péguy, actes du colloque international d'Orléans. *See* 8179. p. 245–52.   8272

Shows that despite comprehension and admiration of Protestant leaders in the years 1914–16 for P.'s work, they did not seek to claim him as one of their own.

———. Péguy pamphlétaire. Neuchâtel, La Baconnière, 1950. 98 p.   8273

Brief analysis of P.'s polemics, from 1900 to 1913. Suggests that P.'s thought moves quickly and naturally from specific events to general truths; it is thus that the polemicist becomes a lyric poet.

Review: A. Martin in ACPFM 12: 11, 1950.

Hardré, Jacques. Charles Péguy et Albert Camus: esquisse d'un parallèle. FR 40: 471–84, 1967.   8274

Establishes some biographical parallels in youthful years of P. and Camus. Remarkable similarities in their political

philosophies (humanitarian socialism), in their notion of evil, in their opposition to military aggression, in their faith in mankind, and in their commitment to justice, individual liberty and truth. P.'s Christian faith in his latter years is seen as the major distinguishing factor.

———. Charles Péguy et la mystique française. *In:* Romance studies presented to William Morton Dey. Chapel Hill, Univ. of North Carolina, 1950. p. 81–85. (University of North Carolina studies in Romance languages and literature, 12) 8275

Defines P.'s notion of "mystique" as opposed to "politique" in terms of spiritual and moral values. Suggests P.'s popularity in France during World War II may have sprung from the fact that he expressed values important to Frenchmen in times of crisis.

Henry, André. Bergson maître de Péguy. Elzévir, 1948. 327 p.   8276

Serious, non-technical comparison; P.'s work seen as an incarnation (and not a deformation) of Bergson's ideas: whereas Bergson presented his opposition to traditional rationalism in a logical mode, P. espoused the opposition in his very style, choosing organic form for his essays on Bergson. A more technical analysis might reveal more contrasts.

Reviews: G. Maire in ACPFM 4: 15–16, 1949; R. Mossé-Bastide in RPFE 162:99–102, 1952.

———. Du vrai sérieux vécu par Péguy au sérieux inauthentique décrit par l'existentialisme athée. ACPFM 18:1–17, 1950.   8277

Interesting effort to distinguish, through the notion of "seriousness," between P.'s Bergsonian position and the existentialist attitude. Sees existentialism as creating its values from apparent, material realities, while P. believes in an inner moral and dynamic life.

Henry, *Sister* Mary. Péguy's debt to Pascal. EspCr 2:55–65, 1962.   8278

Important introduction to Pascal's influence on P. Shows that P. often finds in Pascal a confirmation of his own developing attitudes and a resolution of the fundamental human duality.

Laichter, Frantisek. A la recherche du vrai Péguy. ACPFM 103:9–38, 1963. 8279

Response to H. Guillemin, who had attacked P. in his "Péguy et Jaurès," *supra.* Seeks to demonstrate how Guillemin quoted P. out of context and without sufficient reference to dates, chronology and contemporary events. Guillemin the victim of his own subjective prejudices.

———. Les Cahiers de la quinzaine dans la presse, de 1900 à 1914. CdO 39:8–24 1972. 8280

Good general review of 739 press clippings and articles about P. and his *Cahiers,* collected by P. during his lifetime. Whether criticized or praised, P. seems to have been, in general, honestly understood until 1910; thereafter, politically inspired activity of the Action française seeks to use P. for nationalistic ends, causing misunderstanding of his later work; silence of the socialists and alienation of the Catholics.

———. Une rénovation créatrice et militante. *In:* Péguy reconnu. *See* 8181. p. 429–36. 8281

Witness borne, by a Czech citizen, to the force of P.'s ideas in the world of the 1960's. P. seen as a prophet and as a fighter for truth; his Christian message seen as general and not as specifically Catholic.

Lasserre, Pierre. Charles Péguy. *In his:* Les chapelles littéraires. Garnier, 1920. p. 139–252. 8282

Treats evolution of P.'s thought as an individual case, indicative, however, of the evolution of a segment of public opinion in France. Influences acting upon P.: leftist moralism, Bergsonism, P.'s individual genius.

Mallard, Henri-Victor. La morale de Péguy. Eds. de l'ermite, 1952. 155 p. 8283

Analysis of the double nature of P.'s commitment (socialism, nationalism). Discovery, beneath these two commitments, of a constant affirmation of the values of purity and heroism, even of martyrdom. P.'s unrelenting individualism. P.'s lack of systematic doctrine. Comparison and contrast of P. and the Catholic socialists. P.'s tendency to cruel intolerance.

Review: A. Théry in ACPFM 72:26, 1952.

Marc, Alexandre. Péguy et le socialisme. Presses d'Europe, 1973. 189 p. 8284

Collection of essays, many of which were previously published as articles, on P.'s socialism and on socialism in general. Author advocates Proudhonian politics (libertarianism, individualism, antifascism, antimarxism) and uses P., quite aptly, to defend his position.

Maugendre, L. A. La renaissance catholique au début du XXe siècle. V. I. Beauchesne, 1963. 416 p. V. II. Beauchesne, 1964. 304 p. 8285

Primarily devoted to Georges Dumesnil and the Amitié de France, Volume I traces the relationship of Joseph Lotte's *Bulletin des professeurs catholiques de l'université* to orthodox Catholic circles. Evokes the difficulties that Lotte's faithfulness to P. caused for the *Bulletin* in this relationship. Volume II focuses upon Lotte and expands upon his relationship to P.

Reviews: T. Quoniam in ACPFM 109:31–32, 1964, and in ACPFM 112:36–38, 1965.

May, Etienne. Les cahiers de la quinzaine. Es 1:259–64, 1905. *Also:* ACPFM 80:29–33, 1960. 8286

Favorable contemporary view of P.'s enterprise. Shows sound grasp of what P. was seeking to express through his periodical.

Mounier, Emmanuel. Entretiens. ACPFM 84:7–24, 1961. 8287

Notes taken by Mounier on conversations with J. Maritain, G. Izard, M. Arland, *et al.* (1929–30); valuable, considered judgment of P. by Maritain. Opinions on Malraux, Maurras, Rimbaud, Bernanos, Gide, and others.

———. Péguy ou l'antimodernisme de la charité. *In:* Péguy et la vraie France. *See* 8180. p. 105–19. 8288

P.'s socialistic Catholicism seen as helping to make Christianity acceptable in an age of science and industry.

———, **Marcel Péguy, and Georges Izard.** La pensée de Charles Péguy. Plon, 1931. 424 p. 8289

Three-part work: Mounier on P.'s vision of mankind and the world (Bergsonism; realism and the supernatural); M. Péguy on P.'s political and social thought (stresses the notion that P. was thoroughly anti-democratic); Izard on P.'s religious thought (interdependence of nature and the supernatural; P.'s social gospel). Reviews: H. Massis in RU 44:742-47, 1931; 45:227-30, 1931.

Nugent, Robert. Péguy and charity. Ren 9: 32–35, 1956.   **8290**
Rather disconnected analysis of P.'s use of poetry for the apparent purpose of molding the French national character. P. seen as seeking to recapture a national past, as Proust sought to regain a personal past. Based primarily on the *Saints innocents*.

Onimus, Jean. Incarnation: essai sur la pensée de Péguy. Amitié Charles Péguy, 1952. 269 p. (CACP 6)   **8291**
Fundamental philosophical study. Pursues the spirit-matter dichotomy into all the major realms of P.'s thought: politics (freedom and commitment), epistemology (book knowledge and experiential knowledge), logic (syllogistic and organic modes), metaphysics (materialism, rationalism and élan vital), and theology (God and man, fall and redemption, Incarnation). Non-technical in approach; contains isolated exaggerations. Bibliography. Reviews: A. Béguin in Esp 191: 1064–65, 1952; H. Féret in ACPFM 33:18–24, 1953; W. Orlando in TR 54:129–33, 1952.

———. Le patriotisme de Péguy. ACPFM 57:1–13, 1957.   **8292**
Demonstrates P.'s attachment to French values, rather than to an intellectual concept of the fatherland or to any momentary French government or policy; draws distinctions between P.'s patriotism and that of Maurras.

———. Péguy et le mystère de l'histoire. Amitié Charles Péguy, 1958. 168 p. (CACP 12)   **8293**
Best work to date on one of P.'s principal contributions to intellectual history, his theory of history itself and of historiography. Documents P.'s opposition to the metaphysics of "objectivity" in historiography and to historical positivism; defines the term "event" as P. understood it; explains P.'s Christian notions of history, temporal reality, the living present, and Time. Reviews: T. Quoniam in ACPFM 70:23–24, 1959; J. Robichez in RSH 93:110–11, 1959; G. Zoppi in RHL 4:628–30, 1961.

———. Péguy, la différence et la répétition. *In:* Péguy. *See* 8178. p. 470–90.   **8294**
Important synthesis. Application of Deleuze's categories to P.'s works brings out the principles of P.'s epistemology, ontology and ethics, as well as the relationship of these principles to his stylistic and literary structures. Passing comments on P.'s relationship to Kierkegaard, Nietzsche and Proust.

Péguy, Marcel. La vocation de Charles Péguy. Eds. du siècle, 1926. 127 p. (CahQ 18, no. 2)   **8295**
P.'s son traces in this *Cahier* (the *Cahiers* were taken over by him after the fifteenth series, P. having died in battle) the evolution of P.'s thought. Some militant anti-communist, anti-Semitic bias; but interesting details, especially on P.'s relationship with his wife after his return to the faith. Claims she was not anti-Christian, but that P. remained outside the Church for other reasons. Reviews: J. de Gourmont in MerF 701:396–99, 1927.

———. Pourquoi Péguy fonda les Cahiers. Eds. du conquistador, 1950. 88 p.   **8296**
Pamplet by P.'s son purporting to analyze the evolution of P.'s thought from 1895 to 1900, but in reality attacking the "socio-arrivistes" and presenting P. as an anti-democratic, anti-socialistic partisan of "Christian racism."

Péguy, Pierre. Péguy présenté aux jeunes. Gallimard, 1941. 80 p.   **8297**
Clear and edifying little study of the evolution of P.'s religious and patriotic thought by P.'s second son. Review: Anon. in CACP 2:69, 1948.

Petit, Jacques. Bernanos, Bloy, Claudel, Péguy: quatre écrivains catholiques face à Israël. Calmann-Lévy, 1972. 268 p. **8298**

Suggests the four writers were all victims, to varying extents, of the myths about Jews current in their time. P. alone is seen as having an immediately favorable attitude toward the Jews, but he tended to see them as people or as economic classes, avoiding in this way the deeper theological questions distinguishing Jews from Christians. P.'s arguments against anti-Semitism shown to be superficial and ineffectual. Objective study, but needing further historical documentation on P.

Reviews: J. Bastaire in ACPFM 184: 41–42, 1973; V. Malka in NL 2350: 8–9, 1972.

Peyre, André. Péguy sans cocarde. José Millas-Martin, 1973. 127 p. **8299**

Interview with Roger Secrétain who portrays P. and his ideas favorably while striving to avoid all partisan or sectarian coloration. P. shown as having foreseen some of the problems leading to student unrest of the 1960's. P.'s potential as a spiritual or moral leader for today's youth. Brief comparisons and contrasts with Marcuse, Bergson, De Gaulle and the ideals of the May '68 movement. Preface by Robert Debré. Brief biography of Secrétain by Peyre, and of P. by G. Dalgues.

Prajs, Lazare. Péguy et Israël. Nizet, 1970. 219 p. **8300**

P. seen through modern Jewish eyes. Points out limitations of P.'s knowledge of Judaism. Sees Bernard Lazare as P.'s principal source of information on subject (valuable biographical data on Lazare). Lauds P.'s courage in attacking anti-Semites and in defending Bergson. Review: M. Muratore in SFr 15:188, 1971.

Quoniam, Théodore. La morale de Péguy. ACPFM 87:11–25, 1961; 88:2–10, 1961; 92:3–11, 1962. **8301**

Five papers on a thorny subject, reaching a more favorable assessment than Mallard, *supra*. Author raises the central problems of P.'s stern moralism, of his militant individualism, and of his quest for the natural self. Sees childlikeness as a definitive moral value for P.; sees P.'s political "révolte" as constructive rather than destructive; points out the Pascalian combination of rational and emotional forces in P.'s moral decisions, evoking the dialectic of moral imperatives incarnate in human beings.

————. La pensée de Péguy. Bordas, 1967. 192 p. **8302**

Introductory study with bibliography.

Rabi. Israël. *In:* Péguy reconnu. *See* 8181. p. 331–42. **8303**

P.'s friendship with, and understanding of, Jews praised; P. presented as obsessionally and viscerally opposed to anti-Semitism. Places P.'s conversion to Catholicism in 1910 (cf. however P.'s *Lettres et entretiens*). Suggests P. brought into his Catholicism fundamental elements of Hebrew theology.

Riby, Jules. Péguy et Pascal, notes et souvenirs. *In:* Péguy, Charles. Pascal. Amitié Charles Péguy, 1947. p. 3–24. (CACP 1) **8304**

Riby recalls P.'s assiduous attendance at E. Boutroux's Sorbonne course on Pascal (1897); sees Pascal as P.'s first personal and direct connection with Christianity since the lycée. Essay serves as a preface to a collection of P.'s writings on Pascal.

Rideau, Emile. Péguy et Teilhard de Chardin. ACPFM 133:3–24, 1967. **8305**

Major comparative study; lists common themes (Bergsonism, notion of reality, the Incarnation, notion of spirituality) and points of divergence (historical optimism, notion of evil and of Redemption).

Robinet, André. Péguy entre Jaurès, Bergson et l'Eglise. Seghers, 1968. 349 p. **8306**

Chronological philosophical analysis of P.'s thought, stressing both the discontinuity of P.'s positions with respect to specific events and the constancy of his fundamental outlook, defined as one of exacerbated individualism. Favorable to Jaurès and Bergson; severely critical of P. (for infidelity to Jaurès, for alleged partial deformation of Bergson's thought, for anarchism) and of his apologists (Béguin, Onimus). Sees P. as a coherent thinker, developer of an "aphilosophy," and not as a mystic.

Reviews: S. Fraisse in RHL 70:153–55, 1970; H. Guillemin in Monde 7482:

i–ii, 1969; A. Martin in ACPFM 154: 41–45, 1969.

―――. Péguy lecteur de Bergson: première rencontre. EtBer 8:61–81, 1968.   **8307**

Apparent influence of Bergson on P.'s *Réponse brève à Jaurès* (1900). A certain reading of Bergson seen as primary and early source of P.'s individualism.

Roche, Anne. Péguy et le socialisme scientifique dans les Œuvres posthumes. *In:* Péguy. *See* 8178. p. 407–16.   **8308**

Seeks to show that P.'s socialism was less Utopian and more nearly Marxist than had been assumed on the basis of texts known before 1969.

Rousseaux, André. Le prophète Péguy. Neuchâtel, La Baconnière. V. I, 1942. 112 p. V. II, 1944. 238 p. V. III, 1945. 381 p. (Les cahiers du Rhône, 6, 51, 57)   **8309**

Essential thematic study that treats primarily P.'s poetry. More objective and less hagiographic than the title might suggest.

Review: A. Béguin in CACP 2:74–76, 1948.

Roussel, Jean. Charles Péguy. Eds. universitaires, 1952. 121 p. (Classiques du XXe siècle)   **8310**

Brief introduction to P.'s thought for students. Bibliography.

―――. Mesure de Péguy. Corrêa, 1946. 213 p.   **8311**

Spiritual and intellectual biography of P. with little attention to factual details of his life. Early statement of opposition to those who paint P. either as a leftist or as a rightist. Stresses constant opposition of P. to all forms of materialism: social, political, intellectual, etc. P. described as a pure defender of the liberty of the human spirit. Appendix, p. 193–209, attacks R. Secrétain for having appeared to doubt the sincerity of P.'s Catholicism.

Reviews: G. Lerminier in CACP 2: 84–85, 1948.

Schmitt, Hans A. Charles Péguy, the decline of an idealist. Baton Rouge, Louisiana state univ. press, 1967. 212 p.   **8312**

P. as seen by a noted American historian. P.'s idealism presented as becoming narrow-minded and intolerant because of failure of his Utopian ideas

and his overweening pride and ambition.

Reviews: R. Nelson in ACPFM 152: 11–13, 1969; J. Onimus in RHL 69: 153–55, 1969; J. Ratté in JMH 40: 656–57, 1968; E. Weber in AHR 73: 1171, 1968.

―――. Charles Péguy: the man and the legend, 1873–1953. ChiR 7:24–37, 1953.   **8313**

Summary of the evolution of P.'s idealistic political and philosophical positions; his influence on the political right and left; attempts on both sides, after his death, to claim him as an ideological ancestor. Provides an ambivalent judgment of P. which is somewhat more favorable than that in Schmitt's subsequent book, *Charles Péguy, the decline of an idealist, supra.*

Sorel, Georges. Charles Péguy. Ronda 1:58–63, 1919.   **8314**

A not unfavorable article, connecting P., for the Italian reader, with popular and populist traditions and primitive religious emotions.

―――. Le patriotisme actuel en France. ACPFM 6:10–13, 1949.   **8315**

Originally published in Italian translation, this early review (1910) of P.'s *Notre jeunesse* is here reproduced from Sorel's French manuscript. It shows a clear understanding of P.'s separation from socialism on one hand, and from the Action française on the other.

Steinacker, Eppo. Nietzsche und Péguy. Bren 18:169–76, 1954.   **8316**

A brief philosophical comparison in such areas as attitude toward the "modern world," toward continuity, and toward night. Generally favorable to P., but finds him to remain relatively unknown in Germany.

Suire, Pierre. Le tourment de Péguy. Laffont, 1956. 318 p.   **8317**

Profoundly Christian interpretation of P.'s life and work. Sees P.'s socialism as a search for religion. Includes synoptic table of P.'s life and works and of contemporary political and literary events.

Review: A. Martin in ACPFM 59:9, 1957.

Taylor, Stanley William. Fidélité de Péguy à l'école. *In:* Péguy, actes du colloque international d'Orléans. *See* 8179. p. 42–48.   **8318**

Documented study of primary and secondary education received by P.; effort to show influence of it on P.'s later attitudes.

Tison-Braun, Micheline. Péguy et le traditionalisme héroïque. *In her:* La crise de l'humanisme. V. I, 1890–1914. Nizet, 1958. p. 406–53.   **8319**

P. seen as a solitary ascetic who chose this path instinctively, not rationally. Suggests the unity of P.'s life: even his socialism was Christian in character; points to the reasons for P.'s break with the socialist party. Sees a certain narrow-mindedness in P.'s anti-intellectualism and anti-scientism. (Cf., however, her later opinion, *infra.*)

———. Péguy retrouvé. ACPFM 170:51–57, 1971.   **8320**

The critic redresses the balance of her judgment of P. as expressed in *La crise de l'humanisme,* arriving here at a far more favorable, though not totally laudatory, assessment. Credits J. Viard, *Philosophie de l'art littéraire et socialisme selon Péguy, infra,* with opening her eyes to the real P., beneath the layers of interpretation laid over his work by rightist and leftist dogmatic sects.

Vadé, Yves. Au péril du monde moderne. *In:* Péguy reconnu. *See* 8181. p. 196–215.   **8321**

Brief analysis of P.'s conception of the "modern world," that contemporary collusion of rationalism and materialism, of science and money, with certain political parties, for ideological ends. P.'s metaphysical revolt against the "modern world."

———. Péguy et le monde moderne. Minard, 1965, 113 p. (CACP 16)   **8322**

Most thorough effort to date to define the term "monde moderne" as P. used it, in all its ramifications. Chronological approach shows evolution and broadening of the concept in P.'s mind. Relationship of P.'s Christian outlook to his struggle against the "modern world." Generally favorable to P.

Reviews: J. Bastaire in ACPFM 126: 192–94, 1966; V. Debidour in BdL 284:34–35, 1967.

Van Itterbeek, Eugène. Péguy et Zola. ACPFM 113:25–32, 1965.   **8323**

Superior analysis of P.'s views on Zola as expressed in an 1899 critique of *Fécondité.* While admiring Zola's "classic" prose and his sincere commitment for Dreyfus, P. thought he had misunderstood social problems, had falsely dramatized the ugliness of true poverty, and had replaced Christian religious lies with equally dangerous pantheistic lies.

———. Socialisme et poésie chez Péguy, de la Jeanne d'Arc à l'affaire Dreyfus. Minard, 1966. 232 p. (CACP 17)   **8324**

Erudite analysis of the relationship between P.'s socialism in the later half of the 1890's and his trilogy of plays about Joan of Arc (1897).

Review: E. Cahm in ACPFM 138: 30–32, 1968.

Viard, Jacques. Anarchiste. *In:* Péguy reconnu. *See* 8181. p. 216–39.   **8325**

When P. and the socialist leaders parted company in 1900, did they leave P. or did P. leave them? Viard seeks to show that P. remained constant to the socialist ideal originally shared by all, while Herr, Andler, Jaurès and others moved away from it; these leaders later sought to obfuscate the question, by suggesting that P. had changed.

———. Proust et Péguy, des affinités méconnues. London, Athlone press of the univ. of London, 1972. 68 p.   **8326**

Serious historical documentation brings to light heretofore unsuspected affinities between the two writers: similar esthetic, political and religious preoccupations.

———. Péguy catholique et protestant. CdO 29:3–18, 1969.   **8327**

Study showing how well P. was understood by Protestants and Jews of his time, and how often he was misunderstood by Catholics. P.'s libertarian temperament, combined with Christian faith, may have tended to make P. appear Protestant. Sees in P. a prophet of the ecumenical movement. Article serves as a foreword to the Protestant pastor Roberty's letters to P. *See* 8108.

———. Péguy, Jaurès et la nation. ACPFM 133:25–44, 1967.   **8328**

Attacks notion that P.'s criticism of Jaurès caused Jaurès's murder, and that Jaurès had read Germany's intentions correctly in 1913. Viard presents P.'s *Cahiers* as supporting Dreyfus without being unpatriotic. Defends P.'s anti-pacifist stance of 1913.

———. Péguy le socialiste; du côté de chez Sartre: Péguy aux outrages. ACPFM 97: 3–78, 1962.   **8329**

Vigorous defense of P.'s socalist beliefs and behavior against the attacks of H. Guillemin in TM and Exp, *supra*. P.'s criticism of Jaurès in 1913 is presented as justifiable, because P. was historically right in his judgment of German intentions; the writers of *Les temps modernes* are described as the true heirs of the Intellectual Party properly vilified by P. Moralistic and elitist prejudices seen as the foundations of Guillemin's attacks.

———. Philosophie de l'art littéraire et socialisme selon Péguy. Klincksieck, 1969. 412 p.   **8330**

Major doctoral thesis linking P.'s political thought to that of a long line of humanitarian, non-Marxist social writers, including Rousseau, Balzac, Hugo, Michelet, Proudhon and Weil. Shows relationship between literary form, style and political attitudes; P. related to Proust on this level. Diffuse, yet erudite and exceptionally penetrating, this study tends to imitate the essay form it describes. Reviews: J. Bastaire in NRF 215: 76–79, 1970; P. Duployé in ACPFM 185:40–48; R. Nelson in FR 45:248–50, 1971.

———. Proust et les Cahiers de la quinzaine. ACPFM 180:20–37, 1972.   **8331**

Proust subscribed to P.'s *Cahiers* from 1908 through the last series in 1914; convincing presentation of similarities in political, social and philosophical positions espoused by the two writers.

Weber, Eugen. A persistent prophet—Péguy. FR 27:337–45, 1954.   **8332**

A brief history of P.'s consistently expressed awareness, from 1905 to 1914, that war with Germany was coming; seen as "amazing" in the context of P.'s times.

Wilder, Amos Niven. Péguy, poet of Christian France. *In his:* Modern poetry and the Christian tradition: a study in the relationship of Christianity to culture. Scribner's, 1952. p. 130–37.   **8333**

Superficial and betimes inaccurate vulgarization.

Style, Structure, Themes

Antoine, Gérald. Jalons pour une étude stylistique de Péguy. *In:* Péguy, actes du colloque international d'Orléans. *See* 8179. p. 327–35.   **8334**

Points out need for a sound edition of P.'s complete works (no edition exists). Calls for stylistic and thematic analyses to facilitate accurate, in-depth reading of his work. Suggests need for systematic study of themes using methods proposed by Riffaterre. Cautions against broad and hasty generalization.

———. La joie des mots chez Péguy. *In:* Péguy. *See* 8178. p. 516–36.   **8335**

Valuable comment on P.'s style: his word-play, creation of amusing words, lyric use of everyday words, comic use of archaic words. Explanation of P.'s conception of words as sharing a "geography" (complex of concrete meanings) and a "genealogy" (spiritual relationship to word families), so that each word becomes a microcosmic Incarnation. Hence, the author evokes a potential theology of style applicable to P.'s work and explains in this way the underlying joyous vitality of P.'s prose and poetry.

Balibar, Renée. Charles Péguy: deux mots rayés nuls. NCr 175:8–33, 1966.   **8336**

The multiplicity of styles in P.'s *Jeanne d'Arc* (1897) suggests the heterogeneity of the cultures he absorbed in school. Stylistic analysis of P.'s autobiographical *Pierre, commencement d'une vie bourgeoise*, reveals conflicting levels of style and competing cultural ideals. Suggests need to pursue this sort of investigation.

———. Comment lire Péguy aujourd'hui. NCr 180:81–105, 1966.   **8337**

Scientifically respectable definition of style, stylistic components, and levels of style. Elucidation of moral values explicit in a passage of P.'s *Pierre, commencement d'une vie bourgeoise;* stylistic analysis of the same passage reveals P.'s adoption of stylistic traits taught in French composition classes in the schools of his time. Definition and exemplification of the notions of "contexture" and "extratexte" as applied to P.'s prose. Conflict between explicit moral values in the text and the school morality implicit in the style.

————. Sur le personnage de Madame Gervaise dans Péguy. *In:* Péguy. *See* 8178. p. 225–36. **8338**

Analysis of the teacher-pupil paradigm in P.'s works as exemplified in the Madame Gervaise-and-Jeannette relationship. Stresses similarity of this model to that presented in elementary-school texts in P.'s day, to show that P.'s social, political and moral attitudes, as expressed by Madame Gervaise, are a transmission of bourgeois ideals inculcated in him in primary school.

Barbier, Joseph. L'Eve de Charles Péguy. Eds. de l'école, 1963. 272 p. **8339**

Analysis of P.'s *Eve* for students. *Eve* seen as a contemplation of the work of the Creator and of the work of the Redeemer. More theologically oriented than the work of Béguin (*see* 8342). Review: G. Péguy in ACPFM 101: 35, 1963.

————. Le vocabulaire, la syntaxe et le style des poèmes réguliers de Charles Péguy. Berger-Levrault, 1957. 572 p. **8340**

Essentially technical, descriptive study. Largely a compendium of examples, the study reaches a few tentative conclusions along the way and determines that P. is a unique French poet, using oral style, and that he has worn out the alexandrine verse once and for all. Bibliography.

Reviews: B. Guyon in RSH 90:300–03, 1958; J. Onimus in RHL 59:415–16, 1959; G. Péguy in ACPFM 64:30–31, 1958.

Béguin, Albert. De la Jeanne d'Arc de 1897 au Mystère de 1909. ACPFM 53:7–25, 1956. **8341**

Solid manuscript study tracing the growth of the *Mystère de la charité de Jeanne d'Arc* from a portion of P.'s 1897 drama entitled *Jeanne d'Arc.* Includes a valuable descriptive inventory of all documents and publications containing the successive versions of the text as P. developed them, as well as other related documents.

————. L'Eve de Péguy. Amitié Charles Péguy, 1948. 279 p. (CACP 3–4) **8342**

Superior and original step-by-step exegesis of P.'s last and longest poem. Important data in appendix on manuscripts of *Eve* and on early critical reception of the poem.

Reviews: A. Alter in ACPFM 7:19, 1949; J. Madaule in CahMN 3:118–19, 1949.

Bonenfant, Joseph. L'imagination du mouvement dans l'œuvre de Péguy. Montréal, Centre éducatif et culturel, 1969. 356 p. **8343**

Bachelardian approach to movement in P.'s work. Movement as theme (P. in motion, the road to salvation, dreams of returning, etc.); expression of movement (interpretation of motion imagery). The dynamic associated with emotion and soul, as opposed to static, geometric rationality. Finds two main sorts of motion: horizontal (processions, assaults, etc.) and vertical ("jaillissement," desire to reach the heights, etc.). Occasional undiscerning use of Freud and Bergson.

Reviews: A. Devaux in ACPFM 184:34–37, 1973; S. Fraisse in RHL 71:529–30, 1971; R. Vigneault in EF 4:469–79, 1970.

Bonnot, Jacques. L'itinéraire poétique de Charles Péguy, des Mystères aux Tapisseries. ACPFM 107:5–28, 1964. **8344**

Excellent example of intuitive criticism, explaining by thematics P.'s sudden shift from free verse to alexandrines.

Burac, Robert. L'ennemi de l'intérieur: sur une structure de Péguy. *In:* Péguy. *See* 8178. p. 427–40. **8345**

Treats recurring structure of communion prevented and desired in P.'s imagery; variations on the paradigm of the extremities against the middle, with the middle winning out. Sees this structure as fundamental to P.'s value system and to his definition of the "modern world."

Castelain, Jean-Claude. Notes sur la composition du Porche et des Innocents. ACPFM 162:41–47, 1970.   **8346**

Attempts to describe thematic structure in two long prose poems by P., using modern concepts of theme and "ressort obsessionnel." Diagrammatic analysis of the "Hymne à la nuit," which forms the conclusion of the Porche.

Cauquil, Bernadette. Le style polémique dans les œuvres en prose de Péguy. ACPFM 164:9–22, 1970.   **8347**

Excerpt from a university paper on a seldom-treated subject. Under the headings of Humor, Caricature and Burlesque, this essay treats satire and parody as well. Excellent examples, well analyzed. Superior introduction to a subject which still deserves treatment in detail.

Chabanon, Albert. La poétique de Péguy. Laffont, 1947. 260 p.   **8348**

First book specifically to treat P.'s poetics. Important insights: presents P.'s poetic principles as "classical," founded on soberness and sincerity; discovers the symbolic value of poetic forms, as well as the significance of binary configurations in P.'s poems. Treats prosody, poetic harmony, free-verse forms. P.'s Quatrains are not studied.

Reviews: A. Béguin in CACP 2:87–88, 1948.

Chabot, Jacques. Ordre et ordonnance dans Victor-Marie, comte Hugo. ACPFM 120:36–51, 1966.   **8349**

Best article to date on this essay. As a study of the relationship between essay content and form, this article uncovers principles applicable to many other prose works by P. Treats the essay both as art form and as message.

Dru, Alexander. Péguy. London, Harvill press, 1956. 121 p. Also: New York, Harper, 1957.   **8350**

Suggests P. deserves to be remembered primarily as a poet; treats P.'s world view as related to his poetic art. P.'s creative imagination and his de-

velopment of a language to express it (ch. VIII); interesting parallels with Coleridge. Analysis of P.'s Commentaire d'Eve (from Béguin, L'Eve de Péguy, p. 208–21). Contains numerous biographical details, but the focus is primarily poetic.

Reviews: P. Deasy in Cweal 69:620, 1958; C. Métais in ACPFM 66:32, 1958.

Duployé, Pie. La mélancolie virgilienne. In: Péguy. See 8178. p. 459–69.   **8351**

Discovers, in P.'s works of 1910–1913, a developing treatise on melancholy. Seeks to show that the melancholy tone of Eve is Virgilian in character and an outgrowth of P.'s own state of mind at the time of writing. Tends to neglect the more frivolous and more joyous elements of P.'s work of the period.

Emmanuel, Pierre. Le serviteur du Verbe incarné. In: Péguy reconnu. See 8181. p. 358–73.   **8352**

Relationship between P.'s prose style, his poetic forms, and his thought. Literature as incarnation of idea.

Francis, Raymond. L'humour de Péguy. In: Péguy. See 8178. p. 504–15.   **8353**

Attempts to redress the balance of works painting P. as a stern moralist by stressing P.'s sense of humor; sees P. as maintaining a light-hearted attitude toward the vicissitudes of life and refusing to take himself too seriously. Examples of P.'s stylistic humor.

Gide, André. Journal sans dates. NRF 3:399–410, 1910.   **8354**

Gide's enthusiastic reception of P.'s Mystère de la charité. Valuable intuitions about the nature of P.'s style. Impressionistic analogies. It should be noted that Gide's enthusiasm later waned, and he excluded P.'s work from his Anthologie de la poésie française.

Guyon, Bernard. L'art de Péguy. Amitié Charles Péguy, 1948. 88 p. (CACP 2)   **8355**

First general analysis of P. as literary artist. First work to stress conscious and voluntary nature of P.'s composition; shows P.'s philosophy to be related to his style; treats repetitions as a device, not a weakness.

Reviews: Anon. in ACPFM 4:14–15, 1949.

Khac-Rivière, Lydie Huynh. L'évolution du déchirement tragique à la réconciliation lyrique dans les Mystères de Charles Péguy. ACPFM 156:5–21, 1970. **8356**
Traces parallel evolution of tone and theme from *Mystère de la charité* through the *Porche* and the *Saints-Innocents*. Creative, Christian reading of P.'s three major prose poems.

Le Grix, François. Les livres. RHeb 20:408–24, 1911. **8357**
Review of P.'s *Mystère de la charité de Jeanne d'Arc*. Relatively favorable, although light in tone, tending to suggest that P.'s Joan of Arc was historically unbelievable and not to be taken seriously. Makes light of P.'s style. This little review confirmed in P.'s mind the link between bourgeois commercialism and the Catholic establishment and provoked his vast essay entitled "M. Fernand Laudet, un nouveau théologien."

Louette, Henri. Péguy lecteur de Dante. Minard, 1968. 123 p. (CACP 21) **8358**
Essentially a comparison-and-contrast study of P.'s *Eve* and the *Divine comedy*. Brief presentation of P.'s ideas on creative reading. P.'s opinion of Dante and his attitude toward his own poem. *Eve* seen as a sort of (unintentional) "completion," indeed "couronnement," of Dante's work. Excessive praise of P., called here the "premier Poète de la France."
Review: A. Devaux in ACPFM 173: 16–17, 1971.

Nelson, Roy Jay. Péguy poète du sacré. Minard, 1960. 222 p. (CACP 13) **8359**
Revised doctoral dissertation attempting to categorize P.'s poetic images according to their symbolic value in his work. Poem-by-poem analysis traces development in P.'s poetry of a dualistic symbolic cosmos. Information on circumstances surrounding composition of each poem; remarks on the symbolic value of various poetic forms employed by P.
Reviews: W. Bal in LR 1:59–66, 1964; D. Cooper in Ren 14:51–54, 1961; L. Roudiez in RR 61:72–76,

1961; S. Storelv in ACPFM 81:30–31, 1960.

O'Donnell, Donat (pseud. of Conor Cruise O'Brien). The temple of memory: Péguy. *In his:* Maria Cross: imaginative patterns in a group of modern Catholic writers. Oxford univ. press, 1952. p. 137–66. **8360**
P.'s style as related to time; P.'s theme of suffering. The author's basic hypothesis, that crucifixion has sexual connotations for some Catholic writers, tends to narrow his focus somewhat, making P. appear, out of context, rather obsessed with suffering and death. Interesting analysis of parts of the *Mystère de la charité* and of *Eve*.

Onimus, Jean. Introduction aux Mystères de Péguy. ACPFM 89:10–36; 90:2–44, 1961. **8361**
Basic, traditional literary study, intended to aid students preparing the *agrégation* on P. (1961); biographical details; history of the composition of *Mystère de la charité*, *Porche* and *Saints-Innocents* (cuts, additions, reworking by P.); form; characters. Thorough treatment of themes. Superior introduction to P. as poet.

——. Introduction aux Quatrains de Péguy. Amitié Charles Péguy. 1954. 102 p. (CACP 9) **8362**
Early study of the composition, rhythm, harmony, themes and symbolism of the ballad-like verses first published in the 1941 edition of P.'s *Œuvres poétiques complètes*. Demonstrates convincingly, with manuscript evidence, that the Pléiade has published many stanzas of the poem in reverse order, by groups, so that parts of the text are intelligible only when read backward. See important later study by J. Sabiani (*see* 8367).
Reviews: B. Guyon in RHL 55:530–32, 1955; J. Sauvenay in ACPFM 42:4, 1954; B. Voyenne in RdPF 7–8:81–83, 1955.

——. La genèse de Clio. ACPFM 47:3–35, 1955. **8363**
Essential study showing that P. composed *Clio I* in 1909 and *Clio II* in 1910, with major additions and insertions in 1912 and 1914.

―――. L'image dans l'Eve de Péguy. Amitié Charles Péguy, 1952. 148 p. (CACP 7)   8364

Thorough study of symbolic value of imagery in P.'s longest poem in alexandrine verse.

Reviews: A. Béguin in Esp 191: 1064–65, 1952; H. Féret in ACPFM 33:18–24, 1953; W. Orlando in TR 54:129–33, 1952.

Parent, Monique. La phrase poétique dans Le porche du mystère de la deuxième vertu, de Charles Péguy. *In her:* Saint-John Perse et quelques devanciers. Klincksieck, 1960. p. 83–161. (Bibliothèque française et romane, series C, 1)   8365

Careful syntactic analysis of the *Porche*, dealing with P.'s free verse as Spitzer, *infra*, did with his prose. Phonetic analysis, based on kymographic studies. Definition of P.'s free-verse form; types of thought structure and development; complexity and richness of P.'s means of expression.

Reviews: C. Champroux in RLR 74:222–25, 1961; J. Onimus in ACPFM 92:36–38, 1962; R. Winter in BJR 3:44–45, 1961.

Porché, François. Péguy et les Cahiers de la quinzaine. MerF 108:5–21, 1914. 8366

Clear and sympathetic contemporary presentation of what P. wished to accomplish with his *Cahiers*. Traces the evolution of P.'s choice of literary forms from prose to free verse to alexandrine verse. Sees P.'s Catholicism as a return to the origins of the faith.

Sabiani, Julie. La ballade du cœur, poème inédit de Charles Péguy. Klincksieck, 1973. 276 p. (Publications de l'U.E.R.-Lettres et sciences humaines de l'Université d'Orléans)   8367

Critical edition, with new information on dates of composition, of heretofore unpublished stanzas of P.'s *Quatrains*. Presented in a hypothetical but reasonable order. Important ms. study; brief thematic study suggesting these verses show that P. evolves from consideration of his personal conflict (love for Blanche Raphaël) into a fuller Christian understanding of human love. Completes Pléiade and Onimus, *Introduction aux Quatrains, supra*. Postface by J. Viard.

―――. Les ressourcements du cœur. NRDM 6:610–16, 1973.   8368

Brief comparison of the notion of love in Péguy and Proust.

Scarpati, Claudio. L'antiteatro di Péguy. Brescia, Franciscanum, 1970. 212 p. 8369

The essential work to date on the dramatic character of P.'s *Jeanne d'Arc, Mystère de la charité, Porche,* and the *Saints-Innocents*. Interesting comparison with Claudel. Considers P.'s approach to theater to be consciously anticonventional; shows link between P.'s polemics and his esthetics; includes thematic analysis of the four works and information on their staging. Section on reception of P.'s work in Italy. Bibliography.

―――. Poetica della meditazione nel Mystère de la charité de Jeanne d'Arc di Charles Péguy. Ae 388:323–53, 1964.   8370

Long analysis of the *Mystère* with relatively little original information: the history of its composition seems to be based on the Béguin ed., *supra;* for the thematic structure there is a similar development in Onimus, *Introduction, supra.*

Secrétain, Roger. L'œuvre de Péguy est-elle dans la littérature vivante? Premier exposé de Roger Secrétain. ACPFM 149: 13–32, 1969.   8371

Paper of major importance. Superior brief study on the relationship between style and logic in P.'s work. Shows that P.'s resulting demiurgic style was frequently incomprehensible to his contemporaries. Calls for methodology allowing ordinary reader to enter into direct and literary contact with P., beyond all sectarianism.

Spitzer, Leo. Zu Charles Péguys Stil. *In his:* Stilstudien. V. II. Munich, Max Hueber Verlag, 1961. p. 301–64.   8372

Originally published in 1924, this is one of the earliest linguistic analyses of P.'s style. Treats prose and poetic prose (*Mystère de la charité, Notre jeunesse, Note sur M. Bergson,* etc.). Stresses relationship between P.'s thought and his style. Suggests P. sought to breathe a Bergsonian *élan vital* into his language but failed, partly because of the limitations of language itself. Essential study.

Tricaud, Martial. Les sources de la Jeanne d'Arc de Péguy. ACPFM 37:3–16, 1954.
8373
Superficial treatment of the sources of the 1897 drama and of the *Mystère de la charité.*

Viard, Jacques. Les œuvres posthumes de Charles Péguy. Minard, 1969. 264 p. (CACP 23)
8374
Vital study of mss. (now at Centre Péguy in Orléans) of P.'s posthumous works. Important data on posthumous essays published 1952–55, including accurate dating. Presents texts of numerous fragments and shorter prose works heretofore unpublished, many of considerable importance. Describes P.'s methods of composition with documentary proof.
Reviews: S. Fraisse in RHL 71:128–29, 1971; B. Guyon in RSH 138:333–37, 1970; R. Nelson in FR 45:248–50, 1971.

Vigneault, Robert. L'univers féminin dans l'œuvre de Charles Péguy: essai sur l'imagination créatrice d'un poète. Bruges, Paris, Montreal, Desclée De Brouwer, 1967. 334 p.
8375
Vigneault undertakes, as a literary critic, a Freudian analysis of P.'s attitude toward women in his work (and in his life). Suggests the conflict between purity and passion may have been kept unconsciously alive by P., to nourish his poetic creativity.
Reviews: A. Devaux in ACPFM 138:20–23, 1968; M. Laverty in FS 24:204–06, 1970; L. Mailhot in EF 1:93–96, 1970.

Yvon, Henri. Passés simples dans Eve de Péguy et Mon Faust de P. Valéry. RLiR 25:383–90, 1961.
8376
Finds 42 uses of the *passé simple* in *Eve,* to about 690 examples of the *passé composé;* finds 47 *passés simples* in *Mon Faust,* for 256 *passés composés.* Lists occurrences of the *passé simple* in context. Ascribes (without apparent justification) the choice of this tense generally to the demands of versification.

Reputation and Influence

Ashbourne, *Lady* M. Charles Péguy. DuR 153:353–64, 1913.
8377
P. as observed from Great Britain during his lifetime.

Bonnaud-Lamotte, D. Comment faire aimer Péguy aujourd'hui. ACPFM 130:1–16, 1967.
8378
Includes documents suggesting some interest in P.'s work in Russia and in the People's Republic of China.

Cahm, Eric. Péguy et sa politique vus de l'Angleterre. *In:* Péguy reconnu. See 8181. p. 411–20.
8379
Obstacles to the study of P.'s work in England; reasons why he is relatively little known there. Suggests it is as a seeker after human liberty that P. can best be appreciated in England.

Espiau de la Maëstre, André. La pénétration de Péguy en Allemagne de 1910 à nos jours. *In:* Péguy, actes du colloque international d'Orléans. See 8179. p. 348–64.
8380
Brief, documented history of the publication of P.'s works in the German language and of the vicissitudes of German critical reaction. Notes that P.'s apparently passionate patriotism may have shocked or frightened German public opinion and slowed acceptance of his work in Germany.

Giordan, Henri. Contribution à l'histoire des Cahiers: les premières réactions italiennes. *In:* Péguy, actes du colloque international d'Orléans. See 8179. p. 336–46.
8381
Superior analysis, through a study of the relationships of the *Cahiers* with certain Italian writers (notably Papini, Prezzolini, and the *Voce* group), of the *Cahiers'* role, as a collective institution, in the diffusion of a particular spiritual and fraternal view of human society in Italy. Comparison of the *Cahiers* and *La Voce* in format and organization.

Hardré, Jacques. Péguy aux Etats-Unis. ACPFM 195:14–19, 1974.
8382
Comments on the work of P.'s divers American critics, followed by extensive bibliography, *supra.*

Kelly, Sister Marie-Thérèse. L'influence de Charles Péguy aux Etats-Unis. ACPFM 171:47–51, 1971.   **8383**

Bibliographical information on P. studies in the U. S.

Margenburg, Edith. Charles Péguy: ein Beitrag zur Geschichtsphilosophie, Kulturkritik und Gesellschaftslehre im gegenwärtigen Frankreich. Nendeln/Liechtenstein, Kraus, 1967. 81 p. (Romanische Studien, 42) *Orig. ed.:* Berlin, 1937. **8384**

Interesting analysis, dating from Hitler era, of P.'s social criticism, with emphasis on *Marcel* and with reference to *Clio* and to *L'argent suite.* Portrays a P. perhaps too closely related to the fascist motto: "Travail, Famille, Patrie." Bibliography and table of contents (major articles) for all *Cahiers de la quinzaine* published by P.

Mistral, Gabriela. Pienso en Péguy. Sur 120: 7–12, 1944.   **8385**

The Chilean poetess tells of her debt to P. whom she calls "santo mío y tutor mío."

Prezzolini, Giuseppe. Per la memoria di Carlo Péguy. NA 174:43–48, 1914. **8386**

An important Italian anticlericalist critic takes early note of P.'s work.

Ryan, Mary. Charles Péguy in his prose. DuR 162:71–86, 1918.   **8387**

Reply to the Ashbourne article, *supra,* showing birth of controversy on P. in Great Britain. Discovers that P.'s prose shows his thought in generation, while his poems express its static final state. Author shows broad knowledge of P.'s writings.

Sorel, Georges. Il risveglio dell'anima francese. Voce 2:303, 1910.   **8388**

Quite probably the first published mention of P. in Italy.

CHAPTER XVIII

PAUL VALÉRY
(Nos. 8389–8963)

A. James Arnold*

Bibliography

Arnold, A. James. Le centenaire de Paul Valéry aux Etats-Unis. SFr 18:240–57, 1974. **8389**

Examines the contributions to the centenary published in the U.S.A. between 1970 and 1972. The article contains an assessment of the special number of YFS, 1970, and a brief description of the proceedings of the colloquium held at Johns Hopkins University in November 1971.

———. Paul Valéry and his critics: a bibliography. French-language criticism 1890–1927. Charlottesville, Univ. press of Virginia for the Bibliographical society of the univ. of Virginia, 1970. xxii, 617 p. *Also:* New York, Haskell House, 1973. **8390**

Gives a detailed analysis of writings in French on V., the man and the work, through the year of his reception at the French Academy. The organization of entries is chronological; a substantial index to subjects and titles, as well as names, is included. Criticism in French from the period covered by this volume has not been retained for CBFL. A continuation is currently being prepared by E. M. McHugh.

Reviews: T. Benn and S. Morton in YWMLS 33:214, 1971; C. Chadwick in MLR 68:423–24, 1973; C. Crow in FS 26:476–77, 1972; C. Farrell, Jr. in RR 63:72, 1972; R. Neely in BA 45: 283, 1971.

Bulletin des études valéryennes. Ed. by Daniel Moutote. Montpellier, Université Paul-Valéry, 1974–75. 6 fasc. **8391**

The six fascicles printed between April 1974 and July 1975 show considerable promise. A regular rubric for current bibliography, for dissertations in progress, etc., will make this a valuable research tool.

Catalogue de fonds spéciaux de la Bibliothèque littéraire Jacques Doucet — fonds Valéry. Boston, G. K. Hall, 1972. vii, 445 p. **8392**

A catalog created by photocopying the 14,000 entries in the Valéryanum. As a primary bibliography it is superseded by the collaborative effort of Karaïskakis and Chapon (1976). Two aspects of the catalog are unlikely to be surpassed: the identification of documents in the Valéryanum relative to specific titles and mss. and the list of works on V. available there. In the case of clippings from newspapers and reviews, no breakdown is provided beyond the identification of individual scrapbooks as containing French or foreign clippings and the years covered. The Valéryanum's collection of clippings is so vast that documents catalogued on two index cards (p. 411) have provided the bulk of the material for one critical bibliography with another in progress.

Essai de bibliographie des œuvres de Paul Valéry. Bib 17:18–24, 1949. *And:* Paul Valéry: essai de bibliographie. Bib 36:17–21, 1968. **8393**

A first serious effort to catalog V.'s titles released in French between 1895 and 1948, this list of some 300 entries is nonetheless very incomplete. An attempt was made to update it in 1968. Includes only French items.

*With some assistance from J. V. Arnold and L. J. Austin.

Hoy, Peter C. Carnet bibliographique 1971–1972. *In:* Lectures de Charmes. *See* 8477. p. 199–221. **8394**

A very thorough list of publications of all types from the centennial year inaugurates this new series devoted to V. studies.

Karaïskakis, Georges, and François Chapon. Bibliographie des œuvres de Paul Valéry publiées de 1889 à 1965. Auguste Blaizot, 1976. xi, 580 p. **8395**

This volume, the result of a half century of connoisseurship by the principal author and a decade of meticulous scholarship by the curator of the Valéryanum, is henceforth the cornerstone of V. studies. The arrangement of the bibliography is chronological; a series of tables permits the reader to retrieve individual items with ease. As a reference work it is indispensable and very nearly flawless.

Review: L. Austin in FS 31:223–25, 1977.

Lorenz, Erika. Die Valérykritik im heutigen Frankreich. RJ 7:113–32, 1955–56. **8396**

This critical bibliography is less limited than its title indicates. Works considered date back to Thibaudet and Lefèvre, including publications outside France in German and English. Nonetheless its present value for research is negligible in view of the modifications in V. criticism over the past twenty years.

Editions

Valéry, Paul. Cahiers. Ed. by J. Robinson. Gallimard, 1973–74. 2 v. (Bibliothèque de la Pléiade) **8397**

This edition of the *Cahiers* may ultimately have as great an impact on V. studies as did the original facsimile edition. The editor has followed in detail V.'s second classification of his notebooks by subject, with references to the earlier outline of 1908. The classification, which dates from the 1920's, includes reorganized groupings of almost all the texts written to that date. In attempting to establish an edition in conformity with V.'s intention, a certain amount of subjectivity was unavoidable in making decisions on texts V. had not classified himself. The inclusion in the appendix of both the classifications drawn up by V., and the detailed preface concerning editorial method, provide a sufficient guarantee of excellence in the execution of an exceedingly painstaking project. The notes contain some important rectifications of the CNRS edition of the *Cahiers*.

Reviews: P. de Boisdeffre in NRDM 402–05, July–Sept. 1973; H. L[aurenti] in RLM 413–18:194–96, 1974.

———. Charmes ou poèmes. Ed. by Charles G. Whiting. London, Athlone press, 1973. 147 p. (Athlone French poets, 11) **8398**

The salient feature of this ed. is the decision to follow the text of the original 1922 printing. It is an unfamiliar feeling to encounter "L'abeille" and "Au platane" before "Aurore." A sense of the topical, long absent from the collection, is due to V.'s original dedications of numerous poems to friends and fellow poets and to his wife. Notes are printed as back matter and are primarily intended to inform the English-speaking reader. The twenty-five page introduction in English draws on the editor's previously published articles.

Review: B. Swift in YWMLS 35: 197, 1974.

———. Charmes, poèmes de Paul Valéry commentés par Alain. Gallimard, 1929. xxvi, 248 p. *Also:* 1952. 219 p. **8399**

This first reading of *Charmes* in its entirety has become something of a legend. The principle of the reading is a more or less connected glossing of key words, images and constructions with frequent reference to other poems in the collection. Gloss and text are printed on facing pages, giving Alain's commentary a support without which it would be unreadable. That this commentary still has an impact on more current work is demonstrated by the two contrasting studies of "Au platane" by Lawler and Austin, the former building upon Alain, the latter indirectly refuting him. V.'s preface to this ed. constitutes the original ed. of his "Commentaires de Charmes." *See* 8421 for details leading up to this publication and H. Mondor's role in it.

———. Le cimetière marin. Ed. and translated by Graham Dunstan Martin. Austin, Tex.: Univ. of Texas press; Edinburgh,

Edinburgh univ. press, 1971. v, 99 p. (Edinburgh bilingual library, 1) **8400**

A fine ed. of the poem for readers of English with some French. The translator's introduction and commentary are most successful when dealing with the more technical points of language and style.

————. Le cimetière marin. Ed. by H. Mondor and L. J. Austin. Grenoble, Roissard, 1954. 76 p. unpaginated. **8401**

The critical material is comprised of H. Mondor's "Paul Valéry, élève de philosophie," p. 5–31; and L. J. Austin's "Les manuscrits du Cimetière marin," p. 33–66. The definitive text of the poem without variants follows. Austin's essay draws on his more detailed study of the mss. already published in the *Mercure de France*. Here, however, he presented the entire text (7 strophes) of the original "Mare Nostrum" and established a loose connection with V.'s 1890 sonnet entitled "Cimetière." This material has yet to be reprinted and is of difficult access due to the conditions of the original publication: 976 numbered copies "hors commerce."

————. The collected works of Paul Valéry. Ed. by Jackson Mathews. New York, Pantheon, 1956–1965; Princeton, Princeton univ. press, 1968–1975. 15 v. (Bollingen series, 45) *Also:* London, Routledge and Kegan Paul, 1958–1975. 15 v. **8402**

This is essentially a reader's edition characterized by the excellence of its translations. Notes from the *Cahiers* and elsewhere are used to elucidate the texts for the reader of English. Critical introductions are analyzed under the appropriate headings.

————. Eupalinos and L'âme et la danse. Ed. by Vera J. Daniel. Oxford, Oxford univ. press, 1967. 217 p. **8403**

A very helpful addition to the secondary literature on the two best-known dialogs as well as an excellent ed. of the texts as published jointly in 1923. The general introduction draws together the best of the previously published critical literature on the subject and presents it with admirable clarity. The few variants to the basic texts were taken from V.'s corrected proofs. Forty-five pages of notes grouped at the end of the volume serve to situate concepts and terms in the broader context of V.'s work as well as to clarify specific difficulties. An alphabetical list of classical allusions occurring in the two dialogs will permit students with little or no Greek to orient themselves painlessly.

Reviews: N. Suckling in FS 23:95–96, 1969; P. Walzer in RHL 69:327–28, 1969.

————. La jeune Parque: manuscrit autographe, texte de l'édition de 1942, états successifs et brouillons inédits du poème. Présentation et étude critique des documents par Octave Nadal. Club du meilleur livre, 1957. 464 p. **8404**

The facsimile autograph of the final draft occupies p. 1–68 recto only, followed by Nadal's presentation. The printed text of *La jeune Parque* is the last reviewed by V. in 1942 for the *Poésies*. The critical apparatus (analyzed below under "La jeune Parque") includes a general essay on the composition and a detailed examination of notes, fragments and early mss. of the poem. The volume is completed by the facsimile reproduction of some of the material studied by Nadal.

Reviews: M. Bémol in RHL 59:413–14, 1959; J. Charpier in LetN 6:257–65, 1958; E. Noulet in SynB 13:266–72, 1958; R. Quilliot in RSoc 119:102–04, 1958; J. Tortel in CahS 47:122–26, 1958; R. Wilbur in CL 13:263–68, 1961.

————. La jeune Parque, poème, commenté par Alain. NRF, 1936. iv, 76 p. *Also:* Gallimard, 1953. p. 9–135. **8405**

Still more than in his 1929 commentary of *Charmes,* Alain uses the text of *La jeune Parque* as a springboard to his own reflections. These are not precisely disconnected but their links are not to be found in the text of the poem. This ed. of the poem constitutes as well the original ed. of V.'s "Le philosophe et la jeune Parque." Alain's commentary is itself divided into two parts: a forty-page preface followed by a facing page gloss of the type used in his edition of *Charmes.*

————. Œuvres. Ed. by J. Hytier. Gallimard, 1957–1960. 2 v. (Bibliothèque de la Pléiade) **8406**

For fifteen years this has been the standard ed. of V.'s works. The critical apparatus is ample, particularly in the area of V.'s early poetry. It is probable that in the future a revision of this ed. will be required to account for the voluminous material recently deposited at the Bibliothèque Nationale.

―――. Poésies choisies. Ed. by H. Fabureau. Hachette, 1952. 96 p. (Classiques illustrés Vaubourdolle)   **8407**

This unpretentious school ed. by a critic who cannot be counted among the more fervent Valéryens is still useful. The glosses presented in note form frequently contain good insights for a close reading of individual poems. Otherwise the apparatus of the ed. is not in any real sense critical.

Correspondence

Bibesco [Marthe Lucie (Lahovary)] princesse. Paul Valéry. *In her:* Le confesseur et les poètes. Grasset, 1970. p. 167–215.   **8408**

Among V.'s letters to abbé Mugnier dating from 1923 to 1940, there are two or three of some critical value. One cannot say as much of the princess's presentation.

Gide, André, and Paul Valéry. Correspondance 1890–1942. Ed. by Robert Mallet. Gallimard, 1955. 558 p. *Trans.:* Self-portraits. The Gide/Valéry letters, 1890–1942. Ed. by Robert Mallet. Abridged and translated by June Guicharnaud. Chicago, Univ. of Chicago press, 1966. vi, 340 p.   **8409**

With the V.-Fourment correspondence, published two years later, this constitutes the most important single source of documentary material of a biographical nature on V. The introduction (p. 9–35) is informative without being critically significant in itself. Reviews: A. Anglès in Preu 54:83–87, 1955; F. Millet in MP 65:268–71, 1968; G. Picon in MerF 1105:100–07, 1955; P. Walzer in RHL 57:277–81, 1957; J. Weightman in Obs 9122:27, 1966.

Goffin, Marie-Louise. Paul Valéry selon lui-même. SynB 11:134–54, 1956.   **8410**

The only extensive discussion of the Gide-V. correspondence to have gone beyond the perspective of a review article. The author has gauged the uniqueness of V.'s exchanges with Gide.

Lang, Renée. Rilke, Gide et Valéry. Boulogne-sur Seine, Eds. de la revue Prétexte, 1953. 78 p. *Trans. and rev.:* Rilke, Gide e Valéry nel carteggio inedito. AmL 6: 67–74, 139–46, 215–22, 1958; 7:33–38, 103–10, 169–73, 235–42, 1959; 8:29–35, 1960. *Reprinted as a volume:* Florence, Sansoni, 1960. 7–98 p. (Biblioteca degli eruditi e dei bibliofili, 40)   **8411**

The Italian ed. supersedes the less complete French ed. Using the largely unpublished correspondence of V. and Rilke as her primary material, Lang chronicles the personal and artistic relations of the two poets. In this respect the monograph remains unsurpassed. The commentary on Rilke's translations frequently praises his inspiration to the detriment of V.'s methodical practice of composition. In so far as the text touches on V.'s poetics, presented here so summarily as to be distorted, the result is somewhat less felicitous.

Reviews: M. Baym in RR 45:307–08, 1954; G. Schuler in BA 35:380–81, 1961.

Louys [sic], Pierre, and Paul Valéry. Lettres inédites présentées par Pierre Borel. OLib 147:3–16, 1958.   **8412**

This is actually a florilegium of extracts from selected letters dating for the most part from 1890. The presentation stresses the literary tastes and the self-proclaimed decadence of the new friends. Unfortunately the article has little critical value.

Mondor, Henri. Paul Valéry et Les cahiers d'André Walter (avec des fragments inédits). Nef 23:3–32, 1946. *Also in his:* Les premiers temps d'une amitié, André Gide et Paul Valéry. Monaco, Eds. du rocher, 1947. p. 29–82.   **8413**

Approximately half the article is devoted to the exchange of letters between Gide and V. on the publication of the *Cahiers d'André Walter*. As the interest of the article depends upon the letters themselves rather than on the commentary, the subsequent publication of the Gide-V. *Correspondance* has considerably diminished its value.

Valéry, Paul, and Gustave Fourment. Correspondance 1887–1933. Ed. by Octave Nadal. Gallimard, 1957. 268 p. **8414**

This correspondence has permitted some significant rectifications of our understanding of V.'s spiritual crisis of 1892. Nadal published his findings in articles between 1955 and 1957. *See* 8460, 8461.

Reviews: M. Bémol in RHL 59: 246–48, 1959; R. Lang in BA 32:405, 1958; E. Noulet in SynB 13:262–66, 1958.

Exhibit Catalogs

Catalogue de l'exposition Paul Valéry organisée à l'occasion du soixante-quinzième anniversaire de sa naissance. Ed. by Jules Mouquet. Bibliothèque Sainte-Geneviève, 1946. 19 p. **8415**

The 150 items exhibited are presented in brief bibliographical form without quotations or detailed descriptions. The only present value of the catalog might be to aid in identifying the owner of a given ms. Notes by Gide, J. Hytier and Marie Dormoy complete the catalog.

Collection Richard Anacréon. Ed. by Gabriel Couderc. Sète, Musée Paul Valéry, 1970. 35 p. (unpaginated) **8416**

The Anacréon collection of Valéryana was exhibited in Sète during Nov. 1970. The catalog is the only one prepared for the several exhibits at the Musée Paul Valéry that contains sufficient detail to be of critical value. Numerous items in the collection were exhibited with valuable autograph material.

Paul Valéry. Ed. by Julien Cain. Bibliothèque nationale, 1956. xiv, 96 p. 8 plates. **8417**

This catalog presents the first comprehensive retrospective exhibit of V. manuscripts, eds. and the usual memorabilia. Its interest now is primarily biographical as some of the manuscript materials (those from the *Cahiers* in particular) have since been made public. Otherwise the descriptive commentary on mss. exhibited is generally too succinct for the catalog to remain of much use in the study of texts.

Review: C. Pichois in RHL 58:415, 1958.

Paul Valéry: exposition du centenaire. Ed. by Etienne Dennery et al. Bibliothèque nationale, 1971. xvi, 198 p. 20 plates & frontispiece. **8418**

Unlike the 1956 retrospective, this exhibit was arranged thematically rather than chronologically. This happy decision determined in part the lasting value of the catalog as a critical tool. Most of the entries include descriptive statements, some of which are sufficiently detailed to be of real assistance to the researcher. Occasional blunders were corrected on an errata sheet.

Review: Anon. in BDB 17:27, 1972.

Paul Valéry pré-Teste. Ed. by François Chapon et al. Bibliothèque littéraire Jacques Doucet, 1966. 74 p. **8419**

The great care taken by Chapon in presenting the texts of mss. (particularly those of early poems and unpublished letters) makes this catalog unique. It is indispensable to anyone working on V.'s early writing as it does in fact constitute the first ed. of several poems and variants of poems already known.

Reviews: Anon. in BBF 12:114, 1967; M. Legris in Monde 6811:7, 1966; R. Warnier in SFr 11:390–91, 1967.

Biography

Aigrisse, Gilberte. Psychanalyse de Paul Valéry. Eds. universitaires, 1964. 323 p. **8420**

This study derives from the kind of archetypal analysis practised by Charles Baudoin. It assumes a hierarchy of symbolic values in the formation of personality. V.'s texts are submitted to this analysis in such a way that they are read as documents in a psychoanalysis of their author. Readers of Jung will recognize both the language and the values that organize this study. There are occasional observations on specific poetic texts which can be integrated into commentaries of other types.

Reviews: J. Fonsny in ECl 33:91, 1965; M. Lobet in RG 100:135–37, 1964.

Alain (pseud. of Emile Chartier). Le déjeuner chez Lapérouse. NRF 58:234–44, 1939. **8421**

Alain recounts his first meeting with V., arranged by H. Mondor, after he had read and commented on *Charmes* at Mondor's request. This very artistic luncheon was to prove the springboard to Alain's published commentary on both *Charmes* and *La jeune Parque*. The value of the article is essentially documentary. It was here that Alain related the enthusiasm of his students for V.'s two major poems.

———. Hommage à la poésie. MerF 300: 587–96, 1947. **8422**

Here Alain wished to leave a monument to V., whom he did not hesitate to qualify the greatest poet of all time. Quite naturally his critical views were cut from this same cloth. The best purpose to which this testimony can be put henceforth is as a contribution to V.'s biography by an essayist of considerable reknown.

Arrighi, Paul. Paul Valéry et la Corse avec des documents inédits. RHL 56:392–400, 1956. **8423**

For the most part the documents are of marginal interest, but a note clarifies the mysterious transformation of the family name from Valérj to its present form.

Austin, Lloyd J. Les premiers rapports entre Valéry et Mallarmé. *In:* Entretiens sur Paul Valéry. *See* 8476. p. 39–50. **8424**

A meticulous analysis of the first epistolary exchange between Mallarmé and V. The unique contribution of Austin's paper is to demonstrate that in a very early letter, possibly written prior to 1890 and never sent to Mallarmé, V. represents himself as a disciple of the Huysmans of *A rebours*. V.'s letter of Oct. 20, 1890, printed several times in the past, is studied in the ms. variants of a draft which may date from late Aug. of the same year. The draft is photographically reproduced as plate III in the Acta of the colloquium. Mallarmé's reply of Oct. 25 has been included, with the text of V.'s draft letter, in vol. IV, part 1 of Austin's edition of the Mallarmé *Correspondance*, Gallimard, 1973.

Bastet, Ned. L'enfant qui nous demeure. *In:* Entretiens sur Paul Valéry. *See* 8476. p. 87–97. **8425**

Readers unfamiliar with its basic reference points in psychoanalysis may find this article confusing because of its brevity. Methodologically, however, the approach taken here is identical to that which underlies the author's recent studies of V.'s reflections on the theater. When he gives it adequate scope it will represent a considerable advance over his archetypal reading of 1962.

———. La symbolique des images dans l'œuvre poétique de Valéry. Aix-en-Provence, Publications des annales de la faculté des lettres, 1962. 171 p. mimeo. (Travaux et mémoires, 24) **8426**

The author's declared intention—to reveal a Valéryan psychodrama through the deconstruction of the poetic texts into psychological clusters—brings his work into the orbit of biography. His conceptual framework, largely borrowed from Bachelard and Ch. Baudoin, further suggests comparison with the work of G. Aigrisse which appeared two years later in a more accessible format. Unlike Aigrisse, he practices a form of static analysis in search of a fundamental symbolic truth. From the point of view of either biography or criticism this is doubtless an error. However, the material presented here in a unique form can prove useful to other critics pursuing quite different ends, as it suggests possibilities for comparison which are often far from self-evident.

Beach, Sylvia. My friend Paul Valéry. *In her:* Shakespeare and company. Harcourt, Brace & Co., 1956. p. 158–62. *Also:* London, Faber and Faber, 1959. p. 163–67. *Trans.:* Mon ami Paul Valéry. *In her:* Shakespeare and company. Mercure de France, 1962. p. 173–77. **8427**

A few pages of memories by one who, with Adrienne Monnier, saw much of V. in the days of his return to letters. The most significant detail here is an independent account of V.'s botched attempt at suicide in London, a story V. had related to her.

Bémol, Maurice. A propos du Grand silence valéryen. RHL 59:213–18, 1959. **8428**

Bémol replies directly to Nadal's view of V.'s long period of apparent literary inactivity. His tone is that of an argument pro domo sua since his own thesis of a Great Silence is in question.

Beucken, Jean de. Paul Valéry. SynB 131: 211–27, 1957.   **8429**

Relates in minute detail the circumstances of the commemoration of the fiftieth anniversary of symbolism in Liège on May 27–29, 1936. V.'s address was to become "Existence du symbolisme" in his collected *Ecrits divers sur Stéphane Mallarmé*. These reminiscences deal very little with V.'s text, however, being rather a chronicle of the events. The article concludes with some anecdotes concerning V.'s relations with bibliophiles and publishers.

Breton, André. Prestige de Paul Valéry. *In his:* Entretiens 1913–1952 avec André Parinaud et al. Gallimard, 1952. p. 15–18. *Also:* Gallimard, 1969. p. 15–18.   **8430**

Until such time as their correspondence may be published, these few pages remain the most valuable document concerning the important personal influence of V. on Breton during the years preceding the birth of surrealism (1913–1921). For further information one may consult M. Sanouillet's *Dada à Paris,* which has a good index, or Arnold's *Paul Valéry and his critics* (*see* 8390) where all references to V. in surrealist publications through 1927 have been indexed.

Bussy, Dorothy. Some recollections of Paul Valéry. Hor 13:310–21, 1946. *Also in:* The golden horizon. Ed. by C. Connolly. London, Weidenfeld & Nicolson, 1953. p. 355–66.   **8431**

A valuable chapter from the memoirs of one who frequently saw V. at close quarters in the twenties. These recollections include numerous anecdotes in French, taken down while V. sat for his portrait by the author's husband. In such unguarded moments V. called D'Annunzio a great charlatan and voiced strong objections to Thibaudet's book on him.

Chapon, François. Circonstances d'un poème. BBB no. 1:11–16, 1972.   **8432**

The piece of occasional verse addressed to Adrien Mithouard on Dec. 8, 1918 is probably of less interest than the relation of the circumstances of its composition. Chapon includes a previously unpublished letter from V. in 1901 and an extract of his improvised speech in Mithouard's honor on May 10, 1935.

Dollot, René. Ricordi italiani. Trieste, Ed. dello Zibaldone, 1952. 191 p.   **8433**

At the suggestion of Jules Valéry the author undertook to write a memoir on V.'s maternal grandfather. Dollot had access to the family archives while composing his historical account of the career of Giulio Grassi. He adds to this the genealogical chart of the Lugnani family, the maternal ancestors of Fanny Grassi, V.'s mother. The section of his memoir devoted directly to V. is of largely anecdotal interest.

Duchesne-Guillemin, Jacques. De quelques sigles. *In:* Paul Valéry, 1871–1971. *See* 8487. p. 216–22.   **8434**

An exercise in cryptography which reveals the identity of numerous individuals mentioned in the *Cahiers,* most notably the mysterious Beatrice figures about whom V. scholars had been reluctant to write.

———. Valéry et Léonard. EFL 8:57–71, 1971.   **8435**

This essay is atypical of its author: rambling, mixing the already commonplace with some little-known appreciations of V.'s Leonardo (K. Clark, Heydenreich), then suggesting that for Catherine Pozzi V. became a new Leonardo. Finally the real subject appears: the deciphering of elusive cryptic passages in the *Cahiers* relative to V.'s private life (see preceding entry). The contribution of the essay is to have deflated the fetishism of the 1892 crisis by pointing out that V. recognized at least one other of comparable importance: his break with C. Pozzi in 1921.

Fargue, Léon-Paul. Rue de Villejust. J. Haumont, 1946. 59 p.   **8436**

Fargue's friendship with V. dated from the days of the *Centaure* and Mallarmé's Tuesdays. Here he reminisced shortly after his friend's death, giving one of the best physical portrayals of the man ever written.

Faure, Gabriel. Paul Valéry méditerranéen. Horizons de France, 1954. 131 p.   **8437**

This brief essay has the charm and the faults of those written by friends with an eye toward emphasizing a particular aspect of their author. Nonetheless, this one would suffice to demonstrate the permanence of the Mediterranean in V. if any further proof were required after the enthusiastic testimony of Valery Larbaud in 1927.

Féline, Pierre. Souvenirs sur Paul Valéry. MerF 321:402–28, 1954.   **8438**

Féline's family had lived in the same house as the V. family in Montpellier and toward 1890 P. Féline and V. were fast friends. These reminiscences deal largely with V.'s initiation into mathematics and Wagnerian opera. The later period of their friendship is represented by nine letters from V. dating from 1914 to 1923 and six others from the period 1932 to 1944. The last evokes the liberation of Paris.

Gaède, Edouard. L'amitié de Valéry et de Gide à travers les textes des Cahiers. RHL 65:244–59, 1965.   **8439**

Gaède rendered a service in drawing together, and printing the best of, V.'s reflections on Gide in his *Cahiers*. The harshness of his opinions might shock if one did not know how completely they express V.'s disgust at sentimentality, affected vulgarity, and the evangelical pose. Moreover, there is scarcely a word here that Gide would not have understood (whatever the pain) had he been made aware of it.

Hofmann, Claude. De quelques sources à Paul Valéry. *In:* Entretiens sur Paul Valéry. *See* 8475. p. 135–47.   **8440**

The author uses the psychoanalytic notions of the return of the repressed, the obsessive image, and repetition to find Michelet's *Sorcière* in the disguises of *La jeune Parque*. His methodology caused some consternation at the colloquium; the subsequent discussion, p. 148–61, prolongs the paper in a useful direction.

Lang, Renée B. The Valéry—Rilke friendship revisited. *In:* Paul Valéry centennial. *See* 8485. p. 602–12.   **8441**

The author finds it difficult to forgive V. for not sharing Rilke's boundless enthusiasm for their relationship.

See 8937 for a more complete treatment of the subject.

Lannes, Roger. Appel à Paul Valéry. J. B. Janin, 1947. 93 p.   **8442**

An essay deploring V.'s passing and attempting to grasp his real significance as the quasi-official representative of French culture in the period between the two wars. The critical posture of the author reveals itself on the first page with the assimilation of V. to M Teste.

Larbaud, Valery. Fauteuil XXXVIII Paul Valéry. Alcan, 1931. 119 p. (Les quarante)   **8443**

This volume represents a publishing venture, not a critical activity. Larbaud had already given the best of his appreciation of V. the man and the poet by 1927. The short anthology of V.'s aphoristic writings was culled from other texts. The history of chair 38 at the French Academy is about as artificial as history can be.

La Rochefoucauld, Edmée de. Paul Valéry et l'Italie. *In:* Entretiens sur Paul Valéry *See* 8475. p. 283–97.   **8444**

This paper, read at the 1965 V colloquium at Cerisy, represents the outline of a topic that has been treated more critically by Duchesne-Guillemir and Magnery.

————. Voyages en Angleterre de Pau Valéry. RDM 11:313–23, 1971. *Also* Paul Valéry et l'Angleterre. *In her* L'angoisse et les écrivains. Grasset, 1974 p. 85–115.   **8445**

A fairly complete and detailed serie of notations concerning V.'s relation with England: visits, acquaintances readings, honors. These are treated chronologically as background or docu mentation for a biography. The valu of the article is in the assembling o data previously available only in bit and snatches. Should be complemented by C. Mackworth's essay published i 1974.

Lawler, James R. Valéry et Claudel—u dialogue symboliste. NRF 32:239–61 1968. *Trans. (in part):* Magic and move ment in Claudel and Valéry. *In his:* Th language of French symbolism. Princeton, Princeton univ. press, 1969. p. 112–45.

8446

Using their correspondence and their respective notebooks, Lawler constructs a very plausible argument for the friendship of V. and Claudel having as its basis the most profound dissimilarities. The correspondence is most interesting as are their views on one another's work.

Libero, Libero de. Valéry parente illustre. Milan, All'insegna del pesce d'oro, 1955. 51 p.   8447

The title derives from a conscious attempt to present an intimate portrait of V. to his Italian cousins. For a fortnight in March 1937 the author was in almost daily contact with V., frequently noting his anecdotes and opinions. A page of V.'s thoughts on his interview with Mussolini is noteworthy, as are certain of his reflections on his own work. Enough of the material reported here is confirmed by other sources to establish the author as a reliable witness. His concluding pages have some bearing on a tendency among Italian critics to read V. in terms of their own hermetic tradition.

Mackworth, Cecily. Aestheticism and imperialism: Paul Valéry in London. *In her:* English interludes, Mallarmé, Verlaine, Paul Valéry, Valery Larbaud in England, 1860–1912. London-Boston, Routledge & Kegan Paul, 1974. p. 124–54.

8448

Although rather chatty in style and drawing extensively on V.'s own 1925 account, "My early days in England," this essay will help clarify V.'s association with the Chartered Co. in 1896. The account is both readable and well documented. V.'s very real fascination with C. Rhodes and his imperial ethics is well handled. Beyond filling in this important lacuna in V.'s biography the essay provides an abundance of detail on the literary circles V. frequented in England at that time. It is curious, however, that no mention is made of his attempted suicide.

Magnery, Louis A. Paul Valéry et l'Italie. SFr 13:89–96, 1969.   8449

Argues that whereas V. felt foreign to the cultural nationalism of the new nation-state of Italy, he certainly had a profound attachment to "his" city, Genoa. V.'s attachment to Italy was affective, emotional and maternal—not to be dissociated from his sentiments toward his own mother. Magnery is quite reluctant to admit this. A florilegium of Italian opinions on V. completes the article.

Mallet, Robert. Improvisation. RdL 15–27, Jan.-March 1970.   8450

This improvised speech commemorating the centenary of André Gide contains several details concerning the publication of the Gide-V. correspondence. Its interest is documentary and biographical.

Massis, Henri. Paul Valéry et la nuit de Londres. NL 1679:1, 5, 1959. *Also in his:* De l'homme à Dieu. Nouvelles éds. latines, 1959. p. 414–21. *Issued separately as:* Le suicide de Paul Valéry. Liège, Aelberts-éds. dynamo, 1960. 8 p. (Brimborions, 69)   8451

Massis relates the story, as he remembers V. telling it to a group of friends, of his attempted suicide in London in April 1896. The facts coincide with the few other printed versions of the story. See Sylvia Beach *supra.* Massis adds his customary tone of opprobrium for an immoral act.

Mauron, Charles. Valéry; Valéry: la dormeuse. *In his:* Des métaphores obsédantes au mythe personnel; introduction à la psychocritique. Corti, 1962. p. 81–104; 157–93.   8452

This book has provoked hostile reactions due in large measure to its claim of scientific objectivity which few literary scholars are willing to grant to a psychoanalytic enterprise. In his search of V.'s (unconscious) personal myth, Mauron practices a type of static analysis quite different from that found in Bastet's essay above. For Mauron only the superpositioning of texts (*Le Cimetière marin* and *La jeune Parque* in Pt. II, chapter 5) can reveal the obsessive phantasm. The goals of psychobiography become clearer in Pt. III, chapter 10 as Mauron relates "La dormeuse" to oral affectivity and the sentimental crisis of 1890–1892. "La dormeuse" is seen as a mythical figure having her own place and function in

V.'s personal myth. At this point one might expect a convergence with Bastet and Aigrisse, but they prefer more spiritual solutions which, within their own framework, are incompatible with Mauron's Freudian perspective.
Reviews: A. Blanchet in Et 319: 277–78, 1963; J. Cocking in FS 12:89–90, 1965; M. Milner in RHL 66:353–55, 1966; P.-H. Simon in Monde Aug. 14, 1963.

Mein, Margaret. Valéry and Gide. *In:* Entretiens sur Paul Valéry. *See* 8475. p. 179–202. **8453**
The most thorough presentation of V.'s relations with Gide; it analyzes the *Correspondance* but also the published work of the two men as well as their respective *Journal* and *Cahiers*. The result is a portrayal indicating more deep-seated similarities than previous critics had been willing to grant.

Mercié, Jean-Luc. Paul Valéry et les poèmes pour la sorcière. RUO 42:133–44, 1972. **8454**
This chatty introduction to V.'s poems to and for Mme Muhlfeld (from 1925 onward, Mme Blanchenay) adds a few details to our understanding of V.'s long friendship with the lady who, at the time of his return to letters, could still make a literary career.

Mondor, Henri. Un déjeuner. NRF 1:643–58, 1953. *Also in his:* Propos familiers de Paul Valéry. *See* 8457. p. 47–68. **8455**
Fourteen years after Alain's version appeared in the NRF, Dr. Mondor recounted his experience of the Lapérouse luncheon with V. The value of Mondor's article is to have preserved, as best he could, the actual exchanges between Alain and V.

———. L'heureuse rencontre de Valéry et Mallarmé. Lausanne, Guilde du livre, 1947. 125 p. **8456**
The privileged moment in V.'s life represented by Mallarmé's friendship provided the substance of a solid essay, the best Mondor devoted to V. It comments on V.'s writings on Mallarmé but derives most of its flavor from the author's intimate knowledge of Mallarmé's biography. This may well be the best biography of V. to date for the period 1890–98.

———. Propos familiers de Paul Valéry. Grasset, 1957. 283 p. **8457**
As an admirer of V., Mondor's fervor was equalled only by that of the collector J. M. Monod. The material for this chronicle is drawn from the author's notations of V.'s conversations at society gatherings, dinners or at home between January 1925 and July 1945, just hours before his death. Thus we have here for good or ill, the most complete compilation of opinions, witticisms and asides of the Poet Laureate (unofficial) of the Third Republic.
Reviews: M. Bémol in RHL 58: 561–64, 1958; R. J[udrin] in NRF 6:338–40, 1958; E. Noulet in SynB 13:259–61, 1958.

———. Vie de Mallarmé. Gallimard, 1941–42. 2 v. *New ed. in one vol.:* Gallimard, 1946. 830 p. **8458**
The material on V. and Mallarmé is more accessible in the same author's *L'heureuse rencontre de Valéry et Mallarmé*, 1947.

Monod, J.-P. Regard sur Paul Valéry. Lausanne, Ed. des Terreaux, 1947. 59 p. **8459**
Personal reminiscences by V.'s minister of the pen, originally composed as lectures for a Swiss audience in September 1945.

Nadal, Octave. La jeunesse et l'amitié de Paul Valéry et de Gustave Fourment. MdF 82:33–40, 48, 1957. *Also in:* Valéry, Paul, and Gustave Fourment. Correspondance 1887–1933. *See* 8414. p. 15–30. **8460**
This article is a companion piece to the one published in MerF in 1955. It attempts to explain the prolongation of V.'s 1892 crisis from October to November.

———. Paul Valéry et l'événement de 1892. MerF 323:614–26, 1955. *Also in his:* A mesure haute. Mercure de France, 1964. p. 151–64. **8461**
Noting two conflicting reports by V. himself as to the effective date of his intellectual conversion, Nadal prudently opts for both: the stormy Genoa night of Oct. 4 to 5, 1892 followed by a recurrence of the spiritual crisis in

Paris a month later. Using the correspondence with G. Fourment, he clarifies some ambiguities left in the versions of this traumatic experience as V. had reported it to Gide and to Louÿs. Several pages on Rimbaud and V.'s understanding of his work between 1890 and 1892 round out the most complete relation of this capital period in V.'s life.

——. Paul Valéry—jeunesse et création, Arithmetica universalis. CahS 44:339–47, 1957. *Also in:* Valéry, Paul, and Gustave Fourment. Correspondance 1887–1933. *See* 8414. p. 30–39. *Also in his:* A mesure haute. Mercure de France, 1964. p. 181–90. **8462**

Nadal's thesis, based on two letters to Fourment in 1898, is that V. then envisaged a reduction to definite mathematical variations of all physical, physiological and psychological phenomena.

Pomès, Mathilde. Paul Valéry et l'Espagne. *In:* Paul Valéry centennial. *See* 8485. p. 592–602. **8463**

A composite article: Pomès gives an appreciation of V.'s lecture on Lope de Vega (1935) and details of the manner in which it was written. The complete text of the lecture is reproduced for the first time in French. Details of V.'s travels in Spain, his preferences in Spanish poetry, and some previously unpublished letters complete the article.

Robinson, Judith. Valéry, the anxious intellectual. *In:* Paul Valéry 1871–1971. *See* 8487. p. 118–38. **8464**

A major contribution to V.'s biography in that it combines the expertise of a scholar thoroughly familiar with the *Cahiers* and the analytical tools of Mauron and Aigrisse. Robinson successfully applies the psychoanalytic concept of anxiety to the well known (both to V. and his commentators) unresolved conflicts in V.'s mental life. The results indicate that more work in this area is called for.

Rouart-Valéry, Agathe. L'apologie de la main chez Paul Valéry. *In:* Paul Valéry contemporain. *See* 8486. p. 277–87. **8465**

This contribution to the 1971 Strasbourg colloquium can be read in conjunction with that of G. Antoine (*see* 8611). It is a sensitive portrayal of V. as *homo faber.*

——. Paul Valéry. Gallimard, 1966. 205 p. **8466**

The principal element in this book is the abundant iconography illustrated by V.'s texts both published and previously unpublished. The connecting statements and the organization of the whole are the work of V.'s daughter.

——. Paul Valéry vu par sa fille. FS 23:378–93, 1969. **8467**

V.'s daughter, who had already been of great assistance to scholars, delivered this charming and sometimes moving account of her father in a lecture at Oxford. It will be a document of considerable interest to biographers, most of all perhaps for the discussion of V.'s anxiety as a permanent trait manifesting itself in the most diverse situations.

Saqui, J. Le souvenir de Paul Valéry à Nice. Nice, Félix Bottin & fils, 1946. 37 p. **8468**

As is customary in texts of this type the author devotes more space to the glory of the locality than to V. Details of V.'s relations with the city abound; these doubtless have their place in an eventual biography.

Stravinsky, Igor. Valéry: a memoir. *In:* Valéry, Paul. Plays. New York, Pantheon; London, Routledge & Kegan Paul, 1960. p. xx–xxv. (The collected works of Paul Valéry. V. 3) **8469**

Two valuable anecdotes on matters of some importance are to be found here. The first concerns V.'s criticism of the manuscript version of Stravinsky's 1939 Norton lectures at Harvard. The second involves V.'s intervention on the side of Stravinsky when he disagreed with Gide over their joint *Perséphone* project in 1934. A letter from V. after a performance of *Perséphone* is included. Stravinsky's parting observations on V. as religious thinker in *Mon Faust* are stimulating.

Tosi, Guy. Gabriele D'Annunzio e Paul Valéry. Florence, Sansoni, 1960. 23 p. (Biblioteca degli eruditi e dei bibliofili, 40) **8470**

Tosi has assembled and commented on all available material, published and manuscript, to establish the significance of the V.-D'Annunzio friendship. Quite clearly V. was strongly attracted by the personal charm of the Italian, whatever his judgment may have been of the elder writer's work. Several letters in Italian demonstrate that V. wrote the language less well than he spoke it.

Valéry, Claude. Présence de Paul Valéry. *In:* Paul Valéry contemporain. *See* 8486. p. 289–99. **8471**

This evocation of V. by his elder son proceeds in the manner of the progressive revelations experienced by Proust's Marcel: from the total otherness of his first impression of *La jeune Parque,* read by Gide in the author's absence, to the phases of V.'s literary celebrity, closing upon *La jeune Parque* now understood in quite another way.

Collected Articles

Cahiers Paul Valéry. 1: Poétique et poésie. Ed. by Jean Levaillant. Gallimard, 1975. 243 p. **8472**

Although the first to be conceived, this is the third series to be devoted exclusively to V. since the centenary. Its inception was held up for several years. As a result some articles in this issue have odd references in the footnotes. There is some duplication of effort in bibliography. At present this series contains the most thorough of the current bibliographies. The publication of the V.-Louÿs correspondence moves forward at a snail's pace: eleven letters from V. (1891–92) printed in this issue can now be added to fifteen (1915–17) published privately in 1926. There is still no proper critical edition of this important correspondence in view. Articles of importance have been analyzed separately under the appropriate subject headings.

Centenaire de Paul Valéry. Ed. by Huguette Laurenti. Eur 507:1–157, 1971. **8473**

This special number of *Europe* brings little that is new to V. scholarship. Its organization and conception are oriented toward the multi-faceted values of his work for Europeans of several nationalities. The contents are not analyzed separately.

Les critiques de notre temps et Valéry. Ed. by Jean Bellemin-Noël. Garnier, 1971. 191 p. **8474**

With one exception this volume is composed of reprinted articles and chapters of books which are generally available and well known to V. critics. The "thèse complémentaire" which Jean Levaillant defended in the University of Paris in 1966 has not been published in its entirety despite an indication to the contrary in this volume. The extract printed here (pp 88–95) has been analyzed below (*see* 8809).

Review: W. Ince in FS 27:351–52 1973.

Entretiens sur Paul Valéry. Ed. by Emilie Noulet-Carner. Paris-The Hague, Mouton 1968. 415 p. (Décades du centre culturel international de Cerisy-la-Salle, nouvelle série, 7) **8475**

This volume contains the texts of the seventeen communications to the V. colloquium of September 2 to 11 1965. The individual communications are analyzed under the appropriate headings below.

Entretiens sur Paul Valéry. Actes du colloque de Montpellier des 16 et 17 octobre 1971 (Université Paul-Valéry). Ed. by Daniel Moutote. Presses univ. de France 1972. 194 p. **8476**

This colloquium distinguished itself from other celebrations of the centenary by organizing communications along different lines: "de Montpellier à Paris" (biographical); "permanence des origines" (thematic); "vers l'Europe" (emphasizing V.'s contacts with other nations and literatures). The critical contributions are described under the pertinent headings. The official opening remarks by J. Guitton (Académie française) and P. Laubriet (Univ. Paul-Valéry) have not been retained. Certain communications were too brief or too general to warrant separate entry.

Lectures de Charmes. Ed. by Huguette Laurenti. RLM 413–18:5–223, 1974 (Paul Valéry, 1) **8477**

The first number in a new series devoted to V.'s work. Individual contributions described under the appropriate headings.

Paul Valéry. Ed. by Victoria Ocampo. S 14:7–104, 1945. **8478**

The volume contains an affectionate retrospective by Victoria Ocampo, an offertory by Supervielle, five pages on V.'s themes by E. Noulet, an equal number on the man by H. Steiner, an homage by Pedro Salinas, another—in the form of variations on "La dormeuse"—by J. Guillén. Spanish versions of "La fausse morte" and "Le sylphe", and bilingual presentations of *Mon Faust* (Act II, scene 5) and of V.'s letters to V. Ocampo complete the part of the volume devoted to V. One further item, an extraordinary text by J. Borges, is analyzed below (*see* 8958).

Paul Valéry. Ed. by Wallace Fowlie. QRL 3:210–327, 1947.   8479
   This special number of a literary magazine of high quality is memorable today for its effort to introduce V. to American readers of the postwar period. The articles by Wm. Troy, K. Douglas, A. Coleno, H. H. Watts and W. Fowlie—while good for the time—have all been surpassed. They are not analyzed separately. The translations by W. Fowlie, Roger Shattuck and others continue to read well. T. S. Eliot's biographical statement is reprinted from *Paul Valéry vivant.* In it he made the now celebrated claim for V. as the representative poet, the symbol of the poet, for the first half of the century.

Paul Valéry. EspCr 4:1–48, 1964.   8480
   The five contributions are analyzed under the appropriate headings.

Paul Valéry. CAIEF 17:169–256, 1965.
                                                       8481
   Contains the six communications on V. given at the 1964 meeting of the AIEF. Each is analyzed below under the appropriate subject heading.

Paul Valéry. YFS 44:3–230, 1970.   8482
   The seventeen contributions to this centenary volume make it one of the most important printed between 1970 and 1974. The quality of the articles, analyzed under appropriate headings, deserved better editing. The volume is full of typographical errors and omissions of letters and entire words.
   Reviews: A. Arnold in SFr 18:242–47, 1974; E. Gaède in RHL 73:921–22, 1973; N. Suckling in FS 27:354–55, 1973.

Paul Valéry. NRF 224:1–25, 1971.   8483
   Includes two brief notes on V.'s poetry and poetics by M. Deguy and P. Oster as well as three texts by V.: "Alphabet," "Esquisse d'un poème," (two versions) and eight "Lettres à Jean Paulhan." These have not been analyzed separately.

Paul Valéry. Ed. by Bernard Vannier. MLN 87:539–681, 1972.   8484
   More than any other colloquium devoted to the centenary, this one revealed a deep split between linguistic formalists and practitioners of more traditional scholarly methods. All contributions but two are analyzed under the appropriate headings. Elizabeth Sewell's very personal address, "The work remembered," escapes classification. M. Deguy's variations on the last line of "L'ange" are too diffuse in their suggestion of a formalist poetics in V.'s work.
   Review: A Arnold in SFr 53:249–51, 1974.

Paul Valéry centennial. A look at the man in the poet. Ed. by Ivar Ivask. BA 45:571–626, 1971.   8485
   This commemorative volume prepared for the centenary organized contributions along biographical lines, soliciting reminiscences from writers of different national backgrounds in keeping with the magazine's international outlook. It also includes the complete French text of V.'s 1935 address on Lope de Vega, printed here for the first time. Individual contributions of some substance are described separately. They are complemented by a four-page assessment of V. for the American reader by W. E. McClendon, a personal statement by the editor, and a checklist of books by and about V. reviewed in BA from 1927 to 1971.

Paul Valéry contemporain. Ed. by Monique Parent and Jean Levaillant. Klincksieck, 1974. viii, 401 p. (Actes et colloques, 12)
                                                       8486
   Contains the texts of two of the three major commemorations of the centenary in France: the Strasbourg and Vincennes colloquia of Nov. 1971. Contributions of lasting value are analyzed separately. Others, too brief or too general, include: M. Bilen,

Antinomies et autonomie chez Paul Valéry; M. Dufrenne, *L'esthétique de Paul Valéry;* P. Laurette, *Structures d'ordre proche dans la poésie de Paul Valéry.* The last named offers preliminary results of a computer program analysis; promising but incomplete at present.

Paul Valéry, 1871–1971. Ed. by Judith Robinson. AJFS 8:101–242, 1971.   **8487**

The ten contributions to this Australian celebration of the centenary include some important material; all are analyzed under separate headings.

Paul Valéry, essais et témoignages inédits. Ed. by Marc Eigeldinger. Neuchâtel, A la Baconnière, 1945. 238 p. *Also:* La presse française et étrangère-Oreste Zeluck, 1945.   **8488**

The most significant of the twenty contributions to this volume are analyzed separately under the pertinent headings. A facsimile reproduction of a three-page ms. of "Ébauche d'un serpent" (from the Mermod collection) and the text of a letter from V. to Ed. Jaloux dated Oct. 28, 1927 concerning M. Teste complete the volume.

Paul Valéry vivant. Ed. by Jean Ballard. CahS 7–381, 1946.   **8489**

The numerous contributions to this issue of *Cahiers du sud* in homage to V. are too brief, too general or too dated to require individual analysis. The volume has long been known to V. scholars and is still frequently cited. Review article: T. de Triquou. Paul Valéry méditerranéen. [Casablanca, Imprimerie rapide, 1949.] p. 3–22.

General Studies: Books

Bémol, Maurice. Paul Valéry. Clermont-Ferrand, G. de Bussac; Paris, Les belles lettres, 1949. xvi, 454 p.   **8490**

As the first French state doctoral dissertation devoted to V. this book played an important role in providing a focus for research over the next decade. Its limitations are the direct result of an overly ambitious design: to prove V.'s superiority as contemporary thinker. To this end Bémol has coined the general term "Valérysme"

which he subdivides for analysis under the headings pure method, doctrine and literary "Valérysme." The unifying principle is an ego psychology which, although present in parts of V.'s work, does not account for the contradictions or the paradoxical aspect so characteristic of his thought. These aspects have been more adequately treated by numerous recent studies.

Reviews: G. Martin in FR 24:166–69, 1950; and in RHL 53:255–58, 1953; J. Trouillard in BAGB 3ᵉ série, no. 2:57–61, 1952.

———. Variations sur Valéry. Saarbruck, Publications de l'univ. de la Saare, 1952. 131 p.   **8491**

The seven texts in this collection were written between 1939 and 1950. Four had been published previously in journals most of which could be located today only with the greatest difficulty outside France. They treat V. in relation to esthetics, medicine, technology and the sciences, respectively. All are of good quality without being especially distinguished. Of the three remaining texts two were originally lectures. The second lecture treats V. and Goethe in the manner of French comparatism. The final text in the volume represents an imaginary defense of the author's doctoral dissertations. Individually and collectively they are of marginal importance today.

Reviews: L. Austin in RHL 54:109–11, 1954; L. Bisson in FS 7:372–74, 1953; R. Pouilliart in LR 17:314–16, 1963.

———. Variations sur Valéry. V. 2. Nizet, 1959. 185 p.   **8492**

A dozen of his articles, speeches and book reviews. Those texts which merit special mention are described under the appropriate subject headings.

Bendz, Ernst. Paul Valéry et l'art la prose. Göteborg, Gumpert, 1936. 191 p.   **8493**

V.'s own enthusiasm for this study, which he considered the best book devoted to his work according to documented reports, should have recommended it to scholars. Yet it has long since been forgotten. Its current rarity is certainly a factor, a mere three hundred copies having been printed for sale. The technical approach to style, which V. appreciated to the point of annotating the ms., remains very useful, particularly as it bears on the less studied of V.'s speeches and occasional pieces. Bendz's admiring but thoroughly independent and sometimes irreverent attitude imparts an enduring freshness to his book.

Bendz, E[rnst Paulus]. Till fragan om diktverkets genesis. Ett kapitel ur Paul Valérys estetik. Göteborg, Elanders boktryckeri aktiebolag, 1933. 36 p. **8494**
The dimensions of the essay were much too slim for the general inquiry into V.'s esthetics which the author proposed. His subsequent book in 1936, while it does not treat the poetry, otherwise supersedes this earlier effort.

Benoist, Pierre-François. Les essais de Paul Valéry, poèmes et prose, étudiés et commentés. Eds. de la pensée moderne, 1964. 288 p. (Mellottée-les chefs-d'œuvre de la littérature expliqués) **8495**
A book suitable for students beginning their study of French literature. It has no critical apparatus as such, aiming rather to smooth out problems an untrained mind may encounter in a first reading of V.
Review: R. Lang in FR 40:572–73, 1967.

Berne-Joffroy, [André]. Présence de Valéry précédé de Propos me concernant par Paul Valéry. Brussels-Paris, Raoul Henry-Plon, 1944. 237 p. **8496**
Although this study has lost much of its original interest since the availability and the systematic review of the *Cahiers,* one should note its impact at the time of publication. V.'s "Propos me concernant," p. 11–61, were read variously as his most extensive biographical statement and as a foretaste of the notebooks. Berne-Joffroy's essay is intelligent, frequently witty and interlarded with excellent quotations. It remains quite readable.

Berne-Joffroy, André. Valéry. Gallimard, 1960. 314 p. (La bibliothèque idéale) **8497**
This book has the overall plan and conception imposed by the series in which it appeared: a modest study of the man and his work (p. 9–154) followed by a carefully edited an-

thology of extracts (p. 157–276), judgments by contemporaries (p. 279–92) and a summary documentation. For a book of its type, it is particularly well put together by a writer with an excellent personal sense of V.'s work.
Review: O. de Magny in LetN 8:183–84, 1960.

Bolle, Louis. Paul Valéry. Fribourg, Egloff, 1944. 149 p. *Also:* Paul Valéry, conscience et poésie. Geneva, A. Kundig, 1944. 149 p. **8498**
One of the better studies available in its day, it is rarely cited by contemporary scholars. This is particularly regrettable in that Bolle's chapter on "La logique imaginative" is still fresh. He observed similarities between V.'s critical idealism and Kant which have quite recently been stressed anew by R. Freedman. The chapter on V.'s fascination with correspondences among the arts merits further investigation. His treatment of the question of pure poetry, however, has been superseded in recent years.

Bourbon Busset, Jacques de. Paul Valéry ou le mystique sans Dieu. Plon, 1964. 189 p. (La recherche de l'absolu, 13) **8499**
The title of the book and the series in which it appeared are sufficient indication of its ideological orientation. The old thesis of V. as the cold intellectual is here married to that of the mystic in spite of himself so as to lead V. back to the fold. The level of critical discourse is frequently reminiscent of exchanges between Thomists and agnostics in the twenties.
Reviews: M. Lobet in RGB 100:124–25, 1964; P. Sénart in TR 197:136–37, 1964.

Cain, Lucienne Julien. Trois essais sur Paul Valéry. Gallimard, 1958. 193 p. **8500**
This volume, much discussed at the time of its publication, brings together three separate but related essays: "Edgar Poe et Valéry" (*see* 8923), "V. et l'utilisation du monde sensible," and "L'être vivant selon V." Part of the interest generated by the book was due to the author's close association with V. and his *Cahiers* over a period of years. Since the *Cahiers* were only then beginning to appear, these essays served to whet the appetite and guide the

first steps of critical readers. Certain of the author's observations on V. the man and the thinker remain of some value.

Reviews: L. Aragon in LetF 1, 5, Nov. 27, 1958; M. Bémol in RLC 35:324–25, 1961; J. Mathews in RR 50:233–34, 1959; J. Pommier in RHL 60:259–61, 1960.

Charney, Hanna. Le scepticisme de Valéry. Didier, 1969. 141 p. (Essais et critiques, 7)   **8501**

Sets out to define V.'s dominant intellectual attitude as one of skepticism defined as a simultaneous recognition and condemnation of contemporary intellectual values (Bergsonian and existentialist). As a general statement of V.'s position in contemporary intellectual history, it finds support in the work published in V.'s lifetime. However, the study does not take into account the *Cahiers*. Furthermore, references have not been brought into conformity with the Pléiade ed. of V.'s works. As a result the value of the book for current scholarship is marginal.

Charpier, Jacques. Essai sur Paul Valéry. Seghers, 1956. 223 p. (Poètes d'aujourd'hui, 51)   **8502**

Contains a particularly good introduction to the early years. It condenses the biographical material published by Mondor and the earliest revelations by Nadal. While it does not in itself present any significant critical findings, the essay will competently orient the beginning student of V.

Consiglio, Alberto. Paul Valéry—saggi e ricerche per il centenario, 1871–1971. Naples, G. e M. Benincasa, 1971. 129 p.   **8503**

The essays collected in this volume to commemorate V.'s centenary serve primarily as testimony to V.'s influence on a part of Italian letters in the late twenties. The principal subjects treated are V.'s multiple representation of Leonardo da Vinci and his Narcisse.

Crow, Christine M. Paul Valéry: consciousness and nature. Cambridge, Cambridge univ. press, 1972. xiii, 271 p.   **8504**

The striving for thoroughness which orients this study, while admirable in itself, will possibly be overshadowed by several of its individual contributions. The commentary on sensibility and intellect, for instance, which Crow recognizes as linked in V.'s thought, is set against the best recent discussions which have doubted the centrality of the affective (Hytier, Robinson). Crow's analysis of the idea of love in the *Cahiers* is a valuable contribution to an area which, at the time of her writing, had just been opened up by Walzer and Bastet. On the other hand, her presentation of the importance of biology for V. should be supplemented by Virtanen's historical perspective on the same subject.

Reviews: Anon. in TLS Sept. 29, 1972; C. Chadwick in MLR 70:198–99, 1975; C. Hackett in FS 27:474–75, 1973; H. Laurenti in RHL 74:926–27, 1974.

Doisy, Marcel. Paul Valéry, intelligence et poésie. Le cercle du livre et Eds. Paul Mourousy, 1952. 243 p. (Les univers de la littérature, 4)   **8505**

The general study of the man and his work, with its biographical frame of reference, has never produced much of real value for students of V. This one is a case in point. The lack of any knowledge of the *Cahiers* left the author without a firm ground for his proposed examination of the forms of intelligence in V.'s work.

Duchesne-Guillemin, Jacques. Etudes pour un Paul Valéry. Neuchâtel, A la Baconnière, 1964. 247 p.   **8506**

This volume collects a half dozen important essays, several of which have long been unobtainable in their original published form, most notably those devoted to *La jeune Parque* and *Charmes* (analyzed separately). None of the essays is itself definitive but together they promise to remain of value for some time. The following have not been analyzed separately: "Avant la trentaine" (NRF 61:181–92; 62:374–84, 1958); "Paul Valéry: orgueil et transfiguration" (OrL 10:321–34, 1955); "Valéry et la composition" (Glanes 15–16:33–50, 1950). Chapters six and seven of the present volume, "Le Faust et les *Cahiers,*" and "L'homme et l'œuvre" are original publications of lectures given in 1961–62 and 1964, respectively.

Review: J. Cocking in MLR 62:55–60, 1967.

Fabureau, Hubert. Paul Valéry. Nouvelle revue critique, 1937. 253 p. **8507**

This study undoubtedly represents the most systematic exploitation of the myth of V.-Teste. All of V.'s work is reduced to aspects of Teste (scruples, betrayals, imprisonment, escape, etc.), to such a degree that a more appropriate title might have been "Aventures de M. Teste, vie romancée."

Felici, Noël. Regards sur Valéry. Fernand Hazan, 1951. 93 p. **8508**

The fragmentary nature of this slim volume and the lack of a basic informing principle make it of marginal interest in the present state of V. scholarship. It belongs with that rather large group of writings which set out to demonstrate that V. is not really so hard to read after all.

Fernandat, René. Autour de Paul Valéry, lignes d'horizon. Grenoble, B. Arthaud, 1933. 220 p. *Also (rev.):* Deuxième édition, considérablement augmentée, précédée d'une Lettre-préface de M. Paul Valéry. Grenoble-Paris, B. Arthaud, 1944 [1945]. 283 p. **8509**

The chapters of this essay vary in scope from *L'idée fixe* to "V. devant Maine de Biran et Hegel." Nearly all the chapters have since been surpassed by more complete studies. Pending a truly thorough examination of V. and surrealism, the penultimate chapter will remain of some interest. V.'s letter-preface is frequently cited.

Gaède, Edouard. Nietzsche et Valéry, essai sur la comédie de l'esprit. Gallimard, 1962. 504 p. **8510**

Exhaustive in its scope, exemplary in its methodology, this is clearly one of the best scholarly studies devoted to V. Nietzsche converses with V. here, the one illuminating the other in their differences as much as in their similarities. The impressive results of Gaède's work should encourage a closer formal examination of certain of V.'s major texts with relation to Nietzsche. The notes and the bibliography are exceptionally good.

Reviews: R.-M. Albérès in TR 178: 110–12, 1962; G. Bianquis in EG 19:

296–300, 1964; M. de Diéguez in Cr 210:955–62, 1964; H. Staub in NieS 1:432–40, 1972.

Grubbs, Henry A. Paul Valéry. New York, Twayne, 1968. 153 p. (TWAS, 43) **8511**

This book is somewhat brief for its scope as a general study for non-specialists, but its clear prose and no nonsense approach will doubtless contribute to a better understanding of V. outside the circle of his long-time admirers. Every V. specialist will find something to object to here, but that may be unimportant given the broad audience to which this series appeals.

Reviews: A. Arnold in FR 42:618–20, 1969; P. Walzer in RHL 69:1060–61, 1969; C. Whiting in MLJ 53: 278–79, 1969.

Hytier, Jean. La poétique de Valéry. Colin, 1953. 312 p. *Also:* 1970. *Trans.:* The poetics of Paul Valéry. Trans. by Richard Howard. Garden City, Doubleday, 1966. vi, 353 p. (Anchor book, A13) **8512**

Long considered among the very best books on V., this one is particularly valuable for its exhaustive presentation of the conflicting exigencies of sensibility and intellect in V.'s poetics. Hytier concludes by examining in detail his theory of effects, using the concept of the esthetic infinite to good advantage. This concept, and V.'s theory of ornament (which Hytier presents especially well), might have suggested a parallel with Kantian esthetics. That connection remained unexplored, however, until Freedman's essay in 1972.

Reviews: Anon. in TLS 2704:753–54, Nov. 27, 1953; M. Bémol in RHL 55:249–53, 1955; R. Mucci in Id 5:4, 1953.

Ingrosso, Oronzo. Note su Valéry. Bari, Levante, 1959. 67 p. **8513**

The five short articles in the volume present then current views of V. to the literate Italian reader. The sole study which may have an enduring value draws an interesting parallel between V.'s *L'âme et la danse* and Degas.

Lafont, Aimé. Paul Valéry l'homme et l'œuvre. Marseille, J. Vigneau, 1943. 273 p. **8514**

V.'s letter-preface, reprinted in his *Lettres à quelques-uns,* has long been the most seriously pondered part of the book. It was here that V. wrote in some detail about the composition of *La jeune Parque* and its many drafts. The critical apparatus of Lafont's study appears rudimentary today.

Lanfranchi, G[eneviève]. Paul Valéry et l'expérience du moi pur. Lausanne, Mermod, 1958. 63 p.   8515

The author finds a double attitude toward the concept of the "Moi pur" running through V.'s work, including the early *Cahiers*. The evidence presented here makes it clear how two opposing camps—Catholic and intellectualist—have been able to stake out mutually exclusive claims. According to Lanfranchi, who fortunately avoids the "mystique sans Dieu" mode of expression, both attitudes coexisted in V. without ever achieving a real synthesis. Several recent articles have concluded similarly.

Reviews: M. Bémol in RHL 60:87–88, 1960; M. Lecomte in SynB 150–52:412–13, 1958–59.

La Rochefoucauld, Edmée de. Paul Valéry. Eds. universitaires, 1954. 161 p. (Classiques du XXᵉ siècle)   8516

Occasionally pertinent biographical details and first-hand anecdotes raise this study above the general level of its type; but, on the whole, each subject heading has been treated more thoroughly and in greater depth by recent scholarly investigations.

Latour, Jean de. Examen de Valéry. Essai pour servir d'introduction à son œuvre. Précédé d'une lettre et d'un texte inédits de Paul Valéry. Gallimard, 1935. 263 p.   8517

The organization of this essay was such that it has escaped the common fate of general studies on living writers. The author chose to focus on V.'s critique of values in both its negative and positive aspects. Elements of the essay can be read profitably today.

Lawler, James R. The poet as analyst. Essays on Paul Valéry. Berkeley-Los Angeles-London, Univ. of California press, 1974. xiv, 353 p.   8518

This volume collects ten essays, some of them revised and expanded, original-

ly published between 1963 and 197_ With the exception of the last, concern_ ing the final volumes of the *Cahier_* and an article on V. and Eliot used _ the epilog, all the essays treat aspects _ V.'s poetry. Individual chapters a_ analyzed separately.

Löwith, Karl. Paul Valéry: Grundzüg_ seines philosophischen Denkens. Götti_ gen, Vandenhoeck & Ruprecht, 1971. 1_ p. (Kleine Vandenhoeck-Reihe)   85_

An important essay by a respecte_ writer on European philosophy fro_ Descartes to Nietzsche and Heidegge_ A shorter version was originally pu_ lished as: *Paul Valéry: Grundriss sein_ philosophischen Denkens.* NRs 81:54_ 63, 1970. Löwith is familiar with t_ *Cahiers* and begins his journal artic_ with an examination of V.'s CEM sy_ tem (chapter 3 of the monograph). H_ sees the importance of V.'s "MOI pu_ as a critique of the tradition of tran_ cendental idealism. The journal artic_ concludes with V.'s reflections on la_ guage (chapter 2 of the monograph_ which Löwith considers to be the co_ stant reference point of an otherwi_ generalized skepticism. In this essay _ is not a proto-Saussurian but rather _ contemporary representative of th_ European tradition of reflection _ language. The monograph fleshes o_ the two chapters outlined in the journ_ article. Löwith adds to them chapte_ on V.'s Cartesianism, a very solid piec_ on V.'s critique of history and historiog_ raphy; and on V.'s idea of human co_ struction compared to natural creatio_ This last chapter should be supple_ mented by the more complete study _ C. Crow (*see* 8619).

Mackay, Agnes Ethel. The universal self. _ study of Paul Valéry. London, Routledg_ and Kegan Paul, 1961. iv, 263 p.   852_

A work for the general reader wit_ some French. It does not key referenc_ to the Hytier edition of the *Œuvr_* which had just appeared. In commen_ tary on the poetry, the author's relianc_ on Noulet and Cohen is surprisin_ given the date of publication.

Reviews: G. Burne in C 4:385–8_ 1962; N. Oxenhandler in EspCr 2:43_ 44, 1962.

Noulet, E[milie]. Paul Valéry. Grasset, 1938. lii, 221 p. *Also (rev.):* Brussels, Renaissance du livre, 1951. 199 p. **8521**

The 1938 edition incorporates essays published as early as 1927. It included V.'s "Fragments des mémoires d'un poème" of which this was the original ed. Between 1927 and 1938 Noulet's writings produced an impact on study of V. equal to that of Thibaudet's book. Mme Noulet's insistence on V.'s intellectualism served to draw attention away from the sensual aspects of his poetry, and her presentation of a unity of thought in the major prose works helped to mask the importance of paradox and contradiction for him. Most notably she extended this concept of V.'s architectonics to her interpretation of *Charmes* as a unified whole symbolically representing the very process of poetic creation. Critical opinion remains sharply divided on this point.

Parize, Jean-Henry. Essai sur la pensée et l'art de Paul Valéry. Brussels, Richard-Masse, 1946. 76 p. **8522**

By its very generality, placed well above the level of the individual works, and the relative ignorance of V.'s central preoccupation, this essay falls between the two major types that add to our understanding today. It already belongs to the past.

Pelmont, Raoul. Paul Valéry et les beaux-arts. Cambridge, Harvard univ. press; London, Oxford univ. press, 1949. 196 p. (Harvard studies in Romance languages, 23) **8523**

Most of its several chapters have been surpassed by more specialized monographs, but the whole is still useful as an introduction because of its broad range. Unfortunately all references are to editions of V.'s works which are no longer current, much less standard. The author is successful in his demonstration of the extent to which V.'s thought and work were steeped in the fine arts, or rather in their principles. Compare the 1947 article by W. Weisbach (*see* 8897).

Reviews: L. Bisson in FS 4:88–89, 1950; K. Douglas in BA 24:153, 1950.

Pire, François. La tentation du sensible chez Paul Valéry. Brussels, Renaissance du livre, 1964. 169 p. (La lettre et l'esprit) **8524**

Pire has offered a portrayal of V. in counterpoint to M. Raymond's temptation of the mind. His title invites the comparison and his readers have generally made it, frequently concluding that a more balanced understanding of V. emerges therefrom. The first chapter, devoted to "Esthésique et poïétique," has best stood the test of the book's first decade.

Rang, Bernhard. Paul Valéry. Bonn-Dortmund, Stadtbücherei-Stadtische Volksbüchereien, 1961. 33 p. (Dichter und Denker unserer Zeit, 30) **8525**

This little volume includes five brief notes by Rang on various aspects of V.'s life, work and bibliography, all of an introductory nature. Two pages by V. on poets and books are included in German translation. Perhaps the most valuable contribution is the printing of three German renderings of "Les Pas" (by Rilke, Kraft and Derndarsky) following the original, thus permitting judicious comparison.

Rauhut, Franz. Paul Valéry—Geist und Mythos. München, Max Hueber Verlag, 1930. 312 p. **8526**

Incomplete as a synthesis and inclined toward rapid and insufficiently developed comparisons. Nonetheless, the reading of V.'s political writings in the light of Spengler's contemporaneous work and of V.'s texts on esthetics as complementary to Nietzsche remains noteworthy. Not until Gaède's study thirty years later was the parallel with Nietzsche explored in any depth. The chapter on the Narcissus poems contains observations which are still useful. The stimulating comparison of V.'s view of language with that of his contemporary E. Cassirer has been generally overlooked.

Raymond, Marcel. Paul Valéry et la tentation de l'esprit. Neuchâtel-Paris, A la Baconnière-La presse française et étrangère, Oreste Zeluck, 1946. 304 p. *Also:* Neuchâtel, A la Baconnière, 1964. 167 p. **8527**

All work of a phenomenological nature devoted to V. is in some way tributary to this pioneering study. Although many of Raymond's subheadings have been treated in greater detail by other writers, particularly since the publication of the *Cahiers,* this study remains a pleasure to read and continues to stimulate critical reflection.

Rideau, Emile. Introduction à la pensée de Paul Valéry. Desclée De Brouwer, 1944. 304 p.   8528

This book contributed significantly to a once widespread view that V. should be considered a mystic without God. Like the writings of H. Bremond, who originally launched the concept in the literary press, it falls within the domain of apologetics. The approach to V. is sympathetic without ever losing sight of the conclusion to be reached: Christianity alone provides the foundation for the transcendence which would crown V.'s otherwise antithetical attitudes. How one judges the value of this interpretation will depend on one's attitude toward the ideological system it is meant to reinforce.

Romain, Willy-Paul. Paul Valéry, le poème la pensée. Eds. du globe, 1951. 127 p.   8529

The six studies incorporated here are of uneven quality. Only the exegesis of "Intérieur" (*Charmes*) should hold our attention as one of the few serious readings of the poem.

Scarfe, Francis. The art of Paul Valéry—a study in dramatic monologue. London-Melbourne-Toronto, William Heinemann, 1954. xiii, 338 p.   8530

One aspect of this study deserves renewed interest: V.'s use of dramatic monolog, which the author handles well in his exegesis of *Le cimetière marin.* The rest is fairly dated today.

Reviews: Anon. in TLS 2741:512, Aug. 13, 1954; M. Bémol in RHL 57: 100–02, 1957; R. Gibson in LonM 1: 81–82, 84, 1954.

Sewell, Elizabeth. Paul Valéry, the mind in the mirror. New Haven, Yale univ. press; Cambridge, Bowes & Bowes, 1952. 61 p. (Studies in modern European literature and thought)   8531

The mirrors of the title are at once those of the mind and those objectified (reflecting surfaces of various types) throughout the work. They provide the author with the ideal matrix for her

brief study of V.'s work as an art of, and on, reflection. The motif of this study is what remains today, its details having been improved upon by more thorough investigations.

Review: C. Smith in Montjoie 1: 47–48, 1953.

Soulairol, Jean. Paul Valéry. La colombe, Eds. du vieux colombier, 1952. 215 p.   8532

Among the pages which have not been surpassed by more recent studies are several on V.'s association with the post-Mistral *félibrige,* an aspect of his early life which is generally ignored, perhaps wrongfully.

Review: S. Pitou in BA 28:314, 1954.

Sutcliffe, F. E. La pensée de Paul Valéry— essai. Nizet, 1955. 191 p.   8533

This essay deserves better than the near total silence which surrounds it today, due no doubt in large measure to its publication date—just prior to the successive revelations of the Pléiade edition of the *Œuvres,* then of the *Cahiers.* The first flush of enthusiasm for the analysis of mental process in the *Cahiers* seemed to relegate Sutcliffe to an uninformed past. More recent research indicates that there was considerable merit in his stubborn insistence on the unresolved contradictions between V.'s analytical method and his practice of comprehensive interpretation.

Review: L. Austin in RHL 57:285– 88, 1957.

Tauman, Léon. Paul Valéry ou le mal de l'art. Nizet, 1969. 247 p.   8534

This essay was among the first to utilize systematically the important Gladiator passages in the *Cahiers* of which J. Robinson had done a preliminary study in 1964. The initial chapter draws this method together with the first creature it produced, M. Teste, but in so doing it identifies the creature with the creator in such a way that discriminations become impossible. A corollary of the author's treatment of these creatures—whose only existence is textual—as persons is to set up an imaginary world in which Teste becomes the creator. In this regard, *see* 8802.

Thomson, Alastair W. Valéry. Edinburgh-London, Oliver & Boyd, 1965. 119 p. (Writers and critics, 4) **8535**

A dependable introduction for the general reader with some French. Stresses the poetry and the early prose (Teste, Leonardo), placing V. intelligently in the modern European tradition. The final pages contain some pertinent remarks on judgments by previous English-language critics (Eliot, Wilson, Kermode). Follows Ince in the interpretation of V.'s poetics.

Reviews: M. Dodsworth in NewS 257, Aug. 20, 1965.

Thuile, Jean. Cimetière marin, commémoration. Blaizot, 1948. 117 p. **8536**

A curious book indeed, belonging for the most part to the neglected domain of hagiography. The title notwithstanding, it deals only tangentially with V.'s poem, dwelling instead upon a grandiloquent evocation of the cemetery itself. Despite these major flaws, there are some good insights concerning V. and Pascal which Gaède used to excellent advantage in his 1962 book.

Virtanen, Reino. The scientific analogies of Paul Valéry. Lincoln, Univ. of Nebraska studies, 1974. 99 p. (New series, 47) **8537**

Virtanen approaches V.'s study of the natural and exact sciences from a literary viewpoint, considering functionally the scientific terms which appear in the published work and, to a far greater extent, in the Cahiers. He presents a concise but thorough examination of the broad range of these terms in V.'s lexicon. Indeed, one is tempted to conclude—as some earlier commentators had done—that V.'s centrality in contemporary esthetics is a function of this early synthesizing activity. Frequent pertinent references to other writers, Proust in particular, reinforce this notion in the first chapters. Nonetheless, Virtanen's consecutive reading in the Cahiers demonstrates V.'s growing disquiet centering on the crisis of the image and the concurrent crisis in atomic physics. As he notes, the result for V. is a gradual drift from the exact sciences toward the life sciences as a frame of reference. The present study builds upon but does not duplicate the 1963 book by Robinson. One regrets the absence of any reference to

the related studies by Crow and Jallat (see 8619 and 8629).

General Studies: Articles

Adorno, Theodor W. Valérys Abweichungen. NRs 71:1–38, 1960. **8538**

The article was occasioned by the publication of German eds. of Rhumbs and of V.'s essays on art. Adorno wished to combat a fashionable tendency in Germany, to dismiss V. as merely a reactionary writer on the arts because of his concern with form. For Adorno it is the anti-political position of V. that is interesting; this conservative sketched a model of the production of art for a market economy to which Marx could have subscribed. May be read as a supplement to Goldmann's critique of V.

Alain (pseud. of Emile Chartier). Propos. Gallimard, 1956–1970. 2 v. (Bibliothèque de la Pléiade) **8539**

An excellent analytical index in the first volume and an adequate index of names in the second permit the reader to follow Alain's growing admiration for V. as he expressed it in reviews and occasional remarks in the press from the twenties onward. The value of the Propos today for V. criticism lies in the importance one major writer (and moulder of opinion) placed on another.

Auden, W. H. Valéry: l'homme d'esprit. HudR 22:425–32, 1969. Also (minor variations): Introduction. In: Valéry, Paul. Analects. Princeton, Princeton univ. press; London, Routledge & Kegan Paul, 1970. p. vii–xvii. (The collected works of Paul Valéry, 14) **8540**

There is a refreshing openness in the English poet's essay on the French writer he visibly admires without, as he is quick to admit, always understanding him. But there is something disturbing in Auden's unabashed claim that no English ear will ever really grasp French poetry correctly. This is assuredly one of the most personal appreciations of V. ever made by another writer of stature.

Austin, Lloyd James. The genius of Paul Valéry. In: Wingspread lectures in the humanities. V. I. Racine, Wisc., Johnson foundation, 1966. p. 39–55. **8541**

This is the text of the author's 1963 lecture sponsored by the Johnson Foundation. It is an introduction to V. for a general audience of English speakers. As such it ranks among the best of its type.

———. Paul Valéry: Teste ou Faust? *In:* Paul Valéry. *See* 8481. p. 245–56.   **8542**

The answer to the question posed by the title is: both. Teste already contains the possibility of Faust; Faust is still Teste. The last of V.'s *Cahiers* serves to draw together these two personae. Austin's strategy is to gradually unfold the nature of this bond, which he sees as the gradual evolution of V.'s affectivity coming to accept itself in the unfinished Faust. A particularly sensitive grasp of a fundamental concept.

———. Valéry's views on literature. *In:* Paul Valéry, 1871–1971. *See* 8487. p. 175–92.   **8543**

Austin's inquiry serves to reopen this area of research on the basis of a fuller understanding of V.'s concept of literature. Some of the subheadings in this rich text are: literature as language, the relations of poetry to literature in the broader sense, the notion of composition, and V.'s unpublished views on Flaubert, whom he had grossly misunderstood.

Barrère, Jean-Bertrand. Cassandre—Paul Valéry: un sceptique profond. *In his:* L'idée de goût de Pascal à Valéry. Klincksieck, 1972. p. 239–81.   **8544**

V. is seen as the terminus of a history of taste spanning the high points of French rationalism. After Gide, the last "honnête homme," V.'s skepticism in these matters is highlighted. An eminently readable essay, quite useful in its context for purposes of literary history. However, one notices the absence of any reference to H. Charney's work in the same area, carried out in a similar perspective.

Bastet, Ned. L'expérience de la borne et du dépassement chez Valéry. *In:* Cahiers Paul Valéry. 1: poétique et poésie. *See* 8472. p. 57–90.   **8545**

Research into the prolongations of the opposition limitation/refusal of limitation leads to a new perspective on the "MOI pur," compatible with that

of Derrida but expressed more simply. Having found homeostasis to be a goal of V.'s desire, Bastet unobtrusively notes its similarity to the Freudian death instinct. We are thus led imperceptibly toward Lacan, but in a manner intended not to disturb more traditional literary scholars.

———. Le Faust valéryen et l'aventure humaine. Sud 4:12–25, 1971.   **8546**

The absence of any ed. of the fragments and mss. concerning Faust, the importance of which Bastet first revealed at the 1965 Cerisy colloquium leaves some doubt as to the legitimacy of the claims of this article. How can one reasonably argue that these sketches, notations and incomplete scenes would have constituted the most ambitious and perhaps the only work to express completely the extreme tension of V.'s thought?

Bellemin-Noël, Jean. Le narcissisme de Narcisse (Valéry). Lit 6:35–55, 1972.   **8547**

The article takes as its material "Narcisse parle" (*Album...*), "Fragments du Narcisse" (*Charmes*), and "Cantate du Narcisse." It cannot, however, be considered a thematic study precisely because of its methodology which is hostile to the search for topoi. V.'s Narcissism is taken here to be a stylistic expression of the psychoanalytic concept. An understanding of Lacan's concept of the Mirror Stage is supposed on the part of the reader. The results are rewarding although the necessary investment is considerable. This article represents the next step, methodologically, after the author's contribution "Narcisse parle" in RHL (1970).

Benda, Julien. Conceptions de la vérité chez Proust, Valéry. *In his:* La France byzantine ou le triomphe de la littérature pure. Gallimard, 1945. p. 137–45. *Also* Union générale d'éditions, 1970. p. 13–45. (10/18)   **8548**

V. is a consistent point of reference throughout this condemnation by the arch-intellectualist of the best and most influential literature written between the two world wars. V. stands convicted of romanticism, a crime against the national genius in the eyes of this critic

Blöcker, Günter. Paul Valéry. *In his:* Die neuen Wirklichkeiten. Berlin, Argon, 1958. p. 133–48. **8549**

From our present perspective this essay appears to belong to the past. It represents V. as typical of literary modernism in prewar France. To cite an example of a critical position that can scarcely be upheld today, Blöcker sees the "MOI pur" as V.'s version of the synthetic self of creativity in the tradition of subjective idealism. See Lanfranchi's essay published in the same year for contrasting, but equally unacceptable, views.

Bolle, Louis. Valéry. *In his:* Les lettres et l'absolu. Geneva, Perret-Gentil, 1959. p. 21–73. **8550**

The absolute of Bolle's title is that goal of esthetic modernism, the perfect rendering of an imperfect universe through art. He has sensed that V.'s abandonment of this myth in favor of a fragmentary work, composed entirely of exercises, sketches, commissions and "poèmes abandonnés" signals the end of an order. Yet he attempts to convince his reader that V.'s negative critique of the myth will in fact restore a new importance to poetry. More recent examinations of the period foreclosed by the 1939–45 war reveal the illusory character of this hope. Nonetheless this study represents progress in the critical treatment of the ideal of pure poetry. (Compare the same author's 1944 essay.) The third and fourth chapters focus sharply on V.'s contributions to modernism, his perfection of metaphoric composition and his conception of poetic music.

Bonnefoy, Yves. Paul Valéry. *In his:* L'improbable. Mercure de France, 1959. p. 135–46. **8551**

Bonnefoy identifies V.'s Mediterraneanism with philosophical idealism, citing Plato, Plotinus and Hegel. Over against this tradition he invokes the spirit of an ideal Aristotle whom V. presumably ignored. Bonnefoy then attributes the absolute originality of contemporary French poetry to this latter spirit. One senses that the essay represents that negative movement of thought which is necessary for Bonnefoy to transcend V.

Bounoure, Gabriel. Paul Valéry. *In his:* Marelles sur le parvis—essais de critique poétique. Plon, 1958. p. 89–103. **8552**

Sees V. voyaging ceaselessly between the antinomies of M. Teste and Leonardo. It is in this rhythmic movement that Bounoure finds the originality of *Mon Faust.*
Review: L.-G. Gros in CahS 349: 428–32, 1958.

Brombert, Victor. Valéry: the dance of words. HudR 21:675–86, 1968–69. **8553**

Brombert's tactic is to turn around V.'s choreographic metaphor on style and to demonstrate that the prose, too, is a dance of words. The outstanding qualities singled out by Brombert are flexibility and purpose, which he sets over against the scope and power V. lacks. Style can be summed up in the realism (observation coupled with fine detail) of this self-proclaimed anti-realist. A highly intelligent, urbane introduction to V. as prose writer.

Cattaui, Georges. L'univers de Valéry, un illuminisme néo-pythagoricien. *In:* Paul Valéry, essais et témoignages inédits. *See* 8488. p. 123–42. *Also:* Valéry illuministe néo-pythagoricien. *In his:* Orphisme et prophétie chez les Français, 1850–1950. Plon, 1965, p. 153–77. **8554**

The encyclopedic knowledge of the author finds connections between V. and thinkers both great and small. Unfortunately the promise of the title is never realized, and probably could not be. The best parallel Cattaui draws concerns V. and Thomas Aquinas, affording a plausible explanation for the fascination V. held for French neo-Thomists between the wars.

Champigny, Robert. Valéry on history and the novel. *In:* Paul Valéry. *See* 8482. p. 107–14. **8555**

A closely reasoned examination of V.'s statements on the novel and on writing history leads to a condemnation of V.'s anti-novelistic position. Champigny argues that V. tends to present history as myth, defining the mythical perspective as the confusion of cognitive and esthetic perspectives. This brief article deserves a more thorough development. (Compare the alternative view of F. Usinger; *see* 8589).

Clogenson, Yves. Valéry devant la mystique et l'occultisme. *In:* Entretiens sur Paul Valéry. *See* 8475. p. 229–53.   **8556**

The discussion following communication of the text fairly demolished the thesis that V. secretly nourished any vocation of mysticism in the traditional sense. At most one can make a case for his semi-serious interest in the subject through 1892. A more balanced appreciation of the concept of mysticism in V. is found in W. N. Ince's "Etre, connaître et mysticisme du réel selon Valéry" (*see* 8625).

Cocking, J. M. Towards Ebauche d'un serpent: Valéry and Ouroboros. AJFS 6: 187–215, 1969.   **8557**

On the one hand, this essay confirms Lawler's claim in his 1963 study of *Charmes* that the serpent of V.'s "Ebauche..." owes something to the Ouroboros as symbol of a closed system of sensibility. On the other hand, Cocking's exploration of the symbol in terms of intellectual history leads to Berthelot and Eliphas Lévi. Among the interesting hypotheses established by Cocking is a further extension of the symbol: Ouroboros in (al)chemical writings occupies a position of synthesis between early science and mental reflection.

Damon, Yvonne. Le sens du mystère chez Valéry. Sud 4:31–41, 1971.   **8558**

Damon replies to the growing chorus of voices claiming V. as an ancestor of structuralism. Using the *Soirée...* and *Mon Faust* to good advantage and referring frequently to other parts of V.'s prose work, she establishes V.'s position on the subject of consciousness in a tradition beginning with Kant. In this respect her article complements the 1964 essay by Mossop on V.'s poetics (*see* 8905). The scope of the question clearly invites further development.

Daniel, Vera J. Valéry and his Napoleon. *In:* Paul Valéry, 1871–1971. *See* 8487. p. 206–15.   **8559**

Builds upon Gaède's 1962 study, the conclusions of which are accepted as a point of departure. Daniel adds to the dossier considerable material gleaned primarily from the *Cahiers*. She sees V.'s Napoleon as an artist in whom Dionysus and Apollo are united.

Derrida, Jacques. Les sources de Valéry— qual quelle. MLN 87:563–99, 1972. *Also in his:* Marges de la philosophie. Eds. de minuit, 1972. p. 325–63.   **8560**

A reflection on the frequency of sources ("sources," "Quellen") in V.'s work leads to an examination of *L'idée fixe* and its "implexe," to Freud and the "MOI pur." Sources are refused in their literary-historical as well as in their thematic or symbolic import. An important contribution to a continuing debate.

Dresden, Samuel. Paul Valéry. *In his:* Bezonken aventuren, essays. Amsterdam, J. M. Meulenhoff, 1949. p. 150–60. **8561**

Beginning with the exposition of V.'s early theory of composition, the author introduces the notion of the "MOI pur," which he handles well, gradually moving toward the notion of an intellectual sensibility. Here he stresses the more sensual aspects of the poetry, providing the necessary contrast to his point of departure. In general this essay presents for Dutch readers a perspective on V. rather like that of E. R. Curtius.

Duchesne-Guillemin, Jacques. Jeunesse de Paul Valéry. SynB 10:355–58, 1955. *Also:* Eros et Psyché. *In his:* Etudes pour un Paul Valéry. Neuchâtel, A la Baconnière, 1964. p. 7–12.   **8562**

With this article the author advanced the first serious claims for the equal importance of sensibility and intellect in V.'s work. To illustrate his point he chose the then unpublished "Eros et Psyché" from the *Cahiers*. In this case the terms of the equation are eroticism and attention.

———. Paul Valéry et l'Italie. MLR 62: 48–54, 1967.   **8563**

Draws on the notations concerning Italy, the Italians and their culture to show the extent to which V. felt himself spiritually linked to Italy. The most important element, already mentioned by A. Rouart-Valéry at the Cerisy colloquium, is that Italian was V.'s mother tongue. Italian served likewise as the language of his lovelife in later years, as Duchesne-Guillemin shows in passages concerning R. Vautier and Catherine Pozzi. Two pages on V.'s Italianism in French are also instructive.

Frandon, Ida-Marie. Le modernisme de Valéry: expression littéraire et formulation scientifique. RSH 36:495–510, 1971. **8564**

Useful only as a first step in approaching a subject that has now been studied in greater detail. One might recommend it as an introduction to Robinson's 1963 book on the *Cahiers* from which it borrows liberally. The most serious flaw is the absence of any direct study of the *Cahiers* where the really important material is to be found.

Freedman, Ralph. Paul Valéry—protean critic. *In:* Modern French criticism from Proust and Valéry to structuralism. Ed. by John Simon. Chicago-London, Univ. of Chicago press, 1972. p. 1–40. **8565**

Rigorous pursuit of parallels with Kantian thought. Freedman presents a strong case for V. having wrought a new Kantian revolution in esthetics. The details of his argument offer little that is positively new but its forcefulness makes this a thesis to reckon with. Compare G. Labica (*see* 8868) and Damon (*see* 8558).

Review: A. Aldridge in BA 47:325–26, 1973; G. Bauer in FR 46:424–25, 1972–73; J. Culler in FS 29:114–15, 1975.

Genette, Gérard. Valéry et l'axiomatique littéraire. TelQ 23:75–82, 1965. *Also:* La littérature comme telle. *In his:* Figures. Seuil, 1966. p. 253–65. *Also in:* Les critiques de notre temps et Valéry. See 8474. p. 175–85. **8566**

Genette finds ample data to support the thesis that V. (sometimes) espouses a formalist poetics similar in certain respects to positions of the Russian formalists of the twenties or the American New Critics. Read in its original magazine printing the text reveals a further aim: to accredit the new formalist/structuralist position by claiming as an ancestor one of the idols of the established group of scholars. Ricardou and Todorov have subsequently modified this rapid conclusion.

———. Valéry et la poétique du langage. MLN 87:600–15, 1972. **8567**

Following Barthes' definition of Cratylism—the myth according to which linguistic signs are motivated—Genette undertakes a roundabout demonstration of V.'s relation to this age-old

belief. The greater part of his article leads to V. via Mallarmé and attempts to situate both in this tradition which contemporary Saussurian linguistics refuses. Compare in a similiar vein, A. Rey (*see* 8638).

Gide, André. Paul Valéry. Ar 10:3–17, 1945. *Also in his:* Paul Valéry. Domat, 1947. p. xi–xxxii. *Also in his:* Eloges. Ides et calendes, 1948. p. 101–27. *Also in his:* Feuillets d'automne. Mercure de France, 1949. p. 95–113. **8568**

This is the most detailed statement Gide published concerning his friend of fifty-odd years. The personal revelations are touching and speak eloquently of V.'s strength of mind. In the final page Gide launched the frequently repeated judgment that V.'s prose may ultimately surpass his verse; but he hastened to add that among those who had excelled in both, only Goethe could be compared to V. Following his article Gide printed five of V.'s letters to him, all previously unpublished. These were reprinted in *Pages françaises*, no. 9, Jan. 1946, before being incorporated into the Gide-V. *Correspondance* in 1955.

Gifford, Paul. Dimension humoristique de Paul Valéry. RHL 75:588–607. 1975. **8569**

V.'s humor, like Proust's, is underestimated and ill appreciated by his commentators. The present article is a first step toward rectifying that situation. If the author has easy work in *L'idée fixe,* where Edmond T. is a humorous counterpart to his (apparent) homonym in the *Soirée...,* can we ultimately follow Gifford all the way to the conclusion that the British sense of humor is an appropriate analog to V.'s?

Ince, W. N. Impatience, immediacy and the pleasure principle in Valéry. FMLS 2:180–91, 1966. **8570**

An article conceived as an attempt to draw together for the layman the best current knowledge of V., who emerges as that ideal bridge between the two cultures popularized by C. P. Snow. It stands as a good, brief introduction to the man and his work.

Ireland, G. W. Gide et Valéry précurseurs de la nouvelle critique. *In:* Les chemins actuels de la critique. Plon, 1967. p. 23–36. *Also:* Union générale d'éditions, 1968. p. 23–36. (10/18)   **8571**

The title is perhaps too ambitious. In fact Ireland situates V., alongside Gide, at the watershed from which one slope does indeed direct us toward criticism of a formalist type. What he recalls here quite pertinently is that V. in his practice as critic (notably in *Variété*) most often contradicted the precepts of V. the theoretician.

Jaloux, Edmond. Paul Valéry. *In:* Paul Valéry, essais et témoignages inédits. *See* 8488. p. 23–34.   **8572**

An intelligent statement concerning V.'s varied styles. Jaloux distinguishes V.'s abstract intellectual prose from the sensual estheticism of the nineties. Critically, however, it retains no special value. One may note that Jaloux attributes to V.'s prose precisely that quality refused by Benda above.

Larnac, Jean. Paul Valéry. Pen 5:42–56, 1945.   **8573**

The author's thesis, that V. announces the end of bourgeois thought, i.e. rationalism, has found a more capable exponent in L. Goldmann. Larnac's sociological perspective required at the very least that he accurately describe V.'s class origins, yet he presents V. as a patrician by birth. An equally serious inaccuracy is the statement that V. was basically sympathetic to Freudianism.

Lechantre, Michel. P(h)o(n)étique. *In:* Cahiers Paul Valéry. 1:poétique et poésie. *See* 8472. p. 91–122.   **8574**

Lechantre follows Derrida as well as Ricardou's "impossible Monsieur Texte" in positing the necessity of a dual reading which will deconstruct/reconstruct the work so as to exhibit its logocentric, quasi-theological postulates. As such, the reading is over-determined, inflected ideologically. If the reader can provisionally accept the rules of this game, then the observations on V.'s linguistic concepts (phonetics as basis of poetics, whence the bracketed letters in the title), will be of interest. Lechantre's comparison of V. with Rousseau on these points is stimulating.

Lefèbve, Maurice-Jean. Valéry et ses coquilles. *In:* Entretiens sur Paul Valéry. *See* 8475. p. 45–57.   **8575**

The shells of the title are those which the mollusc creates, both his work and his true home. The article covers a terrain that has been explored many times. Its real contribution is a function of the author's existentialist posture which lights some dark corners. The discussion, p. 58–67, questioned this posture, particularly in its insistence on the importance and value of dream for V.

Loris, Pierre. L'homme et la civilisation de l'entendement. *In:* Entretiens sur Paul Valéry. *See* 8475. p. 299–327.   **8576**

The claim made to the effect that V. can be distinguished by his method from all previous philosophers is ill founded, as J. Ricardou pointed out in his intervention after the communication of this paper to the 1965 Cerisy colloquium.

Maurois, André. Introduction à la méthode de Paul Valéry. Cahiers libres, 1933. 109 p. *Also:* Paul Valéry. *In his:* Etudes littéraires, v. 1. New York, Eds. de la maison française, 1941. p. 7–52. *Also in his:* De Proust à Camus. Perrin, 1964. p. 65–91. *Trans.:* Paul Valéry. *In his:* From Proust to Camus—profiles of modern French writers. Doubleday, 1966. p. 47–70. *Also:* London, Weidenfeld and Nicolson, 1967. p. 47–70.   **8577**

When one counts the translations into German and Spanish it becomes obvious that this is one of the most widely disseminated essays on V., a very respectable record for a lecture that began modestly enough at the Université des Annales on Dec. 13, 1932. (This indication has disappeared from editions subsequent to 1933.) The merits of the text are those of its original forum: clarity and superficiality.

Nussbuam, J.-M. Paul Valéry ou le crépuscule de la philosophie. *In:* Paul Valéry, essais et témoignages inédits. *See* 8488. p. 207–17.   **8578**

This article will appear more timely now than at its publication date, given the general disarray of traditional philosophy. Nussbaum understood that V.'s critique of philosophical activity was tributary to his critique of the solidity of the language of philosophy. Although he apparently did not foresee the devastation that modern linguistic theory would wreak in this domain, his analysis of V.'s critical posture leads in the same direction.

Poulet, Georges. Valéry. *In his:* Etudes sur le temps humain. Edinburgh, Edinburgh univ. press, 1949. p. 350–63. *Also:* Plon, 1950. p. 386–99. *Also:* Union générale d'éditions, 1972. p. 386–99. (10/18) *Trans.:* Valéry. *In his:* Studies in human time. Baltimore, Johns Hopkins press; London, Oxford univ. press, 1956. p. 280–90. 8579

Poulet explores aspects of temporality in V.'s work, opening with M. Teste and working through the dialogs, *Variété*, and the several volumes extracted from his *Cahiers* during V.'s lifetime. The critical position is a logical extension of M. Raymond's. The essay should be read in the same spirit.

Raudive, Konstantin. Paul Valéry. *In his:* Der Chaosmensch und seine Überwindung. Memmingen-Allgäu, Dietrich Verlag, 1951. p. 58–66. 8580

The author's conviction that contemporary art is a manifestation of cultural decadence leads to a peculiar reading of V.'s work. On the whole this analysis is exemplary of the tendentious conclusions drawn by moralizing critics.

Robinson, Judith. New light on Valéry. FS 22:40–50, 1968. 8581

This article serves as a partial "état présent" indicating a fund of new material recently uncovered by the author, much of it only now becoming available to scholars. The principal discovery, in three stages, concerns V.'s plans for the eventual publication of his *Cahiers*. Robinson has just completed that project according to the guidelines presented here. The full range of suggestions opened up by the article defies summary.

Roy, Claude. Paul Valéry. TM 13:1864–78, 1958. *Also in his:* L'homme en question. Gallimard, 1960. p. 151–66. (Descriptions critiques, 5) 8582

A very intelligent essay, full of insights which testify to a deep understanding of V. Among these the commentary on artistic endeavor as the production (laborious, if need be) of epiphanies is noteworthy. Excellent pages on V. and Pascal as well as on the importance of V.'s "poésie brute." May still suggest fruitful areas of research.

Rychner, Max. Paul Valéry. *In his:* Zur Europäischer Literatur zwischen zwei Weltkriegen. Zurich, Manesse Verlag, 1951. p. 159–85. 8583

This essay is an incomplete and strongly ideological introduction to V. for readers of German. Rychner gives particular attention to the Teste cycle but without bringing to it any special insights. He is, however, one of the very few commentators of V.'s "Rapport sur les prix de vertu." He relates the fall of virtue to the eclipse of the individual and to the rise of Hitlerism. In conclusion he contrasts V.'s "Une conquête méthodique" with the *Communist manifesto* as two opposing formulations of the future direction of society. In V. he sees the defender of individualism against totalitarianism.

Sarraute, Nathalie. Paul Valéry et l'enfant d'éléphant. TM 2:610–37, 1947. 8584

Sarraute dared to question the (almost) unchallenged supremacy of the poet laureate of the Third Republic. Comparing the Parque's imminent tear to painful variations on *Les précieuses ridicules* will probably not cause much commotion today. If one could ignore the treachery involved in the systematic practice of truncated quotation, one might find the article quite humorous, an example of journalism employed to bury V. not to praise him.

Schmidt, Julius. Paul Valéry, le Cimetière marin. ZNU 29:433–47, 1930. 8585

V.'s poem serves as the focal point for a generally solid introduction to his work for the German student. Situates the poem in the broader context of the dialogs and essays published to date. Early and necessarily incomplete.

Shattuck, Roger. Paul Valéry: sportsman and barbarian. Delos 1:96–116, 1968. *Also in:* Valéry, Paul. Occasions. Trans. by Roger Shattuck and Frederick Brown. With an introd. by Roger Shattuck.

Princeton, Princeton univ. press, 1970. p. ix–xxx. (Collected works, 11. Bollingen series, 45)   **8586**

This essay concludes with the observation that V. is a myth. Noting the bizarre fact that we still possess no true biography of V., and that for the most part we read him incorrectly (beginning with a fetishistic view of the poetry), Shattuck concludes that the value of V. in actu is to be found in the correspondence and the *Cahiers*. Moreover, he takes V.'s interest in science and mathematics quite seriously, but stops short of wanting to edit order into the *Cahiers*. For this author V. is the indispensable barbarian through whom civilization renews itself.

Starobinski, Jean. Je suis rapide ou rien. *In:* Paul Valéry, essais et témoignages inédits. *See* 8488. p. 143–50.   **8587**

An incisive and valuable essay on the contradictions in V.'s thought, in the course of which Starobinski judiciously points out the limitations of the type of systematic enterprise Bémol was about to complete. Quite appropriately, he presents that aspect Bémol called Valérysme as the Apollonian component of a dialectical movement which is incomprehensible without its Dionysian counterpart.

Thévenaz, Pierre. Valéry, le philosophe malgré lui. *In:* Paul Valéry, essais et témoignages inédits. *See* 8488. p. 163–76.   **8588**

One observation assures the merit of this article: V.'s celebrated intellectualism is but the expression of his instrumentalism. Thus V. appears to the author to be a philosopher in spite of himself because of the very difficulties of maintaining his position. This paradoxical account of a still more paradoxical position is in fundamental agreement with Raymond's more elaborate study.

Usinger, Fritz. Paul Valéry. *In his:* Dichtung als Information. Von der Morphologie zur Kosmologie. Mainz, von Hase & Kochler, 1970. p. 237–45.   **8589**

The author zeroes in on V.'s celebrated refusals: biography, history. At the risk of exaggerating V.'s skepticism, which he sees as all-embracing, he effectively demythologizes V.'s view of

literary activity. The author's insistence on the realm of the mind as V.'s natural home is useful in situating him on the map of contemporary letters and is, in the main, accurate.

Valéry, Claude. Le droit, sa notion et son langage d'après Paul Valéry. *In:* Entretiens sur Paul Valéry. *See* 8475. p. 361–75.   **8590**

These reflections on V.'s views of the law but scratch the surface of his analysis of language, which is where V. considered the real problem to lie.

Verdaasdonk, Hugo. Dérivabilité et référence. Sud 4:60–69, 1971.   **8591**

This contribution to V.'s conception of form and meaning, of signification and sign, benefits from the author's knowledge of contemporary linguistic and philosophical research in several cultures. The orientation is formalist.

Wahl, Jean. Sur la pensée de Paul Valéry. *In his:* Poésie, pensée, perception. Calmann-Lévy, 1948. p. 77–93.   **8592**

Using as his principal reference points *Moralités, Choses tues* and *L'idée fixe,* Wahl attempts to situate V. in the perspective of modernist thought. He first presents V.'s radical critique of all systematic thought. Confronting this generalized skepticism with V.'s position on esthetics, he concludes that the value accorded to artistic creation by V. had been undermined by his own suspicion of all synthesizing activity. One of the best early statements of a problem central to V. studies.

Wilson, Edmund. Paul Valéry. *In his:* Axel's castle. New York-London, Scribner, 1931. p. 64–92. *Also:* London, Collins, 1961. p. 58–79. (Fontana library, 539C)   **8593**

The care Wilson took with this essay is typified by the statement that in 1917 V. married Mallarmé's daughter. Presumably someone set right the identity of Jeannie Gobillard, but as recently as the 1967 printing of the Fontana library edition V.'s marriage to that lady was still dated seventeen years after the fact. A substantial part of the closing section is devoted to praise for A. France's M. Bergeret at the expense of V.'s M. Teste. The incommensurability of these two characters posed no difficulties for Wilson.

Themes

Celeyrette-Pietri, Nicole. Métamorphoses de Narcisse. *In:* Lectures de Charmes. *See* 8477. p. 9–28.   **8594**

This article has one advantage over Sabbagh's on the same subject: a very detailed bibliography of versions, manuscript and published, as well as references to the documents now in the Bibliothèque Nationale. These two scholars are clearly working parallel to one another and their results published to date are in large measure complementary. One of the more important conclusions reached is that the Narcissus project was essentially interminable and that the supposed unity of a given fragment is partially attributable to the critic who chooses to see it as a coherent whole. Consult for contrast to this line of approach, J. Bellemin-Noël (*see* 8547).

Décaudin, Michel. La dimension verticale dans la poésie de Valéry. *In:* Paul Valéry contemporain. *See* 8486. p. 95–103. **8595**

Proposing to read V.'s poetry along the double axis verticality/horizontality, Décaudin makes a number of interesting observations which tend toward a general system. The texts examined are insufficient, however, as are the dimensions given to present his results. The preliminary findings call for more thorough investigation.

Derche, Roland. Les fragments du Narcisse, par Paul Valéry. *In his:* Quatre mythes poétiques. SEDES, 1962. p. 98–106. **8596**

The sole usefulness of this article for V. scholars is in its situation of V. in a long and varied tradition. The context in this case is more valuable than the text.

Faivre, Jean-Luc. Paul Valéry et le thème de la lumière. LR 20:299–318, 1966; 21: 3–27, 103–22, 207–22, 369–75, 1967; 22: 40–58, 133–50, 1968. *Also:* Lettres modernes, Minard, 1974. 152 p. (Thèmes et mythes 13)   **8597**

The goal of this study is the revelation of a spiritual quest using analytical (primarily Jungian) psychology as a tool. The author recognizes a predecessor in N. Bastet's *La symbolique...* Bachelard and the critics of consciousness figure prominently, as does

Aigrisse. V.'s texts are subjected to a thematic fragmentation the goal of which is the establishment of a network of symbols within the overall theme of light. The symbols are considered to have a universal, coded meaning, Jung being the exemplary cryptographer. The value and the limitations of such a study are implicit in the idealist reductionism of its methodology. Somewhat more annoying is the habit of quoting texts at second hand, particularly those taken from the *Cahiers*.

Laitenberger, Hugo. Der Begriff der Absence bei Paul Valéry. Wiesbaden, Franz Steiner Verlag, 1960. vii, 158 p.   **8598**

This thoroughgoing study of the concept of absence in V.'s work combines the linguist's concern for the semantic field of a key lexical term with a rigorous philosophical method. It is a model of its type and should be of considerable value to future scholars. Beginning with an enlightening commentary on "London Bridge" the author proceeds to situate the concept of absence in relation to time, language, the self and the "MOI pur." Particular attention is accorded to the *Soirée avec Monsieur Teste*, the *Introduction à la methode...* and the "Note et digression...", *Eupalinos...*, *L'idée fixe* and the poems "Equinoxe," *Le cimetière marin* and "Les pas." In conclusion the function of absence is contrasted with that of presence. In the final chapter good arguments are presented for seriously revising A. Henry's characterization of absence in V.'s lexicon. The author finds Gmelin to be closer to the mark. Laitenberger uses to excellent advantage the excerpts from V.'s *Cahiers* published during his lifetime, but did not have access to the recently published C.N.R.S. edition.

Review: E. Lorenz in RJ 13:197–98, 1962.

Laurette, Pierre. Le thème de l'arbre chez Paul Valéry. Klincksieck, 1967. 196 p. (BFR, série C: études littéraires, 14) **8599**

This book has escaped the criticism recently leveled against thematic studies of V. by reason of its methodological flexibility. What it gains thereby in scope it tends to lose in depth, with some chapters not exceeding three pages. On balance there is here an ample demonstration of the tree as a reference point, subject of meditation, even as obsession throughout V.'s work. The author has explored the *Cahiers* thoroughly.

Reviews: A. Arnold in FR 42:616–18, 1969; K. Blüher in RFor 80:501–03, 1968; R. Champigny in RR 60:78–80, 1969; P. Walzer in RHL 69:328–29, 1969.

Lawler, James R. Lucidité, Phœnix de ce vertige.... *In:* Paul Valéry. *See* 8484. p. 616–29. *Also in his:* The poet as analyst. *See* 8518. p. 149–65.   **8600**

Lawler traces the motif of the sleeping woman throughout V.'s work, citing some unpublished material. His findings demonstrate certain constant aspects of the motif as it occurs in divers guises. He takes his title from a line not finally retained for *La jeune Parque*.

————. Paul Valéry et Saint Ambroise. *In:* Paul Valéry. *See* 8481. p. 231–43. *Also (rev.):* Il faut être un saint.... *In his:* The poet as analyst. *See* 8518. p. 230–43.   **8601**

Traces the appearance of the name Ambroise throughout V.'s work from his fanciful autobiography to his sonnet for Irene in 1942, Lawler finds in the name a focus for V.'s aspiration to an intellectual sainthood, which he takes to be one of the constants of his mental life.

Levaillant, Jean. Paul Valéry et la lumière. CAIEF 20:179–89, 1968.   **8602**

The thematic value of light, of vision for V. was well known before this study and is not especially altered by it, despite an indisputable mastery of execution by the author.

Meylan, Pierre. Sur l'esthétique musicale de Paul Valéry. *In his:* Les écrivains et la musique. V. 2. Lausanne, Eds. du cervin, 1952. p. 37–48.   **8603**

Written from the perspective of musicology, this article relates V.'s admiration for Wagner (as it could be known in the fifties) and his gradual evolution toward the relative simplicity of Gluck. Meylan attempts to situate *Amphion* in this evolution and has perceptive insights concerning the probable reason for its failure on the lyric stage.

Priddin, Deirdre. L'acte pur des métamorphoses. *In her:* The art of the dance in French literature from Théophile Gautier to Paul Valéry. London, Adam and Charles Black, 1952. p. 126–62. **8604**

Although Priddin assumed that V. was primarily an intellectualist, this fault has not prevented her from commenting intelligently on "Degas, danse, dessin" and *L'âme et la danse*. Her systematic pursuit of a parallelism between V. and Bergson is the more effective because she does not argue for influence. Balanced argument. The author has developed several of the many related functions of the dance in V.'s world. It would surely have improved her book to have known L. Séchan's remarkable study of 1930 on *L'âme et la danse*.

Sabbagh, Céline. Calypso—a theme of ambiguity, a theme of fascination. *In:* Paul Valéry. *See* 8482. p. 106–18.   **8605**

Despite some methodological imprecision (Calypso is alternately presented as image, symbol and theme), the article demonstrates the existence of an affective dualism with important formal ramifications. The author focuses on avatars of Calypso in V.'s writing from 1891 to 1945, thus identifying a central thematic and rhetorical figure. The 1969 article by M. Lechantre (*see* 8635) leads in a similar direction.

————. Les disparitions de Narcisse. *In:* Paul Valéry contemporain. *See* 8486. p. 153–72.   **8606**

The author has undertaken an ambitious and promising project: to study the myth of Narcissus throughout V.'s published work, the *Cahiers* and those unpublished documents to which she has had access. In this section of her dissertation in progress, she has limited the scope to the theme of disappearance (swoon or apotheosis) of the protagonist. See the parallel research of N. Celeyrette-Pietri, *supra*.

Stewart, William McC. Peut-on parler d'un orphisme de Valéry? CAIEF 22:181–95, 1970.   **8607**

Drawing on a quantity of unpublished documents, Stewart presents a strong argument for the centrality and durability of the Orphic theme in V.'s work. Operas on the subject by Gluck and Monteverdi appear to have had an important impact in 1905, reinforcing a much earlier imaginary identification with the proto-poet. The author hints at the importance V.'s loves may have had in keeping alive the ideal of Orpheus/Eurydice.

————. Le thème d'Orphée chez Valéry. *In:* Entretiens sur Paul Valéry. *See* 8475. p. 163–78.   **8608**

From the disguised sonnet published in "Paradoxe sur l'architecte," through the *Cahiers* for 1920–21, to the *Amphion* conceived for the lyric stage, Stewart traces the modifications of this theme in its several guises. Quite significantly, he finds Orpheus associated with the pendular movement of mental life in the *Cahiers* (8, 362). The discussion following communication of Stewart's text brings out the many similarities between V.'s treatment of Orpheus and his multiple renderings of *La jeune Parque* and *Mon Faust.* Should be read in conjunction with author's contribution in CAIEF *supra.*

Suckling, Norman. Paul Valéry and the civilized mind. London-New York-Toronto, Geoffrey Cumberlege-Oxford univ. press, 1954. ix, 285 p. (Univ. of Durham publications)   **8609**

The principal charge that V. critics have brought against this book is that it treats V. as a myth of the civilized mind. Thus freed from the thorny questions of separating a work from a biography, Suckling could unabashedly proclaim "Ebauche d'un serpent" to be the positive cosmology of his own V. In the strict logical sense the position cannot be attacked, but, at the same time, as it confuses creator and creation, it also negates the specific form or tone, in the case of "Ebauche d'un serpent" the burlesque treatment of cosmology. It can be said that the entire book is beside the point, or alternatively that the point of the book is outside V.'s work.

Reviews: L. Austin in RHL 57: 283–85, 1957; W. Fowlie in Poetry 85:300–03, 1955; J. Mathews in RR 45:284–89, 1954; A. Viatte in Eras 10:550, 1957.

Suhami, Evelyne. Paul Valéry et la musique. Dakar, Publications de la faculté des lettres et sciences humaines, 1966. 136 p. (Langues et littératures, 15)   **8610**

Using all of V.'s available texts on, or related to, music, his correspondence and *Cahiers* as well as *Amphion* and *Sémiramis,* the author has constructed an impressive thesis concerning the musical nature of V.'s esthetics or rather the precise esthetic grounding of V.'s notion of music. A tripartite division organizes the study. The most general division, in which the author stresses the importance for V. of Gluck, Wagner and Weber, is the least likely to be superseded by more specialized monographs. The second part, on dance and poetry, is less valuable. The third, which treats V.'s melodramas, sets them off to their best advantage.

Review: P. Walzer in RHL 69:329–31, 1969.

Cahiers

Antoine, Gérald. Quelques linéaments du Traité de la main ou de l'esprit de la main que Valéry rêva d'écrire. *In:* Paul Valéry contemporain. *See* 8486. p. 177–91.   **8611**

There is something both magnificent and futile about this study, which attempts to reconstruct from the most disjointed passages of the *Cahiers* the essential of what V.'s *Traité de la main* might have been. Futile in that the project itself is impossible of realization; magnificent in that the author has a keen grasp of the preeminence for V. of the instrumental organ par excellence, the executor of all things human.

Bastet, Ned. Langage et fracture chez Valéry. *In:* Paul Valéry contemporain. *See* 8486. p. 75–92.   **8612**

Bastet has understood that it is desire that finally links V.'s analysis of language to his construction of works. That the works realized do not equal in perfection those dreamed of troubles him less than it did V., and rightly. Desire so total as V.'s can know no satisfaction. Bastet's merit here is in charting a path beyond the current preoccupations of the structural linguists, while recognizing both their legitimacy and their interest, toward the larger questions of creativity.

————. Œuvre ouverte et œuvre fermée chez Valéry. AFLSHN 2:103–19, 1967. **8613**

Finds a double movement of the mind in V.: an opening outward, and a turning inward which sacrifices the notion of humanity to a rigorous, closed form. Ramifications of the essay are extensive. Replies directly to Genette's 1965 article, claiming that his is a half-truth since it considers only the second movement. At the other pole one encounters the mysticism of the real in V. (*See* Ince *infra.*) There is material here for a thorough examination of V.'s bi-polar mode of thought, which has now been touched upon by several scholars using different but complementary methods of approach.

Bémol, Maurice. Paul Valéry. Cahiers, tome I, 1894–1900 et tome II, 1900–1902. RHL 58:556–61, 1958. *Also in his:* Variations sur Valéry. V. 2. *See* 8492. p. 116–26. **8614**

This review article now has its own place in the history of V. criticism. As a first exploration of the wealth of information offered by the facsimile publication of the first two *Cahiers,* it records the satisfaction of the most eminent French Valéryen of the day at finding his own thesis confirmed. It is also the source of a widely held opinion that V.'s pretensions in mathematics and mathematical physics were just that. Most notable is his characterization of V. as a visionary for attempting to apply mathematics to the functioning of the psyche. In her 1963 study of V.'s methods of analysis in the *Cahiers,* Robinson was to give a more favorable judgment.

————. Paul Valéry. Cahiers [tomes III-X, 1903–1925]. RHL 60:245–59, 1960. **8615**

A long review article which continues the preceding entry. In the criticisms leveled against philosophy and literature by V., Bémol chooses to see an original psychology that V. sought to establish. This reflects his own 1949 thesis. By 1960 Bémol was insisting on the major defects of the C.N.R.S. edition: no table of contents, no indication of chronology, no explanation of the small number of pages for certain years. Other defects (incompleteness, faulty chronology, etc.)

would eventually be recognized and lead to the more orderly, albeit selective, ed. prepared by Robinson.

Blanchard, Anne. Le silence de Paul Valéry. CahS 361:427–45, 1961. **8616**

An intelligent reading of the first four *Cahiers* intended principally to reveal the scope, nature and worth of V.'s reflections during the celebrated great silence. In a literary historical perspective, the essay constituted a sensitive reply to the accusations of Nathalie Sarraute (*see* 8584).

Broglie, Louis de. Préface. *In:* Paul Valéry. Cahiers. V. 1. C.N.R.S., 1957. p. i-iv unpaginated. *Also:* Les cahiers de Paul Valéry. Extraits des cahiers (écrits de 1894 à 1945). [s.l.n.d.] p. i-iv unpaginated. **8617**

The eminent physicist and friend of V., when called upon to preface the *Cahiers,* prudently wrote of V.'s love of the sciences and his preference for frequenting men of science. He declared that the importance of the sciences for V., and his understanding of them, awaited a future generation of scholars.

Celeyrette-Pietri, Nicole. Le jeu du je. *In:* Paul Valéry contemporain. *See* 8486. p. 11–25. **8618**

The frame of reference is post-Saussurian linguistics (Benveniste, Jakobson) and the subject, V.'s analysis of the function of pronouns. V. is seen as an independent discoverer of the triangular structure: "I, you, he," although he is said to have formulated it idiosyncratically. Her conclusion that V.'s concept of the first person singular is close to Lacan's is still not sufficiently prepared, but it does appear here with greater verisimilitude than in Schmidt-Radefeldt's book.

Crow, Christine M. Paul Valéry and Maxwell's demon: natural order and human personality. Hull, Univ. of Hull, 1972. 83 p. (Occasional papers in modern languages, 8) **8619**

The full scope of this monograph is indicated in the subtitle. Beginning with a focus on V.'s understanding of Maxwell's sorting demon, then radiating out from it to his most generalized statements on order and the notion of

universe in the *Cahiers,* the author constructs a model intended ultimately to permit a reading of V.'s poetics in terms of his notions of science, and vice versa. The value of such an effort to describe V.'s interdisciplinary imagination is obvious. More rigorous in its construction and in the presentation of material than R. Virtanen's 1974 essay, it is intended for a specialized audience whereas the general reader may find the latter work more accessible.
Reviews: N. Celeyrette-Pietri in RHL 74:927–28, 1974; W. Ince in MLR 70:430–31, 1975.

Duchesne-Guillemin, J[acques]. Théorie et pratique du langage chez Paul Valéry. *In:* Actes du Xe congrès international des linguistes. V. 3. Bucharest, Eds. de l'Académie de la République socialiste de Roumanie, 1970. p. 83–88.   **8620**
Several years before the speculation on V. as linguist reached its present pitch, Duchesne-Guillemin warned against reconstructing a hypothetical system from the *Cahiers.* This contribution to a colloquium of linguists held in 1967 can be read as anticipatory criticism of much that has recently been written on the subject.

Gaède, Edouard. Le continu et le discontinu dans les Cahiers de Valéry. RMM 70:173–92, 1965.   **8621**
Based on a study of V.'s analysis of, and references to, the celebrated paradoxes of Zeno of Elea which can be found in the *Cahiers* of all periods. Finds that Zeno became for V. something of a symbol for philosophical speculation generally. V. did not take the mathematical approach to these arguments, as is customary. The symbolic function of Zeno is related to the central dilemma of the continuous and the discontinuous which occupied V. all his life.

———. Valéry et la Grèce. *In:* Paul Valéry. *See* 8481. p. 191–201.   **8622**
Gaède argues that although V.'s knowledge of Greek culture was minimal, it functioned as a major reference point in his intellectual life. This contradiction, like so many others, was only apparent since V. used the Greek world primarily as the mask or projection of several of his own fascina-

tions. Some good observations on V.'s sense of the tragic lead in a direction explored more recently by Bastet.

Gaillard, Pol. Paul Valéry critique de Pascal. RSH 36:511–24, 1971.   **8623**
Despite the author's regrettable lack of awareness of Douglas' 1946 article on the subject (*see* 8854), this article should be considered a complement to its predecessor in view of Gaillard's exploitation of the *Cahiers* which had been unavailable to Douglas. Gaillard bases his analysis of V.'s criticisms of Pascal on a deep-seated fascination; his findings confirm those made incidentally by Gaède in his *Nietzsche et Valéry,* 1962.

Ince, Walter N. Le concept du moderne chez Valéry. *In:* Paul Valéry contemporain. *See* 8486. p. 1–10.   **8624**
The exposition reveals a contradiction between V.'s approval of the modern in the domain of thought, and his condemnation of the modern in the arts. The conclusion seeks to dissipate the elements of the contradiction without fundamentally resolving it, thus demonstrating once again, unintentionally perhaps, the centrality of contradiction in V.

———. Etre, connaître et mysticisme du réel selon Valéry. *In:* Entretiens sur Paul Valéry. *See* 8475. p. 203–28. *Also (abridged):* Résurgences du mysticisme. *In:* Les critiques de notre temps et Valéry. *See* 8474. p. 47–61.   **8625**
The present article begins where Robinson had left the subject in the final chapter of her 1963 book. Ince proposes to follow V.'s analysis of the three terms in his title throughout the *Cahiers.* Like Robinson he finds therein a certain mysticism, related not to a faith but to the phenomenon of perception. "London Bridge" is cited as a prime example. Ince mentions both Gestalt psychology and Merleau-Ponty's phenomenology as possible analogies. V.'s alternation between being and knowing is such that V. as analyst can criticize V. as mystic. The discussion following communication of Ince's text leads usefully to a possible comparison with William Blake.

————. Resonance in Valéry. EFL 5:38–57, 1968.   **8626**

A companion piece to his article in RSH *infra*. It examines the field of a group of words, forms of "résonner," which occurs with extraordinary frequency in V. Beginning with reflections on V.'s own link between resonance and physiology, which he observed in his own highly nervous temperament, Ince traces its associations through affectivity and finds it used as pejorative or strongly condemnatory of the human, all too human. But whereas resonance seems at times to cover all that is irrational in psycho-physiological response (V.'s CEM system), it is also used to designate euphoria or the "état chantant" of poesis in its most positive sense. Poetry appears then as a highly organized instance of a phenomenon which, random and uncontrolled, is abhorrent to V.

————. Valéry on Bêtise et poésie: background and implications. *In:* Order and adventure in post-romantic French poetry. Essays presented to C. A. Hackett. Ed. by E. M. Beaumont, J. M. Cocking and J. Cruickshank. Oxford-New York, Basil Blackwell-Barnes & Noble, 1973. p. 136–48.   **8627**

The real subject of the essay is the problematical future of literature in a society that will recognize it as linguistic/fiduciary, as just another myth belonging to the past. The texts on the subject culled from the *Cahiers* are impressive in their consistency over a long period. The overall approach is consonant with that of a number of the structural linguistic reappraisals of V.

Review: B. Swift in YWMLS 35: 197, 1974.

————. La voix du maître ou moi et style selon Valéry. RSH 33:29–39, 1968. **8628**

Starting from an analysis of the semantic field and implication of the two terms "style" and "voix," Ince has adduced an important network of relations which V. manifestly considered to represent the synthesis of self (or identity) in the creative process, "chant" or rather "chanter" representing the third term of synthesis. Taken on its own terms this study is very convincing. A competing theory, quite hostile to this approach, has been advanced by formalists in recent years. Consult A. Rey (*see* 8638).

Jallat, Jeannine. Valéry and the mathematical language of identity and difference. *In:* Paul Valéry. *See* 8482. p. 51–64.   **8629**

Breaks new ground by linking V.'s notations on N[ombres] + S[ubtils] in the *Cahiers* to differential calculus on the one hand and, more importantly, to the elements of a theory of ornament in the arts. Demonstrates convincingly that V. attempted to arrive at the nature of ambiguity through the neutral language of mathematics.

————. Valéry et le langage mathématique de l'identité et de la différence. *In:* Paul Valéry, 1871–1971. *See* 8487. p. 223–29.   **8630**

Continues preceding article. All references to the facsimile *Cahiers* are to v. 1; the bulk of the analysis is based, however, on hitherto unpublished manuscript notes from the period 1892–94. This investigation, when completed, should permit meaningful statements on V. and mathematics.

————. Valéry et le mécanisme—la notion de modèle et la théorie de la construction. SRLF 8:185–241, 1967.   **8631**

In a careful analysis of the references to Kelvin and Thomson, Jallat traces the conception and function of the notion of model in physics and the metaphoric use to which V. put it. Even before physics, architecture had offered V. an analogous system of relations which he translated into the *Introduction à la méthode de Léonard de Vinci*. An important idea, which Jallat does not follow up, is that the constructivism of V.'s poetics can be seen in relation to that of painters and sculptors who were his contemporaries. Central subject of this essay appears in the final pages where V. is treated as a translator of relations from the system of one model to that of another. It is highly probable that the originality of V.'s reflections on the physical sciences and mathematics lies here, not in the domain of the analysis proper to each. Should be read in conjunction with Crow (*see* 8619) and Virtanen (*see* 8537).

La Rochefoucauld, Edmée de. En lisant les Cahiers de Paul Valéry. Eds. universitaires, 1964–67. 3 v. **8632**
This reading of the *Cahiers* was conceived for a general readership and published in article form in the *Revue de Paris* from 1957 to 1967. The author had known V. well and brings her own personal view of him to her examination of the *Cahiers*. Now that so many excellent specialized studies have been based on the *Cahiers*, with more to come, this is best considered as an introduction or an overview. One admirable quality deserves mention: the reader cannot fail to develop a feeling for V. the man from these three volumes, which are indexed to subjects and names at the end of volume three. Review: R. Lang in BA 42:395–96, 1968.

Lawler, James R. Huit volumes des Cahiers de Valéry. RHL 63:62–89, 1963. *Trans.:* Après tout, j'ai fait ce que j'ai pu.... *In his:* The poet as analyst. *See* 8518. p. 244–81. **8633**
This review article on volumes 22–29 (1939–45) of the *Cahiers* completes the series begun by Bémol in 1958. The death of Bémol accounts for the absence of a like review of volumes 11–21. Lawler succeeds admirably in calling to our attention the repetition of motifs and preoccupations and V.'s own retrospective view of his life (including the traumatic events of 1892), as well as details of real interest but of less than major importance. Lawler also begins to counter the opinion circulated by Bémol that V.'s interest in the physical sciences was that of a doodling amateur: rather a way of seeing the world than a system for explaining it. Lawler presents the decoding of some of the abbreviations used systematically by V.: CEM and N+S, a task which Duchesne-Guillemin has pursued with such impressive results. The trait of autophagy, symbolized by the Ouroboros and treated so well by Bastet (*see* 8833), here receives its first tentative mention. Finally, Lawler's own preference for the poet and theoretician of poetics leads him to reveal occasionally unexpected finds: Valéry admirer of Ronsard as well as Balzac, ambivalent toward Hugo and Stendhal, sharply critical of Baudelaire's prose.

Lechantre, Michel. L'hiéroglyphe intérieur. *In:* Paul Valéry. *See* 8484. p. 630–43. **8634**
The title is taken directly from a drawing in *Cahiers* 24, 145 for 1940. This is an article of capital importance for V.'s concept of language, remarkably free of the cant that has begun to cloud discussion of the subject. Lechantre is well aware of V.'s insistence on the phonological primacy of language (citing his neologism, "Phongène") and examines the implications of this attitude without bias. Among the interesting results is a surprising parallel with Rousseau's view of language. For a positive understanding of V.'s relation to contemporary linguistics this is at present the best starting point.

———. Les refuges de Valéry. RevN 447–55, April 15, 1969. **8635**
Lechantre reconstructs from largely fragmentary notations a fundamental movement of withdrawal (from life, from the real, from commitment) which recurs throughout the *Cahiers:* Robinsonism and Caligulism. J. Derrida recognized his debt to Lechantre (*see* 8560).

Liang, Pai Tchin. Idée de symétrie d'après les Cahiers de Paul Valéry et formes de pensée chinoise. *In:* Entretiens sur Paul Valéry. *See* 8475. p. 329–36. **8636**
V.'s use of algebraic formulas is compared to that of a Chinese scholar, T'an Sseu-T'ong. According to the author the concept of symmetry in the equation has a similar function for both writers: to equate is to annul. For the most part V. is used to demonstrate a permanent aspect of traditional Chinese thought.

Noulet, Emilie. Albums d'idées (1934). RUB 205–30, Feb.-April 1968; 291–317, May-July 1968. *Also* (*with some slight additions and an Avant-propos*): Albums d'idées, voilà le titre. Les Cahiers de Paul Valéry. Année 1934. Brussels, Jacques Antoine, 1973. 171 p. **8637**
This chronological reading of the *Cahiers* for 1934 has a dual purpose: to demonstrate that the forthcoming edition of the *Cahiers* by Robinson can never replace the C.N.R.S. edition; and, more importantly, to defend V. against those latter-day critics who make claims

for an irrational element in his work. This critic's conception of V.'s intellectualism is so total that at one point in her essay she warns solemnly against using the term sensibility when speaking of him. The frequent occurrence of the term in the *Cahiers* is accounted for by the hypothesis that sensibility is always the object of an analysis where the intellect holds undisputed sway.

Review: H. L[aurenti] in RLM 413–18:192–93, 1974.

Rey, Alain. La conscience du poète—les langages de Paul Valéry. Lit 4:116–28, 1971.   **8638**

The texts from the *Cahiers* used to establish Rey's position are gleaned from Schmidt-Radefeldt's book and are so acknowledged. In the course of his demonstration that V.'s private research in the area is crude compared to what it could have been had he but read Bröndal or Meillet, Rey sheds some light on the function of the "implexe" in *L'idée fixe* and on V.'s insistence that the arbitrariness of the linguistic sign is of the domain of the irrational. His presentation of V.'s model(s) of the sign is quite helpful. Most disquieting for Rey is V.'s persistence in holding to the phonological primacy of language which, for this branch of stylistics, is anathema. V. is finally rejected as an unrepentant Cratylist. Compare his contribution to the centenary published in 1974.

———. Sens et discours poétique chez Valéry. *In*: Paul Valéry contemporain. *See* 8486. p. 39–48.   **8639**

His exploration of the *Cahiers* for their value as linguistic analysis leads Rey after a few stimulating (but, as he well knows, superficial) comparisons, to observe that the concept of linguistic subject is very nearly that of Lacan. Moreover, despite the evidence that V. refused to take the path of Saussure, Rey in conclusion affirms that V. paved the way for the generative, structural analysis which alone can adequately account for the textuality of texts. This despite Rey's awareness that V. refused to abandon the position of the primacy of language as a sound system, a refusal that for V. relegated writing to the status of a secondary function of language. In this regard

Rey's conclusions appear somewhat hasty and ill founded.

Robinson, Judith. L'analyse de l'esprit dans les Cahiers de Valéry. J. Corti, 1963. 223 p.   **8640**

This first major study of the *Cahiers* has become the reference point for new work in several areas. It will remain a very readable and valuable tool even as some of its findings are modified. Thus, the first chapter on V.'s critique of language tends to situate him parallel to Wittgenstein, the logical positivists and English analytical philosophy (Russell, Ryle, Ayre). Schmidt-Radefeldt has built upon this commentary, extending it to the fundamental principles of structuralist linguistics. His thesis is in turn being challenged in certain respects, and it will doubtless be some time yet before a really clear picture emerges.

Reviews: J. Bellemin-Noël in RHL 65:148–49, 1965; A. Chisholm in AJFS 1:221–22, 1964; E. Noulet in RUB 158–70, Oct. 1964–Feb. 1965.

———. Dreaming and the analysis of consciousness in Valéry's Cahiers. FS 16:101–23, 1962.   **8641**

This first serious examination of V.'s defense against Freudian theory points up the extent to which V. chose to take his stand on linguistic grounds, thus permitting himself to dismiss psychoanalysis as methodologically naive. For a parallel, and very different, reading of the function of Freud in V.'s thought, see Derrida (*see* 8560).

———. Valéry's conception of training the mind. FS 18:227–35, 1964.   **8642**

Among the books V. claimed had had a strong influence on him was *Un officier de cavalerie* by Gen. L'Hotte. Robinson has pieced this biographical puzzle together with disjointed passages in the *Cahiers* marked by the sign "Gladiator" and has demonstrated beyond any doubt that their common theme was the training—*dressage*—of the mind. She has also had access to a collection of notes in V.'s unpublished papers entitled "Gladiator—notes préliminaires au Training-Book." The result, although brief, is an impressive example of V.'s conviction that true philosophy is a matter of mental discipline.

———. Valéry's view of mental creativity. *In:* Paul Valéry. *See* 8482. p. 3–18. **8643**
Continues reflections begun in her 1963 book; considers V.'s view of creativity as paralleling that of experimental psychology in the fifties, specifically as regards V.'s "poïétique" in the broad sense and the concept of divergent thinking.

Schmidt-Radefeldt, Jürgen. Die Aporien Zenons bei Paul Valéry. RFor 83:52–69, 1971. **8644**
This article is less valuable than it would have been had the author consulted Champigny (on the "Cimetière marin") or Gaède, who had written on precisely this subject six years earlier. Only in his concluding pages does the author introduce a new perspective, the relation of V.'s linguistic analysis to this problem, a perspective he had developed more fully in his 1970 book-length study.

———. Paul Valéry linguiste dans les Cahiers. Klincksieck, 1970. 202 p. **8645**
Schmidt-Radefeldt's thesis that V. anticipated the principal positions of structural linguistics (i.e. before the publication of Saussure's *Cours...*) is reinforced through his systematic reading of the *Cahiers.* Even the most reluctant, hard-bitten rationalist will find the reasoning plausible and worthy of careful refutation. The non-linguist will find here an exciting account of those formalist aspects of V.'s esthetics which have appeared as embarrassing loose ends in previous analyses. It is probable that a close examination would oblige one to modify Schmidt-Radefeldt's suggestion that "Narcisse parle" represents Narcissism in the same sense as Lacan's concept of the Mirror Stage.
Reviews: W. McClendon in BA 45:651, 1971; A. Nicolas in RSH 36:675–79, 1971; N. Spence in FS 27:475–76, 1973.

———. La théorie du point-de-vue chez Paul Valéry. *In:* Paul Valéry contemporain. *See* 8486. p. 237–49. **8646**
A capital article that analyzes V.'s concept of perspectivism—point of view—in relation to many potential fields of application from physics to the novel. The study of the *Cahiers* appears to be thorough and the references from other fields are particularly impressive. Situates V. usefully in the development of one of the most fruitful concepts of the twentieth century.

Schön, Nicole [i.e. Nicole Celeyrette-Pietri]. Attente et surprise chez Valéry. EFL 8:72–81, 1971. **8647**
The subject is a broad one, and the results presented here disproportionately slim. The outline of the article could serve as an initial guide to the more thorough investigation which the question deserves.

Virtanen, Reino. Allusions to Poe's poetic theory in Valéry's Cahiers. PMMLA 1:113–20, 1969. **8648**
This paper extends (with some overlap) the author's study of "Au sujet d'Eureka" (*see* 8895). Here Virtanen examines further the evidence provided by the *Cahiers* with which he is manifestly familiar.

Walzer, Pierre-Olivier. Fragments d'esthésique. *In:* Paul Valéry, 1871–1971. *See* 8487. p. 230–42. **8649**
This article draws the conclusions toward which his two preceding ones (1965 and 1970) had been working. Further examination of the evidence has led to an important revision of the judgment that V.'s idea of the physiology of sexuality was that of the ambient culture: here certain of V.'s views compare favorably with the recent findings of J. Piaget and his collaborators. More importantly, the link between the sensual and the esthetic is adequately established by a more complete utilization and understanding of the *Cahiers.*

———. Introduction à l'érotique valéryenne. *In:* Paul Valéry. *See* 8481. p. 217–29. *Also:* Valeurs de l'érotisme. *In:* Les critiques de notre temps et Valéry. *See* 8474. p. 61–73. **8650**
The first of several efforts to properly situate the function of Eros in V.'s world. The starting point is the astonishment expressed in J. Robinson's book at V.'s apparently negative attitude toward both love and sexuality. Walzer pursues the question in detail and concludes that, particularly in later life, V. frequently associated Eros with mysticism. Whereas both phenomena retain an aura of mystery which his earlier

analytical confidence could not adequately account for, both are finally accepted as positive and important.

———. The physiology of sex. *In:* Paul Valéry. *See* 8482. p. 215–30.   **8651**

This contribution is the logical second step in Walzer's analysis of the value of eroticism for V. Here he restricts his scope to the physiological view of sexuality found in the *Cahiers.* He concludes, somewhat hastily perhaps, that none of V.'s basic reflections had gone beyond the investigations current at the turn of the century. Walzer overlooks, however, that in the experimental area V. was looking ahead to the type of work done much later by Masters and Johnson. Walzer does bring out the importance of V.'s inability to proceed analytically from the physiology of sexuality to creativity as a mental phenomenon, despite V.'s awareness that the two are linked.

———. Valéry. Deux essais sur l'amour: Béatrice et Stratonice. RHL 68:66–86, 1968.   **8652**

Analyzing the references to Béatrice and Stratonice in the *Cahiers* for the years 1921 to 1937, Walzer considers the former both as real lover and as a rubric for a future "De l'amour." Stratonice corresponds, however, to a projected text for the theater. This subject is currently being studied by Bastet (*see comment in* 8833). The Walzer article is in no way definitive but remains useful, both for its perceptive comments and for the references to the appropriate sections of the *Cahiers.*

Poetry in General

Austin, Lloyd James. Modulation and movement in Valéry's verse. *In:* Paul Valéry. *See* 8482. p. 19–38.   **8653**

The concepts of modulation and a generative mobility, seen as elements of form, permit Austin to build a strong case for V.'s poetry as an attempt to rival the perfection of the non-referential arts of music and architecture. An important new approach to a basic question.

Bastet, Ned. Valéry et la voix poétique. *In:* Approches—essais sur la poésie moderne

de langue française. Belles lettres, 1971. p. 41–50. (AFLSHN 15)   **8654**

A rigorous study of the semantic field of "voix" and numerous related terms, primarily as V. analyzed them in the *Cahiers.* This short essay goes some way toward identifying the concept of poetic voice which V. considered a phenomenon of total sensibility: i.e. as physiological with psychological and other ramifications. Unfortunately the author had apparently not seen the results of Ince's research into the same area published three years earlier (*see* 8628 et passim).

Bisson, L. A. A study in Le faire valéryen. FS 10:309–21, 1956.   **8655**

The examination of the subject of composition has subsequently been done in greater detail by Ince. The commentary on three poems (*La jeune Parque,* "Pour votre Hêtre suprême," and "Au platane") sets forth the essential steps in V.'s practice of composition: stimulation, maturation, fabrication. The detailed examination of metaphoric structure suggests the transformation of the "vers de circonstance" ("Pour votre Hêtre...") into a mature poem ("Au platane"). Lawler in his 1963 study of "Au platane" (*see* 8771) confirmed Bisson's findings using new mss. material.

Bowra, C. M. Paul Valéry. *In his:* The heritage of symbolism. London, MacMillan, 1943. p. 17–55. *Also:* New York, Schocken Books, 1961. p. 17–55.   **8656**

The principal defects in this essay are a tendency to read *Charmes,* after Noulet, as a connected allegory of the process of creation; and to see in the *Album...* only the immature first efforts of Mallarmé's disciple. Although Bowra continues to read well after some thirty years, the general approach is quite dated.

Celeyrette-Pietri, Nicole. Au commencement sera le sommeil: quelques réflexions sur un poème en prose. *In:* Cahiers Paul Valéry. 1: poétique et poésie. *See* 8472. p. 207–24.   **8657**

This study of a prose poem, first published in *Commerce* (1925) and reproduced here, returns to the Wagnerian notion of leitmotiv as a source of V.'s technique of modulation. It is noteworthy that in this text written for *A.B.C.* V.'s use of modulation is not auditory as in his verse poems, but visual.

Chadwick, Charles. Valéry's return to reality. *In his:* Symbolism. London, Methuen; New York, Barnes & Noble, 1971. p. 44–51. (The critical idiom, 16) **8658**
    This series for the general reader makes extraordinary demands of the author, who must condense in the extreme. Here the strategy used is to refer to major texts in terms of V.'s biography. Thus V.'s work is symbolist despite his return to reality, by which we are to understand his avoidance of both human symbolism and transcendental symbolism, the two poles around which this monograph is constructed. The inadequacy of the demonstration can doubtless be imputed to the format of the series.

Chiari, Joseph. Paul Valéry. *In his:* Contemporary French poetry. Manchester, Manchester univ. press, 1952. p. 13–43. *Also:* New York, Philosophical library, 1952. **8659**
    V. is qualified in the opening paragraph as possibly the most important French poet since Racine. It is in terms of the sustained quality of the poetry that V. is great, whereas Hugo is great by momentary bursts. Chiari considers V. to be a first cousin of existentialism and his concern with phenomenology recalls Raymond's somewhat earlier essay. This remains an eminently readable, if rather dated, introduction by a critic who has a fine sense of the tradition of European poetry. A foreword by T. S. Eliot opens the volume.

Davy, Charles. Words in the mind. London, Chatto & Windus, 1965. p. 13–31. **8660**
    The material on V. appears more or less prominently in the first three chapters of the book. The author is primarily concerned with problems of translation encountered when he undertook English verse renderings of *Le cimetière marin* and *La jeune Parque,* printed in appendix. His account of V.'s poetics is solid enough and, for readers of English, a good supplement to the translation of Hytier's book.

Décaudin, Michel. Narcisse: une sorte d'autobiographie poétique. IL 8:49–55, 1956. **8661**
    In the present state of V. studies this article occupies tne place of chronicle of the group of poems inaugurated by "Narcisse parle." V. had originally conceived a pastoral symphony of which this poem would have represented the prelude. The ms. of the project is reproduced in facsimile.

Duchesne-Guillemin, J[acques]. Valéry au miroir. Les Cahiers et l'exégèse des grands poèmes. FS 20:348–65, 1966. **8662**
    The form of the article, originally delivered as a lecture, lacks something of the rigor that the subject demands. Yet by sheer brilliance it holds together and continues to be of interest. Working back and forth from the *Cahiers* to the major poems the author dredges up biographical references where everyone had affirmed there were none and suggests striking parallels between *La jeune Parque* and *Le cimetière marin.* In the course of his virtuoso performance, Duchesne-Guillemin called into question V.'s profession of literary formalism just at the moment when Genette was giving it new life.

Eigeldinger, Marc. Paul Valéry et la tradition du vers classique. *In his:* Poésie et tendances. Neuchâtel, A la Baconnière, 1945. p. 115–24. **8663**
    Entirely consistent with the following entry; V. is the exemplar of the intrinsic merit of regular prosody.

———. Paul Valéry, poète classique suivi de Stèle pour Paul Valéry. *In:* Paul Valéry, essais et témoignages inédits. *See* 8488. p. 105–16. **8664**
    V.'s death affords an excellent opportunity to consider his accomplishment as poet sub specie aeternitatis, whence the immutable classicism of the title. V. is presented as the major bulwark against change and most especially against the irrational. Of purely historical interest. Compare the diametrically opposing view of Benda (*see* 8548).

Etiemble, [René]. Note adjointe, sur deux ou trois consonnes chez Valéry. *In his:* Poètes ou faiseurs? (1936–1966). Hygiène des lettres, V. 4. Gallimard, 1966. p. 251–57.   **8665**

Etiemble defends V.'s unusually high frequency of repeated consonants against facile charges of imitative harmony. He does not go far in this brief note, which orients the reader toward the research published by Bergeron.

Fromilhague, René. De quelques thèmes chrétiens dans les Poésies de Paul Valéry. *In:* Missions et démarches de la critique.... Klincksieck, 1973. p. 217–26.   **8666**

Starting with the acknowledged neo-Christian *décor* of several pieces of V.'s juvenilia, Fromilhague seeks to extend the idea of a pervasive Christian influence to the *Poésies*. The resulting quasi-liturgical reading will convince only the most faithful. Nonetheless several comments on difficult details are worthy of note.

Gauthier, Michel. L'architecture phonique du langage poétique. *In:* Paul Valéry contemporain. *See* 8486. p. 377–97. **8667**

A study of V.'s poetic practice as primarily the construction of phonemic systems. Such an attempt is appropriate at the moment when the new linguistics —particularly contemptuous of such ideas—is interested in annexing V. to its camp. There remains a strong case to be made along just these lines. The author is quite aware of the delusions of imitative harmony and his thesis is oriented toward something more dear to V., if equally difficult to prove at the moment, the conditioning of physiological response. Much more work needs to be done in this area.

Glauser, Alfred. La jeune Parque et Le cimetière marin. *In his:* Le poème-symbole de Scève à Valéry, essai. Nizet, 1967. p. 181–210.   **8668**

For this critic the symbol-poem is the poet's alter ego, a more perfect body, the identity that life denies. The long poem is more conducive to this project than shorter, fixed forms like the sonnet and a degree of theatricality in presentation is assumed. Using these criteria the author has selected *La jeune Parque* and *Le cimetière marin* as V.'s symbolic embodiment. Glauser would have it that these poems are of necessity formal autobiographies; therefore he extends to *La jeune Parque* the allegoriz-

ing tendency so often found in commentary on *Charmes*. But here, unlike Noulet's commentary on *Le cimetière marin,* the allegory reveals the truth of the poet more than that of the poem. No critic has ever taken more literally Montaigne's dictum on the identity of the man and his style.

Reviews: H. Block in FR 42:789–90, 1969; L. Morice in RR 60:143–47, 1969.

Gmelin, Hermann. Kleines Wörterbuch zu Paul Valérys Gedichten. RFor 60:735–86, 1947.   **8669**

The twenty-seven terms analyzed are presented as a brief lexicon ("absence" to "trésor") including their contextual relations. Those selected are considered to be key words in V.'s poetry. A useful adjunct to the more statistically oriented work of Guiraud and the commentaries by Henry, neither of whom appears to have used Gmelin's work. Gmelin tends to develop the philosophical implications of the semantic field, whereas Guiraud limits himself to a narrower linguistic function.

Reviews: H. Bémol in AUS 1:386–91, 1952; *also in his:* Variations sur Valéry. V. 2. Nizet, 1959. p. 75–83.

Guiraud, Pierre. Index du vocabulaire du symbolisme. V. 2. Index des mots des poésies de Paul Valéry. Klincksieck, 1953. 42 p.   **8670**

Using the 1942 edition of the *Poésies* (but excluding *Pièces diverses, Cantate du Narcisse, Amphion, Sémiramis* and "L'amateur de poèmes"), Guiraud has compiled an exhaustive alphabetical index of the words, including articles, composing the lexicon of V.'s major poems. Each word is keyed by line to the poems in which it occurs. All verbal forms (fin., infin., p.p.) are given, including subjects. Rhyming words are duly noted. No critical apparatus is included since the index was to serve as the statistical matrix for the critical studies entered below. Remains valuable for future research on the poetry.

———. Langage et versification d'après l'œuvre de Paul Valéry. Klincksieck, 1953. 239 p. (Linguistique, 56)   **8671**

Serious critical explorations of V.'s poetry in its phonemic, metric and lexical aspects must begin here. Of the several attempts to approach V.'s work with a linguistic methodology, this is the only one with a sufficiently complete statistical sample to permit generalizations or to function as a ground for critical statements by literary scholars. Of particular interest today is the fifth chapter, devoted to "Le son et le sens." Guiraud reviews the idealist positions from Plato's *Cratylus* to Mallarmé with considerable attention to Jespersen and Grammont. His conclusion, on which he bases statements concerning the possible symbolic function of phonemic structure in the poem, is close to that of Spire and Burnshaw. Guiraud attempts, in effect, to reconcile Saussurian linguists with the neo-symbolist linguistic dilettantes by arguing that the unmotivated linguistic sign is manipulated by poets for particular effects.

Reviews: M. Bémol in RHL 55:390–95, 1955; *also in his:* Variations sur Valéry, v. 2. Nizet, 1959. p. 84–94.

Harth, Helene, and Leo Pollmann. Paul Valéry. Frankfurt, Athenäum, 1972. 253 p. (Schwerpunkte Romanistik, 10) **8672**

This is the first book for readers of German to bring together the results of V. scholarship since the publication of the *Cahiers*. Harth opens this joint study with an overview of V. criticism today in which more recent types of investigation tend to eclipse the more established ones. Pollmann's exegesis of the major poems and *L'idée fixe* is a multi-level pursuit of symbolism in which linguistic expression is considered primary. All in all a useful study, one which has yet to find an appropriate counterpart in either English or French.

Review: N. Suckling in FS 29:111–13, 1975.

Hartman, Geoffrey H. Valéry. *In his:* The unmediated vision. An interpretation of Wordsworth, Rilke and Valéry. New Haven, Yale univ. press; London, Oxford univ. press, 1954. p. 97–124. **8673**

Given the quality of this study, one marvels at its lack of impact on V. criticism. The seven page commentary on "La dormeuse" is among the best to be found, certainly in English. Hartman handles the difficult notions of sound and form particularly well.

Henry, Albert. Langage et poésie chez Paul Valéry. Mercure de France, 1952. 174 p. **8674**

The fate of this book is curious. On the one hand it constitutes the first serious attempt to approach V.'s poetic work using a linguistic methodology; on the other its tripartite division covers subjects that were treated more fully by others within a year of its publication. The brief essay on poetics was eclipsed in 1953 by Hytier's exhaustive treatment of the materials then available. The somewhat longer essay on categories of words in V.'s lexicon is helpful to the novice or the reader seeking a general orientation; but it is selective. Moreover, Guiraud's *Langage et versification...* (*see* 8671) covers some of the same material more rigorously. Finally the lexicon itself (177 words studied on the basis of one or several examples in context) is keyed to the foregoing essay by a number of idiosyncratic signs, each of which applies to a semantic category. The lexicon itself invites detailed comparison with that established by Gmelin.

Reviews: H. Bémol in AUS 1:386–91, 1952; L. Bisson in FS 7:84–86, 1953; A. Gmelin in FM 27:296–97, 1959.

Hytier, Jean. L'esthétique valéryenne du sonnet. AJFS 6:326–36, 1969. **8675**

Hytier's erudition places V.'s reflection on the sonnet form in a nineteenth-century French perspective, demonstrating both his (theoretical) allegiance to a tradition and his own originality. This article is usefully supplemented by W. Mönch's contribution to the Montpellier colloquium (*see* 8680).

Ince, W. N. Paul Valéry—Poésie pure or Poésie cuite? FS 16:348–58, 1962. **8676**

This is probably the most readable short statement on V.'s poetics for the intelligent layman. It avoids the occasional silliness still engendered by the term "poésie pure" and leads the cautious reader to a point at which he might be prepared to accept V. on his own terms.

Jones, Rhys S. The selection and usage of symbols by Mallarmé and Valéry. Triv 1:44–55, 1966. **8677**

The numerous concrete comparisons of metaphor and symbol in the work of the two poets is certainly suggestive and deserves, as the author points out, a more fully developed form. His rapid commentaries on composition and poetics will be found to be of less value than the examples he has so carefully paired.

Laurenti, Huguette. Musique et monologue—notes pour une approche valéryenne du poème. *In:* Lectures de Charmes. *See* 8477. p. 49–66.   **8678**

After her probing study of V.'s reflections on Wagner, in her *Valéry et le théâtre* (1973), the author pursues the notion of composition into the major poems. This first effort to discuss the possible value of the terms score, harmony, modulation is necessarily general and tentative. Further detailed study in this area could well result in a type of criticism that could account for the function in V.'s poetry of sound systems as formal constructs, thus avoiding the conflicts that have arisen repeatedly when the accent has been placed on the linguistic sign as arbitrary signifier. The investigations of Morier, utilized in this manner, could prove invaluable.

Lawler, James R. Les larmes: hélas! c'est bien moi. BA 45:613–19, 1971. *Also in his:* The poet as analyst. See 8518. p. 137–48.   **8679**

The brevity of the piece notwithstanding, one will find here a good case for the affective origin of an important part of V.'s poetry, including *La jeune Parque.* Lawler's approach stresses the progressive effacing of this intimate genesis. The completed poem then strives toward that ideal of impersonal universality which V. and Eliot appear to have shared.

Mönch, Walter. Valéry et la tradition du sonnet français et européen. *In:* Entretiens sur Paul Valéry. *See* 8476. p. 157–72.   **8680**

This extremely useful study places V.'s practice of the sonnet in the European tradition from the Rennaissance to the present. It builds upon J. Hytier's 1969 article in AJFS. The discussion following delivery of this paper at the Montpellier colloquium brought out two useful points: 1) that Mallarmé and V. himself did indeed prac-

tice the Shakespearean sonnet on occasion; and 2) that Ficino may be a useful author to explore concerning V.'s understanding of the golden section in this and other aspects of composition.

Mondor, Henri. Précocité de Valéry. Gallimard, 1957. 442 p.   **8681**

Mondor offered a chronicle of V.'s schoolboy writings, his early poems, and in general his production up to the death of Mallarmé. He presented them with abundant reference to hitherto unpublished documents. Bémol stated lucidly the major objection to be made: convinced of his positivist objectivity, Mondor allowed himself to be gulled, particularly in the latter section concerning Mallarmé, by the psychologism of V.'s own affirmations on the subject. In brief, this is not a history but the groundwork for a history.

Reviews: M. Bémol in RHL 58: 553–56, 1958; R. Lang in BA 34:138, 1960; E. Noulet in SynB 13:261–62, 1958.

———. Les premiers temps d'une amitié, André Gide et Paul Valéry. *See* 8413. 157 p.   **8682**

Valuable for the inclusion of V.'s anthology of ten poems offered to Gide in 1892. The Pléiade edition of the *Œuvres* treats these as variants under the headings for the individual pieces in the *Album....*

———. Le vase brisé de Paul Valéry étudiant. *In:* Paul Valéry, essais et témoignages inédits. *See* 8488. p. 13–19.   **8683**

Mondor relates the circumstances in which V. composed "Pour la nuit" in 1889 and presents the text sent to P. Louÿs in 1890. His commentary is interesting with respect to V.'s early taste in poetry.

Morawska, Ludmiła. L'adjectif qualificatif dans la langue des symbolistes français (Rimbaud, Mallarmé, Valéry). Poznán, Uniwersytet im. Adama Mickiewicza w Poznaniu, 1964. 170 p.   **8684**

A linguistic study of limited interest. V.'s poetry offers material for analysis throughout the book.

Morier, Henri. La motivation des formes et des mètres chez Valéry. *In:* Paul Valéry contemporain. *See* 8486. p. 325–52. **8685**

If one abstracts some naive statements to the effect that V. must have felt the horror of his Pythia, there are very valuable data here, partially analyzed, concerning fixed and free verse forms, metric and rhyme schemes, and their probable psychological connotations. By standing the author's biographical hypothesis on its head in favor of V.'s own theory of effects, it may be possible to develop from just such data workable conclusions concerning the most appropriate way in which to read a poem written in a certain form. Conversely, one will find here some excellent arguments as to V.'s choice of specific formal conditions for a given poem. Not the least of the author's contributions is the result of his investigation into V.'s high frequency of points of exclamation.

Mossop, D. J. Valéry and technical purity. *In his:* Pure poetry—studies in French poetic theory and practice, 1746–1945. Oxford, Clarendon press, 1971. p. 194–248. **8686**

The most complete study in English of V.'s understanding of "poésie pure," valuably set off against two centuries of theory and practice in France. The preceding chapter on Bremond is likewise helpful in relation to the latter's misuse of certain of V.'s notions. The last twenty-five pages on V. are a detailed reading of *Le cimetière marin,* stanza by stanza, organized along thematic lines. While it will prove helpful to readers who have little French, this reading of the poem does not bring anything really fresh to the subject. One further reservation might be made regarding the use of V.'s "MOI pur" in a sense suggestive of Ego psychology. Recent criticism has been generally critical of this interpretation of the term. *See* 8905 for author's briefer statement of V.'s position in the context of neo-Kantian esthetics.
Reviews: R. Champigny in FR 46: 166–67, 1972–73; W. Ince in FS 29: 229–30, 1975.

Nadal, Octave. Poèmes en prose. *In his:* A mesure haute. Mercure de France, 1964. p. 229–46. *Trans.:* Introduction. *In:* Valéry, Paul. Poems in the rough. Trans. by Hilary Corke. Princeton, Princeton univ. press; London, Routledge and

Kegan Paul, 1969. p. xi–xxix. (The collected works of Paul Valéry, v. 2. Ed. by Jackson Mathews.) **8687**

A capital piece on a subject that has yet to be taken up with the necessary rigor and attention of a full-length study. Nadal situates V.'s practice of the prose poem in the tradition beginning with Baudelaire. His originality is in presenting it as an autonomous activity, not as imperfect verse.
Review: J. Fletcher in Spec 224: 386, 1970.

Parent, Monique. La fonction poétique du langage dans Charmes. *In:* Paul Valéry contemporain. *See* 8486. p. 61–73. **8688**

One has the uneasy feeling that the frequent allusions to contemporary structural linguistics, with the prestige of its technical vocabulary, serve as new garb for the thematic study of *Charmes* (see the author's 1970 book). Thus the conclusion that V.'s idea of poetry was structuralist is to be taken with a degree of skepticism. As in Hegel, the end was already present in the beginning.

————, **and Pierre Parent.** Réflexions sur la valeur des motifs de l'eau et du vent dans La jeune Parque et dans Charmes. *In:* Lectures de Charmes. *See* 8477. p. 67–102. **8689**

This essay is in two parts, a ten-page presentation of the location and context of a number of theme words that are associated with one or the other of the themes studied, and a rapid sketch of the semantic/thematic value of these terms throughout La *jeune Parque* and *Charmes.* Each poem is considered under a separate heading. In the conclusion one notes a certain circularity: presuppositions about the poems' meaning are too neatly borne out by the study. Hypotheses concerning the functioning of unconscious processes, although certainly suggestive, are inadequately developed to warrant the claims made. Part of the problem may be in the tendency to regard Jungian archetypes as fixed essences. In this respect the study appears to be a linguistic metacommentary of Aigrisse's analytical method.

Pareyson, Luigi. Le regole secondo Valéry. RdE 7:229–59, 1962. **8690**

The subjects covered in this essay correspond to those in chapters 5 and 6 of Hytier's *Poétique de Valéry:* inspiration and composition. In general the quality of the essay compares well with Hytier's treatment.

————. Suono e senso secondo Valéry. RdE 11:56–98, 1966.   **8691**

The logical continuation of the author's contribution to the same journal in 1962; a sophisticated and well-balanced treatment of the difficult question of phonetic and metaphoric patterns in V.'s poetry. The theory is set forth in more detail than in Hytier's *Poétique de Valéry* and is more carefully examined than in Bergeron (*see* 8752). It should be considered a basic text on the subject.

Paul, David. Valéry and the relentless world of the symbol. SoR 6:408–15, 1970.   **8692**

The notion of symbol used to organize the article is too vast to be useful. The author affirms, without proof, that V.'s "Dormeuse" must have been based upon Giorgione's "Sleeping Venus." A page on the correspondence between poetry and painting does little to raise the level of critical discourse.

Rinsler, Norma. The defence of the self: stillness and movement in Valéry's poetry. EFL 6:36–56, 1969.   **8693**

Pursuing the field of associations of "pur" ("le pur," "pureté") in V.'s work, the author goes well beyond the findings of other researchers to grasp the motivating concept: motion arrested is related directly to the exigency of the supremely self-possessed subjectivity. This finding permits her to adduce a connection between the poetry and Teste, and the connection holds. Surprisingly the investigation then leads to the image of the nape ("nuque") as the nexus of a violent eroticism recurring throughout the work. Through the vulnerable but impersonal nape the other, in sexual love, is kept from assuming the threatening status of subject. The synthesis of these attitudes is found in the image of poetic creation as rape in "Aurore" ("Ces idéales rapines...," VIII, 3). This is a very sophisticated piece of work and has a potential for wide application.

Sauvy, Alfred. Quelques réflexions sur l'har monie dans la poésie de Valéry. *In* Entretiens sur Paul Valéry. See 8475. 377–409.   **869**

Unfortunately shows no awareness c the work already done on the sam subject by Bergeron or Guiraud. As result the question of sound and mean ing barely goes beyond Grammont an imitative harmony, although Sauvy i aware that the answer is not to b found there.

Shaw, Priscilla Washburn. Paul Valéry-th world in the mind. *In her:* Rilke, Valér and Yeats—the domain of the self. Ne Brunswick, N.J., Rutgers univ. press, 196 p. 105–74.   **869**

This study would be worthy o mention if only for the conclusion o *La jeune Parque:* the poem answers th question how the self is, rather tha what it is. The approach to the shiftin relationships of the parts to the whol is in general very competently handle and is accessible to readers with littl or no French. Another merit of thi volume is to have studied the poetry c V., Rilke and Yeats for their importan contrasts. In sum, a very good piece o comparative scholarship.

Spœrri, Théophile. La puissance méta phorique. *In:* Paul Valéry, essais e témoignages inédits. See 8488. p. 177–98   **869**

The treatment of the evolution o metaphor adumbrates a general theor which attempts to mediate betwee early Bachelard and Marx. The com ments on "Palme" and "Les grenades" present V. as a peculiarly modern poe in this perspective. Deserves furthe study and elaboration. In passin Spoerri cites P. Lebrun's "Le cimetièr au bord de la mer," which he contrast with V.'s "Le cimetière marin."

Walzer, Pierre-Olivier. La poésie de Valéry Geneva, P. Cailler, 1953. 498 p. *Also* Geneva, Slatkine reprints, 1966.   **869**

This doctoral dissertation wa printed in the same year that Austi published two major contributions o the *Cimetière marin* (reviewed in ap pendix 3 of this volume) and J Hytier contributed the most thorough study to date of V.'s poetics. Its overal view of the poetry is consequentl

limited. Recent studies of individual poems have regularly referred to Walzer's commentaries.
Review: M. Bémol in RHL 55:385–89, 1955.

Veber, Jean-Paul. Paul Valéry. *In his:* Genèse de l'œuvre poétique. Gallimard, 1960. p. 388–451. 8698
The concept of theme is taken here to be a constant of the writer's psychic life and in this sense is related to the Freudian notion of the complex. However, as Weber practices his brand of thematic criticism, his findings do not necessarily converge with those of Mauron or Aigrisse. Unlike them, he sees V. alternating between two thematic poles, one primary—the Swan; the other secondary—the Breast. For the most part his adaptation of psychoanalysis to criticism has met with little enthusiasm among V. scholars. Weber's work is quite fragmentary, reductionist and frequently gives the impression of gratuitous interpretation.
Review: C. Hackett in YFS 44:148–56, 1970.

Whiting, Charles G. Préciosité in La jeune Parque and Charmes. *In:* Paul Valéry. *See* 8482. p. 119–27. 8699
Argues convincingly that preciosity in V.'s poetry masks a sensuousness perceived as vulnerability (*see* N. Rinsler above). Both are poles of V.'s antithetical imagination. The importance of V.'s "powerful sexual sensuality" excludes any identification of his manner with historical "préciosité," the function of which was quite different. A valuable article.

————. Valéry: development of a poet. AJFS 9:161–66, 1972. 8700
The declared purpose of the article, to see exactly how the early poems evolve toward the poetry of La jeune Parque and Charmes, leads to notations on the evolution of theme and technique in quite a number of poems, too many perhaps to allow for the desired precision. Many of these observations could serve to orient future studies toward a more ample development.

Wills, Ludmilla M. Le regard contemplatif chez Valéry et Mallarmé. Amsterdam, Rodopi NV, 1974. 182 p. 8701
The idea of this comparative study is potentially very fruitful: to define the nature of poetry for V. and for Mallarmé through the fundamental difference in the function of the gaze as constitutive of form. The line of approach is phenomenological; Bachelard is cited prominently, and the study makes good use of Hartman's 1954 book. There are occasional didactic digressions to inform the reader of Bachelard's importance. These could have been excised without affecting the thesis.

Żurowski, Maciej. Paweł Valéry. Młoda Parka i Uroki. PrzH 7:71–81, 1963. 8702
A general introduction to V.'s major poems, *La jeune Parque* and *Charmes,* for Polish readers. The author presents *La jeune Parque* in relation to Mallarmé's "Hérodiade" discussing intelligently the questions of preciosity and mannerism. *Charmes* is given a rapid overview with frequent allusions to competent critics. The conclusion of the article assimilated the final stanzas of the *Cimetière marin* to Bergsonism with an astonishing disregard for the available scholarly treatments of the subject since Thibaudet.

Album de vers anciens

Bellemin-Noël, Jean. En marge des premiers Narcisses de Valéry: l'en-jeu et le hors-jeu du texte. RHL 70:975–91, 1970. 8703
A valuable, highly suggestive but quite dense text analyzing the versions of "Narcisse parle" previously identified by Walzer. The commentary is textual and strives to give equal weight to homophony and rhythm within a Sausserian framework. Methodologically the article proposes to replace the old conceptual explication by a formal unfolding of the text. The real problem, however, is encountered in the "vase" (line 14 of the text published by Monod in 1947) which suggests the possibility/necessity of recourse to an extra-textual frame of reference. The only criterion finally is that of the

cohesiveness and comprehensiveness of the explication. The logical next step in Bellemin-Noël's intertextual reading of the several Narcissus poems was published in *Littérature* for 1972 (*see* 8547).

Brunelli, Giuseppe Antonio. Introduzione alla poesia di Paul Valéry. V. I: Testi. 40 p. V. II: Da Solitude a Intermède (1887–1892). 82 p. Messina, Peloritana editrice, 1964–65.   **8704**

These two slim volumes represent the material prepared for a course at the University of Messina; they are pedagogical rather than critical in nature. The volume of thirty-six texts contains no variants. In the second volume, commentary is limited to notes of one to three pages and focuses on biographical material, not specifically on the forty-eight poems under consideration. A somewhat more polished version was published almost simultaneously. See below.

————. Paul Valéry e il canzoniere (1887–1892). Messina, Peloritana editrice, 1965. 214 p. (Università degli studi di Messina. Istituto di lingue e letteratura straniere.)   **8705**

Here the author has presented on facing pages texts and commentary on the poems written before V.'s revolution of 1892. Fifty poems are studied, in approximately twice the detail as in the previous volume. Nonetheless the critical commentary is very sketchy and largely derivative. The connection between biography and artistic creation is assumed to be self-evident with the usual result that the poems are made to elucidate the life of young V. There are no unpublished texts or other discoveries of note.

Review: E. de Domenico in CulF 13:283–84, 1966.

Dubu, Jean. Valéry et Courbet: origine de La fileuse. RHL 65:239–43, 1965. **8706**

The argument that Courbet's "La fileuse endormie," observed at the Musée Fabre in Montpellier, was the starting point of V.'s poem is highly probable. However, the author's claim that certain images must have been formed on the basis of direct observation supposes a poetics of mimesis that is quite irrelevant. The poem is then presented as an analysis of the Courbet painting, which it patently is not.

Elder, David. E. M. Le finale fragmenté des Narcisses de Valéry. *In:* Cahiers Paul Valéry. 1: poétique et poésie. See 8472. p. 187–206.   **8707**

This study of manuscript sketches for a conclusion to the Narcissus poems should continue Bellemin-Noël's article, which the author seems not to have known. The length of the commentary, seven slight pages, is inadequate to provide a proper assessment. For the present, the value of the article is in its presentation of previously unpublished ms. material now in the Bibliothèque Nationale.

Fasano, Giancarlo. Profusion du soir: genesi di alcune strutture poetiche di P. Valéry. SRLF 4:279–321, 1963.   **8708**

Like Whiting before him, Fasano based a part of his study on a faulty chronology, supposing that "Profusion..." had been written in its definitive form in the nineties. However, the most significant part of his essay does not hinge upon this argument over antecedence. Fasano is more interested in the potential polymorphism of poetic figures and, in this domain, his essay remains the most thorough devoted to the poem. Fasano has given a stimulating contribution to a subject that has yet to be treated extensively: the mutations of basic figures throughout V.'s work.

Giaveri, Maria Teresa. L'Album de vers anciens di Paul Valéry, studio sulle correzione d'autore edite ed inedite. Padova, Liviana editrice, 1969. xii, 156 p. **8709**

To date the only comprehensive study of the poems collected in the *Album...* to examine systematically the formal evolution of V.'s early style. The documentation is thorough, including materials in the *Cahiers,* the Valéryanum of the Doucet Library, and unpublished papers then in the family collection. The chapter on musical technique is very convincing, as is the commentary of early versions of "Narcisse parle." In passing the author notes that her own formal findings coincide with Mauron's concerning the thematic relationship of sleep, purity, death. She thus draws a parallel be-

tween early ("Anne," "La fileuse") and later poems ("La dormeuse," "La fausse morte") in which certain constants subsist. Although it invites further elaboration in several areas, this is clearly the best available book on the composition of the *Album*....
Reviews: C. Cordié in SFr 16:185–86, 1972; I. Gheorghe in RSH 36: 673–75, 1971; N. Suckling in FS 25:233–35, 1971.

Grubbs, Henry A. New light on Valéry's Féeries. MLN 76:755–56, 1961.   8710
Volume 10 of the *Cahiers* confirms the author's hypothesis (*see* 8711) that "Même féerie" represents a subsequent, lateral development of the series "Blanc," "Fée," "Féerie." In the notebook dated Jan.-April 1925 lines 9 and 11 appear in their definitive form, as does line 10 but for one word. A valuable footnote to an important article.

———. La nuit magique de Paul Valéry: étude de Féerie. RHL 60:199–212, 1960.   8711
This is the first, and still the best, attempt to study the four versions of the fairy poem since Hytier grouped them in the first volume of the *Œuvres* in 1957. Grubbs reproduces *in toto* the texts of the 1890 printing of "Blanc" in *L'ermitage*, the 1914 printing of "Fée" in *Les fêtes*, the 1920 printing of "Féerie" in the *Album*... and the 1926 printing of "Même féerie" in *Quelques vers*. The commentary is separated into two parts: the first three texts are considered versions of one poem; "Même féerie," quite paradoxically, given the title, is seen as another poem or, in Grubbs' felicitous expression, another solution of a single poetic problem. Future studies should start with this article.

Laurent, Freddy, S. J. Interprétation d'un poème de Valéry: La fileuse. ECl 26: 272–85, 1958.   8712
A traditional "explication de texte" stressing the grammatical/syntactical articulations in the poem. Its value is exclusively pedagogical.

Lawler, James R. L'ange frais de l'œil nu.... EFL 7:38–69, 1970. *Also in his:* The poet as analyst. *See* 8518. p. 74–116.   8713

At the outset Lawler rectifies Whiting's contention that "Profusion du soir" is a less perfect antecedent of *Le cimetière marin*. In fact, Lawler points out, the poem as it was published in 1926 was in the main composed after *Le cimetière marin*. Whiting's article collapses in so far as he sees the two poems as linked in this way. The same fact of dating likewise demolishes the contention of G. Fasano that "Profusion du soir" is a poor ancestor of *La jeune Parque*. Having cleared the field, Lawler proceeds to demonstrate that "Profusion du soir" is actually a superior poem written with the full authority of V.'s prowess, already sufficiently demonstrated in *Charmes*. Its later date, however, does no more to assure its merit than a supposition of an earlier date could do to prove its inadequacy. The real merit of Lawler's study is in his considering the poem on its own terms.

———. Existe?... Sois enfin toi-même.... AJFS 8:146–74, 1971. *Also in his:* The poet as analyst. *See* 8518. p. 36–73. 8714
This is by far the most complete study of the "Air de Sémiramis;" it is not likely to be surpassed for some time. The commentary covers source material, phonemic structure, effects of exclamatory punctuation, composition—citing the doctrine of *ut pictura poesis* with respect to Degas' painting of Semiramis—and manuscript versions and documents. In a particularly well prepared conclusion, Lawler sees the poem as a hyperbolic myth of the intellect.

———. Saint Mallarmé. *In:* Paul Valéry. *See* 8482. p. 185–98. *Also (expanded):* J'ai adoré cet homme.... *In his:* The poet as analyst. *See* 8518. p. 117–36.   8715
A sensitive comparison of variants of "Valvins" with "Psaume pour une voix" and passages in the *Cahiers* indicates a formal influence of Mallarmé on V.'s texts. The pervasiveness of Mallarmé's moral influence gave this piece its original hieratic title.

Nardis, Luigi di. Voile sur la rivière. *In his:* Il sorriso di Reims e altri saggi di cultura francese. Rocca San Casciano, Cappelli, 1960. p. 219–28.   8716

Studies the original 1897 version of "Valvins" in a biographical context, noting in particular that Berthe Morisot had done a painting on the same Mallarméan motif.

Newman-Gordon, Pauline. Hélène ou la reine triste. *In her:* Hélène de Sparte—la fortune du mythe en France. Debresse, 1968. p. 115–23.   **8717**

The title is given erroneously as "Hélène ou la reine triste" although no published version of the poem includes the conjunction. In the main the text follows that printed in *Chimère* but does not reproduce in all particulars the punctuation of that printing. Consistent with the overall design of the book, the chapter on V. is devoted to content analysis set in a literary-historical context. The concluding page offers a suggestive comment on the terms "écume," "temps," "mémoire" which the author finds similarly associated in this poem and in *La jeune Parque*.

Parent, Monique. Cohérence et résonance stylistiques d'après un poème de Paul Valéry. TLL 3:93–115, 1965.   **8718**

The most detailed analysis of "La fileuse" to date, with a strong accent on its linguistic components. Study of the variants presented in Hytier's ed. of the *Œuvres* reveals gradual replacement of logical association by an association of images wherein phonemic and visual values converge. The concept of structure used here is semantic/syntactic. The study of linear and cyclical aspects of the poem is illuminating in general. The technical aspects of the article are far superior to the few pages on interpretation in which the author falls back on paraphrase.

Schön, Nicole [*i.e.* Nicole Celeyrette-Pietri]. Note sur Un feu distinct de Paul Valéry. FS 26:434–38, 1972.   **8719**

Compares the 1920 version with a draft written in 1897 (*Cahiers* 1, 202) and reproduced here. The author also consulted two intermediary drafts in the family's collection of mss.

Spitzer, Leo. La genèse d'une poésie de Paul Valéry. Rens 2–3:311–21, 1944–45. *Also in his:* Romanische Literaturstudien,

1936–1956. Tübingen, Max Niemeyer, 1959. p. 343–52.   **8720**

The first half of this article on "La fileuse" is devoted to some literary-historical source hunting that has since been discredited. Mondor quipped—in *Les premiers temps d'une amitié...*—that V. could scarcely have known in 1891 a poem (Heredia's "La fileuse") that was published only in 1905. J. Dubu's article establishes the Courbet painting as a starting point far more probable than an obscure epigram by Leonidas or a poem by Chénier. The few pages devoted to stylistic observations are solid, however.

Whiting, Charles G. Femininity in Valéry's early poetry. YFS 9:74–83, 1952.   **8721**

Whiting interprets the most dated elements of the *Album...* in terms of the cultish decadence V. flaunted in pieces like "Le bois amical" and in his correspondence with Gide. The fundamental flaw in the article does not concern the fact of V.'s misogyny, certainly real enough in the nineties, but rather the fact that these poems had been carefully rewritten before publication in 1920.

———. Profusion du soir and Le cimetière marin. PMLA 77:134–39, 1962.   **8722**

As Lawler has pointed out (*see* 8713), the supposition that the published text of "Profusion..." antedates the *Cimetière marin* is false. But it would still be possible to write on the similarities Whiting sees in the two poems (he does not, after all, present the one as an earlier version of the other).

———. Valéry jeune poète. New Haven, Yale univ. press; Paris, Presses univ. de France, 1960. 154 p.   **8723**

In this first volume devoted to the earliest versions of the poems published in the *Album...*, the author has set out to demonstrate the progress in V.'s poetic technique from 1890 to 1900. This avowed intention is sometimes at variance with the thematic grouping of the poems, which are regularly presented in relation to later texts by V. or to the work of other French poets. When he comments on the "content" of the poems, Whiting frequently finds himself explaining changes in subsequent versions in terms of biographical data (as available in the published correspondence, for the most part). The lasting value of this study is doubtless in its intelligent approach to the probable exchanges between V.'s lived experience and his early poetic production.

Reviews: L. Bisson in FS 15:82–83, 1961; J. Frey in EspCr 1:44–45, 1961; J. Parisier-Plottel in RR 53:72–74, 1962; S. Pitou in BA 36:161, 1962; J. Robichez in IL 13:30–31, 1961; N. Suckling in MLR 56:275–77, 1961.

La jeune Parque

Aigrisse, Gilberte. La jeune Parque de Paul Valéry à la lumière de la psychanalyse. *In:* Entretiens sur l'art et la psychanalyse. Paris-The Hague, Mouton, 1968. p. 269–94. (Décades du centre culturel international de Cerisy-la-Salle, nouvelle série, 6)   **8724**

The debate following delivery of this paper at the 1962 colloquium on art and psychoanalysis is today the most valuable aspect of it, the bulk of the text having been incorporated into the author's *Psychanalyse de Paul Valéry.* If one accepts as legitimate the study of thematic material isolated from poetic composition then this paper can be of some value. P. Ricœur and G. Ferdière contributed to the discussion.

Bémol, Maurice. De La bacchante à La jeune Parque. *In his:* Variations sur Valéry. V. 2. *See* 8492. p. 127–50.   **8725**

Bémol argues for a very broad influence of M. de Guérin on *La jeune Parque,* making claims that one cannot take very seriously. Bémol seems to have been so sure of his discovery that he mistook similarities for something of a more positive nature.

———. La Parque et le serpent. Belles lettres, 1955. 127 p.   **8726**

As an essay on forms and myths this monograph falls short of the promise of its subtitle. As a piece of source hunting it does build a good case for V.'s drawing on M. de Guérin's "La Bacchante" while writing *La jeune Parque.* Bémol's commentary on V.'s internal serpent as the source of psychological and mythic unity should be compared to Schroeder's parallel development of the serpent's erotic function in *La jeune Parque.*

Reviews: A. Schneider in RHL 57: 281–83, 1957 and in RLC 32:435–38, 1958.

Campbell, Grace. La synphore dans La jeune Parque de Paul Valéry. University, Miss., Romance monographs, 1975. 65 p.   **8727**

This essay is conceived as a contribution to stylistics taking *La jeune Parque* as the field of investigation. The principal innovation is the neologism of the title, "la synfore," defined as simple juxtaposition of the signified ("signifiés") where two elements are in some respect incompatible. An initial observation suggests that this technical term may be analogous to the standard surrealist definition of metaphor, less the metaphysical overtones, and to Royère's extension of the classical trope catachresis in his commentary on Baudelaire. These "synfores" are seen as molds in which the poet casts his ideas. It is particularly at this point that the usefulness of the essay is doubtful since it supposes a type of poetic composition quite alien to V.

Chisholm, A[lan] R[owland]. An approach to M. Valéry's Jeune Parque. Melbourne, Melbourne univ. press, 1938. 66 p. **8728**

This first monographic study of *La jeune Parque* is still of value, particularly for the thorough grasp of Schopenhauerian categories which informs it. Chisholm is keenly aware that the Parque's drama is related to individuation, and to its opposite, to phenomenal reality, and to the noumenal. His lively exegesis never loses sight of the physiological aspect of the poem and avoids the excessive abstraction which characterizes Alain's commentary. He appears to have been aware of a connection with the Apollonian ideal of Nietzsche. As regards discussion of poetic means, however, numerous recent studies have superseded this one.

Review: G. Milnes in MLR 34:110, 1939.

Cohen, Gustave. Initiation à La jeune Parque. *In his:* Essai d'explication du Cimetière marin suivi d'une glose analogue sur La jeune Parque.... Brussels-Paris, De Visscher-Gallimard, 1946. p. 99–127. **8729**

The first half of the essay is vaguely literary-historical; the remainder is a paraphrase of sections of V.'s poem. It has none of the qualities of lucid exposition and rationalist rigor that have assured the durability of his essay on *Le cimetière marin.*

Dragonetti, Roger. Les larmes ou l'impuissance du langage. *In his:* Aux frontières du langage poétique. Ghent, Rijksuniversiteit te Ghent, 1961. p. 149–56. (Romanica Gandensia, 9)   **8730**

The value of this brief text lies in its relating tears as a thematic device to others of V.'s works, notably the *Dialogue de l'arbre.* As a privileged theme, tears literally express the sense of the tragic, thereby canceling it out. In this respect he is undoubtedly correct in considering that tears signify for V. the powerlessness of language to convey a fundamental experiential reality.

Duchesne-Guillemin, Jacques. Essai sur La jeune Parque. Brussels-Paris, L'écran du monde-itinéraires, 1946. 87 p. *Also in his:* Etudes pour un Paul Valéry. *See* 8506. p. 43–96; 225–45.   **8731**

This essay constitutes the most influential close reading of the poem to date. Two aspects are particularly noteworthy: the reading of the poem as a dramatic construction in two acts, and the responsible use of the musical term modulation to characterize V.'s peculiar mode of composition. This latter contribution has more recently been applied to *Charmes* by L. J. Austin (*see* 8653). Of late there has been pertinent criticism directed at Duchesne-Guillemin's effort to reduce the poem to a chronological construction.

Reviews: D. Alden in RR 39:329–31, 1948; A. Fontainas in MerF 301:131–35, 1947.

———. Introduction to La jeune Parque. *In:* Paul Valéry. *See* 8482. p. 87–105.   **8732**

A genetic study which relates the psychological transformations of the speaker to an affective mode found frequently in the *Cahiers.* The similarities are quite remarkable. Particularly convincing is the treatment of the linking of sleep with death in the poem.

Dutton, K. R. Valéry's La jeune Parque: towards a critical close reading. AJFS 11:83–108, 1974.   **8733**

Analysis in minute detail of the "Harmonieuse MOI" passage and the relation of several of its images to other sections of the poem successfully identify a number of obscure details and situate their function in terms of what the author sees as an organic whole. Throughout his reading he comments pertinently on his predecessors, calling our attention to their respective merits and flaws. The article is intended as the necessary first step toward a complete critical reading. The opening pages, visibly added to justify presentation of the paper in a symposium on critical approaches to literature, are strained and not always helpful.

Fromilhague, René. La jeune Parque et l'autobiographie dans la forme. *In:* Paul Valéry contemporain. *See* 8486. p. 209–35.   **8734**

This contribution to the 1971 colloquium at Strasbourg was some ten years out of date at its conception, since it failed to take into account the manuscript study published by Ireland in 1962. His conclusion is that all is quite simple, a question of elementary geometry, and that the problem of different "MOI" in the poem can be reduced to identity. It is doubtful whether this approach will significantly advance our understanding.

Hytier, Jean. Etude de La jeune Parque. Ar 9:3–44, 1945. *Also in his:* Questions de littérature. New York-London, Columbia univ. press, 1967. p. 3–39.   **8735**

This is among the first extensive scholarly exegeses of the poem, being roughly contemporary with both Sørensen and Duchesne-Guillemin. One important convergence with the latter's interpretation must be noted: the stress placed on the oral aspect of the poem. Hytier's exegesis was the first to treat the poem in musical terms, from the prelude to the finale. Unlike Duchesne-Guillemin, he does not attempt to reconstruct a real chronology.

Ireland, G. W. La jeune Parque—genèse et exégèse. *In:* Entretiens sur Paul Valéry. *See* 8475. p. 85–101.   **8736**

This contribution to the Cerisy colloquium is related to the author's study of V.'s drafts of the sections of the poem, *infra*. Here he has chosen to treat the questions of genesis and exegesis as complementary, using *La jeune Parque* as his frame of reference. The discussion, p. 102–13, brings out aspects of the question not treated in depth in the oral communication.

————. Notes on the composition of La jeune Parque. ZFSL 72:1–27, 1962. **8737**

An important article which has already influenced the best recent studies of the gradual elaboration of *La jeune Parque*. More carefully than Nadal, Ireland scrutinized the typescripts and mss. in the collections of Mme Valéry, Monod and Mondor. Any serious student will have to deal with the article itself, as no résumé can suffice.

Köhler, Hartmut. Poésie et profondeur sémantique dans La jeune Parque de Paul Valéry. Nancy-Saint-Nicolas-du-Port, V. Idoux, 1965. viii, 48 p. (Univ. de Nancy. Publications du centre européen univ. Mémoires, 13) **8738**

Despite the somewhat schematic presentation of the subject imposed by the format of a short thesis, this stylistic examination of metaphoric structure in the poem can be of considerable value. The author proceeds along a dual axis of interpretation: diachronic (etymological) and synchronic (the poem as a duration in process). His work integrates and develops the findings of Sørensen, Schroeder and Nadal as well as an early article by E. Winkler.

Levaillant, Jean. La jeune Parque en question. *In:* Paul Valéry contemporain. *See* 8486. p. 137–51. **8739**

This sketch of a textual reading begins by pointing up the limitations of three types of exegesis that have been applied to *La jeune Parque:* the chronological rewriting (Duchesne-Guillemin); the Jungian analysis (Aigrisse); the intellectual/spiritual (Nadal). All three are dismissed as extra-textual. Perhaps the most telling aspect of this critique is the demonstration that the text cannot be reduced to a thematic center with variations. Study of the variants does bear this out. Without finally answering the question in any

but the most general terms the article invites us to ask ourselves anew how to approach the poem.

Lussy, Florence de. La genèse de La jeune Parque de Paul Valéry: essai de chronologie. Lettres modernes, Minard, 1975. 175 p. (Situation, 34) **8740**

Critical study of the poem enters a new era with the publication of this analysis of the fourteen known drafts. All but one (the final draft, in the Bibliothèque littéraire Jacques Doucet) have been in the collection of the Bibliothèque Nationale since 1972. Lussy has been able to reestablish the chronology and grouping of thirteen successive drafts from some 1450 sheets of paper of the most disparate types and dimensions. She has adopted a descriptive terminology sufficiently flexible to permit meaningful distinctions. This is the necessary first step toward an eventual critical edition to replace Nadal's, now recognized as textually incomplete.

Minard, Michel J. Typographie et littérature, notes de méthode (3). *In:* Lectures de Charmes. *See* 8477. p. 161–89. **8741**

Among these notes on the hazards of the printer's craft and its status in the study of literary texts there are a few pages of pertinent discussion of the "Harmonieuse MOI" (or MOI, or Moi) to be found in autograph, typed and printed versions of the poem. Given the considerable weight of commentary this passage has been made to bear, it is useful to consider by what means, not infrequently accidental, the text came to be printed in a specific type face. These aspects of textual bibliography, generally considered essential in work on earlier literary periods, have been unfortunately disregarded in our time.

Nadal, Octave. Genèse du poème; palettes. *In:* Paul Valéry. La jeune Parque. Club du meilleur livre, 1957. p. 163–205. *Also:* La création chez Paul Valéry. *In his:* A mesure haute. Mercure de France, 1964. p. 191–223. *Also (in part):* Palettes. *In:* Les critiques de notre temps et Valéry. *See* 8474. p. 168–74. **8742**

One of the capital studies of poetic composition; it ranks alongside Austin's commentary on *Le cimetière marin* for its impact on our understanding of V.'s approach to his long poems. Most important is the careful presentation of the "palettes" or range of tones from which V. worked in selecting words as much for their sonority, rhythm, modulation or euphony. Since Ireland's study of the mss., it has been necessary to revise some of Nadal's suppositions concerning states of the poem in course of composition.

————. Les larmes de l'esprit dans La jeune Parque. MerF 331:193–210, 1957. *Also:* Présentation. *In:* Paul Valéry. La jeune Parque. Club du meilleur livre, 1957. p. 75–95. *Also in his:* A mesure haute. Mercure de France, 1964. p. 165–80.   **8743**

Nadal, like Duchesne-Guillemin before him, divided the poem into two parts with the principal division at 1. 325. He stressed the tragic development of a circular dramatic action in which the function of tears is a modulation from the first to the second panel of the diptych. Nadal found the symbolic play of the tragedy to be outside the orbit of Christian symbolism, using a pre-Hellenic identification of the Swan-god with Apollo, the latter being assimilated elsewhere in the poem to the sun itself.

Parent, Pierre. Les leitmotive dans La jeune Parque. TLL 11(2):171–83, 1973.   **8744**

Analyzes the poem using the Wagnerian concept of Leitmotiv in its strict sense to account for a number of modulations, images of natural objects and forces, and other devices. The approach is potentially useful but a truly strong case is not made. Only the 1938 ed. set off the fifteen passages referred to here as distinct parts of the poem. The notions of psychic process are taken directly from Jung whose spiritualized symbolism orients the values assigned to the Leitmotive.

Schroeder, Lisa. Valérys Jeune Parque: Versuch einer Interpretation. Hamburg, Cram, de Gruyter, 1955. 251 p. (Hamburger romanistische Studien, Reihe A, Band 39)   **8745**

A significant study which has been largely ignored or dismissed. On the one hand, Schroeder's identification of M. de Guérin's "La Bacchante" as a source of V.'s poem has been passed over in favor of similar evidence presented the same year by Bémol. More importantly, Schroeder's somewhat exclusive empha-

sis on the erotic ran counter to the dominant trends in V. criticism. Her identification of the "Thyrse" as an a tribute of Dionysus does support her reading, however. Only recently have Walzer and Whiting given new strength to her findings.

Review: M. Bémol in RLC 32:438–40, 1958.

Sørensen, Hans. La poésie de Paul Valéry étude stylistique sur La jeune Parque Copenhagen, Universitetsforlaget i Aarhu nyt Nordisk Forlag—Arnold Busck, 1944 382 p.   **874**

The earliest and most complete stud of style in the poem, this monograph proceeds from Broendal's adaptation o Saussurian linguistics and is therefore remote from current structural analysis While not a literary reading of *La jeun Parque,* it contains the most exhaustiv analysis to date of semantic, syntacti and phonetic elements. Taken on it own terms this study remains of con siderable importance. Fully indexed.

Reviews: S. Johansen in OrL 2:251–64, 1944; K. Knauer in ZFSL 67:112–24, 1956.

Staub, Hans. Lumières de La jeune Parque *In:* Paul Valéry contemporain. *See* 8486 p. 301–23.   **874**

In his study of light as a theme th author was aware of earlier work b Bastet and Levaillant but apparentl did not know the work of Faivre o Lawler. Staub sees the play of phoneme supporting the theme in *La jeun Parque.* His careful distinction betwee light source and object illuminated goe some way toward accounting for som difficult metaphoric shadings. Th method employed permits Staub to ar rive at fundamental distinctions amon the "MOI" in the poem, wherea Fromilhague, in the same volume, at tempted to reduce them to a simplifie unity.

Charmes

Austin, Lloyd James. La genèse du Cimeti ère marin. CAIEF 3–5:251–69, 1953   **874**

This study antedates the author' publication of work on the mss. It i superseded by his two-part essay (*see* 8751).

――――. Les moyens du mystère chez Mallarmé et chez Valéry. CAIEF 15:103–17, 1963.   **8749**

A rapid review of diverse readings of "Ode secrète" opens the half of this brilliant article devoted to V. The author finds in K. Maurer's reading a valuable detail: Hercules is both the subject of the dance and the conqueror of Hercules. Extending this notion to the composition of the poem, Austin traces a movement from personal to impersonal, from intimate to cosmic, which provides both unity and symbolic meaning. Easily the best study of the poem as a whole. See also the 1974 contribution by Köhler which proposes an alternative to the overall symbolism of the poem.

――――. The negative plane tree. *In:* Paul Valéry. *See* 8480. p. 3–10.   **8750**

This article is an excellent complement to Lawler's. After reviewing the allegorizing glosses of "Au platane," Austin draws attention (in part through the adroit use of the *Cahiers*) to a more appropriate sense of symbolism. He agrees with Lawler on the point of the poem's irony, but demurs with respect to any supposition as to the independent life of the tree.

――――. Paul Valéry compose Le cimetière marin. MerF 317:577–608; 318:47–72, 1953.   **8751**

Has become the indispensable point of departure for subsequent scholarship. Analyzes the construction and orientation of three working versions of 7, 10 and 23 strophes respectively, and posits the existence of two unattested intermediary versions of 9 and 18 strophes. As the complete texts of the second and third versions remain unpublished, Austin's analysis stands as the most complete study of its type. Its greatest contribution is in the extremely careful description of substitution, addition and rejection of elements in these working versions.

Bergeron, Léandre. Le son et le sens dans quelques poèmes de Charmes de Paul Valéry. Aix-en-Provence, Ophrys, 1964. 2 v.   **8752**

Three poems are studied in detail: "Aurore" and "Palme" were chosen for their common origin and form; "Ebauche d'un serpent" for the comic opera effect V. attributed to it. The method employed follows rather closely the theoretical position of Guiraud in his *Langage et versification...*, but for the first time attempts to study critically the phonemic structure of complete poems. The results provide a firm basis for critical statements. The conclusions reached are surprisingly slim; clearly more sophisticated research is in order using this study as a point of departure. V. 2 is entirely composed of sets of recordings, one for each poem, in which phonetic transcriptions are superimposed on a reading of sound waves. These physical data are intended to serve as a check on the generalizations made in the study, but their usefulness is far from self-evident.

Bourjea, Serge. L'ombre-majuscule: une exégèse de La ceinture. *In:* Lectures de Charmes. *See* 8477. p. 121–45.   **8753**

Along with the articles by Vannier on *Le cimetière marin* (1972) and Köhler on "Ode secrète" (1974), Bourjea has provided, despite differences in approach, the elements of a study of V. as poet of the solar myth. Bourjea works back and forth among various poems and prose texts, using the *Cahiers* as they apply, in order to show that "La ceinture" has the characteristics of a metaphoric reduction to the essential of those elements that are elaborated more fully in several other texts.

Bouvet, Alphonse. Notes sur La pythie et L'ode secrète de P. Valéry. RSH 33:489–96, 1968.   **8754**

There is no positive attribution of the influence of Decharme's *Mythologie de la Grèce antique* on V.'s "La Pythie" or his "Ode secrète," although one may choose to suppose it from the evidence adduced by Bouvet. One has the gravest reservations about the rationalist reduction that Bouvet performs on V.'s poems. The result of his operation is an indifferent abstract content.

Champigny, Robert. The Zeno stanza. *In:* Paul Valéry. *See* 8480. p. 11–18.   **8755**

This brilliant demonstration of the poetic value of the Zeno stanza in *Le cimetière marin* argues against V.'s claim that the philosophical aspects of the poem merely represent coloring. Champigny points out that the competing claims of the Eleatics (Zeno in the poem) and Heraclitean thought form a symbolic representation of the fundamental oppositions in the poem. In his discussion of Zeno's paradoxes the principal new contribution is to relate the "son" of l. 4 to the paradox of the grain of millet.

Chisholm, Alan Rowland. Moods of the intellect in Le cimetière marin. *In:* Paul Valéry. *See* 8482. p. 72–86. **8756**

An analysis of the poem in terms of the speaker's shifting intellectual moods. While valid on the plane of intellect, this reading needs to be completed by others more concerned with formal devices. Taken on its own terms, a quite admirable essay.

Cohen, Gustave. Essai d'explication du Cimetière marin précédé d'un avant-propos de Paul Valéry au sujet du Cimetière marin. Gallimard, 1933. III p. **8757**

This perdurable essay has exercised its influence for decades despite periodic demonstrations of its inadequacy. Witness the relatively recent Spanish-language edition (1967). The thoroughgoing rationalism of Cohen's classic explication continues to appeal to a view of V. the calculating poet-philosopher, and no amount of argument to the contrary seems capable of dislodging it.

Reviews: E. Gianturco in RR 24: 243–45, 1933; P. Snodgrass in BA 8: 70, 1934.

Curtius, Ernst Robert. Paul Valéry; Gedichte von Paul Valéry in deutscher Übertragung. *In his:* Französischer Geist im zwanzigsten Jahrhundert. Bern-Munich, Francke, 1952. p. 356–82; 383–404. **8758**

The most enduring aspect of Curtius' essay on V. is his identification of the serpent as V.'s special mythological symbol. His interpretation of the poetry is markedly Hegelian; he isolates three fundamental tones in *Charmes:* intellectuality, sensuality and sorrow. This reading works best on "Ebauche d'un serpent." He includes his own German

version of the poem as well as versions of *Le cimetière marin*, "Palme," "Au platane," and "L'abeille." Curtius' essay has had a considerable influence on German-language criticism of V.

Dragonetti, Roger. Rythme et silence chez Paul Valéry. *In his:* Aux frontières du langage poétique. Ghent, Rijksuniversiteit te Ghent, 1961. p. 157–68. (Romanica Gandensia, 9) **8759**

By considering "Les pas" in its relation to, and as an investigation of, the nature and function of rhythm, Dragonetti has freed the poem from the facile paraphrase that has plagued it heretofore. His gloss on the word "lit," which he interprets etymologically as foundation eliminates from the poem the romantic interest that has been found there. Then the steps of the title can be linked, thematically as well as technically, to the phenomenon of Athikté's dance in *L'âme et la danse*. The result is a considerable net gain for the poem as a serious piece. It also demonstrates once again what damage has been done to the shorter poems by monothematic readings of *Charmes*.

Duchesne-Guillemin, Jacques. Etude de Charmes de Paul Valéry. Brussels-Paris, L'écran du monde-Les deux sirènes, 1947. 183 p. *Also (partially) in his:* Etudes pour un Paul Valéry. *See* 8506. p. 97–155. **8760**

The first study to approach the poems from the standpoint of technique: musicality and metrics are the organizing concepts of the opening chapters. An appendix on the order of the poems in the collection was aimed at Noulet's thesis based on a disposition of the poems occurring in one edition only. The chapters mentioned and the appendix, upgraded to a chapter, were reprinted in 1964. The material not reproduced is composed largely of short studies that had been superseded in the intervening years.

Reviews: H. Johnston in FS 3:369–70, 1949; R. Lang in BA 22:277, 1948.

Eigeldinger, Marc. L'art poétique de Paul Valéry—Aurore. *In his:* Poésie et tendances. Neuchâtel, A la Baconnière, 1945. p. 43–54. **8761**

Approaching "Aurore" as an *ars poetica*, Eigeldinger tends to distill its substantial quintessence, which he presents as a generally valid statement concerning poetic composition. His analysis does have the merit of following carefully the sequential and strophic development of the poetic statement. Form is considered only as an aspect of the thematic reflection on poetry, i.e. as the idea of form.

Gelsey, Elizabeth A. de. L'architecture du Cimetière marin. RHL 63:458–64, 1963.
                                                    8762
The significance of this article far exceeds what might be expected of its modest proportions. Roughly half is devoted to a schematic review of the strophic grouping used in the principal readings of the poem. Most importantly perhaps de Gelsey's reading is based on the rhythmic and melodic alternation between two poles. These poles are conceived as thematic, thus permitting the author to assign subtitles to the dominant theme in each grouping. The insistence upon the thematic subgroups is the weak point in an otherwise convincing argument.

Gerstel, Eva-Maria. The creative process in two early manuscripts of Paul Valéry's Fragments du Narcisse. Sym 23:16–37, 1969.   **8763**
There is an initial distortion of perspective in the claim that all V.'s work beginning with Teste is but a version of his Narcissus myth. The article's value is in the presentation of two ms. versions of the "Fragments..." recently acquired by Harvard's Houghton Library. It is unfortunate that the ms. versions are not reproduced within the article which proceeds line by line through the mss. The conclusion offers a schematic representation of both syntactic and phonetic modifications in the poem.

Grubbs, Henry A. Two treatments of a subject: Proust's La regarder dormir and Valéry's La dormeuse. PMLA 71:900–09, 1956.   **8764**
The author's stated intent—to distinguish between narrative technique and poetic form using a given theme—is a laudable one. The results are somewhat marred by a reading of V.'s poem that is not always convincing. Grubbs indulges in conjecture as to which lines

were gifts of the gods (5 and 9 are his best bets).

Huber, Egon. Zu Paul Valérys Gedicht La ceinture. ZFSL 72:155–60, 1962.   **8765**
Huber compares V.'s text with Rilke's translation in an attempt to grasp the reason for some of the oddities in the latter. He adds the still more curious interpretations of Walzer and Noulet, not to mention Alain who had given up in despair. Huber's descriptive paraphrase, however superior to that of his predecessors, shares with them the persistent desire to extract a content which, in this case, is related to a Hegelian portrait of the artist.

Ince, W. N. An exercise in artistry: Valéry's Les grenades. RR 55:190–204, 1964. **8766**
Ince's broader, more synthesizing commentary on "Les grenades" serves as a good counterpoint to Lawler's reading, which develops more fully the formal implications. Ince's hypothesis, that the Petits poèmes MCMXVII contained a version of the poem, was confirmed by Lawler.

——. The sonnet Le vin perdu of Paul Valéry. FS 10:40–54, 1960.   **8767**
Following a suggestion first made by Noulet, Ince pursues a rigorous examination of similarities between the poem as symbol and that part of "La crise de l'esprit" which articulates its root metaphor. Ince finds a common source in Poincaré's enunciation of Carnot's Principle (in La valeur de la science). The sonnet is made to bear the weight of some heavy theorizing in the physical sciences.

Köhler, Hartmut. Interprétation, à la lumière des Cahiers, de quelques poèmes de Paul Valéry. In: Paul Valéry contemporain. See 8486. p. 353–76.   **8768**
The poems under consideration are "Fragments du Narcisse," "Intérieur," and "Ode secrète." The comments on the first two are either fragmentary or lacking in sufficient focus to alter appreciably the reading of those poems. Not so for "Ode secrète," the source of which Köhler believes he has found in W. G. Cox's book; Mallarmé had given a French translation of it entitled Les dieux antiques. Köhler sees the poem as the analog of the solar myth in which

Hercules (in the much debated second half) figures the dying god.

Lausberg, Heinrich. Das Sonett Les grenades von Paul Valéry. Opladen, Westdeutscher Verlag, 1971. 224 p. (Wissenschaftliche Abhandlungen der Rheinisch-Westfälischen Akademie der Wissenschaften, 46) **8769**

A very thorough monographic study of the syntactic, semantic, rhythmic and phonetic structure of the sonnet. The handling of philological method is impeccable; Lausberg strives for a synthesis beyond the minute analyses to which he subjects each element of the poem. In his literary-historical considerations Lausberg draws together materials which illuminate other aspects of V.'s work. Contains a valuable word index printed in appendix. For completeness this is not likely to be surpassed.

Lawler, James R. Form and meaning in Valéry's Le cimetière marin. Melbourne, Melbourne univ. press, 1959. 41 p. *Trans. in his:* Lecture de Valéry.... *See* 8772. p. 193–229. **8770**

Lawler's study is the second to stress the formal aspects of the finished poem and their determination of its meaning. He uses to good effect the manuscript study done by Austin but does not reach the same conclusions in all cases. The idea of form involves a more complex composition of elements for Lawler than it had for Weinberg.

Reviews: E. Noulet in RUB 13:367–71, 1960–61; M. Smith in EspCr 2:47–48, 1962; N. Suckling in AUMLA 13: 87–89, 1960.

————.. An ironic elegy: Valéry's Au platane. FR 36:339–51, 1963. *Also (partially) in his:* Lecture de Valéry.... *See* 8772. p. 40–52. **8771**

Lawler brings to the subject of the evolution from "Pour votre Hêtre Suprême" to "Au platane" the benefit of having consulted an untitled draft dating from June 1918. He comments on the apparent romantic haste and enthusiasm which would give way, in the final version, to what Lawler calls tragic irony: the poignant contrast between desire and the ineluctable negation of desire.

————. Lecture de Valéry, une étude de Charmes. Presses univ. de France, 1963. viii, 271 p. **8772**

The first study of *Charmes* to introduce elements of the Anglo-American "new criticism" into French-language commentary on the major poems. Lawler submits each poem to a close reading in which formal considerations frequently take precedence over commentary on theme or subject. His work thus stands out sharply against that of Cohen and Noulet. Individual exegeses benefit greatly from Lawler's study of unpublished mss. of the poems. Like Noulet and Gallois, Lawler sees a secret architectural unity in the composition of *Charmes,* but he disagrees with both as to its significance. He correctly stresses the great diversity of form (strophic, rhythmic and metric) in *Charmes.*

Reviews: L. Austin in RHL 65:148–49, 1965; A. Chisholm in AJFS 1:222–24, 1964; H. Grubbs in RR 55:306–09, 1964; J. Mathews in MLN 82:128–34, 1967; E. Noulet in MerF 1216:327–31, 1965.

————. The meaning of Valéry's Le vin perdu. FS 14:340–51, 1960. *Also (partially) in his:* Lecture de Valéry.... *See* 8772. p. 183–89. **8773**

Lawler replies directly to Ince, restating the basic points of his argument. The symbolism is transformed from the domain of physics to that of Christianity, as it had been in "La crise de l'esprit." On this point Lawler also finds Maurer unconvincing. He himself reads the poem as "a perfect moment of the creative mind," a position he can integrate to his view of *Charmes* as a unified whole.

Macrí, Oreste. Il cimitero marino di Paul Valéry. Florence, Sansoni, 1947. 115 p. **8774**

The essay on metrics and metaphysics in the *Cimetière marin* happily concentrates on the history of metric variations in odes written in French and in Italian. V.'s metric originality appears to good advantage with V. emerging as a master of the ode. A commentary on V.'s poem follows the text, printed in French and Italian on facing pages. The reading of the poem for the most part follows Cohen while providing some new philological glosses. Macrí is particularly complete in his treatment of the Eleatic tone of V.'s poem.

Maiorana, Maria Teresa. L'ombre d'Hamlet dans Le cimetière marin. RLC 42:346–65, 1968.   8775

The author puts forward the startling claim that the speaker of the *Cimetière marin* is a repressed Hamlet. On the positive side there are a number of striking resemblances in detail: the worm, the dead hour of twelve, V.'s noon corresponding to Shakespeare's midnight, and so on. Such a static analysis cannot account for the metaphoric development of the poem; moreover, the article supposes a (repressed) influence where, in all probability, we are dealing with a striking symbolic isomorphism that arises when two artists approach the theme of life and death with an accent on dramatic monolog.

Maka-De Schepper, Monique. Le thème de la Pythie chez Paul Valéry. Belles lettres, 1969. 276 p. (Bibliothèque de la faculté de philosophie et lettres de l'univ. de Liège, 184)   8776

The first half of the study, the more valuable, is devoted to "La Pythie" as a poem. Even here the author's approach is thematic. The result of her thesis is a relatively complex and very interesting treatment of a poem that had not received its due. This study may change that. Whether or not the Pythia is a dominant theme in V., serving to synthesize others, is still an open question. The approach of Sabbagh (*see* 8605) is broader in range and methodology, promising more shading and less reduction to a dominant element.

Review: R. Geen in RR 63:72–74, 1972.

Maugendre, L.-A. Eusèbe de Bremond d'Ars et Paul Valéry. PenC 71:73–81, 1961.   8777

Maugendre presents a three-page note by Bremond d'Ars, printed *in toto* on p. 79–81. We learn that the latter's poem "Désert" was written to exorcise the Luciferian effect of V.'s "Ebauche d'un serpent." Surely one of the most astonishing manifestations of the fortune of V.'s poetry.

Maurer, Karl. Interpretationen zur späteren Lyrik Paul Valérys. Munich, L. Lehnen, 1954. 252 p.   8778

This dense and supremely scholarly exegesis concentrates almost exclusively on the two short poems "Ode secrète" and "Le vin perdu." The comparative philological method, as Maurer applied it to "Ode secrète," has subsequently provided the point of departure for Austin's sensitive reading. While Maurer's method may be said to weigh down V.'s poems, it does, through contrastive analysis, bring out their originality.

Reviews: M. Bémol in RLC 29:418–19, 1955; S. Johansen in OrL 12:255–56, 1957.

Mossop, D. J. L'architecture du Cimetière marin. IL 16:89–92, 1964.   8779

Mossop accepts the strophic organization recently proposed by de Gelsey. His own contribution to the fundamental question of the relation of the parts to the whole is to refuse her static/thematic analysis of their import. He stresses rather the question of the dynamics of each group of strophes and the direction each takes. This position is both sound and fruitful, as it restores to the poem a measure of the extraordinary inner tension and coherence which characterize it.

Moutote, Daniel. L'égotisme poétique de Valéry dans Charmes. *In:* Lectures de Charmes. See 8477. p. 29–48.   8780

A fundamental presupposition underlies this study: *Charmes* is an organic composition with a unifying principle. Moutote posits an ideal Self as the synthetic construction organizing the larger whole. V.'s egotism is studied in terms of his own application of the concept to Stendhal (1927) and Descartes (1937), as well as the texts of the Teste cycle. It is doubtful, however, in light of several recent contributions to the question, whether this reflexive act of consciousness (egotism) can be assimilated to the "MOI pur" as Moutote attempts to do.

Noulet, Emilie. Aurore, essai d'exégèse. *In:* Lectures de Charmes. See 8477. p. 103–19.   8781

Noulet extends to the exegesis of "Aurore" the theory of the thematic unity of *Charmes* that she has defended against all challengers since 1927. The absolute preeminence of theme for Noulet can be seen in this typical claim: the reason for the odd-numbered metric foot (seven syllables) and the odd number of stanzas (nine) corresponds to the theme of the poem: in the early light of dawn thought, like light, is unstable, uncertain, in flux. Whence the choice of strophic form and of meter. The non sequitur seems not to trouble this critic's certainty of being in the right.

————. Tone in the poems of Paul Valéry. *In:* Paul Valéry. *See* 8482. p. 39–50. *Also in her:* Le ton poétique. Corti, 1971. p. 167–83. **8782**

Relies heavily on the notion of a conceptual architecture (i.e., in the disposition of the poems) in *Charmes* to support the argument that tone is a fusion of the general theme and its momentary variation in a specific rhythm and meter. This article runs counter to most recent criticism in positing the primacy of the idea in the poem as the element from which form derives. The article reads better in the original French of the 1971 printing.

Onimus, Jean. Lectures du Rameur. *In:* Lectures de Charmes. *See* 8477. p. 147–60. **8783**

A literary-historical introduction leads to the working hypothesis that "Le rameur" is an allegory and, as such, readable on many levels. Onimus reviews several readings: psychoanalytic (Bastet), metaphysical (Walzer), and mystical (his own). There is little here that is really fresh, but the article is useful as an orientation for further reading and reflection.

Parent, Monique. Cohérence et résonance dans le style de Charmes de Paul Valéry. Klincksieck, 1970. 223 p. **8784**

The first of the two major divisions of the book, devoted to the associations ("résonance") among elements of V.'s lexicon, is open to serious criticism. A statistical table of images found in *Charmes* is used to regroup thematic material around two poles, the elemental and the human. These are commented on as successive units following a principle of association which frequently results in the impression that *Charmes* is to be considered a forest of symbols. Further, the commentary in most cases reduces V.'s most successfully ambiguous symbols to one-dimensional images. The second major division, concerning the means used by V. to obtain coherence in *Charmes,* is on more solid ground. Again, the method used is drawn from linguistics and is intended to build upon the contributions of Guiraud and Henry. Here the commentary on stylistic devices is generally reliable.

Reviews: W. Ince in FS 27: 352–53, 1973; M. Lecuyer in RR 64:315–16, 1973; D. Parris in MLR 68:424–25, 1973; Y. Scalzitti in MP 71:105–07, 1973.

Pieltain, Paul. Métamorphoses d'un fragment du Narcisse de Paul Valéry. CahAT 4:29–37, 1962. **8785**

Studies in detail the transformation of that part of "Narcisse parle" (1891) which V. incorporated in the first of three "Fragments du Narcisse" in *Charmes.* Attention is given as well to the intermediary version of *L'album de vers anciens* (1920). The final version is judged superior in all respects, although the reasons for this superiority (musicality is preferable to preciosity, etc.) are not altogether convincing.

Pommier, Jean. Le cimetière marin de Paul Valéry. AUS 10:213–228, 1961. *Also in his:* Dialogues avec le passé. Nizet, 1967. p. 197–217. **8786**

Accepting the documentation and commentary provided by Austin in his edition of the *Cimetière marin* (1954), Pommier queries whether V.'s visit to Cette in July 1914 may not have provided the experience which later found its way into the poem. A further thought linking the early title "Mare nostrum" with the Italian campaign of autumn 1917 provides a reasonable hypothesis for V.'s return, at that very date, to the theme of the resting place of his Italian forebears. Most of the commentary deals with the appropriateness of, and occasionally the literary echoes found in, specific images.

Schmitz, Alfred. Valéry et la tentation de l'absolu. Essai d'analyse du Cimetière marin. Gembloux, J. Duculot, 1964. 140 p. 14 pl. **8787**

The principal contribution of this reading of *Le cimetière marin* is in the diagram, p. 137–39, in which the concepts of the return, of immanence as point of departure and terminus after several "temptations" of the absolute (transcendence), are set forth in an easily readable format. A further advantage is that Schmitz has grasped the poem in its dynamics and has avoided the reductions of static analysis. His attempt to tie the movement and articulations of the poem to Bergsonian thought is much less likely to meet with critical acceptance.

Tauman, Léon. Réflexions sur *Le cimetière marin.* EFL 1:59–71, 1964. **8788**

This essay is a free play of associations radiating out from the images and terms of the poem, through other poems —verse and in the rough—on through the *Cahiers,* and back again. A certain gratuitousness pervades the whole.

Thomas, Jacques. Source de *La fausse morte* de Paul Valéry. RHL 61:238–42, 1961. **8789**

The author proposes that the source of V.'s poem is to be found in the third strophe of Mathurin Régnier's *Stances:* "O mourir agréable!" The very concept of source as it is used here is doubtful, as V. himself pointed out with acerbic wit.

Vannier, Bernard. Horlogerie. *In:* Paul Valéry. *See* 8484. p. 669–81. **8790**

There are a number of useful observations of detail: in its overall construction *Le cimetière marin* is a day poem 24 (hours/stanzas) x 60 (minutes/feet); the paradox of the Zeno stanza is verbal/rhythmic rather than philosophical; the noonday sun is identified with Apollo. These observations need to be incorporated in a more complete reading, something the present article does not pretend to be.

Venettis, Jean. Exégèse poétique de l'Ebauche d'un serpent de Paul Valéry. Eds. de la palladienne, 1941. 54 p. **8791**

The bulk of the essay is in the form of an *explication de texte* which proceeds from a view of poetry that is both rationalist and mimetic. The author re-

fuses to read the poem as a burlesque piece despite his awareness of V.'s statement to that effect to Fr. Porché. This critical posture leads to considerable commentary on V.'s philosophical errors and to the inevitable conclusion that, in this poem, he is but a neo-Mallarméan virtuoso.

Wäber, G. Le rameur: eine Gedichtinterpretation zu Paul Valéry, Charmes. ZFSL 75:365–74, 1965. **8792**

The close reading, stanza by stanza, and pertinent remarks on form make this the most thorough commentary on the poem to date. Future studies will be obliged to begin here.

Weinberg, Bernard. An interpretation of Valéry's *Le cimetière marin.* RR 38:133–58, 1947. *Also in his:* The limits of symbolism. Chicago-London, Univ. of Chicago press, 1966. p. 322–52. **8793**

Weinberg's method is one of immanent reading characteristic of the new Aristotelians; it seeks a principle of unity and a poetic justification of the form (poetic structure here being conceived as different from any other). The principle of unity is found in the tripartite extended metaphor—sea, cemetery, spectator—and is pursued in terms of a binomial surface/depth tension. The chief weakness may be the inability to account for the centrality of the sun and its relation to the repeated images of circularity. Nor does this method allow for commentary on the extraordinary exploitation of the phonemic qualities of language in the poem.

Review: C. Rosenberg in ArQ 23: 374, 76, 1967.

———. Valéry—Les grenades. *In his:* The limits of symbolism. *See* 8793. p. 353–64. **8794**

The real contribution of this close reading is to have situated the poem in the tradition of the sonnet, the symbolist sonnet in particular. Weinberg concludes that "Les grenades" is not only a perfectly traditional sonnet, it is a distinguished one. The analysis of metaphoric structure is exemplary of this critic's approach to poetry. It shares both the strengths and the weaknesses of his earlier study of *Le cimetière marin.*

Pièces Diverses & Miscellaneous

Gheorghe, Ion. Le mythe de la création par la musique chez Paul Valéry et Lucien Blaga. RSH 34:275–82, 1969.   **8795**

This article on "Amphion" can usefully be considered in terms of a mythic elaboration of the synthetic function of poetic activity analyzed by Ince earlier (*see* 8624). Consult also the two studies by Stewart (*see* 8607, 8608) and Devoto's "De Amphion a Eupalinos" (*see* 8927).

Lawler, James R. A la fontaine de Psyché. Bib 36:12–16, 1968.   **8796**

The focus of the article is on "Equinoxe" in terms of V.'s concept of the complementarity of sensation, affect and abstraction. The dynamic structure of the poem is set forth in a sequential commentary of the twelve stanzas.

————. Light in Valéry. AJFS 6:348–75, 1969. *Incorporated in:* O roi des ombres fait de flamme.... *In his:* The poet as analyst. *See* 8518. p. 166–200.   **8797**

An essay on "Neige," "A l'aurore," and "Heure." Each poem is concerned with a different quality of light: first light in "Neige;" dawn as a loving woman in "A l'aurore;" the dazzling light of a divine visitant in "Heure." The study of the mss. is exemplary. Lawler notes that, as theme, light for V. is frequently linked to violence of feeling, and is not exclusively the focus of mental control and formal discipline.

————. The serpent, the tree and the crystal. EspCr 4:34–40, 1964. *Also* (*rev.*): Valéry's pureté. *In his:* The language of French symbolism. Princeton, Princeton univ. press, 1969. p. 185–217.   **8798**

The point of departure is the oft-noted paradox between V.'s ultra-rationalism and a certain ill-defined mysticism. A synthesis is suggested in the metaphoric complex of the title: serpent, tree, crystal, the appearance, function and meaning of which are traced throughout the *Cahiers*. These are taken to be the imaginary objects in which the divided mind creates its unity. The tree metaphor has since been treated exhaustively by Laurette (*see* 8599). In the study of "Equinoxe" which makes up the bulk of the article,

Lawler adduces an organic connection with several poems of *Charmes* through the recurrence of the three imaginary objects.

————. The Shipwreck of Paul Valéry. EFL 3:38–64, 1966. *Also* (*revised*): Je vois le Christ... *In his:* The poet as analyst. *See* 8518. p. 1–35.   **8799**

In his analysis of "Sinistre," Lawler does a convincing job of adducing an intention to commemorate the twenty-fifth anniversary of V.'s traumatic Genoa night. He places V.'s shipwreck motif in the illustrious company assembled by Auden in *The enchafèd flood*, then adds another name—Arthur Gordon Pym. Within the poem Lawler finds a pattern of references to "Le bateau ivre" which he exploits systematically in the commentary on the first ms. version. Poe's mariner is considered to be a kind of conceptual motif. The final pages are especially successful in communicating the force of the poem.

————. Valéry's later poetry. AJFS 4:295–322, 1967. *Also:* Je pense..., je sens... *In his:* The poet as analyst. *See* 8518. p. 201–29.   **8800**

Lawler treats directly the poems "L'oiseau cruel," "Sonnet d'Irène," "Chanson à part," and "Le philosophe et La jeune Parque." One may query, after reading Lawler's skillful exegeses, whether these poems finally merit the importance he ascribes to them.

Nadal, André. Abeille spirituelle, poème inconnu et art poétique de Paul Valéry. Nîmes, Chastanier frères et Bertrand, 1968. 32 p.   **8801**

A detailed explication of the most frequently cited of the *Douze poèmes* first published by O. Nadal in 1959. Numerous parallels with the poems of *Charmes* serve to situate it in the V. canon. The claim made for "Abeille spirituelle" as an *ars poetica*, however, is exaggerated.

Narrative: Teste Cycle

Crow, Christine M. Teste parle—the question of a potential artist in Valéry's M. Teste. *In:* Paul Valéry. *See* 8482. p. 157–68.   **8802**

Taking M. Teste as one of V.'s principal masks, Crow investigates the dilemma of non-verbal creation for the writer. The critical point of view adopted tends to treat V.'s art as mimetic and Teste as a person. Some distortion of perspective results.

Goldmann, Lucien. Valéry: Monsieur Teste. *In his:* Structures mentales et création culturelle. 2nd. ed. Eds. Anthropos, 1970. p. 171–78.   8803

Useful in pointing up the type of importance Descartes has for V.'s hero of the mind. Goldmann's conclusions may appear unconvincing; they are not sufficiently prepared; but the path he has opened here is worthy of further exploration.

Hackett, C. A. A note on the Album de Monsieur Teste. FS 18:33–35, 1964. 8804

This brief note deserves mention for its indication of an area that has yet to be adequately explored: V.'s nine illustrations for the *Album de Monsieur Teste,* published months before V.'s death. Hackett's summary description of the illustrations completes his presentation.

———. Teste and La soirée avec Monsieur Teste. FS 21:111–24, 1967.   8805

The article functions mainly to draw together intelligently and in easily digestible form the best that had previously been published on the subject. Hackett's commentary on the *Soirée...* adds a useful generic category: the mock-heroic narrative.

Ince, W. N. Composition in Valéry's writings on Monsieur Teste. *In:* Paul Valéry. *See* 8480. p. 19–27.   8806

Concentrates on V.'s authorial strategy in *La soirée...* and in the *Lettre de Madame Emilie Teste.* The article is distinguished by its focus on stylistic devices rather than on psychology and some other subjects (Cartesianism, Bergsonism) which have for so long dominated criticism of this work.

———. La promenade avec Monsieur Teste. *In:* Paul Valéry. *See* 8482. p. 169–84.
8807

An examination of the manuscript variants of "La promenade avec M. Teste" has revealed several important

details. A ms. from 1897 or 1898 contains the unusual expression "le vent simple" which reappears in the opening line of *La jeune Parque.* A drawing accompanying one ms. presents the relation Self/World through an image of container/contained using contiguous circles. Another represents Teste as a Parisian Heraclitus, an image which Ince interprets as a very un-Testian mystical reconciliation of opposites. This last prelogical, non-analytical representation suffices to explain why this text was not to figure in V.'s Testian canon.

Lecuyer, Maurice A. Etude de la prose de Paul Valéry dans La soirée avec Monsieur Teste. Lettres modernes, Minard, 1964. 56 p. (ALM, 55)   8808

The linguistic orientation of the study and its very limited scope—the analysis of three paragraphs—restrict its range of application. Certain of the author's remarks, notably those concerning rhythm and the production of phonemes, will be found useful in further explorations of V.'s prose style.

Reviews: J.-Cl. Chevalier in FM 34: 315–16, 1966; H. Grubbs in MLJ 49:264, 1965; F. Jenkins in RPh 19: 392–93, 1965–66.

Levaillant, Jean. [Teste]. *In:* Les critiques de notre temps et Valéry. *See* 8474. p. 88–95.   8809

In this extract from a recent Paris doctoral dissertation, Levaillant finds Narcissism not as a theme or a metaphor but inscribed stylistically in the syntax of the narrative. If the thesis can be made to hold it will represent a significant advance for formalist stylistics in V. studies. These few pages are for the moment an insufficient test of its validity.

Rey, Alain. Monsieur Teste de haut en bas. Poét 9:80–88, 1972.   8810

In spite of a rather precious style, this textual reading of the *Soirée...* (with allusions to the rest of the cycle) promises to alter our view of a part of V.'s work that had become overgrown with redundant commentary. This short article ranks with the recent discussion of mss. as a first rate analysis.

Vogel, Christine. Monsieur Teste et quelques-uns de ses précurseurs (recherche de quelques traits constants du héros cérébral; esquisse d'une évolution). *In:* Paul Valéry contemporain. *See* 8486. p. 251–76.   **8811**

The article concerns itself primarily with situating Ed. Teste in a tradition beginning with Poe's Dupin (discovered many times before), Huysmans' Des Esseintes and Villiers' Tullia Fabriana in "Isis;" R. de Gourmont's hero in *Sixtine* and Mallarmé's in "Igitur." If one takes these as the author intends—not as sources but as more or less similar types—the article has considerable merit. V.'s Teste then appears to us as the perfection of a type that had been tried and modified an impressive number of times.

Narrative: Other Texts

Dazzi, Manilo. Meditazione su un testo di Paul Valéry: London Bridge. RasI 3: 307–16, 1948.   **8812**

This reading of "London Bridge" stresses the function and significance of the visual reduction of the phenomenal world. The author underscores quite admirably a fundamental aspect of V.'s poetics, but his neo-realist position leads him to question certain of their implications. Despite the skepticism of Dazzi's conclusion, the value of his article is assured by the quality of the analysis.

Loubère, J. A. E. Valéry utopiste. RSH 36: 525–42, 1971.   **8813**

Among the *Histoires brisées,* Loubère gives special attention to "L'île Xiphos" and to those in which the character named Gozon appears. He is considered as a link to V.'s conception of utopia. This article constitutes a very interesting first approach to a fascinating subject that has received little attention. The author is aware that the *Histoires brisées* are fragmentary creative extensions of V.'s politics of mind.

Noulet, Emilie. Un texte inédit de Paul Valéry—Agathe. BARLLF 35:108–16, 1957. *Also:* SynB 12:145–51, 1957. *Also in her:* Suite valéryenne. Brussels, Eds. des artistes, 1959. p. 9–84. *And in her:*

Suites—Mallarmé, Rimbaud, Valéry. Nizet, 1964. p. 185–96.   **8814**

V.'s *Agathe* has yet to stimulate much significant commentary, probably because of its publication in a limited ed. Noulet's article made no claim other than to present a long-awaited text.

Raymond, Marcel. Sur une définition de la poésie. *In:* Paul Valéry, essais et témoignages inédits. *See* 8488. p. 37–47.   **8815**

Raymond adumbrates a comparison with Bergson's *Le rire.* Finding the results inconclusive, he falls back on V.'s theory of sensibility as a locus of exchange, concluding that expressivity in poetry is an ideal equivalence or equilibrium which relies on something akin to Eliot's objective correlative. Brief but profitable.

Dialogues

Bonfanti, Giosue. Motivi per un esame di Eupalinos. Aut 41:443–60, 1957.   **8816**

An essay for the general reader proceeding by gradual approaches to the dialog, from the exterior aspect to its inner workings. Useful only as an introduction in view of the more thorough scholarly commentary on *Eupalinos....*

Cassina, Gino. Paul Valéry, poète de la danse. *In:* Paul Valéry, essais et témoignages inédits. *See* 8488. p. 95–103. **8817**

Sketches briefly but accurately the centrality of bodies in motion, the pure act of metamorphosis, to V.'s poetics. Working back and forth from *L'âme et la danse* to *Poésies,* he establishes convincingly the importance of this concept for affective form in V.'s work.

Daniel, Vera J. Eupalinos: rencontre de thèmes anciens. *In:* Entretiens sur Paul Valéry. *See* 8476. p. 113–24.   **8818**

This communication to the 1971 Montpellier colloquium should be read as the logical extension of her 1967 article. It incorporates the findings of Jallat's 1967 study of "Valéry et le mécanisme" (*see* 8631). For Daniel the ideal of construction as it appears in *Eupalinos...* is the necessary complement to V.'s abstract analysis of the model. Built finally upon nothing—not a material edifice—it stands in relation to death in V.'s world.

———. Valéry's Eupalinos and his early reading. FS 21:229–35, 1967.   **8819**

This short article is a complement to the critical apparatus in the author's edition of *Eupalinos*... and *L'âme et la danse,* published in the same year. It examines at close range the relevance, for V.'s dialog on the architect, of his readings in Owen Jones' *Grammar of ornament* as well as his somewhat better known reading of Viollet-le-Duc. Daniel concludes that both were undoubtedly present as available source material when V. composed his *Eupalinos*....

Duchesne-Guillemin, J. L'âme et la danse revisitées. FS 23:362–77, 1969.   **8820**

Duchesne-Guillemin attempts to situate *L'âme et la danse* with respect to V.'s works roughly contemporaneous with it. He accounts for the particular erotic flavor in terms of notations in the *Cahiers* and biographical data on V.'s liaison with Catherine Pozzi. These are in turn related to the physiological motif by the successive metaphoric expressions of Athikté's dance, the core metaphor of the work.

———. Les dialogues de Paul Valéry. CAIEF 24:75–91, 1972.   **8821**

Drawing extensively on the *Cahiers* the author reconstructs a history of V.'s preoccupation with dialog as a form. He demonstrates that V.'s theater is itself an extension of this genre into which V., like Lucian, consistently injected comedy. Poe is cited as an early model. V.'s liaison with Renée Vautier is linked to both *L'idée fixe* and the project of a tragedy on the theme of Stratonice.

Fehr, A. J. A. Les dialogues antiques de Paul Valéry, essai d'analyse d'Eupalinos ou l'architecte. Leiden, Universitaire Pers, 1960. 182 p.   **8822**

A major contribution to the study of *Eupalinos,* this essay sums up the best previous work on the subject in scholarly fashion. Fehr's study of techniques of composition permits him to make useful comparisons with *L'âme et la danse* and *Dialogue de l'arbre.* He wisely eschews any generalized source hunting in Plato but does point

out convincing parallels between the opening of the *Symposium* and the *Phaedrus* and that of V.'s *Eupalinos*.... One of the most significant general observations concerns the apparent similarity between V.'s use of the negation of opposites and the Hegelian dialectic. Reviews: H. Decker in Sym 17:66–68, 1963; E. Noulet in RHL 62:283–85, 1962; J. Robinson in MLR 56:278–79, 1961; R. Wiarda in LT 722–25, 1960.

Got, Maurice. Assomption de l'espace: à propos de l'Ame et la danse. Cercle du livre, 1957. 123 p. *Also:* SEDES, 1966. 103 p.   **8823**

This work is a commentary on the dance and on the soul. It bears little direct relation to V.'s dialog, which serves rather as a pretext. The one worthwhile area of research proposed here (a comparison with certain concepts of Vedantic Yoga) scarcely proceeds beyond the stage of introducing the appropriate Sanskrit terms. One is left wondering whether there exist grounds for a proper comparison. Reviews: V. Daniel in FS 21:372–73, 1967; M. Décaudin in IL 20:135, 1968.

Lévy, C. Les termes d'architecture dans l'Eupalinos de Paul Valéry. FM 26:113–23, 1958.   **8824**

Lévy's presentation of the terms (common as well as technical) used by V. to discuss architecture may prove a useful complement to the more historical approach of V. J. Daniel. The observation that in his vocabulary V. distinguishes clearly between material and the construction of materials is noteworthy.

Parisier-Plottel, Jeanine. Les dialogues de Paul Valéry. Presses univ. de France, 1960. 106 p.   **8825**

This study has chosen to stress V.'s thought as expressed in the dialogs rather than to explore the unique form of the genre. Since more complete studies of V. as thinker are available, the usefulness of this one is limited by its own scope. Duchesne-Guillemin's recent contribution is more likely to serve as a model for future investigation. Reviews: L. Bisson in FS 15:80–82, 1961; R. Lang in BA 35:41, 1961; E.

Noulet in RHL 62:283–85, 1962; W. Stewart in RR 52:149–51, 1961; J. Robinson in MLR 56:277–78, 1961.

Robinson, Judith. Words and silence in L'idée fixe. MLN 87:644–56, 1972. **8826**

The only scholarly article exclusively devoted to this most theatrical of V.'s dialogs. Robinson's study of the use of silence leads her to suggest V. as a predecessor of the theater of silence in Beckett, Pinter, Ionesco. More importantly, she grasps clearly V.'s exteriorization of his annoyance with psychoanalysis in a very ironic manner. This aspect of her article overlaps with Derrida's in the same number of MLN.

Séchan, Louis. L'âme et la danse de Paul Valéry. *In his:* La danse grecque antique. E. de Boccard, 1930. p. 273–313. **8827**

Still the most thorough study of V.'s dialog in relation to the dance of classical antiquity. The author follows Lévinson (in his 1927 essay) in arguing for a literary-historical source in M. Emmanuel's *La danse grecque antique d'après les monuments figurés* (1895). His comments on the Ludovici Throne and Botticelli's Graces in the Primavera are also suggestive. Séchan was among the first to have considered seriously the implications of Nietzsche's *The birth of tragedy* for V.'s esthetics.

Stevens, Wallace. Chose légère, ailée, sacrée. *In:* Valéry, Paul. Dialogues. New York, Pantheon, 1956. p. xxii–xxviii. (The collected works of Paul Valéry. V. 4.) *Also:* London, Routledge & Kegan Paul, 1958. **8828**

Drawing on Séchan's 1930 essay for the possible influence of Nietzsche on V., Stevens affirms quite peremptorily that V.'s own genius was Apollonian and that consequently the Dionysian did not accord with it. In a brilliant non sequitur he further affirms that *L'âme et la danse* is a lesser work than *Eupalinos...* because it does not contain an equal proliferation of ideas. As in the case of his appreciation of *Eupalinos...* this preface tells us substantially more about the poet Stevens than about V.'s dialog.

———. Gloire du long désir, Idées. *In:* Valéry, Paul. Dialogues. New York, Pantheon, 1956. p. ix–xxi. (The collected

works of Paul Valéry. V. 4) *Also:* London, Routledge & Kegan Paul, 1958. **8829**

For Stevens *Eupalinos...* is a masterpiece of constructivist art, one of the most perceptive texts of modern times. He insists upon the intellectual rigor with which V. approaches the fundamental problems of art in his time. This little essay will not tell us much we do not already know about V.'s dialog; it is, however, a document of some importance concerning the qualities that drew one major poet to the work of another.

Weinberg, Kurt. Zu P. Valérys Dialogue de l'arbre: das Gedicht von den Antipoden Valéry und Gide. *In:* Interpretation und Vergleich: Festschrift für Walter Pabst. Ed. by E. Leube and L. Schroder. Berlin, E. Schmidt, 1972. p. 331–55. **8830**

Seeing the dialog as the realization of a project V. had articulated in a letter to Léautaud (May 1905), the author explores with tact and an excellent sense of form the embodiment of V.'s rationalism in Lucrèce and, in Tityre, his interpretation of Gide. The result is far removed from the tradition of source hunting. It adds an unexpected dimension to the dialog; biographical questions become inseparable from formal considerations.

Wheelwright, Philip. Introduction. *In:* Valéry, Paul. Idée fixe. New York, Pantheon; London, Routledge & Kegan Paul, 1965. p. xiii–xxiii. (The collected works of Paul Valéry, 5) **8831**

Rather than a commentary on this dialog, Wheelwright's introduction is an exploration of the conditions of dialog for V. His best insight is in distinguishing *L'idée fixe* from the Socratic dialogs as an art of conversation in which no Socrates-figure finally wins the day. Wheelwright understands the centrality of paradox for V., but this introduction by its very nature cannot take the advanced student very far.

Drama

Bastet, Ned. Faust et le cycle. *In:* Entretiens sur Paul Valéry. *See* 8475. p. 115–34. *Also (abridged):* [Faust]. *In:* Les critiques

de notre temps et Valéry. *See* 8474 p.
95–107.   8832
At the center of Bastet's 1965 communication, which has been widely discussed in the intervening decade, is
the concept of the cyclical nature of
all existence, physical and mental. The
Cahiers testify to V.'s having felt this
to the point of exacerbation. V.'s Faust
is then situated, within the myth of
the Eternal Return, as a cultural
archetype.

————. Stratonice and the rejection of
tragedy. *In:* Paul Valéry. See 8482. p.
128–47.   8833
Finds in the unfinished *Stratonice*
(1922–43) a Valéryan definition of
tragedy which draws on both Wagner
and Nietzsche. But V.'s originality is
in the rejection of the tragic mode
through a heightened awareness which
transcends tragedy. Bastet's article compares favorably with Laurenti's chapter
on *Stratonice* in her general study.

————. Valéry et la clôture tragique. *In:*
Paul Valéry, 1871–1971. *See* 8487. p.
103–17.   8834
Complements the preceding article.
Again drawing upon unpublished materials, especially the "dossier tragédie,"
Bastet examines in comprehensive terms
the significance for V. of the tragic
play in its spatio-temporal dimensions.

Blanchot, Maurice. Valéry et Faust. Ar 3:
92–102, 1946. *Also in his:* La part du
feu. Gallimard, 1949. p. 273–88.   8835
In the opening pages Blanchot situates the Faust brilliantly in V.'s work
as a whole, notably in relation to his
Teste and Leonardo. His essay on the
play is among the very best. For Goldmann the fragmentary nature of the
Faust testifies to its sociological significance; whereas for Blanchot this is
the ambiguous mark of its artistic
perfection.

Blüher, Karl Alfred. Strategie des Geistes—
Paul Valérys Faust. Frankfurt am Main,
Klostermann, 1960. 134 p. (Analecta
Romanica, 10)   8836
Here V.'s Faust is considered appropriately as the final contribution to
his "comédie de l'esprit." The author
sets the fragments of *Mon Faust* over
against early works, most notably the

Teste cycle and the Leonardo essays.
His philological commentary (on "sensibilité," Lust, etc.) is particularly fine,
as is his treatment of the memory motif
in "Lust." The discursive style of this
monograph renders it more useful for
most purposes than von Richthofen's
fragmented gloss. Some confusion exists
concerning the unidentified fragments
of V.'s Faust to which Blüher refers.
Unfortunately Blüher makes no use of
the *Cahiers*.
Reviews: E. von Richthofen in
Archiv 199:349–51, 1962; F. Sutcliffe
in RJ 12:195–97, 1961.

Butler, E[liza] M[arian]. Conclusion. *In
her:* The fortunes of Faust. Cambridge,
At the univ. press, 1952. p. 344–48. 8837
Sees the import of V.'s Faust as
charting the course taken by the triumph of rationalism over religion, the
traditional struggle of this topos. Compare the conclusions of Goldmann's
article in 1965.

Charney, Hannah, and Maurice Charney.
Doctor Faustus and Mon Faust: an
excursus in dualism. Sym 16:45–53, 1962.
                                           8838
The ground for comparison of V.
with Thomas Mann is their respective
preoccupation with dualism, above and
beyond all that otherwise separates
them. In this respect V.'s Faust and
Mann's Leverkühn are seen to be
similar. The comparison illuminates
Mann's character more than V.'s.

Dabezies, André. Paul Valéry et la fin du
monde de Faust. *In his:* Visages de Faust
au XXᵉ siècle—littérature, idéologie,
mythe. Presses univ. de France, 1967. p.
321–60. (Publications de la faculté de
lettres et sciences humaines de Paris-
Sorbonne; série recherches, 33)   8839
An intelligent and systematic use of
the published *Cahiers* provides the best
relation to date of the early conception
of V.'s Faust and the progress of the
writing from a fascination with the
Devil to a new, personal and timely
Faust. Questions of style are properly
accentuated. The previous research of
Müller, Blüher and occasionally von
Richthofen, is used to advantage. The
result is an excellent assessment of the
stylistic and intellectual import of V.'s
Faust.

Goldmann, Lucien. Valéry et la dialectique —à propos de Mon Faust. MédF 163:33–40, 1965. *Also in his:* Structures mentales et création culturelle. Eds. Anthropos, 1970. p. 153–69.   **8840**

For Goldmann V.'s Faust is a final effort to confront the dialectical positions of Goethe (in "Lust") and of Nietzsche (in "Le solitaire"). This project necessarily found its expression in a fragmentary form since, according to Goldmann, V.'s rationalism recognized its own inability to alter exterior reality. Compare Robinson in AJFS (*see* 8846).

Grubbs, Henry A. Paul Valéry and the emperor Tiberius. FS 14:224–31, 1960. **8841**

Based primarily upon the author's readings in the *Cahiers,* the article draws together V.'s youthful reflections on Tiberius as the subject of a projected tragedy along with numerous notations made through 1908. He concludes with an allusion to similarities found in Camus' *Caligula.* In light of recent investigations into V.'s idea of tragedy, this documentation is best coordinated with the work of Bastet and Laurenti.

Hell, Victor. Le style, c'est le diable (P. Valéry, Mon Faust)—création et satanisme dans Mon Faust de Paul Valéry et dans le Dr. Faustus de Thomas Mann. *In:* Paul Valéry contemporain. *See* 8486. p. 193–208.   **8842**

Continues logically the article of H. and M. Charney, yet it is incomparably richer in both subject matter and methodology. Hell seeks to illuminate differences as well as similarities and especially to bring out the function of these two Fausts, in the work of their respective authors, but more importantly perhaps in a civilization that seems to have rendered Faust henceforth impossible.

Laurenti, Huguette. Paul Valéry et le théâtre. Gallimard, 1973. 539 p. (Bibliothèque des idées)   **8843**

This weighty tone would have been inconceivable before publication of the *Cahiers,* from which the author draws her best material. Only half the study is devoted to V.'s plays, libretti, etc. (completed or projected). The dialogs which have been staged are not con-

sidered. A lucid exposition of V.'s thoughts on the conditions of theater (space, time, poetry, music, audience, etc.), all of which have ramifications for his work as a whole. A good lexicon of a dozen terms basic to V.'s analysis completes the study, which is destined to be the cornerstone of future constructions.

Lhote, Marie-Thérèse. Le Faust wagnérien de Paul Valéry. RLC 46:272–84, 1972.   **8844**

Basing her point of departure upon V.'s life-long admiration for Wagner, the author builds an hypothesis for a Wagnerian Faust on notations in the *Cahiers* for 1944 (28, 217) and 1945 (29, 804). That V. had a heightened interest in mysticism in his last years is undeniable. That his Faust derives in any direct way from Wagner is not proven by this article.

Richthofen, Erich von. Commentaire sur Mon Faust de Paul Valéry. Presses univ. de France, 1961. 139 p.   **8845**

The choice of critical apparatus (a page by page gloss of the 1946 Gallimard ed. and the fragment published by Ballard in *Paul Valéry vivant*) limits the scope of the commentary to the range of concerns of literary history, principally source, influence and reminiscence. Quite possibly the most useful aspect is to be found in the systematic checking of the *Cahiers* (through vol. 23 inclusively) for references to *Mon Faust.* Richthofen formally excludes as useless any consideration of Nietzsche for the general climate of "Le solitaire," preferring allusions to an impressive array of romantic writers. Compare Blüher and Goldmann on this point.

Robinson, Judith. Valéry's Mon Faust as an unfinished play. AJFS 6:421–39, 1969.   **8846**

This reading assumes the position developed by Bastet (*see* 8613) to the effect that V. was equally drawn to synthesize and to leave in fragmentary form the works of the mind. Consequently Robinson finds an individual/psychological cause for the phenomenon Goldmann had attributed to a transpersonal/collective need. For her, fragmentation was in effect the form required of this play for V., a paradox of which V. himself could have been proud.

Roussillon-Bartell, Simone. Lust, la demoiselle de cristal. Quelques réflexions sur la langue de l'œuvre. FM 33:37–49, 1965. **8847**

Examines the language V. has placed in the mouth of each character in an effort to ascertain whether there is a manifest attempt to achieve a properly theatrical effect. An examination of popular, familiar and quite ungrammatical expressions yields some positive results. The appropriate conclusion is drawn concerning V.'s discrimination of language by social role and a suggestion is made that the success this text encountered on the stage may well be due to just such considerations.

Yvon, H. Les expressions négatives dans Mon Faust, de Paul Valéry. FM 30:13–34, 1962. **8848**

Studies the frequency of types of negation (*non, ne, ni,* etc.) and their grammatical function in V.'s *Mon Faust* which thus appears as pretext rather than as literary text. *Mon Faust,* according to this grammarian, offers a somewhat literary image of contemporary spoken language. To have any value for literary scholars the raw data presented here would require systematic reinterpretation.

Essays: *Variété*

Bémol, Maurice. La méthode critique de Paul Valéry. Belles lettres, 1950. 174 p. *Also:* Clermont-Ferrand, G. de Bussac, 1951. *Also:* Nizet, 1960. **8849**

This study is a complement to the author's principal state doctoral thesis (*see* 8490). The first section, comprised of some seventy pages, is a condensation of materials presented therein. The second half presents as a specialized type of "Valérysme" the essays on writers collected in the several volumes of *Variété* as well as a number of V.'s prefaces and occasional pieces. This study is subject to the same criticisms as the "grande thèse" and lacks its wealth of documentation. The doctrinaire aspect of Bémol's concept of

"Valérysme" is even more in evidence here.

———. Paul Valéry et la critique littéraire. RE 7:366–77, 1954. *Also:* Paul Valéry et la méthode scientifique en critique littéraire. *In his:* Variations sur Valéry. V. 2. *See* 8492. p. 63–74. **8850**

It is a curious experience to find V.'s name coordinated with the concept of science in literary criticism when one realizes that the author was treating that most positivistic of disciplines, literary history. Once again the fundamental problem is the atypical nature of *Variété* with respect to V.'s idea of criticism.

———. Valéry et Sainte-Beuve—contribution à l'étude de leurs méthodes critiques. AUS 1:48–59, 1952. *Revised and expanded:* Le valérysme de Sainte-Beuve. *In his:* Variations sur Valéry. V. 2. *See* 8492. p. 11–46. **8851**

The thesis that V. is very like Sainte-Beuve in practicing a biographical/psychological criticism derives from the author's exclusive reliance on essays in the *Variété* series. To the reader today this conclusion may rather suggest that the essays used for documentation represented a marginal and alimentary form of literary activity for V.

Cioran, E. M. Valéry before his idols. (Mallarmé, Poe, Leonardo). HudR 22:411–24, 1969. *Also:* Valéry face à ses idoles. NRF 17:801–19, 1969. *And:* L'herne, 1970. 45 p. **8852**

This short essay was originally conceived as a preface to *Leonardo/Poe/Mallarmé,* v. 8 of *The collected works of Paul Valéry,* but did not appear there. It is easy to see why: V. is presented as a closet autobiographer and, alternatively, as the galley-slave of the nuance.

Reviews: R. Lang in BA 45:280, 1971; J. Piatier in Monde May 30, 1970.

Diéguez, Manuel de. Valéry et la critique technique. *In his:* L'écrivain et son langage. Gallimard, 1960. p. 103–23. (Les essais, 97) **8853**

Although quite dated today, this chapter has the distinction of having placed V.'s criticism at the source of all contemporary practice. On the one hand, the critics of consciousness and, on the other, the technicians. The problem, as this writer saw it, was that both lines of V.'s descendants were neglecting questions of style that he had prized so highly.

Douglas, Kenneth N. Paul Valéry on Pascal. PMLA 61:820–34, 1946.　　**8854**

In a probing essay on V.'s published statements on Pascal (in *Variété* and in Lefèvre's *Entretiens avec Paul Valéry*), Douglas reached the conclusion that V.'s antagonism proceeded from some secret affinity. The idea was taken up by Gaède in his *Nietzsche et Valéry*. This 1946 study must now be supplemented by the findings of Gaillard (*see* 8623).

Frank, Joseph. Paul Valéry: masters and friends. SR 75:393–414, 1967. *Also:* Introduction. *In:* Valéry, Paul. Masters and friends. Princeton, Princeton univ. press; London, Routledge & Kegan Paul, 1968. p. ix–xxxiii. (The collected works of Paul Valéry, 9)　　**8855**

To introduce an English-speaking public to the author of so many divergent essays called for a broad-based approach. Consequently Frank produced little that had not been said before. His best pages situate V. with respect to Nietzsche, following the direction traced by Gaède.

Review: J. Parisier-Plottel in FR 42: 765–66, 1969.

Germain, Gabriel. Le mystère créateur dans l'expérience poétique de Valéry. RdM 68: 373–87, 1955.　　**8856**

Drawing almost exclusively on the pertinent texts published in the volumes of *Variété*, Germain reaches conclusions similar to those of Hytier in his appreciation of "l'infini esthétique." However, his suggestion of a parallel between V.'s experience as poet and certain aspects of yogic supermind would doubtless have met with V.'s disapproval. Overall one senses keenly at twenty years' distance that, without the complement of the *Cahiers, Variété* is not a very adequate source from which to reconstruct V.'s poetics.

Girard, René. Valéry et Stendhal. PMLA 69:347–57, 1954.　　**8857**

The thesis of this article can be summed up in the claim: M. Teste is the antithesis of Stendhal. Perhaps Girard would have done better, since after all we are dealing with fictions in both cases, had he written: V.'s Stendhal is the antithesis of his Edmond Teste, a statement which might help us understand what troubled V. in Stendhal. A particularly well written article.

Essays on Poetic Theory

Auden, W. H. The creation of music and poetry. MidCR 2:18–27, 1959.　　**8858**

Auden opens with a comparison of V.'s "Poésie et pensée abstraite" and Stravinsky on music. He establishes a formal perspective from which to make meaningful statements on the two art forms, poetry and music: word:interval::rhythm:rhythm. The article essentially suggests possible lines of inquiry for a comparative criticism that might take us beyond the loose analogies of the type used by V. himself in discussing poetry and music.

Delbouille, Paul. Paul Valéry et le mythe des sonorités. ZFSL 70:129–38, 1960.　　**8859**

Despite its laudable intention—to study V.'s concept of the function of sound in poetry—this article is doubly flawed. First it supposes that the essential elements are to be found in essays like "Questions de poésie" and "Poésie et pensée abstraite," rather than in V.'s poetic practice. Second and doubtless more prejudicial to its future value, the article makes no use whatever of the *Cahiers*.

Eliot, T. S. Introduction. *In:* Valéry, Paul. The art of poetry. New York, Pantheon; London, Routledge & Kegan Paul, 1958. p. vii–xxiv. (The collected works of Paul Valéry, 7) *Also:* New York, Vintage books, 1961.　　**8860**

This last statement on V. by Eliot will in the long run be his most influential as well. The 1961 reprinting of this volume in paperback format has had a considerable impact on the Anglo-American reading of V.

Reviews: K. Burke in KR 20:529–46, 1958; H. Corke in List 62:451,

453, 1959; N. Frye in HudR 12:124–29, 1959.

Gerlötei, Eugène. Méditations valéryennes: principes de recherches conformes à la poésie classique. RE 10:65–76, 1957. **8861**

V. is taken seriously as esthetician and his theoretical writings are used to define a classical poetics broad enough to incorporate Pindar, Sophocles, Hölderlin, Keats and V. himself. This classicism appears eternal, an idea and an ideal. It is doubtful whether such a definition finally does justice to V., or to the poetic tradition of the West.

Gibson, Robert. Valéry. *In his:* Modern French poets on poetry—an anthology.... Cambridge, At the univ. press, 1961. p. 115–25 and *passim.* **8862**

The section on "poetic ends" contains a good connected anthology of ten pages of V.'s own statements on the subject. They can serve as a complement to Hytier's book; their purpose is more pedagogical than critical. Fully indexed.

Hytier, Jean. Autour d'une analogie valéryenne. CAIEF 17:171–89, 1965. *Also in his:* Questions de littérature. New York-London, Columbia univ. press, 1967. p. 159–72. **8863**

Starting from V.'s analogy poetry: prose::dance:walking, Hytier gives a virtuoso performance on the history of this and related analogies to account for the differences between the two modes. His conclusion relates V.'s formulation of it, several times revised, to the long and illustrious tradition of a rhetorical figure.

———. The refusals of Valéry. YFS 11: 105–36, 1949. *Also:* Les refus de Valéry. *In his:* Questions de littérature. New York-London, Columbia univ. press, 1967. p. 56–81. *Reprinted in part as:* Les dangers de la métaphysique. *In:* Les critiques de notre temps et Valéry. *See* 8474. p. 28–35. **8864**

An essay originally conceived as a contribution to a volume on criticism and creation. In that context Hytier set forth a principle, shared by Bémol, that the commentator should gauge the degree to which his method would meet with the approval of the author in question. This methodological gambit

leads to a discussion of V.'s views on philosophy, mysticism, and the sciences, followed by the acknowledgement of V.'s refusal to grant any significance whatever to literary history or criticism. The aspects of V.'s poetics covered by this article are much better known today; therefore the article can best serve as an introduction to V.'s "Théorie poétique et esthétique."

Ince, W. N. The poetic theory of Paul Valéry—inspiration and technique. Leicester, Leicester univ. press, 1961. ix, 187 p. *Also:* 1970. **8865**

Except for a note appended to the table of contents, the 1970 printing of this study is unchanged from the original, which was not only conceived before publication of the *Cahiers* but prior to the standard edition of the *Œuvres* as well. Like Hytier he has presented V.'s poetics in such a way as to avoid the intimations of cold intellectuality that had characterized much earlier commentary. Nonetheless Ince has a predilection for the *homo faber* in the poet.

Jallat, Jeannine. Léonard, la figure et le texte. *In:* Paul Valéry contemporain. *See* 8486. p. 125–35. **8866**

Seeks to establish in V.'s work the ground for a general rhetoric, a theory of ornament or of figures. The methodological position is roughly that of J.-F. Lyotard in *Discours, figure* (1971). The present article is only a working paper on a subject of considerable significance.

———. Valéry et les figures de rhétorique. *In:* Cahiers Paul Valéry. 1: poétique et poésie. *See* 8472. p. 149–85. **8867**

The most valuable part of the article treats V.'s notion of metaphor and metonymy in terms of Lacanian condensation/displacement, using J.-F. Lyotard's *Discours, figure* as a mediating text. Jallat is the first critic to have drawn attention to Lacan's comment on "Au platane" in his *Ecrits.*

Labica, Georges. Introduction à la méthode de Paul Valéry—autopsie d'une esthétique. CahALC 1:70–94, 1966. **8868**

Labica has attempted to construct the model of V.'s concept of consciousness, and the criticism which derives therefrom, without reference to the *Cahiers* or the commentary based upon them. The results are coherent and self-consistent, therefore utilizable. When one compares the conclusions reached by Labica with recent commentary on the *Cahiers*, one is obliged to consider that in his notebooks V. laid the groundwork for a structuralist theory of mental activity that is in important respects incompatible with his own criticism of consciousness. The current schism in V. criticism appears, from this perspective, to be the extension of an unresolved conflict existing within V.'s own work.

La Rochefoucauld, Edmée de. Images de Paul Valéry. Strasbourg-Paris, F.-X. Le Roux, 1949. 119 p.   8869

Two sections of this book (otherwise composed of brief notes and reminiscences) deserve to be retained. The chapter entitled "La poétique selon Valéry" was drawn from notes taken by the author at the Collège de France. V. had reviewed the text, suggesting emendations. This very condensed journalistic version of the first year and a half of the course does little more than sketch in a number of the subjects covered. Nonetheless it remains one of the rare first-hand accounts of this aspect of V.'s work. For the same reason the chapter "Paul Valéry professeur sous l'occupation" should be consulted for V.'s last views of "la politique de l'esprit."

Mathews, Jackson. The poïetics of Paul Valéry. RR 46:203–17, 1955.   8870

Using the available material on V.'s course at the Collège de France, Mathews set out to reveal the implicit system from which all V.'s mental constructions follow. His article can be read today as a prime example of that modernist tradition of the synthesizing mind against which a branch of linguistic formalism has reacted so sharply in recent years. The article continues to stand as the best study of its type devoted to the subject.

N. D. L. R. Paul Valéry et Voltaire, propos inédits. RHL 68:382–400, 1968.   8871

A brief note introduces the edited text of V.'s "cours de poïétique" for March 9, 1945. He had been ill and unable to prepare the material for the course. Having recently read Voltaire's correspondence, doubtless for his "Discours sur Voltaire," he chose to improvise on that subject. The accompanying note has no critical value other than to present and explain the nature of this previously unknown text.

Passeron, René. La poïétique. RE 24:233–46, 1972.   8872

Passeron establishes a useful distinction between esthetics (the consumption or reception of art by its public) and poïetics (the making of art) based upon V.'s "cours de poïétique" at the Collège de France. Seen in this light V.'s use of the term poïetics constituted a healthy reaction against the confusion that continues to reign in literary studies concerning the use of the term esthetics.

Pietra, Régine. Si l'esthétique pouvait être…. RE 25:315–33, 1972.   8873

A logical extension of Passeron's article in the same journal. To V.'s use of "poïétique" Pietra adds his neologism "esthésique," by which V. intended the private phenomenon of pleasure occasioned by art. The greatest usefulness of this excellent study is to have called attention to V.'s annoyance with the so-called lower senses (smell being the most treacherous). Taking up V.'s critique, she links the lower orders of sensation with the irrational; vision, the only sense to receive V.'s full approbation, is linked to reason and especially to self-control.

Read, Herbert. The poet and his muse. ErJ 31:217–48, 1963. *Also* (*in part*) *in:* BJA 4:99–108, 1964.   8874

After considering the position of Blake, Shelley and Wordsworth with respect to poetic inspiration, the author takes up the jilting of the Muse by Poe and V. For him, V. replaces the concept of inspiration with that of the constructing self (with reference to "Au sujet du Cimetière marin"). There is a unity in all this, however, as all the poets studied recognize the creative state by the presence of a self superior to the ordinary self. A very readable essay, but one which adds little to Hytier's treatment of the question. It broader scope is definitely in its favor

Roe, G. M. W. Paul Valéry as a literary critic: theory and practice. NFS 13:23–32; 73–84, 1974. **8875**

Attempts a comprehensive survey of an important subject. Limited by the author's having missed the most important recent contributions to its several aspects.

Todorov, Tzvetan. Valéry's poetics. *In:* YFS 44:67–71, 1970. *Also:* La poétique de Valéry. *In:* Cahiers Paul Valéry. 1: poétique et poésie. *See* 8472. p. 123–32. **8876**

Counsels against a hasty assimilation of V.'s poetics to structuralist activity. Having noted a theoretical affinity, he then details the methodological divergence in practice. Compare with Rey (*see* 8639) and Ricardou (*see* 8907).

Yeschua, Silvio. Substitutions et poétique chez Paul Valéry. *In:* Cahiers Paul Valéry. 1: poétique et poésie. *See* 8472. p. 133–48. **8877**

Faced with the now celebrated contradiction between V.'s skepticism and his constructive poetic, Yeschua used substitution systematically as the mediating term. This is accurate as far as it goes, and Yeschua has provided some good illustrations.

Other Essays

Adorno, Theodor W. Valéry Proust Museum. NRs 64:522–63, 1953. **8878**

Comments on V.'s essay "Le problème des musées" in the context of living, evolving culture versus the mausoleum effect of the museum. While recognizing V.'s cultural-political conservatism, Adorno finds all the more striking his criticism of the cultural economics of museums. As he was to do seven years later, he presents those aspects of V.'s critique that are most compatible with a Marxist analysis of the function of contemporary culture (*see* 8538).

Boudot, Pierre. Nietzsche et Valéry. *In:* Quinze années d'études nietzschéennes en France. RLM 76–77:57–62, 1962–63. *Also:* La parole comme totalité—Paul Valéry. *In his:* Nietzsche et l'au-delà de la liberté—Nietzsche et les écrivains fran-

çais de 1930 à 1960. Aubier-Montaigne, 1970. p. 27–33. **8879**

Commenting briefly on V.'s introduction to his *Quatre lettres au sujet de Nietzsche* (1927), Boudot attributes V.'s lack of interest to his temperament and to the intellectual climate in France in the first decade of the twentieth century. He sees in V.'s critical attitude a Cartesian analytical posture, but does not recognize the special complexity of his fascination with Nietzsche.

Cooper, Douglas. Introduction. *In:* Valéry, Paul. Degas Manet Morisot. New York, Pantheon; London, Routledge & Kegan Paul, 1960. p. ix–xxxiv. (The collected works of Paul Valéry, 12) **8880**

An excellent essay on the contradictions in V.'s approach to the visual arts. Fairly but critically, the author presents V. the literary man torn between the principles of his criticism and the digressions that so frequently violate them. We see V. the writer on art in a very similar light to V. the literary critic in *Variété*. Cooper does not give V. the same status as professional art critic that G. de Traz accorded him.

Croce, Benedetto. Il mondo presente. *In his:* Conversazioni critiche, serie quarta. Bari, Laterza, 1932. p. 294–96. **8881**

This brief note on *Regards sur le monde actuel* is worthy of mention only because of the author's own importance. Croce attacked V. quite vehemently for his lack of historical perspective on a sharply divided modern world.

Ferré, André. Paul Valéry et l'enseignement. GraR 562–83, June 1935. **8882**

Except for an allusion to V.'s 1927 lecture "Education du sens poétique," published only in résumé, Ferré's material did not touch upon V.'s texts specifically treating education. Nonetheless he found throughout the published work to date the elements of a pedagogy not very different from that which one can derive from his explicit statements on the subject.

Chaix-Ruy, J. Paul Valéry et le thème du retour éternel. RdM 15:261–75, 1955. **8883**

The strategy of the article is to reduce V.'s views on history to those of Vico by way of Nietzsche's Zarathustra.

The author can then conclude that V. was an unoriginal thinker. He cites Croce's judgment approvingly. It is doubtful whether the argument for Vico as a source can be made to stand, and the significance and function of Nietzsche for V. have been better handled by Gaède and others.

Cocking, J. M. Valéry's Hellenism. AJFS 4: 287–94, 1967.   **8884**

Cocking's title is misleading in that he was actually writing on V.'s "Inspirations méditerranéennes" (in *Essais quasi politiques*) which should not be confused with Hellenism (*see* 8622). The principal thrust of this article concerns V.'s sensualism as it pertains to his view of the Mediterranean world.

Fosca, François (pseud. of Georges de Traz). Valéry. *In his:* De Diderot à Valéry—les écrivains et les arts visuels. Michel, 1960. p. 269–83.   **8885**

Fosca, whose criteria for excellence are severe, considers V. an art critic of fine professional calibre. He singles out the pages on drawing in "Degas Danse Dessin" and the essays on Corot and Delacroix, but judges "Tante Berthe" harshly. Fosca's high praise derives in part from his approval of V.'s very conservative view of the more innovative contemporary artists. Compare the judgment of D. Cooper above.

Review: A. Thérive in EPar 197: 119–27, 1961.

Geen, Renée. Valéry and Swedenborg. FS 20:25–32, 1966.   **8886**

Primarily a straightforward reading of V.'s brief essay on Swedenborg in *Etudes philosophiques,* the article combines his further observations on St. John of the Cross to make a case for V. regarding the mystic as poet. An argument that should be considered carefully by those who prefer to see V. the poet as mystic.

Guyot, Charly. En relisant l'Introduction à la méthode de Léonard de Vinci. *In:* Paul Valéry, essais et témoignages inédits. *See* 8488. p. 83–93.   **8887**

Accurately situates the *Introduction...* at the source of all V.'s central concerns, showing clearly that its importance transcends the scope of V.'s "Théorie poétique et esthétique." More complete studies have, however, gone beyond this commentary in all areas.

Macrí, Oreste. Paul Valéry, uomo europeo. RasI 4:1007–24, 1949.   **8888**

In most respects this article is superseded by Roulin (*see* 8890), but the intelligent handling of Croce's opposition to V. is without equal.

Madariaga, Salvador de. Introduction. *In:* Valéry, Paul. History and politics. New York, Pantheon; London, Routledge & Kegan Paul, 1962–63. p. xxi–xxxvi. (The collected works of Paul Valéry, 10) **8889**

Only a few pages are really to the point, but they are excellent. De Madariaga attributes to V.'s intellectualized view of politics an inability, or unwillingness, to distinguish between majority rule and freedom, between benign dictatorship and the human need for liberty.

Review: H. Charney in RR 55:309–10, 1964.

Roulin, Pierre. Paul Valéry témoin et juge du monde moderne. Neuchâtel, A la Baconnière, 1964. 268 p.   **8890**

It is odd that V.'s writings on the contemporary scene, so abundantly and sometimes hotly debated from 1932 to his death, should have awaited 1964 to receive their first scholarly treatment. Roulin has made a solid contribution.

Reviews: F. Desponds in EdL 9: 111–12, 1966; J. Mathews in Enc 20: 95, 1963; H. Nicolson in Obs 8349, June 10, 1951; P.-H. Simon in MondeH 828, Aug. 27–Sept. 2, 1964; J. Weightman in Enc 20:84, 86, 88, 1963.

Rychner, Max. Une conquête méthodique. *In:* Paul Valéry, essais et témoignages inédits. *See* 8488. p. 199–205.   **8891**

A very solid and impressive commentary on V.'s essay in *Essais quasi politiques,* which had appeared prophetic to survivors of two global conflicts. While indicating the flaws in V.'s theoretical position, Rychner stressed the essential accuracy of his detailed analysis. Further, Rychner recognized that this analysis was inseparable from V.'s own concrete situation. Easily the best treatment of "Une conquête méthodique" before Roulin's book.

Speranza Armani, Ada. Paul Valéry e l'insegnamento. RCVS 4:11–12; 5:12–13, 1967. **8892**

Treats seriously, in a journal by and for educators, the three essays grouped under the heading "Enseignement" in V.'s *Œuvres*, v. 1, as well as others related more or less directly to teaching. The result is a remarkable demonstration of the relationship of these texts—which have been considered purely occasional pieces—to major themes in V.'s thought.

Valéry, François. Preface. *In:* Valéry, Paul. History and politics. New York, Pantheon; London, Routledge & Kegan Paul, 1962–63. p. ix–xx. (The collected works of Paul Valéry, 10) **8893**

The only substantial statement on V.'s politics by a member of his family. V.'s son presents the conservative anarchist as a dialectician of the real, but alien to Hegel or Marx. The V. who emerges here has much in common with Nietzsche.

Review: H. Charney in RR 55:309–10, 1964.

Vilar, Jean. Un entretien avec André Malraux. MagL 54:10–24, 1971. **8894**

Were it not for the importance of the writer interviewed, the remarks on V. would be of marginal interest. With respect to the *Regards sur le monde actuel,* Malraux placed V. next to Spengler in importance as an historical essayist. He related his impressions of a lecture by V. given under the auspices of the Union pour la vérité.

Virtanen, Reino. The irradiations of Eureka: Valéry's reflections on Poe's cosmology. TSLL 7:17–25, 1962. **8895**

Skillfully traces V.'s attitude toward Poe's cosmology from the first burst of enthusiasm in 1892 to his trenchant irony in the 1921 essay "Au sujet d'*Eurêka*" (in *Etudes philosophiques*). An excellent knowledge of the *Cahiers* and of V.'s published work fills out this examination in breadth.

Wais, Kurt. D. H. Lawrence, Valéry, Rilke in ihrer Auseinandersetzung mit den bildenden Künsten. GRM n.F. 2:301–24, 1952. *Also:* Die zeitgenössische Dichtung und die bildenden Künste. *In his:* An den Grenzen der Nationalliteraturen.

Berlin, W. de Gruyter, 1958. p. 296–301. **8896**

Situates V.'s attitude toward the plastic arts with respect to the positions of Lawrence and Rilke. Valuable as a first step toward a thoroughgoing comparative study.

Weisbach, Werner. Gedanken Paul Valérys zur bildenden Kunst. NSR n.F. 14:579–99, 1947. **8897**

Considers V.'s texts on artists and the plastic arts as representative of his notion of the mind as a creative faculty. The strength of the article lies in the breadth of material it treats; its weakness, in an excessively stable and idealist concept of the self ("Moi") in V.'s work.

Yeschua, Silvio. Le Yalou: énigmes, forme, signification. *In:* Paul Valéry contemporain. *See* 8486. p. 105–23. **8898**

This very learned article marks the literary-historical as well as the personal boundaries of a curious text (in *Regards sur le monde actuel*) that has never received its due. In all probability more attention will be paid to it in future. For all the erudition displayed here the author seems to have overlooked the fact that V. considered publishing "Le Yalou" among the texts of the Teste cycle.

Valéry in Literary History

Arnold, A. James. La querelle de la poésie pure. RHL 70:445–54, 1970. **8899**

In an effort to show that the quarrel which began in 1925 on the occasion of V.'s election to the Academy had its roots in the esthetics of an earlier day, the article focuses on the symbolist ideal of a fusing of the arts. It can be read in conjunction with Mossop's essay which provides the broader perspective on the background of modernist esthetics.

Berne-Joffroy, [André]. Destin de la rhétorique: Stendhal, Valéry, Paulhan. CahS 300:272–98, 1950. **8900**

A convincing demonstration that, in his writings on V. (*Les fleurs de Tarbes* and "Un rhétoriqueur à l'état sauvage"), Paulhan had invented his own V. whom he equated with the modern

"rhétoriqueur." Numerous anti-rhetori-
cal statements by V. are cited to acquit
him of the charge. This article is a
document of lasting value in a debate
which has been reopened on other
grounds in recent years. The final section defends V.'s view of Stendhal
against Paulhan's objections.

Decker, Henry W. Pure poetry, 1925–1930:
theory and debate in France. Berkeley-
Los Angeles, Univ. of California press,
1962. viii, 131 p.   **8901**

This first attempt at a scholarly
summation of the debate sometimes
confuses theory with tactics and occasionally misreads V.'s notion of pure
poetry. There are a few errors of fact
regarding the pre-original publication
dates of certain of Lefèvre's *Entretiens
avec Paul Valéry.* Fully indexed.

Ince, W. N. Valéry and the novel. AJFS 8:
193–205, 1971.   **8902**

Ince builds upon the articles by
Zants and Ricardou. His contribution is
the exploration of the *Cahiers* for further material on the novel as a genre.
Ince recognizes that the constructive
value of V.'s attitude is limited by his
extraordinary hostility to the form (or,
in V.'s view, the formlessness) of the
novel. Very readable, but does not alter
our understanding of the question as
Ricardou has analyzed it.

Leonard, Albert. La poésie pure. *In his:* La
crise du concept de littérature en France
au XXᵉ siècle. Corti, 1974. p. 91–107.
                                                8903

V.'s conception of pure poetry is
subordinated to that of Bremond,
which is presented in the version given
by Clément Moisan. Consequently V.'s
role in this major debate does not receive its full measure of importance.
The value of this contribution to the
question is in its scope: the crisis of the
concept of literature is traced from
Mallarmé to structuralism.

Michaud, Guy. Paul Valéry, poète pur. *In
his:* L'univers poétique. Message poétique
du symbolisme. V. 3. Nizet, 1947. p. 555–
74. *Also (in one vol.):* Nizet, 1961. p.
555–74.   **8904**

Michaud reinforces the misunderstanding surrounding the term pure poetry and V.'s relation to it. Specific ob-

servations are often pertinent, yet the
overall effect is a continued distortion.
A far more analytical approach has
been taken since Mossop's 1964 essay.
Michaud's use of the designation V.-
Teste is likewise lacking in analytical
precision.

Mossop, D. J. The origins of the idea of pure
poetry. Durham, Univ. of Durham, 1964.
21 p.   **8905**

Although V. is considered here as but
the conclusion of an esthetic movement
which grew with the influence of Kant's
Critique of judgement, the essay is a
valuable contribution to this still murky
question. The term pure poetry clearly
gains in being abstracted from the historical quarrel and set in the context of
modernist esthetics.

Pommier, Jean. Paul Valéry et la création
littéraire. Eds. de l'encyclopédie française,
1946. 44 p.   **8906**

Pommier's task was a most delicate
one: to praise the contradictor of literary history in his inaugural lesson from
a chair of literary history. His tactic can
be summed up in one piquant phrase.
Recalling V.'s witticism to the effect
that the lion is composed of assimilated
lamb, Pommier replied: we name the
lambs.

Ricardou, Jean. Le nouveau roman est-il
valéryen? *In:* Entretiens sur Paul Valéry.
See 8475. p. 69–83.   **8907**

Essentially Ricardou answers yes to the
question posed by his title: yes, for the
agreement in principle to condemn description in the novel; maybe, insofar as
the naked fact may play its part in a
(formal) network of relations that might
make of "La marquise sortit à cinq
heures" a Valéryan phrase. He offered a
more detailed analysis of the question
in 1969.

———. Valéry ou l'impossible Monsieur
Texte. SynB 277–78:11–24, 1969. *Also in
his:* Pour une théorie du nouveau roman.
Seuil, 1971. p. 59–90.   **8908**

Ricardou unfolds his impossible V. in
four parts: the detractor of romanticism; the writer of self-contradiction;
the detractor of the (old) novel; the
impossible Monsieur Texte [sic]. The essay is rich and does not easily lend itself
to condensation. Ricardou's strategy is
to intensify the elements of contradic-

tion, refusing to prefer one element to another. Synthesis, a dirty word in this perspective, is out of the question. Therefore, of necessity, V. appears in conclusion as a transitional writer.

Sanouillet, Michel. Dada à Paris. J.-J. Pauvert, 1965. 646 p. **8909**
Although the arrangement of the book does not lend itself to a separate treatment of V. and dada, Sanouillet has provided a good introduction to V.'s relations with Breton, Aragon and others in the years immediately preceding the official birth of surrealism. Fully indexed.

Simond, Daniel. Reconnaissance à Valéry. *In:* Paul Valéry, essais et témoignages inédits. *See* 8488. p. 49–64. **8910**
This text is a warm hymn in praise of a mentor. It is peculiarly Swiss in its flavor and represents one type of influence V. had on younger writers.

Walzer, Pierre-Olivier. Paul Valéry. *In his:* Le XXᵉ siècle. I. 1896–1920. Arthaud, 1975. p. 310–23; 427–28. (Littérature française. V. 15) **8911**
A very rare publication; a literary history informed by the best recent scholarship on V. Can be recommended to the serious student for purposes of orientation.

Zants, Emily. Valéry and the modern French novel. EspCr 7:81–90. 1967. **8912**
The notion of situating V. with respect to the New Novel was surely a laudable one but, for several reasons, this article does not quite achieve its goal. A more direct approach to poetics would have been necessary in order to avoid falling into the dualist trap of form and content. Compare the approach of J. Ricardou.

Influence and Comparison

Alexander, Ian W. Valéry and Yeats. The rehabilitation of time. ScotP 1:77–106, 1947. **8913**
Initially Mallarmé is taken as mediator between V. and Yeats but gradually the younger poets develop in directions more compatible with one another. Finally, Yeats's gyre, like V.'s ouroboros, symbolizes the rehabilitation of time which is denied in Mallarmé. In devel-

oping V.'s position in poetics the author makes a number of probing observations which situate V. between neo-Kantian Idealism and phenomenology. The article deserves serious consideration.

Arbour, Romeo. Bergson et la poésie moderne. *In his:* Henri Bergson et les lettres françaises. Corti, 1955. p. 326–32. **8914**
Arbour relates the history of the question of V.'s Bergsonism to date, agreeing in the main with O'Neill's article. He brings nothing new to the question.

Balatti, Marina. Sulla nozione di poesia come oggetto chiuso in Paul Valéry. SRLF 12:393–408, 1973. **8915**
Places V.'s formalism, his notion of the work as a closed system, in its literary-historical context with special reference to the late nineteenth century and to Mallarmé in particular. Significantly the same concept has begun to orient historical and stylistic approaches to V.'s work (see Laurenti and Bastet on V.'s theater).

Batterby, K. A. J. Valéry and the poetic climax. *In his:* Rilke and France, a study in poetic development. London, Oxford univ. press, 1966. p. 140–84. (Oxford mod. langs. and lit. monographs) **8916**
The extensive chapter on V. is the best analysis of V.'s influence on Rilke in terms of language and style. An extended commentary on Rilke's translation of *Le cimetière marin*, its techniques and characteristics, is particularly helpful. Numerous references to previous considerations of the question, mostly in German.
Review: G. Tracy in Monats 61: 401–402, 1969.

Bémol, Maurice. Goethe et Valéry: leurs vues comparées sur la comparaison littéraire. RLC 32:173–84, 1958. *Also:* Valéry, Goethe et la comparaison. *In his:* Variations sur Valéry. V. 2. *See* 8492. p. 95–109. **8917**
The very concept of comparative literature is placed in question through the conjunction of the peculiarly French notion of comparing national literatures and V.'s own conviction that literature is in its essense a linguistic phenomenon. Similarly, translation is supposed to be either impossible or pointless, or both. No resolution of this slippery problem is attempted.

―――. Rilke et Valéry. *In his:* Variations sur Valéry, V. 2. *See* 8492. p. 159–74.
8918

The text of a 1950 lecture preceding the extensive study of the V.-Rilke relationship. Bémol's approach is similar to that of R. Lang who pursued the question much farther in her study of their correspondence.

―――. Valéry et l'Italie. AUS 5:260–70, 1956. *Also in his:* Variations sur Valéry. V. 2. *See* 8492. p. 47–62.   **8919**

The tentative suggestions made here concerning V.'s debt to Italy have been explored in greater depth in recent years.

Bisson, L. A. Valéry and Virgil. MLR 53: 501–11, 1958.   **8920**

Writing on the "Variations sur les *Bucoliques,*" Bisson develops a good case for V.'s distaste for Virgil being due, at least in part, to Huysmans's representation of the Latin poet in *A rebours.* His correspondence with Gide in 1891 would indicate a more positive attitude and the fact that V. reread Virgil in 1929 leads to a hypothesis that, in the "Variations sur les *Bucoliques,*" V. exaggerated the element of dislike, perhaps to justify the liberty he took in the translation of Virgil, adopting an attitude encountered fifty-odd years earlier in Des Esseintes. For Bisson V.'s "Dialogue de l'arbre" is Virgilian in about the same sense as *Eupalinos* is Platonic.

Bonnet, Marguerite. André Breton: naissance de l'aventure surréaliste. Corti, 1975. 460 p.   **8921**

No section of this book is specifically devoted to V., although his presence is important in the chapters concerning Breton's literary debut in the neo-symbolist circle of Jean Royère. Bonnet cites extended passages of the early exchange of letters between V. and Breton in 1914. Partially indexed.

Bonneville, Georges. Un Valéry américain: Conrad Aiken. PoCp 81:37–42, 1967.   **8922**

An intelligent attempt to present to the French reader an important American poet, V.'s junior by some eighteen years, in whose work certain Valéryan concerns and privileged motifs do in-

deed occur prominently. Suggestions of possibilities for further exploration.

Cain, L. Julien. Edgar Poë et Valéry. MerF 309:81–94, 1950. *Also in her:* Trois essais sur Paul Valéry. Gallimard, 1958. p. 131–50.   **8923**

In her approach to Poe's influence on V., Lucienne Cain demonstrated that V. praised Poe as the supremely conscious poet at precisely the time when he considered himself to be a decadent after the manner of Huysmans.

Charney, Hannah. Monsieur Teste and der Mann ohne Eigenschaften: homo possibilis in fiction. CL 27:1–7, 1975.   **8924**

Explores the possibility of a conceptual similarity between V.'s hero of the intellect and Musil's Ulrich. Attempts to go beyond the obvious stylistic dissimilarity, of which Musil himself was aware. In view of the recent position on the novel as form taken by Umberto Eco (in *Opera operta*), V. can indeed be seen as a precursor in the *Soirée....*

Ciplijauskaité, Biruté. Jorge Guillén y Paul Valéry, al despertar. PSA 267–94, June 1964.   **8925**

The theme of waking is studied in V.'s "Aurore" and Guillén's "Más allá." Since the theme is fundamental to the work of both poets, it has been chosen to direct a comparative study which stresses the differences between them. An intelligent analysis based upon a sound method.

Cruickshank, John. Valéry and Pascal: order and adventure. *In:* Order and adventure in post-romantic French poetry. Essays presented to C. A. Hackett. Ed. by E. M. Beaumont, J. M. Cocking and J. Cruickshank. Oxford, Basil Blackwell; New York, Barnes & Noble, 1973. p. 120–35.   **8926**

The latest contribution to the debate over V.'s harsh criticism of Pascal assumes two incompatible approaches to rationality. It finds Gaède's argument inadequate. Taken on its own terms, a very thorough essay.

Review: B. Swift in YWMLS 35: 197, 1974.

Devoto, Daniel. De Amphion a Eupalinos. RLC 46:415–27, 1972.   **8927**

Article in Spanish. Starting from V.'s association of architecture with music in both *Amphion* and *Eupalinos...,* Devoto compares his position with that of the Spanish novelist Juan Valera. An excursus into musicology considers the essential role of specific instruments in the myth of the poet-architect. Beyond these positive details there is an intention—far more debatable—to demonstrate that like Valera, V. had rediscovered the arcane foundation of both music and architecture in number, in the same numerical relations. While V. may well have been aware of such a tradition, it is doubtful whether he conceived his work (including his "filles du nombre d'or") in this neo-Pythagorean tradition. For a similar attitude, consult G. Cattaui (*see* 8554).

Eliot, T. S. From Poe to Valéry. Harcourt, Brace, 1948. 32 p. *Also in his:* To criticize the critic and other writings. London, Faber and Faber, 1965. p. 27–42. **8928**
This is the most celebrated of many essays on the subject of Poe and V. Eliot considered V.'s debt to Poe in two parts: his self-consciousness as poet and the practice of pure poetry. For Eliot, V. represented the terminus of a tradition originating with Poe as well as a valuable guide to Poe's importance for modern poetry.

Eschmann, Ernst Wilhelm. Paul Valéry. Herrliberg-Zurich, Bühl-Verlag, 1948. 55 p. (Bühl-Verlag-Blätter, 25) **8929**
Although the brevity of this essay does not permit a thorough general study, the author has succeeded in contrasting V. with Rilke and *Mon Faust* with Goethe's Faust. His best comments are frequently no more than notations which would require further amplification.

Garrigue, François. Goethe et Valéry. RLM 12:32–64; 13:113–23; 14:191–224; 15: 241–55; 16:337–66, 1955. *Also:* Lettres modernes, Minard, 1955. 140 p. (Confrontations, 1) **8930**
The essay is in two parts. The first treats V.'s allocutions on Goethe in 1932 with frequent references to *Regards sur le monde actuel.* The second is devoted to the Goethean ramifications of *Mon Faust.* Throughout his study Garrigue reinforces his parallel theses by using V.'s aphorisms as commentaries on Goethe, or the latter's conversations

with Eckermann to highlight his own commentary on V. The fundamental guiding principle is that of Goethe as a mirror for V. from 1932 to his death. Garrigue is at his best in demonstrating the important formal differences between Goethe's and V.'s Fausts.
Reviews: M. Bémol in EG 12:65, 1957; W. Paulsen in BA 31:43, 1957; J. Theisen in Ant 33–35, April 1956; R. Warnier in Ant 41–43, Nov. 1956.

Gaulmier, Jean. Paul Valéry lecteur de Gobineau. *In:* Mélanges de linguistique, de philologie et de littérature offerts à Monsieur Albert Henry. Strasbourg-Paris, Klincksieck, 1970. p. 61–68. **8931**
Establishes a very probable case for V. having read, around 1906, Gobineau's *Histoire des Perses;* according to this thesis, Gobineau must be considered a contributor to V.'s skepticism toward the writing of history.

Germain, Gabriel. D'un humanisme intégral, oppositions et positions. CahS 349:417–27, 1958. **8932**
Develops the argument that, in *Agathe,* V. was pursuing something analogous to the mystical quest that opens onto the infinite. Germain cites the example of Yoga and of Buddhist mysticism as reference points. This perspective, however dubious, does provide a means for understanding the profound attraction V. exercised on the proto-surrealists during the period prior to 1924.

———. Valéry au seuil du Yoga—son expérience du Moi Pur et son échec spirituel. *In:* Yoga, science de l'homme intégral. Ed by J. Masui. Cahiers du sud, 1953. p. 322–40. **8933**
Sketches a bold comparison of V.'s theory of the "MOI pur" with the thirteenth chapter of the *Bhagavad-Gita.* Unfortunately, the parallel is not sufficiently developed to really make a strong case. As long as the notion of V.'s mysticism continues to be debated this essay will have to be taken into account.

Gershman, Herbert S. Valéry and Breton. *In:* Paul Valéry. See 8482. p. 199–206. **8934**

Traces the origins of Breton's disaffection with V., whom Breton had considered a master. A useful comparison of their respective anti-literary positions provides the background. Gershman argues correctly that, for Breton, V. was a myth, the spiritual father of M. Teste and, quite unwittingly, a precursor of surrealism. Further work on this subject must await the publication of the important V.-Breton correspondence.

Jones, Rhys S. Hegel and French symbolism —some observations on the Hegelianism of Paul Valéry. FS 4:142–50, 1950. **8935**

After so many attempts to argue for the positive influence of "x" on V., Jones sees in the categories of Hegelian logic, the first triad in particular, an opportunity to account both for the apparent likeness of some of V.'s thoughts to those of illustrious predecessors, and the manifest ternary structure of a number of major poems, notably "Ebauche d'un serpent." Eschewing the positivistic approach, he argues for a heuristic acceptance of V.'s "Hegelianism" on the grounds that it is the rational system capable of transforming all others. The argument's major weakness is the absence of so much evidence of a different sort which had to await the publication of the *Cahiers*.

Köhler, Hartmut. Valéry und Baudelaire. *In:* Beitraege zur vergleichende Literaturgeschichte. Festschrift fuer Kurt Weis. Tuebingen, Niemeyer, 1972. p. 209–24. **8936**

A critical examination of V.'s judgments on Baudelaire in his correspondence, in the various articles on Mallarmé, in "Situation de Baudelaire" and in the *Cahiers*. Köhler finds some contradiction among these and a desire on V.'s part to minimize a Baudelairean influence that had in fact been quite strong in his youth. This article should help rectify a long-standing misconception based upon the uncritical reception of some of V.'s harsher statements on Baudelaire.

Lang, Renée. Ein fruchtbringendes Missverständis: Rilke und Valéry. Sym 13:51–62, 1959. **8937**

The thesis is contained in the title. It is one R. Lang has developed on

several occasions. Here she concentrates on Rilke's translations of V.'s "Fragments du Narcisse" in a biographical context. See A. Robinet de Clery below.

Laurenti, Huguette. Orphée et Wagner. *In:* Entretiens sur Paul Valéry. See 8476. p. 79–85. **8938**

A sketch of the more ample development Laurenti devoted to Wagner and V. in her *Paul Valéry et le théâtre*.

Lawler, James R. T.-S. Eliot et Paul Valéry. MerF 341:76–101, 1961. *Also incorporated in:* Epilogue: two confrontations. *In his:* The poet as analyst. See 8518. p. 282–306. **8939**

Lawler studies in detail the five texts Eliot devoted to V. between 1920 and 1958. As early as 1922 Eliot sought to interest the English-speaking world in V.'s poetry, and his own interest in him, although never devoid of reservations, continued undiminished over a period of nearly forty years. Ultimately Eliot came to appreciate V. as a critic; on this point Lawler attempts to combat Eliot's judgment that V.'s criticism was flawed because it contained no criterion of seriousness.

LeSage, Laurent. Paul Valéry and Jean-Paul Sartre—a confrontation. MLQ 32:189–205, 1971. **8940**

Considerable evidence is put forward to the effect that Sartre borrowed liberally from V., from *Le cimetière marin* specifically, in *L'être et le néant*. The type of influence is otherwise a negative one, with Sartre reacting strongly to V. and his intellectual position.

Loubère, J. A. E. Borges and the wicked thoughts of Paul Valéry. MFS 19:419–31 1973. **8941**

Argues persuasively for a complex form of influence of V. on Borges. The evidence in Borges' "Pierre Menard autor del Quijote" is such that V. becomes an important component in the make-up of this fictional twentieth-century author of *Don Quixote*. Much useful material is found in *Tel Quel* and *Mauvaises pensées et autres*.
Review: Anon. in YWMLS 35:198, 1974.

Maurer, Karl W. Goethe and Valéry. UnivP 9:33–47, 1967. **8942**

The spider metaphor of "Au sujet d'Adonis" is likened to a mandala, thus drawing the commentary in the direction of an archetypal pattern of growth (compatible, it would seem, with the type of analysis done by Aigrisse). The author then moves, rather too quickly, toward the comparison with Goethe's symbol of organic growth. The article may account for aspects of V.'s rather abstract interest in Goethe, but it tends to exaggerate its importance.

Mercanton, Jacques. Valéry et Rilke. *In:* Paul Valéry, essais et témoignages inédits. *See* 8488. p. 69–81. **8943**

Treating V. as a catalyst rather than an influence, Mercanton makes a good case for Rilke's affinity to V. He locates the common ground of the affinity in an aspect of modernism, from which both poets diverge each in a personal manner. A good, though brief, comparative study.

O'Neill, James C. An intellectual affinity—Bergson and Valéry. PMLA 66:49–64, 1951. **8944**

The review of statements on V.'s supposed debt to Bergson is solid and the rejection of this approach is certainly correct. But, in light of current research on V., the author's willingness to reaffirm an affinity, however misunderstood by V. himself, appears overly hasty and insufficiently analytical. See Robinson's contribution to the question in 1965.

Petroni, Liano. De poète à poète: Giuseppe Ungaretti interprète de Paul Valéry. *In:* Entretiens sur Paul Valéry. *See* 8476. p. 179–89. **8945**

Until the publication of this article the relatively abundant commentary on V. by Ungaretti had gone unnoticed outside Italy. A welcome introduction to a question of significance for comparative studies.

Robinet de Cléry, Adrien. Paul Valéry. *In his:* Rilke traducteur. Geneva, Georg, 1956. p. 85–137. **8946**

The author studies in detail Rilke's translation of "Aurore," "Cantique des colonnes," *Le cimetière marin,* and "Fragments du Narcisse." Using line by line comparisons, he demonstrates the

high price Rilke had to pay in order to render the form of each poem faithfully. A good starting point for further investigation. See K. Wais's contribution to this question in 1967.

Robinson, Judith. Valéry critique de Bergson. *In:* Paul Valéry. *See* 8481. p. 203–15. **8947**

This very solid piece uses the *Cahiers* to excellent advantage in demolishing the thesis of Bergson's positive influence. There is also an implicit refutation of O'Neill's 1951 article in the presentation of V.'s hostility—frequently on linguistic grounds—to Bergson's whole metaphysical concept of the world. Concerning the possibility that V. may in fact have misunderstood Bergson, see the discussion with Alexandre, p. 298–300.

Roudinesco, Dr. A. Les derniers vers de Paul Valéry: les Bucoliques de Virgile. NRF 32:193–95, 1955. **8948**

This brief note relates the circumstances surrounding V.'s most ambitious project as translator and his last major effort as poet.

Rychner, Max. Dichtung und Theorie der Dichtung. Merk 17:1021–36; 1131–42, 1963. **8949**

A wide-ranging essay on poetics in which V. is considered largely in terms of his early understanding of Poe. Without developing the idea Rychner affirms the importance of V. for G. Benn and he relates R. Borchardt's estimation of V.'s work in the twenties. Rychner sees a striking parallel between the thirteenth strophe of the *Cimetière marin* and the ninth canto of Dante's *Inferno.* The general interest of this article lies in the centrality of V.'s position in Western poetics, according to Rychner.

Schneider, Albert. Les méthodes d'invention de Lichtenberg et de Valéry. AUS 1:60–82, 1952. **8950**

Does not claim any influence of Lichtenberg on V. and recognizes such influence is improbable. Constructs a detailed series of parallelisms on the double theme of critical and heuristic mental processes as the basis of creativity. Resultant similarity of view on several points is striking. The best point made is that both writers prized a rhetoric of forms.

Smith, Rowland. Roy Campbell and his French sources. CL 22:1–18, 1970. **8951**

V. is said to have been a decisive influence (through "Palme" and "Cantique des colonnes" specifically) on Roy Campbell's poetry written in Provence between 1930 and 1933.

Sutcliffe, F. E. Hegel and Valéry. FS 6:53–57, 1952. **8952**

Sutcliffe went straight to the heart of the question posed by Jones two years earlier. Citing the importance of the "combinatoire" in V. as in Hegel, he suggested that Jones's parallels, however striking, are purely formal. Concerning Jones's application of the first triad to a poem like *La jeune Parque,* Sutcliffe points out that, whereas in Hegel's logic the notion of finality dominates all other operations, this notion is alien to V.'s poem.

Torrens, James, S. J. T. S. Eliot and the austere poetics of Valéry. CL 23:1–17, 1971. **8953**

Except for a regrettable tendency to assimilate V.'s notion of pure poetry to that of Bremond, this is an intelligent statement of what V. represented in the eyes of his Anglo-American counterpart.

Vitale, Mario. L'Ulisse dantesco: Dante e Paul Valéry. Naples, L. Loffredo, 1971. 29 p. **8954**

This brief essay considers the Eleatic flavor of the *Cimetière marin* as counterpoint to Canto XXVI of the *Inferno.* It demonstrates no exceptional grasp of this aspect of V.'s poem, which serves to illuminate the Italian work. V.'s speaker is presented as an analog to Dante's Ulysses.

Wais, Karin. Studien zu Rilkes Valéry-Übertragungen. Tübingen, Max Niemeyer Verlag, 1967. iv, 164 p. **8955**

The necessary complement to Batterby's study of V.'s stylistic influence on Rilke. Wais examines Rilke's translations from the viewpoint of comparative technique and form, with an eye for the finest detail. A book intended for the specialist in comparative stylistics.

Review: E. Mason in Arca 4:102–05, 1969.

Reception and Reputation

Barboza, Enrique. El pensamiento de Paul Valéry. CA 139:180–202, 1965. **8956**

At its best an adequate introduction to V.'s thought for readers of Spanish. It is superficial, however, in presenting V. as a specialized type of the Cartesian (i.e. French) mind. Formulas lead to unsubstantiated generalizations.

Bendz, Ernst. Paul Valéry; nägra minnesord. Göteborg, Gumperts Förlag, 1945. 87 p. **8957**

The text of an address delivered at the Stockholms Högskola on Oct. 15, 1945 during an official binational commemoration. It is of interest primarily as a document on V.'s reception in Sweden.

Borges, Jorge Luis. Valéry como símbolo. *In:* Paul Valéry. *See* 8478. p. 30–32. *Also in his:* Otras inquisiciones. Buenos Aires, Emecé editores, 1960. p. 105–07. *Trans.:* Valéry as symbol. *In his:* Other inquisitions. 1937–1952. Austin, Univ. of Texas press, 1964. p. 73–74. *And in his:* Labyrinths. New York, New directions, 1964. p. 197–98. **8958**

Despite its extreme brevity this text has a history by virtue of the celebrity of Borges. Its principal significance is to have proclaimed, on the morrow of V.'s death, that he was as much a myth as was Edmond Teste. This immortal quality, according to Borges, assured his permanence alongside poets who were superior to him: Yeats, Rilke, Eliot, Joyce and S. George.

Díez-Canedo, Enrique. El poeta Paul Valéry en la capital de España. *In his:* Conversaciones literarias, tercera seria: 1924–1930. México, J. Mortiz, 1964. p. 9–15. **8959**

Reminiscences of V.'s two lectures in Madrid in May 1924: "Baudelaire et la postérité" and "L'esprit de la Pléiade." The text is detailed and contains one of the best descriptions of V. as public lecturer. Its current value is exclusively documentary.

Fiumi, Lionello. Note su Paul Valéry con alcune traduzione di liriche. Verona, Accademia di agricoltura scienze e lettere, 1967. 59 p. **8960**

The nearly thirty pages of essays vary in type from personal recollections of V. in Paris (1930–1940) to presentations of critical works to an Italian public (H. Fabureau, G. Faure, E. de La Rochefoucauld). In the case of the latter's reading of the *Cahiers,* Fiumi stresses beyond all measure the importance of V.'s reflections on Christianity with the result that V. is made to return to the fold. The volume is completed by Fiumi's Italian rendering of nine poems from *Charmes.* A letter from V. to Fiumi, in Italian, concerning the translation of "Anne" includes interesting details on the phonemic structure of the poem.
Reviews: Costa du Rels in RdP 74: 154–55, Sept. 1967; L. Losito in CulF 14:159–60, 1967; L.-A. Magnery in SFr 12:190–91, 1968.

Lozano, Rafael. Señas de Paul Valéry. *In:* [Valéry, Paul] Poesía de Paul Valéry. Mexico, Editorial prisma, 1943. p. 13–36.
                                                                      8961
The introduction to this anthology of poems translated by Lozano presents V. as one of the great lyric poets of the ages. The concept of pure poetry is treated at some length and is linked closely to Poe. It is the architectonic quality of V.'s poems that Lozano stresses most, attempting to convey it in his translations, which he considers the execution of the same music on a different instrument. This brief essay is best

considered today as one measure of the reception of V. in Spanish America.

Simond, Daniel. Paul Valéry et la Suisse. *In:* Entretiens sur Paul Valéry. *See* 8476. p. 139–55.   **8962**
A very useful contribution to the 1971 Montpellier colloquium; it contains a bibliography of V.'s works published in, or on, Switzerland and a list of Swiss articles, monographs and collective volumes devoted to V. The text of the communication stresses V.'s lectures, travels and personal encounters in Switzerland.

Speranza Armani, Ada. Croce e Valéry. Stu 40:237–56, 1966.   **8963**
This is a very valuable article in that it draws together for the first time the usually devastating criticisms levelled against V. by the most authoritative Italian esthetician of his day. The careful documentation will make it possible to find the pertinent Croce texts. But the article also proposes to make sense of Croce's hostility, directed especially against any supposition of logical rigor in V.'s thought. Speranza Armani finds the fundamental element of division in V.'s negation of esthetics as science, the very point on which Croce's reputation had been built. She concludes that Croce had misunderstood V.'s poetry which is quite compatible with his own notions.

CHAPTER XIX

SAINT-JOHN PERSE

(Pseud. of Marie René Alexis Saint-Leger Leger)

(No. 8964–9348)

René Galand*

Bibliography and Indices

Freitag, Ruth S. Saint-John Perse: A list of his writings in the collections of the Library of Congress. *In:* Emmanuel, Pierre. Saint-John Perse: praise and presence. Washington, Library of Congress, 1971. p. 25–80.　　　　　　　　　**8964**

Lists the 191 titles of P.'s published writings represented in the Library of Congress. 52 additional entries for unpublished papers which are individually described and summarized.

Little, Roger. Saint-John Perse: A bibliography for students of his poetry. London, Grant and Cutler, 1971. 80 p.　　**8965**

A complete listing of P.'s poetry, criticism, tributes, speeches, and correspondence published prior to December 30, 1970. Also includes 50 books, periodicals, and theses wholly or substantially devoted to P., as well as 866 other articles and references. No attempt is made to differentiate between the significant and the inconsequential.

————. Word index of the complete poetry and prose of Saint-John Perse. Durham, Durham univ., 1965. 290 p. (mimeographed). Supplement A. Southampton, univ. of Southampton, 1966. 42 p. (mimeographed).　　　　　　**8966**

Useful instrument for stylistic and thematic studies. Some of the most common words have been omitted (e.g., *avoir, être, avec, dans, par...*). No statistics are given.

Reviews: C. Hackett in FS 22:261–62, 1968; G. Rees in MLR 62:134–35, 1967.

Saint-John Perse. Bibliographie sélective. *In his:* Œuvres complètes. *See* 8968. p. 1347–92.　　　　　　　　　**8967**

Includes a detailed list of editions and translations of P.'s poetic works, and a selected, but extensive, bibliography of critical studies.

Edition

Saint-John Perse. Œuvres complètes. Gallimard, 1972, xlii, 1415 p. (Bibliothèque de la Pléïade)　　　　　　　**8968**

With a few minor exceptions, this volume includes all of the previously published poems, tributes, speeches, statements, and correspondence of P., as well as a considerable amount of previously unpublished writings. Biography, bibliography and notes were prepared by P. himself. Variants or early versions are not included. Published writings by P. not included in this volume are listed below as separate entries.

Review: P. de Boisdeffre in RDM 149–51, Jan. 1973.

Miscellaneous Texts and Correspondence

Saint-John Perse. [Extracts from three letters to the publisher of L'ordre des oiseaux]. *In:* L'ordre des oiseaux. Saint-John Perse. Georges Braque. Exposition des manuscrits et eaux-fortes. 17 décembre–17 janvier 1963. Bibliothèque nationale.　**8969**

Extracts from three letters by P. dated January 26, March 5, and March 10, 1962.

————. [Fragments of letter and translation from Pindar]. *In:* Noulet, Emilie. Le ton

* Occasional assistance from Carol Rigolot.

dans la poésie de Saint-John Perse. SynB 10-20, Sept.-Oct., 1968. *Also in:* Noulet, Emilie. Le ton poétique. Corti, 1971. p. 185-203. **8970**

Contains fragments of letter and translation by P. from Pindar's "First Pythian ode," with original notes.

————. [L'Homme], [Textes et documents], [Annexe]. *In:* Honneur à Saint-John Perse. *See* 9022. p. 603-12, 653-67, 685-793. **8971**

These two sections contain letters, some of which constitute major poetic or political statements, addressed by P. to P. Béarn, L. Blum, R. Caillois, W. Churchill, General de Gaulle, M.-P. Fouchet, D. Hammarskjöld, G. Huppert, A. MacLeish, F. de Miomandre, K.-J. Müller, F. D. Roosevelt. Included are also letters addressed to or concerning P. from: Admiral Auboyneau, Alain-Fournier, L. Barthou, G. Bidault, W. Churchill, P. Claudel, Colette, General de Gaulle, T. S. Eliot, L. E. Evans, L.-P. Fargue, A. Fontaine, G. Frizeau, A. Gide, J. Giraudoux, F. Jammes, V. Larbaud, F. de Miomandre, A. de Noailles, Paul-Boncour, R.-M. Rilke, J. Rivière, F. D. Roosevelt, R. Schuman, J. Supervielle, A. Tixier, P. Valéry, R. Vitrac. P.'s letters have been reprinted in his *Œuvres complètes* (*see* 8968), but only a few of the letters addressed to him have been included in the notes of this edition.

————. [Letter to Octavio Barreda.] EtC 7:16-17, 1961. **8972**

This letter to the Mexican translator of *Anabase* is reproduced in facsimile between pages 16 and 17.

————. [Letter to Shlomo Elbaz.] *In:* Little, Roger. Preface to a new translation of Anabase. ArlQ 2:111, 1970. **8973**

Letter to author of a master's thesis at the University of Jerusalem.

————. [Selected fragments from Amers]. *In:* Clergue, Lucien. Genèse. Pierre Belfond, 1973. Unpaginated. **8974**

Fragments from *Amers* selected by P. to accompany 50 photographs by Lucien Clergue, on the double motif of woman and the sea.

————. Témoignages littéraires. Témoignages politiques. Lettres. *In his:* Œuvres complètes. *See* 8968. p. 547-1083. **8975**

These sections contain letters addressed to: Alain-Fournier, G.-J. Aubry, P. Béarn, P. Berthelot, F. Biddle, Mrs. R. W. Bliss, L. Blum, A. Bosquet, W. Brandt, Dr. Bussière, R. Caillois, J. J. Castro, K. J. Chapin, J. Charpier, W. Churchill, P. Claudel, J. Conrad, A. Conty, E. E. Cummings, Mina Curtiss, J. Damour, T. S. Eliot, M.-P. Fouchet, G. Frizeau, G. Gallimard, General de Gaulle, A. Gide, P. Guerre, D. Hammarskjöld, A. Henry, E. Herriot, G. Huppert, F. Jammes, J. F. Kennedy, V. Larbaud, J. F. de Launay, Madame Saint-Leger Leger, E. Lindegren, A. MacLeish, L.-A. Marcel, M. Martins, F. de Miomandre, A. Monnier, G.-A. Monod, K. J. Müller, O. Nadal, Mrs. K. Nehru, J. Paulhan, H. Peyre, L.-M. Raymond, J. Rivière, F. D. Roosevelt, A. Rousseaux, I. Stravinsky, J. Supervielle, the King of Sweden, A. Tate, and G.-C. Toussaint. In the notes are included letters addressed to P. by W. Churchill, P. Claudel, General de Gaulle, A. Gide, E. Herriot, J. F. Kennedy, V. Larbaud, F. de Miomandre, A. Monnier, F. D. Roosevelt.

Biography

[Annexe]. *In:* Honneur à Saint-John Perse. *See* 9022. p. 681-789. **8976**

Provides detailed information on P.'s diplomatic service in China, as Secretary General for Foreign Affairs, and on his American exile. Includes the text of the 1940 and 1941 decrees depriving P. of his French citizenship, confiscating his property, and expelling him from the Order of the Legion of Honor. Includes journalistic accounts of his removal from his post of Secretary General in May 1940.

Beucler, André. Rencontre avec Saint-John Perse. Iô 2:1-8, 1964. **8977**

Describes a meeting with P. to whose office the author had been brought by his friend Léon-Paul Fargue.

Cameron, Elizabeth R. Alexis Leger dans l'histoire diplomatique. *In:* Honneur à Saint-John Perse. *See* 9022. p. 739-52. **8978**

Detailed account of P.'s diplomatic activity from 1925 to 1940.

————. Fighters for lost causes: Alexis Saint-Leger Leger. *In:* The diplomats: 1919–1939. Ed. by Gordon A. Craig and Felix Gilbert. Princeton, Princeton univ. press, 1953. p. 378–405. *Trans. in:* Honneur à Saint-John Perse. See 9022. p. 739–52.   **8979**

Detailed account of P.'s diplomatic activity from 1925 to 1940.

Chapin, Katherine Garrison. St.-John Perse: an American view. SSW Feb. 20, 1961. *Trans. in:* Honneur à Saint-John Perse. See 9022. p. 286–91. *Also in:* Œuvres complètes. See 8968. p. 1247–52.   **8980**

A revealing portrait of P. by a close American friend.

Courrent, Jacques. Autour d'un pseudonyme: Saint-John Perse. VL 120:278–79. 1961.   **8981**

Suggests a possible source of P.'s pseudonym: in the first *Supplément* of the *Grand dictionnaire universel du XIXᵉ siècle* by Pierre Larousse, the word Saint-Leger is immediately preceded by the name of the English writer Saint-John (Percy.)

Devlin, Denis. Saint-John Perse à Washington. *In:* Saint-John Perse. See 9026. p. 86–89. *Also in:* Honneur à Saint-John Perse. See 9022. p. 71–73.   **8982**

Personal recollections by the Irish poet who translated the poems of *Exil* into English. Stresses P.'s interest in grammar and linguistics.

Fouchet, Max-Pol. Rencontre de l'exact. *In:* Saint-John Perse. See 9026. p. 140–43. *Also in:* Honneur à Saint-John Perse. See 9022. p. 131–35. *Also:* Un chant de force pour les hommes. *In his:* Les appels. Mercure de France, 1967. p. 121–26.   **8983**

Brief summary of three interviews with P. in Washington in the fall of 1948. Stresses P.'s rejection of the Judeo-Christian tradition and his exact mastery of language as a means of asserting man's authority over the world of things.

Guerre, Pierre. Dans la haute maison de mer. Rencontres avec Saint-John Perse. *In:* Saint-John Perse, homme de vigie. See 9027. p. 344–54. *Also in:* Honneur à Saint-John Perse. See 9022. p. 168–80. *Also in:* Œuvres complètes. See 8968. p.

1332–42. *Trans.:* YR 50:308–17. 1960. Sur 268:18–28, 1961.   **8984**

Relates visits and conversations with P. in his house on the Presqu'île de Giens. Revealing glimpse of the poet and his numerous interests: botany, zoology, geology, medicine, ethnography, philology, history, law.

Guillou, Jean. Karukéra, île natale de St. John Perse. FR 39:281–87, 1965.   **8985**

Compares P.'s vision of his native island with his own experience of Guadeloupe, which is strongly influenced by his awareness of racial and economic problems.

Hoppenot, Henri. D'Alexis Leger à Saint-John Perse. FL 759:1, 6, 1960. *Also:* D'Alexis Leger à Saint-John Perse. Liège, Dynamo, 1960. 15 p. *Also in:* Honneur à Saint-John Perse. See 9022. p. 803–07.   **8986**

Personal recollections of P. by a former colleague and friend in the French diplomatic service.

Mazars, Pierre. Une journée avec Saint-John Perse. FL 759:1, 6, 1960. *Also:* Une journée avec Saint-John Perse. Liège, Eds. Dynamo, 1961. 14 p. *Also in:* Honneur à Saint-John Perse. See 9022. p. 618–23. *Also in:* Œuvres complètes. See 8968. p. 575–77.   **8987**

In this interview, P. touches upon a number of topics: his collaboration with Briand, his encounter with Hitler, the publication of *Anabase,* the selection of his pseudonym, his reasons for writing, the significance of *Anabase* and *Exil,* his poetic vocabulary, Claudel and Valéry, the interest in poetry evinced by modern scientists and philosophers.

McCormick, James. Just an impression. KR 23:336, 1961.   **8988**

Candid description of the ceremonies of the Nobel Prize award.

Morand, Paul. Alexis Leger en 1916. Il n'a jamais failli sur l'essentiel. *In:* Honneur à Saint-John Perse. See 9022. p. 616–17.   **8989**

Brief recollections of P. in the diplomatic service by a fellow diplomat.

————. Journal d'un attaché d'ambassade. 1916–17. La table ronde, 1949. p. 21–22, 88, 200–01, 294.   **8990**

Vivid evocation of a farewell party in honor of P., who was leaving for China. Brief mentions of P.'s friend, Misia Sert, of a letter written by P. to Berthelot, of Céleste [Albaret]'s opinion of P.'s poetry.

Offner, Jacques. Le nom de Saint-John Perse. VL 121:181–85, 1962. **8991**

Inclines to accept the explanation suggested by Jacques Courrent, *supra*, for P.'s pseudonym.

Raymond, Louis-Marcel. Eloge de Saint-John Perse. ECF 9:61–108, 1961. *Also in:* Honneur à Saint-John Perse. *See* 9022. p. 624–28. **8992**

Recalls conversations with P. on a number of topics: natural history, geography, personal incidents and travels, Larbaud, Gide, differences between French and English, the role of literary critics, P.'s methods of writing. Good illustration of P.'s talent as conversationalist.

Rougemont, Denis de. Saint-John Perse en Amérique. *In:* Honneur à Saint-John Perse. *See* 9022. p. 614–15. **8993**

Tells of the speech given by P. in memory of Briand in 1942, and of P.'s life in America during the first years of his exile.

Saint-John Perse. Biographie. *In his:* Œuvres complètes. *See* 8968. p. ix–xlii. **8994**

This detailed biography was prepared by the author himself. Provides the most complete information available on the events of his life and the composition of his works.

Schlumberger, Jean. Rencontres. Visite de L.-L. conduit par Jacques Rivière. NRF 176–268–71, 1967. **8995**

Pages written in 1911 after a visit from P., during which Schlumberger and P. appear to have found but little in common.

Strömberg, Kjell. La petite histoire de l'attribution du prix Nobel à Saint-John Perse. *In:* Saint-John Perse. Œuvre poétique. Monaco, Rombaldi, 1965. p. 9–19. **8996**

Anecdotes pertaining to P.'s selection (recommendations by Hammarskjöld, T. S. Eliot, Mauriac), and to the Nobel ceremony (P. eschewing the decorations attributed to Alexis Leger). [CR]

Victoria, Marcos. La musique dans la nuit. *In:* Honneur à Saint-John Perse. *See* 9022. p. 280–85. **8997**

Recounts anecdotes told by P., one of which is alluded to in *Anabase* ("un enfant triste comme la mort des singes," Canto IV).

Tributes

Allan, Blaise. Jeanne et l'Anabase. *In:* Saint-John Perse. *See* 9026. p. 52–54. **8998**

Brief anecdote about a French woman who worked as a cook for a New York publisher and who was fascinated by P.'s poetry.

American Academy and National Institute of Arts and Letters. Citation officielle. *In:* Honneur à Saint-John Perse. *See* 9022. p. 640–41. **8999**

Text read upon the election of P. as honorary member of the Academy in 1960.

Andrade, Jorge Carrera. [Tribute to P.] *In:* Hommage international de Combat. *See* 9021. *Also in:* Honneur à Saint-John Perse. *See* 9022. p. 157–58. **9000**

P.'s poetry is characterized as an impersonal epic celebrating the great adventure of human civilization and as the expression of a new classicism equalled only by the great poems of antiquity.

Arts. June 12, 1957. **9001**

Tribute to P. upon the publication of *Amers*. Contributions by Roger Caillois and Paul Morand.

Berger, Yves. Raisons d'aimer. *In:* Honneur à Saint-John Perse. *See* 9022. p. 234–36. **9002**

Lists a number of reasons, mostly subjective, for praising the poetry of P.

Char, René. A Saint-John Perse *In:* Saint-John Perse. *See* 9026. p. 33. *Also in:* Honneur à Saint-John Perse. *See* 9022. p. 23. **9003**

Char states his own affinity with the author of *Anabase, Eloges,* and *Exil.*

Cruchaga, Juan Guzman. Pluies. *In:* Saint-John Perse. *See* 9026. p. 42. *Also in:* Honneur à Saint-John Perse. *See* 9022. p. 28. **9004**

Poem written as a tribute to P.

Fargue, Léon-Paul. Lettre. *In:* Saint-John Perse. *See* 9026. p. 30. *Also in:* Honneur à Saint-John Perse. *See* 9022. p. 20. 9005

Brief letter to P., expressing his admiration for *Vents*.

Guillén, Jorge. Je vivrai dans mon nom. *In:* Saint-John Perse. *See* 9026. p. 36–40. *Also in:* Honneur à Saint-John Perse. *See* 9022. p. 25–27.   9006

Translation of a poem in honor of P. which brings together many of P.'s most characteristic motifs and images.

Lambrichs, Georges. L'appel de mai 42 ou La splendeur de vivre. *In:* Honneur à Saint-John Perse. *See* 9022. p. 233. 9007

Recalls his discovery of *Exil* during World War II as an answer to the reality of the time.

Larbaud, Valery. Come a maestro. NRF 236:760, 1933. *Also in:* Honneur à Saint-John Perse. *See* 9022. p. 403.   9008

Lists P. among the four authors he considers as having had the greatest personal influence on his literary formation.

————. Préface pour une édition russe d'Anabase. NRF 148:64–67, 1926. *Also in:* Saint-John Perse. Anabase. New York, Brentano's, 1945. n.p. *Also in:* Honneur à Saint-John Perse. *See* 9022. p. 426–28. *Also in:* Œuvres complètes. *See* 8698. p. 1236–37. *Trans. in:* From the NRF. An image of the twentieth century from the pages of the Nouvelle revue française. Ed. with an introd. by Justin O'Brien. Farrar, Strauss and Cudahy, 1958. p. 136–40.   9009

P., Claudel, Jammes, Valéry and Fargue, are singled out as the only five significant poets of the period 1895–1925. P. is praised for introducing a new geographic, historical, and human dimension into French poetry.

Lindblad, Bertil. Présentation de Saint-John Perse. *In:* Honneur à Saint-John Perse. *See* 9022. p. 643–44.   9010

Brief tribute to P. at the Nobel Banquet.

Lucchese, Romeo. Eloge de Saint-John Perse. *In:* Honneur à Saint-John Perse. *See* 9022. p. 259–61.   9011

Tribute to P. based on some of P.'s motifs: the island, the sea, the tree, the emblem of Shiva.

MacLeish, Archibald. Official presentation to the American Academy and the National Institute of Arts and Letters. *In:* Honneur à Saint-John Perse. *See* 9022. p. 633–34. *Also in:* Œuvres complètes. *See* 8968. p. 1158–59.   9012

Text accompanying the presentation to P. of the Award of Merit Medal for Poetry in 1950.

Malraux, André. Allocution. *In:* Honneur à Saint-John Perse. *See* 9022. p. 639. *Also in:* Œuvres complètes. *See* 8968. p. 1161.   9013

Speech given upon the award of the Grand Prix National des Lettres to P. in 1959.

Monnier, Adrienne. Poème pour Saint-Leger Leger et Saint-John Perse. *In:* Honneur à Saint-John Perse. *See* 9022. p. 613. 9014

Brief tribute to P. in 1923.

Morand, Paul. Saint-John Perse. Arts June 12, 1957. *Also in his:* Monplaisir. I. Gallimard, 1967. p. 241–45. *Also in:* Honneur à Saint-John Perse [extract] *See* 9022. p. 616–17.   9015

Brief tribute to P., whose integrity and dignity are highly praised. In *Anabase,* notes the refusal of facile exoticism and the rejection of facile lyricism.

Ocampo, Victoria. Desacuerdos (a propósito de Saint-John Perse y de una ardilla). Sur 270:92–94, 1961.   9016

Justifies the attribution of the Nobel Prize to P. because of his love of language, his refusal of sadness, and his celebration of life to its extreme limits. Telling anecdote about a squirrel that came to P.'s window in Washington.

Oster, Pierre. Le seul maître. *In:* Honneur à Saint-John Perse. *See* 9022. p. 214. 9017

Brief tribute to P. by a poet whose work has been influenced by P.

Proust, Marcel. Il y avait manque de transition... *In:* Honneur à Saint-John Perse. *See* 9022. p. 383.   9018

Fragment from *A la recherche du temps perdu* in which mention is made of the "poèmes admirables mais obscurs de Saint-Leger Leger" [*Eloges*].

Schehadé, Georges. Voici l'île. *In:* Saint-John Perse. *See* 9026. p. 41. *Also in:* Honneur à Saint-John Perse. *See* 9022. p. 28.   9019

Poem written in tribute to P., largely inspired by *Eloges.*

Yale University. Citation officielle. *In:* Honneur à Saint-John Perse. *See* 9022. p. 638–39. 9020
Citation read upon the conferring of the Doctor of Letters degree upon P. in 1959.

Collected Articles

Hommage international de Combat. Comb May 16, 1957. *Also in:* Honneur à Saint-John Perse. *See* 9022. p. 145–164. 9021
Includes tributes to P. by Pierre Jean Jouve, Conrad Aiken, Jean Cassou, Miguel Angel Asturias, Pierre Emmanuel, Henry Miller, Jean Grosjean, Michel de Ghelderode, Marcel Arland, Jorge Carrera Andrade, Julien Gracq, Léon-Gabriel Gros, and Alain Bosquet.

Honneur à Saint-John Perse. Hommages et témoignages littéraires suivis d'une documentation sur Alexis Leger diplomate. Introd. de Jean Paulhan. Gallimard, 1965. 817 p. 9022
This impressive and indispensable work brings together nearly 150 articles, essays, notes, and tributes to P. Texts, speeches, and letters by P. are also included, as well as 10 photographs. Contains much of the most significant research on P. up to date of publication. Important articles have been analyzed separately under the appropriate headings.
Reviews: R. Lacôte in LetF June 24, 1965; C. Nelson in FR 39:652, 1966; S. Pitou in BA 40:293, 1966.

Livres de France V. 10, January 1959. 9023
Special issue on P. Includes bibliography, portraits, illustrations, and the reproduction of one page in P.'s handwriting.

Mungen. No. 15. Feb. 1, 1964. 9024
Special issue on Saint-John Perse. Includes Japanese translations of *Anabase* by Rikutaro Fukuda, *Exil* by Masaki Katayama, *Oiseaux* by Komao Naruse, *Poésie* by Komao Naruse; discussion of P.'s work by Rikutaro Fukuda, Hajimi Sato, Küchiro Mizuta, Komao Naruse, Isamu Kurita; the poetics of Saint-John Perse by Komao Naruse; *Exil* by Masaki

Katayama; texts by Roger Caillois, trans. by Küchiro Mizuta; Allen Tate, trans. by Yozo Tokunaga; Gabriel Bounoure, trans. by Reiko Yokokura; Albert Béguin, trans. by Chimako Tada; with four portraits of P.

Poesia española. Número especial dedicado a Saint-John Perse. Nov. 1960. 9025
Includes: José García Nieto, *Saint-John Perse:* José G. Manrique de Lara, *Mundo poético de Saint-John Perse; Poemas de Saint-John Perse (Crónica, Amistad del príncipe, Exilio)* trans. by Manuel Alvarez Ortega; *Cronologia de Saint-John Perse;* texts by Emile Henriot, André Rousseaux, Alain Bosquet, René Massat, A. Rolland de Renéville trans. by Jesús Acacio.

Saint-John Perse. CahP 10. Gallimard, 1950. *Also in:* Honneur à Saint-John Perse. *See* 9022. p. 11–140. 9026
Includes tributes to P. by: André Gide, T. S. Eliot, Léon-Paul Fargue, Herbert Steiner, René Char, Jules Supervielle, Jorge Guillén, Georges Schehadé, J. G. Cruchaga, Valery Larbaud, Blaise Allan, Pierre Jean Jouve, Paul Claudel, André Breton, A. Rolland de Renéville, Albert Béguin, Giuseppe Ungaretti, Denis Devlin, Jorge Zalamea, Roger Caillois, Gabriel Bounoure, M.-J. Lefebve, Archibald MacLeish, Stephen Spender, Renato Poggioli, L.-M. Raymond, Friedhelm Kemp, Denis de Rougement, Max-Pol Fouchet and Allen Tate. The significant articles have been analyzed under the appropriate headings. Blaise Allan's article has been omitted in *Honneur à Saint-John Perse.*

Saint-John Perse, homme de vigie. CahS 352, 1959. *Also in:* Honneur à Saint-John Perse. *See* 9022. p. 165–206. 9027
Contributions by Pierre Guerre, André Rousseaux, and Luc-André Marcel. The significant articles have been analyzed under the appropriate headings.

A tribute to Saint-John Perse. BerR 1, Winter 1956. 9028
Includes: *Une lettre de Saint-John Perse sur la poésie moderne* (French text and English translation); Arthur J. Knodel, *On approaching a difficult poet: Saint-John Perse;* René Girard, *Winds and poetic experience;* George Huppert,

Poem to a stranger: a study in symbolic structure; Fragment of Amers: Etroits sont les vaisseaux (II and VI) (French text and English translation). The significant articles have been analyzed separately under the appropriate headings.

General Studies

Albe. Franse letteren: Saint-John Perse. DWB 8:492–96, 1959.   **9029**

General presentation of P. and his works from *Eloges* to *Amers* on the occasion of the award of the Prix international de poésie.

Alyn, Marc. Un poète de sang bleu. Dém Oct. 6, 1960. *Also in:* Honneur à Saint-John Perse. *See* 9022. p. 518–19.   **9030**

Characterizes P.'s vision of history, which combines allusions to contemporary events with a remote past, as an attempt to capture the cosmic movement at work within man and within the universe.

Amer, Henry. Saint-John Perse, poète de la distance. *In:* Honneur à Saint-John Perse. *See* 9022. p. 236–38.   **9031**

P.'s poetry, instead of seeking the closest intimacy with the innermost recesses of individual experience, of consciousness or the unconscious, keeps at a distance from singular events, beings, or things. This distance may be expressed in various ways (geographical exile, spiritual askesis, ceremony of language), but it does not prevent the poet from sharing in the sufferings or the joys common to all men.

Anex, Georges. Poète du seuil et du songe. *In:* Honneur à Saint-John Perse. *See* 9022. p. 241–45.   **9032**

P.'s poetic space extends between the threshold and the dream, between security and adventure, between the immobility of the shore and the movement of the wind and the call of the sea.

Aragon, Louis. Car c'est de l'homme qu'il s'agit... LetF 848:1, 5, 1960. *Also in:* Honneur à Saint-John Perse. *See* 9022. p. 576–84.   **9033**

Refutes the legend of P.'s obscurity. P.'s poetry speaks of man in all the urgency of his aspiration, which seeks its ultimate fulfillment through the exaltation of human love. A highly personal reaction to P.'s poetry, with occasional barbs aimed at Aragon's political enemies.

Arnold, Fritz. Saint-John Perse. Merk 119: 92–95, 1958.   **9034**

General presentation of P. Traces P.'s evolution from *Eloges* to *Amers:* personal reminiscences in *Eloges*, historical and mythical aspects in *Anabase*, mythic figure of the Alien in the poems of *Exil*, the juncture of earth and sea, of home and exile, of the spirit transcending its human bonds in *Vents* and *Amers*.

Audejean, Christian. Avez-vous lu Perse? Esp 1:181–83, 1961.   **9035**

Sees each of P.'s works as a stage in the poet's spiritual quest. Praises P. for his literary dignity.

Auden, W. H. A song of life's power to renew. TBR 1, 12, July 27, 1958. *Trans. in:* Honneur à Saint-John Perse. *See* 9022. p. 502–03.   **9036**

Sees an affinity with Rimbaud and Whitman, but the comparison is mostly with Pindar. Whereas Pindar's world was small and its history provincial in scale, P. celebrates the whole universe of Man, the author of Universal History, and life's power to renew itself in spite of all disasters, natural or manmade.

Balaschow, N. Cen-Jon Perse nakhodit Orientiry. VLit 3:132–44, 1961.   **9037**

General presentation of P.'s life and works. Sees *Anabase* as the key to P.'s poetry.

Baldner, R. W. St.-John Perse as poet-prophet. PPNCFL 17:123–29, 1966.   **9038**

The germ of the motif of the poet-prophet appears in *Anabase*, but it is only in the poems of exile that it is fully developed. *Vents* characterizes the poet as "homme assailli du Dieu." In *Amers*, the poet, from prophet, becomes an oracle. He no longer interprets the god; he merely transmits the essence of the message.

Béguin, Albert. Une poésie scandée. *In:* Saint-John Perse. *See* 9026. 78–80. *Also in:* Honneur à Saint-John Perse. *See* 9022. p. 65–67. *Also in his:* Poésie de la présence. Neuchâtel, La Baconnière, 1957. p. 313–18. *Trans. in:* Saint-John Perse. Winds. Pantheon, 1953. p. 239–41. (Bollingen series, 34.) **9039**

In P.'s poems, recurrent words and sentences create a highly individualized rhythmical structure which echoes the movement of human time through the ages.

Berger, Pierre. Saint-John Perse; ou, les pleins pouvoirs de la poésie. Preu 33:58–62, 1953. **9040**

Examines the main themes to be found in P.'s poetry: exoticism, the harmony of man with the cosmos, the sense of the sacred.

Bernard, Suzanne. Saint-Léger Léger ou les débuts de Saint-John Perse; Saint-John Perse et la fidélité à la notion de poème. *In her:* Le poème en prose de Baudelaire jusqu'à nos jours. Nizet, 1959. p. 599–601, 755–62. **9041**

With P., poetry recovers its ritual function, the celebration of a universal order, which is reflected in the formal organization of the poem.

Blanch, Antonio. Saint-John Perse, premio Nobel. RyF 755:479–83, 1960. **9042**

Brief presentation of P.'s poetry upon the award of the Nobel prize.

Blin, Georges. Littérature française moderne. AnCF 69:534–38, 1969–70. **9043**

According to the poetic theory expressed in *Vents,* the poem keeps the promise that it makes, much like the Greek oracles of antiquity. Examines the motif of prophecy in *Vents* and other writings.

Blöcker, Günter. Saint-John Perse: Dichtungen. *In his:* Kritisches Lesebuch. Literatur unserer Zeit in Probe und Bericht. Hamburg, Leibniz-Verlag, 1962. p. 426–29. **9044**

Brief presentation of P.'s life and works.

Boisdeffre, Pierre de. Le destin de Saint-John Perse. JdG Oct. 25, 1959. *Also in:* Honneur à Saint-John Perse. *See* 9022. p. 573–75. **9045**

Although P.'s poetry conveys the sense of the Sacred, it does not, unlike Claudel's, lead to religious faith. Includes a brief survey of P.'s poetry from *Eloges* to *Amers.*

———. Saint-John Perse n'est plus un exilé. *In his:* Une histoire vivante de la littérature d'aujourd'hui. Perrin, 1968. p. 657–66. **9046**

Brief survey of P.'s poetry from *Exil* to *Chronique.* Although no reference is made to a transcendental God, few works, according to Boisdeffre, convey a stronger sense of the Sacred.

———. Saint-John Perse, prix Nobel. RDM 455–61, Dec. 1, 1960. **9047**

Brief presentation of P., general and somewhat superficial.

———. Souveraineté de Saint-John Perse. RDM:174–81, Nov. 15, 1966. **9048**

General survey of P.'s works from *Eloges* to *Chronique.* Stresses P.'s belief in the greatness and power of man, his secular faith in the Cosmos, his celebration of the splendor of the world, his trust in the sovereignty of poetry.

Bol, V.-P. Essai d'introduction à l'œuvre de Saint-John Perse. RevN 25:161–72, 1957. **9049**

Characterizes P.'s use of vocabulary and syntax, his celebration of the world, his preference for a certain human type. Brief analysis of *Vents.*

Bollack, Jean. Anderswo. NRs 71:310–17, 1960. *Trans.:* Ailleurs. *In:* Honneur à Saint-John Perse. *See* 9022. p. 338–44. **9050**

Traces the symbol of the sea from *Eloges* to *Amers,* as it changes from the call of absence to the restoration of a lost presence, from the obsession of Nothingness to the exaltation of Being, from an initial division to eventual reconciliation.

Bosquet, Alain. L'œuvre de Saint-John Perse. RdP 67:128–36. 1960. **9051**

Brief survey of P.'s evolution from *Eloges* to *Chronique,* stressing P.'s refusal of any hierarchy of values, his sense of a life principle at work in the cosmos, and his rehabilitation of man and the forces against which he struggles.

———. Saint-John Perse. Seghers, 1953. 207 p. (Poètes d'aujourd'hui, 35) *Also:* 1967 and 1971. **9052**

Good introduction to P.'s poetry in spite of the limited anthology and sketchy bibliography. Good biographical section. 16 photographs are included. Bosquet characterizes P.'s evolution from *Eloges* to *Chronique* as the gradual fusion of the poetic theme, the creative activity of language, and the elaboration of a poetics. Interesting sections on imagery, metrics, syntax, and P.'s literary affinities. The updated, revised ed. is to be preferred. Review: L. Estang in PenF Nov., 1957. *Also in:* Honneur à Saint-John Perse. *See* 9022. p. 569–72.

————. Saint-John Perse. LivF 10, no. 1: 3–6, 14, 1959.   **9053**
Bosquet sees three conditions which poets must fulfill in order to meet the demands of today: the creation of a personal idiom, the elaboration of an ethic, the establishment of a solidarity with the elemental world. P.'s poetry has the rare power to do so.

————. Saint-John Perse ou la rhétorique rédemptrice. *In his:* Verbe et vertige. Situation de la poésie. Hachette, 1961. p. 131–48. *Also in:* Honneur à Saint-John Perse. *See* 9022. p. 363–77.   **9054**
Stresses P.'s refusal of Cartesian logic, his rejection of any hierarchy of values, and his creation of a synthesis in which the real, the imaginary and the activity of language share the same authority. P.'s central motif is identified as the principle of cosmic energy which causes the self, the world, and the word to merge in the epic trinity of the poem.

————. The works of Saint-John Perse. *In:* Saint-John Perse. Exile and other poems. Bilingual ed. Trans. by Denis Devlin. Pantheon, 1949. p. 154–60. (The Bollingen series, 15.)   **9055**
Eloges praises the world and life. *Anabase* is a long epic poem recounting the expedition of a prince who is both captain and prophet. In *Exil*, the exiled prince has lost his power and his kingdom, and the poet is no longer master of his poem. *Vents* is the poem of man confronted with the violence of history and the violence within himself, both of which he fears and loves.

Bounoure, Gabriel. Saint-John Perse et l'ambiguïté poétique. *In:* Saint-John Perse. *See*

9026. p. 106–11. *Also in:* Honneur à Saint-John Perse. *See* 9022. p. 91–97. *Trans. in:* Saint-John Perse. Winds. Bilingual ed. Trans. by Hugh Chisholm. Pantheon, 1953. p. 242–47. (Bollingen series, 34)   **9056**
P.'s ambiguities are the sign of a fundamental ambivalence. The revelation of reality can only be achieved through the magical and mystical operation of poetry which requires a detour through nothingness.

Breton, André. Le donateur. *In:* Saint-John Perse. *See* 9026. p. 68–70. *Also in:* Honneur à Saint-John Perse. *See* 9022. p. 53–55.   **9057**
Breton evokes his early admiration of P.'s imagery, celebration of desire, and praise of human activities for other than utilitarian motives. This tribute may explain why Breton called P. a "surréaliste à distance" in his 1924 *Manifeste du surréalisme.*

————. Surréaliste à distance... *In:* Honneur à Saint-John Perse. *See* 9022. p. 384 **9058**
Fragment from the 1924 *Manifeste du surréalisme* in which P. is listed as a "surréaliste à distance".

Brodin, Pierre. Saint-John Perse. *In his:* Présences contemporaines, 2. Debresse, 1955. p. 393–411. *Also (rev.):* New York, French and European, 1972. p. 183–95.   **9059**
General presentation of P.'s poetry, mostly based on current criticism (Caillois, Noulet, Guerre...).

Caillois, Roger. Dichter der Kultur. Antaios 1:61–63, 1959.   **9060**
P. is seen as a poet who defends the order of culture against the disorder of nature. Each and everything receives its place and rank in ceremonies and rituals which he celebrates.

————. Poétique de Saint-John Perse. Gallimard, 1954. 212 p. *Also (rev.):* 1962.   **9061**
This book contains a considerable amount of material previously published or translated in: Hém 1:8–14, 1943; Font 34:406–12, 1943 and 41:78–83, 1945; SR 53:198–206, 1945; *Saint-John Perse. Exile and other poems.* New York, Bollingen series XV, 1949. p. 147–53; CahP 10:97–105, 1950;

Sur 7–8:10–20, 1950; TR 72:53–70, 1953; CahNo 98–99:284–92, 1953–54; Preu 36:28–32, 1954; *Honneur à Saint-John Perse*. Gallimard, 1965. p. 80–90. Best available study of P.'s vocabulary, syntax, stylistics, poetic structures, themes and symbols. Reviews: Anon. in Arts 461:5, 1954; V. Crastre in Preu 54:87–89, 1955; M. Dassonville in RSH 113:79–86, 1964; M. Dolan in Sur 294:107–09, 1965; L. Estang in PenF Nov. 1957 (*also in: Honneur à Saint-John Perse. See* 9022. p. 569–72); E. Noulet in her *Alphabet critique* III. Brussels, Presses univ., 1965. p. 241–45.

Cano, José Luis. Saint-John Perse, poeta de la soledad. CHA 138:391–94, 1961. **9062**

Brief presentation of P. on the occasion of the Nobel prize award.

Chapin, Katherine Garrison. Perse on the sea within us. NRep 139, no. 17:19–20, 1958. **9063**

Each of P.'s long poems expresses the drama of man facing his own mystery through the cosmic elements of the outer world: man's intellectual sterility and need for revivification in *Pluies*, the cold loneliness of exile in *Neiges*. In *Amers*, the sea represents what is creative in the heart of man. Various levels at which the poem can be read are suggested: as a ceremonial poem in honor of the sea, as a poem concerned with poetic inspiration, as a poem of being, as a love poem in which the sea is the symbol for the passion between man and woman.

————. Poet of wide horizons: a note on Saint-John Perse. QJLC 27:104–08, 1970. **9064**

Brief evocation of her friendship with P. Characterizes P.'s world as concrete and actual; his poetry, rooted in the lived experience, is free from abstraction as well as from pessimism and frustration.

————. Saint-John Perse: notes on some poetic contrasts. SR 50:65–81, 1952. **9065**

Contrasts the "aristocratic" and the "primitive" personalities of the poet.

————. Saint-John Perse: some notes on a French poet and an epic poem. SR 66: 33–43, 1958. **9066**

On one level, *Vents* relates to the Shivaic belief that life moves in cycles, that destruction and disintegration bring about a rebirth. It expresses P.'s faith in the power of man to overcome the sterility and spiritual emptiness of a closing era. On another level, it celebrates the god-like power of poetic inspiration. Includes a discussion of P.'s metrics, as well as general information about P.'s life, works, and interests.

————. St. John Perse: time confronted. NRep 145, no. 24:21–22, 1961. **9067**

In the history of man's spiritual drama, *Chronique* follows the progress of man through time and space in his quest to pierce the mystery of his future and of his own being. Traces the theme of time and waiting from *Eloges* to *Amers*.

Charpier, Jacques. Saint-John Perse. Gallimard, 1962. 299 p. **9068**

Contains recollections of encounters with P. by Alain-Fournier, Gide, Archibald MacLeish, Allen Tate, et al., a detailed biography, a critical essay on P.'s poetry, brief analyses of individual poems, an extensive anthology, interviews with P., critical appraisals by Valery Larbaud, Claudel, Breton, et al., a bibliography, iconography, musicography, cinematography, phonography and discography. Twenty-five photographs are included.

————. Saint-John Perse and the fertile woman. YFS 11:101–05, 1953. **9069**

Contrasts the image of Woman in the works of P. with other views of Woman in the Western tradition.

————. Saint-John Perse l'Américain. BSPFA 31–37, 1961. **9070**

Studies the increasing importance of the American scene in P.'s poetry from *Exil* to *Vents*. In *Vents*, America embodies the conquering spirit of Western civilization and the excesses to which it may lead.

Chiari, Joseph. Saint-John Perse and Henri Michaux. *In his:* Contemporary French poetry. Manchester, Manchester univ. press, 1952. p. 153–60. **9071**

Both P. and Michaux are characterized as poets who cannot be fitted into any movement or group. P.'s poetry is a spoken meditation. The poet's imagination unfolds scenes, landscapes and thoughts in which the real world and the world beyond the senses are subtly blended.

Chocheyras, J. A propos d'une expérience: traduction, poésie et style. RLC 41:385–400, 1967.   9072

Examines the problems of translation by means of a comparison between T. S. Eliot's and Anthony Hartley's translations of *Anabase* ("A la moisson des orges...").

Churchman, Anne. L'énumération chez Saint-John Perse, à propos d'une page de Vents. *In:* Studies in modern French literature presented to P. Mansell Jones. Manchester, Manchester univ. press, 1961. p. 61–70. *Also in:* Honneur à Saint-John Perse. *See* 9022. p. 480–88.   9073

Discusses P.'s use of enumeration, which enables the poet to grasp each thing in its individuality as well as the totality of the universe without submitting to any logical structure. From *Eloges* to *Vents*, P.'s enumerations become less and less subject to spatial and temporal limits. The only connecting link between their constituting elements is their oneiric unity.

Cioran, E.-M. Saint-John Perse ou le vertige de la plénitude. NRF 8:1076–81, 1960. *Also in:* Honneur à Saint-John Perse. *See* 9022. p. 220–25.   9074

In opposition to Valéry or T. S. Eliot, P. does not celebrate the purity of Nothingness: his poetic activity aims at a lyrical justification of man's destiny in the universe.

Claudel, Paul. Lettres à Saint-John Perse. *In:* Honneur à Saint-John Perse. *See* 9022. p. 463–65.   9075

Expresses his admiration for *Vents* and announces the completion of an essay on this poem. His main points: *Vents* is an epic poem and P. is a pagan or rather a pre-Christian.

Clémot, Michael. L'œuvre de Saint-John Perse. MSpr 56:297–318, 1962.   9076

General presentation of P. stressing the celebration of life, the human power for greatness in the face of exile and nothingness, and his vision of poetry as a means of accomplishing the union of man and the world.

Cogo, Bernardino. Saint-John Perse itinerante definitivo. Letture 16:243–62, 1961.   9077

General survey of P.'s works from *Eloges* to *Chronique*. Clear and well informed.

Colt, Byron. St.-John Perse. Acc 20:158–69, 1960.   9078

On the motif of primitive magic in the works of P.

———. St.-John Perse. MLQ 21:235–38, 1960. *Also in:* Honneur à Saint-John Perse. *See* 9022. p. 589–92.   9079

Discusses P.'s affinities with Nietzsche and Rimbaud.

Cranston, Mechthild. L'activité du songe in the poetry of Saint-John Perse. FMLS 2:356–67, 1966.   9080

Traces the conflict of two principles from *Images à Crusoé* to *Amers*: violence, which rules the world of action, and acquiescence, which governs the sphere of dreams. This conflict is seen as P.'s metaphor for the struggle between life and death. Its resolution culminates in the victory of life, which embraces both dream and death.

———. Alexis et Alice au pays des merveilles: un éloge de Saint-John Perse. RLMC 21:61–73, 1969.   9081

Close reading of section XIII of *Eloges* ("La tête de poisson ricane...") along Bachelardian lines. The scene where even the grinning head of a dead fish or the carcass of a dead cat are seen as objects of beauty accomplishes the synthesis of opposites in which life and death merge in the splendor of lyrical vision. Includes a detailed comparison with Baudelaire's "Une charogne."

———. Saint-John Perse: La tête de poisson ricane... *In her:* Enfance mon amour. La rêverie vers l'enfance dans l'œuvre de Guillaume Apollinaire, Saint-John Perse et René Char. Debresse, 1970. p. 85–153.   9082

Thematic study of the sea along Bachelardian lines. The sea is linked to two conflicting principles, action and dream, which command two sets of words and images associated with this motif. Contains a close reading of section XIII of *Eloges* ("La tête de pois-

son ricane...''). Includes material previously published; see 9080 and 9081.
Reviews: M. Décaudin in RLM 166–69:186–87, 1967; A. Sonnenfeld in FR 47:210–11, 1973.

Curnier, Pierre. Saint-John Perse: Amers. *In his:* Pages commentées d'auteurs contemporains. I. Larousse, 1963. p. 211–22. **9083**
Brief remarks on P.'s encyclopedic knowledge, his vision of the unity of the universe, and the theme of reconciliation between man and nature, followed by a short explication of the opening two cantos of *Amers*.

Deguy, Michel. Le chant de Saint-John Perse. Cr 20:507–15, 1964. *Also in:* Honneur à Saint-John Perse. *See* 9022. p. 226–32. **9084**
P.'s poetry brings the entire world into the French language. The universe thus becomes a text through which it yields its meaning.

Diéguez, Manuel de. Une critique créatrice. Comb Jan. 19, 1961. *Also in:* Honneur à Saint-John Perse. *See* 9022. p. 529–32. **9085**
The main themes discussed by P. in his Stockholm address are also the major problems raised by contemporary creative criticism: the relationship between poetry and science, metaphysics, religion and history. Poetry appears as the only possible synthesis of these areas.

Dumur, Guy. Note sur Saint-John Perse. TR 39:149–53, 1951. **9086**
General comments on P.'s poetry upon the publication of the special tribute in CahP 10, 1950.

Duncan, Robert. The poetic vocation: a study of Saint-John Perse. Jub 9:36–40, 1961. **9087**
Examines P.'s concept of poetry as a living, personal force in constant process. Contrasts P.'s vision of the world with a Christian vision, Dante's *Divine comedy*.

Eigeldinger, Marc. Saint-John Perse. *In his:* Poésie et tendances. Neuchâtel, La Baconnière, 1945. p. 77–82. **9088**

Characterizes P.'s style as rigorous, sober, condensed, and briefly mentions some similarities linking him to Supervielle and La Tour du Pin. [CR]

Emmanuel, Pierre. Saint-John Perse: Praise and presence. Washington, Library of Congress, 1971. 82 p. **9089**
An illuminating study which characterizes P.'s work as the proclamation of a self-sufficient esthetic humanism and optimistic agnosticism, and his art as a magic action through which the world is sublimated into praise. P.'s poetry is found lacking in one respect: it fails to evoke the dimension of suffering and evil, to exorcise the demoniac.

Erba, Luciano. Di alcune ragioni e suggestioni delle enumerazioni di Saint-John Perse. Ae 35:507–09, 1961. **9090**
Compares P.'s use of enumeration with its use in the epic poems of antiquity, in Marino's *Adone* or in *La Gerusalemme liberata,* and in surrealism.

Ethier-Blais, Jean. Saint-John Perse. Toujours recommencée. *In his:* Signets. I. Ottawa, Le cercle du livre de France, 1967. p. 185–89. **9091**
P.'s poetry is actually a cosmology, and language the instrument through which he creates a world as new as the universe of Einsteinian relativity.

Etiemble, René. Saint-John Perse en exil. *In his:* Poètes ou faiseurs? Hygiène des lettres. IV. Gallimard, 1966. p. 143–48. **9092**
Stresses the influence of Chinese rhetoric in P.'s use of parallel constructions, and the influence of Littré in P.'s use of words.

Fowlie, Wallace. A note on St. John Perse. Poetry 74:343–48, 1949. **9093**
General presentation of *Exil, Poème à l'étrangère, Pluies,* and *Neiges,* occasionally too much influenced by Saillet, as in his reading of the second verse of *Exil* as a reference to the swastika and to the French who escaped from France in 1940. Relates P. to Mallarmé, Rimbaud and Claudel. Stresses P.'s preoccupation with language.

——. Poems that sing of man. SatR 47: 22–23, 1960. **9094**

Brief survey of P.'s life and works. From *Eloges* to *Chronique,* P. describes the condition and destiny of man at this moment of history. In spite of P.'s affinities with Claudel, Mallarmé or Rimbaud, his poetry is unique. It magnifies the legend of man's attainments in time and space, and reassesses the nature and function of poetry which is a pledge and a sign for the future of man.

————. Saint-John Perse. Poetry 79:31–35, 1951–52.   9095

Defines P.'s poetry as the act of seizing the intimate and essential unity and combining all diversity, all antinomy. His poetry thus becomes a transcription of reality outside of time. Includes a biographical sketch, a brief survey of P.'s works from *Eloges* to *Vents,* and a discussion of P.'s scansion and language. P.'s poetic ambition recalls the examples of Rimbaud, Lautréamont, and Claudel's *Cinq grandes odes.*

Friedrich, Hugo. Saint-John Perse. *In his:* Die Struktur der modernen Lyrik. Hamburg, Rowohlt, 1956. p. 146–48.   9096

Some observations on the sensuous unreality of P.'s world, in which exotic landscapes, lost civilizations and strange myths are presented with the most detailed precision. Compares P. with Rimbaud and Lautréamont.

Galand, René. A prophet for our times: Saint-John Perse. ASLHM 43:143–58, 1972.   9097

Most of P.'s poems echo cosmogonic myths of the Eternal Return. Recurrent motifs and images linked to decay and regeneration are more than a symbolic representation; like myths and rituals, they serve to ensure the actualization of what is represented. Their power may cause men to turn the poet's vision into reality.

————. Saint-John Perse. Twayne, 1972. 172 p. (Twayne world authors series, 294)   9098

This study attempts to illuminate the deep relationships between the poet's metaphysical concept of Being, his psychological understanding of literary creation, his dominant themes and motifs, and the formal structures of his poetic language. Each cycle of poems is analyzed for its particular theme, its individual setting, and its symbolic structure as well as for the specific moment which it marks in P.'s spiritual drama.

Reviews: C. François in WCM 41–42, summer 1973; J. Houston in FR 47:440, 1973; M. Schaettel in RSH 1: 182–83, 1974.

Gali, Christian. Quatre heures avec St. J Perse. Arts 794:3, 1960.   9099

For P., poetry is essentially a mode of life enabling him "to live better, and farther". In the poem, he seeks the maximum of precision and verbal concentration. The final texts of *Anabase, Vents,* and *Amers* are only one third of the original versions. P. also discusses the interest in poetry manifested by such scientists and philosophers as Einstein and Heidegger, and expresses his admiration for a painter, Braque, and a poet, René Char.

Garaudy, Roger. D'un réalisme sans rivages Picasso, Saint-John Perse, Kafka. Plon 1963. 250 p.   9100

In P., the duality between the poet and the diplomat is explained through the Marxist concepts of alienation and reification. P.'s poetry is interpreted as the effort to overcome the duality which separates the individual from the world and from other men in a capitalistic society, and to bring about a new civilization which would sum up the totality of human history in its Hegelian unity.

Reviews: R. Kanters in FL 936:4 1964; P. Simon in his: *Diagnostic de. lettres françaises contemporaines.* Brussels, La renaissance du livre, 1966. p. 355–61.

Gaskell, Ronald. The poetry of Saint-John Perse. LonM 1, no. 12:49–56, 1962. 9101

Brief presentation of P.'s work from *Eloges* to *Chronique.*

Gaster, Beryl. Saint-John Perse. ContR 199 129–31, 1961.   9102

Brief survey of P.'s life and works.

Gattegno, Félix. Saint-John Perse. Fic 29 88–94, 1961.   9103

General presentation of P. upon the award of the Nobel prize, characterizing him as the poet of truth and presence rather than a metaphysical poet.

Gaucheron, Jacques. Amour de la poésie. Eur 367–68:230–33, 1959. **9104**

Brief presentation of P.'s poetry stressing the themes of exile, separation, and yearning for the absolute.

Gide, André. Dignité du langage... *In:* Honneur à Saint-John Perse. *See* 9022. p. 394. **9105**

Brief praise of P.'s use of language.

————. Don d'un arbre. *In:* Saint-John Perse. *See* 9026. p. 23–26. *Also in:* Honneur à Saint-John Perse. *See* 9022. p. 14–17. **9106**

Gide recalls his early admiration for *Eloges,* the errors which marred the text published in the NRF, the special reprinting which he arranged as a form of reparation, and the ingenious way in which P. thanked him by having Gide's name given to a palm tree.

Girard, René. L'histoire dans l'œuvre de Saint-John Perse. RR 44:47–55, 1953. *Also in:* Honneur à Saint-John Perse. *See* 9022. p. 548–57. **9107**

P. uses history not only to cast the shadow of a mysterious past over the present, but also to ruin the Hegelian vision of a world order centered around Western civilization. The formal and symbolic structures of his works create a poetic order which, as is suggested by the motifs of rite and caste, evoke a universe where a pervading sense of the sacred looms behind nothingness and chaos. Provocative study, with some penetrating remarks on *Pluies* and *Anabase.* Sees affinities between P.'s and Malraux's vision of history.

Glissant, Edouard. De l'un à l'univers. *In his:* L'intention poétique. Seuil, 1969. p. 95–124. **9108**

Traces a progression from Segalen to Claudel and P., each corresponding to a different stage in the dialectical relationship of the Self and the Universe: total estrangement, total communion, and the assumption of exile and perpetual becoming.

Goffin, Robert. Une conversation de mandarins. Quelques observations. *In his:* Fil d'Ariane pour la poésie. Nizet, 1964. p. 221–31. **9109**

In P., poetry creates a new form of knowledge. Some observations on P.'s rhythms and techniques.

————. Métabolisme de la poésie: de Saint-John Perse à Robert Vivier. BARLFF 37:125–34, 1959. *Also in his:* Fil d'Ariane pour la poésie. Nizet, 1964. p. 214–20. **9110**

The key to P.'s poetry is found in his letter to the *Berkeley review* where the goal of French poetry is defined as "un jeu, très allusif et mystérieux, d'analogies secrètes ou de correspondances, et même d'associations multiples, à la limite du saisissable."

Grassin, Jean-Marie. Saint-John Perse: poète des deux rives atlantiques. PFr 2:12–34, 1971. **9111**

Intelligent introduction, stressing *Eloges* and the influence of the New World on P.'s poetry: Antillean geography, the American myth of innocence and purity in opposition to Old World corruption. [CR]

————. Western trails: the American scene in Saint-John Perse's poems. CentR 15:99–125, 1971. **9112**

Identifies the imagery and themes inspired by America in P.'s poetry.

Gros, Léon-Gabriel. Royaumes d'avant-soir. CahS 358:436–44, 1960. *Also in:* Honneur à Saint-John Perse. *See* 9022. p. 520–21. **9113**

In *Anabase,* P. follows the progress of mankind personified as a single hero. In *Chronique,* he proceeds beyond the succession of civilizations to a cosmogony reminiscent of that of Lecomte du Nouÿ or Teilhard de Chardin. *Chronique* accomplishes the transformation of anguish into beauty in the face of death.

Guenther, Charles. Prince among the prophets. Poetry 93:332–35, 1959. **9114**

General study of *Amers,* which is linked with P.'s reference to the rheism of the Pre-Socratics in his letter to R. Caillois dated January 26, 1953.

Guerre, Pierre. Saint-John Perse et l'homme. Gallimard, 1955. 92 p. **9115**

Lists P.'s fundamental attitudes and motifs, from the passive animal enjoyment of nature to the active struggle to master it, from the enthusiastic acceptance of the world to the conquering surge of human pride, from the rupture with a dying past to the heroic search for a new greatness. The poet plays a major role in this conflict as he guides man to the frontier of an unknown future. Good general classification, but the analysis remains somewhat limited. Review: C. Ernoult in LetN 762–63, May 1955.

Guicharnaud, Jacques. L'homme de vigie. *In:* Honneur à Saint-John Perse. *See* 9022. p. 250–52. **9116**

P.'s poetry, and especially *Amers,* appears as a relentless indictment of all that tends to degrade man and the world.

Guissard, Lucien. Saint-John Perse, prix Nobel de littérature 1960. Tend 8:549–64, 1960. **9117**

Stresses P.'s respect for the French language and its traditional rhythms, his celebration of life and of the hidden forces at work in the world of things and within man, his humanistic wisdom.

Gustafson, Ingemar. Le poète sortant de ses chambres millénaires. Aft Dec. 5, 1956. *Also in:* Honneur à Saint-John Perse. *See* 9022. p. 471–72. **9118**

Brief presentation of Erik Lindegren's partial translation of *Eloges, Anabase, Exil, Vents* (Saint-John Perse. *Jord. Vindar. Hav.* Stockholm, Albert Bonniers, 1956). Underlines P.'s epic and mythic inspiration, his vision of the universe as a constant process of destruction and recreation.

Haack, Hanns-Erich. Hebung des Wertniveaus. Zu den Dichtung von Saint-John Perse. DRs 86:229–36, 1960. **9119**

Brief presentation of P.'s life and dominant themes. Discussion of German translations of his works.

————. Saint-John Perse. MSpr 54:377–83, 1960. **9120**

Brief presentation of P. and his poetry.

Hahn, Karl Josef. Saint-John Perse. Hoch 52:492–94, 1960. **9121**

P. is seen as standing apart from the late romantic and symbolist climate which prevailed in French poetry around 1900. Brief presentation of P. and his work.

Hartley, Anthony. Saint-John Perse. Enc 16, no. 2:41–44, 1961. **9122**

Finds in P. an attitude of impassioned acceptance of the world somewhat similar to what can be found in Gide's *Nourritures terrestres,* in Péguy's *Eve,* or in the works of the impressionists and post-impressionists. Stresses the mythopoeic quality of *Eloges* and the sense of loss which underlies *Images à Crusoé. Anabase* expresses man's unquenchable ambition to possess the world and conveys the sense of the cyclic quality of man's destiny. Contrasts the epic devices and the impersonal tone with the romantic figure of the poet which appears in P.'s works.

Heer, Friedrich. Saint-John Perse. *In his:* Offener Humanismus. Berne-Stuttgart-Vienna, Alfred Scherz Verlag, 1962. p. 98–115. **9123**

P. is compared with Teilhard de Chardin and Ernest Bloch for his faith in the future of man and his sense of the sacred in the elemental world. *Amers* describes a cosmic liturgy in which the Sea takes the place of Christ and his Mother. Poetry is a form of initiation to a higher life.

Henry, Albert. Storia e critica interna. SCr 5:80–86, 1968. **9124**

Warns against the dangers of historical interpretation, using the opening verses of *Exil* as example.

Holmquist, Bengt. [Perse est-il le plus grand poète de notre époque?]. DagN Dec. 5, 1956. *Trans. in:* Honneur à Saint-John Perse. *See* 9022. p. 565–66. **9125**

Attempt to characterize P.'s originality in contrast to Rimbaud and Claudel. Sees affinities with Mallarmé.

Huppert, George. Poem to a stranger: a study in symbolic structure. *In:* A tribute to St.-John Perse. *See* 9028. p. 53–64. **9126**

Studies P.'s technique of symbolic association between distinct motifs and image-groups. The exegesis occasionally appears somewhat forced, as in the association of green with evil (apparently because German soldiers wore green uniforms in World War II). Interesting comparison with the *Book of Tobit.*

Ibert, Jean-Claude. Un grand poète: Saint-John Perse. RduC 160:412–15, 1953. **9127**
Brief presentation of P. and his poetry.

Jaccottet, Philippe. Trop de beauté. Complément. *In his:* L'entretien des muses. Gallimard, 1968. p. 33–41.   **9128**
Expresses a preference for the verses in which the outside world is revealed in all its particularity and intimacy. Elsewhere, the excess of imagery appears as a means to cover a void, to exorcise the threat of a loss of contact with Being.

Jacobson, Brigitte. Saint-John Perse. *In:* Lange, Wolf-Dieter. Französische Literatur der Gegenwart. Stuttgart, Alfred Kröner Verlag, 1971. p. 57–77.   **9129**
General study of P.'s life and works, stressing the encyclopedic range of his poetry, his paganistic celebration of the world, the motifs of nothingness and rebirth. Examines P.'s stylistics, poetics, and dominant themes.

Jaeckle, Erwin. Wer mit Trägheit und Gewohnheit bricht: Saint-John Perse. *In his:* Zirkelschlag der Lyrik. Zurich-Stuttgart, Fretz und Wasmuth, 1967. p. 171–74.   **9130**
Brief presentation, stressing the prophetic and ritual aspect of P.'s poetry, its celebration of man and the earth.

Janzon, Ake. [L'étranger majestueux.] SvenD Dec. 5, 1956. *Trans. in:* Honneur à Saint-John Perse. *See* 9022. p. 567–68.   **9131**
P.'s poetry appears as an expression of trust in the inexhaustible energy of life embodied by an archetypal figure, the Prince, the Stranger.

Jouve, Pierre Jean. Six lectures de radio. TR 35:48–60, 1950.   **9132**
P.'s poetry is seen as a highly refined verbal construct which has the power to express the highest intellectual speculations as well as the most instinctual drives, wisdom as well as violence.

Kanters, Robert. Saint-John Perse. RdP 71: 103–13, 1964.   **9133**
Indicates P.'s poetic affinities with Hugo, Nerval, Baudelaire and Rimbaud at their most classical. P.'s poetry is characterized as an attempt to express

the language of things through the idiom of poetry.

Kemp, Friedhelm. Atem der Welt. Ein Vortrag über Saint-John Perse. Hoch 54:116–27, 1961. *Also:* GuG 7:7–34, 1961. **9134**
General presentation of P. stressing his estrangement from the Western tradition, his nomadic outlook, his encyclopedic knowledge of the world, his communion with the sacred and living unity of Being. P.'s poetry is related to the Vedas and to pre-Socratic philosophers.

———. Renaissance du poème. *In:* Saint-John Perse. *See* 9026. p. 133–35. *Also in:* Honneur à Saint-John Perse. *See* 9022. p. 122–25.   **9135**
The main sources of P.'s poetic power are found in his dominant themes (the sense of mythical and historical origins, the coupled motifs of decadence and of the birth of new empires), in the wealth of his vocabulary, in the musicality and the rigor of his syntax, and, most of all, in the originality of his vision.

Knabenhans, Brigitte. Saint-John Perse. *In her:* Le thème de la pierre chez Sartre et quelques poètes modernes. Zürich, Juris-Verlag, 1969. p. 85–89.   **9136**
Sketchy survey of the stone as poetic motif in the works of P. The stone appears in a friendly conjunction with the elemental forces of the sea, the rain, and the wind, and with man himself.

Knodel, Arthur J. Notes on an illustrious bibliophobe: Saint-John Perse. Coranto 4:3–15, 1966.   **9137**
Traces the motif of aversion to books in P.'s life and works and describes some of the most remarkable editions of P.'s poems.

———. On approaching a difficult poet: Saint-John Perse. *In:* A tribute to Saint-John Perse. *See* 9028. p. 26–33. **9138**
Defends P. against charges of excessive obscurity, demonstrating that his poetry presents no syntactical barriers, contains few purely literary allusions, uses a vocabulary which is not excessively recondite, and that all anthropological, mythological, geographical, and historical references have their

roots in external reality and actual chronicle.

——. Prolifique l'image, et le mètre, prodigue. HudR 11:437–42, 1958. *Trans. In:* Honneur à Saint-John Perse. *See* 9022. p. 504–08.   **9139**

Detailed description of *Amers*. Challenges C.A. Hackett's characterization of P.'s poetry as "essentially literary".

——. Saint-John Perse: a study of his poetry. Edinburgh, Edinburgh univ. press, 1966. 214 p.   **9140**

Full-scale study of P.'s life, works, and poetics, based on thorough research. The readings provided are generally sound and well documented, although somewhat limited in their exploration of symbolic dimensions.

Reviews: Anon. in TLS 65:537, 1966; P. Mansell Jones in FS 21:79–80, 1967; C. Nelson in MLN 83:650–53, 1968, and in FR 40:853–54, 1967.

——. The unheard melody of Saint-John Perse. RR 50:195–201, 1959. *Trans. In:* Honneur à Saint-John Perse. *See* 9022. p. 659–64.   **9141**

Detailed commentary of P.'s letter on poetry published in BerR, 1956, which throws considerable light on P.'s own poetic practice.

Köhler, Erich. Nobelpreis für Literatur. RupC 29:8–10, 1961. *Also in his:* Esprit und arkadische Freiheit. Frankfurt am Main, Athenäum, 1966. p. 244–29. **9142**

Brief presentation of P.'s life and works, stressing the spiritual unity of his evolution.

Konûpek, Jiri. Temnotný Saint-John Perse. Plamen 10:80–85, 1966.   **9143**

Discusses P.'s reputation for obscurity, stressing the objectivity, concreteness, and even realism of his poetry.

L., L. de. Saint-John Perse. PSA 56:201–03, 1960.   **9144**

Brief presentation of P. upon the award of the Nobel prize.

Lefebve, Maurice-Jean. La revanche de la poésie. *In:* Saint-John Perse. *See:* 9026. p. 112–15. *Also in:* Honneur à Saint-John Perse. *See* 9022. p. 98–103.   **9145**

Provocative attempt to define the ideological significance of the *verset* and the originality of its use by P.

Lhong, Henry. Saint-John Perse. *In:* Primault, M., H. Lhong and J. Malrieu. Terres de l'enfance: le mythe de l'enfance dans la littérature contemporaine. Presses univ. de France, 1961. p. 126–30.   **9146**

Brief and rather superficial discussion of the theme of childhood in the early poems of P.

Little, Roger. The image of the threshold in the poetry of Saint-John Perse. MLR 64:777–92, 1969.   **9147**

Studies the ritual and metaphysical significance of the threshold symbol in the works of P.

——. Language as imagery in Saint-John Perse. FMLS 6:127–39, 1970.   **9148**

Thorough examination of P.'s use of language; the bee and the sea as sources of imagery.

——. Saint-John Perse. London, Athlone, 1973. 139 p.   **9149**

General presentation of P. and his works. Biographical sketch, brief analyses of P.'s poems, critical essays, and correspondence. Indicates P.'s influence on French, English and American writers. Brief but well-documented study; throws light on P.'s use of archetypal patterns.

Review: Anon. in TLS 1562:Dec. 21, 1973.

——. Saint-John Perse and music. FS 25:305–13, 1971.   **9150**

Thorough study of references to music in P.'s poetry. Examines all facts known about P.'s relations with music and musicians, four articles written in 1909 and 1910 on the conductor Edouard Brunel and the pianist Paul Maufret, and P.'s friendship with Stravinsky.

Loranquin, Albert. Saint-John Perse. Gallimard, 1963. 221 p.   **9151**

General essay tracing P.'s evolution from lyrical nostalgia to epic celebration, from the reality of action to the realm of dream and to their eventual reconciliation. Includes a survey of P.'s poetic craft: vocabulary, verbal constructions, stylistic and sound devices, general themes and motifs. Failure to take advantage of existing scholarship appears responsble for a number of misreadings. Reviews: M. Chavardès in Monde 9, Jan. 18, 1964; M. Deguy in CahS 380: 304–06, 1964; X. Grall in SigT 4:37, 1964; A. Guibert in Preu 156:86–87, 1954; R. Kanters in FL 936:4, 1964; J.-B. Morvan in PoCp 68:57–58, 1964; C. Nelson in MLN 81:97–99, 1966; E. Noulet in BARLLF 42:29–46, 1964 and in her *Alphabet critique III*. Brussels, Presses univ., 1965. p. 75–79.

Lundkvist, Arthur. [Vision du monde et chant suprême.] MorTid Dec. 5, 1956. *Trans. in:* Honneur à Saint-John Perse. *See* 9022. p. 562–64. **9152**

Survey of P.'s poetry from *Eloges* to *Amers*. Sensible, but unoriginal.

MacLeish, Archibald. The living spring. SatR 32, 29:8–9, 1949. *Also in his:* A continuing journey. Boston, Houghton-Mifflin, 1967. p. 313–17. *Trans. in:* Honneur à Saint-John Perse. *See* 9022. p. 443–46. *Also in:* Saint-John Perse. *See* 9026. p. 443–46. *Also in:* Saint-John Perse. Œuvres complètes. *See* 8968. p. 1258–61. **9153**

P.'s modernism is compared to that of Sandburg and Pound. P. is that rare poet in his generation capable of praise. *Exil* is read as a poem about the poet and the inescapable demand of poetry.

———. A note on Alexis Saint-Leger Leger. Poetry 59:330–37, 1942. *Rev. and expanded in:* Saint-John Perse. Eloges and other poems. Norton, 1944. p. 9–14. *Also in:* Exile and other poems. Pantheon, 1949. p. 143–46. (The Bollingen series, 15). *Trans. in:* LetFB 7–8:9–14. *Also in:* LetG 2:18–23, 1944. **9154**

Biographical sketch. Includes major pronouncements by P. on poetic creation. Stresses the importance of the unconscious and the need for the subconscious to be mastered by reason. Contains fragments of a personal letter to MacLeish (complete text in: Œuvres complètes. *See* 8968. p. 549–51) in which P. mentions his hatred of literary exoticism, his hostility to culture, his total identification with France and the French language and the deep impression made upon his childhood by the animal and vegetable life of the tropics.

———. Le temps de la louange. *In:* Saint-John Perse. *See* 9026. p. 116–19. *Also in:* Honneur à Saint-John Perse. *See* 9022. p. 104–06. **9155**

Recollects his first reading of P.'s poetry in the twenties with *Anabase* and his first encounter with P. himself, in 1940, when the poet sought refuge in America.

Manrique de Lara, José G. Mundo poético de Saint-John Perse. PoeE 95:5–9, 1960. **9156**

Tribute to Nobel prize recipient, including a schematic, oversimplified exposé of P.'s debt to Mallarmé, surrealism, Claudel, Fr. Düss, and the French language. [CR]

Margoni, Ivos. Saint-John Perse. Bel 16:64–84, 1961. **9157**

General indictment of P. from a Marxist perspective. P. is described as one of the last representatives of the post-romantic tradition of hermeticism originating with Rimbaud and Mallarmé, and characterized by the Platonic refusal of the "apparences du monde" and the search for ideal archetypes.

Martins, Wilson. A poesia de Saint-John Perse. RLA 2:19–46, 1961. **9158**

Like the poetry of Valéry and Claudel, P.'s poetry is viewed as a modern form of academicism, fundamentally opposed to the surrealist goals of provocation and rebellion, or to automatic writing. Stresses the autobiographical aspects of P.'s poetry from *Eloges* to *Chronique,* examines the nature of its obscurity, and notes recurrent images, themes, attitudes, motifs, and constructions.

Maxence, Michel. Saint-John Perse, ou la tentation de la démesure. TelQ 4:57–64, 1961. **9159**

Accuses P. of attempting to replace reality by Platonic archetypes, history by myth, and contemporary decadence by a false archaism.

Miomandre, Francis de. Miracle des mots. NL Sept. 26, 1957. *Also in:* Honneur à Saint-John Perse. *See* 9022. p. 459–60. **9160**

Praises P.'s mastery of language.

Mœller, Charles. Saint-John Perse, prix Nobel. RevN 32:593–600, 1960. *Also in:*

Honneur à Saint-John Perse. *See* 9022. p. 585–88.   **9161**

P.'s discovery of the historical dimension which carries all civilizations to their doom does not lead to despair, but to an unwavering faith in the cyclical forces of Becoming. Sees affinities between Indian Shivaism, Chinese tao, Nietzschean *amor fati*, and the cosmic pulsation of *Vents* and *Amers*.

Muner, Mario. Saint-John Perse, Char, and La poésie irresponsable. AUMLA 19:5–20, 1963.   **9162**

Irresponsible poetry is defined as the poetry that the author strives to leave free to flow from his soul without any constrictive intervention of thought. Both P. and Char are seen as abdicating the task of building valid poetic structures out of the fragmentary poetic embryos provided by inspiration.

Murciaux, Christian. Saint-John Perse. Eds. universitaires, 1960. 128 p. *Also in:* TR 156:9–37, 1960. [chapter I only].   **9163**

Brief but adequate survey of P.'s life and works. Short sketch of P.'s poetics: vocabulary, rhythm, imagery. Suggests possible spiritual or literary affinities: Segalen, Whitman, Hölderlin, Nietzsche, Spengler, Toynbee, Teilhard de Chardin. Reviews: Anon. in RFB 4:9, 1961; G. d'Aubarède in TR 163:130–31, 1961; C. Nelson in BA 36:375–78, 1962.

Narusa, Koma. Saint-John Perse. Ron. Mungen 15:168–04, 1964.   **9164**

Essay on P.'s poetics.

————, **Rikutaro Fukada, Küchiro Mizuta, Hajimi Sato and Isamu Kurika.** Zadankai: Saint-John Perse. wo megutte. Mungen 15:147–67, 1964.   **9165**

Round-table discussion on P.

Nemerov, Howard. The golden compass needle. SR 67:94–109, 1959. *Also in his:* Poetry and fiction: essays. New Brunswick, Rutgers univ. press, 1963. p. 366–81.   **9166**

Generally unfavorable criticism of *Amers*, which is compared to Hugo's *La légende des siècles* and Leconte de Lisle's evocations of primitive civilizations. Some perceptive remarks about the ritual structure of P.'s poems, which have as their purpose the purgation

and renewal of the present. W. Fowlie's translation is found to be too literal, often stilted and unidiomatic.

Nimier, Roger. Saint-John Perse, le plus secret des grands poètes ouvre la saison. Arts 787:1,3,1960. *Also in:* Honneur à Saint-John Perse. *See* 9022. p. 515–17.   **9167**

Ranks P. with the greatest lyrical poets and characterizes *Chronique* as the poem of encounter with age and history.

Noulet, Emilie. Les chants d'amour de Saint-John Perse. Marg 129:6–12, 1969.   **9168**

The woman who sings, in "Chanté par Celle qui fut là," is seen as the symbol of poetry, of the voice of inspiration that has spoken to the poet during all his life. A similar symbol in *Amers*, where poetry, the woman, and the sea are one.

————. Le nominalisme de Saint-John Perse dans Amers. BARLLF 40:291–302, 1962. *Also in her:* Alphabet critique. 1924–64. IV. Brussels, Presses univ. de Bruxelles, 1965. p. 43–54.   **9169**

For P., as for many poets, language and reality merge with one another. There is no separation between the real sea, the past, present, and future experience of the sea by the poet (actual or dreamed), and the celebration of the sea in the poem itself. Repetition, litany, enumeration and anaphora are techniques used to recreate the presence of the sea.

————. Saint-John Perse, poète d'aujourd'hui. RUB 5:225–32, 1953. *Also in her:* Alphabet critique. 1924–64. III. Brussels, Presses univ. de Bruxelles, 1965. p. 24–32.   **9170**

Praises P.'s objective poetry, which gives an epic dimension to his vision of the outside world. Relates P.'s style to the baroque. Some reservations about P.'s rhetoric.

Nysenhole, A. La phrase nominale dans Amers de Saint-John Perse. FM 37:198–211, 1969.   **9171**

Close analysis of the sentence structure in *Amers*, which tends to confirm the tendency of modern French to replace verbs by substantives is especially strong in poetry. This use of nominal sentences is explained by their possibly having greater affective value than verbal assertive sentences.

Osterling, Anders. Présentation de l'œuvre de Saint-John Perse. *In:* Honneur à Saint-John Perse. *See* 9022. p. 641–43.   **9172**
Text accompanying P.'s presentation for the Nobel prize. Praises the universality of P.'s poetry, his celebration of human creativity and continuity, his faith in the power of poetry, the integrity of his poetic attitude, and the prophetic value of his message.

――――. Saint-John Perse en suédois. StTd Dec. 8, 1956. *Trans. in:* Honneur à Saint-John Perse. *See* 9022. p. 457–58.   **9173**
Brief presentation of Erik Lindegren's partial translation of *Eloges, Anabase, Exil,* and *Vents* (Saint-John Perse: *Jord. Vindar. Hav.* Stockholm, Albert Bonniers, 1956).

Parent, Monique. L'imagination poétique dans l'œuvre de Saint-John Perse. EF 1:5–25, 1965.   **9174**
General survey of P.'s life and works. Sees P.'s main theme as the human experience through space and time, the evolution of man toward a mysterious form of transcendence. The poet is the man who can seize external reality not only in all its concreteness, but also in its spiritual significance.

――――. Saint-John Perse et quelques devanciers: études sur le poème en prose. Klincksieck, 1960. p. 163–245.   **9175**
Parent distinguishes three stages in P.'s poetry: the celebration of the past (*Eloges*), power (*La gloire des rois, Anabase*), and the elements (*Pluies, Neiges, Vents*). For each stage, a study of the main themes is completed by a detailed semantic and syntactical analysis of shorter fragments. Well documented; throws light on many obscurities in P.'s poetry.
Reviews: Anon. in RFB 3:13, 1961; C. Camproux in RLR 74:222–25, 1961; J. Onimus in ACPFM 92:36–38, 1962; M. Otten in LR 176–79, May 1965; R. Pouillart in RBPH 41:1263–66, 1963; R. Winter in BJR 3:44–45, 1961.

Paulhan, Jean. Enigmes de Perse. NRF 119: 773–89, 1962; 121:74–83, 1963; 133:6–17, 1964. *Also in his:* Œuvres complètes.

v. 4. Le cercle du livre précieux, 1969. p. 163–94.   **9176**
The enigmas are three: an epic without a hero, a celebration without assured motivation, a rhetoric without language. Paulhan's explanation appears equally enigmatic and suggests an implicit analogy with the surrealists' quest: P.'s work is seen as a Bible in which all contradictions are resolved, including the opposition of dream and reality, spirit and matter, praise and blame, past and future.

Paz, Octavio. St. John Perse: poet as historian. Nat 192:522–24, 1961. *Trans. in:* Honneur à Saint-John Perse. *See* 9022. p. 253–58.   **9177**
From *Eloges* to *Anabase,* P.'s poetry appears as the epic of an age. It conveys the meaning of human life within the current of history. Its sense of the sacred, however, makes it more similar to the ancient sacred books of the Orient or to Mayan cosmogonies than to traditional epic poems.

Peschechera, Vito. L'adolescenza di Perse. Cen 17:344–48, 1968; 18:17–21, 1969.   **9178**
Brief study of *Images à Crusoé* and *Eloges,* stressing the dionysiac love of nature.

Peyre, Henri. Saint-John Perse. Eloges. 2. [Pour fêter une enfance]. Poème à l'étrangère (1942). Pluies VIII (1943). *In:* The poem itself. Ed. by Stanley Burnshaw. Cleveland and New York, Meridian, 1962. p. 92–97.   **9179**
Brief but incisive comments on fragments from three poems.

Picon, Gaëtan. Le plus hautainement libre... *In:* Saint-John Perse. *See* 9026. p. 71–74. *Also in:* Honneur à Saint-John Perse. *See* p. 56–60. *Also in his:* L'usage de la lecture I. Mercure de France, 1960. p. 155–59. *Trans. in:* Saint-John Perse. Winds. Pantheon, 1953. p. 235–39.   **9180**
Like myth and religion, P.'s poetry expresses the secret and sacred sense of the challenge of life to death.

――――. Saint-John Perse. *In his:* Panorama de la nouvelle littérature française. Gallimard, 1949. p. 158–161.   **9181**

Stresses P.'s attention to composition, the brilliant precision of his language, and the scope of his vision.

Pieltain, Paul. Introduction à la lecture de Saint-John Perse. CahAT 3:5–30, 1961. **9182**

Brief, but precise explications of fragments taken from *Eloges, La gloire des rois, Anabase,* and *Exil.*

Pieyre de Mandiargues, André. A l'honneur de la chair. NRF 113:872–75, 1962. *Also in:* Honneur à Saint-John Perse. *See* 9022. p. 216–19. *Also in his:* A l'honneur de la chair. Liège, Dynamo, 1963. 20 p. *Also in his:* Troisième belvédère. Gallimard, 1971. p. 243–46. **9183**

Praises P.'s celebration of sexuality.

Poggioli, Renato. Nouveauté de Saint-John Perse. *In:* Saint-John Perse. *See* 9026. p. 122. *Also in:* Honneur à Saint-John Perse. *See* 9022. p. 108–09. **9184**

P.'s use of narrative is epic and mythic, rather than anecdotic or episodic; his lyricism is emblematic, not autobiographical. He changes words into oracles, not into idols or music, and the most subjective experience into the most highly objective poetry.

——. The poetry of Saint-John Perse. YFS 1:5–33, 1948. *Also in his:* The spirit and the letter. Cambridge, Harvard univ. press, 1965. p. 229–53. *Trans:* Inv 3:28–49, 1950. **9185**

Detailed reading of P.'s works from *Eloges* to *Vents.* Stresses P.'s sense of the organic world in its continuous metamorphoses from a dying past to a new future and of human history in its transition from conquest to exile.

Portelaine, Henri de. Saint-John Perse: poète lyrique. RduC. 244:443–55, 1960. **9186**

General survey of P.'s work. Poorly documented: the author confuses Long Island (New Jersey), mentioned in *Exil,* with Long Island (New York).

Poulet, Georges. Saint-John Perse. *In his:* Etudes sur le temps humain. III. Le point de départ. Plon, 1964. p. 160–186. *Also in:* Honneur à Saint-John Perse. *See* 9022. p. 298–315. **9187**

In P.'s poetic universe, the harmonious coexistence of man and things, of spirit and world, is only a transitory stage. Space and time are first experienced as a dynamic continuity converging toward a center, the poet's consciousness, but their movement carries them beyond his reach as they vanish into an empty expanse which reduces them to insignificance.

Printz-Påhlson, Göran. Skummet på diktens läppar. En studie i Erik Lindegren stora tolkning av Saint-John Perses Lyrik. BLM 26:607–11, 1957. **9188**

Discusses Erik Lindegren's translation of P. published under the title Saint-John Perse: *Jord, vindar, hav.* Stockholm, Albert Bonniers, 1956 [Saint-John Perse: *Earth, winds, sea*].

Raine, Kathleen. The higher meteorology of Saint-John Perse. NRep 2003:17–18, 1953. *Trans. in:* Honneur à Saint-John Perse. *See* 9022. p. 468–70. **9189**

Stresses the primitive aspect of P.'s poetry, which does not differentiate significantly between the creations of man and those of nature. *Vents* appears closer to the Vedic hymns than to Homer; P. celebrates a pagan order rising to a vision of ecstatic joy in the face of death and destruction.

——. St. John Perse: poet of the marvellous. Enc 29:51–61, 1967. *Also in her:* Defending ancient springs. London, Oxford univ. press, 1967. p. 176–92. **9190**

Stresses the relationship of P.'s poetry to the contemporary expericence. In *Anabasis,* the migrant tribe is Western man, and the country which he must leave the civilization of his past. *Vents,* an epic description of the fall of civilization, is also a poem of setting out. *Amers* summons man to the fullest attainable experience, to immersion in the immortal and indivisible life of the cosmos. Discusses P.'s English translations and the complexity of his imagery.

Raymond, Louis-Marcel. Lecture de Saint-John Perse. ActU 14:255–77, 1948. *Also in:* Saint-John Perse. *See* 9026. p. 123–32. *Also in:* Honneur à Saint-John Perse. *See* 9022. p. 110–21. **9191**

Biographical sketch followed by a brief survey of P.'s poetry which is found to be firmly rooted in a concrete reality familiar to botanists and geographers.

Raymond, Marcel. En marge du surréalisme. *In his:* De Baudelaire au surréalisme. Corti, 1940. *Also (rev.):* 1947. p. 320–22. *Also in:* Honneur à Saint-John Perse. *See* 9022. p. 430–32. **9192**

Brief remarks on P.'s use of rhythmic prose and key words, on the communion between man and nature. Sees P.'s *Anabase* and Valéry's *La jeune Parque* as two different attempts to reconcile symbolism and classicism.

Rhodes, S. A. The poetry of Saint-John Perse. SR 44:25–50, 1936. *Trans. in:* Honneur à Saint-John Perse. *See* 9022. p. 543–47 [partial text only]. **9193**

P.'s poetry brings the knowledge of a world which is simple and real, but which retains its mystery. Faced with suffering or joy, beauty or ugliness, his art resolves all conflicts and creates a harmonious reflection of the universe. Sees affinities with Lautréamont, Rimbaud, and Mallarmé. P. is also linked with Claudel and Whitman.

Richard, Jean-Pierre. Saint-John Perse, poète de la vivacité. CahS 364:253–86, 1961–62. *Also in his:* Onze études sur la poésie moderne. Seuil, 1964. p. 31–66. *Also in:* Honneur à Saint-John Perse. *See* 9022. 1965. p. 593–600 [Partial reproduction only]. **9194**

A penetrating study of P.'s imaginary universe. Examines various symbolic manifestations of a basic struggle between the tempting security offered by a closed world and an established order, and the yearning for the conquering violence of action. Elemental forces are called upon to overcome traditional boundaries. Conversely, the deadly perfection of Nothingness awakens man's nostalgia for the fullness of Being.

Roditi, Edouard. Commerce with Saint-John Perse. Ad 300:186–91, 1963–65. **9195**

Tells of his translating *Anabase* into English at the age of 16, of his subsequent meetings with Eliot who was then engaged in a similar undertaking, and of his efforts, in later years, to have the German translation of Walter Benjamin published. P. is seen as an heir of the Parnassians rather than as a great visionary on a par with Nerval, Baudelaire, Rimbaud, or Lautréamont.

Rolland de Renéville, André. Actualité de Saint-John Perse. RduC 125:148–52, 1949. **9196**

P.'s poetry is seen as reflecting the mental structure of a primitive race. Through the drama of the human race, he also expresses the personal tragedy of a poet faced with history.

———. D'une chronique miraculeuse. *In:* Saint-John Perse. *See* 9026. p. 75–77. *Also in:* Honneur à Saint-John Perse. *See* 9022. p. 61–64. **9197**

P.'s poetry appears difficult to place in relation to the European poetic tradition. It may owe much of its singularity to its hesitation between modern Europe and the ancient East, between modern civilization and the primitive mental structures from which this civilization evolved.

Roudaut, Jean. Notes sur le réalisme de Saint-John Perse. CahS 376:265–75, 1964. **9198**

P. accomplishes the synthesis of the world of things and the world of language. His imagery is characterized by its perfect appropriateness to reality. Poetry is used as the most effective means of accomplishing the identification of man with the world, of establishing a link between man and the very movement of Being.

Roudiez, Léon S. The epochal poetry of Saint-John Perse. ColF 4, no. 4:27–31, 1961. **9199**

General survey of P.'s life, works and literary reputation. Points to the contrast between the closed world of *Eloges* and the restlessness of *Anabase* and *Vents,* between the sea experienced as a frontier in *Eloges* and as the ultimate goal in *Amers.*

Rougemont, Denis de. Saint-John Perse et l'Amérique. *In:* Saint-John Perse. *See* 9026. p. 136–39. *Also in:* Honneur à Saint-John Perse. *See* 9022. p. 126–30. **9200**

Both the westward impulse which created America and the lyrical force which created the poem *Vents* express the epic of the human soul, its dynamism, its conquering violence, and its vision of a new City of man.

Rousseaux, André. Dans l'empire des choses vraies. *In:* Saint-John Perse, homme de vigie. *See* 9027. p. 181–92. *Also in:* Honneur à Saint-John Perse. *See* 9022. p. 181–92.   **9201**

Places P. among the poets who, in reaction against the excesses of symbolism, have forged a new alliance with the earth. Poetry is the instrument of this union between man and the world: it brings to light the latent truths hidden within the heart of things.

————. Gloire et distance de Saint-John Perse. *In his:* Littérature du XXᵉ siècle. V. Albin Michel, 1955. p. 95–104.   **9202**

Stresses the remoteness of P.'s poetry and its aristocratic and esoteric power.

————. Saint-John Perse, roi de la terre. *In his:* Littérature du XXᵉ siècle. VII. Albin Michel, 1961. p. 23–42.   **9203**

In contrast with Mallarmé's struggle against the material world, P.'s poetry is seen as a return to concrete reality, as sealing an alliance with the earth, and as a celebration of the secret forces hidden within the heart of things.

Roy, Claude. Saint-John Perse. CahS 293: 33–44, 1949. *Also in his:* Descriptions critiques. Gallimard, 1949. p. 133–45.   **9204**

P. accomplishes for himself the work of time by recapturing the essence of a fabulous antiquity and recreating the tone of ancient sacred books, proverbs, or liturgies whose meaning is no longer known or fully understood. Brief survey of P.'s main themes from *Eloges* to *Vents* which are interpreted as the death sentence of bourgeois society. Includes an interesting pastiche.

Saillet, Maurice. Saint-John Perse, poète de gloire. Cr 17:291–304, 1947; 18:406–18, 1947; 19:494–504, 1947; 21:108–26, 1948. *Also in his:* Saint-John Perse, poète de gloire. Mercure de France, 1952. 190 p.   **9205**

First general study in French of P.'s works from *Des villes sur trois modes* to *Vents*. The commentary remains rather superficial, the sources far-fetched, and some of the interpretations appear dubious (e.g., *Exil* and *Pluies* are dismissed as Resistance poems). Fails to see the continuity of P.'s spiritual evolution and the deeper unity of his symbolism.

Reviews: R. Caillois in NRF 14:289–93, 1954. *Also in his: Poétique de Saint-John Perse.* Gallimard, 1954. p. 191–98; L. Guillaume in FrA 79:1121–24, 1952.

Schlocker, Georges. Kritik der Übersetzung: Saint-John Perse. Ant 6:200–06, 1958.   **9206**

Focuses on Friedhelm Kemp's translation of P. (Darmstadt-Berlin-Neuwied, Hermann Luchterhand Verlag, 1957) which is found less sharp and concise than the original. Stresses the encyclopedic character of P.'s poetry, its description of a surreal world peopled with superhuman creatures, and its epic transformation of history.

Seguin, Marc. Saint-John Perse, poète de la mer. BAGB 2:236–48, 1963.   **9207**

Traces the increasing importance of the theme of the sea from *Eloges* to *Amers.*

Selma, José Vila. Saint-John Perse. FMod 1:93–101, 1961.   **9208**

Brief presentation of P.'s life and works, with some considerations on P.'s place in contemporary French poetry.

Senghor, Léopold Sedar. Saint-John Perse, ou poésie du royaume d'enfance. TR 172: 16–36, 1962. *Also in his:* Liberté I. Seuil, 1964. p. 334–53.   **9209**

Relates P.'s vision to African cosmogonies and to the theories of Teilhard de Chardin. Includes good study of the poet's use of rhythms, sounds, and symbols.

Smith, William Jay. In praise of childhood. NRep 136, no: 8:18–19, 1957.   **9210**

Stresses the sustained psalm-like fervor of the tone, the sensuous imagery, the long, winding *versets.* Some interesting remarks on the symbolism of the door.

Spada, Marcel. Saint-John Perse poète de la mer *In:* Studi in onore di Vittorio Lugli e Diego Valeri. II. Venezia, N. Pozza, 1961. p. 899–914.   **9211**

Traces the motif of the sea in P.'s poetry from *Eloges* to *Amers. Amers* is seen as the crowning achievement in P.'s poetic evolution. After his spiritualizing progress from the earth to the rain, the snow, and the winds, the poet finds in the sea the perfect symbol of pure spirit.

Stakenburg, Joan Th. Saint-John Perse. Streven 14:1038–48, 1961. **9212**
General presentation of P.'s life and works from *Eloges* to *Vents*.

Steiner, Herbert. Amitié du prince. *In:* Saint-John Perse. *See* 9026. p. 31–32. *Also in:* Honneur à Saint-John Perse. *See* 9022. p. 21–22. *Trans. in his:* Begegnungen mit Dichtern. Hamburg, Trajanus-Presse, 1957. p. 58–59. **9213**
Recalls Valéry's and Larbaud's admiration for P. Stresses the scope and the lucidity of the poet's vision and his sensitivity to cosmic rhythms. Sees P. as the creator of his own myth and hierarchy.

Tate, Allen. Homage to St. John Perse. Nine 2:78–80, 1950. *Also:* Poetry 75:213–16, 1950. *Trans.:* Mystérieux Perse. *In:* Saint-John Perse. *See* 9026. p. 144–50. *Also in:* Honneur à Saint-John Perse. *See* 9022. p. 136–40. **9214**
Recalls his first encounters with P. Underlines differences between Whitman and P. Sees *Vents, Pluies* and *Neiges* as opening a new symbolic domain for poetry.

Truffaut, Louis. Saint-John Perse et le thème du poète. NS 3:105–09, 1961. **9215**
The figure of the poet, which appears only briefly in *Anabase*, assumes an increasing importance in P.'s later works where he is seen as a prophet, a leader of men, and an interpreter of oracles.

Turnell, Martin. The epic of Saint-John Perse. Cweal 70:376–78, 1959. **9216**
Traces the theme of exile in *Images à Crusoé, Anabase, Exil, Vents,* stressing the epic character of P.'s poetic undertaking. In *Amers,* the sea stands for forces present in the soul of man. The struggle between the male and female principles, between man and the elements, between the poet and language is resolved in a final harmony.

Ungaretti, Giuseppe. Histoire d'une traduction. *In:* Saint-John Perse. *See* 9026. p. 81–85. *Also in:* Honneur à Saint-John Perse. *See* 9022. p. 68–70. **9217**

Attempts to define the "indéfini," the mysterious and indefinable power of P.'s poetry.

Van Rutten, Pierre. Oiseaux, ou l'esthétique de Saint-John Perse. HAB 15:40–44, 1964. **9218**
Stresses the ambivalence of P.'s poetry, which is a reconciliation of opposites: birds belong both to the earth and the sky. The perception of their objective existence by the artist leads to the revelation of a mystery, the archetypal Order which presides over the organization of the cosmos.

Verspoor, Dolf. Saint-John Perse. Eras 1: 287–93, 1946. **9219**
Brief presentation of P.'s work from *Eloges* to *Exil*.

Viatte, Auguste. St.-John Perse, prix Nobel. RUL 15:502–06, 1961. **9220**
General presentation of P. upon the award of the Nobel Prize. Stresses the themes of the great forces of Nature and Exile.

Vigée, Claude. La quête de l'origine dans la poésie de Saint-John Perse. *In his:* Révolte et louanges. Corti, 1962. p. 199–218. *Also in:* Honneur à Saint-John Perse. *See* 9022. p. 345–62. **9221**
Penetrating and convincing analysis of P.'s spiritual drama from *Eloges* to *Amers*. The confrontation with the creative power of poetic inspiration leads to the metamorphosis of demonic possession into a nuptial union. Includes a revealing anecdote on P.'s religious attitude as told to the author by P. himself.

Waïs, Kurt. Alexis Leger (Saint-John Perse): Leben und Werk. DF 2:226–56, 1957. **9222**
Detailed examination of P.'s life and work from *Images à Crusoé* to *Vents*. Close analysis of *Exil, Pluies, Neiges,* and *Vents*.

————. Die lyrischen Jugendwerke von Saint-John Perse. *In his:* Französische Marksteine von Racine bis Saint-John Perse. Berlin, W. de Gruyter, 1958. p. 335–62. **9223**
Traces P.'s spiritual progress from *Eloges,* where tropical nature is seen as an earthly paradise, to *Vents* where it

is treated with contempt and the poet yearns for the purity of the high mesas. Similar oppositions are examined in *La gloire des rois* and *Anabase.*

Walravens, Jan. Saint-John Perse, dichter op het hoogste vlak. VlG 45:133–35, 1961.
9224

Praises P. for avoiding the possible danger of a new "pompiérisme" akin to Déroulède through his personal vision of man and history, his imagery, and his themes. Suggests a comparison of P. with Ezra Pound.

Wilder, Amos N. Nature and the immaculate word in St.-John Perse. *In his:* Modern poetry and the Christian tradition: study in the relation of Christianity to culutre. Scribner, 1952. p. 103–11.   **9225**
The theme of *Anabase* is the "world-old caravan of man." Modern man gathers up the relics of millenia of racial memory. In the poems of *Exil,* seas, snows and rains suggest the theme of cleansing and obliteration. Nature teaches the poet to strip off the past in order to make room for a new song, to shed society, history and the self in order to seek beyond the human, but against the impulse to seek beyond the human, there is always the contrary movement back.

Willige, Wilhelm. Der Dichter Saint-John Perse. NS 3:127–29, 1958.   **9226**
Brief presentation of P.'s German translation by Friedhelm Kemp.

Yoyo, Emile. Saint-John Perse ou le conteur. Bordas, 1971. 112 p.   **9227**
Interesting attempt to show that P.'s poetry is deeply rooted in the culture of the Antilles, its speech, its vocabulary, its syntax, its customs, and its beliefs. The demonstration is often forced (e.g., "celui qui laque en mer" is a Chinese craftsman, not a West Indian fisherman, p. 17). Includes a provocative comparison between P. and Césaire.
Reviews: M. Quaghebeur in LR 36: 300–02, 1972; C. Rigolot in MLN 88: 924–25, 1973.

Zalamea, Jorge. La consolation poétique. *In:* Saint-John Perse. *See* 9026. p. 90–93. *Also in:* Honneur à Saint-John Perse. *See* 9022. p. 74–78.   **9228**

Stresses the healing power of P.'s poetry and its creation of a world able to resist the contagion of evil.

Amers

Blanchet, André. Le masque d'or de Saint-John Perse. Et 295:337–53, 1957. *Also in:* Honneur à Saint-John Perse. *See* 9022. p. 496–501. *Also in his:* La littérature et le spirituel. III. Aubier, 1961. p. 155–76.
9229

A reading of *Amers* by a Catholic critic. The people assembled on the seashore are seen as the confrontation of man with the mystery of divinity. The poet leads the procession of men to a communion with the sacred. For P., divinity is not a transcendental God; it is identified with the material universe.

Bosquet, Alain. Amers de Saint-John Perse. Preu 89:80–82, 1958.   **9230**
Amers is seen as an epic poem whose purpose is to praise a memorable event, which is not the exploit of a hero, but the universe in its cosmic, human, and verbal forms. In the poem, the sea, the poet, and language are in constant correspondence.

Clayre, Alasdair. Poet of the sea. T&T 43, no. 24:27, 1962.   **9231**
Review of *Amers.* The poem juxtaposes the decaying world of human order and the creative forces within and without man which destroy the works of man and inspire new creations through the poet, the actresses or the lovers.

Ferreira da Silva, Dora. Nota sobre Amers. Dial 16:83–90, 1964.   **9232**
Summary and general commentary on *Amers,* mentioning Nietzschean characteristics of narrator, the paradox of P.'s style (austerity and luxuriance), and the contrasting movements of "Etroits sont les vaisseaux" (majestic and rapid). [CR]

Fowlie, Wallace. L'œuvre pure de Saint-John Perse. *In:* Honneur à Saint-John Perse. *See* 9022. p. 262–65.   **9233**
Amers appears as the crowning achievement in P.'s poetic development for its synthesis of human history, its celebration of the great human themes, its mythic dimension, its combination of

the idyllic and the epic, and the splendor and musicality of its form.

————. Saint-John Perse's quest. *In his:* Climate of violence. Macmillan, 1967. p. 87–101. **9234**

In *Amers,* the poet's effort to establish the communion of man and nature and the reconciliation of man and time finds its culmination in the fundamental unity of the world. Brief explication of *Amers* and some of its motifs (the winged beast, the relay, woman).

Gros, Léon-Gabriel. Epopée ou opéra fabuleux. CahS 343:453–61, 1957. **9235**

Amers is an epic poem in which the poet, instead of using a theme borrowed from a known epic matter, invents his own, the human response to the sea. It is also a mystic poem in which the sea symbolizes the goal of human desire. It can above all be described in Rimbaud's terms as an "opéra fabuleux," a work which encompasses an entire culture.

Guicharnaud, Jacques. Vowels of the sea: Amers, by Saint-John Perse. YFS 21:72–82, 1958. **9236**

Stresses the "secular mysticism" of P.

Guillou, Jean. Amers de Saint-John Perse, obscurité ou clarté? BSPFA 13–23, 1968. **9237**

Analyzes various types of obscurity in *Amers.*

Guthrie, Ramon. Hazard of the sea. Nat 187:175–76, 1958. **9238**

Although *Amers* contains echoes of Baudelaire, Mallarmé, Whitman, Rimbaud, Pindar, the *Song of songs,* and Valéry's "Cimetière marin," it is P.'s most highly personal poem. The structural unity of the poem reinforces its symbolic power; P.'s sea combines the mystic and the physical. It is a real sea, and also a symbol of completeness, of fertility, of total liberation, and of the oneness of conflict and harmony.

Henry, Albert. Amers de Saint-John Perse: une poésie du mouvement. Neuchâtel, La Baconnière, 1963. 180 p. **9239**

Fragments of this book were previously published in NRF 76:696–704, 1959 and NRF 77:879–87, 1959. Essayistic but generally sound study. Henry examines the general structure of the poem, the significance of the variants, the symbolic value of the sea (*Amers* is at the opposite pole of Bachelard's *L'eau et les rêves*), the vocabulary, imagery and syntax, and suggests possible affinities between P. and the Baroque. Sees *Amers* as the final stage in P.'s spiritual evolution.

Reviews: J. Bourguignon in RLR 27:496–97, 1963; F. Chanel in EdL 7:194–96, 1964; M. Deguy in CahS 380:304–06, 1964; F. Jenkins in RPh 22:72–78, 1968–69; J. Keegstra in BJR 9:42–44, 1964; E. Noulet in BARLLF 42, 29–46, 1964. *Also in her: Alphabet critique.* III. Brussels, Presses univ., 1965. p. 293–304.

Kaplan, H. J. St. John Perse: the re-creation of the world. Repo 20:32–35, 1959. **9240**

General discussion of *Amers* read as a celebration of man's subtle, ambiguous and unconquerable activity.

Kemp, Robert. Un grand événement littéraire. NL Aug. 1, 1957. *Also in:* Honneur à Saint-John Perse. *See* 9022. p. 493–95. **9241**

Compares P. with Pindar, Aeschylus and Claudel, and considers *Amers* as the most magnificent celebration of the sea and of love ever written. Stresses the Hellenic character of P.'s poetry: the sea which it praises becomes a goddess, as did Cybele the earth.

Koch, Kenneth. St.-John Perse's new poem. EvR 2:217–19, 1959. *Trans. in:* Honneur à Saint-John Perse. *See* 9022. p. 509–11. **9242**

Praises *Amers* for its form, its distance toward the world, its choral technique, its musicality, and the exactness of its metaphors.

Marcel, Luc-André. Quelques raisons de louer... *In:* Saint-John Perse, homme de vigie. *See* 9027. p. 365–76. *Also in:* Honneur à Saint-John Perse. *See* 9022. p. 193–206. **9243**

In *Amers,* the source of P.'s imagery is found in the originality of his vision and in the multiple links which it establishes between words, rhythms, and things.

Marshall, John. The greatest living French poet. YR 48:142–48, 1958. **9244**

A study of *Amers*. Discusses the civilization described in the poem, the meaning of the title, and the form of the poem. The action of the poem culminates in the Strophe, where the act of love is an act of rebirth, recovery, and renewal.

Ménard, René. Poésie et nouvelle alliance. Cr 123–24:685–97, 1957. **9245**

Both Char in *Les compagnons dans le jardin*, and P. in *Amers* are seen as major figures in the struggle between the two great modern myths: poetry considered as a way to knowledge and truth and the belief in the infinite perfectibility of the human condition through the conquest of matter by human reason. Char restores the sense of the Sacred in Nature; in *Amers*, the celebration of the Sea is a celebration of the Sacred.

Noulet, Emilie. L'octosyllabe dans Amers. *In:* Honneur à Saint-John Perse. *See* 9022. p. 316–26. *Also in her:* Alphabet critique. 1924–64. III. Brussels, Presses univ. de Bruxelles, 1965. p. 55–65. **9246**

The high incidence of coupled octosyllabic rhythms in the "Invocation" and the "Chœur" of *Amers* is interpreted as a return to classical equilibrium.

———. Saint-John Perse: Amers. SynB July 1957. *Also in her:* Alphabet critique. 1924–64. III. Brussels, Presses univ. de Bruxelles, 1965. p. 33–42. **9247**

Commentary upon the opening section of *Amers*, stressing the use of rhythms, vocabulary, echoes and repetitions.

Paulhan, Jean. Amers. Notice de présentation. *In:* Œuvres complètes. *See* 8968. p. 1131. **9248**

Text written for an exhibition of the monumental edition of *Amers*. Stresses the originality of this work, which is both an epic and hymn, a combination not to be found previously in literature.

Perregaux, Béatrice. Amers de Saint-John Perse—étude de la Strophe. CahS 376: 276–84, 1964. **9249**

Close reading of the third section of *Amers*, the "Strophe," which is both the vision of the dream and the linguistic creation which gives concrete reality to

the vision. The unity of Being is accomplished in the poem through the fusion of reality and imagination.

Roy, Claude. Saint-John Perse dans Amers. Lib May 29, 1957. *Also in:* Honneur à Saint-John Perse. *See* 9022. p. 491–92. **9250**

Although the theme of the sea has been extensively used in French poetry in recent times (Hugo, Baudelaire, Mallarmé, J. Verne, Corbière), P. belongs to another tradition, the learned and refined poetry of Maurice Scève, Cavafis, Ezra Pound or T. S. Eliot.

Anabase

Attal, Jean-Pierre. Une image de Saint-John Perse. CahCh 5:82–86, 1969. *Also in his:* Une image métaphysique et autres essais. Gallimard, 1969. p. 443–46. **9251**

Brief commentary confirming the exactness of the image in *Anabase*, VII, where the hills appear as "chamelles douces sous la tonte."

Berrie, Anne. Sur l'Anabase de Saint-John Perse. TLL 7:197–210, 1969. **9252**

Stresses the psychological interpretation of *Anabase*, which is seen as a conflict between reality and the dream, between the beauty of the concrete world and the yearning for the absolute, between the perishable attraction of woman and the eternity of death.

Blomdahl, Karl-Birger. [Le compositeur suédois commente son oratorio: Anabase]. Roster i Radio 50, Dec. 9–15, 1956. *Trans. in:* Honneur à Saint-John Perse. *See* 9022. p. 433–34. **9253**

The poem is interpreted as the conquering expedition of a nation of horsemen whose destiny is embodied by an anonymous chief.

Bogan, Louise. Asian exoticism. *In her:* Selected criticism. Noonday, 1955. p. 81–82. **9254**

Sees *Anabase* as exemplifying a new Asian exoticism which stresses harshness, barrenness, cruelty and strength, much like T. E. Lawrence's *Seven pillars of wisdom*. A penetrating summary of *Anabase* which is characterized as dealing with the beauty and terror of the earth, the beauty and brutality of the civilizations which man imposes upon it, and man's spiritual journey.

Carmody, Francis J. Saint-John Perse. Several Oriental sources. CLS 2:125–51, 1965. **9255**

Lists Oriental motifs which P. might owe to Plutarch, Herodotus, Ammianus Marcellinus, Strabo. Well-documented source study on *Anabase.*

Crevel, René. Anabase de Saint-John Perse. Phil March 1925. *Also in:* Honneur à Saint-John Perse. *See* 9022. p. 415–16. **9256**

A surrealist interprets *Anabase* as expressing man's yearning for the "terre arable du songe."

————. Pour la liberté de l'esprit. MesO April 1931. *Also in:* Honneur à Saint-John Perse. *See* 9022. p. 416–18. **9257**

For the surrealists, *Anabase* expresses the rejection of Western rationalism in favor of the surreal represented by Oriental thought.

Eliot, T. S. Lettre à Saint-Leger Leger. *In:* Honneur à Saint-John Perse. *See* 9022. p. 149. **9258**

Letter accompanying his translation of *Anabase.*

————. Lettres à Saint-John Perse. *In:* Œuvres complètes. *See* 8968. p. 1141–44. **9259**

Letters and fragments of letters dating from 1927 to 1929, relating to Eliot's translation of *Anabase.*

————. Preface. *In:* Saint-John Perse. Anabase. Bilingual ed. London, Faber and Faber, 1930. *Also (rev.):* 1959. *Also (rev.):* New York, Harcourt, Brace, 1938 and 1949. p. 9–12. *Also in:* Saint-John Perse. Anabase. New York, Brentano's, 1945. n. p. *Trans. in:* Honneur à Saint-John Perse. *See* 9022. p. 420–22. **9260**

Anabase is seen as a series of images of migration and conquest. The obscurity of the poem is explained through the suppression of explanatory and connecting matter, a method which does not prevent sequences of images from obeying the logic of imagination. Eliot adopts Fabre's tentative synopsis of the action of the poem. Believes *Anabase*

to be as important as Joyce's *Anna Livia Plurabelle.*

Fabre, Lucien. Publication d'Anabase. NL Aug. 23, 1924. *Also in:* Honneur à Saint-John Perse. *See* 9022. p. 406–11. **9261**

First significant study of *Anabase* which is interpreted as the epic and lyrical relation of a military expedition led by a warrior prince. Stresses the elliptic and allusive character of P.'s art and compares his obscurity with Valéry's and Fargue's. Contains a dubious attempt to reconstruct the action described in *Anabase.*

Hoffmannsthal, Hugo von. [Préface pour une édition allemande d'Anabase] NSR May 1929. *Trans. in:* Commerce 20, 1929. *Also trans. in:* Saint-John Perse. Anabase. New York, Brentano's, 1945. n.p. *Also trans. in:* Honneur à Saint-John Perse. *See* 9022. p. 423–25. **9262**

Sees P. as the most recent link in a chain of poets who have sought to renew French lyricism: Baudelaire, Rimbaud, Mallarmé, Claudel, Valéry.

Jammes, Francis. Lettre à Saint-Leger Leger. *In:* Honneur à Saint-John Perse. *See* 9022. p. 405. **9263**

Letter thanking P. for sending him *Anabase,* but expressing strong reservations about the obscurity of the imagery and the use of a Claudelian *verset.*

Knodel, Arthur J. Towards an understanding of Anabase. PMLA 79:329–43, 1964. **9264**

The effort to guard against runaway interpretation may have prevented the critic from paying sufficient attention to the symbolic value of key motifs: the tree and its leaves; water, flowing or still; the interrupted flight; the feminine star... The documentation is remarkably thorough. Part of it was provided by P. himself.

Larbaud, Valery. Lettres à Saint-John Perse (1922–24). *In:* Œuvres complètes. *See* 8968. p. 1233–35. **9265**

Letters mostly concerned with the publication of *Anabase.*

Little, Roger. Anabasis. Translation with a preface. ArlQ 2:108–35, 1970. **9266**

Stresses the psychological presentation of man's inner conflict between the desire to found a human order, the City, and the passion for new experience and discovery, between the nomad Leader and the Stranger, between stasis and dynamism.

———. Une image de la dialectique mouvement-stasis dans l'Anabase de Saint-John Perse. RSH 142:229–35, 1971.   **9267**
Contrasts the tree and grass motifs as symbols of stagnating immobility and dynamic change.

Micha, René. Au sujet du mouvement dans l'Anabase. *In:* Honneur à Saint-John Perse. *See* 9022. p. 246–49.   **9268**
Sees possible analogies between the use of movement in *Anabase,* in Eisenstein's films, and in the painting of the Quattrocento.

Papatzonis, T. C. Saint-John Perse vu par un Hellène. *In:* Honneur à Saint-John Perse. *See* 9022. p. 292–96.   **9269**
Anabase combines the epic breadth, the tragic depth and the classical measure of ancient Greek art. P.'s poetry describes a pagan paradise, a world anterior to the concepts of good and evil, and a cosmic order which excludes metaphysical anguish.

Parent, Monique. La fonction poétique dans deux textes de Saint-John Perse. TLL 9: 347–57, 1971.   **9270**
Applies Jakobson's structuralist method to the opening and closing cantos of *Anabase.* Close study of semantic, syntactical and rhythmical parallels and contrasts, of the themes and their organization, of the metaphors and metonymies, and of the symbols.

Raine, Kathleen. In praise of the earth. NewS 1482:170, 1959.   **9271**
Review of *Anabase,* stressing P.'s equal glorification of death and life, the pure and the impure, the generative power of woman and the violence of the warrior. Emphasizes classical precision of P.'s perception. Sees affinities with Gauguin, Rimbaud, Claudel, and the Joyce whose sense of glory and wonder delighted in the multiplicity of life.

Srinivasa Iyengar, K. R. St.-John Perse's Anabase: a study. AryP 33:15–18, 57–62, 1962.   **9272**

In the nomadic conqueror, the lure and thrill of adventure, the boredom and satiety of success, and the desire for fresh adventure are seen as prototypical of the perennial human situation. P.'s *Anabase* is universal history in miniature: it achieves the fusion of the epic and lyric modes. As in the *Mahabharata,* the epic drama is played in the desert Mongolia of the human soul. Parallels are suggested with Byron's *The deformed stranger,* Eliot's *Waste land,* Pound's *Cantos,* MacLeish's *Conquistador,* W.C. Williams' *Destruction of Tenochtitlan* and Seferis' *Mythistorima.*

Taubman, Robert. Under the turpentine tree. Spec 6833:862, 1959.   **9273**
Anabase appears as an attempt to evoke from a remote barbaric past images capable of communicating a sense of life which modern civilization no longer possesses. Finds numerous allusions to different religions, mythologies, sciences and cultures. Sees affinities with Rimbaud, Mallarmé and even the prose of Malraux.

Thibaudet, Albert. L'Anabase de Saint-John Perse. EN Aug. 9, 1924. *Also in:* Honneur à Saint-John Perse. *See* 9022. p. 412–13.   **9274**
Places *Anabase* in relation to Lautréamont's *Chants de Maldoror,* Rimbaud's *Illuminations* and Claudel's *Connaissance de l'est.* Stresses the Asiatic character of the poem.

Ungaretti, Giuseppe. [Préface pour sa traduction italienne d'Anabase] Fronte 2, 1931. *Also in:* Traduzioni. Rome, Novissima, 1936. *Trans. in:* Honneur à Saint-John Perse. *See* 9022. p. 429.   **9275**
Anabase is interpreted as the successful attempt to combine the historical drama of a people with the individual history of the Stranger who appears in the poem.

Vitrac, Roger. Publication d'Anabase. JLit Sept. 1924. *Also in:* Honneur à Saint-John Perse. *See* 9022. p. 414.   **9276**
A surrealist opposes *Anabase* to the poetry which he would reject: Valéry, Jules Romains, Tristan Derème and Paul Claudel.

Waïs, Kurt. Deux manières d'exister dans l'œuvre de Saint-John Perse. *In:* Honneur à Saint-John Perse. *See* 9022. p. 266–72.
9277

P.'s *Anabase* leads beyond Nietzsche's *Zarathustra* to a new spiritual conquest followed, in the poems of exile, by a return to the elementary forces of nature and the eventual triumph over time.

Watts, Harold H. Anabase: the endless film. UTQ 19:224–34, 1950.   **9278**

Analysis of *Anabase* viewed as a means of providing the reader with the materials needed to discover new truths about the historical becoming of man and to question the historical schemes fostered by Western culture.

Weinberg, Bernard. L'Anabase de Saint-John Perse. *In:* Saggi e ricerche di letteratura francese. I. Milan, Feltrinelli, 1960. p. 209–68. *Trans:* ChiR 15:75–124, 1962. *Also in his:* The limits of symbolism. Chicago and London, Univ. of Chicago press, 1966. p. 365–419.   **9279**

Addresses itself to fundamental problems: Is *Anabase* a narrative or a lyric poem? Who is speaking, and to whom? What is the chronology of the events? Weinberg concludes that *Anabase* is a lyric poem in which a narrator recounts his adventure and quotes various speakers, but with occasional comments which must be ascribed to the poet who intervenes directly in the poem.

Zeltner-Neukomm, Gerda. St.-John Perse als Dichter der Fremdheit. *In:* Überlieferung und Gestaltung. Festgabe für Theophil Spoerri zum sechzigsten Geburtstag am 10. Juni 1950. Zürich, Speer Verlag, 1950. p. 187–206.   **9280**

A study of *Anabase* concentrating on the motif of the stranger which is related to the use of similar motifs in other poems.

Chronique

Benamou, Michel. Le chant de la terre dans Chronique. FR 34:480–82, 1961. *Also in:* Honneur à Saint-John Perse. *See* 9022. p. 522–25.   **9281**

The poet's progress through life (his travels) and literature (his poems) parallels the history of mankind and the succession of geological eras. The birth of the poem, the origin of man, and the creation of the world are equally shrouded in mystery, but the absence of a visible cause (God) needs no other compensation than the permanence of the earth and the perenniality of life.

Charpier, Jacques. Saint-John Perse. Exp 26–27, Dec. 29, 1960. *Trans.:* AyL 3, no. 4:77–82, 1960.   **9282**

Chronique is seen as the final reply in the poet's dialog with Time and as a confirmation of the unity of work which preserves the memory of its own past.

Fowlie, Wallace. Chronique by St. John Perse. Poetry 99:194–96, 1961.   **9283**

General study of *Chronique* which is more the history of humanity, the story of man as a race, than the personal history of the poet.

Hemley, Cecil. Onward and upward. HudR 15:314–17, 1962.   **9284**

Chronique is interpreted as an attempt to sum up history, to assess the human adventure. Generally unfavorable view of the vision of history presented in *Chronique* which is found to be rather depressing.

Khan, Ansar. St. John Perse's Chronique—an Asian view. FrA 181:1021–25, 1963.
9285

Chronique is sharply criticized for its ideology which is seen as racist in its praise of European civilization, a theme which cannot be developed without racial arrogance. Forced interpretation according to which *Chronique* is primarily a glorification of colonial conquest.

Ménard, René. Saint-John Perse: Grand âge et Poésie. Cr 169:483–91, 1961. *Also in:* Honneur à Saint-John Perse. *See* 9022. p. 533–39.   **9286**

Discusses the main motifs of *Poésie:* poetry as a means of knowledge, as a mode of life and as a revelation of Being. *Chronique* is read as an illustration of *Poésie,* as the passionate acceptance of human reality.

Noulet, Emilie. Saint-John Perse: Chronique. CahdM 1–4, March 1966. *Also in her:* Alphabet critique. 1924–64. III. Brussels, Presses univ. de Bruxelles, 1965. p. 66–71.
9287

Brief analysis of *Chronique* as a salute to old age, human life and the earth.

Parent, Monique. Les thèmes poétiques de Saint-John Perse dans Chronique. BJR 6:5–13, 1962.   **9288**

Discussion of earth, time and man in P.'s earlier works and then in *Chronique,* showing how the poet's intuition of the proximity of death colors his vision and inspires his quest for immortality and eternity. An important contribution to the understanding of the evolution of P.'s poetry. [CR]

Eloges

Ashton, Dore. St.-John Perse's Guadeloupe. KR 23:520–26, 1961.   **9289**

Description of a visit to Guadeloupe in search of the atmosphere described by P. in *Eloges,* much of which seemed to have changed but little since the 1890's.

Galand, René. En marge d'Eloges. FR 46, special issue no. 5:112–19, 1973.   **9290**

The early poem "Des villes sur trois modes" is seen as a first presentation of P.'s basic motif, the conflict of Nature and Culture. The pirates described in this work are linked to the Barbarians who appear in the writings of Verlaine, Gide and Nietzsche. Like ritual orgies in primitive religions, their actions liberate the creative violence of untamed Nature.

Goldmann, Lucien. Eloges III. Saint-John Perse. RISULB 3:53–59, 1960. *Also in his:* Structures mentales et création culturelle. Anthropos, 1970. p. 369–79. **9291**

An intriguing although not entirely convincing application of genetic structuralism. The method involves three steps: 1. the formulation of a semantic model describing the global system of relationships between men, other men, and the universe; 2. the genesis of this model in the collective conscience of certain social groups; 3. the verification that the microstructures of the poem (semantic, rhythmic, syntactical...) reflect the structure of the global model.

Reviews: Anon. in Marg 137:69–70, 1971; A. Akoun in QL 19–20, Feb. 16,

1971; R. Lauverjat in RLR 79:182–86, 1971.

Güiraldes, Ricardo. Un canto. Proa 9, April 1925. *Trans. in:* Honneur à Saint-John Perse. *See* 9022. p. 386–89.   **9292**

Relates *Eloges* to the increasing significance of exoticism in French literature (Levet, Larbaud, Loti, Farrère, Claudel, Morand). Stresses the importance of the key phrase: "Je parle dans l'estime." Includes translation in Spanish of "Pour fêter une enfance."

Henry, Albert. Les images à Crusoé et la méthode philologique. TLL 9:329–46, 1971.   **9293**

A stylistic comparison of the early and final versions of *Images à Crusoé.* Three main tendencies are noted in P.'s revisions: the elimination of phrases suggesting excessive sentimentality or emotionalism; the omission of exotic terms too closely linked to definite plants or animals; a constant search for greater stylistic concentration and consistency.

Jammes, Francis, and André Gide. Correspondance. *In:* Honneur à Saint-John Perse. *See* 9022. p. 609–10.   **9294**

Letters dated 1911, discussing Larbaud's interest in P. and the publication of *Eloges.*

Larbaud, Valery. Eloges. Phal Dec. 1911. *Also in:* Saint-John Perse. *See* 9026. p. 45–51. *Also in:* Honneur à Saint-John Perse. *See* 9022. p. 32–38. *Also in:* Œuvres complètes. *See* 8968. p. 1227–32.   **9295**

The first important article on P. by a major literary figure. With Valéry, Fargue and Claudel, P. is presented as a direct successor of Rimbaud. Stresses the authenticity and exactness of P.'s perception.

Little, Roger. Saint-John Perse et le parler créole. RSH 139:467–71, 1970.   **9296**

Uses the studies of Elodie Jourdain (*Du français au parler créole* and *Le vocabulaire du parler créole de la Martinique*) to explain a number of words and idioms used in *Eloges.* Does not, however, examine the Creole words to be found in the first version of *Eloges.*

Rosenfeld, Paul. The poet Perse. Nat 158: 570, 572, 1944. **9297**

P. in *Eloges* is seen as the opposite of Gide in *El Hadj* or *Corydon*. The form is the free-verse mold reminiscent of Claudel and built on obsessive rhythms. Praises the sumptuous verbal texture and the sense of the divinity immanent within the rhythm and color of earthly objects.

Exil

Aiken, Conrad. Whole meaning or doodle: Rains by Saint-John Perse. NRep 1585: 512, 1945. *Trans. in:* Honneur à Saint-John Perse. *See* 9022. p. 441–42. **9298**

Opposes two procedures open to the poet: whole meaning (linear development of a theme) and "doodle" meaning (improvisation, proceeding from one associational smoke ring to another). *Pluies* combines the advantages of both. The poet takes the history of man in terms of rain (rain as fertilizer, as purifier, as the principle of life and change) as the central stem, but allows himself the dispersed exfoliation of imaginative reference evoking the many-faced past of man.

Backlund, Percival. Saint-John Perse: Den vindburne diktaren. Hori 13:27–30, 1966. **9299**

Brief analysis of *Vents*.

Bienamé, Dora. Exil di Saint-John Perse. Let 58–59:101–18, 1962. **9300**

Thematic analysis of the seven cantos of *Exil* stressing the contrast between the vanity and the exaltation of human action and creation.

Bollack, Jean. En l'an de paille. Arg 3: 1960. *Trans.* NRs 71:757–66, 1960. *Also in:* Honneur à Saint-John Perse. *See* 9022. p. 473–79. **9301**

A penetrating study of *Vents* as a theory of Being and Becoming, as the quest for the violent force which destroys and renews, which restores the original Chaos in order to restore its primeval fertility. The winds symbolize not only the force of Becoming and the violence of History, but also the prophetic violence of poetic inspiration.

Cesbron, G. Etude d'un texte de Saint-John Perse: lecture bachelardienne d'Exil IV. IL 5:233–41, 1974. **9302**

Meditating on the presence of earth, fire, water, lightning, thresholds, grottos and shores in *Exil*, the author concludes that P.'s poem is based not only on a historical exile, but also on psychic archetypes. Relies heavily on J.-P. Richard. [CR]

Claudel, Paul. Un poème de Saint-John Perse: Vents. RdP 56:3–15, 1949. *Also (rev.) in:* Saint-John Perse. *See* 9206. p. 58–67. *Also in:* Honneur à Saint-John Perse. *See* 9022. p. 43–52. *Also in his:* Œuvres en prose. Gallimard, 1965. p. 613–27. *Trans.:* HudR 14:396–408, 1951. *Also in:* Saint-John Perse. Winds. Pantheon, 1953. p. 223–34. (Bollingen series, 34) **9303**

Vents is characterized as an epic poem recounting the Poet's rejection of the past, his conquest of a new world and his search for the sea from which he returns with a message for other men. Suggests that P.'s quest, in spite of his rejection of religion, may actually be a search for God.

Dolamore, Charles. The love and aggression of Saint-John Perse's Pluies. FMLS 7:211–20, 1971. **9304**

In *Pluies*, the rains are imbued with two contrasting sets of qualities: love and fertility, war and aggression. They symbolize the qualities which can elevate man above the everyday plane of his existence.

Fowlie, Wallace. The poetics of Saint-John Perse. Poetry 82:345–50, 1953. **9305**

General study of *Winds* as an affirmation of the power and mission of poetry.

Girard, René. Winds and poetic experience. *In:* A tribute to Saint-John Perse. *See* 9028. p. 46–52. **9306**

Vents is a poem which is also the record of its own genesis. The poet appears successively as the Narrator, the Traveler, the Exile, the Stranger, and the Prodigal, the Enchanter. The Narrator recognizes that destruction must precede rebirth. The Traveler freed from allegiance to all past civilizations and creeds becomes the Exile, the Stranger. Nihilism is justified as a stage beyond which he must proceed: he returns as the Prodigal, as the initiator of new ways. Finally, he is the Enchanter, the magician of language whose poetic evidence testifies to the transmutation of nihilism into a new version of things.

Jouve, Pierre Jean. Exil. *In:* Saint-John Perse. *See* 9036. p. 55–57. *Also in:* Honneur à Saint-John Perse. *See* 9022. p. 39–42.   **9307**
Examines P.'s verbal imagination and his use of vocabulary and sound in Canto VI of *Exil* to convey the sense of metaphysical loss and to praise man's abiding greatness.

Katayama, Masaki. Saint-John Perse Ryutaku no bunseki. Mungen 15:195–99, 1964.   **9308**
Explication of *Exil*.

Knodel, Arthur J. The imagery of Saint-John Perse's Neiges. PMLA 70:5–18, 1955. *Trans. in:* Honneur à Saint-John Perse. *See* 9022. p. 447–56.   **9309**
Thorough analysis of *Neiges* (structure, typographical disposition, use of sound, syntax and relationship to previous poems). Special emphasis is placed on the imagery. Pioneering, well-researched study, but somewhat limited in its conclusions.

Koerber, Cecile. Saint-John Perse: Neiges. FR 37:22–30, 1963.   **9310**
A Christian reading of *Neiges:* the figure of the mother is somewhat arbitrarily identified with a Beatrice-like Lady, the Virgin Mary, and the Muse. The poem itself is compared with Dante's *Paradiso*.

Little, J. Roger. Elements of the Jason-Medea myth in Exil by Saint-John Perse. MLR 61:422–25, 1966.   **9311**
Persuasive study of possible, but by no means certain, sources of *Exil* in the story of Jason and Medea.

McMahon, Joseph H. A question of man. Cweal 73:407–09, 1961.   **9312**
Attempts to examine the impact of wartime Washington on P.'s personal and spiritual drama. *Vents* is read as the poet's humanist response to the threat posed by immensely powerful forces: war and technocracy, as they combined to produce the atom bomb.

Noulet, Emilie. Exil. LetFB Feb. 1943. *Also in her:* Alphabet critique. 1924–64. III. Brussels, Presses univ. de Bruxelles, 1965. p. 20–21.   **9313**
In spite of its verbal splendor and its poetic intensity, P.'s style does not appear totally free from echoes of Claudel and D'Annunzio.

———. Saint-John Perse: Exil suivi de Poème à l'étrangère; Pluies; Neiges. Font Nov. 1947. *Also in her:* Alphabet critique. 1924–64. III. Brussels, Presses univ. de Bruxelles, 1965. p. 22–23.   **9314**
Praises P.'s lyrical power and poetic technique, but makes some reservations about an excessive use of echoes and contrasts.

Ogburn, Charlton. Comment fut écrit Pluies. *In:* Honneur à Saint-John Perse. *See* 9022. p. 273–79.   **9315**
Informative account of a driving trip through South Carolina and Georgia in the company of P. Throws light on the circumstances under which *Pluies* was written.

Parent, Monique. Le thème de l'orage dans Exil de Saint-John Perse. BdF 19:209–16, 1960.   **9316**
Studies the symbolic meaning of the storm which is linked to the destructive, but also to the purifying and creative aspects of violence in history and poetry. On the sands of exile, the god of the thunderstorm suddenly pounces upon the poet-heroes whom he would press into his service, as Iphigenia was abducted to serve as the priestess of Diana in the distant land of Taurida.

R. Le poète en exil. CahLib 2: Dec. 22, 1943. *Also in:* Font Oct. 1944. *Also in:* Honneur à Saint-John Perse. *See* 9022. p. 438.   **9317**
Brief review of *Exil* in a Resistance paper.

Saget, Justin. Vents. MerF 1006:326–29, 1947.   **9318**
Sees neither an organizing principle nor an underlying concept in *Vents*. The poem is dismissed as a long piece of eloquence in which the poet alternates between renunciation and resentment, and hides an inner emptiness beneath the pomp and ornamentation of his style.

Strauss, Walter A. Saint-John Perse, poet of celebration. EUQ 14:100–11, 1958.   **9319**

Brief study of one fragment of *Exil* (the first three stanzas of Canto III), followed by general remarks stressing the motif of celebration: the lyric celebration of P.'s tropical experience, the epic of man's conquering and civilizing activity, the cosmic rhapsodies in honor of the natural forces — rains, winds, snows — and culminating in a paean to the sea. The conquest of poetic language is seen as analogous to the conquest of nature.

Van Rutten, Pierre. Présentations de Pluies. FMonde 85:30–34, 1971.   **9320**

In this *explication de texte,* the usual elements of the poem are examined: the circumstances under which the poem was written, both personal and historical; the prosody; the tone; the general structure; the imagery; the combination of the two main themes associated with the rains, fertility and purification. In *Pluies* as in most of P.'s poems, natural phenomena are read as symbolic messages.

La Gloire des Rois

Bienaimé Rigo, Dora. La gloire des rois di Saint-John Perse. Gal 13:16–27. 1963.   **9321**

In *La gloire des rois,* the dominant themes of later poems make their first appearance: solitude and exile, the traveler, the Nietzschean desire to go beyond all limits and to change the face of the earth.

Goldmann, Lucien. La gloire des rois. Saint-John Perse. RISULB 3:60–69, 1969. *Also in his:* Structures mentales et création culturelle. Anthropos, 1970. p. 381–92.   **9322**

The global model of the cycle *La gloire des rois* is seen as the historical process in which the impersonal order of nature ("Récitation...") is successively followed by the legitimate order of culture ("Amitié du Prince"), by its violent overthrow ("Histoire du Régent"), by the advent of life and violence ("Chanson du présomptif"), by the failure of this new reign and the return to the legitimate order embodied

by the figure of the King ("Berceuse"). Provocative and brilliant, but not altogether convincing.

Oiseaux

Brombert, Victor. Perse's avian order. HudR 19:494–97, 1966.   **9323**

Discusses the genesis of *Birds* in the works of Braque and P., where the motif of the bird is related to the themes of space, movement, and migration. In spite of its opulent thematic texture and its bold imagery, *Birds* occasionally falls into verbosity and pompousness. Includes brief survey of the theme of the bird in Western literature.

Chapin, Katherine Garrison. Perse in flight. NRep 157, no. 13:26–28, 1967.   **9324**

Birds is a meditation on the experience of flight, a poetic dream born of the view of birds in flight. It is also a meditation on the art of Braque in the series of 12 color etchings of birds which the painter executed for the de luxe edition of the poem.

Raine, Kathleen. St.-John Perse's Birds. SoR 3:255–61, 1967.   **9325**

The poem has a double theme, nature and art, and the bird appears as the unifying image of nature and poetic imagination. Stresses the austerity of its imagery and its vocabulary. Includes a discussion of the English translation.

Affinities and Parallels

Achard Abell, Marcelle. Heidegger et la poésie de Saint-John Perse. RMM 71:292–306. 1966.   **9326**

Detailed comparison of Heidegger and P.: both consider poetry and philosophy as means of seeking the revelation of Being; both reject the supremacy of science, logic, and reason; both explore the very basis of human speech; both have shown interest in pre-Socratic philosophers; both reject abstraction and seek a return to concrete experience; both advocate a constant questioning of reality; both see language as an essential instrument in the revelation of Being; both see man as limited by the unfolding mystery of Being.

Baligand, Renée A. Lautréamont et Saint-John Perse, chantres de la mer. RULau 2, no. 3:5–16, 1970.   9327

For Lautréamont, the sea is associated with death and evil; for P., the sea is the symbol of life, fertility and sexual ecstasy.

Boer, Jo. De dichter Saint-John Perse. Eras 1:163–72, 1946.   9328

Examines affinities between P. and the works of L. Couperus and E. Du Perron which are attributed to similar childhood experiences.

Bonnefoy, Yves. L'illumination et l'Eloge. *In:* Honneur à Saint-John Perse. *See* 9022. p. 327–37.   9329

Impressive study of affinities and contrasts between P. and Rimbaud in relation to a number of themes: childhood, the natural world, Christianity, the value of human work and play.

Connell, Allison B. Saint-John Perse and Valery Larbaud. FR 41:11–22, 1967.   9330

Well-documented study of P.'s friendship with Larbaud. Discusses Larbaud's writings on P. and P.'s tributes to Larbaud as well as possible affinities and mutual influences.

Detharé, Vincent. Saint-John Perse et Alain-Fournier. *In his:* Images et pèlerinages littéraires. Vieux colombier, 1962. p. 161–63.   9331

Brief note showing Alain-Fournier as one of the first to recognize P.'s poetic talent in 1911. [CR]

Eliot, T. S. Un feuillet unique. *In:* Saint-John Perse. *See* 9026. p. 27–29. *Also in:* Honneur à Saint-John Perse. *See* 9022. p. 18–19.   9332

Tribute to P. T. S. Eliot acknowledges P.'s influence on some of the poems which he wrote after translating *Anabase*.

Horry, Ruth N. Paul Claudel and Saint-John Perse. Parallels and contrasts. Chapel Hill, Univ. of North Carolina press, 1971. 132 p.   9333

Detailed comparison of Claudel and P.'s metaphysical concepts of reality, their views of the poet's function as re-creator of the cosmos and their use of the *verset*. Both have created epic visions of the universe, but whereas Claudel views the world as a continuous manifestation of divine will, P. regards the created world as an end in itself. The conclusion does not clearly indicate whether P.'s original principle is immanent or transcendent. A competent, but narrowly focused study.

Review: J. Houston in FR 45:727, 1972.

Itterbeek, Eugene van. Saint-John Perse over Dante. DWB 111:137–43, 1966. 9334

P.'s vision of Dante stresses his fidelity to the earth, his attachment to life, his sense of the unity and universality of man, which enabled him to transcend the limits of his age and overcome the chains of religious tradition.

Kemp, Friedhelm. Saint-John Perse: Winde. Merk 104:973–82, 1956.   9335

The translation of *Vents* (Book I, Cantos 1, 2, 4, 5 and 6) is preceded by a brief introduction in which P.'s poetry is compared with Hugo (in his *Légende des siècles*), Walt Whitman, Theodor Däubler (in his *Nordlicht*), Ezra Pound (in his *Cantos*) and Pablo Neruda (in his *Canto general*). Stresses the close control and discipline to which the creative spirit is subjected in P.'s poetry and the resulting poetic tension.

Knodel, Arthur J. Marcel Proust et Saint-John Perse, le fossé infranchissable. RdP 76:80–92, Dec. 1969.   9336

Examines the relationship between P. and Proust: Proust's admiration for *Eloges,* P.'s lack of interest in Proust's work and the possible reasons for it. The explanation offered is Proust's rejection of reality unmediated by art.

Leyris, Pierre. Quand T. S. Eliot parle Perse. MNo 96:73–79, 1956.   9337

Discusses P.'s translation of Eliot's *The hollow men.*

Little, Roger. Saint-John Perse, poète anglais. RCL 46:505–13, 1972.   9338

Examines P.'s relationship with Conrad, Eliot, Auden, MacLeish and others, the influence of English on P.'s poetry, and P.'s views on fundamental differences between English and French poetry.

———. T. S. Eliot and Saint-John Perse. ArlQ 2:5–17, 1969. **9339**

Examines P.'s influence on Eliot and studies Eliot's translation of *Anabase* which is found somewhat wanting.

Madariaga, Salvador de. Alexis Leger. *In:* Honneur à Saint-John Perse. *See* 9022. p. 675–77. *Also in:* Œuvres complètes. *See* 8968. p. 1153–55. **9340**

Compares the diplomatic styles of Philippe Berthelot and P.

Nelson, C. E. Saint-John Perse and T. S. Eliot. WHR 17:163–71, 1963. **9341**

Discusses affinities and contrasts between P. and Eliot. Eliot is a poet of separation and dissociation of poet and society. P.'s personae may be separated, but not alienated from society; they come to terms with modern man's situation without having to seek God. A similar opposition is noted in their attitude toward love and sex. Examines how this opposition subtly distorts Eliot's translation of *Anabase*.

Nieto, José García. Saint-John Perse, premia Nobel. PoeE 95:1–4, 1960. **9342**

Brief introduction and bibliography, unconvincingly mentioning similarities between P. and Juan Ramón Jiménez (path from immediate to universal; preoccupation with language) and P. and Unamuno (renovation of language).

Noulet, Emilie. Le ton dans la poésie de Saint-John Perse. SynB 10–20, Sept.-Oct. 1968. *Expanded version in her:* Le ton poétique. Corti, 1971. p. 185–203. **9343**

Compares the tone in *Amers* and in Pindar's *Odes*, making use of previously unpublished documents: a letter and extracts from P.'s translation of Pindar with original notes. Detailed analysis of devices used to create P.'s characteristic tone: repetition, inner rhyme, refrain, metagrammatism, enumeration and litany. Includes the text of "Des villes sur trois modes" in the version originally published in 1908.

Palm, Göran. Havet, ett kommunikationsproblem. OB 74:9–13, 1965. **9344**

Sketchy comparison of the motif of the sea in Baudelaire, Neruda, P. and Lautréamont.

Peschechera, Vito. Per Dante o per sé? Osservazioni sull' allocuzione fiorentine di Saint-John Perse. *In:* Studi di letteratura francese. I. Florence, Olschki, 1967. p. 163–74. **9345**

P.'s portrait of Dante is found to be an expression of P.'s own fundamental concerns: the rejection of mysticism, the primacy of language, the humanistic message of poetry and the vision of poetic creation as a form of historical action.

Piontek, Heinz. Saint-John Perse. WuW 13: 39–40, 1958. **9346**

Brief survey of P.'s life and works. Compares P.'s verse with Jean-Paul's "Streckvers" and the spirit of his poetry with Pound, Rilke and Gottfried Benn. Stresses the image of the poet as the magic conqueror of the world.

Spender, Stephen. Un bas-relief. *In:* Saint-John Perse. *See* 9026. p. 120–21. *Also in:* Honneur à Saint-John Perse. *See* 9022. p. 107. **9347**

Observes P.'s influence on W. H. Auden, Archibald MacLeish and T. S. Eliot. Compares each fragment of *Exil* or *Vents* to a bas-relief and relates P.'s works to the Biblical and Hellenic traditions.

Thomas, Henri. Une œuvre d'un seul tenant. NRF 7:120–23, 1953. *Also in:* Honneur à Saint-John Perse. *See* 9022. p. 558–61. **9348**

Suggests similarities between P. and Whitman for their cosmic vision, between P., Whitman and Hugo for their use of enumeration, and between P., Gide, Michaux and Lewis Carroll for their descriptions of imaginary travels. Underlines the unity and continuity of P.'s work.

CHAPTER XX

SURREALISM

(Nos. 9349–9869)

Anna Balakian, Micheline Tison-Braun, Julia F. Costitch, Hélène Laroche Davis, Hiam Finkelstein, Roger M. Isaacs, J. Theodore Johnson, Jr., Carlos Lynes, Jane W. Malin, Marie Naudin, Elmer Peterson, Jeanine P. Plottel, Laure Rièse, and Hannah C. Zinni

Surrealism in General
(Nos. 9349–9495)

Marie Naudin*

Bibliography and Etat Présent

Gershman, Herbert S. A bibliography of the surrealist revolution in France. Ann Arbor, Univ. of Michigan press, 1969. 63 p.   **9349**
A valuable work which includes books and articles, periodicals, collective tracts and manifestoes.
Reviews: P. Ray in JML 1:33–37, 1970; R. Short in FS 25:351–54, 1971; S. Taylor in NYRB 14, no. 1–2:41–45, Jan. 29, 1970.

Hardré, Jacques. Present state of studies on literary surrealism. YCGL 27, 9:43–66, 1960. *Also in:* The present state of French studies: a collection of research reviews. Ed. by Charles Osburn. Metuchen, N. J., Scarecrow press, 1971. p. 713–52.   **9350**
A very valuable critical summary of articles and books which have appeared internationally and which deal with surrealism from the publication of the first manifesto in 1924 through 1960.

Le Sage, Laurent. The direction of studies on surrealism. EspCr 8:230–39, 1968. *Also in:* The present state of French studies. Ed. Charles B. Osburn. Metuchen, N.J., Scarecrow press, 1971. p. 753–63.   **9351**
Emphasis on the serious aspect of analysis requested and undertaken for the works of a dead movement. Reviews of books by Matthews, Alquié,

Browder, Caws, Heppenstall and Roussel.

Matthews, John H. Forty years of surrealism (1924–1964); a preliminary bibliography. CLS 3:309–50, 1966.   **9352**
Important beginning for a universal bibliography of surrealism. Divided in two parts, surrealism in the Americas and surrealism in Europe, this article enumerates publications by and about surrealists, surrealist reviews, reviews which have devoted a special number to surrealism, other collective publications, important catalogs of surrealist exhibitions, books and articles on surrealism.

———. Literary surrealism in France since 1945. BA 36:357–64, 1962.   **9353**
An excellent, annotated list of works (1945–1962) including eds, or new eds. of works by Breton, Eluard, Péret, etc., surrealist periodicals, critiques of surrealism. Also gives an account of firms devoted to surrealist publications.

Papenbrock, Jürgen von. Surrealismus und Wirklichkeit. BRP 6:291–306, 1967. *And:* Surrealismus und Unterbewusstsein. BRP 7:30–44, 1968. *And:* Surrealismus und Poesie. BRP 7:277–85, 1968.   **9354**
Series of articles on: 1) Surrealism and reality; 2) Surrealism and the subconscious; 3) Surrealism and poetry. In all of these, Papenbrock seeks to show why surrealism was foredoomed to failure. [MBA]

A selection of surrealist works. *In:* Surrealism. *See* 9415. p. 175–85.   **9355**

*With assistance from Martha B. Alden, Anna Balakian, Agnes Porter Beaudry, and Margarete Mattson.

Divided into (1) history, commentary and critical studies; (2) surrealist periodicals; (3) surrealism in art; (4) works by writers discussed in this special issue devoted to surrealism; (5) other surrealist texts.

Sullerot, François. Aperçu analytique des livres consacrés au mouvement dada jusqu'à 1962. RAEMD no. 1:75-80, 1965. **9356**

A valid critical and analytical review of books on dada (1936-1961).

Books

Abastado, Claude. Introduction au surréalisme. Paris-Montreal, Bordas, 1971. 251 p. (Littérature française) **9357**

A serious work, accurately titled, with a chronology to 1939, a good bibliography of French critical works, a list of reviews and bio-bibliographical notices.

Review: Anon. in BCLF 27:902, 1972.

Alexandre, Maxime. Mémoires d'un surréaliste. La jeune Parque, 1968. 222 p. **9358**

A minor participant in the surrealist movement reveals his innermost thoughts and feelings during the height of the movement (1923-1933). Valuable also as a recollection of the disagreement between Breton and Aragon, the role of Jean Arp, and the stages of the movement. [APB]

Alquié, Ferdinand. Philosophie du surréalisme. Flammarion, 1955. 234 p. *Trans.:* The philosophy of surrealism. Trans. by Bernard Waldrop. Ann Arbor, Univ. of Michigan press, 1965. viii, 196 p. **9359**

This is not a surrealist philosophy, as the author emphasizes, but a philosophical examination of the surrealist "theory of love, of life, of the imagination, of the relations between man and the world." Refers to the work of several surrealists while focusing on Breton. A professor of Cartesian philosophy, Alquié attempts to bring about a rapprochement between Descartes and Breton, and sever both hermeticism and Hegelian dialectics from surrealist thought. Yet a stimulating and thought-ful study that offers a broad philosophical frame of reference. [AB]

Reviews: Anon. in TBR 32, Feb. 1, 1966; Anon. in TLS 528, June 16, 1966; A. Balakian in SatR 33-34, March 12, 1966; J. Brun in RMM 61:360-69, 1956; M. Carrouges in MNo 102:88-102, 1956; J. Lanes in NRep 155, no. 25:28-30, Dec. 17, 1966; L. Le Sage in EspCr 18:230-39, 1968; J. H. Matthews in Sym 20:187-89, 1966; R. Melville in NewS 1849:267, Aug. 19, 1966.

Audoin, Philippe. Les surréalistes. Seuil, 1973. 191 p. (Ecrivains de toujours, 93) **9360**

Short history of the movement. Emphasis on the various members both permanent and successive as well as on their meeting places, diverse exhibitions and magazines. For Audoin, Breton's death and May 1968 mark the last attempts at cohesion for the group, and he pays them tribute for their 50 years of life.

Reviews: S. Arnold in BA 48:733, 1974; J. Bertrand in RGB 10:95-96, Dec. 1973; F. Bott in Monde 9023:14, Jan. 18, 1974 and MondeH 1317:14, Jan. 17-23, 1974; G. Cesbron in LR 28:415-17, 1974; J. Piel in Cr 331:1131-33, 1974; G. Raillard in FM 104:52-53, 1974.

Balakian, Anna. Literary origins of surrealism. A new mysticism in French poetry. King's crown press, 1947. 171 p. *Also:* New York univ. press, 1966. 171 p. **9361**

The works of the romantics, Baudelaire, Rimbaud, Lautréamont, Mallarmé, the symbolists, Gide, Apollinaire, Supervielle and the dadaists viewed intelligently as foreshadowing surrealism. Bibliography and index of names quoted.

Reviews: P. Mansell Jones in FS 2:97-98, 1948; J. Matthews in MLJ 59:439-41, 1966; B. Morrissette in MLN 63:63-68, 1948.

———. Surrealism: the road to the absolute. Noonday press, 1959. 221 p. *Also:* Dutton, 1970. 256 p. *Also:* London, Allen and Unwin, 1972. 256 p. **9362**

Much less concerned than Bédouin with the continuation of surrealism after the Second World War, Balakian discusses the movement beginning with

Lautréamont, Hegel and Freud and going from Saint-Pol-Roux, Apollinaire, Reverdy, up to the *Entretiens* of Breton in 1952. Very good material on the surrealist image and the influence of surrealism on post-surrealist literature. Useful for any student of literature. Lacks a bibliography. Includes (p. 112–141 or p. 140–69) her "The surrealist image," RR 44:273–81, 1953.
Reviews: Anon. in TLS 72:713, 1973; H. Block in C 5:84–86, 1963; S. Gray in EspCr 1:43–44, 1961; C. Hackett in FS 27:357–58, 1973; K. Rexroth in TBR 44, April 24, 1960; E. Vassylkivsky in RR 51:310–13, 1960.

Bancquart, Marie-Claire. Paris des surréalistes. Seghers, 1972. 230 p. (L'archipel)
9363

Some reflections rather than a penetrating study, but they are quite valuable and can make possible subsequent research inasmuch as the work is especially focused on the parallel and contrasting visions of Breton and Aragon. Desnos and Soupault are only briefly dealt with and Bancquart concentrates her study between the years 1920–40. Chronology and index of places in Paris that were mentioned.
Reviews: Anon. in BCLF 28:525, 1973; H. Béhar in RHL 74:147–48, 1974; P. Dhainaut in CahIS 22–23: 116–17, 1973; H. Juin in Monde 8666: 15, Nov. 24, 1972; J. Malrieu in Sud 13:115–16, 1974.

Bédouin, Jean-Louis. La poésie surréaliste. Seghers, 1964. 362 p. *Also:* 1970. 364 p.
9364

Brief introduction insisting on the fact that outside the psychic automatism babbling underneath, the poetry of these 55 poets is neither an essence nor a form different from that of all authentic poetry. Good anthology. The poems chosen are preceded by a biographical notice and by a bibliography of some works properly surrealistic.
Reviews: A. Jouffroy in Exp 680: 27–28, June 25, 1964; R. Kanters in FL 957:2, Aug. 20, 1964.

————. Vingt ans de surréalisme. 1939–1959. Denoël, 1961. 324 p. **9365**
Historical panorama completing that of Nadeau and showing the consolidation of the surrealistic movement in the international, political, artistic and literary domains. Includes six manifestoes published during this period. Perhaps biased but interesting for the study of the vitality of a tendency which could have seemed dominated at that time by the existentialist current.
Review: H. Block in JAAC 18:174–82, 1959–60.

Béhar, Henri. Etude sur le théâtre dada et surréaliste. Gallimard, 1967. 361 p. (Les essais, 131)
9366

A very clear work divided into three parts: precursors and fringe writers, dada, surrealism. Preceded by an introduction on the manifestations of dada. Includes a bibliography of the plays studied and of the critical works referred to in the notes as well as a repertory of productions. In presenting each of the plays, the author tends to emphasize the positive innovations of the dadaist and surrealist theater.
Reviews: M. Arrivé in RHL, 69: 883–84, 1969; H. Baudin in RTG 1: 45–47, May 1970 and in BCLF 23: 108, 1968; G. Cerutti in SFr 13:387, 1969; M. Décaudin in IL 21:42, 1969; P. Dhainaut in QL 42:14–15, Jan. 1–15, 1968; H. Gershman in MD 11:449, 1968–69; M. Le Bot in CahDS 3:85–90, 1968; R. Lorris in FR 42:163–64, 1968; J. van Rees in FrB 49:31–32, 1970; M. Sanouillet in CahDS 3:85–88, 1969 and in ELit 1:445–48, 1968.

Bigsby, C. W. E. Dada and surrealism. London, Methuen, 1972. 99 p. (The critical idiom, 23)
9367

The originality of this simple but solid study is the way in which it establishes contrasting parallels between these two movements and the various literary tendencies which preceded and followed them. A valuable selected bibliography and an index of names.

Bo, Carlo. Bilancio del surrealismo. Padua, Cedam, 1944. 116 p.
9368

As the title suggests, this book proposes an overview of surrealism with some allusions to its roots in Lautréamont and Nerval through to Eluard and Breton. Its two central parts deal with the poetic results of the movement and its practical applications especially in the field of politics. The volume in cludes a bibliography of surrealist and critical works complete through 1939.

————. Il surrealismo. Torino, Ed. radio italiana, 1953. 163 p. (Saggi 4. Etichette del nostro tempo, v. 1) **9369**
This work, originally designed as a radio program, is a good introduction to the surrealist movement. It presents clearly the evolution of surrealism from its links with dada to the post World War Two period. It gives us a glimpse of the prophets of surrealism in the twentieth century, an insight into the work of Breton and Eluard and a critical appraisal of the movement.

Bohrer, Karl Heinz. Die Gefahrdete, Phantasie, oder Surrealismus und Terror. Munich, Carl Hanser, 1970. 106 p. (Reihe Hanser, 40) **9370**
Based on the discoveries of French surrealism, a study of the relation between art and life, according to a combinative and prophetic method advocated at first in early German romanticism. Two essays concern the esthetic side of the problem of the contradiction between fancy and daily life; two others describe the resulting political dilemma.
Review: M. Sperber in Merk 25: 998–99, 1971.

Bréchon, Robert. Le surréalisme. Colin, 1971. 224 p. (U²/Synthèses, 159) **9371**
Excellent exposé of surrealist doctrine and esthetics. Chronology. Bibliography lacks works of foreign critics. Index.
Reviews: Anon. in PFr 5:198, Autumn 1972; P. Berthier in Et 336: 628–29, 1972; R. Cardinal in FS 28: 230–31, 1974; L. Le Sage in FR 45: 913–14, 1972; L. Losito in CulF 20:168, 1973; A. Mingelgrün in RBPH 51:415–16, 1973.

Burgër, Peter. Der französische Surrealismus. Studien zum Problem der avantgardistischen Literatur. Frankfurt am Main, Athenäum, 1971. 207 p. **9372**
A contrasting comparison of Tzara and Valéry followed by studies of dadaism and surrealism. Emphasis on *Le paysan de Paris, Nadja* and *Le château d'Argol*. Bibliography. Index.
Reviews: W. Babilas in RJ 23:256–61, 1972; H. Rück in NS 22:505–06, 1973; G. Schmigalle in KrL 3:24–27,

1974; N. Schwab-Bakman in RHL 73: 154, 1973.

Cardinal, Roger, and Robert Stuart Short. Surrealism. Permanent revelation. London, Studio Vista; New York, Dutton, 1970. 165 p. **9373**
A survey of some of the main aspects of the movement. Especially interesting for the numerous photographs and reproductions of paintings and for its last chapter which deals with the surrealist destiny. A rather incomplete bibliography. Index of names mentioned.
Reviews: C. Hackett in FS 3:355–56, July 1973; J. Lyle in A&A 6, no. 5:59–60, 1971.

Caws, Mary Ann. The poetry of dada and surrealism: Aragon, Breton, Tzara, Eluard and Desnos. Princeton, N. J., Princeton univ. press, 1970. 236 p. **9374**
Serious but debatable study. For each author, Caws first analyzes the theoretical writings, then the poetic collections in chronological order, claiming that the poems inevitably illustrate the theories, and that an author's work does not evolve, even if he moves from dadaism to surrealism and on to political involvement. Includes bibliography of works consulted.
Reviews: A. Balakian in MLQ 33: 208–10, 1972; P. Broome in AUMLA 36:249–50, 1971; J. Duncan in MLR 67:427–28, 1972; C. Hackett in FS 3:355–59, 1973; S. Lawall in MR 12: 354–59, 1971; A. Mingelgrün in RBPH 52:669–72, 1974; B. Morrissette in MP 70:174–78, 1972; R. Riese-Hubert in FR 46:165–68, 1972; Van Meter Ames in JAAC 29:282, 1970–71.

————. Surrealism and the literary imagination. A study of Breton and Bachelard. The Hague-Paris, Mouton, 1966. 85 p. (Studies in French literature, 12) **9375**
An interesting study which shows that Bachelard's theory of the dynamic literary imagination is closely related to the surrealist attitude as formulated by Breton, and that many similarities between the two men are manifestations of a certain 20th-century temperament not yet dead.
Reviews: A. Balakian in RR 40: 156–59, 1969; L. Le Sage in EspCr 8:230–39, 1968; J. Matthews in Sym 22:289–90, 1968.

The dada painters and poets. Ed. Robert Motherwell. Wittenborn, Schultz, 1951. 431 p. (The documents of modern art, 8) *Also* (*rev.*): 1967.   **9376**

Although more concentrated on painting, this is a superb anthology of manifestoes, texts and recollections from the dada school from an international viewpoint. Excellent introduction. Long bibliography.

Dictionnaire abrégé du surréalisme. Galerie des beaux-arts, 1938. 75 p. *Also:* Corti, 1969. 76 p.   **9377**

An amusing collection of quotes taken from the surrealists as well as from their predecessors and critics. Numerous illustrations.

Reviews: E. Kanceff in SFr 16:183, 1972; R. Short in FS 25:351–54, 1971.

Durozoi, Gérard, and Bernard Lecherbonnier. Le surréalisme: théories, thèmes, techniques. Larousse, 1972. 286 p. (Thèmes et textes)   **9378**

A fine reflective work on the value of surrealism placed in its historic perspective with a subtle critique not only of its weaknesses but also of its greatness. A critical bibliography of French works.

Reviews: W. Babilas in RJ 23:256–61, 1972; H. Rück in NS 22:505–06, 1973; G. Schmigalle in KrL 3:24–27, 1974; N. Schwab-Bakman in RHL 73:154, 1973.

Ey, Henri. La psychiatrie devant le surréalisme. Centre d'éditions psychiatriques, 1948. 52 p.   **9379**

With the help of precise examples, a demonstration that surrealism does not depend on psychiatry and that, in general, the artistic products of the insane are clearly inferior to the most automatic productions of the surrealists.

Gaunt, William. The surrealists. Putnam, 1972. 272 p.   **9380**

An excellent, well-documented popular work, with a clear, balanced exposition, giving an historical account as well as a critical view, including very beautiful illustrations, biographies, chronology, bibliography (unfortunately incomplete as far as the literary works of painters and sculptors are concerned) and index.

Review: V. Raynor in WPBW 7, no. 52:8, Dec. 24, 1972.

Gauthier, Xavière. Surréalisme et sexualité. Gallimard, 1971. 279 p. (Idées)   **9381**

Confronts the works of Marx, Lenin, Lacan and Freud. An excellent study because of its analysis of texts and paintings dealing with the fight for sexual freedom undertaken by surrealism. Points to a partial failure, especially in literature. Valuable bibliography. Twenty illustrations.

Reviews: F. Bott in Monde 8428:14, Feb. 18, 1972; M. Chapsal in Exp 1068:61, Dec. 27-Jan. 2, 1972; P. Dhainaut in CahIS 21:106–08, 1972; G. Lapouge in QL 136:13–14, March 1, 1972; J. Martinet in Mat 14:4, May 1972; C. Mauriac in FL 1335:25, Dec. 17, 1971; R. Riese-Hubert in FR 46:639–40, Feb. 1973; F. Savater in RO 115:109–12, 1972.

Gershman, Herbert S. The surrealist revolution in France. Ann Arbor, Univ. of Michigan press, 1969. 267 p.   **9382**

Excellent balance sheet that is both temperate and humorous. Interesting chapter concerning the early literature of surrealism. More dense than the work of Balakian. Two appendices give a selective chronology of surrealism and a schematic view of its foundations. Numerous helpful footnotes. No bibliography.

Reviews: A. Balakian in MLQ 33:165–71, 1972; P. Brians in YCGL 19:78–81, 1970; J. Carmody in RR 62:73–74, 1971; M. Caws in FR 44:255–56, 1970–71 and EspCr 10:150–56, 1970; W. Hoffmann in MLN 85:626–34, 1970; S. Kantarizis in AUMLA 34:349–51, 1970; T. Marshall in WCR 4, no. 2:59–60, 1969; J. Matthews in BA 43:186–88, 1969; M. Pops in C 11:389–91, 1969; R. Shattuck in TBR 34:4–5, July 20, 1969; R. Short in FS 25:351–53, 1971; A. Viatte in CulF 18:46, 1969.

Grossman, Manuel L. Dada. Paradox, mystification and ambiguity in European literature. Pegasus, 1971. 192 p.   **9383**

The interest of this study, which assumes the historic framework of Hugnet's book, is to be found in the chapter analyzing the literary innovations of Ball, Tzara, Picabia, Arp and of French group *Littérature*. Grossman shows that integral elements of surrealism were already present in dada.

Selected bibliography and index of names mentioned.
Reviews: Anon. in YCGL p. 135, 1971; L. Rosenfield in Clio 2, no. 1: 81–82, 1972.

Halicka, Alice. Hier; souvenirs. Eds. du pavois, 1946. 304 p.   9384
The author and her husband, Louis Marcoussis, were artists in Montmartre during the first quarter of the century. They knew virtually all members of the cubist-surrealist group. The author explains who each one was, rather than assuming we already know them. The last half of the book is of no literary interest. [APB]

Hausmann, Raoul. Courrier dada. Le terrain vague, 1958. 157 p.   9385
A restatement, principally by way of Hugnet, of the true dada character in Berlin. An additional view by Huelsenbeck of the role of the other members of the group, notably the author's, who interestingly describes his own contributions, quotes his manifestoes, and gives a complete bibliography of his work.

Hercourt, Jean. La leçon du surréalisme, suivie de Jules Supervielle. Geneva, Le verbe, Louis Penet, 1947. 62 p.   9386
Interesting perspective which underscores the importance of scientific evolution as a conditioning factor in the development of poetry. Examples drawn primarily from Eluard and Supervielle, poets of the contemporary world, and from Jouve, a reactionary poet.

Hugnet, Georges. L'aventure dada (1916–1922). Galerie de l'Institut, 1957. 134 p. *Also:* Seghers, 1971. 238 p.   9387
Although a bibliography is missing, this work contains precise information concerning the dada school in Zurich, Berlin, Cologne, Hanover, New York and Paris. Excellent introduction by Tzara. 32 illustrations emphasizing painting, collages and dadaist photographs.
Review: A. Pieyre de Mandiargues in NRF 9:1100–02, 1957.

Kyrou, Ado. Le surréalisme au cinéma. Arcanes, 1953. 290 p. (Ombres blanches)
9388

A work which retraces the history of films between 1900 and 1950 in light of a critique which is both subjective and surrealist. Ch. 7 is devoted to the study of dada and surrealist films, ch. 8 to Buñuel.

Légoutière, Edmond. Le surréalisme. Masson, 1972. 232 p. (Ensembles littéraires)
9389
Excellent commented anthology highlighting extracts of the principal dada and surrealist manifestoes. Eighteen authors grouped as follows: precursors, dadaists, surrealists, tail end of surrealism. Texts from poetry, prose and the theater. Concise bibliography.
Reviews. Anon. in BCLF 28:908, 1972; M. Galb in Exp 1076:63–64, Feb. 21–27, 1972; P. Morelle in Monde 8428:13–14, Feb. 18, 1972, and in MondeH 1218:14, Feb. 24–March 1, 1972; B. Pivot in FL 1345:1, 3(13–15), Feb. 26, 1972.

Matthews, John H. An introduction to surrealism. University Park, Pennsylvania state univ. press, 1965. 192 p.   9390
An excellent work which clarifies and demonstrates the concordance of the major elements of surrealism (dream, automatic writing, chance, imagination, the miraculous, love) by confronting the texts of writers and painters. Incredibly scanty bibliography but the footnotes are excellent. Index of names mentioned.
Reviews: M. Beaujour in EspCr 6: 131–32, 1966; J. Gaulmier in BFLS 45:376–77, 1966–67; M. Kozloff in Nat 201:504–05, Dec. 20, 1965; L. Le Sage in EspCr 8:230–39, 1968; C. Lynes in FR 39:951–54, 1966; P. Ray in JAAC 24:446–48, 1965–66.

————. Surrealism and film. Ann Arbor, Univ. of Michigan press, 1971. 210 p.
9391
An excellent study, especially of Luis Buñuel's work. Equal tribute to those scenarios brought to the screen and to those that were not. Solid documentation. No bibliography but precise footnotes. Index of names and works cited.
Reviews: P. Ilie in Diac 2, no. 4: 520–23, 1973–74; J. Manchip White in 54–59, 1972; M. Kushnir in JML 3:

Sym 27:165-72, 1973; N. Watanabe in FR 46:630-31, 1972-73.

————. Surrealism and the novel. Ann Arbor, Univ. of Michigan press, 1966. 197 p.   **9392**

Study of eight novels and collections of short stories by Crevel, Desnos, Gracq, Leiris, Mansour, Fourré and Jouffroy in light of Breton's critique of this genre and his particular novelistic preferences. An interesting work, full of pertinent information but incomplete because of weak bibliography. The list of novels which demonstrate the surrealist esthetic is also found lacking.

Reviews: Anon. in TLS 3428:1062, Nov. 9, 1967; A. Balakian in RR 60: 158-59, 1969; M. Beaujour in FR 41:431-33, 1967; R. Bellé in Person 49:423-24, 1968; M. Caws in Novel 1:192-94, 1968; H. Gershman in BA 41:342-43, 1967; R. Heppenstall in LonM 17, no. 12:90-94, 1968; J. Lanes in NRep 155, no. 25:28-30, Dec. 17, 1966; R. Navarri in Eur 475-76:34-44, 1968.

————. Surrealist poetry in France. Syracuse, N.Y., Syracuse univ. press, 1969. 254 p.   **9393**

Serious work intended to complete Nadeau's and Bédouin's studies. Analyzes new ideas added to poetic language by the surrealists of several generations. Concrete examples taken from the surrealistic works of Soupault, Aragon, Péret, Desnos, Vitrac, Leiris, Arp, Eluard, Char, Rosey, Mayoux, Jouffroy, Mansour, Cabanel, Dhainaut and Bounoure.

Reviews: A. Balakian in MLQ 33: 208-10, 1972; G. Bonicatto in SFr 15:384, 1971; H. Gershman in FR 44:605-06, 1971; S. Kantarizis in AUMLA 34:347-48, 1970; S. Lockerbie in FS 26:92-93, 1972; H. Peyre in Sym 24:380-82, 1970; S. Sellin in BA 44:630-31, 1970; S. Watson Taylor in TBR 14, nos. 1-2:41-45, Jan. 29, 1970.

————. Theatre in dada and surrealism. Syracuse, N.Y., Syracuse univ. press, 1974. 300 p.   **9394**

A critical continuation of Béhar's book, dismissing the precursors and adding the names and works of Isvic,

Duprey, Pierre, Auquier and Aelberts. Matthews confronts the dramatic and theoretical works of the authors and, unlike Béhar, puts more emphasis on surrealism than dada. Although there is no bibliography, the footnotes are sufficient to take its place.

Monnerot, Jules. La poésie moderne et le sacré. Gallimard, 1945. 207 p. (Les essais, 16)   **9395**

A quite valid account of surrealism, particularly with respect to poetry and painting. Contrasted parallels between the surrealists and the gnostics on one hand, and the primitives on the other. A postscriptum on Rimbaud.

Reviews: M. Blanchot in Ar 8:98-104, 1945; A. Hoog in Esp 112:253-59, 1945; P. Grison in FrA 52:256-57, July 1950.

Nadeau, Maurice. Histoire du surréalisme. Seuil, 1945. 370 p. Also: Seuil, 1954. 358 p. Also: Club des éditeurs, 1958. 391 p. Also: Seuil, 1964. 524 p. Also: Seuil, 1970. 191 p. (Points, 1) Trans.: The history of surrealism. Trans. by Richard Howard. Macmillan, 1964. 1965, 1968. 351 p. Also: London, Cape, 1968. 351 p.   **9396**

Not a complete history, this work stops at the Second World War. But it is very useful in following the increasing dilemma at the heart of the movement between literary and political activities. Some good studies of surrealist works.

Reviews: Anon. in TLS 482:1306, Nov. 21, 1968 and in TLS 72:546, 1973; J. Berger in NSoc 314:500, Oct. 3, 1968; V. Crastre in TM 38:290-313, 1948; A. Darack in SatR 59, Oct. 30, 1965; I. Hamilton in ILN 6745: 32-33, Nov. 9, 1968; M. Kozloff in Nat 201:504-05, Dec. 20, 1965; J. Lanes in NRep 155, no. 25:28-30, Dec. 17, 1966; J. Matthews in Sym 20:187-88, 1966; H. Read in YP 999:6, May 12, 1966; J. Weightman in Gua 38,025:9, Oct. 11, 1968 and in TBR 15, no. 6:8, 10, 12, Oct. 28, 1965.

Pierre, José. Le futurisme et le dadaisme. Lausanne, Rencontre; Paris, SPADEM, 1966. 208 p. (Histoire générale de la peinture)   **9397**

Deals especially with painting and principally with Italian futurism and German dadaism. A few interesting pages where the major futurist and dada manifestoes can be found in French. Brief but useful glossary. Solid introduction by Ph. Soupault. Review: R. Hausmann in QL 23: 12–13, March 1, 1967.

Ray, Man. Self-portrait. Boston & Toronto, Atlantic-Little, Brown, 1963. 402 p. *Trans.:* Autoportrait. Trans. by Anne Guérin. Laffont, 1964. 360 p. **9398**

The author, a photographer, was an intimate member of the surrealist clan, including Breton, Soupault, Aragon, Marcel Duchamp. He also knew Picasso, Matisse, Braque, Picabia, and Brancusi. [APB]

Ribemont-Dessaignes, Georges. Déjà jadis ou du mouvement dada à l'espace abstrait. Julliard, 1958. 299 p. (Lettres nouvelles) **9399**

A subjective and uneven work. Naturally its largest interest resides in the personal memories of Ribemont-Dessaignes about the avant-dada, dada and surrealist periods.

Reviews: N. Arnaud in Cr 14:900–03, 1958; W. Babilas in Archiv 195: 361-63, 1959.

Richter, Hans. Dada—Kunst und Antikunst. Der Beitrag Dadas zur Kunst des 20. Jahrhunderts. Cologne, Verlag M. DuMont Schauberg, 1964. 259 p. *Trans.:* Dada: Art and anti-art. London, Thames and Hudson, 1965. 246 p. [The world of art library: Modern movements] *Trans.:* Dada—art et anti-art. Brussels, Eds. de la connaissance, 1965. 218 p. **9400**

A critical and historically compelling narrative. Using first-hand information, the author emphasizes the Zurich group, a literary and artistic personality of the stature of Schwitters, contemporary inheritors in the United States, new realism, pop art, assemblage, etc., elements borrowed from dada by later movements, and the post-dada period in various countries.

Reviews: Anon. in Times 3355:528, June 16, 1966; Anon. in TLS 56, 570: 15, March 3, 1966; J. Bersani in Cr 231–32:780–81, 1966; A. Causet in ILM 248, no. 6605:33, March 5, 1966; R. Hughes in SunT 7448, Feb. 20,

1966; E. Lucie-Smith in List 75, no. 1929:399–400, March 17, 1966; N. Lynton in Gua 37, no. 210:9, Feb. 25, 1966; W. Oliver in YP 36, 931:89–90, Feb. 21, 1966; A. Powell in DaiT 34480:22, March 3, 1966; J. Selz in QL 4:17, May 1, 1966; P. Toynbee in Obs 9111:26, Feb. 20, 1966.

Sanouillet, Michel. Dada à Paris. Pauvert, 1965. 644 p. **9401**

Fundamental work concerning the study of the spirit of the avant-garde which stirred Paris from 1915 to 1924. Some errors and partial judgments with a chauvinistic tendency to minimize the role and the work of Tzara. On the other hand, numerous examples and excellent footnotes. Ample bibliography and appendix of 171 pages including the correspondence of Breton, Tzara, Picabia and various other documents.

Reviews: Anon. in BCLF 20:955, 1965; Anon. in TLS 3460:14–15, June 20, 1968; J. Bersani in Cr 225:99–117, 1966; M. Caws in EspCr 6:296–97, 1966; M. Décaudin in CahD 2:208–10, 1968; P. Dhainaut in CahS 61: 161–62, 1966; S. Dresden in FrB 36:126–27, 1966; J. Gaugeard in LetF 5, July 1–7, 1965; H. Gershman in BA 40:423, 1966; R. Guiette in RBPH 44:1037–39, 1966; P. Moreau in RLC 41:473–77, 1967; P. Prigioni in RJ 17: 225–27, 1966.

Schuster, Jean. Archives 57/68. Batailles pour le surréalisme. Eric Losfeld, 1969. 205 p. (Le terrain vague). **9402**

Series of essays and articles especially interesting for the political evolution of a die-hard surrealist and for his unflinching defense of esthetic and philosophical positions of Breton during his whole life.

Review: J. Matthews in BA 44:258, 1970.

Somville, Léon. Devanciers du surréalisme: les groupes d'avant-garde et le mouvement poétique 1912–1925. Geneva, Droz, 1971. 215 p. (Histoire des idées et critique littéraire, 116) **9403**

Extremely valuable for its bibliography, its inventory of magazines from the first half of the century and its analysis of manifestoes showing new tendencies between 1909 and 1920: integralism, impulsionism, dynamism, paroxysm, dramatism, synchronism. An

appendix giving characteristic texts of Beauduin, Barzun and Fabri.
Reviews: M. Caws in RR 14:234–35, 1974; S. Fauchereau in Cr 318: 997–1012, 1973; R. Geen in MLJ 56:513–14, 1972; J. Goldenstein in ELit 4:374–77, 1971; M. Goosse in RBPH 52:222–23, 1974; A. Lebois in Lit 19:161, 1972; C. Tournadre in RHL 74:146, 1974.

Thirion, André. Révolutionnaires sans révolution. Laffont, 1972. 578 p. *Trans.:* Revolutionaries without revolution. Trans. by Joachim Neugroschel. Macmillan, 1975. 507 p.   **9404**
Proceeding from an autobiographical account, interesting information on the behavior of the surrealists living on the rue du Château and rue Fontaine, and of the habitués of the Cyrano and of the cafés in Montparnasse. A no less interesting criticism of French and Russian communism during the years 1925–1955. Many references to the political publications of Breton and his acolytes. No bibliography. Index of names.
Reviews: P. de Boisdeffre in RDM 167–70, April-June 1972; C. Bourniquel in Esp 414:1094–95, 1972; B. Pivot in FL 1345:1, 3, 13, 15, Feb. 26, 1972.

Tzara, Tristan. Lampisteries, précédées des sept manifestes dada. Pauvert, 1963. 149 p.   **9405**
Valuable book. Complete bibliography of the author's other works, the manifestoes of the dada school, 23 literary and artistic critical essays where names such as Reverdy, Apollinaire and Picabia dominate. Ideas relevant to the work of art as a world in itself.
Reviews: S. Fauchereau in Cr 311: 375–84, 1973; R. Lacôte in LetF 2, Nov. 28, 1963.

――――. Le surréalisme et l'après-guerre. Nagel, 1947. 88 p. *Also:* Nagel, 1966. 96 p.   **9406**
Extremely clear historical account of the parallel development of poetry and history. Condemnation of surrealism's inability to deal with the problems created by the Second World War. Precise definition of what contemporary poetry should be. Valuable tonic work

which includes the text of the lecture "La dialectique de la poésie" given in December 1946 and February 1947 at Bucharest and Prague.

Vovelle, José. Le surréalisme en Belgique. Brussels, André De Rache, 1972. 373 p.   **9407**
An important work with a careful bibliography and divided into two major parts: the history of the surrealist movement in Belgium and an analysis of the paintings of Magritte, Delvaux, Mesens, Graverol, Baes, etc. Also a selection of texts. Distinguishes originality and differences of the Belgians in relation to French surrealism. Emphasis on the importance of Magritte.
Reviews: M. Bodart in RGB 108, no. 10:83–85, 1972; H. Juin in MagL 72:45–48, Jan. 1973.

Collected Articles

Cahiers de l'Association internationale pour l'étude de dada et du surréalisme. No. 1– 1966–   **9408**
An occasional publication, now taken over by the publisher Minard. Usually each number is devoted to a special topic.

Dada/Surrealism. Flushing, N.Y., Queen's college press, 1972–   **9409**
An occasional publication, edited by Mary Ann Caws. Somewhat difficult to identify, technically speaking, because issues often lack volume numbers and dates.
Review: A. Walter in FR 47:830–31, 1974.

Entretiens sur le surréalisme. Ed. by Ferdinand Alquié. Paris, The Hague, Mouton, 1968. 568 p. [Décades du Centre culturel international de Cerisy-la-Salle, nouvelle série 8]   **9410**
Articles by various hands on varied aspects of surrealism.
Reviews: A. Arnold in FR 44:976–78, 1971; M. Caws in EspCr 10:150–56, 1970; P. Dhainaut in CahIS 17–18: 111–12, 1969; M. Guiomar in RE 19:429–33, 1966; J.-Cl. Margolin in RdS 57–58:144, Jan.-June 1970; J.

Matthews in Sym 24:382–83, 1970;
C. Van Rees in LT 311–12, 1971.

Essays on surrealism. TCL 21:1–58, 1975.
9411
Contents: Mary Ann Caws, *The poetics of a surrealist passage and beyond* (p. 24–36); Edith Kern, *Surrealism, the language of unthought* (p. 37–47); J. H. Matthews, *The manifesto of surrealism* (p. 1–9); Eric Sellin, *Simultaneity: Driving force of the surrealist aesthetic* (p. 10–23).

Le groupe; la rupture. Change 5:1–221, 1970. **9412**
The significant articles have been analyzed separately under the appropriate headings.

The language of surrealism. Sym 24:293–386, 1970. **9413**
A series of articles by various hands on surrealism and language.

Permanence du surréalisme. CahXXs 4:8–158, 1975. **9414**
Articles on a wide range of subjects related to surrealism.

Surrealism. YFS 31:1–186, 1964. **9415**
The significant articles have been analyzed separately under the appropriate headings.
Reviews: M. Bonnet in RHL 66:349–53, 1966; A. Licari in SFr 10:589, 1966.

Surréalisme. Eur 475–76:1–302, 1968. **9416**
On various aspects of surrealism.
Review: R. Lacôte in LetF 2164:8, 11, Dec. 31, 1972.

Surrealist literature. EspCr 6:1–51, 1966. **9417**
Includes: Anna Balakian, *The significance of the surrealist manifestoes* (p. 3–13); Pierre Dhainaut, *Machines à écrire: à propos de Raymond Roussel et de quelques surréalistes* (p. 14–22); John H. Matthews, *Mechanics of the marvellous: the short stories of Benjamin Péret* (p. 23–30); Eric Sellin, *Antonin Artaud and an objectified language of the stage* (p. 31–35); Laurent Le Sage, *Michel Butor: techniques of the marvelous* (p. 36–44); Renée Riese-Hubert, *Les surréalistes et Picasso* (p. 45–51).

Articles

Adorno, Theodor W. Rückblickend auf den Surrealismus. *In his:* Noten zur Literatur I. Frankfurt, Suhrkamp Verlag, 1958. p. 153–60. **9418**
The author refuses to accept the surrealists' own definition of their movement as being associated with dreams, with the unconscious of the psychoanalysts and as a collection of literary and pictorial illustrations of the theories of Freud and Jung. In fact, surrealism reifies the human content of things, and montage is the real model of its artistic processes.

Alquié, Ferdinand. Révolte surréaliste et déréalisation. CahS 327:255–65, 1955. **9419**
A fine study of the crisis of the object, the subject and of reality in the surrealists' works, of the effective, technical means of disintegrating reality but also of revealing man in his concrete mystery.

———. Le surréalisme et la psychanalyse. TR 108:145–49, 1956. **9420**
Parallel analysis of the theories of Freud and Breton, giving credit to surrealism which, according to Benveniste, found the language, sought by Freud, that could join opposites.

Amadou, Anne-Lisa. De franske surrealister og deres syn på diktekunsten. Vin 15:28–36, 1961. **9421**
Entitled "The French surrealists and their view of poetry." After a general survey of surrealism which Amadou regards as a now dead movement, she compares the surrealists' notion of inspiration as passive "recueillement" with similar views held by the German romantics, Nerval, Baudelaire and Rimbaud. In reality, the surrealists had a very limited view of poetry and the proof of this is that many important poets moved out of surrealism to a higher and broader inspiration. [MM]

Angenot, Marc. Discordance, image, métaphore. RUB 22:359–69, 1970. **9422**
Series of pertinent observations on the principal stylistic devices of dada and surrealism which revolved around the image and evolved from dissonance to utopia, from the deceptiveness of

dada to universal analogy, from world disorder to a new intelligibility.

————. L'esprit contre la raison. Approche de l'irrationalisme surréaliste. RaiP 14: 75–83, 1970.   **9423**
Systematic account of passages in which different surrealists criticize reason and logic, emphasize revelation and insanity, and find in the Hegelian sense of the term "esprit" their beacon light.

————. Qu'est-ce que le surréalisme? RSH 139:455–66, 1970.   **9424**
An amusing article regrouping all the definitions of surrealism by its followers, its sympathizers, the unconcerned and its enemies.

————. Rhétorique surréaliste des jeux phoniques. FM 40, no. 2:147–61, 1972.
                                   9425
Systematic study of the various perversions to which the surrealists subject classic prosody. Notes their desire to obtain the greatest deviation possible from the norm.

————. Le surréalisme noir. LR 26:181–93, 1972.   **9426**
An account, with the aid of quotes, of the importance of the black adjective in surrealist vocabulary.

Arnaud, Noël. Les métamorphoses historiques de dada. Cr 134:579–604, 1958.
                                   9427
With regard to the publication of the works of Hausmann, Huelsenbeck, Werkauf, Buffet-Picabia, an historic panorama (including even Italy, Yugoslavia, Belgium, Holland) of a movement irreducible to any other preceding or subsequent.

Balakian, Anna. The metaphysical gamut of surrealism. FR 18:202–08, 1945.   **9428**
To the scientific materialism developed by Gonzague Truc in *Une crise intellectuelle,* Balakian opposes the mystic atheism of surrealism extolling knowledge of the concrete through disorder, chance, contradiction, the concretization of nothingness and the abandonment of the symbol.

————. The significance of the surrealist manifestoes. *In:* Surrealist literature. *See* 9417. p. 3–13.   **9429**

An intelligent commentary emphasizing the influence of these manifestoes on contemporary poets as well as on the subsequent new novelists.

Bataille, Georges. Le surréalisme et Dieu. Cr 4, no. 28:843–45, 1948.   **9430**
A review of the *Documents surréalistes* published by Nadeau, and of *A la niche les glapisseurs de Dieu* by Breton. Emphasis on the paradox between surrealism, which seeks an absence of words, and the assembling of texts, so that by the negation of things surrealism has become a thing.

————. Le surréalisme et sa différence avec l'existentialisme. Cr 1, no. 2:99–100, 1946.
                                   9431
A very subtle and laudatory article for surrealism highlighting automatism as a source of liberty in the moment. Differing from the existentialism of Sartre, surrealism gives a character of existence to liberty. The outburst of words is the image of free existence which is never given except in the moment.

————. Texte envoyé à 3ᵉ convoi. *In:* Le groupe. *See* 9412. p. 100–02.   **9432**
A subtle critique of surrealism and of automatic writing.

Beaujour, Michel. De l'océan au château: mythologie surréaliste. FR 42:353–70, 1969.   **9433**
An interesting study of the contradictory and ambivalent itinerary followed by surrealism between opening and occultism, public revelation and esoteric revelation in order to grapple with Being.

Binni, Lanfranco. Surrealismo. Il manifesto del '24. Ponte 27:699–718, 1971. **9434**
A reexamination of the first manifesto. Binni restates the definition of Breton and points out that it has never been rejected by other surrealists or subsequent writers with surrealist tendencies. He underlines similarities between surrealism and romanticism and defines the limits of the relationship of surrealism with Freud and Bergson.

Blanchot, Maurice. Quelques réflexions sur le surréalisme. Ar 2, no. 8:98–104, 1945. *Also:* Réflexions sur le surréalisme. *In his:*

La part du feu. Gallimard, 1949. p. 92–104. **9435**

A very fine study full of praise for the paradoxes posed by surrealism which, in 1945, according to Blanchot, is no longer here or there but everywhere. At the same time, critical review of *La poésie moderne et le sacré* of Monnerot.

Block, Haskell M. Surrealism and modern poetry: outline of an approach. JAAC 18:174–82, 1959. **9436**

Valid defense of the revaluation of the best international poetry of the 20th century in the vein of surrealism. Numerous references to Jean Epstein's *La poésie d'aujourd'hui.*

Bo, Carlo. Riflessioni critiche. Let 9:125–37, 1947. **9437**

A good critical view of surrealism touching on the goals of the surrealists and the impact of the movement on world literature. Defines the position of the surrealist poet toward his poetry by comparison with the French romantics and symbolists. Probes the question of the vitality of surrealism in 1947.

Bol, Victor P. La poésie. Le surréalisme. RevN 17:199–207, 1953. **9438**

A highly favorable view of surrealism which somewhat supports Blanchot. Amends judgments of Claude Mauriac and Sartre. An expressed belief in vitality of surrealism.

Brun, Jean. Philosophie du surréalisme. RMM 61:360–69, 1956. **9439**

A defense of Ferdinand Alquié's *Philosophie du surréalisme* which offers certain reflections on the surrealist undertaking, reflections that can lead the reader to a deeper understanding of philosophy itself. Takes the opportunity to discuss Sartre's judgments on the surrealist object.

Calas, Nicolas. The rose and the revolver. YFS 1, no. 2:106–11, 1948. **9440**

A testimony to surrealism by comparison with both traditional and existential poetry.

Carrouges, Michel. Le surréalisme à l'écoute. RevMus 210:123–35, 1952. **9441**

The first part of this article deals with the relationship between the surrealists and music. The second is devoted to Roussel and Kafka. Some very pertinent notations regarding the attitude of Breton toward music.

———. Le surréalisme et les philosophes. Cr 108:438–45, 1956. **9442**

An extensive review of *Philosophie du surréalisme* by Alquié, with criticism of comparisons made between Breton and Descartes, and of differences between Breton, Hegel and Marx.

Champigny, Robert. Analyse d'une définition du surréalisme. PMLA 81:139–44, 1966. **9443**

A very subtle analysis and critique of the contradictions in the definition of surrealism as given by Breton in his first manifesto.

Chavardès, Maurice. Grandeur et frontières du surréalisme. VI 15, no. 2:91–103, 1947. **9444**

Somewhat akin to the article by Claude Mauriac to which he refers several times. Chavardès points out different contradictions which the surrealists have encountered and praises their role as trailblazers, but affirms that they also have reached the threshold of humanism and belief.

Cohn, Ruby. Surrealism and today's French theatre. *In:* Surrealism. *See* 9415. p. 159–65. **9445**

Brief but pertinent study of the surrealist elements in Artaud, Vitrac, Cocteau, Schehadé, Audiberti, Pichette, Vauthier, but especially in the big four absurdist playwrights: Adamov, Beckett, Genet and Ionesco.

Cornell, Kenneth. On the difficulty of a label. *In:* Surrealism. *See* 9415. p. 138–44. **9446**

A valid panorama of the poetry parallel to, or subsequent to, the surrealist wave insisting on the importance of the latter.

Corvin, Michel. Le théâtre dada existe-t-il? RHT 23:217–87, 1971. **9447**

An excellent study of the plays of Ribemont-Dessaignes and Tzara, occasionally pointing out their metaphysical intentions. In the works of Ribemont-

Dessaignes notes the frequent use of parable and in Tzara's the respect for structure and traditional scenic requirements. This study is followed by Tzara's *Première et deuxième aventures célestes de M. Antipyrine* and *Le cœur à gaz.*

Cortet, Jean. Du surréalisme à l'existentialisme une double impasse. RduC 116:335–52; 117:42–59, 1955.   **9448**

A debatable but interesting and valid comparative study of many aspects of the two important movements of the 20th century.

Cranston, Mechthild. Breton, Eluard and Char: Ralentir, travaux, Elective affinities? RLMC 24:133–50, 1971.   **9449**

The first detailed discussion of the pattern of collaborative writing of a chain of surrealist poems, *Ralentir travaux*, by Breton in conjunction with Eluard and Char. Minute attention given to the functioning of the thirty poems; the author supports the longstanding assumption that Breton is a better prose writer than a poet with the unauthenticated statement that "by 1930 he had distinguished himself chiefly as a novelist and journalist." (These were two forms of writing despised by Breton!) [AB]

Crastre, Victor. Le mysticisme surréaliste. *In his:* Poésie et mystique. Neuchâtel, La Baconnière, 1966. p. 153–81. (Langages)   **9450**

Starting with some of Breton's conversations of 1952 and works of Carrouges and of Alquié, the author defines with reasonable accuracy the characteristics, both mystical and atheistic, of theoretical surrealism while establishing the superiority of the latter over the catastrophic view of the universe presented by the cubist poets.

Decottignies, Jean. L'œuvre surréaliste et l'idéologie. Lit 1:30–47, 1971.   **9451**

Not about surrealist ideology as such but, rather, the problems raised by the intrusion of ideology in literary forms that are conceived as narrative or lyrical. Points to the opposed ideologies underlying surrealism (individual vs. revolutionary poet) and concludes that the surrealist œuvre cannot exist on any ideological level other than the surrealist discourse. Examines Breton's

proclamations concerning dialectical materialism and finds in them a basic contradiction involving an implied rejection of Marxism for being an orthodoxy opposed to the individual revolt. Analyzes the significance of the ideological content of *Nadja* and *Les vases communicants.* [AB]

Fowlie, Wallace. Surrealism in 1960: a backward glance. PoetryR 95:365–72, 1960. *Also in his:* Age of surrealism. Bloomington & London, Indiana univ. press, 1960. p. 193–203.   **9452**

A rapid but quite valid account. However, Fowlie does not adequately consider the continuity of the evolution of Breton's thought or that of his new followers which is easily discernible from 1945 on.

Review: J. Matthews in YFS 31:145–53, 1964.

Garelli, Jacques. L'écriture automatique conçue comme réceptivité créatrice. *In his:* La gravitation poétique. Mercure de France, 1966. p. 157–63.   **9453**

Very interesting study of the similarity of the surrealists' concept of the poetic imagination to Heidegger's theory of transcendental imagination.

Gershman, Herbert S. L'affaire Pastoureau. *In:* Surrealism. *See* 9415. p. 154–58.   **9454**

Explanation and bibliographical note on the ambiguous attitude of Breton concerning Carrouges whom the other surrealists wished to eject between 1945 and 1951.

———. Futurism and the origins of surrealism. It 29:114–23, 1962.   **9455**

Seeks to prove a relation between Italian futurism and dada by showing that Marinetti, the major exponent of futurism, and some of his followers were not unknown to the dadaists and often contributed to French avant-garde publications.

Green, Paul. The relevance of surrealism with some Canadian perspectives. Mos 2, no. 4:59–70, 1969.   **9456**

A brief but valuable article indicating ways in which surrealist techniques and attitudes can catch fire in contemporary poetry. A short summary of sur-

SURREALISM

realist symptoms, principally in Anglo-Saxon poetry.

Hackett, C. A. Les surréalistes et Rimbaud. *In his:* Autour de Rimbaud. Klincksieck, 1967. p. 61–80. **9457**
    With respect to the life and work of Rimbaud, this chapter reviews in turn Breton, Eluard and Char and concludes that the surrealists have not offered an elucidation of the Rimbaud mystery. A short but valuable analysis.

Hodin, J. P. The future of surrealism. JAAC 14:475–84, 1956. **9458**
    Based on an analysis of the pictorial and sculptural works displayed at the Venice biennial in 1954, some reflections on the fact that the first, or Freudian, phase of surrealism has ended and that the second, or Jungian, is in the middle of its development. A quality article.

Hoog, Armand. Le surréalisme et la damnation laïque. Nef 27:115–19, 1947. **9459**
    Valid reflections on surrealism and its combative ancestors from the obscure patrimony of romanticism.

Houdebine, Jean-Louis. Méconnaissance de la psychanalyse dans le discours surréaliste. TelQ 46:67–82, 1971. **9460**
    Amplified repetition of the position taken by Starobinski in the special number of *L'arc* devoted to Freud showing that Breton preferred Myers to Freud and idealism to materialism.

Ilie, Paul. Surrealism and cinema. Diac. 2, no. 4:54–59, 1972. **9461**
    A harsh but interesting criticism of J. H. Matthews' *Surrealism and film.* Gives additional importance, as surrealist films, to *Alphaville* by Godard, *Le sang d'un poète* by Cocteau and to the films of Polanski, Bergman and Hitchcock.

Jouffroy, Alain. Société secrète de l'écriture. *In:* Le groupe. *See* 9412. p. 30–45. **9462**
    An article with a twofold purpose that relates Breton's and Jouffroy's conversations and reports between 1946 and 1966, and demonstrates how automatic writing, as asocial as it is, is a very close representation of thought

Kantarizis, Sylvia. Dada and the preparations for surrealism. AJFS 8:44–61, 1971. **9463**
    Interesting article tending to show, with the support of texts published between 1917 and 1920, that, contrary to the opinion of Sanouillet and Gershman, dadaism is not the source of surrealism. Unfortunately, references to the dada movement concern only Tristan Tzara.

———. Surrealism, communism and love. EFL 7:1–17, 1970. **9464**
    Relevant study of surrealist texts between Jan. 1927 and March 1930, dealing with politics and love, resulting in the formulation by the surrealists of love as a point of inspiration of the revolution in the individual and its ultimate collective aim.

Kanters, Robert. Du surréalisme comme scandale et comme initiation. RdP 74, no. 1:123–31, 1967. **9465**
    Concerned with the disappearance of Breton and the reprinting of several of his works and of the critical works of Richter and Waldberg. This article stresses the importance of dreams, esoteric doctrines and materialism advocated by surrealism. Comparisons with the opinions of Carrouges and Guénon.

Klossowski, Pierre. De Contre-attaque à Acéphale. *In:* Le groupe. *See* 9412. p. 103–07. **9466**
    A study of the reciprocal approaches and estrangements of Breton and Bataille.

Martineau-Genieys, Christine. Autour des images et de l'érotique surréaliste: L'union libre, étude et synthèse. *In:* Réflexions et recherches de nouvelle critique. Les belles lettres, 1969. p. 171–86. (AFLSHN, 8) **9467**
    Applies Barthes' "règle d'exhaustivité" ("dans l'œuvre tout est signifiant") to "L'union libre." Examines the title for its significance by commenting on the surrealist context of love, eroticism, marriage, and points to a fundamental convergence between the act of love and the poem. Examines closely the images with occasional references to surrealist films and paintings. Concludes that the poem assembles "all the principal ideas, all the preoccupations, all the themes —

in short, the whole moral of love — of Breton and his group." The poem is not just a list of stunning images but a classically organized composition. [AB]

Matthews, John H. Poetic principles of surrealism. ChiR 15, no. 4:27–45, 1962.   **9468**

Written upon the occasion of the appearance in *Bief,* June 1959, of an "Art poétique" signed by Breton and Schuster, this is a very pertinent analysis, supported by direct references to surrealist texts.

————. The right person for surrealism. YFS 35:89–96, 1965.   **9469**

A very clear and concise study of Sade's influence on the surrealists and their constant respect for his work.

————. Romanticism taken by the tail: the surrealist approach. Sym 23:294–302, 1969.   **9470**

Borrowing part of the title of Picasso's work, *Desire taken by the tail,* Matthews retraces in the romantic period the origins of desire emphasized in surrealism.

————. Some post-war surrealist poets. *In:* Surrealism. *See* 9415. p. 145–53.   **9471**

Presents and analyzes the works of young surrealists, notably Legrand, Mansour, Cabanel, Malrieu, Dhainaut, Tarnaud, Silbermann, Duprey, Flamand and Lebel.

————. Surrealism and England. CLS 1: 55–72, 1964.   **9472**

A pertinent study of why surrealism failed to become established in England. Refers to the works of Read, Davies and Gascoyne. Enumeration and analysis of English periodicals which dealt with surrealism between 1936–1947.

————. Surrealism and the cinema. C 4: 120–33, 1962.   **9473**

Analyzes only the scenarios of those surrealists who were Breton's adherents. After a period of activity from 1924 to 1930 efforts ceased only to begin again after 1945. For the surrealists the cinema is only a means of experience and financial difficulties prevented them from using it for continued development.

Mauriac, Claude. Surréalisme et révolution. TR 4:716–36; 5:862–900, 1948.   **9474**

A rather sardonic but accurate analysis of Breton's attitudes toward war and revolution. Brings out texts which contradict each other. Contrasting parallels with actions and writings of other contemporary writers, in particular Malraux and Sartre.

Middleton, J. C. Bolshevism in art: dada and politics. TSLL 4:408–30, 1962.   **9475**

A good study summarizing and rectifying the works of Hugnet and Haussman. Aside from a brief attraction for Bolshevism in Germany in 1919, most of the dada members and groups showed little interest in politics in general or in communism in particular.

Morot-Sir, Edouard. The new novel. *In:* Surrealism. *See* 9415. p. 166–74.   **9476**

Detection in the new novel of typical surrealist traits, notably the quest of chance, a dark and heavy humor, and the giving birth to a new universe thanks to the magic power of words.

Nelli, René. Des troubadours à André Breton. CahS 309:303–10, 1951.   **9477**

A comparison of the surrealist poets and the troubadours, not in terms of their poetic techniques but, rather, their attitudes regarding love and eroticism. Attempts to find in both "le même courant souterrain de l'esprit d'amour." More about the surrealists in general than specifically. [AB]

Newton, Robert P. Dada, expressionism, and some modern modes. RUS 55, no. 3:163–84, 1969.   **9478**

A fine article discussing the origins of, and contemporary sequels to, dada as well as the principal innovations brought forth by the movement itself in Zurich. It fortunately completes Richter's work by which it is inspired.

Peyre, Henri. The significance of surrealism. YFS, 1, no. 2:34–39, 1948. *Also in:* Surrealism. *See* 9415. p. 23–36.   **9479**

A warm homage to surrealism which is seen as one of the most far-reaching attempts at changing not only literature and painting, but psychology, ethics and man himself.

Raible, Wolfgang. Der Surrealismus oder die innere Reise. *In his:* Moderne Lyrik in Frankreich. Stuttgart, Berlin, Cologne, Mainz, W. Kohlhammer, 1972. p. 50–57. (Sprache und Literatur, 77)   **9480**
Refers to Monnerot's *La poésie moderne et le sacré* as the most authoritative work on the surrealist movement. Its most typical representative, the group of *Le grand jeu*, was really much more promising in its exploration of the hereafter, than Breton's orthodox surrealism. Its principal theme was the journey and one of its most characteristic poets Henri Michaux.

————. Sprachliches. *In his:* Moderne Lyrik in Frankreich. Stuttgart, Berlin, Cologne, Mainz, W. Kohlhammer, 1972. p. 29–38. (Sprache und Literatur, 77)   **9481**
Analysis of modern developments in poetry including the Italian futurists, Cravan, dadaists, Apollinaire, Reverdy. Mallarmé's and Maeterlinck's skepticism about language turns into an extreme nominalism in the hands of the surrealists, reintroducing syntactic connections, while making 20th-century lyricism conscious of its linguistic medium.

————. Surrealismus und kein Ende? *In his:* Moderne Lyrik in Frankreich. Stuttgart, Berlin, Cologne, Mainz, W. Kohlhammer, 1972. p. 57–64. (Sprache und Literatur, 77)   **9482**
For Raible the fruits of surrealism have been most promising, whenever surrealism became an important ingredient of an already existing poetry, whereas Breton's pure surrealism has been fairly repetitive and sterile.

Revol, Enrique Luis. Una cultura de la imaginación. RHum 1:45–57, 1958.   **9483**
Very laudatory article, based in part on the work of Alquié. Considers surrealism as the only ethic accounting for the multiple facets of man, an ethic still intact and valid to this day.

Riese-Hubert, Renée. Les surréalistes et Picasso. *In:* Surrealist literature. *See* 9417. p. 45–51.   **9484**
A successive analysis of judgments made by Artaud, Breton, Leiris, Desnos, Eluard and Tzara.

Riffaterre, Michael. La métaphore filée dans la poésie surréaliste. LFr 3:46–60, 1969.   **9485**
A structuralist analysis which aims to prove that surrealist images are strictly determined by verbal sequence. Examples from Breton and Eluard.

Robert, Bernard-Paul. Pour une définition du surréalisme. RUO 43:297–306, 1973.   **9486**
Valid study comparing texts of Pierre Janet, notably *L'automatisme psychologique,* with the first manifesto by Breton and other surrealist documents.

Rottenberg, Pierre. Esquisse cartographique du mouvement: surréalisme. TelQ 46:41–58, 1971.   **9487**
Negative criticism of the revolutionary movement begun by surrealism in that Breton, a disciple of Hegel (and Freud), revives his totalitarian thought, depends sexually on him and does not bring about the movement of phallic transcendence advocated by Marx, Engels, Lenin, Mao-Tse-Tung. Analysis of certain passages of Breton and Crevel in the light of these assertions.

Roussel, Jean. Mais avant André Breton? AgN 37:69–77, 1949.   **9488**
Anticipating the work of Somerville, Roussel considers Marcello-Fabri the forerunner of surrealism. However, in focussing on Fabri, he commits certain injustices towards Breton and surrealism.

Sartre, Jean-Paul. Situation de l'écrivain en 1947. TM 20:1410–29; 21:1606–41; 22:77–114, 1947. *Also in his:* Qu'est-ce que la littérature? Gallimard, 1948. p. 203–374. (Idées) *Also in his:* Situations II. Gallimard, 1948. p. 202–330.   **9489**
A comparative study of three generations of writers in the 20th century. The second, dominated by surrealism, arouses a rather fierce indictment in terms of both existentialism and Marxism.

Schmidt, Albert-Marie. Destinée du surréalisme. RSH 45:62–74, 1947.   **9490**
For Schmidt, surrealism is one of the last forms emanating from the baroque, where the liberation of the word is com-

plete. However, he points out the failure of this social, political, and esthetic revolt, and a winding down in its attempt at reconciliation with literature.

Soupault, Philippe. Traces which last. *In:* Surrealism. *See* 9415. p. 9–22. **9491**

A narration of Soupault's adherence to dada and surrealism in which the we of the team replaces the I of the individual. Also explains his withdrawal from the group in order to maintain an attitude of liberation which for him characterizes true surrealism.

Tzara, Tristan. Le surréalisme et l'après-guerre. Ad 162–63:7–13, 1946. **9492**

A first-hand account of the dada adventure and its goals. Notations on surrealism and an inquiry into the development of the movement which, according to Tzara, should evolve (in 1946) towards a more optimistic literary humanism.

Viatte, Auguste. Bilan du surréalisme. RUL 3:233–39, 1948. **9493**

Upon the occasion of Nadeau's work, a sympathetic but tendentious look at surrealism which brings forth the facets assimilable to and by religion.

Vigée, Claude. L'invention poétique et l'automatisme mental. MLN 75:143–54, 1960. **9494**

An interesting study of the connections between image and language, and between dream and poetry. Objects that Breton's automatism is the sign of an extreme nominalism whose origin goes back to Rimbaud and Hegel. In fact, for Vigée, the real functioning of poetry is not accomplished in the words alone, but prior to their selection, in their direction, and is completed in the end by their medium.

Virmaux, Alain. La tentation du cinéma chez les poètes au temps du surréalisme, d'Artaud à Supervielle. CAIEF 20:257–74, 1968. **9495**

Traces a curve of infatuation and hope up until 1930 and the advent of the sound film; thereafter, a withdrawal of the intentions proclaimed at the outset of the movement.

Jean Arp
(i.e. Hans Arp)
(Nos. 9496–9503)

ROGER McKENZIE ISAACS

Giedion-Welcker, Carola. Jean Arp. London, Thames and Hudson, 1957. 122 p. **9496**

This must be considered the invaluable source work, the basic text for all A. studies. Not only is it beautifully illustrated, it also contains an excellent bibliography and a comprehensive catalog of A.'s sculptures up to 1957.

Isaacs, Roger. Arp and Bachelard: the fire as father. *In:* Dada/Surrealism. Ed. by Mary Ann Caws. Flushing, N.Y., Queens College press, 1972. p. 55–66. **9497**

An examination of the pivotal role played by the element Fire in both the poetic texts and the plastic works. The author proposes a system whereby the element can be recognized in both worlds and then discusses its uses and abuses.

———. L'érotisme spatial et temporel dans la poésie de Jean Arp. Sym 27:19–34, 1973. **9498**

An examination of the important part sex plays in A.'s universe. Sex is seen as a highly moral act which contributes to the continuity of both human and objectal elements in the world.

Last, Rex. German dadaist literature: Kurt Schwitters, Hugo Ball, Hans Arp. New York, Twayne publishers, 1973. p. 116–83. **9499**

The importance of this long article lies in the fact that it develops some of the themes outlined in *The poet of dadaism* and hints at a moral structure in A.'s universe. Last also expresses the hope that the artist's work will be studied in a more systematically thematic fashion.

———. Hans Arp: The poet of dadaism. London, Oswald Wolff, 1969. 128 p. **9500**

Even though this monograph deals almost exclusively with A.'s German poetry, it still makes an important contribution to an understanding of the artist's work in French. Last recognized that A. was a man dissatisfied with the human condition of the twentieth century. He also saw that A., contrary to what is normally thought of as being the dadaist style, was a conscious and conscientious creator.

Matthews, John. Jean Arp (1887–1966). *In his:* Surrealist poetry in France. Syracuse, N. Y., Syracuse univ. press, 1969, p. 72–101. **9501**

This article is mainly concerned with A. as a practitioner of the surrealist "marvelous." It also shows the artist as a man constantly in search of a new and more dynamic poetic language.

Read, Herbert. The art of Jean Arp. London, Thames and Hudson, 1968. 216 p. **9502**

This is one of the best illustrated books on A. In it, the author has clearly shown just how futile an experience it would be to try to separate A.'s writings from his plastic works. However, he does not come to terms with any of the specific themes which could serve as a basis for comparison.

Trier, Eduard. Jean Arp: Sculpture: His last ten years. London, Thames and Hudson, 1968. 145 p. **9503**

This work continues and complements Carola Giedion-Welcker's. The catalog of sculptures and the selected bibliography date from 1957. The illustrations are most laudably presented in that Trier very often takes great pains to show the same work from several different angles, and this is vital for the student of A.'s plastic works.

André Breton
(Nos. 9504–9578)

HIAM FINKELSTEIN and ANNA BALAKIAN

Bibliography

Prigioni, Pierre. André Breton et le surréalisme devant la critique (1952–1962). RJ 13:119–48, 1962. **9504**

A very informative survey of books and essays devoted mostly to B. that have appeared in the years 1952–1962. Offers concise and usually meaningful comments on the works of Victor Crastre, René Nelli and the *Cahiers du sud* group, Yvon Belaval, Ferdinand Alquié, Gérald Schaeffer, Jean Gaul-

mier, etc. Comments extensively on B. and surrealism in literature devoted to occult philosophy. Also introduces five major books about B. and surrealism published before 1952 (Monnerot, Gracq, Carrouges, Eigeldinger). The survey is not exhaustive, though, and is limited to French critics. [HF]

Sheringham, Michael. André Breton: a bibliography. London, Grant and Cutler, 1972. 122 p. (Research bibliographies and checklists, 2) **9505**

Bibliography of primary material (including translations into English), secondary material (books and articles), and an index of all of B.'s publications. Quite exhaustive (cut-off date 1971) and useful. [HF]

Edition

Breton, André. Ode à Charles Fourier: édition présentée avec une introduction et des notes par Jean Gaulmier. Klincksieck, 1961. 99 p. **9506**

Introduction consists of three parts: 1. "Naissance du poème" — generally useful information concerning the genesis of the poem (some of it communicated by B. to the editor). 2. "Surréalisme et Fouriérisme" — introduction to Fourier's philosophical and social system, a perceptive discussion of the basic propositions shared by B. and Fourier. 3. "Fouriérisme et littérature." A good study, although Fourier is treated with greater discernment than B. [HF]

Biography

Breton, André. Entretiens (1913–1952) avec André Parinaud et al. Gallimard, 1952. 317 p. *Also:* Nouvelle ed. rev. et corr. Gallimard, 1969. 315 p. (Le point du jour) **9507**

Radio interviews with Parinaud, recorded in 1950 and broadcast in 1952, and later revised and rewritten by B. The interviews cover B.'s life and work chronologically from early youth ("Avant 1914") to 1950 ("Derniers regards en arrière"). Followed by several interviews conducted between 1941 and 1952. Useful source of biographical material; interesting for the insight it offers into B.'s attempt at retrospection. [AB]

Duits, Charles. André Breton a-t-il dit passe. Denoël, 1960. 195 p. (Dossiers des Lettres nouvelles) **9508**

Memories of a young French-American boy who met B. in New York in 1942. Glimpses of the life of exiles in New York. [AB]

Review: M. Chapelan in FL 23, June 30–July 6, 1969.

Paz, Octavio. André Breton ou la recherche du commencement. *In:* André Breton et le mouvement surréaliste. *See* 9527. p. 606–19. *Trans.:* André Breton or the search for the beginning. STC no. 3:41–50, 1969. **9509**

Paz reminisces on his close friendship with B. who looms in his eyes as one of the unusual men and poets of our time, in the position of a mediator between the degraded state of current civilization and future restoration of an eidetic reality. He leaves open the question of the paradoxical predilection of B. for both Rousseau and Sade. [AB]

General Studies: Books

Alexandrian, Sarane. André Breton par lui-même. Seuil, 1971. 190 p. (Ecrivains de toujours, 90) **9510**

A portrait and a panorama of work and thought. Phrases, sentences and whole passages taken out of B.'s writing (mostly prose) and incorporated in an interpretative context, which succeeds in being quite faithful to B. Developed on the whole thematically. A useful reference. [AB]

Reviews: Anon. in TLS 442, April 21, 1972; F. Bott in Monde 11, Sept. 3, 1971; G. Cesbron in HumCL 29–32, Nov, 1972; P. Kyria in Comb 7, Sept. 23, 1971; A. Marissel in Esp 412:517–19, 1972.

————. Le surréalisme et le rêve. Gallimard, 1974. 505 p. (Connaissance de l'inconscient) **9511**

A pretentious book which starts out under the semblance of scientific documentation and ends in the anecdotal files of surrealism. The central figure is of course B., whose work and intentions are constantly equated with the collective purposes of surrealism. Dreams are reported and explained but the author does not aim at a level of comprehension of the relation of the mechanics of dreaming and of its functional power in the work of art. Perhaps part of the reason is that surrealism is considered as a methodology applicable to the search of knowledge in diverse areas of human behavior rather than for its literary harvest. Strictly a lay approach to the psychological background of B.'s work, the point of view is that of an "insider" professing to know the innermost intentions of B. and his entourage. [AB]

Audoin, Philippe. Breton. Gallimard, 1970. 255 p. (Pour une bibliothèque idéale) **9512**

A good, concise and very comprehensive guide to B. Includes: 1. Biography. 2. The work, seen in terms of qualities exhibited by the work of Duchamp, Ernst, Matta; considered in relation to several major themes: life, reality and "le peu de réalité;" "le merveilleux;" castles and fantoms; the quest (affinities with the medieval "matière de Bretagne"); poetry and automatic writing; love and human liberty. 3. Individual comments on B.'s writings; brief yet articulate presentation of their essence and content. [HF]

Balakian, Anna. André Breton, magus of surrealisme. Oxford univ. press, 1971. 289 p. **9513**

Analytical study of B.'s life and work. Structured both chronologically and thematically, the book offers a view of B.'s work in its totality, while accounting for changes in B.'s thought and writing in various stages of his career. Contains a wealth of information about hitherto neglected aspects of his work (influence of Janet's notion of psychic automatism on B.'s thought and terminology; the influence of hermetic literature); offers an interesting reading of poems, while often referring to the hermetic sources of their content and imagery. A moving account of B.'s last years. An indispensable critical biography. [HF]

Reviews: Anon. in TLS 422, April 21, 1972; Anon. in WPBW 5:6–7, Aug. 8, 1971; L. Bersani in TBR 15–16, May 30, 1971; M. Caws in FR

46:422–23, 1972; J. Matthews in MLQ 33:327–44, 1972.

Browder, Clifford. André Breton, arbiter of surrealism. Geneva, Droz, 1967. 214 p.
9514
A comprehensive and systematic study of B.'s life, thought and work, too dry and objective to be really inspiring. Following an extensive "life" chapter, the book examines in detail several major themes (revolt; surreality; automatic writing; dreams and the surrealist object; objective chance and love; Marxism, Utopianism and magic; humor). An excellent bibliography of both primary and secondary sources (up to date of publication). [HF]
Reviews: M. Bonnet in CahDS 3: 80–84, 1969 (1970); E. Deberdt-Malaquais in RR 61:73–75, 1970; L. Le Sage in FR 41:751–52, 1968.

Carrouges, Michel. André Breton et les données fondamentales du surréalisme. Gallimard, 1950. 334 p. (Les essais, 43) *Also:* 1967. 378 p. (Idées, 121) 9515
Defines the main facets of B.'s œuvre as the discoveries of the link between automatism and poetry, and the link between subjective or personal automatism and universal automatism (or between the personal unconscious and the collective or even cosmic unconscious.) An extensive exploration of the hermetic and occultist sources underlying surrealism. An impassioned vision of surrealism's rejection of the arbitrary in all its forms and its ideal of regaining harmony between man and the cosmos. Concludes that surrealism retains a point of view which encompasses and unites science and revolution, psychology and historical materialism, sociology and metapsychology, that leads man toward the "supreme point," thereby defining surrealism as "dialectical humanism." Offers an extensive literary and scientific frame of reference. A stimulating study. [HF]
Review: Anon. in TLS 2530:461–62, July 28, 1950.

Caws, Mary Ann. André Breton. Twayne, 1971. 135 p. (TWAS, 117) 9516
A brief note about "life" and a briefer one about the surrealist movement create the framework for a more detailed discussion of B.'s writing: manifestoes; essays (chapters devoted to *Les pas perdus, Point du jour, La clé des champs, Le surréalisme et la peinture,* each subdivided into topics such as "Freedom and risk," "Art and language," etc.); longer prose works. Poetry is introduced through topics such as: reading a surrealist poem; the linking of theory and poetry; words. Concludes with the discussion of three essays dealing with life and the imagination: "Il y aura une fois," "Situation surréaliste de l'objet" and "Du surréalisme et ses œuvres vives." A useful introductory guide to B.'s writing.
Reviews: V. La Charité in FR 45: 912–13, 1972; J. Matthews in MLQ 33:327–34, 1972.

———. Surrealism and the literary imagination: a study of Breton and Bachelard. The Hague and Paris, Mouton, 1966. 88 p. 9517
Introduces Bachelard and his evolution from surrationalism to the phenomenology of the imagination. Compares the surrealist temperament with that of Bachelard to find that the difference is mostly one of "style." Attempts to demonstrate that B. and Bachelard are similar in their poetic theory and in their belief in the union of the super-real and the real and in the power of the imagination to transform the universe. [HF]
Reviews: A. Balakian in RR 60: 156–59, 1969; D. Baudoin in CahDS 3:91–98, 1969 (1970).

Crastre, Victor. André Breton. Arcanes, 1952. 197 p. 9518
A homage and general study of B.'s life and activities. Consists of a detailed account of B.'s youth ("Le compagnon de Jacques Vaché"), the dada and the trance periods (the years 1924–25 considered the richest period in the history of surrealism), and a perceptive account of the group and of the authority exercised by B. Offers an interesting and detailed reading of *Nadja,* and relates surrealism to Freud, Bergson, modern science, esoterism. Considers B.'s mysticism a synthesis of Hegelian idealism and Freudian and Marxist materialism. One main interest is the somewhat scattered account of

the relationship with the Communist Party. Crastre was a member of the communist *Clarté* group, and was active in forming contacts with the surrealists. [HF]

––––––. André Breton: Trilogie surréaliste: Nadja, Les vases communicants, L'amour fou. Société d'édition d'enseignement supérieur, 1971. 111 p.   **9519**
Nadja examined against the background of "surrealist life" and the quest for the "merveilleux." The main themes of *L'amour fou* are broached in a rather uninspiring manner. The best discussion is reserved for *Les vases communicants*. Crastre, a member of the *Clarté* group, succeeds in weaving into his analysis interesting details about surrealism and Marxism, the tension in surrealism between absolute idealism and historical materialism, and the distinction between Freudian psychoanalysis and the surrealist project. [HF]

Durozoi, Gérard, and Bernard Lecherbonnier. André Breton: L'écriture surréaliste. Larousse, 1974. 255 p. (Thèmes et textes)   **9520**
Examines some of B.'s works with the declared purpose of shedding light on their ambitions and aims and on the kind of reading activity they call for, and follows up by considering the notion of "l'écriture surréaliste." Strays at times from its declared purpose, but may still serve as quite a useful reader's guide. [HF]

Gracq, Julien. André Breton, quelques aspects de l'écrivain, avec un portrait d'André Breton par Hans Bellemer. José Corti, 1948. 209 p.   **9521**
Not a comprehensive critical study, but what amounts at times to a poetic meditation or reflection utilizing something akin to B.'s own poetic prose to communicate thoughts of a very personal nature. Examines the phenomenon of the group and finds that at its height surrealism echoes the dawning of an aborted religion. Offers an interesting discussion of B.'s syntax and prose style. An intelligent, powerful work. [HF]

Lenk, Elisabeth. Der springende Narziss: André Bretons poetischer Materialismus.

Munich, Rogner & Bernhard, 1971. 269 p.   **9522**
Examines surrealism as a sociocultural phenomenon symptomatic of the disintegration of bourgeois culture and characterized by the group-principle and the shift from esthetic individualism to collectivism. Explores the inner dynamics of the group by focusing on B. as a prototype of the surrealist artist, and attempts to show how the different stages of his development as a poet reflect the larger issue of the movement as a social phenomenon. Explores in detail B.'s early poetry, the search for a new poetic form and the development of surrealist collective esthetics (games, dream practice, etc.). [HF]

Massot, Pierre de. André Breton ou le septembriseur. Le terrain vague, 1967. 48 p. (unnumbered)   **9523**
An extended homage and eulogy. Offers glimpses into life and work, but the rhetoric precludes deeper insights. [HF]

Matthews, J. H. André Breton. Columbia univ. press, 1967. 48 p. (Columbia essays on modern writers, 26)   **9524**
A short introduction to B. presenting its material in a very clear, concise and informative manner. Comprises a chronological survey of activities, theory, prose writings. B.'s art criticism serves as a point of departure for the discussion of poetry. Encompasses a lot more than its small format suggests. [HF]
Reviews: L. Allen in N&Q 15:316–17, 1968; H. Gershman in FR 41:581–82, 1968.

Mauriac, Claude. André Breton; essai. Eds. de Flore, 1949. 358 p. *Also:* Grasset, 1970. 327 p.   **9525**
A long and very minute study which strives to give the impression that after all B. is not so alien to the spirit of the author's Catholic father. Portrays a man to whom liberty is more important than anything else, to whom a moral point of view is essential. Mauriac's B. is aware of the errors of his youth and has a "mauvaise conscience" about his youthful Luciferian perspectives regarding the problem of evil; his vocabulary reveals a quasi-

religious attitude close to Christian mysticism. Mauriac subjects surrealist theory to a rigorous logical analysis in order to extricate from it errors and contradictions, thereby also depriving it of some of its most fundamental aspects. [HF]

Review: N. Oxenhandler in FR 46: 421–22, 1972.

Collected Articles

André Breton; essais et témoignages. Ed. by Marc Eigeldinger. Neuchâtel, La Baconnière, 1950. 246 p. *Also (rev.):* André Breton; essais. Avec quatre portraits. Ed. by Marc Eigeldinger. Neuchâtel, La Baconnière, 1970. 287 p. (Langages) **9526**

Contains a few relatively unknown early texts and poems by B., and a few articles, some of which are very good. The more significant articles have been analyzed separately under the appropriate headings.

André Breton et le mouvement surréaliste. NRF 172:589–964, 1967. **9527**

A special number published following B.'s death. Divided into: 1. "Hommages"; 2. "Témoignages"; 3. "L'œuvre"; 4. "Le mouvement surréaliste". The more significant articles have been analyzed separately under the appropriate headings.

Bonnet, Marguerite. Les critiques de notre temps et Breton. Garnier, 1974. 190 p. (Les critiques de notre temps) **9528**

Excerpts from essays and books on B. with an introduction and section prefaces by Bonnet. Comprises six sections: Souvenirs and portraits, the surrealist project, dream and automatism, "constantes," ideology, studies of specific works. The texts vary in importance, and the excerption often detracts from their usefulness. It is also to be regretted that the book incorporates only criticism in the French language. Includes good critical B. bibliography.

General Studies: Articles

Balakian, Anna. André Breton as philosopher. *In:* Surrealism. *See* 9415. p. 37–74. **9529**

Considers B. as "sole philosopher of surrealism." Distinguishes between B. and humanistic philosophies of the West in terms of their conception of man's weakness and potential; animism or deistic philosophies and B.'s notion of an everlasting unity in creation; B.'s imagination and Bergson's intuition; Freudian psychology and its preoccupation with abnormalities and B.'s call to reclaim the unused resources of human consciousness. [HF]

———. André Breton et l'hermétisme, des Champs magnétiques à La clé des champs. CAIEF 15:127–39, 1963. **9530**

Traces references and allusions to occultism in B.'s writing. Considers conflicting views (Carrouges and Alquié) regarding the place of hermeticism in surrealism. Examines in detail several poems and essays revealing the extent of B.'s hermetic orientation from the beginning of his career. [HF]

———. Breton in the light of Apollinaire. *In:* About French poetry from Dada to Tel quel: text and theory. Ed. by Mary Ann Caws. Detroit, Wayne state univ. press, 1974. p. 42–53. **9531**

Explores the significance of the relationship of B. and Apollinaire in terms of B.'s personal development and of the destiny of surrealism in general. According to this study, not the use of the word "surrealist" but his redefinition of the word "poet" gave Apollinaire the major role in the avantgarde of surrealism, following the fortuitous encounter of the disparate life-styles of Apollinaire and B. [HF]

———. Metaphor and metamorphosis in André Breton's poetics. FS 19:34–41, 1965. **9532**

Differentiates between the "correspondences" (Baudelaire, romantic poetry) and alchemical transmutation as translated into poetry, where transcendence is replaced by metamorphosis. Focuses on B.'s notion of the imagination as the act of creating images. [HF]

———. Breton and the surrealist mind — the influence of Freud and Hegel. *In her:* Surrealism: the road to the absolute [1970]. *See* 9362. p. 123–39. **9533**

Concise and informative survey of Freud's influence on B.'s thought and on surrealist experimentation, the distinction between the surrealist project and Freud's, and B.'s objection to Freud's separation of material reality from psychic reality. The affinity between Freud and Hegel in terms of the impact both had on B. and the surrealists. [HF]

Beaujour, Michel. André Breton, mythographe: Arcane 17. EF 3:215–33, 1967. *Also in:* André Breton; essais. *See* 9526. [1970] p. 221–40.   **9534**

An interesting and well-written examination of the "mythe nouveau" that B. brings to life in *Arcane 17*. The author traces the links connecting the Melusine myth to the symbolism of the *Arcane 17* of the Tarot and then to the myth of Osiris and Isis, and states that all those myths have a common origin in the myth of "l'amour fou." [HF]

———. André Breton ou la transparence. *In:* Breton, André. Arcane 17, enté d'ajours. Suivi de André Breton ou la transparence par Michel Beaujour. [Union générale d'éditions, 1965]. p. 161–83. (Le monde en 10/18)   **9535**

Places *Arcane 17* in the context of B.'s growing interest in "la haute magie." Quotes from "Poisson soluble" and *Nadja* to introduce B.'s notion of a transparent universe. Explains the symbolism of the Tarot and traces the movement of the book from opacity, "obscurantisme" and "brouillard" of the early years of the war towards a transparence and crystallization, through the intervention of B.'s "femme-enfant." [HF]

———. De l'océan au château: mythologie surréaliste. FR 42:353–79, 1969.   **9536**

Considers the two myths of the ocean and the castle as the two cardinal points of surrealist thought and activity. Traces in B.'s writing the ocean myth signaling the psychic unconscious, an interior sea common to all of humanity beyond time and space, with its accompanying images of submersion and abdication of individual identity. The castle myth is related to B.'s call for the "occultation" of surrealism and to the cult of Sade and the "roman noir."

Concludes that each myth carries a hidden heresy; the ocean myth has led some surrealists away from poetry towards revolutionary struggle, whereas in the second myth the temptation is diametrically opposed to it. [HF]

Bonnet, Marguerite. Le surréalisme d'André Breton: un projet d'existence. IL 1:24–29, 1971.   **9537**

Considers B.'s writing under the three headings of "Plutôt la vie," "Changer la vie," and "Le grand porteur des clés," in terms of his affirmation of life, his conception of political action, and the notion of "désir" as the privileged means of "connaissance." Attempts to encompass too much for its allotted space. [HF]

Brown, Frederick. Creation versus literature: Breton and the surrealist movement. *In:* Modern French criticism from Proust and Valéry to structuralism. Ed. by John K. Simon. Chicago, Univ. of Chicago press, 1972. p. 123–47.   **9538**

A general introduction to the special ambiance of surrealist poetics that centers on B. but encompasses the whole movement. Considers surrealism as a mythopoeic adventure whose central dream is a dream of being, whose state is transparency and its symbol the crystal. Places the word "concrete" at the center of surrealist ideology and develops the notion of surrealist poetry as "a locked, reflexive universe where language exists,... *on its own terms...*" [HF]

Butor, Michel. Heptaèdre héliotrope. *In:* André Breton et le mouvement surréaliste. *See* 9527. p. 750–79.   **9539**

An interesting adoption of B.'s interpretation of dreams and waking dreams in *Les vases communicants* and his interrogation of the manifestations of objective chance in *L'amour fou.* Butor extracts texts from B.'s writing, correlates them to B.'s personal history and creates an intricate maze of correspondences and coincidences in which B. the writer becomes both subject and object of his experiences. [HF]

Cardinal, Roger. André Breton: the surrealist sensibility. Mos 1:112–26, 1968.   **9540**

A brief and rather superficial look into B.'s sensibility in terms of his esthetic appreciation and view of beauty. [HF]

Caws, Mary Ann. Breton. *In her:* The poetry of dada and surrealism: Aragon, Breton, Tzara, Eluard and Desnos. Princeton, Princeton univ. press, 1970. p. 69–94. **9541**

An examination of B.'s poetic vision and of several notions underlying his poetics and themes (rejuvenation of words and the surrealist image, play of analogies, multiplicity and unity, doubling and distance, etc.). Combines discussion of theoretical and critical texts and analysis of individual poems. [HF]

Champigny, Robert. Une définition du surréalisme. *In his:* Pour une esthétique de l'essai: analyses critiques (Breton, Sartre, Robbe-Grillet). Lettres modernes, Minard, 1967. p. 7–28. (Situation, 15). **9542**

The first chapter, devoted to B.'s definition of surrealism in the *Manifeste,* analyzes the exact wording to find illogicalities and contradictions. Points out that this text defines an enterprise and its means, while claiming to define psychic automatism. Suggests that B.'s formula: "le fonctionnement réel de la pensée" is a limiting one and, indeed, a contradiction in terms. While not very sympathetic to the definition, Champigny tends to accept the validity of the technique. [HF]

Chesneau, Albert. André Breton et l'expérimentation poétique. FR 42:371–79, 1969. **9543**

Speculates on the process by which B. creates his poetry. Believes that B.'s poetry is not sufficiently communicative to the readership and therefore is not sufficiently universal in appeal. [AB]

Eigeldinger, Marc. L'art de brûler la chandelle par les deux bouts. *In:* André Breton; essais. *See* 9526. [1970] p. 175–206. **9544**

An examination of what the author refers to as B.'s phenomenology of the imagination: the imagination as a "puissance métamorphosante et révolutionnaire" which forces the poet to rethink the sense and structure of the world. Followed by a comprehensive discussion of the surrealist image in relation to the imaginative faculties, perception and representation, surreality, etc. A perceptive introduction to the poetics of B. and surrealism. [HF]

Firchow, Peter Edgerly. Nadja and Le paysan de Paris: two surrealist novels. WSCL 6:293–307, 1963. **9545**

Not recognizing surrealism's redefinition of poetry, the author judges *Le paysan de Paris* and to a lesser degree *Nadja* as poorly written novels destined to gather the dust of oblivion. He seeks authoritative support to his contentions by references to a historical study of the contemporary French novel whose relevance to these two works is nil. [AB]

Fowlie, Wallace. Breton: the manifestoes. *In his:* Age of surrealism. The swallow press, and William Morrow and co., 1950. p. 102–19. *Also:* Bloomington, Indiana univ. press, 1960. **9546**

A generalized summary of the main tenets of surrealism as promulgated by B. Followed by a very short survey of the surrealist movement and a few paragraphs about *Nadja.* [HF]

Fraigneux, Maurice. André Breton et l'humanisme surréaliste. RGB 87:758–70, 1952. **9547**

A spirited defense of love and human communion as gleaned in the philosophy of B. The pursuasiveness of the author's theme is somewhat flawed by the lack of footnotes to quotations in support of his view. [AB]

Gaulmier, Jean. Remarques sur le thème de Paris chez André Breton, de Nadja à L'amour fou. TLL 9:159–69, 1971. **9548**

An interesting panoramic view of B.'s Paris as reflected in his writings. [HF]

Gracq, Julien. Spectre du Poisson soluble. *In:* André Breton, essais. *See* 9526. [1970] p. 207–20. **9549**

Gracq finds that it is not so much the incoherence of automatism that should surprise us in "Poisson soluble" as the "remarkable coherence of certain sequences and the astonishing plausibility of many of the images." B.'s unique poetic universe in this text is well illustrated by an inventory list of its many images. [HF]

Gros, Léon-Gabriel. André Breton ou la leçon du cristal. CahS 294:299–308, 1949.   **9550**

A brief survey of B.'s poetry (following publication of the Gallimard *Poèmes*). Focuses on the image and attempts to distinguish between images that merely break rational constraints and the more powerful images in B.'s poetry that answer the formula: "Reconnaître le merveilleux précipité du désir." [HF]

Houdebine, Jean-Louis. André Breton et la double ascendance du signe. NCr 212: 42–51, 1970.   **9551**

A long and somewhat laborious critique of B. and surrealism which is one of several attempts on the part of Marxist oriented critics to "déconstruire" B.'s œuvre and thought. [HF]

Hubert, Renée-Riese. Miró and Breton. *In:* Surrealism. *See* 9415. p. 52–59.   **9552**

The first study of the parallel creations of Miró and B., called *Constellations,* within a time lag of sixteen years between the artist's work and the poet's response. The elements that conciliate the two creative works are seen to be the benign irony, the gravitation toward unity between man and nature, their synchronization creating a cosmic reality of harmony. The study is descriptive in nature rather than typological in the linking of these works from separate media. A very useful listing of the whereabouts of Miró's twenty-two gouaches with exact specifications is a very useful resource. [AB]

Morel, Jean-Pierre. Aurélia, Gradiva, X: Psychanalyse et poésie dans Les vases communicants. RLC 46:68–89, 1972.   **9553**

A very thorough and interesting interrogation of the relationship between *Vases* and Freud's theory. Analyzes the types of autoanalysis that B. performs in the book and the difference between B.'s conclusions and Freud's, with the conclusion that B. moves closer to literature. Finds that B.'s deviations from Freud transform dream into the equivalent of a literary work. Relates "la poésie du rêve" to the process of condensation which, in *Vases,* applies to the transfer of love from one woman to another, with the mysterious X as chief player. Comparisons with Nerval's *Aurélia* and Jensen's *Gradiva* (which were on B.'s mind while writing *Vases*). [HF]

Navarri, Roger. Une autre lecture du Signe ascendant. NCr 69–70, Sept. 1970.   **9554**

Houdebine has dogmatically applied a rigorous analysis to a text which is not strictly "theoretical" but, rather, poetical: a passionate plea for the analogical method in which conceptual rigor is not of primary importance. *See* 9551. [HF]

Pastoureau, Henri. Des influences dans la poésie présurréaliste d'André Breton. *In:* André Breton; essais. *See* 9526. [1970] p. 45–80.   **9555**

Quite a thorough study of B.'s early poetry (1914–1919), and the influence of symbolism, Mallarmé, Valéry, Apollinaire, Vaché, Reverdy, Rimbaud, Jarry, Lautréamont. [HF]

Plouvier, Paule. Breton, Jung et le hasard objectif. Eur 475–76:103–08, 1968. **9556**

Points to an irreducible opposition of B.'s and Freud's interpretations of the interaction of desire and the real in the manifestations of chance, in spite of a common point of departure. Sees a greater affinity between B.'s objective chance and Jung's concept of synchronicity. This notion has merit, although the essay offers a limiting perspective of B.'s concept, which does not account for the greater complexity of B.'s thought. [HF]

Starobinski, Jean. Freud, Breton, Myers. ArcL 34:87–96, 1968. *Also in:* André Breton; essais. *See* 9526. [1970] p. 153–71. **9557**

Shows how B. searching for psychological theory which, unlike Freud's, would view automatic phenomena positively, turned to Myers, whose *The human personality and its survival of bodily death* provided him with many of the details used in "Le message automatique." Concludes by placing B. between Freudian rationalism and spiritualist parapsychology. A good penetrating essay. [HF]

Explications

Brandt, Per Aage. The white-haired generator. Poetics 6:72–83, 1972.   9558

Brilliant study which finds a three-tiered structure in B.'s *Le revolver à cheveux blancs,* which the author views as a passage from reality to dream and to a potential re-entry into "political" reality. Concrete, scientifically geared analysis, commanding by the author's knowledge of logistics as well as poetics. [AB]

Cardinal, Roger. Breton: Au beau demi-jour de 1934. *In:* The art of criticism; essays in French literary analysis. Ed. by Peter H. Nurse. Edinburgh, Univ. press, 1969. p. 255–71.   9559

Justifies this attempt at an "explication de texte" of a surrealist poem by assuming that even irrational texts tend to mean something, and that readers with the same cultural background will react more or less in the same way to given irrational images or symbols. Encapsulates surrealist poetics and investigates syntax and structure, atmosphere and mood, imagery and visual patterns. On the terms proposed by Cardinal, this exhaustive analysis makes good sense. [HF]

Chénieux, Jacqueline. Pour une imagination pratique. André Breton: Il y aura une fois... IL 24:230–36, 1972.   9560

An interesting analysis of B.'s text "Il y aura une fois" as a call for an "imagination pratique" and as a guide enabling the reader to utilize the imagined for the enhancement of life. [HF]

Hubert, J. D. André Breton et le paradis perdu. FR 37:200–05, 1963.   9561

Close reading and analysis of two poems of B.: one from *L'air de l'eau* ("On me dit que là-bas") in the light of an earlier one from *Clair de terre* ("Les coqs de roche passent dans le cristal"). The author demonstrates the difference between B. and Baudelaire in their evocation of lost paradises. [AB]

Schaeffer, Gérald. Un petit matin de 1937. *In:* André Breton; essais. *See* 9526. [1970] p. 241–78.   9562

A study of "Ode à Charles Fourier." Considers subject (Fourier in relation to the twentieth century), form (images,

prosody, structure), and historical and personal context (the war, the new direction given to surrealism by B., B.'s personal situation, etc.). Provides a close examination of the text. Thorough and intelligent. [HF]

Vielwahr, André. Explication de texte: L'union libre d'André Breton. NTLTL 2: 20–28, 1972.   9563

Demonstrates that the images of "L'union libre" may be considered arbitrary only when taken out of context and that coherence appears to be the main feature of the poem, with the conclusion that no automatic writing was at work here. [HF]

Novel

Beaujour, Michel. Qu'est-ce que Nadja? *In:* André Breton et le mouvement surréaliste. *See* 9527. p. 780–99.   9564

An excellent essay about *Nadja* as a book "battant comme une porte," whose separate elements can be shuffled like playing cards. Investigates its special narrative mode and its anti-literary techniques of verification (photographs). Considers anecdotes of a particular kind found in *Nadja* as its basic narrative elements and points to its dialectics of order and disorder, organic plan and chance. Some of the basic questions posed by *Nadja* are related to Leiris' *L'Afrique fantôme.* [HF]

Cardinal, Roger. Nadja and Breton. UTQ 41:185–99, 1972.   9565

Proposes a series of questions: "Was Nadja more than an object of passionless curiosity to B.? Was he involved in the development of her madness? Could he have helped her; did he let her down? Should he have intervened when she was put in the asylum? Finally, are his actions defensible on conventional, or again on surrealist terms?" Looking for evidence (hints, hidden or implied meanings) in the text itself, Cardinal reveals contradictions in B.'s defense of his actions and points to antagonism in B.'s personality between the free-thinking surrealist and the puritan, still bound by the prejudices of a bourgeois background. Concludes that B. failed *himself* as a surrealist. [HF]

Champigny, Robert. The first person in Nadja. *In:* About French poetry from Dada to Tel quel: text and theory. Ed. by Mary Ann Caws. Detroit, Wayne state univ. press, 1974. p. 242–53.   **9566**

Finds that the first person pronoun is used in *Nadja* in both a narrative mode (*Nadja* as autobiography and history) and a gestural or dramatic mode, involving oratorical and emotive phraseology. B. is seen both as a historical person who makes a historical report about Nadja and himself and, on the other hand, as a *persona* performing a dramatic role. As a result there is a confusion between history and fiction. The dramatic ego interferes and the story of B. and Nadja becomes part of the dramatic role. [HF]

Hubert, Renée-Riese. The coherence of Breton's Nadja. ConL 10:241–52, 1969.   **9567**

Discovers the coherence of *Nadja* in a pattern of repetition, analogies, and chance encounters (revealing links between apparently disconnected incidents which become disquieting as soon as they are viewed in a sequence); the constituent elements being people, signs, words, names, etc. Creates an analogy between the non-linear structure of the novel and the film *L'étreinte de la pieuvre* with its repetitions, multiplications, and the image of the eight tentacles of the octopus, like the eight episodes of the film, which are all attached to one body. Interesting study. [HF]

Jones, Louisa. Nadja and the language of poetic fiction. CahDS 3:45–52, 1972.   **9568**

Considers *Nadja* a typically surrealist variation on the conventions of poetic fiction as formulated in the late nineteenth and early twentieth centuries. Examines those conventions while relating them to *Nadja:* the split lyrical *I*, and the self as the *other* ("Qui suis-je?"); tension between autobiography and novel, and the mingling of action simply recorded with action created imaginatively, which leads to a notion of the plot as enigma; the blending of linear time and spatial organization in the same basic structure of the book. The book is also related to the earlier tradition of the prose poem. [HF]

Jouanny, Robert-A. Nadja: André Breton: analyse critique. Hatier, 1972. 80 p. (Profil d'une œuvre)   **9569**

The most systematic, thorough and objective analysis of B.'s central work that has yet appeared. Intended for the classroom, the organization is scholastic; the study relates the work of B. to the totality of his philosophy and writings. Excellent as an introduction to the text of B. but surpassing by its intelligence and sagacity its introductory objective. [HF]

Levy, Sydney, André Breton's Nadja and automatic writing. CahDS 28–32, 1972.   **9570**

Asserts that *Nadja* is structured and read like an automatic text (read in the sense of establishing relationships among the elements). "Meaning [in *Nadja*] is the accumulation of fragments, and these fragments are themselves organized like the automatic text." References (events, actual happenings) behave as images and there is, consequently, no distinction between signified and referent, a confusion between event and image. [HF]

Lynes, Carlos. Surrealism and the novel: Breton's Nadja. FS 20:366–87, 1966.   **9571**

Points to a changed conception of the novel, one that offers the concentration and shock of emotion found in poetry and ignores the "moments nuls" to evoke only the "moments privilégiés." Relates this new form to the accomplishments of romanticism in transforming the writing of poetry and the poem itself into an *experience*, and suggests reading *Nadja* in the perspective of Nerval's *Sylvie* and *Aurélia*. Follows with a very detailed and interesting reading of the novel, with certain analogies continuously drawn with *Aurélia*. A remarkable essay. [HF]

Martin, Claude. Nadja et le mieux-dire. RHL 72:274–86, 1972.   **9572**

Questions the reason for the numerous important modifications of the original *Nadja* in the new 1962 edition. Martin finds that those differences "témoignent d'égards au mieux-dire" (which B. himself admits to in the Preface), and that the book is well-structured and obeys the classical laws of balance, symmetry and harmonious distribution of its parts. [HF]

Matthews, J. H. Désir et merveilleux dans Nadja d'André Breton. Sym 27:246–68, 1973.   9573

The best part of the essay concerns the complex role played by photographs in *Nadja*. Their banality, says Matthews, is in a sense a homage to the "merveilleux;" they are the surface which draws the reader into "marvelous depths perceived by the imagination." [HF]

Navarri, Roger. Nadja ou l'écriture malheureuse. Eur 528:186–95, 1973.   9574

Claims that the reason *Nadja* is B.'s most popular work also implies a certain paralysis of the critical spirit. There is nothing spontaneous about *Nadja,* Navarri maintains; nothing is less innocent, more concerned with producing an effect. Writing *Nadja* is the only possible course for a man who cannot be anything but a spectator of that which some "individus privilégiés" experience. [HF]

Shattuck, Roger. The Nadja file. CahDS 1:49–56, 1966.   9575

Interprets the action of the novel as an allegory of personality. The essay pivots on the story of Monsieur Delouit who haunts himself. In haunting Nadja, B. was pursuing his own identity — "[a] vampire-like quest for himself [which] destroys her and establishes in her place his identity, the *toi* that has solved the enigma." The "Qui suis-je?" opening of *Nadja* is answered by the fusion of the *toi* in the last pages with the elusive *moi* of the beginning. [HF]

Steinwachs, Gisela. Mythologie des Surrealismus oder die Rückverwandlung von Kulture in Natur: eine strukturale Analyse von Bretons Nadja. Berlin, Luchterhand, 1971. 189 p.   9576

A structural analysis of *Nadja* that is built upon the concepts of "culture" and "nature" as they appear in modern structuralism. Introduces structural esthetics and examines the theories of Saussure and Lévi-Strauss. Evaluates dream and automatism as interpreted by B. and Freud, and investigates myth from a pathological point of view. The basic question of madness vs. lucidity in

Nadja is perceived in the context of the "reversion" from culture to nature. [HF]

Testud, Pierre. Nadja ou la métamorphose. RSH 144:579–89, 1971.   9577

Points to the unsettling nature of a work that undergoes complete metamorphosis, in which the transparency of the beginning turns into the opacity of the last pages. Investigating the book in detail in the light of the above, Testud concludes that the arrogance of the "Qui suis-je?" is repudiated in the last part and replaced by an absolute humility in the presence of passion; a "recherche égocentrique" has become "communion amoureuse." [HF]

Wylie, Harold. Breton, schizophrenia and Nadja. FR 43, special issue no. 1:100–06, 1970.   9578

A meticulous analysis of the nature of madness identified in *Nadja*. Very close reading of parts of the text brings out specific symptoms of schizophrenia in B.'s delineation of the character of Nadja; these are considered in relation to B.'s ambivalence toward her love. One of the best of the increasing number of pieces on *Nadja*. [AB]

René Crevel
(Nos. 9579–9605)

Carlos Lynes

Republished Texts

Crevel, René. Le clavecin de Diderot. 1932. Présentation de Claude Courtot. Jean-Jacques Pauvert, [1966]. 105 p. (Collection Libertés, 38)   9579

The "présentation" gives a generally accurate but somewhat tendentious biographical outline, followed by a note denouncing the Oct. 1965 number of *Action poétique* for minimizing C.'s activity in the surrealist movement and exaggerating his role in the A.E.A.R. and the Communist party; a second part exalts the significance of *Le clavecin de Diderot* as the expression of surrealist total revolt and as an arm of action against what C. already called "l'opportunisme contemporain."

———. L'esprit contre la raison suivi de Dali ou l'anti-obscurantisme et de Nouvelles vues sur Dali et l'obscurantisme, Solitude variée, Pour la simple honnêteté et Au carrefour de l'amour, la poésie, la science et la révolution. Préface de Marcel Jouhandeau. Textes réunis par Jean Schwartz. Tchou, 1969. 151 p.   **9580**

In the preface, 34 years after his brief but sensational note on C.'s suicide, Jouhandeau insinuates again—most improbably—that, at the end, C. may have been concerned with religious problems. The rest of this preface is very personal, sometimes sentimental, filled with veiled or open attacks harking back to another age, subject to caution for some of the biographical facts or interpretations. The "Note bibliographique" of Jean Schwartz is sober in tone and reliable.

————. Mon corps et moi. Préf. de Jean Frémon. Suivi d'un dossier de textes réunis et présentés par Michel Carassou et Jean-Claude Zylberstein. Jean-Jacques Pauvert, 1974. 251 p.   **9581**

The preface gives a young present-day novelist's appreciation of C. and his second novel, originally published in 1925 and here presented in a handsome new edition. The dossier, intelligently introduced by Carassou, brings together some 20 texts published by C. in little magazines (1923-1926), including several which are preliminary versions of passages reworked in *Mon corps et moi*.

————. Mon corps et moi. La mort difficile. Préf. de Robert Kanters. Lausanne, Eds. rencontre, 1963. 251 p. (Prix Rencontre)   **9582**

The preface to this Swiss edition of C.'s second and third novels, which had long been out of print, is perceptive and sympathetic; like most other essays on C., however, it is more concerned with the "mythical" figure of the author than with critical examination of his texts.

————. La mort difficile. Préf. de Salvador Dali. Suivi d'un dossier de textes réunis et présentés par Michel Carassou et Jean-Claude Zylberstein. Jean-Jacques Pauvert, 1974. 255 p.   **9583**

The preface (which, though not so stated here, had appeared in 1954 in *La Parisienne* as "La mort de René Crevel") is more of a curiosity than a

critical essay or completely reliable biographical memoir; it is pertinent to C.'s third novel only if the book is read as transposed autobiography. Carassou, presenting the dossier, emphasizes (excessively, if one wishes to read C.'s *texts* rather than his "legend") the autobiographical content; the dossier gives C.'s little "Autobiographie" (1925) and 14 very frank letters to Marcel Jouhandeau as two other expressions of the same "vérité" concerning the author.

————. Les pieds dans le plat. Préf. de Ezra Pound. Suivi d'un dossier de textes réunis et présentés par Michel Carassou et Jean-Claude Zylberstein. Jean-Jacques Pauvert, 1974. 317 p.   **9584**

Translated from a text published in *The Criterion* in 1939, this "preface" is typical of Pound—highly personal, filled with unorthodox and provocative judgments, not exempt from error, but striking for its insights and vigor. *Les pieds dans le plat*, a "*Comédie humaine* in one volume," is called absolute proof of C.'s genius as an "écrivain né" who developed his gifts in an admirable series of novels. Pound insists that, from 1938 on, all young writers *must* read C., that he will be read more and more, whereas "on délaissera les grands noms gonflés de vent de ses aînés qui acceptent la pourriture." The dossier presents unpublished letters to Tzara and other texts which throw light on C.'s politics and his attitude toward Breton in 1934-1935.

Special Numbers

Crevel, René. Choix de textes. ActP 28-29: 17-42, 1965.   **9585**

Published to mark the thirtieth anniversary of the Congrès de Paris pour la défense de la culture and C.'s suicide, on the eve of this congress, the texts emphasize C.'s Marxist activity at the end of his life. They are preceded by two editorials (signed Gilbert-M. Duprez and Henri Deluy), which recall C. primarily to try to answer the question: "Trente ans après la mort de Crevel, où en sommes-nous?" Another text, "Qui est René Crevel?" by Denise Miège is a rather elementary introduction, with a brief chronology limited to political events.

René Crevel. Textes réunis et présentés par Jean-Jacques Lévêque. TemM 10–11:Oct. 1954. 64 p. **9586**

Tributes, mostly brief, collected by a French student, poet, and budding art critic who, not yet twenty, was fascinated by his discovery of some of C.'s books. Among the texts which throw some light on C. and his works are those of the young editor himself, Jacques Baron, François Beloux, Jean Breton, Michel Leiris, Henri Pastoreau, Claude Peronne, André de Richaud, J. H. Sainmont, Philippe Soupault, and Tristan Tzara.

General Studies

Bataille, Georges. Crevel (René). Le clavecin de Diderot. CritS 7:50, 1933. *In his:* Œuvres complètes. V. 1. Gallimard, 1970. p. 326–27. **9587**

Attempting to produce a pamphlet against bourgeois society, C. reveals his own "sottise" and also "la profonde insuffisance intellectuelle du surréalisme auquel il se réfère;" C.'s inept citations from Marx, Engels, Lenin have absolutely nothing in common with his own "littérature de malade énervé."

Breton, André. Entrée des médiums. Litt 1–16, Nov. 1, 1922. **9588**

Famous article, describing C.'s role as initiator of the experiments in hypnotic sleep conducted by Breton and his group; includes the "stenographic" record of one of C.'s "rêves parlés" dated Oct. 7 (1922).

————. Sur la mort de René Crevel. NRF 23:291–93, 1935. **9589**

Replying to Jouhandeau's text in the preceding issue of the NRF, Breton protests less against the "criminal" accusation against him than against the attempt to reduce the multiplicity of possible reasons for C.'s suicide to one improbable motive; Breton also rejects the insinuation that C. may have been turning toward religious faith—this in spite of the fact that one of his last published texts was a violent attack against the repressive role of the church ("A l'ombre conjuguée de la mître et

de la matraque," MondeB June 20, 1935).

Carré, Marie-Rose. René Crevel: surrealism and the individual. YFS 31:74–86, 1964. **9590**

A well-informed general presentation which tries to define C.'s unique place in surrealism and suggests—less convincingly—analogies with the writings of Beckett, Ionesco, even Camus. The critic (author of an unpublished "biographie intérieure" of C., presented at the Sorbonne in 1963 as a thesis for the *doctorat d'université*) tends to read C.'s texts, even his six novels, as documents on the problematic figure of the author, and does not resist the temptation to propose a symbolic interpretation—plausible, perhaps, but overly simple and at best unprovable—of C.'s suicide.

Charensol, Georges. Les vingt à trente ans. René Crevel. NL 218:5, Dec. 18, 1926. **9591**

Less a review of *La mort difficile,* which had just appeared, than a brief presentation of C. and his activity up to that point; the second half consists of characteristic quotations from C.'s writings.

Courtot, Claude. René Crevel. Etude de Claude Courtot, avec un choix de textes... Seghers, 1969. 189 p. (Poètes d'aujourd'hui, 182) **9592**

Lively, often polemical and truculent essay, generally well informed, interesting above all as a third generation surrealist's reading of C. and his works. The history of C.'s relations with surrealism and with Marxism and the Communist party needs further investigation by someone who is not a militant supporter of either camp. This volume, even in the 97 pages of its excellent "choix de textes," rightly does not try to present C. as a "poet" in the conventional sense.

Faÿ, Bernard. René Crevel: Etes-vous fous? REur 300–01, Sept. 1, 1929. **9593**

Perceptive comments on C.'s fifth novel, but based on the debatable premise that C. is already a "légende vivante" and that the author's personality is the source of the fascination exerted by his writings.

Gaillard, André. Portrait contemporain: René Crevel. CahS 43:332–35, 1956. (Reprint of text which appeared in *Cahiers libres*, Oct. 1926, and in Gaillard, André. Œuvres complètes. Marseille, Cahiers du sud, 1941.)   **9594**

Three years before his own suicide, Gaillard, who found himself and the other ardent, despairing young men of his generation in C.'s writings, wrote this sensitive, moving appreciation of *Mon corps et moi.*

Gauthier, Xavière. Surréalisme et sexualité. Gallimard, 1971. 381 p. (Collection Idées)   **9595**

In chapter on homosexuality, especially p. 234–37, the author of this provocative study explains the lack of male chauvinism in C.'s attitude toward women—atypical of the surrealists—largely by his homosexuality.

Jouhandeau, Marcel. René Crevel. NRF 23:121–22, 1935.   **9596**

Appearing two weeks after C.'s suicide, this brief text accused André Breton, almost literally, of being criminally responsible for the tragic event: "Il meurt pour avoir trop cru en quelqu'un..."

Lynes, Carlos. René Crevel vivant. EnLA 3–12, Spring 1956.   **9597**

Reproduces, 21 years after the event and for the first time, the exact text of the two suicide notes left by C., reports of his telephone conversation with Eluard some hours before his fatal act, and above all proposes a reading which, recognizing the difficulty of separating the writings from the man who produced them, nevertheless insists that what is still alive, ready at least to live again, is not the pathetic or tragic "legend" of the man, but "la voix émouvante et émue qui nous parle dans ses livres." This essay also calls for new editions of C.'s books, long out of print and thus little read.

———. Solitude de René Crevel. FS 12:125–42, 1958.   **9598**

A tragic obsession with solitude—"mal dont nul ne saurait guérir" (*Mon corps et moi*)—dominated C.'s life and his writings, never being assuaged or sublimated, in love or friendship, in poetic creation, in the ardent quest for a surrealist "monde nouveau," or in Marxist revolutionary action. This essay sees the departure point of the obsession in C.'s childhood family situation, links it to "le malheur essentiel de la conscience" (Alquié), to romantic "ennui" and to "l'inquiétude moderne" (Daniel-Rops); it devotes itself primarily, however, to a close analysis of the forms assumed by this anguished solitude in the thematic organization of C.'s six novels.

———. Tel qu'en lui-même... CahS 43:336–44, 1956.   **9599**

Written for the "fronton" marking—one year late—the 20th anniversary of C.'s suicide, and based on the preliminary draft of a book which was to have been entitled "René Crevel ou le quatorzième convive," this essay proposes a study of the "réseau d'obsessions" constitutive of the "personnalité essentielle" of the author as revealed in his language and in the "univers imaginaire" of his works; with emphasis on C.'s six novels, it then suggests—and describes—three "stages" in the development of this "personality" and in the writings which permit the reader to actualize this figure.

Matthews, J. H. René Crevel and Robert Desnos. Babylone (1927). La liberté ou l'amour! (1927). *In his:* Surrealism and the novel. Ann Arbor, Univ. of Michigan press, 1966. p. 59–74.   **9600**

Invokes against C. (but, paradoxically, not against Desnos) an almost classical notion of genre, unity of tone, mood, atmosphere, even the autonomy of the work of art, to pass a severe judgment on C.'s fourth novel (*not* his "first"). This study proposes a very incomplete reading, confuses the *voix surréaliste* of the text with that of an intrusive author, ignores the major themes suggested by C.'s earlier tentative title "La femme et la ville" and the chapter heading "Ressusciter le vent," and draws—without fully assuming it—this tendentious conclusion: "In the resignation displayed in *Babylone* some may see foreshadowed an ultimate capitulation marked by its author's suicide."

Morin, Louis. Le jour n'a rien repeint (René Crevel et le surréalisme). NRF 15:953–61, 1967.   **9601**

Emphasizes C.'s ambivalence toward surrealism, a certain distrust of the powers of language, his failure, in spite of an anxious striving, to find in surrealism or, toward the end, in militant Marxism viable solutions to the problems which obsessed him. The tone of this sensitive essay suggests identification with C.'s blinding lucidity and his anguished solitude; an editorial note at the end reports that two days after bringing his text to the NRF, the author, 28 years old and preparing a thesis on C., took his own life.

Rottenberg, Pierre. Esquisse cartographique du mouvement: surréalisme. TelQ 46: 41–58, 1971. **9602**

In this study forming part of *Tel quel's* collective endeavor to "de-construct" surrealist theory and practice, C.'s understanding of Marxism and his commitment to revolution, from *Le clavecin de Diderot* (1932) on, are contrasted with Breton's inability to free himself from idealism. Rottenberg's complex theoretical analysis of texts by these two writers is not easy to follow unless the reader is familiar with *Tel quel's* research during the years immediately preceding this publication.

Soupault, Philippe. René Crevel. *In his:* Profils perdus. Mercure de France, 1963. p. 24–36. **9603**

A biographical memoir-portrait of C. by a contemporary who knew him well, especially during the early years of his literary activity.

Tzara, Tristan. René Crevel. Etoiles 1, 5, Sept. 18, 1945. **9604**

Ten years after C.'s suicide on the eve of the Congrès international des écrivains pour la défense de la culture, his close friend and associate in the avant-garde and revolutionary movements of 1920–1935 pays tribute to C. as one of the purest representatives of the generation of writers for whom "la vie et la poésie devaient s'identifier." Tzara shows close knowledge of all C.'s writings and finds his specific quality in his brilliant amalgamation of polemical violence and extreme freedom in the imaginative interpretation of the external world.

Zeltner-Neukomm, Gerda. Zur Bedeutung des Wortes in einem surrealistischen Roman. Trivium 5:114–30, 1947. **9605**

In *Mon corps et moi*, words reveal their emptiness when they are used in the most banal sense, and the autobiographical narrator-protagonist ends with the lucid recognition of solitude and *néant*. In *La mort difficile*, without such devices as automatic writing, the "word" (language) is liberated and becomes productive in the poetic and surrealist sense; at the end of his novel, however, speech gives way to silence, liberty becomes the night, the night becomes Pierre's "difficult" death. For the critic, C.'s surrealist use of language reflects the dilemma of modern poetry.

Robert Desnos
(Nos. 9606–9673)

HÉLÈNE LAROCHE DAVIS

Bibliography

Gaubert, Serge. Bio-bibliographie. *In:* Desnos. *See* 9607. p. 229–35. **9606**

Valuable bibliography because it is up to date and follows closely D.'s life as well as the writing and publication of his works year by year. The most detailed bibliography of D. existent. Includes all his contributions to various reviews.

Special Numbers

Desnos. Eur 517–18:3–291, 1972. **9607**

Special number. Contents analyzed separately.

Robert Desnos. Sim 22–23:1–173, 1956. **9608**

Special number. Contents analyzed separately.

Vous avez le bonjour de Robert Desnos. SigT 5:2–53, 1951. **9609**

Special number entirely devoted to D. Each article is very short and pays homage to the poet. Short poems written for him alternate with the articles. One significant article has been analyzed here separately: "Les deux cantates" by A. Smoular.

Biography

Bédouin, Jean Louis. La poésie surréaliste. Seghers, 1964. p. 142–50.   **9610**

Short biography, followed by a selection of poems. Emphasizes the poet at work, his ability to manipulate language.

Berger, Pierre. Mon copain Robert Desnos. Poé 26–27:31–38, 1945.   **9611**

Accounts of Berger's first meeting with D. and of their relationship. D. had a power of hope. D. and the young poets who came to see him. His attitude toward life, his success due to a "mariage systématique du conscient et de l'inconscient."

————. Robert Desnos. Une étude... œuvres choisies, bibliographie... Seghers, 1949, 1960. 221 p. (Poètes d'aujourd'hui, 16) *Also:* Robert Desnos. Une étude de Pierre Berger. Avec un choix de poèmes... Chronologie bibliographique... Seghers, 1970. 192 p. (Poètes d'aujourd'hui, 16)   **9612**

Token of friendship to a man Berger knew well. More than a biography. Also chronology of D.'s works accompanied by comments. Striking portrait of the man and the poet. The second part of the book includes unpublished poems and a good selection of texts. Follows the various steps of D.'s career.

Desnos, Youki. Les confidences de Youki. Fayard, 1957. 238 p.   **9613**

Autobiography which gives details on the life among journalists, writers and artists of the 1920's. Her experience with painter Foujita, then with D. Circumstances in which D. composed and published his poems. Quarrels within the surrealist movement. Various jobs of D. How he was arrested by the Gestapo and suffered in the Nazi concentration camps. All is told with great simplicity. Includes D.'s first poem "Aquarelle" as well as letters from Germany; interesting documents.

Dumas, Marie Claire. Avant-propos. *In:* Desnos. *See* 9607. p. 3–14.   **9614**

Biographical details of D. no one else has mentioned, the writing of "Prospectus" and "Les Nouvelles Hébrides" for instance. Contains "Chanson," an original text which dates from 1916. Sheds light on D.'s separation from the

surrealist movement. Interesting facts on D.'s work on the radio. Clarification of D.'s political evolution. Excellent article by a scholar who knows the poet more thoroughly than any other and who directed this issue of *Europe* dedicated to D.

Fraenkel, Théodore, and Samy Simon. Biographie de Robert Desnos. Cr 215–28, Aug.–Sept. 1946.   **9615**

First part by Fraenkel presents D. before the war. Details on his temperament; his talent for automatic writing, his individualism and strong need for independence. Second part by Simon, tells of his activity in the underground and in captivity, how generous he was with the other prisoners.

Ganzo, Robert. Robert Desnos. *In his:* Cinq poètes assassinés. Minuit, 1947. p. 92–126.   **9616**

Among the five poets killed by the Germans, D. is the prophet announcing the liberation. Presents the life of D. in the concentration camps, his courage and his talent in uplifting the morale of his comrades. The selection of poems emphasizes the two important aspects of D.: the poet of love and the virtuoso of language.

Hugnet, Georges. Souvenirs de l'occupation nazie. *In:* Robert Desnos. *See* 9608. p. 60–71.   **9617**

Biographical details. Friendship with Hugnet at the time of German occupation.

Jeander. Le pas qui ne pourra jamais s'éloigner. *In:* Robert Desnos. *See* 9608. p. 33–35.   **9618**

Homage to D. after his death. Details on the film "Bonsoir Mesdames, Bonsoir Messieurs."

Jeanson, Henri. Desnos 1918. *In:* Robert Desnos. *See* 9608. p. 29–31.   **9619**

Original details on D.'s life which are not found anywhere else.

Juin, Hubert. Robert Desnos. Marg 115:11–24, 1967.   **9620**

General and rapid survey of D.'s life. Paints the background of the period and stresses the influence of Allain and Souvestre's *Fantômas* as well as the district of Paris where D. spent his childhood. D. marked by the "langage du faubourg." When D. wrote "The night of loveless nights," he was born as a poet. D.'s evolution from dream to earth related.

Kroupa, Adolf. Desnos est mort sans poème. LetF 1347:3–5, 1970. **9621**
Revealing article; proves that the "Dernier poème" was never written by D. His last texts are those from Compiègne. Scholars specializing in D. agree.

Laurence, Robert. Souvenirs de déportation avec Robert Desnos. *In:* Desnos. *See* 9607. p. 138–45. **9622**
Biographical notes on the life in the camps with this friend D., first Compiègne, then the odyssey to the concentration camps.

Manzini, Gianna. Il sogno di Desnos. *In her:* Ritratti e pretesti. Milan, Il saggiatore, 1960. p. 31–34. **9623**
Analyzes the dream in which D. sees himself as a number falling into a blank page; dream which dates from 1916. She imagines what the dream could be; stresses the serious and even dangerous oneiric power of D. which influenced his destiny. One mistake: D. did not die at Auchwitz but at Terezin.

Salacrou, Armand. Desnos et la publicité radiophonique. *In:* Robert Desnos. *See* 9608. p. 39–41. **9624**
Biographical details on how Salacrou and D. worked together in radio advertising.

General Studies

Bachat, Charles. Tradition et subversion poétique chez Desnos. *In:* Desnos. *See* 9607. p. 35–40. **9625**
Shows how D. uses and transgresses the poetic tradition. His preoccupation with form, from the word games to the opera. Shows how D. plays with the old forms of the language following the same process explained by Freud in *Le mot d'esprit et ses rapports avec l'inconscient.* Rapid and technical look at "Siramour." D. as a romantic surrealist.

Bertelé, René. Préface. *In:* Desnos, Robert: Corps et biens. Gallimard, 1968. p. 5–14. **9626**
Sensitive preface that asserts that *Corps et biens* is the most important work of the first period of surrealism and contains all of D.'s essential intentions.

Boisdeffre, Pierre de. Quatre poètes français à l'heure allemande. MerF 1128:645–63, 1957. **9627**
During the German occupation, the poet's voice defends freedom. Summary of D.'s career: his turning away from his early beliefs in dream to use reason and his conviction that poetry must serve the needs of the real world. Emphasizes the hope in the poems of captivity. One mistake: Boisdeffre writes *Quarts de veille* for *Etat de veille.*

Bouvier, Michel. Les ombres sur la place. *In:* Desnos. *See* 9607. p. 84–91. **9628**
Obscure article, too abstract and without quotations. Attempts to show that the ideal situation for creating is expressed, in D.'s work, by the image of deserted places, of uniformity, which leaves room for chance and spontaneous birth. Same privileged role of obscurity.

Breton, André. Sur Robert Desnos. *In his:* Perspective cavalière. Gallimard, 1970. p. 168–70. **9629**
Describes Breton's first meeting with D.

Buchole, Rosa. L'évolution poétique de Robert Desnos. Brussels, Palais des académies, 1956. 238 p. **9630**
Good chronological survey of life and works of D. Rapid analysis of major poems, always relating them to historical background. Follows the evolution of D. from passive fascination with the subconscious to the lucid effort toward controlled rhythm and harmony. Excellent bibliography, at least for works published until 1956. Review: M. Otten in LR 4:363–65, 1960.

Caws, Mary Ann. Poems and surrealist poems: Becker, Frénaud and Robert Desnos. ConL 12:88–97, 1971. **9631**
D. as "the most extreme of the surrealist experimenters with language."

Contrasts grammatically standard poetic language of Becker and Frénaud to surrealist poetic language of D. Commentary on D.'s "Un jour qu'il faisait nuit," "Au Mocassin le berbe," and "Désordre formel."

―――――. Robert Desnos. In her: The poetry of dada and surrealism. Princeton, Princeton univ. press, 1970. p. 170–203.   **9632**

Emphasis on D.'s self-involvement on narcissism. His language is "constantly self-referential." Good interpretation of D.'s poems, especially "A la Mystérieuse." Extensive quotations with English translations.

―――――. Robert Desnos and the flasks of night. YFS 50:108–19, 1974.   **9633**

Certain recurring structures in D.'s poetry are the evidence of intoxicated vision or speech. The "liquid source" for the word play is analyzed in passages from *Deuil pour deuil, La liberté ou l'amour* and *Siramour.* The intoxication becomes metaphor and leads to the "fixed gaze" or obsession. Intoxication is the most valuable source of D.'s lyricism but it is dangerous because it can "entail the denial of the poem."

Dadoun, Roger. Grandes images du grand livre poète Robert Desnos. In: Robert Desnos. See 9608. p. 78–98.   **9634**

Thematic study based on central images. Relationship between the theme of the street and the theme of night. Evolution of style from the abyss—sea, night, dream, erotic climate of hard and soft—to the labyrinth—star, hand, street. Esthetic and social sublimation. Symbolism of the diamond as the utmost of hardness and purity.

Darle, Juliette. La cantate pour l'inauguration du Musée de l'homme. In: Desnos. See 9607. p. 41–50.   **9635**

D. is still present and recaptured in other arts. Tells how lines of D.'s poetry are reproduced in the tapestries of Marc Saint Saens and in the tapestries of Jean Picart Le Doux and Lurçat of which four photographs are included. Other examples from music and film cited.

Dumas, Marie Claire. Desnos et R. Roussel. In: Desnos. See 9607. p. 179–83.   **9636**

Introduction to D.'s articles on Roussel. D. defends the playwright of *L'étoile au front* with strong polemic tones.

Fowlie, Wallace. Robert Desnos. In his: Mid-century French poets. Twayne, 1955. p. 198–201.   **9637**

Short introduction to a choice of poems by D. Rapid summary of D.'s life. His importance as an authentic surrealist poet. Gift of automatism and importance of eroticism. One mistake at the beginning of the article: the poem supposedly found on D. at his death would be called "J'ai rêvé tellement fort *de* toi" and not "*à* toi". Besides, there never was such a poem, as A. Kroupa proves.

Gaubert, Serge. Desnos et le naufrage. In: Desnos. See 9607. p. 15–34.   **9638**

Excellent insight into D.'s poetic universe. Original article which studies D.'s predilection for what is beyond the mirror, for the plunge to the bottom of the sea and the marvelous. Study of the various plunges: hypnotic sleep, cinema, love, death. But the sea is night, anguish and the poet changes his course: "Le naufrage ou l'abandon devient exploration et découverte des noyaux d'énergie." Return to earth to live among men and drag surrealism to the "domaine public."

Greene, Tatiana. Les bottes de sept lieues de Robert Desnos: Son langage poétique. Sym 24:320–29, 1970.   **9639**

This article contains the most interesting commentary on *C'est les bottes de sept lieues cette phrase "Je me vois,"* which is an attempt at instant self-analysis. The article traces two opposite tendencies through D.'s poetry: delirium and lucidity. It follows D.'s high points as a surrealist poet. Notes that the quality of his automatic writing which is satirical can also be lyrical. Includes excellent quotations and studies briefly D.'s "poétique de l'amour."

―――――. Le merveilleux surréaliste de Robert Desnos. FR 50:193–203, 1967.   **9640**

Sensitive article with good and numerous quotations and a definition of D.'s "merveilleux" as well as a demonstration of its sources.

Gros, Léon Gabriel. Deux morts exemplaires. CahS 297:306–13, 1949.   **9641**
Parallel between André Gaillard and D.

Lartigue, Pierre. Le dernier carnet de Robert Desnos. LetF 1277:3–5, 1969.   **9642**
Interesting article written by a scholar sensitive to D.'s literary texture. Follows his poetic style up to the more classical volume of *Contrée.* The article clarifies the point of D.'s last texts. Written in captivity, they are "Sol de Compiègne" (a manuscript facsimile of this poem appears in the article) and a text on painting.

Légoutière, Edmond. Robert Desnos. *In his:* Le surréalisme. Masson, 1972. p. 181–90.   **9643**
Short introduction to a selection of texts by D. Insists on the latter's predominant role in the surrealist movement at the time of the hypnotic sleep. Excellent remarks before each text. Rapid biographical summary.

McFarlane, I. D. Love and the accessoire poétique in the poetry of Robert Desnos. *In his:* Order and adventure in post-romantic French poetry. Oxford, Blackwell, 1973. p. 231–43.   **9644**
Stresses distance between dream and attainment in D.'s poetry. Gap must be filled by poetic means. How archetypal symbols are formed. Rapid inventory of recurring images in D.'s poetic world.

Matthews, John. Robert Desnos (1900–1945). *In his:* Surrealist poetry in France. Syracuse, Syracuse univ. press, 1969. p. 55–67.   **9645**
Considers only the period during which D. was with the surrealist movement. Chooses poems which mark the important steps in D.'s evolution and studies his linguistic explorations.

Meuris, Jacques. Robert Desnos ou le voyant de l'amour. Marg 33:39–45, 1953.   **9646**
Freedom, love and voyance are the leading forces for D. See, e.g., *La liberté ou l'amour* and *The night of loveless nights.*

Ory, Carlos Edmundo de. Robert Desnos y Federico García Lorca. IndAL 174:3–7, 1963.   **9647**
Both visionary poets still preserve their balance as human beings. This article reviews the imaginary universe of both poets and is illustrated by drawings of D. and of Lorca. It also contains a poem written by D. for the Spanish republicans "Sangre y sombra." Mentions that D. wrote a "Cantate to the memory of Lorca."

Ottavi, André. De la poésie aux poèmes. *In:* Desnos. *See* 9607. p. 75–83.   **9648**
This article refutes the vain polemic which opposes rhetoric and the imaginary. Numerous quotations support the arguments. See kinship with Bachelard and Mircea Eliade. Rich analysis of the tree image because "la rhétorique et l'imaginaire coïncident en leur structure arborescente." Excellent remarks on "La ville de Don Juan."

Plantier, René. L'écriture et la voix. *In:* Desnos. *See* 9607. p. 51–74.   **9649**
This article takes to task Bertelé's introduction to D.'s *Corps et biens.* Importance given to the poetic inventions of the word games and to the work of the artisan, "l'ouvrier poète." Technical study of "Rrose Sélavy," "L'Aumonyme" and "Langage cuit." Reveals the creative processes behind these poems. The article follows D.'s struggle with language, especially until "A la Mystérieuse."

Rebourcet, Gabriel. L'archinon et Robert Desnos. *In:* Desnos. *See* 9607. p. 125–28.   **9650**
Poetic article, surrealistic style. Witnesses the second death of the poet when Les Halles of Paris were destroyed. Evocation of D.'s hypnotic sleep creations and his spirit of revolt.

Rousselot, Jean. Robert Desnos. *In his:* Panorama critique des nouveaux poètes français. Seghers, 1953. p. 303–12.   **9651**
Presents mainly one aspect of D.: the poet of everyday life. Insists on his neo-humanism without philosophical pretension. Gives great importance to militant poetry. Above all D. is "le poète humain."

Scheler, Lucien. Un texte de Robert Desnos signé Paul Eluard. LetF 12–13, March 14, 1972.   **9652**
Demonstrates how an article, "Le génie sans miroir," on the artistic creation of insane people, was written by D. and not by Paul Eluard. A photo of an almanac page with Eluard's signature stands as proof of it.

Simon, Samy. Robert Desnos pionnier de la radio. *In:* Robert Desnos. *See* 9608. p. 36–38.   **9653**
D. and Deharme discover a new poetic language. New revolutionary techniques of radio drama. D. leads technology toward poetry. He is a virtuoso of the advertising slogan.

Tortel, Jean. Robert Desnos aujourd'hui. Cr 219–20:718–37, 1965.   **9654**
A poet writing on a poet; understanding of the deep work. Asks what place D.'s language has in the present world of poetry. Stresses the work of D. on language, his "poétique." The surrealist images have lost some of their strength now because we are accustomed to them, yet his poetry has ambiguity and is alive.

Individual Poems or Collections

Angenot, Marc. La complainte de Fantômas et La complainte de Fualdès. EF 4:424–30, 1968.   **9655**
D.'s poem very faithful to the serial of Allain and Souvestre. Also imitation of a popular song written in the 19th century about the assassination of Fualdès.

Bellemin-Noël, Jean Sur un poème de Desnos: Les quatre sans cou. PoE 29: 84–87, 1965.   **9656**
D.'s position at the time (1933); his journalistic work and his detachment from the surrealist movement. Explanation of the poem, based on D.'s life.

Caws, Mary Ann. Robert Desnos: structuration des Ténèbres. SiEc 1:85–102, 1974.   **9657**
Structural approach to the poems of *Ténèbres,* study of their architecture ("architexture"). Shows how repetitions are manipulated to create various

effects: obsession, irony, suspension of time, movement and negation. Sheds a penetrating light on the difficult poems of *Ténèbres.*

Elsass, Michèle. L'étoile et la sirène. *In:* Desnos. *See* 9607. p. 91–96.   **9658**
Studies the theme of woman in D.'s *Corps et biens* and in *Fortunes.*

Favre, Robert. Desnos danse Des Esseintes. *In:* Desnos. *See* 9607. p. 105–12.   **9659**
Interesting and detailed commentary of the poem "Elégant cantique de Salomé Salomon" from "Langage cuit."

Girod, Manuela. Mécanique métaphysique: Rrose Sélavy (1922–1923). *In:* Desnos. *See* 9607. p. 97–104.   **9660**
Study of "Rrose Sélavy." Clever style, plays on words, using D.'s own method to understand the aphorisms, to discover "ce qui se trame derrière le mur du langage" which, actually, is brittle. Technical study which reveals the structure of D.'s language in "Rrose Sélavy" and thus discovers what is behind it: Rrose, a flower, a mermaid, eros (eRros), or D. himself.

Pelinq, Mireille. Quelques points de rencontre du cinéma et de la poésie en 1923 dans L'Aumonyme de Robert Desnos. RSH 130:296–305, 1968.   **9661**
The profound source of the poem is dream structured so that it corresponds to the vision of the spectator with a passion for the cinema. The poem might be the poetical sketch of a possible film, richer than a scenario. Good analysis of the first poem of *L'Aumonyme.* Same theme and structure to be found in "The night of loveless nights."

Smoular, Alfred. Robert Desnos. Deux cantates. *In:* Vous avez le bonjour de Robert Desnos. *See* 9609. p. 2–16.   **9662**
Presentation of "Cantate pour l'inauguration du Musée de l'homme" et "Les quatre éléments."

Prose Fiction

Caws, Mary Ann. Techniques of alienation in the early novels of Robert Desnos. MLQ 28:473–77, 1967.   **9663**

Stimulating and original article. Study of the structure of denial in *Deuil pour deuil* and *La liberté ou l'amour*. Sterility of the written and its incapacity to render life.

Matthews, J. H. René Crevel et Robert Desnos: Babylone (1927), La liberté ou l'amour (1927). *In his:* Surrealism and the novel. Ann Arbor, Univ. of Michigan press, 1966. p. 59–73. **9664**

Compares Crevel's novel *Babylone* and D.'s *La liberté ou l'amour* to uncover the difficulties encountered by a surrealist novelist. Sees Crevel's failure due to compromises and D.'s success to a total "lack of concern for rational developments."

Cinema

Belz, Carl I. The film poetry of Man Ray. Cr 2:117–30, 1965. **9665**

Mainly on Man Ray, but three pages on D. and the film "L'étoile de mer" based on a short unpublished poem of D.

Cohn, Bernard. Desnos le frénétique. NL 12, Jan. 5, 1967. **9666**

On the publication of *Cinéma*. D. judges films as a poet, as an adventure which leads to the absolute in action. D. is against all censorship, moral or intellectual. Surprise and humor play an important part in his scenarios.

Dumas, Marie Claire. Calligraphies et autres jeux de Robert Desnos. QL 3–5, Jan. 15–31, 1975. **9667**

Short article on D.'s play on words and letters in "Rrose Sélavy" where the language is fascinated by itself and liberates the pleasure principle of Eros. Letters and drawings have a similar role. The article reproduces drawings and calligraphies which D. jotted down in little notebooks. Includes two unpublished poems, "Le canapé de Paméla" and "Demi-rêve."

———. Un scénario exemplaire de Robert Desnos. EtCi 38–39:135–39, 1965. **9668**

Shows the influence of the surrealist manifesto on the scenario "Minuit à quatorze heures." The marvelous changes and becomes modern; cinema is the "merveilleux moderne." The

imaginary is present in the midst of everyday life.

Gauthier, Guy. Le cinéma selon Robert Desnos. *In:* Desnos. *See* 9607. p. 129–35. **9669**

Notes the importance of cinema for D. and lack of recognition in the field. D.'s instinctive approach as a film critic. This article is followed by a text from *Autoportrait* by Man Ray which describes D.'s poem "L'étoile de mer" and tells how Man Ray made a film with it.

Jalard, Michel Claude. Desnos au cinéma. QL 1–101, Jan. 31, 1967. **9670**

About the publication of *Cinéma;* texts by D. presented by Tchernia. The film criticism which shows the surrealist approach to cinema is most interesting. Its goal: "déréaliser le quotidien."

Drama

Béhar, Henri. Robert Desnos ou les portes battantes. Notes sur La place de l'étoile. *In his:* Le théâtre dada et surréaliste. Gallimard, 1967. p. 266–74. **9671**

Written in 1927 and revised in 1944, the play evolves from a drama to an *anti-poème*. A tragedy of love, it draws a parallel with the love of D. for Yvonne George. The objects and characters have a magic power, and D. contrasts the mediocre life of wakefulness and the marvelous life of dream.

Esslin, Martin. La place de l'étoile. *In his:* The theatre of the absurd. Revised and enlarged ed. Harmondsworth, Penguin books in association with Eyre & Spottiswoode, 1968, c 1961. 336 p. (Pelican books, A929) **9672**

D.'s play *La place de l'étoile* foreshadows the theater of the Absurd; it is an anti-poem similar to the *antipièce* of Ionesco.

Gelas, Bruno. Le lyrisme du spectacle. *In:* Desnos. *See* 9607. p. 113–24. **9673**

A study of D.'s only play *La place de l'étoile* and some characteristics shared by his scenarios. The "lyrisme du spectacle" awakened by the cinema is prevalent in texts which have a great potential force on the spectator's imagination. D. completed an "opera-film" which would have been a "spectacle total."

Yvan Goll
(i.e. Iwan Goll)
(Nos. 9674–9681)

JULIA F. COSTICH

Brion, Marcel. A poesia di Claire e Yvan Goll. Anh 19:14–22. **9674**
Brief survey of the works of both poets in Portuguese.

Brion, Marcel; Francis Carmody; Richard Exner; Jules Romains. Yvan Goll: quatre études. Seghers, 1956. 222 p. (Poètes d'aujourd'hui, 50) **9675**
Very useful introduction to life and work. Diverse responses to G.'s texts and ideas emphasizing his transcendence of personal and general problems. Followed by selection of texts.
Review: L.-G. Gros in CahS 337: 427–31.

Carmody, Francis J. The poetry of Yvan Goll. A biographical study. Caractères, 1956. 212 p. **9676**
Comprehensive study of G.'s poetry as it reflects the "inner causes" and "external events" of life. Situation of G. in relation to literary movements; useful treatment of less familiar works in French and German. List of poems by G. and bibliography of his works.

Exner, Richard. Surrealist elements in Yvan Goll's Franco-German poetry. Sym 11: 92–99, 1957. **9677**
Notes dream images, breaking of sense unities, visual elements, automatism, the supernatural as surrealist aspects. G. as coalescence of expressionism and surrealism. Even-handed treatment of controversial subject.

Goll, Claire. Goll et Breton. Eur 475–76: 109–10, 1968. **9678**
Highly partisan account of controversy and reconciliation between G. and Breton. Finds G. surrealist before the movement.

Kushner, Eva. Yvan Goll: deux langues, une âme. *In:* Proceedings of the fourth congress of the international comparative

literature association. The Hague, Mouton, 1966. p. 576–87. **9679**
Discusses implications of French and German usage in G.'s work. Finds him to be a truly bilingual poet.

Perkins, Vivien. Yvan Goll. An iconographical study of his poetry. Bonn, H. Bouvier u. Co. Verlag, 1970. 204 p. **9680**
Highly specialized review of possible sources for G.'s esoteric imagery, countering the biographical and concrete views of his texts. Suggests a vast background in occult and Biblical material and notes its personal use in specific poems.

Raymond, Louis-Marcel. Yvan Goll: choix de poèmes, précédé de la vie et l'œuvre d'Yvan Goll. Saint-Jean, P.Q., L'imprimerie Le Canada-Français, 1948. 50 p. **9681**
Reviews G.'s work in light of literary and biographical trends; includes a selection of texts.

Francis Picabia
(Nos. 9682–9699)

J. THEODORE JOHNSON, JR.

Biography

Everling, Germaine. L'anneau de Saturne. Fayard, 1970. 205 p. **9682**
Reproduces much of the material published previously in OLib and contains poems and letters by P. and Germaine and occasional brief texts by others. These, plus the numerous anecdotes, provide an invaluable insight into both the personal life of P. and the spirit of the times. Considerable space is given to anecdotes surrounding P. and his relations to dada, to other artists, writers, and musicians, down to *Relâche*. Emphasis on the fourteen years that run from the first encounter in 1917 down to the difficult years of rupture in the early 1930's.

Everling-Picabia, Germaine. C'était hier: Dada... OLib n.s. 109:119–78, 1955. **9683**
Lively, personal account of P. and his circle from 1917 to the early 1920's. Numerous letters and extracts from texts by P. and others. Appears much

expanded in *L'anneau de Saturne* 15 years later.

Guth, Paul. Francis Picabia ou le dadaïste en retraite. *In his:* Quarante contre un. Corrêa, 1947. p. 211–17. **9684**

An interview. Furnishes little biographical information but does provide good portrait of the man.

Le Bot, Marc. Picabia devant la guerre. RAEMD 1:33–44, 1965. **9685**

Biographical material concerning P. and the dada position towards World War I.

Sanouillet, Michel. Francis Picabia et *391*. V. 2. Eric Losfeld, 1966. 287 p. **9686**

A vast and scholarly introduction to the re-edition of the entire run of the review *391* published by Sanouillet six years previously. Contains important and richly documented background chapters on P.'s life from his birth to *291*, with special emphasis on the period of the Armory Show, the Stieglitz group, the reviews *291* and *391* as well as P.'s connections with Apollinaire. The bulk of the volume is an invaluable critical analysis and background of each number of *391* as it moves from Barcelona to New York, Zurich and Paris, as well as extensive notes to each page of each number of this most typographically complex dada review. A brief concluding chapter traces P. from the days of *391* down to his death in 1953. Extensive appendices include reproductions of the reviews *Cannibale* (nos. 1 and 2) and *La pomme de pins,* table of contents of the reviews *Camera work, 291, Cannibale, La pomme de pins, 491, 591, 691* and *Anthologie dada,* a genealogical tree of the P. family, unpublished letters and diverse documents relevant to the review *391* or to such P. productions as the ballet *Relâche,* an excellent bibliography, and a table of contents of the review *391,* and alphabetical index of texts and illustrations of *391,* and an index of proper names cited in this second volume by Sanouillet. An indispensable work not only for P. and his circle but for dada and other movements in the arts during the period 1917–24.

Reviews: M. D[écaudin] in RLM 183–88:252–55, 1968; P. Dhainhaut in CahDS 2:210–13, 1968; H. Gershman in BA 42:230–31, 1968.

Literary Work

Arnaud, Noël. La religion et la morale de Francis Picabia. [Verviers (Belgium), 1958. 34 p. Association Temps mêlés.] **9687**

A paean to P. and dada originally presented as a lecture, written in the appropriate dada manner, and abundantly illustrated with works by P. A mixture of nonsense, gibberish, and perceptive remarks.

Bonnet, Marguerite. A propos de Cortège: Apollinaire et Picabia. RLM 85–89:62–75, 1963. **9688**

The image that opens chapter two of P.'s *Jésus Christ Rastaquouère,* that of the bird who lays her eggs in the air, comes from Apollinaire's "Cortège" of 1912. Discusses similarities and connections between Apollinaire and P., and concludes that although he used an image from Apollinaire, P. found his "esprit nouveau" in 1920 to be rather timid. Although Apollinaire exercised considerable influence on P., it was perhaps P., his "Fille née sans mère" and his interest in machines, that influenced Apollinaire.

Caradec, François. Dada sans/avec parangon. CahDS 3:51–62, 1969. **9689**

Demonstrates through an analysis of "Une nuit d'échecs gras," a page composed for P.'s *391* by Tristan Tzara, that dada really did not upset typography but rather fully exploited its possibilities.

Hunt, Ronald. The Picabia/Breton axis. Artf 5, no. 1:16–25, 1966. **9690**

A very general survey of P.'s life and work from 1913 to 1922, the year of the closest relationship between Breton and P. Breton was then editor of *Littérature* to which P. contributed cover designs and poems. Principal contributions of Duchamp and P. to surrealism include the mechanomorphic and its derivative the ironic/erotic. Suggests that P. was amenable to the nature surrealism was assuming in 1924, but as surrealism embraced the politics of communism, P. converted to the values of capitalism.

Massot, Pierre de. Francis Picabia. Seghers, 1966. 192 p. (Poètes d'aujourd'hui, 146)
9691
An anthology of poetic texts, presented without critical apparatus, from various collections and periods beginning with *Cinquante-deux miroirs* (1917) down to the posthumous *Poèmes de Dingalari* (1955). Massot was a personal friend of P., and his lengthy introductory essay (p. 11–54) which focuses principally on P. the man, provides some useful biographical glimpses. References to the artistic climates through which P. passed, or as with the case of dada, which he helped to generate; only occasional connections attempted between the visual and verbal works. Bibliography lists works by P., including book illustration, principal studies on P., and a bibliography of the works of Pierre de Massot. Eight photographs of P.
Reviews: P. Dhainaut in CahS 53: 135–36, 1966; J.-J. Lebel in QL 13: 4–6, Oct. 1–15, 1966.

Revault D'Allonnes, Olivier. La rupture avec le passé: Francis Picabia à l'époque Dada. *In his:* La création artistique et les promesses de la liberté. Klincksieck, 1973. p. 119–41.
9692
Reviews selective biographical material and discusses summarily such topics as machines and particularly dada. Attempts, through a cursory analysis of certain literary pieces, to identify the creative mechanisms at work in P. Reproduces and discusses briefly the previously unpublished poem "Huile de foie de morue" of 1919.

Painting

Aisen, Maurice. The latest evolution in art and Picabia. CamW 41:14–21, June 1913.
9693
Somewhat pretentious assertions based in part on statements made by P. to the author. Concerns pictures exhibited at the Armory Show and at the Stieglitz Gallery "291." P.'s art awakens the psychic sense in us and reveals the realm of the *pensée pure* or infinity.

Camfield, William A. Francis Picabia. Salomon R. Guggenheim museum, 1970. 165 p.
9694
An exhibition catalog containing a lengthy, well-documented introductory essay tracing life of P. and relating his work to various movements and personalities in the arts and literature. Numerous reproductions, some in color, are accompanied by full references to exhibitions and critical studies. Excellent bibliography (p. 149–56) as well as a brief chronology and a list of exhibitions. A basic work.
Review: Anon. in A&A 6:48–53, 1971.

———. The machinist style of F. Picabia. ArtB 3–4:309–22, 1966.
9695
An authoritative article, constituting one of the most significant critical pieces on P. published to date as well as an extremely useful contribution to the question of machinism in 20th-century literature and art, the influences and consequences of which are explored in this article. Provides wealth of information with references to painters and poets. Examines the theme of machinism and explores its sexual symbolisms, particularly in the pictorial work of P.

Homer, William Innes. Picabia's Jeune fille américaine dans l'état de nudité and her friends. ArtB 57:110–15, 1975.
9696
A detailed analysis of the 1915 picture which seemingly presents American femininity in the guise of a spark plug but is perhaps a symbolic portrait of Mrs. Agnes Meyer, the spark that ignited new energies within the Stieglitz group. Evokes the 1913–15 period in P.'s life. Eleven illustrations.

Le Bot, Marc. Francis Picabia et la crise des valeurs figuratives. 1900–1925. Klincksieck, 1968. 208 p.
9697
An important and thorough examination of the most significant phases of P.'s art as it moved from impression through abstraction and Orphism to machinism and beyond. Relates P. to cubism and concentrates on the Armory Show, the Stieglitz group in New York, and the publication of the reviews *291* and *391*. Although the approach is biographical and historical in the main, stressing the pictorial aspects of P., several chapters examine P.'s literary

production both independently and as it relates to works by Apollinaire, Cendrars, Barzun and the context of dada. Emphasis on the psychological and thematic aspects of P.'s poetry, and points up influence of Nietzsche on P.'s thought. Appendices include a general chronology of the career and works of P. as well as a bibliography covering the period 1879 through 1924. 56 black and white reproductions.
Reviews: P. Dhainaut in CahDS 3: 77–80, 1969; J. Gauchon in Eur 475–76:356–57, 1968; H. Gershman in BA 43:223–24, 1969.

Mousseigne, Alain. Francis Picabia et le sphinx. GazBA 80:305–11, 1972.   **9698**
A good analysis of the Oedipus theme in a gouache of *Le sphinx* (1923) and a second painting (1926) of the theme. Interrelates this theme to P.'s writings and to his concern with the androgynous being in these works of his transparent period. Some references to the overt homosexuality in the *boîtes de nuit* of the 1920's.

Sanouillet, Michel. Picabia. L'œil du temps, 1964. 175 p.   **9699**
An abundantly illustrated succinct biography of P. with emphasis on his artistic production. Some plates in color; very limited references to contemporary writers. Contains a "Préface illusion" consisting of sentences drawn from the writings of P. by Sanouillet, and a chronology and an extensive bibliography by Poupard-Lieussou (p. 149–75). The latter includes works, reviews directed, scenarios and ballets, and numerous collaborations as well as homage volumes and article studies devoted to P., a list of exhibitions (down to 1964) and of books he illustrated. Reviews: Anon. in TLS 40, Jan. 21, 1965; J.-J. Lebel in QL 13:4–6, Oct. 1–15, 1966.

Georges Ribemont-Dessaignes (Nos. 9700–9709)

Laura Rièse

Arnaud, Noël. Déjà jadis. Cr 137:900–03, 1958.   **9700**
Speaks of R.'s career and his relationship with the dada movement. *Déjà*

jadis retraces the author's association with the surrealists and the modern tendencies in art. An interesting article on the continuation of the dada movement.

Béhar, Henri. Georges Ribemont-Dessaignes ou le Démon de l'absolu. *In his:* Etude sur le théâtre dada et surréaliste. Gallimard, 1967. 358 p. 110–45.   **9701**
Shows R. as a dadaist playwright although his first play *L'empereur de Chine* is in free verse and classical in construction. Each act is dedicated to a hero and corresponds to a certain point of view. R. succeeds, however, in creating through language a real dada manifesto. *Le serin muet* is a work of great clarity but were it not for the ways of non-communication, it could hardly be declared a dadaist play. A complete and intelligent analysis of R.'s place in the world of dada.

Corvin, Michel. Georges Ribemont-Dessaignes et Autant-Lara: l'affaire des prix. CahDS 1:183–91, 1966.   **9702**
Exchange of letters between R. and Mme Autant-Lara. Biographical details.

———. Georges Ribemont-Dessaignes et le laboratoire Art et action. CahDS 1:160–82, 1966.   **9703**
R. was most prolific contributor to the Laboratoire Art et action. We are given an account of the scenic realization of the plays, full of ideograms and geometric synthesis. Too great a concentration leading to obscurity. The presentation, however, satisfied the author.

———. Georges Ribemont-Dessaignes: Larmes de couteau. CahDS 1:144–59, 1966.   **9704**
Text presenting R.'s play, *Larmes de couteau.* Play was received coldly and criticized for its accumulation of clichés and metaphors. Possibly some lack of comprehension.

Esslin, Martin. The tradition of the absurd. *In his:* The theatre of the absurd. Doubleday, 1969. p. 345–49.   **9705**
Places R. as the chief dadaist and speaks of his participation in the movement. Shows how in his early plays he tries to create a poetic universe through nonsense and violence which meant

liberation for the dadaists. A precise appreciation.

Hommage à Georges Ribemont-Dessaignes. Marg 152:1–60, 1973.   **9706**

The entire issue is dedicated to R. Ayguesparse shows him as a poet, novelist, playwright, a witness of his time, and not just a destructive writer but an inventor of new ideas. R. gives his autobiography. Some see his diversity, others the role he played between dadaists and surrealists. He was ahead of his time. The influence of his play *L'empereur de Chine* in Italy brought with it the dada movement. His influence upon others is studied. An important number for the understanding of the man.

Jotterand, Frank. Georges Ribemont-Dessaignes. Présentation par Frank Jotterand. Choix de textes. Seghers, 1966. 192 p. (Poètes d'aujourd'hui, 153)   **9707**

Takes too long to portray R. in his property in the south of France. Many passages of *Déjà-jadis* quoted rather than appreciated. Too short a chapter on R. as dadaist painter. The same fault when he discusses him as a musician and his liking for contemporary music. His chapter on R.'s theater is neither informative nor critical. Differs very much from Béhar. We have also a skeleton idea of the theme of his novels. The last chapter gives a better personal appreciation of R.'s poetry. The book has importance since it reveals his manifold trends and affiliations with dada and surrealism. A choice of texts follows. Provides information about the man rather than literary criticism.

Review: A. Noël in QL no. 23:13–14, 1967.

Queneau, Raymond. Conversation avec Georges Ribemont-Dessaignes. *In his:* Bâtons, chiffres et lettres. Gallimard, 1965. p. 35–45.   **9708**

Queneau succeeds in getting out of R. his ideas on surrealism and the importance of language. R. explains how he composed his successive books. Very revealing for understanding of art of R.

Sanouillet, Michel. Dada à Paris. Pauvert, 1965. 649 p.   **9709**

R. is mentioned throughout the book. Insights into the role he played in the dada movement; his numerous contribu-tions, his friendships and quarrels; his relationship with Picabia and his paintings. R. is seen as a very eclectic character playing a role in practically every field. Much biographical information dispersed throughout book.

Raymond Roussel
(Nos. 9710–9766)

JEANINE P. PLOTTEL

Special Number

Raymond Roussel. Ed. by Jules Ferry. Biz 34–35:1–160, 1964.   **9710**

One of the most important volumes devoted to R. Significant articles have been analyzed separately under the appropriate headings.

Reviews: G. Deleuze in AeLet 18: 12–13, Jan. 26–Feb. 1, 1966; P. Guyotat in FrOb 742:13, July 23, 1964; O. Hahn in Exp 696:70–71, Oct. 25, 1964 and in TM 218:163–72, 1964; R. Lacôte in LetF 1044:2, Sept. 3–9, 1964.

Biography

Caburet, Bernard. Raymond Roussel. Contribution à une étude par Bernard Caburet, avec un choix de textes... Seghers, 1968. 188 p. (Poètes d'aujourd'hui, 180)   **9711**

A general study of R. dealing with language, representation of reality, personality of the writer, his suicide, and the hermetic component of the work which Caburet links to obsession with time, secrecy, and identity. Caburet includes an interesting anthology of R.'s own texts and a useful chronology and bibliography.

Caradec, François. Vie de Raymond Roussel. Pauvert, 1973. 400 p.   **9712**

Detailed, fastidious examination of any and all facts known about R.'s life and the circumstances of publication and performance of his works.

Reviews: Anon. in TLS 67:415, 1973; J. Frémond in NL 2371:5, March 5, 1973; R. Kanters in FL 1401:16, March 24, 1973; J.-J. Levèque in NL 2371, March 5, 1973; O. de Magny in QL 161:5–6, April 1, 1973; P. Toutain in NL 2371:4, March 5, 1973.

Chatard, Jean, and Robert Momeux. Interview de Michel Ney, duc d'Elchingen. *In:* Raymond Roussel. *See* 9710. p. 98–105. **9713**

An interview with R.'s nephew and heir, which is a source for much information found in lengthier works. Ney believes R. killed himself because he had no money left, and hints that R.'s letters may have been kept hidden by his publisher, Alphonse Lemerre.

Cocteau, Jean. Fac-similé d'une carte de Jean Cocteau à Jean-Jacques Pauvert. *In:* Raymond Roussel. *See* 9710. p. 34–35. **9714**

This short article establishes that Cocteau knew R. and held *Impressions d'Afrique* and *Locus solus* to be masterpieces. The suggestion that perhaps *Les enfants terribles* owes a certain flavor to R. bears further investigation.

Jacob, Max. Lettres de Saint-Benoît-sur-Loire. Barb 6:35–38, 1968. **9715**

Useful for those interested in R.'s relationship with surrealism.

Janet, Pierre. De l'angoisse à l'extase. V. 1. Félix Alcan, 1928. 132–36, 146–47. *Also (partial reprint) in:* Roussel, Raymond. Comment j'ai écrit certains de mes livres. Jean-Jacques Pauvert, 1963. p. 127–32. **9716**

R. was a patient of Janet who wrote up his "case history" changing his client's name to Martial. He quotes R. extensively and comments on the writer's feelings of glory and of having attained the absolute as well as on his anxiety, his hatred of newness and change, and the rituals of his existence.

Ricardou, Jean. Disparition élocutoire. *In:* Sciascia, Leonardo. Actes relatifs à la mort de Raymond Roussel. Eds. de l'Herne, 1972. p. 9–30. **9717**

Ricardou adjusts facts surrounding R.'s death to fit significant words and signs of the writer's life script so that, in the tradition of Plato's Cratylus, reality emblematizes language.

Roussel, Raymond. Comment j'ai écrit certains de mes livres. A. Lemerre, 1935. 477 p. *Also:* Jean-Jacques Pauvert, 1963. 323 p. **9718**

The title essay sets forth most of the biographical facts about R. More im-

portant, however, is the key, the "meta-text," the higher explanation of all R.'s works. In summary, his procedures were to select two almost identical words, to take each in a sense other than its obvious one, and to link it to the other such words, seeking always the highest degree of arbitrariness possible.

Sciascia, Leonardo. Atti relativi alla morte di Raymond Roussel. Con un saggio di Giovanni Macchia. Palermo, Ediz. Esse, 1971. 79 p. *Trans.:* Actes relatifs à la mort de Raymond Roussel. Trad. de l'italien par Giovanni Joppolo et Gérard Julien Salvy. Textes de Jean Ricardou et Gérard Julien Salvy. Eds. de l'Herne, 1972. 91 p. **9719**

Sciascia prints the Italian police inquest of the circumstances of R.'s probable suicide. The Italian novelist, fascinated by the mysterious death of a mysterious artist, shows how the inconsistencies, contradictions and incongruities take shape as in a detective story.

Review: C. Ambroise in Monde 8213:23, June 11, 1971.

General Studies

André, Robert. La stèle de Raymond Roussel. *In:* Raymond Roussel. *See* 9710. p. 89–92. **9720**

The existential dilemma of R.'s aspirations as exemplified by one of his earliest works, *La doublure.*

Attal, Jean-Pierre. L'image métaphysique. MerF 1208:270–95, 1964. *Also in his:* L'image métaphysique et autres essais. Gallimard, 1969. **9721**

Interesting essay showing R.'s place in modern sensibility.

Blanchot, Maurice. Le problème de Wittgenstein: Roussel. NRF 22:866–75, 1963. *Also in his:* L'entretien infini. Gallimard, 1966. p. 493–97. **9722**

A brilliant essay comparing R.'s approach to language and reality with positions of Wittgenstein and Flaubert. How do words express things? Are there too many things and not enough words, or too many words seeking out things? Is language an adequate expression of reality?

Borzic, Jean. Roussel en Sorbonne. *In:* Raymond Roussel. *See* 9710. p. 67–72.
9723
A theoretical appraisal of the relationship between language and reality in the works of R. and Mallarmé. Interesting speculations on meaning and poetic structure.

Breton, André. Fronton-virage. *In:* Ferry, Jean. Une étude sur Raymond Roussel. *See* 9710. p. 9–34. *Also in his:* La clé des champs. Pauvert, 1967. p. 218–43.   **9724**
Breton suggests that although at present we read R. with pleasure and little understanding, comprehension would increase our enjoyment. The key should be sought in traditions of alchemy and initiatory literature.

———. Raymond Roussel. *In his:* Anthologie de l'humour noir. Eds. du sagittaire, 1940. p. 180–83.   **9725**
Especially interesting for students of surrealism.

Butor, Michel. Sur les procédés de Raymond Roussel. *In his:* Répertoire. Eds. de minuit, 1960. p. 173–85. *Also in his:* Essais sur les modernes. Gallimard, 1960, 1964. p. 199–221.   **9726**
A good general introduction to R., and useful for studying sources of literary techniques of the "nouveau roman."

Caradec, François. La machine à imprimer Roussel ou l'impression des Impressions. *In:* Raymond Roussel. *See* 9710. p. 58–62.   **9727**
The original editions of many of R.'s works were meant to be read without cutting any pages. Typographical and formal presentation were linked to contents: for R. as for Mallarmé a book's physical appearance mattered greatly and reflected intentions expressed both by message and medium.

———, **and Juan Esteban Fassio.** La machine à lire Roussel, ou la machine à lire les Nouvelles impressions d'Afrique. *In:* Raymond Roussel. *See* 9710. p. 63–66.
9728
Describes a machine for reading R., influenced by a previous one built for the Surrealist Exhibition of 1937 by J. B. Brunius.

Carrouges, Michel. Une étude sur Raymond Roussel. MNP 73:29–34, 1953.   **9729**
Does not believe that R.'s works have a third secret meaning beyond the implicit and explicit ones, but that all meanings stated comprise the sense and signification of the inner text which has no key. "L'homme qui a perdu son ombre," such is R.

———. Raymond Roussel. *In his:* Les machines célibataires. Arcanes, 1954. p. 66–92.   **9730**
Examines bachelor machines of *Locus solus* and *Impressions d'Afrique,* and compares them with those of Duchamp, Kafka, Jarry. As in Kafka, transgression of the Law causes heroes to be struck down, but redemption is always possible through illumination ultimately brought about by cataclysm and catastrophe.
Review: J. Mayoux in Biz 1–2, May–Oct. 1955.

Cocteau, Jean. [Raymond Roussel] *In his:* Opium. Stock, 1930. p. 186–98. *Also:* Raymond Roussel. *In his:* Poésie critique I. Gallimard, 1959. p. 133–40.   **9731**
A brilliant appraisal of R. that many critics quote.

Dali, Salvador. Raymond Roussel. Nouvelles impressions d'Afrique. Le surréalisme au service de la révolution. 6, 1933. 41 p.
9732
R. was just about Dali's favorite writer so that this article should be noted by students of surrealist art and literature.

Dhainaut, Pierre. Machines à écrire. A propos de Raymond Roussel et de quelques surréalistes. EspCr 6:14–22, 1966.   **9733**
An interesting article and one of the first to appear in an American journal.

———. Raymond Roussel oseur d'influence. *In:* Raymond Roussel. *See* 9710. p. 73–74.
9734
An excellent study of R.'s influence on Marcel Duchamp.

Dinguirard, Jean-Claude. La logique de Roussel. SubP 6:60–68, 1968.   **9735**
An analysis of the first canto of *Nouvelles impressions d'Afrique.* Among the most intelligent articles about R.

showing the mechanisms underlying his poetic structures.

Dujardin, Edouard. Le cas de Locus solus. *In:* Raymond Roussel. *See* 9710. p. 56–67. **9736**

That a precursor of James Joyce, the originator of the stream of consciousness technique, was one of R.'s early admirers seems one of the ironies of modern literary criticism. The kinship between R. and Joyce manifests itself not only through their common conception of language as generating thought, but through their link to Dujardin, author of *Les lauriers sont coupés*. Reprinted from RevEp May 1923.

Eluard, Paul. Raymond Roussel, l'étoile au front. *In:* Raymond Roussel. *See* 9710. p. 34. **9737**

A prose poem on R., of interest to students of surrealist sensibility. Reprinted from *La révolution surréaliste* 4, 1925.

Ferry, Jean. L'Afrique des Impressions. Jean-Jacques Pauvert, 1967. 207 p. **9738**

A marvelous guide to R.'s *Impressions d'Afrique* combining erudition and literary insight with whimsey and wit. Ferry examines the work's structure, its geography, chronology, characters, philology, and philosophy with bravado worthy of Lewis Carroll.

———. Analyse de deux ouvrages de Raymond Roussel. *In:* Anthologie de l'humour noir. Ed. by André Breton. Eds. du sagittaire, 1940. *Also:* Pauvert, 1970. [c. 1966]. p. 183–88. **9739**

Contains an outline of the structure of *Locus solus*. An indispensable guide for critics and readers.

———. A propos de Flio: premières constations. *In:* Raymond Roussel. *See* 9710. p. 14–17. **9740**

Ferry describes a ms. of R. published in the same issue of *Bizarre* which seems to be a typed first draft full of typographical errors, but which may eventually prove to be the Rosetta stone of R. studies.

———. Une autre étude sur Raymond Roussel. *In:* Raymond Roussel. *See* 9710. p. 106–57. *Also:* Une autre étude sur Raymond Roussel. Leçons de petit apparat

sur les chants 1, 3 et 4 des Nouvelles impressions d'Afrique. Collège de Pataphysique, 1964. 54 p. **9741**

An intelligent, penetrating and extremely amusing exegesis of a very difficult work, cantos I, III, and IV of *Nouvelles impressions d'Afrique* (canto II was the subject of an earlier Ferry book), an important, but neglected text of modern French literature, which should be read by all interested in R. and surrealism.

———. Une étude sur Raymond Roussel. Précédé de Fronton virage par André Breton. Arcanes, 1953. 215 p. **9742**

An impressive study of the second canto of *Nouvelles impressions d'Afrique*, "Champ de bataille des Pyramides," showing how R.'s structures function and generate their own logic. Ferry anticipates concerns of present literary criticism, and many of his examples may serve as illustrations of theoretical speculations on poetic production.

Foucault, Michel. Raymond Roussel. Gallimard, 1963. 210 p. (Le chemin) **9743**

Foucault believes that R.'s work defines its spatial language as it seeks to explore the hidden duality of the visible and the visible duality of the hidden: visible and invisible repeat themselves, and this constant dissociation coincides with language itself.

Reviews: Anon. in TLS 17–18, Jan. 9, 1964; P. Berger in LetF 981:3, June 6–11, 1963; P. Dhainaut in EnLA 23:54–57, 1964; G. Ferdière in CahGFM 31–33, Dec. 1964; H. Juin in NL 1879:2, Sept. 5, 1963; G. Macchia in CdS Aug. 30, 1963; J. Rampolla in Aus 19:39–42, 1963; A. Robert in NRF 129:489–94, 1963; R. Sorin in Biz 34–35:75–76, 1964; J. Starobinski in LetN 11:207–09, 1963.

Guerrero Zamora. Raymond Roussel y los objetos insólitos. *In his:* Historial del teatro contemporáneo. V. 1. Barcelona, Juan Flors, 1961. p. 43–53. **9744**

Very interesting article which suggests several parallels between R. and Iberian literary and metaphysical tradition not found elsewhere.

Heppenstall, Rayner. Raymond Roussel. A critical guide. London, Calder & Boyars,

1966. 97 p. *Also:* Raymond Roussel. A critical study. Berkeley & Los Angeles, Univ. of California press, 1967. 97 p.
9745

An excellent introduction to R. in English. Chapters are devoted to the life, early poems and stories, *Impressions d'Afrique, Locus solus, L'étoile au front* and *La poussière de soleils, Nouvelles impressions d'Afrique, Flio* and *Documents pour servir de canevas* and to a review of bibliographical material. Reviews: Anon. in TLS 1061, Nov. 24, 1966; J. Ashbery in TBR 58–60, 62, Oct. 29, 1962; M. Douglas in List 2059:328–30, Sept. 12, 1968; J. Duncan in MLR 65:913–14, 1970; J. Matthews in FR 41:430–31, 1967; P. O'Connor in TC 1032:42–43, 1967; G. Steiner in NY 206–12, Oct. 28, 1967; J. Weightman in Obs 9153:27, Dec. 11, 1966.

Héroult, Michel. Ciel naturel et position astrologique de Raymond Roussel. *In:* Raymond Roussel. *See* 9710. p. 34–35.
9746

One of very few serious articles applying astrology to literary analysis.

Jean, Marcel, and Arpad Mezei. Raymond Roussel et le problème du langage. Le maître du temps. La pierre philosophale. *In their:* Genèse de la pensée moderne. Corrêa, 1950. p. 175–215.   **9747**

Analysis of R.'s use of language within the structure of the relationship between time and ego. The suggestion is that R. belongs to a hermetic, astrological tradition, and is a link in the chain of Western philosophy of language that includes Plato's *Cratylus,* Rabelais' *Pantagruel,* Leibnitz, Fabre d'Olivet. Three very important essays.

Jenny, Laurent. Structure et fonctions du cliché. A propos des Impressions d'Afrique. Poét 12:495–517, 1972.   **9748**

An important application of Barthes' and Riffaterre's theories on clichés. Jenny believes that R.'s "procédé" did not allow him to generate original literary productions, but only to formulate cultural and literary stereotypes of predetermined social structures.

Kristeva, Julia. La productivité dite texte. Comm 11:59–83, 1965. *Also in her:*

Sémèiotiké: recherches pour une sémanalyse. Seuil, 1969. p. 208–45.   **9749**

An important contribution to the problematics of text grammar. Is it possible for a text to generate its own meanings without reference to any other reality except that of its own language? R.'s *Impressions d'Afrique* is used as a case in point.

Leiris, Michel. Conception et réalité chez Raymond Roussel. Cr 89:821–35, 1954. *In:* Roussel, Raymond. Epaves. Ed. by François Caradec. Pauvert, 1973. p. 9–34. *Trans.:* Conception and reality in the work of Raymond Roussel. A&L 2:12–26, 1964.   **9750**

Most important source for students, scholars and critics dealing with R. Leiris, an early admirer, knew the writer well and had preserved the work for posterity. Perhaps the best single article on R. to date.

————. Le voyageur et son ombre. *In:* Raymond Roussel. *See* 9710. p. 77–78.
9751

An article which quotes several R. letters written during his trips to Australia, Tahiti and Persia. Reprinted from *La bête noire* 1: April 1, 1935.

Macchia, Giovanni. L'ultima macchina di Roussel ovvero la luce, l'estasi e il sangue. *In:* Sciascia, Leonardo. Atti relativi alla morte di Raymond Roussel. Palermo, Ediz. Esse, 1971. p. 6–33.   **9752**

Macchia reconciles the contradictions of R.'s works: *homo faber* and *homo ludens,* reactionary and precursor of surrealism, an admirer of machines and a seeker of ecstasy.

Matthews, J. H. Raymond Roussel. *In his:* Surrealism and the novel. Ann Arbor, Univ. of Michigan press, 1966. p. 41–55.
9753

An intelligent appraisal of R.'s place in the history of the surrealistic novel.

Montesquiou, Robert de. Un auteur difficile. *In his:* Elus et appelés. Emile Paul, 1921. p. 189–223.   **9754**

One of the earliest articles about R. and one that has not been appraised fairly. Very worthwhile reading for an insight into the "decadent" aspect of R.'s sensibility.

Plottel, Jeanine P. Analecture d'un conte. Nanon. Le manifeste et le caché, langages surréalistes et autres. SiEc 1:125–32, 1974. **9755**
An analysis of one of R.'s earliest works, combining a linguistic and a psychoanalytic approach.

————. Roussel's mechanisms of language. CahDS 2:23–27, 1972. **9756**
The study of R.'s mechanisms of language is given a linguistic and psychoanalytical orientation.

————. Structures and counterstructures in Raymond Roussel's Impressions d'Afrique. CahDS 5:11–19, 1975. **9757**
An article showing how multiple meanings destroy meaning, annihilate the referent, but, from a psychoanalytic perspective, express reality.

Ricardou, Jean. L'activité roussellienne. TelQ 39:78–99, 1969. *Also in his (rev.):* Pour une théorie du nouveau roman. Seuil, 1971. p. 91–117. **9758**
A study of how R.'s techniques and works are relevant to the "nouveau roman" and to modern literature.

Robbe-Grillet, Alain. Enigmes et transparence chez Raymond Roussel. Cr 199:1027–33, 1963. *Also in his:* Pour un nouveau roman. Eds. de minuit, 1963. p. 70–76. *Trans.:* Riddles and transparencies in Raymond Roussel. *In his:* Snapshots and Towards a new novel. Trans. by Barbara Wright. London, Calder & Boyars, 1964. p. 97–102. *Also in his:* For a new novel; essays on fiction. Trans. by Richard Howard. New York, Grove press, 1966. p. 79–87. **9759**
An especially interesting article for the student of the "nouveau roman" as it shows the development of its technique through R. and surrealism.
Review: J. Ferry in Biz 34–35:72, 1964.

Rousselot, Jean. La logique implacable de Raymond Roussel. *In his:* Mort ou survie du langage. Société générale d'éditions, 1969. p. 137–46. **9760**
Deals unsuccessfully with R. in the context of Valéry's statement that literature aims to "nous défaire par la parole de l'oppression de ce que nous sommes."

Schifres, Alain. Entretiens avec Arrabal. Belfond, 1961. p. 117–18. **9761**
Arrabal reveals R. as an important influence. Interesting for appraising R.'s impact on modern literature.

Schneider, Pierre. La fenêtre ou piège à Roussel. CahS 306:290–306, 1951. **9762**
One of the earliest and best articles on R.

Sollers, Philippe. Logicus solus. *In his:* Logiques. Seuil, 1968. p. 124–32. **9763**
A penetrating article by a leading French novelist.

Veschambre, Christiane. Sur les Impressions d'Afrique. Poét 1:64–78, 1970. **9764**
An excellent article studying technique, structure, and textures of R.'s book.

Vitrac, Roger. Raymond Roussel. NRF 173:162–76, 1928. *Also in:* Raymond Roussel. *See* 9710. p. 79–84. **9765**
A long study of R. by a surrealist who calls him a "Marcel Proust du rêve." Essential article for the study of surrealist literary taste and criticism.

Drama

Ashbery, John. Les versions scéniques d'Impressions d'Afriques et de Locus solus. *In:* Raymond Roussel. *See* 9710. p. 19–67. **9766**
Ashbery believes that while R. himself seems to have adapted *Impressions d'Afrique* for the stage, the version of *Locus solus* was written by Pierre Frondaie, a successful novelist of the Twenties. The article compares novels and plays, summarizes critical reception, and includes programs and pictures of performances as well as the documents under consideration.

Philippe Soupault
(Nos. 9767–9783)

HANNAH C. ZINNI

Biography

Breton, André. Entretiens 1913–1952. Gallimard, 1952. 317 p. *Also:* Gallimard, 1969. 315 p. **9767**

References to S. *passim*. Most important are found on p. 36–37 where Breton discusses S.'s original approach to poetry, his acute sense of what is modern, and his refusal to modify his works once written. Later (p. 56–58) discusses *Les champs magnétiques* and the plays which S. coauthored with him.

Reviews: P. Emmanuel in RduC 15: 179–81, 1953; A. Parinaud in Arts 384:1, 4, 1952; A. Rousseaux in FL 2, Oct. 11, 1952.

Guth, Paul. Philippe Soupault et le surréalisme. RdP 59:135–42, 1952.   **9768**

Excellent, comprehensive description of the surrealist movement from S.'s point of view as obtained through interview. Includes S.'s role in the beginnings of surrealism and the reasons for his later separation from the group. For S., surrealism is total liberation and the beginning of a new era in poetry.

————. Philippe Soupault n'aime pas les bourgeois. *In his:* Quarante contre un. V. 1. Corrêa, 1947. p. 261–67.   **9769**

Short, witty sketch of S.'s life and works through World War II. Numerous direct quotes from S. References to his relationship with Apollinaire, Breton, Eluard and Aragon. Remarks concerning his family history and his fierce rejection of the bourgeois way of life.

Mabire, Jean-M. Entretien avec Philippe Soupault. EtCi 40–42:29–33, 1965.   **9770**

Very interesting interview in which S. reveals the possibilities surrealists saw in film and the disappointments they encountered. Ideally, film is the best mode of expression for dreams, but commercial problems and the deformation of surrealism in films by Cocteau and Dali were discouraging. S. still believes, however, in the unique non-intellectual seeing power of the camera.

Mora, Edith. Poésie 58, 8: Philippe Soupault. NL 1619:1, 7, 1958.   **9771**

Based on interview. S.'s life and works are a search for liberty. For him, surrealism is the poet's determination to speak the truth in his own inner language. Surrealism has had an earth-shaking effect, and it survives in the works of artists such as Ionesco and

Boulez. Complete in one part although a second part is indicated at conclusion.

Rajk, Etienne. Rencontre avec Philippe Soupault. Paru 14:17–20, 1946.   **9772**

Interview concerning S.'s writings during World War II, in particular his book on Eugène Labiche. His various journalistic activities during the war are recounted, including his work in the U.S.A. and South America.

Ribadeau-Dumas, François. Carrefour de visages; Philippe Soupault. RMon 174: 268–73, 1926.   **9773**

Interesting, though overly critical, portrait of S. based upon an interview. Despite his anti-bourgeois protestations, S. seems to be bourgeois in taste and education. His sensitivity and active spirit are responsible for his individuality. At heart, he is a generous young poet whose political activity should not be taken seriously.

Romus, André-Marie. Entretien avec Philippe Soupault. MRo 14:109–20, 1964.   **9774**

Comprehensive interview touching on many important subjects: the necessity of scandal in poetry, the origin of *Les champs magnétiques*, the break with the surrealist group and the vocation of journalism, the creative process, the influence of Reverdy and Lautréamont, the experiences with Proust and Joyce. S. responds well to all questions, giving up a generous view of himself as poet.

Soupault, Philippe. Gide et nos vingt ans. RdP 54:140–45, 1947.   **9775**

Describes personal reaction as young man to Gide and his works.

————. Journées d'apprentissage. RdP 52: 85–90, 1945.   **9776**

Effects of prison life, as witnessed and experienced by S. during World War II.

————. Que reste-t-il de nos amours? Réa 166:82–88, 120–21, 1959.   **9777**

S. discusses origins and importance of dadaist movement. Describes his reactions to Apollinaire, whom he considered a *voyant*, and to the Russian Revolution. Speaks of Breton, Aragon, and Théodore Fraenkel and of their postwar ideas about literature. Illustrated.

General Studies

Dupuy, Henry-Jacques. Philippe Soupault. Présentation de Jacques Dupuy. Choix de textes, bibliographie... Seghers, 1957. 221 p. (Poètes d'aujourd'hui, 58) **9778**
Thorough and perceptive account of S.'s life and works with detailed attention to his role in the surrealist movement. Excerpts from S.'s prose and poetical works follow text. Chronological bibliography included. Bits of contemporary criticism also. Sketches and photos appropriate.
Review: E. Noulet in her *Alphabet critique 1924–1964.* V. 2. Brussels, Presses univ. de Bruxelles, 1965. p. 63.

————. Philippe Soupault ou la poésie spontanée. Rens 17:142–45, 1945. **9779**
Sensitive study of S.'s style. Its semantic simplicity, sounds, and rhythm seem to arise spontaneously from a mind at ease but open to infinitely diverse impressions.

Grossman, Manuel L. Dada. Paradox, mystification, and ambiguity in European literature. Bobbs-Merrill, 1971. 192 p. **9780**
In chapter on dada movement in Europe, recalls S.'s war experiences, his disillusionment and suffering. Tells how S. and his friends Breton and Aragon came to know dada and to include it in their review *Littérature.* Also describes his part in provocation demonstrations staged by the dadaists. When dada failed, S. found it hard to give up.

Heist, Walter. Erinnerung an Philippe Soupault. NRs 82:519–28, 1971. **9781**
A treatment of S.'s literary role in Germany, his literary efforts with Breton, a discussion of his novels, and a consideration of his systematic traveling as a *Tagesschriftsteller.*

Légoutière, Edmond. Le surréalisme. Masson, 1972. 232 p. (Ensembles littéraires) **9782**
Six short pages include a brief biographical note, concise commentaries on *Rose des vents* and *Westwego,* and

annotated excerpts from these two collections.

Matthews, J. H. Philippe Soupault (1897–). *In his:* Surrealist poetry in France. Syracuse, Syracuse univ. press, 1969. p. 17–30. **9783**
Discusses S.'s place in history of surrealism and demonstrates Apollinaire's great influence on him. A study of examples reveals how the poet transforms reality in accordance with his needs and aspirations. A sensitive article which includes English translations of poems cited.

Tristan Tzara
(pseud. of Sami Rosenstock)
(Nos. 9784–9845)

ELMER PETERSON AND
MICHELINE TISON-BRAUN

Bibliography

Bibliographie des œuvres de Tristan Tzara. Berggruen, 1951. 13 p. **9784**
This plaquette lists only 35 books and 8 prefaces written by T. between 1916 and 1950 and is therefore very incomplete. [EP]

Editions and Texts

Béhar, Henri. Inédits de Tristan Tzara. *In:* Tristan Tzara. *See* 9789. p. 56–112. **9785**
The following unpublished texts by T. are briefly introduced and presented: "L'homme à branches" (a poetic text); two lectures (one on a dada exhibition, the other on Jarry); a lecture on a dada exhibition in 1958; another article on Jarry; six poems; an article by T. on the meaning of anagrams. [MTB]

Tzara, Tristan. Œuvres complètes. V. 1. Ed. établie, présentée et annotée par Henri Béhar. Flammarion, 1975. 752 p. **9786**

In process of publication. [EP]

————. Sept manifestes dada. Jean Budry, 1924. 97 p. *Also (rev.):* Sept manifestes dada, lampisteries. Pauvert, 1963. 154 p. **9787**
The 1963 Pauvert edition is the most important because, in addition to these

essential dada manifestoes, it includes the *lampisteries* section, a selection of 23 short dada notes written by T. between 1917 and 1922. [EP]
Review: R. Lacôte in LetF 1005:2, 1963.

Special Numbers

Hommage à Tzara. Str 2:1–42, 1964. **9788**
The significant articles have been analyzed separately. [EP]

Tristan Tzara. Eur 555–56:3–280, 1975. **9789**
Special number. Contents analyzed separately. [MTB]

Biography

Aragon, Louis. L'aventure terrestre de Tristan Tzara. LetF 1010:1, 6–7, Jan. 2–8, 1964. *Also in:* Tristan Tzara. *See* 9789. p. 8–17. **9790**
Meditating on T.'s death, Aragon recalls his meeting with "this small man of quicksilver" and their lifelong friendship. [MTB]

————. L'homme Tzara. *In:* Tristan Tzara. *See* 9789. p. 18–38. **9791**
Comments on the notes in *Seeds and bran* showing how T. was led to revolution by his meditations on language; stresses T.'s loyalty to the Party, with which he did not always agree but which represented his hope for the future. [MTB]

B., J. Une conférence de Tzara. Esp 132:659–61, 1947. **9792**
Fascinating account of T.'s Sorbonne speech which was heckled by André Breton. [EP]

Codrescu, Andrei. Introducing Tristan Tzara 1. Works 2, no. 3:12–15, 1970. **9793**
Interesting discussion of the pre-dada T., his Romanian influences, and his collaboration with the literary magazine ONE. [EP]

Fauchereau, Serge. Le dadaïsme parisien. Cr 318:997–1012, 1973. **9794**
Thorough study of T.'s activities in Paris in the early 1920's. Valuable for references to Romanian reviews to which T. contributed. [EP]

————. En songeant à Tristan Tzara. *In:* Tristan Tzara. *See* 9789. p. 145–51. **9795**
Notes, among random memories, how T.'s Romanian poems show a slight estrangement which later evolved into dada's full-blown revolt. [MTB]

————. Tristan Tzara, dada et l'expressionnisme. Cr 303–04:752–80, 1972. **9796**
Excellent résumé of the Zurich years, the importance of Hugo Ball, and German expressionism on T. [EP]

————. Tristan Tzara et l'avant-garde roumaine. Cr 300:416–29, 1972. **9797**
Important article treating T.'s pre-Zurich literary influences and efforts. [EP]

Gaucheron, Jacques. Esquisse pour un portrait. *In:* Tristan Tzara. *See* 9789. p. 33–55. **9798**
A profile of T. after the Second World War, stressing human elements in his works that go far beyond dada. [MTB]

————, **and Henri Béhar.** Chronologie de Tristan Tzara. *See* 9789. p. 231–40. **9799**
A list of biographical and bibliographical data presented year by year. [MTB]

Lindsay, Jack. Tristan Tzara. *In his:* Meetings with poets. London, Frederick Muller, 1968. p. 211–27. **9800**
Anecdotes about author's meetings with T. between 1947 and 1963, and their common efforts in the peace movement. Author translates *Une route seul soleil* and describes T.'s poetry as a "movement from deliberate chaos" to "final linking of the lonely poet's struggle with the struggle for the classless society in which alienation can be overcome." [EP]

Soupault, Philippe. Souvenir de Tristan Tzara. *In:* Tristan Tzara. *See* 9789. p. 3–7. **9801**
Recalls T.'s arrival in Paris in 1919, the rowdy years of dada and how Soupault's friendship with T. endured in spite of political and literary schisms within the group. [MTB]

Vitrac, Roger. Tristan Tzara va cultiver ses vices. *In:* Tristan Tzara. *See* 9789. p. 135–37. **9802**

Answering an interview (*Journal du peuple,* April 14, 1923) on the subject: "Why do you write," T. asserts his intention to destroy both literature and individuality in order to achieve communication of "elements of life" by each man to all the others. [MTB]

General Studies

Cassou, Jean. Preface. *In:* Tzara, Tristan. Morceaux choisis. Bordas, 1947. p. 5–12. **9803**

Slim but useful volume which gives some idea of the range of T.'s poetic career. [EP]
Reviews: L.-G. Gros in CahS 284: 646–49, 1947; G. Ribemont-Dessaignes in Cr 28:778–87, 1948.

Caws, Mary-Ann. Quelques approximations de Tzara. *In:* Tristan Tzara. *See* 9789. p. 192–201. **9804**

A stylistic study, based on corrections in T.'s mss., showing his effort towards order and concentration, his habit of constructing a poem from one nucleus and his frequent linking of elements by sound rather than sense. [MTB]

————. Tristan Tzara. *In her:* The poetry of dada and surrealism. Princeton, Princeton univ. press, 1970. p. 95–135. **9805**

Excellent analysis of thematic links in T.'s poetry such as vivid color, motion, a certain direction or grouping, geometrical figures, and light or its variants. [EP]
Reviews: C. Hackett in FS 3:355–59, 1973; D. Nyren in LJ 95:2262, 1970; R. Shattuck in NYRB 23–24, June 1, 1972.

————. Introduction. *In:* Tzara, Tristan. Approximate man & other writings. Detroit, Wayne state univ. press, 1973. p. 17–37. **9806**

Excellent translations. Valuable notes explain T.'s creative process. Lucid introduction traces the evolution of T.'s poetry detailing structure and themes and explaining how "poetry is for T. the transcendence of language from its tragic incompetence and necessary artifice into the purest demonstration of mental freedom." [EP]

Clancier, G.-E. Itinéraire de Tristan Tzara. Font 61:479–86, 1947. **9807**

Brief but penetrating résumé of T.'s career, insisting on the fact that while the work is nurtured by the history of our times, it never descends to becoming a simple lyrical commentary on those times. [EP]

Gaucheron, Jacques. Pour dire adieu à Tristan Tzara. Eur 419–20:263–65, 1963. **9808**

Short eulogy in which Gaucheron discusses the importance of Spain in T.'s poetry and the significance of T.'s poetic theories as expressed in *Grains et issues, Le surréalisme et l'après-guerre,* and the prefaces to eds. of Villon, Rimbaud, Corbière, Apollinaire, Eluard, etc. [EP]

Grossman, Manuel. Montage in the dada poetry of Tristan Tzara. DadaS 4:53–56, 1974. **9809**

T.'s manifestoes used as a point of departure for an interesting discussion of cinematic simultaneity from Eisenstein to Brakhage. [EP]

Jaccottet, Philippe. L'outrage des ans. NRF 105:502–06, 1961. **9810**

Starting with a review of the *Poètes d'aujourd'hui* ed. on T., author criticizes his poems as being "deplorably precious, redundant, and boringly extravagant." [EP]

Juin, Hubert. Préface. *In:* Tzara, Tristan. L'homme approximatif. Gallimard, 1968. p. 5–15. **9811**

Stresses the positive aspects of dada and situates *L'homme approximatif* as a great surrealist work. [EP]

Lacôte, René. Tristan Tzara. Présentation par René Lacôte. Choix de textes... Seghers, 1952. 229 p. (Poètes d'aujourd'hui, 32) *Also* (*rev.*): Présentation par René Lacôte and Georges Haldas. Seghers, 1960. 230 p. **9812**

The first *poètes d'aujourd'hui* volume suffers from incompleteness because it was published eleven years before T.'s death. The second ed., although more complete, unfortunately does not include any of T.'s pre-dada poetry. [EP]

Review: P. Jaccottet in NRF 105: 502–06, 1961.

Peterson, Elmer. Tristan Tzara. New Brunswick, Rutgers univ. press, 1970. 259 p. **9813**
Analysis of T. as an interpreter of modern esthetics rather than as a poet. The focus is on the manifestoes and the critical essays. [EP] Reviews: Anon. in LJ 96:480, 1971; A. Balakian in FR 46:627–28, 1973; R. Shattuck in NYRB 18, no. 10:10, 1972.

Ribemont-Dessaignes, Georges. Tristan Tzara, la poésie et la révolte. Cr 28:778–87, 1948. **9814**
Review of eight books by T. published in 1946 and 1947. [EP]

Rousselot, Jean. Une approximation et un souvenir. *In:* Tristan Tzara. *See* 9789. p. 140–44. **9815**
Shows how T. evolved from cultivation of chaos to a form of order independent of logic. [MTB]

————. Pégase ou dada? *In his:* Mort ou survie du langage. Société générale d'éditions, 1964. p. 163–69. **9816**
Penetrating article in which the author describes a constant struggle in T. between a nostalgia for a precivilized world and a wish to make a new world of men. The whole poetic effort of T. seen as an "enterprise of conciliation." [EP]

————. Tristan Tzara, ou: la poésie dépouillée de la misère des mots. *In his:* Présences contemporaines. N[ouvelles] E[ditions] D[ebresse], 1958. p. 231–41. **9817**
Important essay which describes T.'s poetry as a "très consciente querelle entre la nostalgie d'un chaos cosmique... et celle d'un monde à la mesure de l'homme... entre un instinctif besoin de supprimer — à commencer par le langage — et le moins instinctif désir de rejoindre ses semblables et leur joie." [EP]

Schwarz, Arturo. Tristan Tzara, théoricien. Dada. *In:* Tristan Tzara. *See* 9789. p. 165–73. **9818**
T.'s poetic adventure is seen as a permanent revolution against all beliefs and systems in art, literature, ethics, politics and science. T. is linked to the young Marx by his belief that the revolution is a first step towards the fulfillment of man's potentialities. [MTB]

Won, Ko. Buddhist ideas possibly prevailing in Tzara's philosophy. DadaS 4:50–52, 1974. **9819**
A properly cautious attempt to find commonality in dada and Zen. [EP]

Individual Works

Béhar, Henri. A mots découverts. *In:* Tristan Tzara. *See* 9789. p. 95–112. **9820**
T.'s patient deciphering of Villon's secret code is related to his assertion that traditional poetry serves as transition between directed and undirected thought by means of its manipulation of language. T.'s preoccupation with anagrams is compared to that of de Saussure. Anagrams can also be detected in T.'s own poems, confirming his interest in poetry as a game of pluridimensional arrangement of words and letters. [MTB]

Browning, Gordon. Tristan Tzara and decomposition. DadaS 4:27–34, 1974. **9821**
Sensitive explication of a key T. poem, *Le géant blanc lépreux du paysage.* [EP]

————. Tristan Tzara, Poèmes inédits. PoE 42–43:226–37, 1970. **9822**
Introduction and presentation of six poems by T. written in Romanian between 1913 and 1915 and translated by Colomba Voronca. Unfortunately the poem, *Le cierge et la vierge,* which is discussed in some detail in Browning's introduction, is not printed. [EP]

————. Tzara et La grande complainte de mon obscurité. *In:* Tristan Tzara. *See* 9789. p. 202–13. **9823**
A commentary of T.'s "Complainte" (I, II, III), showing the mode of insertion of Nostradamus's predictions into the text, the ambiguous use by T. of the theme of obscurity and his dazzling use of obscure phrases. [MTB]

Caldwell, Ruth. A step on Tzara's road to communication. DadaS 4:35–41, 1974. **9824**

Intelligent discussion of *L'indicateur des chemins de cœur* as a transitional volume for T., marking the passage from dada to a deep *surréalisant* need for communication. [EP]

Caws, Mary Ann. Tristan Tzara: the circus of language. *In her:* The inner theatre of recent French poetry. Princeton, Princeton univ. press, 1972. p. 51–75. **9825**
An extremely sensitive reading of T.'s poetry which concentrates on his *25 et 1 poèmes.* Author finds structure in these poems, giving the lie to dada's words in a hat theory of poetry. [EP]

Dobzynski, Charles. Le secret de François Villon. LetF 803:1, 2, Dec. 17–23, 1959. **9826**
Very important article which announces the as yet unpublished 2 v. study of Villon to which T. devoted four years of patient scholarship. Author claims that the key discovered by T. and used to decipher some 1,500 anagrams in Villon's work is "une des plus vertigineuses surprises littéraires du siècle." [EP]

———. Tristan Tzara: le signe qui persiste. *In:* Tristan Tzara. *See* 9789. p. 153–58. **9827**
T.'s study of Villon's anagrams as a means of hiding one form of reality behind another is seen as a symbol of T.'s own effort to express an ever-changing reality in his poems. [MTB]

Dufournet, Jean. Tzara et les anagrammes de Villon. *In:* Tristan Tzara. *See* 9789. p. 113–34. **9828**
Analyzes T.'s method of deciphering Villon's anagrams and quotes numerous examples showing T.'s findings concerning the murder of Ph. Sermoise. (*See,* in 9820, an unpublished text by T. on this subject.) [MTB]

Duvignaud, Jean. Optique Tzara. Eur 35: 104–06, 1948. **9829**
T.'s *Le surréalisme et l'après-guerre* used as a point of departure for a discussion of the relationship between poetry and revolution. [EP]

Gaucheron, Jacques. Chronique poétique: Tristan Tzara. Pen 20:87–94, 1948. **9830**
Author praises T.'s *Morceaux choisis* and his *Surréalisme et l'après-guerre,*

agreeing with him that "la poésie est plongée dans l'histoire jusqu'au cou...." [EP]

———. Tristan Tzara: De mémoire d'homme ou l'homme est en train de changer. Pen 42:234–39, 1952. **9831**
Review of *De mémoire d'homme* in which the author pleads that T. not always be immediately associated and defined by dada since his poetry demonstrates a constant evolution. [EP]

Gorunescu, Elena. L'itinéraire roumain de Tristan Tzara. *In:* Tristan Tzara. *See* 9789. p. 159–64. **9832**
Quotes from a few Romanian poems, especially "Le chant du déserteur," in which dada's iconoclastic spirit is clearly foreshadowed. [MTB]

Guérir, Alain. Notes de lecture: Parler seul. Eur 60:117–18, 1950. **9833**
Excellent review of *Parler seul* with a discussion of its preparation in the psychiatric hospital of Saint-Alban. [EP]

Impey, Michael H. Tzara's first poems. DadaS 4:66–72, 1974. **9834**
English translations of eight Romanian poems not included in the Sernet anthology. These as well as the other poems in the second ed. of *Primele poeme ale lui Tristan Tzara* suggest that "the matrix of T.'s surrealist poetry is more Romanian than hitherto has been thought possible." [EP]

Leiris, Michel. Présentation de La Fuite. Laby 17:9, 1946. *Also:* Str 2:24–27, 1964. *Also in his:* Brisées. Mercure de France, 1966. p. 96–100. **9835**
Brilliant analysis of the place of *La fuite* in T.'s work. [EP]

Sernet, Claude. Introduction. *In:* Tzara, Tristan. Les premiers poèmes, suivis de 5 poèmes oubliés. Seghers, 1965. p. 7–34. **9836**
Insists on the maturity of these early poems, discovering in them all the essential traits which are found much later in *L'homme approximatif* and *Midis gagnés.* Stresses the continuity of a poetic career that began and developed before dada and that continued long after. [EP]

Drama

Béhar, Henri. Tristan Tzara. *In his:* Etude sur le théâtre dada et surréaliste. Gallimard, 1967. p. 146–75.   9837
Excellent chapter on T. Particularly good analysis of *Mouchoir de nuages.* [EP]

Han, Jean-Pierre. La fuite ou le mouvement de la vie. *In:* Tristan Tzara. *See* 9789. p. 228–30.   9838
In *La fuite,* a dramatic work related to the historical reality of 1940, T. expresses his trust in the movement of life. [MTB]

Robbins, Aileen. Tristan Tzara's Handkerchief of clouds. DramR 16:110–29, 1972.   9839
Brief study of *Handkerchief of clouds* followed by an excellent translation of the play. [EP]

Singer, Leslie. Tzara's Gas burning heart and all that. ChiR 20–21:44–46, 1969.   9840
Very sympathetic reading of *Le cœur à gaz* in its English version, describing it as "magnificent, uncompromising nonsense, tinged with subtle and wry humor." Reviewer sees the play as one of the last examples of dada innovation giving way to surrealism which became "successful, prosperous, respectable and inane." [EP]

Wilson, Ruth. The plays of Tristan Tzara. YT 4:124–51, 1973.   9841
Notes on T. and dada followed by fine translations of the two "celestial adventures." [EP]

Painting

Leuwers, Daniel. Tzara critique d'art. *In:* Tristan Tzara. *See* 9789. p. 214–28.   9842
Shows how T.'s views on art evolved from absolute revolt to acceptance of a political creed, showing faithfulness in spite of "the breach." [MTB]

Influence

Lista, Giovanni. Tristan Tzara et le dadaïsme italien. *In:* Tristan Tzara. *See* 9789. p. 173–92.   9843
Studies dada's influence in Italy from 1919 to 1921, the publication of T.'s early dada poems, the resistance of the Marinetti group and the eventual creation of a shortlived dada movement in Italy, with Cantarelli, Evola and the magazine Blue. [MTB]

Osgood, Eugenia V. Two journeys to the end of the night: Tzara's L'homme approximatif and Vicente Huidobro's Altazór. DadaS 4:57–61, 1974.   9844
Excellent comparison of two volumes of dada/surrealist and creationist poetry, both published in 1931 by two former Presidents of Dada. [EP]

Won, Ko. A comparison of dada manifestoes by Takahashi and Tzara. DadaS 4:42–49, 1974.   9845
Interesting comparison of T.'s influence on a pioneer Japanese dada poet. [EP]

Roger Vitrac
(Nos. 9846–9869)

Jane Wofford Malin

Editions

Vitrac, Roger. Dés-lyre. Ed. by Henri Béhar. Gallimard, 1964. 221 p.   9846
Béhar has collected and presented V.'s poetry after a meticulous search of mss., pamphlets and magazines.
Reviews: M. Alyn in FL 20:6, Jan 21–27, 1965; H. Béhar in NRF 25:330–33, 1965; A. Bosquet in Monde 9, Jan. 16, 1965; C. Ernoult in LetN 146–48, Oct.–Nov. 1965; R. Lacôte in LetF 2, Dec. 31, 1964–Jan. 6, 1965; P. Robin in MerF 353:503–08, 1965.

———. Théâtre. Ed. by Henri Béhar. Gallimard, 1946–1964. 4 v.   9847
Carefully presented material collected from mss., periodicals, etc.
Reviews: H. Béhar in MerF 353:509–12, 1965 and in NouvO n.s. 25, Feb. 11, 1965; R. Hubert in FR 38:809–10, 1964–65.

General Studies

Abirached, Robert. Un jeune auteur nommé Vitrac. Et 376–79, Dec. 1962.   9848

Sensitive commentary on V.'s *Victor* with a brief discussion of the change in the role of language in the avant-garde, the frequently delayed acceptance of its authors, and the significance of Jean Anouilh's staging of *Victor*.

Anouilh, Jean. Cher Vitrac. *In:* Vandromme, Paul. Un auteur et ses personnages. [On cover: Jean Anouilh, un auteur et ses personnages.] Essai suivi d'un recueil de textes critiques de Jean Anouilh. Table ronde, 1965. p. 171–73. **9849**

Associates V. both with Jarry and Molière. Anouilh admits he unconsciously plagiarized *Victor* in *Ardèle*. *Victor* is a play twenty years before its time.

Artaud, Antonin. Lettres à Vitrac. *In his:* Œuvres complètes. V. 3. Gallimard, 1961. p. 197–201, 244–51. *Also in:* Béhar, Henri. Vitrac, un réprouvé du surréalisme. *See* 9854. p. 281–301. **9850**

Four letters or projected letters concerning *Le coup de Trafalgar*, Artaud's reaction to the play during its composition and his analysis of it.

————. Lettres d'Artaud à Vitrac, sur la dernière manifestation du Théâtre Alfred Jarry. Ed. by Henri Béhar. NRF 23:765–76, 1964. *Also in:* Béhar, Henri. Vitrac, un réprouvé du surréalisme. *See* 9854. p. 281–301. **9851**

Béhar makes a convincing case to establish that *Le théâtre Alfred Jarry et l'hostilité publique* is by V. and not by Artaud.

————. Œuvres complètes. V. 2. Gallimard, 1961. 287 p. **9852**

Volume contains essential and detailed material concerning the Théâtre Alfred Jarry and Artaud's staging of V.'s plays *Les mystères de l'amour* and *Victor*.

Béhar, Henri. Etude sur le théâtre dada et surréaliste. Gallimard, 1967. 358 p. (Les essais, 131) **9853**

Excellent and provocative study. See particularly "Vitrac ou les lueurs de l'incendie," p. 245–65, and "Le théâtre Alfred Jarry: Antonin Artaud," p. 227–44, for a study of the surrealist aspects of V.'s theater and his involvement with the ideas of Artaud. Good general background for the period. Bibliography.

Reviews: J. Jakubowicz in RW 6: 105–11, 1971; M. Sanouillet in CahS 3:85–88, 1969; C. van Rees in FrB 40: 31–32, 1970.

————. Vitrac, un réprouvé du surréalisme. Nizet, 1966. 329 p. **9854**

Only book-length study of V. Admittedly discreet in personal details and incomplete in analysis of works, it is, nevertheless, a good basic work, suggestive of further studies to be done. Bibliography.

Reviews: Anon. in BCLF 22:727, 1967; R. Bellet in Eur 275–76, June–Aug. 1968; M. Corvin in CahS 2:216–18, 1968; M.-C. Dumas in RHL 70: 347–48, 1970.

Copfermann, Emile. A Bourges: Victor ou les enfants au pouvoir. LetF 19, Oct. 22–29, 1968. **9855**

Good brief study of the Théâtre Alfred Jarry. Sensitive analysis of the significance of V.'s *Victor* as well as of the Bourges production.

Dort, Bernard. Victor ou les enfants au pouvoir. ThP 48:126–31, 1962. **9856**

Somewhat different point of view of V.'s *Victor*. V. has never put into question the real privileges of the middle-class family of 1900. *Victor* is an anti-boulevard play on the boulevard.

Gascoigne, Bamber. A time when anything goes. Obs 20, Aug. 9, 1964. **9857**

Victor is a silly play that pretends to be serious; the clown playing Hamlet. Incompetent and childish, pseudo-childish even.

Gross, John. Darkness risible. Enc 23:41:43, Oct. 1964. **9858**

Points out the good and bad aspects of *Victor*. Situates black comedy and anti-comedy as typical of our age. V. was a very funny man who mistrusted laughter. A contrasting point of view from other criticisms of *Victor*.

Matthews, J. H. Antonin Artaud and the Théâtre Alfred Jarry. *In his:* Theatre in dada and surrealism. Syracuse, Syracuse univ. press, 1974. p. 133–54. **9859**

Solid study of the ideals Artaud and V. held in common concerning the theater and their experiences with the performances of the Théâtre Alfred Jarry.

————. Vitrac. *In his:* Surrealist poetry in France. Syracuse, Syracuse univ. press, 1969. p. 68–79.   **9860**

Traces the development of V.'s poetry from symbolist to surrealist: the function of words, the play of humor and various other aspects are discussed briefly.
Reviews: H. Peyre in Sym 24:380–82, 1970; E. Sellin in BA 44:630–31, 1970.

————. Vitrac. *In his:* Theatre in dada and surrealism. Syracuse, Syracuse univ. press, 1974. p. 109–32.   **9861**

Treats only the plays which can be associated clearly with surrealism: in *Victor* and those preceding it. Valuable as a corrective to existing scholarship, especially Béhar.

Moussy, Marcel. De Victor à Jacques ou de la révolte à la soumission. CRB 29:27–28, 1960.   **9862**

An extensive number of parallels apparent between plays of V. and Ionesco.

Sanouillet, Michel. Dada à Paris. Pauvert, 1965. 646 p.   **9863**

Numerous references to V. in the course of the study of the development of the dada movement in Paris. Bibliography.

Sénart, Philippe. La revue théâtrale: Le coup de Trafalgar. RDM 682–84, June 1972.   **9864**

Good presentation of both V.'s play and its staging. Touches particularly on the importance of the real and of the character of Simon.

Surer, Paul. Vitrac. *In his:* Cinquante ans de théâtre. Société d'édition d'enseignement supérieur, 1969. p. 53–56.   **9865**

V.'s interest in the cinema. Discusses also V. as the only surrealist playwright. Cites influences of Jarry, the guignol and black humor.

————. Vitrac. *In his:* Le théâtre français contemporain. Société d'édition d'enseignement supérieur, 1964. p. 81–87.   **9866**

Good brief discussion. V. has best brought surrealism to the stage, and his farces express horrendous truth.

Swerling, Anthony. Strindberg's impact in France 1920–1960. Cambridge, Trinity lane press, 1971. p. 59–61.   **9867**

Finds parallels between Strindberg's and V.'s *Mystères de l'amour.* Treats also V.'s and Artaud's interest in Strindberg during the period of the Théâtre Alfred Jarry. Details of comparison are so meticulously drawn up that by that very fact they are rendered less convincing.

Vielhaber, Gerd. ...der von Neunzehnhundertundspäter Vs Erstaufführung in Bochem. FAZ 15, Nov. 25, 1970.   **9868**

Good discussion of *Le coup de Trafalgar* and the place of V. in the surrealist movement.

Zand, Nicole. A Villeurbanne: Le coup de Trafalgar de Vitrac. Monde 17, Dec. 8–9, 1968.   **9869**

The creation starts from the real in order better to show the apparent incoherence of the gestures of daily life. The irrational erupts where one least expects it.

CHAPTER XXI

PAUL ELUARD

(pseud. of Eugène Grindel)

(Nos. 9870–10108)

ANNE HYDE GREET

Bibliography

Jean, Raymond. Eluard aujourd'hui. *In:* Rencontres avec Paul Eluard. *See* 9925. p. 7–11. **9870**
A brief bibliographical résumé, often perceptive, but with a surprising lack of fastidiousness in omissions and inclusions, considering the author's own literary preoccupations.

Piscopo, Ugo. Eluard en Italie. *In:* Rencontres avec Paul Eluard. *See* 9925. p. 212–19. **9871**
A fine bibliographical essay, emphasizing surrealist affiliations, translations of E., reviews of his work, and his affinity with the Italian school of hermetism. Some mention also of the scanty critical literature on E. which exists in Italy.

Scheler, Lucien. Esquisse bibliographique d'un addenda aux Œuvres complètes d'Eluard. CahPE 1:2–10, 1972. **9872**
Valuable addition to Scheler's Pléiade ed. of complete works. 1) E.'s contributions (such as book reviews) to various periodicals, for the most part surrealist. 2) "Le fou," sequence of three early poems, (p. 9–10). 3) *Inédits,* in the category "Poèmes retrouvés ..." All documents (reviews, letters, poems, etc.), classed under the title of the periodical where they first appeared, with the exception of "Le fou" which is published in full, and not to be found elsewhere.

Editions

Eluard, Paul. Œuvres complètes. Préf. et chronologie de Lucien Scheler. Textes établis et annotés par Marcelle Dumas et

Lucien Scheler. Gallimard, 1968. 2 v. (Bibliothèque de la Pléiade) **9873**
A masterful presentation of a complex work. The only solid ed. of E. and an outstanding achievement among Pléiade eds.
Reviews: Anon. in TLS 3526:1095–97, Sept. 25, 1969; P. Bigongiari in ApL n.s. 43:127–30, 1968; M. Chapsal in Exp 885:45–46, June 24–30, 1968; J. Couvreur in Monde 7302:July 6, 1968; V. Dhainault in CahDS 3:72–77, 1969; G. Dumur in MédF 55–59, July 1968; J. Gaucheron in Eur 475–76:354–55, 1968; H. Gershman in BA 44:59–61, 1970; R. Jean in Monde 7302:July 6, 1968; V. Jean in QL 61:12–13, Nov. 16–30, 1968; R. Lacôte in LF 1240:July 10, 1968; E. Mora in NL 2135:4, Aug. 22, 1968; C. Roy in NouvO 187:34–36, June 12–18, 1968.

————. Poesie. Introduzione e traduzione di Franco Fortini. Testo francese a fronte. Turin, G. Einaudi, 1955, 1966. 557 p. (Nuova collana di poeti tradotti con testo a fronte, 7) 573 p. *Also (rev.):* Poesie. Con l'aggiunto di alcuni scritti di poetica. Introduzione e traduzione... Cronologia della vita dell'autore e del suo tempo. Milan, A. Mondadori, 1969. 572 p. **9874**
A bilingual edition of E. The introduction, primarily for the layman, figures among the best general studies of E. in Italian.
Reviews: C. Fabbri in Id 30:6, 8, July 23, 1950; Canceff in SFr 15:591, 1971.

————. Poésies choisies et présentées selon l'ordre chronologique par Claude Roy. Iconographie de Jean Hugues. Dessins de Picasso. Club du meilleur livre, 1959. 328 p. (Club du meilleur livre. Poésies) **9875**

A fascinating but unobtainable volume.

————. Le poète et son ombre. Textes inédits présentés et annotés par Robert D. Valette. Seghers, 1963. 207 p.   **9876**

Important collections of *inédits* and first versions: poems, prose poems, art and literary criticism, surrealist texts of various kinds, lectures, at least one scenario, etc.

Reviews: C. Audejean in Esp 32: 685–86, 1964; R. Lacôte in LF 1012:2, Jan. 16–22, 1964.

————. Ultime poesie d'amore. [Le dur désir de durer, Le temps déborde, Corps mémorable, Le phénix] Introd., traduz., note e bibliografia a cura di Vincenzo Accama. Milan, Lerici, 1965. 289 p. (Poeti europei, 21)   **9877**

A critical ed., primarily for the layman, of poems written around Nusch, E.'s instability after her death, and his later love for Dominique.

Review: F. Piselli in Ponte 23:277, 1967.

Unpublished Texts

Eluard, Paul. Chanson inédite pour Gala (1950). LetF 1208:15–19, Nov. 15–21, 1967.   **9878**

————. Un poème inédit de Paul Eluard. VoiN 2:May 1958.   **9879**

————. L'ultime Donner à voir. Créa 1: 62–65, 1971.   **9880**

Correspondence and Diary

Bouissounouse, Janine. Quand Paul Eluard me racontait ses rêves. FL 1126:10–11, Nov. 13–19, 1967.   **9881**

Quotations from E.'s letters (not republished) to the author.

————. Sur des lettres de Paul Eluard. *In:* Paul Eluard. *See* 9923. p. 209–14.   **9882**

Quotations from E.'s letters (not republished).

Eluard, Paul. Choix de lettres à sa fille (1932–1949) présenté par R. V. [Valette]. *In:* Paul Eluard. *See* 9924. p. 21–33.   **9883**

16 letters, with brief introduction by Valette, emphasizing the continuity in E.'s relationship, not only with his daughter Cécile but with his former wife Gala. Four of these letters appeared also in LetF Nov. 22, 1962 and letters 12–16 in TelQ 2:6–18, 1960.

————. Huit inédits de Paul Eluard. Prés. par Anna Szabo. LF 1343:3, July 15–21, 1970.   **9884**

Of biographical interest. Poem and seven letters to Erica M., dated 1949, during and after third trip to Hungary, in July. Nusch dead; Dominique not yet on the scene; E. vulnerable to the possibility of a new love.

————. Lettres à Joë Bousquet. Préf. et notes de Lucien Scheler. Editeurs français réunis, 1973. 136 p.   **9885**

Introduction to life of Bousquet (p. 9–24). E.'s letters, 1928–1935, rich in biographical details (p. 27–95). Admirable annotation (p. 115–34). Appendix suggests that additional letters, on a more intimate level, exist, from E. to Bousquet.

————. Lettres d'il y a 30 ans, sur Munich: un brouillon non daté de Paul Eluard. PolA iii, Jan. 1969.   **9886**

Reproduction of a manuscript page, evoking the memory of a free Prague, and offered for publication by E.'s widow Dominique.

————. Lettres de jeunesse avec des poèmes inédits de Paul Eluard. Documents recueillis par Cécile Valette-Eluard, présentés et annotés par Robert D. Valette. Cover by Picabia. Seghers, 1962. 223 p.   **9887**

Introduction (p. 7–16) and excellent notes throughout.

Reviews: Anon. in RFB 3:4, 1962; M. Alyn in TR 178:117–19, 1962; H. Meschonnic in Eur 399–400:203–05, 1962.

————. A poet's theories: extracts from the diary of Paul Eluard. Trans. by David Wise. Granta no. 1216:29–30, 1962. **9888**

Translations from E.'s as yet unpublished diary concerning his poetics.

Poulenc, Francis. Correspondance 1915–1963. Réunie par Hélène de Wendel. Préf. de Darius Milhaud. Seuil, 1967. 276 p.   **9889**

Letters from E. often furnishing titles for song cycles, *passim*.

Iconography

Europe. No. 91–92:1953 and no. 403–04: 1962. Europe et Les éditeurs français réunis, 1972. 362 p. **9890**

A reprint of all the iconography from both issues (40 p. illustrations), many of the articles from the 1953 no. and all those from the 1962 no. Criticized by G. Poulin (see below) as a slanted selection, slighting the surrealist works and stressing the political poems. Review: G. Poulin in EF 9:55–64, 1973.

Exposition, Paul Eluard 1895–1952. Préf. de Jean Marcenac. Prés. de Colette Caubisens. Catalogue, Ville de Saint-Denis, Musée municipal d'art et d'histoire, 1963. 96 p. **9891**

Reviews: J. Couvreur in Monde 7302:July 6, 1968; V. Fradisse in LetF May 8–14, 1957; R. Lacôte in LetF 12, April 4, 1963.

Paul Eluard, 1895–1952. Exposition, Maison Pulliérane, Pully 5–28 sept. 1969. Catalogue. Pully [Vaud]:1969. 56 p. **9892**

Reviews: Anon. in LetF 32, Sept. 3, 1969; A. K. in GazL Sept. 6–7, 1969.

Ségalat, Roger-Jean: Album Eluard. Iconographie réunie et commentée. Gallimard, 1968. 322 p. (Bibliothèque de la Pléiade. Album, no. 7) **9893**

Interesting visual biography with 467 illustrations; unusually objective attitude towards the poet. Reviews: Anon. in TLS 3526:1095–97, Sept. 25, 1969; P. Bigongiari in ApL n.s. 43:127–30, 1968; M. Chapsal in Exp 885:45–46, June 24–30, 1968; J. Couvreur in Monde 7302:July 6, 1968; V. Dhainault in CahD 3:72–77, 1969; R. Jean in QL 61:12–13, Nov. 16–30, 1968; C. Roy in NouvO 187: 34–36, June 12–18, 1968.

Valette, Robert D. Eluard. Livre d'identité. Tchou, 1967. 249 p. **9894**

Outstanding iconography, accompanied by documents and, notably, by extracts from unpublished correspondence. Reviews: Anon. in MagL 13:36–39, 1967; C. Audejean in Esp 35:941–42, 1968; A. Ayguesparse in Marg 126: 112–13, 1969; P. Daix in LetF 1208:18–19, Nov. 15–20, 1967; P. Dhainault in CahDS 3:72–77, 1969; H. Gershman in

BA 42:397:1968; R. Jean in QL 61: Nov. 16–30, 1968; P. Loriot in NouvO 164:31, Jan. 3–9, 1968; J. Rousselot in NL 2117:7, March 28, 1968.

Biography

Aragon, Louis. Discours à l'inauguration du lycée Paul Eluard à Saint-Denis, le 29 mai 1965. HumanD 877:June 13, 1965. **9895**

Biographical details, particularly concerning relationship between E. and Aragon.

————. L'homme communiste. V. 2. Gallimard, 1953. p. 113–205. **9896**

Four documents of principally biographical interest, concerning the friendship between E. and Aragon and the role of Communism in their lives and in the practice of their art.

Breton, André. Les pas perdus. Nouvelle revue française, 1924. 212 p. (Les documents bleus) *Also (rev.):* Gallimard, 1970. 182 p. (Idées, 205) **9897**

Passim. Notably Desnos' remarks about E. under hypnosis.

Caute, David. Communism and the French intellectuals 1914–60. London, André Deutsch, 1964. p. 371–88. *Trans.:* Le communisme et les intellectuels français 1914–60. Trans. by Magdeleine Paz. Gallimard, 1967. 471 p. **9898**

Reference to E., *passim.* Informative background material, in a controversial area, some knowledge of which is necessary for an understanding of the poet's development.

Décaudin, Michel. Eluard et dada. *In:* Paul Eluard. *See* 9924. p. 50–52. **9899**

E.'s opposition to Breton's group in 1919–1920.

Decaunes, Luc. Eluard inconnu. Marg 88: 8–11, 1968. **9900**

An illuminating attempt to place the poet's character in perspective. Brief but useful.

————. Paul Eluard. Biographie pour une approche, suivie de notes jointes et d'un essai de bibliographie des œuvres publiées en langue française. Rodez, Eds. Subervie, 1965. 159 p. **9901**

Since a biography at once comprehensive and objective is still lacking, with the exception of Velikovskii's which remains untranslated, Decaunes' work is one of the few authoritative comments available on the poet's life and works. Many omissions.
Review: A. Ayguesparse in Marg 103–04:90–91, 1965.

Ehrenberg, Ilya. Post-war years 1945–1954. V. 6 of Men, years, life. Trans. by Tatiana Shebunina in collaboration with Yvonne Kapp. London, MacGibbon and Kee, 1966. p. 284–92.   **9902**
Although subjective, some biographical data and acute observations.

Fouchet, Max-Pol. Un jour, je m'en souviens... Mémoire parlée. Mercure de France, 1968. 236 p.   **9903**
E.'s courage during the Occupation. History of publication of "Liberté" (p. 87–89).
Reviews: Anon. in ParM 1017:134, Nov. 2, 1968; Anon. in TLS 3477: 1180, Oct. 17, 1968; Y. Berger in Monde 7368:Sept. 21, 1968; H. Chabrier in AeLo 75:20, March 1–7, 1967; M. Lobet in RGB 9 (Nov. 1968), 35–47; F. Nourrissier in NL 2139:2, Sept. 19, 1968.

————. Paul Eluard auteur de Liberté. MagL 77:18–20, 1973.   **9904**
Interview by Jean-Jacques Brochier. Account of the writing and publishing of "Liberté," but also an illuminating *témoignage* concerning E., as seen by a contemporary.

Fournier, Albert. Demeures poétiques d'Eluard. *In his:* Demeures du temps retrouvé. Editeurs français réunis, 1971. p. 351–71.   **9905**
Biographical information on the poet's habitations.
Review: P. Gamarra in Eur 510: 221–23, 1971.

Gaucheron, Jacques. Notes sur deux poètes en guerre avec la guerre. Léon Moussinac et ses guerres. Paul Eluard au temps du Devoir. Eur 421–22:146–55, 1964.   **9906**
An essay concentrating mainly on Moussinac. A bibliography of *Devoir* and the meaning of the title.

Josephson, Matthew. Life among the surrealists, a memoir. Holt, Rinehart and Winston, 1962. *passim.*   **9907**
Of some biographical value, although gossipy. Indexed.

Kroupa, Adolf. Eluard et la Tchécoslovaquie. *In:* Paul Eluard. *See* 9924. p. 221–38.   **9908**
In particular, E.'s affiliations with the Czechoslovakian poet, Vitezslav; also, with Sima. E.'s tracing of Apollinaire's journey, accompanied by Breton (1935). The possibility of an earlier trip (1923). His popularity in translation.

Lacôte, René. La vie et l'œuvre. *In:* Paul Eluard. *See* 9923. p. 15–34.   **9909**
A concise résumé, especially of E.'s relation to the surrealist movement and his role during the Occupation.

Marcenac, Jean. Eluard et l'amour. *In:* Rencontres avec Paul Eluard. *See* 9925. p. 85–96.   **9910**
Of value as a *témoignage* rather than as literary criticism. The subsequent discussion (p. 96–100) contributes nothing new to the theme of love, but contains an interesting biographical detail.

————. Les progrès de l'espérance. Eur 52: 9–17, 1950. *Also in:* Parrot, Louis. Paul Eluard [1952]. *See* 9935. p. 219–33. **9911**
This article, concerning E.'s political evolution after Nusch's death, is of a general nature, using the rhetoric of sentimentality.

Parrot, Louis. Paul Eluard et ses amis. *In his:* L'intelligence en guerre. Panorama de la pensée française dans la clandestinité. Jeune Parque, 1945. p. 101–34, 263–75, 289, 335 *et passim.*   **9912**
Valuable biographical commentary of E.'s activities during the war. Also his role in *Lettres françaises, L'éternelle revue* and in publishing house "Aux Portes de France."

Roy, Claude. Cours naturel d'Eluard. *In his:* Nous. Gallimard, 1972. p. 153–80. (*His:* Somme toute: Tome II)   **9913**
Biographical study of author's friendship with E. Sufficiently objective and unsentimental to be a valuable portrait of the poet and of those close to him, especially during the Occupation.

———. Eluard jusqu'à la fin. NRF 231: 56–71, 1972. *Also in his:* Nous. Gallimard, 1972, p. 519–36. (*His:* Somme toute: Tome II) **9914**
Biographical study of the years with Dominique.

Sadoul, Georges. Portraits du poète à plusieurs âges de sa vie. *In:* Paul Eluard. *See* 9923. p. 39–50. **9915**
Although a "témoignage," some valuable biographical notations; especially lively on communist affiliations.

Scheler, Lucien. Max Jacob parle d'Eluard. LetF Feb. 26–March 5, 1953. **9916**
Excerpts from six of fifteen letters, dated 1942, to E. from Jacob: an interesting assessment of the younger poet and an indirect confrontation of their somewhat diverse attitudes.

———. Un texte de Robert Desnos signé Paul Eluard. LetF 1426:12–13, March 8–12, 1972. **9917**
The events which led up to the text "Le génie sans miroir" (Pléiade II, p. 785–92).

Valette, Robert D. Le fil de la tendresse humaine. *In:* Paul Eluard. *See* 9924. p. 8–21. **9918**
Biographical notes on E.'s trip to the South Seas and the Orient in 1924 and on his love for Gala. The author takes the point of view that Gala remained the great love of the poet's life.

Velikovskii, Samariĭ Izrailevich. K. Gorizontu vsekh lĭudeĭ. Put' Poliâ Elĭuara. Moscow, Izdatel'stvo Khudozhestvennaia literatura, 1968. 232 p. [Published by "Art Literature"] **9919**
A finely written psychological biography of E., all from the Marxist point of view. Reminiscent of J. Moore's essay (*see* 10003) on poetry of commitment is a concluding statement: "It was given to him...to bring together art and revolution, artistic pursuit and communism, his personal truth and the Promethean truth of the XXth century." Reviews: T. Motyleva in NovM 44: 283–84, 1968 and 166–69, April 1969.

Collected Articles

Cahiers Paul Eluard. No. 1, May 1972; no. 2, Dec. 1972; no. 3, May 1973. **9920**
Difficult to obtain, but extremely useful. Consists, so far, of three numbers.

Eluard et les problèmes de l'art engagé. Promesse no. 6, 1963. **9921**
Special number. Fifty-one brief reactions, many of them personal, to the problem of commitment in poetry. See, under separate entry, Decaunes, Rousselot.

Paul Eluard. Les éditeurs français réunis, 1972. 92 p. **9922**
Contains a preface by Roland Leroy and three lectures, by Besse (*see* 9951), Bonnafé, Marcenac, given at Pully-Lausanne, 25 Sept. 1969, to wind up an exhibition of the life and work of E. organized by Pully in collaboration with the Musée d'art et d'histoire at Saint-Denis. The book introduces little that is new; it consists of popular lectures, not of learned papers.

Paul Eluard. Eur no. 91–92, 1953. 265 p. **9923**
Special number. Many illustrations of iconographic interest. Mainly commemorative in nature; some biographical studies, usually subjective. Many justifications of the political poetry. Review: C. Bo in FLe 40:1, Oct. 4, 1953.

Paul Eluard. Eur no. 403–04, 1962. 378 p. **9924**
Special number. Many illustrations of iconographic interest. Mainly consists of critical essays. Some concerned with continuity versus change; general view of E. as evolving from surrealism to communism. Studies of poetic techniques. Bibliography and chronology, Scheler (see also Pléiade ed.).

Rencontres avec Paul Eluard. Colloque de Nice (19–21 mai 1972). Eur 525:7–326, 1973. **9925**
Papers from the colloquium during the 4th Festival du Livre (p. 1–152), followed by a number of additional articles on E. (p. 154–242). Considering the present high status of E. in France, this curiously uneven collection reflects contemporary and conflicting vogues in criticism. To some extent, E. becomes lost in the shuffle. The problem arises, not from the methodologies applied but from the influence of logical positivism which results in a scrupulous

avoidance, on the part of some linguists, of formulating any kind of "value judgment." As a result, findings which have significance seem, all too often, a form of academic gymnastics rather than an intelligent reaction to "the poem itself." Most papers and articles are included, here, as examples of varied approaches which make some contribution to our understanding of E. For essays of special interest, see, under separate entry, Balakian, Décaudin, Gurdj, Poulet and Vajda.

General Studies: Books

Carrouges, Michel. Eluard et Claudel. La symbolique des deux poètes. Seuil, 1945. 149 p. (Pierres vives)　　　**9926**

E. (p. 35–78): La révolte, La destruction, La métamorphose, La métamorphose de l'homme, Le désespoir, L'amour. The first essay of distinction on E.'s poetics. A thematic approach.

———. La mystique du surhomme. Gallimard, 1948. p. 107–08, 148–50. (Bibliothèque des idées)　　　**9927**

An essay on prophetic imagery. Metamorphosis (bird, flight, ubiquity) in E.'s poetry (p. 107–08); "Wonderland" (power of light, fusion of sky and earth, light's source in nature or in man) (p. 148–50). Most quotes from *Capitale de la douleur*.

Eglin, Heinrich. Liebe und Inspiration im Werke von Paul Eluard. Bern and Munich, Francke, 1965. 599 p.　　　**9928**

Freudian study of poetic inspiration. E.'s dominant preoccupation, the possibility or impossibility of writing poetry, in particular, his esthetic (*Donner à voir*), inextricably linked to love and also to friendship, that is, to a triangle between poet, lover and friends, called by Eglin the complex of Candaules and interpreted literally as a voyeur's gift of his wife to his friends. The argument is weakened by a lack of historical or literary perspective. No reference to surrealist ideas on love or to poems written after Nusch's death. Concentration on theoretical sources of inspiration; neglect of actual texts (erotic metaphors, images). Significant omissions in bibliography, such as Richard, Pantanella. Reviews: A. Fonteyne in RBPH 46: 540–45, 1968; F. Formerod-Chanel in

EdL série II, 10:59–60, 1967; M. Nerlich in RFor 80:511–15, 1968; J. Onimus in RSH 332–34, 1967; J. Papenbrock in BRP 1:180–86, 1968; J. Starobinski in RHL 71:139–40, 1971; N. Suckling in Eras 18:294–99, 1966; T. A. van Dijk in FrB 39:105–06, 1969.

Gaffé, René. Paul Eluard. Paris, Brussels, A l'enseigne du cheval ailé, 1945. 151 p.　　　**9929**

Presentation of E. through his chapbooks, from *Poèmes* (1941) to *Poésie et verité* (1942). Sympathetic but dated.

Guyard, Marie Renée. Le vocabulaire politique de Paul Eluard. Klincksieck, 1974. 285 p.　　　**9930**

A useful and thorough study, based on structural linguistics, of vocabulary with political overtones, including words in titles to poems. Indices. Contexts of key words (p. 141–284). Analyses of key words; notably "HOMME, pivot de l'énoncé politique d'E." (p. 105–28). Bibliography, (p. 133–37) of linguistic studies.

Jean, Raymond. Paul Eluard par lui-même. Seuil, 1968. 188 p. (Ecrivains de toujours, 79)　　　**9931**

Valuable iconography. Linking of scanty biography to rich analysis of work and thought of poet. Notable passages on imagery (based on article "Les images vivantes dans la poésie d'E."), style, role of objects, and transformation as a poetic function. For strong refutation, see Bosquet review, *infra*.

Reviews: Anon. in BCLF 23:797, 1968; C. Audejean in Esp 35:941–42, 1968; A. Ayguesparse in Marg 121: 97–98, 1968; A. Bosquet in Monde 7302:4, July 6, 1968; M. Caws in BA 43:215–16, 1969; P. Chappuis in NRF 32:843, 1968; M. Doumond in ELit 3:260–63, 1970; J. Gaucheron in Eur 475–76:355, 1968; A. Grini in CulF 15:213–14, 1968; G. Poulin in Rel 336:83–86, 1969; T. A. Van Dijk in FrB 39:106–07, 1969.

Jucker-Wehrli, Ursula. La poésie de Paul Eluard et le thème de la pureté. Zurich, Juris-Verlag, 1965. 121 p. (Diss. Zurich, 1965)　　　**9932**

Influenced by Richard, this may be the most ambitious and distinguished book of literary criticism yet devoted to the poet. Emphasis on metaphysical aspects of his vision as expressed through imagery.

Meuraud, Maryvonne. L'image végétale dans la poésie d'Eluard. Lettres modernes, Minard, 1966. 83 p. (Langages et styles, 4)   **9933**

A comprehensive examination of plant imagery; technical aspects of E.'s imagery generally (such as its relation to an idea or its lack of visual perspective) ; plant imagery linked to the theme of love; an investigation of its symbolic overtones.

Reviews: Anon. in BCLF 22:200, 1967; D. Bouverot in FM 36:240–41, 1968; M. Caws in BA 42:63–64, 1968; J.-C. Chevalier in IL 19:83, 1967.

Nugent, Robert. Paul Eluard. New York, Twayne, 1974. 153 p. (TWAS, 322)   **9934**

An introduction to E. touching on the major aspects in a general way: 1) his evolution; 2) his imagery; 3) the theme of love; 4) surrealist techniques; 5) his poetics; 6) the problem of "poésie engagée"; 7) E.'s place in the European, especially French, literary tradition.

Parrot, Louis. Paul Eluard. Préface, étude, choix de textes... Seghers, 1944. 175 p. (Poésie, 44). *Also:* 1945. 199 p. Poètes d'aujourd'hui, 1. Poésie, 45). *Also (rev.):* 1951. 237 p. *Also (rev.):* Parrot, Louis, and Jean Marcenac. Paul Eluard. Nouvelle éd. augm. Préf. de Parrot. Postface de Marcenac. Seghers, 1952. 237 p. (Poètes d'aujourd'hui, 1)   **9935**

In 1952 ed., observations by two friends of E. both literary critics. Parrot concentrates on the years of formation; Marcenac, on the years of political involvement. Subsequent eds. in the 60's fluctuate in pagination but not in substance.

Review: J. Amrouche in Ar 12:133–34, 1945–46.

Perche, Louis. Paul Eluard. Eds. universitaires, 1964. 123 p. (Classiques du XXe siècle, 63)   **9936**

Part I: Biography. II–IX: Idealism, sensations, woman, language, imagery, reality and imagination (sources of po-

etry), ethics. An examination in detail of many poems constitutes the major value of this classic work on E., a stylistic analysis of the poet's evolution from surrealist to political poetry. Perche's discussions of important passages and the distinctions he draws between the chapbooks illustrate both evolution and an underlying continuity.

Poulin, Gabrielle. Les miroirs d'un poète. Images et reflets de Paul Eluard. Montreal, Bellarmin; Paris, Desclée De Brouwer, 1969. 170 p. (Essais pour notre temps, 7)   **9937**

The image of mirrors, with its related imagery of reflections, eyes, vision, crystal, as a key to E.'s thought and a reflection of events in his life, especially in poems concerning love and death, but also in the late poems. Interesting, but simplistic.

Reviews: R. Dionne in Rel 339: 175–77, 1969; R. Finch in UTQ 359–61, 1969–70.

General Studies: Articles and Brief Mention

Albouy, Pierre. Volonté d'y voir clair. *In:* Paul Eluard. *See* 9923. p. 139–53. **9938**

Distinctions between surrealist and "didactic" images. Defense of latter. E.'s theory of poetry postulates active expression, such as communism.

Alquié, Ferdinand. Philosophie du surréalisme. Flammarion, 1955. *passim.* (Bibliothèque de philosophie scientifique) *Trans.:* The philosophy of surrealism. Trans. by Bernard Waldrop. Ann Arbor, Univ. of Michigan press, 1965. viii, 196 p.   **9939**

E.'s place in surrealist thought.

———. Une seule pensée. Act March 23, 1945.   **9940**

Discusses "Liberté" and the ethical humanistic basis of surrealism which made inevitable the development of E. and Aragon into poets of political commitment.

Arcangeli Marenzi, Maria Laura. La parola di Paul Eluard. *In her:* Linguaggio e poesia. Venice, Libreria universitaria editrice, 1966. p. 7–48.   **9941**

E.'s vocabulary: its generality, musicality, luminosity. Influence of Paulhan, of "l'amour courtois"; roles of Gala,

Nusch, Dominique; problem of occasional verse. Scholarly and perceptive.

Bachelard, Gaston. L'air et les songes. Corti, 1950. 306 p.   **9942**
An essay on the poetic imagination and its use of dynamic imagery. In "Le ciel bleu" (first publ. in Confl no. 25), discussion of "dématérialisation" and the poetic power of reverie in "La dame de carreau" (p. 191–94). In "Les nuages," the role of cloud imagery in E.'s writing on art (Ernst, Masson) (p. 216–18).

————. Germe et raison dans la poésie de Paul Eluard. *In:* Paul Eluard. *See* 9923. 115–19. *Also in his:* Le droit de rêver. [2ᵉ partie: Littérature...] Presses univ. de France, 1970. p. 169–75.   **9943**
Dominant role of humanistic and didactic images in E.'s poetry.

Baissette, Gaston. Les poètes et les cosmogonies. Seghers, 1953. p. 69–75.   **9944**
E.'s cosmic awareness. An interesting idea, poorly yet provocatively presented through brief references to scattered poems.

Balakian, Anna. The post-surrealism of Aragon and Eluard. YFS 2:93–102, 1948. *Also in her:* Surrealism: the road to the absolute. Noonday press, 1959. p. 165–87. *Also* (*rev.*): Dutton, 1970. p. 213–30.   **9945**
A pioneer essay on the later poetry of Aragon and E. Both tended to divide their efforts between circumstantial and interpretative verse concerning political events. Discussion of *Poésie ininterrompue* (p. 175–77). The author, one of the first to postulate "the aesthetic continuity of surrealism," even in occasional verse, and to affirm that post-surrealism was an evolution rather than a change. At the same time, she indicates the loss of perspective, with political involvement, and the disastrous influence of communism on such texts as *Les sentiers et les routes de la poésie.*

Benayoun, Robert. Erotique du surréalisme. Jean-Jacques Pauvert, 1965. p. 143–47. (Bibliothèque internationale d'érotologie 160)   **9946**
E. and love, compared to attitude of other surrealists.

Benjama, Mustapha. L'eau et le feu dans la poésie de Paul Eluard. *In:* Paul Eluard. *See* 9924. p. 211–21.   **9947**
Two ubiquitous images, especially as they appear in poems of the 20's. Their union, in various manifestations, indicates little evolution in E.'s imagery, notably the symbolic role of such antimonies as water and fire, snow and warmth, throughout his poetry.

Benoit, Leroy J. Poetic themes of Paul Eluard. MLQ 12:216–29, 1951.   **9948**
A résumé of the poet's work, dated, yet useful.

Bernard, Suzanne. Les poèmes d'Eluard. *In her:* Le poème en prose de Baudelaire jusqu'à nos jours. Nizet, 1959. p. 679–87 et *passim.*   **9949**
Important study of E.'s techniques in prose poetry (analysis of "La dame de carreau") and its relation to his esthetic which differs from that of the surrealist esthetic.

Besse, Guy. Eluard, amour-premier. Eur 483–84:155–62, 1969.   **9950**
Continuity in E.'s work: theme of first love revealed in love poems and poetry of circumstance.

————. L'enfance maîtresse. *In:* Paul Eluard. *See* 9922. p. 21–39.   **9951**
A study of the poet as child, revealed in such themes as dream, revolution (or newness), confidence, innocence (or purity).

Bigongiari, Piero. Eluard après Rimbaud. *In:* Paul Eluard. *See* 9924. p. 183–95. *Also:* Eluard dopo Rimbaud. *In his:* Poesia francese del Novecento, 1968. Florence, Vallecchi, 1968. p. 77–91. (La cultura e il tempo, 19)   **9952**
On numerous levels E.'s philosophical position of moral responsibilities is presented as it relates to the more esthetic concerns of Lautréamont, Hugo and especially Rimbaud. Provocative but debatable.

————. Eluard dalla belleza amara alla verità pratica. *In his:* Poesia francese del Novecento. *See* 9952. p. 65–95.   **9953**
A series of thematic and esthetic studies of a general or deductive nature, not always clear: *Eluard e le "règles d'exception"* (p. 65–68); *Poesia come natura* (p. 69–76); *Eluard dopo Rim-*

baud (p. 77–91); *L'utilità della poesia* (p. 92–95).

Boisdeffre, Pierre de. Paul Eluard (1895–1952) ou l'éternel printemps. Monde 9, Dec. 3, 1952. *Also in his:* Des vivants et des morts. Témoignages 1948–1953 suivis d'une lettre de Pierre Emmanuel. Paris-Brussels, Centre culturel et universitaire d'Outre-Mer, 1953. p. 317–28. *Also:* Eds universitaires, 1954. **9954**
E.'s travels in 1924. Loss of power in late poems. Interesting on E.'s evolution.

Boulestreau, Nicole. Eluard et les nouveaux proverbes. *In:* Rencontres avec Paul Eluard. *See* 9925. p. 154–61. **9955**
A study of the Eluardian proverb. Many references to Paulhan. Emphasis not on poetic context but on a structure, analogical to surrealist dreams, and, eventually, to an Eluardian dialectic. Observations, often interesting, but organization somewhat untidy.

Bourguignon, Claire. Eluard et le feu. CahS 381:89–99, 1965. **9956**
The image of fire, presented in terms of its associations with other images, notably water, light and painting, and with abstract themes, such as fraternity, childhood, love. Ends with a series of juxtaposed passages from E. and from Ronsard.

Brée, Germaine. Twentieth-century French literature. Macmillan, 1962. p. 315–24. **9957**
Presentation of eight poems by E., dating 1924–1944 (p. 315–24). *Explication* of "Tout aiguisé de soif, tout affamé de froid" (p. 320–21).

Brodin, Pierre. Paul Eluard. *In his:* Présences contemporaines. V. I. Debresse, 1954. p. 103–20. **9958**
Bibliography. Brief survey of life and works. E.'s stature, according to contemporary critics.

Caminade, Pierre. Image et métaphore. Un problème de poétique contemporaine. Bordas, 1970. 159 p. (Etudes supérieures) **9959**
An examination into distinctions between image and metaphor, as set up by the author. References to E., *passim*. Coexistence of image and metaphor in E.'s verse (p. 128–29).

Caws, Mary Ann. Paul Eluard. *In her:* The poetry of dada and surrealism: Aragon, Breton, Tzara, Eluard, and Desnos. Princeton, Princeton univ. press, 1970. p. 136–69. **9960**
An intelligent summing up of E.'s esthetics. Some textual discussion, but mostly general. Noteworthy comparison of E. and Tzara.

Couvreur, J. Paul Eluard devant la mort. Thy 55:479–83, 1962. **9961**
E.'s reaction to Nusch's death: although unsatisfactory on *Corps mémorable* and E.'s political development, the author points out that *Voir* and *Picasso à Antibes* indicate a new, or renewed, involvement.

Decaunes, Luc. [Eluard et les problèmes de l'art engagé]. *In:* Eluard et les problèmes de l'art engagé. *See* 9921. p. 23–28. **9962**
The problems of "engagement" and of evolution in E.'s work: committed poetry, esthetically valid ("la beauté est essentiellement militante"); close relation between early (World War I) and late poems.

———. Paul Eluard fidèle à lui-même. CahS 296:139–43, 1949. **9963**
Premiers poèmes, Corps mémorable, Poèmes politiques. Underlines continuity from early to late poems, in theme and style.

Dubois, Hubert. Paul Eluard. CahS 16:41–54, 1929. **9964**
Thematic commentary, to some extent still valid.

Dubois, Jacques. La leçon de Paul Eluard. NCr 42:68–79; 43:105–21, 1953. **9965**
Partly, a Marxist presentation of E.'s vision. Mainly, a precise attack against such "bourgeois" critics as Boisdeffre, Paulhan, Mauriac, Bédouin, Carrouges. A classic example of how quickly E.'s poetry came to be treated as a football by two groups of critics rather than as a work of art.

Dupeyron, Georges. Paul Eluard et la confiance. *In:* Paul Eluard. *See* 9924. p. 53–58. **9966**
Aspects of E.'s optimism: the value of present time, imagery of light and its associations, poetry of action. The author takes issue with Béguin.

Duval, Jean. Cahiers. Préf. par Jean Cassou. José Corti, 1968. p. 98–101, 210–13. **9967**
E. the embodiment of his own imagery. His admission of Breton's influence. Analysis of E.'s poetics (p. 210–13).

Ehrenbourg, Ilya. Paul Eluard. *In his:* Cahiers français. Fasquelle, 1961. p. 237–53. **9968**
Continuity of E.'s poetry. His relation to symbolism and surrealism. His use of language.

Eigeldinger, Marc. Surréalisme et dynamisme de l'imagination. Paul Eluard et le dynamisme de l'imagination. *In:* L'imagination créatrice. Rencontre internationale organisée par la Fondation pour une entraide intellectuelle européennee, Pigny-la-Forêt, 9–13 oct. 1970. Actes mis en forme par Roselyne Chenu. Av.-propos de Pierre Emmanuel. Neuchâtel, Eds. de la Baconnière, 1971. p. 165–77; entretien: p. 178–80. **9969**
A remarkably objective and illuminating evaluation of E.'s place in modern poetry.

Emmanuel, Pierre. Le Je universel chez Paul Eluard. FrL 67:21–31, 1946. *Also:* G.L.M., 1948. 45 p. (Théorie, 2) *Also in his:* Le monde est intérieur. Essais. Seuil, 1967. p. 132–60. **9970**
Continuity of image, symbol, theme. Role of pronouns *je, tu.* Explication of "Pour vivre ici" (*cf. his* commentary on same text. *In:* Paul Eluard. *See* 9924. p. 44–50).

Fabre-Dive, Andrée. Eluard et l'enfant. RSH 142:237–60, 1971. **9971**
An analysis of texts on childhood and on ramifications of the theme, which comment on E. himself. The child as an expression of love and of human continuity; childhood as an attitude of joy and wonder; those who have renewed their childhood: the lover, the militant, the poet and, of course, the surrealist.

Ferenczi, László. Je m'obstine à mêler des fictions aux redoutables réalitiés. ALitASH 14:131–44, 1972. **9972**
The function of imagery in E.'s poetry, viewed in the context of 19th and 20th century influences. The relation of his poetics to surrealism and dada. His linguistic experiments. An explication

of "Je te l'ai dit...," etc. Interesting, if somewhat rambling and inconclusive study.

Fowlie, Wallace. Eluard: the doctrine of love. *In his:* The age of surrealism. Swallow press and Wm. Morrow & Co., 1950. *Also:* Bloomington, Indiana univ. press, 1950, 1960. p. 138–56. **9973**
General essays containing analyses of "Première du monde," "Celle de toujours, toute" and "Nous sommes." On a popular rather than a scholarly level and perhaps not so successful as the essays on Cocteau, Breton, Mallarmé, but endowed with Fowlie's unique approach.

Garavito, Julian. Paul Eluard et les poètes hispano-américains. *In:* Rencontres avec Paul Eluard. *See* 9925. p. 220-26. **9974**
Although E., as distinct from other surrealists, did not have a specific influence on Spanish-American poets, his later poetry is in the same vein as that of Vallejo, Carrera Andrade, Octavio Paz, and others. The main interest of this study lies in the many juxtaposed texts quoted at length.

Gaucheron, Jacques. Eluard et la morale. *In:* Paul Eluard. *See* 9924. p. 98–114. **9975**
E.'s poetry, in opposition to "la morale," taken in its pejorative (or Nietzschean) sense. The poet's need to invent a new humanistic (Marxist) "morale," based not on dualism but on a fidelity to life which E. discovered in communism. Ethical implications of *la pureté.*

———. En marge des derniers livres de Paul Eluard. *In:* Paul Eluard. *See* 9923. p. 260–65. **9976**
The Marxist approach: E.'s poetic theory has its source in the early World War I poems and becomes dominant only in the verse inspired by communism and World War II.

Gaudric, Marianne. Le Paris d'Eluard. *In:* Rencontres avec Paul Eluard. *See* 9925. p. 161–73. **9977**
Paris, in E.'s writing, varies according to whether his poetry is oriented toward political action or personal lyricism. An essay, divided by many subtitles which are self-explanatory and somewhat repetitive. Emphasis on im-

age of the city and its political and social overtones, mainly in the later poems.

Gaulmier, Jean. Continuité de Paul Eluard. *In:* Paul Eluard. *See* 9924. p. 68–73. **9978**

An attack against "bourgeois" critics who compared *Poèmes politiques* to previous work. The attempt to demonstrate in *Capitale...*, themes of later books: for example, implicit in the theme of the world's revelation through love is, through love, the revelation of liberty.

Gibson, Robert. Paul Eluard and surrealism. *In:* Studies in honour of A. R. Chisholm. Melbourne, Hawthorne press, 1969. p. 294–305. (Spec. no. of AJFS 6, no. 2–3, 1969) **9979**

Clear distinction between E.'s attitude and that of other surrealists (primarily Breton) toward poetry and the poet's role.

Gide, André. Interviews imaginaires. Gallimard, 1942. p. 148–49. **9980**

Gide's sceptical but open reaction to surprise and mystery in E.'s poetry. "E. m'inquiète. C'est l'ouverture sur l'inconnu; le départ vers on ne sait quoi, et peut-être vers nulle part."

Griot-Campeas, Claire. Le surrationalisme d'Eluard. *In:* Rencontres avec Paul Eluard. See 9925. p. 174–87. **9981**

Bachelard's expression "le surrationalisme" as it is expressed in E.'s life and thought. An interesting point of departure which, unfortunately, leads its author into recapitulating well-known biographical facts rather than clarifying her fresh interpretation of a much-debated poetic evolution.

Gros, Léon-Gabriel. La langue au service de l'amour. CahS 16:57–64, 1929. **9982**

To some extent, still valid. E.'s style seen as parallel to literary preoccupations of the era, rather than controlled by them. An anticipation of those later critics who find E.'s surrealism distinctly individual and independent.

Guedj, Colette. La métaphore chez Paul Eluard, essai méthodologique. *In:* Rencontres avec Paul Eluard. *See* 9925. p. 226–31. **9983**

Brief but excellent application of linguistic method to the analysis of Eluardian metaphor.

———. Peut-on utiliser une méthode linguistique dans l'explication d'un texte poétique. CahPE 3:1–7, 1973. **9984**

Interesting postulation of a linguistic method, using as an example, "Les représentants tout-puissants du désir," from *L'amour la poésie.* In spite of the objective presentation, conclusions are drawn which constitute, in reality, value judgments.

Guyard, Marie-Renée. Les connotations politiques du vocabulaire de la végétation chez Paul Eluard. Lit 4:63–67, 1971. **9985**

An unusual approach to the study of Eluardian imagery. Reprinted in her *Le vocabulaire politique...*, supra.

———. Eluard et la lumière. *In:* Rencontres avec Paul Eluard. *See* 9925. p. 66–71. **9986**

Recurrence of the word *lumière* in specific chapbooks dating from 1939 to 1953. Linguistic study of the poet's various uses of the word, interesting, in particular, for the method used.

Hubert, Renée Riese. Characteristics of an undefinable genre: the surrealist prose poem [Breton, Eluard, Desnos]. Sym 22: 25–34, 1968. **9987**

An evaluation of E.'s prose poems in *Capitale....*

Hugnet, Georges. Introduction. *In:* Petite anthologie poétique du surréalisme. Jeanne Bucher, 1934. p. 83–97. **9988**

Still remains one of the finest essays on surrealist poetry.

Ingrassia, Antonin. Eluard et Baudelaire. Aix-en-Provence, La pensée universitaire, 1962. 125 p. multigraphié. (Publications des Annales de la Faculté des lettres, Aix-en-Provence. Série Travaux et mémoires, 23) **9989**

A largely thematic comparison of the role of good and evil in poems of Baudelaire and E. Technical and philosophical issues avoided. Somewhat arbitrary conclusion that E. follows Baudelairean rather than Mallarmean tradition.

Jaccottet, Philippe. Une règle lumineuse. *In his:* L'entretien des muses. Gallimard, 1968. p. 67–71.   **9990**
Elliptic, provocative evocation of "rapports" in E.'s poetry, from the point of view of the author's taste.

Jean, Raymond. Les images vivantes dans la poésie d'Eluard. *In:* Paul Eluard. *See* 9924. p. 118–35. *Also in his:* La littérature et le réel. De Diderot au nouveau roman. Eds. Albin Michel, 1965. p. 99–124. *Also in his:* Paul Eluard par lui-même. *See* 9931. p. 53–80.   **9991**
Important study of E.'s imagery. Categories studied: *place; barque; bateau; vitres; fenêtres; pierres; cailloux; yeux; paupières; rire; branches; buissons; rayons; filets.* Compare with Richard.

Kittang, Atle. D'amour de poésie. Essai sur l'univers des métamorphoses dans l'œuvre surréaliste de Paul Eluard. Minard, 1969. 118 p. (Situation, 12)   **9992**
A detailed analysis of E.'s imagery (1922–1938) which illuminates the poet's esthetic.
Reviews: R. Campagnoli in SFr 16: 191, 1972; R. Cardinal in FS 26:355–56, 1972; M. Doumont in ELit 3:263–65, 1970; A. Mingelgrün in RBPH 49: 111–15, 1971.

Laude, Jean. Notes sur la poésie de Paul Eluard. CahS 329:98–114, 1955.   **9993**
Problems of finding a poetic language which fuses thought, word and action. Places E.'s search for a language in the context of symbolism and after.

Launay, Michel. Index chronologique des œuvres de Paul Eluard. Index des premiers écrits 1908–1916. CahPE 1:22–73, 1972; 2:24–52, 1972; 3:19–72, 1973.   **9994**
Lexicological index of all words (especially nouns, verbs, adjectives) in E.'s work, arranged alphabetically and classified chronologically according to individual texts or, occasionally, groups of poems.

Lecoq, Paul. La mort vécue. *In:* Paul Eluard. *See* 9924. p. 88–97.   **9995**
The theme of death in E.'s poetry, especially in relation to Nusch.

Leiris, Michel. Art et poésie dans la pensée de Paul Eluard. *In:* Paul Eluard. *See*

9923. p. 50–57. *Also in his:* Brisées. Mercure de France, 1966. p. 169–78. **9996**
Two aspects of E.'s esthetics: his ideas on language in relation to the imagination, plastic arts, poetry; and his evolution from a personal towards a militant poetry.

Marcenac, Jean. L'amour chez Eluard et Aragon. NCr 87–88:174–205, 1957. **9997**
A Marxist essay which opposes, to a "traditional" association between love and death, a linking of erotic and fraternal love, as expressed by Aragon and E.

Matthews, J. H. Paul Eluard (1895–1952). *In his:* Surrealist poetry in France. Syracuse, Syracuse univ. press, 1969. p. 102–13.   **9998**
A valuable, if at times unclear or unconvincing, essay on the Eluardian esthetic.

Mazaleyrat, J. La tradition métrique dans la poésie de Eluard. *In:* Le vers français au 20e siècle. Colloque organisé par le Centre de philologie et de littérature romanes de l'Université de Strasbourg. Klincksieck, 1967. p. 25–33, discussion p. 34–42.   **9999**
Brilliant paper. The problem of "rupture" or lack of continuity in E.'s verse, an illusion, from point of view of prosody. Traditional rhythmic structures and metrical formulae, ubiquitous, and based, especially, on the Alexandrine. Most examples taken from *Capitale...* Valuable discussion.

Meschonnic, Henri. Eluard, poète classique. *In:* Paul Eluard. *See* 9924. p. 135–50. *Also in his:* Pour la poétique. V. 2. Une parole écriture. Gallimard, 1973. p. 117–43.   **10000**
E. a classical poet and, essentially, not a surrealist. Emphasis on later didactic poetry which the author sees as supporting his theory. The significance of chapbooks of the 20's, relegated to those prefaces which express an esthetic concern reconcilable with E.'s later work.

————. Un langage-solitude. Les formes-sens de La vie immédiate d'Eluard. *In his:* Pour la poétique. V. 3. Une parole écriture. Gallimard, 1973. p. 179–274.   **10001**

These essays, as a whole, follow a method which mingles, in a disconcerting fashion, linguistic analysis and the study of imagery or themes, with the result that, although useful and illuminating to the Eluardian, it is highly obscure for anyone not thoroughly acquainted with E.'s writings and, perhaps also, with Meschonnic's general procedures, as they have evolved in the past few years.

————. Prosodie et langage du couple dans La vie immédiate d'Eluard. LFr 7:45–55, 1970.   **10002**
Exploiting both structuralist and more traditional approaches, this study tantalizes by its brevity.

Moore, John. Poetry betrayed? Approaches to commitment in French poetry between 1930 and 1942. NFS 4:28–40, 1965.   **10003**
An outstanding presentation, distinguished for its perception, intelligence, and objectivity, of twentieth-century "poésie pure" and "poésie engagée," and their eventual fusion. E. seen as successful in writing poetry of commitment because of the "texture" of his ideas. All poetry is considered committed poetry. Thus, the lengthy debate between bourgeois and Marxist European critics is turned to ridicule without ever being noticed.

Mounin, Georges. La communication poétique, précédé de Avez-vous lu Char? Gallimard, 1969. 296 p. (Les essais, CXLV)   **10004**
E.'s materialistic humanism in "Trois poètes et la dialectique." Analysis of "Où se fabriquent les crayons" and enigmas in "Toilette" and "La notion de situation en linguistique et la poésie."

Nelli, René. Poésie ouverte, poésie fermée. Essai. Les cahiers du sud, 1947. p. 30–34, 129–30.   **10005**
Especially E.'s "poésie fermée": relation of image to idea, of style to emotion.

Neri, G. Il primo Eluard. Cont 56–57:55–69, 1963.   **10006**
Dated, but still meaningful evaluation of bibliographical highlights: notably *Lettres de jeunesse* (and the anticipatory article in TelQ), Eur spec.

nos., 1953 and 1962, and M. Décaudin's "Eluard et dada." Discussion of the idea that "the principle of contradiction," seen by some critics as central in E.'s verse, was inspired by dada.

Nicoletti, Gianni. Eluard poetà ininterrotto. Sit 7–8:50–55, 1956. *Also in his:* Saggi e idee di letteratura francese. Bari, Adriatica editrice, 1965. p. 341–48. *Also in:* Saggi e idee.... Seconda edizione, 1967. p. 407–13.   **10007**
A brilliant presentation of continuity in E.'s poetry and of E. as exemplifying a general evolution in 20th-century poetry from subjectivity to collectivism. Sources of this evolution found in symbolist poets.

Nugent, Robert. Eluard's use of light. FR 34:521–30, 1961.   **10008**
The image of light as it relates to such themes as harmony, love, life, poetry, "the problem of purity," morality. Nugent proposes a *métaphysique de la lumière* comparable in its universal applicability to Richard's *métaphysique du regard*. His concerns are also related to those of Jucker-Wehrli and Poulet. This essay was among the first thematic studies of the poet.

Onimus, Jean. Les images de Paul Eluard. AFLSHA 37:131–48, 1963.   **10009**
An impressive, valuable study. After an introduction on the concreteness and visibility of Eluardian images, Onimus groups them into positive images (luminous, *aérien*, pure and, generally, transparent) and negative images (shadows, night, fog and rain, boundaries, ice, aridity). He discusses the various possible juxtapositions of these two groups and their effect upon the reader, thus justifying an emotional or intuitive interpretation of images which seem, at first, complex or obscure. One of the finest studies of E.'s poetics.

————. La pureté poétique: Eluard. *In:* Souillure et pureté. Ed. by Michel Adam. Toulouse, Privat, 1972. p. 176–89. **10010**
Although, for the most part, a polished résumé of ideas to be found elsewhere, the final section presents a fascinating and original attack on E., usually considered a major humanist poet.

Pantanella, R. L'amour et l'engagement d'après l'œuvre poétique de Paul Éluard. Aix-en-Provence, La pensée universitaire, 1962. 217 p., multigraphié. (Publications des Annales de la Faculté des lettres. Travaux et mémoires, 22)   **10011**

A conscientious thematic study showing continuity and evolution in E.'s love poetry, from intimate lyrics to poems of social commitment. Texts are used to demonstrate E.'s state of mind; thus, "Giorgio de Chirico," interpreted as an expression of the poet's depression (p. 28); "L'Amoureuse," a poem to Gala, as concerned primarily with the theme of virginity; poems to Nusch and Dominique, as indications of the poet's "progress" toward a social reality. E.'s basic tenet remains constant: "l'amour ne peut être que révolutionnaire" (p. 207).

Papenbrock, Jürgen von. Vers und Rhythmus im Werk Paul Eluards bis 1938. RITL 20:473–85, 1971.   **10012**

Interplay of modern "free" forms and stricter "classical" forms in E.'s pre-1938 poetry (including prose poems). Frequent references to individual texts, notably "Il y a tant de choses" and "Tes yeux sont revenus d'un pays arbitraire."

————. Zur Lyrik Paul Eluards. BRP 3. no. 2:44–69, 1964.   **10013**

A discussion of E.'s early work in relation to surrealism, from a Marxist viewpoint (i.e., the utilitarian function of art in society). Emphasis on formal elements; on influence of 19th-century poetry, particularly of Baudelairean esthetic. Contrast between E.'s middle-class idealist attitude in surrealist poems, and later revolutionary proletarian stand, less mythical, more realistic and socially-oriented, in poems of World War II era. Analysis of "Avis" illustrates Papenbrock's most interesting point: E.'s adaptation of early techniques to new themes. The most comprehensive of Papenbrock's articles, containing the essence of nearly all his subsequent work (which leans so heavily on this first study). Difficult style.

Passeron, René. Paul Eluard et le mythe d'Icare. AeLet 1:423–37, 1946.   **10014**

An early application of Bachelard's ideas to Eluardian imagery of eyes, reflections, landscapes, and especially mirrors. In contrast to Bachelard's emphasis on aerial imagery, Passeron notes that air and water often mingle (as in cloud images) and that, usually, E.'s aerial quality implies a subsequent fall or "chute." His discussion of light and purity anticipates Jucker-Wehrli.

Picon, Gaëtan. Tradition et découverte chez Paul Eluard. Font 58:962–74, 1947. Also in his: L'usage de la lecture. Mercure de France, 1960. p. 89–104.   **10015**

Review of new ed. of Choix de poèmes. Emphasizes E.'s continuity: sees not rupture but evolution along a path discernible since first poems. E.'s poetry an expression of man's relation to world. Few derivations from specific predecessors, but, as distinct from surrealists, a traditional lyricist: expresses in an original manner traditional human sentiments. His innovation: he is not nostalgic, like forerunners, but emphasizes the present moment and "les jeux de la prophétie." Lucid presentation of E.'s originality.

Pierre, Rolland. Le vocabulaire de Paul Eluard. In: Paul Eluard. See 9924. p. 161–78.   **10016**

The importance of language as a point of departure in studying E.'s poetics. The growth of his vocabulary. Linguistic categories indicate a change in his attitude toward human realities around 1936. By 1942 his vocabulary is formed. At the same time, verbal categories suggest that "le fonds verbal," although it becomes enriched, preserves continuity with the poet's past.

Piscopo, Ugo. Eluard e la Resistenza. In his: Novecento e tradizione. Naples, La provincia editrice, 1967. p. 86–132.   **10017**

General survey of E.'s poetry, verging on the sentimental. "La poesia di sempre" (E.'s poetics), p. 86–116. "La lotta" (poetry of the Resistance), p. 117–32. The final seven pages refer to war poetry.

————. La poesia di Eluard e la cultura italiana. Rome, Tripoli, Copitelli, 1965. (Quaderni dell'Istituto italiano di cultura di Tripoli, pubblicati in collaborazione con Il veltro. No. 2)   **10018**

Five studies of E.: 1) his Baudelairean or symbolist heritage; 2–4) his evolution and continuity; 5) his relation to

Italian poets, especially Ungaretti and Quasimodo.

Reviews: L. Ajello in CulF 14:115–17, 1967; F. Piselli in Ponte 23:277, 1967.

Poulet, Georges. La lumière éluardienne. Cr 209:815–35, 1964. *Also in his:* Etudes sur le temps humain. V. 3. Le point de départ. Plon, 1964. p. 128–60.   **10019**

Originally a review of *Poèmes pour tous* (1963), *Le poète et son ombre* (1963), *Derniers poèmes d'amour* (1963) and *Europe*, special issue of 1962. Poulet does not review them but provides a key essay for Eluardian studies, complementary to that of Jean-Pierre Richard, covering some of the same material, but more abstract.

———. Paul Eluard et la multiplication de l'être. *In:* Rencontres avec Paul Eluard. *See* 9925. p. 36–55.   **10020**

The theme of self-awareness in its various avatars. Fascinating application of Poulet's thematic preoccupations to the evolution of E.'s poetry.

Rendu, Denise. Eluard ou le langage réconcilié. EspL 2:29–47. 1955.   **10021**

E. as a surrealist, in a changing historical context. The basic continuity and inevitable evolution of his poetry, for this critic, are obvious and imply no paradox or ambiguity.

Rhodes, S. A. Aspects of Paul Eluard. FR 30:115–20, 1956.   **10022**

A brief introduction to the poet. Many themes touched upon, although none is explored in depth: reality and dream, form and movement, love, despair, E.'s imagery, his subjectivity.

Richard, Jean-Pierre. Paul Eluard. *In his:* Onze études sur la poésie moderne. Seuil, 1964. p. 105–39. (Pierres vives)   **10023**

The best single essay on E.'s esthetic; his themes and imagery, his imaginary universe. Concise, beautifully written, it is the point of departure for all subsequent Eluardian studies.

Riffaterre, Michael. La métaphore filée dans la poésie surréaliste. LFr 3:46–60, 1969.   **10024**

A study, in the structuralist vein, of a "logique de mots" to which we are unaccustomed in surrealist imagery. Convincing examples from E. (p. 52–

55). Interesting commentary on the mechanics of surrealist metaphor.

Rolland de Renéville, André. En lisant Paul Eluard. *In his:* Univers de la parole. Gallimard, 1944. p. 115–26.   **10025**

Three dominant themes: E.'s independence from surrealism; love as a metaphysical postulation; relation of image to idea.

Roy, Claude. Descriptions critiques: Paul Eluard. Poé 30:35–44, 1946. *Also in his:* Descriptions critiques. V. 1. Gallimard, 1949. p. 35–43.   **10026**

In part, a "témoignage," in part, a commentary. One of best descriptions of poet in relation to his work.

———. Vues sur Paul Eluard. *In:* Paul Eluard. *See* 9923. p. 57–71.   **10027**

Fragments from an unfinished ms. Principal themes: love poetry and the experience of happiness; metaphysics (encompassing the surreal) as the unsayable which demands expression; idealism and dialectic materialism. Among other precious bits of information, it seems that Goya's *Los caprichos* was one of E.'s favorite books. A tantalizing study not to be overlooked.

Ruff, Marcel. Eluard and Baudelaire. *In:* Etudes baudelairiennes. V. 3. Neuchâtel, A la Baconnière, 1973. p. 201–13.   **10028**

An intriguing, if not completely convincing, confrontation between two temperaments and between the attitudes of the hero poets. Ruff covers, most eloquently, numerous themes including "la femme," "le voyage," "l'engagement politique," and, by far the most significant, "la peinture."

Rustan, Marie-Josèphe. Le temps poétique de Paul Eluard. CahS 322:461–70, 1954.   **10029**

Human time, contrasted to poetic time. Characteristic of E.'s poetry is an emphasis on the present (and, paradoxically, eternal) moment.

Sandre, Yves. Rythmes et structures chez Paul Eluard. *In:* Paul Eluard. *See* 9924. p. 152–60.   **10030**

Lucid, unusual analysis of E.'s prosody: its differences from the past, its debt to tradition. Implicit association of technical preoccupations with surrealist desire to involve the reader in a new vision.

Showalter, English, Jr. Biographical aspects of Eluard's poetry. PMLA 78:280–86, 1963.   **10031**

An ingenious analysis of autobiographical aspects of the poems, particularly those in *Capitale...* relating to Ernst and Dali, at times when those artists may have been involved with Gala. Many lucid comments on E.'s early poems to a number of other painters. The author, however, tends to quote out of context, as proof of his contention that the poet speaks for himself and not for Chirico, Masson, Klee, Braque, Miró. Both the drawback and the advantage of such a study lie in its narrow interpretation of E.'s poetry and of his esthetics.

Soupault, Philippe. Il y a dix ans, Paul Eluard. Le poète de la douceur. FL 865: 1, 5, Nov. 17, 1962.   **10032**

Soupault sees E. as not following the surrealist line because he was, by temperament, too sweet and sentimental. He believes E.'s best poetry is contained in *Capitale...* and condemns the later political poems.

Spire, André. Paul Eluard et le vers libre. *In:* Paul Eluard. *See* 9923. p. 35–38.   **10033**

Some acute technical observations by a poet with similar preoccupations.

Thiessing-Specker, Lotte. Zur Lyrik Paul Eluards. Triv 3:99–120, 1945.   **10034**

The idea of reality as it evolves in E.'s work is linked with a syntactical evolution in the poems. Abundant examples.

Tzara, Tristan. Paul Eluard et les images fraternelles. LetF 594:1, 5, Nov. 17–23, 1955.   **10035**

Surprise and inevitability of E.'s imagery. Their place in the poem.

Vajda, Andras. Dada dans la poésie d'Eluard. *In:* Rencontres avec Paul Eluard. *See* 9925. p. 231–42.   **10036**

Of great interest, for several reasons: an unusually subtle appreciation of dada and a fascinating application of the dada esthetic to some surprising poems from *Les animaux et leurs hommes...* as well as more typical texts from *Les né-*

cessités... and *125 Proverbes;* secondly, and perhaps more significantly, a method which reconciles opposing tendencies in contemporary Eluardian criticism. Repeatedly, a logical schema is applied to an irrational text and subsequently interpreted, with restraint and finesse, through the medium of the author's own poetic sensibility. Refreshingly well-written: clear, precise, polished.

Vaksmakher, Maurice. Paul Eluard en U.R.S.S.: Ainsi doit parler la vérité même. *In:* Paul Eluard. *See* 9924. p. 238–46.   **10037**

Comments on the difficulty of translating E.'s poetry into Russian. Survey of Eluardian critics in Russia.

Whiting, Charles G. Eluard's poems for Gala. FR 41:505–17, 1968.   **10038**

A useful biographical interpretation of the early poems, often illuminating, at times simplistic. The poems to Max Ernst seen as comments on an affair between Gala and the painter and not as verbal reactions to a plastic vision.

——. Verlainian reflections in Eluard's poetry. RR 61:182–86, 1970.   **10039**

Verlaine's influence seen from the early poems through *Capitale...* in such techniques as alliteration, assonance, internal rhyme, repetition. Both poets use the *chanson;* they stress emotion, sensation, dream, and their work has a confessional quality.

Zumthor, Paul. Poésie médiévale et poésie moderne, continuité et différences. CahS 372:270–83, 1963.   **10040**

A linguistic comparison, unconvincing in that the poems and the poets (E. and Adam de la Halle) seem, from a literary point of view, chosen arbitrarily.

Zurowski, M. Paul Eluard et la tradition. KN 8:265–78, 1961.   **10041**

A stimulating, often enlightening confrontation between E. and some of his forebears, marred only by the dubious use of the highly debatable term "cubist poets" for Jacob, Apollinaire and Reverdy.

Art and Music

Bachat, Charles. Picasso et les poètes. Eur 492–93:165–77, 1970.   **10042**

Picasso as a source of E.'s poetry of commitment. Relationship between E.'s vocabulary and Picasso's "motif plastique": "le regard," "l'œil intérieur." E. as Picasso's Marxist interpreter (p. 174–77).

Bruyr, José. Le poète et son musicien: Paul Eluard et Francis Poulenc. *In:* Paul Eluard. *See* 9924. p. 246–51.   **10043**

E.'s principal composers. Poulenc's favorite poets. E.'s poems set to music by Poulenc. Discussion of "Le travail d'un peintre" with reference to Poulenc's taste in art. An informative essay couched in a difficult style.

Charbois, Nicole. Eluard et Picasso. *In:* Rencontres avec Paul Eluard. *See* 9925. p. 188–207.   **10044**

A comparison of two temperaments which have, according to the author, much in common, in terms of taste, aspirations, essential motivation. Charbois attempts to equate Picasso's visual techniques (especially in "Guernica") with E.'s ideas. What the author has, in fact, demonstrated rather neatly is Picasso's art as one source of E.'s inspiration.

Décaudin, Michel. Le travail du peintre ou Le poète, la peinture et la musique. *In:* Rencontres avec Paul Eluard. *See* 9925. p. 101–06.   **10045**

Some useful observations on E. and the *livre de peintre,* followed by an examination of Poulenc's song cycle based on seven poems for painters chosen from *Voir.* Not a close analysis of text, music or their interplay, but rather a series of general conclusions based primarily on the meter of the poems with reference to the rhythmic values of the music. Brief discussion of Poulenc's impressions of E., his choice of texts, the structure of the cycle (in terms of tone and texture). A pioneer study in a little-explored area: the *mélodie* as a complex relationship between words and music.

Gateau, Jean-Charles. Morale de la lumière. A propos du poème de Eluard A Chastel. SFr 46:87–90, 1972.   **10046**

A study of E.'s manner of transmuting a painter's world into verbal imagery, important for its information, its interpretation and the method used.

———. Picasso ou l'anti-Baudelaire. RSH 36:261–70, 1971.   **10047**

Biographical background. Analysis of E.'s third poem to Picasso in 6 parts ("Les uns ont inventé l'ennui d'autres le rire"), particularly the sources of imagery and Picasso's significance for E.

Greet, Anne Hyde. Paul Eluard's early poems for painters. FMLS 9:86–102, 1973. *Also in:* Literature and the plastic arts 1880–1930. Seven essays. Ed. by Ian Higgins. Edinburgh, London: Scottish academic press, 1973. p. 86–102.   **10048**

An attempt to indicate, by interdisciplinary approach, relationships between poetry and painting. Analyzes, from this point of view, the early poems to Braque, Chirico, Arp, Klee and Miró. Some discussion of E.'s intentions in the composition of *Voir* and of his ideas, generally, on esthetics.

Hubert, Renée Riese (in collab. with J. D. Hubert). Une collaboration surréaliste: Les malheurs des immortels. *In:* Surréalisme/Surrealismo. Rome, Bulzoni; Paris, Nizet, 1974. p. 203–19. (Quaderni del novecento francese)   **10049**

Witty, brilliant, interdisciplinary study of relationships between collages and texts. Analyses of: *Rencontre de deux sourires, Mon petit Mont Blanc, Conseils d'ami, A la recherche de l'innocence, Les plaisirs oubliés* and, notably, *Les ciseux et leurs pères.* Illustrated.

———. Eluard's A Fernand Leger. Expl 24:54, 1966.   **10050**

A detailed interpretation of the poem in the light of Leger's theories about line, form and color, as an objective description of a vision (or a philosophy) most unlike the poet's own.

———. Ernst and Eluard, a model of surrealist collaboration. KRQ 21:113–21, 1974.   **10051**

An interdisciplinary study of *Répétitions.* Illuminates the affinities between poet and artist, and explores the possibilities of the *livre de peintre* as a genre. Illustrated.

———. Georges Braque and the French poets. BA 385–90, 1963.   **10052**

Analysis of "Georges Braque" (p. 386–87), delicate and skillful. Striking interpretation of the negations in first and affirmations in second stanza as an indication that E. shares Breton's reservations about Braque as a painter.

――――. Le langage de la peinture dans le poème en prose contemporain [Reverdy, Breton, Eluard]. RSH 105:109–16, 1962.
10053

E.'s reaction to surrealist art, expressed by vocabulary and juxtapositions. E. and Miró, Tanguy, Man Ray, Masson, Dali. Excellent interdisciplinary study.

――――. Les surréalistes et Picasso. EspCr 6:45–51, 1966.
10054

Valuable insights concerning E.'s evaluation of Picasso during and just after World War II, as a contemporary indication of the poet's own preoccupations. Not a commentary on the poems.

Jean, Marcel. Histoire de la peinture surréaliste. Seuil, 1959. 382 p.
10055

Passim: E.'s relation to the painters.

Jean, Raymond. Eluard et Picasso. Eur 493–95:37–41, 1970.
10056

A brief but lucid comment on a friendship and a shared esthetic.

Penrose, Roland. Picasso, his life and work. New York, Schocken books, 1958, 1962. 410 p. *Also* (*rev.*): Penguin, 1971. *Also:* New York, London, Harper and Row, 1973. 518 p. (Icon editions)
10057

Passim, detailed account of relationship and collaborations between E. and Picasso. Invaluable as biography and for its commentary on E. and the visual arts.

Poulenc, Francis. Journal de mes mélodies. Grasset, 1964. 110 p.
10058

Poulenc's important commentary on his *mélodies:* the settings of E.'s poetry, in particular, are discussed.

――――. Moi et mes amis. Confidences recueillies par Stéphane Audel. Paris, Geneva, La Palatine, 1963. 206 p.
10059

Biographical material on E. Of special interest for his influence on P.'s *mélodies* and choral music.

Strachan, W. J. Chastel's illustrations for Le bestaire. Typ 4:30–35, [1950?]
10060

A workmanlike study of the artist's approach to the problem of illustrating E.'s poetry.

Thomé, J. R. La saison des amours de Paul Eluard, avec douze eaux-fortes, et un emboîtage en peau de daim de Johnny Friedlander. CoGr 43:26, 1950.
10061

A discussion of the relationship between text and etchings.

Waldberg, Patrick. Présentation et préface. *In his:* Max Ernst, peintures pour Paul Eluard. De Noël, 1969. p. 5–16. (Publié à l'occasion de l'exposition Max Ernst, à la galerie André François Petit, en 1969)
10062

Reproduction of fragments of murals by Ernst for E.'s house at Eaubonne, near forest of Montmorency. Perceptive juxtaposition of the paintings with verse by the poet dating from the same period. Illuminates the relationship between Ernst and E. in an unexpected manner.

Individual Poems and Collections

Balakian, Anna. Etude des poèmes en prose: Les dessous d'une vie ou La pyramide humaine. *In:* Rencontres avec Paul Eluard. *See* 9925. p. 59–65.
10063

Valuable analysis of three prose poems, especially of the first. The role of epigraphs from Edward Young. Influence on Mallarmé, Rimbaud. Comparison with Breton, emphasizing the complexity of surrealism and the diversity between individual surrealists.

Beaujour, Michel. Analyse de Poésie ininterrompue. *In:* Paul Eluard. *See* 9924. p. 74–87.
10064

Postulates a change of direction in E.'s development. This notion is emphasized in a detailed, comprehensive analysis of the poem which is seen as the turning point towards poetry of commitment. A distinguished essay.

Béguin, Albert. Paul Eluard: poésie et morale. *In his:* Poésie de la présence de Chrétien de Troyes à Pierre Emmanuel. Neuchâtel, A la Baconnière; Paris, Seuil, 1957. p. 325–68. (Les cahiers du Rhône— Série blanche, 95)
10065

A study of the opposition between didacticism and lyricism in Une leçon de morale.

Bertelé, René. Paul Eluard ou de la critique de la vie à la critique de la poésie. Confl n.s. 2:200–05, 1945.
10066

Review of *Au rendez-vous allemand.*
E.'s evolution from personal poetry to
poetry of commitment.

Borel, Jacques. Un Eluard nocturne. NRF
175:92–104; 176:291–98, 1967. **10067**
On *Capitale de la douleur* and *Amour
de la poésie.* Instead of the usual association by Eluardian critics of night
with loneliness and day with communication, night is ˋassociated with the
lovers, and day, with separation. Sight,
as for Richard (see 10023), is the
privileged sense, but also, the most en-
dangered, because necessarily reciprocal.

Bounoure, G. Eluard. *In his:* Marelles sur
le parvis. Essais de critique poétique. Plon,
1958. p. 262–71. **10068**
I. Dreams, light and darkness, cyclic
imagery, especially in *Capitale....* II.
Review of *A toute épreuve.* Contrast
with *Capitale....* Increasing emphasis on
solitude and on doubts of the powers of
love poetry.

Carmody, Francis J. Eluard's rupture with
surrealism. PMLA 76:436–46, 1961.
10069
E.'s break with Breton in 1938 seen
as not uniquely political. Some distinctions indicated between surrealist
and later imagery, but the emphasis is
on the relation of E.'s poetry to literary
history. Detailed analysis of *Quelques-
uns des mots qui, jusqu'ici, m'étaient
mystérieusement interdits.*

Carrard, Philippe. Un poème de Paul Eluard, essai d'approche linguistique et littéraire. EdL 2:234–51, 1969. **10070**
A purely linguistic approach to the
study of *La terre est bleue comme une
orange.*

Cassou, Jean. Pour la poésie. Corrêa, 1935.
p. 268–78. **10071**
Reviews of *L'immaculée conception,
L'amour la poésie* and *La vie immédiate.* The second review discusses the
relationship of surrealist to precious
imagery.

Chiari, Joseph. Paul Eluard. *In his:* Contemporary French poetry. Philosophical
library, 1952. p. 125–52. **10072**
Comprehensive essay: emphasis on
theme of love; analysis of passages from
La rose publique and *Poésie ininter-*

rompue. Chiari sees two aspects, one
"purely lyrical" and the other, "social,
or... human." "E. has succeeded in
integrating in his poetry his social and
political views," in contrast to Aragon
and Auden, partly because he loves
individuals, not groups or concepts, and
speaks, when he is moved, not as a
mouthpiece. Thus he remains a great
lyricist, reminding Chiari of Scève or
Donne.

Cichocki, Marcel. Texte commenté: Le jeu
de construction [Capitale de la douleur].
HumCLm 3–7, June 1963. **10073**
Interesting "explication de texte."

Claessens, Francis. Introduction à la lecture
d'Eluard. CahAT 2:21–43, 1960. **10074**
A provocative reading of passages
from *La rose publique;* the relationship
of E.'s poetic practice to his theory of
"interpénétration" and to Breton's de-
ˋscription of "le point sublime" (the
latter, philosophically unsound, according to Claessens).

Cranston, Mechthild. Breton, Eluard and
Char: Ralentir travaux. Elective affinities?
RLMC 24:133–50, 1971. **10075**
An unusually fine study of a difficult
subject; of value to all scholars of E.,
Char, and Breton. Analysis of the text,
of each poet's role in the collaboration,
of their relationships to each other as
revealed by the text. Illuminating comments on E.'s style and on his influence,
at the time, upon Char.

Crevel, René. Au carrefour.... CahS 337,
Oct. 1956. *Also in his:* L'esprit contre la
raison, suivi de Dali ou l'anti-obscurantisme et de Nouvelles vues sur Dali et
l'obscur, Solitude variée, Pour la simple
honnêté et Au carrefour de l'amour, la
poésie, la science et la révolution. Préf. de
Marcel Jouhandeau. Textes réunis par
Jean Schwartz. Tchou, 1969. p. 125–46.
10076
An essay on poetry as intellectual
action centering on E.'s *La rose publique.* Probably written spring 1935.

Curnier, Pierre. Paul Eluard: Poésie ininterrompue. *In his:* Pages commentées
d'auteurs contemporains. V. 2. Larousse,
1965. p. 87–103. **10077**
A parallel is drawn between E.'s ideas
on poetic imagery and his political adherence to communism, between the

structure of *Poésie ininterrompue* and the Marxist dialectic. Analysis of Part I, lines 182–220. An interesting study.

Dhainault, Pierre. Les Exemples d'Eluard. *In:* Au temps de dada. Problèmes du langage. Lettres modernes, 1970. p. 27–43. (CahDS 4)   **10078**

E.'s search for a poetic language, coincident with, but independent from, dada, as shown by his originality in *Exemples*. Influence of Paulhan. Investigation of vocabulary, syntax, assonance and alliteration, rhythm, imagery. Detailed analysis of "l'exemple:" parallels in visual art.

Ducros, Franc. Combinaison, fonction métalinguistique et référents. Réflexions sur quelques images poétiques. RLR 78:85–96, 1969.   **10079**

Sketchy, linguistic examination, out of context, of the verse "Solitude, beau miel absent" (L'or et l'eau froide) and of a quatrain for which an incorrect page reference is given in Scheler.

Gallo, Laurence. La mort, l'amour, la vie de Paul Eluard, étude stylistique. *In:* Réflexions et recherches de nouvelle critique. Les belles lettres, 1969. p. 187–206. (AFLSHN 8, 1969)   **10080**

A linguistic analysis which unfortunately does not include the text. Given the dryness of the approach and the author's non-literary preoccupations, this painstaking essay has importance to those interested in a methodology rather than in poetry.

Gateau, Jean-Charles. Eluard et les îles. *In:* Rencontres avec Paul Eluard. *See* 9925. p. 125–31.   **10081**

Interesting analysis of "Dans mon beau quartier," which finds the sources of this prose poem not only in texts of the 20's but also in the Carné and Prévert film *Les portes de la nuit.*

Gaucheron, Jacques. Paul Eluard. Pen 24:113–17, 1949.   **10082**

Reviews *Le meilleur choix...* and *Poèmes politiques.* Primarily a Marxist justification of the political poems.

———. Poésie et imagination, étude sur *Ailleurs ici partout. In:* Rencontres avec Paul Eluard. *See* 9925. p. 20–35.   **10083**

Perhaps the only study devoted uniquely to these lines, it takes the text

as a point of departure for a commentary on "les problèmes de l'imagination." Some attention is paid, as well, to structure and style. Unfortunately, overflowing with digressions and lacking in clarity.

Gershman, Herbert S. Valéry, Breton and Eluard on poetry. FR 38:332–36, 1965.   **10084**

Useful confrontation of aphorisms from Valéry's "Littérature" (1929) and their parody by Breton and E. in "Notes sur la poésie" (1929), which clarifies, according to Gershman, differences between Valéry and the surrealists.

Gros, Léon-Gabriel. A l'épreuve du temps. CahS 311:120–26, 1952.   **10085**

A review of *Première anthologie.* Interesting not only as a comment on E.'s literary tastes but for the important biographical data omitted (i.e., E.'s exposure to a private collection of French poetry during World War II).

———. L'œuvre exemplaire de Paul Eluard. CahS 248:566–72, 1942. *Also in his:* Poètes contemporains. V. 1. Les cahiers du sud, 1944, p. 63–70.   **10086**

A review of *Choix de poèmes.* The role of love in E.'s esthetic.

———. Royaumes d'avant-soir. CahS 358:436–44, 1960–61.   **10087**

Reviews *Le dur désir...* and *Le temps déborde.* E. and the theme of death.

———. Ta bouche aux lèvres d'or... CahS 315:191–96, 1952.   **10088**

A review of *La jarre peut-elle être plus belle que l'eau?* E.'s evolution presented in a confrontation of texts from early and late chapbooks.

———. Le témoin poétique. La nuée du brasier. CahS 306:307–14, 1961.   **10089**

This review of *Une leçon de morale* stresses continuity in E.'s work: the difference between "poésie personnelle" and "poésie engagée" is arbitrary. Even more significant: "E. appartient à cette génération surréaliste qui s'est refusée à tenir la poésie pour un genre littéraire... "

Groupe u [J. Dubois, F. Edeline, J.-M. Klinkenberg, P. Minguet, F. Pire, and H. Trinon]: Rhétorique poétique. Le jeu des figures dans un poème de Paul Eluard. RR 63:125–51, 1972. **10090**

A fine structuralist essay, valuable as a comment on E.'s style, in the winter of 1940–41, which hovers between surrealist imagery of love and a simpler language of political commitment.

Kibédi Varga, A. Syntaxe et rythme chez quelques poètes contemporains [Du Bouchet, Prévert, Eluard, Reverdy]. *In:* Le vers français au XXe siècle. Colloque organisé par le Centre de philologie et de littérature romanes de l'Université de Strasbourg. Klincksieck, 1967. p. 175–88; discussion, p. 189–95. **10091**

A suggestive and important study of prosody in modern poetry, containing analyses of two poems by E.: "Au premier mot limpide" and "A peine défigurée," the first being the more detailed. Valuable discussion.

Launay, Michel. Analyse du premier écrit d'Eluard: Volé! nouvelle inédite [1908]. *In:* Approches. Essais sur la poésie moderne de langue française. Les belles lettres, 1971. p. 165–74; Annexe: Index de Volé, p. 172–74. (AnN 15:1971) *Also in:* CahPE 1:11–21, 1972. **10092**

An exercise in the application of word lists and frequencies to trace E.'s development from an early text. Contrast between a "sociocritical" reading of first part of text with a "psychocritical" reading of the latter part. A stated concern to reconcile history with linguistics, to reconcile a scientific attitude with what the author conceives to be a "poetic" one.

―――. La mort, l'amour, la vie. Proposition pour une lecture. Lit 1:48–61, 1971. **10093**

A linguistic approach which attempts to impose "scientific" techniques upon a poem, resulting in a complex, antiintuitive analysis. Unfortunate reliance upon paradoxical (and undefined) terms: "forme-sens," "lecture-écriture," "testament-monument." An admirable but not altogether successful experiment.

Laurent, M. Explication française. Un poème de Paul Eluard. Ec May 27, 1960. **10094**

An unusual, perceptive commentary of "Si tu aimes l'intense nue."

Nadeau, Maurice. Paul Eluard moraliste. *In his:* Littérature présente. Corrêa, 1952. p. 260–313. **10095**

Like Béguin, Nadeau sees a didactic poetry splitting off from E.'s powerful lyricism in *Une leçon de morale.*

Noulet, Emilie. Eluard, Paul: Poésie ininterrompue II. *In her:* Alphabet critique, 1924–64. V. 2. Brussels, Presses universitaires de Bruxelles, 1965. p. 99–101. (Univ. libre de Bruxelles, Travaux de la Faculté de philologie et lettres, XXVI) **10096**

A review of *Poésie ininterrompue II,* interpreting the text as a fusion of poetics and ethics. Stresses inseparability of E. from his convictions, whether based on surrealist esthetic or political commitment.

Onimus, Jean. Pour lire Répétitions de Paul Eluard. IL 25:18–25, 1973. **10097**

A remarkable study, for its lucid and perceptive presentation of a pre-surrealist esthetic. Exceptional among analyses of individual works.

―――. Pour un enseignement de la poésie. Essai de commentaire de texte. L'amour la poésie. Comme une image, IV. O.C. t. 1, p. 256, Pléiade, 1968. CahPE 3:9–18, 1973. **10098**

A most helpful analysis of imagery and of associations of ideas in a hermetic poem, "Armure de soie le parfum noir rayonne" (7 stanzas and 62 verses), constituting a major part of *L'amour la poésie.* Written with the author's usual clarity and in his usual muted style, this concise study illuminates the text and the poet's thought.

Peyre, Henri. Paul Eluard (1897–1952). *In:* The poem itself. Ed. by Stanley Burnshaw. Holt, Rinehart, and Winston, 1960. xiv, 337 p. *Also:* Hammondsworth, Penguin books, 1969. 340 p. (A pelican original) **10099**

Mildly disappointing commentaries by a distinguished scholar, in an unusually fascinating book. "La dame de carreau" (p. 104–05). "A peine défigurée"; "Mon amour..."; "Je cache les sombres trésors" (p. 106–07). "Amoureuse..."; "Le baiser": "Je n'ai envie que de t'aimer"; "Couvre-feu" (p. 108–09).

Raymond, Marcel. Un poème d'Eluard [poème liminaire de Facile 1935]. *In his:* Être et dire; études. Neuchâtel, Eds. de la Baconnière, 1970. p. 257–65.   **10100**
Analysis of "Tu es l'eau détournée de ses abîmes," interesting not only for its ideas but for its approach.

Robin, Pierre. La poésie française au service de la Résistance. 1. Problèmes français quatrième série. Beyrouth, Société d'impression et d'édition, 1944. p. 22–27.   **10101**
Mainly concerned with *Poésie et vérité* (1942).

Saillet, Maurice. Moralisme et poésie. MerF 309:117–21, 1950.   **10102**
A review of *Une leçon de morale* which emphasizes change and continuity in E.'s poetry. An unusual and fascinating evaluation of the theme of love: a seemingly objective awareness of E.'s weaknesses and talents; above all, a refreshingly well-written attack on the didacticism of the poet's later verse, in which the author reveals no political bias but simply takes an esthetic stand.

Scheler, Lucien. Le choix du cœur et l'univers poétique. *In:* Paul Eluard. *See* 9923. p. 134–39.   **10103**
A review of E.'s *Première anthologie* as an illustration of "poésie impersonnelle." Especially significant because of the relation between poet and editor at the time of the anthology's composition.

Seeley, Carol. The poetry of Paul Eluard. WR 14:29–41, 1949.   **10104**
Review of *Poésie ininterrompue* containing a résumé of a number of Eluardian themes. One of first critics to comment on poems to painters (Arp, Magritte and Picasso).

Södergard, Osten. Etude sur le vocabulaire de Capitale de la douleur de Paul Eluard. SN 32:106–16, 1960.   **10105**
A fascinating statistical analysis which finds the early E.'s vocabulary as rich as that of symbolists, of Valéry, or of Apollinaire, but less erudite, more concrete.

Tortel, Jean. Paul Eluard dans son grand souci de tout dire. CahS 315:201–12, 1952.   **10106**
An attempt to reconcile the later, overtly didactic poems of *Pouvoir tout dire* with E.'s earlier work. Less convincing than Gros' article in the same issue (*see* 10088).

Vernier, Richard. Poésie ininterrompue et la poétique de Paul Eluard. The Hague, Mouton, 1971. 180 p. (De proprietatibus litterarum, series practica, 27)   **10107**
A comprehensive study of the poem, seen in the context of E.'s entire work, with abundant reference to earlier texts, biographical data and other critics. Especially noteworthy are the chapters on themes and imagery, and on the reconciliation between E. the poet and E. the political idealist (with priority given to the former). At once sensible, perceptive and well-written. One of the few books devoted to E. which have distinction.

Wake, C. H. Eluard: L'extase. *In:* The art of criticism. Essays in French literary analysis. Ed. by Peter H. Nurse. Edinburgh, Univ. press, 1969. p. 287–99.   **10108**
A fine analysis, exemplifying one way of approaching E.'s imagery.

CHAPTER XXII

POETRY BEFORE 1940 (PART TWO)

(Nos. 10109–10484)

Dominique Baudoin, Claude Bouygues, Mary Ann Caws, Julia F. Costich,
Robert W. Greene, Tatiana Greene, Mortimer Guiney, Renée Riese Hubert,
Claire Schub, Claude Senninger, Dina Sherzer, and Jean-Claude Vilquin

Pierre Albert-Birot
(Nos. 10109–10132)

Dominique Baudouin

Iconography

Pierre Albert-Birot, Angoulême 22 avril 1876, Paris 25 juillet 1967. Musée d'Angoulême, Exposition du 28 juin au 15 octobre 1969. Angoulême, Musée d'Angoulême, 1969. 24 p. (Catalogue rédigé par Arlette Albert-Birot.) **10109**
The preface (J. A. Catala, *Un Charentais méconnu, Pierre Albert-Birot, 1876–1967, Souvenirs d'une enfance angoumoisine*, p. 3–10) includes lengthy excerpts from an unpublished autobiography of the poet. A list of A.-B.'s works follows including: *Peintures* (No. 12 should read "Autoportrait"), *dessins, gravures, sculptures, livres, documents, manuscrits, photographies.*

Special Numbers

Connaissance de Pierre Albert-Birot. Témoignages, hommages, études, notes. Textes... suivis d'un chapitre inédit de Grabinoulor. Ed. by Max Pons. Barb 6, spec. no. 7, 1–139, 1968. **10110**
Authors: M. Pons, A. Albert-Birot, C. Aveline, P. Béarn, A. Beucler, Chapelain-Midy, H. Chopin, R. Datheil, Y. Deletang-Tardif, M. J. Durry, J. Follain, L. Guillaume, M. Janet, B. Jourdan, A. Lebois, M. Nicoletti, P. Pia, J. Rousselot, R. Roussot, G. Severini, B. Wright, Zadkine. *Grabinoulor,* livre III, chap. 4. A 6-page bibliography of works of and studies on A.-B. (omits *La Panthère noire,* major volume of poetry, 1938. For more details see *French XX,* 67305, 74367).

Pierre Albert-Birot: études, dossiers, inédits, bibliographie. Ed. by Arlette Albert-Birot. F 2–3:1–155, n.d. [1973] **10111**
Significant articles are analyzed separately, but the whole issue is an indispensable contribution to A.-B. studies. Bibliography contains works and studies on A.-B.

Pierre Albert-Birot l'homme de la pierre à feu. Ed. by Arlette Lafont. Alt 44:n.p. [50 p.], 1959. **10112**
Reminiscences and "témoignages" by various hands. Contains poems of A.-B., including three previously unpublished.

General Studies

Albert-Birot, Pierre. Naissance et vie de SIC. LetN 17:843–59, 1953. *Also (rev.):* A propos du drame surréaliste d'Apollinaire. Marg 62–63:29–39, 1958. **10113**
Confidences on his artistic and literary self-education before 1914. Conspectus of the history of his periodical SIC: origins in 1916, intents, contents by issues, sudden suspension in 1919. Origins and performance, thanks to himself, of Apollinaire's *Mamelles de Tirésias,* and birth of the word "surrealism." More details about it in second article. Anecdotal presentation, nevertheless indispensable on this writer and his literary magazine. SIC, which appeared from Jan. 1916 to Dec. 1919, has been reprinted (SIC. Eds. de la Chronique des lettres françaises, 1973. 527 p.)

Baudouin, Dominique. La Panthère noire de Pierre Albert-Birot. EsDXX 5:28–40, 1975. **10114**

To date the only comprehensive study of the poet's probably best volume, in which through contrasted optimism and pessimism he reaches the maturity of a philosophical poetry of man's fate. A thorough thematic analysis.

Chopin, Henri. Notes à propos de l'œuvre de Pierre Albert-Birot. Taf 3–7, Oct. 1963. *Also in:* CCIEP 47:13–18, n.d. (Nov. 1963). *Also in (rev.):* Connaissance de Pierre Albert-Birot. *See* 10110. p. 38–42. *Also in (rev.):* Pierre Albert-Birot. *See* 10111. p. 19–27.   **10115**

The first three articles briefly present A.-B.'s varied attempts as those of a prisoner announcing multiple new ways in poetry. The first two items add annotated excerpts from his theater. The last and more important one places A.-B. in a poetical trend issuing from the Zutists, Jarry, futurists; situates him parallel to dada; sees him as a precursor of lettrism, of sound, and concrete or objective poetry.

Follain, Jean. Pierre Albert-Birot. Présentation par Jean Follain, choix de textes... Seghers, 1967. 192 p. (Poètes d'aujourd'hui, 163)   **10116**

Follain's essay outlines the short literary career of the founder of SIC at the time of futurism; then the different aspects of his work, theater, poetry, prose. Good survey, though limited (39 p.). Valuable mostly for insights on the poetic tensions of the work: between the everyday and eternal, the ego, its adamic double and universal, joy of real and epic fantasy. Excellent choice of texts in 130 p. by Arlette Lafont. Bibliography of works of and on A.-B.

Reviews: D. Baudouin in CahDS 3: 90–92, 1969; M. Décaudin in RLM 183–88:256, 1968.

Grey, Roch. Pierre Albert-Birot. Maint 2: 186–93, 1946.   **10117**

A portrait of the man and a brief overview of his work's variety, emphasizing the poet's egocentrism. Otherwise laudatory evocation with suggestive formulas, by a woman of letters who was the only constant witness to the poet's intellectual adventure since the time of SIC.

Jourdan, Bernard. Approche de Pierre Albert-Birot ou le poète et son double. Cr 177:121–33, 1962.   **10118**

After a brief literary orientation, follows the construction of the *autre moi* through its masks: an ego deriving from the primitive Adam (*Mémoires d'Adam*, etc.), and chiefly taking after *Grabinoulor* the superman of a baroque cosmogony, archetype and anagram of his creator. Succinct critical appraisal with tactful and refined formulas, at times reticent. Tends to lock the poet in a disdainful egotism.

Lebois, André. Passeport pour l'île Albert-Birot. *In:* Albert-Birot, Pierre. Grabinoulor amour. Limoges, Rougerie, 1955. p. 7–41. (L'espace poétique)   **10119**

Underlines the diversity and literary audacities of the "pyrogène." Stresses primitivism, the quest for joy as both exaltation and transfiguration of reality, the concern for problems of poetic language. Against the reproach of egocentrism, shows A.-B.'s sense of human sympathy. Sketches the major traits and numerous literary affinities of the multiform prose epic *Grabinoulor*. Not systematic, this brilliant presentation, under the guise of a laudatory "flânerie anthologique," is based on a thorough knowledge of the work, with a wealth of critical insights.

Perez-Jorba, J. Pierre Albert-Birot. Bibliothèque de l'instant, 1920. 45 p.   **10120**

Along with exalted praise, offers useful views on A.-B.'s avant-garde esthetics or *nunisme*. Draws already valuable conclusions on the main traits of the work, from the first poems and plays, and the beginnings of *Grabinoulor*. Indispensable as a first critical testimony.

Rousselot, Jean. Albert-Birot ou l'écriture réinventée. *In:* Pierre Albert-Birot. *See* 10111. p. 28–33. *Also (partly) in:* Albert-Birot et la convenance du dire. *In his:* Mort ou survie du langage. Paris-Brussels, Sodi, 1969. p. 133–36.   **10121**

Sees *Grabinoulor* as an epic prose poem borrowing its stylistic characteristics from several genres. Presents little known texts from A.-B.'s prose works concerning his conceptions of the "langue en barre" without punctuation, and of poetic language. Short but documented and worthwhile sketch of an important aspect of the writer.

Poetry: Specific Studies

Baudouin, Dominique. Une lecture des Poèmes à l'autre moi. *In:* Pierre Albert-Birot. *See* 10111. p. 101–16.   **10122**
Studies the thematic structures of the work: its synthesis between spiritual double and physical ego, reaching beyond narcissism; its sur-realism or balance between real and surreal oriented towards poetic transgression through temporal and spatial dilatation. Defines, as expressed in the dual character of A.-B.'s poetic verb, a poetry of human ambivalence. A systematic and thorough analysis of this, A.-B.'s major volume of poetry.

Bosquet, Alain. Aux trente-deux vents, poèmes de Pierre Albert-Birot présentés par Albert-Birot. TR 92:21–28, 1955.   **10123**
Reminds one of the work's abundance and disconcerting variety. Underlines its ambiguous mixing of irony and anxiety before the absurd. This poet shares and goes beyond his generation's *tics,* prefiguring Ponge and Supervielle. Short general presentation, but well-informed and concentrated with penetrating insights.

Burgos, Jean. Pour un portrait de Pierre Albert-Birot. *In:* Pierre Albert-Birot. *See* 10111. p. 7–15.   **10124**
The wonderstruck ingenuity of the young poet, in a Douanier Rousseau's fashion, should not distract the reader from A.-B.'s sense of time, death, solitude and strangeness. Shows the poet's evolution towards a more complex awareness of the relationship of man and the world. Offers comparisons with Michaux and Supervielle. Judicious and penetrating critical views, though sketchy at times. The best comprehensive appreciation of A.-B.'s poetry in this special issue.

Lassaque, Roger. La joie du verbe et des sept couleurs. *In:* Pierre Albert-Birot. *See* 10111. p. 89–100.   **10125**
Examines certain verbal traits of the long poem of 1919 (rhyme plays, utterances, onomatopoeias, use of *et* and *il y a,* the scenery-poem, the poster-poem) as many bridges linking the world and the poem, which is nevertheless re-creation, not imitation. Methodical but partial views with no pretense of attempting a comprehensive evaluation of the whole poem.

Lebois, André. La poésie de Pierre Albert-Birot. MerF 318, no. 1078:239–45, 1953.   **10126**
An introduction to A.-B.'s *Dix poèmes à la mer,* which follow, p. 246–55. Brief but suggestive outline of the main traits of his inspiration: transgression of spatial and temporal categories; a positive spirit of childhood and joy, of love of life and language, not unacquainted with the tragic; a poet of the city too. Developed in Lebois' *Passeport...* (*see* 10119).

———. Préface. *In:* Albert-Birot, Pierre. Poésie, 1916–1924. Gallimard, 1967. p. 1–17.   **10127**
Brief view of A.-B.'s literary situation, stressing the interest of his poetic chronicles; relates him mostly to the early century poets, without much attention to possible relations or comparison with futurism, dada, surrealism. Points out the multiple facets of this poetry. A lively invitation to reading by one of the best connoisseurs of the work.

Mora, André. En hommage à Pierre Albert-Birot. *In:* Pierre Albert-Birot l'homme de la pierre à feu. *See* 10112. n.p.   **10128**
Among the 25 contributions to this special issue, this one stands out as a very valuable sketch of the expansion of a poetic space which extends from everyday reality to cosmic dimensions.

Verhesen, Fernand. La courbe de ce poème qui nous recrée et Pierre Albert-Birot. CCIEP 47:7–12, n.d. [1963].   **10129**
Underlines the metaphysical dimensions of an apparently superficial and common exteriority. The most penetrating view on a paradoxical poetic space among the three contributions to this special issue.

Prose

Abastado, Claude. Jeux et visée d'un texte parodique, Grabinoulor. *In:* Pierre Albert-Birot. *See* 10111. p. 67–78.   **10130**

Reveals a fine example of parody of literary fiction conventions; parody by contamination of the structures and themes of the epic, the philosophical tale, the personal diary; by questioning space, time and logical categories; by play on writing styles and on narrative perspectives. Then a quick sketch on positive significations. Striking suggestion of approach by ways of recent critical grids of a swarming text, which however would most likely elude every grid and method.

Lebois, André. Grabinoulor redivivus. Thy 67:317–23, 1965.   **10131**

About the 1964 Gallimard ed. of *Grabinoulor;* stresses its fragmentary character. Points out some traits of this modern epic of the poetic imagination: freedom and humor of its mythical dimensions, satirical realism, moral richness, full-flavored language. Short appreciative study with many a useful suggestion.

Theater

Décaudin, Michel. De l'utilité de Pierre Albert-Birot au théâtre. *In:* Pierre Albert-Birot. *See* 10111. p. 47–54.   **10132**

Draws from different issues of SIC and from other texts the conceptions of the nunist theatre. Stresses their consonance with Apollinaire's dramaturgy in *Les mamelles de Tirésias.* Reviews several of A.-B.'s plays to show their variety. Brief but methodical and reliable overview which does justice to a neglected precursor of the innovations in the new theater. Includes a bibliography of A.-B.'s theater and views on theater.

Joë Bousquet
(Nos. 10133–10156)

CLAUDE BOUYGUES

Correspondence

Bousquet, Joë. Lettres à Carlo Suarès. Préf. de Marc Thivolet. Limoges, Rougerie, 1973. 175 p.   **10133**

Contains most of the letters to Carlo Suarès and covers the 1928–38 period during which B. became aware of the

powers of *l'écriture.* By far some of the most revealing letters on the poet's personal tragedy and literary ideals.

———. Lettres à Poisson d'Or. Préf. de Jean Paulhan. Gallimard, 1967. 232 p.   **10134**

An illuminating and a moving collection of documents dated from 1937 to 1949. Invaluable pieces of information about B. the man, the poet, the philosopher, and his favorite readings.

Reviews: Anon. in TLS 66:898, 1967; C. Audejean in Esp 35:1110–12, 1967; C. Cordié in Pai 23:73–74, 1968; R. Jean in QL 29:10, June 1, 1967; R. Kanters in FL 1097:17–18, April 24, 1967; A. Miguel in NRF 30:105–09, 1967; J. Piatier in Monde 6896:i–ii, March 15, 1967.

General Studies: Books

André, Suzanne; Hubert Juin; and Gaston Massat. Joë Bousquet. Trois études par Suzanne André... Choix de textes... Seghers, 1958. 222 p. (Poètes d'aujourd'hui, 62)   **10135**

André's introduction is a not too convincing investigation of B.'s ontological system. Juin establishes close relationships between the poet and his works, and wrongly likens B.'s experience to Pascal's. Massat's contribution to the volume is a very detailed and accurate biography. Choice of texts could be better; does not do justice to such capital works as *Traduit du silence* and *La connaissance du soir.*

Review: M.-J. Rustan in CahS 349: 58, 1959.

Maurette, Michel. Joë Bousquet. Présenté par Michel Maurette. Lettres inédites. Bibliographie. Rodez, Subervie, 1963. 128 p. (Visages de ce temps, 10)   **10136**

Présentation by Maurette heavily stresses the biographical and the anecdotic. Choice of texts is fairly good but scanty. Best part of the volume is the bibliography, especially as regards B.'s texts printed in publications from 1928 (*Chantiers* 1, 2) to 1955. Tendency to be apologetic.

Reviews: J. Guichard-Meili in Esp 32:188–89, 1964; J. Lebrau in LetF 5, Jan. 2, 1964; P. Loubière in EnLA 23:53–54, 1964.

Special Numbers

Joë Bousquet. CahS 303:177–231, 1950. **10137**
One third of this issue is an homage to B. Contributing are F. Alquié, P. Guerre, G. Massat, R. Nelli, J. Paulhan. Also included are texts by B.: *Fragments de journal* and *Caractéristique* (p. 207–31). Significant articles have been analyzed separately.

Joë Bousquet ou le recours au langage. CahS 362–63:1–115, 1961. **10138**
115 p. out of 176 devoted to B. Various contributors. Texts by B. (p. 101–15) are *Correspondance avec M., Fers de lance, Fragments de journal. Correspondance* and *Fragments* have been gathered by J. Ballard. *Fers de lance* is a collection of maxims of capital interest put together by R. Rovini. This issue contains the first examples of criticism based primarily on the texts, and is therefore of signal importance. Significant articles are analyzed separately.

General Studies

Alquié, Ferdinand. Joë Bousquet et la morale du langage. CahS 303:187–90, 1950. **10139**
On B.'s conception of poetry: not a means to avoid or forget the terrible consequences of his war wound, but to get to the core of this tragic event and assume its full significance on the ontological level.

Burucoa, Christiane. Tableau de la conscience infiniment privée. *In:* Joë Bousquet ou le recours au langage. *See* 10138. p. 84–90. **10140**
Endeavors to unmesh the intricate relationships between language, reality (*l'événement*), consciousness and the absolute with particular reference to B.'s *Les capitales ou de Jean Duns Scot à Jean Paulhan,* and through the use of B.'s correspondence with Burucoa. Notes interesting similarities between B.'s and the surrealists' experience of language.

Gros, Léon-Gabriel. Joë Bousquet ou l'avènement de la sensibilité. *In his:* Poètes contemporains. Deuxième série. Marseille, Cahiers du sud, 1951. p. 34–51. **10141**

Attempts to describe the ideological foundations of B.'s poetry. B. evolved from a surrealistic emphasis on dream, to a metaphysical conception of language, to a viewpoint (expressed in *La connaissance du soir*) rather close to that of Francis Ponge in *Le parti pris des choses.*

Juin, Hubert. L'homme à l'intérieur du langage. Essai sur l'œuvre et la pensée de Joë Bousquet. CahS 318:289–300, 1953. **10142**
Centered around the philosophical problem of the relationships between language, thought and being. Similarities between André Gaillard's and B.'s ways to reach poetical knowledge and sense of unity (going beyond the Life-Death contradiction). The ontological dimension of B.'s conception of language is what sets him apart from Duns Scot and Paulhan. Clearly organized text, but will seem at times unnecessarily abstruse to the average reader. Worth the effort, though, as it deals with capital problems lying at the core of B.'s works.

Massat, Gaston. Reconnaissance à Joë Bousquet. *In:* Joë Bousquet. *See* 10137. p. 201–06. **10143**
Two main divisions: 1) the author's and B.'s debt to the surrealists; 2) elucidation of the problem of love: B. is said to follow the tradition of courtly love, but his cult for woman, both so intricately and extremely mystical and carnal at the same time, is beyond the troubadours' ideal.

Nelli, René. Joë Bousquet et son double. *In:* Joë Bousquet. *See* 10137. p. 177–86. **10144**
Penetrating study by a close friend of B. and one of his best critics. A convincing attempt to trace the major steps in the evolution of B.'s basic concerns, from destiny and man's attitudes towards it, to love and femininity, and to the relationship between language, reality and consciousness.

———. Le style de Joë Bousquet ou l'aventure du langage dans l'esthétique de la poésie. *In:* Joë Bousquet ou le recours au langage. *See* 10138. p. 8–31. **10145**
Points out some influences by the surrealists, and an interesting tendency of B. to promote the analogical and

the poetical to the detriment of the logical (new criticism would compare with Lautréamont, among others). Distinguishes two manners in B. To the *récits* or prose works corresponds a *poésie-fiction* style, whereas *poésie-langage* prevails in the poems. Reference is made in a note to a lecture given by the author on the same topic (Narbonne, July 1960). A very rewarding study.

Paulhan, Jean. A l'abeille d'hiver. *In:* Joë Bousquet. *See* 10137. p. 191–97. *Also in:* LetF 1174:3–4, March 16, 1967. *Also (rev.):* Préface. *In:* Bousquet, Joë. Lettres à Poisson d'or. *See* 10134.   **10146**

Obviously not meant as a preface to *Lettres...* but nevertheless important since written by a man whose influence on B. is undeniable. Parts II and III (p. 12 and 14 of the preface to *Lettres ...*) deal with the capital question of whether language precedes thought.

Robbe-Grillet, Alain. Joë Bousquet le rêveur. Cr 9:819–29, 1953. *Also in his:* Pour un nouveau roman. Eds. de minuit, 1963. p. 82–94.   **10147**

Points out that with B. the creator's powerlessness and the vitality of his creation are in a cause-effect relationship. Makes reservations, as expected, about B.'s mysticism which is based upon, and unavoidably derived from, the poet's idea of Totality (reference to God in the final analysis). B. should state explicitly that inventing, re-creating a world cannot be the way to the essence of things as writing is strictly an individual's personal experience and must be started over and over again. Imagination is the only medium between man and the outside reality. An articulate and forceful analysis.

Rovini, Robert. Joë Bousquet, la chance du néant. *In:* Joë Bousquet ou le recours au langage. *See* 10138. p. 37–65.   **10148**

The first thorough study based on B.'s key texts (*Le meneur de lune, La connaissance du soir, Traduit du silence, La neige d'un autre âge, Le mal d'enfance, Iris et petite fumée, Les capitales, Il ne fait pas assez noir*). Interesting parallels drawn between the poet and Georg Frankl, Mallarmé and the surrealists. Contradicts H. Juin's point of view on language as a transcending power. Numerous and opportune quotations. Well organized, rewarding study.

Rustan, Marie-Josèphe. Joë Bousquet et le temps. *In:* Joë Bousquet ou le recours au langage. *See* 10138. p. 70–83.   **10149**

From *le Temps hideux* (or *Temps-perdition*) to *le Temps-Salut*. Main divisions are self-explanatory: *La durée-passion, La durée ontologique, Entre le Temps-rupture et le Temps-destin, L'Instant-illumination, L'Absence réalisante.* Followed by a short note on B. and opium. An important thematic and philosophical contribution.

Thivolet, Marc. Préface. *In:* Bousquet, Joë. Lettres à Carlo Suarès. *See* 10133. p. 7–26.   **10150**

Detailed historical account of the relationship between B. and C. Suarès. An important piece of criticism on B.

Individual Works

Emié, Louis. Méditation sur La connaissance du soir de Joë Bousquet. CahS 289:454–61, 1948.   **10151**

The first important essay on the relationship between language and thought in B. with reference to *La connaissance* only. Reflections and comments on what is a potential *Ars poetica* with B.: "Le poème n'est pas l'expression de l'homme qui a reçu le langage, mais de l'homme qui le reçoit." Language is a means to investigate the self considered both as a reality and as a surreality.

Kanters, Robert. La passion de Joë Bousquet. FL 1097:17–18, April 24, 1967.   **10152**

Critical commentary on *Lettres à Poisson d'or*, and an attempt to recreate the Carcassonne background of B. Also a brief analysis of B.'s philosophy as illustrated in his *Lettres*. Not a capital text, but may help approach B.

Miguel, André. Joë Bousquet et le mythe de l'androgyne. NRF 175:105–09, 1967.   **10153**

Besides a review of *Lettres à Poisson d'or*, an interesting and convincing essay on sexual ambivalence in B.'s love letters. Femininity and virility are experienced as successive and even at times simultaneous phases of love relationships.

Noulet, Emilie. Bousquet, Joë. La connaissance du soir. *In her:* Alphabet critique. V. 1. Brussels, Presses de l'univ. de Bruxelles, 1964. p. 194–97. **10154**

La connaissance contains the foundations of an ethics of imagery and rhythm, a formula for modern poetry, and an *Ars consolationis.* Interesting, though highly impressionistic views. Tendency to be excessively apologetic.

Patri, Aimé. Existentialisme, platonisme et surréalisme chez Joë Bousquet. Cr 5:400–03, 1946. **10155**

An analysis of the matter of B.'s *Le meneur de lune* (1946). Points out strikingly Sartrian formulas in the book, and tries to define B.'s blend of mysticism and Platonism. B. goes beyond the surrealists' experience of dream, and eventually develops a metaphysics of language. A short but illuminating study.

Rustan, Marie-Josèphe. Les capitales de Joë Bousquet. CahS 338:115–21, 1956. **10156**

A short and rather sharp analysis of B.'s *Les capitales ou de Jean Duns Scot à Jean Paulhan.*

René Daumal
(Nos. 10157–10195)

Claire Elizabeth Françoise Schub

Editions

Daumal, René. L'évidence absurde. Essais et notes I (1926–1934). Ed. by Claudio Rugafiori. Gallimard, 1972. 286 p. (*First edition:* Chaque fois que l'aube paraît. Essais et notes I. Gallimard, 1953.) **10157**

Important essays, notes, and articles from *Le grand jeu, Cahiers du Sud, N.R.F.*

———. Les pouvoirs de la parole. Essais et notes II (1935–1943). Ed. by Claudio Rugafiori. Gallimard, 1972. 282 p. **10158**

Essays and notes from *Recherches philosophiques, Mesures, Verve, Cahiers du sud, Fontaine.* On movement, space, India, the absolute, poetry. Includes "Pour un métier poétique," "Le message de la Bhagavad-Gîtâ," etc.

———. Tu t'es toujours trompé. Ed. by Jack Daumal. Mercure de France, 1970. 253 p. **10159**

Short introduction by D.'s brother. D.'s powerful, angry text, written around 1926–28, deals with "l'éveil perpétuel de la conscience" (p. 25), metaphysics, pataphysics, laughter, the absolute, the word "Dieu," India. Underlying idea of true thought being revolutionary. Ends with short article by Benjamin Crémieux about the anguish of youth and hope for a new humanism: "Le désarroi de la jeunesse intellectuelle française en 1925."

Correspondence

Daumal, René. Lettres à ses amis I. Gallimard, 1958. 374 p. **10160**

Letters from 1915–32. The beauty and strength of his friendships as well as D.'s unique imagination are revealed here.

Reviews: J. Roudat in Cr 144:410–12, 1959; A. Rousseaux in FL 650:2, Oct. 4, 1958.

Collected Articles

Le grand jeu. Ed. by Marc Thivolet. Minard, 1968. 214 p. (Les cahiers de l'Herne) **10161**

Excellent presentation of the three published issues of *Le grand jeu* and of the fourth issue which was never published.

Hommage à René Daumal. Ed. by Max-Pol Fouchet. Font 52:778–807, 1956. **10162**

Includes a short tribute to D. who was a member of the editorial committee of *Fontaine* and a short biography by Fouchet (p. 779). Also "Sur René Daumal" by Henri Hell (p. 780–87), "La guerre sainte" and part of chapter 4 of *Le Mont Analogue* by D.

Il y a dix ans, René Daumal. CahS 322:345–404, 1954. **10163**

Very favorable articles by Manuel Rainoird, Léon-Gabriel Gros, Bernard Dort, Jacques Masui. Texts by D.: "Le mensonge de la vérité;" poems from *Poésie noire, poésie blanche;* letters to Jacques Masui; translations from Laws of Manu and the *Bhagavad Gîtâ.* Significant articles are analyzed separately under appropriate headings.

René Daumal. Ed. by Philippe Vaillant. Grive 135–36:2–50, 1967. **10164**

Tribute to D. Sensitive, beautiful portrait of D. by Valentine Hugo on the cover. Includes articles by André Dhôtel, Jacques Lepage, Pierre Minet, Luc Perin, Michel Random, Jean Pies, Camille Lecrique, Philippe Vaillant, "Précisions nécessaires" — an interview with Jack Daumal. Also bibliography of D. by Gérard Mavel, and D. chronology by P. Vaillant, portraits by Valentine Hugo of D. and of Roger Gilbert-Lecomte. Significant articles are analyzed individually under appropriate headings.

La voie de René Daumal du Grand jeu au Mont Analogue. Ed. by Jacques Masui. Minard, 1967–1968. 138 p. (Les cahiers Hermès, 5) **10165**

Includes *Manifeste du Grand jeu* by Roger Gilbert-Lecomte and articles dealing with D.'s life and work by Michel Random, Jean Biès, Jacques Masui, Jean Richer, Jean Roudaut, Pierre Minet, Raymond Christoflour. Also excerpts from essays, articles, letters and translations from Sanskrit by D. Very impressive and important. Significant articles are analyzed individually under appropriate headings.

Biography

Biès, Jean. René Daumal et l'expérience Gurdjieff. *In:* La voie de René Daumal. *See* 10165. p. 35–47. **10166**

Stresses the importance of Gurdjieff the "Master" to an understanding of D. Summary of teachings (the Work), including the need to kill one's personality to discover the Essence, the use of shock, the "stop" exercise, will, movement. D. takes this "chemin de l'indésirable." *Le Mont Analogue* seen as a diary of the Gurdjieff adventure towards self-discovery.

Lobet, Marcel. L'expérience spirituelle de René Daumal. RGB 4:79–85, 1968. **10167**

"René Daumal apparaît comme un témoin des temps futurs..." Literature, for D., was "une exploration de l'invisible." Stresses similarities between D. and Rimbaud as seekers of the absolute,

as mystics. Sees young people today as "une génération en quête d'un nouveau Graal" and wonders if this generation will rediscover D.

Masui, Jacques. L'expérience spirituelle de Daumal et l'Inde. *In:* La voie de René Daumal. *See* 10165. p. 56–67. **10168**

The importance of India in understanding D.'s inner life, through unpublished letters and Masui's memories. D.'s conviction that there is an absolute truth in the music, poetry, language, philosophy and sacred books of India.

———. Préface. *In:* Daumal, René. Bharata. L'origine du théâtre. La poésie et la musique en Inde (traductions de textes sacrés et profanes). Gallimard, 1970. p. 7–12. **10169**

Preface by Masui throws light on D.'s discovery of the Hindu tradition through René Guénon and his attitude toward it; his rediscovery of "le trésor perdu de la première grammaire"—our mother language, Sanskrit. Explains the sciences of the language which are connected with the Vedas; "les sciences du langage comme moyen de libération." Review: M.-T. Bodart in SynB 287: 102–05, 1970.

———. René Daumal et l'Inde. *In:* Il y a dix ans, René Daumal. *See* 10163. p. 380–86. **10170**

The value of an idea, for D., exists only if it can be lived. His knowledge of Sanskrit, which he considered to be the sacred language, the language of his own being. Masui explains D.'s attitude toward the Eastern mentality, especially in his approach to translating. For D., the teachings of ancient India were realized by Gurdjieff.

Minet, Pierre. La défaite. Confessions. Sagittaire, 1947. 274 p. *Also:* Brussels, Jacques Antoine, 1973. **10171**

Dedicated to D., among others. Minet, who was, according to Michel Random in *Le grand jeu,* "l'enfant vadrouilleur du siècle," lived a life of complete freedom, on the streets of Paris. He was a friend of D. and Roger Gilbert-Lecomte: "ils étaient mes dieux." Minet considered D.'s devotion to Gurdjieff as treason, but he continued to admire him. Mostly, a lyrical, fascinating "confession" of Minet's youth of running away to Paris, adventure, visions, rebellion, freedom, dreams, bars, streets, and poetry.

――――. Sur René Daumal. *In:* La voie de René Daumal. *See* 10165. p. 105–07.

10172

A very loving memory of the young D.—his humor, his quality of being so different from others.

Pauwels, Louis. Monsieur Gurdjieff; documents, témoignages, textes et commentaires sur une société initiatique contemporaine. Seuil, 1956. 533 p. *Trans.:* Gurdjieff. With paintings by Felix Labisse, Georges Rohner, Ferro. Douglas (Isle of Man), Times press, 1964. 457 p. **10173**

Fascinating account of Gurdjieff and those who became involved with him. "Part IV: Literature" occurs only in French edition. Includes mostly D.: D. on friendship, on poetry. Letter by Pierre Minet: how D. became "moins un homme qu'un automate" because of Gurdjieff's view of man as a machine.

――――. Une société secrète: les disciples de George Gurdjieff. Arts 357:5, May 1–7, 1952. **10174**

Explains the inevitable destructiveness of Gurdjieff's teachings. Includes a biography of Gurdjieff, and a summary of his teachings: Man is a machine, a puppet. Man has no permanent "self." For Pauwels, who was a member of a Gurdjieff group and who almost destroyed himself, the teachings go against the forces of life and of inspiration. For D. and for Luc Dietrich, the teachings changed their lives. *Le Mont Analogue* as an allegory of the Gurdjieff experience. Includes photographs of D., Luc Dietrich, Lanza del Vasto, Katherine Mansfield.

Random, Michel. Le grand jeu. Denoël, 1970. 2 v. **10175**

1: Background of *Le grand jeu,* its history. D. from *Le grand jeu* to Gurdjieff's teachings. Direction and ideals of *Le grand jeu:* "la métaphysique expérimentale," dream, "révolution-révélation," parapsychology, influence of René Guénon, writers surrounding the movement, struggle against surrealism. Some photographs. 2: Texts dealing with *Le grand jeu* and the lives of those involved. Letters and notes from *Les Phrères Simplistes,* articles

from *Le grand jeu.* Articles by D. (p. 63–88): "Une expérience fondamentale," "Liberté sans espoir," and other important texts. Includes "Petit glossaire du *Grand jeu.*"

――――. Les puissances du dedans. Luc Dietrich, Lanza del Vasto, René Daumal, Gurdjieff. Denoël, 1966. 441 p. **10176**

Extremely interesting and important study of the struggles of the three artists and their encounter with the teachings of Gurdjieff. Lanza del Vasto's rejection of Gurdjieff's work. The ironic and sad destruction of Dietrich and Daumal. Concentrates on the destructive aspect of Gurdjieff and of the creative person. Includes good photographs. "Mémorables," "La guerre sainte" by Daumal.

――――. René Daumal et Le grand jeu. *In:* La voie de René Daumal. *See* 10165. p. 15–27. **10177**

Le grand jeu as a call to "révélation-révolution." The adventure, intensity, and youth of the movement. Excellent summary of this period of D.'s life.

――――. Roger Gilbert-Lecomte, René Daumal et Le grand jeu. *In:* René Daumal. *See* 10164. p. 29–33. **10178**

About "les années magiques" for D. and Gilbert-Lecomte between 1922 and 1932. The intensity of their experiences, the great adventure of *Le grand jeu.* Discovery of ancient texts: a return to the source. "Nerval le nyctalope," psychic adventures. "Le soleil noir" or revelation of another world.

General Studies

Biès, Jean. René Daumal. Seghers, 1967. 192 p. (Poètes d'aujourd'hui, 69) *Also:* 1973. **10179**

Sensitive, poetic study of D.'s life and writings. Texts by D. include parts of *La grande beuverie, Le Mont Analogue, Chaque fois que l'aube paraît, Poésie noire, poésie blanche, Lettres à ses amis,* translations from the *Rig-Veda.*

――――. René Daumal, témoin de la fin d'un monde. *In:* René Daumal. *See* 10164. p. 34–40. **10180**

We are in the dark age, the Kali Yuga of the Hindu cosmic cycle. D. understands this and shows the dark age in *La grande beuverie.* D. has no pity for the false artists, the profane scientists. Influence of René Guénon and Gurdjieff. Excellent understanding of *La grande beuverie.*

Bodart, Marie-Thérèse. René Daumal: du surréalisme au cristal de la dernière stabilité. SynB 263–64:115–21, 1968. **10181**
The importance of *Le grand jeu.* The break with surrealism. Perhaps D. accepted Gurdjieff as only a confirmation of "certaines réalités." Beauty as an objective factor: "mystère d'unité et d'amour."

Entretiens du polyèdre. L'itinéraire spirituel et littéraire de René Daumal. Et 328: 701–23, 1968.   **10182**
Interesting discussion among writers and critics: André Dhôtel, Jean Follain, Jacques de Bourbon Busset, Henri Thomas, Jean Mambrino.

Gros, Léon-Gabriel. René Daumal et Le grand jeu. *In:* Il y a dix ans, René Daumal. *See* 10163. p. 353–57.   **10183**
The ideals of *Le grand jeu* and the importance of spiritual development.

Lepage, Jacques. Un poète de la connaissance: René Daumal. Esp 5:1011–17, 1961.   **10184**
D., Michaux, Milosz as three "poètes mystiques sans Dieu." D.'s belief in man's "trésor de vérité" and in "l'absolue réalité de la poésie." "Création, connaissance, intégration" and the use of negation in D.'s poetry.

————. René Daumal ou l'expérience fondamentale. *In:* René Daumal. *See* 10164. p. 14–17.   **10185**
Essentially same text as 10184.

Nimier, Roger. René Daumal. *In his:* Journées de lecture. Gallimard, 1965. p. 111–19.   **10186**
The importance of D. by an admirer.

Noulet, Emilie. Les cahiers de la Pléiade (Constellation, numéro spécial, 1946). *In her:* Alphabet critique 1924–1964. V. 1 (A–C). Brussels, Presses univ. de Bruxelles, 1964. p. 219–25.   **10187**
Noulet deals critically with D.'s exploration of higher worlds through visions induced by carbon tetrachloride. For Noulet, a state of narcosis does not lead to a perception of the beyond and she sees D. as misinterpreting what she

perceives as a "spectacle mental" which can easily occur.

Rolland de Renéville, André. Deux poètes de la connaissance. *In his:* Univers de la parole. Gallimard, 1944. p. 159–70. **10188**
D. and Roger Gilbert-Lecomte used poetry as a vehicle for religious experience. The attempt of *Le grand jeu* to connect their own experiences with the great mystical tradition; D.'s poems in his *Le contre ciel* as a series of negations to reach the self.

Poetry

Lecrique, Camille. Poésie noire, poésie blanche. *In:* René Daumal. See 10164. p. 41–44.   **10189**
D. as conqueror of new psychic spaces.

Roudaut, Jean. L'attitude poétique de René Daumal. *In:* La voie de René Daumal. *See* 10165. p. 98–104.   **10190**
Explores D.'s well-defined feelings about poetry; poetry should be oral, useful, conscious. Poetry has meaning in "cette absolue parole-non-parlée." D.'s idea of "la poésie noire et la poésie blanche." Poetry as alchemy. The poem as spiritual experience.

Novel

Attal, Jean-Pierre. René Daumal et le véritable mode d'emploi de la parole. Cr 253:558–68, 1968.   **10191**
Comparison of D. (mostly *Une expérience fondamentale* and *Le Mont Analogue*) and Dante (*La vita nuova*).

Daumal, Vera. Postface. *In:* Daumal, René. Le Mont Analogue. *See* 10194. p. 193–96. *Also in:* Daumal, René. Mount Analogue. *See* 10195. p. 148–51. **10192**
Very important because it summarizes the end of the novel which D. did not finish.

Richer, Jean. Sur le sentier de la montagne: René Daumal conteur. *In:* La voie de René Daumal. *See* 10165. p. 87–97.   **10193**
Le grande beuverie and *Le Mont Analogue* as forms of "récit initiatique." The *Odyssey*, the Grail legend as pro-

totypes. Influence of Rabelais. *La grande beuverie* as a pataphysical, moral and metaphysical work.

Rolland de Renéville, A. Préface. *In:* Daumal, René. Le Mont Analogue. Récit véridique. Gallimard, 1952. p. 11–23. **10194**

Interesting preface giving background — *Le grand jeu, La grande beuverie, Le contre-ciel,* Sanskrit, etc. Letter from D. to Raymond Christoflour explaining *Mount Analogue* as the symbolic mountain "qui est la voie unissant le Ciel à la Terre; voie sans quoi notre situation serait sans espoir." (Note: other critics consider this novel to be autobiographical.)

Shattuck, Roger. Introduction. *In:* Daumal, René. Mount Analogue; a novel of symbolically authentic non-Euclidean adventures in mountain climbing. Trans. by Roger Shattuck. Pantheon, 1960. p. 11–34. **10195**

Excellent introduction traces the themes of *Mount Analogue* "through D.'s brief life and long work."

Jean Follain
(Nos. 10196–10225)

Mortimer Guiney

Special Numbers

Hommage à Jean Follain. NRF 222:1–128, 1971. **10196**

Special number. Important articles analyzed separately.

Jean Follain. Contr 3:1–38, 1972. **10197**

Special number. Important articles analyzed separately.

Visages de Jean Follain. Inédits de Jean Follain. Bibliographie-iconographie. Textes réunis et présentés par Max Jacob. Barb 11–12:7–70, 1971. **10198**

Special number. Important articles analyzed separately.

Biography

Albert-Birot, Arlette. Sous le signe de Grabinoulor. *In:* Visages de Jean Follain. See 10198. p. 35–38. **10199**

Comments about the friendship between F. and Pierre Albert-Birot. Also compares very interestingly the painting of F.'s wife, Madeleine Dinès, and his poetry.

Béalu, Marcel. Le palais souterrain. *In:* Hommage à Jean Follain. *See* 10196. p. 16–18. **10200**

A few interesting remembrances of F. by another poet.

Dujardin, Raoul. Jean Follain. MancheL Dec. 17, 1961. **10201**

Shows a bit of what the people in F.'s home town thought of him and of his poetry. Interesting primarily because of the importance of this region in F.'s writing.

Frontenac, Yves. Première rencontre avec Jean Follain. Dia 14–16, Jan. 1967. **10202**

An interview with F. after his return from Peru where he had gone in 1961. He reveals a remarkable knowledge of the country, criticizes the exploitation of the Indians and has a few words to say about the Latin American policies of the United States.

Guillevic, Eugène. Jean Follain. LetF 1377:8, March 17–23, 1971. **10203**

A long time friend of F., the poet Guillevic speaks of their friendship which, in spite of their different political attitudes, was always very warm. Time and space were F.'s obsessions and, if he can be called a poet of things, it is only in the way a drowning man will grasp anything.

———. Jean Follain. RdL 29–31, April-June 1971. **10204**

Written by a major poet who was, for many years, a close friend of F. Explains his personal debt to F. and the importance of the latter's break from the surrealist esthetic. Also emphasizes how each poem is born of the terrible anxiety which F. lived with all his life.

Pons, Max. [Texte liminaire] *In:* Visages de Jean Follain. *See* 10198. p. 7–12. **10205**

A long time close friend of F. reminisces about him more interestingly and more intelligently than most who have published their memories of him.

General Studies

Borel, Jacques. Jean Follain. *In:* Hommage à Jean Follain. *See* 10196. p. 42–57.
10206

Emphasizes the fact that F.'s poems are almost always written in the present in spite of his supposed attraction for the past. Notices the progressive depersonalization of his poetry.

Bosquet, Alain. Jean Follain ou le délire du comédien. NRF 91:308–12, 1960.   10207

Compares F. to Ponge. Sees a major change in the poetry beginning with *Exister* in 1947. Implies that F.'s evolution led him from phenomenology to idealism.

Decaunes, Luc. Jean Follain ou la possession du temps. Marg 77:6–13, 1961.
10208

Like Decaunes, those who write best about F. are poets themselves. Emphasizes time in F.'s poems and compares them to the snapshot of the photographer. Sees an important key to the poetry in the prose. Full of excellent insights not always as fully developed as one might hope.

Dhôtel, André. Jean Follain. Présentation par André Dhôtel. Choix de textes... Eds. Pierre Seghers, 1956. (Poètes d'aujourd'hui, 49) *Also:* Jean Follain. Une étude de André Dhôtel. Choix de textes... Seghers, 1972. (Poètes d'aujourd'hui, 49)
10209

Excellent short introduction to F.'s poetry with strong emphasis on its relationship to his childhood. A bit skimpy on biography. Photographs of F., friends and family and excerpts from his major works. The 1972 ed. is basically the same but with different photographs.

Dumaine, Philippe. Voyeur-voyant. *In:* Visages de Jean Follain. *See* 10198. p. 27–31.   10210

Valuable and intuitive critical remarks about F.'s "art poétique."

Durry, Marie-Jeanne. Propos de Jean Follain recueillis par M.-J. Durry. *In:* Visages de Jean Follain. *See* 10198. p. 53–55.   10211

A very valuable series of comments made by F. while participating in a discussion with the author on prose and poetry.

Emmanuel, Pierre. Jean Follain. MancheL Nov. 7, 1971.   10212

Discusses the role of memory in F. and its relationship to the creation of a new space in the poem. Also rejects the notion that F.'s poetry is impersonal and objective and calls it "one of the most personal in our literature."

Gros, Léon-Gabriel. Jean Follain ou le vertige du microcosme. *In his:* Poètes contemporains, deuxième série. Cahiers du sud, 1951. p. 165–82.   10213

Emphasizes F.'s revolutionary break with the traditions in French poetry since surrealism. Sees the poems as an attempt to overcome solitude in both poet and reader. A perceptive early view of F.

Jaccottet, Philippe. Une perspective fabuleuse. *In his:* L'entretien des muses. Gallimard, 1968. p. 131–38.   10214

Extremely sensitive study, by an excellent poet, of F.'s evocation of childhood in his poetry. Emphasizes spatial and temporal perspective as basis of his poetry.

Jourdan, Bernard. Jean Follain ou les saisons des choses. Cr 155:302–11, 1960.
10215

A rapid review of the evolution of F.'s poetry notable for its occasional insights. For example, blames Max Jacob's influence for the tendency to exaggerate word plays. Sees a basic difference between the prose and the poetry in spite of superficial similarities.

La Rochefoucauld, Edmée de. Jean Follain. *In her:* Courts métrages. Grasset, 1970. p. 119–44.   10216

Argues that F. is not a regionalist. Compares his prose and poetry from point of view of stylistic differences. Much biographical information. Discusses his attitude towards time. Somewhat disappointing and lacking in critical insights.

Lorho, Robert. Les insidieux moments de Jean Follain. Eur 513–14:206–12, 1972.
10217

A good discussion of the relationship in F.'s poetry of the ephemeral and how it leads to an understanding of permanence.

Onimus, Jean. Jean Follain ou les profondeurs de l'insignifiant. AFLSHN 15: 127–41, 1971. **10218**

An important short study which discusses F.'s use of things in his poetry and the ·underlying desperate anxiety which is the real source of his inspiration.

Schaettel, Marcel. Lecture et rêverie selon Gaston Bachelard. RMM 72:231–42, 1967. **10219**

A Bachelardian reading of "Hors durée" by F. emphasizing that the reader must respond directly to the elements of the poem. A few interesting insights.

Thomas, Henri. Un monde d'enfance et de mort. *In:* Hommage à Jean Follain. *See* 10196. p. 32–34. **10220**

A sensitive poet and close friend of F. offers a few critical intuitions and a portrait of F. Short but apt.

———. Preface. *In:* Follain, Jean. Exister, Territoires (preface). Gallimard, 1969. p. 7–12. **10221**

A good poet and long time friend of F., Thomas emphasizes — a bit exaggeratedly — F.'s freedom from the metaphor. Shows, too, how F. avoids the temptations of lyricism and uses common language in his poems.

Individual Works

Dhôtel, André. Jean Follain D'après tout. Et 139–41, Jan. 1968. **10222**

A long review, by one of F.'s most perceptive critics, of his volume *D'après tout.* Discusses the poet's attitude towards time, his brutality, his unrelenting hope for mankind and, finally, the fact that, occasionally, a poem seems to succeed and create a new reality outside of the contingencies of time as duration. Sees more pessimism and discouragement in the later poems.

———. Poésie médiatrice. NRF 116:286–90, 1962. **10223**

An important review of *Poèmes et proses choisis.* Develops ideas of poetry as a mystical mediation leading from man's world to God. Debatable but very interesting.

Mambrino, Jean. Un cahier de poésie. Et 719–26, May 1971. **10224**

A sensitive, intelligent review of *Espaces d'instants* by a Jesuit. Sees an evolution in F.'s poetry toward greater compassion and awareness of suffering.

Wolken, Karl Alfred. Jean Follain: Gedichte. NDH 121–22, Sept.-Oct. 1963. **10225**

A review of translation of some of F.'s poems into German. An interesting, slightly different perspective from the French. Sees F. as a poetic rationalist.

Michel Leiris
(Nos. 10226–10259)

DINA SHERZER

General Studies

Bersani, Jacques. Michel Leiris. *In his:* La littérature française depuis 1945. Bordas, 1970. p. 447–56. **10226**

Excellent brief presentation of the life and works of L. containing short extracts and illustrations, and emphasizing the main preoccupations of L.

Boyer, Alain-Michel. Michel Leiris. Eds. universitaires, 1974. 125 p. **10227**

Excellent book presenting L.'s work of his surrealist period, poetry, dream accounts, *Aurora* and autobiographical works. Shows that these works form an indivisible whole which can be considered as a general anthropology to elucidate man. Many provocative and insightful remarks make this book very stimulating.

Review: R. Jean in QL 185:13–14, 1974.

Chambers, Ross. Michel Leiris et le théâtre orphique. SRLF 8:243–308, 1967. **10228**

Very good article developing the idea that the dialectic of theater and life, and of the self and the world is the problem which will haunt L.'s entire life. Three themes are studied: poetry, death, and love. The discussion on the labyrinth and autobiography raises very interesting problems. Shows that the unity of L.'s work rests on a certain number of constants.

Dort, Bernard. Dans les eaux de la mémoire. CahS 332:121–27, 1955.   **10229**

Shows how both Proust and L. are looking for their past which reveals itself thanks to certain sensitive elements. Points out the difference between the two experiences, Proust's leading to a total revelation, L.'s to an interrogation and even to a confrontation.

Glissant, Edouard. Michel Leiris ethnographe. LetN 43:609–21, 1956.   **10230**

L. is presented as one of those Europeans who is a writer and an ethnographer and who offers two types of works: those that express an experience in Western society and those that are total approaches to non-Western societies. Argues that one cannot study L.'s literary work without knowing his ethnographic work since both ethnographer and writer have the same preoccupation: to understand one's own being and to conquer knowledge of man.

Gobin, Pierre. L'érotisme et la fête: Bataille, Leiris, Vaillant. Mos 1:87–102, 1968.   **10231**

Very good article analyzing the concept of eroticism in the works of the three writers, stressing their debt to Freud, Hegel, Sade and emphasizing the particular importance of Marcel Mauss' *Essay on the gift.*

Juliet, Charles. La littérature et le thème de la mort chez Kafka et Leiris. Cr 126:933–45, 1957.   **10232**

Both Kafka and L. are haunted by the idea of death. The two attitudes are compared. Contains interesting remarks on language play.

Mauriac, Claude. Michel Leiris. *In his:* L'alittérature contemporaine. Albin Michel, 1969. p. 69–88.   **10233**

Emphasizes L.'s desire to debase himself and his fear of death. Mentions the importance of language. Exploitation of words analogous to those of Joyce. L. expresses "une angoisse existentielle" which is intimately ours.

Nadeau, Maurice. Michel Leiris et la quadrature du cercle. Julliard, 1963. 130 p.   **10234**

Indispensable excellent general presentation of L.'s works, life and ideas, showing the value of autobiography, the importance of language, and L.'s interest in order, ritual, and ceremony. Very interesting remarks on L.'s creation of a personal mythology. Notices that L.'s work announces the possibility of dealing with literature as a means and as an end in itself.

Reviews: R. Berger in LetF 1000:9, 1963; J. Pache in RdBL 5:21–22, 1963; G. Raillard in FMonde 22:20–21, 1964; J. Terdjean in TR 200:136–38, 1964.

Peyre, Henri. Literature and sincerity. New Haven and London, Yale univ. press; Paris, Presses universitaires de France, 1963. p. 271–75.   **10235**

General presentation of L., surrealist, poet, autobiographer. As a self-analyst L. is seen as a fervent addict to sincerity, and as an enemy of esthetic pastime. Very insightful remarks on the style of L.

Ronat, Mitsou. Une ethnographie particulière: Leiris. Change 7:73–83, 1970.   **10236**

Ethnography and poetry are two faces of one double activity. Interesting analysis of these two types of experience in L.'s life, showing their interrelationship and complementarity.

Surrealism and Poetry

Bachelard, Gaston. La terre et les rêveries de la volonté. Corti, 1948. 232 p.   **10237**

In the chapter on the labyrinth, notices that L.'s images of labyrinth are in between Huysmans' images, which express hardness, and Nerval's, which express easiness, smoothness. L.'s images show hardening, petrifying. Examples from *Le point cardinal.*

———. La terre et les rêveries du repos. Corti, 1948. p. 125–28.   **10238**

Interesting remarks on the house in *Aurora* attracting attention to the complexity of the images.

Blanchot, Maurice. Rêver, écrire. NRF 102:1087–96, 1961. *Also in his:* L'amitié. Gallimard, 1971. p. 162–70.   **10239**

Very important article dealing with the relationships between dreaming and writing. L.'s account of dreams, *Nuits sans nuits,* is seen as an interrogation and a liberation of the self, during which the writer becomes aware of the multiplicity of the self. The same simplicity, precision, and modesty appear both in L.'s account of dreams and his autobiography. These qualities are the signs of interrogation-liberation with which L. makes his life. L.'s way of writing is compared to Proust's.

Chappuis, Pierre. Michel Leiris. Une étude de Pierre Chappuis. Avec un choix de textes... Seghers, 1973. 190 p. (Poètes d'aujourd'hui, 216) **10240**

Excellent study focusing primarily on L.'s use of language and on his poetry. Sees an evolution from a surrealist type of writing to a type of writing which is indebted to Roussel. Shows the similarities between L.'s poetry and his prose. Analyzes several poems and provides a choice of texts. One of the best studies on L.

Review: R. Jean in QL 185:13–14, 1974.

Durand, Xavier. Michel Leiris et la substance verbale. CahDS 4:79–92, 1970. **10241**

On *Glossaire: j'y serre mes gloses.* Examines how such a glossary can be explained and justified, and how such verbal games function. Good study.

Hoog, Armand. Le surréalisme et la damnation du laïque. Nef 4:115–19, 1947. **10242**

In this general article on surrealism, places *Aurora* in the perspective of other works such as *Nadja* and *Au château d'Argol.* Is of the opinion that despite some weaknesses *Aurora* is attractive because of the appetite for damnation, suicide, and strange tortures that L. displays in it.

Matthews, J. H. Michel Leiris. *In his:* Surrealism and the novel. Ann Arbor, Univ. of Michigan press, 1966. p. 107–23. **10243**

Detailed summary of the content of *Aurora* emphasizing its similarities with Huysmans' and Gracq's novels and with Roussel's technique of word manipulation. The title and the dominant image of the philosopher's stone indicate the optimistic message of the novel.

————. Michel Leiris. *In his:* Surrealist poetry in France. Syracuse, Syracuse univ. press, 1969. p. 80–89. **10244**

Good presentation of L. as a poet whose faith in the poetic word has been developed by surrealism. L.'s conception of *fureur* and epilepsy in the poetic experience is studied. Points out L.'s sensibility to the potentialities of language.

Monnier, Adrienne. A propos d'Aurora: une lettre de Michel Leiris. LetN 4:509–12, 1953. **10245**

L. explains in detail why he chose the title *Aurora* for his novel, and he provides information about the mythical character of his heroine. Essential to the reading of the novel.

Autobiographies

Blanchot, Maurice. Le combat avec l'ange. NRF 38:288–99, 1956. *Also in:* L'amitié. Gallimard, 1971. p. 150–61. **10246**

Penetrating reflections on *L'âge d'homme, Biffures,* and *Fourbis.*

————. Regards d'outre-tombe. Cr 11:291–301, 1947. *Also in his:* La part du feu. Gallimard, 1949. p. 247–58. **10247**

L'âge d'homme is viewed as one of the central works of modern literature because its intentions, i.e., to escape *gratuité,* to accomplish a real act, to understand oneself and to inform the others about oneself, to free oneself from one's obsessions, to write a dangerous book which shows the back of the stage, are problems inherent in literature. Very interesting discussion of the book as a work of confession, and of its construction. A few remarks on *Aurora* which contains the themes which will be shown to be vital in *L'âge d'homme.* An essential and extremely valuable essay.

Borel, Jacques. Problèmes de l'autobiographie. *In:* Positions et oppositions sur le roman contemporain. Ed. by Michel Mansuy. Klincksieck, 1971. p. 79–90. **10248**

General and rather wordy study on autobiography dealing with various writers. L. is presented as somebody who has an unhappy conscience, who is haunted by the nostalgia of risk and punishment, and for whom exposing oneself is the equivalent of a political choice and commitment.

Bréchon, Robert. L'âge d'homme de Michel Leiris. Hachette, 1973. 94 p. (Poche critique)   **10249**

Very interesting book dealing essentially with L'âge d'homme, but containing also remarks on previous works. Notices that L.'s reference to the bullfight makes him akin to Bataille in that literature is viewed as a ritual prostitution. Mentions the importance of L.'s surrealist experience which gave him a desire for systematic profanation linked to the feeling of sacredness. Underlines the importance of ethnographic research which helped L. to talk about himself. Considers L. as a modern hero of introspection along with Joyce and Proust.

Butor, Michel. Une autobiographie dialectique. *In his:* Répertoire 1. Eds. de minuit, 1960. p. 261–70.   **10250**

L'âge d'homme is a classical autobiography in which L. describes himself in different periods of his life presented in a chronological order. La règle du jeu, on the other hand, is a dialectical autobiography in that themes that are merely mentioned in Biffures are developed in more detail in Fourbis. Argues that L. gets closer to himself, cures himself and in so doing he makes the reader discover himself and appreciate his relationship with other men and things.

Duvignaud, Jean. Off limits. NRF 168: 1060–65, 1966.   **10251**

Essay on Fibrilles which is placed in the context of the other works by L. Insists on the "dépassement de soi" in the autobiography inspired by travel and ethnography. The aborted suicide and the return to writing are manifestations of this "dépassement de soi."

Lanes, Jerrold. Langage, acte, acte de mourir: L'esthétique de L'âge d'homme. Sym 4:340–53, 1970.   **10252**

In his preface to L'âge d'homme, L. advocates taking risks, committing oneself; in this sense his book is not a rupture with surrealism, but a return to the ideals that animated the movement at the beginning. The difference between Breton and L. is that L. keeps the surrealist's free associations, but

unlike Breton he does not indulge in images of an optimistic and vivid beauty but rather exposes bare realities using an objective style which is even debasing. In L'âge d'homme there is a dialectic between death and love but this dialectic has no resolution.

Levinas, Emmanuel. La transcendance des mots. TM 44:1090–95, 1949.   **10253**

Interesting remarks by a philosopher on Biffures. Stresses the importance of thought association and the exploitation of all the possibilities of thought coming into contact with the matter of words.

Magny, Olivier de. Michel Leiris ou le moi fraternel. MNP 95:126–31, 1955. **10254**

On L'âge d'homme, Biffures, and Fourbis seen as forming an immense poem at times very abstract, but which strike us to the marrow when certain notions are looked at closely. Thinks that since Montaigne no attempt goes so far.

Picon, Gaëtan. Michel Leiris et la règle du jeu. *In his:* L'usage de la lecture. V. 2. Mercure de France, 1961. p. 147–53. **10255**

Presentation of Fourbis. Qualifies the tone of L. as one of somebody who discovers and perceives at the moment he speaks and whose words communicate the shock of revelation. Stresses the beauty of the pages devoted to death and analyzes what a book which describes a succession of failures brings to its author and to the reader.

Pontalis, J. B. Michel Leiris ou la psychanalyse interminable. TM 925–33:1139–46, 1955–56.   **10256**

Remarks on La règle du jeu and Aurora. Interesting comparison of stagnation in L. and Proust. Proust does not give the feeling of sterility; temporality implies degradation but also metamorphosis. In L. nothing moves. L. is not searching for the key to a secret, but his repetitions, his detours and debates are the mark of the desire to escape from a circular jail.

Schneider, Claude. Michel Leiris au pied du mur. Preu 192:75–79, 1967.   **10257**

Studies the development of the three volumes of La règle du jeu and shows that L. is a man caught in the middle of ramifications that defy all attempt at expression.

Sontag, Susan. Michel Leiris' Manhood. *In her:* Against interpretation. Dell, 1965. p. 61–68.   **10258**

L. is in the lineage of Montaigne and Rousseau, but he writes anti-literature which is literature. Self-laceration and self-exposure similar in Mailer, but Mailer's motivation is spiritual, L.'s desperate. Only the cold and impersonal fascinates L. L.'s book yields boredom which is the most creative stylistic feature of modern literature.

Wollheim, Richard. On self-exposure. List 2033:350–52, 1968.   **10259**

In *Manhood* sees a link between Freud's method and L.'s pursuit of associations and following up of concatenated images and scenes. The book is judged sophisticated and subtle but superficial, yet having the poignancy of a book totally written outside moral values.

Georges Limbour
(Nos. 10260–10263)

JEAN-CLAUDE VILQUIN

Dhôtel, André. L'œuvre de Georges Limbour. Cr 34:195–205, 1949.   **10260**

A perceptive review of L.'s works from *Soleils bas* to *Le bridge de Madame Lyane* with emphasis on the elements of magic, dream, myth, allegory and imagery.

————. Le rêve de Georges Limbour. NRF 219:98–104, 1971.   **10261**

A short note on the importance of dreams, images and metaphors in L.'s work.

Hubert, Renée Riese. Limbour et la poétique de Masson. RomN 12:1–4, 1970.   **10262**

This interesting note looks at L.'s art criticism, with special reference to his writings on André Masson from 1924 to 1965.

Roudaut, Jean. Il y avait un mérou. Cr 204:387–402, 1964.   **10263**

A brilliant imagerial analysis that attempts to disentangle the intricacies

of L.'s poetic prose and the polysemous character of the elusive "mérou." *La chasse au mérou* is seen here as the essential key to L.'s earlier works. One of the most suggestive essays on that author to date.

Henri Michaux
(Nos. 10264–10345)

RENÉE RIESE HUBERT

Bibliography

Place, Georges. Henri Michaux. Eds. de la Chronique des lettres françaises, 1969. 41 p.   **10264**

Important bibliographical and reference data on both the writer and the artist.

General Studies: Books

Badoux, Laurent. La pensée de Henri Michaux. Zurich, Juris-Verlag, 1963. 96 p.   **10265**

Classifies M. in the Kierkegaard, Husserl, Heidegger and Sartre tradition due to revolt, anguish and quest. Stresses forgetfulness which permits one to view world in the light of novelty.

Bellour, Raymond. Henri Michaux ou une mesure de l'être. Gallimard, 1965. 279 p.   **10266**

Attributes to M. search of self-knowledge without narcissism. Shows fusion of autobiographic and imaginary elements. The poet constantly renews his itinerary towards being. Extensive discussion of the distance between language and meaning and use of pronouns related to the very essence of M.'s poetry. A major study.
Review: R. Hubert in FR 40:717–18, 1967.

Bertelé, René. Henri Michaux. Une étude, un choix de poèmes... Seghers, 1946. 221 p. (Poètes d'aujourd'hui, 5) *Also (rev.):* 1963. 224 p.   **10267**

Emphasizes M.'s opposition to rhetoric and formal literature, for which he substitutes the direct chronicle of experience and a relentless interrogation of life. In his works which include mystic, scientific and metaphysical phases, the poet informs us about man and myth today.

Bowie, Malcolm. Henri Michaux, a study of his literary works. Oxford, Clarendon press, 1973. 212 p.   10268

Discusses M. as poet of being in conflict with world searching for adequate linguistic means. Considers M. both a primitive and sophisticated mind who creates only small and unenduring structures, who, endowed with energy of mind, refuses to serve general principle. Most comprehensive literary study. Outstanding in conception of poetry, existentialist and linguistic problems. Reviews: Anon. in TLS Feb. 15, 1974; R. Ellmann in NewS 86:120–21, July 27, 1973; M. Graham in LonM 13:139–41, 1973.

Bréchon, Robert. Henri Michaux. Gallimard, 1959. 239 p.   10269

Discusses M.'s opposition to literature. The poet deals with emotions in the raw. His texts have nevertheless the coherence of a scientific work. Uses also thematic approach as he analyzes the effect of alienation and nightmare. Considers work as quest for self, where literature has a cleansing effect as it tends to restore man to his full potential. Similar problems were dealt with by René Bertelé. A sound full-length study. Reviews: G. Neri in Verri 4:103–06, 1960; J. Pénard in Cr 15:943–51, 1959.

Coulon, Philippe de. Henri Michaux poète de notre société. Neuchâtel, La Baconnière, 1949. 276 p.   10270

Shows that M. reveals man deprived of support, forced to descend into the darkness of his body and of matter. As the poet rejects the outer world he creates an imaginary realm on which, however, he cannot lean. Poetry points towards a reorganization of our world. An early study based on a limited number of books.

Engler, Winfried. Henri Michaux. Das Michauxbild 1922–59. Tübingen, Fotodruck Präzis, 1964. 312 p.   10271

Thesis tracing evolution from book to book; belongs to both Geistesgeschichte and esthetics. Sees change from existentialist attitude to Buddhist type of contemplation.

Gide, André. Découvrons Henri Michaux. Gallimard, 1941. 53 p.   10272

Situates M. beyond conventions. Mysteriously absent from his most personal pages, he establishes a poetic complicity with his reader. Not very probing study.

Loras, Olivier. Rencontre avec Henri Michaux au plus profond des gouffres. Chassieu, J. et S. Bleyon, 1967. 151 p.   10273

Writes from scientific psychoanalytical point of view; engages in a medically oriented diagnosis of behavior under intoxication. Mescaline has a disembodying effect whereby time stops, action is paralyzed and the poem even loses relation with author. Review: V. La Charité in FR 43: 167–68, 1969.

Murat, N. Henri Michaux. Eds. universitaires, 1967. 123 p. (Classiques du XXᵉ siècle, 88)   10274

Attributes to M. a search for humanism. Raises the issue of writing as form of action against procrastination. Writing is a transgression rather than an accomplished or finishable product.

Special Number

Cahier Henri Michaux. Ed. by Raymond Bellour. Minard, 1966. 460 p. (Cahiers de l'Herne)   10275

Principal articles have been analyzed separately.

General Studies: Articles

André, Robert. Un hérétique de la sensation. *In:* Cahier Henri Michaux. *See* 10275. p. 172–81.   10276

Considers that M.'s language is an instrument of torture that multiplies the horrors of nightmare. M.'s quest pushes him into drug experience which modifies existing structures instead of creating new ones.

Beaujour, Michel. Sens et nonsens. Glu et gli, et le grand combat. *In:* Cahier Henri Michaux. *See* 10275. p. 133–43.   10277

Demonstrates that nonsense poems endowed with great intensity give flexibility to the ordinary "petrified" language of books. Convincing study.

Belaval, Yvon. Introduction à la poésie expérimentale. *In his:* Poèmes d'aujourd'hui. Gallimard, 1963. p. 108–32.   **10278**

Sees M. exploring the functioning of the mind. Shows how mescaline creates ruptures in space and time but leaves the center intact.

————. Une magie rationnelle. *In his:* Poèmes d'aujourd'hui. Gallimard, 1963. p. 93–108.   **10279**

Rational magic refers to scientific thought processes which extend into the domain of dream, a world which has its own bestiary yet relates to cosmic forces.

Bellour, Raymond. La double énigme. TM 227:1903–13, 1965.   **10280**

Sees one and the same character always in motion throughout M.'s writing and art, both of which constitute a meditation on language.

————. La passion de Narcisse. *In:* Cahier Henri Michaux. *See* 10275. p. 49–80.   **10281**

Relates self-questioning, self-awareness, reflections on the process of knowing and writing to Narcissus. Excellent study exploring also Narcissus myth in some other writers. Probing comment on poetic humor.

Bense, Max. Textes. *In:* Cahier Henri Michaux. *See* 10275. p. 241–56.   **10282**

Studies consciousness of thought in relation to expression; sees consciousness in terms of progression; the equivalent of an act. Philosophical approach leaning on Husserl and Wittgenstein. Penetrating essay emphasizing metaphysical preoccupations.

Bernard, Suzanne. L'univers d'Henri Michaux. *In her:* Le poème en prose de Baudelaire jusqu'à nos jours. Nizet, 1959. p. 715–23.   **10283**

M. evokes the inner drama of man in revolt against his condition and incites to an act of spiritual liberation. Yet he is not truly the master of the very creatures to whom he gives life. Does not really stress prose poem as genre.

Bienaimé, Dora Rigo. Michaux et l'Italie. RLMC 21:143–51, 1968.   **10284**

An account of the reception of M. in Italy alluding to critical studies and translations. Sees in poetry and painting parallel visions, but only the latter constitutes a territory of recuperation for the artist.

Bigongiari, Piero. Il discorso su Michaux è il discorso di Michaux. *In his:* Poesia francese del novecento. Florence, Vallecchi, 1968. p. 139–47.   **10285**

Examines paradoxical situation of coherence and incoherence produced by M.'s willed destruction of common sense as well as the consciousness of the absolute or infinite during drug experiments.

Bishop, Lloyd. Michaux's clown. FR 36:152–58, 1962.   **10286**

Compares extensively M.'s character to Prufrock; neither can admit that he is not a hero. M.'s clown is the real man shorn of pretentions and rationalizations.

Blanchot, Maurice. Du merveilleux. Ar 27–28:120–33, 1947.   **10287**

Essay which exemplifies M.'s juxtaposition of purely imaginary and critical comments in our world.

————. L'infini et l'infini. *In:* Cahier Henri Michaux. *See* 10275. p. 80–89.   **10288**

Discusses the poet shifting the field of reality; history becomes revolution and man an undefinable creature warring against self.

Boschère, Jean de. Henri Michaux—le poète d'après le voyage au pays de magie. CahS 284:605–13, 1948.   **10289**

Compares M. to Baudelaire and Lautréamont because of revolt against modern crowds. Lauds interpenetration of M.'s creatures and his poetic concepts.

Bosquet, Alain. Henri Michaux ou l'impossibilité d'être. TR 80:155–59, 1954. **10290**

Believes that M.'s man affirms himself through constant self-assassination. Negation and destruction give birth to a new mythology.

————. Michaux le refus de naître. *In his:* Verbe et vertige. Hachette, 1961. p. 149–64.   **10291**

M.'s poetry has the characteristics of scientific prose and of a first version of a poem. It can make revelations on the obscure regions of our mind.

Bounoure, Gabriel. Le Darçana d'Henri Michaux. NRF 53:875–83, 1957. **10292**

Attributes to M. freedom which permits even to destroy or deny space. Claims need to master objects stems from play instinct, not from wish for possession.

————. Henri Michaux. *In his:* Marelles sur le parvis. Plon, 1958. p. 251–54. **10293**

Sees in M. relation with Thomism, dadaism, Heraclitian scepticism, Lewis Carroll and Rimbaud.

Bréchon, Robert. L'espace, le corps, la conscience. *In:* Cahier Henri Michaux. *See* 10275. p. 181–94. **10294**

Discusses confrontation with obstacle and aspiration toward wide open spaces. Knowledge of space is visceral and muscular. Imaginary space created by language has liberating effect.

————. Parcours d'Henri Michaux. Cr 125: 219–28, 1957. **10295**

Stresses role of poet who, in a hostile universe, seeks constantly to recapitulate the forces of the self. He becomes a seer not for the sake of knowledge but for the authenticity of being.

Brée, Germaine. Le monde peuplé de Michaux. KRQ 17:19–28, 1970. **10296**

Sees in the poet a Proteus who glides behind all faces to get hold of them. A sort of Knight, he belongs to an epic which turns burlesque.

Broome, Peter. The introversion of Henri Michaux: his aims, techniques and shortcomings. NFS 1:34–44, 1962. **10297**

Sees in M. a rebel poet who seeks total liberty and a future spiritual Utopia. Concentration and imagination become sources of new power.

————. Michaux and the exorcism of God. AJFS 2:191–220, 1965. **10298**

Finds in the author both saintliness and revolt, for he creates his own miracles, which he subsequently replaces by scientific pretenses and lucidity.

————. Poetry and event in the work of Henri Michaux. AJFS 4:344–78, 1967. **10299**

M.'s poetry diagnoses the moral and scientific degeneration of our age in which fact has outstripped imagina-

tion. Its exorcism leads to revolution or saintliness. Excellent article.

Cleyet, G. Henri Michaux. TCS 5:17–24, 1970. **10300**

Discusses M.'s analysis of society and its relation to the writings of Sartre and Camus. Calls poet a brain engineer who examines what goes on in the mind.

Darrault, Ivan. La ralentie. Essai de description sémantique. Promesse 19–20:37–45, 1967. **10301**

Applies Greimas' structural semantics to a three phase ("réduction," "normalisation," "structuration") description of the poem.

Ellmann, Richard. The ductile universe of Henri Michaux. KR 9:187–98, 1949. **10302**

Shows that M. casts psychological insights into physical terms. Compares his simplification of human figure to Klee. Stresses disintegration of world and hope for millenium.

Engler, Winfried. Henri Michaux: Dichtung der Grenzsituation. Antaios 1:413–19, 1960. **10303**

Considers M. a poet of existential philosophy who shows how man lives and how his existence could be changed. Shows his concern with power, totalitarianism and his allusions to many cultures and religions.

Goth, Maja. Henri Michaux et Kafka. *In his:* Franz Kafka et les lettres françaises. Corti, 1956. p. 65–69. **10304**

Sees similarity of the two authors in a fantastic world where man is degraded; their liberation from the nightmare stems from creation. Both authors exemplify the quest of the self. Comparison not too revealing in regard to M.

Gros, Léon-Gabriel. Henri Michaux ou L'homme en proie aux monstres. *In his:* Poètes contemporains. 2ᵉ série. Cahiers du sud, 1951. p. 83–98. **10305**

Outlines man confronting with lucidity his unavoidable disintegration. M.'s spiritual dilemmas take physical shapes.

Guennier, N. La création lexicale chez Henri Michaux. CdL 2:75–87, 1968. **10306**

Analyzes originality of M.'s vocabulary in relation to linguistic norms. Poet borrows from foreign languages and technical vocabulary and creates a kind of "esperanto." Methodical study.

Guette, Jean. Michaux et la mescaline. LetN 36:398–406, 1956. **10307**

Shows that author does not have recourse to his customary literary techniques when he writes under the influence of mescaline which diminishes the sensual quality of images.

Hackett, C. A. Michaux and Plume. FS 17: 40–50, 1963. **10308**

Analysis of *Plume* as stories in the Rabelais, Voltaire, Swift tradition. Shows that *Plume* is partly autobiographical. Relates book to M.'s art and essays on art.

Heissenbüttel, Helmut. Exerzitien der metaphysischen Not. Merk 16:280–87, 1962. **10309**

Sees in M.'s poetry a plausible logic which contradicts itself. Claims M. is a teacher, a methodologist rather than a poet.

Houdebine, Jean-Louis. Description d'un portrait. Promesse 19–20:8–36, 1967. **10310**

Explains M.'s texts as tension between continuity and discontinuity, dispersion and unification. Views Meidosems as hypersensitive creatures in an aggressive milieu.

————. Essai de lecture réflexive d'un texte de Michaux à ses différents niveaux d'énonciation. *In:* Greimas, A. J. Essais de sémiotique poétique. Larousse, 1972. p. 155–78. **10311**

A structural analysis of a passage from *Meidosem.* Methodology based on the theories of A. J. Greimas, Emile Benveniste, Julia Kristeva; touches on problems of syntax, metrics, phonetics, narration and dialog.

————. Note sur l'aspect proprement scriptural des écrits sur la drogue. Promesse 19–20:65–79, 1967. **10312**

Explains that M.'s drug experiences are not based on pleasure principle but search for knowledge which results in information on abnormal psychology. Explores in depth the relation between writing and experience and their necessary distances.

Jaccottet, Philippe. Commentaire de L'espace aux ombres. *In his:* L'entretien des muses. Gallimard, 1968. p. 105–12. **10313**

M. giving accounts of both real and imaginary voyages uses different types of language. Jaccottet stresses "style d'onde" characterized by mobile and fluid elements.

Jouffroy, Alain. En quoi Michaux est-il révolutionnaire? *In his:* La fin des alternances. Gallimard, 1970. p. 194–215. **10314**

Stresses the relation between M. and Lautréamont. M.'s poetic text is an agglomeration of signs. His writing records the mobility of the world and gives the reader the opportunity to change as he becomes his own screen.

Kuentz, Pierre. Clefs sans serrure, analyse de Dans la nuit de Michaux. Lit 6:56–65, 1972. **10315**

Confronts the text like an object, which cannot be exhausted by reading. Shows the interaction of graphic and phonic elements. The word "nuit" appearing in the text by means of declensions is destroyed in the process.

Kuhn, Reinhard. The hermeneutics of silence—Michaux and mescaline. YFS 50: 130–41, 1974. **10316**

A convincingly lucid study of M.'s drug inspired literature. M. is not in search of paradise but interested in examining the mind's processes during intoxication and even more so, detoxication. Comparing M.'s writings before, during and after drug experimentation, Kuhn proves that mescaline did not bring about radical changes in the poetry.

————. Prismatic reflections: Michaux. *In:* About French poetry. Detroit, Wayne state press, 1972. p. 186–204. **10317**

An examination of the process of disintegration and of the efforts towards unity or inner reconciliation. Kuhn reveals striking analogies with some Mallarmé texts which include recurrent echoes and reflections. Excellent study containing a discussion of the simultaneity of drawing and text which singularizes *Paix dans les prisements.*

Kushner, Eva. L'humour de Michaux. FR 36:495–504, 1965.   **10318**

Shows that humor is the equivalent of a nervous reaction. M. mocks his inner monster, as he splits not into actor and spectator but into two enemies.

Lascault, Gilbert. Les monstres et l'Unheimliche. *In:* Cahier Henri Michaux. *See* 10275. p. 214–27.   **10319**

Loss of self and removal from God give rise to monsters and experience of uncanny. Discourse is repeated act of aggression and transgression of all norms.

Laude, Jean. Ecritures et calligraphies chez Michaux. Liberté 9:25–41, 1969.   **10320**

Is concerned with the rapidity of the creator's gesture which the reader recreates on a metaphoric level. Poetry and painting do not express the same thing by different means, even if both constitute an exploration of the self. Highly original.

————. Voyages. *In:* Cahier Henri Michaux. *See* 10275. p. 159–66.   **10321**

Relates the voyage to the act of writing; one can substitute for the other as a form of exploration of our consciousness. Writing also establishes the necessary link between the realm of the real and imaginary.

Le Clézio, J.-M.-G. Sur Henri Michaux. Fragments. CahS 380:262–69, 1964.
10322

Sees in M.'s poetry and painting a last attempt to break the walls of silence and claustrophobia. Writing becomes a biological act and the cry the essence of language.

Lefort, Claude. Sur une colonne absente. *In:* Cahier Henri Michaux. *See* 10275. p. 227–38.   **10323**

M., denouncing all fictions and in revolt against language, creates a distance between self and writing. This distance is even greater in the texts written under the influence of mescaline.

Legros, Georges. Un poème de Michaux: Repos dans le malheur. CahAT 8:48–60, 1960.   **10324**

Shows how "malheur" is at once an abstraction and a character; at once hostile, yet close to the poet.

Leonhard, Kurt. Henri Michaux. Dichter und Maler. NRs 77:70–84, 1966.   **10325**

Classifies both poetry and art by genres between which comparisons can easily be made. Neither one points towards reality, but towards possibilities which cannot become reality.

Lupasco, Stéphane. Michaux et la folie. *In:* Cahier Henri Michaux. *See* 10275 p. 96–100.   **10326**

Claims that M.'s drug experiments were aimed at understanding normal phenomena. Is convinced that states of madness do not lead to conflict and contradictions. In M. madness, scientific observation and poetic perception live side by side.

Mansuy, Michel. Henri Michaux. *In his:* Etudes sur l'imagination de la vie. Corti, 1970. p. 108–39.   **10327**

Interesting Bachelard oriented study. Sees sickness and anger as fertile forces in imagination and vision; describes M.'s attempt to seek peaceful relations with inert and even unstructured elements.

Menemencioglu, Melehat. La recherche de l'expressivitié dans la poésie d'Henri Michaux. *In:* Le vers français au XXᵉ siècle. Ed. by Monique Parent. Klincksieck, 1967. p. 219–31.   **10328**

M.'s poetry expresses with intensity the inexpressible by means of rhythmic syncopation and concise syntax. He tortures the very word in order to make it reveal truth.

Micha, René. Plume et les anges. *In:* Cahier Henri Michaux. *See* 10275. p. 143–59.   **10329**

Considers Klee and Chaplin as sources of inspiration and analyzes the affinities of their works with *Plume.*

Noguez, Dominique. Les voyages imaginaires de Michaux. Liberté 11:7–18, 1966. **10330**

Stresses language used to relate different imaginary voyages. M. enlarges the realm of language so that it can express the full exploration of the mind.

Onimus, Jean. Peur et poésie chez Henri Michaux. Et 292:217–37, 1957.   **10331**

Sees man infinitely reduced; can only hope for the end of consciousness which creates isolation and misery.

Paz, Octavio. Courant alternatif. NRF 102: 1011–34, 1961. **10332**
Considers writing an outburst of dizziness without reference to ideas. Under the impact of mescaline, moral values and compensations, unrelated to our reality, are established. Illuminates the links between various aspects of work.

Picon, Gaëtan. Sur Henri Michaux. Font 60:279–92, 1947. **10333**
Sees in M. the survival of an archetypal diversity without search for structural unity. Represents a world where reality is either lacking or excessive, a testimony of the tragedy of our times.

———. Unité et pluralité chez Henri Michaux. In his: L'usage de la lecture. V. 1. Mercure de France, 1962. p. 105–20. **10334**
M.'s poetry can serve as testimony of our age, for the poet cannot retrieve the unity of his divided self. His imaginary world reveals the real one as it destroys illusions.

Potvin, André. Henri Michaux ou la solitude enragée. RGB 4:89–99, 1958. **10335**
The poet is a fragmented being in constant search of new experiences. The poem is the thread which leads out of the labyrinth and provides relief from existential anger.

Poulet, Georges. Henri Michaux et le supplice des faibles. In: Cahier Henri Michaux. See 10275. p. 166–72. **10336**
Conceives of M.'s being as weak, almost reduced to nothing, yet lucid and burdened by a Jansenist feeling of shame. New interpretation.

Rolland de Renéville, André. Henri Michaux. In his: Univers de la parole. Gallimard, 1944. p. 102–15. **10337**
Focusses on elements of violence and refusal of a universe not created by the poet. Relatively early, but perceptive study on problems of knowledge and language developed subsequently by other critics.

Rosolato, Guy. Les voix. In: Cahier Henri Michaux. See 10275. p. 115–22. **10338**

Applies categories established by Jakobson and especially Benveniste to M. Insists on an anonymous voice by which the 'I' or subject establishes its movements within the discourse and relates it to myth as it presupposes and supersedes the Absolute voice, that of the dead Father.

Roudaut, Jean. Notes à propos d'un livre d'Henri Michaux. In: Cahier Henri Michaux. See 10275. p. 205–14. **10339**
Discusses various realms of space such as voyages beyond death, passage from inner to outer space and psychological exploration. Relates concepts of space to discontinuity of time and being.

Saillet, Maurice. Henri Michaux et le voyage imaginaire. MerF 304:213–17, 1948. **10340**
M. is incapable of acting in conformity with his sense of revolt. Poetry constitutes only exorcism possible.

Steinmetz, Jean-Luc. La poésie d'Henri Michaux. Promesse 19–20:80–96, 1967. **10341**
Sees in M. a poet who relates in depth the word to the object and makes it the equivalent of a gesture. He carries language to its full potential, to the borderline where nonsense takes on meaning. Convincing study.

Temkine, Raymonde. De Baudelaire à Michaux. Eur 456–57:234–44, 1967. **10342**
Compares Baudelaire's and M.'s reactions to drugs. Contrary to Baudelaire, M. repudiates mysticism and morality, his infinite is but the rejection of the finite.

Terrasse, Jean. Henri Michaux: de l'être du langage au langage de l'être. SynB 275: 70–87, 1969. **10343**
Concentrates on problems of writing, a kind of self-annihilation. Language too slow to capture reality, but necessary to maintain the continuity of our being. Poet aware of inadequacy of language in regard to communication.

Todorova, Delphine. Les cordobes. In: Cahier Henri Michaux. See 10275. p. 122–28. **10344**
Opposes two types of description, pictural to inner or abstract, by ex-

amining the role of phonic, rhythmic, syntactic and semantic elements.

————. La structure linguistique du narrateur. *In:* Cahier Henri Michaux. *See* 10275. p. 108–15.   **10345**

Discusses presence of narrator and his various relations to reader as well as shifting association between traveller-narrator-author. Shows M.'s texts correspond to both categories: stories and discourse. Applies most effectively linguistic categories to text.

Benjamin Péret
(Nos. 10346–10365)

MARY ANN CAWS AND JULIA F. COSTICH

Bailly, Jean-Christophe. Au-delà du langage: une étude sur Benjamin Péret. Eric Losfeld, 1971. 112 p. (Le désordre, 13)   **10346**

Lively study of P.'s surrealist poetry and prose. Finds linguistic approach inadequate; analyzes several important themes. [JFC]

Bédouin, Jean-Louis. Benjamin Péret. Présentation par Jean-Louis Bédouin. Choix de textes... Seghers, 1961. 208 p. (Poètes d'aujourd'hui, 78)   **10347**

Very sympathetic essay on P. by a fellow surrealist. Elegiac in tone and largely concerned with biography. Followed by selected texts. [JFC]

Bevilacqua Caldari, Franca. Una lettura di Le grand jeu di Benjamin Péret: Les temps révolus. *In:* Surréalisme; surrealismo. Rome, Bulzoni; Paris, Nizet, 1974. p. 49–74. (Quaderni del novecento francese, 2)   **10348**

Study of syntax, phonics, and structures of the text, of its oppositions and its linkings, its concern for the natural, the objective and the concrete as well as the common, befitting the "integral primitivism" which was P.'s aim. [MAC]

Blanquaert, Marie-Odile. Le mythe de l'amour sublime dans Feu central de Benjamin Péret. CahDS 1:57–72, 1965.   **10349**

Study of images of liberty: figures of birds, abundance of fruit. Hatred of night and solar myth of "amour sublime" against closed world. Play of contraries, where erotic central fire corresponds with explosion of revolutionary surging, "femme-lumière" imbedded in pagan cult of life, of sun, of love. [MAC]

Caws, Mary Ann. Benjamin Péret: a plausible surrealist. YFS 31:105–11, 1964.   **10350**

General introduction to P.'s surrealism. Emphasizes P.'s readability and suggests readings. [JFC]

————. Benjamin Péret's game and gesture. *In her:* The inner theater of recent French poetry. Princeton, Princeton univ. press, 1972. p. 75–105.   **10351**

Presents P.'s sense of play and physical movement as primary elements in his poetry. Excellent analyses of individual texts. [JFC]

————. Péret and the surrealist word. RomN 11:233–37, 1969.   **10352**

Analyzes P.'s attitudes toward language through a study of selections from his poetry; illustrates the postulate that "the poet's views on language are as clearly revealed in the language of his poems as anywhere else." [JFC]

————. Péret's amour sublime: just another amour fou? FR 40:204–12, 1966.   **10353**

P.'s theory of love is distinguished from Breton's because while for Breton, ultimate achievement of "l'amour fou" is not possible in the world, for P. "l'amour sublime" can be consummated in real human life. [JFC]

Costich, Julia F. The poem in the world of change: Péret's Quatre à quatre. RomN 15:410–15, 1974.   **10354**

Analysis of an important poem as it reflects the operation of change in P.'s surrealist world. [JFC]

Courtot, Claude. Introduction à la lecture de Benjamin Péret. Le terrain vague, 1965. 195 p. (Association des Amis de Benjamin Péret) *Also:* Losfeld, 1965. 196 p.   **10355**

Careful documentation: letters, photographs. Eulogy of "forgotten" poet, who realized hopes of Breton. Breton's horizontal line, P.'s vertical one; interesting comparisons. P.'s constancy, his creation. Study of poetic technique interspersed with theoretical propositions on coincidence, description of humor and familiarity of vocabulary and images, balanced with analysis of syntax, of tenses. Satisfactory study and versatile. [MAC]

Eluard, Paul. L'arbitraire, la contradiction, la violence, la poésie. *In his:* Œuvres complètes. Gallimard, 1968. p. 817–25. **10356**
Beautiful appreciation of the surrealist poet by another who later left the group, drawing attention to the coalescence of qualities particular to poetry and surrealism in P. [JFC]

Hanchett, Elizabeth Jackson. The cosmic imagination of Benjamin Péret: a reading of Une île dans une tasse. DadaS 2:41–44, 1972. **10357**
Interesting brief study of an important text. [JFC]

———. Poésie activité de l'esprit: a study of Atout trèfle by Benjamin Péret. FR 44:1036–47, 1971. **10358**
Going beyond the limits of analysis of a single text, this article is useful as an example of the technique of reading a surrealist poem. Analysis of "tonal variations" and structural connections merging with thematic and syntactic elements. [MAC/JFC]

Matthews, J. H. Benjamin Péret. *In his:* Surrealist poetry in France. Syracuse, Syracuse univ. press, 1969. p. 42–54. **10359**
Emphasizes the importance of P. in any appraisal of surrealism. Studies metamorphosis and transmutation. Characteristic nature of P.'s poetry in a future mode said to be prophecy. Disorientation in a self-sufficient statement; his attack on limits and his superiority over Eluard as poet; his relation to revolution. [MAC/JFC]

———. Benjamin Péret: marvelous conjunction. *In:* About French poetry from Dada to Tel Quel: theory and text. Ed. by Mary Ann Caws. Detroit, Wayne state univ. press, 1974. p. 126–38. **10360**
Study of the grammatical form in its poetic significance: joining elements against the rational. [MAC]

———. Invective et merveilleux dans Je ne mange pas de ce pain-là de Benjamin Péret. KRQ 18:409–21, 1971. **10361**

Makes the important point that this collection is poetically remarkable in its fusion of political protest with a surrealist awareness of the marvelous. [JFC]

———. Mechanics of the marvellous: the short stories of Benjamin Péret. EspCr 6:23–70, 1966. **10362**
Study of normality and distance (in Le gigot) from that concept and from logical principles, of irony and familiarity in style, a combination said to be disturbing rather than reassuring. P. shown to "borrow from the real to elaborate the surreal." [MAC]

Mayoux, Jehan. Benjamin Péret, ou la fourchette coupante. SurM 2:150–58; 3:53–58, 1957. **10363**
The first comprehensive study of P.'s surrealism. Highly sympathetic; notes important ideas and images. Same style and tone as Courtot. The "unknown" P., the vitality of his life and work, aggressivity, freedom, revolution, anticlericalism. Breton constructs surrealism from inside; P. opposes it to outside. [MAC/JFC]

Prigioni, Pierre. Péret: das Gewissen seiner Zeit. GRM 14:188–97, 1964. **10364**
Views P. as representative not only of surrealism, but also of important political tendencies of his time. [JFC]

Rosemont, Franklin. An introduction to Benjamin Péret. RadA 4:1–13, 1970. **10365**
Survey of P.'s surrealism from the point of view of an American surrealist. This issue includes several translations into English of works by P. [JFC]

Francis Ponge
(Nos. 10366–10390)

CLAUDE SENNINGER

Special Number

Hommage à Francis Ponge. NRF 8:385–425, 1956. **10366**
Significant articles analyzed separately.

Biography

Bousquet, Joë. A Francis Ponge. *In his:* Correspondance. Gallimard, 1969. p. 99–102.   **10367**

Text established and presented by Suzanne N. André. It contains three letters to P.

General Studies

Bigongiari, Piero. Le parti pris de Ponge. CahS 344:109–16, 1958. *Also in:* Hommage à Francis Ponge. *See* 10366. p. 417–21.   **10368**

His work plunges into "the sedimentary layers of the subconscious." He twists his syntax like a Mallarmé but his poetry is never as hard as the symbolic object. On the contrary it acquires the unavoidable character of the thing for itself.

————. Ponge e la funzione del linguaggio. ApL 31:121–26, 1965.   **10369**

Apropos of "Pour un Malherbe," Bigongiari makes a short sketch of the Pongian poetic.

Bosquet, Alain. Rêverie sur le premier Ponge. NRF 28:98–106, 1966.   **10370**

Bosquet underlines the logical nature of P.'s poetic process where "subjectivity is at the service of the object" and "when the comparison game is like a mathematical intoxication."

Camus, Albert. Lettre au sujet du Parti pris. *In:* Hommage à Francis Ponge. *See* 10366. p. 386–92.   **10371**

Extremely stimulating article in which Camus attempts to show that P. has, thanks to his search for the right word and his insistence upon describing things, accepted the failure of the world. Through this insistant quest, P. reaches an "intolerant humanism" and a "passionate relativism."

Carner, José. Francis Ponge et les choses. *In:* Hommage à Francis Ponge. *See* 10366. p. 409–12.   **10372**

P., who would like to express things in the way they would express themselves if they could, is at the same time, classic and modern in his approach.

Carrouges, Michel. La mappemonde de Ponge. Preu 18–19:13–16, 1952.   **10373**

Carrouges insists here on the homologous quality of the natural and the man made, of the small and the big, of nature and man (at the level of nature) in P.'s poetry which he compares and contrasts with the world of Claudel and Eluard.

————. La rage de l'expression, L'araignée par Francis Ponge. MNP 66:99–102, 1953.   **10374**

P.'s poetic method establishes a new liberty in the use of forms beyond those already employed. The structure and typography of *L'araignée* makes one think of the famous Mallarmean *Coup de dés*.

Chappuis, Pierre. L'ivresse lucide de Ponge. NRF 178:667–71, 1967.   **10375**

Very interesting interpretation of *Le savon* by P. The connection between soap and water would be comparable to that of language and poetry.

Clancier, G. E. Un poète dans tous ses états. CahS 372:283–89, 1963.   **10376**

The young P. had defined the essence of his talent this way: "Definitions-descriptions esthetically and rhetorically adequate." For Clancier the title of a second volume *Méthode* should be a modern *Discours de la méthode*.

Denat, A. Après le grand recueil ou le Ponge de l'Objeu. SynB 204:76–87, 1963.   **10377**

The article is like a mosaic when the author's commentaries cut across passages of P.

Duché, Jean. Francis Ponge et le langage. SynB 50:224–28, 1950.   **10378**

Duché interviews P. who explains that like Braque he considers himself a temporary reconciliator between man, society and nature.

Etiemble, René. Ponge. *In his:* C'est le bouquet! Gallimard, 1967. p. 90–97. (Hygiène des lettres, 5)   **10379**

Etiemble performs a Malherbian investigation on three of P.'s poems: *L'œillet, La guêpe, Le mimosa.* He comments on the words used and their juxtaposition, and sees in P.'s work a unique method composed of words, etymologies, anagrams and rhythms.

———. Ponge. *In his:* Poètes ou faiseurs? Gallimard, 1966. p. 178–87. (Hygiène des lettres, 4) **10380**

Etiemble had earlier seen in P. a reconciliation of science and mystical experience. In this article, he realizes that he was wrong and explains that the unity of the work is based on rhetoric and that there is no objective vision *per se.*

Farasse, Gérard. La portée de L'abricot. Comm 19:186–94, 1972. **10381**

By dint of the metaphor of music, the author presents a very accurate semantic study of P.'s poetry. The two figures of speech at work in this semantic prosody are metonymy and oxymoron.

Ferrier, Jean-Louis. La musique du pré. Exp 1030: 70, April 11–15, 1971. **10382**

Ferrier explains the genesis of the poem in which "Ponge's fundamental project is to modify life through disgust, by dint of reinventing the usage of words."

Greene, Robert W. Ponge, metapoet. MLN 85:572–92, 1970. **10383**

Through a semantic and phonetic analysis of *La fable, Le soleil placé en abîme, Objeu* and *Le pré,* Greene shows that P.'s poems are not works in progress but works *on* the progress of writing (which he calls metapoems).

Jaccottet, Philippe. A propos du Grand recueil. *In his:* L'entretien des muses. Chroniques de poésie. Gallimard, 1968. p. 115–20. **10384**

Enthusiastic article which studies the images of *Le grand recueil* and insists on a certain lucidity of these images which goes beyond surrealism.

———. Malherbe comme modèle. *In his:* L'entretien des muses. Gallimard, 1968. p. 121–28. **10385**

Jaccottet observes that P. has discovered hitherto unknown aspects of Malherbe and in doing so has sketched a portrait of himself.

———. Remarques sur Le soleil. *In:* Hommage à Francis Ponge. *See* 10366. p. 396–405. **10386**

In the work *Soleil,* about which Jaccottet says a few words, P. presents the reader not with a finished product, as before, but with the product in the process of being created, with its errors, its rough drafts and its corrections.

Pieyre de Mandiargues, André. Le feu et la pierre. *In:* Hommage à Francis Ponge. *See* 10366. p. 406–08. **10387**

By dint of eroding away concepts and images and exploiting what is left, P. succeeds in creating not only an "objective poetry," a genre which is again coming into fashion, but a "secondary" poetry which underlines the object and goes as far as rediscovering it.

Walther, Elisabeth. Francis Ponge: eine ästhetische Analyse. Cologne-Berlin, Kiepenheuer & Witsch, 1965. 182 p. **10388**

A philosophical study concentrating on the phenomenological and semiotic aspects of P.'s work. It analyzes P.'s epistemology as it relates to his esthetic and sees in P. a harmonization of opposing ontological views of Heidegger and Husserl. His morality, however, is closer to Diderot and the encyclopedists than to Sartre or Camus. Whitehead's concept of unity in diversity and his categories are also influential in P.'s thought.

———. Ponge. Analytische Monographie. Ein Beitrag zur semantischen und statistischen Ästhetik. Stuttgart, Die Reprographie, 1961. 174 p. **10389**

The author became interested in P. when she set out to translate him. She discovered that philosophical rather than literary ideals governed his work. The book discusses ontology, semantics, communication and semiotic theory. A section is devoted to individual works. Appendices, notes, bibliography and charts of word frequency.

Willard, Nancy. The common life with a star. *In her:* Testimony of the invisible man. Columbia, Mo., Univ. of Missouri press, 1970. p. 43–60. **10390**

An extremely pleasant account of P.'s poetry, written in simple terms for the layman.

Pierre Reverdy
(Nos. 10391–10426)

ROBERT W. GREENE

Edition & Correspondence

Reverdy, Pierre. Œuvres complètes. Ed. by Etienne-Alain Hubert, Maurice Saillet, Stanislas Fumet. Flammarion, 1967– .
15 v.   **10391**

Only collected ed. of R.'s works. To date 8 v. have appeared: *Plupart du temps* (1967), *Le voleur de talan* (1967), *Le gant de crin* (1968), *La peau de l'homme* (1968), *Flaques de verre* (1972), *Risques et périls* (1972), *Cette émotion appelée poésie* (1973) and *Note éternelle du présent* (1973). Appendices to first 3 v., prepared by M. Saillet and S. Fumet, particularly informative as regards R.'s life and esthetic principles.

————. Trente-deux lettres inédites à André Breton 1917–192[4]. ELit 3:97–120, 1970.   **10392**

Letters dealing with Breton's contributions to *Nord-Sud,* founding of *Littérature* and R.'s opinion of some of his contemporaries.

Special Numbers

Hommage à Pierre Reverdy. Ed. by Luc Decaunes. Entre 20:1–206, 1961. **10393**

Important homage collection. Contains selections from R.'s writings and correspondence, and contributions from a number of scholars, critics, friends and fellow poets.

Pierre Reverdy, 1889–1960. Ed. by Maurice Saillet. MerF 344:1–384, 1962. **10394**

Premier homage collection to date. Contains selections from R.'s writings and correspondence, and contributions from a number of critics, writers, artists, friends and fellow poets. Major essays by Brassaï, Gabriel Bounoure, Georges Poulet, Jean-Pierre Richard, Stanislas Fumet and Daniel-Henry Kahnweiler.

Biography

Bounoure, Gabriel. Pierre Reverdy et sa crise religieuse de 1925–27. *In:* Pierre

Reverdy, 1889–1960. *See* 10394. p. 192–222.   **10395**

Sympathetic, informed account of R.'s religious crisis. Contrasts poet's Catharist-tinged faith with Max Jacob's more flamboyant if equally sincere Catholicism.

Brassaï (pseud. for Gyulia Halasz). Reverdy dans son labyrinthe. *In:* Pierre Reverdy, 1889–1960. *See* 10394. p. 159–68. **10396**

Stunning word-portrait of R. the man by world-renowned photographer.

Duché, Jean. Visite à Pierre Reverdy. FL III:1, 3; 112:1, 4, 1948.   **10397**

Transcript of interview with poet on occasion of publication of *Le livre de mon bord* (1948).

Fumet, Stanislas. Histoire d'une amitié. *In:* Pierre Reverdy, 1889–1960. *See* 10394. p. 312–34.   **10398**

Primary source for a life of R. Contains lengthy excerpts from previously unpublished letters (from R. to author).

Guth, Paul. Pour Pierre Reverdy, poète du présent, l'homme est imperfectible jusqu'à l'infini. FL 524:4, May 5, 1956. **10399**

Transcript of interview with poet on occasion of publication of *En vrac* (1956).

Stojkovic-Mazzariol, Emma. En marge d'une correspondance. *In:* Pierre Reverdy, 1889–1960. *See* 10394. p. 84–96. **10400**

Article based on (and with copious quotes from) correspondence author had with R. in years 1947–52.

General Studies

Admussen, Richard L., and René de Costa. Huidobro, Reverdy and the editio princeps of El espejo de agua. CL 24:163–75, 1972.   **10401**

Clarifying summary of half century of debate over question of whether Chilean poet Vicente Huidobro, contributor to R.'s review *Nord-Sud* in 1917, anticipated or imitated French poet's style.

Attal, Jean-Pierre. Sens et valeur du mot main dans l'œuvre poétique de Pierre Reverdy. Cr 179:306–29, 1962. *Also in his:* L'image métaphysique et autres essais. Gallimard, 1969. p. 101–31. **10402**

Exhaustive analysis of single facet of R.'s *œuvre.* Unique in approach to poet.

Bachat, Charles. Reverdy et le surréalisme. Eur 475–76:79–100, 1968.   **10403**
Well-documented study of R.'s relations with dada-surrealist group during decade beginning 1916–17.

Bernard, Suzanne. Pierre Reverdy. *In her:* Le poème en prose de Baudelaire jusqu'à nos jours. Nizet, 1959. p. 637–50.
10404
Enthusiastic, penetrating analysis of R.'s prose poetry. Discusses R.'s notational style, literary cubism, images and essential mystery of "stories" recounted in prose poems.

Caminade, Pierre. Image et métaphore. Un problème de poétique contemporaine. Bordas, 1970. p. 10–33. (Etudes supérieures, 36)   **10405**
Virtually entire book, certainly first half, explicitly glosses R.'s theory of image. Enlightening, both historically and conceptually.

Cornell, W. Kenneth. The case for Pierre Reverdy. *In:* Essays in honor of Albert Feuillerat. Ed. by Henri Peyre. New Haven, Yale univ. press, 1943. p. 267–78. (Yale romanic studies, 22)   **10406**
Earliest essay published on R. in America. Retains usefulness as general introduction to poet.

Daniel, Martin. The poetry of Pierre Reverdy. MLR 48:184–90, 1963.   **10407**
Solid introduction to R.

Du Bouchet, André. Envergure de Reverdy. Cr 47:308–20, 1951.   **10408**
Empathetic demonstration of R.'s breadth by distinguished fellow poet.

Fongaro, Antoine. La poétique de Pierre Reverdy. CahS 327:265–86, 1955. **10409**
First serious attempt to codify R.'s poetic theory. Still useful.

Fumet, Stanislas. Pierre Reverdy ou le lyrisme de la réalité. MerF 304:439–57, 1948.   **10410**
Sensitive treatment of R.'s attitude towards everyday things, objects. Parallels with Cubist painters indicated.

Geay, Jean-Pierre. La quête du réel dans l'œuvre poétique de Pierre Reverdy. RE 23:189–203, 1970.   **10411**
In pursuit of real throughout his life, R. ends up with nothingness. Rapid but comprehensive survey of entire *œuvre.*

Greene, Robert W. The moralism of Pierre Reverdy. FS 21:323–35, 1967.   **10412**
Traces evolution in form and substance of R.'s moralistic aphorisms from *Le gant de crin* (1927) through *Le livre de mon bord* (1948) to *En vrac* (1956).

————. Pierre Reverdy, poet of nausea. PMLA 85:48–55, 1970.   **10413**
Relates recurrent images of collapse in R.'s poetry to imagery and thematics of *La nausée* and *Le mythe de Sisyphe.*

————. The poetic theory of Pierre Reverdy. Berkeley and Los Angeles, Univ. of Calif. press, 1967. 108 p. (Univ. of Calif. publications in modern philology, 82)   **10414**
Chronological analysis of R.'s theoretical writings. Situates R.'s poetic theory in relation to cubism, surrealism, *poésie pure* tradition, Valéry and Ponge. Extensive documentation.
Reviews: R. Admussen in EspCr 9:59–60, 1969; K. Cornell in RR 60: 226, 1969; R. Federman in CL 23:74–77, 1971; L. Pronger in FR 42:166–67, 1968; C. van Rees in Neo 52: 436–37, 1968; C. Wake in FS 25:239, 1971.

Grossvogel, David I. Pierre Reverdy: the fabric of reality. YFS 21:95–106, 1958.
10415
Nuanced study of R.'s stance *vis-à-vis* material reality, his "cubist" techniques and anguish specific to his poetry.

Guiney, Mortimer. La poésie de Pierre Reverdy. Geneva, Georg, 1966. 264 p.
10416
Long, uneven study. Examines at great length handful of poems with view to placing R. in broad cultural and philosophical context. Suggestive rapprochements between R. and Camus. Other links between R., Bergson and Jung less convincing. Ambitious, often fascinating if only partially successful

attempt to fuse literary exegesis with critical biography.

Reviews: R. Admussen in EspCr 9:60–61, 1969; C. Cordié in SFr 12: 588–89, 1968; R. Greene in FS 22: 262–64, 1968; A. Greet in FR 42:458–59, 1969; R. Hubert in CLS 5:208–10, 1968; V. Lee in BA 42:62, 1968; E. Marks in RR 60:225–26, 1969; L. Somville in EL 2:257–59, 1969; R. Vernier in MLQ 29:376–77, 1968.

Hubert, Renée Riese. L'évolution du poème en prose dans l'œuvre de Pierre Reverdy. MLN 75:233–39, 1960. *Also In:* Hommage à Pierre Reverdy. *See* 10393. p. 55–62.   **10417**

Convincingly shows increasing simplicity and purity of R.'s prose poetry across *Poèmes en prose* (1915), *Étoiles peintes* (1921), *La balle au bond* (1928) and *Flaques de verre* (1929).

Kahnweiler, Daniel-Henry. Reverdy et l'art plastique. *In:* Pierre Reverdy, 1889–1960. *See* 10394. p. 169–77.   **10418**

Brief, laudatory survey of R.'s writings on plastic arts by foremost art dealer-historian of cubist age.

Picon, Gaëtan. Poétique et poésie de Pierre Reverdy. MerF 324:16–35, 1957. *Also in his:* L'usage de la lecture. Mercure de France, 1960. p. 239–62.   **10419**

Heuristic if somewhat selective confrontation of R.'s theory and practice. Stresses central paradox of R.'s attachment to things and his obsession with inner life.

Poulet, Georges. Reverdy et le mystère des murs. *In:* Pierre Reverdy, 1889–1960. *See* 10394. p. 228–44. *Also in his:* Le point de départ, études sur le temps humain. Plon, 1964. p. 187–209.   **10420**

Commentary, rich in telling detail and example, on varied, obsessive images of confinement in R.'s poetry.

Richard, Jean-Pierre. Reverdy, entre deux mondes. *In:* Pierre Reverdy, 1889–1960. *See* 10394. p. 253–74. *Also in his:* Onze études sur la poésie moderne. Seuil, 1964. p. 13–29.   **10421**

Subtle exploration of dolorous kingdom between heaven and hell that constitutes R.'s poetic realm, his *interland*.

Rizzuto, Anthony. Style and theme in Reverdy's Les ardoises du toit. University, Alabama, Univ. of Alabama press, 1971. 204 p.   **10422**

Rigorous stylistic analysis of *Les ardoises du toit* (1918). Chapters on "Vocabulary," "Word Order," "Intensification," "Metaphor," "Rhyme and meter" and "Visual verse." Revealing treatment of objective lyricism peculiar to R.'s poetry and its unique blend of private and universal themes.

Reviews: R. Admussen in Style 7: 227–30, 1973; M. Caws in RR 63:241, 1972; M. Guiney in MLJ 56:471–72, 1972; R. Horry in CLAJ 15:93–95, 1971; Y. Scalzitti in MP 70:277–78, 1972–73.

Rousselot, Jean, and Michel Manoll. Pierre Reverdy. Présentation par Jean Rousselot suivi d'un essai par Michel Manoll. Œuvres choisis... Seghers, 1951. 240 p. (Poètes d'aujourd'hui, 25) *Also (rev.):* Pierre Reverdy. Une étude de Jean Rousselot, un essai de Michel Manoll. Avec un choix de poèmes. Seghers, 1970. 190 p. (Poètes d'aujourd'hui, 25)   **10423**

Includes selections from R.'s writings and other documents. Manoll's essay on ascetic impulse in R.'s *œuvre* especially illuminating.

Saillet, Maurice. La nature de Reverdy. MerF 309:418–36, 1950. *Also in his:* Sur la route de Narcisse. Mercure de France, 1958. p. 55–79.   **10424**

Careful examination of R.'s images, style, dates and circumstances of composition of certain collections.

Stojkovic, Emma. L'œuvre poétique de Pierre Reverdy. Padua, Cedam, 1951. 128 p.   **10425**

First book-length study of R. Contains letter-preface from poet dated 18/12/1948. Modest, sympathetic, still useful appraisal. Concentrates on R.'s theory and practice of image, his prose poems, and two collections: *Les épaves du ciel* (1924) and *Sources du vent* (1929).

Review: A. Patri in MNP 56:88–89, 1952.

Novel

Somville, Léon. Les romans autobiographiques de Pierre Reverdy. EL 3:21–45, 1970.   **10426**

Study of *Le voleur de talan* (1917), *La peau de l'homme* (1926) and *Risques et périls* (1930) as autobiographical novels and as important documents in history of literary, artistic avant-garde Paris *circa* 1916–17.

Jules Supervielle
(Nos. 10427–10484)

TATIANA GREENE

Iconography

Jules Supervielle. Manuscrits. Documents divers. Editions originales et illustrées. Photographies. Souvenirs. Peintures. Aquarelles, dessins, sculptures. Steff, 1958. 20 p. (Bibliothèque littéraire Jacques Doucet)   **10427**
Presentation by Octave Nadal.

Autobiographical Texts

Supervielle, Jules. Boire à la source. Corrêa, 1933. 229 p.   **10428**
This lyrical and factual text constitutes a partial autobiography. A charming and at times almost laconic book. Indispensable for understanding *l'homme et l'œuvre*, and the very special role and nature of memory for S.

———. En songeant à un art poétique. *In his:* Naissances, poèmes suivis de En songeant à un art poétique. Gallimard, 1951. p. 57–71.   **10429**
En songeant... is a long footnote to S.'s brief text for the NRF's *Tableau de la poésie en France* (Nov. 1933). This penetrating self-analysis shows S. as leaning toward a modicum of wisdom and reason. An interesting text on inspiration, reason, the dream, light and obscurity in poetry.

Supervielle, Jules, and Octave Nadal. Conversation. *In:* Hommage à Supervielle. *See* 10434. p. 617–30.   **10430**
Another dialog, after those with Etiemble and Mallet (*see* Etiemble, Supervielle) and the numerous interviews (*see* Greene, Etiemble). S. tells of his admiration for Jaurès whom he considers a poet in prose. Talks of the healthy poets (as opposed to Poètes maudits). Says that *A la nuit* is his best book of poems.

Supervielle, Jules, and [René] Etiemble. Correspondance 1936–1959. Edition critique. Texte établi, annoté, préfacé par Jeannine Etiemble. Société d'édition d'enseignement supérieur, 1969. 199 p.   **10431**
Preface speaks of what war and fascism meant for these two self-exiled writers. Two independent men's views on the world, literature, prosody, the state of their health. There are 60 letters by S. and 35 by Etiemble.
Review: M. Chapalan in FL Sept. 15–21, 1969.

Special Numbers

Homenaje a Supervielle. Sur 266:1–40, 1960.   **10432**
Not a special number but a large section of the regular number. Articles by Borges, Rafael Alberti, Gloria Alcorta and Etiemble [extracts from his book]. Introductory note by Marcel Jouhandeau.

Hommage à Jules Supervielle. GdC 5–76, March 1945.   **10433**
Very interesting contributions by Alain Bosquet, Robert Elie, Etiemble, Elie de Grandmont, Gilles Hénault, Marie Raymond and Guy Sylvestre.

Hommage à Jules Supervielle. NRF 20:193–213, 1954.   **10434**
Brief texts by Roger Caillois, Paul Claudel, Henri Michaux, Armand Robin, and Georges Schehadé. Two slightly longer articles by Gabriel Bounoure and Etiemble.

Hommage à Jules Supervielle. NRF 94:586–787, 1960.   **10435**
This long *hommage* honoring the poet who died in 1960 contains poems by Gabriel Cousin, Jean Laugier, Jean-Philippe Salabreuil, Jean Tardieu, Jules Tordjman, and Claude Vigée and short tributes by Georges Anex, Jean Cocteau, André Dhôtel, Jean Dutourd, Jean Follain, Roger Judrin and Robert Lorho. Important articles are by Yves Berger, Maurice Blanchot, Jean Cassou, Jean Grosjean, Franz Hellens, Philippe Jaccottet, Monique Klener, Jean Le Louet, René Micha, André Pieyre de Mandiargues, Georges Poulet, A. Rolland de Renéville, Claude Roy, Jean Schlumberger, Jules Supervielle and

Octave Nadal, Henri Thomas and Jean Tortel.

Jules Supervielle. AvP 1–63, 1935.   **10436**
This, the first of several special homage issues, contains most interesting contributions by Armand Bernier, Jean Cassou, Marie Gevers, Christian Sénéchal, Henri Michaux, Maurice Carême, Edmond Vandercammen, A. Rolland de Renéville et al., as well as texts by S.

Reconnaissance à Supervielle. Reg 21:1–111, 1938.   **10437**
In addition to poems by S. and a bibliography by Sénéchal, this special issue has forty-six contributors.

Biography

Nadal, Octave. Conversation avec Supervielle. *In his:* A mesure haute. Mercure de France, 1964. p. 257–68.   **10438**
Important, perhaps indispendable text. Speaks of his feeling of kinship with all men, of his desire to appeal to the understanding of all readers, of the notion of "le poète sain."

[Rilke, Rainer-Maria, and Jules Supervielle]. Correspondance Rilke-Supervielle. LetP 13:48–55, 1952.   **10439**
Three letters to Supervielle quoted in part by Fernand Lot, Claude Roy or Elisabeth Stübel (who read them at the Rilke Archives in Weimar). (Also see Greene *infra.*, p. 309–11)

General Studies: Books

Blair, Dorothy S. Jules Supervielle. Oxford, Blackwell, 1960. 186 p.   **10440**
The principal merit of this work, originally a doctoral thesis at the University of the Witwatersrand, is the study of S.'s language. It examines all of the poet's work, except *Le corps tragique* (1959). Sensitive and keen analyses marred by uneven writing and errors in quotations (31 for S., one for Verlaine), unsubstantiated statements by critics, misspelled names (as: Pierre Seguers) and errors of information. In her introduction, dated 1959, she writes that only three studies were published "to date in French"; T. Greene's (1958) was a fourth one. Interesting and informative.

Review: M. Benamou in Sym 16: 307–10, 1962.

Ehrsam, Kurth. Die Novelle Jules Supervielles. Zurich, [no publisher], 1956. 138 p.   **10441**
Studies a few stories from the first two collections of tales, and one story, *Orphée,* from the last. Compares S. with Maupassant, an unexpected contrast. Mixes, somewhat helter-skelter, considerations such as the problem of death, the symbol of the tree, etc, in this doctoral thesis supervised by Th. Spoerri.

Etiemble, [René]. Supervielle. Gallimard, 1960. 327 p. (La bibliothèque idéale) *Also (rev. and shortened):* Gallimard, 1968. 256 p. (Pour une bibliothèque idéale)   **10442**
Written by an admirer and a friend of many years, this very useful presentation begins with briefly sketched portraits of S. by Henri Michaux, Christian Sénéchal, Claude Roy, Marcel Jouhandeau and Georges Schehadé. The book includes S.'s answers to the *Questionnaire de Marcel Proust,* chapters titled "Les jours" (a brief biography) and "L'œuvre" (with sub-chapters "La poétique," "La prose" and "Les poèmes"), "Les livres" (a summary of each publication), "Pages" and "Phrases" (excerpts from S.), then three conversations, one with Etiemble, the other two with Robert Mallet on French radio May 8 and 15, 1956, "Reflets" (these being texts by Eluard, Emmanuel, Mallet, Hellens, Jouhandeau, Roy, Gros, Estand, Bousquet, Noulet, Jaccottet, Hourcade and others). A useful bibliography is followed by the very interesting lists titled "Iconographie", "Musicographie" and "Phonographie." Photographs and documents. A lively and likeable study.
Reviews: A. Loranquin in BdL 222: 405, 1960; E. Noulet in her *Alphabet critique. 1924–1964.* V. 1. Brussels, Presses univ. de Bruxelles, 1964. p. 121–24.

Greene, Tatiana. Jules Supervielle. Geneva, Droz; Paris, Minard, 1958. 441 p. **10443**
Examines all of S.'s work including verse, tales, novels and plays in their successive stages up to the texts of 1956. Attempts to determine what constitutes S.'s originality and studies

his work from the psychological, then from the esthetic point of view. Claims that an author's biography, the study of his main themes, moods, keywords, symbols, images, dialog and prosody acquire their full significance only when the reader can see their interdependence, and those aspects are therefore all studied here. The writings in the different genres are examined successively. Possible relationships with other writers or movements are studied: Laforgue, Lautréamont, Romains, Francis Thompson, Rilke, Valéry, and S.'s position in relation to surrealism. Extensive bibliography of S.'s writings and studies and reviews of his works. Appendices include a systematic list, for each book title, of those texts in it which had appeared in one or more pre-original versions, some with different titles; analyses of variants of the poems; a frequency list of key words (nouns); a summary of the main works and articles on S. from 1919 to 1956; and of five letters to T. Greene.

Reviews: M. Benamou in Sym 16: 307–10, 1962; R. Pelmont in RR 51: 75–77, 1960; R. Pouilliart in LR 17: 187–90, 1963.

Hiddleston, James A. L'univers de Jules Supervielle. José Corti, 1965. 238 p.
10444

Originally a doctoral diss. (1962) at the University of Edinburgh. Considers all of S.'s work, including *Le corps tragique* (1959). Best contribution is the study of the dream and its expression, such as the frequent use of clouds; sees S.'s "true originality" in spontaneous dreaming and his way of apprehending the depth of the outer world or the self. The last chapter is entitled "La synthèse impossible." This sensitive study does not bring a really new analysis or interpretation of S.'s inspiration, nor of his language, and its approach is reflected in the disparate chapter titles. Reviews: J. Duncan in MLR 62: 537–39, 1967; J. Raymond in Monde June 1, 1966.

Jones, Louisa E. Poetic fantasy and fiction, the short stories of Jules Supervielle. The Hague and Paris, Mouton, 1973. 84 p.
10445

The short stories had been studied by Ehrsam and by Stübel, as well as by Blair and Greene. Jones attempts to examine them in the light of recent works on the esthetic of fiction, and, in her bibliography, she cites Buber, Jakobson, Chomsky, Todorov and Genette. Her text does not, however, establish clear connections between her criticism and their thought. Omits Greene's work on S. in her bibliography, while including three unpublished theses. Nice observations on S.'s language in the short story.

Roy, Claude. Jules Supervielle. Une étude par Claude Roy. Inédits, œuvres choisies... Seghers, 1949. 177 p. (Poètes d'aujourd'hui, 15)
10446

A useful, somewhat impressionistic 85 p. essay, followed by then unpublished texts of S. A good introduction to him, though the dramatic works are not mentioned. The tone and main themes of the verse works are described in a keen manner.

Review: L. Gros in CahS 300:304–11, 1950.

Sénéchal, Christian. Jules Supervielle, poète de l'univers intérieur. Essai précédé de vers inédits du poète, Campagnons du silence. Jean Flory (Les presses du hibou), 1939. 238 p.
10447

A work of real worth, it examines with respect and sympathy the central themes of the self, the heart, and the hands. Sénéchal sees above all in S. a poet of the inner world. He gives exegeses of poems, cites numerous statements by S. on his poetry, sees the importance of dream for S. with its accompanying "explosion d'irréel" (S.) and a greatly increased activity of the senses. An admiring and searching study of the poet's modes of expression, Sénéchal's work does not examine the prose works, nor the dramatic production.

Specker, Lotte. Jules Supervielle, eine Stilstudie. Zurich, Emil Ruegg, 1942. 220 p.
10448

This doctoral essay, written under Th. Spörri, contains a perspicacious study of S.'s language, particularly of his use of metaphor. The author sees S. as evolving more and more toward the form of the fable, and as replacing Baudelaire's *correspondances* with metamorphoses. Gives precise and detailed analyses of images and style, draws conclusions from the variants of *Gravi-*

tations as to the direction of S.'s thought toward the concrete, and supports her findings with abundant illustrations.

Viallaneix, Paul. Le hors-venu ou le personnage poétique de Supervielle. Klincksieck, 1972. 175 p.   **10449**

The *hors-venu* is also the title of a poem in *Les amis inconnus*. There are eleven chapters on the themes, rhythms and affective content of the volumes of verse. Viallaneix sees in S. a brother of Jean-Jacques, of Socrates (who exerted an hypnotic influence on those around him), and of du Bellay who was also an orphan like S. Studies the role of memory, the night, and S.'s love for silence. Goes to the core of the poet's persona. Applies in his criticism criteria and terms used by Joubert.

Vivier, Robert. Lire Supervielle. José Corti, 1972. 211 p.   **10450**

An admirer of S. for many years, Vivier gives a sensitive portrait of the poet and a sympathetic presentation of the poetry. No bibliography; only incomplete references given for the numerous quotations; lines misquoted; contains erroneous information. Sometimes unclear. His book's merit lies in perspicacious characterization, as in his lines on the intensity of S.'s vigilance, or on a lordliness which gives events, in S.'s poetry, a ritual quality. The prose and drama works are mentioned briefly.

General Studies: Articles

Alcalde, Leopoldo Rodriguez. Prólogo. *In:* Supervielle, Jules. Poemas, selección, traducción y prólogo. Madrid, Ed. RIALP, Adonais, 1948. p. 7–19.   **10451**

In his introduction to his beautiful translations, Alcalde contrasts S.'s poems with the "vaga fluidez onírica" of automatic writing, seeing S.'s texts as lucid, sensitive and more expressive in their bareness than the verbal excesses of many surrealists.

Béguin, Albert. Jules Supervielle, poète des deux nuits. *Postface to:* Supervielle, Jules. A la nuit. Neuchâtel, A la Baconnière; Paris, Seuil, 1947. p. 51–66. (CahRh 68) *Also in his:* Poésie de la présence de Chrétien de Troyes à Pierre Emmanuel. Neuchâtel, A la Baconnière; Paris, Eds. du seuil, 1957. p. 285–99.   **10452**

Béguin, as ever a penetrating critic, sees S. as subordinating vocabulary, syntactical invention, prosody, punctuation and all other details of form to a dominant search for melodic continuity. Even a short poem by S. appears to last long because the unity of the poem is, primarily, a vocal unity.

Blair, Dorothy S. Jules Supervielle's use of imagery. MLR 55:580–83, 1960.   **10453**

Studies various versions of poem "L'appel."

Blanchet, André. Jules Supervielle, poète de l'espace. Et 307:145–62, 1960. *Also in his:* La littérature et le spirituel. Vol. III. Classiques d'hier et d'aujourd'hui. Paris, Aubier, Eds. Montaigne, 1961. p. 135–54.   **10454**

Sees no hermeticism in S., but a forgetting of the self, different from that of mystics. One of the best texts on S.'s originality, which is described as partly bucolic, partly cosmic, as well as a love for that which is newest and most tender (as a new-born fawn). In S.'s world of eternity and gaping spaces, one loses one's footing. "Supervielle n'est pas chrétien," writes Blanchet in this Jesuit journal. S. was baptized and married in a Catholic church but had not been made to learn the catechism. Says S. did not know that he was praying and always believed that he did not believe.

Blanchot, Maurice. Oublieuse mémoire. *In his:* L'entretien infini. Gallimard, 1969. p. 459–64.   **10455**

In his essay "Oublieuse mémoire" (the title of S.'s 1949 book of poems), Blanchot approves the coupling of these two words, since, forgetting is "the very vigilance of memory," the unconscious memory of origins. Blanchot's text is a skillful fugue on the theme and the words *oubli, oublier,* etc. S. remains close to a "profonde mémoire immémoriale" which begins in legendary time.

Bo, Carlo. Ancora Supervielle. LAC 2, no. 10:52–57, 1951. *Also in his:* Della lettura e altri saggi. Florence, Vallecchi, 1953. p. 473–81.   **10456**

Sees "the error of a critic" in Gaëtan Picon's perplexity before S.'s poetry and cautions against too facile a reading of S.

Borel, Jacques. Supervielle l'évasif. NRF 209:641–62, 1970.   **10457**

Referring to "Le portrait" (*Gravitations*), says that S.'s poetry, seemingly so open, is one in which he attempts to change centripetal forces to centrifugal ones, and thus deflect it in the direction of outer space. Walls dissolve; all is porous; stones and the poet float, as in Chagall. The "évasif" poet has left his self, in a saving flight, and a saving confusion. S. is neither a stranger nor a captive. A graceful text, which goes to the core of S.'s poetic processes.

Bosquet, Alain. Jules Supervielle ou l'amitié cosmique. RdP 124–31, Sept. 1956. **10458**

S. occupies an important place in the poetic production of the first half of our century, according to Bosquet. The "crucial problem" is the why of his "constant commerce with immensity" and with an ungraspable elsewhere.

Bounoure, Gabriel. Jules Supervielle. CahS 101:329–42, 1928.   **10459**

Sees primarily a voyager in S. S. is the poet of relativity and refuses our ordinary manner of perceiving the world. All spatial conditions are described by him in a new way and form a universal ballet. This early, original, and accurate criticism shows S. to be close to the concrete world and its dimensions. S. is deemed closer to the Montevidean Lautréamont than to Laforgue and the gravity of Maldoror inspires his "féerie."

―――――. Tentatives modernes de poésie cosmique. GraR 12:276–86, 1932. **10460**

Studies "sentiment cosmique" in Pierre Guéguen, Jules Romains, Jules Supervielle and Théo Varlet, and sees S. as moving in a metapsychic and metaphysical world where identity and determination lose their precision. Says that life, death, time and space exist, for S., in a reversible dimension, and that a dream-like freedom is at the root of both the creation of the universe, and its erasing, in S.'s poetry.

Caceres, Ester de. Significación de la obra de Jules Supervielle en la cultura uruguaya. IESM 63–81, Nov. 1943.   **10461**

Examines the significance of S.'s writings in Uruguayan culture, and finds that, unlike Laforgue and Lautréamont, the other two Uruguayan-born French poets, S. preserves the memory of the Uruguayan landscape, people, and way of life in his themes.

Chiari, Joseph. Contemporary French poetry. Manchester, Manchester univ. press, 1952. p. 45–70. *Also:* New York, Philosophical library, 1952.   **10462**

Chiari's praise is partly founded on opinions one does not readily share. S. reminds him of Sartre's existentialism: the observation that the *Poèmes de Guanamiru* sequence "seems to contain most of his bad poetry" is rather brutal and perhaps unfair. But real insights compensate for this.

Couffignol, Robert. 1938-Jules Supervielle: La fable du monde. *In his:* "aux premiers jours du monde..." La paraphrase de la Genèse de Hugo à Supervielle. Lettres modernes, Minard, 1970. p. 309–23.   **10463**

Sees the presence of the divine in short stories such as *Le bœuf et l'âne de la crèche* in the volume of verse *La fable du monde* or in the farce *La première famille.* Notes S.'s capacity for marveling, his para-biblical creation of the world, his humor. Quotes verses from Isaiah, Job and the Psalms which S. seems to echo.

Cranston, Philip E. Jules Supervielle: Livre de fables. FR 46, special issue 5:95–102, 1973.   **10464**

Gives us the ur-Supervielle. Cranston has examined S.'s very first work, *Livre de fables,* written in 1893, when S. was 10, on a little *registre de comptes,* and containing two poems in French, two in Spanish, grammar and arithmetic exercises, conjugations and translations. Texts which one could not otherwise obtain are given in their entirety, such as comptine-like pieces in Spanish. These very early lines prefigure many of S.'s subjects and themes.

Eliot, T. S. Foreword. *In:* Chiari, Joseph. Contemporary French poetry. *See* 10462. p. vii–xi.   **10465**

About S. and Saint-John Perse, Eliot writes "there are no two poets of their generation in France of whose permanence I feel more assured...."

Etiemble, [René]. L'évolution de la poétique chez Supervielle entre 1922 et 1934. *In:* Hommage à Jules Supervielle. *See*

10434. p. 63–76. *Also* Val 6:51–71, 1946. *Also:* TM 59:532–47, 1950. *Also in his:* Poètes ou faiseurs? (1936–1966). Hygiène des lettres IV. Gallimard, 1966. p. 298–322.   **10466**

Describes *Gravitations* as having an unsure kind of surrealism and speaks of the "modest" *Débarcadères*. Yet both these works are bold, assertive, and, in great part, very original. Etiemble sees S. as giving to poetry its rightful complexity, between spontaneity and the conscious craftsmanship evidenced in his reworking his poems. Thus is born "the hope of a new classicism," after Mallarmé's "desperate attempts" and the excesses of the surrealists. Etiemble notes how, through various rewritings, S. holds on to his original rhythmical scheme.

————. Il faut de tout pour faire une Fable du monde. TM 31:1880–97, 1948. **10467**

Incorporates his article "Supervielle et le sens de la nuit" LetFB 5:18–25, 1942. Presenting S. as an antidote to Rimbaud, Etiemble admires him for navigating a straight course in spite of having been tempted by the irrational world of dreams. He steered close to the haven of reason. "S. or the remedy against surrealism," writes the author of *Le mythe de Rimbaud*. Does Etiemble force S.'s thought to suit his own profound conviction? To him S. demonstrates that "without cruel intelligence, there is no poetry" and is the most human, the best tempered of to-day's poets.

Fluchère, Henri. Jules Supervielle. FS 4: 345–53, 1950.   **10468**

Fluchère says that S.'s most unexpected metaphors rest upon a solid base ("un point d'équilibre"); he sees S. as an authentic, if involuntary, heir to Apollinaire's humanistic attitude (as expressed in *La jolie rousse*), and one who has reconciled tradition and adventure in his writings.

Fontainas, André. Le sens de l'exotique dans la poésie française. RevAL 4–15, May, 1922.   **10469**

Sees S. as a poet of South America more "in the nervous nonchalance of his images..., his drawn-out rhythms" than in his descriptions of the pampas. There are interesting, accurate and perceptive remarks, especially in view of

the vaunted exotic quality critics had seen in S.'s works (principally in his *Poèmes* and the volume *Débarcadères*).

Garibaldi, Fernando. El arte de Jules Supervielle. Mor 1:137–42, 1947.   **10470**

Referring to the tale "La piste et la mare" (in *L'enfant de la haute mer*), with its blind murder, attempts to analyze the "transfiguration of realism" in this very good study of S.'s subtle details, both tragic and humorous. Says S.'s narrative cancels solitude and shows man, unable to speak, but surrounded with witnesses and presences, such as animals. An original text which shows S.'s awareness of an enigmatic world and his "diaphanous limpidity."

Hourcade, Pierre. Jules Supervielle, poète de la mort et de la vie. EIP 14–15:56–70, 1955–56.   **10471**

Says that, while mysticism is alien to S., still, all things, to him, become *phantasmes* and enter the world of his dreaming. S. is described as both fraternal and distant, and impervious to a fashion which consists in seeing myths everywhere in poetry. A certain absent-mindedness preserves him as one of the truest poets. Followed by "Poesie di Supervielle tradotte de Fernando Capecchi," p. 71–84.

Hubert, Renée Riese. Jules Supervielle in stageland. YFS 29:102–07, 1962.   **10472**

Many details are given on S.'s plays and their performances. His plays, which do not have "the solid anguish of Beckett's creatures," are not devoid of dramatic tension, since fairytale characters or mythical ones are sometimes confronted in them with our complex modern world.

————. Les mythologies intimes de Supervielle. Sym 13:300–06, 1959.   **10473**

Asserts that S. has no systematic, biographic, or histrionic system and that he expresses no judgment upon the world's creatures. Sees an organic, rather than a pantheistic, animism in S.'s poetic world. Not only does S. render non-existent the frontiers which separate life and death, but he also brings together different periods of time, or "the shell" and "the ear" which listens to it. Myth and metamorphosis rejoin memory, and human existence is linked to an enigma. A penetrating study of major themes.

Lot, Fernand. Tentatives modernes de poésie cosmique. GraR 20:276–86, 1932. **10474**

Sees in S.'s writings a marvelous ubiquity. One moves back or forward in time or space in this poetry of potential miracles and dream-like freedom.

Mansuy, Michel. Jules Supervielle. *In his:* Etudes sur l'imagination de la vie. J. Supervielle, H. Bosco, A. Robbe-Grillet, H. Michaux, J. Rostand, P. Teilhard de Chardin. José Corti, 1970. p. 15–44. **10475**

Sees in S. a Saint Francis of Assisi. Sees also a certain idealism in S., akin to that of Novalis, because living beings, for S., are sometimes an incarnation of an idea, and because of his faith in metempsychosis says that, on one hand, S.'s creations have an objective reality for him, but on the other hand, his attachment to the corporeal devalues the spiritual. Sees in S. (as in Bosco) an oceanic consciousness of the I.

Martin, Graham. Metaphors in Supervielle's poetry. MLR 59:579–82, 1964. **10476**

Examines metaphor and symbol in several poems by S.

Monteiro, Adolfo Vitor Casais. Descoberta no mundo interior: a poesia de Jules Supervielle. Pôrto, Ed. Presença, 1938. 55 p. *Also in his:* A poesia de Jules Supervielle, estudo e antologia. Lisboa, Ed. Confluência, [1946?] 156 p. (Antologia de autores portugueses e estrangeiros) **10477**

First study in book form on S. Sees a special psychic climate in S.'s poetry, with memories of a childhood spent near the pampas which exert their magic power, and believes that South America remains for S. an ever-present foundation. Monteiro's analysis and description of S.'s works are among the most discerning. He thinks that the discovery of new relationships between things causes S. to give a new value to many words. Sees an atmosphere of contrasts at the same time as a union of the outside world and the poet's conscience, the latter being best aware of itself, though non-narcissistic, when it is most aware of the presence of the outside world within itself. Sees S.'s

accent, tone and melody as especially able to express the creation of a new world. Not a metaphysical poet, S. is one who believes in the reality of dream.

Nadal, Octave. Jules Supervielle ou le rêve surveillé. MerF 334:584–91, 1958. *Also in his:* A mesure haute. Mercure de France, 1964. p. 269–75. **10478**

Speaks of S. as of a born dreamer, who wants to give his poetry an intelligible expression, and of S.'s poetics as inseparable from an ever deeper, yet always controlled, reverie. Says that S. has created a new figure of speech, elliptic allegory, which deprives allegory of any intellectuality.

Orr, John. Foreword and introduction. *In:* Supervielle, Jules. Contes et poèmes. Edinburgh, At the univ. press, 1950. p. ix–xxi. (Edinburgh univ. texts. Language and literature, 2) **10479**

Considers S. one of the greatest contemporary French authors, who combines characteristics of La Fontaine, Lewis Carroll and Milton. He sees in S. "a mind uncurtained by tradition," open to new analogies. Orr's analysis of S.'s language is among the best. He connects S.'s sensibility and sympathy with his poetics. His choice of texts, together with his sympathetic criticism, gives the reader an accurate and balanced view of S.'s manifold art and imagination.

Poulet, Georges. Superveille. *In his:* Etudes sur le temps humain. V. III. Plon, 1964. p. 109–27. **10480**

Studies memory in S.'s poetry, saying that S. remembers little and also does not always recognize what he remembers. This gives rise to many metamorphoses and quid-pro-quos. Like some authors of science-fiction, S. imagines a cosmic oblivion after the disappearance of human memory. S.'s images, he thinks, break and cease at every instant, and the continuity of his poetry is the continuity of the abyss, just as the real strong presence in it is that of absence. Poulet's text reads as a poem of penetrating precision. He concludes that in space are found the simultaneity and the lucidity which recompose our world and where each thing is in its true place. Original if at times surprising statement on S.

Raymond, Marcel. De Baudelaire au surréalisme. Corrêa, 1933. p. 381–87.   **10481**

Sees S. as influenced by Laforgue, Claudel, Rimbaud, Whitman and Rilke, and believes the motivating force of his poetry is metaphysical anguish. In his authoritative work, Raymond gave an important place to S. at a relatively early time.

Rousseaux, André. Jules Supervielle, poète de la nostalgie. *In his:* Portraits littéraires choisis. Geneva, Skira, 1947. p. 325–34. *Also in his:* Littérature du vingtième siècle. V. 3. A. Michel, 1949. p. 106–15.   **10482**

A good description of one of S.'s principal moods. Describes S. as liking precision, anxious in the face of uncertainty. He moves as in limbo, but constantly toward more clarity. When he speaks of the soul, it is as of a subtle reality reached through dream.

Saillet, Maurice. Jules Supervielle. MerF 302:127–31, 1948.   **10483**

Speaks of S.'s use of everyday words. Says that S. is the poet of "échanges" between the landscapes of the earth and those of the soul. Of the other two Uruguayans, says that while Lautréamont's dominant trait was his cruelty, and Laforgue's a lunar memory, S.'s is his "mansuétude," his kindliness and gentleness, his discretion and a clairvoyance of the heart.

Stübel, Elisabeth. Einführung in die Novellen von Jules Supervielle. ZFSL 65:311–36, 1944.   **10484**

Is mainly interested in the volume's *L'enfant de la haute mer* and *L'arche de Noé.* Studies their psychological substructure, speaks of their "pseudo-reality." Says that, in *Antoine du désert,* S. found a medium ground between *conte* and *nouvelle.* Finds in Jung an explanation of certain themes and symbols.

CHAPTER XXIII

PAUL CLAUDEL

(Nos. 10485–11041)

Chapter Coordinator: Douglas W. Alden

Valentini Brady-Papadopoulou, William Bush, Jean-Pierre Cap, Calvin Claudel, John F. Erwin, Jr., Lynne L. Gelber, Sharon E. Harwood, Nina Hellerstein, Tobin H. Jones, Volker Kapp, William Howard Matheson, Moses M. Nagy, Norman H. Paul, Michel Rybalka, and Harold M. Watson

Bibliography

Benoist-Méchin, Jacques, and Georges Blaizot. Bibliographie des œuvres de Paul Claudel de Tête d'or au Soulier de satin 1890–1929, précédée de Fragment d'un drame (1891). Auguste Blaizot et fils, 1931. 185 p. **10485**

Detailed bibliography of C.'s works in their chronological order, with dates of reprints and translations in other languages. Last chapter gives a reasonably complete list of books and articles on C.'s work, in France and abroad. Though incomplete, still a useful reference. [MMN]

Bibliographie des œuvres de Paul Claudel. Ed. by Jacques Petit and Andrée Hirschi. Les belles lettres, 1973. 191 p. **10486**

Chronologically arranged listing of all works by C. up to 1971. Includes all publications of a text prior to inclusion in collection, those of special interest even after publication in collection, all eds. of a work containing modifications and/or additions, all eds. of collections. Extensive title index includes title changes cross-referenced. Indispensable scholarly tool. Additions to index published in BSPC and annual volumes of C. series in RLM. [LLG]

Labriolle, Jacqueline de. Claudel and the English-speaking world. A critical bibliography. London, Grant & Cutler, 1973. 172 p. **10487**

An excellent bibliographical tool, this volume lists everything published, located, performed or broadcast in Great Britain and the U.S. up to 1972–73. Materials are intelligently subdivided, and many, though far from all, entries

are accompained by bibliographer's own critical notes. [JFE]

Reviews: R. Rancœur in BBB 19: 475–76, 1974; G. Shurr in ClaudelS 1:83–84, 1974.

Wilhelm, Julius. Paul Claudel in deutscher Darstellung und Forschung. *In:* Paul Claudel zu seinem hundertsten Geburtstag. *See* 10610. p. 37–58. **10488**

A survey of C. research in Germany. Wilhelm chooses those works which appear interesting to him and gives short summary of contents. Despite many lacunae this is a useful introduction to the history of German research up to 1969. [VK]

Editions

Brunel, Pierre. L'échange de Paul Claudel: première version, introduction... Les belles lettres, 1974. 252 p. (AnLUB, 161) **10489**

Reproduction and analysis of variant mss. and drafts in standard format adopted for Besançon series. Complete standard text is not reproduced. Brunel's introduction and commentary are fascinating for their range and erudition. [JFE]

Claudel, Paul. Au milieu des vitraux de l'apocalypse. Dialogues et lettres accompagnés d'une glose. Ed. établie par Paul Claudel et Jacques Petit. Gallimard, 1966. 426 p. **10490**

C. at his best in characteristic exegesis, first in the form of dialogs with his "daughter," then in letters to her. [JFE]

Reviews: M. Deguy in NRF 30:869–75, 1967; J. Madaule in Esp 35:129–

34, 1967; J. Maia in Brot 84:231–36, 1967; E. Roberto in CahCC 5:185–98, 1967.

———. Connaissance de l'Est. Ed. by Gilbert Gadoffre. Mercure de France, 1973. 390 p.　　　　　　　　　　　**10491**

An excellent critical ed. based on 1914 ed. The editor's introduction is a gem of careful, reasoned scholarship, and includes superb chapters on Renard and Mallarmé as C.'s "inspirers" and examples; on C.'s use of analogy; on forms and structures within the work; and on history of publication of texts, with critical assessments of previous and subsequent editions. Four "poèmes inachevés" are appended to original text. [JFE]

Reviews: P. Brunel in BSPC 51:19–20, 1973; A. Espiau de la Maëstre in RFor 85:216–18, 1973; J. Grosjean in NRF 251:95–97, 1973; N. Hellerstein in ClaudelS 2:108–10, 1975.

———. Figures et paraboles. Ed. by Andrée Hirschi. Les belles lettres, 1974. 240 p. (AnLUB, 160)　　　　　　　　　**10492**

Sound, scholarly presentation of texts, variants and mss. of *Figures et paraboles* not including *Richard Wagner* and *La légende de Prâkriti* of C.'s 1936 ed. (both done separately in Besançon series), and with the addition of "A la rencontre du printemps" (1936) and "Une visite à Bâle" (1938). Editor's main concern for each text, beyond normal critical apparatus, is the "parabole," its form and elucidation, since the ideas in each are seen as having already been expressed elsewhere by C. [JFE]

———. Journal I (1904–1932). Introd. par François Varillon. Ed. by François Varillon and Jacques Petit. Gallimard, 1968. xc, 1499 p. (Bibliothèque de la Pléiade, 205)　　　　　　　　　　　**10493**

Introd. by Varillon attempts explanation of C.'s personality, motives for keeping a journal, evolution of form and content, discrepancies with other works or between *Journal* entries, and reasons for periods of silence or subjects omitted. Diary is indispensable document for understanding life, nature of judgments, sources of works or style. Notes and chronology by J. Petit. [LLG]

Reviews: Y. Florenne in QL 70:10–11, 1969; L. Guichard in RHL 73:

728–31, 1973; P.-H. Simon in Monde Feb. 22, 1969.

———. Journal II (1933–1955). Introd. par François Varillon. Ed. by Jacques Petit. Gallimard, 1969. xxi, 1360 p. (Bibliothèque de la Pléiade, 213)　**10494**

Notes and chronology of Petit offer excellent, extensive comparisons with other C. works. Also suggest influences, explain events, names and places mentioned in entries, point out recurring themes and images. Indexes of names and characters, places, musical, literary and artistic works, Biblical quotes and references. [LLG]

———. La légende de Prâkriti. Ossements. Le bestiaire spirituel. Ed. by Andrée Hirschi. Les belles lettres, 1972. 207 p. (AnLUB, 139)　　　　　　　　**10495**

Good ed. of these three texts, grouped by editor despite their different dates of original publication because of similar themes and interests. [JFE]

Reviews: A. Espiau de la Maëstre in RHL 74:733–34, 1974; J. Mouton in BSPC 50:63–64, 1973; J. Pallister in ClaudelS 1:87–88, 1973.

———. Œuvre poétique. Introd. par Stanislas Fumet. Gallimard, 1957. xxviii, 993 p. (Bibliothèque de la Pléiade) *Also (rev.):* 1967. lvii, 1246 p.　**10496**

Excellent notes by Fumet. 1967 ed. extensively annotated by Petit and contains index to themes and images, as well as a bibliography. [LLG]

[———]. Œuvres complètes de Paul Claudel. Gallimard, 1950–74. 27 v.　**10497**

Texts accompanied by notes and glosses, sometimes extensive. [LLG]

———. Œuvres en prose. Gallimard, 1965. xlvii, 1627 p. (Bibliothèque de la Pléiade)　　　　　　　　　　　**10498**

Collection of essays on art, music, literature, and foreign cultures, some of which not previously published. Introd. by Petit contains discussion of C.'s notion and use of prose. Includes chronology of prose texts and travels. Notes especially helpful in establishing similarities between texts. [LLG]

———. Le pain dur. Ed. by Jacques Petit. Les belles lettres, 1975. 150 p. (AnLUB, 170)　　　　　　　　　　　**10499**

Excellent reproduction and analysis of variant mss., notes and drafts, but which, as with other eds. in this series, does not include standard text. In its place is a plasticene "compte-lignes" for use with the current Pléiade edition. Petit's introduction treats various themes in the play and is especially good on treatment of the play as "carnaval." [JFE]

―――――. Le poète et le Shamisen. Le poète et le vase d'encens. Jules ou l'homme-aux-deux-cravates. Ed. by Michel Malicet. Les belles lettres, 1970. 310 p. (AnLUB, 116)   **10500**

An excellent critical ed. Each of the three texts, grouped together because of similarities of form, inspiration and date of composition, receives a thorough introduction by the editor, and is accompanied by a virtually overwhelming plethora of notes, variants and commentary. [JFE]
Reviews: P. Brunel in BSPC 45:29–31, 1972.

―――――. Richard Wagner, rêverie d'un poète français. Ed. critique et commentée par Michel Malicet. Les belles lettres, 1970. 179 p. (AnLUB, 110)   **10501**

In his introd., the editor cautiously but convincingly reconstructs C.'s interest in, and changing attitudes toward, Wagner. The text of *Richard Wagner* is well presented with a useful appendix and a short selective bibliography. [TJ]

―――――. Théâtre. [Tome I] Ed. by Jacques Madaule. [Gallimard, 1947] xlii, 1013 p. (Bibliothèque de la Pléiade) *Also:* [Gallimard, 1967] lx, 1366 p. (Bibliothèque de la Pléiade, 72)   **10502**

1967 ed. includes versions of *L'échange* and *Partage de midi* written after 1947. Madaule introd. traces evolution of plays from frivolity of first group, to somberness of middle plays influenced by love affair and religious vocation, to harmonious resolution of internal conflicts in better structured later plays often suggested by others. Notes by Petit include circumstances of publication and production, updated bibliography, variants for *Tête d'Or*, *La jeune fille Violaine*, and *Partage*, as well as C.'s diagrams for staging *Choéphores*. [LLG]

―――――. Théâtre. [Tome 2] Ed. by Jacques Madaule. [Gallimard, 1948] 1336 p. (Bibliothèque de la Pléiade) *Also:* Gallimard, 1965. 1549 p. (Bibliothèque de la Pléiade, 73)   **10503**

1965 ed. adds two plays not included in 1948 ed. as well as variants for *L'histoire de Tobie et de Sara* not previously published. Notes include dates and circumstances of composition, description of original ed. and list of later eds. Also updates bibliography on each play, list of principal productions, C.'s published correspondence and commentary on theater. [LLG]

―――――. La ville. Ed. by Jacques Petit. Mercure de France, 1967. 442 p.   **10504**

Excellent critical ed. and study of *La ville* in its three stages (1890 version, 1894–95 partial revision and 1897–98 second version), reproducing and analyzing all mss. and published variants. Critical introd., a masterful piece of scholarship, situates the play in the development of C.'s *œuvre* in the light of his personal experience and contacts, and literary and historical sources. [JFE]
Reviews: Anon. in BCLF 22:725, 1967; J. Lefèbvre in LR 25:407–08, 1971; J. Madaule in Esp 35:125–26, 1967; J. Robichez in BSPC 27:7–11, 1967.

Roberto, Eugène. L'endormie de Paul Claudel ou la naissance du génie. Ottawa, Univ. d'Ottawa, 1963. 203 p. (CahCC, 1)   **10505**

Establishes corrected and annotated text from handwritten ms. Not a line by line analysis. Includes study of author's alienation from Creation. Broad discussion of sources. Special attention to qualities of style and image seen in this first play which are repeated in later works. [LLG]
Reviews: A. Espiau de la Maëstre in RFor 77:190–92, 1965; J. Onimus in RSH 119:467–69, 1965.

Present State of Claudel Studies

Espiau de la Maëstre, André. Bilan de la critique claudélienne de langue française (1908/1968). *In:* Paul Claudel zu seinem hundertsten Geburtstag. *See* 10610. p. 16–36.   **10506**

Enumerates the monuments of mummified C. clichés in French research. [VK]

Moreau, Pierre. Etat présent des études claudéliennes en France. IL 22:24–32, 1970.   **10507**
Although somewhat dated remains most helpful for critical bibliographical data. Sources of information abound on critical eds., biographical studies, texts on C.'s relation to the world beyond France and the present, on analyses of C.'s poetry and theater, and the baroqueness of C.'s themes and language. Does not include more recent structuralist considerations. Does point out lack of studies relating C. to the other arts, especially music. [LLG]

Roberto, Eugène. Réflexion littéraire: Claudel. RUO 35:342–56, 1965.   **10508**
Text of a lecture in which the editor of the *Cahiers canadiens Claudel* discusses problems of C. research as they relate to the text, to sources, and to biographical information. [DWA]

Correspondence

[Claudel, Paul]. Claudel homme de théâtre. Correspondances avec Copeau, Dullin, Jouvet. Ed. by Henri Micciollo and Jacques Petit. Gallimard, 1966. 327 p. CahPC, 6)   **10509**
129 letters between C. and Copeau from 1903–1938 form the bulk of this scholarly ed. and reveal their long personal and professional friendship. The break over production of *L'annonce* at the Comédie-Française leads to correspondence with Dullin and Jouvet who were also unsuccessful at satisfying the author's dramatic exigencies. Appendix of press reviews on *L'échange* in 1913. [NHP]

————. La porte ouverte. Lettres inédites de Paul Claudel. Introductions de Maurice Zundel et Jacques Madaule. Images de Paul Claudel et Itinéraire de France du Guéraud. La Pierre-qui-vire (Yonne), Les presses monastiques, 1970. 69 p.   **10510**
Selection of C. letters from 1936–1950 to Mlle France du Guéraud, a paralysis victim who appealed to C. for spiritual guidance. Example of his mis-

sionary zeal and spiritual concern. [NHP]

————, and André Gide. Correspondance, 1899–1926. Ed. by Robert Mallet. Gallimard, 1949. 399 p. *Trans.:* The correspondence, 1899–1926, between Paul Claudel and André Gide. Ed. by Robert Mallet. Pref. and trans. by John Russell. Pantheon, 1952. 299 p.   **10511**
Epic spiritual struggle reflecting the conflict between authority and the individual enliven this exchange of professional reflections on life and literature. [NHP]
Reviews: F. Bruno in Id 31:2, 1950; C. Duffy in Eras 8:2, Jan. 10, 1955; M. Carrouges in VI 18:369–74, 1950; F. Catalano in Bel 5:346, 1950; F. Lockquell in RevD 66:327–32, 1950; H. Massis in BdL 115:55–57, 1950; C. Mauriac in TR 28:104–16, 1950; F. Mauriac in TR 24:1842–46, 1949; M. Ryan in Bl 31:474–83, 1950; M. Turnell in Cweal 57:284–86, 1952.

————, and Aurélien-François Lugné-Poe. Claudel homme de théâtre. Correspondance avec Lugné-Poe. 1910–1928. Introduction de Pierre Moreau. Avant-propos de Jacques Robichez. Notes de René Farabet. Gallimard, 1964. 317 p. (CahPC, 5)   **10512**
91 letters between the dramatist and his first director trace the development of C.'s education in theater production, the start of a close involvement which lasted a lifetime. [NHP]
Review: P. van Rutten in CahCC 5:202–04, 1967; P. Simon in MondeH Jan. 6, 1965.

————, and Darius Milhaud. Correspondance Paul Claudel—Darius Milhaud. 1912–1953. Préf. de Henri Hoppenot. Ed. by Jacques Petit. Gallimard, 1961. 369 p. (CahPC, 3)   **10513**
Some 300 letters, mostly on problems of theater production and music composition, reflect their long and fruitful collaboration. Exceptionally good notes. [NHP]

————, and Jean-Louis Barrault. Correspondance Paul Claudel/Jean-Louis Barrault. Préf. de Jean-Louis Barrault. Ed. by Michel Lioure. Gallimard, 1974. 411 p. (CahPC, 10)   **10514**
Some 200 letters from 1939–1954. The friendly and professional exchange

reveals much interesting information on the performances and interpretations of C.'s plays. Detailed notes. [NHP]

————, and Louis Massignon. Paul Claudel —Louis Massignon (1908–1914). Correspondance. Ed. by Michel Malicet. Desclée De Brouwer, 1973. 265 p. **10515**

The correspondence of two religious thinkers. Editor's introduction gives a good and highly detailed sketch of their friendship and gradual separation, as well as a summary, with significant excerpts, of their limited correspondence after 1914. [JFE]
Review: Anon. in NL 2411:4, Dec. 10, 1973.

————, Francis Jammes, and Gabriel Frizeau. Correspondance. 1897–1938. Avec des lettres de Jacques Rivière. Ed. by André Blanchet. Gallimard, 1952. 465 p. **10516**

Correspondence with three of C.'s more famous converts. Some 350 letters of largely spiritual interest. [NHP]

Claudel et l'Amérique II. Lettres de Paul Claudel à Agnès Meyer (1928–1929). Note-Book d'Agnès Meyer (1929). Ed. établie avec introd. et notes par Eugène Roberto. Ottawa, Eds. de l'univ. d'Ottawa, 1969. 322 p. (CahCC, 5) *See* 10589. **10517**

These 66 letters of C. to Agnes Meyer, from March 31, 1928 to Dec. 24, 1929, provide precious insights on C. the man and the dramatist, with special background on the Ysé crisis and aftermath. In lieu of her letters, obediently destroyed, generous extracts from her Notebook (May 25, 1929 to April 27, 1930) and her numerous commentaries on his letters furnish continuity for the most intense period of a special friendship. Although some letters remain difficult to date, and despite a few textual errors and inadequate notes, these are documents of considerable literary merit. [HMW]
Reviews: A. Blanc in RHL 70:342–43, 1970; A. Espiau de la Maëstre in RFor 82:190–92, 1970; J. Houriez in RSH 139:495–99, 1970; J. de Labriolle in RLC 44:141–42, 1970; R. Nelson in FR 43:513–14, 1970; F. Vial in ClaudelN 6:19–22, 1970.

Du Sarment, A. (Sœur Marie-Agnès). Lettres inédites de mon parrain Paul Claudel. J. Gabalda, 1959. 140 p. **10518**

Selection of their correspondence from 1925. A young admirer who became a nun after reading the C. correspondence with Jacques Rivière. [NHP]

Petralia, Franco. Lettre inedite di Paul Claudel a Paterne Berrichon. RLMC 8: 229–50, 1955. **10519**

Twenty-one letters from C. to Rimbaud's brother-in-law and editor; texts in French, notes in Italian; Berrichon ed. of Rimbaud (Mercure de France, 1912) has famous preface by C. [WHM]

Rivière, Jacques, and Paul Claudel. Correspondance. 1970–1914. Plon, 1926. 264 p. *Trans.:* Lettres to a doubter. Trans. by Henry Longan Stuart. Boni, 1927. 261 p. **10520**

Mostly spiritual and personal in nature, with preface by Isabelle Rivière; little concern with literary problems. [NHP]

Suarès, André, and Paul Claudel. Correspondance. 1904–1938. Ed. by Robert Mallet. Gallimard, 1951. 270 p. **10521**

Most of the 165 letters are dated before 1915 and trace the religious discussion and ideological differences which ended in the failure of C. to convert Suarès. [NHP]

Commentaries on Correspondence

Davignon, Henri. La correspondance de Claudel et de Gide. *In his:* De la Princesse de Clèves à Thérèse Desqueyroux. Brussels, Palais des académies, 1963. p. 51–76. **10522**

These 1950 lecture notes offer a cursory summary of the "spiritual essence" of the C.-Gide correspondence. Useful as introduction, but rather superficial. [HMW]

Etat des lettres publiées par Paul Claudel. Les belles lettres, 1975. 160 p. (AnLUB, 178) **10523**

Systematic list of all C. letters published to 1975; entries are grouped chronologically from 1891 to 1955, with complete index of correspondents appended. An extremely useful tool, especially for locating letters contained in other than volumes of collected correspondence. [JFE]

Klossowski, Pierre. En marge de la correspondance de Claudel et de Gide. TM 56:2152–74, 1950. *Also in his:* Un si funeste désir. Gallimard, 1963. p. 55–88.   **10524**

Two specific questions are discussed: the interpretation by Gide of the Gospels and of the figure of Christ; and the problem of Gide's homosexuality. Biographically informative. [VB]

Lawler, James. Valéry et Claudel: un dialogue symboliste. NRF 189:239–61, 1968.   **10525**

Perceptive commentary on the C.-Valéry correspondence, abundantly quoted, in which the esthetic and the biographical are inextricably intertwined. [VB]

Mauriac, François. A propos de la correspondance Claudel-Gide. *In his:* Lettres ouvertes. Monaco, Eds. du rocher, 1952. p. 81–90. *Trans.:* Letters on art and literature. Philosophical library, 1953. *Also:* Port Washington, N.Y., Kennikat press, 1970. p. 75–84.   **10526**

An "open letter" to the deceased—therefore presumably "saved"—Jacques Rivière, concerning the initial publication of the C.-Gide correspondence. Mauriac examines their attitudes, their reasons (as divined by him) for allowing publication, then ends with a prayer to Rivière to enlighten Gide. [JFE]

Nokermann, J. Paul Claudel et André Gide: a propos de la correspondance. LR 6:57–62, 1952.   **10527**

Through an analysis of letters of C. and Gide and of C.'s *Journal*, author concludes that the letters written in 1905 are not in their proper order in Robert Mallet's ed. of C.-Gide correspondence (*see* 10511). [SEH]

Rousseaux, André. La correspondance Gide-Claudel. *In his:* Littérature du vingtième siècle. V. 6. Albin Michel, 1958. p. 36–44.   **10528**

Points out importance of evolving nature of letters. Shows how, in spite of C.'s pretentiousness, correspondence is a key to literary renaissance of 20th century. [LLG]

Iconography

[Gillet-Maudot, Marie-Jeanne] Paul Claudel. Gallimard, 1966. 187 p.   **10529**

Iconography of interest to scholar wishing visual connections between C.'s work and the landscapes in which he grew up, lived and worked. Also contains familial influences, family tree, map of peregrinations, handwriting samples and photos of friends and associates. [LLG]

Biography: Books

Bibesco, [Marthe Lucie (Lahovary)] Princesse. Echanges avec Paul Claudel. Nos lettres inédites. Mercure de France, 1972. 210 p.   **10530**

Agreeably written commentary but entirely anecdotal. Correspondence also pleasant reading but not fundamental to study of C. [DWA]

Reviews: Y. Florenne in Monde April 28, 1972; J. Mouton in BSPC 46:20–22, 1972; L. Roche in RDM no. 4:247–50, 1972.

Bouchard, Isabelle, p.m. L'expérience apostolique de Paul Claudel d'après sa correspondance. Montreal, Fides, 1969. 203 p.   **10531**

Very systematic and thoroughly documented account of C. in his self-assigned apostolic role. Although interested in the more edifying cases of conversion to Catholicism such as those of Gabriel Frizeau, Francis Jammes, Agnes Meyer or Odile R., the author devotes an entire chapter each to Rivière, Gide and Suarès, only the first of whom became a convert, and mentions in some detail other important figures like Ghéon, Maritain and Rolland. On this particular subject, this is an authoritative work. [DWA]

Review: L. Fèvre in BSPC 40:18–19, 1970.

Chaigne, Louis. Vie de Claudel et genèse de son œuvre. Tours, Maison Mâme, 1961. 282 p. *Trans.:* Paul Claudel: the man and mystic. Trans. by Pierre de Fontnouvelle. Appleton-Century-Crofts, 1961. 280 p.   **10532**

An admiring chronological biography by acquaintance. Includes personal anecdotes. Strong psychological bias in attempting explanations for personal decisions, for influences of family, friends milieu and literature. Extensive quotes demonstrate major themes. Especially helpful for religious influences and developing attitudes toward art and politics. [LLG]

Reviews: G. Cattaui in TR 162:22–25, 1961; E. Henriot in Monde March 15, 1961; A. Loranquin in BdL 228: 195–97, 1961; A. Viatte in RUL 16: 31–35, 1961. ˋ

Claudel, Paul. Claudel parle, entretiens enregistrés... Société Paul Claudel, 1965. 35 p. **10533**

Transcript of recorded conversations between C., Pierre Schaeffer and Jacques Madaule held at Brangues in February and March 1944. [JFE]

―――. Mémoires improvisés recueillis par Jean Amrouche. Gallimard, 1954. 349 p. *Also:* Mémoires improvisés. Quarante et un entretiens avec Jean Amrouche. Texte établi par Louis Fournier. Gallimard, 1969. 380 p. (Coll. Idées) **10534**

Rich, enthralling, indispensable mine of background information and reflection on C.'s work, life and literary contacts, subtly guided by Amrouche in a series of 41 radio interviews in 1951–52. Subject to some caution, however, because of C.'s occasionally deforming memory, although many passages are remarkably consistent with corresponding ones in his Journal. The new edition corrects numerous errors of transcription but is too cheaply bound to survive one reading. The original recordings are also available on seven LP discs. [HMW]

Review: A. Espiau de la Maëstre in ECl 41:68–99, 1973.

Daniel-Rops (pseud. of Henri-Jules Petiot). Claudel tel que je l'ai connu. OLib 121: 3–30, 1956. *Also:* Strasbourg, F.-X. Le Roux, 1957. 112 p. **10535**

The author's portrait of C. based on their long friendship and his personal reminiscences of their association: recollections of their conversations on Biblical, liturgical and literary subjects, as well as C.'s memories of his own dual career. Book version contains an unusually interesting and large number of photographs, many taken from the author's private collection. [JFE]

Francis, Eve. Un autre Claudel. Grasset, 1973. 339 p. **10536**

A highly readable book which, against the interesting backdrop of Eve Francis' dramatic career during which she was C.'s favorite actress and close friend, relates how she interpreted C.'s plays from the *première* of *L'otage* in 1914 to the Hébertot version of *L'annonce* in 1948. The style is lively because of her habit of recreating long dialogs with C. which have an authentic ring, though obviously invented. She was twice startled to find the poet-diplomat confessing his love for her (the second episode is documented by a letter), a love which she did not reciprocate and on which she does not comment, for she avoids confession on her own account. [DWA]

Review: J. Petit in BSPC 51:27–28, 1973.

Guillemin, Henri. Le converti Paul Claudel. Gallimard, 1968. 241 p. **10537**

Psycho-biography focuses on faith, seeks roots of "conversion" in family life and intellectual climate of 1880's and 1890's. Questions nature and suddenness of religious renewal and desire to enter monastery. Presents C. texts relating conversion and examines sincerity and meaning of images by which presented. Elucidates contradictions between life and texts. Incomplete because 10 page essential chapter on drama of 1901–04 is omitted. Earlier version published as "La conversion de Paul Claudel" Ecl 25:5–64, 1957. [LLG and WHM]

Reviews: Y. Florenne in QL 70:10–11, 1969; P. Kyria in RdP no. 1:157–58, 1969; P. Oster in NRF 17:458–60, 1969; J. Petit in Monde Nov. 2, 1968; J.-N. Segrestaa in BSPC 34:14–17, 1969.

Biography: Articles

Barrault, Jean-Louis. Paul Claudel, notes pour des souvenirs familiers. *In:* Paul Claudel et Christophe Colomb. *See* 10607. p. 45–87. **10538**

First-hand, but superficial information on *Christophe Colomb* and more generally on C. Barrault wrote two other short articles in the same number. [MR]

Bésineau, Jacques. Claudel au Japon: souvenirs et documents inédits. Et 311:345–51, 1961. **10539**

Memories of C. gathered from various Japanese friends (Yamanouchi, Miyajima); first publication of a text by C. as preface to the Japanese translation of *Connaissance de l'Est;* C.'s distress over the bombing of Japan. [WHM]

Chapon, François. Claudel, collaborateur de L'occident. BSPC 36:3–46, Nov. 1969–Jan. 1970. **10540**

Tells about C.'s early literary efforts in his contributions to *L'occident,* the monthly literary review, and his associations with famous writers. A number of C.'s letters to François Chapon, editor, are presented. This correspondence during the first decade or so of this century reveals the spiritual renaissance in France away from naturalism. [CC]

Du Bos, Charles. Commentaires au bas d'un grand texte, Ma conversion par Paul Claudel. *In his:* Approximations. Fayard, 1965. p. 1159–1241. **10541**

Takes as a basis the text that C. published in 1913 about his conversion to Catholicism. Important document on C.'s religion and on his influence upon other believers. [MR]

Espiau de la Maëstre, André. A propos des deux éditions des Mémoires improvisés de Paul Claudel. ECl 41:68–99, 1973. **10542**

Essential essay for the study of the two versions of the *Mémoires* (1954 ed. and the later 1969 ed., based on the original interview tapes). [WHM]

———. Paul Claudel. WuWe 11:433–48, 1956. *Also in:* Lob der Schöpfung und Ärgernis der Zeit. Moderne christliche Dichtung in Kritik und Deutung. Ed. by Karlheinz Schmidthüs. Freiburg, Basel, Vienna, Herder, 1959. p. 39–58. (Herder-Bücherei, 45) **10543**

An attempt to destroy the traditional view of C. through a different representation of the biographical facts such as the conversion and the call to become a monk. Essentially the same ideas expressed in author's book. [VK]

Fassbinder, Klara Marie. Der Briefwechsel zwischen Paul Claudel und Deutschen. Hoch 57:157–72, 1964. **10544**

Personal testimony of the relationship of Fassbinder to C. and at the same time a documentary abstract of C.'s correspondence with Germans. [VK]

Gelber, Lynne L. Claudel on Rodin: sweet vengeance to bitter memory. ClaudelS 3, no. 1:30–36, 1976. **10545**

Tells of C.'s lifelong animosity toward Rodin who took advantage of his talented sister Camille and was somewhat responsible for her tragic mental breakdown. [CC]

Guillemin, Henri. Claudel: propos. *In his:* Pas à pas. Gallimard, 1969. p. 443–61. **10546**

A collection of various of C.'s *dicta* garnered from Guillemin's repeated conversations with him. [JFE]

———. Pas si simple, Claudel. NRF 189:216–38, 1968. **10547**

Psycho-biographical reflections on C.'s career after his marriage in 1906: professional success, support of Franco and the Fascists, self-adulation. Severity of Mauriac, contempt of Bernanos. Guillemin attempts to soften the portrait with a few carefully chosen quotations favorable to C. [VB]

Guyon, Edouard-Félix. Paul Claudel à la découverte de la Chine. RHD 88:193–209, 1974. **10548**

This rapid representative survey of C.'s impressions of China, both as artist and as diplomat, draws on various correspondences, on *Connaissance de l'Est* and on *Sous le signe du dragon.* [JFE]

Lefèvre, Frédéric. L'entretien du 18 avril 1925. *In his:* Les sources de Paul Claudel. Libr. Lemercier, 1927. p. 131–64. *Also:* Une heure avec Paul Claudel. *In his:* Une heure avec... Cinquième série. Gallimard, 1929. p. 110–17. **10549**

Answering the questions of Lefèvre, C. gives an overall view of his literary activities in Japan between 1921 and 1927. Most valuable part is C.'s outline of his views on the depth and originality of Japanese art. Pertinent references to his own poetry and to the dangers of the Action française. Concludes with a remark on Hindu philosophy. Short but valuable text. [MMN]

Massis, Henri. De Claudel à Chesterton. TR 143:31–57, 1959. **10550**

Massis' recollections of his conversations with C. during a month-long retreat both made at the Dominican monastery of Saulchoir in Belgium. Conversations centered exclusively on C.'s religious ideas. Second half of this article is devoted entirely to Massis' reactions to, and opinions about Chesterton, in whom he became interested initially as a result of C.'s remarks on him. [JFE]

Rivière, Jacques. La visite de Claudel. BSPC 61:1–8, 1976. **10551**

Unpublished account of a visit and discussions with C. who had a great influence on Rivière's spiritual life. The period is from 1909 to 1911. [CC]

Roche, Louis. Paul Claudel à l'ambassade de Bruxelles (1933–1934). RHD 85:65–85, 1971. **10552**

Interesting, anecdotal, inside look at C. the poet-diplomat with emphasis on the diplomat — his habits, personality, fondness for the Belgians — by a member of C.'s embassy staff at the time. [JFE]

General Studies: Books

Barbier, Joseph. Claudel, poète de la prière. Tours, Mame, 1962. 329 p. **10553**

Religiously oriented work whose main purpose seems to be edification, and whose commentary consists mainly in transitions between long excerpts from C.'s various works. No literary criticism, little literary judgment, but rather an attempt to condense and synthesize religious aspects of C.'s thought and writings. [JFE]

Barjon, Louis. Paul Claudel. Eds. universitaires, 1953. 139 p. (Classiques du XXe siècle, 9) **10554**

A less than objective introduction to C.'s thought and work with much emphasis on religious aspects. [JFE]

Review: L. Pamplune in Ren 8:37–39, 1955.

Berchan, Richard. The inner stage. An essay on the conflict of vocations in the early works of Paul Claudel. East Lansing, Michigan state univ. press, 1966. 118 p. **10555**

Interesting view of the first two decades of C.'s artistic life through *Partage de midi* and *Cinq grandes odes*. Sees the works of those years as expressions

of the conflict between his religious and poetic vocations and as illustrations of his quest for a reconciliation between them. [JFE]

Reviews: G. Cattaui in TR 226: 153–54, 1966; R. Geen in RR 59:315–16, 1968; R. Hubert in ClaudelN 6: 16–18, 1970; R. Nelson in FR 40:303–04, 1966–67; H. Waters in EspCr 8: 252, 1968.

Bindel, Victor. Claudel. Vrin, 1934. 180 p. **10556**

In analyzing the complete works of C., Bindel evaluates his literary and spiritual evolution. An excellent and comprehensive study of C.'s spiritual message. [MMN]

Blanc, André. Claudel. Bordas, 1973. 256 p. (Présence littéraire, 814) **10557**

Useful introduction to C., with a chronology, a summary and analysis of each work, some critical perspectives, and a bibliography. Meant for students rather than for scholars. [MR]

Review: J.-N. Segrestaa in BSPC 54: 15–16, 1974.

———. Claudel, le point du vue de Dieu. Eds. du centurion, 1965. 220 p. **10558**

Intelligent synthesis of C.'s thought by a less than impartial analyst, in order to show always and everywhere in his work the importance of C.'s Catholic faith and belief. [JFE]

Reviews: G. Franceschetti in SFr 9: 585, 1965; A. L. in RUL 20:559, 1965–66.

Duhamel, Georges. Paul Claudel. Le philosophe, le poète, l'écrivain, le dramaturge. Suivi de Propos critiques. Mercure de France, 1919. 281 p. **10559**

Stresses from the outset that C. does not yield to a common measure; his characters force us to think in new terms. They all appear to share the spirit of his *Art poétique* which is a lyrical presentation of certitude. Duhamel further emphasizes that C. reintegrates lyricism in theater, and by that he becomes comparable to Aeschylus and Shakespeare. Very good analysis by a great author who does not hide his admiration. [MMN]

Eméry, Léon. Claudel. Lyon, Cahiers libres, 1967. 139 p. **10560**

Syllogistic reflections on C.'s philosophy whose cosmic vision suggests juxtaposition of eternal truths and his times. Dense but richly suggestive in sources for esthetics, especially influences on visual and musical in C.'s work. No textual analysis. [LLG]
Review: H. Waters in FR 42:615–16, 1969.

Espiau de la Maëstre, André. Das göttliche Abenteuer. Paul Claudel und sein Werk. Salzburg, Otto Müller, 1968. 380 p. **10561**
A polemical essay aimed at the usual C. cult and critical of the optimistic view of the poet in Germany and France. A preliminary stage of Espiau de la Maëstre's unpublished doctoral dissertation, *Humanisme classique et syncrétisme mythique chez Paul Claudel.* Gives an existentialist interpretation of C. by bringing the theme of revolt in the early works into relation with the later Biblical commentaries. The problem of evil symbolized by the Biblical figure of Job and the motif of failure are investigated through C.'s collected works; complaints against God and against the indulgence of this God are basic motifs of his research. He claims to replace the baroque Catholic by a fearful doubter. [VK]
Reviews: H. Jourdan in RFor 81: 250–61, 1969; J. de Labriolle in IL 23: 39–40, 1971; O. von Nostitz in SZ 183:68, 1969; J. Petit in BSPC 37:18–19, 1970; J. Wilhelm in RHL 71:131–32, 1971 and in ZFSL 78:368–71, 1968.

Fowlie, Wallace. Paul Claudel. New York, Hillary house, 1957. 111 p. *Also:* London, Bowes & Bowes, 1957. 112 p. (Studies in modern literature and thought)   **10562**
Still a worthwhile, if selective, introduction to aspects of C.'s thought and work. Useful primarily for those who know little or nothing about him. [JFE]
Reviews: Anon. in List March 20, 1958; R. Gilman in Cweal 68:499, 1958.

Francia, Ennio. Paul Claudel. Brescia, Morcelliana, 1947. 195 p.   **10563**
General study of C.'s theology, *Art poétique,* influence of Rimbaud and Mallarmé, style and technique, and theater. Some interesting discussion

and some paraphrase. Bascially Catholic approach. [NH]

Friche, Ernest. Etudes claudéliennes. V. 1. Porrentruy, Eds. des portes de France, 1943. xxvi, 241 p.   **10564**
The original attempt at a systematic study of Thomistic elements in C.'s work. Though somewhat dated in comparison to more recent studies, it is still a good starting point for C.'s philosophical orientation. V. 2 was never published. [JFE]
Review: J. Duggan in Month 183: 314–15, 1947.

Fumet, Stanislas. Claudel. Gallimard, 1958. 311 p. (La bibliothèque idéale) *Also:* 1968. 252 p. (Pour une bibliothèque idéale)   **10565**
Format and treatment which are relatively standard for this series: synopses, commentaries, numerous selected texts, chronology, and a varied and interesting choice of photos (latter not included in 1968 ed.). Overall, a good introduction to C. [JFE]

Guillemin, Henri. Claudel et son art d'écrire. Gallimard, 1955. 195 p.   **10566**
Published shortly after C.'s death, this study by one of the poet's confidants in his later life is still worth consulting, though much of it has been superseded by more recent work. Drawing heavily from C.'s then unpublished *Journal* and from his own conversations with C., Guillemin treats, in untechnical fashion, his subject's temperament, techniques and intentions. [JFE]

Guyard, Marius-François. Recherches claudéliennes. (Autour des Cinq grandes odes). Klincksieck, 1963. 115 p.   **10567**
Series of highly interesting essays on C. and etymology, on the biographical, Biblical and liturgical sources for *Cinq grandes odes,* and on the effects of C.'s reading of Coventry Patmore. Also includes variant translations by C. of four Patmore poems. [JFE]
Reviews: M. D[écaudin] in IL 17: 211, 1965; G. Gadoffre in FS 20:209–11, 1966; J. Petit in BSPC 16:15–16, 1964.

Jahier, Piero. Con Claudel. Milan, All'insegna del pesce d'oro, 1964. 119 p.   **10568**

Collection of reprinted writings on C., ranging from 1913 to 1964 and including poetic impressions, resumé of *Art poétique* in Italian, correspondence, recollections. Historical interest based on Jahier's role as discoverer and translator of C. in Italy. Correspondence shows debate between C. as Catholic missionary and Protestant Jahier. [NH]

Jouve, Raymond. Comment lire Paul Claudel. Aux étudiants de France, 1946. 87 p.
10569

Brief, intelligent summary of major aspects of C.'s works. Remains on general level; therefore introduction rather than specific analysis. Major emphasis on religious dimension. Rapid, basic insights into C.'s ideas and esthetics; however, division of subject matter into chapters rather awkwardly done. C.'s influence on later writers exaggerated. [NH]

Lesort, Paul-André. Paul Claudel par lui-même. Seuil, 1963. 191 p.   **10570**

Probably the best and most complete general introduction available to C.'s life and work. Lesort's ability to synthesize and the generally high quality of his critical commentary raise this study several notches above the usual introductory work. [JFE]
Reviews: A. Blanchet in Et 317: 281–82, 1963; C. Borgal in TR 191: 134–35, 1963; R. Brulez in NVT 16:767–72, 1963; J. Petit in BSPC 14:11–12, 1963; H. Waters in Sym 20:189–91, 1966.

Madaule, Jacques. Claudel et le Dieu caché. Desclée De Brouwer, 1969. 169 p. (Foi vivante, 107)   **10571**

Introductory study containing many of Madaule's notions on C., but with specific orientation toward the religious, as befits both title and series. (Part I previously published in author's *Reconnaissances.* Desclée De Brouwer, 943). [JFE]
Reviews: R. de Boyer de Ste. Suzanne in RdP 76:116, 1969; J. Lefèbvre in LR 24:190–91, 1970.

———. Le drame de Paul Claudel. Desclée De Brouwer, 1936. 340 p. *Also:* 1947. 495 p.; 1952. 497 p.; 1964. 428 p.
10572

Remarkably clear analysis of works in chronological order. For years the standard introduction to C., this study is still one of the best, and perhaps the best of all. [JFE]
Reviews: J. Gaucheron in Eur 431–32:279–82, 1965; R. Legaré in Cul 25:506, 1965; J. Petit in CahPC 6:303–04, 1966; XY, "Wagner in letters," TLS 65:254, 1965.

———. Le génie de Paul Claudel. Desclée De Brouwer, 1933. 460 p.   **10573**

The first comprehensive study of C.'s works. Although recent scholarship has further evaluated C.'s works, Madaule's book, in its ensemble, offers enjoyable reading, even today, and remains indispensable for those who desire an overall grasp of C.'s creative genius. [MMN]

Molitor, André. Aspects de Paul Claudel. Desclée De Brouwer, 1945. 336 p. (Temps et visages)   **10574**

Collection of seven disparate essays on life and works of C. Most valuable from a literary point of view are chapter III on *Le soulier de satin,* described as a symphonic composition, a synthesis of C.'s message, and a good example of C.'s masterly style in avoiding declamatory bombast; chapter IV, *La femme et l'amour humain dans l'œuvre de Claudel;* chapter V, *Paul Claudel et l'Ecriture sainte;* and chapter VI, *Les conversations dans le Loir-et-Cher.* [SEH]

Mondor, Henri. Claudel plus intime. Gallimard, 1960. 330 p.   **10575**

Collection of reminiscences, anecdotes and remembered conversations, all suffused in the especially warm glow of Mondor's enthusiasm for C. Characteristically, Mondor looks everywhere for evidence of the influence of Mallarmé in C., and some of his discoveries are questionable at best. Most important is his reproductions of a variant ms. of *La jeune fille Violaine,* thought by him to pre-date the standard *première version,* and of conversations between C. and Valéry to which he was witness. [JFE]
Review: F. Fabre in LR 16:98–100, 1962; R. Judrin in NRF 14:333–34, 1960; L. E. in FL June 25, 1960; A. Loranquin in BdL 222:410–11, 1960; P. Moreau in CahPC 3:258–64, 1961; S. Pitou in Ren 15:212–18, 1963.

Perche, Louis. Paul Claudel, une étude... Seghers, 1948. 223 p. (Poètes d'aujourd'hui, 10) *Also:* 1958. 215 p. **10576**

Perche's treatment of C. is standard for this well-known series: life, work, some critical assessment, selected excerpts, then chronology and bibliography. On the whole, intelligently handled. [JFE]

Truc, Gonzague. Paul Claudel. Eds. de la Nouvelle revue critique, 1945. 174 p. **10577**

Study centers on C.'s Catholicism and reaction to rationalism. Extensive quotes. Points out didactic nature of plays and essays and moral consequences on reader. Most valuable in review of critical reception. [LLG]

Varillon, François. Claudel. Bruges, Desclée De Brouwer, 1967. 143 p. (Les écrivains devant Dieu, 14) **10578**

Psychological-historical approach to works of C. Sketchy and frequently superficial study of influences on C.'s development as a thinker and writer. Part II reproduces extracts from works alluded to in text. [SEH]
Reviews: A. Blanchet in Et 328:154, 1968; J. Fonsny in ECl 36, no. 2:185–86, 1968; C. Martin in BSPC 29:15–16, 1968; G. Robotti in CulF 16:9–11, 1969 and in Studi Claudeliani (*see* 10613), p. 127–29.

Wahl, Jean. Défense et élargissement de la philosophie. Le recours aux poètes. Claudel. Centre de documentation universitaire, 1958. 292 p. (Les cours de Sorbonne) **10579**

Wahl's course at the Sorbonne in which he treats the philosophical import of C.'s thought. Comparisons and contrasts are drawn with Aristotle and Heidegger as Wahl follows C. brilliantly through treatments of space, time, simultaneity, life, being, causality and related concepts. [JFE]

Waters, Harold A. Paul Claudel. New York, Twayne, 1970. 176 p. **10580**

Chatty, comprehensive, and consequently rather cursory presentation of C.'s life and times. The works are discussed in chronological order, not without a certain flair, in the three genre chapters. Fair and useful introduction to C. for the uninitiated,

despite some minor errors and excessive condensation. [HMW]
Reviews: C. Claudel in ClaudelS 1: 59–60, 1972; J. Freilich in FR 47:433–34, 1973.

Willems, Dom Walther. Paul Claudel, rassembleur de la terre de Dieu. Brussels, Renaissance du livre, 1964. 255 p. **10581**

Series of essays on C.'s faith and how it was manifested in personal dramas revealed in *L'annonce, Partage,* and especially *Soulier.* Includes list of important biographical and bibliographical dates and author's memories of meetings with C. [LLG]

Zinke, Ludger. Paul Claudel: Ansätze indirekter Verkündigung. Würzburg, Echter Verlag, 1968. 317 p. (Schriften zur Religionspädagogik und Kerygmatik, 5) **10582**

A dissertation which tries to analyze the theological content of C.'s work, especially his theatrical pieces, as a statement of an indirect announcement of belief. Misses the definition of the specific acknowledgement of belief of C. which more recent study has brought out. In the theological understanding of the poet Zinke does not equal Pryzwara or Balthasar. [VK]

Collected Articles

Actualité de Claudel. TR 194:1–188, 1964. **10583**

Collection of excellent articles preceded by C.'s La cité prophétique. Studies focus on importance of work, language, imagery, themes, style, and theater. [LLG]

Archives claudéliennes (Archives Paul Claudel). **10584**

A series included within ALM. The first four C. items in ALM did not bear a separate designation. Beginning with Kempf's first *Etudes sur la trilogie*, the volume in the ALM series also bore the designation *Archives claudéliennes 5.* Beginning with Becker's *Tête d'or et La ville*, the designation became *Archives Paul Claudel 9.* [DWA]

Bulletin de la Société Paul Claudel. 13, rue du Pont Louis-Philippe, Paris. 1958– . **10585**

Publishes short articles and *inédits,* excellent reviews, exhaustive bibliographies, and news about Claudel societies and events worldwide. Valuable guide to C. scholarship and activity. Quarterly since 1966. [HMW]

Bulletin régional, Société Claudel en Belgique. Hannut. 1956– 10586
Annual. Although concerned primarily with Belgian interests in C., an occasional special number has wider appeal. [HMW]

Claudel: A reappraisal. Ed. by Richard Griffiths. London, Rapp and Whiting, 1968. 197 p. *Also:* Chester Springs, Pa., Dufour, 1970. x, 197 p. 10587
Collection attempts to explain C.'s greatness and contributions to English-speaking world. Variety of essays show how C. made symbolist theater a success. Examines Biblical influence on verse form and the ways in which unorthodox beliefs and problems they engendered contribute to effect of plays. [LLG]
Reviews: E. Beaumont in MLR 65: 175–76, 1970; E. Berchan in ClaudelN 8:9–19, 1971; M. F. Guyard in FS 25:103–04, 1971; W. Ince in Month 227:379–80, 1969; W. Matheson in FR 44:607–08, 1971.

Claudel diplomate. Gallimard, 1962. 362 p. (CahPC, 4) 10588
Indispensable documents on career and world travels show international influence of people and events on poet, including C.'s own reactions. Most items published in the 30's and 40's. [LLG]
Reviews: H. Amer in BSPC 13:11–12, 1963; A. Blanchet in Et 317:281–82, 1963; J.-N. Segrestaa in RHL 64: 325–26, 1964.

Claudel et l'Amérique. Ottawa, Eds. de l'univ. d'Ottawa, 1964. 265 p. (CahCC, 2) *See* 10517. 10589
Collection of articles detailing experiences in Boston, New York, Washington, and Rio de Janeiro. Commentaries on works written by C. reflecting those travels and posts, images used to express views of America, and friendship with Agnes Meyer. Significant articles analyzed elsewhere. [LLG]

Claudel-Milhaud. CRB 88:1–125, 1975. 10590

Reproduces part of special number of CRB 1, 1953, with an additional text by Barrault and excerpts from the correspondence addressed to Darius Milhaud. Valuable number stressing *Christophe Colomb* and C.'s relationship to music. [MR]

Claudel Newsletter. University of Rhode Island, Kingston, R. I. April 1968—no. 9, February 1972. 10591
Semiannual. Small (18 to 32 pages) mimeographed periodical devoted to C. scholarship and news, especially in the U.S. [HMW]

Claudel Studies. University of Dallas, Irving, Texas. 1972– 10592
Semiannual (beginning with second number, 1973). Successor to *Claudel Newsletter,* with enlarged scope and appeal. [HMW]

Connaissance de Paul Claudel. Julliard, 1955. 128 p. (CRB, 12) 10593
Text of presentation at Marigny just after C.'s death. Series of quotes, especially from *Partage,* to elucidate meaning of images, significance of certain ideas, places, role of poet, oppositions, successive influences. [LLG]
Review: M. La Vallée in Ren 8:202–08, 1956.

Les critiques de notre temps et Claudel. Garnier, 1970. 189 p. 10594
This thematically arranged survey of the critical literature on C. contains an excellent choice of articles, previously published elsewhere, to demonstrate the scope and influence of C.'s life and works. His attitudes toward, and relations with, the world of music are neglected. A short bibliography and a list of important biographical dates are included. Significant articles have been analyzed separately. [LLG]
Review: R. Nantet in BSPC 41:19, 1971.

Entretiens sur Paul Claudel. Ed. by Georges Cattaui and Jacques Madaule. Paris, The Hague, Mouton, 1968. 333 p. 10595
This important volume reproduces papers and discussions of conference held at the Centre Culturel International de Cerisy-la-Salle in July of 1963; quality of contributions is generally excellent. Significant articles have been analyzed separately. [JFE]

Reviews: Anon. in BCLF 24:1050, 1969; P. Brunel in BSPC 35:13–14, 1969.

La figure d'Israël. Gallimard, 1968. 423 p. (CahPC, 7)   10596

Includes C. texts, studies of anti-Semitism in France, centrality of Israel in his works, stages in attitudes, examination of his vision of it primarily as dramatic figure. Also appends documents linked to German occupation, extermination camps, complicity of Vichy government, new state of Israel. [LLG]

Formes et figures. Ottawa, Eds. de l'univ. d'Ottawa, 1967. 204 p. (CahCC, 5)   10597

A series of articles of generally high quality loosely grouped around the subtitle of "Formes et figures." Significant articles have been analyzed separately. [JFE]

Review: J. Petit in BSPC 31:12–14, 1968.

The France of Claudel. Ed. by Henri Peyre. RNL 4, no. 2:1–125, 1973.   10598

Significant articles are reviewed separately. [SEH]

Review: A. Espiau de la Maëstre in RHL 76:130, 1976.

Géographie poétique de Claudel. Ottawa, Eds. de l'univ. d'Ottawa, 1966. 232 p. (CahCC, 4)   10599

Explores literary, spiritual and geographical sources of images. Childhood scenes, illustrations in *Le tour du monde,* and imaginary voyage offered as inspirations of *Tête d'or.* Predominance of sea and earth, awareness of space and horizon, Biblical sites evoked in poetry and plays examined by several critics. Mostly continues work of Poulet, Michaud and Vachon. [LLG]

Reviews: J. Lévi-Valensi in RSH 33:510–11, 1968; W. Matheson in FR 41:749–50, 1968.

Grandeur de Paul Claudel. NRF 29, no. 279:933–91, 1936.   10600

In 1935 the French Academy refused the candidacy of C. NRF devoted its Dec. 1936 issue to him with articles by Jammes, Ramuz, Schlumberger, Cingria, Massignon and Weidlé. [MMN]

Hommage à Paul Claudel. VI 37:6–207, 1935.   10601

Some 31 prominent authors, French and foreign, participated in the making of this issue, which—the editorial tells us—was not meant to respond to the negative vote of the French Academy. The issue consists of two sections, "L'homme et le chrétien" and "L'œuvre et les œuvres," both containing short essays whose scholarship has often been superseded by later publications. Valuable survey of C.'s life and works. [MMN]

Hommage à Paul Claudel. NRF 33:387–640, 1955.   10602

The volume is divided in six parts, the last part consisting of a number of unpublished short texts (some letters, psalms, a supplement to the Apocalypse, a fragment from a diary). Contributions by Saint-John Perse, Blanchot, Jean Wahl, Starobinski, Etiemble, Poulet, et al. [VB]

[Paul Claudel]. TR 88:9–136, 1955.   10603

Commemorative number containing mostly brief and eulogistic articles. Of particular note: Romain Rolland: "Sur *L'annonce faite à Marie;*" Jean Variot: "*L'annonce faite à Marie* au Théâtre de l'Œuvre en 1912;" Jean Dardenne: "Protée à la Comédie de Paris." Also selection of letters to Marie Kalff, Louis Gillet, and Henri de Waroquier. [JFE]

Paul Claudel. EspCr 13:1–92, 1973.   10604

Special number containing some important articles, plus a previously unpublished letter from C. to Pierre Kijno, an interesting postscript to the C.-Gide relationship. Significant articles have been analyzed separately. [JFE]

Reviews: M. Nagy in BSPC 54:17–19; F. Vial in ClaudelS 1:89–90, 1974.

Paul Claudel 1–   .   10605

A series of special numbers included in RLM. Began in 1964 and reached number 11 in 1974. Did not appear in 1975 or 1976. Special numbers bore following titles: 1. *Quelques influences formatrices.* 2. *Le regard en arrière: Quelques drames et versions successives.* 3. *Thèmes et images.* 4. *L'histoire.* 5. *Schémas dramatiques.* 6. *La première version de La ville.* 7. *La poésie de la nuit.* 8. *Le double.* 9. *Structures du Soulier de satin.* 10. *L'enfer selon Clau-*

del: Le repos du septième jour. 11. *Les images dans Le soulier de satin.* Significant articles have been analyzed separately. [DWA]

Paul Claudel 1868–1955. Bibliothèque Nationale, 1968. xxiv, 174 p.   **10606**
Catalog of the Bibliothèque Nationale's 1968 Exposition Paul Claudel. A listing, often descriptive, of the 652 items contained in the exposition. By far the bulk of these items were mss. on display. The great value of this volume lies in the wealth of background material assembled by the staff of the Bibliothèque Nationale to serve as commentary. [JFE]

Paul Claudel et Christophe Colomb. [Presentation by Jean-Louis Barrault] CRB 1: 9–114, 1953.   **10607**
Has a text by C. and three by Barrault (giving memories and critical appreciation); additional articles by A.-M. Carré, André Frank, Darius Milhaud, André Alter, and Jacques Soustelle. A facsimile of a C. ms. is reproduced. Interesting from a documentary point of view. Major part of this number is reprinted in CRB 88: 1975. [MR]
Review: M. La Vallée in Ren 8:39–44, 1955.

Paul Claudel. Premières œuvres 1886–1901. Bibliothèque littéraire Jacques Doucet, 1965. 66 p.   **10608**
The catalog of the library's C. exhibition (November 23–December 23, 1965). Contains description of the 126 items displayed, mostly from the library's own collection, the Archives de la Société Paul Claudel, and private sources. Useful for verifying dates of early texts. Notes by François Chapon. [JFE]

Paul Claudel. Tête d'or. Le soulier de satin; Claudel aujourd'hui. Julliard, 1958. 127 p. (CRB, 25)   **10609**
Recollections and brief comments on C. and his theater. Most valuable are Barrault's recollections of his associations with C. and his work; a partial transcript of a rehearsal of *Le soulier de satin* which reproduces Barrault's comments to his cast; and the text of Barrault's ms. of the third version of *Tête d'or.* [JFE]

Paul Claudel zu seinem hundertsten Geburtstag. Stuttgart, Deutsche Verlagsanstalt, 1970. 206 p. (Sonderdruck der Reihe Deutschland-Frankreich, Ludwigsburger Beiträge zur Problem der Deutsch-Französischen Beziehungen)   **10610**
Proceedings of a meeting of the Ludwigsburg Institute devoted to C. Principal communications are analyzed separately. [VK]

Prague. Gallimard, 1971. 408 p. (CahPC, 9)   **10611**
Covers encounter with Bohemia, 1909–11, and the baroque, its influence on his work, political and cultural events, friendships, religious and professional life. Detailed examination of consular problems C. dealt with. Annotated correspondence with Zdenka Braunerová and Milos Marten. Careful, extensive documentation. [LLG]
Review: F. Vial in ClaudelS 1, no. 2:68–69, 1973; H. Waters in FR 46: 624, 1973.

Le rire de Paul Claudel. Gallimard, 1960. 295 p. (CahPC, 2)   **10612**
Nature and extent of laughter in C.'s work. Extracts from little-known works by C. included. Other better-known works set into relief. Attempts by major critics to analyze C.'s humor in search of his philosophy of laughter. Significant articles analyzed separately. [LLG]
Review: S. Pitou in Ren 15:212–18, 1963.

Studi Claudeliani. Ed. by Ida Rampolla. Palermo, Vittorielli editore, 1972. 163 p.   **10613**
Diverse, uneven collection of essays in French and Italian by various hands. Volume contains reviews of several books on C., translation to Italian of two poems, and extensive bibliographies. [SEH]
Review: Y. Batard in BSPC 49:47–48, 1973.

General Studies: Articles

Béguin, Albert. Grandeur de Claudel. *In his:* Poésie de la présence: de Chrétien de Troyes à Pierre Emmanuel. Neuchâtel, La Baconnière; Paris, Eds. du seuil, 1957. p. 225–43.   **10614**

Well written and thoughtful account of the whole work. Recommended. [MR]

Blanchot, Maurice. Claudel et l'infini. *In his:* Le livre à venir. Gallimard, 1959. p. 83–97.   **10615**

One of the finest essays on C. by a leading critic of our time. Presents C. as a "génie orageux," an elementary force, who takes conversion in his stride and struggles even with the infinite. It is interesting to note the importance which Blanchot attaches to C.'s "faute majeure" and also his remark in a footnote about C.'s vengeance on womankind. [DWA]

Cattaui, Georges. La symbolique de Claudel. *In his:* Orphisme et prophétie chez les poètes français 1850–1950. Plon, 1965. p. 179–229.   **10616**

A loose-jointed assemblage of Cattaui's musings about C. Mostly adulatory and of doubtful value. [JFE]

Curtius, Ernst Robert. Die literarischen Wegbereiter des neuen Frankreich. Potsdam, G. Kiepenheuer, 1919. p. 115–60. *Also in his:* Französischer Geist im zwanzigsten Jahrhundert. Bern-Munich, Francke, 1952. p. 115–56.   **10617**

First appreciation of C. by a German Romance scholar. The essay is still readable today because, in addition to a summary interpretation of the early dramas, it contains remarks on *Vers d'exil* and C.'s symbolism which have not been superseded. [VK]

Divoire, Fernand. La bonhomie de Claudel. MerF 113:58–67, 1916.   **10618**

In C. the sublime is unthinkable without the tangible reality and a certain "bonhomie." The formidable universe of God is seen in the joy of this humor. A highly recommended reading. [MMN]

Ducasse, Christian. Le paradis perdu dans l'œuvre de Paul Claudel. *In:* Hommage à Paul Claudel. *See* 10601. p. 100–14.   **10619**

The paradise lost or to come and its everlasting joy are symbolized by the Moon whose gentleness liberates man from the oppressing reality of the physical world. Penetrating study. [MMN]

Espiau de la Maëstre, André. Der Sinn und das Absurde. Salzburg, Otto Müller, 1961. p. 135–259, 344–53, 381–87.   **10620**

First attempt of Espiau de la Maëstre to break through the clichés of traditional C. worship in Germany. Most of these theses have been carried over into his later book (see 10561). The various conceptions of the Violaine material take up the greater part of this essay. [VK]

———. Probleme der Claudel-Forschung. SZ 179:179–268, 1967.   **10621**

A general essay preliminary to Espiau de la Maëstre's book. Treats fanaticism and nationalism, and themes such as anthropology, love and Thomism. [VK]

Etiemble, [René]. Paul Claudel et le vin des rochers. *In his:* Poètes ou faiseurs? (1936–1966). Hygiène des lettres. V. 4. Gallimard, 1966. p. 258–74.   **10622**

Argues that the early tortured "symboliste" expression seen in C.'s work gives way increasingly to simplicity and coherence; C.'s later work, Etiemble feels, has affinities with certain advertising campaigns (le Vin des Rochers) in its clarity and persuasiveness. [JFE]

Fowlie, Wallace. Claudel and the problem of sacred art. Acc 14:3–21, 1954.   **10623**

Explains C.'s Aquinian esthetics as a natural, concrete expression of the sacred. Thomistic faith extended to collaboration of the artist and the world through the poet's use of metaphor. A long biographical sketch precedes the central question of C.'s use of language to express fundamental bond of theology, symbolism and life. [LLG]

Gagnon, Paul. Situation de Paul Claudel. RUSh 5, no. 1:3–16, 1964.   **10624**

The author shows that C. was formed as a positivist and a materialist, very much aware of the contemporary world, but broke with this formation through his reading of Rimbaud. Moreover, through his attempt to present joy born of suffering as the most distinguishing characteristic of Christians, C. transcends the temporality of the modern world to touch upon the eternal preoccupation of man. [WB]

Guitton, Jean. Claudel et Renan. *In his:* Journal, I. Etudes et rencontres, 1952–1955. Plon, 1959. p. 93–97. *Trans.:* The

Guitton journals, 1952–1955. London, Harvill, 1963. **10625**
Recollections of Guitton's only meeting with C. Guitton's comparisons of the C.-Gide and C.-Renan relationships; C.'s thoughts on Rimbaud; and an interesting description of C. the person. [JFE]

Hatzfeld, Helmut. A critical revision of Claudel as a Catholic poet. CCur 5:101–14, 1955. **10626**
Thematic study of C.'s fusion of faith and poetry and his importance for the Catholic revival. Likens to Dante in use of themes of nature, love, and sacrifice, and to Calderón in missionary zeal and devotional didacticism. [LLG]

Juin, Hubert. Paul Claudel dans l'avant-siècle. *In his:* Ecrivains de l'avant-siècle. Seghers, 1972. p. 153–62. **10627**
Lively account of the early C., situating him in relation with the symbolist movement. [MR]

Lalou, René. Paul Claudel. RdP 43:357–82, 1936. **10628**
C., poet of cosmic joy. [MMN]

Madaule, Jacques. La Bible et Paul Claudel. TR 107:178–85, 1956. **10629**
Solid assessment of C.'s inspiration — liturgical rather than Biblical, scripture entering his work primarily through the liturgy — and of his approach in later years to the exegesis of scripture. [JFE]

———. Situation de Paul Claudel. RGB 90:1291–1302, 1954. **10630**
Eminently well-written, if very general, essay by one of the better commentators on C. Emphasizes the literary importance of C.'s work which is classic in spite of the author's anticlassicism. [DWA]

Merleau-Ponty, Maurice. Sur Claudel. *In his:* Signes. Gallimard, 1960. p. 391–97. *Also in:* Les critiques de notre temps et Claudel. *See* 10594. p. 17–22. **10631**
Existential criticism is well represented by this examination of C.'s seemingly contradictory nature. Difficulties with Gide and Rivière traced both to confusion by C.'s friends between a man's acts and his writings and to C.'s belief that need for evil in world comes after imperative in each individual to act to avoid and contradict evil. Each must undergo his own act of sacrifice. No one can intercede, not even a genius, in lieu of that act. [LLG]

Michaud, Guy. Paul Claudel, poète cosmique. *In his:* Messages poétiques du symbolisme, 3. Nizet, 1961. p. 595–629. *Also (excerpt) in:* Les critiques de notre temps et Claudel. *See* 10594. p. 72–78. **10632**
Helpful examination of reputation, biographical and literary influences, and major critical opinion. Rimbaud's search for the absolute and creative language, Mallarmé's symbolic structure of the world, and study of St. Thomas led to C.'s fusion of poetry and religion. Discovery in Bible of primacy of the Word is key to symbolism. Examines use of water, trees, and fire as recurring images in the plays, poems, and essays. [LLG]

Peyre, Henri. Le classicisme de Paul Claudel. NRF 20:432–41, 1932. *Also in:* Les critiques de notre temps et Claudel. *See* 10594. p. 136–43. **10633**
External criticism is used to make the case for C. as a classic based on his role as abstract philosopher and dialectitian. His didacticism links him to Virgil, Lucretius, and Aeschylus. Internal evaluations by Cattaui and Batard have since, and more convincingly, classified C. as a baroque artist. [LLG]

———. Paul Claudel, a romantic in spite of himself. PAPS 114:179–86, 1970. **10634**
An article which shows, as usual, Peyre's somewhat unexpected admiration for C. Here he defines C. as a romantic who became convinced that "his own temperament required that his spiritual balance be maintained by submitting to strict rules." Hence his orthodoxy. [DWA]

Rang, Bernhard. Paul Claudel. *In:* Christliche Dichter der Gegenwart. Beiträge zur europäischen Literatur. Ed. by Hermann Friedmann and Otto Mann. Heidelberg, Wolfgang Rothe Verlag, 1955. p. 267–72. *Also (rev.):* Ed. by Otto Mann. Bern and Munich, Francke, 1968. p. 84–108. **10635**
Appreciative essay which usefully treats C.'s personality and creative work but does not advance research. [VK]
Review: V. Kapp in StG 23–24:286–94, 1971.

Salvi, Elvira Cassa. La lirica di Claudel e il suo realismo transfiguratore. HumB 10: 575–93, 1955.   **10636**

Strikingly well-wrought essay on C.'s "realismo magico e metafisico;" the impact of Croce's tempered judgments on C.'s reputation in Italy; sense of the *danger* in reading C.; the tonality of C.'s voice. [WHM]

Untereiner, René. Notes pour servir à la lecture de Paul Claudel. BAGB no. 3:77–100, 1955.   **10637**

Advice on how to approach C. and a succinct and intelligent overview of his work. Obviously intended for the uninformed but not for the intellectually incompetent. Suitable reading even for a specialist. [DWA]

Varillon, François. Paul Claudel. La conquête du monde. Et 223:308–26, 1935. *And:* La consécration du monde. Et 223: 461–74, 1935.   **10638**

By scope of his work, C. deserves comparison with Pindar, Virgil, Dante and Shakespeare. Appreciation of the most cosmic of C.'s plays, *Le soulier de satin.* In the second part of his essay, the author explains how C. shows the road to follow by teaching the necessary transcendental fulfillment. Good theological analysis of C.'s thought. [MMN]

Poetry: Books

Angers, Pierre. Commentaire à L'art poétique de Paul Claudel, avec le texte de L'art poétique. Mercure de France, 1949. 383, [8] p.   **10639**

Though a diss. at the Université catholique de Louvain, this is the work of a master critic who has managed to obliterate the more formal trappings of scholarship under a distinguished style and whose dense commentaries require as much reflection as the somewhat obscure document which they aim to elucidate. Unquestionably one of the more important works on C., but not for the uninformed who should begin by reading Ryan's chapter on the same subject. [DWA]

Antoine, Gérald. Les cinq grandes odes de Claudel ou la poésie de la répétition. Minard, 1959. 94 p. (Langues et styles)   **10640**

Proceeds from analysis of poems to understanding of psychological impulse which gave rise to the poetry. Esthetic and metaphysical considerations included in study of meaning and use of recurrent sounds, ideas and motifs. Shows C.'s essential combativeness and questioning nature and extent to which poetic creation is a mirror of divine creation. Intelligent, important study. [LLG]

Review: R. Pieltain in MRo 11:51–59, 1961.

Beaumont, Ernest. L'ode claudélienne; deux exégètes: H. J. W. van Hoorn et A. Maurocordato. Lettres modernes, 1958. 40 p. (ALM, 8)   **10641**

Careful, intelligent critical comparison and analysis of two relatively early studies of C.'s odes. [JFE]

Chonez, Claudine. Introduction à Paul Claudel. Albin Michel, 1947. 242 p.   **10642**

Decidedly partisan. Applauds and explains C.'s poetic contributions by linking language and rhythm to universe and human physiology. Accumulation and repetition in work results from joy in physical forms and desire to persuade. Comic elements reinforce link between physical and spiritual. Study more thematic than rhetorical. [LLG]

Colleye, Hubert. La poésie catholique de Claudel. Liège, Soledi, 1946. 205 p.   **10643**

Study of C.'s "Catholic" poetry— *Cinq grandes odes, Cantate à trois voix,* etc. Doctrinaire religious approach; generalizations, paraphrase and quotations rather than critical analysis. [NH]

Hoorn, H. I. W. van, O.F.M. Poésie et mystique. Paul Claudel, poète chrétien. Geneva, Droz; Paris, Minard, 1957. 159 p.   **10644**

Although purporting to be a scholarly work, this book is very amateurish in its basic design in spite of a heavy overlay of erudition, including many quotations in Dutch and German. The first 68 pages set up a definition of poetry as mysticism and then of religion as mysticism, for the ostensible purpose of proving that one can be both a poet and a religious person. Instead of proving this with respect to C., Hoorn then gives only a summary of *L'art poétique* followed by a lengthy commentry on one ode. [DWA]

Kapp, Volker Werner. Poesie und Eros. Zum Dichtungsbegriff der Fünf grossen Oden von Paul Claudel. Munich, Fink, 1972. 180 p. (Freiburger Schriften zur romanischen Philologie, 20)   **10645**

Shows for the first time the symmetrical construction of the *Odes,* the center being the third ode, which in its turn is symmetrically constructed to show the "conversion" of the poet. A semantic analysis of each of the five odes proves that this "conversion" is considered as a poetological problem, and is traced back to the meeting with the woman (Eros). Under the influence of Eros a change is effected in the poems from a Christian influenced poetic in the first ode to a decidedly Christian conception of poetry in the fifth ode. The odes treat five stages of this development; they are connected to each other and build each other up, so that they form a unity. [VK] Reviews: W. Babilas in RHL 75: 864–65, 1975; A. Espiau de la Maëstre in RFor 84:444–46, 1972; A. Fuss in BSPC 51:21–22, 1973; J. Wilhelm in ZFSL 84:189–91, 1974; M. Wood in FS 29:492–93, 1975.

Maurocordato, Alexandre. L'ode de Paul Claudel. Essai de phénoménologie littéraire. Geneva, Droz; Lille, Giard, 1955. 232 p.   **10646**

Covers *Vers d'exil, Les cinq grandes odes, La cantate à trois voix, Cantique de Mesa, Cantique de la lune,* and *Feuilles des saints.* Although somewhat verbose, this work is a detailed explication of C.'s poems and can usefully be consulted by specialists and general readers. Explication, which fills a large part of the book, does not develop into a method, but the preliminary observations about C.'s versification are systematic and constitute a major contribution on this subject. [DWA] Reviews: Y. Le Hir in RHL 57:276, 1957; K. Maurer in RFor 69:160–62, 1957.

————. L'ode de Paul Claudel. Essai de phénoménologie littéraire. Lettres modernes, 1974. 124 p. (ALM, 152)   **10647**

First part of a projected longer work. Author claims that it should not be confused with his earlier work on the same subject, now out of print. An uneven and disappointing study, frequently given to sentimentality, speculation and chattiness. There is some excellent analysis of C.'s language and linguistic structures, especially in *Cinq grandes odes* and in *La cantate à trois voix,* but also frequent digressions on tangential considerations. [JFE] Reviews: Anon. in BCLF 30:94267, 1975; M. Dorian in PA 49:728, 1975.

Moreau, Pierre. L'offrande lyrique de Paul Claudel. L'époque des Grandes odes et du Processional. Lettres modernes, 1969. 46 p. (ALM, 100)   **10648**

Excellent and highly concentrated commentary on *Les cinq grandes odes,* much more readable than some of the longer ones on the subject, but not new in method or conclusions, except for the initial insistence that C. remains essentially dramatic even during this lyrical interlude in his literary career. [DWA] Reviews: J. Petit in BSPC 37:18, 1970; J.-N. Segrestaa in RHL 72:326, 1971.

Olivero, Federico. La concezione della poesia in Paul Claudel. Turin, Chiantore, 1943. 173 p.   **10649**

Various aspects of C.'s poetry, such as joy of sacrifice, role of metaphor, treatment of nature. Traditional religious perspective. Extensive quotes and paraphrase. Remains on general level throughout. [NH]

Perche, Louis. Claudel et les Cinq grandes odes. Périgueux, Eds. Pierre Fanlac, 1946. 109 p.   **10650**

Short study examines each ode and its images, thought and religious background, as well as some major themes. Technique confusing; lacks unity of interpretation. Some perceptive questions, but also vague clichés and obvious generalizations. Some errors of fact. [NH]

Ryan, Mary. Introduction to Claudel. Cork, Cork univ. press, 1951. 111 p. *Also:* Westminster, Md., Newman press, 1951.   **10651**

The title is totally misleading since the book deals only with C.'s lyrical poetry. After a short biographical chapter, and then a summary of *L'art poétique,* there are seven chapters treating C.'s collections of poetry in chronological order. Each poem is described and recounted but there is no literary analysis. Designed to ease the layman into a reading of C.'s poetry but of little use to the scholar. [DWA]

Poetry: Articles

Angers, Pierre. Le prélude de L'art poétique de Paul Claudel. LR 2:117–31, 1948. **10652**

Maintains that *L'art poétique* offers first organic synthesis of C.'s feelings about nature. After a brief introduction outlining C.'s belief in the unity of all creation, author reproduces the text of *Prélude*. Commentary on salient ideas and images in footnotes. Uses *explication de texte* method. Obvious and often repetitive. [SEH]

Balthasar, Hans Urs von. Herrlichkeit. Eine theologische Ästhetik, I. Schau der Gestalt. Einsiedeln, Johannes Verlag, 1961. p. 385–91. *Trans.:* La gloire et la croix. Les aspects esthétiques de la révélation. V. 1. Trans. by Robert Givord. Aubier, 1965. (Théologie; études publiées sous la direction de la Faculté de théologie S. J. de Lyon-Fourvière, 61) **10653**

Interprets *La sensation du divin* and *Sur la présence de Dieu* from *Présence et prophétie* as two complementary pieces to *L'art poétique.* If C. sees in *L'art poétique* existence as not-being-God, then the later essays take up again the problem of existence from the point of view of the experience of the convert. A brief discussion which adds much to the understanding of C.'s poetry. [VK]

————. Paul Claudels lyrisches Werk. *In:* Claudel, Paul. Gesammelte Werke. Bd. 1: Gedichte. Einsiedeln, Zurich, Cologne, Benziger; Heidelberg, Kerle, 1963. p. 573–601. **10654**

A brief but richly documented survey of C.'s collected poetic work. Balthasar goes through the various collections, outlines their worth in the totality of the creative work, and picks out several important moments. [VK]

Blanchet, André. Psaumes de David et de Claudel. Et 325:681–87, 1966. **10655**

Review of C.'s *Psaumes* (1966). C.'s will not become the "authorized version" but are magnificent. A close reading of the texts. [WHM]

Bruckberger, R. Paul Claudel and theology. Ren 8:189–95, 1956. **10656**

Although the author purports to study the poetry, he relies on C.'s essays to show that Claudelian poetry is Thomistic in its esthetics, not Augustinian, and that C. is in Maritain's lineage. [LLG]

Buffum, Imbrie. The critical principles of Paul Claudel. YFS 2:34–42, 1949. **10657**

C.'s beliefs concerning poetry based on rejection of bourgeois self-satisfaction, conservatism, insularity and desire for total control. Explains thereby dislike of Voltaire, Boileau, the Alexandrian, classical taste and 19th century determinism. Imaginative theoretical article. [LLG]

Chiari, Joseph. Paul Claudel. *In his:* Contemporary French poetry. New York, Philosophical library, 1952. *Also:* Manchester, Manchester univ. press, 1952. p. 71–94. **10658**

Clear but hasty explanation of ideas in *Cinq grandes odes* and in plays. Sees belatedly romantic poetic prose as striving to name insights captured from midst of movement and disorder to reach God. Considers poetry flawed by lack of humanity and humility, dramatic poetry as more successful than purely lyrical poems. [LLG]

Du Bos, Charles. Corona benignitatis anni Dei de Claudel. *In:* Grandeur de Claudel. *See* 10600. p. 973–91. *Also in his:* Approximations. Fayard, 1965. p. 1386–1412. **10659**

Describes how C. integrates the liturgical cycle of the year into the natural cycle of the seasons. C.'s poetry invites the reader to ascend into this divine cycle of the spiritual existence. Interesting comparative study. Could be further developed. [MMN]

Espalza, M. de. El simbolismo literario de Paul Claudel. RyF 172:241–48, 1965. **10660**

A study of symbolic language in poetry using C. as an exemplary poet. The author argues that despite the unifying esthetic effect and the archetypal vision inherent in C.'s symbolic language, the readership of C.'s poetry must by necessity be a highly cultured minority. [TJ]

Estang, Luc. Paul Claudel: the poet's poet. Ren 8:171–76, 188, 1956. *Also:* Ren 25: 202–08, 1973.   **10661**
This essay tries to explain the basic tenets of *L'art poétique* and to give meaning to the two treatises, *La connaissance du temps* and *La connaissance au monde et de soi-même*. It depends more on religious than on esthetic or literary judgments. [LLG]

Fuss, Albert. Gedanken zur zweiten Ode Paul Claudels. ZFSL 83:20–45, 1973. **10662**
Investigates the link between biography, poetics, and cosmological speculation especially in the beginning of the two odes. Gives special attention to the symbolism of spirit and water, to questions of syntax, and to the conception of time. [VK]

Gagnon-Mahony, Madeleine. Un aspect du symbolisme structural des Cinq grandes odes. CahUQ 24:91–123, 1970. **10663**
Analyzes structures and interrelations of *Odes* through identification of different speakers, addressees and their gradual fusions. Good idea, subtle development, but somewhat unsatisfying. [NH]

González Padilla, María Enriqueta. Paul Claudel y sus cinco grandes odes. Abs 29: 375–99, 1965.   **10664**
Good generalities about themes and poetic forms of *Les cinq grandes odes,* but not a close study of texts. [DWA]

Guyard, Marius-François. La Bible et la liturgie sources du Magnificat de Claudel. RHL 61:72–80, 1961.   **10665**
Close study of third *Ode*. Emphasizes liturgical reading during seasons in which poem written, importance of Latin in Vulgate to understand C.'s style, and coinciding birth of daughter, Marie, as sources of emotions, images and themes. [LLG]

Howells, B. P. Connaissance de l'Est: an introduction to some prose poems by Claudel. AJFS 4:323–43, 1967.   **10666**
An outstanding contribution to C. studies. In spite of later disavowals, C., in writing the prose poem *Connaissance de l'Est,* was strongly influenced by the symbolists and by Mallarmé in particular in his "aspiration to a rarified spirituality." Furthermore, he was still in a predominantly sensual period of his life (in this period he invented his *verset* which Howells calls an "erotic experience"). Gradually he was able to give a religious dimension to this Dionysian experience. [DWA]

Hubert, Renée Riese. Claudel, poète en prose. FR 35:369–76, 1962.   **10667**
C.'s prose poems in *Connaissance de l'Est* differ considerably from works of similar nature by Baudelaire, Rimbaud, Mallarmé, Reverdy. C.'s ambition takes on cosmic proportions as he attempts to depict the universe rather than specific scenes or events. [SEH]

Kapp, Volker Werner. Claudel und die Modernität. LJGG 14:421–44, 1973. **10668**
Investigates the influence of the "modernity" of Baudelaire, Rimbaud, and Mallarmé on C.'s literary esthetic. With help from Auerbach's *Figura-Studien,* shows by means of examples from *Le soulier de satin* how C.'s presentation of reality means a reacceptance of the eastern reinterpretation of the cross of Christ as a sign of triumph and yet results in showing it as defeat and paradox. [VK]

———. Paul Claudels Cinq grandes odes als Werk des Übergangs. ZFSL 83:129–51, 1973.   **10669**
Adds some diachronical aspects to his book about the *Odes* in order to clarify the causes and results of C.'s artistic crisis. He sees as the main cause the antimony of art and religion, influenced by Mallarmé, which is overcome by drawing the historical dimension into the *Odes*. The result is the production of a religious lyric of a liturgical character and a new dramatic form taking into account historical dimensions. [VK]

Krings, Hermann. Die Kraft des Wortes. Zum Problem der Ästhetik bei Paul Claudel. LJGG 10:161–73, 1969.   **10670**
Krings thinks through, as a philosopher, C.'s thesis of the changing of the world through the word. He includes in this thesis C.'s claim to challenge mankind through art. Fears that the picture of the world through art may only be beautiful appearance since C. views the world as non-being and presents love as separation. [VK]

Laine, Barry. Tradition and innovation in Paul Claudel's Cent phrases pour éventails. FR 49:234–46, 1975.   **10671**

A perceptive analysis of these oriental poems to point out the degree to which C. follows the model of the Japanese haiku. An interesting case of transference from an oriental poetic form into a highly original occidental form. [DWA]

La Vallée, M. Marthe. Claudel, poet believer. Ren 8:177–88, 1956.   **10672**

This shows clearly that C.'s Art poétique is not about art or poetry but is a cosmology that explains C.'s role as a poet. Maintains that C.'s vision derives from a war between Christian and pagan. Characteristics of the verset and the structure of the Odes are analyzed in terms of C.'s two-fold vision. [LLG]

Lawler, James. Claudel's art of composition. In his: The language of French symbolism. Princeton, Princeton univ. press, 1969. p. 146–84.   **10673**

Excellent study of genesis and composition of La cantate à trois voix, based on various mss., brouillons, and on internal structures and evidence. [JFE]

————. Claudel's art of provocation. EFL 1:30–58, 1964.   **10674**

Very thorough analysis of the poem Ballade from the point of view of biographical source, structure and style, based partly on comparison of original ms. and final version. [DWA]

Marie-Antoinette, sœur. Vers claudélien; recréation poétique du monde. RUL 20: 636–56, 1966.   **10675**

Proposes to study C.'s transpositions of material realities into a poetic universe, as well as how the Claudelian verse breaks with French tradition. Contrasts C.'s objectives with those of Baudelaire, Mallarmé and Aeschylus. Sees C.'s basic aim as that of shaping his verse in a pattern conforming to the rhythm of the universe. [WB]

Méroz, Lucien. L'art poétique de Paul Claudel. NeV 16:397–416, 1941.   **10676**

Protests against attempts of critics to reduce the Art poétique to a logical system. The Art poétique is rather a series of intuitions: the intuition of creation, the intuition of the magnificence of nature, and the intuition of divine love. Very clearly expressed. [DWA]

Naughton, A. E. A. Claudel, image-maker and iconoclast. FR 28:385–94, 1955.   **10677**

C.'s Réflexions et propositions sur le vers français is more illuminating than his Art poétique in revealing the poet's ideas on the nature of poetry and on the problems of versification and poetic technique. C., the iconoclast, attacked the traditional French verse forms and called for an intermingling of prose and poetry. Naughton concludes that C.'s example, more than his theorizing, led to a wider appreciation of poetic prose. [SEH]

Neumeister, Sebastian. Paul Claudel, Ite missa est. In: Die französische Lyrik, von Villon bis zur Gegenwart. V. 2. Ed. by Hans Hinterhäuser. Düsseldorf, Bagel, 1975. P. 225–33, 395–97.   **10678**

Interpretation of the poem with reference to Auerbach's Figura-Studien as an unsuccessful attempt to carry out again the comparison of figure and reality which was last accomplished in the baroque period. [VK]

————. Zur Poetik Claudels. NS 67:398–405, 1968.   **10679**

With reference to Auerbach's Figura-Studien, criticizes baroque qualities of C.'s poetry. [VK]

Porché, François. Paul Claudel. In his: Poètes français depuis Verlaine. La nouvelle revue critique, 1929. p. 123–39.   **10680**

Refuses to accept the principles of C.'s versification, for this verse is measured only by the rhythm of the breath. C.'s poetry becomes so personal that it should be identified with his physical life. Some good remarks, but they are spoiled by radical conclusions. [MMN]

Raible, Wolfgang. Paul Claudel. La muse qui est la grâce, strophe I. In his: Moderne Lyrik in Frankreich. Darstellung und Interpretationen. Stuttgart, Berlin, Cologne and Mainz, Kohlhammer, 1972. p. 129–36.   **10681**

Interpretation of the passage in terms of form and content. In the analysis of form, the article contains several new aspects which aid in the understanding of the verse. [VK]

Rivière, Jacques. Paul Claudel, poète chrétien. *In his:* Etudes. Gallimard, 1924. p. 65–121. *Also:* Gallimard, 1944. p. 55–98. *Also in:* Les critiques de notre temps et Claudel. *See* 10594. p. 48–53.   **10682**
Originally published in *L'occident* 1907). Sensuality˙ as a source of C.'s poetic and dramatic style are revealed by numerous specific examples. One of the earliest studies to appreciate C.'s innovative style and its relation to his philosophy of art. [LLG]

Robidoux, Réjean. Claudel, poète de la connaissance. La muraille intérieure de Tokyo. *In:* Formes et figures. *See* 10597. p. 15–52.   **10683**
Excellent study of C.'s notion of poetry as instrument for self-knowledge, knowledge of the world, and as means of reaching God. "La muraille intérieure de Tokio" is treated as a condensation and distillation of C.'s thought throughout his work. [JFE]

Spitzer, Leo. Interpretation of an ode by Paul Claudel. *In his:* Linguistics and literary history; essays in stylistics. Princeton, Princeton univ. press, 1948. p. 193–236.   **10684**
An important work linking linguistics and literary history through close textual study of first stanza of "La Muse qui est la grâce." Theme and rhythm linked through analysis of repetition and shifts of tone to demonstrate effort at harmonizing conflict, embodied in linguistic form, between Christian and pagan, between C.'s Christian ode and Ronsard's paganistic ones, between modern artist and ancient form. [LLG]

———. A linguistic and literary interpretation of Claudel's Ballade. FR 16:134–43, 1942.   **10685**
Brief, but incisive close reading of C.'s *Ballade*. Spitzer analyzes vocabulary, structure, and metrics of the text as a means of elucidating the central theme: the necessary acceptance of the inevitability of death. Traces affinity between C. and François Villon. [SEH]

Viatte, Norbert. Sur La cantate à trois voix de Paul Claudel. NeV 21:209–16, 1946.   **10686**

Poem is found to have a rose-like structure. [DWA]

Vigini, Giuliano. L'ode jubilaire in memoria di Dante di Paul Claudel. SFr 40:101–06, 1970.   **10687**
C.'s *Ode* reveals a continuation of Dante's voyage in ideas, images and symbols. Understanding of growing tension of *Divine comedy* mirrored in C.'s poem, but C. desired to unite with infinite while Dante understands place of man is on earth among the finite. [LLG]

Whitaker, Marie-Joséphine. Le vitalisme de Claudel dans les Cinq grandes odes. BSPC 51:1–15, 1973.   **10688**
Whitaker shows the life-affirming sides of C.'s poetry in which literature and science find a common ground with such optimistic writers as Fabre, Péguy, Bergson, Marcel, and C. himself whose broad Catholicism, in keeping with the Psalmist, portrays "a God of the living and not the dead." [CC]

Wilhelm, Julius. Paul Claudels Cantate à trois voix. *In:* Studia romanica. Gedenkschrift für Eugen Lerch. Ed. by Charles Bruneau and Peter M. Schon. Stuttgart, Port Verlag, 1955. p. 431–53. *Also in his:* Beiträge zur romanischen Literaturwissenschaft. Tübingen, Niemeyer, 1956. p. 214–31.   **10689**
Analyzes the *Cantate* and classifies it in C.'s collected work. [VK]

———. Paul Claudels Cantique du Rhône. *In:* Syntactica und Stilistica. Festschrift für Ernst Gamillscheg zum 70. Geburtstag, 28 Oktober 1957. Tübingen, Niemeyer, 1957. p. 691–99. *Also in his:* Beiträge zur romanischen Literaturwissenschaft. Tübingen, Niemeyer, 1956, p. 194–213.   **10690**
Similar to preceding study and a supplement to it. [VK]

Theater in General: Books

Alter, André. Paul Claudel. Seghers, 1968. 189 p. (Théâtre de tous les temps, 8)   **10691**
Typical of the introductory works in this Seghers series: includes introductory remarks, comments on C.'s concept of drama, his language, synopsis of plays, and general conclusion. "Textes et documents" section contains interesting quotes from C., a variety of

critical judgments by others, chronologies and a bibliography. [JFE]
Review: Anon. in BCLF 24:15, 1969; H. Gouhier in BSPC 33:9–10, 1969.

Bastien, Jacques. L'œuvre dramatique de Paul Claudel. Reims, chez l'auteur, 1957. 262 p.   10692

Well-written and particularly well-printed overview of theater, more descriptive than analytical but worth perusing. Prefers *La jeune fille Violaine* to *L'annonce faite à Marie*, criticizes *Partage de midi*, and finds esthetic weaknesses in *Le soulier de satin*. [DWA]
Review: F. Cassiers in LR 13:113–15, 1959.

Becker, Aimé. Tête d'or (1889) et La ville (1890–1891): la dissonance fondamentale et le drame de la conversion. Lettres modernes, 1971. 103 p. (ALM, 120; APC, 9)   10693

Compact, densely documented examination of the biographical components of C.'s spiritual conflict (1886–1890) mirrored in the protagonists and certain themes of the first versions of these early plays. Although esthetic scrutiny is lacking, Becker clarifies many obscurities in meaning by his methodical marshaling of parallel evidence from the two dramas and other sources to show poetic transpositions of C.'s adolescent anguish and tortured conversion. [HMW]
Reviews: E. Beaumont in FS 27:471–72, 1973; W. Matheson in FR 46:626, 1973.

Chiari, Joseph. The poetic drama of Paul Claudel. P. J. Kennedy, 1954. 186 p.   10694

Examines relation of C.'s art to age of Rimbaldian symbolism. Provides brief synopsis of plays, judges structure, symbolic value of characters and speeches, theme as expounded by story and actions. Considers most plays inferior as dramatic works but poetically great. Characters primarily poetic representations of conflicting aspects of C.'s personality. Undertakes discussion of C.'s theology. Judges him a master of vast visions. Study weak in analysis of poetic language because remains theoretical. Bibliography. [LLG]

Reviews: Anon. in TLS Oct. 15, 1954; D. O'Donnell in NSN 49:617–18, 1955; L. Pamplune in Ren 8:37–39, 1955.

Claudel, Paul. Mes idées sur le théâtre. Ed. by Jacques Petit and Jean Pierre Kempf. Gallimard, 1966. 256 p. *Trans.:* Claudel on the theater. Trans. by Christine Trollope. Coral Gables, Fla., Univ. of Miami press, 1972. xxii, 190 p.   10695

Text includes photos and C.'s stage diagrams. Main themes and problems outlined in preface and index. [LLG]
Review: J. Madaule in Esp 362:125–34, 1967.

Farabet, René. Le jeu de l'acteur dans le théâtre de Claudel. Minard, Lettres modernes, 1960. 162 p. (Théâtre, 2)   10696

Onstage and behind-the-scenes glimpse into the problems encountered by actors portraying C.'s roles. Worthwhile study offering valuable insights into C.'s theater from the technical point of view of the actor. Appendix contains list of performances of C.'s plays from 1912–59 indicating directors, actors, theater. Additional, valuable notes on C.'s ideas on this subject are found in his correspondence with Barrault (*see* 10514). [SEH]
Review: S. Pitou in Ren 15:212–18, 1963.

Landau, Edwin Maria. Paul Claudel. Velber bei Hannover, Friedrich, 1960. 179 p. (Friedrichs Dramatiker des Welttheaters, 22)   10697

Survey of C's total theatrical work from the pen of C.'s German translator. The book contains photos of scenes from C.'s play productions and is meant for a wide public. Landau goes through all of C.'s plays in chronological sequence and occasionally discusses content and sketches a brief interpretation. [VK]

Lioure, Michel. L'esthétique dramatique de Paul Claudel. Armand Colin, 1971. 674 p.   10698

Important, weighty study which aims at a definition of C.'s dramatic esthetics while describing his dramatic theory and genius. C.'s sources, theory, practice and experiences are reviewed and analyzed with utmost intelligence and

perception seasoned with liberal doses of imagination. [JFE]
Reviews: H. Naughton in EspCr 13: 89–91, 1973; J.-N. Segrestaa in RHL 74:135–37, 1974; A. Veinstein in BSPC 56:13–15, 1974.

Madaule, Jacques. Paul Claudel, dramaturge. L'arche, 1956. 158 p. (Les grands dramaturges, 15) **10699**
Introduction to C.'s theater by one of his most enthusiastic commentators; contains summaries and commentaries for all major plays taken in alphabetical order. Especially good for those knowing C.'s theater only slightly. [JFE]

Marcel, Gabriel. Regards sur le théâtre de Claudel. Beauchesne, 1964. 176 p. **10700**
All chapters, except introductory one, are reprints of articles published in late '30's and early '40's, mostly in NL. Believes the poet is found in the characters of the early plays. His drama and conflicts form bases of the plots. Later plays remove him, concentrate on dogma, and lose vibrancy. Commentaries on individual plays. Especially helpful on organizing principles of plays. [LLG]
Reviews: J. Andrieu in SynB 227–28:486–87, 1965; C. Galpérine in CahPC 6:304–07, 1966; M. Parent in BFLS 424–26, Feb. 1965.

Mercier-Campiche, Marianne. Le théâtre de Claudel, ou la puissance du grief et de la passion. Pauvert, 1968. 277 p. **10701**
Exegesis of plays, done in context of entire body of C. dramatic creations. Includes ample discussions of major critical opinion. Attention to limits of link between plots and C.'s life, difficulties, parallels and oppositions in plays, as well as imagery and language. Considers resemblances between C. and Nietzsche. Extensive notes. [LLG]
Reviews: Y. Florenne in QL 70:10–11, 1969; H. Gouhier in BSPC 35:14–16, 1969.

Müller, Klaus. Die Frühdramen Paul Claudels (L'endormie, Fragment d'un drame, Tête d'or, La ville). Stuttgart, Offsetdruck, 1965. 169 p. (Diss., Tübingen) **10702**
Points out that, in the early plays, the division into three acts is a commonplace. Within the acts he observes an increase in the tension curve up to the end. Deduces connections between Fragment d'un drame and Partage de midi as well as between L'endormie and L'ours et la lune respectively and Protée. [VK]

Stiel, Siglinde. Die Erneuerung des Mysterienspiels durch Paul Claudel. Munich, 1968. 167 p. (Diss.) **10703**
Stiel investigates L'annonce faite à Marie, Le soulier de satin, Le livre de Christophe Colomb, Jeanne d'Arc au bûcher, L'histoire de Tobie et de Sara and La sagesse ou la parabole du festin in order to demonstrate surface resemblances with medieval mystery plays. [VK]

Taviani, Ferdinando. La parabola teatrale. Un saggio sul teatro di Paul Claudel. Florence, F. Le Mounier, 1969. 207 p. **10704**
Well-written, scholarly essay (unfortunately marred by numerous misprints in French quotations) on the form and style of the Claudelian drama with particular emphasis on its symbolist origins. [DWA]

Tricaud, Marie-Louise. Le baroque dans le théâtre de Paul Claudel. Droz, 1967. 281 p. **10705**
Examines nature of baroque in art, literature and religous history. Explores extent of its use in C.'s themes, theatrical technique and language — both written and spoken — as basis of study of its use in his plays. Concludes baroque in form and content used as means of catharsis for emotional and overwhelming personal experiences. Thorough and conclusive so long as primary definitons are accepted. Bibliography. [LLG]
Reviews: J. Boly in LR 23:190, 1969; H. Waters in FR 41:750–51, 1968.

Theater in General: Articles

Arnold, Werner. Grundformen europäischer Dramatik bei Claudel. ZFSL 72:161–68, 1962. **10706**
Sees a relationship of C. with three basic forms of the European theater: 1. the late medieval miracle play in L'annonce faite à Marie; 2. the baroque theater in Le soulier de satin; 3. the classical theater in the Trilogy. [VK]

Attoun, Lucien. Le théâtre. Eur 474:289–95, 1968.   **10707**

Problems of presenting C.'s plays to modern audiences: anti-modern aspects of C.'s Catholicism, choice of emphasis on poetic text or physical representation, anti-religious dimension of *Tête d'or*, role of history in *L'otage*. In context of review of Barrault's *Tête d'or* and Serreau's *L'otage*. Valuable commentary on other recent productions. [NH]

Barrault, Jean-Louis. Paul Claudel. *In his:* Nouvelles réflexions sur le théâtre. Flammarion, 1959, p. 200–76.   **10708**

A worthwhile and highly readable collection of personal insights into the man and his esthetic and moral visions. Barrault's account of the staging and production problems and his collaboration with C. are fascinating. The personal account is supplemented with documentation including letters and personal notes from C. to the author. The account of the production of *Soulier de satin* and *Partage de midi* is of particular interest to the student of the stage versions of C.'s drama. [TJ]

————. Souvenirs pour demain. Seuil, 1972. 381 p. *Trans.:* The memoirs of Jean-Louis Barrault. Memories for tomorrow. Trans. by Jonathan Griffin. Dutton, 1974. 336 p.   **10709**

Moving, intimate descriptions of productions of *Soulier, Partage, Echange, Colomb,* and *Tête d'or.* Technical and spiritual collaboration reveals much about C.'s attitudes towards plays and reasons for rewrites. Essential text for students of 20th-century theater. [LLG]

Flower, J. E. Claudel. *In:* Forces in modern French drama. Studies in variations on the permitted lie. Ed. by John Fletcher. London, Univ. of London, 1972. p. 33–48. **10710**

Examines successive influences, especially Barrault's, on C.'s theatrical expression. Considers relationship of Catholicism to imaginative creativity, of innovations to limitations. Helpful study of historical importance of C.'s theater and of attitudes of major critics. [LLG]

Fontana, Oskar Maurus. Die Paul Claudel-Aufführungen in Wien. MuK 6:297–318, 1960.   **10711**

Report of an eyewitness to productions of C.'s plays in Vienna from 1918 to 1960. Occasionally lists names of cast and type of interpretation given in the production of the play. [VK]

Lumley, Frederick. The discovery of Claudel. *In his:* Trends in 20th century drama; a survey since Ibsen and Shaw. London, Rockliff, 1956. p. 63–79. *Also in his:* New trends in 20th century drama; a survey since Ibsen and Shaw. London, Barrie and Rockliff, 1967. p. 61–77.   **10712**

A survey of C.'s contributions to living traditions of stage. His Catholicism and anti-naturalism renewed contemporary drama. Article of more popular than scholarly value. [LLG]

Morisot, Jean-Claude. De Tête d'or au Repos du septième jour: Dieu et la peur de Dieu. RLM 180–82 (PCl 5), 7–24, 1968.   **10713**

Constants of C.'s early dramas: misunderstanding between man and woman; women as presences or poetic figures rather than living beings; Kierkegaardian tension between religion and despair. Difficult but rewarding survey. [HMW]

Paul Claudel 1868–1968. RHT 20:255–358, 1968. *See* 10715.   **10714**

Proceedings of the first day of the Claudel Centennial Colloquium (April 18, 1968) at the Université de Nancy. [JFE]

Paul Claudel. Interprétations et interprètes. RHT 21:7–84, 1969. *See* 10714.   **10715**

Bulk of the proceedings of the C. centennial colloquium (April 19–21, 1968) at the Université de Nancy, centering primarily on C.'s theater as stageable — problems, practices and solutions of practitioners of the theater, with limited contributions from some foreign directors, translators and academics. Especially useful for an understanding of recent attitudes and perceptions of practicing theater people towards C. [JFE]

Petit, Jacques. En art il n'y a pas de définitif... RLM 114–16 (PCl 2):7–24, 1965.   **10716**

C. never considered his works as finished or perfect because he thought nothing was ever definitive in art. C. rewrote his plays to make them clearer and easier to stage. Excellent explanation of C.'s attitude toward artistic creation. [JPC]

Peyre, Henri. The drama of Paul Claudel. Thou 105:185–202, 1952. **10717**

Characterizes C.'s work as a drama of love and suffering to be endured as a means of attaining peace and joy in union with God. Analyzes by means of plot summary three most important plays of C.'s career: *Tête d'or, Partage de midi, Le soulier de satin.* Contains some germinal ideas but largely superseded by more recent criticism. [SEH]

Prévost, Jean. Les éléments du drame chez Paul Claudel. NRF 188:593–609, 1929. **10718**

C. may create some of his most realistic characters with what one can find in the lowest regions of the human soul. Traces the roots of Claudelian drama back to Aeschylus. As for form, C. refuses to follow the classical theater, but reinstates the prerogatives of the spirit. [MMN]

L'Annonce faite à Marie

Aaraas, Hans. L'annonce faite à Marie: vision de l'histoire. RevR 2:158–74, 1967. **10719**

Excellent explication of the play in terms of the "conventional" historical background: a Middle Ages which is disintegrating but also going towards a future and wider unity. [DWA]

Allen, Peter. L'annonce faite à Marie à Hellerau en 1913. TLL 6, part 2:201–10, 1968. **10720**

Detailed and thoroughly documented article on the staging of *L'annonce* in German at Hellerau. Lugné-Poe's staging of *L'annonce* in 1912 in the shabby Salle Malakoff, rented for the purpose, was a discouraging experience for C., whereas the impressive and expert staging at Hellerau the following year was a revelation to him and sparked his interest in dramaturgy. [DWA]

Bellemare, Rosaire, o.m. Le drame de Violaine. RUO 15:247–64, 1965. **10721**

Proposes to study the dogmatic basis for *L'annonce faite à Marie,* defending C.'s works against Massis' accusation of "anarchiques." [WB]

Boly, Joseph. L'annonce faite à Marie. Etude et analyse. Eds. de l'école, 1957. 140 p. **10722**

Evidently intended for school use. Not very satisfactory in its analysis of the play itself, but contains some interesting accessary information such as the biographical background (including a photograph of Combernon), circumstances of writing the various versions, stage productions, and particularly an elaborate and useful "Tableau synoptique des différentes versions de L'annonce faite à Marie." [DWA]

Broilliard, Jacqueline. La réhabilitation de Mara. RLM 114–16 (PCl 2):73–93, 1965. **10723**

The importance of Mara's evolution increases in the first three versions. It is shown to correspond to dramatic and theological logic. [JPC]

Delfor Mandrioni, Hector. Paul Claudel: El significado de la Anunciación a Maria. Segunda edición. Buenos-Aires, Artibus, 1970. 261 p. **10724**

Detailed commentary concerned only with religous interpretation. C. apparently approved of the text. Appendix includes separate articles dealing with C.'s work in general: "La sublimación del amor," "Los dos cuidades," and "Algunos personajes femeninos de los dramas de Paul Claudel." [DWA]

Dessaintes, Maurice. Paul Claudel et L'annonce faite à Marie. Brussels, A. de Boeck, 1951. 126 p. **10725**

C. for Belgians. Only the second half of the volume is devoted to *L'annonce,* the first half being life and works in general. Acceptable presentation useful only as a summary introduction to C.'s work. [DWA]

Deuel, Mildred. The structure of the different versions of L'annonce faite à Marie. MLR 67:543–49, 1972. **10726**

Traces history of compositon of *L'annonce* and C.'s changing vision of universe and dramatic form. Secondary characters and speeches overdeveloped in earliest two versions cause lack of organization. Later C. eliminated these to provide focus to structure and wider Christian context. [LLG]

Espiau de la Maëstre, A. Paul Claudel: L'annonce faite à Marie. LR 16:3–26; 149–71; 241–65, 1962.   **10727**

Argues that the progressive transformation of *L'annonce* over a period of more than fifty years corresponds to important stages in the life and religious thought of C. Aim is to study the relationship of the three principal figures— Violaine, Pierre de Craon and Mara— to C.'s life and thought, but article lacks precision, coherence, and focus. [SEH]

Goldmann, Lucien. Le problème du mal. A propos de Rodogune et de L'annonce faite à Marie. Méd 3:167–75, 1961. *Also in his:* Structures mentales et création culturelle. Anthropos, 1970. p. 135–51. **10728**

Sees *L'annonce faite à Marie* as version of the Faust legend, an intriguing idea which leads to grave distortions of the play. Effort to force the work into preconceived mold on the problem of the creator in modern, production-oriented society. [NH]

Jones, Tobin H. The alchemical language of Paul Claudel's L'annonce faite à Marie. Sym 27:35–45, 1973.   **10729**

In spite of the title, author focuses on how symbolism and imagery, rather than language, reflect medieval alchemy. Considers prolog a figurative representation of hermetic principles. [LLG]

Lowe, Robert W. La doctrine du corps mystique dans L'annonce faite à Marie. RUL 14:579–84, 1960.   **10730**

Short article gives scriptural basis for C.'s presentation of Violaine as the sacrificial victim as well as for Anne Vercor's symbolic role as the man whose prayers are salutary. [WB]

Mavrocordato, Alexander [*sic. i.e.* **Maurocordato, Alexandre**]. The tidings brought to Mary and medieval drama. *In:* The medieval drama and its Claudelian revival. Papers presented at the Third symposium in comparative literature held at the Catholic University of America April 3 and 4, 1958. Ed. by E. Catherine Dunn, Tatiana Fotitch, Bernard M. Peebles. Washington, D. C., Catholic univ. of America press, 1970. p. 52–65.   **10731**

Excellent scholarly article on medieval background of play in spite of author's intention to stylize subject. The play is divisible into the three mansions of the medieval stage: Earth, Heaven and

Hell. The two solstice myths are present, "that of birth, in its white winter garb ...and that of death, in its hideous summer guise, leprosy." The details of the miracle come from a German legend concerning Mechtilde von Magdeburg. [DWA]

O'Flaherty, Kathleen. Paul Claudel and the tidings brought to Mary. Preface by Paul Claudel. Cork, Cork univ. press; and Westminster, Md., Newman press, 1949. 141 p.   **10732**

Perhaps not a work for scholars in spite of the scholarly background of the author, but, for the layman, a remarkably lucid exegesis of the play. If one were starting to read up on C., this would be an excellent place to begin. Appendix (p. 122–41) contains a convenient plot summary of C.'s other plays, but, lacking critical comment or analysis, this part will not substitute as a general introduction to C.'s theater. [DWA]

Review: C. Girdlestone in FS 3: 370–72, 1949.

Pallister, Janis L. Presentation motifs in the prologue of Claudel's L'annonce faite à Marie. ClaudelN 7:23–29, 1971. *Also:* RomN 13:409–13, 1972.   **10733**

Discussion of meaning and importance of four presentations by Violaine. Special emphasis on importance of naming and preparation of themes of justice, renunciation and sacrifice. Interesting addendum to Waters article (*see* 10736). Note that author in RomN version, disclaims ClaudelN version as deformation by editor of that publication. [LLG]

Segrestaa, Jean-Noël. L'annonce faite à Marie: analyse critique. Hatier, 1973. 80 p. (Profil d'une œuvre)   **10734**

Detailed, but superficial study of the play. Tries to define its various dramatic elements and to propose different readings (psychological, historical and symbolic). Ambitious, but disappointing in its results. [MR]

Theisen, Josef. Paul Claudels Annonce faite à Marie: Opfer oder Sühnedrama. NS 11:509–20, 1962.   **10735**

Investigates the motivation of Violaine's kiss in the different versions of the play, with the conclusion that C.

made Violaine guilty and that the play is therefore a drama of atonement and not of sacrifice. [VK]

Waters, Harold A. Possible sources for Claudel's Violaine. Ren 22:99–107, 1970. **10736**

Valuable for those interested in literary history and as a well-written study on the probable models for Violaine (Saint Colette of Corbie) and Pierre de Craon (Pierre de Reims). The study of the Christmas Miracle is less convincing since it relies heavily on external evidence. [LLG]

Dramatic Oratorios

Dubois, E. T. Léon Bloy, Paul Claudel and the revaluation of the significance of Columbus. *In:* Currents of thought in French literature. Essays in memory of G. T. Clapton. Oxford, Basil Blackwell, 1965. p. 131–44. **10737**

Presents Columbus as C.'s most triumphant dramatic figure whose vocation is to be conqueror, leader, and gatherer of the whole universe. [LLG]

Labriolle, Jacqueline de. Les Christophe Colomb de Paul Claudel. Klincksieck, 1972. 245 p. **10738**

Dense, complete analysis. Approaches study from historic, critical, comparative, esthetic, stylistic and thematic points of view. Studies variants, vast range of sources, internal and external structure, language, and imagery. Various productions and own translation into English also examined. Excellent notes and charts, chronology of composition, editions, bibliography. [LLG]
Review: G. Blumenthal in FR 47: 208–09, 1973.

———. Les oratorios dramatiques de Paul Claudel. RLM 180–82 (PCl 5): 83–100, 1968. **10739**

Perceptive and clear presentation of the qualities shared by C.'s *oratorios dramatiques: Le livre de Christophe Colomb, Jeanne au bûcher, L'histoire de Tobie.* Author proposes to elucidate the structural similarities in the three plays by commenting on common characteristics. [SEH]

———. Pourquoi deux Christophe Colomb? RLM 271–75 (PCl 8):33–51, 1971. **10740**

Succinct, at times too terse discussion of C.'s use of the technique of *dédoublement* to make *Le livre de Christophe Colomb* a baroque spectacle on two levels. The two figures of Colomb personify the Thomistic division between essence and existence and vividly portray the conflict between two aspirations: Colomb, like C. himself, felt at once the desire to possess the earth and the urge to be dispossessed of the secular world. [SEH]

L'Echange

Ly-Thi-Nhi, Madeleine. L'échange et le mobile de L'échange. ClaudelS 1, no. 3:63–72, 1973. **10741**

Concerning the play as a satire of materialistic values in America. [CC]

Waters, Harold A. A propos de la seconde version de L'échange. RLM 114–16. (PCl 2):95–109, 1965. **10742**

America and the problems which had preoccupied C. when he wrote the first version, became quite distant in the second. According to Waters' convincing study, in the revision the play lost unity of style and composition and especially poetry. [JPC]

L'Orestie

Aquilon, Pierre. Claudel traducteur d'Eschyle. RLM 101–03 (PCl 1):7–43, 1964. **10743**

A detailed and technical evaluation of C.'s translation by a scholar with a keen sense of poetry. According to Aquilon, C. was a grammarian in the strict sense of the word. He never betrayed the meaning nor distorted the poetry. He was able to give Aeschylus' work new life in French. Superb study of a translation. [JPC]

Guyard, Marius-François. Deux collaborateurs de l'Orestie claudélienne: Leconte de Lisle et Verrall. TLL 2, part 2:137–43, 1964. **10744**

In the preface to his translation of the *Orestie,* C. belittles the earlier translations of Leconte de Lisle and A. W.

Verrall, the latter into English. Guyard asserts that C.'s debt to them was considerable and proves by extensive quotation that C.'s stage directions were a direct translation of Verrall. [DWA]

Matheson, William H. Claudel and Aeschylus. A study of Claudel's translation of the Oresteia. Ann Arbor, Univ. of Michigan press, [1965]. 231 p.   **10745**

A major scholarly work, somewhat arduous to read, which first goes into the history of translation of Aeschylean drama and then examines the accuracy of C.'s translation. C. receives a high mark for his thorough comprehension of Aeschylus, but Matheson does not stop there. He considers Aeschylus to be central to C.'s concept of drama, and he studies particularly the Aeschylean parallels in *Tête d'or* in *Protée* and in the trilogy where the influence of Aeschylus is particularly strong. [DWA]

Reviews: P. Aquilon in BSPC no. 25, 1967; A. Podlecki in ClaudelN 5:226–28, 1970.

Trousson, R. Paul Claudel traducteur de l'Orestie. BAGB no. 4:489–501, 1965.   **10746**

Despite C.'s announced desire to remain absolutely faithful to the original and despite the fact that C. specialists have applauded this apparent fidelity, a close study comparing the translation with the original reveals that C. unconsciously stretched Aeschylus in the direction of his own Christianity with a resulting distortion of the meaning. [DWA]

Partage de midi

Antoine, Gérald. L'expression du tragique dans Partage de midi. *In:* Le théâtre tragique. Ed. by Jean Jacquot. Centre national de la recherche scientifique, 1962. p. 439–50.   **10747**

Detailed study of *Partage de midi* as a tragedy on the fatality of love in the manner of *Phèdre*. Not as useful as Madaule's paper at the same Royaumont colloquium. [DWA]

Brady, Valentini. The blazing firmament: the symbolic substructure of Partage de midi. ClaudelS 2:80–93, 1976.   **10748**

Approaches the play from an archetypal point of view and attempts to elucidate its meaning through the study of median and cosmic symbols detectable in the play. *Partage de midi* emerges as the drama of the division of the Self and of hesitation. [VB]

Brereton, Geoffrey. Claudel: Partage de midi. *In his:* Principles of tragedy. A rational examination of the tragic concept in life and literature. London, Routledge and Kegan Paul, 1968. *Also:* Coral Gables, Univ. of Miami press, 1968. p. 225–43.   **10749**

Partage as a 20th-century example of concept of tragedy as unresolvable conflict between two powers that influence human existence: religion and passionate human love. [LLG]

Czaschke, Annemarie. Der Cantique de Mesa in Paul Claudels Drama Partage de midi. Münster, Aschendorff, 1964. 189 p. (Forschungen zur romanischen Philologie, 13)   **10750**

Makes an inventory, according to H. Lausberg's method, of all elements of the *Cantique* and compares them with those places in which, since ancient times, similar ideas have been expressed, in order to study the traditional aspects of this poem. Czaschke divides the poem into two main parts: 1–19 and 20–79. [VK]

Reviews: J. Boly in LR 20:373, 1966; A. Espiau de la Maëstre in BSPC 18:12, 1965, and in RFor 77:188–90, 1965; K. Weinert in RJ 16:237–39, 1965; M. Wood in FS 19:315–16, 1965.

Deuel, Mildred. A study of the dramatic structure of Partage de midi from 1905–1949. FR 45:964–70, 1972.   **10751**

The evolution of the three versions of *Partage* in terms of character development and modifications of tone, mood, and style. Concludes that the 1948 version is the most suitable for staging. [SEH]

Lee, Vera. The revising of Partage de midi. FR 38:337–48, 1965.   **10752**

Meticulous comparison of the three versions of *Partage de midi* showing the influence of the director Jean-Louis Barrault on the evolution of the play from the extremely lyrical first version in 1905 to the more colloquial and prosaic "versions scéniques" of 1948 and 1949. [SEH]

Lioure, Michel. Ombre et lumière dans Partage de Midi de Paul Claudel. TLL 13, part 2:725–39, 1975.   **10753**

Excellent and extremely accessible, Lioure's article examines the various manifestations of chiaroscuro in *Partage de midi,* relating them to other works of C. [JFE]

Viatte, Auguste. Paul Claudel et sa tragédie du péché. RUL 3:596–602, 1949.   **10754**

General article on *Partage de midi,* pointing out that in it adultery is seen neither from the lover's point of view nor from that of voluptuousness, but rather from that of the forbidden. Shows that C. has given us a tragic theater where severity holds its own with the sublime. [WB]

Watanabé, Moriaki. La création du personnage d'Amalric. ELLF 1:42–58, 1962.   **10755**

Interesting comparison of three early mss. of *Partage de midi.* Defines gradual emergence of function of Amalric in relation to other characters, and describes their development and increasing association with mythical images. Some confusion in logical development of argument, but effective in showing stages of C.'s creation of dramatic structure and characters. [NH]

———. Le don ou la logique dramatique de Partage de midi. RLM 180–82 (PCl 5), 25–57, 1968.   **10756**

Show how the thematic structure of *Partage de midi* grew from the opposition "exchange/impossibility of exchange" in the early mss. to the complex 1906 configuration of gift of self or communion, identity or communication crisis (co-naissance au monde), and intrusion of a transcendent force (God/Ysé: love) leading to the fall and redemption pattern. Comparisons with other plays of C. reveal many echoes. Indispensable. [HMW]

Waters, Harold A. Claudel's Partage desacralized. *In:* Paul Claudel. *See* 10604. p. 14–23.   **10757**

An excellent study of just what is implied in title — that *Partage de midi* can be seen from catholic as well as Catholic viewpoints. [JFE]

Le Repos du septième jour

Berg, Bruno Walter. Claudel. Le repos du septième jour. *In his:* Der literarische Sonntag. Ein Beitrag zur Kritik der bürgerlichen Ideologie. Heidelberg, Winter, 1976. p. 204–08. (Studia Romanica, 25)   **10758**

Interprets the descent of the emperor to the underworld in *Le repos du septième jour* as an unrealistic representation of the bourgeois Sunday. While in bourgeois ideology Sunday is a formal or moral interpretation of the Sabbath commandment, which is deceptive about actual relationships, C.'s piece refers to the real need of the working man. [VK]

Brunel, Pierre. Un drame chinois de Paul Claudel: Le Repos du septième jour. IL 26:17–23, 1974.   **10759**

Proves that C.'s grasp of things Chinese was greater than previously thought. [JFE]

———. L'évocation des morts et la descente aux enfers: Claudel, Homère, Virgile, Dante. RLM 366–69 (PCl 10):45–64, 1973.   **10760**

Although the three epic poets had some influence on the composition of *Le repos du septième jour,* C. was, for the most part, independent of his predecessors. The influence of Dante is seen in the list of astonishingly diversified punishments, in the presence of guides for the travelers, and in the architecture of Hell. Major difference between C.'s Empereur and Ulysses, Aeneas, and Dante is that the Empereur does not merely observe, but rather actively participates in torments of Hell. [SEH]

Houriez, Jacques. Etudes sur la genèse. RLM 366–69 (PCl 10):9–44, 1973.   **10761**

Tripartite study of origins and development of *Le repos du septième jour.* In first part, "L'élaboration du drame," Houriez examines influence of China on the work, role of the Emperor, and his evolution as a character. Part II reproduces C.'s considerations on such problems as dramatic representation of Hell and characteristics of four divisions of Hell. The final section, "Claudel lecteur de St. Thomas," suggests that C., a religious poet and a man of faith, is closer to the mystics than to the theologian St. Thomas Aquinas. [SEH]

Malicet, Michel. Le repos du septième jour, ou la sublimation d'un rêve de désir. RLM 366–69 (PCl 10):89–129, 1973. **10762**

Written in conjunction with unpublished thesis "Les personnages féminins dans l'œuvre de Claudel," this article is a psychoanalytical interpretation of the role of la Mère. [SEH]

Petit, Jacques. Structures du drame. RLM 366–69 (PCl 10):65–87, 1973. **10763**

Considers problems encountered in rendering dramatic a theme that is essentially epic or elegiac. Two major themes are discussed briefly: theme of sacrifice and complicity of Hell. Final section treats the structure of the dialog as a reflection of the structure of the four divisions of Hell. [SEH]

Potter, Louise Mahru. Man and mediator in Repos du septième jour. Ren 22:207–17, 1970. **10764**

The fundamental problem of this play, man's nature, purpose and destiny and the question of sin, is clearly developed. [LLG]

Saulnier, Zoël, and Eugène Roberto. Le repos du septième jour. Sources et orientations. Ottawa, Eds. de l'univ. d'Ottawa, 1973. 176 p. (CahCC, 7) **10765**

Succinct and thorough study in three chapters. The first chapter discusses Chinese sources; the second covers Christian sources, particularly Thomas Aquinas; the third shows how C. amalgamates the two traditions in his play. The appendix (p. 127–76) reproduces parts of Prémare's 18th century Vestiges des principaux dogmes chrétiens tirés des anciens livres chinois used by C. as a source. [DWA]

Le Soulier de satin

Angers, Pierre. Dona Musique et la poésie de Paul Claudel. In: Formes et figures. See 10597. p. 54–74. **10766**

Perceptive study of Dona Musique as expression of man's profound soul, and as revelation of the true spiritual character of the play. [JFE]

Balthasar, Hans Urs von. Nachwort zur deutschen Übertragung. In: Claudel, Paul. Der seidene Schuh. Salzburg, Müller, 1939. p. 425–65. Also: Freiburg, Herder Bücherei, 1965. p. 353–83. (Herder-Bücherei, 199/200) **10767**

Most important contribution of German criticism from the pen of the translator of the play. Balthasar treats four aspects: 1. The horizon as center, which explains the intended meaning of the work; the problem of necessity and impossibility of existence in this horizon. 2. The love between Rodrigue and Prouhèze seeks the elimination of contradiction between godly and wordly love. 3. Just as Prouhèze has love as a center, so Rodrigue has the world. Also in him the permeation of the world by the divine is shown. 4. The union of both main characters as the problem of love and world-assignment brings about the manifestation of the individual as supra-individual destiny. [VK]

Barko, Ivan. Le soulier de satin: ouverture et référent. Deg 1, no. 4:i/1–i/15, 1973. **10768**

An important study of the structure of Le soulier de satin. Because of the various stages in the writing of the play and in spite of unifying themes, the play retains many characteristics of improvisation on which C. himself insisted. The principal unifying force is the metaphor of "ouverture," culminating in the supreme opening onto the infinite which concludes the evolution of Rodrigue. [DWA]

Baudot, Alain. Le soulier de satin est-il une anti-tragédie? EF 5:115–37, 1969. **10769**

Excellent study of tragic and anti-tragic elements in Soulier de satin. Liberation of form and human will from tragic fatality represent Christian optimism, but characters' suffering and enormity of sacrifice remain almost impossible to comprehend and accept. Perceptively defines relationship of tragedy as genre to play. Convincingly substantiated argument, although influence of romantics perhaps overemphasized. [NH]

Berthenoux, Michel. L'espace dans Le soulier de satin. RLM 310–14 (PCl 9):33–66, 1972. **10770**

Essay on the dynamics of space in Le soulier. Space such as a screen, a wall, an enclosed area provokes an opening. The dilation of space is associated with the accomplishment of human beings. [HMW]

Birn, Randi Marie. The comedy of disrespect in Claudel's Soulier de satin. FR 43, special issue no. 1:175–84, 1970. **10771**
Stating that there is an intimate link between comedy and cosmology in C.'s works, the author proceeds to demonstrate that C. uses a mocking sardonic comedy to deflate the self-esteem of vain and pretentious characters of *Soulier* who are incapable of feeling joy and confidence in the goodness of divine creation. Intriguing idea, but the author frequently insists on the obvious and resorts to plot summary to make a point. [SEH]

Bounoure, Gabriel. Le soulier de satin de Paul Claudel. NRF 208:129–41, 1931. **10772**
Calls C.'s plays parables, because they explore—as in the mystical literature—the secret correspondence between two orders of facts in the ineffable universe. To reach his goal, C. gives up the form of the classical tragedy to adopt a more poetical, jubilant and universal form. Instead of passion, he suggests speaking of the music of the passions. Excellent analysis of C.'s masterpiece. [MMN]

Brunel, Pierre. Le soulier de satin devant la critique. Dilemme et controverses. Minard, 1964. 127 p. (Situations, 6) **10773**
After discussing various critical misinterpretations of the play, Brunel corrects numerous erroneous concepts about human and divine love in this play, which he sees as less baroque than pre-baroque. A final chapter surveys and explains Gabriel Marcel's contradictory views of *Le soulier de satin*. A useful corrective, now largely superseded. [HMW]
Reviews: M. Décaudin in IL 18, no. 2:79, 1966; E. R[oberto] in *Géographie poétique de Claudel* (*see* 10599), p. 219–22.

Buovolo, Huguette. A propos d'une analyse structurale de la quatrième journée. RLM 310–14 (PCl 9):68–88, 1972. **10774**
An incomplete but helpful study (condensed from a thesis) of some ambiguities and contradictions in certain themes and characters of the last act of *Le soulier de satin*. [HMW]

Chambers, Ross. La quatrième journée du Soulier de satin. EFL 7:70–87, 1970. *Also:* CRB 80:11–37, 1972. **10775**
An outstanding article which gives a very interesting and plausible interpretation of this final division of *Le soulier de satin* which has always startled readers by its change of pace and tone, as well as by its comic elements. Chambers maintains that this continuation is logical. Rodrigue, the world conqueror, is not only the travesty of himself, he has become *the* artist. All this is error on his part; he is cured at the end when he is brought down in the most humiliating disgrace and is taken over by the sea, which was the dominant theme of this fourth day. [DWA]

Dosedal, Maria. Claudel, Der seidene Schuh; ein Deutungsversuch. Gelsenkirchen-Buer, Post, 1948. 115 p. **10776**
Adapted from lectures in connection with the 1947 performance of the play in Cologne, this book is an interesting document on the reception of C.'s work in postwar Germany. It compares C.'s dramatic characters with Goethe and Gertrud von Le Fort and interprets, contrary to the contemporary view, Camille's redemption as dependent upon the renunciation of Prouhèze. Superseded by later research. [VK]

Forkey, Leo O. A baroque moment in the French contemporary theater. JAAC 18: 80–89, 1959. **10777**
Nonlinear structure of *Soulier,* a play of dependent subplots, places C. in baroque tradition. Musical score and ideology contribute to this quality. Argument based on comparison of drama with baroque art and on Wölfflin's definitions. Historical parallels also drawn for further proof of baroqueness. [LLG]

Freilich, Joan S. Paul Claudel's Le soulier de satin. A stylistic, structuralist, and psychoanalytic interpretation. Toronto, Univ. of Toronto press, 1973. xvi, 227 p. **10778**
A careful reader-centered analysis of stylistic factors determining effect on imagery. Highly influenced by Riffaterre's work on text as metaphor. Shows ways in which images are combined and

effect of patterns on narrative, religious and emotional levels of meaning. Unity of levels found in psychocritical interpretation of structure: pursuit of forbidden desires leads to frustration and guilt; happiness only in surrender to parent figures. Charts of patterns of occurrence, glossary of terms, selected bibliography included. [LLG]

Henriot, Jacques. Le thème de la quête dans Le soulier de satin. RLM 310–14 (PCl 9):89–116, 1972.   **10779**

Thirsting for happiness (love, land, peace, profit), each character is on a quest for Unity, which begins as a simple solidarity of individual destinies and is fulfilled in the general communion of humanity. Several schemas are used to clarify the argument and the structuring of this theme. [HMW]

Ince, W. N. The unity of Claudel's Le soulier de satin. Sym 22:25–53, 1968. **10780**

Reviews critical acceptance; acknowledges complex of emotions at play's source and compound nature of structure and tone. Rejects notion of intellectual message existing in the play. Finds basic unity in tone of joy and global subject of conquest. [LLG]

Landau, Edwin Marie. L'énigmatique Soulier de satin. ClaudelN 7:30–32, 1971.   **10781**

Some light is thrown on the explanation of the title Le soulier de satin, which seems to derive from a game aboard ship called "Hunt the slipper." The theme harks back possibly to C.'s experiences portrayed in Partage de midi. [CC]

Landry, Jean-Noël. Chronologie et temps dans Le soulier de satin. RLM 310–14 (PCl 9):7–31, 1972.   **10782**

Time is chronologically dispersed and dramatically organized as verisimilitude is sacrificed to poetic interest. Scenes that can be fixed in time contain most of the drama, as tension diminishes in the chronologically vague scenes, which are often dream or burlesque. [HMW]

Lerch, Emile. Versuchung und Gnade. Betrachtungen über Paul Claudel und sein Schauspiel Der seidene Schuh. Vienna, Heiler, 1965. 140 p.   **10783**

First monograph of a German Romance scholar about the play. Treats

contents and meaning as well as the relation between belief and form, each in one chapter. Most statements in the book are in conformity with more recent research. [VK]

Review: G. Zeltner in SchR 58: 184–86, 1958–59.

Lindemann, Reinhold. Kreuz und Eros. Paul Claudels Weltbild im Seidenen Schuh. Vienna, Heiler, 1956. 140 p.   **10784**

Sees the passion of crucified Eros presented in Le soulier de satin and the course of the drama as the consequence of the contrast between Christian and human Eros. The book is typical of the false interpretation of C. as an unproblematic total Catholic. [VK]

Review: H. von Balthasar in NZZ 261:29, 1956.

Malicet, Michel. La peur de la femme dans Le soulier de satin. RLM 391–97 (PCl 11):119–87, 1974.   **10785**

Penetrating, scintillating, authoritative psychoanalytical reading of the female imagery in this play, but based on a systematic study of all of C. Wisely reminds one, though, that by itself a psychoanalytical reading is no more complete than any other. [HMW]

Mazzega, Anne-Marie. Une parabole historique: Le soulier de satin. RLM 150–52 (PCl 4):43–59, 1967.   **10786**

While C. had made a serious effort at documentation, he recreates history as an artist, giving it a style and meaning. For C., Europe's calling to conquer and evangelize the world corresponds to the will of God. Mazzenga does not believe C. justified in deliberately altering history, especially with evident anchronisms. [JPC]

Petit, Jacques. Les jeux du double dans Le soulier de satin. RLM 310–14 (PCl 9): 117–38, 1972.   **10787**

Petit sees a major element of this drama in the abundance of doubles and pairings, used consciously as a refusal and denunciation of theatrical illusion. Good analysis, but questionable conclusions. [HMW]

————. Pour une explication du Soulier de satin. Lettres modernes, 1965. 59 p. (ALM, 58)   **10788**

Focuses on C.'s intentions in writing this play. Essay organized around key scenes which show influence on plot and characters of notions of sacrifice, metaphysics of love and contradictions. Discusses contributions, misunderstandings and limitations of other critics. Invaluable study. [LLG]

————. Le soulier de satin, somme claudélienne. RLM 180–82 (PCl 5):101–11, 1968. **10789**

Studies a dozen situations or structures similar to dramatic patterns used in earlier C. plays; concludes that for the first time C. succeeded in "saving" both halves of his personality by at last resolving the conflict between the spiritual and the victory of violence first posed in *Tête d'or*. By making the play a catharsis or exorcism, instead of a celebration of a resolution, Petit seems to contradict his conclusion in his book (p. 7), *supra*. [HMW]

————. et al. Etude des images. RLM 391–97 (PCl 11):7–53, 1974. **10790**

Most of the images in *Le soulier de satin* are ambivalent, occurring in sets of parallel oppositions. Contradictions persist on the level of images, themes, and even in the movements of certain scenes. Since C. was less interested in reconciling opposites than in making them coexist in the same work, critics should not impose one interpretation over another. A surprising if sensible conclusion, but perhaps too simplistic. [HMW]

————. et al. Index des images. RLM 391–97 (PCl 11):54–118, 1974. **10791**

A listing of all images of any importance, alphabetically by the key word in the *verset*, as an appendix to the article, "Etude des images." [HMW]

Przywara, Erich. Über den Sinn von Claudels Seidener Schuh. Bes 6:210–15, 1951. *Also:* Weltbild Claudels (im Seidenen Schuh). *In his:* In und Gegen. Stellungnahmen zur Zeit. Nuremberg, Glock und Lutz, 1955. p. 145–51. **10792**

Drawing upon a comprehensive knowledge of the literary as well as the philosophical and theological tradition of the West, Przywara studies in this brilliant essay the peculiarities of C.'s picture of the world and the structure of the drama in *Le soulier de satin*. Concludes that the drama produces a lack of order which is contrary to the principle of order in Eastern tradition. For further discussion, see his *Humanitas. Der Mensch gestern und morgen* (Nuremberg, Glock und Lutz, 1952), p. 194–97. [VK]

Sagrestaa, Jean-Noël. Regards sur la composition du Soulier de satin. RLM 180–82 (PCl 5):59–81, 1968. **10793**

Clarifies the rigorous but hidden plot structure of this baroque tapestry, sadly truncated in the stage version which distorts the triumph of the finale into a feeling of martyrdom. The sometimes tenuous pursuit of the red, green, and blue threads through all 52 scenes, however, cries out for a diagram or résumé. [HMW]

Selna, Barbara. Paul Claudel. Prison and the satin slipper. Ren 7:171–80, 1955. **10794**

A well-documented article showing how the paradox of the imprisonment of men in the will of God brings freedom. The prison image as seen in scenery, theme and characters forms the overriding structure of *The satin slipper*. The author claims that this image is relevant to the poetry as well, but this point is inadequately developed. [LLG]

Watson, Harold. Fire and water, love and death in Le soulier de satin. FR 45:971–79, 1972. **10795**

Sensitive, perspicacious treatment of the images of fire, the sea, and the stars as symbolic of the dual process of Rodrigue's salvation: his purification from earthly love and his eternal liberation in death. [SEH]

Weinrich, Harald. Le soulier de satin. *In:* Das französische Theater, vom Barock bis zur Gegenwart. V. 2. Ed. by Jürgen von Stackelberg. Dusseldorf, Bagel, 1968. p. 187–205, 394–98. **10796**

Interprets *Le soulier de satin* in terms of a love-duty and love-honor conflict whose central function in the play leads to a comprehensive view of the main action. Stituates this conflict in the literary and philosophical-theological tradition, showing its relation to the symbolism of the work. Excellent essay to be read in connection with Weinrich's article in GRM. [VK]

————. Das Zeichen des Seidenen Schuhs. GRM 12:268–72, 1962. **10797**

Important article which complements his 1968 study. [VK]

Wiese, Benno von. Liebe und Welt in Claudels Drama Der seidene Schuh. GRM 1: 35–47, 1951. *Also in his:* Der Mensch in der Dichtung. Studien zur deutschen und europäischen Literatur. Dusseldorf, Bagel, 1958. p. 261–76.   **10798**

The relationship to the world and to divine order as shown in Prouhèze's love for Rodrigue. This interpretation is a useful approach to the work, but does not plumb its depths. [VK]

Wood, Michael. The theme of the prison in Le soulier de satin. FS 22:225–38, 1968.   **10799**

Explores meaning of imprisonment for Camille, Prouhèze, Dona Honoria, Pélage. Traces use of body as jail and earth as prison throughout play until Prouhèze escapes through death's door and Rodrigue in chains finds freedom in God. [LLG]

Tête d'or

Blanchet, André. Tête d'or est-il païen? Et 303:289–305, 1959.   **10800**

The play is "un cocktail... des différentes variétés de l'alcool païen," with, however, Christian values; worth reading, if only to wonder how Blanchet can arrive at his summation: that *Tête d'or* is essentially Christian, "mais de la bonne manière, c'est-à-dire sans rien renier des valeurs païennes." [WHM]

Bozon-Scalzitti, Yvette. Le verset claudélien. Une étude du rythme, Tête d'or. Minard, 1965. 72 p. (ALM, 63)   **10801**

A worthwhile and intelligent analysis of tonic, musical and prosodic rhythm in *Tête d'or*, containing frequent references to C.'s *Soulier de satin*. [JFE]
Reviews: D. Bouverot in FMonde 35:314–15, 1967; J. Piemme in RLV 34:211–12, 1968.

Brady-Papadopoulou, Valentini. The archetypal structure of Claudel's Tête d'or. RR 67:187–99, 1976.   **10802**

Attempts explanation of manner in which symbols are organized and interrelate. Uses mythic, anthropological, structural and psychoanalytic devices to examine imagery of four elements and

hero's relationship to them. Opposition between symbols presented as thesis-antithesis which resolves into synthesis. [LLG]

Brunel, Pierre. Tête d'or 1949. RLM 114–16 (PCl 2):47–71, 1965.   **10803**

C.'s aversion to *Tête d'or* grew out of the hero's resemblance to Hitler. In 1951 C. recognized that the play was too difficult to adapt to a contemporary context, that of the World War II concentration camps. If the play is not entirely successful, it is in part because C. is ill at ease in the popular language he chooses to use. [JPC]

Chujo, Shinobu. La signification du Caucase dans Tête d'or de Paul Claudel. ELLF 16: 27–40, 1970.   **10804**

Collection of interesting data on role and historical reasons for choice of Caucasus. Location is symbol of border between materialistic Europe of C.'s youth, conquered by Tête d'or, and spiritual, mysterious Asia revealed by Princess. Informative on C.'s readings, though somewhat superficial. [NH]

Fragonard, Marie-Madeleine. Tête d'or ou l'imagination mythique chez Paul Claudel. Association des Amis de l'E.N.S. [1968?] 68 p. (Collection de l'Ecole normale supérieure de jeunes filles [ex Sèvres])   **10805**

A study in four parts of C.'s first complete play tracing its heritage back to Aeschylus, Shakespeare, Nietzsche, Wagner, Lautréamont, Rimbaud. Close textual analysis, study of the imagery, with abundant quotations and frequent reference to a broad mythological and even anthropological perspective for the interpretation of the motifs of Fire, Earth, Sun and Vegetation. Original and suggestive treatment, without, however, proposing a central structuring principle for the interpretation of the mythological dimension. A must for the archetypal critic. [VB]
Review: J. Petit in BSPC 29:19–20, 1968.

Horry, Ruth N. Claudel's Tête d'or. FR 35: 279–86, 1962.   **10806**

Rapid survey of the symbolism of *Tête d'or*, which Horry sees as the overture to all of C.'s later works. Good general treatment of themes and symbols but article lacks profundity. [SEH]

Lamiral, Jean. Tête d'or de Paul Claudel ou la royauté théâtrale de la parole. *In:* Approches. Essais sur la poésie moderne de langue française. Les belles lettres, 1971. p. 25–40. (AFLSHN no. 17, 1971) 10807

Well-written but essentially lyrical commentary which conveys little objective meaning except for a suggestion that the play is polyphonic, a point which is belabored but not proved. [DWA]

Morisot, Jean-Claude. L'histoire et le mythe dans Tête d'or. RLM 150–52 (PCl 4):7–29, 1967. 10808

Morisot strives to decipher through *Tête d'or* the meaning which C. saw in History as it pertains to the relationship between the individual and the masses, the West and the East. Between History, which is oriented toward the past, and myth, turned toward the future, C. chose the latter. [JPC]

————. Tête d'or ou les aventures de la volonté. RLM 44–45:113–96, 1959. 10809

Well-written running commentary on the play which may be of use to someone specializing in the subject but which leaves much to be desired because of its impressionistic nature and failure to present any conclusions. [DWA]

Oswald, Werner. Die symbolische Bezüge in P. Claudels Tête d'or. NS 2:61–72, 1963. *Trans.:* Les références symboliques dans Tête d'or. CRB 65:27–44, 1968. 10810

Investigates the symbolic relations in the three main characters of the play and reaches the conclusion that the play represents C.'s own conversion as allegorical, religious morality. Article is a condensation of conclusions of Oswald's dissertation. [VK]

Paoletti, Floriane. Tête d'or 1889–1894. RLM 144–16 (PCl 2):25–45, 1965. 10811

Does not make an esthetic judgment on the two versions of the play but attempts to explain C.'s intentions. C. sought greater precision of meaning. [JPC]

Paul Claudel. Gallimard, 1968. 120 p. (CRB, 65) 10812

An interesting but not indispensable number containing articles on *Tête d'or*

by Henri Pichette, Camille Bourniquel, Werner Oswald and Jean Duvignaud as well as the third version of the play as contained in C.'s ms. [JFE]

Paul Claudel devant Tête d'or. René Julliard, 1959. 126 p. (CRB, 27) 10813

Contains a group of mildly interesting articles, some excerpts from the C.-Copeau correspondence, and a letter from C. to Florent Schmitt concerning possible staging of *Tête d'or*. [JFE]

Rivière, Charles. Le roi des abeilles. VL 225:699–701, 1970. *And:* Interrogations sur le vocabulaire local de Claudel dans Tête d'or. VL 256:375–81, 1973. *And:* Claudel et l'inspiration rurale dans Tête d'or. VL 267:341–44, 1974. *And:* Claudel et la vie rurale dans Tête d'or. VL 268:403–11, 1974. *And:* Claudel et les travaux des champs dans Tête d'or. VL 269:465–71, 1974. 10814

An unsystematic but interesting series of articles on rustic side of *Tête d'or*, ranging from C.'s knowledge of bees, to the Tardenois vocabulary, descriptions of local customs, and allusions to local history such as the battle of Valmy. [DWA]

Robert, Catherine. La nuit et la terre dans Tête d'or. RLM 245–48 (PCl 7):25–40, 1970. 10815

Reliable summary of the use and meaning of these two elements but with no apparent order or conclusion. [HMW]

Simon, Alfred. Tête d'or: pour un théâtre barbare. Esp 279:778–83, 1959. 10816

Sees *Tête d'or* as a foreshadowing and prophecy of later works of C. The play should not be dismissed merely because it is a youthful work and one which C. later in life believed was not representative of him. [SEH]

Tête d'or et les débuts littéraires. Gallimard, 1959. 263 p. (CahPC, 1) 10817

Important collection of documents essential for knowledge of early works. Includes remarks on early influences, in particular Mallarmé's, and the brief correspondence with him, as well as the correspondence with Pottecher. Letters from father offer fascinating insight into paternal influence. Letters kept by C. showing contemporary reaction to *Tête d'or* also provide view of literary in-

fluences and relations. Important articles by Varillon on symbolism of doors and by Wahl on time as applied to nature and paintings of nature in C.'s works. [LLG]
Reviews: C. Bourniquel in Esp 279: 783–86, 1959; J. Madaule in Eur 367–68:261–68, 1959.

Tissier, André. Tête d'or de Paul Claudel, étude analytique et dramaturgique. Société d'éd. d'enseignement supérieur, 1968. 333 p.   **10818**
Thorough, excellent study of C.'s first complete play. Genesis of the text, discussion of its three versions and of the problems involved in its performance. Includes a study of the symbolism, Biblical and pagan, implicit in the characters and the main themes, and a study of style, dramatic form and content, carried out in a sequential analysis, line by line, of certain key passages of the play. The most complete study of Tête d'or. [VB]

The Trilogy

Augst, Bertrand. L'otage de Paul Claudel. RR 53:32–51, 1962.   **10819**
Examines themes, structure and sources of play as well as critical opinion. Points out links with classics and myth of Job in major theme of revolt and conflict between man and God. [LLG]

Avré, Barna M. L'otage de Paul Claudel: essai de psychologie littéraire. Préface de Henri Guillemin. Avant-propos de Paul Bonnet. Ottawa, Quebec, Le soleil, 1961. 122 p.   **10820**
Superficial, but well documented study of L'otage, with reference to mss., sources, and bibliography. [MR]
Review: H. Waters in Ren 15:54–56, 1962.

Brunel, Pierre. L'otage de Paul Claudel ou le théâtre de l'énigme. ALM 53:1–48, 1964.   **10821**
Remarkably clear and scholarly analysis of the play both from the point of view of its conscious artistic structure and meaning and from the point of view of the inadvertencies and intentional anachronisms. Highly recommended to anyone concerned with this play. [DWA]

Cattaui, Georges. Le cycle des Coûfontaine et le mystère d'Israël. Desclée De Brouwer, 1968. 252 p. (Temps et visages)   **10822**
A misleading and frequently disappointing study in a series normally devoted by publisher to works with religious or spiritual tone: misleading because much of it rambles in generalities and disappointing because of its frequent lack of depth. [JFE]
Reviews: L. Bolle in Cr 262:287–88, 1969; C. Cordié in SFr 13:186, 1969; A. Delcampe in LR 25:320–22, 1971; C. Galpérine in BSPC 33:8–9, 1969; W. Matheson in FR 43:172–73, 1969–70; R. Tavernier in RdP 75, no. 12:36, 1968; R. Tedjan in TR 250:225, 1968; M. Wood in FS no. 3:310–11, 1970.

————. La symbolique de Claudel et le Cycle des Coûfontaine. Cr 99:675–90, 1955.   **10823**
Describes C.'s passage from the subjective and personal vision in his works to the constructive, objective view, with composition dominating poetic inspiration. Insists on the interpenetration of the natural and the supernatural in thematic terms and traces the development of love and beatitude in the Coûfontaine cycle through references to the Beatrice and Tristan and Isolde models. [TJ]

Gouhier, Henri. La trilogie. RLM 150–52 (PCl 4):31–42, 1967.   **10824**
C.'s trilogy is to French theater what Shakespeare's Histories are to the English. While indifferent to the historicity of his episodes, C. sought to find the true meaning of history. His is a poeticized history. [JPC]

Kempf, Jean-Pierre, and Jacques Petit. Etudes sur la Trilogie de Claudel. 1: L'otage. [M. J. Minard], 1966. 67 p. (ALM 69; Archives claudéliennes, 5)   **10825**
Brief exposition of origins, sources, and influences of L'otage. Numerous quotations from C.'s Journal and letters trace the evolution of ideas and writing process. Compares different versions by juxtaposing lines of dialog from various mss. and by tracing psychological development of characters. [SEH]
Review: M. Lioure in RHL 68:330–31, 1968.

————. Etudes sur la Trilogie de Claudel. 2: Le pain dur. [M. J. Minard], 1967. 47 p. (ALM 77; Archives claudéliennes, 6) **10826**

Cursory notes on sources, influences, structure, theme, origins and religious meaning of *Le pain dur*. Points to personal circumstances of author as influential factor in genesis of play. [SEH] Review: A. Tissier in RHL 69:879, 1969.

————. Etudes sur la Trilogie de Claudel. 3: Le père humilié. [M. J. Minard], 1968. 47 p. (ALM 87; Archives claudéliennes, 7) **10827**

Historical and symbolic themes had little importance in the play's genesis since C. did not intend to elaborate a situation or a symbol so much as to prolong the destinies of the characters. Consequently, the play tends to become a dialog, the dramatic action being limited to two encounters between Orian and Pensée (II,2; III,2). The fundamental oppositions of life/death and the future/the past dominate the structure, characters, themes and images, anticipating the esthetics of *Le soulier de satin*. [HMW]

Wolff, Ernst Georg. Dogma, Geschichte und Mythos im neuzeitlichen Drama. L'Otage von Paul Claudel. Zurich, Beer, 1956. 42 p. **10828**

Tries to justify in a philosophical and theological way the inherent problems of the drama. Some rather interesting remarks about the play are lost in the general thought process. [VK]

La ville

Coquet, Jean-Claude. Le système des modalités et l'analyse transformationnelle du discours: La ville de Paul Claudel (première et deuxième versions). *In his:* Sémiotique littéraire. Maison Mame, 1973. p. 147–254. **10829**

By eschewing literary and biographical criticism and using a system of modals (the verbs *savoir, pouvoir, vouloir*) and a system of pro-forms (the pronouns *je, on, ça*) to discover the basic identity of the characters through their transformations of quality/function features, Coquet discovers amazingly simple linguistic structures underlying both versions of this often bewildering play. Although these findings frequently diverge from Petit's (*see* 10504 and 10834), they do not so much invalidate as complement them. An exemplary, essential study. [HMW]

Emmanuel, Pierre. Au cœur de La ville. Esp 234:77–83, 1956. **10830**

An interpretative review of Jean Vilar's production of *La ville* in 1956 in Avignon. In arguing that the character Lâlâ occupies the play's thematic center, the author treats event and character as the fragmentary elements of a dramatic language which communicates an absolute and ideal vision. The author presents C.'s technique and vision of the spiritual theater as a form of the symbolist esthetic. [TJ]

Malicet, Michel, and Jacques Petit. L'hermétisme claudélien. RLM 209–11 (PCl 6):55–78, 1969. **10831**

These intrepid sleuths not only trace many of the arcane allusions and images in *La ville I* to things seen and read— the Bible, the classics (Homer, Virgil, Seneca, Dante), the Kalevala, Japanese legends, and even Mark Twain— but suggest why and how C.'s creative mind worked in elaborating certain hermetic patterns. [HMW]

————. Quelques obscurités de La ville. RLM 209–11 (PCl 6):79–98, 1969. **10832**

This catalog presents a page by page list and clarification of a hundred mystifications. A handy résumé and extension of their preceding article, despite great variations in the importance and persuasiveness of the entries. [HMW]

Marie, Dominique. Les images. RLM 209–11 (PCl 6):9–33, 1969. **10833**

Distilling the essence of a vaster, systematic analysis, this study groups the manifold images of the first version of *La ville* under the themes of ennui, dreams of peace, and revolt. Finds the unique structure of the drama and much of the characterization subtly built on the imagery. Variations of an image or a theme replace evolution of the characters here and reveal an early obsession by C. with certain images and situations. [HMW]

Petit, Jacques. La structure. RLM 209–11 (PCl 6):35–53, 1969. **10834**

Deepens analysis given in his critical ed. (*see* 10504) and embroidered by D. Marie, *supra*. Sees it as the drama of C.'s hesitations before his conversion, with most of the characters acting out one of C.'s reactions between 1886–1890. Masked by this movement of dispersal is a linear movement opposing Besme, Bavon, Ligier to Avare and Ivors and foreshadowing the "antagonistic couple" structure of subsequent dramas... and especially the multiplicity of *Le soulier de satin*. Penetrating insights; persuasive hypothesis. [HMW]

Minor Plays

Barrault, Jean-Louis. Sous le vent des îles Baléares. CRB 80:3–10, 1972.   **10835**
Thoughts on his production of the play. Barrault on C. is always worth reading. [WHM]

Delcourt, Marie. Claudel et Euripide. RHL 61:599–602, 1961.   **10836**
Source study of *Protée*. Shows departures as well as borrowings from the Odyssey. Suggests influence of German translations of Euripides on C. [LLG]

Mettra, Jacques. Le mythe d'Hélène dans le Protée de Claudel. *In:* Actes du IVᵉ congrès de l'Association internationale de littérature comparée, Fribourg, 1964. V. 2. The Hague and Paris, Mouton, 1966. p. 1084–96.   **10837**
Competent analysis of a minor play. [MR]

Nagy, Moses M. Conversations dans le Loiret Cher at Carré Thorigny. ClaudelS 1, no. 4:50–59, 1974.   **10838**
Account of this somewhat amorphous drama in poetic prose which had a great success in 1974 with 150 performances at Carré Thorigny. The stage version was arranged by Silvia Monfort from a much longer original. [CC]

Petit, Jacques. Le premier drame de Claudel: Une mort prématurée. Les belles lettres, 1970. 117 p. (AnLUB, 117)   **10839**
Attempts to trace images and themes of fragmentary first play in the light of Claudelian symbolism of later plays. Juxtaposes lines from *Une mort* with lines from other dramas in order to suggest the subject and structure of the early play and to trace the evolution of such images as night, the illusions of the world, explosions, the trap, and such themes as the separation of lovers, exile, death, Satan. [SEH]
Review: J.-N. Segrestaa in RHL 73: 924–25, 1973.

Roberto, Eugène. Le jet de pierre. *In:* Formes et figures. *See* 10597. p. 75–96.   **10840**
Superb study of sense, structure, form and gesture in C.'s play of that title. [JFE]

Minor Prose

Biard, Joseph. Les sept transfixions de Notre Dame, d'après L'épée et le miroir de Paul Claudel. Tournai, Casterman, 1948. 152 p.   **10841**
An almost devotional attempt to provide scriptural background and commentary for C.'s text, written by a cleric who claims frequently to have used Claudelian texts in his sermons. [JFE]

Blanchet, André. L'élaboration par Claudel de son article sur Rimbaud. RHL 67: 759–75, 1967.   **10842**
Examines sources of C.'s knowledge of Rimbaud's life. Concludes C. saw in the other a double, equally resistant, who then capitulated to conversion. Traces changing attitude from Rimbaud as mystic to that of prophet to explain why, after early refusals, C. finally agreed to write about him. Compares two versions of article and shows centrality of Bremond's influence. [LLG]

Busser, Bernard. Des questions que je me pose à moi-même...: les formes du dédoublement intérieur dans les Commentaires bibliques. RLM 271–75 (PCl 8): 125–47, 1971.   **10843**
Concise and thoughtful essay demonstrating that the dramatic genius of C. is clearly evident in the structure and style of his *Commentaires bibliques*. Basing his arguments on well-chosen citations from the various Biblical commentaries, Busser maintains that C. uses the techniques of dialog, interrogation, and prosopopoeia to portray the "dédoublement intérieur" of C. as he reveals his attitudes and beliefs concerning the Bible. [SEH]

Lubac, Henri de. Claudel théologien. RechD p. 25–29, 1969. *Also in:* Les critiques de notre temps et Claudel. *See* 10594. p. 54–58. **10844**
The convergence of opposites as a basis of C.'s Biblical exegesis studied here provides a helpful clue to C.'s understanding of the Bible and to his linking of Old and New Testament. [LLG]

Madaule, Jacques. Claudel, contemporain de la Bible. RdP 74, no. 7–8:43–57, 1967. **10845**
Succinct, thought-provoking appreciation of C.'s translations of the Psalms. By using simple, straightforward language and style, C. invites his readers to participate in his own prayer. C.'s translations have the value of original compositions as he works diligently with the text of the Vulgate in order to make his rendition meaningful to his contemporaries. [SEH]

Moreau, Pierre. A propos de La lanterne aux pivoines de Paul Claudel. RLC 42: 445–48, 1968. **10846**
Compares 1912 and 1942 version of Chinese tale, the former imbued with realistic fantasy not unlike Mérimée's work. Interesting note on stylistic changes made by calmer, older writer. [LLG]

Petit, Jacques, and Charles Galpérine. Claudel prosateur. RdP 72, no. 5:65–75, 1965. **10847**
Repetitious and prolix review of C.'s prose compositions: his "conversations" and his "paraboles." Cites C.'s contrast between prose and poetry: the aim of prose is instruction, the aim of poetry, delight. Attempts, with limited success, to distinguish various types of prose compositions in C.'s work. [SEH]

Riffaterre, Michael. The art criticism of Paul Claudel. ASLHM 30:151–64, 1959. **10848**
A general overview. Treats C.'s subjective art criticism as attention to a painting's creation, as another way of reaching God. Examines esthetic and metaphysical principles of the poetic criticism in *L'œil écoute.* Suggests use of satire is stylistic tool to bring out salient feature of a painting which makes C.'s art criticism a personal drama. Super-

seded by Mouton's *Les intermittences du regard chez l'écrivain.* [LLG]

Vigée, Claude. Paul Claudel et l'Apocalypse: Le poète comme témoin du sacré. *In his:* Révolte et louange: essais sur la poésie moderne. Corti, 1962. p. 71–81. **10849**
C.'s commentary on the *Apocalypse* interpreted as an identification of C.'s own "activité poétique" with the "opération de l'esprit divin à travers l'histoire humaine." [DWA]

———. Paul Claudel, the Apocalypse, and Israel. Ren 8:196–202, 1956. **10850**
A review article of *Paul Claudel interroge l'Apocalypse* which helps to clarify the contradictory nature of C.'s attitude towards the role of Israel. It points out that C. states both that Israel will be ascendant over the Christian and also that the Jew will merge into the Christian. [LLG]

Special Topics: Books

Andersen, Margaret. Claudel et l'Allemagne. Ottawa, Eds. de l'univ. d'Ottawa, 1965. 358 p. (CahCC, 3) **10851**
Shows influence of Germanic thought on C.'s dramas and effect of his theater in Austria, Germany and Switzerland. C. considered representative of Catholicism and European culture, a model of theatrical innovation for expressionists, Sorge, and Brecht, a bearer of Christian comfort for postwar Germans desiring expiation. Important study. Extensive bibliography of translations and works about C. in German. [LLG]
Review: S. Jauernick in GRM 18: 215–16, 1968.

Andrieu, Jacques. La foi dans l'œuvre de Paul Claudel. Presses univ. de France, 1955. 195 p. (Nouvelle recherche) **10852**
A major study on C., thoroughly documented, admirably written, and objectively presented, although the author clearly shares C.'s views and regards C.'s work as "un véritable bréviaire de mystique chrétienne." After a preliminary chapter on "Les nourritures terrestres," which underlines Gidean similarities in the period of *Tête d'or* defined as C.'s representation of man without faith, the critic passes on to C.'s conversion and then spends the rest of his book defining C.'s theology which he seems to regard as entirely orthodox.

Very useful for a clear definition of C.'s views on religion, this study, except to draw occasional examples, belies its title by a total lack of attention to the literary works. [DWA]

Review: M. LaVallée in Ren 8:202–08, 1956.

Babilas, Wolfgang. Das Frankreichbild in Paul Claudels Personnalité de la France. Münster, Aschendorff, 1958. 111 p. (Forschungen zur romanischen Philologie, 4)
10853

Makes an inventory, according to H. Lausberg's method, of each element of this secondary poem and studies all passages known to him since ancient times in which similar thoughts have already been presented. Though he studies certain aspects of C.'s image of France before the Second World War, this minute philological work on the poem adds little to our understanding of C. For further treatment of this subject see his "Zu Claudels Frankreichbild" in Archiv 195:144–53, 1959 and his "Zur Interpretationen von Claudels Personnalité de la France" in Archiv 196:36–60, 1960. [VK]

Reviews: J. Boly in LR 14:176–77, 1960; J. Petit in RHL 60:261–62, 1960.

Beaumont, Ernest. The theme of Beatrice in the plays of Claudel. London, Rockliff, 1954. ix, 102 p. *Trans.:* Le sens de l'amour dans le théâtre de Claudel: le thème de Béatrice. Trans. by Huguette Foster. Lettres modernes, 1958. 161 p. (Thèmes et mythes, 5)
10854

Sees recurrent theme of C.'s dramas as the transmutation of human into divine love through the spiritualizing effect of woman. Compares C.'s heroines, all of whom become an "image de la Beauté éternelle," to Dante's Beatrice. Two chapters added to French ed. deal with role of woman in early plays of C. and in his works of Biblical symbolism. Selections previously published as "La femme dans les premières pièces de Claudel" in RLM 30:425–56, 1957. [SEH]

Becker, Aimé. Claudel et l'interlocuteur invisible. Nizet, 1974. 346 p.
10855

Excellent, careful, systematic and well-documented study of the theme of "l'appel" in C.'s dramatic work prior to *Partage de midi,* but particularly in the first and second versions of each of the

three plays *Tête d'or, La ville* and *La jeune fille Violaine.* The author makes a strong case for greater patristic influence in these plays than previous critics have, and though his religious prejudice shows through occasionally, this is basically a fine piece of scholarship. [JFE]

Reviews: P. Berthier in Et 343:308, 1975; H. de Lubac in BSPC 58–59:28–30, 1975.

Donnard, Jean Hervé. Trois écrivains devant Dieu: Claudel, Mauriac, Bernanos. Société d'éd. d'enseignement supérieur, 1966. 55 p.
10856

Comparative analysis in three writers of rivalry between faith and poetic inspiration. C. influenced by Balzac, haunted by doubt, and tortured by need to regain God. Versions of *Violaine,* trilogy, and *Soulier* exemplify both temptation of literature and its use as means to sing God's praises. Interesting examination of problems inherent in Catholic literature. [LLG]

Du Sarment, Agnès. Claudel et la liturgie. Bruges, Desclée De Brouwer, 1946. 188 p.
10857

Examines influence of Catholic liturgy and religion and Biblical inspiration on C. from orthodox religious viewpoint. Thorough inventory of themes, symbols, ideas; discussion of form much less complete. Extensive quotations and paraphrase with little analysis. [NH]

Egli-Hegglin, Alice. Le thème du totum simul dans l'œuvre de Paul Claudel. Zurich, P. G. Keller, 1969. xi, 85 p. **10858**

A somewhat dry and loose-jointed, though accurate, examination of spatial and temporal simultaneity, a theme treated at much greater length by others. [JFE]

Reviews: Y. Bozon-Scalzitti in MP 69:95, 1971–72; J. Erwin in RR 65:142, 1974; A. Espiau de la Maëstre in RFor no. 1–2:189–90, 1970.

Gadoffre, Gilbert. Claudel et l'univers chinois. Gallimard, 1968. 393 p. (CahPC, 8)
10859

Excellent, comprehensive study of influence of Far East on C. and his work, his attitudes toward Eastern culture and religions, his contributions to Western understanding. Juxtaposes official consular duties and reports with creative

works inspired by travels. Maps, extensive bibliographies, including manuscript sources, chronological listing of C. works linked to China. [LLG]
Reviews: E. Beaumont in MLR 65: 175–76, 1970, and in FS 25:104–05, 1971; G. Cesbron in LR 24:300–02, 1970; Y. Florenne in QL 70:10–11, 1969; J. Freilich in ClaudelS 6:23–26, 1970; M.-F. Guyard in BSPC 34:10–11, 1969; H. Waters in FR 43:684–85, 1970; J. Wilhelm in ZFSL 80:183–84, 1970.

Halter, Raymond. La Vierge Marie dans la vie et l'œuvre de Paul Claudel. Tours, Mame, 1958. 237 p.   **10860**
Focuses on C.'s religious thought as seen in his works. Basic idea valid: C.'s Virgin Mary is ideal image of virtues of purity, charity, sacrifice; mediates between humanity and God. Exaggerates Mary's role and religious interpretation at the expense of other concepts. Second part on Biblical commentaries more original. Selections of C.'s writings on Mary valuable, but too separate from preceding study. Some errors of fact. [NH]

Mennemeier, Brigitta. Der agressive Claudel. Eine Studie zu Periphrasen und Metaphern im Werke Paul Claudels. Münster, Aschendorff, 1957. xvi, 188 p. (Forschungen zur romanischen Philologie, 2)   **10861**
By making an inventory of aggressive figures of speech with the help of H. Lausberg's method, Mennemeier concentrates on C.'s critique of the distance of humanity from God and on his critique of time. Aim of the investigation is the grasping of the points of attack and the recognition of the points of reference. C.'s aggressivity is inflamed above all by positivism and scholarly credulity, by Protestant Germany and Soviet Russia. Ideological bases for the critique and consequent points of reference are intransigent Catholicism and nationalism. [VK]
Reviews: M. Bémol in RHL 59:562–63, 1959; C. Cordié in Pai 88–89, 1964; J.-M. Gautier in RFor 69:473–74, 1957.

Petit, Jacques. Claudel et l'usurpateur. Desclée De Brouwer, 1971. 211 p.   **10862**
A brilliant essay, elegantly written, completely devoid of jargon, and yet reducing C. to a formula of which any structuralist would be proud. Unquestionably one of the most significant books on C. C.'s theater is dominated by the usurper, the character who takes all—Tête d'or, Léchy, Mara, Turelure, Camille. Even though the usurper might represent Satan, C.'s real sympathies go to him, because—as Petit finally explains—his subconscious life was dominated by his personal struggle with the usurper, his own sister Camille. In his theater, C. is emotionally both the usurper and the victim—Camille and Rodrigue. [DWA]
Review: L. Bourke in ClaudelN 9: 22–23, 1972.

Plourde, Michel. Paul Claudel. Une musique du silence. Montreal, Presses l'univ. de Montréal, 1970. xviii, 393 p.   **10863**
Uneven but important study of silence as an essential condition of C.'s poetry, as a central concern in his theater, and as a constant preoccupation in his art criticism and in "prayer," his literary and personal communications to God. [JFE]
Reviews: E. Beaumont in FS 26:350–52, 1972; A. Blanc in ELit 4:121–24, 1971; P. Claudel in BSPC 40:17, 1970; M. Deuel in MLR 68:663–64, 1973; A. Espiau de la Maëstre in RFor 83: 640–41, 1971; M. Lioure in RHL 71: 530–31, 1971; J. P. in EthF p. 29–31, May–June 1971; L. Somville in Cul 31:364–66, 1970; J. Streignart in ECl 39:400–01, 1971; H. Waters in FR 44:609–10, 1970/1971.

Roy, Paul-Emile, C. S. C. Claudel, poète mystique de la Bible. Montreal and Paris, Fides, 1957. 141 p.   **10864**
A well-printed but totally unsophisticated study, not very useful for assessing C.'s use of the Bible, but interesting for one essential criticism: that C. reads the Bible as a poet and totally rejects, as part of 19th-century scientism, the modern exegesis of the Bible approved by Pius XII. [DWA]

Vachon, André. Le temps et l'espace dans l'œuvre de Paul Claudel. Expérience chrétienne et imagination poétique. Seuil, 1965. 455 p.   **10865**
Brilliant study, centering on the two themes indicated in the title, but covering virtually the entire breadth and scope of C.'s work and thought. Time

and space are first examined in their various figurations in C.'s writings, then expand to become the human and divine dimensions of his universe. Required for serious work on C. [JFE]

Reviews: A. Blanchet in Et 322:435–36, 1965; J. Madaule in BSPC 19:9–11, 1965, in CahPC 6:308–12, 1966, and in Esp 117–26, Jan. 1965; J. Petit in BSPC 27:12–15, 1967; J.-N. Segrestaa in RHL 67:170–71, 1967.

Watson, Harold. Claudel's immortal heroes. A choice of deaths. New Brunswick, N.J., Rutgers univ. press, 1971. xv, 200 p. **10866**

Interesting but uneven and unbalanced study of death and its roles in *Tête d'or, Partage de midi, L'annonce faite à Marie,* and *Le soulier de satin* (with passing reference to C.'s trilogy). Commentary and analysis are especially good in treatment of *Partage de midi.* [JFE]

Reviews: E. Beaumont in FS 27:470–71, 1973; P. Brunel in BSPC 49:58–59, 1973; E. Dubois in MLR 69:423–24, 1974; J. Freilich in ClaudelN 9:23–26, 1972; W. Matheson in MLJ 57:50–51, 1973; M. Nagy in ABR 2:214–25, 1972, and in SCB 33:33, 1973; L. Rièse in MD 15:342–43, 1972–73; H. Waters in FR 46:625–26, 1972–73; M. Wood in RR 66:81–82, 1975.

Special Topics: Articles

Antoine, Gérald. L'art du comique chez Claudel. *In:* Le rire de Paul Claudel. *See* 10612. p. 104–54. **10867**

Major analysis of diversity and richness of C.'s appetite for orgiastic verbal expressions which produce laughter. Numerous examples of plays with letters and words, repetition, incongruous images, use of satire and fantasy. [LLG]

———. L'image de la femme chez Claudel. *In:* Entretiens sur Paul Claudel. *See* 10595. p. 273–88. **10868**

Penetrating presentation of woman as seen primarily in C.'s *Cinq grandes odes* and in *Partage de midi:* woman as mystery; Erato/Ysé; woman as Muse and as Grace. [JFE]

———. Parabole d'Animus et d'Anima: pour faire mieux comprendre certaines

œuvres de Paul Claudel. TLL 13, part 2: 705–23, 1975. **10869**

This penetrating study goes beyond Morisot's *Claudel et Rimbaud* in its treatment of the Animus/Anima theme. Antoine deals with various figurations of the couple in C.'s work, tracing the sense of conflict they represent across three different levels: the poetic and prosodic, the "rimbaldien," and the Biblical. [JFE]

Batard, Yvonne. Claudel critique de la peinture flamande et néerlandaise. *In:* Société française de littérature comparée. Actes du second congrès national. Lille, 30 mai - 2 juin 1957. Didier, 1958. p. 179–84. **10870**

A helpful introduction to C.'s relation to painting. Maintains themes and language are also guides to his pictorial criticism. Choice of subjects often based on affinities with C.'s own style in *L'œil écoute.* [LLG]

Beauvoir, Simone de. Le deuxième sexe, 1. Gallimard, 1949. 510 p. *Trans.:* Claudel and the handmaid of the Lord. *In:* The second sex. Trans. and ed. by H. M. Parshley. Knopf, 1953. p. 224–31. *Also:* Harmondsworth, Penguin, 1972. p. 254–61. **10871**

Original version has no separately entitled subsection and material is spread out in Pt. III of v. 1. Represents feminist view of C. for whom woman is a passive auxiliary, a temptation necessary for salvation. Man, the active partner, heads family and accomplishes God's plans on earth. Examples from several plays. [LLG]

Becker, Aimé. Poésie et mystique: le thème claudélien des sens spirituels. RSRel 43:118–48, 1969. **10872**

Studying C.'s sources and his explications in his writings, particularly in his theater, Becker is pursuing, from his point of view, a theological subject, but, for the literary scholar, he is at the same time organizing in an erudite manner the theme of the "senses" in C.'s work. [DWA]

———. Le premier théâtre de Claudel ou les équivoques de la liberté. RSRel 44:241–87, 1970. *And:* Le drame de la connaissance et de la communion dans le théâtre de Claudel: Du Repos du septième jour (1896) à la seconde Jeune fille Violaine (1898). RSRel 44:363–408,

1970. *And:* L'inexorable appel ou le drame de la vocation de Claudel. RSRel 45:1–44, 1972. **10873**

Scholarly study of C.'s religious vocation from the conversion to the crisis of *Le partage de midi* as seen in his work. From a literary point of view, this amounts to the study of a theme. [DWA]

——. Les sources d'un thème poétique. RSRel 44:34–48, 1970. **10874**

C.'s reading of the Bible and his utilization of the church fathers. An erudite article related to his previous one on the "sens spirituels," adding details but no new ideas. [DWA]

Bernard, Raymond. La description de la mer dans Partage de midi et dans Le soulier de satin. RLM 134–36 (PCl 3):39–48, 1966. **10875**

The sea, one of the original elements and a vital source, is seen as a fundamental reality. It is frequently an element of *Le soulier de satin* although C. does not describe it at length. [JPC]

Brunel, Pierre. Jeux de cartes. RLM 180–82 (PCl 5):123–33, 1968. **10876**

A fascinating look at C.'s use of whist as a dramatic device in *Le pain dur* and of playing card symbols and puns for stylization and irony in *Jeanne d'Arc au bûcher* and other works. [HMW]

——. Der Krieg, la méditation claudélienne sur l'antagonisme franco-allemand. RLM 150–52 (PCl 4):61–82, 1967. **10877**

C. considered separately each of the three wars which took place during his existence and saw no pattern running through them. Mindful of the architecture of history—"la strophe, l'antistrophe et la catastrophe"—he could only hope and pray for peace between the two peoples. [JPC]

——. La nuit dans les Proses bibliques. RLM 245–48 (PCl 7):53–63, 1970. **10878**

Traces C.'s references to light images in his commentaries on the Bible, particularly on the Book of Genesis. C. follows St. John of the Cross in attributing a paradoxical nature to darkness which leads the soul to the contemplation of the Light of God. Well-ordered, sensitive approach to the theme. [SEH]

Bucher, Bernadette. Paul Claudel et le monde amérindien. *In:* Claudel et l'Amérique. *See* 10589. p. 85–121. *Also (excerpts):* L'arrière-plan amérindien de l'Echange. *In:* Actualité de Claudel. *See* 10583. p. 112–33. **10879**

Contends plays of American cycle—*Echange, Soulier,* and *Colomb*—depict pre-New World continent, themes of death, cross, and gold, and historicoreligious spirit of conquest and adventure. Examines sources of, and contradictions in, attitude towards America. Details link in *Echange* between animals and Indians to suggest cosmic backdrop and fundamental religious piety. Laine's failure caused by fatal destiny and lack of moderation. Superficial references to *Soulier* and *Colomb* which abandon nostalgia for past to prepare future through conquest which is destruction of devil. [LLG]

Bugliani, Ann. The theme of love at first sight in Claudel's theater. ClaudelS 3, no. 1:23–29, 1976. **10880**

Love at first sight is often found in the male characters of C.'s drama who are under a compulsion to satisfy a rather impossible ideal or female "soulimage." Bugliani concludes that "this type of love relation is very unstable." [CC]

Burckhardt, Carl J. Paul Claudel und der Ferne Osten. NRs 68:283–97, 1957. *Also in his:* Bildnisse. Frankfurt a.M., Fischer, 1958. p. 167–90. **10881**

Studies C.'s fascination with the Far East and gives biographical details of his sojourn there. Superseded by Gadoffre. [VK]

Cattaui, Georges. Claudel et l'âme juive. *In:* Hommage à Paul Claudel. *See* 10601. p. 58–67. **10882**

Analyzes images relating to Israel. Many of C.'s works become clearer in the light of these remarks. The vocation of Israel, the redemptive mission of Christ, the spirit who carries out the message of the Old Testament show that Israel is the image of the whole human family. Short and concise study, orthodox in tone. [MMN]

Cesbron, Georges. Paul Claudel: cosmos et communion. TLL 10, part 2:149–70, 1972. **10883**

A well-documented essay on what would seem to be an obvious point: that C.'s vision of the universe unites the macrocosm with the microcosm and is the basis both of his poetics and his theology. Perhaps the most interesting part is the passing remark that C. shares this point of view with the Romantics and with Georges de Bouhélier and the poets of the Abbaye. [DWA]

Chambers, Ross. La femme aux yeux bandés —Claudel et le masque de la cécité. RLM 391–97 (PCl 11):189–226, 1974. **10884**

To the two traditional values of the blind (to teach mankind the centrality of the divine, invisible to the sighted; to be a microcosm of a closed universe, whose secret is accessible only to the eye of the spirit), C. adds that of a mask—the blind, or blindfolded, woman who both symbolizes and concretizes the presence of God, a hierophany of truth cloaked in error. Rewarding if limited study of a central image and its ramifications, including C.'s view of the theater and the world. [HMW]

Claudel, Pierre. La bonne humeur claudélienne. *In:* Le rire de Paul Claudel. *See* 10612. p. 73–88. **10885**

Excellent study of C.'s humor as safety valve. Physical and spiritual nature of gaiety and audacity fundamental aspects of C.'s nature. Faith and joy inseparable. [LLG]

Cousin, Françoise. La scène du refus. RLM 180–82 (PCl 5):113–22, 1968. **10886**

Interesting résumé of an unpublished dissertation analyzing the recurring elements, variations, and evolution of the triple refusals so prominent in *L'otage* but present to some degree in most of C.'s dramas. [HMW]

Crubellier, M. Géographie claudélienne. VI 14, no. 5:118–43, 1946. **10887**

Well-written essay on C.'s geography in a poetic and religious sense. An interpretation rather than an inventory of geographical allusions. [DWA]

Espiau de le Maëstre, André. L'ambiguïté de la femme dans la Bible et chez Claudel. ECl 42:176–96, 1974. **10888**

Excellent study of Lâla, as both Wisdom and Madness; Lâla, like Léchy (*L'échange*) is both "sapientiale" and "satanique." Both traditions can be traced back to the Bible. [WHM]

——. Claudel et la musique. LR 13:145–76, 1959. **10889**

C. found in music a metaphysical significance offering at least temporary response to his questions on religion and human destiny. C. was influenced by symbolists' appreciation of music and by Wagner. It is, however, extremely difficult to see impact of Wagner or of any musician on C. in this article. [SEH]

——. De l'art poétique à la célébration orphique de la terre dans la philosophie esthétique de Paul Claudel. ECl 43:179–90, 1975. **10890**

Meticulous examination of developing "musicalization" of C.'s inspiration from the time of the highly "visual" *Art poétique* to the end of his life. [JFE]

——. Job et le problème du mal dans l'œuvre de Claudel. *In:* Entretiens sur Paul Claudel. *See* 10595. p. 301–19. **10891**

Careful, excellent examination of C.'s life-long wrestling with the problem of evil. In tracing C.'s thought on evil from *Tête d'or* to his death, Espiau de la Maëstre concludes the existence of "another" C., one who does not conform to the patent image of a ubiquitously galloping Catholic. [JFE]

——. Le rêve dans la pensée et l'œuvre de Paul Claudel. Lettres modernes, 1973. 63 p. (ALM, 148) **10892**

Extremely interesting, clear and well-written study of oneiric elements in C.'s work, his opinion of, and conscious or unconscious relation to, Freudian thought. Through these elements, C. is linked, in a larger sense, to the Romantic and especially German Romantic tradition. Includes an interesting, if debatable, treatment of *Connaissance de l'Est* and its dream elements. [JFE]

——. Le tragique claudélien. SFr 51:438–49, 1973. **10893**

Rejects monolithic, Madaule-influenced view of C. as optimistic Catholic. Interesting corollary to Merleau-Ponty and Blanchot psycho-criticism. "Tragic" as conflict between muse and grace, art and faith shown extensively in C.'s work. Contends C. fails personally as hero, priest or saint and thus is relegated to role of artist, ever hopeful of finding synthesis of both worlds and ever doubtful of succeeding. [LLG]

Evans, Arthur R., Jr. Firmitas et robur: the column and its meaning in Claudel's work. Sym 19:306–15, 1965.　　　　**10894**

Uses key symbol to examine universality of poet's imagination and verticality of movement and vision in works. Includes broad cultural implications of tree-column symbol. Detailed notes. [LLG]

Gadoffre, Gilbert. La filiation mallarméenne de Paul Claudel. *In:* Entretiens sur Paul Claudel. *See* 10595. p. 33–45.　　**10895**

Excellent examination of the lesson learned by C. from Mallarmé and the symbolist group: the transposition of Wagneresque ideas and practices to a poetic theater. [JFE]

Gandillac, Maurice de. Scission et connaissance d'après l'art poétique de Claudel. RMM 71:412–25, 1966. *Also (rev) in:* Entretiens sur Paul Claudel. *See* 10595. p. 115–30.　　　　　　**10896**

Dense but excellent article on C.'s conception of being. Evaluates some of C.'s debt to Aristotle and makes comparisons of his perception with that of Bergson. [JFE]

Halter, Raymond. Sagesse et Vierge Marie dans l'œuvre de Paul Claudel. TR 129: 114–28, 1958.　　　　　　**10897**

A relatively detailed treatment of C.'s maryology. Mary is seen as having been identified with *Sagesse* from the time of C.'s initial reading of the Bible immediately after his conversion to her final stature as *Reine de l'Univers.* The author, himself a member of the Marianist order, frequently waxes enthusiastic over his subject. [JFE]

Kimura, Reiko. Le thème du feu dans les premières pièces de Paul Claudel. ELLF 20:53–69, 1972.　　　　　**10898**

Examines fire image as expression of central structure and movement of early plays and its ambivalent role as destructive force which brings rebirth. Oversimplifies pattern; presents simple list with little effort at synthesis, al-though basic idea is valid. Excessive repetition and summarizing of contents of plays. [NH]

Labriolle, Jacqueline de. Le thème de la rose dans l'œuvre de Paul Claudel. RLM 134–36 (PCl 3):66–103, 1966.　　**10899**

This theme is related to C.'s major themes (the tree, water, fire) by its religious aspects. Though less prominent, it occurs frequently in C.'s work. The rose symbolizes asceticism in the conquest of joy. Excellent study. [JPC]

Lesort, Paul-André. L'amour et la vallée de larmes. *In:* Entretiens sur Paul Claudel. *See* 10595. p. 81–103.　　**10900**

Important treatment of love and separation throughout C.'s work. [JFE]

Lioure, Michel. Claudel et l'Allemagne. ZFSL 78:346–62, 1968; 79:4–31, 1969.　　　　　　　　**10901**

Thoughtful, well-researched study of the evolution of C.'s attitude toward Germany. [SEH]

Madaule, Jacques. Le tragique chez Claudel. *In:* Le théâtre tragique. Ed. by Jean Jacquot. Centre national de la recherche scientifique, 1962. p. 421–38.　**10902**

Begins with the definition: "Est tragique tout ce qui relève du *fatum,* de la nécessité, ce qui met radicalement en échec la liberté humaine." In this sense, C. had an early obsession with death which came out in his unfinished play *Une mort prématurée* and in *Tête d'or.* After his conversion, C. gradually put this fatalistic tragedy behind him and substituted a new concept of the "libre réponse de l'homme à l'invitation de Dieu." A very thorough study which covers the theme of tragedy in C.'s entire dramatic work. [DWA]

Malicet, Michel. Orphée et Eurydice ou l'histoire d'une image. RLM 245–48 (PCl 7):65–104, 1970.　　　　**10903**

Perspicacious and sensitive article tracing the evolution of C.'s attitude toward woman and his identification of woman and night in the figure of Eurydice. [SEH]

Mettra, Jacques. La bacchanale dans la poésie de Claudel. CahOr no. 6:64–77, 1966.　　　　　　　　**10904**

Thorough study of the bacchanalian theme in C.'s works. This is not an example of complaisance on C.'s part, but an attempt to make "de la pulsation fiévreuse...un déploiement cérémonial, une liturgie." [DWA]

Meylan, Pierre. Variations sur le nom de Claudel. *In his:* Les écrivains et la musique II. Les modernes français. Etudes de musique et de littérature comparées. Lausanne, Ed. du Cervin, 1952. p. 49–61. **10905**

C.'s pre-conversion interest in Wagner, his greater interest in Beethoven because of his friendship with Romain Rolland, and then his eventual violent repudiation of Wagner. Mentions also his collaboration with Milhaud and Honegger. Brief study which has been filled in more thoroughly by other commentators. [DWA]

Moreau, Pierre. Des parfums, des couleurs et des sons chez Paul Claudel. BSPC 26: 9–13, 1967. **10906**

Stresses C.'s keen portrayal of all senses and sensations on the physical as well as spiritual levels, in keeping with symbolist doctrine and new transcendental values, which reacted sharply around 1900 against previous age of mechanistic rationalism. [CC]

Mouton, Jean. Paul Claudel et la peinture. *In:* Entretiens sur Paul Claudel. *See* 10595. p. 153–71. *Also (rev.) in his:* Les intermittences du regard chez l'écrivain. Desclée De Brouwer, 1973. p. 223–49. **10907**

Excellent analysis of C.'s assessment of, and ideas on, a sister art: painting as "magic mirror" linking visible and invisible worlds; time and space in painting; the reproduction of the "vivant;" light and its significance; graphic art and its relation to God in C.'s thought. [JFE]

Nagy, Moses. La condition surnaturelle de l'homme et la souffrance terrestre dans le théâtre de Claudel. RUL 15:131–51, 1960. **10908**

Chapter IV of thesis on *La joie dans l'œuvre de Paul Claudel.* Touches upon *Tête d'or* and *La ville* but is largely devoted to suffering in *Partage de midi* and alterations in the versions of the theme of *La jeune fille Violaine.* Sees lack of critical understanding of C.'s joy to be based upon a failure to see

the supernatural vocation which C.'s characters undertake. [WB]

Petit, Jacques. A propos d'une fantaisie de Claudel: L'escargot, la coquille et la spirale. RLM 134–36 (PCl 3):7–25, 1966. **10909**

L'escargot is studied in the context of C.'s *bestiaire spirituel* and through all the aspects of his esthetic experience. Petit shows C.'s *inquiétude* and depth. Original perspective. [JPC]

————. Claudel et le double: esquisse d'une problématique. RLM 271–75 (PCl 8):7–31, 1971. **10910**

Rapid survey in general terms of the technique of "dédoublement" of characters in C.'s work. Good introduction to more specialized studies of the theme, but the wide range of topics treated in the article does not lead to a cogent conclusion. [SEH]

————. Le décor nocturne. RLM 245–48 (PCl 7):7–24, 1970. **10911**

After listing nocturnal images in thirteen plays, attempts to determine the dramatic value of the "décor nocturne." Contrasts the different attitudes toward night in the various plays and endeavors to establish the fundamental cause of the differences. Intriguing and potentially fertile idea, but the article is inconclusive. [SEH]

————. L'histoire dans la lumière de l'Apocalypse. RLM 150–52 (PCl 4):83–100, 1967. **10912**

According to C., the Apocalypse gives a meaning to the Bible as a whole. Turning to the future in his attempts to interpret history, C. has an apocalyptic perspective. The Apocalypse is at the core of his exegetic and historical thought. It also had an influence on his dramatic work.

————. La pensée religieuse de Claudel. RechD p. 47–57, 1964. *Also:* Claudel, lecteur de la Bible. *In:* Les critiques de notre temps et Claudel. *See* 10594. p. 58–71. **10913**

An important commentary on C.'s poetic religion. The use of "répétition" as both recurrence and rehearsal for Biblical understanding and exegesis adds a dimension to Rywalski's study. The Bible's dramatic force in C.'s life is examined in the *Journal* as a source of the increasing centrality of religion in all his writings. [LLG]

Petriconi, Hellmuth. Das Meer und der Tod in drei Gedichten von Mallarmé, Rimbaud, Claudel. RJ 2:282–95, 1949. *Also in:* Interpretationen französischer Gedichte. Ed. by Kurt Wais. Darmstadt, Wissenschaftliche Buchgesellschaft, 1970. p. 334–52. (Ars interpretandi, 3) **10914**

Studies C.'s *Ballade* together with Rimbaud's *Bateau ivre* and Mallarmé's *Brise marine* in order to clarify the connection between the presentation of the ocean and the yearning for death. He sees in the *Ballade* the human death wish treated without relation to Christianity. [VK]

Pinguet, Maurice. Claudel's Japan. *In:* The France of Claudel. *See* 10598. p. 47–56. **10915**

Sensitive, provocative article tracing C.'s ambivalent attitude toward the country which fascinated him throughout his life. C.'s relations to the principal religions of Japan: Buddhism and Shintoism. [SEH]

————. Paul Claudel exégète du Japon. ELLF 14:1–19, 1969. **10916**

Informative article studies numerous Japanese-inspired texts on general level. Many valuable insights. Perceptive and original explanation of C.'s general attitude and ambivalence towards Japan. [NH]

Place, Jacques. Approche du thème du refuge chez Paul Claudel. *In:* Le refuge (II); études et recherches réunies par Jean Burgos. Circé 3:105–75, 1972. **10917**

Part of a series of studies on the "refuge," i.e. the return to the womb in a psychoanalytical sense. Unconsciously C. used images of refuge: his churches were usually crypts and, under Japanese influence, he finally took refuge in an oriental garden. Valid and well-documented essay which claims only to have scratched the surface. [DWA]

Poulet, Georges. Claudel. *In his:* Les métamorphoses du cercle. Plon, 1961. p. 477–99. *Also (in part):* Les métamorphoses du cercle. *In:* Les critiques de notre temps et Claudel. *See* 10594. p. 79–86. **10918**

This intriguing study of C. forms part of a major analysis of circularity in esthetic perception and consciouness.

C.'s view of Being and Man is examined from that viewpoint, especially as it relates to his notions of time and space. [JFE]

Rousset, Jean. La structure du drame claudélien: l'écran et le face à face. SFr 5:220–30, 1958. *Also in his:* Forme et signification; essais sur les structures littéraires de Corneille à Claudel. José Corti, 1961. p. 171–89. **10919**

Occasionally abstruse article which identifies the preestablished design of C.'s theater as the paradox of the lovers' situation—they find union only in separation. Devices used by C. to maintain contact between the lovers while at the same time keeping them apart include the use of a screen, the presence of a character from outside the natural world, and the image of the sea, omnipresent in C.'s theater and considered by Rousset to be the perfect screen which both separates and unites. Intriguing concept, but vague terminology and lack of focus make the article difficult to follow. [SEH]

Seznec, Jean. Paul Claudel and the sarcophagus of the muses. *In:* Perspectives of criticism. Ed. by Harry Levin. Cambridge, Harvard univ. press, 1950. p. 1–17. **10920**

Commentary on the ode "Les muses," which, as C. himself pointed out in a note, is inspired by a sarcophagus in the Louvre. Discusses C.'s description and use of the muses and then compares C.'s speculations on poetry with the ancients' interpretation of the muses. [DWA]

Soucy, Claudel. L'inspiration platonicienne et ses limites dans le théâtre de Paul Claudel. Essais sur la liberté religieuse. RechD 50:132–39, 1965. **10921**

Intriguing basic idea: C.'s characters have Platonic function as doubles of true essence and divine meaning. Translated theatrically by recurrence or repetition of major scenes in ideal, unreal form. Remains sketchy and general; insufficient analysis of complex philosophical problem or of plays as examples. [NH]

Vetö, Odile. La rédemption et l'amour. TR 191:49–64, 1963. **10922**

Excellent study of subject, occasioned by an analysis of *Paul Claudel interroge le Cantique des cantiques*. Vetö systematically links notions of human and divine love and their role in redemption as seen therein to expressions of similar concepts throughout C.'s work. [JFE]

Vial, Fernand. Le bergsonisme de Paul Claudel. PMLA 60:437–62, 1945. **10923**
Important study. First to note influence of Bergsonian space, time and intuition, especially in *L'art poétique.* Also discusses limits of Thomistic scholasticism in C.'s work. Article valuable for study of parallels and contrasts between Thomism and Bergsonian psychology, as well as detailed indications of Bergsonian theory in plays and poems. [LLG]

————. Symbols and symbolism in Paul Claudel. YFS 9:93–102, 1952. **10924**
Examines links to, and limits of, symbolist school in C.'s work. Considers him a realist and his philosophy strictly Thomistic when compared to other symbolist poets. Details use of images, especially the tree, for literary, natural, metaphysical and liturgical symbolism. An important article enriched and extended by Michaud's *Messages poétiques du symbolisme,* 3. [LLG]

Viprey, Gilbert. Images de la mort. RLM 134–36 (PCl 3):27–37, 1966. **10925**
Studied here are the three principal images of death, a theme which occupied C. a great deal: decay, death through fire or explosion, peaceful and accepted death ("le déliement"). [JPC]

Wahl, Jean. Time in Claudel. IPQ 3:493–505, 1963. **10926**
Lucid examination of movement, time and space. Comparisons with Bergson help clarify concept of universal simultaneity as mediator between permanence and flight. Expanded version of author's article in CahPC 1. [LLG]

Waters, Harold A. Paul Claudel and the sensory paradox. MLQ 20:267–72, 1959. **10927**
Interesting examination of symbolic and allegorical uses of epigrammatic contradictions. Physical impossibilities and confusion of senses considered to be non-temporal (spiritual) qualities discussed by C. in temporal (material) terms in order to demonstrate object of all physical perceptions is non-temporal

grace. Central themes of blindness and music carefully applied to this argument. [LLG]

————. Justice as a theme in Claudel's drama. Ren 17:17–28, 1964. **10928**
Explores the complex notion of human justice as man's free will to righteousness and the ways in which it coincides with and parallels divine justice. Waters traces the historical development of the connection between justice and charity in C.'s mind as revealed in his literary work up to its culmination in *L'annonce.* [LLG]

Wilhelm, Julius. Die Freude (la joie) im dramatischen Werk von Paul Claudel. ZFSL 71:1–14, 1961. *Trans.:* La joie dans l'œuvre dramatique de Paul Claudel. AFLSHA 33:41–54, 1959. **10929**
Goes through C.'s theater to ascertain the role of "la joie." Conclusion: natural joy belongs only to children. Joy as pleasure is seen negatively. The spiritual conception of joy is closely connected with the role of woman and is unattainable after great effort. [VK]

————. Motiv und Symbol der Rose in den Dichtungen von Paul Claudel. *In:* Im Dienste der Sprache. Festschrift für Victor Klemperer zum 75. Geburtstag am 9. Okt. 1956. Ed. by Horst Heintze and Erwin Silzer. Halle, Niemeyer, 1958. p. 435–52. **10930**
Shows that in C. the rose symbolizes the totality of existence, the essence of things, but above all the soul of mankind and especially of woman. Points out the meaning of the perfume of the rose as a symbol for the concept of restitution. [VK]

Wissmann-Moon, Margarete. Mysterium des Fleisches. Zur Metaphysik der Geschlechter in den Dramen Paul Claudels. WuWe 11:30–39, 1958. **10931**
Article deriving from Wissmann-Moon's unpublished diss. *Das metaphysische und psychologische Problem der Geschlechter in den Dramen Paul Claudels* (Tübingen, 1948). A metaphysical interpretation of C.'s picture of woman in his theater that is typical of the early reception of the poet in Germany. Greatly superseded by later research. [VK]

Wood, Michael. The melody of the world: Claudel's doctrine of necessity. FR 39: 523–32, 1966. **10932**
Stimulating discussion of C.'s conviction of the homogeneity and harmony that exist in the universe. Elucidates C.'s theory of the interdependence of all beings in the light of ideas expressed in his *Art poétique* and *Partage de midi*. The article is particularly illuminating in revealing the relationship between the two works and in tracing the innermost sentiments of C. regarding his conversion and his love of God. [SEH]

——. A study of fire imagery in some plays by Paul Claudel. FS 19:144–58, 1965. **10933**
Repos du septième jour, Ville, and *L'annonce* compared for differing use of fire imagery: hell, destruction and leprosy. A tightly reasoned article showing life and desire of all kinds are a flame and both are sources of danger in C.'s plays. [LLG]

Stylistics

Antoine, Gérald. D'un geste linguistique familier à Claudel. RLM 114–16 (PCl 2):111–25, 1965. **10934**
C. wished to shake loose the tyranny of the "logical development" in French syntax through ante- or post-positioning of elements. Antoine presents a statistical analysis of the 160 occurrences of this "geste linguistique." He unfortunately does not offer conclusions. [JPC]

Arnold, Werner. Stil- und Formelemente der Liturgie in der neueren französischen Dichtung. Tübingen, 1966. 132 p. (Diss.) **10935**
A formal esthetic investigation of the assumption of liturgical forms and elements by literature at the turn of the century. Treats the late lyrical work of C., as well as the *Liturgies intimes* of Verlaine, and the lyrical work of Francis Jammes, Marie Noël and Henri Ghéon. [VK]

Brodeur, Léo A. Le corps-sphère: clef de la symbolique claudélienne. Sherbrooke, Canada, Cosmos, 1970. 365 p. **10936**
Recondite study of Claudelian symbolism based on scientific, phenomenalistic method. Sees circular-spherical images as representation of perfection and unity in C.'s cosmos. Work relies exclusively on texts of C.'s works; not related to any previous trends in scholarship and criticism. [SEH]

Chaillet, Jean. Paul Claudel: inventaire poétique du monde. *In his:* Etudes de grammaire et de style. V. 2. Bordas, 1969. p. 317–32. (Coll. Etudes supérieures) **10937**
Brilliant grammatical analysis of "L'esprit et l'eau" from *Les cinq grandes odes* bringing out some basic characteristics of C.'s style. Should be read by anyone making a stylistic analysis of C. [DWA]

Chonez, Claudine. Paul Claudel, le poète au grand corps. Nef 29:26–32, 1947. **10938**
A rather compelling essay on C.'s metrics/prosody and their total significance. [WHM]

Dugas, Pierre-Marie, and Robert Guého. Claudel, L'ode des muses. ECl 34:260–78, 373–93, 1966; 35:56–75, 1967. **10939**
Line-by-line explication of the first Ode. Good cross references to other texts of C. Long-winded but close reading, "telling the story" of the Ode in a competent fashion. [WHM]

Farabet, René. La diction claudélienne du texte écrit au texte parlé; l'action verbale. RLM 44–45:197–240, 1959. **10940**
Very interesting discussion, important for any interpretation of the Claudelian *verset*. Well documented with C.'s own observations, by remarks of actors interpreting C.'s works, and by remarks of critics who liked or disliked the acting of a particular actor or actress. An unusual document in the history of the theater in general. [DWA]

Guyard, Marie-François. Claudel et l'étymologie. CAIEF 11:286–300, 1959. **10941**
Like Hugo, C. was afflicted with *étymologite*. As a symbolist in literature and as a Catholic accustomed to explicating the Bible, he was constantly seeking, or attributing, meanings to words. In fact, many of his linguistic barbarisms become clear only when confronted with the Latin text of the Vulgate from which they derive. [DWA]

Ionesco, Eugène. Ce que j'aurais voulu mieux vous dire. *In:* Le rire de Paul

Claudel. *See* 10612. p. 26–28. *Also in:* Les critiques de notre temps et Claudel. *See* 10594. p. 123–25.   **10942**

Peasant mockery and sarcasm offer C. a means of gaining power over his characters. Reduced to insignificance, evil characters are thus not dangerous. This ingenious explanation of the use of comedy to make the devil comic, and therefore, sainthood tragic, reinforced by C.'s verbal richness, is a lucid addition to C. scholarship. [LLG]

Lechanteur, Jean. Analyse fragmentée d'une page de Claudel. CahAT 13:36–53, 1971.   **10943**

Analyzes passage from "le porc" from *Connaissance de l'Est* according to traditional method of *explication de texte*. Seventeen-page commentary on a seventeen-line passage. Obviously a thorough application of the method for what it may be worth. [DWA]

Lefèbvre, André. Les mots sauvages de Paul Claudel. VL 243:343–50, 1972.   **10944**

Useful commentary on miscellaneous local words, particularly in *L'annonce faite à Marie*. See articles on same subject by Charles Rivière. [DWA]

Lorigiola, P. Les grandes odes de Claudel. ECl 27:152–73, 273–92, 383–406, 1959; 28:30–50, 1960.   **10945**

Detailed study of the five *Odes* as central to Claudelian themes and techniques. Exegesis more ethical/moral than esthetic. [WHM]

Madaule, Jacques. Claudel et le langage. Desclée De Brouwer, 1968. 316 p.   **10946**

C.'s theory of language derived from study of both how he uses language and what he thinks of it. Explores image, time, ryhthm, extent of relation of universe to time, signifier to signified, the oral to written. Focuses on dual nature of iambic rhythm, its use in poetry and drama, especially *L'échange*. Important work. [LLG]

Reviews: E. Beaumont in FS 25: 230–31, 1971; A. Blanc in BSPC 34: 12–14, 1969, and in RHL 70:341–43, 1970; Y. Florenne in QL 70:10–11, 1969.

Malicet, Michel. La scène de transe. RLM 271–75 (PCl 8):69–117, 1971.   **10947**

Well-written, thought-provoking article analyzing the "scènes de transe"

that appear in many of C.'s plays. The hypnotic, hallucinatory quality of these scenes vividly portrays one of the chief characteristics of C.'s theater: the passage from the physical world to the spiritual, from the visible to the invisible. [SEH]

Maurocordato, Alexandre. Les miroirs magiques: prolégomènes à une étude sur la corrélation objective dans le grand lyrisme claudélien. RLM 271–75 (PCl 8):149–67, 1971.   **10948**

Rapid presentation of themes and images in C.'s *Grandes odes* and *Cantate* that appear as "objective correlatives" offering a key to C.'s symbolism. Although the basic premise of the article is intriguing, the author does not develop the ideas fully. [SEH]

Naughton, A. E. A. A poet looks at his work, or Claudel répond ses drames. RR 52:27–35, 1961.   **10949**

Examines why C. so often reworked his texts, especially *Partage*. Concludes that since all existence is fraught with meanings which he desires to uncover, poet's questioning nature extends to his own creations. [LLG]

Oswald, Werner. Entwicklung und Funktion des Metaphorik in Claudels Tête d'or und Otage. Munich, 1962. 133 p. (Diss., Univ. München)   **10950**

Shows that C. uses metaphors quite differently in both dramas: in *Tête d'or* metaphors yield no characterization of the characters, whereas in *L'otage* they are part of the structure of the action. Concludes from this that the four main characters in *Tête d'or* embody different principles of a single problem and are connected to C.'s biography. [VK]

Pearson, Yvonne Alfandari. Aspects du baroque claudélien. Bay 16:323–96, 1963.   **10951**

Baroque elements in several plays but mainly in *Le soulier de satin*. [VB]

Petit, Jacques. La vérité avec le visage de l'erreur. A propos d'une structure dramatique claudélienne. *In:* Paul Claudel. *See* 10604. p. 3–12.   **10952**

Excellent treatment of the interplay of truth and illusion by means of a recurring structure — the "jeux de l'illusion" — throughout C.'s dramatic work. [JFE]

Pfeifer, Joseph. L'acte du choix et son importance structurelle dans le drame claudélien. *In:* Missions et démarches de la critique. Mélanges offerts au professeur J. A. Vier. Klincksieck, 1973. p. 227–35. **10953**
For Pfeifer, the central scene in C.'s plays is the scene of the choice. Descriptive more than critical. [MR]

Pfenniger, Claire. L'expression juste: un outil claudélien pour participer à la création. *In:* Paul Claudel. *See* 10604. p. 34–43. **10954**
Sound stylistic analysis of selected passages from *L'annonce faite à Marie,* examining C.'s techniques of expression and their link with his notions of the poet's function. [JFE]

Prescott, E. Kerrigan. Paul Claudel: the transcendence of temporal flux. MLQ 25: 338–45, 1964. **10955**
C. an exception to contemporaries' use of nonnaturalistic style in order to rise above limits of time in world viewed as chaotic. His metaphor replaces temporal syllogism of 19th century with new logic in which infinite and finite are conjoined. Spatial form of his poetry results from symbolic view of material world in which poet imitates God. Closely reasoned article helpful in placing C.'s style in larger context. [LLG]

Roberto, Eugène. Visions de Claudel. Marseilles, Leconte, 1958. viii, 281 p. **10956**
Thorough and careful study of images in C.'s work — primarily his theater — which project his thought on God, man and the world. The author's method, "explication analogique," is highly successful. Required reading for work on imagery in C. [JFE]
Reviews: M. Hougardy in RBPH 39: 869–70, 1961; S. Pitou in Ren 13:92–96, 1961; J. Wilhelm in ZFSL 70:110–12, 1960.

Samson, Joseph. Paul Claudel, poète-musicien, précédé d'un argument et d'un dialogue de Paul Claudel. Milieu du monde, 1948. 286 p. **10957**
C.'s use of free verse placed in historical context, as inevitable evolution towards awareness of uses of rhythm, similar to parallel evolution among musicians. Notes influence of religious ceremony and earlier poetry on versed rhythms. Extensive study of timbre, accent, intonation, longs and shorts as well as harmony between expression and meaning in poems and plays. [LLG]

Strauss, Claude André. Origine et sens du vers claudélien. PMLA 64:15–26, 1949. **10958**
Lucid examination of C.'s contribution to development of poetry. Iambic basis of *verset* seen in historical context as compromise between free verse and traditional forms based on accent. Desire to imitate universal order which is movement leads poet to awareness of physical determinants of the breath, rhythm of speech and contrasting rhythmic values. [LLG]

Streignart, Joseph. Le cantique du Rhône, l'un des dix de La cantate à trois voix. ECl 38:90–115, 1970. **10959**
Detailed explication of the text. Good on rhythms and versification, composition, audio-visual correspondences. Probably not ultimately a crucial item. [WHM]

Comparison and Influence: Books

Berton, Jean-Claude. Shakespeare et Claudel. Le temps et l'espace au théâtre. Geneva, Paris, La Palatine, 1958. 224 p. **10960**
Relatively chatty treatment of perceptions of time and space and their importance in the works of C. and Shakespeare. Outdated to a great extent by more recent studies. [JFE]
Reviews: E. Mathis in CahPC 2: 287–88, 1960; S. Pitou in Ren 13:92–96, 1961; M. Schrickx in RBPH 39: 105–07, 1961.

Brunel, Pierre. Claudel et le satanisme anglo-saxon. Ottawa, Eds. de l'univ. d'Ottawa, 1975. 230 p. (CahCC, 8) **10961**
The misleading title seems to mean that C. regards Protestantism as satanical (and, continuing the syllogism, that anything Anglo-Saxon is satanical). What Brunel really does is demonstrate a continuing interest on C.'s part in Anglo-Saxon literature and thought from Otway to Joyce (hardly Anglo-Saxon, however) and Spencer to Wells. In most cases, Brunel has proof that C.

read the authors in question. However, he goes much further and develops a systematic catalog of C.'s ideas on these "satanical" subjects, relating each of them to Anglo-Saxon writers whom he explains in such detail that C. himself gets submerged. Furthermore these interesting comparisons are not particularly productive since the question of direct influence on a particular text is seldom raised. [DWA]

―――. Claudel et Shakespeare. A. Colin, 1971. 269 p.   **10962**

A masterful parallel reading of the two dramatists, skillfully combining both the synchronic and diachronic approaches in cogent analyses that are fully cognizant of the role of symbolist and other intermediaries in C.'s debts to Shakespeare and other Elizabethans. Brunel sees Shakespeare as a ferment of renewal for C., from *Tête d'or* to *Soulier de satin,* and maintains that C.'s admiration for Shakespeare did not taper off but waxed and waned in his later works, often mingling with irritation as C. sought more ultimate dimensions and solutions to universal problems. [HMW]

Reviews: G. Cesbron in LR 26:412–15, 1972; M.-F. Guyard in BSPC 43:15–16, 1971; L. Perche in Liv 182:46, 1972; J. Petit in RHL 73:926–27, 1973; L. Witherell in ClaudelS 1, no. 2:69–71, 1973.

Festa, Bianca Maria. Motivi di ispirazione dantesca in un poeta moderno: Paul Claudel. Milan, Gastaldi, 1961. 106 p. **10963**

Parallels between C. and Dante as seen in C.'s *Ode jubilaire* on Dante, and elsewhere. Generalizations lack specific proof or precision, e.g. quotes from Dante to illustrate comparisons. Many ideas assumed to be Dante's influence are purely C. [NH]

Horry, Ruth N. Paul Claudel and Saint-John Perse: parallels and contrasts. Chapel Hill, Univ. of North Carolina press, 1971. 132 p.   **10964**

More of a poetic communion than a critical analysis, replete with superficial generalities and some basic misinterpretations. Still, a pleasant introduction to their theory and stylistic similarities. [HMW]

Reviews: A.-M. Hamburg de Moret in CLAJ 15:248–50, 1971; J. Houston

in FR 45:727, 1972; R. Little in FS 28:102–03, 1974; Y. Scalzitti in MP 71:235–36, 1973; H. Watson in MLJ 57:363, 1973.

Lubac, Henri de, and Jean Bastaire. Claudel et Péguy. Aubier-Montaigne, 1974. 183 p. **10965**

An interesting rapprochement of the two writers, showing their different points of view, their different approaches, their opinions of, and reservations about, each other. Balance of the treatment of each is less than equal, since the authors seem often to be attempting a "justification" of Péguy, treating C. in relation to him. Entire C.-Péguy correspondence, limited as it was, is reproduced and analyzed. [JFE]

Reviews: G. Antoine in BSPC 55:24–25, 1974; J. Bertrand in RGB 110:97, 1974; V.-H. Debidour in BdL 35:373–74, 1974; E. Kanceff in SFr 19:186, 1975; J. Mambrino in Et 341:147, 1974; T. Quoniam in NRDM 4:758–59, 1974.

MacCombie, John. The prince & the genie. A study of Rimbaud's influence on Claudel. Amherst, Univ. of Massachusetts press, 1972. xxi, 197 p.   **10966**

Careful study of C. and Rimbaud, approaching them as "kindred spirits." Particularly good on analysis of similar imagery. Some claims are debatable, but book is worth consulting on the whole. [JFE]

Reviews: A. Carter in FR 46:419–20, 1973; A. Fongaro in SFr 50:312–14, 1974; L. Forestier in RLM 323–26:123–35, 1972; R. Horry in ClaudelS 1:58–59, 1972.

Maurocordato, Alexandre. Anglo-American influences in Paul Claudel. I. Coventry Patmore. Geneva, Droz, 1964. 161 p. **10967**

Generally unconvincing attempt to trace the influence of Patmore on style, technique and choice of themes in C.'s verse. Bases arguments primarily on the fact that C. translated poems of Patmore and on the existence of superficial analogies between the works of the two writers. [SEH]

Review: C. Claudel in ClaudelN 1:12–15, 1968.

Morisot, Jean-Claude. Claudel et Rimbaud: étude de transformations. Minard, 1976.

654 p. (Bibliothèque des lettres modernes, 22)   **10968**

Thorough, detailed study of Rimbaud's influence on C., seen as "transformation" according to C.'s own needs and inner logic. Projection into myth of Rimbaud permits C. to integrate conflicting desires: acceptance of religion versus revolt, direct contact with reality versus search for supernatural. Overlong, repetitive; perhaps exaggerates Rimbaud's role in C.'s works. Perspective somewhat negative. Little purely literary analysis; method is inference from works to life and vice versa. Effective as reconstructing reality behind well-known generalities. Many perceptive insights. [NH]

Review: M. Décaudin in RLM 323–26:125–27, 1972.

Comparison and Influence: Articles

Ages, Arnold. L'image de Renan dans l'œuvre de Paul Claudel. RUL 19:931–35, 1965.   **10969**

Nothing that Renan's name appears at least twenty-five times in C.'s work, the author examines Renan's place in C.'s formation at the Lycée Louis-le-Grand. Also quotes pertinent comments made by C. on Renan. Rather general. [WB]

Allen, Louise D. The literary background for Claudel's Parabole d'Animus et Anima. MLN 62:316–20, 1947.   **10970**

Rejects both Tertullian and Lucretius as sources of C.'s parable because each makes animus or anima servant to the other element of the soul. C.'s more evenly matched personifications represent conflict of faith and reason in religion, inspiration and mechanical technique in art. No longer confined to narrow classical context, they have no fixed literary source. [LLG]

Allen, Peter. Claudel et Wagner. BJR 14:30–40, 1966.   **10971**

Although C. assumed an esthetic stance which held Wagner's works in distaste during the later years, his earlier dramatic works reflected a strong Wagnerian influence. The author points up similarities between C.'s Simon Agnel in Tête d'or and Siegfried and between Tristan and Partage de midi. [TJ]

Amer, Henry. Le hasard, l'homme et les dieux dans le théâtre de Corneille, Racine Claudel. NRF 147:410–33, 1965.   **10972**

Excellent study of the effect of the secularization of Greek tragedy by Corneille and Racine, vigorously rejected by C., who returns to a mode of tragedy in which all is determined by supernatural forces and Fate. In Le soulier de satin, he reworks Racine's Bérénice with a new depth obtained by the presence of the sacred. [VB]

Babilas, Wolfgang. Paul Claudel und Aragon. In: Paul Claudel zu seinem hundertsten Geburtstag. See 10610. p. 119–60.   **10973**

Rich historical presentation of the relationship of the two poets which covers all periods of Aragon's creativity. [VK]

Bauer, Roger. Paul Claudel et Richard Wagner. OrL 11:197–214, 1956.   **10974**

Begins with a study of C.'s numerous references to Wagner, first in his preconversion period when his admiration was unbounded and then in his postconversion period when he continued to refer to Wagner but could no longer appreciate his earlier enthusiasm. Continues with a discussion of strong Wagnerian influences: Tête d'or as Siegfried and purification through love as a central Wagnerian theme in C. Purification theme is particularly visible in Partage de midi where Ysé stands for Yseut. [DWA]

Becker, Aimé. Claudel lecteur de Ruysbroeck l'Admirable. LR 27:111–49, 1973.   **10975**

Carefully documented and persuasive study of the influence of the fourteenth-century Flemish mystic on the thought and works of C. [SEH]

Birn, Randi Marie. Claudel's L'annonce faite à Marie and Genet's Le balcon: similarities in ritual theater. RomN 13:1–7, 1971.   **10976**

Clearly notes how Genet's theater is a reflection of C.'s despite ideological differences. Both break with traditional structures, use ritual, supplement dialog with music, dance, gesture and rhythm. Sacrifice of a martyr for whom death is liberation is central to both. [LLG]

Brunel, Pierre. A la recherche d'une influence: l'image de l'orchestre et la tentation symphonique chez Walt Whitman et Paul Claudel. RLM 134–36 (PCl 3):49–63, 1966 (2).   **10977**
    Brunel shows that it is possible to see C. in his *Cinq grandes odes* as a "prodigious continuator" of the poetic symphony inaugurated by Whitman. [JPC]

————. Claudel et Edgar Poe. RLM 101–03 (PCl 1):99–130, 1964.   **10978**
    C. felt admiration for Poe as well as fear and regarded his verse (along with Keats') as the most beautiful in English. Although Poe's *Eurêka* inspired C. with horror for infinity, in *L'art poétique* and in *Cinq grandes odes* there was a dialog betwen Poe and C., rather than a filiation. A very judicious influence study. [JPC]

————. Claudel lecteur et juge de Milton. RLC 49:249–59, 1975.   **10979**
    In a brief but interesting survey, Brunel shows S.'s various readings, misreadings and judgments of Milton from November 1907 on. His judgment is seen as focused by his rigid view of England in general and by his natural prejudice against the religion of the "poète puritain" in particular. [JFE]

Černý, Václav. Le baroquisme du Soulier de satin. RLC 44:472–98, 1970.   **10980**
    C. discovered Calderón's allegorical drama and the baroque in Prague. Examines extent to which each of these is present in *Soulier* and how these interpenetrating influences made C. a great baroque poet. Interesting complement to work of Tricaud. [LLG]

Decreus, Juliette. Claudel et le Nô japonais. CLS 19:11–17, 1946.   **10981**
    A short but interesting study of the thematic and technical similarities between the Nô and C.'s later drama, specifically *Le soulier de satin* and *Le livre de Christophe Colomb*. [TJ]

Dufrenoy, Marie-Louise. Le renoncement selon Paul Claudel et André Gide. RTC 38:187–95, 1952.   **10982**
    Interesting comparison of Alissa in *La porte étroite* and Violaine in *L'annonce faite à Marie*. Concludes that while Alissa attempted to narrow the doorway through which her beloved might enter the City of God, Violaine

attempted to enlarge the entry to give access to everyone. [WB]

Erwin, John F. Claudel and the lesson of Mallarmé: the theme of absence. *In:* Paul Claudel. See 10604. p. 44–54. **10983**
    Mallarmean antecedents for the varieties of absence in C.'s work: the "sacrament of absence" for lovers, absence as "technique" and as philosophical and poetic concept. [JFE]

Espiau de la Maëstre, André. Paul Claudel, Jean-Paul Richter et le romantisme allemand. RFor 80:249–80, 1968.   **10984**
    Rambling, disjointed overview of C.'s beliefs in the role of God in man's life as expressed in his early poetry and in the first versions of *Tête d'or* and *La ville*. Only passing references are made to Richter's influence or to the impact of Naturphilosophie of German Romanticism on C.'s work. [SEH]

Etiemble, [René]. Aragon et Claudel. NRF 95:881–89; 96:1102–09, 1960. *Also in his:* Poètes ou faiseurs? (1936–1966). Hygiène des lettres, v. 4. Gallimard, 1966. p. 275–97.   **10985**
    In spite of the opposition between the Communist and the militant Catholic, Aragon and Claudel are linked by their love of country, by a certain nihilism, by their recourse to Rimbaud, by their eventual refuge in marriage, by their fanaticism and intolerance. [VB]

Gadoffre, Gilbert. Claudel et la Chine du Tao. MerF 1145:95–106, 1959.   **10986**
    Clear study of progressive influence of Taoism. Eastern notion of rhythmic order and creative void seen in *Connaissance de l'Est, L'art poétique, Repos du septième jour,* and *La ville*. When integrated later with Thomistic metaphysics, Yang and Yin become internal metronome. Influence manifested in themes and in use of iamb explained with numerous examples. [LLG]

————. Claudel et Lafcadio Hearn. *In:* Studies in modern French literature presented to P. Mansell Jones by pupils, colleagues and friends. Ed. by L. J. Austin, Garnet Rees and Eugène Vinaver. Manchester, Manchester univ. press, 1961. p. 104–08.   **10987**
    The prose poem on the Chinese legend of the bell maker in *Connaissance de l'Est* has its source in Lafcadio

Hearn's *Some Chinese ghosts.* For some reason C. did not use the slipper found in the Hearn version, but he later made it the subject of *Le soulier de satin.* [DWA]

——. Claudel et le héros wagnérien. *In:* Paul Claudel zu seinem hundertsten Geburtstag. *See* 10610. p. 161–72. **10988**
The relationship between C.'s theatrical figures and Wagner's heroes. For the first time, Gadoffre attributes French understanding of Wagner at the turn of the century to C. An original study. [VK]

——. Claudel et des philosophes taoïstes. RG no. 7:51–60, 1970. **10989**
During his first residence in China, C. read Lao-tseu and expressed his concepts of "le Vide et le non-Agir" in *Le repos du septième jour* and in *La ville.* On his return to the Orient as ambassador to Tokyo, C. was strongly influenced by his reading of Tchouangtseu. The most distinct allusions to the Taoist philosopher are found in *L'oiseau noir dans le soleil levant.* [DWA]

——. Les trois sources de l'analogie claudélienne. FS 13:135–45, 1959. **10990**
Studies C.'s symbolism in the light of the influence of Mallarmé, St. Thomas Aquinas, J. K. Huysmans' *La cathédrale.* Sketchy survey of influence of first two writers; section on Huysmans is well researched and enlightening. Concluding paragraphs mention in passing impact of Chinese philosophy and traditions on C. [SEH]

Giordan, Henri. Bernanos et Claudel. CahH 2:93–98, 1962. *Also:* Paul Claudel dans l'œuvre de Bernanos. RLMC 15:220–25, 1962. **10991**
Study of their inimical relationship; respect gives way to hostility, particularly over their different sides in the Spanish civil war. [WHM]

Guillemin, Henri. Claudel et Zola. CahNat 5:518–25, 1959. *Also in his:* Zola, légende et vérité? Julliard, 1960. p. 169–87. *Also in his:* Précisions. Gallimard, 1973. p. 331–43. **10992**
Although Zola probably never heard of C., it was impossible that C., an avid reader in his pre-conversion youth, had not read Zola. Guillemin thinks that, at one point, C. even had the ambition to outdo Zola in the novel. He finds evidence for naturalism in C.'s work, particularly in *La ville,* as well as many cases of distinct reminiscences of Zola. [DWA]

Guyard, Marius François. De Patmore à Claudel, histoire et nature d'une influence. RLC 33:500–17, 1959. **10993**
Patmore provided with lyric freedom what C.'s Catholicism lacked: the centrality of Jesus for the completeness of the universe and discipline to order the world. An interesting study of how and when C. discovered the horror of the infinite, and the spiritual marriage of the soul and its God in *Unknown Eros.* [LLG]

——. Sur une image claudélienne de l'Angleterre. *In:* Connaissance de l'étranger. Mélanges offerts à la mémoire de Jean-Marie Carré. Libr. Didier, 1964. p. 267–72. **10994**
Considers C.'s profound debt to English writers and thinkers in contrast to scarcity of images of that country. England presented as significant Other, as both object of fear and as a seduction. Examples primarily from *Soulier* where England's relation to Spain also considered. Interesting thesis. [LLG]

Hanf, Irmgard. Leopold Sedar Senghor. Ein afrikanischer Dichter französischer Prägung. Munich, Fink, 1972. p. 119–74. **10995**
Comparison of a passage from C.'s fourth *Ode* and Péguy's *Le porche du mystère de la deuxième vertu* with Senghor's *Elégie des circoncis* with respect to versification and form, rhythm and sound, syntax, punctuation, typography, vocabulary and metaphors. [VK]

Hue, Bernard. Ibsen et Claudel. *In:* Missions et démarches de la critique. Mélanges offerts au professeur J. A. Vier. Klincksieck, 1973. p. 411–21. **10996**
Sees *Le soulier de satin* as the Catholic counterpart of Ibsen's *The lady from the sea.* Competent comparison. [MR]

Lawler, James R. Claudel and symbolism: *In:* The France of Claudel. *See* 10598. p. 34–46. **10997**
Some intriguing analogies and contrasts between C. and the symbolists are

presented here, but the essay is so brief and the author attempts to cover so many ideas that the article merely skims the surface of the subject. [SEH]

———. Magic and movement in Claudel and Valéry. *In his:* The language of French symbolism. Princeton, Princeton univ. press, 1969. p. 112–45.   **10998**
Comparison and contrast of C. and Valéry, excellently done, treating their personal contact, opinions of each other and of each other's esthetics. Includes penetrating comparative analysis of their respective texts entitled "Abeille." [JFE]

Luytens, David Bulwer. The dilemma of the Christian dramatist: Paul Claudel and Christopher Fry. TDR 6:118–24, 1962.   **10999**
Examines problems shared by two Christian playwrights in non-Christian age and their reactions to non-believing audiences. [LLG]

Madaule, Jacques. Baudelaire et Claudel. Eur 456–57:197–204, 1967.   **11000**
C.'s admiration for Baudelaire early in his career. Author also notes profound differences in the basic philosophy of life of the two poets. Well written, cogent arguments. [SEH]

———. Claudel et Teilhard de Chardin. RdP 70, no. 2:85–95, 1963.   **11001**
Dense, thought-provoking essay that compares and contrasts the basic religious and metaphysical ideas of C. and Teilhard de Chardin. [SEH]

Marie-Julie, sœur. Paul Claudel et Eschyle. RUL 16:645–57; 741–53, 1962.   **11002**
Traces C.'s early biography and his encounter with Aeschylus, and gives reasons for the place the Greek dramatist held in C.'s affection. [WB]

Milhaud, Darius. Ma collaboration avec Paul Claudel. Eur 51:398–401, 1927. *Also:* Eur 533–34:64–67, 1973.   **11003**
Good insight into how a musician uses a poet's language. Composer traces stages of work with C. (1911–27) who showed how to avoid dangers of impressionistic music by attention to daily, humble life and whose poems reflected rhythms which sustained their concentrated dramas. [LLG]

Pollmann, Leo. Paul Claudel und Stéphane Mallarmé. ZFSL 76:1–9, 1966.   **11004**
Illuminates C.'s dialog with Mallarmé with the aid of the poem "Jour d'automne," which Pollmann interprets as the answer to Mallarmé's "Les fenêtres." The common denominator of both poets lies in the struggle to express the unthinkable; the difference lies in the weaving of eternity into time. [VK]

Moscovici, Jacques. Paul Claudel et Richard Wagner. NRF 140:323–34, 1964.   **11005**
An unsubstantiated but valid parallel is established between Wagner's musical and C.'s verbal expression, while a similarity, well-documented this time, is shown between characters of C.'s works and Wagnerian characters. No conclusion, but an interesting rapprochement. [VB]

Mullins, Stanley G. A propos de l'influence d'Eschyle sur Claudel. RULau 1:80–84, 1968.   **11006**
Differentiates between C.'s view of role of the chorus and the choruses of Aeschylus, quoting from unpublished notes on C.'s ties with Aeschylus sent the author by C. in 1948. Sees in C.'s lines "La fécondité indéfinie de l'acte mauvais qui implique et engendre spontanément sa propre sanction, laquelle n'est autre qu'un fil d'une même lignée familiale, qu'un égal crime" a perfect résumé of Aeschylus' influence, with C.'s heroes and heroines, like those of his Greek master, totally submitted to a hidden divinity. [WB]

Naughton, A. E. A. Claudel and Mallarmé. RR 46:258–74, 1955.   **11007**
Important and clearly written influence study. Helpful analysis of shared interest in lexicographical predilections, typographical presentation, etymological use of words. Explores common characteristics of syntax and belief in power of sound to suggest meaning. [LLG]

Petit, Jacques. Claudel et Virgile. RLM 101–03 (PCl 1):45–66, 1964.   **11008**
Although in C.'s eyes Virgil was one of the greatest poets of humanity and although there are numerous reminiscences of Virgil in C.'s work, "no episode, no important text seems to have been inspired by Virgil" and C. never wrote on Virgil. [JPC]

Peyre, Henri. Claudel and the French literary tradition. *In:* The France of Claudel. *See* 10598. p. 11–33. *Also in his:* French literary imagination and Dostoevsky and other essays. University, Ala., Univ. of Alabama press, 1975. p. 115–37. (Series in the humanities, 10) **11009**

Rapid survey of foreign influences and models. Interesting background notes, but offers little specific information. [SEH]

Plourde, Michel. Le silence et le Nô japonais dans le théâtre de Claudel. RUL 21:3–18, 1966. **11010**

Behind the baroque and loquacious C., Plourde finds another C. who founds his philosophy and his dramatic structure on a principle of silence (inherited from the symbolists). Philosophically silence is the principle for divine communication. Esthetically C. found a model for this principle in the Japanese Nô which dramatized this communication between the divine and the human. This article is of prime importance because it goes into detail on the specific influence of the Nô on C.'s theater. [DWA]

Raymond, Marcel. La rencontre de Claudel. *In his:* Etudes sur Jacques Rivière. Corti, 1972. p. 27–83. *Also (in part):* Les premières lectures de Claudel par Jacques Rivière. *In:* Littérature et société. Recueil d'études en l'honneur de Bernard Guyon. Desclée De Brouwer, 1973. p. 307–20. **11011**

Important and well-documented study, more interesting, however, for Rivière than for C. [MR]

Reboul, Yves. Dante et Claudel: les damnés du Repos du septième jour. RLC 44:73–81, 1970. **11012**

Close, careful examination of extent of parallel between *Divine comedy* and *Repos.* Second act of *Repos* a variation on Dante's seven deadly sins with envy an original creation by C. and pride a greater sin. *Divine comedy*'s influence largely external because Dante's hell limited to the senses. [LLG]

Roberto, Eugène. Le livre des merveilles de Nathaniel Hawthorne et Claudel. RUO 37:139–45, 1967. **11013**

As a child, C. was an avid reader of *Le livre des merveilles* translated by Léonce Rabilton. Not only did this reading inspire C. with a love for myth in general, but it instilled in him the habit of mixing the real and the mythical, as Hawthorne did by telling his myths in the real setting of Tanglewood. [DWA]

———. Le théâtre chinois de New-York en 1893. *In:* Formes et figures. *See* 10597. p. 109–34. **11014**

Excellent study of Chinese theater as played in New York during C.'s consular assignment there, and of his verifiable and probable contact with it long before his first departure for the Orient. [JFE]

Rohde, Hartmut. Der Einfluss des Thomas von Aquin auf das Werk Paul Claudels. NS 6:283–90, 1965. **11015**

Looks for parallels to statements of C. in the work of Thomas Aquinas and, after a series of such general parallels, comes to the conclusion that St. Thomas is a key to the understanding of C.'s work. Questionable from the point of view of method, but not uninteresting on account of the material. [VK]

Senghor, Leopold. African poetry and Claudel: analogies and convergence. *In:* The France of Claudel. *See* 10598. p. 57–62. **11016**

Senghor notes similarities between the works of C. and of Black poets. [SEH]

———. La parole chez Paul Claudel et chez les négro-Africains. Dakar, Nouvelles éds. africaines, 1973. 55 p. *Also:* BSPC 49:9–39, 1973. **11017**

Text of Senghor's address to International Congress on C. held at the château de Brangues on July 27, 1972. An interesting comparison of what he sees as "convergences" between C. and "négro-Africain" poets in notions of "parole," of the verset as poetic form, and of ontology. [JFE]

Simon, Pierre-Henri. Claudel ou l'esprit du monde. *In his:* Témoins de l'homme. La condition humaine dans la littérature du XXᵉ siècle. Payot, 1967. p. 69–91. (Original ed.: Colin, 1951) *Also in (in part):* Les critiques de notre temps et Claudel. *See* 10594. p. 164–80. **11018**

Relates C. to literary movements and figures and while agreeing he is a baroque artist, considers him a poet and unclassifiable. [LLG]

Sofer, Johann. Claudel und die französische Klassik. GRM 11:295–319, 1961. **11019**
Investigates C.'s evaluation of the French classicists Descartes, Malebranche, La Fontaine, Molière, Boileau, Corneille and Racine. Assembles C.'s remarks on each and adds a commentary. [VK]

————. Claudels Stellung zu England. NS 2:65–78, 1964. **11020**
By juxtaposition of C.'s texts, Sofer shows C.'s wavering judgments about English writers and thinkers. [VK]

————. Claudels Stelling zu Pascal und Bossuet. GRM 13:23–38, 1963. **11021**
Pascal and Bossuet as philosophical and theological mentors of C. Demonstrates by comparison of various statements of the poet that C.'s relation to Pascal underwent many changes whereas his relation to Bossuet remained stereotyped. [VK]

————. Claudels Urteile über die U.S.A. MSpra 2:1–9, 1963. **11022**
Studies C.'s statements about the U.S.A. by system of juxtaposition of passages. [VK]

————. Dante und Claudel. ZFSL 71:231–44, 1961. **11023**
Collects passages in which C. mentions Dante and shows that the poet fills those parts which he takes over from Dante's creations with his own spirit. This is especially true of Beatrice whose figure C. uses for the clarification of his differently oriented conception of love. [VK]

Trépanier, Estelle. L'hispanisme dans le théâtre de Paul Claudel. RLC 36:386–403, 1962. **11024**
Religious ideology of Spanish Renaissance used in themes, theatrical technique, structure and symbolic characters of C.'s plays, especially *Soulier* and *Partage*. Hispanic primitivism of the 16th century colored by medieval realism seen in problem of grace and free will treated by Lope de Vega and Calderón retained and renewed by C. because his personality predisposed him to similar faith in absolute authority

and creature's relation to Creator. [LLG]

————. The influence of the Noh on the theater of Paul Claudel. LE&W 15, no. 4–16, no. 1 & 2:616–31, 1971–72. **11025**
Examines discovery and use of Taoism, Zen Buddhism, Tao Te Ching, and work of Chuang Tzu in poems, plays and *L'art poétique* as corroborated in *Journal* references. C.'s fusion of art and religion traced to ceremony, gesture, spirituality and slowness of Japanese technique. Intelligent article but printed text disconcerting in number of illogical skips. [LLG]

Vetö, Odile. Claudel et Dante. Ode jubilaire et L'introduction à un poème sur Dante. RLM 101–03 (PCl 1):67–98, 1964. **11026**
Although C. had a great admiration for Dante, he claimed not to have been influenced by him. Actually Dante's view of a unified and organized world and his treatment of Biblical themes did inspire C. Vetö also sees Dante's influence in *Le repos du septième jour*. Long digressions on Dante. [JPC]

Viscusi, Anthony I. Order and passion in Claudel and Dante. FR 30:442–50, 1957. **11027**
Concise, thought-provoking article stressing the belief shared by the two Catholic poets in the existence of divine order amid God's vast creation. They differ, however, in their manner of portraying creation. Viscusi concludes that C. and Dante agree on dogma but differ in temperament. Well-chosen citations from the works of both authors illustrate salient points. [SEH]

Watanabé, Moriaki. Claudel et le nô. ELLF 6:61–77, 1965. **11028**
C.'s gradually developing conception of *nô* as seen in *Journal* and essays. C. interprets *nô* as intrusion of past and of supernatural into present, through dream; *Soulier de satin* and later works show influence. Generally interesting, but often somewhat confusing. [NH]

Watson, Harold. Baudelairian realism in Claudel's early drama. *In:* Paul Claudel. *See* 10604. p. 55–65. **11029**
Interesting article on Baudelairian overtones in C.'s early plays, primarily

Tête d'or, but with frequent reference to later works as well. [JFE]

Reputation

Bloom, Edward A. The vatic temper in literary criticism. C 5:297-315, 1963. **11030**

Quickly dismisses C. as critic of Patmore and Chesterton because his value system is extra-literary and their intention not primarily theological. Judgments based on doctrine irrelevant as literary standard. Example of New Criticism's rejection of Christian school of criticism. Historical survey using examples primarily from Anglo-Saxon tradition. [LLG]

Cattaui, Georges. Intinéraires de Claudel. Cr 95:291-303, 1955. **11031**

A eulogy upon the death of C. in which the author attempts to situate C.'s work and describe its relevance in the context of contemporary concerns. Suggests an affinity between C. and Gerard Manley Hopkins. [TJ]

Duhamel, Georges. Claudel. MerF 1100: 577-82, 1955. **11032**

Interesting homage by friend after C.'s death. Poetic innovations and influence on himself and young generation recalled. [LLG]

Florenne, Yves. Claudel mort et vivant. RevHM 105:39-43, 1955. **11033**

Well-written article penned at time of C.'s death. Expresses opinion that C. might benefit from an eclipse after the recent exaggerated praise of his work. Article merits special attention because it ends with a thorough analysis of the shortcomings of the current performances of *L'annonce faite à Marie* at the Comédie-Française. [DWA]

Giordan, Henri. Paul Claudel en Italie, avec la correspondance Paul Claudel/Piero Jahier. Eds. Klincksieck, 1975. 167 p. **11034**

Well-annotated study on influence and reputation of C. in Italy, beginning with case of direct influence on D'Annunzio and concentrating particularly on the interest shown in C. by the group of *La voce.* Under the imprint of *La voce,* Jahier published in 1912 his

translation of *Partage de midi* at a time when C. was trying to conceal his text in France (even though published in a limited ed.). [DWA]

Gregh, Fernand. Paul Claudel. RDM 8:577-91, 1955. **11035**

Brief commemorative summation of one critic's opinion of C. and his work, written shortly after C.'s death. Contains some interesting, if not unique, reservations about individual works. [JFE]

Landau, Edwin-Marie. Paul Claudel et l'Allemagne. RGB no. 7:27-46, 1967. **11036**

Excellent article by translator of C. into German. Noting that nine of C.'s plays were presented in German before being produced in France, Landau attributes this interest to the "Faustian" side of C.'s work. Mentions influence of C. on Stefan George, Hugo von Hofmannsthal, Reinhard Johannes Sorge, Carl Einstein, Bertolt Brecht, Friedrich Dürrenmatt and Reinhold Schneider. [DWA]

Lasserre, Pierre. M. Paul Claudel et le claudélisme. *In:* Les critiques de notre temps et Claudel. *See* 10594. p. 44-47. **11037**

Originally published in *La minerve française* in 1919. Helpful for an understanding of early opinion of C.'s influence. Criticizes reaction of admirers, notably Duhamel and Rivière, and warns that some opinion reveals more about the critics than about C. Objects to Rivière's interpretation that C.'s poetic rhythm has a sensual source, and finds C.'s work full of obscurities. [LLG]

Ponge, Francis. Prose de profundis à la gloire de Claudel. *In:* Hommage à Paul Claudel. *See* 10602. p. 398-403. *Also in his:* Le grand recueil. [V. 1] Lyres. Gallimard, 1961. p. 27-33. **11038**

Ponge's "hommage" at the time of C.'s death. The poet pays characteristic tribute to C. and his grasp of reality, characterizing him humorously as "tortue." [JFE]

Romane, Jacques. Malentendus devant Claudel. RGB 22:591-601, 1947. **11039**

Defends C. as a great writer but also criticizes him for having tried to "asservir la langue française à des influences étrangères, nordiques et orientales." [DWA]

Warnach, Walter. Paul Claudel. Hoch 47: 381–84. 1955.   **11040**

Memorial to the dead poet. Document of historical interest because of independent judgment of poet who has been understood as total Catholicism. [VK]

Waters, Harold. Situation de Claudel aux États-Unis. BSPC 50:34–38, 1973. **11041**

Lack of interest in C. in the United States before 1968. With the formation of the Paul Claudel Society in the United States, the establishment of the *Claudel Newsletter* and then of *Claudel Studies,* the increase in masters theses and doctoral dissertations on C., interest in the U.S. on the rise. [CC]

CHAPTER XXIV

DRAMA BEFORE 1940

(Nos. 11042–11506)

Simona Akerman, Jean-Pierre Cap, Earle D. Clowney, David A. Coward, Renée Geen,
Naomi Greene, Sharon E. Harwood, Robert Emmet Jones, Vera G. Lee,
June M. Legge, Jane M. Malin, David B. Parsell, Norman H. Paul, Laure Rièse,
and William T. Starr

Drama in General Before 1940 *
(Nos. 11042–11174)

Vera G. Lee and Norman H. Paul

Overview

Aylen, Leo. Greek tragedy and the modern world. London, Methuen, 1964. 376 p. **11042**

Two-thirds of this articulate and readable work is devoted to the exposition of Greek tragedy and the possibility of modern tragedy. In 80 p., the author adequately analyzes plays of Cocteau, Gide, Giraudoux, Sartre, Anouilh and Ghéon. [NHP]

Bishop, Thomas. Pirandello and the French theatre. New York Univ. press, 1960. 170 p. *Also:* 1966. **11043**

Logically presented study of Pirandello's influence on French playwrights of the 20's and 30's and on certain postwar playwrights. Treats the reception of Pirandello's theater in France, presents Pirandellian themes of reality and illusion, and analyzes these themes in plays of French writers. Bishop's study is an honest and important one. [VGL]

Reviews: F. Anders in RHT 1:58–61, 1961; K. White in MD 4:437–39, 1962.

Brisson, Pierre. Le théâtre des années folles. Geneva, Eds. du milieu du monde, 1943. 224 p. **11044**

A survey of French drama and stage from before World War I until the early forties. Brisson's book still exudes the charm of a bedtime story well told. An exciting chronicle, narrated with in-

sight, humor and literary flourish. Competent when treating the *cartel* or the Comédie Française, the author seems especially at home discussing the boulevard and casinos. [VGL]

Champion, Edouard. La Comédie-Française. 1ᵉʳ janvier 1927–31 décembre 1932. Années 1933 et 1934. Année 1935. Nogent-le-Rotrou, Imprimerie Daupeley-Gouverneur, 1934, 1935, 1936. 463, 490, 408 p. Année 1936. Librairie Stock, 1937. 489 p. Année 1937. Librairie Munier, 1938. 382 p. **11045**

Indispensable reference for the historian; continuation of work by Joannidès and Couet; statistics and records of every performance; selections from play reviews; critical bibliography of current books on theater; index. [NHP]

Reviews: A Bellesort in JdD July 29, 1935; G. Boissy in Comoedia March 11, 1935; Colette in Journ March 24, 1935; B. Crémieux in Can March 23, 1935; Dussane in Journ March 27, 1935; M. Martin du Gard in NL March 23, 1935; Orion in ActF Sept. 21, 1935.

Chiari, Joseph. The contemporary French theatre: the flight from naturalism. London, Rockliff, 1958. 242 p. **11046**

Verbose, commonplace and dogmatic survey of plays and authors. [NHP]

Coindreau, Maurice Edgar. La farce est jouée: vingt-cinq ans de théâtre français. 1900–1925. New York, Eds. de la maison française, 1942. 305 p. **11047**

Urbane play-by-play account of theater in the first quarter of the century, including chapters on popular theater, religious theater and on Copeau and the *cartel*. Some classifications may

* Some entries continue beyond this date.

surprise, e.g., Sacha Guitry considered with Octave Mirbeau as theater of "social satire," but the book is generally informative. [VGL]
Review: H. Peyre in FR 16:345–47, 1943.

Cornevin, R[obert]. Le théâtre en Afrique noire et à Madagascar. Le livre africain, 1970. 335 p.   **11048**
Encyclopedic survey of vast and neglected subject; excellent reference and valuable bibliography. [NHP]

————. Le théâtre haïtien des origines à nos jours. Ottawa, Eds. Leméac, 1973. 301 p. (Coll. Caraïbes)   **11049**
Good introductory perspective; half the text deals with contemporary theater; excellent source. [NHP]

Daniels, May. The French drama of the unspoken. Edinburgh, Edinburgh univ. press, 1953. vii, 263 p.   **11050**
Considers as a group and individually writers classified as dramatists of *l'inexprimé*. Analyzes works of Maeterlinck, Vildrac, Amiel and J.-J. Bernard. Indicates not only the value but the limitations of the "silent" approach. [VGL]
Review: D. Knowles in FS 8:182–83, 1956.

Doisy, Marcel. Le théâtre français contemporain. Brussels, Les lettres latines, 1947. 286 p.   **11051**
Divided into two parts, "Les animateurs" and "Les créateurs," the book treats theater of the first half of the century. Especially useful is the shorter first part, describing the evolution of modern French *mise en scène*. From such close range some evaluations are, understandably, blurred; for example, only a few lines devoted to Montherlant but pages to J.-R. Bloch. [VGL]

Encyclopédie du théâtre contemporain. Dirigée par Gilles Quéant. I (1850–1914). Publications de France, 1957. 208 p. ill.; II (1914–1950). Olivier Perrin, 1959. 212 p. (Théâtre de France) **11052**
Profusely and richly illustrated; accurate and informative essays on principal figures and movements; adequate bibliography. [NHP]

Fowlie, Wallace. Dionysus in Paris: a guide to contemporary French theater. Meridian,

1960. 314 p. *Also:* Gloucester, Mass., P. Smith, 1971.   **11053**
Comprehensive, factual account of French theater through the late 50's. The book is structured logically rather than chronologically: drama is categorized as tragic, religious, philosophical or experimental. [VGL]
Reviews: F. Anders in RHT 1:90, 1962; E. McAnany in MD 4:331–32, 1961.

Grossvogel, David. The self-conscious stage in modern French drama. Columbia univ. press, 1958. 378 p.   **11054**
Experimental drama from Jarry to Beckett. The subject and focus of the book are clarified in its provocative title. An essay on laughter serves as the introduction, and no conclusions are offered. Some judgments appear unduly negative or arbitrary. Extensive bibliography. Treats Adamov, Anouilh, Apollinaire, Beckett, Claudel, Cocteau, Crommelynck, Giraudoux, Ionesco, Sartre *et al.* [VGL]
Reviews: G. Brée in RR 50:310–12, 1959; O. Puccini in MLN 75:77–82, 1960; W. Strauss in FR 33:623–24, 1959–60.

Guicharnaud, Jacques. Modern French theatre from Giraudoux to Beckett. In collaboration with June Beckelman. New Haven, Yale univ. press, 1961. 304 p. (Yale romanic studies, 7) *Also (rev.):* Modern French theatre from Giraudoux to Genet. In collaboration with June Guicharnaud. New Haven and London, Yale univ. press, 1967. 383 p.   **11055**
A classic in its genre, the Guicharnauds' critical survey of modern French theater offers many cogent insights throughout its clear and broadreaching presentation. Treats Anouilh, Beckett, Camus, Claudel, Cocteau, Genet, Ghelderode, Giraudoux, Ionesco, Montherlant, Salacrou, Sartre *et al.* [VGL]
Reviews: F. Anders in RHT 2:204–05, 1965; C. François in FR 37:246–47, 1963; R. Hubert in SFr 25:121–22, 1965; D. Knowles in FS 17:190–92, 1963; L. LeSage in EspCr 2:199–200, 1962.

Jones, Robert Emmet. The alienated hero in modern French drama. Athens, Georgia, Univ. of Georgia press, 1962. 137 p. (Univ. of Georgia monographs, 9) **11056**

Psychological study of themes of perversity and maladjustment in French drama since 1920, with special emphasis on homosexuality. Treats Anouilh, Curel, Giraudoux, Lenormand, Montherlant, Sartre *et al.* [VGL]
Reviews: F. Anders in RHT 2:204–05, 1965; T. Bishop in MD 6:469–70, 1963–64; D. Knowles in FS 18:291–93, 1964; L. Pronko in RR 55:153–56, 1964.

Knowles, Dorothy. French drama of the inter-war years, 1918–39. London, Harrap, 1967. 334 p.   **11057**
The author distinguishes between experimental or "studio" theater and "boulevard" fare, and she devotes the major part of her book to a history and description of the former. The text is particularly useful for its information concerning plots, chronology and circumstances surrounding French drama of this period.
Review: P. Ginistier in FS 23:207–08, 1969.

————. La réaction idéaliste au théâtre depuis 1890. Droz, 1934. 558 p. (Coll. Bibliothèque de la Société des historiens du théâtre, 4)   **11058**
Excellent scholarly study of this post-Antoine movement, its theoreticians, dramatists and interpreters. Reliable, authoritative reference work of this period. [NHP]

Lalou, René. Le théâtre en France. Presses univ. de France, 1951. 126 p. (Que sais-je?)   **11059**
A concise, clearly classified and sub-classified chronicle of French theater productions of the first half of the century. [VGL]

Lilar, Suzanne. The Belgian theater since 1890. New York, Belgian government information center, 1950. 67 p. *Also:* New York, 1957. 68 p. *Trans.:* Soixante ans de théâtre belge. Brussels, La renaissance du livre, 1952. 108 p.   **11060**
Brief but very informative and intelligent survey of major figures. [NHP]

Lioure, Michel. Le drame. A. Colin, 1963. 420 p. (Coll. U) *Also (rev.):* Le drame de Diderot à Ionesco. A. Colin, 1973. 280 p.   **11061**
Useful, well-documented textbook for first year French university students;

traces history of genre from 18th century. Second section is an anthology of critical texts, followed by selections from plays, a chronology and a critical bibliography. [NHP]
Review: J. Kneller in FR 37:362–63, 1964.

Matthews, J[ohn] H[erbert]. Theatre in dada and surrealism. Syracuse, Syracuse univ. press, 1974. 286 p.   **11062**
Scholarly and readable account of this little known, often unperformed, heretical theater and its problematic influence on contemporary dramatists. [NHP]

Raymond, Marcel. Le jeu retrouvé. Montreal, L'arbre, 1943. xiii, 242 p.   **11063**
Historical and eulogistic study of French theater figures of 20th century. One-third of book devoted to Copeau and the Vieux-Colombier; sees his influence in work of Baty, Pitoëff, Dullin, Jouvet, Ghéon and Chancerel. [NHP]
Review: Etiemble in LetFB 11:74–75, Jan. 1, 1944.

Sée, Edmond. Le théâtre français contemporain. A. Colin, 1928. 204 p. *Also:* 1950. 218 p.   **11064**
Encyclopedic, largely uncritical history of dramatists from Théâtre Libre to Giraudoux. Useful reference, especially for minor names. [NHP]

Serreau, Geneviève. Histoire du nouveau théâtre. Gallimard, 1966. 190 p. (Idées, 104)   **11065**
The point of departure—a "new theater" which seeks to redefine realism—loosely joins chapters of a critical history of twentieth-century French theater from Antoine to theater artists of the mid-sixties. Treats Adamov, Beckett, Genet, Ionesco, Schehadé, Vauthier, *et al.* [VGL]

Surer, Paul. Le théâtre français contemporain. Société d'édition et d'enseignement supérieur, 1964. 516 p.   **11066**
General overview of French theater from 1918 through the 50's. Except for section on "quatre maîtres" (Anouilh, Claudel, Cocteau and Giraudoux), authors are grouped in such familiar categories as "comic" or "psychological." Short biographical notice introduces each author or director. Illustrated. Surer sees current anguish,

pessimism and nihilism as impoverishing elements in drama. [VGL]

Versini, Georges. Le théâtre français depuis 1900. Presses univ. de France, 1970. 128 p. (Que sais-je? 461)   **11067**
Format very similar to Lalou's panorama. Versini adds some minimal lines concerning some playwrights produced since 1950. [VGL]
Review: Anon. in SFr 44:386–87, 1971.

Voltz, Pierre. La comédie. A. Colin, 1964. 472 p. (Coll. U)   **11068**
Useful, well-organized textbook for first year French university students; traces history of genre from the Middle Ages to date. Second section is an anthology of critical texts from Peletier du Mans to Ionesco, followed by selections from plays, a chronology and a critical bibliography. [NHP]

Memoirs

Lenormand, Henri-René. Les confessions d'un auteur dramatique. Albin Michel, 1949, 1953. 2 v.   **11069**
Anecdotal memoirs of a long career; hundreds of references to authors, actors and critics form a lively picture of theatrical life in the period between the wars. [NHP]
Review: P. Blanchart in RHT 1:93, 1950.

Lugné-Poe, [Aurélien]. Dernière pirouette. Sagittaire, 1946. 219 p.   **11070**
Anecdotal memoirs; most interesting for notes on early Claudel productions. [NHP]

Producers

Borgal, Clément. Metteurs en scène (Copeau, Jouvet, Dullin, Baty, Pitoëff). Fernand Lanore, 1963. 222 p.   **11071**
Objective general studies and well documented biographies, followed by useful selected bibliographies and repertories. [NHP]
Review: H. Gouhier in TR 198–99: 135–36, 1964.

Brasillach, Robert. Animateurs de théâtre. Corrêa, 1936. 224 p. *Also:* La table ronde, 1954. 270 p.   **11072**

Anecdotal and critical essays on Copeau, Jouvet, Dullin, Pitoëff, Baty and Rouché, supplemented by Brasillach's play reviews from 1936–1944 and an appendix listing the productions and roles of Jouvet, Dullin, Baty and Pitoëff. [NHP]

Gontard, Denis. La décentralisation théâtrale en France, 1895–1952. S.E.D.E.S., 1973. 542 p.   **11073**
Scholarly, elegantly published, very well documented and organized, readable rewrite of thesis; historical and critical chapters on early 20th-century efforts, Gémier, Copeau, Jouvet, Dullin, and post-World War II development of provincial companies. Indispensable reference and excellent bibliography. [NHP]

Hort, Jean. Les théâtres du Cartel et leurs animateurs. Geneva, Skira, 1944. 208 p.   **11074**
First intensive study; solid historical and critical work; serious lack of table of contents and index. [NHP]

Rouché, Jacques. L'art théâtral moderne. Cornély, 1910. 83 p.   **11075**
First important study in French of European *metteurs en scène* Fuchs, Erler, Meyerhold, Stanislavsky, Craig and Appia: a fecund influence on French theater. [NHP]
Review: J. Copeau in NRF 24:798–801, 1910.

Collections of Articles and Reviews

Artaud, Antonin. Le théâtre et son double. Gallimard, 1938. 155 p. (Métamorphoses, IV) *Also in his:* Œuvres complètes IV. Gallimard, 1964. p. 11–171. *Trans.:* The theater and its double. Grove press, 1958. 160 p.   **11076**
Landmark collection of essays, including the two manifestoes of the Theater of cruelty, widely and often confusedly interpreted. His concepts of ritual theater are found in Genet, of cosmic symbolism in Barrault's Claudel productions, of the fragility of the rational world in Ionesco, Beckett, Planchon and others. [NHP]
Review: Anon. in TLS 64:214, March, 18, 1965.

Aux sources de la vérité du théâtre moderne (Mallarmé, Zola, Claudel, Antoine, Lugné-Poe, Rouché, Copeau, le Cartel). Actes du Colloque de London (Canada), 1972. Texte établi par James B. Sanders. Lettres modernes, 1974. 224 p. (Situation, 30)　　　　**11077**

Papers presented by H. Block, J. Doat, P. Gobin, J.-M. Guieu, N. Paul, J. Petit, L. Rièse, J. Robichez and J. Sanders. Concise critical studies and analyses of principal contributors to modern theater. The significant articles have been analyzed separately under the appropriate headings. [NHP]

Azaïs, [Marcel]. Le chemin des gardies. Nouvelle librairie nationale, 1926. 509 p.　　　　**11078**

Collection of various articles, including author's play reviews in his *Essais critiques* from 1920–1924. [NHP]

Barrault, Jean-Louis. Réflexions sur le théâtre. Jacques Vautrin, 1949. 205 p. *Trans.*: Reflections on the theatre. London, Rockliff, 1951. xi, 185 p. *Also:* New York, Macmillan, 1952.　　　　**11079**

Autobiographical and critical notes form a valuable contribution to the history of French theater from 1931–1949; particularly revealing chapters on Artaud and Claudel. [NHP]
Review: L. Chancerel in RHT 1: 90–91, 1950.

Baty, Gaston. Rideau baissé. Bordas, 1949. 229 p.　　　　**11080**

Collection of essays on medieval origins of theater, Shakespeare, Racine, and the *metteur en scène;* all previously published (including famous chapter "Sire le mot") under other titles: *Le masque et l'encensoir,* 1921; *Visage de Shakespeare,* 1928; *Phèdre et la mise en scène des classiques,* 1939; *Le metteur en scène,* 1944. [NHP]
Review: L. Chancerel in RHT 1:95, 1950.

Brisson, Pierre. Au hasard des soirées. 1925–1935. N.R.F., 1935. 460 p.　　　　**11081**

Collection of Brisson's critical articles and play reviews in *Figaro.* [NHP]
Reviews: H. Bidou in Temps Sept. 9, 1935; R. Brasillach in RU 124, Oct. 1, 1935; P. Scize in Comœdia Aug. 24, 1935.

————. Du meilleur au pire. Gallimard, 1937. 260 p.　　　　**11082**

Collection of reviews in *Temps* and *Figaro* from 1930–37. [NHP]

Cahiers de la compagnie Madeleine Renaud-J.-L. Barrault. Julliard, 1953–　　　　**11083**

An irregular periodical usually consisting of special numbers mentioned elsewhere. [VGL]

Claudel, Paul. Mes idées sur le théâtre. Préface et présentation de Jacques Petit et J.-P. Kempf. Gallimard, 1966. 254 p. (Pratique du théâtre) *Trans.*: Claudel and the theatre. Coral Gables, Fla., Univ. of Miami press, 1972. 192 p.　　　　**11084**

Selection of Claudel's correspondence, newspaper articles, radio interviews, notes and lectures from 1894–1954, reflecting his intensely personal preoccupation with production of his plays. [NHP]

Colette, [Sidonie Gabrielle]. La jumelle noire. [Première-quatrième] année de critique. J. Ferenczi, 1934–38. 4 v. *Also in her:* Œuvres complètes. V. 10. Flammarion, 1949. 547 p. (Le fleuron)　　　　**11085**

Collection of Colette's play reviews in various newspapers from 1933–1938; chatty, rather gentle remarks. [NHP]

Copeau, Jacques. Critiques d'un autre temps. Gallimard, 1923. 252 p.　　　　**11086**

Collection of Copeau's critical essays and reviews from 1904–13, including the 1913 manifesto of the Théâtre du Vieux-Colombier. [NHP]
Reviews: Azaïs in EssCr 53:86–93, 1924; H. Béraud in MerF 170:753–54, 1924; H. Bidou in JdD July 23, 1929; P. Bost in NRF 132:202–04, 1924; P. Vandérem in RFran 4:401, 1924.

Dullin, Charles. Ce sont les dieux qu'il nous faut. Ed. établie et annotée par Charles Charras. Gallimard, 1969. 316 p. (Pratique du théâtre)　　　　**11087**

Collection of out-of-print essays, speeches and notes on theater from 1911 to 1949, plus outline of a proposed history of the Atelier. Good period document. [NHP]

Ghéon, Henri. L'art du théâtre. Montreal, Serge, 1944. 219 p. *Trans.*: The art of the theatre. Hill & Wang, 1961. 100 p. *Also:* Dramaturgie d'hier et de demain. Lyon, E. Vitte, 1963. 182 p.　　　　**11088**

Four lectures on poetic theater at the Vieux-Colombier in 1923, plus retrospective comments in 1938 in Montreal, presented by Jacques Reynaud. Valuable historic document. [NHP]
Reviews: P. Blanchart in RHT 2: 188–89, 1964; R. Cogniat in Comœdia May 5, 1923.

Hanoteau, Guillaume. Ces nuits qui ont fait Paris. Fayard, 1971. 670 p.   **11089**
Critical and anecdotal accounts of twenty-two memorable theater evenings over the past fifty years. Readable, informative recollections of premières of *Pelléas et Mélisande, Cyrano,* the Ballets russes, plays produced by Copeau, Dullin, *et al.* [NHP]
Review: A. Brincourt in FL March 12, 1971.

Jouvet, Louis. Réflexions du comédien. Nouvelle revue critique, 1938. 211 p. (Choses et gens de théâtre) *Also (rev.):* Rio de Janeiro, Americ-Edit, 1941. 235 p. *Also:* Librairie théâtrale, 1952. 235 p.   **11090**
The actor-director comments on Beaumarchais, Hugo and Becque, and then ponders on the problems of the director and on theater in general. More revealing of Jouvet's experiences than of the position of theater. [NHP]

———. Témoignages sur le théâtre. Flammarion, 1952. 251 p. (Bibliothèque d'Esthétique)   **11091**
Fascinating notes and commentary on Jouvet's productions of Molière, Romains and Giraudoux. Excellent analyses of the creation of roles and relations of actor and author. [NHP]

Léautaud, Paul. Le théâtre de Maurice Boissard. Gallimard, 1958. 2 v.   **11092**
Collection of Léautaud's critical articles and play reviews in MerF, NRF, and NL; noted for his vitriolic, partisan views. [NHP]

Le lieu théâtral dans la société moderne. C.N.R.S., 1963. 248 p. (Le chœur des muses)   **11093**
Colloquium at Royaumont in 1961 with J. Jacquot, D. Bablet, B. Dort, J. Duvignaud, P. Sonrel, A. Villiers, J. Meilziner, J. Vilar, E. Piscator and others. Examines popular theater, its architectural and theatrical definitions and its role in society. Many original

proposals and good historical summaries of present efforts. [NHP]
Review: E. Kongison in RHT 2: 210–12, 1965.

Marcel, Gabriel. L'heure théâtrale. Plon, 1959. 230 p.   **11094**
Collection of 51 play reviews for *Nouvelles littéraires* and *Europe nouvelle* from 1933–1959; grouped around work of Giraudoux, Montherlant, Anouilh, Camus and Sartre. [NHP]

———. Théâtre et religion. Lyon, E. Vitte, 1959. 107 p.   **11095**
Collection of essays on plays by Claudel and Sartre; reveals antipathy to Sartre's lack of humility, the key to great art. A short bio-biography of author. [NHP]

Martin du Gard, Maurice. Soirées de Paris. Flammarion, 1932. 283 p.   **11096**
Collection of play reviews in NL from 1930–31. [NHP]

Mauriac, François. Dramaturges. Librairie de France, 1928. 160 p. (Cahiers d'Occident, II, 5)   **11097**
Collection of play reviews in the *Revue hebdomadaire* from 1920–23. [NHP]

Mortier, Alfred. Quinze ans de théâtre (1917–1932). Albert Messein, 1933. 588 p.   **11098**
Collection of play reviews and critical articles in various magazines. [NHP]

Motley: Today's theatre. YFS 14:1–104, 1954–55.   **11099**
Begins curiously with views of Kierkegaard on farce in 19th-century Berlin. This is followed by a few articles on contemporary French theater in general and by analyses of various playwrights including Adamov, Anouilh, Beckett, Claudel, Cocteau, Neveux, Sartre *et al.* [VGL]

Pitoëff, Georges. Notre théâtre. Textes et documents réunis par Jean de Rigault. Messages, 1949. 112 p.   **11100**
Collection of excerpts from articles and speeches on stage production in general and program notes on Pitoëff's own repertoire; lists of plays and roles he interpreted and bibliography. [NHP]
Review: P. Blanchart in RHT 1:93–94, 1950.

Revue d'histoire du théâtre. Publications de la société du théâtre, 1948–   **11101**
Contains primarily articles on theater before the 20th century, but occasionally publishes pieces on contemporary theater. [VGL]

Simon, Pierre-Henri. Théâtre et destin. A. Colin, 1959. 224 p.   **11102**
Eight eminently readable lectures on the moral and social significance of the plays of Montherlant, Giraudoux, Anouilh, Mauriac, Camus, Sartre, Claudel and Salacrou, followed by a critical appreciation of Touchard's *Dionysos.* [NHP]
Review: K. Rühl in MD 4:218–19, 1961.

Le théâtre contemporain. RechD n.s. 2:1–258, 1952.   **11103**
Interesting collection of essays inspired by a debate on atheism organized by the Centre catholique des intellectuels français. Writers such as Marcel, Gouhier, Chancerel and Maulnier discuss theater in general and, more particularly, religion in theater. G. Lerminier, A. Béguin and others treat works by contemporary Catholic playwrights. [VGL]

Le théâtre en France. Eur 396–97:1–299, 1962.   **11104**
Largely a retrospective by various theater artists. Except for one article on the T.N.P. at Avignon, the issue mainly concerns major events of the French stage from Antoine to World War II. Contains a chronology of theater production in France from 1900 to 1939 (p. 202–10). [VGL]

Villiers, André. Théâtre et collectivité. Flammarion, 1953. 268 p. (Bibliothèque d'esthétique)   **11105**
Two colloquia of the Centre d'études philosophiques et techniques du théâtre on the collective expression and problem of leisure. Papers by Villiers, Gouhier, Jamati, Vilar, Friedmann, Roche, Rollan, Chapeau, Poysti, Darcante, Ambrière and Julien discuss moral and social role of theater. [NHP]

Vincent, Vincent. Rideau. Lausanne, Vaney-Burnier, 1929. 227 p.   **11106**
Collection of play reviews in *Comœdia* and various Swiss newspapers from 1926–29. Particularly interesting

for reviews of Les Copiaus in Burgundy and Switzerland, plus chapter of comments on French theater magazines. [NHP]

Werrie, Paul. Théâtre de la fuite. Brussels-Paris, Les écrits, 1943. 234 p.   **11107**
Collection of play reviews in Belgian magazines from 1930–42; particularly interesting for wartime productions. [NHP]

Special Topics

Aykroyd, Phyllis. The dramatic art of La compagnie des quinze. London, Eric Partridge, 1935. 63 p.   **11108**
First critical and historical study of this company; has the advantage of including interviews with M. Saint-Denis and other actors of the group. [NHP]

Blanchart, Paul. Survivances d'une tradition. *In:* Théâtre. Quatrième cahier. Eds. du pavois, 1945. p. 261–98.   **11109**
Traces use of *commedia dell'arte* techniques and themes in plays of Achard, Anouilh, Cocteau, Crommelynck, Giraudoux, Romains and others: credits influence of Copeau, Dullin and Jouvet for its modern reappearance and development. [NHP]

Block, Haskell M. Mallarmé and the materialization of the abstract in the modern drama. *In:* Aux sources de la vérité du théâtre moderne. *See* 11077. p. 41–51.   **11110**
Concise study of parallels and affinities between this aspect of Mallarmé's work and that of Ghelderode, Genet and Beckett. [NHP]

Cary, Joseph. Futurism and the French théâtre d'avant-garde. MP 57:113–21, 1959.   **11111**
Intriguing study of limited, mostly unintentional influence of Marinetti's militant, nationalist theories on plays by Apollinaire and Cocteau. [NHP]

Copeau, Jacques. Le théâtre populaire. Presses univ. de France, 1941. 64 p. (Bibliothèque du peuple) *Also:* 1942. *Also in his:* Registres I. Appels. Gallimard, 1974. p. 277–313. *Excerpts:* ThP 36:79–114, 1959. *Trans.:* Once again: style. TDR 7:180–91, 1963.   **11112**

At once a summing up and a prophecy as Copeau urges artists to rejoin society in order to regenerate it and their work. Socio-philosophical essay whose program seems to have emerged in the Maisons de la culture during Malraux's term of office. [NHP]

Cor, Laurence W. French views on language in the theater. FR 35:11–18, 1961.   **11113**

Stimulating comparison of use of language in the novel, the theater and the cinema; studies form and function, different patterns imposed by the genre, and the specific particularities of theater production that make a play primarily an aural and emotional experience. [NHP]

————. Inward music in the theater. FR 37:637–45, 1964.   **11114**

Analysis of silence or non-verbal communication on the part of actors and authors, with special reference to J.-J. Bernard and the "théâtre du silence." [NHP]

————. The literary theater in France. MLR 58:350–54, 1963.   **11115**

Good discussion of distinction between theater as spectacle and as literature; compendium of opinions from Copeau, Jouvet and Giraudoux. [NHP]

————. Phonic aspects of language in the theater. FR 37:31–40, 1963.   **11116**

Quotes from various authors and actors underscore this study of the impact of aural communication. Artaud's anti-literary theories and Decroux' use of mime are intelligently presented. [NHP]

Davril, R[obert]. Elizabethan drama and modern French theater. TQ 2:94–105, 1959.   **11117**

Good general discussion of the work of directors from Antoine to Vilar in the stage reforms which resulted from their production of the Elizabethan dramatists. Essentially same text republished as "Les pionniers" in EA 13:162–71, 1960. [NHP]

Dominique, Léon. Le théâtre russe et la scène française. Trans. by Nina Nidermiller and Michèle Wiernik. Olivier Perrin, 1969. 253 p.   **11118**

An account of Russian productions in France. Adapted from the author's reviews published in a Russian journal. [VGL]

Dubech, Lucien. La crise du théâtre. Librairie de France, 1928. 214 p.   **11119**

Informative and critical analysis of the theater of the 1920's; harsh comments on commercial theater. High praise for Copeau's Vieux-Colombier and for the work of the Cartel directors. [NHP]

Evans, Calvin. Mallarméan antecedents of the avant-garde theater. MD 6:12–19, 1963.   **11120**

Good attempt to show prophetic suggestions for future theater in the poet's essay, "Crayonné au théâtre." [NHP]

Fluchère, Henri. Shakespeare in France: 1900–1948. In: Shakespeare survey. Ed. by Allardyce Nicoll. Cambridge, At the univ. press, 1949. p. 115–25.   **11121**

Good historical survey of principal critical works and translations done in French. [NHP]

Gide, André. L'évolution du théâtre. Erm 15:5–22, May 1904. Also: Manchester univ. press, 1939. 37 p. Also in his: Nouveaux prétextes. Mercure de France, 1911. p. 7–27.   **11122**

Incisive critique of the weaknesses of the naturalist and symbolist dramas; a call for a more authentic theater. A manifesto for his own theater as well as that of the inter-war years, especially in the productions of Copeau and the Cartel. The 1939 ed. is supplemented by the notes of Carl Wildman. [NHP]

Jacquot, Jean. Shakespeare en France. Le temps, 1964. 142 p. (Théâtre, fêtes, spectacles)   **11123**

Brief chapter on productions before 1900; emphasis is on new stagings and interpretations from Antoine to Planchon; sees a return to Elizabethan stage as beneficial to contemporary theater. [NHP]

Review: Anon. in CRB 46:126, 1964.

Jouan, F. Le retour au mythe grec dans le théâtre français contemporain. BAGB 3:62–79, 1952.   **11124**

Analyses of almost all the plays with Greek themes by dramatists from Gide to Camus; good general reference. [NHP]

Knepler, Henry. Translation and adaptation in the contemporary drama. MD 4:31–41, 1961.   **11125**

Practical and sensitive discussion of the problems which require cultural as well as linguistic abilities; examples from Anouilh, Genet and Giraudoux. [NHP]

Lakich, John J. The ideal and reality in the French theater of the 1920's. MLQ 31:64–77, 1970.   **11126**

Good study of mostly forgotten plays shows how these two themes in Anouilh, Giraudoux, Cocteau, Camus, Sartre and others can be found in works by Sarment, Bernard, Neveux, Salacrou, Vildrac and Pellerin. [NHP]

Lee, Vera. The ideal of harmony in modern French theater. FR 36:482–90, 1963.
                                                   11127

Lucid, well-documented presentation of the accomplishments and failures of French producers from Copeau to Vilar in promoting new authors and inspiring great theater. [NHP]

Lelièvre, Renée. Le théâtre dramatique italien en France (1855–1940). A. Colin, 1959. 650 p.   **11128**

Ponderous thesis style with many typographical errors rescued by an informative background section of Franco-Italian cultural relations and accounts of the influence of D'Annunzio and Marinetti on French theater. The Pirandello experience has been more thoroughly examined by Bishop (*see* 11043). [NHP]

Review: Y. Batard in RHT 1:74–76, 1962.

Lerminier, Georges. Engagement et disponibilité du critique dramatique. *In:* Le théâtre moderne. Hommes et tendances. Ed. by J. Jacquot. Eds. du Centre national de la recherche scientifique, 1978. v. 1. p. 37–42.   **11129**

The then drama critic of *Le parisien libéré* treats the evolution of the French theater critic's role from the 19th century to mid-20th century. Résumé of discussion on the subject is appended. [VGL]

Ludovicy, E. Le mythe grec dans le théâtre français contemporain. RLV 22:387–418, 1956.   **11130**

Scholarly critical study of plays by Gide, Claudel, Giraudoux, Sartre, Yourcenar, Cocteau and Anouilh; excellent supplement to article by Jouan. [NHP]

Melcher, Edith. The use of words in contemporary French theater. MLN 77:470–83, 1962.   **11131**

Largely derivative study of plays by Claudel, Giraudoux and Audiberti as opposed to the anti-literary plays of Ionesco, Adamov, Beckett, Vauthier and Tardieu. [NHP]

Nelson, Robert J. Play within a play. New Haven, Yale univ. press, 1958. 182 p. (Yale Romanic studies: second series, 5)
                                                   11132

Inspired by Francis Fergusson's *The idea of a theater*, Nelson examines some classic and modern dramatists' use of the mirror technique in expressing their conceptions of theater. Sees Anouilh as more influenced by Gide than Pirandello. [NHP]

Romilly, J. de. Légendes grecques et théâtre moderne. MerF 321, no. 1089:71–87, 1954.   **11133**

Good study of plays by Gide, Giraudoux, Cocteau, Anouilh and Sartre which reinterpret the classics to reflect the modern world. [NHP]

Salvan, J. L. L'esprit du théâtre nouveau. FR 14:109–18, 1940.   **11134**

Author explains how the techniques of the Cartel draw away from a realistic, psychological portrayal to a stylized and suggestive staging. [NHP]

Simon, John K. The presence of Musset in modern French drama. FR 40:27–38, 1966.   **11135**

Thoughtful study of the analogy between theme, pattern and style in Musset's plays and those of Giraudoux, Anouilh, Camus and Sartre. [NHP]

Solntsev, Nicolas. Rencontres de Constantin Stanislavski avec Paris. RHT 4:327–36, 1962.   **11136**

Historical account, with translated excerpts from the Russian, of Stanislavsky's various visits to Paris from the 1880's to 1934. Interesting comments on Sarah Bernhardt and traditional interpretations of Molière at Comédie Française. [NHP]

Veinstein, André. Du Théâtre libre au Théâtre Louis Jouvet. Billaudot, 1955. 284 p. (Librairie théâtrale)   **11137**

Scholarly study of the periodicals published by the art theaters of Antoine, Paul Fort, Lugné-Poe, Copeau, Baty, Dullin and Jouvet. An indispensable and intelligently prepared critique of the aims and accomplishments of these little theaters. [NHP]

Reviews: L. Chancerel in RHT 3–4: 366, 1955; R. Saurel in CRB 13:121, 1955.

Wathelet-Willem, J. L'irréel dans le théâtre contemporain: réflexions sur quelques pièces. MRo 4:25–34, 1954.   **11138**

Rapid history of use of unreal in French theater, followed by sketchy catalog of authors and plays transcending or evading reality. After various digressions on fate of theater threatened by film, author cites influence of directors and of foreign theater in trend toward the unreal. [VGL]

Stage and Stagecraft

Allen, Elizabeth S. Eurythmics for the theatre. ThAMo 3:42–50, 1919.   **11139**

Historical and critical presentation of Emil Jaques-Dalcroze's method, with four drawings, encouraging American directors to follow lead of Copeau in its use as training technique for actors. [NHP]

Annuaire du spectacle. Eds. Raoult, 1946–   **11140**

Listing of theater, film, radio and T.V. artists, administrators and technicians. Information on unions and other professional associations. Data on salaries, theater halls and repertoire. Contains a collection of full-page professional photographs. [VGL]

Arnold, Paul. L'avenir du théâtre. Savel, 1947. 203 p. (Esthétique)   **11141**

General historical study of stage architecture, production, costuming and makeup; good introduction to subject. [NHP]

Reviews: R. Gouhier in RevTh 9–10:124–26, 1948; R. Thomas in RHT 1–2:73, 1948.

Aslan, Odette. L'art du théâtre. Seghers, 1963. 680 p.   **11142**

Encyclopedic anthology of quotes on dramatic theory and technique by critics, actors and dramatists from Plato to Ionesco. Imaginative selection of sources. [NHP]

Review: M. Gravier in RHT 2:190, 1964.

Bablet, Denis. Esthétique générale du décor de théâtre de 1870 à 1914. Eds. du Centre national de la recherche scientifique, 1965. 443 p.   **11143**

Comprehensive history of stage design in France and the effect of foreign theories on its evolution. Investigation of principles governing various styles of décor. Well illustrated. Thorough bibliography. [VGL]

———. La mise en scène contemporaine. I: 1887–1914. La renaissance du livre, 1968. 101 p. (Dionysos)   **11144**

A more compact history treating the same general period as preceding entry and concentrating on *animateurs* rather than décor. [VGL]

———. La plastique scénique. *In:* L'année 1913. I. Ed. by L. Brion-Guerry. Klincksieck, 1971. p. 789–822.   **11145**

Historical, well-documented presentation of pre-World War I development of *mise en scène;* underscores novelty of participation of painters, technicians and directors. [NHP]

Boll, André. La mise en scène contemporaine, son évolution. Eds. de la nouvelle revue critique, 1944. 145 p. (Choses et gens de théâtre)   **11146**

Highly informative and readable history of contemporary stage production in France. Ends by discussing the problem of creativity of authors in relation to directors and public. [VGL]

Chancerel, Léon. Panorama du théâtre, des origines à nos jours. A. Colin, 1955. 224 p.   **11147**

Selective and provocative survey of the esthetics of theater; sympathetic to theatrical rather than literary aspects, with praise for efforts of Copeau and Jouvet. [NHP]

Review: P. Quémeneur in RHT 3–4:372, 1955.

———. Le théâtre et la jeunesse. Préface de Charles Vildrac. Eds. Bourrelier, 1941. 186 p.   **11148**

Rather musty and quaint for today's reader, the book explains, in the light of the author's experience, how to stage plays with young students. Interesting sections on the use of mask (p. 127–39, 175–79). [VGL]

Copfermann, Emile. Le théâtre populaire, pourquoi? Maspero, 1965. 167 p. (Cahiers libres, 69) **11149**
Contains a short history of French popular theater. Account of intrigues at the T.N.P. Examines very subjectively and controversially questions of political theater, of theater as business and of the value of cultural houses. [VGL]

Dhomme, Sylvain. La mise en scène contemporaine d'André Antoine à Bertolt Brecht. Fernand Nathan, 1959. 349 p. **11150**
Useful as a history of the development of stage production in France since 1887. Sections on the contributions of Germany (in particular, Brecht's), Russia and the U.S., although the question of influence is not broached. Discusses the ideas of Artaud and the experience of Barrault. [VGL]

Dorcy, Jean. A la rencontre de la mime et des mimes: Decroux, Barrault, Marceau. Suivi de textes inédits d'Etienne Decroux; Pour le pire et pour le meilleur; Jean-Louis Barrault, La mime tragique; Marcel Marceau, Le halo poétique. Neuilly-sur-Seine, Cahiers de danse et culture, 1958. 152 p. *Trans.:* The mime, and essays by Etienne Decroux, Jean-Louis Barrault, and Marcel Marceau. Trans. by Robert Speller, Jr., and Pierre de Fontnouvelle. New York, R. Speller, 1961. 116 p. **11151**
Good anecdotal history of the genre in the twentieth century. [NHP]
Review: A. Boll in RHT 1:57, 1960.

Dullin, Charles. Souvenirs et notes de travail d'un acteur. O. Lieutier, 1946. 154 p. **11152**
Reminiscences, advice to young actors, thoughts on improvisation and esthetics, from an eminent professional. [NHP]

Duvignaud, Jean. L'acteur, esquisse d'une sociologie du comédien. Gallimard, 1965. 304 p. (Bibliothèque des idées) **11153**
Comprehensive and intelligent historical study of development of the actor's place in society and the degree of his identification with the role. [NHP]

———. Spectacle et société. Denoël, 1970. 165 p. (Bibliothèque médiations) **11154**
The function of the imaginary in society from the Greek theater to the happening; study of the major theatrical forms as essentially representative of the societies in which they were created. [NHP]
Review: M. P. in MRo 20, no. 3: 95–96, 1970.

Epstein, Alvin. The mime theatre of Etienne Decroux. Chry 11:3–13, 1958. **11155**
Brief history of the genre as preface to an intelligent study of Decroux's methods. [NHP]

Fougère, Valentine. Masques, mimes et marionnettes. Tend 34:225–48, 1965. **11156**
General history and description of mask, mime and puppetry on the modern French stage. [VGL]

Gouhier, Henri. L'essence du théâtre. Plon, 1943. 236 p. (Présences) **11157**
Philosophical essay on definition of theater, its dependence on actors, technicians and directors; discussion of religion in history of theater. Short introductory notes by Pitoëff, Dullin, Jouvet and Baty. [NHP]

———. L'œuvre théâtrale. Flammarion, 1958. 218 p. (Bibliothèque d'esthétique) **11158**
Third volume of a philosophical investigation into the meaning of theater; well-documented psychological analyses of artistic creation of plot and characters, dramatic unity, action and time in Bergsonian terms. [NHP]
Review: P. Van Tieghem in RHT 1:57–59, 1959.

———. Le théâtre et l'existence. Aubier, 1952. 222 p. (Philosophie de l'esprit) *Also:* Vrin, 1973. 224 p. **11159**
Second volume of trilogy on a philosophical study of theater; well-documented study of dramatic genres and their historic evolution. [NHP]

Kowzan, Tadeusz. Littérature et spectacle. Warsaw, Eds. scientifiques, 1970. 196 p. **11160**

Pellucid and stimulating study of the esthetic, thematic and semiological rapports between the dramatic text and theatrical production; a masterful and substantial overview, with some bias shown for the theater as spectacle. [NHP]
Review: J. Robichez in RHT 3:297–98, 1973.

Larthomas, Pierre. Le langage dramatique, sa nature, ses procédés. A. Colin, 1972. 478 p.   **11161**
Solid, well-written examination of stylistics from the 17th century to date; excellent exposition of linguistic and psychological nature of para-verbal and verbal elements; sentient and fecund views of familiar plays. [NHP]
Review: J. Roubine in RHL 74: 161–63, 1974.

Lorelle, Yves. Les transes et le théâtre. CRB 38:67–86, 1962. *Also in:* Aslan, Odette. L'art du théâtre. Seghers, 1963. p. 463–65.   **11162**
Provocative socio-psychological study of the process by which actors create roles, with comparisons to role-playing techniques in various religious ceremonies. [NHP]

Mariel, Pierre. Les Fratellini, histoire de trois clowns. Société anonyme d'éditions, 1923. 271 p.   **11163**
Preface by J. Copeau, who admired the tradition of the commedia dell'arte as represented by these artists; anecdotal and analytic account of the profession. [NHP]

Moussinac, Léon. Traité de la mise en scène. Massin, 1948. 179 p.   **11164**
Excellent handbook, including brief history of contemporary stage production with practical outline of basic elements of organization. [NHP]
Review: L. Chancerel in RevTh 9–10:122, 1948.

Piemme, Jean-Marie. L'organisation de l'espace scénique et les problèmes du lieu théâtral. RLV 34:245–60, 1968.   **11165**
Development of thoughts on reading of Bablet (*see* 11143) and Jacquot (*see* 11093); also a short survey of recent trends. [NHP]

Saint-Denis, Michel. Theatre: the rediscovery of style. Theatre arts books, 1960. 110 p.   **11166**
Five readable and penetrating lectures on the importance of classical discipline in actor training, of style, its definition and influence on modern realism, and a brief history of the Old Vic theatre school. [NHP]
Reviews: F. Anders in RHT 1:88–89, 1962; H. Knepler in MD 6:101–03, 1963; O. Larson in ETJ 13:135–36, 1961.

Temkine, Raymonde. L'entreprise théâtre. Cujas, 1967. 498 p.   **11167**
Detailed account of subsidization and decentralization of French theater. The background and operations of national theaters, *centres dramatiques* and *maisons de la culture,* and, lastly, a brief glance at the French public. [VGL]

Van Tieghem, Philippe. Les grands acteurs contemporains. Presses univ. de France, 1960. 128 p. (Que sais-je?)   **11168**
Useful compendium of some two hundred short biographies; more encyclopedic than critical. [NHP]

Veinstein, André. La mise en scène théâtrale et sa condition esthétique. Flammarion, 1955. 394 p. (Bibliothèque d'esthétique)
                                                11169
One of the more serious publications on the concept of stage production as it relates to French theater. Problems of the stage are analyzed from historical, esthetic and psychological points of view. At the heart of the study lies the quarrel of drama as spectacle versus drama as literature. [VGL]

———. Le théâtre expérimental: tendances et propositions. La renaissance du livre, 1968. 118 p. (Dionysos)   **11170**
Striking presentation of technical aspects of stage production. French producers and stage designers contribute information on equipping and designing experimental theaters and staging productions. While the text includes commentary on foreign theater, it is concerned mainly with France. Amply and clearly illustrated with sketches and photos. [VGL]

Villiers, André. La psychologie de l'art dramatique. A. Colin, 1951. 224 p.   **11171**

Lucid analysis and formulation of the principles of theatrical production in all its extraliterary aspects: acting, *mise en scène*, stage architecture, etc. Excellent handbook. [NHP]

——. La psychologie du comédien. Odette Lieutier, 1946. 328 p.   **11172**
Scholarly, readable and well-documented examination of the making of an actor: technique, skill, sensitivity, intelligence, emotions, physique, social background, etc. Excellent analysis of Diderot's *Paradoxe* and selected bibliography. [NHP]

——. La recherche d'un nouvel espace théâtral en 1913. *In:* L'année 1913. I. Travaux sous la direction de L. Brion-Guerry. Klincksieck, 1971. p. 769–87.   **11173**
Scholarly and detailed description of three theatrical events in 1913 which marked the evolution of stage architecture: inauguration of the Théâtre des Champs-Elysées, the Théâtre du Vieux-Colombier, and the Claudel production at Hellerau, Switzerland. [NHP]

Les voies de la création théâtrale. Ed. by J. Jacquot and D. Bablet. Eds. du Centre national de la recherche scientifique, 1970–72. 3 v.   **11174**
Luxurious, highly detailed, beautifully and voluminously illustrated volumes on staging of *créations* in France. Mainly foreign plays, but Genet's *Paravents* in v. 3, p. 11–107. [VGL]

Marcel Achard
(Nos. 11175–11188)

LAURE RIÈSE

General Studies

Achard, Marcel. Discours sous la coupole. Discours de réception à l'Académie française et réponse de Marcel Pagnol. Nagel, 1960. 73 p.   **11175**
Traces life of A. and how he came to write comedies. Cites many critics of A.'s comedies. Compares his theater to some of Shakespeare's light comedies.

Ambrière, Francis. Le théâtre de Marcel Achard. An 97:20–32, 1958.   **11176**
The author traces the life, vocation, tendencies of the first plays. Influence

of Jouvet and Dullin. How A. became a poet and moralist, complete with illustrations.

Barrault, Jean-Louis. Marcel Achard ou la poésie et le cirque. *In his:* Une troupe et ses auteurs. Vautrain, 1950. p. 75–81.   **11177**
The influences in A.'s poetry; his bitter drollery and temperament. Analysis of first scene of *Malbrough s'en va-t-en guerre* as an example of "comédie-chanson."

Knowles, Dorothy. Studio theatre: fantasy, fairytale. *In her:* French drama of the inter-war years 1918–39. Barnes & Noble, 1968. p. 183–87.   **11178**
Presentation of A.'s plays from 1923–1964, his early influences, his classical approach to love and friendship, a not too perfect return to tradition. His flashback technique and Hollywood influence on him. His use of melodrama and satire. Poetry in his early plays; then a world of reality and dream. An approach to A.'s theater differing somewhat from the French critics. Shrewd and critical information.

Mignon, P. L. Achard. *In his:* Le théâtre d'aujourd'hui de A jusqu'à Z. Michel Brient, 1966. p. 11–14.   **11179**
Critical information on author, his plays. Useful commentaries on the writer and several of his works.

Surer, Paul. La comédie romantique. B. Marcel Achard. *In his:* Cinquante ans de théâtre. SEDES, 1969. p. 95–101.   **11180**
After a short biography and bibliography the author discusses the evolution of A.'s plays.

——. Etudes sur le théâtre français contemporain. IX. Les lunaires. IL 10, no. 5:190–97, 1958.   **11181**
Important place given to A.'s work, his tradition, his way of handling laughter to hide suffering, his taste for youth. His speciality, love in all its phases, and how A. uses it.

Individual Plays

Bourget-Pailleron, Robert. Marcel Achard: Machin-Chouette. RDM 21:136–38, 1964.   **11182**

How A. succeeds in exploiting a very banal theme and is able to provide unforseen fantasy. He uses a circus process which may lose its efficacy. Author points out the shortcomings.

—————. Marcel Achard: Patate. RDM 727–29, Feb. 1957.   11183
Mentions how A. manipulates hatred. Contrary to Druon, sees here a theater of convention.

Brisson, Pierre. Marcel Achard. I. Jean de la lune au théâtre. II. Jean de la lune à l'écran. *In his:* Au hasard des soirées. Gallimard, 1935. p. 362–74.   11184
The most complete criticism of the play—weighing good and bad qualities of theme and plot. Second article is an interesting analysis of the play compared with the more dramatic presentation in the film.

Criticus (pseud. of Marcel Berger). Marcel Achard: le style au microscope. OLib 424: 51–70, 1962. *Also:* Marcel Achard. *In his:* Le style au microscope. Dramaturges. Calmann-Lévy, 1952. p. 9–36.   11185
Acknowledges the success of *Jean de la lune.* Shows intentions of author and comments especially on the first act. A most original and useful "exposition de texte."

Druon, Maurice. Les raisons d'un succès: M. Achard et Patate. Nef 4:61–63, 1957.
11186
Important departure in A.'s theater. A detailed study on friendship and human relations. Very useful to the understanding of the play.

Poirot-Delpech, Bertrand. L'idiote de Marcel Achard. *In his:* Au soir le soir. Mercure de France, 1969. p. 45–48.   11187
An interesting and analytical account of A.'s technique in making the play pass from comedy to tragic verisimilitude.

Simiot, Bernard. Le théâtre. RevHM 42: 163–64, 1950.   11188
La demoiselle de petite vertu interpreted as a comedy fighting the realistic slice of life plays.

Antonin Artaud
(Nos. 11189–11266)

NAOMI GREENE

Editions

Artaud, Antonin. Œuvres complètes. Gallimard, 1965–74. 13 v.   11189
Extensive critical ed. of A.'s works with notes giving time and place almost everything was written. V. 8 contains letters from Mexico. V. 9, 10, 11 contain letters from Rodez.

Correspondence

Artaud, Antonin. Lettres à Génica Athanasiou. Gallimard, 1969. 377 p.   11190
Letters from A. to a woman he was in love with during his early years in Paris.

Biography

Armand-Laroche, Dr. Jean-Louis. Antonin Artaud et son double. Périgueux, Pierre Fanlac, 1964. 157 p.   11191
Psychoanalytical study of A. by a psychiatrist who is convinced of A.'s schizophrenia.
Review: H. Hécaen in JPNP 1:115–16, 1964.

Brau, Jean-Louis. Antonin Artaud. Eds. de la table ronde, 1971. 277 p.   11192
This first full-length biography of A. is somewhat disappointing since it brings to light little that is new. But it is well written and the author is evidently enthusiastic about his subject.

Breton, André. La révolution surréaliste. *In his:* Entretiens. Gallimard, 1952. p. 103–14.   11193
Several interesting pages describing Breton's memories of the young A. at the time he joined the surrealist group.

Bugard, Pierre. Le comédien et son double. Stock, 1970. 237 p.   11194
One may not agree with the author's tendency to analyze A. from a psychological viewpoint but he does bring to light some of A.'s answers to medical questionnaires concerning his use of drugs. See esp. p. 159–80.

Henric, Jacques. Artaud travaillé par la Chine. *In:* Artaud, 10/18. *See* 11205. p. 213-44. **11195**

Polemical attempt to make A. "revolutionary" and link him to materialism and to the thought of Mao Tse-tung. Provocative — especially in its comparisons of A. and other surrealists — though often distorts A.

Hort, Jean. Antonin Artaud: le suicidé de la société. Geneva, Eds. connaître, 1960. 148 p. **11196**

Reminiscences of A.'s years in the theater in Paris during the 1920's by a fellow actor. Unfortunately, Hort did not really understand A. nor did he sympathize with A.'s dislike of Western theater.

Isou, Isidore. Antonin Artaud torturé par les psychiatres (les ignobles erreurs d'André Breton, Tristan Tzara, Robert Desnos et Claude Bourdet dans l'affaire de l'internement d'Antonin Artaud). Suivi de: Qui est le docteur Ferdière? par Maurice Lemaître. Lettrisme, 1970. 160 p. **11197**

Study of A.'s stay at Rodez. Just as A. condemns Van Gogh's doctors, Isou wants to show how A.'s encounters with doctors (particularly Ferdière) during his stay in institutions resulted in the "physical destruction and physical-psychic tortures of Antonin Artaud." In comparison with Isou's book, A.'s own condemnation of psychiatry appears fairly mild.

Malausséna, Marie-Ange. Antonin Artaud. RevTh 23:39-57, 1953. **11198**

Biographical notes by A.'s sister who tends to emphasize A.'s happy childhood and devotion to his mother, and who assigns a determining role to the illness which first struck when A. was five.

Marowitz, Charles. Artaud at Rodez. EvR 12:65-67, 81-86, 1968. **11199**

Marowitz brings to light some interesting facts about A.'s visit to Ireland and his stay in various institutions. But since his article does contain some errors, one wonders if all the new facts are totally correct.

Nin, Anaïs. The diary of Anaïs Nin. Ed. and with an introd. by Gunther Stuhlmann. II, 1934-1939. New York, The swallow press & Harcourt, 1967. 357 p. *Also:* London, Owen, 1966. **11200**

Interspersed pages devoted to an account of Nin's friendship with A. in the 1930's. According to Nin, A. was in love with her, but she resisted him, fearing to be drawn into his "madness." Similar, but fictionalized, account of her meetings with A. in the chapter *Je suis le plus malade des surréalistes* of her book *Under a glass bell* (London, Editions Poetry, 1947).

Thévenin, Paule. Antonin Artaud dans la vie. TelQ 20:25-40, 1965. *Trans.:* A letter on Artaud. TDR 9:99-117, 1965. **11201**

Discussion and reminiscences concerning her own friendship with A. which began shortly after his release from Rodez and lasted until his death. Thévenin relates how A. worked on the poems he wrote in the course of these last two years (the importance of sound, of breathing, etc.), and tells of the discovery of his final illness.

Special Numbers

Antonin Artaud et le théâtre de notre temps. CRB 22-23:3-254, 1958. **11202**

Collection of essays and reminiscences concerning A. by Jean-Louis Barrault, Arthur Adamov, Maurice Blanchot, René Daumal, André Masson, Claude Mauriac, Paule Thévenin, et al. Important biographical notes by Paul Thévenin.

Antonin Artaud, l'homme et son message. NP/PP 20:7-146, 1971. **11203**

Interviews with Robert Aron, Jean-Louis Barrault, Gaston Ferdière and Henri Thomas, as well as a number of articles on A.

Antonin Artaud, ou La santé des poètes. TourF 63-64:3-226, 1959. **11204**

Collection of articles and reminiscences concerning A. The editors wanted to discuss, and perhaps destroy, some of the controversies that had sprung up around A. Was he an atheist? Had he been persecuted by Dr. Ferdière? But in general they inflamed disputes rather than calmed them. Of special interest are the bio-bibliographical notes by his sister, Marie-Ange Malausséna, and an article by his doctor at Rodez, Gaston Ferdière.

Artaud. Ed. by Philippe Sollers. Union générale d'éditions, 1973. 306 p. (10/18)
11205
Assemblage of papers, followed by discussions, delivered at a colloquium on A. and Bataille held in July, 1972 at the Centre culturel international of Cerisy-la-Salle directed by Philippe Sollers. Interpretation of A. along the lines of *Tel quel* textual/political criticism: A. as a "subversive" force as far as writing, society, madness and knowledge are concerned. Papers by Philippe Sollers, Julia Kristeva, Marcelin Pleynet, Pierre Guyotat, Xavière Gauthier, Jacques Henric and Guy Scarpetta.

Artaud sans légende. MagL 61:8–29, 1972.
11206
This issue, devoted largely to A., contains a good bio-bibliography of A., short articles by Alain Virmaux (A. and the theater), Jean-Louis Brau (A. and the cinema), Laurette Véza (A. the poet) among others. Also a text by A. long believed lost: *Point final.*

De la contradiction au sommet ou pour en finir avec Artaud. TourF 69:9–68, 1961.
11207
Series of articles and reminiscences mainly concerned with A.'s stay in Rodez, and his last two years in Paris. Contains letters by A.

Hommage à Antonin Artaud. FrA 1–138, Sept. 1948.
11208
Volume which appeared soon after A.'s death. Contains laudatory articles by J. de Boschère, A. Patri, J. Rousselot and M. Bataille.

Revue de la poésie, K. 1–2:1–138, 1948.
11209
Review which appeared shortly after A.'s death. Articles show reactions of his former friends and colleagues: writers such as Adamov and Audiberti, men of the theater such as Roger Blin and Charles Dullin. Helpful factual article on A.'s connection with cinema by Gaston Bounoure and Caradec.

Spécial Antonin Artaud. QVQ 5–6:97–151, 1948.
11210
Short texts by friends of A. such as Arthur Adamov, Paule Thévenin, Jean Paulhan, Roger Blin, Marthe Robert and one by Gide concerning a talk given by A. at the Vieux Colombier theater.

Il teatro della crudeltà. Sip 230:1–100, 1965.
11211
Issue of *Sipario* devoted to international manifestations of the "theater of cruelty," especially in France, England, Germany, Italy and the United States. Interviews with Peter Weiss and Julian Beck. Considerations of "cruelty" in the cinema and on television.

General Studies

André-Carraz, Danièle. L'expérience intérieure d'Antonin Artaud. Librairie Saint-Germain-des Prés, 1973. 184 p.
11212
This book concentrates on A.'s mystical aspirations — his search for Being and for Unity, his experience of the Void — and how they are reflected in his poetry, theater and later writings.

Blanchot, Maurice. Artaud. NRF 8:873–81, 1956. *Also in his:* Le livre à venir. Gallimard, 1959. p. 45–52. *Also:* Gallimard, 1971. p. 53–62. (Idées, 246)
11213
Brief but important, dense study of the impossibility of writing in A. and the relationship between thought and language.

Brotherston, J.G. Revolution and the ancient literature of Mexico, for D. H. Lawrence and Antonin Artaud. TCL 18:181–89, 1972.
11214
Concise description of the differences and similarities in A.'s and Lawrence's view of Mexico.

Caws, Mary Ann. Artaud's myth of motion. *In her:* The inner theater of French poetry. Princeton, Princeton univ. press, 1972. p. 125–40.
11215
Interesting thematic analysis of A.'s work in terms of motion and mobility, although one doubts if A.'s world view can be explained in terms of any single concept.

Charbonnier, Georges. Essai sur Antonin Artaud. Seghers, 1959. 217 p. (Poètes d'aujourd'hui, 66) *Also* (*rev.*): Antonin Artaud, un essai de Georges Charbonnier. Seghers, 1970. 220 p. (Poètes d'aujourd'hui, 66)
11216

Unfortunately Charobonnier has pushed his admiration of A. to the point where his style is a poor imitation of A.'s own and often more confusing. But he has assembled a number of texts that should serve as a good introduction to A.'s work.

Review: A. Loranquin in BdL 209: 271–72, 1959.

Copfermann, Emile. Le théâtre pour comprendre et exercer la vie. *In his:* La mise en crise théâtrale. Maspero, 1972. p. 13–47. **11217**

Rapid glance at A.'s life and work but surprisingly detailed descriptions of the production of Le théâtre Alfred Jarry.

Derrida, Jacques. La parole soufflée. TelQ 20:41–67, 1965. *Also in his:* L'écriture et la différence. Seuil, 1970. p. 253–92. **11218**

Interesting article even if it sheds more light on Derrida's metaphysical/linguistic criticism than on A. Analyzes the nature of writing and our relationship to the work as well as the relationship between madness and metaphysics in A. Discusses A.'s feelings that his thoughts and words — and hence his life — were being "stolen" in metaphysical terms.

Durozoi, Gérard. Artaud: l'aliénation et la folie. Larousse, 1972. 231 p. (Thèmes et textes) **11219**

Despite its title, this book does not concentrate on the question of A.'s "madness," but serves as an excellent introduction to A.'s life and work. Informative, clear, impartial (yet sympathetic), if not profound. The author is the first to discuss the different critical approaches that have been taken in connection with A.'s work. Good critical bibliography.

Foucault, Michel. Histoire de la folie. U. G. E. [Union générale d'éditions], 1971. p. 301–04. (10/18) *Also:* Gallimard, 1972. p. 554–57. **11220**

Several pages toward the end of this study analyze the relationship between A.'s madness and his work. When Foucault talks of A.'s madness as "the absence of the work," he is less clear than when he expresses his admiration for the works of genius produced by "madmen" like Nietzsche, Van Gogh and A.

Hahn, Otto. Portrait d'Antonin Artaud. Le soleil noir, 1968. 137 p. **11221**

Analysis of A. along the lines of Sartrean existentialist criticism. Hahn is at his best when dealing with A.'s earlier texts like "Héloïse et Abélard." Originally published in two parts in TM 192:May 1962; 193:June 1962.

Review: P. Pia in Car Feb. 5, 1969.

Henric, Jacques. Une profondeur matérielle. Cr 278:616–25, 1970. **11222**

A. from the perspective of materialism. Emphasizes A.'s condemnation of Western idealism and dualism. Interprets A.'s statements that his intellectual sufferings were felt in his body and his demand for a non-verbal theater as examples of materialism. Interesting, although in his desire to prove his thesis, Henric seems to ignore some of the contradictions in A.'s thought, especially his leanings toward mysticism.

Joski, Daniel. Artaud. Eds. universitaires, 1970. 124 p. (Classiques du XXe siècle) **11223**

Ordered, logical and easily readable, if far from profound, introduction to A.'s life and work. Unfortunately, the author inveighs against A.'s cultish followers and then proceeds to join their ranks.

Reviews: A. Ayguesparse in Marg 139:82, 1971; A. Marissel in Esp 399: 168–71, 1971.

Knapp, Bettina. Antonin Artaud: man of vision. David Lewis, 1969. 233 p. **11224**

Somewhat confusing, but enthusiastic study of A.'s life and work. The author attempts to show how many of A.'s ideas — especially in the theatrical realm — had an influence on later developments.

Reviews: A. Amoia in FR 42:683–84, 1970; G. Wellwarth in RR 52:155–56, 1971.

Kristeva, Julia. Le sujet en procès. TelQ 52:12–30, 1972; 53:17–38, 1973. *Also in:* Artaud. *See* 11205. p. 42–133. **11225**

Very difficult, technical analysis of A. somewhat along the lines of Lacanian psychoanalysis. Sees A., like Mallarmé and Joyce, as part of a literary "avant-garde" which has attacked the concept of a unified self as well as the structures, especially the linguistic ones, surrounding it.

Laporte, Roger. Antonin Artaud ou La pensée du supplice. NoCo 12:19–36, 1968. **11226**

Analysis of the fundamental problems, expressed in A.'s early works, concerning thought and being, life and literature.

Leroy, Jacques. Ecrire artaudien, écrire Artaud: la mauvaise foi de la parole. SubS 7:89–100, 1973. **11227**

The problem of thought and language in A. along the lines put forward by Jacques Derrida (theft of language, relation between body and thought).

Lyons, John D. Artaud: intoxication and its double. YFS 50:120–29, 1974. **11228**

Lyons examines the relationship between A.'s search for a new system of communication and his experiences with the drugs which destroy the boundaries established by verbal language.

Mauriac, Claude. Antonin Artaud. *In his:* L'alittérature contemporaine. Albin Michel, 1958. p. 33–48. *Trans.:* The new literature. George Braziller, 1959. p. 35–50. **11229**

Interesting discussion of A. in a work devoted to a number of contemporary writers including Kafka, Beckett and Michaux. Brief analysis of some of A.'s earlier writings; sees A.'s madness in a metaphysical dimension as "the impossibility of being, the horror of essential solitude."

Review: C. Burucoa in EnLA 13:37–38, 1958.

Sontag, Susan. Approaching Artaud. NY 13:39–79, May 19, 1973. **11230**

Introduces relatively little new material on A. but does place him in the context of larger literary trends, in particular that of modernist literature.

Theater

Arnold, Paul. The Artaud experiment. TDR 8:15–29, 1963. **11231**

Good impartial analysis of several of A.'s ideas on theater. Arnold discusses some of the major problems and contradictions in A.'s theatrical theories.

Artaud directs Les Cenci. TDR 2:90–145, 1972. **11232**

Documents by A. concerning the production of this play by the Theater of Cruelty. Articles, interviews and reviews concerning the play drawn from Parisian newspapers which covered its opening.

Béhar, Henri. Le théâtre Alfred Jarry. *In his:* Roger Vitrac: un réprouvé du surréalisme. Nizet, 1966. p. 131–59. **11233**

Good information concerning A.'s collaboration with Roger Vitrac and "Le théâtre Alfred Jarry." Also contains an appendix with unpublished letters by A. to Vitrac. For similar information, seen in a larger context, see, by the same author, *Etude sur le théâtre dada et surréaliste.* Gallimard, 1967.

Brustein, Robert. Antonin Artaud and Jean Genet. The theatre of cruelty. *In his:* The theatre of revolt. An approach to modern drama. Boston, Toronto, Little, Brown, 1962. p. 363–411. *Also:* London, Methuen, 1965. **11234**

Discusses the "theater of cruelty" in terms of movements (dadaism) and men (Nietzsche) prior to A., and later playwrights (especially Genet). Constitutes a brief introduction to A.'s ideas on theater.

Chiaromonte, Nicola. Antonin Artaud. Enc 29:44–50, 1967. *Trans.:* Antonin Artaud et sa double idée du théâtre. Preu 205:8–17, 1968. **11235**

Important article relating A.'s concept of theater to his own struggle with language and writing. Penetrating analysis of what A. means by the theater's "double" and by "cruelty." The author points out a fundamental dichotomy between spirituality and physicality in A.'s concept of theater.

Demaitre, Ann. The theater of cruelty and alchemy: Artaud and Le grand œuvre. JHI 33:237–50, 1972. **11236**

Interesting, well-documented study of intellectual structure at core of Theater of Cruelty. Uses A.'s writings to show that alchemy, though not rigorously developed, superseded notion of cruelty; helps explain elusive "double," and expresses dualism in A.'s personality. The five stages of alchemical process parallel his idea of a theater and (admittedly debatable) Jungian theory of alchemy as a work of personal salvation and redemption through suffering. [LB]

Derrida, Jacques. Le théâtre de la cruauté et la clôture de la représentation. Cr 22: 595–618, 1966. *Also in his:* L'écriture et la différence. Seuil, 1970. p. 341–68.
11237
Derrida defines the "theater of cruelty" as "life itself insofar as everything that cannot be staged is concerned." According to this definition, the true "theater of cruelty" can never take place, and thus A.'s theater also betrayed its principles.

Dort, Bernard. L'avant-garde en suspens. ThP 18:41–48, 1956. *Also in his:* Théâtre public (1953–1966). Seuil, 1967. p. 243–54. (Pierres vives)
11238
Sees A.'s theatrical ideas as idealist insofar as he does not have a definite public in mind. Dort thinks in terms of the anti-bourgeois theater rather than in terms of the total, gestual, primordial (and, in effect, classless) theater envisaged by A.

Duvignaud, Jean. Le théâtre et après. Casterman, 1971. 148 p. (Mutations-orientations)
11239
Duvignaud does not discuss A. directly but analyzes the tradition of "cruelty" in Western theater from the Elizabethans to the theater of the absurd and "happenings." Thus, from Duvignaud's perspective, A.'s thought is not radically different, but very much in the mainstream of Western theater.

Fanchette, Jean. Antonin Artaud et le théâtre moderne. *In his:* Psychodrame et théâtre moderne. Buchet-Chastel, 1971. p. 148–88.
11240
A.'s work in the theater seen from a psychological viewpoint and in the light of a "therapeutic" theater.

Gouhier, Henri. Antonin Artaud et l'essence du théâtre. Vrin, 1974. 252 p.
11241
Study of A.'s theater which, acccording to the author, aims at a kind of spectacle which ultimately goes beyond theater. Concludes by seeing A. in relation to Nietzsche and Brecht. Solid if not provocative.

Grotowski, Jerzy. Il n'était pas entièrement lui-même. TM 251:1885–93, 1967. **11242**

Grotowski agrees with A. concerning the central role of myth in theater and the importance of purification. Although many people have spoken of Grotowski's theater in terms of A., the Polish director himself feels that his own theater differs from that envisaged by A. insofar as he believes in systematic training, the need of a text, the absence of music, and in the all-important role of the actor.

Orenstein, Gloria Feman. The dialectics of transformation: André Breton, Antonin Artaud. *In her:* The theater of the marvelous: surrealism and the contemporary stage. New York univ. press, 1975. p. 17–31.
11243
Interesting study of the long ignored aspects of magic, occultism and alchemy in A.'s concept of theater. Provocative comparison between A. and Breton.

Piemme, Jean-Marie. Le théâtre sans texte ou la parole convertie. MRo 19:91–99, 1969.
11244
Good, brief analysis of the similarities and differences among A., Grotowski, the Living Theater and Happenings. Unlike many critics, Piemme is careful to point out where and how A.'s concept of theater is different from the later phenomena.

Pleynet, Marcelin. La matière pense. TelQ 52:31–40, 1972. *Also in:* Artaud. *See* 11205. p. 135–50.
11245
Difficult analysis bearing in part on the way A. used the theater as an "occasion" to capture the self.

Scarpetta, Guy. Brecht et Artaud. NCr 25: 60–68, 1969.
11246
Marxist view of Brecht and A. Scarpetta believes that, in spite of his declared materialism, Brecht is still involved in idealism. A., on the other hand, may serve as a point of departure for a truly materialist theater where theory and practice meet and where life itself is involved.

Sellin, Eric. The dramatic concepts of Antonin Artaud. Chicago and London, Univ. of Chicago press, 1968. 190 p. **11247**
Scholarly, serious inquiry into A.'s theatrical ideas and writings. The author shows the relationship of primitive theater to A.'s concept of drama as well as the influence A.'s ideas have

exerted upon contemporary theater.
Reviews: R. Chambers in AUMLA 31:119–21, 1969; A. Demaitre in FR 43:325–26, 1969.

Seymour, Alan. Artaud's cruelty. LonM 3: 59–64, 1964.   **11248**
Harsh appraisal of A.'s ideas on cruelty. Perhaps an antidote to all those who have made the "theater of cruelty" into a cult.

Sollers, Philippe. La pensée émet des signes. TelQ 20:12–24, 1965. *Also in his:* L'écriture et l'expérience des limites. Seuil, 1968. p. 88–105.   **11249**
Discussion of A.'s refusal to separate thought from being, of his desire to make word and body coincide. For Sollers, A.'s theater is the place where "thought can find its body," where the body can be a sign among other signs, as a word is a sign among other words. A.'s cruelty, says Sollers, comes from this desire to capture thought, just as his rejection of Western dualist culture stems from his desire to unite body and mind.

Sontag, Susan. Marat/Sade/Artaud. PR 32: 210–19, 1965. *Also in her:* Against interpretation. Dell, 1967. p. 163–76.   **11250**
Consideration of A. in relation to recent dramatic events such as Peter Brook's *Marat/Sade* and "happenings."

Temkine, Raymonde. Fils naturel d'Artaud. LetN 127–37, May–June 1966.   **11251**
Largely an analysis of the ways Grotowski's theater puts A.'s ideas into practice. Notes that it is not a question of influences but of "confluences."

Todorov, Tzvetan. L'art selon Artaud. *In his:* Poétique de la prose. Seuil, 1971. p. 212–24. (Poétique)   **11252**
Interesting analysis of *Le théâtre et son double* seen in the general context of "language," especially "symbolic" vs. "verbal" language. Todorov appears to equate symbolic language with the kind of theatrical language demanded by A. In Todorov's view, such a theatrical language has a double effect. Actors and gestures lose their "materiality;" they cease to be "substance présente pour devenir signe." Secondly, signs are no longer abstract but make us aware of their physical presence.

Tonelli, Franco. L'esthétique de la cruauté: étude des implications esthétiques du Théâtre de la cruauté d'Antonin Artaud. Nizet, 1972. 156 p.   **11253**
The book opens with a comprehensive analysis of A.'s theatrical concepts, particularly those of "cruelty," "catharsis" and "double." Following chapters are devoted to writers or playwrights sharing aspects of A.'s sensibility or ideas. Such writers including Sade, Vitrac, Ghelderode, Beckett and Arrabal.

Vilar, Jean. Le metteur en scène et l'œuvre dramatique. RevTh 3:297–320, 1946. *Also in his:* De la tradition théâtrale. Gallimard, 1955. *Also:* Gallimard, 1966. (Idées)   **11254**
The director Jean Vilar seems one of the few who did not consider A.'s theoretical conceptions impossible to realize. Emphasis placed on A.'s "physical" language.

Virmaux, Alain. Antonin Artaud et le théâtre. Seghers, 1970. 348 p. (L'archipel)   **11255**
Thorough and comprehensive treatment of A.'s ideas on theater. Shows A.'s influence on directors and dramatic theorists, his relationship to other dramatic schools. Detailed examination of texts. Includes photographs (some of *Les Cenci*), several texts not yet published in A.'s *Œuvres complètes,* and the most complete list to date of A.'s cinematic and theatrical roles. Excellent bibliography.

Poetry and Style

Blanchot, Maurice. La cruelle raison poétique. CRB 22–23:66–73, 1958. *Also in his:* L'entretien infini. Gallimard, 1969. p. 432–38.   **11256**
Still one of the best essays yet written on A. Blanchot analyzes the all-important question of the relationship between being and poetry in A., as well as A.'s search for "le sacré."

Deleuze, Gilles. Le schizophrène et le mot. Cr 255–56:731–45, 1968.   **11257**
Study of Lewis Carroll, A.'s translations of some poems by Carroll, and the relationship between linguistic "non-sense" and schizophrenia. Even if one disagrees with Deleuze's interpreta-

tion, the article is well thought out and interesting.

Greene, Naomi. Antonin Artaud: poet without words. Simon & Schuster, 1970. 256 p.   **11258**

Study of A.'s work carried out through an examination of several themes that appear in much of his writings (i.e., his hatred of verbal language, his ambiguous feelings about corporeality). Analyses of important passages in some of his later poems.
Reviews: B. Gill in NY May 8, 1971; E. Sellin in Diac 21–26, Winter 1971.

Koch, Stephen. On Artaud. TriQ 6:29–37, 1966.   **11259**

Penetrating discussion of A.'s desire to unite language and being, to erase the gap between subject and object. Important comments on the relationship between intellect and physicality in A.'s last poems.

Magny, Olivier de. Ecriture de l'impossible. LetN 32:125–38, 1963.   **11260**

Interesting article concerning the problem, or perhaps the impossibility, of language and writing in contemporary literature. A. seen in relation to other writers such as Beckett, Blanchot and Michaux.

Ménard, René. Antonin Artaud et la condition poétique. Cr 19:299–310, 1957.   **11261**

A study of the vital relationship between writing and being, between poetry and inner reality in A.

Sojcher, Jacques. La démarche poétique. Eds. rencontre, 1969. 232 p.   **11262**

Discussion of the nature of poetry in metaphysical terms close to those of Heidegger and Blanchot. For Sojcher, the poet protests against the world which has lost its sense of sacredness and has fallen into a "degraded" language. A., along with Rilke, Nietzsche, Char, Breton and Rimbaud, is one of the poets most frequently and extensively discuused.

Thévenin, Paule. Entendre/voir/lire. TelQ 39:31–63, 1969; 40:67–99, 1970.   **11263**

Two very important textual analyses of the layers of meaning in A.'s later poems, mainly through a detailed and exhaustive study of some of the words

they contain. Thévenin contends that only an analysis of this sort will enable us to approach the poems for what they are, and not in the light of A.'s "madness" or "illness." The second article concentrates on *Le retour d'Artaud le Momo*. Even if one thinks Thévenin over-interprets these texts, her articles constitute a vital step in the exegesis of A.'s poetry.

Fiction

Dadoun, Roger. Le nom d'Héliogabale dans le texte d'Artaud. Lit 3:64–78, 1971.   **11264**

Extremely detailed and erudite analysis of the various meanings suggested by the name Héliogabale in A.'s *Héliogabale*. Draws on A.'s etymological analyses which are revealing in their own right.

Gauthier, Xavière. Héliogabale, travestissement. *In:* Artaud, 10/18. *See* 11205. p. 187–95.   **11265**

One of the few essays devoted to A.'s *Héliogabale,* an important and revealing work. Gauthier analyzes the sexuality and confusion of sexuality (castration, hermaphroditism) in this work.

Cinema

Virmaux, Alain. Une promesse mal tenue: le film surréaliste. EtCi 38–39:103–33, 1965.   **11266**

Good discussion of A.'s cinematic theories and of his work in film. Establishes the importance of his film, *La coquille et le clergyman,* in the history of surrealist filmmaking. Somewhat the same discussion in English in Virmaux's article "Artaud and film" in TDR 15:154–65, 1966.

Henry Bataille
(Nos. 11267–11286)

Renée Geen

General Studies

Amiel, Denys. Henry Bataille. Sansot, n.d. 64 p.   **11267**

First serious study of B. and basis for later works. Stresses the importance of

B.'s life on his work and the unity between his poetry and theater. Comparison with Ibsen. Amiel sees B.'s originality in his attempt to reveal the subconscious aspects of modern sensitivity through lyricism and sincerity. Appended critical judgments on individual plays are useful.

Besançon, Jacques Bernard. Essai sur le théâtre d'Henry Bataille. The Hague, J.-B. Wolters, 1928. 299 p.   **11268**

Most extensive and scholarly treatment of B.'s life and works. Besançon analyzes in detail each of B.'s plays and in an overall judgment evaluates B.'s limitations as a psychologist, moralist and dramatist. Showing that B.'s intuitive vision of man is more poetic than dramatic, and underlining the discrepancy between B.'s theory and practice of the drama, Besançon concludes that B. is a "literary melodramatist." Bibliography of B., selected critical bibliography and index.

Review: E. Sée in his *Le mouvement dramatique, 1929–1930*. Eds. de France, 1930. p. 56–59.

Biondolillo, Francesco. Il teatro di Henri [sic] Bataille. RdI 18:49–90, Jan. 1915.   **11269**

Study of B.'s major plays from *L'enchantement* to *La phalène*, stressing simplicity of plots, individuality of characters, and lyrical expression of tragedy, but also some psychological incoherences and esthetic flaws.

Blanchart, Paul. Henry Bataille, son œuvre. Eds. du Carnet critique, 1922. 68 p.   **11270**

Places B.'s theater between the symbolist tragedy and the *pièce à thèse*. Sees an esthetic conflict in B. stemming from a poet-dramatist-merchant "trinity." Chronological bibliography of B.'s works and casts of first performances are useful. Critical bibliography is incomplete.

Catalogne, Gérard de. Henry Bataille ou le romantisme de l'instinct. Eds. de la pensée latine, 1925. 70 p.   **11271**

Uncritical praise. Catalogne feels that thanks to his psychological insight, his sincerity and poetic gifts, B. attained his ideal of "lyricisme exact."

Coindreau, Maurice Edgar. Le théâtre de la passion. *In his:* La farce est jouée, vingt-cinq ans de théâtre français, 1900–1925. New York, Eds. de la maison française, 1942. p. 93–122.   **11272**

Good summary of B.'s weakness and originality.

Gaubert, Ernest. Henry Bataille. MerF 597–612, April 16, 1908.   **11273**

B.'s poetry foreshadows both the style and content of his theater.

Géraldy, Paul. La marche nuptiale d'Henry Bataille. An 52:37–49, 1955.   **11274**

Reminiscences of a friend which shed light on B.'s tormented personality, his poetic vocation and the autobiographical nature of several of his plays.

Lacour, Léopold. Le théâtre d'Henry Bataille. RdP 125–50, May 1, 1910.   **11275**

Differences between B. and Porto-Riche. *La vierge folle* is singled out as a masterpiece of modern tragedy.

Lemaître, Jules. Ton sang [and] La lépreuse. *In his:* Impressions de théâtre, 10ᵉ série. Société française d'imprimerie et de librairie, 1898. p. 227–37, 361–73.   **11276**

Lemaître considers the former the transposition of a bourgeois drama into a lyrical "nosography" and the latter a primitive and naive poem in the guise of a medieval legend.

Lemonnier, Léon. Le théâtre d'Henry Bataille. GraR 244–62, Apr. 1922.   **11277**

Focuses on contrasts in B.: a delicate poet who likes to torture and even disgust his audience; a fervent idealist who does not shy away from moral obscenities; a subtle psychologist who uses every trick of his craft.

Lièvre, Pierre. Henry Bataille. Marg 203–12, Dec. 15, 1918.   **11278**

B.'s drama as the antithesis of poetic theater since it presents, in Lièvre's opinion, false emotions, i.e. exceptional in nature or unconvincingly developed, in a setting which attempts to be realistic.

Revon, Maxime. Henry Bataille. MerF 38–60, Nov. 15, 1922.   **11279**

Perhaps the best summary of criticism against B. Revon claims that B.'s vague idealism, cumbersome lyricism and exasperated sense of life are left uncontrolled by the demands of dramatic art. His melodramatic theater is seen in direct opposition to the search for simplicity and truth which characterize the previous generation of dramatists.

Seillière, Ernest. L'évolution morale dans le théâtre d'Henri [sic] Bataille. Boivin, 1936. 152 p.   **11280**

The title of this work is somewhat misleading since Seillière sees practically no moral evolution in B.'s theater. On the contrary, he denounces in each main work studied the religious, social and psychological dangers inherent in B.'s mysticism of passion, together with the incoherence and sophistry of B.'s moral theories. Although Seillière succeeds in relating B.'s moral stance to the ideological currents of time, his own *parti pris* is too well established to make this an impartial study.

Thiébaut, Marcel. Henry Bataille. RdP 608–29, Aug. 1, 1922.   **11281**

This mediocre article nonetheless raises some interesting points, e.g. the visual perspective of B. as painter and dramatist, the importance of women in his theater. Thiébaut gives B. an important part in the development of modern drama.

Individual Plays

Allard, Roger. Henry Bataille ou la quadrature du faux art. NRF 14:537–44, 1920.   **11282**

This devastating review of *La quadrature de l'amour,* condemned for its stupidity, pretentiousness and bad taste, is an excellent example of anti-B. criticism.

Basch, Victor. L'Amazone de M. Henry Bataille. *In his:* Etudes d'esthétique dramatique; première série. Vrin, 1929. p. 211–21.   **11283**

In the evolution of B.'s theater, Basch considers *L'Amazone* a continuation of the esthetic and ideological shift, started in *Les flambeaux,* from the concerns of individuals to those of the collectivity.

Copeau, Jacques. Henry Bataille. *In his:* Critiques d'un autre temps. Troisième édition. Eds. de la Nouvelle revue française, 1923. p. 93–118.   **11284**

Reprints of Copeau's articles on *Le scandale, La vierge folle* and *Le songe d'un soir d'amour* which appeared in *La grande revue* from 1909 to 1910. Copeau's wish that B. be more self-disciplined comes as no surprise.

Rageot, Gaston. Un renouveau d'Henri [sic] Bataille. RevPL 636–37, Oct. 15, 1932.   **11285**

Minor article but interesting in showing evolution of B. criticism. A revival of *Le scandale* shows that B. still appeals as a dramatist despite his manner and style which are outmoded.

Poetry

Roulhac, Georges-Albert. La poésie d'Henry Bataille. GraR 263–74, Apr. 1922. **11286**

A most unconvincing attempt at rehabilitating B.'s poetry.

Jean-Jacques Bernard
(Nos. 11287–11294)

RENÉE GEEN

Bernard, Jean-Jacques. Mon ami le théâtre. Albin Michel, 1958. 255 p.   **11287**

Personal history of the theater from the Vieux-Colombier to the Cartel. Chapters 10 through 15 deal specifically with B.'s own plays.

————. Mon père Tristan Bernard. Albin Michel, 1955. 269 p.   **11288**

In this tribute to his father, B. includes some autobiographical data of interest.

Daniels, May. Jean-Jacques Bernard. *In her:* The French drama of the unspoken. Edinburgh, Univ. press, 1953. p. 172–237.   **11289**

Thorough and scholarly study, but somewhat unsympathetic to the basic premises of the dramatists of the unspoken. Underlines differences between Maeterlinck's and B.'s conception of "dialogue sous-jacent." Divides B.'s theater into "plays concerned with unexpressed emotions of which the character is aware, and plays dealing with sentiments and desires submerged in the subconscious." Sees a diminishing effectiveness of the unspoken after *L'âme en peine* and concludes that, on the whole, B.'s "is a miniature art, a theatre of intimacy, sometimes perfect of its kind, but restricted and monotonous." Selected bibliography, reviews of individual plays, index.

Frith, John Leslie. Introduction. *In:* Bernard, Jean-Jacques. The sulky fire; five plays: The sulky fire, Martine, The springtime of others, Invitations to a voyage, The unquiet spirit. Trans. by John Leslie Frith. London, Jonathan Cape, 1939. p. 7–11. **11290**

Short introduction traces the fortunes of B.'s plays in England.

Lemonnier, Léon. Le théâtre de Jean-Jacques Bernard. RMon 166:292–96, 1925. **11291**

Although brief, this article makes several pertinent points on B.'s classicism and modernism.

Palmer, John. J.-J. Bernard and the theory of silence. FortR 121:46–58, 1927. **11292**

Despite its title, this article convincingly shows the dramatic merits of B.'s plays, quite apart from theory.

Rhodes, S. A. Jean-Jacques Bernard. BA 16:134–38, 1942. **11293**

Brief summary of B.'s plays. Rhodes is particularly sensitive to their "subtle music" and "pure drama."

Surer, Paul. Etudes sur le théâtre français contemporain; le théâtre intimiste. IL 5:178–86, 1952. **11294**

Surer's tendency to view B.'s plays primarily as illustrations of an esthetic theory is not entirely justifiable.

Paul Géraldy
(pseud. of Paul Le Fèvre)
(Nos. 11295–11308)

SIMONA AKERMAN

Brisson, Pierre. Le théâtre des années folles. Geneva, Eds. du milieu du monde, 1943. 224 p. (Bilans) **11295**

In chapter VI, "Le Boulevard et ses environs," plays termed "pathétiques et légères" are treated as well as the generation gap. G. is criticized as being too lyrical, although sincere, in the tradition of Rostand, Bataille and even Marivaux.

Doisy, Marcel. Esquisses; Paul Géraldy, Jean Sarment, Sacha Guitry. A Flament, 1950. p. 1–90. **11296**

Love is seen as the main theme of G.'s three important plays, *Aimer, Robert et Marianne* and *Christine*. Doisy focuses on the inner poetry of G.'s theater, but neglects his poems.

Dubech, Lucien. Les chefs de file de la nouvelle génération. Plon, Nourrit, 1925. 241 p. **11297**

Concludes that G. is not simple. He reproaches him for certain complications of the heart and imagination. The author thinks that he was at his best in "la comédie légère."

Duhamel, Georges. Deux poètes de l'amour. *In his:* Les poètes et la poésie. 1912–1914. 4th ed. Mercure de France, 1922. p. 261–75. **11298**

A whole chapter is devoted to G. and Maurice Magre. G. is considered solely the poet of love.

Garnier, Christine. L'homme et ses personnages. Confidences d'écrivains. Prédédé d'une lettre à l'auteur. Grasset, 1955. p. 75–98. **11299**

G. answers a letter sent by Garnier and explains himself. Expresses his deep love for the theater and for love in general, comments upon his contemporaries, and voices his preference for the simple people of Paris. The whole thing amounts to a personal confession.

Géraldy, Paul. Les auteurs et leurs livres: Toi et moi. An n.s. 10:52–63, 1951. **11300**

Appreciates his book of poems as a hymn to love. Subjective treatment of his own work.

Guth, Paul. Paul Géraldy. RdP 57:127–34, 1950. **11301**

Biographical, impressionistic treatment. G. is seen as a true Parisian. His relationship with Colette is also reviewed. G. defines the role of the actor, of poetry, of the heart. The whole endeavor is seen as "une course vers soi-même."

Jaloux, Edmond. Perspectives et personnages. Plon, 1931. 253 p. (L'esprit des livres, sér. 3) **11302**

In a chapter called "Deux livres sur l'amour," G. and Henri de Régnier are dealt with. In *Toi et moi,* G. displays an optimistic vision.

Knowles, Dorothy. French drama of the inter-war years 1918–1939. London, Harrap, 1967. 339 p. *Also:* New York, Barnes & Noble, 1968. 334 p. **11303**
Chapter X deals with the Boulevard theater: the sex play and the play of manners and character: Henry Bataille, Henry Bernstein, André Josset and Paul Géraldy. G. gives greater emphasis to the sentimental aspects. There is no action and no story because G. believes that life is continuous.
Review: H. Block in MD 12:100, 1969.

Mégret, Christian. Paul Géradly qui a réussi ses tâches et ses jours. Car 835:23, Sept. 14, 1960. **11304**
G.'s relationship with Péguy, Henry Bataille and Colette. Analyzes favorably the poet and the playwright.

Palmer, John. M. Paul Géraldy and the play of sex. *In his:* Studies in contemporary theatre. London, Secker, 1927. p. 151–62. **11305**
G. is considered as a typical author for the 1925 contemporary play on sex. But sex is for him only an excuse or a motive.

Sée, Edmond. Le théâtre français contemporain. Colin, 1928. p. 143, 152–54. (Section de langues et de littératures, 106) **11306**
G. compared to Becque. The play *Aimer* is seen as his masterpiece and certain Racinian accents are detected.

Surer, Paul. Etudes sur le théâtre français contemporain. III. Le théâtre intimiste. IL 5:178–86, 1952. **11307**
Vildrac, J.-J. Bernard and Denys Amet are analyzed as well as Paul Géraldy. The latter is seen as characteristic of the "théâtre intimiste."

———. Le théâtre français contemporain. Société d'édition et d'enseignement supérieur, 1964. p. 155–59. **11308**
G. is seen as promoter of the "théâtre intimiste." His intense, pathetic simplicity is praised.

Henri Ghéon
(pseud. of Henri Vangeon)
(Nos. 11309–11330)

JEAN-PIERRE CAP

Autobiography and Texts

Ghéon, Henri. A bâtons rompus. Ma vocation. Florilège 44–48, June 1933. **11309**
A concise account of G.'s early calling to the theater at age eight, his first writings, his participation in the NRF and the Vieux-Colombier, the influence of his friends Gide and Vielé-Griffin. G. claims that his esthetics, based on reality, remained the same throughout his career as a dramatist.

———. Dramaturgie d'hier et de demain; essai sur l'art du théâtre. Lyon, E. Vitte, 1963. 182 p. *Trans.:* The art of theatre. Introd. by Michel-Saint-Denis. Trans. by Adele Fiske. Hill and Wang, 1961. 100 p. **11310**
A synthesis of G.'s concept of the theater. Indispensable for any study of G.'s dramatic theory.
Review: P. Blanchart in RHT 2:188–89, 1964.

———. L'homme né de la guerre. Témoignage d'un converti. Eds. de la N.R.F., 1919. 228 p. *Also:* Bloud et Gay, 1923. **11311**
An autobiography up to 1917 in which G. explains the circumstances of his conversion and of the changes it caused in his life and in his art. He also deals extensively with his experience of the war.

———. Nos directions; réalisme et poésie, notes sur le drame poétique, du classicisme, sur le vers libre. Eds. de la N.R.F., 1911. 239 p. **11312**
Contains G.'s most important articles published in the NRF from 1909 to 1911. Essential to assess G.'s esthetic principles as well as those of the NRF.

———. Partis pris. Réflexions sur l'art littéraire. Nouvelle librairie nationale, 1923. 240 p. **11313**
Essays reflecting G.'s post-conversion esthetic principles. They are marked by his strong religious and nationalistic convictions.

General Studies

Anglès, Auguste. Une cellule amicale: le premier groupe de la Nouvelle revue française 1908–1914. *In:* Cahiers André Gide 3. Le centenaire. Gallimard, 1972. p. 117–32. **11314**

On the spirit animating the founders of the NRF, including G., and their working relationship. The best article on the subject.

Brochet, Henri. Henri Ghéon. Préf. de Michel Richard. Les presses de l'Ile de France, 1946. 180 p. **11315**

Deals primarily with G.'s life and works after his conversion in 1915. Lacks precision but useful. Brochet worked with G. for over 20 years.

Les cahiers de la Petite Dame [Maria van Rysselberghe] 1918–1929. Préf. d'A. Malraux. Gallimard, 1973. passim. (Cahiers André Gide 4) **11316**

Through this chronicle of Gide's life, one can better understand how he and G. drifted apart from each other.

Cap, Biruta. Stefan Zweig as agent of exchange between French and German literature. CLS 10:252–62, 1973. **11317**

Documents the interest in G.'s *Le pain* by S. Zweig, Oscar Fried and Max Reinhardt, and the actual negotiations between the author and his foreign collaborators.

Cap, Jean-Pierre. Henri Ghéon critique de Paul Claudel. ClaudelS 1:14–27, 1972. **11318**

Evaluates the respective dramatic concepts of the two writers and the distance which separated them due to G.'s affiliation with the Action française.

Coindreau, Maurice. La farce est jouée. New York, Eds. de la maison française, 1942. p. 185–91. **11319**

General appreciation of G.'s dramatic career until 1925, stressing the main characteristics of his dramatic concepts and the qualities and defects of his plays.

Corre, François. Un père fondateur: Henri Ghéon. EspCr 16:172–76, 1974. **11320**

Vigorously states G.'s role as founder of the NRF, as critic, poet, dramatic innovator. One of the best general evo-

cations of G.'s literary career and his friendship with Gide.

Deléglise, Maurice. Le théâtre d'Henri Ghéon. Contribution à l'étude du renouveau théâtral. Sion (Suisse), 1947. 407 p. *Also:* Le théâtre d'Henri Ghéon. Billaudot, 1951. 407 p. **11321**

The most extensive and thorough study of G.'s drama. Deléglise views G.'s Christian production very sympathetically. Though he admits some plays were written too rapidly, he points to G.'s many achievements based on a keen understanding of dramatic theory and staging as well as on the concept of "celebration" to which masses are sensitive. He also sees G. as having been successful in his attempt at returning poetry to the theater. D. does not see, as others did, proselytism as a potentially weakening factor in G.'s drama.

Duhamelet, Geneviève. L'homme né de la guerre: Henri Ghéon. Brussels, Eds. Foyer Notre Dame, 1951. 16 p. (Conversions du XXᵉ siècle) **11322**

A study of G.'s radical change in esthetics and in his life after his conversion in 1915.

Fassbinder, Klara Marie. Henri Ghéon. *In her:* Der versunkene Garten. Begegnungen mit dem geistigen Frankreich des entredeux-guerres 1919–1939. Wiederbegegnungen nach dem zweiten Weltkrieg. Heidelberg, F. H. Kerle Verlag, 1968. p. 117–22. **11323**

Situates G. in French letters and recalls an interview revealing of G.'s personality and attitude toward literature since his conversion which, as translator of his religious plays, Fassbinder had with G. in his "atelier."

Gide, André. Eloges. Neuchâtel-Paris, Ides et calendes, 1948. 147 p. **11324**

Explains why he and G. ceased seeing each other: G. was a militant Catholic and Gide a convinced skeptic. But there had been no break between them. Gide states that the more G. became a committed writer, the less he paid attention to his art. This damaging comment has since become a cliché.

Henri Ghéon, 1875–1944. JTP 104:1–60; 1945. **11325**

This special issue contains articles by Jacques Copeau, Léon Chancerel, J. Reynaud and Ch. Forot. Contains the first bibliography (incomplete) of G.'s dramatic works.

Praviel, Armand. Du romantisme à la prière. Perrin, 1927. p. 175–200. **11326**
Praviel shows that before his conversion G. was moving towards naturism and afterwards towards neoclassicism. His notion that G. was a primitive is correct to some extent. Though inconclusive, this study is still useful.

Reynaud, Jacques. Henri Ghéon. 1875–1944, étude et bibliographie. Avec une lettre inédite de Gide. Assoc. des amis d'Henri Ghéon, 1960. 46 p. (Nos spectacles, no. 75, supplément) **11327**
A very sympathetic biography. Contains some errors on G.'s career before his conversion. The list of G.'s works (p. 29–46) is the best available except for G.'s criticism, of which only volumes are listed.

Saint-Clair, M. (pseud. of Maria van Rysselberghe). Ghéon. NRF 8:306–13, 1956. **11328**
A very warm article on G. by someone who knew him well for almost four decades.

Sylvestre, Guy. Henri Ghéon. In his: Poètes catholiques de la France contemporaine. Pref. by Jean Bruchési. Montreal, Fides, 1943. p. 81–93. **11329**
Very general, dealing primarily with G. as poet.

Tintignac, Claude. Le thème du renoncement dans la Vie de Saint Alexis et sa personnalité dans les lettres françaises. Nizet, 1973. 80 p. **11330**
Useful for G.'s Le pauvre sous l'escalier.

Henri-René Lenormand
(Nos. 11331–11377)

ROBERT EMMET JONES

Biography

Blanchart, Paul. In memoriam. RHT 2:167–76, 1951. **11331**
Biographical information. L.'s theatrical repertory. Bibliographical recommendations and indications. L.'s nontheatrical articles.

Gillois, André. Henri-René Lenormand. In his: Qui êtes-vous? Gallimard, 1953. p. 34–40. **11332**
Interview with L. Biographical and critical remarks by L. who speaks of role of fear in his works. Sees his plays as modern tragedies of internal rather than external fatality. Says his plays are exorcisms of his demons. Gillois notes the humor and irony in the plays.

Lenormand, H.-R. Les confessions d'un auteur dramatique. Albin Michel, 1949, 1953. 2 v. **11333**
Most important and essentially only biographical source for study of L. Brilliant autobiography. Fine background book for study of theater from 1900 to 1940. This work may be L.'s masterpiece.

Sheffer, Eugene J. An autobiographical notice of H.-R. Lenormand. FR 15:501–04, 1942. **11334**
Statement obtained from L. on his only visit to the U.S.A. The biographical notes, lists of interests and comments on the theater were important in 1942, but L.'s Confessions have superseded and expanded this material.

General Studies

Antonini, Giacomo. Henri-René Lenormand. In his: Il teatro contemporaneo in Francia. Milan, Corbaccio, 1930. p. 187–216. **11335**
Sees L. as most original dramatist of his time. Some good insights into individual plays. Considers Les ratés to be one of the most important French plays of the period. Shows importance of occultism, psychoanalysis, animism, and fatalism in the plays. Points out the difference between what L.'s characters are and what they believe themselves to be. Overrates some of the plays, but his views are generally valid.

Behrens, Ralph. L'inconnu as object of desire in the plays of Lenormand. FR 31:152–54, 1957. **11336**
Attacks Jones' article on desire and death in L.'s plays.

Berton, Claude. L'homme et son fantôme (Le théâtre de H.-R. Lenormand) NL 390:June 27, 1915. **11337**

Fine study of L.'s themes, obsessions, techniques.

Blanchart, Paul. H.-R. Lenormand: dramaturge d'apocalypse. RevTh 4:9–14, Jan-Feb. 1947. **11338**

Claims L.'s universe is the antithesis of Claudel's. It is closed to grace and hope. Presents strange idea that L. introduces to theater what Proust does to the novel. Sees two poles of L.'s art as suggestion and poetry. L.'s theater is one of decadence of all sorts. L. is a prophet whose studies of humanity have a pitiless lucidity.

———. Le théâtre de H.-R. Lenormand. Masques, 1947. 248 p. **11339**

Best book on L. although author tends to overestimate L.'s worth as dramatist. Comparisons with Shakespeare, Aeschylus, Racine far-fetched. Good, often excellent analyses of the plays and prose works (fiction, memoirs, criticism). Sees most of plays as metaphysical, climatic, or psychological tragedies, but word "tragedy" is misused. Sees the two keys to L.'s works as poetry in sense of prophecy, and psychoanalysis, but claims Freudian influence is overrated by critics.

Criticus (pseud. of Marcel Berger). H.-R. Lenormand. *In his:* Le style au microsope. V. 3. Calmann-Lévy, 1952. P. 237–59. **11340**

Analysis of the first tableau and part of the second of *Le simoun.* Discusses advantages of tableaux rather than acts. Shows that the style demonstrates presence of a great dramatist who translates psychological substance of a character through a word, a gesture, or even silence. Sees L. as a fine stylist who does not repudiate *vraisemblance* or rationalism. Valuable study.

Daniel-Rops (pseud. of Henry-Jules Petiot). Sur le théâtre de H.-R. Lenormand. Eds. des cahiers libres, 1926. 152 p. **11341**

Three short essays on aspects of L.'s work. Concerned as much with L. as with his plays. Author sees "inquiétude" as basis of L.'s theater. Discusses importance of time, climate, the psychological unknown. Valuable essay on

values and dangers of Freud's theories in literature. More philosophically than esthetically oriented. Still worthwhile although somewhat dated.

Dickman, Adolphe-Jacques. Le mal, force dramatique chez M. Lenormand. RR 19:218–31, 1928. **11342**

Fine study of evil in L.'s plays. Nature gives us an example of evil which goes against man's moral sense. Reality is thus the reality of the unconscious. Good triumphs through reason, evil through instincts. Evil becomes the dramatic force in L.'s plays. Analysis of five plays in the light of the concept of evil. L. tries to restore an equilibrium by expressing man's anxieties and neuroses. Conclusion is questionable.

Doisy, Marcel. Henri-René Lenormand. *In his:* Le théâtre français contemporain. Brussels, Eds. La Boétie, 1947. p. 197–201. **11343**

Good, if brief, study of influences on L. Relates him to Maeterlinck, Poe, Pirandello, Freud. Calls L. a metaphysical dramatist who shows the beauty and poetry of a domain previously reserved for psychiatrists. Points out influence of cinema. Claims justly that artifice plays a part in L.'s theater and often is difficult for the rational mind to accept. Birth date given is wrong.

Dubech, Lucien. Romantisme de M. Lenormand. RU 18:252–55, 1924. **11344**

Claims L. is the basis for his characters. He is prey to a powerful and disorganized imagination. Gets rid of his ghosts by portraying them on the stage. Artistic creation is an exorcism for him. L.'s plays are transpositions of dreamed novels. Comments on novelistic techniques are weak.

Glicksberg, Charles I. Depersonalization in the modern drama. Person 39:158–69, 1958. **11345**

Deals essentially with the role of the unconscious. Most of article treats authors other than L. Says L. questions bases of reality, norms of sanity. L. deals with abnormalities of the sexual instinct. Personalities of his characters are split into segments. L. is haunted by relativity of time. Good but limited analysis.

Jones, Robert Emmet. Desire and death in the plays of Lenormand. FR 30:138–42, 1956. **11346**

Study of two themes that form the basis and *raison d'être* of L.'s theater. Shows that desire becomes synonymous with life and leads inexorably to death and destruction.

————. The lower depths. *In his:* The alienated hero in modern French drama. Athens, Univ. of Georgia press, 1962. p. 43–57. **11347**

L.'s characters are not tragic. They are too self-centered, too often lack humanity, and avoid action. Characters are emotional rather than rational. Desire replaces and conquers love in the plays. Absurdity dominates those who attempt to flee desire. Characters are essentially solitary and alienated from society. Evil is dominant force in the plays.

Palmer, John. H. R. Lenormand and the play of psychology. NCA 100:594–607, 1926. **11348**

Finds L.'s plays original and forward-looking. Sees dominance of active power of evil. Evil has its own logic, is perpetually creative. L. is a romantic who recoils from realities too hard to accept. He creates a world of illusions as a refuge. Sees a conflict between artist and moralist.

————. M. H.-R. Lenormand and the play of psycho-analysis. *In his:* Studies in the contemporary theatre. Boston, Little Brown, 1927. p. 65–93. **11349**

Sees L. as profoundly original author despite fact his ideas are those of Freud. L. is obsessed with active power of evil. Essentially a study of evil in literature. Deals too much with reactions of other authors to evil. Well-written, informative essay, but too many generalizations and often too discursive.

Posen, R. Aspects of the work of Henri-René Lenormand—Part I. NFS 6:30–44, 1967. **11350**

Somewhat disorganized but good insights. Study of *Le réveil de l'instinct* as precursor of the later works, e.g., *Le simoun* where nature reflects man's evil instincts. Plays reflect L.'s travels and life. Article more biographical than study of works. Shows relation between prose works (fiction) and plays. L.

shows complexity of human character and is master of theatrical technique. The latter concept is not always well demonstrated.

————. Aspects of the work of Henri-René Lenormand—Part II. NFS 7:25–38, 1968. **11351**

Much better than preceding article in insights and organization. Studies L.'s main interests: psychological aberrations and their cure, environment as an influential factor and agent of destruction, supernatural forces. Shows very convincingly that Freud's influence was greater than is commonly supposed.

Radine, Serge. Grandeur et misère de l'œuvre de H.-R. Lenormand. ChrS 594–96, July-Aug. 1951. **11352**

Good brief essay on L.'s importance. Sees L.'s originality in breaking away from Boulevard theater and incorporating nature into the human drama.

————. Lenormand. *In his:* Anouilh, Lenormand, Salacrou. Geneva-Paris, Trois collines, 1951. p. 55–96. **11353**

Personal, moralizing view of L. the artist who is seen as an important but ultimate failure. More attention to the man than the work. Emphasizes relation to Freudian theories, but shows that L. is concerned only with the dark side of man's character. Hence limitations of the plays. Finds L. not objective enough, too romantic in his subjectivity. Too many quotes from L. Limited and often superficial analyses of the plays.

Rageot, Gaston. Entre le cinéma et la science. *In his:* Prise de vues. La nouvelle revue critique, 1928. p. 137–47. **11354**

Sees many modern plays as film scenarios rather than theater. *Les ratés* is the first important play of this type, the most cinematographic realization of a psychological study.

Surer, Paul. Henri-René Lenormand. *In his:* Le théâtre français contemporain. SEDES, 1964. p. 187–201. **11355**

Finds too much pessimism in L.'s universe yet sees him as an essentially original author. An incisive essay.

White, Kenneth. Toward a new interpretation of Lenormand's theatrical ethos. MD 2:334–48, 1960.   11356

Attacks critics who claim L.'s works are repetitions of Freud's ideas. L. is more influenced by Strindberg. Crucial theme of plays is love of life vs. anguish caused by aimlessness of modern existence. Prefigures works of Anouilh, Sartre, Camus, Beckett. Sees basic conflict in plays between spiritual and rational aspects of man. Exaggerates the spiritual aspect too much.

Individual Works

Brisson, Pierre. H.-R. Lenormand. *In his:* Au hasard des soirées. Gallimard, 1935. p. 304–13.   11357

Examines mostly unfavorably *Mixture* and *Une vie secrète*. Characters in *Une vie secrète* are abstractions. *Mixture* is "invraisemblable." Some good comments but overly harsh.

Dubech, Lucien. Le simoun. *In his:* Le théâtre 1918–1923. Plon-Nourrit, 1925. p. 153–57.   11358

Bizarre article dismissing L.'s dramatic talent. Dislikes *Le simoun* as a play. Suggests L. write novels instead of plays.

Dussane (pseud. of Béatrix Couloud [Dussan]). Les confessions d'un auteur dramatique par H.-R. Lenormand. MerF 307:511–13, 1949.   11359

Claims that L.'s autobiography throws light on the psychoanalysis of inspiration. The work brings back a whole epoch in vivid form. Finds much value in L.'s theater especially in light of the *Confessions*.

Florenne, Yves. Confessions et correspondance dramatiques. TR 68:141–43, 1953.   11360

Finds L.'s *Confessions* to be a masterly work comparable to those of Rousseau and Gide. L. treats with sincerity and truth himself, the process of dramatic creation, and man in general. Notes that L., not Artaud, is the inventor of the term "theater of cruelty." Brief, but important, study of the *Confessions*.

Frank, André. Georges Pitoëff et H.-R. Lenormand, son témoin. RevTh 29:20–25, 1952.   11361

Illustrations by L. (?) of Pitoëff's sets for *Les ratés.* Important for understanding of the play.

George, André. Le théâtre: M. H.-R. Lenormand et L'amour magicien. LetP 121–30, Jan. 1927.   11362

L'amour magicien is claimed to be L.'s masterpiece. This opinion is now dated.

Jamati, Georges. H.-R. Lenormand: L'homme et ses fantômes. *In his:* La conquête du soi. Flammarion, 1961. p. 261–62.   11363

Praises style, dramatic technique and psychological insights of L. Likes the play better than most critics. Some valuable insights.

———. H.-R. Lenormand: Le simoun. *In his:* La conquête du soi. Flammarion, 1961. p. 256–61.   11364

Sees play as a philosophical rather than psychological drama. Excellent analysis of L.'s concepts of good and evil and their peculiarities. Notes importance of mystery and suggestion in the play.

Kemp, Robert. Le simoun. *In his:* La vie du théâtre. Albin Michel, 1956. p. 26–33.   11365

Discusses role of fatalism in the play. Compares Laurency to Oedipus but finds that L.'s mechanics are too obvious. Sees *Le simoun* in tradition of well-made play.

Lemarchand, Jacques. Théâtre et merveilleux. NRF 53:903–07, 1957.   11366

Questions wisdom of reviving *Le temps est un songe*. Finds it still an interesting play because it shows the metaphysical anxiety of its epoch. Sees it as dated, however. Important comments on the influence of Einstein's theory of relativity.

Martin du Gard, Maurice. Lenormand, Baty et Cézanne. *In his:* Carte rouge. Flammarion, 1930. p. 222–30.   11367

Written on occasion of revival of *Le simoun*. Finds three distinct subjects in *Le simoun* which do not gell. Finds the incest disgusting; criticizes the thirteenth scene as too literary. Article reflects Victorian morality, and is now dated.

Orrok, Douglas Hall. Lenormand's Don Juan. L&P 6, no. 3:87–89, 1956. **11368**
Feels *L'homme et ses fantômes* should not be interpreted only with reference to homosexual element. Don Juan is really androgynous in the Platonic sense and can only be understood as such. He seeks unity and knowledge as well as the one woman from whom he has been separated. Interesting but bizarre concept that often goes beyond the bounds of credibility.

Seillière, Ernest. Un autre cas d'impérialisme artistique. *In his:* La religion romantique et ses conquêtes. Champion, 1930. p. 261–69. **11369**
Provocative study of *La* (sic) *vie secrète.* Shows Nietzschean influence and sees the Dionysian orgy as inspiration for L.'s esthetics. Places L. in line of Romantic German, French Christian, and Rousseauistic thinkers. Compares the play with Maugham's *The moon and sixpence.*

Vax, Louis. La séduction de l'étrange. Presses univ. de France, 1965. p. 100–01. **11370**
Discussion of *L'amour magicien.* L., because he is writing a psychological drama, explains too much of the mystery. Hence the play fails. Valid study.

Influence and Rapprochement

Belli, Angela. Lenormand's Asie and Anderson's The wingless victory. CL 19:226–39, 1967. **11371**
Deals with the importance of myth in the two plays. Good analysis.

Gravier, Maurice. Strindberg et H. R. Lenormand. MuK 10:603–10, 1964. **11372**
Excellent study showing similarities between artistic temperaments of L. and Strindberg. Much proof is drawn from L.'s *Confessions.* Especially good on comparison between *L'homme et ses fantômes* and *Road to Damascus.* Claims that L. is only great French expressionist dramatist and most authentic disciple of Strindberg.

Lelièvre, Renée. Le théâtre dramatique italien en France: 1855–1940. La Roche-sur-Yon, Imprimerie centrale de l'Ouest, 1959. 650 p. **11373**

Mostly isolated references to L.'s comments on productions of Italian plays in France. Shows L.'s debt to Coraccio in *Le simoun.* Discusses influence of D'Annunzio, Pirandello, and the futurists on French theater with scattered, brief references to L.

Oria, José A. El teatro de Lenormand, antes y despues de la influencia de Freud. Buenos Aires, Talleres gráficos de la penitenciaría nacional, 1935. 23 p. **11374**
Presents convincing evidence that the same themes are found in L.'s works before and after he had read Freud in 1917.

Swerling, Anthony. Strindberg's impact in France 1920–1960. Cambridge, Trinity Lane press, 1971. 238 p., passim. **11375**
Gives many comments by L. on Strindberg's works. Shows convincingly influence of Strindberg's *Simoon* on L.'s *Le simoun* in choice of characters, situation, setting. Remarks on influence of *The dance of death* on *Les ratés,* of *To Damascus* on *L'homme et ses fantômes.* Influence study is valuable, but author tends to dismiss L. too abruptly. Indexed.

White, Kenneth. Visions of a transfigured humanity: Strindberg and Lenormand. MD 5:323–30, 1962. **11376**
Shows L.'s debt to Strindberg. Both try to portray the nightmare of life illuminated by flashes of regained purity. Sees search for redemption in many of L.'s plays. L. is the poet of man's blackest anguish and highest aspirations. Good study.

Novel

Sheffer, Eugene. Poule de luxe. Nat 172, no. 22:522–23, June 2, 1951. **11377**
Review of L.'s novel *Renée.* Sees parallels between this novel and the plays. Good, if limited, analysis.

Georges Neveux
(Nos. 11378–11397)

JANE WOFFORD MALIN

Theater

Ambrière, Francis. Les spectacles. MerF 299:133–36, Jan. 1, 1947. **11378**

Good short article on *Plainte contre inconnu* of N. The play is above the average of contemporary plays and one can see indications of a great poet unafraid of stirring up some commonplaces.

Béhar, Henri. Le rêve actualisé: Georges Neveux, Georges Hugnet. *In his:* Etude sur le théâtre dada et surréaliste. Gallimard, 1967. p. 281–95. (Les essais, 131) **11379**

Excellent and provocative study placing N. against the background of his period. Bibliography.

Reviews: J. Jakubowicz in RW 6: 105–11, 1971; M. Sanouillet in CahDS 3:85–88, 1969; C. van Rees in FrB 40: 31–32, 1970.

Bishop, Thomas. Pirandello's influence on French drama. *In:* Pirandello, a collection of critical essays. Ed. by Glauco Cambon. Englewood Cliffs, N. J., Prentice-Hall, 1967. p. 43–65. (Twentieth century views) **11380**

Brief but thoughtful discussion of Pirandello's influence on the drama of N., in particular illusion and reality and self-confrontation.

Brée, Germaine. Neveux, a theatre of adventure. YFS 14:65–70, 1954–55. **11381**

Perceptive article discussing N.'s theater as being deliberately anti-tragic, not a theater of action but one of simple adventures. Highly theatrical in the best sense of the word, N. has no message and no theory, but deals in the essential questions of love, life and death.

Cézan, Claudel. Au Théâtre de l'œuvre, Aldous Huxley va faire sourire la Joconde. NL 27:8, Jan. 20, 1949. **11382**

N. explains the difference between adapting and translating a work. In any case, one must conserve the internal nerve channels which are present in any writing.

Jamet, Claude. Mythologie pas morte. *In his:* Images mêlées de la littérature et du théâtre. Eds. de l'élan, 1947. p. 41–46. **11383**

Review of a production of N.'s *Thésée* at the Mathurins. N. is a dramatist of promise although *Thésée* is no masterpiece. Staging is excellent and the modern Greek costumes a real find.

Malin, Jane W. Neveux, dramaturge surréaliste? Bay 23:405–13, 1959. **11384**

Principal plays of N. treated in the light of their relationship to basic surrealist techniques as defined in the article. Overly emphatic introduction detracts from basic study. Dated.

Neveux, Georges. Jean Vilar, vous exagérez! Arts 1, 4, Dec. 5–11, 1952. **11385**

Pinpoints relationships between author, actor and director. Interesting and vehement.

———. Prendre la vie au tragique, jamais au sérieux. AvSc 7, March 15, 1961. **11386**

On the *Voleuse de Londres*.

Pronko, Leonard C. Neveux, the theatrical voyage. DramS 3:244–52, 1963. **11387**

N. attempts to find an inner reality, a hidden truth, a controlled, delicate, tasteful and sensitive fantasy. N.'s is pure theater, dealing with eternal themes and delicately balanced between drama and farce. N. dramatizes the acceptance and the affirmation of life. *Juliette, Thésée, Zamore* and *Plainte contre inconnu* are discussed in some detail.

Roy, Claude. Lettre à Anton Tchékov pour lui présenter Neveux. CRB 6:3–10, 1954. **11388**

Warm appreciation of N.'s poetic qualities, his lucidity and his compassion. Retraces his theatrical career with some detail on the first presentation of *Juliette.*

Swerling, Anthony. Strindberg's impact in France 1920–1960. Cambridge, Trinity lane press, 1971. p. 59–61. **11389**

Finds parallels between *Miss Julie* and N.'s *Les demoiselles du large.* Details of comparison are so meticulously drawn up that by that very fact they are rendered less convincing.

Tillier, Maurice. Neveux s'est fait plus dostoïevskien que Dostoïevski. FL 22:13, March 2, 1967. **11390**

Interview with N. discussing *Et moi aussi j'existe* and other plays. N. states that two tendencies alternate in him which lead him to yield either to complete dreaming or to an imperious need of sincere confession.

Weyergans, Franz. Neveux. *In his:* Théâtre et roman contemporains. Eds. universitaires, 1957. p. 261–69. **11391**

Includes an excerpt from *Plainte contre inconnu.* N.'s principal accomplishment is to have captured the mystery of human beings in a sturdy theatrical construction.° Suggestive though somewhat vague and poeticized.

White, Kenneth S. Two French versions of A midsummer night's dream. FR 33:341–50, 1960. **11392**

Judges N.'s French text of Shakespeare's play to be inferior to that of Supervielle. A fairy play has become sardonic whimsy. N.'s version is shorter, more personal, more Gallic while Supervielle's is more accurate and more faithful to the original.

Poetry

Smith, F. R. Neveux and the oral element in modern poetry. AJFS 5:84–103, 1968. **11393**

Excellent study on a much neglected aspect of N.'s work. Sensitive evaluation of poetry.

Television

Bordaz, Robert. Neveux et Vidocq. RDM 615–20, March 1971. **11394**

The television serial is a return to the imagination. Public participation makes it a collective work. N. has renewed the serial and reinvented Vidocq.

Neveux, Georges. Contre une télévision amnisique. CRB 47–48:90–94, 1964. **11395**

Television has no memory as yet, and one cannot see a program again as one can reread a novel. N. pleads for the necessity of a television library, not for the sake of reruns, but in order to improve television by creating for it those works which cannot be done as well in another medium.

——. J'ai inventé Vidocq! NL 45:1, Jan. 26, 1967. **11396**

N. explains his penchant for the serial which is, for him, an enterprise of collective poetry revealing the legends

and myths dormant in us all. Television is the ideal medium.

——. Le spectateur at le public. NL 27:8, April 7, 1949. **11397**

Discusses his views as opposed to those of Armand Salacrou concerning the interaction which must take place between the public and the stage.

André Obey
(Nos. 11398–11412)

EARLE D. CLOWNEY AND JUNE M. LEGGE

Biography and Interview

Copeau, Jacques. Lettres inédites de Jacques Copeau à Jean Schlumberger, Xavier de Courville et André Obey. RevTh 5:15–28, summer 1950. **11398**

Last eight pages of article contain very informative account of O.'s association with Copeau, expressed through Copeau's response to plays O. submitted for his observation, criticism, suggestions and praise. Works discussed are *L'homme de cendres, Bataille de la Marne, Ultimatum, Revenu de l'étoile, La nuit des temps, Les amis de la dernière heure.*

Mignon, Paul-Louis. La pièce sur commande. WoTh 8:225–35, 1959. **11399**

Claude Santelli and O. discuss advantages and disadvantages of writing commissioned plays.

Obey, André. Le travail de l'aube. Ver 1:14–19, 1947. **11400**

O. mentions his indebtedness to Copeau for being shown the magic of the theater: harmonious marriage between drama and scenery. Sees contemporary French theater as one of becoming — rather than one of being. Ends with biographical sketch of O.

Obey, Nicole. Mémoires de mon père. Ver 1:20–25, 1947. **11401**

Nicole Obey's fond recollection of her father.

Generalities

Crumbach, Fr. H. Revenu de l'étoile. *In his:* Die Struktur des epischen Theaters. Braunschweig, Waisenhaus-Buchdruckerei

und Verlag, 1960. p. 121-29.   **11402**
O.'s *Revenu de l'étoile* proves the total range of artistic expression of epic theater.

Fergusson, Francis. Noah: the theater-poetic reality of the myth. *In his:* The idea of a theater. Princeton, N. J., Princeton univ. press, 1949. p. 203-10.   **11403**
Detailed analysis of *Noah* and aspects of O.'s dramatic technique. Compares poetry in *Noah* to that in Chekhov's *The cherry orchard*. Mentions Copeau's obvious influence on O. in *Lucrèce* and *Noah* with the excellent use of the highly trained acting company and the strict adherence to the older dramatic tradition.

Gandrey-Retz, J. Vers l'inversion de Don Juan. Arts 244:7, 1950.   **11404**
Discusses Freudian nihilistic and existential significances of *L'homme de cendres*.

Ghéon, Henri. Lucrèce chez les Quinze. JTP 7:210-14, 1931.   **11405**
Informative article, praising O.'s conversion of Shakespeare's poem to a very convincing drama.

————. Noé chez les quinze. JTP 5:144-78, 1931.   **11406**
An excellent source for critical examination of all facets of O.'s *Noé*. Extremely helpful information on staging, costuming, structure, plot and character analysis. Concludes with an historical bibliography on Noah in the theater (15th through 19th centuries).

Kim, Jean-Jacques. La Bible et les écrivains contemporains. TR 107:187-97, 1956.   **11407**
Section on O.'s use of Lazarus as the prototype of man meditating on Bible and philosophical problems.

Lerminier, Georges. Le théâtre: Maria. Esp 122:839-40, 1946.   **11408**
Attempts to defend O.'s *Maria* from almost unanimous adverse criticism.

Lumley, Frederick. The stage of the drama: France. *In his:* Trends in twentieth-century drama. Fair Lawn, N. J., Essential books, 1956. p. 230, 239, 240.   **11409**
Brief discussion of O.'s early promise in *Le viol de Lucrèce, Noé* and *La*

bataille de la Marne and his subsequent failure to fulfill this promise.

Neveux, Georges. Lazare d'André Obey. Arts 335:9, 1951.   **11410**
Describes O.'s *Lazare* as a play appealing to our metaphysical sensitivity. Has praise for certain features of play: scene between Lazarus and Jesus, Jesus as pupil rather than teacher.

Say, Michael. Une première mondiale à Baden-Baden: Revenu de l'étoile, par André Obey. Ver 2:76-79, 1947.   **11411**
Enthusiastic praise for the world premiere of *Revenu de l'étoile* in Baden-Baden, with special mention of Valentine Tessier and A. M. Julien.

Simon, Alfred. Passions pour mourir. Esp 204:78-81, 1953.   **11412**
Short analysis of the play *Une fille pour du vent*. Focuses on the death of Iphigenia. Some criticism of O.'s methods, in particular those learned from Copeau.

Marcel Pagnol
(Nos. 11413-11451)

DAVID A. COWARD

Bibliography and Filmography

Bibliographie. AvSc 105-06:96, 1970.   **11413**
Invaluable, especially for early articles on P. and contemporary reviews of his films.

Biofilmographie de Marcel Pagnol. AvSc 105-06:88-93, 1970.   **11414**
Accurate survey of the whole field.

Bibliographie des œuvres de Marcel Pagnol. Bib 21, no. 2:15, 1953.   **11415**
Usefulness limited by date. Some gaps. To be used with caution.

Brion, Patric, and Jean Kress. Filmographie. CduC 173:72-73, 1965.   **11416**
Complete and detailed filmography established under the supervision of P. An essential tool.

Marcel Pagnol: bibliographie. LivF 15-16, March 1964.   **11417**
Sound and reliable guide.

Editions

Pagnol, Marcel. Œuvres complètes. Club de l'honnête homme, 1970–71. 12 v. **11418**
Definitive edition of major and minor works, some not available hitherto. Assembles numerous prefaces previously published in various periodicals which are essential for understanding P.'s life, aims and art. Articles republished are: "Les nouveaux souvenirs de Marcel Pagnol" FL Aug. 3, 10, 17, 24, 31, Sept. 7, 1963 (repr. in LectPT March 1965 and AlP 2:209–27, Aug. 1964); "Marcel Pagnol raconte comment est né Monsieur Topaze" FL Aug. 6, 13, 20, 27, 1964 (repr. in AlP 8:246–76, Feb. 1965 and LectPT March 1965); "Marcel Pagnol raconte ses débuts au cinéma" FL Oct. 21, 28, Nov. 4, 1965 (repr. in AlP 31:76–106, Jan. 1967); "Comment je suis devenu poète" ParM 1068:148–55, Oct. 25, 1969.

———. Les sermons de Marcel Pagnol. Choisis et présentés par Norbert Calmels. Provence, Robert Morel, 1967. 123 p. **11419**
Introduction contains reflections on the art of the sermons preached by P.'s curés. Useful guide to a little-studied subject.
Reviews: L. Chaigne in NL 13, April 18, 1968; D. Petrone in OsR 6, Feb. 16, 1968.

Biography

Achard, Marcel. Marcel Pagnol, mon ami. *In his:* Rions avec eux. Les grands auteurs comiques. Fayard, 1957. p. 298–328. **11420**
Amiable anecdotage, but some biographical details and views on P.'s style. Contains an extract from an early verse tragedy, *Catulle*. Versions of this chapter appeared in various periodicals.

Antoine, André-Paul. Marcel Pagnol, Marcel Achard, Henri Jeanson. RDM 12: 521–33, 1962. **11421**
Valuable information on "les moins de trente ans," a literary group of which P. was a member. Brief remarks in defense of P.'s literary achievement.

Audouard, Yvan. Audouard raconte Pagnol. Stock, 1973. 247 p. **11422**

Pleasant reminiscences. Non-chronological and gossipy. Some scattered background information and a few comments on the plays.

Blavette, Charles. Ma Provence en cuisine. Préf. de Marcel Pagnol. Eds. France-Empire, 1961. 315 p. **11423**
Recollections illuminating P.'s temperament and working methods from *Jofroi* to *Le schpountz*. Value limited by chatty approach.

Fernandel (pseud. of Ferdinand Contandin). Mon ami Marcel Pagnol. CinF 24:Nov. 19, 1937. *Also:* AvSc 105–06:85–86, 1970. **11424**
Fernandel on his association with P. Information on P.'s unorderly working methods.

Fieschi, Jean-André, Gérard Guégan, and Jacques Rivette. Une aventure de la parole: entretien avec Marcel Pagnol. CduC 173:24–37, 1965. **11425**
Interview. Important for P.'s discussion of his technique as film-maker.

———, **G. Guégan, et al.** Pagnol au travail par ses collaboratuers. CduC 173: 56–62, 1965. **11426**
Interviews with members of P.'s film-making team of the thirties. Provides important insights into P.'s methods of work and his aims as a film-maker.

Gautier, Jean-Jacques. Un écrivain vous parle: Marcel Pagnol. Réa 203:153–61, 181–84, 1962. **11427**
Interview. Comments by P. on various aspects of his work and attitudes. Useful indications.

Mourgeon, Jacques. La leçon des choses de Pagnol. NL Dec. 31, 1973, Jan. 6, 1974. **11428**
Brief but fair assessment of P.'s life and personality based on the six television interviews of autumn 1973.

Pour nos cinquante ans. CahS 373–74:1–248, 1963. **11429**
Series of articles by the Fortunio group which set up the *Cahiers du sud* in 1925. J. Ballard, L. Brauquier, M. Brion and G. d'Aubarède recall their youthful idealism and provide valuable glimpses of the early P.

General Studies

Bagge, Dominique. Le mythe de Judas dans la littérature française contemporaine. Cr 108:423–37, 1956. **11430**

A valuable thematic article situating P.'s use of Judas against that of Claudel, P. Bost and others. The author argues that P. advances "le pari de l'obéissance."

Caldicott, C. E. J. Notice bibliographique et judiciaire sur la collaboration de Jean Giono avec Marcel Pagnol. RUO 41: 563–66, 1971. **11431**

Account of Giono's suit of plagiarism heard on October 14, 1941 in the Troisième tribunal civil de Marseille. Brief analysis of P.'s debt to Giono's story.

Combaluzier, Louis. Le jardin de Pagnol. Les œuvres françaises, 1937. 188 p. **11432**

Strong on anecdotes which contain occasional biographical information, but equally strong on trivialities. Pompous, self-important book of little worth.

Knowles, Dorothy. French drama of the inter-war years, 1918–1939. London, Harrap, 1967. p. 269–71. **11433**

Cast P. resolutely as a "boulevardier," follows his cinema career, and concludes that his return to the theater in 1955–56 was "less well-inspired."

Koëlla, Charles E. Les Marseillais de Marcel Pegnol. FR 24:307–24, 1951. **11434**

Little more than a plain summary of the trilogy. A few undeveloped insights, but conclusions are few.

Rostaing, C. Le français de Marseille dans la trilogie de Marcel Pagnol. FM 10: 29–44; 117–31, 1942. **11435**

Scholarly investigation of P.'s language. Provençalisms are carefully measured and occur chiefly in vocabulary. Serious attempt to relate linguistic analysis to a general view of his work.

Vial, Fernand. Provence and Provençals in the works of Marcel Pagnol. ASLHM 35: 29–47, 1964. **11436**

Superficial survey of P.'s output with a few suggestive hints.

Theater

Ambrière, Francis. César. *In his:* La galerie dramatique, 1945–1948. Le théâtre français depuis la libération. Corrêa, 1949, p. 136–39. **11437**

Enthusiastic presentation of *César* (Théâtre des variétés, Dec. 18, 1946) which brings out the unity of the trilogy and offers reflections on P.'s adaptation of his original film script.

Brisson, Pierre. Le théâtre des années folles. Geneva, Eds. du milieu du monde, 1943. p. 94–96. **11438**

Some harsh but fair criticism of P.'s theater. P. not forgiven for forsaking stage for screen. Captures the mood of the polemical thirties.

Surer, Paul. La comédie satirique. IL 8: 179–89, 1956. *Also in his:* Le théâtre français contemporain. Société d'édition d'enseignement supérieur, 1964. p. 108–17. *Also in his:* Cinquante ans de théâtre, Société d'édition et d'enseignement supérieur, 1969. p. 75–80. **11439**

Distinguishes P.'s "veine satirique" from his "veine romantique." The early P. is savage, but the trilogy is less effective as satire. Short and superficial appraisal of his dramatic qualities.

Cinema

Bazin, André. Le cas Pagnol. *In his:* Qu'est-ce que le cinéma? V. 1. Eds. du cerf, 1959. p. 119–25. **11440**

Develops ideas suggested in earlier articles. A lucid and objective account of P.'s place in the history of cinema. Stresses his instinctive approach, but is less impressed by other aspects of his amateurism. The most constructive of many histories of cinema.

———. Les lettres de mon moulin et le cas Pagnol. FrOb 234:Nov. 19, 1954. **11441**

Review of great penetration which develops into a general discussion of P. as "cinéaste."

———. Théâtre et cinema. Esp 180:891–905; 181:232–53, 1951. **11442**

P.'s views on "théâtre filmé" taken a a pretext for a lucid and wide-ranging discussion. Criticizes P.'s theory but sit uates his films as neo-realist. Fair and discriminating essay.

Beylie, Claude. Marcel Pagnol. Seghers, 1974. 190 p. (Cinéma d'aujourd'hui, 80) **11443**

Well-researched historical survey of P.'s films and theories, the fullest critical appraisal to date (p. 9–118). Enthusiastic but discriminating. Includes extracts, very detailed filmography and bibliography.

Clair, René. Légitime défense. In his: Réflexion faite. Gallimard, 1951. p. 164–67, 172–73, 193–96. Also (rev.): Cinéma d'hier, cinéma d'aujourd'hui. Gallimard, 1970. p. 222–32, 258–59, 260–65. (Collection "idées") Trans.: Reflections on the cinema. Trans. by Vera Traill. London, William Kimber, 1953. **11444**

Clair's tolerant account of his esthetic battle with P. in the thirties over the "visual" as opposed to the spoken. Important reflections on "théâtre filmé" and P.'s place in the history of cinema.

Jeanne, René, and Charles Ford. La France en face du cinéma parlant. MerF 333: 215–39, 1956. **11445**

Hard on "l'homme-théâtre du cinéma." Restates the view that P. underestimated the visual in favor of his text and "authorship." His films are cinematographically uninteresting and owe their success to Raimu. Well-informed discussion.

Labarthe, André S. Pagnol entre centre et absence. CduC 173:66–70, 1965. **11446**

Rejects the criticism of "théâtre filmé," and does justice to P.'s "cinématurgie." Indicates a number of useful approaches to P.'s films.

Leprohon, Pierre. Marcel Pagnol. In his: Présences contemporaines. Debresse, 1957. p. 210–23. **11447**

Perceptive discussion of P.'s films and especially the collaboration with Giono.

Renoir, Jean. Ecrits 1926–1971. Pierre Belfond, 1974. 314 p. (Les bâtisseurs du XXe siècle) **11448**

Useful perspective on P. the filmmaker. Important interview with P. on location shooting.

Prose Fiction

Georges Yvonne. Les provençalismes dans L'eau des collines. (La Provence dans L'eau des collines, roman de Marcel Pagnol: étude de langue.) Aix-en-Provence, 1967. 240 p. (Publications des Annales de la Faculté des lettres, Aix-en-Provence. Série: Travaux et mémoires, 42) **11449**

Detailed linguistic analysis. Conclusions scant, unambitious and disappointing. Provençalisms more frequent than in the trilogy, but are strongest in vocabulary.

Mongrédien, G. Autour du Masque de fer. RDM 421–27, Oct. 1965. **11450**

Although well-researched, Le masque de fer is a novel. As an historian, P. needs to accept resignation in face of the unknowable.

Rat, Maurice. Succulence des romans de Pagnol. VL 144:147–50, 1964. **11451**

Cursory nod towards the evocative qualities of P.'s prose plus a few etymological notes on provençalisms in L'eau des collines. No reservations concerning the surface value of P.'s vocabulary.

Stève Passeur
(Nos. 11452)

Sharon E. Harwood

Ratiu, Basile. L'œuvre dramatique de Stève Passeur. Didier, 1964. 253 p. **11452**

Concise survey of P.'s theater. Tone of plays dictated by "esprit de contradiction." Love, treated in a cynical and brutal manner, is dominant theme. Author devotes a chapter each to: themes and ideas, characterization, mise en scène, dramatic techniques. Appendices contain list of plays performed, plot summaries of plays and extensive bibliographies.

Armand Salacrou
(Nos. 11453–11481)

Juris Silenieks

Bébon, Philippe. Salacrou. Eds. universitaires, 1971. 125 p. (Classiques du XXe siècle) **11453**

Aside from occasional anecdotal material, study adds little to S. criticism. Arbitrary omissions of significant material; poor organization.

Review: G. de Mallac in BA 47:98, 1973.

Brodin, Pierre. Armand Salacrou. *In his:* Présences contemporaines. V. 1. Eds. Debresse, 1954. p. 221–35.   **11454**

Chronological survey of plots, themes, characters. Critical comment limited to generalities about S. as observer of contemporary mores, his craftsmanship, and reasonable pessimism.

Bunjavec, Milan. Le problème du temps dans L'inconnue d'Arras d'Armand Salacrou. TLL 8:117–42, 1970.   **11455**

Well-documented, exhaustive analysis of S.'s flashback technique, its historical analogues and philosophic and esthetic implications. Although study deals with one play, its serves as introduction to S.'s dramatic techniques in general.

Charmel, André. Essai sur le théâtre d'Armand Salacrou. Eur 27:101–11, 1949.   **11456**

Attempt at definition of S.'s esthetics as symptomatic of *mal du siècle,* existentialist anguish, and conflict between reason and sensibility. Analysis of S.'s dramaturgical innovations, his rejection of plausibility in favor of "anarchie organisée."

Esch, José van den. Armand Salacrou, dramaturge de l'angoisse. Eds. du temps présent, 1947. 340 p.   **11457**

First comprehensive study of S.'s work up to 1947. Sees S. as existentialist writer of great promise. Emphasizes S.'s philosophical anxieties and dramaturgical innovations. Good specimen of postwar criticism reflecting existentialist ambiance.
Review: Anon. in BCLF 3:131, March 1948.

Franco, Fiorenza di. Le théâtre de Salacrou. Gallimard, 1970. 170 p.   **11458**

Thematic approach along five basic philosophical preoccupations oversimplifies and categorizes S.'s work and results in repetitions. Neglects analysis of dramatic forms. Revealing interviews with S.
Review: J. McLaren in FR 45:504–05, 1971.

Got, Maurice. Savonarole, le masculin à l'état pur: étude de La terre est ronde. *In*

his: Théâtre et symbolisme. Le cercle du livre, 1955. p. 280–93.   **11459**

Psychological probings into the character of Savonarola, attempting to explicate psychological determinism in terms of conflict between asceticism and human love, spirit and blood. Of limited interest.

Guicharnaud, Jacques. Man in time and space: Armand Salacrou. *In his:* Modern French theatre, from Giraudoux to Genet. In collaboration with June Guicharnaud. New Haven, Yale, univ. press, 1967. p. 87–97.   **11460**

Traces evolution of S.'s attempt to graft philosophical themes of universal meaning on variously amplified naturalist forms. Judges reconciliation of political commitment with metaphysical concerns not successful. Selective but original study.

Hahn, Paul. Introducing Armand Salacrou. ETJ 3:2–10, 1951.   **11461**

Laudatory survey of plays written before 1950 to arouse interest among American producers. Biographical notes, plots, main philosophical themes, S.'s theatrical fortunes and contemporary relevance.

Hobson, Harold. Armand Salacrou. *In his:* The French theatre of today. London, Harrap, 1953. p. 128–68.   **11462**

Sympathetic survey of selected major plays. Biographical sketches, anecdotal accounts of critical reception and theatrical fortunes. Analysis of expressionist and surrealist elements. Attributes S.'s pessimism to loss of faith and his concern over bourgeois mores.

Homburger, René. Ein Dramatiker: Armand Salacrou. Ant 4, no. 4:52–60; no. 5:37–45, 1956.   **11463**

Well-documented extensive biographical sketch, detailed accounts of plots, copious quotes from critical notes. Study presents little original critical analysis.

Hosbach, Johanna D. Armand Salacrou: Les nuits de la colère. *In:* Das moderne französische Drama. Ed. by Walter Pabst. Berlin, Erich Schmidt Verlag, 1971. p. 205–19.   **11464**

Extended analysis of S.'s Resistance play, its genesis and structure with alternating realist and surrealist elements, its relationship to other S. plays and contemporary analogues.

Knowles, Dorothy. Studio theatre: the school for cynicism. *In her:* French drama of the inter-war years 1918–39. London, Harrap, 1967. p. 143–58.   **11465**

Survey of major plays. Judges S. for his radical pessimism and inquiry into life's absurdity as precursor of existentialism. Examines dramatic techniques in light of his surrealist learnings.

Lumley, Frederick. This fever called living — Armand Salacrou and Jean Anouilh. *In his:* Trends in 20th century drama. London, Rockliff, 1956. p. 164–75.   **11466**

Sees S. as a radically romantic pessimist longing for faith and purity. Biographical account and detailed analyses of major plays. Early surrealist plays and new dramatic techniques regarded as erratic experimentations.

Lusseyran, Jacques P. La malédiction de la solitude chez Anouilh et Salacrou. FR 39:418–25, 1965.   **11467**

Thematic affinities and divergences in two plays by S. and Anouilh. Analysis of solitude is limited in scope and provides little insight into works of the two authors.

Marcel, Gabriel. Singularité d'Armand Salacrou. Th 3:59–78, 1945.   **11468**

One of the first extensive studies of S.'s originality, emphasizing his search for new dramatic forms and his commitment to orient theater to metaphysical themes. Many later critics follow Marcel's approach.

Maulnier, Thierry. A la recherche de la tragédie. Ar 24:92–97, 1947.   **11469**

Analysis of S.'s *Les nuits de la colère* as attempt to create modern tragedy through formalistic devices such as flashbacks, chronological distortions. Play succeeds in creating *Verfremdungseffekt*, but lacks poetic qualities necessary to tragedy.

Mignon, Paul-Louis. Salacrou. Gallimard, 1960. 318 p. (La bibliothèque idéale)   **11470**

Substantive survey with extensive biography, bibliography, texts and critical comments. Sees S. as innovator of dramatic forms and playwright of

"grands sujets," with little interest in psychology or mores. Valuable source book.

Review: Anon in RFB 2:7, 1961.

Poujol, Jacques. Salacrou l'inquiéteur. FR 27:428–36, 1954.   **11471**

Sees S.'s theater as didactic confrontation with spectator to impart existential anguish over absurdity of human condition, death, old age, freedom of choice, happiness. Analysis of dramatic techniques.

Radine, Serge. Armand Salacrou. *In his:* Anouilh, Lenormand, Salacrou, trois dramaturges à la recherche de leur vérité. Geneva, Eds. des trois collines, 1951. p. 99–140.   **11472**

Exhaustive analyses of selected plays dealing with their philosophical import. Considers S. as impenitent romantic, his work uneven, beautiful and banal, replete with contradictions and artistic deficiencies. Great potential not realized because of S.'s intellectual shortcomings. Somewhat dogmatic criticism.

Salacrou, Armand. Dans la salle des pas perdus. C'était écrit. Gallimard, 1974. 317 p.   **11473**

First installment of recollections, dealing with S.'s early career, interspersed with meditations from the vantage point of a writer who has renounced the world.

————. Les idées de la nuit. Arthème Fayard, 1960. 259 p. (Le grenier des Goncourt)   **11474**

In addition to articles and *pièces à lire* previously published, collection contains recollections and essays of some autobiographical import elucidating S.'s work.

————. Impromptu délibéré. Entretiens avec Paul-Louis Mignon. Gallimard, 1966. 180 p. (Le manteau d'Arlequin)   **11475**

Conversations ranging over variety of subjects, reexamining S.'s philosophic and esthetic positions, basic themes in his works, their meaning and geneses in relation to personal experiences.

Silenieks, Juris. Circularity of plot in Salacrou's plays. Sym 20:56–62, 1966. **11476**

Analysis of relationship between themes of human unchangeability and plots without essential development as dramaturgical illustration of determinism and life's absurdity.

―――. Themes and dramatic forms in the plays of Armand Salacrou. Lincoln, Nebr., Univ. of Nebraska, 1967. 170 p. (University of Nebraska studies: n.s. 35) **11477**

Chronological survey tracing evolution of S.'s plays from subjective philosophical concerns to growing social consciousness, from early surrealist experiments to Brechtian epic forms.

Simon, Pierre-Henri. L'athéisme anxieux d'Armand Salacrou. *In his:* Théâtre et destin. Armand Colin, 1959. p. 119–41.
11478

Penetrating study of S.'s pessimism and conflicting philosophical anxieties over predestination, search for God, absence of moral standards. Examines affinities with Gide, Giraudoux, existentialist thought.
Reviews: E. Jahiel in Sym 16:159, 1962; K. Rühl in MD 4:218–19, 1961.

Surer, Paul. Armand Salacrou. *In his:* Le théâtre français contemporain. Société d'édition et d'enseignement supérieur, 1964. p. 120–29. **11479**

Good specimen of negative criticism. Brief biography, bibliography, summaries of plots. Judges S.'s attempt to create metaphysical theater least successful. His talent never fully matured.

Ubersfeld, Annie. Armand Salacrou. Seghers, 1970. 190 p. (Théâtre de tous les temps, 13) **11480**

Imposing study of S.'s work emphasizing alternating concerns over personal anxieties and social realities. Sees evolution toward Marxist-oriented social criticism denouncing bourgeois order, immorality of capitalism. Provides good contrast with other interpretations. Richly documented.

―――. Salacrou: un théâtre du scandale. Pen n.s. 100:69–81, 1961. **11481**

Stresses evolution of S.'s attitudes from metaphysical concerns to social consciousness. Sees S.'s theater as provocation of bourgeois spectator and accusation of social order and capitalist immorality.

Jean Sarment
(Nos. 11482–11493)

DAVID B. PARSELL

Delpit, Louis. Jean Sarment. *In her:* Paris-théâtre contemporain. Northampton, Mass., Smith college studies in modern languages, 1924–25; 1938–39. Part I, 1924–25, p. 99–100; Part II, 1938–39, p. 149–51.
11482

In two parts, Delpit offers a general introduction to S.'s dramatic art followed by useful summaries of his plays in chronological order of performance. Appreciative but not effusive; most helpful in assessing S.'s early success and prominence.

Doisy, Marcel. Jean Sarment. *In his:* Esquisses. Flament, 1950. p. 91–170. **11483**

A sympathetic, uncritical reading of S., using material from his novels and poems to amplify themes expressed in his plays. Study is useful for its plot summaries and for coverage of S.'s minor works, but analysis lacks objectivity and is often laudatory to the point of fulsomeness.

Knowles, Dorothy. Jean Sarment. *In her:* La réaction idéaliste au théâtre depuis 1890. Droz, 1934, p. 499–500. **11484**

In her brief analysis, author examines S.'s opposition of the real to the ideal and sees it as symptomatic of the neo-romantic spirit that emerged in the 1920's.

―――. Studio theatre: the new romantics. *In her:* French drama of the inter-war years 1918–39. London, Harrap, 1967. p. 161–81. **11485**

Discusses S.'s plays in conjunction with those of Anouilh, isolating neo-romantic elements in each. Treatment combines plot summaries of major plays with useful historical data, showing that the neo-romanticism of S.'s characters leads either to blatant escapism or clandestine revolt. Conclusion states that S. failed to meet the promise of his earliest efforts.

Lakich, John J. The ideal and reality in French theater of the 1920's. MLQ 31: 64–77, 1970. **11486**

Includes S. among certain supposedly "neo-romantic," "escapist" playwrights whose work is due for re-evaluation a a legitimate artistic response to social and psychological realities. Lakich accurately situates S. and his contemporaries as precursors of Giraudoux and Anouilh.

Palmer, John. M. Jean Sarment and the new romance. *In his:* Studies in the contemporary theatre. Boston, Little, Brown, 1927. p. 112–36. *Also:* Freeport, N. Y., Books for libraries press, 1969.   **11487**

Prolix discussion of S.'s early plays, heavily dependent upon extended quotations and preceded by a long meditation on Romance in its various forms. Perhaps the weakest essay in this collection; adds little to one's knowledge of S.

Rhodes, S. A. Jean Sarment. *In his:* The contemporary French theater. New York, Crofts, 1942. p. 383–86.   **11488**

Solid, generally sympathetic introduction to life and career of S., intended for advanced American students. Dated in its estimate of S.'s overall importance but useful for details.

Salomé, René. Jean Sarment. Et 702–11, 1925.   **11489**

Cautious but appreciative treatment of S.'s early plays, almost prophetic in its assessment of his major strengths and weaknesses as a dramatist.

Storer, Mary Elizabeth. Jean Sarment and the French theatre. RR 26:26–29, 1935.   **11490**

Encourages affirmative reappraisal of S.'s plays. Dated, but useful to an understanding of S.'s prominence between World Wars. Includes solid analytical summaries of major plays.

Surer, Paul. Etudes sur le théâtre contemporain: IX: Les lunaires. IL 10:190–93, 1963. *Also in his:* Le théâtre français contemporain. Société d'édition et d'enseignement supérieur, 1964. p. 131–38.   **11491**

Excellent, incisive analysis of S.'s plays, showing major themes and dominant influences. Isolates as a serious weakness S.'s use of two-part interior monolog as a substitute for actual dialog. Conceding the merits of S.'s best-known plays, author concludes that S. has nonetheless failed to measure up to his models or to fulfill the promise of his early success. Includes comprehen-sive list of plays with years of first performance.

Vier, Jacques. Le théâtre de Jean Sarment. *In his:* La littérature à l'emporte-pièce. Eds. du cèdre, 1958. p. 84–102.   **11492**

Solid, well-documented analysis of S.'s major plays, stressing recurrence of themes from Shakespeare's *Hamlet*. Sympathetic without indulgence, Vier's study is useful for its analysis and presentation of S.'s dramatic art.

Werrie, Paul. Jean Sarment: Le Pêcheur d'ombres ou le pirandellisme avant Pirandello. *In his:* Théâtre de la fuite. Brussels, Les écrits, 1943. p. 150–56.   **11493**

Adapted from a newspaper review, Werrie's article examines the stated play as a sample of S.'s better work, concluding that the masochistic suffer-ing of S.'s characters leads to an impasse rather than to a renewal of French dramatic art. Good discussion, limited only by its confinement to a single play.

Charles Vildrac
(pseud. of Charles Messager)
(Nos. 11494–11506)

WILLIAM T. STARR

Biography and Miscellaneous

Beattie, A. H. Vildrac and the Abbaye de Créteil. FR 29:219–27, 1956.   **11494**

Several pages devoted to V.'s youth, but mostly about the Abbaye de Créteil and his part in its realization and organization.

Bouquet, Georges, and Pierre Menanteau. Charles Vildrac. Présentation... Choix de textes. Bibliographie, portraits, fac-similé. Seghers, 1959. 223 p. (Poètes d'aujourd'hui, 69)   **11495**

The first part is a leisurely, informal biography, setting forth the principal facts of V.'s life and insisting on his appreciation of life. Special notice is given to his role in the founding and existence of the Abbaye de Créteil. There is an adequate discussion of his literary ideas and an examination of his *Notes sur la technique poétique* (Georges Duhamel was co-author). The study of his poetry is very good; his debt to

Verhaeren and Verlaine is noted, and the author insists that V. was not a "unanimiste," but a strong individualist, especially in his poetry. The effect of the war of 1914–18 on the poetic production is briefly discussed. Judgments of various writers, contemporaries of V., are provided.
Review: R. Lacôte in LetF 807:2, Jan. 14–20, 1960.

Küchler, Walter. Charles Vildrac. DFR 1: 100–16, 1928.   **11496**
Discusses V.'s writing and its relation to classical French tradition. The poetic ability of V. is illustrated by careful analyses of various poems, and a detailed comparison of V.'s "Les deux buveurs" with "Un jeune homme" by Francis Jammes, which remains banal and unpoetic. The dramas are then studied in a series of rather sensitive analyses, which insist on their philosophical aspects. V.'s art combines a refined realism of outward circumstances with the inner spiritual life.

Vildrac, Charles. Pages de journal 1922– 1966. Gallimard, 1968. 284 p.   **11497**
Interesting reading as well as helpful for an understanding of the man and the writer. The author's selections reveal much about himself and his life, events, associations, friends, attitudes, beliefs (social and political as well as esthetic and moral).

Poetry

Duhamel, Georges. Charles Vildrac et les hommes. VPr 24:104–09, 1911. *And in his:* Propos critiques. Figuière et Cⁱᵉ, 1912. p. 63–81.   **11498**
A sensitive analysis of V.'s poetry, especially the poems in *Le Livre d'amour,* by a friend and associate. Echoing his own tendencies, Duhamel finds in them a true religion of humanity, a realism that is lucid, but tender and mitigated by a robust optimism.

Hermann, Yvonne. Charles Vildrac. Marg 5:161–66, 1950.   **11499**
Homage to a man considered to be a great poet. Extensive quotations from Luc Durtain, Jacques Copeau, Lucine Jacques, and V.

Pondrom, Cyrena A. The road from Paris: French influence on English poetry, 1900– 1920. Cambridge, At the university press, 1974. p. 122–25, 203–04.   **11500**
Sees in V. a poet who loves men and life, and who brings love and imagination to bear on human wretchedness, no matter how trivial or sordid the circumstances. Includes a critique of V.'s lecture on French poetry at Grafton Galleries, Nov., 1912, and a good analysis of "Une auberge."

Theater

Daniels, May. Charles Vildrac. *In her:* The French drama of the unspoken. Edinburgh, Edinburgh univ. press, 1953. p. 121–43.   **11501**
The main facts about V. and the Abbaye de Créteil are set forth. The principal influences on the group, including V. (Whitman, Wm. James, Bergson), and their reaction to symbolism and naturalism are examined. Studies V.'s plays from the standpoint of the "drama of the unspoken," which is carefully defined. There is some discussion of V.'s place in general in the French theater.

Fechter, Paul. Das europäische Drama. Geist und Kultur im Spiegel des Theaters. III. Vom Expressionismus zur Gegenwart. Mannheim, Bibliographisches Institut, 1958. p. 283–84.   **11502**
A brief but interesting discussion of *Le Paquebot Tenacity,* and V.'s theatrical art, which is compared to Pagnol's.

Knowles, Dorothy. Studio theater: the unspoken. *In her:* French drama of the interwar years 1918–1939. London, Harrap, 1967. p. 112–28.   **11503**
A good but rather brief survey of V.'s work as a dramatist. *Le Paquebot Tenacity* is discussed as a minor masterpiece, and certain Tolstoyan traits are pointed out in his other works. His principal merit is his simplicity and accurate, direct observation.

Savitzki, Ludmila. Charles Vildrac et le théâtre contemporain. MerF 163:289– 305, 1923.   **11504**
Considers V. an excellent dramatist, exceptional among his contemporaries.

Ponders the reasons for V.'s choice of characters and praises their simplicity. Notes the differences between his characters and those of the so-called realists. Analyzes each of the plays to that date, and praises V.'s ability to create characters without the aid of picturesque slang, mores, or surroundings.

Surer, Paul. Etudes sur le théâtre français contemporain. III. Le théâtre intimiste. IL 4:178–86, 1952. **11505**

Defines and discusses the "théâtre intimiste," then examines the works of four dramatists, among whom V. V. represents the *théâtre d'intimité* in its purest and most perfect form. Taking people in a modest condition for his subject, V. reveals penetratingly their sentimental and psychological life. Positive and negative criticisms of his theater are reviewed.

————. Le théâtre français contemporain. Société d'édition et d'enseignement supérieur, 1964. p. 161–65. *Also in his:* Cinquante ans de théâtre. Société d'édition et d'enseignement supérieur, 1969. p. 107–10. **11506**

A brief biography and a discussion of the principal qualities of V.'s theater, poetic and intimate.

CHAPTER XXV

JEAN GIRAUDOUX

(Nos. 11507–11721)

AGNES G. RAYMOND

Assisted by Paul Mankin

Bibliography and Etat Présent

Albérès, René Marill. Etat présent des études sur Jean Giraudoux. IL 5:190–200, 1957. **11507**

This updates and summarizes the findings published in the critical bibliography accompanying Albérès' doctoral diss., *Esthétique et morale chez Jean Giraudoux* (p. 527–47), published the same year.

Body, Jacques. Giraudoux, Jean. *In:* Dizionario critico della letteratura francese. V. 1. Turin, Unione tipografico torinese, 1972. p. 489–92. **11508**

Beginning with a rapid sketch of G.'s life and works, this article is primarily an *état présent* of G. studies. Brief bibliography.

LeSage, Laurent. L'œuvre de Jean Giraudoux. Essai de bibliographie chronologique. Paris, Nizet, and University Park, Pennsylvania state univ. library, 1956. 48 p. **11509**

An indispensable tool of research for G. scholars. All the different publications of G.'s writings appearing between 1904 and 1955 are listed here in chronological order with alphabetical index by titles and all the necessary cross references. Needs to be updated to include *La menteuse* and several minor *inédits*.

———. L'œuvre de Jean Giraudoux. t. 2. University Park, Pennsylvania state univ. library, 1958. 188 p. mimeographed. **11510**

A critical bibliography in French of just about everything that has been written about the author, including dissertations, appearing between 1909 and 1955. Since this is not selective, the critical remarks are more in the nature of a summary of contents. This is a sequel to his bibliography of G.'s works (1956). A very valuable contribution.

Nobutoshi, Ando. Giraudoux au Japon. HumC 3:114–16, 1968. **11511**

G. is becoming known in Japan, largely through the success of *Ondine* and the work of two Japanese writers who have been influenced by him. In 1953 M. Kato published *Le monde giraldien*, a critical appreciation, and in 1960 Prof. J. Kawashima published *Les œuvres théâtrales de Jean Giraudoux*. M. S. Nakamura translated *Suzanne et le Pacifique* (1946) and *Combat avec l'ange* (1967). [PM]

Edition

Giraudoux, Jean. Théâtre complet. Neuchâtel and Paris, Ides et calendes, 1945–53. 16 v. **11512**

V. 12-15 contain variants of the plays. Most of the volumes have a frontispiece in color by Christian Bérard. While this is not a critical ed., the fine quality of paper and print and the four volumes of variants make it the preferred ed. of scholars.

Miscellaneous Texts

Body, Jacques. Deux chroniques oubliées: Giraudoux et Proust, Giraudoux et Claudel. SFr 33:457–67, 1967. **11513**

Introduces two articles concerning Proust and Claudel which G. wrote for the *Feuillets d'art*, of which he was literary editor during its brief existence from 1919 to 1922. New insights and material on G.'s critical methods.

Giraudoux, Jean. Carnet des Dardanelles. Introd. et notes de Jacques Body. Le bélier, 1969. 125 p. **11514**

Rough notes which G. recorded between March 1915 and January 1916. By reprinting an extract from *Adorable Clio* which relates this same period of World War I in literary form, the editor provides a valuable means of comparing G.'s actual experiences and reactions with his published version of them. Running commentary by Body accompanies this *inédit*.

Review: J. Onimus in RSH 140: 651–52, 1970.

LeSage, Laurent. La culture allemande et les universités américaines: an unpublished manuscript of Jean Giraudoux. HLB 13:114–24, 1959. **11515**

LeSage presents a carefully annotated version of an *inédit* dating from 1911–12. Of interest to scholars researching G.'s impressions of his first sojourn at Harvard and his prewar ideas on German culture.

Correspondence

Giraudoux, Jean. Lettres de Jean Giraudoux. Présentées et annotées par Jacques Body. Klincksieck, 1975. 279 p. (Les publications de la Sorbonne) **11516**

This volume is composed almost entirely of new letters. They are presented chronologically and grouped according to following categories: I. *Lettres de jeunesse*, 1902–1908; II. *Dans les écluses de la vie*, letters to his parents and wife, 1908–1937; III. *Correspondances littéraires*, 1909–1939; IV. *Suppléments aux voyages de l'inspecteur Giraudoux*, 1919–1938; V. *Générations*, 1938–1942, letters to his son and his mother.

Biography

Albalat, Antoine. Trente ans de quartier latin. Malfère, 1930. p. 79–88. **11517**

Reminiscences of G.'s early years as a journalist between 1908–1910.

Aucuy, Jean-Marc. La jeunesse de Giraudoux: souvenirs de Marc Aucuy recueillis par son fils. Spid, 1948. 171 p. **11518**

Marc Aucuy was G.'s classmate at the lycée de Châteauroux and more briefly at the lycée Lakanal. Not particularly informative, but the text is supplemented by some interesting photos and extracts from some of G.'s class exercises.

Barillon-Le Mehauté, Annick. Le séjour du lieutenant Giraudoux à Harvard 1917. RLMC 21:131–43, 1968. **11519**

Well documented account that makes use of some little known lectures by André Morize.

Beucler, André. Giraudoux top secret. RDM 514–31, Oct. 15, 1962. **11520**

Details of G.'s duties as Commissaire général à l'information. His plenipotentiary powers were limited to his voice and pen. Quotes conversations with G. relative to a secret mission to Hungary, Austria and Germany on which he sent Beucler to do a little reconnaissance.

————. Les instants de Giraudoux et autres souvenirs. Eds. milieu du monde, 1948. 213 p. **11521**

Indispensable reading for those who wish to savor G.'s conversation and become acquainted, however superficially, with the man as well as the author. Whether Beucler reconstituted these precious moments from notes or a prodigious memory, his own creative genius has undoubtedly refurbished them for our pleasure. They span the years 1924–1944.

Review: L. Fiumi in Caro 70:74–76, 1964.

Bourdet, Denise. Edouard Bourdet et ses amis. La Jeune Parque, 1946. p. 26–31. **11522**

Memories of dinners, excursions, and poker parties in which G. figured between 1906–11.

Bourin, André. Elle et lui. Chez Madame Jean Giraudoux. NL Nov. 16, 1950. **11523**

Rare and important interview with G.'s widow.

Charensol, Georges. Comment écrivez-vous, Jean Giraudoux? NL Dec. 19, 1931. *Also*

in his: Comment ils écrivent. Montaigne, 1932. p. 103–16.   **11524**
Reveals G.'s views on style and composition. A much quoted interview.

Cocteau, Jean. Souvenir de Jean Giraudoux. Confl 113–15, Sept.–Oct. 1944. *Also:* J. Haumont, 1946. 22 p.   **11525**
Cocteau's farewell to G. accompanied by his drawing of the death mask. The drawing appears in Chris Marker's *Giraudoux par lui-même,* facing p. 170.

Dumur, Guy. Giraudoux le menteur. NouvO 253:36–39, Sept. 15–21, 1969.   **11526**
Thoughts inspired by reading *La menteuse.* Contains an *inédit,* a speech written by G. to inaugurate the building of a new lycée in Bellac. Also some unfamiliar photographs. Defends reading this *roman inédit* for the pleasure of the intellectual exercise.

Ganne, Gilbert. Jean-Pierre Giraudoux: un fils régent en exil. NL 2204:1, 11, Dec. 18, 1969. *Also in his:* Tels que les voient leurs héritiers. Plon, 1972. p. 69–90. **11527**
An interview with G.'s son, followed by an unpublished letter dated Sept. 12, 1940, one of the rare examples of G.'s epistolary style. Both interview and letter are of biographical interest.

Géraldy, Paul. Féeries. RdP 54–61, Jan. 1946. *Also:* Eds. de la Nouvelle revue critique, 1946. 43 p.   **11528**
An homage that contains a penetrating character sketch of G.

Giraudoux, Jean-Pierre. Le fils. Grasset, 1967. 311 p.   **11529**
These semi-fictionalized memoirs contain significant details and character sketches of the family life of G.'s son; likewise a judgment of his father's work and his own responsibility to it.

——. Père et fils: secrets d'un visage. Monde 7678:5, Sept. 20, 1969.   **11530**
An intimate portrait of G. by his son, who is a writer. Details on father and son traveling through France. Relation of G. to politics and to the fictional characters he created.

Guinle, Alexandre. Jean Giraudoux à Lakanal et à Normale. Comœdia Feb. 19, 1944.   **11531**
Memories of a classmate and lifelong friend of G.

Lefèvre, Frédéric. Une heure avec. 1ʳᵉ série. Gallimard, 1924. p. 141–51. 4ᵉ série, 1927. p. 113–27.   **11532**
Each series contains two interviews originally published in NL. In the first series, G. defends the Service des œuvres françaises à l'étranger against the accusations of the press and defines his position as a writer. The second series begins with a biographical sketch and then elaborates G.'s views on literature. These are probably the most significant and valuable interviews on record.

LeSage, Laurent. Giraudoux's German studies. MLQ 12:353–59, 1951.   **11533**
Well-documented account ranging from G.'s studies at the lycée to the beginning of his career in the diplomatic service.

Lestringuez, Pierre. Notre ami Jean Giraudoux. *In:* Jean Giraudoux. *See* 11597. p. 29–36.   **11534**
Recollections of his friendship with G. from 1922 to the time of his death.

Maclean, Mary. Jean Giraudoux and Franz Wedekind. AJFS 4:97–105, 1967.   **11535**
Fills a gap in G.'s biography prior to his first trip to Harvard. Demonstrates a significant influence.

Martin du Gard, Maurice. Mon journal de Giraudoux. 1943–44. EPar 92–101, Sept. 1964.   **11536**
Factual testimony of a contemporary of G. on his pregnant silence under the Nazis a few months before his death.

Morand, Paul. Giraudoux, souvenirs de notre jeunesse. Suivi de Adieu à Giraudoux avec des lettres et documents inédits. Geneva, La Palatine, 1948. 158 p. *Also in his:* Mon plaisir en littérature. V. 1. Gallimard, 1967. p. 145–217. **11537**
Memories of Munich, Paris and World War I (1905–1918) with some rare examples of G.'s correspondence. Also contains an homage first published in 1944 (Lausanne, Portes de France). Indispensable reading for G.'s biography. It is unfortunate that Morand has not updated these memoirs.

——. Journal d'un attaché d'ambassade 1916–1917. Gallimard, 1963. 300 p. **11538**
From August 16, 1916 to July 31, 1917, Morand was assigned to the Paris office of the Ministry of Foreign

Affairs. This diary records his impressions of important political personages like Philippe Berthelot and Jules Cambon as well as social relationships. G.'s name does not figure as frequently as those of Cocteau and Proust since he was at Harvard during part of this time, but Morand does publish four short letters from G. and makes some passing references. No index. Adds little to what he tells us in his book on G.

Morize, André. Témoignage d'un ami. HumC 3:19–22, 1968. **11539**

Text of a talk given July 26, 1949 in G.'s apartment, 89 Quai d'Orsay. A tender remembrance by an old friend and member of the team when G. was Commissaire général à l'information (1939–1940). [PM]

Pierrefeu, Jean de. Comment j'ai fait fortune. Eds. de France, 1926. p. 159–65. **11540**

Contains an anecdote about G.'s youthful financial ambitions which corroborates Franz Toussaint's chapter "L'homme à la perle" (*Sentiments distingués*). Also some nostalgic recollections of the Pension Laveur, which he and G. frequented about 1908–1910. The first three chapters are full of insights into the psychology of their generation before World War I.

Ratel, Simone. Entretiens avec Jean Giraudoux. Est-ce le commencement d'un romantisme français? Comœdia June 18, 1928. *Also in her:* Dialogues à une seule voix. Le tambourin, 1930. p. 9–16. **11541**

Interview in which G. elaborates on his affinity with the German romantics.

Sudreau, Pierre. Giraudoux et l'esprit de l'urbanisme. RDM 1:9–23, 1960. **11542**

The author, Minister of Construction at the time of writing this article, summarizes G.'s views on urbanism and quotes him profusely to further the cause of city planning and urban renewal throughout France.

Toussaint, Franz. Sentiments distingués. Robert Laffont, 1945. 341 p. **11543**

The last half of this volume of reminiscences contains anecdotes which portray the young G. flirting with big business, teaching Latin grammar to a pretty girl in the park, masquerading as a guide in the Louvre to a couple of ravishing American tourists, and substituting for a public letter writer for a damsel in distress. Although his veracity cannot be vouched for, Toussaint is an inimitable story teller.

———. Giraudoux et Giraudoux. Lyon, Audin, 1948. 73 p. **11544**

An adventure in Portugal during World War I. Introduction by Alexandre Guinle.

———. Jean Giraudoux. Arthème Fayard, 1953. 235 p. **11545**

Includes the above item plus a number of other anecdotes published separately but not listed in this bibliography. Preface by René Lalou.

Warnod, André. J'ai épousseté le buste d'Electre, nous dit Jean Giraudoux. Fig May 11, 1937. **11546**

G. tells how he researched the Electra theme and how he envisages it.

Wattelet, Paul (pseud. of Louis Aragon). Jean Giraudoux et l'Achéron. Confl 35:116–31, 1944. **11547**

A revealing portrait of G. as Commissaire général à l'information, in charge of censorship among other things. Regards him as naïve and ineffectual with no sense of reality and more preoccupied with style than content.

Weil, Simone. Draft of a letter to Jean Giraudoux 1939 or 1940. *In her:* Seventy letters. Trans. and arranged by Richard Rees. London, Oxford univ. press, 1965. p. 110–11. **11548**

Of interest only because it gives a rare glimpse of G. in his function of Minister of Propaganda. Reaction of this distinguished conscientious objector to one of G.'s speeches is significant.

General Studies

Albérès, René-Marill. Esthétique et morale chez Jean Giraudoux. Nizet, 1957. 559 p. (Diss., Paris) **11549**

A monumental work and still the definitive study on G. Thoroughly documented and supplemented by a critical bibliography and appendices containing official documents relating to G.'s studies, his diplomatic career, and notes and variants of *Intermezzo, Judith,* and

Supplément au voyage de Cook. The critic's emphasis is primarily philosophical. He attaches more importance to G.'s relations with the cosmos than with the real world and sees a coherent pattern of thought in G.'s work. Ignores G.'s impish humor and profound distrust of abstractions. His esthetic analysis suffers from his tendency to sublimate concrete reality. This same tendency prevents him from ever really coming to grips with the tragic aspect of G.'s thought, even in the last part of his work, which is devoted to social and political preoccupations. Reviews: D. Knowles in FS 14:81–82, 1960; F. Müller in Archiv 196:228–29, 1960; A. Pizzorusso in RLMC 12:91–93, 1959; A. Rousseaux in FL Sept. 28, 1957.

————. La mort de Giraudoux n'aura pas lieu. NL Dec. 18, 1969. **11550**

Evaluation of the Grasset edition of the *Œuvre dramatique, La menteuse, Carnet des Dardanelles* and *Or dans la nuit,* all appearing in 1969. Testifies as to the authenticity of posthumous works, which he helped to edit, and to the relevancy of G.'s work for the contemporary reader.

Bidal, M. L. Giraudoux tel qu'en lui-même. Corrêa, 1956. 205 p. **11551**

Mme Bidal has penetrated more perceptively than most critics the Apollonian mask of G. For the reader who is already conversant with G.'s works, this long essay reconciles many of the puzzling quirks and contradictions in G.'s view of the human condition, without ever separating form from substance. It deserves careful reading.

Body, Jacques. Jean Giraudoux et l'Allemagne. Marcel Didier, 1975. 521 p. (Les publications de la Sorbonne) **11552**

Probably the most important scholarly work to date, this is an exhaustive study of G.'s personal, literary, and political relations with Germany. The first part is exclusively biographical, taking the author up to World War I. The second part deals with the philosophical and esthetic influences of German literature on G.'s novels, his role in World War I and his account of it in his published works, followed by an analysis of *Siegfried et le Limousin* and *Bella.* The third part is devoted to the

theater and would appear to be largely political in emphasis. The bibliography contains a list of German publications on G. up to 1944, and there are some minor biographical documents in the appendix.

————. Nationalisme et cosmopolitisme dans la pensée de Jean Giraudoux. *In:* Actes du 4ᵉ congrès de l'Association internationale de littérature comparée. The Hague, Mouton, 1966. p. 534–40. **11553**

Beautifully written article which tries to resolve the contradictions between G.'s ideological nationalism and his cosmopolitan experience.

Bory, Jean-Louis. L'île Giraudoux. *In his:* Pour Balzac et quelques autres. Julliard, 1960. p. 161–77. **11554**

Essay inspired by Sartre's famous article in the NRF and special issue of *Confluences* devoted to G. in 1944. The critic sees G.'s entire work as a *choix des élus.* Discusses its *surréalité* as distinguished from surrealism.

Bourdet, Maurice. Jean Giraudoux: son œuvre, portrait et autographe. Eds. de la Nouvelle revue critique, 1928. 61 p. **11555**

Bears witness to solid reputation which G. enjoyed in France prior to becoming a playwright. Gives a rapid but complete picture of G.'s life and works including a bibliography of his writings, translations of his books, and articles of criticism until 1928. Still a good source of information on the first stage of G.'s literary career.

Brodin, Pierre. Jean Giraudoux. *In his:* Les écrivains français de l'entre-deux-guerres. Montreal, Valiquette, 1945. p. 137–71. **11556**

Except for the date of G.'s death, the chronology which introduces this chapter has not been updated and it ends with a discussion of *Pleins pouvoirs.* The critic places G. in the tradition of La Fontaine, Marivaux, and Musset.

Brunet, Etienne. Programmes de statistique linguistique écrits en langage PL/I. CUMFID 1, 2, 3, 4, 6, 7, 8. Nice, 1970–73. **11557**

For scholars versed in the technology of computer programming this highly specialized revue prints the actual programs used to tabulate the data and make the calculations upon which statistical research is based. Etienne Brunet is an editor of this revue, and G. is the subject of most of his research. Seven out of eight of the early numbers are devoted to analyses of G. texts. Computer language used to produce these statistics is probably not compatible with computer systems used in the United States.

————. Le traitement des faits linguistiques et stylistiques sur ordinateur. Texte d'application: Giraudoux. *In:* Statistique et linguistique. Klincksieck, 1974. p. 105–37. (Actes et colloques, 15) **11558**

An extremely important article, not only because of the author's findings but for what it tells us about the state of computer studies in stylistics and the tools available for this type of research. The findings are based on a dictionary of G.'s vocabulary with word frequencies compiled from sixteen G. texts put in machine readable form for the Trésor de la langue française. This corpus was augmented by seven prose texts, four of which are only samplings from the longer novels. The chronological spread of these texts and the equal ratio of novels to plays make it possible to study G.'s stylistic evolution both chronologically and in relation to the different literary genres. The author summarizes the research previously published in the *Cahiers des utilisateurs de machines à des fins d'information et de documentation.* A less technical presentation of his findings was published in the *Cahiers Jean Giraudoux,* 2–3, 1973–74 under the title *Le vocabulaire d'Ondine.*

Cheval, René. Jean Giraudoux und Deutschland. NS 12:619–25, 1970. **11559**

Cheval points to G.'s cultural and literary ties to Germany, inspired by the teachings of Charles Andler and a prolonged stay in Munich (1905–06). The contrast between Germany and France, as shown in *Siegfried,* is well analyzed. So is G.'s serious pacifism and his quest for an objective evaluation of the two countries. [PM]

David, Aurel. Vie et mort de Jean Giraudoux. Le roman d'une idée. Flammarion, 1967. 252 p. **11560**

The subtitle is significant. The author of *Structure de la personne humaine* and *La cybernétique et l'humain*

applies his theories to an analysis of G.'s work by tracing the life and death of an idea which dominates his prose writings on the subconscious level until 1927. This study presupposes a knowledge of cybernetics as well as of G. Although some of the critic's premises and conclusions are highly debatable, this is a thought provoking work which stimulated a flood of reviews.

Reviews: C. Cluny in LetF Feb. 16–21, 1967; A. Maurois in NL April 8, 1967; A. Raymond in FR 41:898–900, 1968.

Debidour, V. H. Giraudoux. Eds. universitaires, 1955. 128 p. **11561**

A thematic treatment of G.'s work with emphasis on pessimism and escapism.

Druon, Maurice. Lettre à Jean Giraudoux sur l'immortalité. *In:* Le 41e fauteuil. Perrin, 1971. p. 239–47. **11562**

One of a collection of essays devoted to great writers who were not admitted to the French Academy. This is an exquisitely written tribute to Jean Giraudoux, a masterpiece of the genre.

Du Genêt, Gabriel. Jean Giraudoux ou un essai sur les rapports entre l'écrivain et son langage. Jean Vigneau, 1945. 75 p. **11563**

Accuses G. of having created a false world of essences and coincidences based on a poetry of childlike innocence. Not a stylistic study. Discusses G.'s use of irony. Too general and superficial to be of value.

Durry, Marie-Jeanne. L'univers de Giraudoux. Ar 2:108–22, 1944. *Also:* Mercure de France, 1961. 57 p. **11564**

The author expresses various reservations about G.'s art, his sincerity, and the durability of his works.

Reviews: R. Albérès in TR 161:135–37, 1961; G. Piroué in MerF 341:748–51, 1961.

Fink, Werner. Jean Giraudoux, Glück und Tragik. Basel, Helbing & Litchtenhahn, 1947. 127 p. **11565**

Happiness and tragedy are the axis of this rapid study of G.'s novels and theater.

Lamont, Rosette. Giraudoux's Hector: a hero's stand against heroism. *In:* The persistent voice. Ed. by Walter G. Langlois. New York univ. press, 1971. p. 145–56.   **11566**

A masterful refutation of Sartre's article reproaching G. for an obsolete Aristotelianism. Portrays G. as a writer as profoundly *engagé* as Sartre but haunted by a prophetic sense of destiny which overrides rationalism. Defines G.'s anti-hero as a man who refuses to give up the absurdity of his hope and the rationality of his respect for life.

Lemaître, Georges. Jean Giraudoux. The writer and his work. Frederick Ungar, 1971. 220 p. *Also in his:* Four French novelists: Marcel Proust, André Gide, Jean Giraudoux, Paul Morand. London and New York, Oxford univ. press, 1938. p. 209–300. *Also:* Port Washington, N. Y., Kennikat press, 1969.   **11567**

An expanded and updated version of the critic's 1938 essay written primarily for the layman, this book contains the frankest and most complete biography of G. yet published, although certain details of his personal life are open to question. The major additions to the original essay are two chapters dealing with G.'s prose fiction and his theater, both of which are analyzed title by title in chronological order. From the standpoint of the specialist, the critic leans too heavily on biographical data for his interpretations and makes little use of recent scholarship. His bibliography contains a list of English translations of G.'s works.

Reviews: T. Bishop in SatR 55:59, Feb. 5, 1972; M. Gallant in TBR Jan. 30, 1972.

LeSage, Laurence. Jean Giraudoux, surrealism, and the German romantic ideal. Urbana, Univ. of Illinois press, 1952. 80 p. (Illinois studies in language and literature 36, 3)   **11568**

This is still the only important published work relating G. to the surrealists and the German romantics. Seen in the light of his German predecessors, G.'s preciosity, his irony and his anti-realism take on a new significance. A concise and thoroughly documented study that is more illuminating and covers more ground than many a more voluminous work. The reader should be forewarned of one unfortunate error repeated on pp. 3, 5, and 13 where the

critic quotes from the "Soliloque sur la colonne de juillet" under the mistaken impression that it was authored by G. The "Soliloque" is correctly listed in the LeSage bibliography as being a pastiche by Yves Gandon. The chapter on surrealism is devoted to establishing its affinity with German romanticism and clearing up certain misunderstandings on the part of the surrealists about the German romantics.

Reviews: E. Lohner in CL 6:271–74, 1954; G. May in RR 46:156–57, 1955.

LeSage, Laurent. Jean Giraudoux. His life and works. State College, Pennsylvania State univ. press, 1959. 238 p.   **11569**

The most scholarly overall study to appear in English. The first three chapters deal with G.'s life and works in chronological order so that the reader has a thoroughly integrated picture of the man and the writer. Three more chapters are devoted to themes, philosophy, technique and style. The concluding chapter, G.'s work before the critics, shows the evolution of critical thought from Gide to Albérès. Except for quotations, which are in French, the clear incisive style of the critic makes this study accessible to the layman as well as to the specialist. No bibliography.

Reviews: W. Frohock in RR 51:73–74, 1960; J. Hardré in PBSA 54:75–76, 1960; D. Inskip in FS 15:188–90, 1961.

Lewis, Howard D. The dramatic theory of Jean Giraudoux: the primacy of style. NFS 12:63–73, 1973.   **11570**

The author demonstrates with copious documentation from G.'s pronouncements on the theater that this playwright rejects an intellectual approach to his audience and stresses the paramount role of style. For G. theater is synonymous with imagination and language.

Magny, Claude-Edmonde. Précieux Giraudoux. Seuil, 1945. 124 p. *Also:* 1965.   **11571**

An important essay which has influenced most critical thought on G. Analyzes G.'s stylistic peculiarities and probes the social and metaphysical reasons for its esthetic appeal. Compares G. to Heraclitus. Concludes that the use of precious rhetoric is justified by the fundamental ambiguity of the universe, which only the poet and the philosopher have the means to express adequately.

Marker, Chris. Giraudoux par lui-même. Seuil, 1952. 192 p. **11572**

Follows the usual format of the series. The commentary of the critic is illustrated by excerpts from the author's work, including some schoolboy verses, p. 63–64. Especially interesting for the iconography. Sympathetic treatment of G.'s life and work.

Martin du Gard, Maurice. Feux tournants: nouveaux portraits contemporains. Camille Bloch, 1925. p. 193–214. **11573**

Some early opinions about G. by a critic who always appreciated him for his true worth (reprints articles from NL Jan. 31, 1925 and Feb. 7, 1925).

————. Giraudoux l'enchanteur. *In his:* Les libéraux de Renan à Chardonne. Plon, 1967. p. 69–76. **11574**

Dated Mar. 8, 1944, this homage praises G.'s detachment from impure and vulgar things. Attributes to G. the grace of Marivaux and the spirit of revolt of Agrippa d'Aubigné.

May, Georges. Jean Giraudoux: academician and idiosyncracies. YFS 3:24–33, 1949. **11575**

G.'s literary criticism avoids academic banalities and focuses on those traits of the writer which make him a kindred spirit.

Messières, René de. Le rôle de l'ironie dans l'œuvre de Giraudoux. RR 373–83, 1938. **11576**

G. uses irony to impose a human order on nature and thus escapes from the temptation of the romantics to take his work too seriously. G. has the poetic vision of the *poètes voyants* but not their excesses. An early study often quoted.

Pizzorusso, Arnaldo. Tre studi su Giraudoux. Florence, Sansoni, 1954. 191 p. **11577**

Written for specialists and emphasizing in G.'s work the autogenesis of the word, this book gives a subtle analysis of G.'s rhetoric, thematic mode (the conflict between myth and hu-

manity) and multiple narrative techniques. Pizzorusso is familiar with both G.'s prose and theater and makes ample use of G. criticism. The first study (on rhetoric) is probably the most valuable, going beyond Gabriel du Genêt's study of 1945. In a brief appendix dealing with *Contes d'un matin,* Pizzorusso traces some of G.'s later writings.

Review: R. de Cesare in RHL 57: 103–04, 1957.

Rousseaux, André. Giraudoux ou l'éternel printemps. RHeb 156–73, July 14, 1934, and 325–54, July 21, 1934. *Also in his:* Ames et visages du XXe siècle, sér. 2: Le paradis perdu. Grasset, 1936. p. 109–56. *Also (rev.):* 1946. *Also in his:* Portraits littéraires choisis. Geneva, Skira, 1947. p. 79–129. **11578**

A much quoted article analyzing G.'s *préciosité* as an expression of his Edenic vision. 1946 ed. enlarged to include a previously published article, *Jean Giraudoux choisit des élues* (p. 161–68).

Roy, Claude. Jean Giraudoux. *In his:* Descriptions critiques. V. 1: Gallimard, 1949. p. 87–106. **11579**

Judgment of a communist critic whose remarks on the advantages and disadvantages of writing from the Marxist viewpoint are as interesting as what he has to say about G. Accuses G. of always having kept his distance from controversial issues by his refusal to take sides, to choose, to act. G.'s saving grace, according to this critic, is his solidarity with mankind.

Sertelon, Jean-Claude. Giraudoux et le moyen âge. Pensée universelle, 1974. 304 p. **11580**

This surprising subject is thoroughly prepared by an introduction enumerating the numerous allusions to the Middle Ages in G.'s writings and their sources in his Limousin heritage and his academic background. Sertelon traces G.'s insistence on the primacy of language back to the "art clos" of the troubadours. His preciosity, his use of symbols and allegory, his themes, especially his preoccupation with purity, are likewise reminiscent of the esthetic, moral and metaphysical norms of medieval literature. In his desire to transfigure human existence, G. is a direct descendant of medieval poets.

Thibaudet, Albert. Autour de Giraudoux. NRF 1064–76, Dec. 1, 1919. *And:* Le voyage intérieur. Sur Suzanne et le Pacifique. NRF 332–36, Sept. 1, 1921. *Also in his:* Réflexions sur le roman. Gallimard, 1938. p. 82–90; 149–52.
11581

This distinguished critic was one of the first to recognize G.'s literary genius, which he finds more akin to the manner of the Goncourts than to either the classic or romantic writers.

Thiébaut, Marcel. Jean Giraudoux. RdP 397–426, Nov. 15, 1934. *Also in his:* Evasions littéraires. Gallimard, 1935. p. 9–49.
11582

An important general study of G. as a novelist, playwright, and critic. Stresses the escape theme.

Trevisan, Anna. Littérature, mon beau souci. Note su Giraudoux critico letterario. ACF 7:170–83, 1968.
11583

G. is seen as a rhetorician more than *idéologue* whose singular concern with style colors his literary criticism. Carefully researched, with frequent quotes from G.'s essays, this article, which contains 95 footnotes in eleven pages, continues the exposure of G. as an "essentialist." [PM]

Special Numbers

Lets cahiers bourbonnais et du Centre. 2, 1972.
11584

Contains articles relating to the childhood and family life of G. The one based on memories of a relative of G.'s mother is continued in the third and fourth issues of the *Cahiers* for the year 1972.

Cahiers Jean Giraudoux, 1. Grasset, 1972. 99 p.
11585

This is the first publication of the Société des amis de Jean Giraudoux, founded in 1971. The contributions of note are largely of a biographical nature: an homage by G.'s son; an early *inédit* presented by Colette Weil; three essays on *Les enfances Giraudoux* by Françoise Guinle, who assembles the known facts about G.'s sojourn at Harvard in 1907 and again in 1917;

some brief notes from G. to his cousins, which are of considerably less interest than the introductory remarks by Jacques Body.

Cahiers Jean Giraudoux, 2 and 3. Grasset, 1973–74. 141 p.
11586

Except for two *inédits* and a short bibliography for 1972, this double issue is devoted to *Ondine* and contains just about everything one needs to know about the text and the performance of the play. Of particular note are Jacques Body's article, *Sources allemandes d'Ondine,* taken from his forthcoming book, *G. et l'Allemagne,* and an interesting example of computerized research by Etienne Brunet in his statistical study of *Le vocabulaire d'Ondine.*

Cahiers littéraires de l'O.R.T.F. 10, Feb.–March 1969. p. 2–10.
11587

Special issue containing brief articles by Jean-Louis Barrault, André Beucler, Eugène Ionesco, and Chris Marker, among others.

Connaître Giraudoux. CRB 36, Nov. 1961. 126 p.
11588

An important issue inspired by the Renaud-Barrault production of *Judith* in 1961. Contains extracts from previously published works by Robert Brasillach, Paul Claudel, Laurence LeSage, and Jean-Paul Sartre, as well as the reprint of a newspaper interview with G. in 1931 and quotes from a lecture he gave two weeks after the première of *Judith.* Also G.'s own list of 19 works inspired by the story of Judith and a manuscript copy of the author's summary of a primitive version of his play, both *inédits.* Some interesting background material on the apocryphal tale including a sample of Babylonian theater. An illustrated article by J.-L. Vaudoyer on images of Judith by great painters. An irrelevant *inédit* by Jean Cocteau and articles by Jacqueline Capek, Jean-Pierre Faye, Elisabeth de Fontenoy, Jean-Pierre Giraudoux, Maurice Mercier, Francis de Miomandre, and Claude Roy.

Giraudoux issue. TDR May 1959. 137 p. (Distributors: Hill and Wang, New York)
11589

Opens with a translation of Jean Anouilh's tribute to G., first published in the *Chronique de Paris,* Feb. 1944. Articles by Germaine Brée, Mary Douglas Dirks, Eugene Falk, Wallace Fowlie, John Gassner, and Oreste Pucciani. Also two one act plays: G.'s *Song of songs,* translated by John Raikes and the *Paris impromptu,* translated by Rima D. Reck.

Giraudoux parmi nous. HumC 3. Belles lettres, 1968. 131 p. (Publication périodique des Jeunes de l'Association G. Budé) **11590**

Special issue containing a brief introduction by Jacques Body followed by three *inédits* later collected in *Or dans'la nuit,* a volume of *inédits* which he published in 1969. Articles by Jacques Body, André Morize, Lise Gauvin, etc., listed separately in this bibliography. [PM]

La guerre de Troie n'aura pas lieu. AvSc 479, Sept. 15, 1971. 37 p. **11591**

Contains the complete text of the play with photos and critical appraisals of the Jouvet production of 1935, the T.N.P. production of 1963, and the recent one at the Théâtre de la Ville. Short statement by Jean Vilar.

Hommage à Giraudoux. Ed. by René Tavernier. Lyon, Confluences. Sept.-Oct. 1944. 131 p. **11592**

The most prestigious and informative volume of homages containing twenty articles on a variety of subjects. Of special interest are those by Louis Aragon (under the pseudonym Paul Wattelet), André Beucler, Jean Blanzat, Jean Cocteau, Jean Prévost, Claude Edmonde Magny, André Roussin, and Jean Thomas.

Hommage à Giraudoux. CahEq 5:8–33, Feb. 1945. **11593**

Eight short articles on style and themes.

Hommage à Giraudoux. Châteauroux, Langlois-Prévost, n.d. 96 p. **11594**

Published by the Lycée de Châteauroux to commemorate its change of name to the Lycée Jean Giraudoux. Contains a brief introduction by André Beucler followed by texts of speeches by five government functionaries. It includes five class exercises by Jean Giraudoux which were filed in the Cahier

d'honneur du lycée. Date of ceremony June 18, 1949.

Review: J. Guéhenno in FL Aug. 8, 1952.

Hommages à Jean Giraudoux. Comœdia Feb. 5, 1944. *Also in:* Voici 14–15, June 1944. **11595**

Contains short paragraphs by a galaxy of notables: Arland, Audiberti, Cocteau, Colette, Crommelynck, Bourdet, Fargue, Grenier, Halévy, Jouhandeau, Mondor, Sartre, and Vaudoyer.

Intermezzo. CRB 3:2–22, 1955. **11596**

Only the first twenty-two pages are devoted to the play. Essentially reprints of previously published articles by Edmond Jaloux, Edouard Bourdet, and René Lalou.

Jean Giraudoux. Cahiers Comœdia-Charpentier. Publications techniques et artistiques, 1944. 42 p. **11597**

Reminiscences and homages by Marcel Arland, Alexandre Arnoux, Lucien Bonzon, Edouard Bourdet, Paul Claudel, Pierre Lestringuez, Marcel Raval, and François de Roux. The articles by Bonzon, Claudel, and Lestringuez are of biographical interest.

Jean Giraudoux. EspCr 9:71–145, 1969. **11598**

Begins with a reprint of a brief homage by Jean-Paul Sartre and G.'s "Prière sur la Tour Eiffel," followed by an analysis of the text by Agnes G. Raymond. Articles by Neal Oxenhandler, Will L. McLendon, Lawrence Harvey, and Bryan G. Dobbs.

Jean Giraudoux et Pour Lucrèce. CRB 2: 1953. 128 p. **11599**

Issue inspired by production of this posthumous play made public for the first time. Fourteen articles, five of which are extracts from previously printed works. The only one having to do specifically with the play is "A la recherche de *Pour Lucrèce*" by J. L. Barrault.

Mémorial du centenaire du lycée Jean Giraudoux. Châteauroux, Association des anciens élèves du lycée, 1954. 287 p. **11600**

Reminiscences and photos of G.'s high school days related by classmates and former students of the lycée de Châteauroux renamed in 1949 for its distinguished alumnus.

Le monde des livres. Sept. 20, 1969. 11601
An important special issue of *Le Monde* to commemorate the twenty-fifth anniversary of G.'s death. Some articles listed separately.

Que reste-t-il de Giraudoux? MagL 33:8–23, Oct. 1969. 11602
Five, for the most part, unfriendly articles. A biographical sketch by Jean-Louis Bory, a disenchanted critic who calls G. the Joconde of the rue d'Ulm and the Quai d'Orsay; a review of *La menteuse* and *Or dans la nuit* comparing G.'s style to trapeze acts on a spider web; Gilles Sandier gives an unsympathetic review of G.'s theater; four pages of judgments by André Beucler, Edwige Feuillère, Madeleine Ozeray, Robert Sabatier, etc., in which G. is scrutinized both by birds of a feather and birds of prey.

Tombeau de Giraudoux. Ar 105–31, March 1944. 11603
Contains an homage by André Gide, Marie-Jeanne Durry's essay on *L'univers de Giraudoux,* a short article about a performance of *La guerre de Troie* at Prague by Jiri Mucha, and a judgment by Jean Amrouche concerning G.'s place in literary history.

Theater in General

Aylen, Leo. Cocteau, Gide, Giraudoux. *In his:* Greek tragedy and the modern world. London, Methuen, 1964. p. 258–77. 11604
According to this critic, these writers treat themes of Greek tragedy in the tradition of sophisticated boulevard comedy. The dialog resembles the conversation of diplomats. But in spite of the many changes in form, their plays illuminate our understanding of Greek tragedy and achieve an effect somewhat analogous.

Brasillach, Robert. Le théâtre de Jean Giraudoux. RU 313–35, 1933. *Also in his:* Portraits. Plon, 1935. p. 123–63. 11605
Written in 1932, this early essay still holds good today. Praises G.'s attempt to restore theater to its liturg-ical role, his gift for comedy, and the refusal of his heroes and heroines to be corrupted by superior forces. They always maintain their distance and their dignity in the face of an inexorable fate.

Cohen, Robert G. Giraudoux. Three faces of destiny. Chicago, Univ. of Chicago press, 1968. 164 p. 11606
An ambitious treatment of G.'s theater beginning with an attempt to outline the ideological substructure of his dramaturgy. The plays are classified as sexual, metaphysical, or political. The concluding chapter gives a valuable perspective on G.'s theater by evaluating it in relation to his immediate predecessors and successors.
Reviews: R. Goodhand in MLJ 53: 515–16, 1969; L. LeSage in MLQ 30: 463–65, 1969; A. Raymond in FR 43:335–37, 1969.

Florenne, Yves. Du côté du théâtre. La tragédie apprivoisée. Monde Sept. 4, 1969. 11607
Good but conventional appraisal of G.'s plays. Interesting reference to Paul Claudel and Aurel David's controversial interpretation of G.'s revolutionary vision. Includes an amusing drawing of G. as an antique but bespectacled Apollo.

Grossvogel, David I. Jean Giraudoux. *In his:* The self-conscious stage in modern French drama. Columbia univ. press, 1958. p. 68–105. 11608
Defends the dramatic quality of a literary theater created entirely by language.

Guerrero Zamora, Juan. Giraudoux cristalizado. *In his:* Historia del teatro contemporaneo. V. 3. Barcelona, Flors, 1962. p. 191–213. 11609
The themes of G.'s theater are all translated into love relationships, according to this critic, who therefore examines the theme of the couple. He sees G. obsessed by a nostalgia for purity and paradise lost. Judith, Lucile and Electre personify this *ensimismamiento.* However, the playwright's wit constitutes a blasphemy against the esthetics of true tragedy.

Guicharnaud, Jacques. Theatre as proposition: Jean Giraudoux. *In his:* Modern

French theatre from Giraudoux to Beckett. New Haven, Yale univ. press, 1961. p. 19-47. *New ed.:* Modern French theatre from Giraudoux to Genet. New Haven and London, Yale univ. press, 1967. p. 17-43. **11610**

Maintains that G.'s theater is not one of ideas. The debates in his plays are not discussions but an esthetic equilibrium between contrary definitions. G. had complete confidence in the human logic of language as a means of accounting for the universe.

Houlet, Jacques. Le théâtre de Jean Giraudoux. Pierre Ardent, 1945. 187 p. **11611**

A superficial study of themes and dramatic technique. Reads like a hasty attempt to capitalize on the interest in G.'s theater created by his recent death.

Inskip, Donald. Jean Giraudoux: the making of a dramatist. London, Oxford univ. press, 1958. 194 p. **11612**

Though not the most recent, this is by far the best work to date on G.'s theater. Not only does it give an in-depth analysis of all the plays, including the variants, but it treats in considerable detail G.'s relations with Louis Jouvet, who staged most of his plays. In fact, Inskip manages to take into account many of the significant factors which influenced the creation of each play as well as the reaction of the public and the critics. A straightforward presentation in a clear and easy style and an attractive format with nine illustrations make G.'s theater accessible to the general reader as well as to the specialist.

Reviews: P. Mankin in FR 33:90-91, 1959-60; F. Müller in Archiv 196: 237, 1959.

Kinsella, Thomas. Dressing Giraudoux for the market. KR 29:698-704, 1967. **11613**

While reviewing Roger Gellert's reasonably faithful, if occasionally awkward, translations of *Amphitryon 38, Intermezzo,* and *Ondine,* the critic makes some probing comparisons with the adaptations by S. N. Behrman and Maurice Valency. He concludes that the latter, for all their liberties and infidelities to the original, are preferable from the standpoint of producing them for American audiences.

Lumley, Frederick. A dramatist of optimism: Jean Giraudoux. *In his:* New trends in twentieth century drama. A survey since Ibsen and Shaw. London, Barrie & Rockliff, 1972. p. 36-59. (Previous eds. 1956, 1960, 1961, 1967) **11614**

Superficial observations on French theater, G.'s life, and on each of his plays. This chapter was written for the 1960 ed.

Mander, Gertrud. Jean Giraudoux. Velber, Friedrich Verlag, 1969. 158 p. **11615**

An excellent introduction for the general German public of G.'s dramatic work. All quotes are in German. Shows appreciation for G. as "hochgebildeter Humanist" and as a "poetic impressionist." No new critical insights but a lucid presentation of themes and a concise analysis of twelve plays. A brief final chapter of collected critical judgments is woefully incomplete, as *Judith* and *Pour Lucrèce* are ignored. [PM]

Mankin, Paul. Precious irony. The theatre of Jean Giraudoux. The Hague and Paris, Mouton, 1971. 195 p. (Studies in French literature, 19) **11616**

Surprisingly little has been written on G.'s use of irony since René de Messière's article in 1938. This book gives a key subject the ample treatment it deserves. By devoting a chapter to each of the major plays and by presenting the quotations first in French and then in his own English translation, Mankin has provided the reader with the necessary context for the fullest appreciation of G.'s humor as well as his own skillful interpretation of it. Especially well done are his chapters on *Amphitryon 38* and *La guerre de Troie n'aura pas lieu.* His chapter on *Judith* has some thought provoking remarks on accusations of anti-Semitism. A very readable and useful book as well as a scholarly one.

Mauron, Charles. Le théâtre de Giraudoux. Etude psychocritique. José Corti, 1971. 275 p. **11617**

This study was written in 1964 and published posthumously (Mauron died in 1966). It claims to be the first psychocritical analysis of G.'s theater. The method as defined by the author consists of superimposing texts of different periods to reveal a basic pattern of underlying structures. Mauron sees a personal conflict manifesting itself in the dominant themes of the break-up of the couple and the flight from anguish. Claims that G. failed to adapt his personal myth to reality. Denies the importance of political themes in G.'s work. Contributes nothing new to Giralducian scholarship.

May, Georges. Jean Giraudoux: diplomacy and dramaturgy. YFS 5:88–99, 1950.
11618

G.'s career as diplomat not only suggested some timely topics for his plays but the art of diplomacy and compromise proved useful in winning over or regaining a public alienated by what the critics maliciously labeled a literary play.

Mercier-Campiche, Marianne. Le théâtre de Giraudoux et la condition humaine. Domat, 1954. 303 p. *Also:* Del Duca, 1969. 269 p.
11619

A philosophical approach to Giralducian themes which brings G. in line with existential thought. Precise and chronological treatment of plays.
Reviews: L. LeSage in RR 46:76–77, 1955; N. Smith in Eras 23–24:734–36, 1956.

Moraud, Yves. Jean Giraudoux, auteur tragique: la dialectique du verbe et de l'action. RSH 34:283–303, 1969. **11620**

An eloquent and persuasive attempt to rehabilitate G. as a classical dramatist and to defend his concept of tragedy as a sort of rhetorical contest.

Ozeray, Madeleine. A toujours, Monsieur Jouvet. Buchet-Chastel, 1966. 256 p.
11621

G. also figures in this autobiography which centers around her career with Jouvet. The actress tells us why she did not get the role of Isabelle in *Intermezzo*, how G. came to write an adaptation of *The constant nymph,* how she inspired the role of Ondine and influenced the stage setting, and how she insisted on Jouvet for the role of Hector and Hans. See especially p. 33–38, 50–52, 82–88, 108–10, 114–20, 129–40, 198–99, 244.

Raymond, Agnes G. Giraudoux devant la victoire et la défaite. Nizet, 1963. 226 p. *Trans.:* Jean Giraudoux. The theater of

victory and defeat. Amherst, Univ. of Massachusetts press, 1966. 196 p. **11622**

This is the first serious attempt to study the work of G. in its historical context. Limited in scope, it analyzes the author's reaction to the victory of 1918 and the defeat of 1940 as reflected in the Siegfried cycle, *Sodome et Gomorrhe,* and *La folle de Chaillot,* using his political writings to illuminate his theater. A final chapter which exposes the hoax of *Les hommes-tigres* links the two periods and shows that the anti-capitalist bias of *La folle* goes back to World War I. The political approach explains the sources and the evolution of the Siegfried myth from the novel through the variants of the play. The interpretation of *Les hommes-tigres* aroused some controversy (cf. J. Body CALC 1:15–21, 1966). The English version of the book is slightly altered for the benefit of the Anglo-Saxon reader and all quotations are translated into English.
Reviews: Anon. in Choice 3:906, 1966; G. Barberet in RR 56:76–77, 1965; B. Knapp in RR 59:317–18, 1968; L. LeSage in FR 38:124–25, 1964–65; P. Mankin in BA 41:225, 1967; L. Rosenfield in CLS 4:336–38, 1967.

Ready, Wayne. Giraudoux aux Etats-Unis. HumC 3:117–26, 1968. **11623**

An account of G. productions in the United States including a review of *Judith* in the APA production of 1965, which points out the ambiguities of the play. [PM]

Sørensen, Hans. Le théâtre de Jean Giraudoux: technique et style. Aarhus, Universitetsforlaget; Copenhagen, Ejnar Munksgaard, 1950. 276 p. (Acta Jutlandica, Aarskrift for Aarhus universitet, XXII supplementum, Humanistisk serie 35) **11624**

A play by play analysis using the variants. Has a strict academic knowledge of the technique of the theater and seems to think that G.'s revisions were chiefly for stylistic purposes. Gives an interesting interpretation of *La guerre de Troie n'aura pas lieu* showing its relevance to events of 1935.
Reviews: A. Boase in FS 6:270–71, 1952; L. LeSage in RR 43:67–69, 1952.

Amphitryon 38

Cellier, Léon. Structure d'Amphitryon 38. *In his:* Etudes de structure. Minard, 1964. p. 21–30. (ALM 56) **11625**

Like Racine's *Phèdre*, G.'s play falls into two parts at the exact center in the middle of Act II, Scene III when Mercure announces Jupiter's intention to visit Alcmène. What precedes is fairly traditional; what follows is pure Giraudoux.

Eustis, Morton. Jean Giraudoux, playwright, novelist, and diplomat. ThA 22: 127–33, 1938. **11626**

An account of G.'s reaction to the New York première of *Amphitryon 38* which he attended at the Shubert Theater during an unheralded trip to the U.S.A. in 1937.

Jasinski, René. Deux Alcmènes: de Molière à Giraudoux. *In:* De Jean Lemaire de Belges à Jean Giraudoux. Nizet, 1970. p. 413–29. **11627**

Jasinski perceives all the nuances in these two versions of the Amphitryon legend. He successfully lays to rest the popular verdict that Molière's *Amphitryon* was nothing more than a court ballet and that the G. version is only a frothy comedy. After reading this article it is difficult to say who displayed the greater psychological acumen, the critic or the two authors.

Lemarchand, Jacques. Deux Amphitryon (Kleist et Giraudoux) par le Schiller Theater et le Schlosspark Theater de Berlin. FL June 18, 1963. **11628**

Plautus emphasized the farcical in his treatment of the myth. Molière did an elegant drawing room comedy. Kleist accentuated the purity of Alcmène. In contrast G.'s play seems polite and artificially brilliant. The German production accents the Parisian style and cheapens the play.

Lindberger, Orjan. Amphityron 38. *In his:* The transformations of Amphitryon. Stockholm, Almqvist & Wiksell, 1956. p. 167–202. (Acta Universitatis Stockholmiensis) **11629**

Chapter 9, devoted to G., is probably the most exhaustive study that has ever been made of the dramatic representations of the Amphitryon theme from Plautus to Kaiser in 1944. Shows that G. was a scholarly poet and had actually studied the history of the Amphitryon motif before writing his own version. This scholarly critic also shows that G. redid the course of action more than anyone else between him and Plautus. Defends G.'s preciosity as the literary counterpart of diplomacy and equally necessary for dealing with complex and ambiguous situations in the theater as in foreign affairs. A valuable study unfortunately not readily available in our libraries.

Ryan, Lawrence. Amphitryon, doch ein Lustspielstoff! *In:* Kleist und Frankreich. Ed. by Walter Müller-Seidel. Berlin, Erich Schmitt, 1969. p. 83–121. **11630**

Ryan takes issue with Wittkowski's article and insists on the comedic aspects of *Amphitryon 38*. [PM]

Six, André. Explication française. Giraudoux: Amphitryon 38 (Acte II, Scène 2). IL 21:47–50, Jan.–Feb. 1969. **11631**

This is the famous debate between Alcmène and Jupiter on immortality vs. the human condition, which is better explicated by René Jasinski (*see* 11627).

Wittkowski, W. Der neue Prometheus. Kleist's Amphitryon zwischen Molière und Giraudoux. *In:* Kleist und Frankreich. Ed. by Walter Müller-Seidel. Berlin, Erich Schmitt, 1969. p. 33–82. **11632**

The Kleist memorial year 1961 brought forth articles about G.'s debt in *Amphitryon 38*. The author shows G.'s Alcmène to be a revolutionary figure protesting religious authoritarianism. A carefully researched paper that traces the Amphitryon myth in Molière, Kleist and G. [PM]

Electre

Albert, Walter. Structures of revolt in Giraudoux's Electre and Anouilh's Antigone. TSLL 12:137–50, 1970. **11633**

Defends G. against the accusation that his intellectual and moral powers were inferior to his artistic gift by showing the revolutionary morality of his *Electre* as compared with the polite fatalism of Anouilh's *Antigone*.

Auber, Michael. A propos d'Electre. NRF 88:754–59, 1960. **11634**

Cites a number of cuts in the production by the Comédie française and indicates how this surprising censorship, which he attributes to the actors, rendered the text almost unrecognizable.

Brunel, Pierre. Analyse d'Electre. In his: Le mythe d'Electre. Colin, 1971. p. 228–32. (Collection U2) **11635**

A scene by scene résumé of G.'s play, of interest because of its context. The book contains twenty-one plays on the Electra theme, including one each by G. and his son. The section devoted to great moments of the Electra story as depicted by different writers provides additional material for comparison.

Burdick, D. M. Concept of character in Giraudoux's Electre and Sartre's Les mouches. FR 33:131–36, 1959. **11636**

Critique of the psychological and philosophical base of these two versions of the Electra theme. The critique is couched in Sartrian terminology.

Electre 1937 et 1939. FL Oct. 31, 1959 and Nov. 7, 1959. **11637**

The production of Electre by Pierre Dux at the Comédie française marks the first real entrance of G. into the national repertory. The only other play produced there was his Cantique des cantiques in 1938. The October article compares the Jouvet and Dux productions with photos of Act II, Scene I.

Gauvin, Lise. Giraudoux et le thème d'Electre. Minard, 1969. 40 p. (ALM 108) **11638**

Shows that G.'s treatment of the legend is faithful in spirit if not in detail to his Greek models. Summarily dismisses G.'s remark that Electre is a "tragédie bourgeoise." Does not deal with the anachronistic elements of the play. No mention of political overtones.

Herrmann, M. Se déclarer. Zur Bedeutung eines Schlüsselwortes in Giraudouxs Electre und Racines Bajazet. NS 277–82, June 1969. **11639**

An involved speculation on the interpretation of this verb with specific references to Racine's play. Electre's act of "declaring herself" is in direct contradiction to her potential marriage while Bajazet, Roxane and Atalide declare themselves with love and marriage

in mind. Obviously Racine is more traditional. [PM]

La folle de Chaillot

Clurman, Harold. Lies like truth. Theatre reviews and essays. Macmillan, 1958. p. 213–18. **11640**

Reviews of Broadway production of The madwoman of Chaillot and The enchanted. Shows a thorough-going appreciation of G.'s timeliness and laments the uninspired, semi-literate direction of these two plays.

La folle de Chaillot à travers le monde. Centre Culturel Jean Giraudoux, Bellac, 1971. 21 p. mimeo. **11641**

Catalog of an exhibition. Especially valuable for its list of revivals of the play in France and productions abroad.

Jouvet, Louis. A propos de la mise en scène de la Folle de Chaillot. De Molière à Giraudoux. In his: Témoignages sur le théâtre. Flammarion, 1962. p. 148–56, 185–213. **11642**

In the first essay Jouvet maintains that great theater does not need a stage set or lighting effects. The second essay contains a commentary on two variants of a scene from La folle de Chaillot, which he quotes.

LeSage, Laurent. Giraudoux and big business: an element of reminiscence in La folle de Chaillot. FR 31:278–82, 1958. **11643**

Suggests the influence of Jean de Pierrefeu on G. Bases his assumption on an amusing account of G.'s affairomanie in Pierrefeu's book Comment j'ai fait fortune.

Lestringuez, Pierre. Quand Jouvet répète La folle de Chaillot. XXs Dec. 13, 1945. **11644**

Relates some prophetic remarks by G. about this play one month before his death.

Maulnier, Thierry. La folle de Chaillot. Essor Jan. 5, 1946. **11645**

Not as great a play as Judith, Electre or Ondine. This is nothing more than a divertissement, which must be very irritating and disappointing to the militant revolutionaries, who were expecting a more serious indictment of those responsible for the defeat of 1940.

Reboussin, Marcel. Giraudoux and the Madwoman of Chaillot. ETJ 13:11–17, 1961.
11646
Text of a lecture given to introduce a production of the play in the U.S.A. Points out sources of the play in *Pleins pouvoirs* and identifies some of the allusions to places and people.

Retablo, El Trujamán del. De la segunda salida de nuestra ingeniosa loca Madame Aurélie de Chaillot. EstLit 337:14–15, Feb. 12, 1966.
11647
Review of TNP performance of *La folle de Chaillot* with a detailed description of the staging and a sketch of the quarter, which in its present polluted state belies the happy ending of the play.

La Guerre de Troie

Beck, William. Some French plays in translation. HudR 9:280–83, 1956. **11648**
On Christopher Fry's translation of *La guerre de Troie*, which he finds far superior to Maurice Valency's adaptations. Praises direction of Harold Clurman. Shows a genuine understanding and appreciation of G.'s style and dramatic technique.

Bentley, Eric. A great bronze gong. *In his:* What is theatre? Essays 1944–1967. London, Methuen, 1969. p. 73–77. **11649**
Thinks G. is decadent and his *préciosité* insufferable. Nonetheless he was captivated by Clurman's production of *Tiger at the gates.* Praises the way in which this director adds action to the stream of rhetoric. Is surprised by the relevance of this twenty year old play which he considers the best anti-war theater since Brecht's *Mother Courage.*

Body, Jacques. Sur des sources grecques et françaises de la Guerre de Troie n'aura pas lieu. HumC 3:104–09, 1968. **11650**
Shows that G.'s early concern for man's struggle against destiny goes back to 1911. Mentions the names of two acquaintances who might have influenced him, Louis Séchan, a fellow Normalien, and Henri Chabrol, a personal friend and Hellenist, author of *L'ambassade amoureuse* (1936), a play

about Menelaus that has many points in common with *La guerre de Troie.*

Broadway's big beginning. Life 39, no. 16: 161–68, 1955. **11651**
Of interest for pictorial material on Audrey Hepburn in *Tiger at the gates.*

Frois, Etienne. La guerre de Troie. Profil d'une œuvre. Hatier, 1971. 80 p. **11652**
An analysis of G.'s play, probably prepared for use in the lycées when this play was on the program of the *baccalauréat.* Contains information about acting and staging as well as content and stylistic analysis.

Newman-Gordon, Pauline. Claudel et Giraudoux. *In her:* Hélène de Sparte. La fortune du mythe en France. Debresse, 1968. p. 149–58. **11653**
An interpretation of *La guerre de Troie n'aura pas lieu* which achieves an excellent balance between the poetic and satirical aspects of the play. The critic treats other uses of the myth such as *La belle Hélène,* which is often mentioned in connection with G.'s play.

Intermezzo

Blinoff, Marthe. Remarques sur le comique de Giraudoux. FR 32:337–40, 1959.
11654
A limited treatment of a key subject that is much neglected. Analyzes the comic elements in the first act of *Intermezzo.*

François, Carlo. Le thème de la sorcière dans Intermezzo. FR 33:462–68, 1960.
11655
The critic sees an analogy between Michelet's popular work, *La sorcière,* and the character of Isabelle in G.'s play, *Intermezzo.*

Giraudoux, Jean. Intermezzo. Introduction and notes by Ethel E. Tory. London, Harrap, 1970. 129 p. **11656**
Presentation of original Grasset edition has been rationalized and corrected. Considerable geographical information relative to the setting of the play. No analysis of structure or style.
Review: E. Ratcliff in FS 27:98–99, 1973.

Lalou, René. Quand le rideau se leva. NL March 4, 1933. *Also:* CRB 10:20–21, 1955. **11657**

Sees an analogy between G.'s *Intermezzo* and *A midsummer night's dream* with Isabelle as Titania and the Inspecteur as Bottom.

Schneider, Marcel. Fantastique poétique: Jean Giraudoux. *In his:* La littérature fantastique en France. Arthème Fayard, 1964. p. 374–75. **11658**

Intermezzo is his favorite work by G. because of the childish myth of Arthur and the Ensemblier. The latter is a personification of the Leibnizian idea that all is for the best in the best of all possible worlds. Arthur is a more personal devil, who creates minor annoyances.

Judith

Brustein, Robert. Bagatelles. Judith by Jean Giraudoux. APA repertory company. *In his:* The third theatre. Knopf, 1969. p. 157–59. **11659**

Not only was the critic unimpressed by this performance but G. at best strikes him as an extremely fragile fantasist, as artificial as costume jewelry and not the least bit interested in the subjects he debates so endlessly. This article is itself a bagatelle, but it suffices to convey Brustein's thoughts on G.'s theater.

Clurman, Harold. A director prepares. ThA 47:16–19, 75–76, April 1963. **11660**

The director of the American production of *Tiger at the gates* and *Judith* publishes his notes on how he conceived the performance before it went into rehearsal, his aim being to make G.'s theater acceptable to English speaking audiences without diluting it by adaptation. Devoted primarily to *Judith,* these pages give an interesting insight into the mind of an exceptionally perceptive director.

Leefmans, Bert. Giraudoux's other muse. KR 16:613–26, 1954. **11661**

The critic examines the nature of tragedy in *Judith* in order to determine why this is the only one of G.'s plays that he labeled a tragedy. The metaphysical interpretation which he offers is less illuminating than a single fact

he failed to note, namely that this is the only full length play that closed after sixty-one performances. In terms of critical and popular success *Judith* was indeed G.'s only tragedy.

Moraud, Yves. Judith ou l'impossible liberté. Minard, 1971. 64 p. (ALM 108) **11662**

An in-depth analysis of G.'s *Judith* which illuminates every facet of the play by situating it in reference to tradition and the present. The sort of study that needs to be done for each individual work before a definitive *étude d'ensemble* can be made.

Roy, Claude. Giraudoux et Dieu. CRB 36: 27-36, 1961. **11663**

Describes Claudel's wrath on reading a review of G.'s blasphemous play, *Judith.* This article gives the background for Claudel's poem, "Judith," reprinted in the same issue (p. 75–84).

Ondine

Another triumph for Audrey. Life 26, no. 10:60–64, 1954. **11664**

Of interest for pictorial material on Audrey Hepburn in the role of Ondine.

Brosse, Monique. Personnages et situations mythiques dans Ondine. RLMC 22:181–203, 1969. **11665**

Profound and sensitive parallel study of G.'s play and the tale by La Motte-Fouqué.

Clavin, Judith S. The GBSsence of Jean Giraudoux. ShawR 5:21–35, 1962. **11666**

Sees an analogy between *Saint Joan* and *Ondine,* two ideal women; between Father Keegan and Countess Aurelia, the hyper-sane lunatics. *Judith* and *The enchanted* have traces of the Life Force. The two playwrights looked upon theater as a purveyor of universal truths and a vehicle for educating the public. No proof of influence.

Gerstenlauer, Wolfgang. Undines Wiederkehr: Fouqué — Giraudoux — Ingeborg Bachmann. NS 514–27, Oct. 1970. **11667**

Inspired by a master's thesis he wrote on Fouqué, G. transformed the German novella into a symbolic and surrealistic play *Ondine,* eliminating the problem of the nymph's soul and focusing on the conflict with her human partner. Gerstenlauer praises G.'s originality and contrasts his version to Ingeborg Bachmann's *Undine geht.* [PM]

Ozeray, Madeleine. Les poireaux de Mortefontaine. LetF May 22-28, 1958. *Also in her:* Le rêve et la vie de Gérard de Nerval. Published jointly with René Lacôte. Pierre Seghers, 1958. p. 7-15. **11668**
A fascinating and authoritative account of the genesis of *Ondine.*

Siegfried

Albérès, René Marill. La genèse du Siegfried de Giraudoux. Bibliothèque des lettres modernes, 1963. 156 p. **11669**
An abridged ed. of a 2 v. complementary thesis. Albérès calls this the story of a sly, ironic and disciplined submission to the laws of successful playwriting in the interest of which G. sacrificed his poetic and cosmic inspiration. Emphasis is on dramatic technique with almost no reference to historical reality, which would have provided a much better explanation of many of the variants.
Reviews: R. Pouilliart in LR 20: 372-73, 1966; A. Virmaux in RHL 66: 747-48, 1966.

Crémieux, Benjamin. Jean Giraudoux et le théâtre. NL April 28, 1928. **11670**
This article by one of G.'s most understanding critics, who encouraged him to write for the theater and reviewed all his plays, contains some interesting information about the production of *Siegfried* and some prophetic insights into G.'s career as a dramatist.

Inskip, Donald. Jean Giraudoux and Le mérite des femmes. MLQ 18:211-14, 1957. **11671**
Tracks down an allusion in *Siegfried* to the work of an obscure 18th-century writer and shows the significance of G.'s ironic choice. A fascinating detail.

————. The stylist in the theatre. Some remarks on a passage of Jean Giraudoux's Siegfried. MLR 53:218-21, 1958. **11672**
A study of four different versions of a passage from *Siegfried et le Limousin* shows that, in adapting the novel for the theater, G. was ever conscious of the cadences of the spoken work and the speech rhythms of the actor.

————. Some notes on the first production of Jean Giradoux's Siegfried. FS 12:143-46, 1958. **11673**
Compares the printed text of *Siegfried* as it appeared in the *Petite illustration* with the text used for production on file in the library of the Société des Régisseurs de théâtre in Paris. Changes bear the stamp of theatricality and Jouvet's suggestions.

Muller, Henry. Reprise de Siegfried. RevHM 77:584-85, 1952. **11674**
Recollections of the first performance of *Siegfried* and G.'s reaction.

Richard, Lionel. Giraudoux entre deux nationalismes. Quelques aspects de la réception critique de Siegfried. Mos 5:103-08, 1972. **11675**
Stresses the political bias of the reviewers, who accused G. of being anti-French or anti-German and who generally avoided an analysis of the dramatic structure of the play. Neither Richard nor the early critics recognized the three faces of Germany incarnated by Siegfried, Eva, and Zelten, who represent the forces seeking to control the future of that country and of Europe.

Other Plays

Caminade, Pierre. Sub specie rosae. HumC 3:127-31, 1968. **11676**
Speculative remarks about G.'s feminism as seen in *Sodome et Gomorrhe.* [PM]

Capek, Jacqueline. Un inconnu: Jean Giraudoux. CRB 36:57-65, Nov. 1961. **11677**
An account of Gilbert Pineau's televised version of G.'s *Cantiques des cantiques,* broadcast August 1, 1961 on French television.

Fenzl, Richard. Giraudoux, la critique qui entre, la critique qui sort. Aus L'impromptu de Paris, scène 3. PNU 16:146-52, 1969. **11678**
Fenzl cogently discusses an excerpt from this G. playlet, not performed since 1938, indicating that Jouvet, attacking theatre critics, is G.'s spokes-

man. The brief passage is analyzed structurally, showing G.'s highly developed style, here an antithetical parallelism, probably based on scene 1 of Molière's *Impromptu de Versailles*. Fenzl concludes that *L'impromptu de Paris* is dramatically weak, quoting F. W. Müller (NS 1957, p. 71). [PM]

Lalou, René. Vérité et poésie. Gav May 1, 1947.   **11679**

A review of *L'Apollon de Bellac*. This excellent critic sees the poetic genius of *Intermezzo* in G.'s last one act play.

Parturier, Françoise. Jouvet nous parle de L'Apollon de Marsac. Ep April 16, 1947.   **11680**

An interview with Jouvet relative to the South American production of *L'Apollon de Bellac*.

Yon, André. Giraudoux's use of four verses from Vigny's La colère de Samson. MLN 76:757–59, 1961.   **11681**

This brief note on a flagrant case of literary borrowing which the critic uncovered in the *Supplément au voyage de Cook* provides a fascinating insight into G.'s method of composition and into his use of language.

Prose Fiction

Berthier, Philippe. Suzanne et le Pacifique ou l'anti-Robinson Crusoé. RSH 35:127–39, 1970.   **11682**

Points out the satire implicit in G.'s Edenistic account of life on a desert isle as opposed to Defoe's prosaic description of survival tactics.

Blanc, Henri. D'un récit en espalier. RSH 143:437–57, 1971.   **11683**

The configuration of *Elpénor* suggests an analogy with a tree growing against a wall, the wall being Homer's *Odyssey*. The critic gives the most detailed analysis of G.'s travesty of an unheroic episode and offers an hypothesis to explain the motivation behind this particular parody.

Gaby, Mathieu. Du côté du roman: un pays hors du temps. Monde Sept. 20, 1969.   **11684**

Keen investigation of G.'s fiction based on sensations and impressions.

Believes G.'s novels are not outdated but foretell the *nouveau roman*.

Gide, André. Provinciales. NRF 463–66, June 1, 1909. *Also in his:* Nouveaux prétextes. Mercure de France, 1911. p. 300–04.   **11685**

Of interest because it is the most favorable of the four reviews of G.'s first publication under his own name. Gide's seal of approval gave G. an immediate entry to the elite circles of French publishing. Gide is more generous in his praise of the young author than he is in his homage ("Tombeau de G.," *Arche*, March 1944). G.'s chief merit according to Gide is having pulled French literature out of the rut of naturalism. But while he appreciated G.'s style, he was annoyed by what seemed to him to be an irrational treatment of such serious themes as war and peace.

Goodhand, Robert. Langage inarticulé de l'amour dans l'œuvre romanesque de Jean Giraudoux. RomN 5:106–09, 1964.   **11686**

Lovers in G.'s novels assume an indirect language of tenderness. Documents his hypothesis more by interpretation than by concrete examples.

———. Psychological development in Jean Giraudoux's Eglantine. FR 38:173–79, 1964.   **11687**

Attempts to refute the generally held critical opinion that G. shows no capacity for depicting psychological development in his fictional characters. Shows convincingly that *Eglantine* is an exception. More importantly, he notes a new technique in character analysis which occurs in other G. novels, namely the materialization of the subconscious impulses of his characters as they move through the stages of a malaise.

Knapp, Luther. Le mythe de la province, première forme de messianisme dans l'œuvre de Giraudoux. HumC 3:23–38, 1968.   **11688**

An analysis of early idealism as seen in G.'s novels, especially *Juliette au pays des hommes* and *Simon le pathétique*. [PM]

Lerch, Emile. Giraudouxs posthumer Roman La menteuse. SchR 69:326–33, 1970.   **11689**

La menteuse is characterized as typical with special emphasis on G.'s art with words and rhetoric. The novel itself, written in 1936 and discovered in 1968, deals with a Proustian heroine, Nelly, whose meanderings between fantasy and reality defy a plot analysis but are a delight to the G. specialist. Lerch fits into that category. [PM]

LeSage, Laurent. Forgotten stories of Jean Giraudoux. FR 24:97–104, 1950. **11690**
Preview of the volume of short stories, which G. published in various newspapers between 1906 and 1911, usually under a pseudonym, collected and presented by LeSage under the title *Contes d'un matin* (Gallimard, 1952).

Magny, Claude-Edmonde. Le Nijinsky du roman, Jean Giraudoux. *In her:* Histoire du roman français depuis 1918. Seuil, 1950. p. 146–68. **11691**
A chapter full of paradoxical views and unresolved contradictions. At one point G. is presented as the greatest of realist writers. On the other hand, his novels reveal a rampant romanticism like that of Gérard de Nerval, but eminently humanistic. All in all the critic finds G.'s novels annoying, disappointing, monotonous, and generally unsatisfying as compared with Stendhal, Balzac or Proust.

McLendon, Will L. A compositional aspect of Giraudoux's novels: the offshoot chapter. OrL 23:233–46, 1968. **11692**
Treats G.'s predilection for gratuitous variations on a theme, using as illustration the numerous fragments in which the heroine of his novel *Bella* figures. These are strong evidence that G. was concerned with composition and structure in his novels. The offshoots also indicate G.'s experimental method before giving final form to the novel. This same compositional habit was carried over to the theater.

———. Giraudoux and the split personality. PMLA 73:573–84, 1958. **11693**
In his study of the "episodism" of G.'s fictional characters and the recurrence of doubles, the critic attempts to penetrate the author's sentimental façade. McLendon combs the major part of G.'s work in his search for autobiographical detail to compose a discreet and convincing portrait of the man.

———. Un mutilé de Giraudoux. Simon le pathétique. FR 31:91–108, 1957. **11694**
Shows how G. reordered the chapters of this novel in the 1926 ed. and suppressed certain key passages, which the critic reprints from the ms. This wilful deformation of his fictional characters is a striking accompaniment to his style and demonstrates his tenet that "le roman est la déformation de la vérité en une affabulation de longue ambition."

Meylan, Jean-Pierre. Jean Giraudoux. *In his:* La Revue de Genève, miroir des lettres européennes, 1920–1930. Geneva, Droz, 1969. p. 236–43. **11695**
Analysis of "Hélène et Touglas ou les joies de Paris," a fragment of his novel *Bella* which G. contributed to RdG in April 1925. The critic situates the novel as well as the fragment in the context of G.'s political and literary life.

Piatier, Jacqueline. Entre Bella et Ondine: La menteuse. Monde Sept. 20, 1969. **11696**
Important comprehensive article on this posthumous novel.

Pierrefeu, Jean de. Les beaux livres de notre temps. Plon, 1938. p. 31–55. **11697**
Contains two remarkable reviews, one of *L'école des indifférents*, first published in *Opinion*, April 1911, and "Jean Giraudoux magicien," an article relative to *Elpénor*, first published in the *Journal des débats*, Oct. 26, 1919. Defends G. against the uncomprehending critics of this early period with a perceptiveness which must have come from an intimate acquaintance with the author and his literary aims. Pierrefeu and G. both wrote short stories for *Le matin* from 1908–1910.

Publication de deux romans inédits, réédition de l'œuvre théâtrale, Roy Prior, un Canadien, lance l'opération Giraudoux. FL Sept. 1–7, 1969. **11698**
Detailed account of how Roy Prior discovered and prepared for publication the second half of *La menteuse*.

Raymond, Agnes G. Première ébauche d'un profil stylistique de Jean Giraudoux. Lang&S 6:39–47, 1973.   **11699**

This is an experiment in lexical statistics based on an analysis of G.'s "Prière sur la Tour Eiffel." Statistics bear out the fact that G., like his model Renan ("Prière sur l'Acropole"), used abnormally few adjectives as compared with Corneille and Racine.

Sartre, Jean-Paul. M. Jean Giraudoux et la philosophie d'Aristote. A propos de Choix des élues. NRF 54:339–54, 1940. *Also in his:* Situations I. Gallimard, 1947. p. 82–98. *Trans.:* Jean Giraudoux and the philosophy of Aristotle. *In his:* Literary and philosophical essays. London, Hutchinson, 1955, 1968. p. 42–55.   **11700**

Probably the most quoted essay on any of G.'s writings, it is primarily a book review of G.'s last novel, *Choix des élues* (1939). Sartre brands it as the revelation of a schizophrenic mentality, which on the philosophical plane is akin to an Aristotelian view of the universe with its fixed concepts and archetypes. Sartre expresses puzzlement at this fictional representation of an outmoded philosophy.

Stuart, Eleanor. More about Simon le pathétique. FR 31:554–57, 1958.   **11701**

Letter to the editor refuting McLendon's article (*see* 11694). Does not think G. ever showed much interest in motivating his characters and reasons for his changes and deletions are not always clear. An interesting debate.

Thibaudet, Albert. Réflexions sur le roman. Gallimard, 1938. p. 82–90; 149–52.
11702

Contains reprints of two early articles, "Autour de Giraudoux" (1919) and "Le voyage intérieur. Sur Suzanne et le Pacifique" (1921). Thibaudet was one of the first to recognize G.'s literary genius, which he finds more akin to the manner of the Goncourts than to either the classical or romantic writers.

Style and Themes

Baldensperger, Fernand. L'esthétique fondamentale de Jean Giraudoux. FR 18:2–10, 1944.   **11703**

A probing article on the affinity between Giraudoux and the German romantics, especially as regards heroines and their relationship to nature.

Brunet, Etienne. Le traitement des faits linguistiques et stylistiques sur ordinateur. Texte d'application: Giraudoux. *In:* Statistique et linguistique. Actes et Colloques, Klincksieck, n.d. 15:105–37.   **11704**

Extremely important article on state of computer studies in stylistics and the tools available for this type of research. The findings are based on sixteen G. texts put in machine readable form for the Trésor de la langue française and on a dictionary of G.'s vocabulary with word frequencies compiled from these materials. This corpus was augmented by seven prose texts, four of which are samplings of the longer novels. The chronological spread of these texts and the equal ratio of novel to theater make it possible to study G.'s stylistic evolution in relation to the literary genre. This is only one of a number of statistical studies which Brunet has devoted to G. Most of them have appeared in publications not readily available in this country such as *Cahiers des utilisateurs de machines à des fins d'information et de documentation* (published by U.E.R., Lettres et sciences humaines, Nice).

Celler, Morton M. Giraudoux et la métaphore. Une étude des images dans les romans. The Hague, Mouton, 1974. 150 p.   **11705**

The G. metaphor is an inexhaustible subject, but this study adds little to LeSage (*see* 11711) although it is twice as long and uses some statistical documentation, which is unexplained and unacceptable by today's sophisticated standards. Celler still thinks G. wrote the "Soliloque sur la Colonne de juillet," which he quotes p. 40, 42, and 143.

Review: L. LeSage in FR 48:790–91, 1975.

Gandon, Yves. Jean Giraudoux ou plaisirs et jeux du style. *In his:* Le démon du style. Plon, 1938. p. 136–46. *Also:* 1960. p. 145–55.   **11706**

Stresses the gratuitous features of G.'s style, which characterize the writer who tries to recreate the world in his own image.

————. Soliloque de Jean Giraudoux sur la Colonne de juillet. NL Aug. 27, 1929. *Also in his:* Mascarades littéraires. M. P. Trémois, 1930. p. 21–32. **11707**

A very clever pastiche of G.'s literary mannerisms inspired by his "Prière sur la Tour Eiffel."

Ganz, Arthur. Human and suprahuman ambiguity in the `tragic world of Jean Giraudoux. PMLA 87:284–94, 1972. **11708**

The author discerns in G.'s tragedies a paradoxical pattern: an image of destruction through a quest for the ideal. In trying to make these plays conform to his pattern, the author raises more questions than he answers.

Gauvin, Lise. Giraudoux et le Canada. HumC 3:110–13, 1968. **11709**

G. had been to Canada in January 1908 and was fascinated by "un ensemble de détails pittoresques et un symbole poétique d'une grande richesse." There are several references to Canada in *Siegfried* and *Les aventures de Jérôme Bardini*, all imbued with a sense of poetry and peace. [PM]

Hansen, Anne Chaplain. Les deux univers de Jean Giraudoux. OrL 6:1–51, 1948. **11710**

A stylistic study which hypothesizes that G. tried to resolve the basic dualism of the abstract and the concrete through the power of language. Detailed discussion of the different figures of speech and a vocabulary of contrastive pairs, which characterize G.'s style.

LeSage, Laurence. Metaphor in the nondramatic works of Jean Giraudoux. Eugene, Univ. of Oregon press, 1952. 75 p. **11711**

While this monograph does not include the theater, it is still the most exhaustive study on a key aspect of G.'s style. It is also important since it treats the still neglected part of G.'s work, his novels. By situating G. between the symbolists and the surrealists, LeSage illuminates some of the metaphysical implications of the metaphor; and by pointing out certain well-defined patterns in G.'s metaphors, he gives the reader an insight into the author's method. This study provides a much needed literary perspec-

tive on G.'s esthetics. Same *caveat* on the "Soliloque sur la colonne de juillet," quoted on p. 13 and 17 (*see* 11568).

May, Georges. Marriage vs. love in the world of Giraudoux. YFS 11:106–15, 1953. **11712**

In spite of the fact that G.'s two most successful plays pay tribute to conjugal happiness and fidelity, a complete catalog of his works shows that love and marriage rarely go together.

McDonald, Ruth Elizabeth. Le langage de Giraudoux. PMLA 13:1029–50, 1948. **11713**

The use of the metaphor and the recurrence of certain key words are the stylistic characteristics singled out for study by this critic.

McLendon, Will L. Giraudoux and the impossible couple. PMLA 82:197–205, 1967. **11714**

Refutes critics who label G. a *précieux* and an *illusionniste*. Stresses the solitary pessimistic nature of his characters throughout his work culminating in a fusion of stoicism and idealism. In his catalog of impossible couples he rules out Alcmène as being a close relative to the *vierge giralducienne* and ignores Andromaque entirely. Considers *Pour Lucrèce* a microcosm of G.'s life and art. See also McLendon's other stylistic studies (*see* 11692, 11693 and 11694).

Meister, Guido. Gestalt und Bedeutung der Frau im Werk Jean Giraudoux'. Basel, Helbing & Lichtenhahn, 1951. 159 p. **11715**

This is still the only full scale study of G.'s heroines. It ranges from the symbolism of the young girl, who usually represents the flight from reality, to the woman who becomes the instrument of destiny. It concludes with the role of the perfect couple, on whom earthly paradise depends.

Moraud, Yves. La pédagogie selon Giraudoux ou la politesse envers la création. IL 22:136–47, 1970. **11716**

Under the section "Documentation pédagogique," the critic studies G.'s conception of the child and of pedagogy as it is revealed in *Les aventures de Jérôme Bardini* and *Intermezzo*.

The result is a stinging condemnation of the French educational system and a Rousseauistic attitude towards the rights of the child.

Müller, Franz W. Die idées obsédantes im Werke Jean Giraudoux'. NS 3:106–17, 1955; 4:165–73, 1955.   **11717**

Carefully researched article in which the author points to G.'s obsessions with macabre and mysterious motifs in the posthumously discovered *Les contes du matin* and insists that G. the novelist was fascinated by catastrophe in all its symbolic forms. In the dramatic works *Siegfried, Judith, Amphitryon 38,* and *Pour Lucrèce* are singled out for their "idées obsédantes" of disaster and the word "glisser" in *Electre* is analyzed in that context. Müller refutes much of Laurent LeSage's more bland criticism. [PM]

Spacensky-Kester, Denyse. Les cinq tentations de Giraudoux. Essai sur le héros de roman. HumC 3:39–103, 1968. **11718**

An important critical article showing G.'s metaphysical approach to ideological positions via five temptations: "la tentation du sublime," "la tentation du dépaysement," "la tentation du tragique," "l'orgueil," and "le néant."

G.'s tenderness and sensitivity are emphasized. [PM]

Influence and Rapprochement

Body, Jacques. Jean Giraudoux entre Gide et Charles-Louis Philippe. RHL 73:1029–40, 1973.   **11719**

This article is of interest for the light it throws on the influence of Charles-Louis Philippe and G.'s relations with the group of writers of the N.R.F. Documented with new material, four letters from G. to Gide and one to Charles-Louis Philippe.

Jaloux, Edmond. D'Eschyle à Giraudoux. Fribourg, Egloff, 1946. p. 305–13. **11720**

Places G.'s theater in the tradition of Marivaux and Musset.

LeSage, Laurent. A Danish model for Jean Giraudoux: J. P. Jacobsen. RLC 26:94–105, 1952.   **11721**

Presents compelling evidence from some unpublished notebooks that G. read Jacobsen when he was a student in Germany and imitated him in one of his early short stories, *L'ombre sur les joues.*

CHAPTER XXVI

JEAN COCTEAU

(Nos. 11722–11893)

Debra Popkin*

Correspondence and Autobiographical Writings

Cocteau, Jean. Les armes secrètes de la France. *In his:* Poésie critique. II. Gallimard, 1960. p. 221–45. **11722**

Speech given by C. before Queen Elisabeth of Belgium, somewhat repetitious of earlier speeches, in which he discusses his role as a poet—recipient of messages transmitted to him by the "invisible Lord" and other mysterious forces.

————. Des beaux-arts considérés comme un assassinat. *In his:* Essai de critique indirecte. Grasset, 1932. p. 97–262. **11723**

A continuation of the essay on Chirico, *Le mystère laïc,* in which C. compares Chirico's paintings to great poetry. C. expresses his ideas on the role of the true artist or poet as a pure, free individual who is held under suspicion by the public at large. States the need for the poet to remain invisible, to have a style without any characteristic mannerisms.

————. Carte blanche. Eds. de la sirène, 1920. 117 p. *Also in his:* Le rappel à l'ordre. Stock, 1926. p. 77–145. *Also (with introd.):* Lausanne, Mermod, 1953. 161 p. (Collection du bouquet, 55) **11724**

Includes sketches, watercolors, and photographs. Series of articles (published in ParMi March 31 to Aug. 11, 1919) in which C. discusses the new spirit in the arts. Contains witty aphorisms on C.'s esthetics.

————. Colette; discours de réception à l'Académie royale de langue et de littérature françaises de Belgique. Oct. 1, 1955.

Grasset, 1955. 123 p. *Also in his:* Poésie critique. II. Gallimard, 1960. p. 107–36. *Trans.:* A speech on Colette. LonM 3:16–24, 1956. **11725**

C.'s homage to Colette after his election to fill the seat left vacant by her death. C. discusses his close relationship with Colette and with the Countess Anna de Noailles. Reminiscences about C.'s encounters with Colette, her interest in his stories, and her influence on him.

————. Le coq et l'arlequin: notes autour de la musique. Eds. de la sirène, 1918. 74 p. *Also in his:* Le rappel à l'ordre. Stock, 1926. p. 11–75. *Trans.:* Cock and harlequin. London, Egoist press, 1921. 57 p. *Also in his:* A call to order. London, Faber and Gwyer, 1926. p. 1–77. *Also:* New York, Henry Holt, 1927. **11726**

In addition to promoting the new music of Erik Satie and the French Six, C. formulates his own personal esthetics, which include clarity, simplicity, precision and a return to native French sources of inspiration.

————. Le cordon ombilical (souvenirs). Plon, 1962. 81 p. **11727**

Short book about relationship between C. and his characters. Many other matters alluded to, including the prize-fighter Al Brown. Six sonnets are included. Some remarks of interest, but generally repetitious.

————. Démarche d'un poète. *In his:* Poésie critique. II. Gallimard, 1960. p. 9–17. **11728**

Discussion of C.'s difficulty in maintaining his "freedom," his refusal to take sides.

*Assisted by Michael Popkin and Marianne Meijer.

———. La difficulté d'être. Morihien, 1947. 277 p. *Also:* Monaco, Eds. du rocher, 1953. 252 p. *Also:* Union générale d'éditions, 1964. 183 p. *Trans.:* The difficulty of being. Introduction by Ned Rorem. London, Peter Owen, 1966. 160 p. *Also:* New York, Coward McCann, 1967. **11729**

A collection of mature essays, written in a direct style without puns or aphorisms, in which C. reminisces openly about his past and the people close to him. Of special interest are the essays on pain and death, and the two essays in which C. explains his method of work, *Des mots* and *De mon style.*

———. Discours de réception de M. Jean Cocteau à l'Académie française, et réponse d'André Maurois. Gallimard, 1955. 126 p. *Also in his:* Poésie critique. II. Gallimard, 1960. p. 137–71.   **11730**

C. discusses apparent contradiction of his becoming an Academician in view of his reputation for frivolity as a jack-of-all-trades. Continues with remarks on poetry and eulogy of Jérôme Tharaud.

———. Le discours d'Oxford. Gallimard, 1956. 57 p. *Also in his:* Poésie critique. II. Gallimard, 1960. p. 173–99. *Trans.:* Poetry and invisibility. LonM 4:29–44, 1957.   **11731**

General remarks on poetry. Concludes with brief autobiographical sketch of himself and influences on his own development as a poet.

———. Discours sur la poésie. *In his:* Poésie critique. II. Gallimard, 1960. p. 201–19.   **11732**

Speech given in Brussels on Sept. 19, 1958. Somewhat repetitious of earlier speeches, especially the *Discours d'Oxford.* Speaks of own mistaken notion about the nature of poetry in his early youth, before reaching the age of twenty. Criticizes Sartre for calling him a counterfeiter. Attacks Sartre as accomplice of the Encyclopedists who does not belong to the race of persecuted poets.

———. D'un ordre considéré comme une anarchie. (Allocution prononcée au Collège de France le jeudi 3 mai 1923.) *In his:* Le rappel à l'ordre. Stock, 1926. p. 235–60. *Also in his:* Poésie critique. I. Gallimard, 1959. p. 67–88. *Trans.:* Order considered as anarchy. *In his:* A call to order. London, Faber and Gwyer, 1926.

p. 181–208. *Also:* New York, Henry Holt, 1927.   **11733**

C. proposes that writers should have "style" rather than a particular style. Discussion of C.'s own works and of influence of Radiguet.

———. Entretiens avec André Fraigneau. Bibliothèque 10/18, 1965. 173 p. **11734**

Not as essential as the volume of conversations on the cinema, also with Fraigneau, because the material here will be familiar to all readers of C.'s autobiographical work. Fraigneau himself is thoroughly familiar with that work and is a most compliant interviewer, sometimes feeding C. lines and always agreeing with him. These interviews were broadcast on French radio in early 1951 and thoroughly cover all C.'s work up to that date.

———. Le foyer des artistes. Plon, 1947. 231 p.   **11735**

A collection of mildly interesting newspaper articles, many on the theater, published in *Ce soir* 1937–38 and in *Comœdia* during the occupation. Some articles about C.'s own work in progress.

———. Journal d'un inconnu. Grasset, 1953. 238 p. *Trans.:* The hand of a stranger. London, Elek books, 1956. 187 p. *Also.:* New York, Horizon press, 1959. **11736**

A collection of essays on various themes including invisibility, friendship, liberty, injustice, the death penalty, and even permanent waves. C. discusses his own works, his contemporaries, and problems of both major and minor concern.

———. Lettre à Jacques Maritain. Stock, 1926. 70 p. *Also in his:* Poésie critique, II. Gallimard, 1960. p. 19–63. *Trans.:* Letter to Jacques Maritain. *In:* Art and faith: Letters between Jacques Maritain and Jean Cocteau. New York, Philosophical library, 1948. p. 11–70. **11737**

C. states that closeness to childhood links him to Maritain. C. maintains that it is false to speak of his own Catholicism in terms of a conversion and claims that Maritain pushed him toward God when he was hesitant. C. expresses enthusiasm for a religion of love; sees God in everything, including what had been attributed to the devil; favors the idea of following the principles of Christianity to the letter.

———. Lettre aux Américains. Grasset, 1949. 102 p. *Also in his:* Poésie critique. II. Gallimard, 1960. p. 67–106. *Trans.:* Letter to Americans. *In:* Cocteau's world. Ed. by Margaret Crosland. London, Peter Owen, 1972. p. 397–411. *Another ed.:* New York, Dodd, Mead, 1973. **11738**

C. relates his impressions of Americans as gathered during a visit to New York in 1949. Discusses reception of his own films in America.

———. Lettres à André Gide. Préf. et commentaire de Jean-Jacques Kihm. La table ronde, 1970. 219 p. **11739**

Well-written preface by Kihm states that the lack of a real dialog between C. and Gide stems from a basic difference in the temperaments of the two writers. Includes letters from Gide to C. Letters reveal C.'s desire to establish a relationship with Gide and Gide's cool, aloof attitude.

———. Maalesh; Journal d'une tournée de théâtre. Gallimard, 1949. 235 p. *Trans.:* Maalesh; a theatrical tour in the Middle-East. London, Peter Owen, 1956. 136 p. **11740**

A diary written during a theatrical tour, through Egypt and Turkey, on which C. staged plays by other dramatists as well as *La machine infernale* and *Les parents terribles.* Less specifically related to theater than the diary of *Beauty and the beast* was related to film, but one performance of *Britannicus* is described at length, as seen from backstage. Brilliant observations—on Christian Bérard, Jean Genet, and Loti, among others—are scattered throughout, and one receives a very sharp overall impression of what theater meant to C.

———. Mon premier voyage; tour du monde en quatre-vingts jours. Gallimard, 1936. 231 p. *Trans.:* Round the world again in eighty days. London, Routledge, 1937. 250 p. *Another trans.:* My journey round the world. London, Peter Owen, 1958. 175 p. **11741**

Account of C.'s journey around the world in eighty days in celebration of Jules Verne's centenary. Describes his chance encounter with Charlie Chaplin on a Japanese cargo boat and speaks of kinship with Chaplin, whose childlike nature and pity for humanity C. admires.

———. Le mystère laïc. Eds. des quatre-chemins, 1928. 81 p. *Also in his:* Essai de critique indirecte. Grasset, 1932. p. 3–96. **11742**

In addition to praising Chirico as a painter of mystery and miracles without the faith, C. expresses his own views on art and poetry. Regards poetry as a closed world to which very few are admitted. Insists on absolute freedom for the artist. Among the aphorisms is C.'s famous definition of poetry as a kind of numerical precision. André Fermigier says (*see* 11793) that this book was directed against surrealism.

———. Opium, journal d'une désintoxication. Stock, Delamain & Boutelleau, 1930. 264 p. *Also:* Le club français du livre, 1957. 294 p. *Trans.:* Opium. London and New York, Longmans, 1932. 188 p. *Also:* London, Peter Owen, 1957. 176 p. *Also:* New York, Grove press, 1958. 167 p. **11743**

C. discusses the benefits he derived from smoking opium: a new sense of time and space, freedom from the need for constant companionship, a feeling of calm and physical well-being, inspiration for the poems in *Opéra.* Random notes on C.'s own career are interspersed with criticism of C.'s contemporaries and writers of the past. Includes brief account of C.'s acquaintance with Proust and praise for Raymond Roussel. Drawings by C. are among his most imaginative and provocative.

———. Poésie de journalisme. Pierre Belfond, 1973. 140 p. **11744**

C.'s newspaper articles are reprinted in *Portraits-souvenir, Tour du monde en quatre-vingts jours* and *Le foyer des artistes.* This anthology is comprised of material not published in those volumes, but it is not the bottom-of-the-barrel assortment one would expect. The daily articles about a boat trip along the Mediterranean coast are charming, and the articles omitted from *Le foyer des artistes* (see analysis under that heading) are quite as interesting as those included there. As usual, remarks on C.'s own work are scattered throughout.

———. Portraits-souvenir, 1900–1914. Grasset, 1935. 252 p. *Trans.:* Paris album 1900–1914. London, W. H. Allen, 1956. 175 p. **11745**

Collection of essays on C.'s contemporaries, on music, and on the theater (published in Fig Jan. 19 to May 11, 1935). Contains personal reminiscences and drawings by C. This is the most readable of C.'s autobiographical volumes, and almost every discussion of C.'s youth quotes from these essays or (in biographies) plagiarizes them.

————. Préface à Les chevaliers de la table ronde. In his: Les chevaliers de la table ronde. Gallimard, 1937. p. 11–16. Also in his: Théâtre. I. Gallimard, 1948. p. 71–75. Trans.: Preface to The knights of the round table. In his: The infernal machine and other plays. Norfolk, Connecticut, New directions, 1963. p. 181–84. **11746**
C. explains his dream-like inspiration to write the play. Insists upon the fact that he remains outside of this particular drama.

————. Préface de 1922 à Les mariés de la Tour Eiffel. OLib 21:351–61, 1923. Also in his: Les mariés de la Tour Eiffel. Gallimard, 1924. Also: Gallimard, 1927. Also in his: Théâtre. I. Gallimard, 1948. p. 41–49. Trans.: Preface. In his: The infernal machine and other plays. Norfolk, Connecticut, New directions, 1963. p. 153–60. **11747**
C. defines his esthetic of *poésie de théâtre*, a special theatrical poetry, which he contrasts with the traditional use of poetry in the theater. C.'s poetry of the theater is an attempt to use everyday objects that are larger than life and make them bright in a new context.

————. Le secret professionnel. Stock, 1922. 79 p. Also: Au sans pareil, 1925. 107 p. Also in his: Le rappel à l'ordre. Stock, 1926. p. 175–233. Trans.: Professional secrets. In his: A call to order. London, Faber and Gwyer, 1926. p. 107–80. Also: New York, Henry Holt, 1927. **11748**
Essay on C.'s personal esthetics. Contains aphorisms on poetry and role of the poet. C. sees true poets as those who renew clichés and make them fresh again. C. urges young artists to be true to themselves.

Déon, Michel. Jean Cocteau peint et se dépeint. RDM 4:645–52, 1957. **11749**
Praises C. for opening new paths by insulting tradition. In an interview, C. and Déon discuss C.'s work painting

Chapel in Villefranche-sur-Mer. C. gives general comments on his work as a painter. C. expresses an interest in new science-fiction writers.

Fifield, William. The art of fiction XXXIV. Jean Cocteau: an interview. ParR 32:13–37, 1964. Also in: Writers at work: the Paris review interviews. Third series. Viking press, 1967. p. 57–81. **11750**
Fifield's interview with C. shortly before C.'s death. C. discusses major influences on his writing: Stravinsky, Satie, Picasso, Radiguet. C. stresses importance of unconscious, external inspiration in his creation.

————. Excerpts from conversations with Jean Cocteau. MalR 7:5–13, 1968. **11751**
Wide-ranging discussion by C. of literature, film and theater. C. talks about his adaptations of Shaw's *Dear liar* and of Tennessee Williams' *A streetcar named desire*. Some comments on C.'s conception of true creativity.

Biography

Bibesco, [Marthe Lucie (Lahovary)] la Princesse. Jean Cocteau, mon collègue. RGB 91:541–50, 1955. **11752**
Light and entertaining accounts of lunch with C., C.'s career, C.'s friendship with Radiguet, and C.'s virtuosity as mime, illusionist, actor and magician.

Brown, Frederick. An impersonation of angels: a biography of Jean Cocteau. Viking press, 1968. 438 p. **11753**
Denigrates C. by portraying him as a parasite living off the achievements of the men in his life. Interesting depictions of Edouard de Max, Catulle Mendès, Robert de Montesquiou, Stravinsky, Diaghilev, Erik Satie, Picasso and Radiguet. Excellent historical overview of the period. Witty, engrossing, and as full of negative comments as all C.'s French detractors put together. Inadequate in evaluating C.'s achievements, but highly recommended for anyone who is not put off by its splenetic tone.
Reviews: P. Anderson in Spec 223:444, 1969; M. Battersby in A&A 5:68, 70, 1970; H. Clurman in Nat 208:88–89, 1969; W. Fowlie in Cweal 98:622, 1969; B. Knapp in JML 1:746–48, 1970 supplement; L. Roudiez in SatR

52:95, 1969; F. Steegmuller in TBR 6, Dec. 22, 1968; J. Weightman in Obs 9, 292:33, 1969.

Cassou, Jean. Discours de M. Jean Cassou (éloge de Jean Cocteau, Nov. 6, 1965). BARLLF 43:203–16, 1965.   **11754**

Tribute to C. by his successor at the Royal Belgian Academy, with emphasis on C.'s high regard for friendship, good-heartedness, and desire to be well liked. A poetic, highly stylized account of C.'s life and works. Considers C.'s grace the fruit of serious reflection and patient labor.

Crosland, Margaret. Jean Cocteau, a biography. London, Peter Nevill, 1955. 206 p. *Also:* New York, Knopf, 1956. 243 p.   **11755**

A sketchy and incomplete biography. Attempts to depict C.'s entourage. No discussion of C.'s works. Not a scholarly work but one of excessive adulation toward C. Information was taken directly from C. himself.

Reviews: Anon. in List 53:347, 1955; E. Eaton in SatR 39:18, 1956; G. Freedley in LJ 81:1695, 1956; J. O'Brien in RR 49:313–14, 1958.

Desonay, Fernand. Jean Cocteau, mon ami. MRo 13:111–18, 1963.   **11756**

An account of C.'s funeral at Milly-la-Forêt by the professor who had welcomed C. to the Royal Academy of Belgium. Contains personal recollections of encounters and friendship with C. stressing C.'s warmth and kindness.

Fumet, Stanislas. Jean Cocteau ne joue plus. TR 191:9–14, 1963.   **11757**

Tribute to C. after his death with references to C.'s life as middle-class Parisian, C.'s "conversion" and relationship with Jacques Maritain and his wife, and C.'s rejection by Breton and the surrealists. Regards C. as a sort of talent scout, extraordinary craftsman, and author of maxims and witty sayings rather than as a great poet.

Garnier, Christine. Evocation de Jean Cocteau. RDM 21:108–15, 1963.   **11758**

After C.'s death, the author recalls an interview with C. in which they discussed the nature of death, C.'s career, and other matters. Reprints also an earlier article (*see* 11759).

———. Jean Cocteau me parle de lui. RevHM 104:514–21, 1955.   **11759**

Interview with C. in which C. stresses his need for constant activity. The public of 1955 is viewed as too cautious to be scandalized by anything. C. discusses his early writings and importance of influences of Stravinsky, Picasso and Radiguet.

Jacob, Max. Choix de lettres de Max Jacob à Jean Cocteau, 1919–1944. Paul Morihien, 1949. 158 p.   **11760**

Letters reveal close friendship between Jacob and C. as well as Jacob's need for love and approval. Of special interest are Jacob's discussion of his Catholicism and his positive reaction to C.'s letter to Jacques Maritain. Jacob expresses admiration for C.'s poetry and for the critical works, *Carte blanche* and *Le rappel à l'ordre,* emphasizing C.'s clarity and freshness of insight. Praises *Orphée* as a masterpiece of invention. Final letter is a pathetic plea for help as Jacob is being deported to a concentration camp.

La Charmondière. Autour de Jean Cocteau. Un double scandale. RevD 62:41–46, 1956.   **11761**

An attack on C.'s election to the French Academy and the speech he made there as well as the speech he delivered before the Royal Belgian Academy. Regards both speeches as hypocritical and full of errors. While admitting that C. was a prodigy in his youth, calls C.'s old age a highly immoral and "grimacing affectation".

Magnan, Jean-Marie. La machine à signification. RdP 72:51–65, 1965.   **11762**

A discussion of C.'s fascination with Picasso's method of putting everyday objects to new, unexpected use in his canvasses as C. himself later did in his poetic works. This discussion was later included in Magnan's book, *Cocteau* (1968). Article also includes 32 letters from C. to Jean-Marie and Claude Magnan (July 8, 1956 to Sept. 3, 1963) in which C. speaks of his *Corrida du premier mai,* his work as a painter, plans for film *Le testament d'Orphée,* and poems *Cérémonial espagnol du Phénix* and *Requiem.*

Maritain, Jacques. Réponse à Jean Cocteau. Stock, 1926. 71 p. *Trans.:* Response to

Jean Cocteau. *In:* Art and faith: letters between Jacques Maritain and Jean Cocteau. New York, Philosophical library, 1948. p. 71–135. **11763**

In his reply to *Lettre à Jacques Maritain,* Maritain discusses his own background as a Thomist philosopher and his concern with angels. Maritain finds in C.'s esthetic pronouncements, such as *Le coq et l'arlequin,* the laws of self-purification and self-destitution that rule over any spirituality, but considers C. to be in danger from opium and sin.

Martin du Gard, Maurice. Jean Cocteau dans mon Journal. RevHM 89:38–49, 1953. **11764**

Entries in author's Journal from 1921, 1927, and 1928 dealing with C. the man. Anecdotes on C.'s relationship with musicians of the French Six, with theater-going Parisian society, and with the critic Henri Béraud. Discusses C.'s efforts to promote Jean Desbordes who could never really replace Radiguet in C.'s affections.

Massis, Henri. De Radiguet à Maritain; hommage à Cocteau. Liège, Eds. dynamo, 1963. 12 p. (Brimborions, 117) **11765**

Reminiscences about C.'s love for Radiguet and grief at Radiguet's death. Discusses dinner with C. at Maritain's house, arrival of Père Charles Henrion, and C.'s subsequent conversion to Catholicism. Sees C. as man who had a "vision" to the end of his life.

Mauny, Erik de. A little guide to Jean Cocteau. LonM 2:68–77, 1955. **11766**

Aims to dispel myths and legends about C. by tracing his background and literary career. Emphasizes freshness and subtle use of irony in C.'s poetry. Discusses angelism—inner spirit which inhabits the poet and forces him to write often in spite of himself. Praises C.'s devotion to his craft as a poet.

Mauriac, Claude. Une amitié contrariée. Grasset, 1970. 280 p. **11767**

Excerpts from thirty years of diary entries. Mauriac selected (from thousands of pages) all the passages dealing with C. and presents them here in the form of a Proustian novel. The order is non-chronological, and Mauriac follows most passages with comments written in 1969. Letters from C. and comments by him are quoted at length. An analysis of Mauriac's contradictory attitudes toward C. would make an excellent book, but this is not it. Some interesting criticism of individual works, but also many tedious pages of self-evident observations about Time. Essential for the student of Claude Mauriac, but of marginal interest for the student of C.

Reviews: J. Piatier in Monde 8059: 15, Dec. 11, 1970 and in MondeH 1155:12, Dec. 10–16, 1970.

Muller, Henry. Jean Cocteau ou la sirène à queue verte. RevHM 112:589–94, 1955. **11768**

Account of C.'s reception by the French Academy with details of C.'s elaborate costume and of his acceptance speech as newly elected member. Refers to C. as an enchanter who put everyone under his spell. Includes discussion of Maurois' reply to C.

Peters, Arthur King. Cocteau et Gide: lettres inédites. *In:* Jean Cocteau 1. *See* 11783. p. 54–67. **11769**

A brief introduction by Peters on the stormy relationship beween C. and Gide is followed by a series of sixteen previously unpublished letters dated 1913 to 1946. Subjects of the letters include style, the position of the artist before posterity, and the problems of criticism. Some of these letters are reprinted in Peters' book (1973), which gives a full analysis of C.'s relationship with Gide.

———. Jean Cocteau and André Gide; an abrasive friendship. New Brunswick, N.J., Rutgers univ. press, 1973. 426 p. **11770**

A well-documented, in-depth study of relationship between C. and Gide. Probes similarities and differences between two rivals. Analyzes Gide's impact on C.'s development as a writer. Studies their ambivalent friendship as it is reflected in their correspondence.

Putnam, Samuel. Child in a dark room (Jean Cocteau). *In his:* Paris was our mistress. Viking press, 1947. p. 172–78. **11771**

Description of a visit to C.'s dark, opium-filled bedroom by translator of *Les enfants terribles.* Considers C.'s boyhood memoirs in *Portraits-souvenir 1900–1914* as essential to understanding of C. as child fond of game-playing and make-believe who refused to grow up.

Sachs, Maurice. Le sabbat. Corrêa, 1946. 443 p. *Trans.:* Witches' sabbath. Stein and Day, 1964. 315 p. *Abridged trans.:* Day of wrath. London, Arthur Barker, 1953. 223 p. **11772**

The classic attack on C. as a misleader of youth. The writer, as a young man, literally prayed to C.'s picture. Highly untrustworthy, and excessively negative as literary criticism, but fascinating. C. is mentioned frequently, and his portrait is drawn at length, based on personal experience. According to C., who was deeply stung by this book, Sachs wanted to withdraw what he had written but died before he could do so.

Sprigge, Elizabeth, and Jean-Jacques Kihm. Jean Cocteau: the man and the mirror. Coward-McCann, 1968. 286 p. *Also:* London, Victor Gollancz, 1968. **11773**

This sympathetic biography of C. is entertaining reading even for the layman. Well documented and illustrated, it gives a fair treatment of C.'s relationships with those artists and writers who influenced him. Includes material from C.'s correspondence with J.-J. Kihm and a thorough account of C.'s activities during the last few years of his life. Not as detailed as biography by Steegmuller.

Reviews: L. Bates in Punch 254:284, Feb. 21, 1968; S. Gavronsky in WPBW 10, Apr. 28, 1968; I. Hamilton in ILN 252:32–33, Feb. 17, 1968; R. Heppenstall in Spec 7283:104–05, Jan. 26, 1968; P. Toynbee in Obs 9, 211:31, Jan. 28, 1968.

Steegmuller, Francis. Cocteau: a biography. Boston, Little, Brown, 1970. 583 p. *Also:* London and Bastingstoke, Macmillan, 1970. *Trans.:* Cocteau. Trans. by Marcelle Jossua. Buchet-Chastel, 1973. 408 p. **11774**

The definitive biography of C. in any language. Almost all preceding biographies of C. relied heavily (sometimes without acknowledging the fact) on C.'s own autobiographical writings. The research that went into this volume corrects innumerable errors and half-truths and makes many of the preceding biographies virtually obsolete. Thoroughly footnoted, with an extensive bibliography. Gives an excellent picture of many celebrities such as Max Jacob, Radi-

guet, Jean Marais, etc. Provides concise critical evaluations of every significant work by C., evaluations that are rigorous but fair. Highly readable, exhaustive in scope, and possibly the best biography of a contemporay French writer.

Reviews: Anon. in TLS 3594:56, Jan. 15, 1971; Anon. in VQR 47:xxxvi, 1971; N. Bliven in NY 130–34, Mar. 13, 1971; C. Brown in Gua 14, Nov. 26, 1970; C. M. Cluny in QL 176; 18–19, 1973; C. Connolly in SunT 7695:31, Nov. 22, 1970; A. Lejeune in B&B 15:21–22, Nov. 1969; R. Mazzocco in NYRB 16:29–33, 1971; P. Quennell in Spec 225:768, Dec. 12, 1970; Y. Quintin in FR 45:914–15, 1972; M. Schorer in TBR 6–7, Sept. 27, 1970; M. Turnell in NewS 80: 805–06, Dec. 11, 1970; J. Wain in Obs 9, 358:30, Nov. 22, 1970; J. Weightman in ChiTBW 4:4, Oct. 18, 1970.

Collected Articles

Adam 300; a special edition of Adam published in memory of Jean Cocteau. London, Curwen press, 1966. 200 p. **11775**

Personal recollections of encounters and correspondence with C. by various friends and acquaintances like Rosamond Lehmann, translator of *Les enfants terribles*, André Germain, Milorad, Ronald Duncan and Rollo Myers. Articles give impression of C. as brilliant conversationalist with great powers of persuasion.

Autour de Jean Cocteau. TR 94:1–185, 1955. **11776**

Special issue of this periodical devoted to C. Contains many brief but interesting articles by various writers, critics, and friends of C. Personal reminiscences by Poulenc and Auric and brief discussion of themes in C.'s poetry by Alain Bosquet are of special interest.

Cahiers Jean Cocteau. I. Gallimard, 1969. 122 p. **11777**

Tributes to C. by Georges Auric, Paul Morand and André Fraigneau. The letters from Marcel Proust and Maurice Sachs to C. are of interest primarily as a biographical supplement. The letters from C. to his mother are of exceptional interest, since they presumably show C. at his most unpretentious. Those letters are charming and even touching, particularly when he urges her not to believe all the rumors about him.

Cahiers Jean Cocteau. II. Gallimard, 1971. 150 p.   **11778**

The major critical essay in this volume is a psychological analysis of C.'s myths (Oedipus, Antigone, Orpheus) by Milorad. Articles by Emmanuel Berl, Claude Michel Cluny and Arthur K. Peters, and excerpts from *Le passé défini*, C.'s unpublished diary, dealing principally with *Bacchus*. Of interest to students of *Thomas l'imposteur* will be the account of its composition (by Pierre Chanel) and several dozen dedications written by C. for the copies of that novel that were given to his friends when the novel was published.

Cahiers Jean Cocteau. III. Gallimard, 1972. 123 p.   **11779**

Tributes to C. as film-maker, notably by Robert Bresson and Henri Langlois. Another fascinating essay by a writer (Yvon Belaval) who was young and impressionable when he knew C. in the late 20's. Most importantly, this series continues to publish hitherto unpublished (and even unknown) essays and letters by C. Future volumes can therefore be as highly recommended as the three published thus far.

Crosland, Margaret. Cocteau's world. London, Peter Owen, 1972. 489 p. *Also:* New York, Dodd, Mead, 1973.   **11780**

An anthology of C.'s writings translated from the French, edited, and introduced by Crosland.

Hommage à Jean Cocteau, prince des poètes. 72 p. PoCp Special issue: 1–72, 1961.   **11781**

A collection of essays by different writers reprinted from various sources. Each essay is followed by a poem by C. Of special interest are H. Agel's essay on C.'s films, *Image de Jean Cocteau*, and Anouilh's tribute to C.

Jean Cocteau. Emp 3–168, May–June–July 1950.   **11782**

This special issue of *Empreintes* had an enormous influence. Prior to its publication only the books by Claude Mauriac and Roger Lannes had examined C. in depth, and the book by

Mauriac was highly negative. This volume has tributes from Jean Genet and Georges Auric, among others, as well as essays by many critics who later wrote whole volumes on C. There are facsimiles of letters from Gide, Proust, Apollinaire, Picasso, etc. Selections from C.'s writing and the first serious attempt at a bibliography. No single item is irreplaceable, but this volume laid out the main lines of C. criticism for many years to come.

Jean Cocteau 1 (1972). Cocteau et les mythes. Ed. by Jean-Jacques Kihm and Michel Décaudin. RLM 298–303, 1972. 195 p.   **11783**

Includes an incomplete but helpful bibliography on C. The significant articles have been analyzed separately under appropriate headings.

Spécial Cocteau. Les mariés de la Tour Eiffel, Les chevaliers de la Table Ronde. AvSc 365–66:3–86, 1966.   **11784**

Reprints C.'s 1922 preface to *Les mariés* and C.'s preface to *Les chevaliers* as well as Anouilh's article from *Points et contrepoints* (1961) and texts of both C. plays. Some brief critical comments by Milhaud on music for *Les mariés* and by Jacques Pradère on rediscovery of original musical score. Includes remarks on audience's favorable reaction to *Les chevaliers* in 1966 by André Camp, detailed notes on C.'s theatrical career, casts of all his plays, photographs, and brief critical excerpts on C. from 1920's to 1960's.

General Studies

Azpúrua Ayala, Ricardo. Apunte sobre Jean Cocteau. RNC 9:106–12, 1948.   **11785**

A discussion of some recurrent themes and character types in C.'s works.

Bancroft, David. Cocteau's creative crisis, 1925–1929; Bremond, Chirico, and Proust. FR 45:9–19, 1971.   **11786**

C.'s rejection of the Abbé Bremond's conception of poetry as inseparable from prayer (as developed in Bremond's *Debate on pure poetry*) leads to discussion of C.'s admiration for Chirico who gave expression to his own intuitive perception of the world. Emphasizes C.'s admiration for Proust for having attained perfect marriage of style and thought; latent influence of Proust on C. is described.

Bo, Carlo. Resistenze in una voce umana. *In his:* In margine a un vecchio libro. Milan, Bompiani, 1945. p. 67–73. **11787**

A generally negative appraisal of C.'s achievements. Regards C. as sharing in Voltaire's shortcomings of coldness and sterility despite excellent craftsmanship. Praises *La machine infernale* for suggesting possibilities of inner metamorphosis. Criticizes *La fin du Potomak* for containing all of C.'s vices.

Borgal, Clément. Cocteau: Dieu, la mort, la poésie. Eds. du centurion, 1968. 216 p. **11788**

A history of C.'s spiritual evolution as evidenced in his works. Gives brief survey of C.'s works in all domains with focus on certain recurring themes: the search for God, the poet as interpreter of mysteries, and C.'s obsession with death. Relies heavily on quotations from texts by C. including C.'s *Entretiens avec André Fraigneau.* Links C. to mysticism and Gnosticism.

Brosse, Jacques. Cocteau. Gallimard, 1970. 251 p. [Pour une bibliothèque idéale, 10] **11789**

The best critical study available. Although the essay portion of the book is brief, original insights into C.'s work are frequent. Use is made of psychoanalytical criticism to examine the themes that reappear in different forms throughout C.'s work. Particularly good on the Oedipus story and on C.'s view of himself as a poet. Discussions of individual works and a thorough bibliography, as well as some brief excerpts from other writers.

Reviews: M. Galey in Exp 1009:52–53, Nov. 9–15, 1970; A. Marissel in Esp 400:442–43, 1971; J. Piatier in Monde 8059:15, Dec. 11, 1970.

Clouard, Henri. Les constantes de Jean Cocteau. RdP 69:80–92, 1962. **11790**

Traces four permanent characteristics of C.'s works: constant revolution; desire to dazzle (to be in the forefront); the neo-classicism of Radiguet's influence; and C.'s personal truth as revealed in his books on his travels and his accounts of his own personal suffering. Deplores C.'s cheap tricks and inten-

tional obscurity while admiring C.'s sense of man's tragic fate.

Decreus, Juliette. Aux limbes du drame: Jean Cocteau. ML 34:18–21, 1952. *Also (rev.):* FIV 34:3–8, 1953. **11791**

An analysis of C.'s adherence to images of childhood and dreams throughout his works. Discusses C.'s amoral, abnormal characters with their latent tendencies toward incest and their stress on friendship. Regards the exploration of the unconscious as the essential element in C.'s dramatic and poetic works.

Etiemble, René. Jérôme et Jean Cocteau. *In his:* Le péché vraiment capital. Gallimard, 1957. p. 55–74. **11792**

Negative reaction to C.'s *Discours de réception à l'Académie française.* Accuses C. of being an opportunist who tries to please all sides at once. Asserts that in C.'s references to his predecessor at the French Academy, Jérôme Tharaud, C. failed to understand Tharaud's works, which were pro-colonial and anti-Semitic. Criticizes C.'s *Lettre aux Américains* and *Maalesh* for containing errors and incongruities worse than those in works of Tharaud.

Fermigier, André. Introduction. *In:* Cocteau, Jean. Entre Picasso et Radiguet. Hermann, 1967. p. 9–33. **11793**

This anthology of C.'s writings on art has an excellent introduction by André Fermigier, analyzing the major artistic currents in France after World War I and their influence on C. Good discussion of Picasso, Stravinsky and the surrealists. The volume contains several illustrations as well as a 60-page facsimile of the 1917 edition of *L'ode à Picasso.*

Fifield, William. Jean Cocteau. New York, Columbia univ. press, 1974. 48 p. (Columbia essays on modern writers, 70) **11794**

This brief essay analyzes C.'s image as victim and explains the ways in which C. helped foster that image through his need to submit and his choice of "heartless" men as his models. Special attention is given to Picasso, Dargelos, and Radiguet and their incorporation into C.'s works. Fifield suggests that at times C. came close to developing the style of Ionesco's theater of the absurd and of Robbe-Grillet's new novel. Concludes with discussion of C.'s plays, in which he deplores use of stage trickery.

Fongaro, Antoine. Jean Cocteau: mensonge et poésie. RLM 6:534–48, 1956.   **11795**

Pleads for serious interpretation of C.'s works rather than fascination with his colorful life. Insists on importance of words and language in C.'s creation of the unexpected and the fantastic. Traces three constant themes: destiny and free will, the mystery of poetic creation, and the passage of time which is linked with theme of love. Views all C.'s works as a meditation on death. Many typographical errors.

Fowlie, Wallace. Jean Cocteau: the history of a poet's age. Bloomington, Indiana univ. press, 1966. 181 p.   **11796**

A compassionate but somewhat superficial study of C.'s life and works in all fields. Ranks C. with the great classical and contemporary writers. Interesting for analysis of Picasso's influence on C. and for description of a meeting with C. Includes selected bibliography of C.'s writings.

Review: N. Oxenhandler in FR 41: 161–62, 1967.

Fraigneau, André. Cocteau par lui-même. Seuil, 1957. 192 p. (Ecrivains de toujours, 41) *Trans.:* Cocteau. New York, Grove press, 1961. 192 p.   **11797**

Traces C.'s career in all fields by means of extensive quotations from C.'s writings, illustrations by C. and photographs. Fraigneau's excessive admiration for C. as a man of "genius and heart," which has its source in his first meeting with C., prevents this study from being objective criticism. Every work by C. is praised and defended for its beauty and nobility of style.

Hellens, Franz. Adieu au poète Jean Cocteau. Liège, Dynamo, 1963. 12 p. (Brimborions, 118)   **11798**

Speaks of the movement in the arts of the 1920's to which both Hellens and C. belonged. States that C. had completed his essential works at age of thirty, and that C. then went on to repeat himself. Considers C. to have written three great works: *Clair-obscur, Le grand écart, Le secret professionnel.*

Jean, Raymond. Le style de Jean Cocteau. FrA 14:26–31, 1957.   **11799**

An examination of C.'s style and the priority C. gave to form over content. Regards the cinema as the medium in which C. revealed his true genius. Discusses C.'s fondness for romantic décor and his keen sense of the visual.

Kautz, Hans Rudolf. Dichtung und Kunst in der Theorie Jean Cocteaus. Heidelberg, Offsets-druck-Fotodruck, 1970. 331 p.   **11800**

A well-documented dissertation on C.'s esthetics. Analyzes both the classical elements (such as strictness of form) and the romantic elements (such as personal freedom for the artist) that mark C.'s style. Discusses C.'s conception of the creative process and his debt to Rimbaud and Mallarmé. Includes an account of the rivalry between C. and the surrealists. A rather thorough bibliography of criticism on C. and on the surrealists is provided.

Kihm, Jean-Jacques. Cocteau. Gallimard, 1960. 323 p. (Bibliothèque idéale)   **11801**

In a 100-page essay C. is "painted only through his work." There is some original research (Kihm found the class records from the Lycée Condorcet) but usually Kihm closely follows C.'s own accounts. Like most works that do so, this one contains many half-truths. Little effort is made to distinguish major works from minor ones. Divided into sections on each of C.'s genres, including a good discussion of C. as a painter. The apparatus (work-by-work discussions, excerpts, brief opinions, good bibliography) is much more extensive than in the volume by Brosse, which replaced this work in the same series. But the Brosse volume has a better essay.

————, **Elizabeth Sprigge, and Henri C. Béhar.** Jean Cocteau, l'homme et les miroirs. La table ronde, 1968. 477 p.   **11802**

A greatly expanded (almost twice as long) version of the English book by Sprigge and Kihm. Béhar had originally been chosen to translate the text for Kihm to correct, but he and Kihm did additional research, stressing matters such as homosexuality and opium that were glossed over in the English version. Primarily a biography with little literary criticism. The first biography to use C. archives at Milly-la-Forêt. Some fascinating material in the appendices: notably an "astrological portrait of C.," excerpts from a school revue on which C. collaborated in 1906, and many excerpts from *Je suis partout,* which attacked C. throughout 1941. The best biography in French, full of valuable material.

Review: J. Piatier in Monde 7440: vii, Dec. 14, 1968.

Knapp, Bettina L. Jean Cocteau. New York, Twayne publishers, 1970. 179 p. (Twayne's world authors series, 84)
11803

A relatively brief, introductory survey of C.'s life and works, similar in scope to study by Fowlie. Emphasizes C.'s obsession with originality and need for a catalyst (Radiguet, Picasso, etc.) to set C.'s creativity in motion. Argues that C. was not a true creator but a powerful force in the areas of the novel, drama, and film. Includes selected bibliography of works by and about C.

Reviews: A. Amoia in FR 44:604–05, 1971; T. Rees in JML 1:748–50, 1971 supplement.

Koch, Stephen. Cocteau. Mid 8:111–26, 1968. **11804**

Criticizes C. for his desire to please and his craving for publicity. Attributes C.'s need for self-examination and self-justification to his feelings of guilt over his homosexuality. Discusses combination of two metaphors in C.'s life: poet as performer, life as art. Considers these metaphors most successfully integrated in *Thomas l'imposteur.*

Lannes, Roger. Jean Cocteau. *In his:* Jean Cocteau. Une étude par Roger Lannes, un choix de poèmes et une bibliographie établie par Henri Parisot. Seghers, 1948. 301 p.; essay p. 11–95. (Poètes d'aujourd'hui, 4) *Also:* Seghers, 1955. p. 7–90. *Also:* Seghers, 1966. p. 9–77. *Also:* Seghers, 1969. p. 5–92. **11805**

In every edition, the essay by Lannes, written in 1945, is unchanged, but the poems by C. and the photographs vary greatly. In the 1966 and 1969 editions, a brief essay on C. by Pierre Seghers is added to bring the volume more up-to-date. Lannes' essay, introducing selected poetry by C., aims at dispelling the

myths about C. as a frivolous avant-garde figure. After a brief biographical sketch, Lannes analyzes each of C.'s works, emphasizing C.'s very personal style with its bareness, sensitivity, and keenness of perception. As a compassionate friend, Lannes explains C.'s need for freedom from any controlling doctrine and for self-renewal.

Macris, Pierre. L'ange et Cocteau. *In:* Jean Cocteau 1. *See* 11783. p. 71–90. **11806**

An analysis of C.'s conception of "angelism" emphasizing the relationship between the poet and the Angel who tortures him and forces him to write. Includes a discussion of the "angelic" beings, typified by Dargelos, who caused C. personal suffering in real life and who are characterized by a rebellious nature and an innocent lack of morality.

Magnan, Jean-Marie. Cocteau. Bruges, Desclée De Brouwer, 1968. 187 p. (Les écrivains devant Dieu, 17) **11807**

Study of C.'s ambivalent attitude toward religion as reflected in his writings. Followed by selected texts by C. Discusses C.'s need for, and fear of, order, C.'s fascination with beauty, mystery, and the diabolical. Attempts to explain C.'s ultimate rejection of Catholicism and acceptance of "le Seigneur inconnu" as shown in *Sept dialogues avec le Seigneur inconnu qui est en nous.*

Review: H. Sutcliffe in FS 24:209–10, 1970.

Mauriac, Claude. Autour de Jean Cocteau. NRF 54:787–804, 1940. **11808**

An abbreviated version (selected and edited by Jean Paulhan) of the arguments presented by Claude Mauriac in his book *Jean Cocteau; ou la vérité du mensonge.* Claude Mauriac himself felt that the passages had been crudely yet shrewdly selected and that the inner harmony of his text had been destroyed.

————. Jean Cocteau ou La vérité du mensonge. Odette Lieutier, 1945. 184 p. **11809**

The first book-length study devoted to C. and a bitter disappointment to C., who expected great things of it. Mauriac's analysis of C.'s work, liberally quoting from that work, is often obscure but more frequently scathing. C. is not a genuine poet; he is amusing but never profound. Mauriac is correct on many scores, particularly on the matter of C.'s repetitiousness, and his dissection of *L'ange Heurtebise* is a convincing demonstration of the mechanical nature of much of C.'s poetry. But Mauriac was not yet a very good writer, and this book is less of a work of criticism than an attempt to exorcise a personal demon.

Meunier, Micheline. Jean Cocteau et Nietzsche; ou, La philosophie du matin. J. Grassin, 1971. 46 p.   **11810**

Attempts to prove that C. is the only true descendant of Nietzsche. Complains that her earlier study of C. was ignored by other critics and bibliographers. States that Nietzsche can only be understood by reading C.'s works and vice versa.

————. Méditerranée ou les deux visages de Jean Cocteau. Debresse, 1959. 301 p.   **11811**

Difficult, estoeric study of C.'s works, not for the uninitiated. Presupposes a familiarity with all of C.'s works and a knowledge of classical and modern philosophy. Considers C. as "new man" under Nietzsche's definition. Praises C. as deep thinker. Stresses classical elements in C.'s writings: nobility of characters, search for grandeur. Indicates similarities between C.'s works and works of ancient Greeks.

Review: J. Baumann in Thy 61:314 ff., 1959.

————. Présence de Jean Cocteau, ou le sang d'un poète. Lyon, E. Vitte, 1964. 95 p.   **11812**

Considers herself the only critic really to understand C. Admires C. as creator of "new world of words." Praises C. for having revealed secrets and mysteries of the universe and for being clear rather than obscure. Repeats arguments expressed in her earlier full-length study *Méditerranée*.

Meylan, Pierre. Jean Cocteau témoin d'une époque musicale. *In his:* Les écrivains et la musique. Tome II. Lausanne, Eds. du Cervin, 1951. p. 103–17.   **11813**

A discussion of C.'s role as publicist and source of inspiration for the French Six and of the personal and esthetic harmony between C. and Satie. Criticizes C.'s own theatrical texts as not as successful as his theoretical works. Examines C.'s admiration for Ravel after the Six had disbanded.

Millecam, Jean-Pierre. L'étoile de Jean Cocteau. Précédé d'une lettre de Jean Cocteau à l'éditeur. Monaco, Eds. du rocher, 1952. 129 p.   **11814**

Defends C. against his detractors. Discusses C.'s "invisibility." Considers C. "the first existentialist thinker of our time." Includes exegesis of *L'ange Heurtebise, La Crucifixion,* and *Les enfants terribles.*

Mourgue, Gérard. Jean Cocteau. Eds. universitaires, 1965. 125 p. (Classiques du XXe siècle, 73)   **11815**

Good introductory study of C.'s works in all fields: the novel, criticism, poetry, theater, essay, cinema, and fine arts. Interesting for students who are not yet familiar with C.'s works. Contains broad use of quotations from C.'s texts with explanations and plot summaries. Includes analysis of C.'s last poem *Le requiem.*

Review: J.-M. Andrieu in SynB 233:124–25, 1965.

————. Permanence de la mythologie de Jean Cocteau. RubR 32:30–38, 1967.   **11816**

A discussion of C.'s repeated use of myths and his treatment of characters as mythological figures. Reprints material from his NRF article *Poésie de dessin chez Cocteau* (May 1965), which also appeared in his book *Jean Cocteau* (1965). Examines the manner in which C. turned his themes (the theme of the imposter, the theme of poetry) into myths. Regards C.'s ideas as unchanging since C. was always in favor of the individual who is persecuted by society. Praises C.'s courage, revolt, and genius.

Polanšćak, Antun. Jean Cocteau est mort en automne. SRAZ 15–16: 227–33, 1963.   **11817**

Tribute to C. after his death stressing C.'s link to all the new arts in Paris and C.'s role as animator of all international art movements of his era. Discusses C.'s high regard for friendship and for hard work and craftsmanship. Contains a superficial summary of C.'s achievements in all fields. Regards *Le Potomak* as forerunner of the "new novel."

Rašín, Vera. Les Six and Jean Cocteau. M&L 38:164–69, 1957. **11818**

Briefly discusses the links, "spiritual and social as well as links of technique," between the six composers and C. The two-page listing of C.'s works in collaboration with "Les Six" is useful but incomplete.

Rees, Thomas. Notes on the aesthetics of Jean Cocteau: Clair-obscur, conscious-unconscious. STC 7:51–70, 1971. **11819**

A discussion of the role of the unconscious or involuntary inspiration in C.'s works is followed by a discussion of C.'s efforts to impose a degree of conscious control over his inspiration. Regards C. as follower of Nietzsche who sought to unite Dionysian (romantic and unconscious) with Apollonian (classical and conscious) elements in art. Focuses on convergence of these tendencies in *Clair-obscur*.

Roy, Claude. Jean Cocteau ou vingt ans en 1913. Confl 28:63–70, 1944. **11820**

Stresses importance of the year 1913 in the theater and the arts. Praises C.'s critical intuition as expressed in *Le rappel à l'ordre*. Discusses duality of C. as both man of the theater and serious "inner" man. Compares C.'s closeness to death, love, and poetry to that of Racine. Asks that serious attention be given to *Allégories, Plain-chant,* and *Renaud et Armide*.

Rueff, Jacques. Discours sur Jean Cocteau. *In his:* Discours de réception à l'Académie française et réponse de M. André Maurois. Gallimard, 1965. p. 11–54. **11821**

Tribute to C. by his successor at the French Academy, the economist Jacques Rueff. Stresses C.'s enormous influence in all fields for over fifty years. Expresses gratitude to C. for returning poetry to its etymological meaning; regards all true creators (artists and scientists) as poets.

Turnell, Martin. The achievement of Cocteau. Cweal 45:309–11, Dec. 21, 1956. **11822**

Analysis of C.'s idea of poetry as stemming from late nineteenth century theory of poetry as vision. Regards C. as more important as a publicity artist for other artists than as true creator in

his own right. Second of two articles on C.

———. The legend of Jean Cocteau. Cweal 45:285–87, Dec. 14, 1956. **11823**

Discussion of C.'s early background stressing the importance of the theater and the circus in C.'s boyhood and C.'s beginnings as a poet. Mentions rivalry with Gide for influence over the young. Regards C. as incarnation of the extravagance and caprice of the 1920's. Follows C.'s career to 1955, the year of his election to the French Academy. First in a series of two articles on C.'s artistic achievement.

Vanni, Itale. Jean Cocteau o della giovinezza poetica. NA 493:50–69, 1965. **11824**

A discussion of C. as typical society artist as opposed to the cloistered artist. Considers C. as a seeker of novelties, a great conversationalist, but one who never possessed the gift of being a real poet. Traces C.'s career in all fields, stressing his fondness for theatricality and artificiality, and his unsatisfied desire to be a pure poet.

Novel

Bancroft, David. The poetic wonderland of Cocteau's Thomas l'imposteur. AJFS 3:36–50, 1966. **11825**

An analysis of three basic formula-themes: the Oedipus theme, the Orphic theme, and the theme of a childhood wonderland. *Thomas l'imposteur* is seen as C.'s first successful exposition of the world of childhood as a direct reflection of the world of poetry. Regards the hero Thomas as representative of ideal poetic state for C. because of his innocence and acceptance of things he had never attained for himself.

———. Some notes on the Album des Eugènes in Cocteau's Potomak. AJFS 8:36–43, 1971. **11826**

Analysis of *Le Potomak* as story of a crisis, which began in visual form with the creatures drawn in the *Album des Eugènes*. Regards the innocent couple, the Mortimers, as partial projection of C. himself as he was prior to crisis of 1913. In submitting to the Eugènes, C. is seen as submitting to dictatorship of new forces in the creative world.

Cocteau, Jean. Autour de Thomas l'imposteur. NL 2:1, Oct. 27, 1923. *Also in his:* Le rappel à l'ordre. Stock, 1926. p. 261–69. *Trans.:* Notes concerning Thomas l'imposteur. *In his:* A call to order. London, Faber and Gwyer, 1926. p. 209–18. *Also:* New York, Henry Holt, 1927.
11827

C. defends his novel as not mere showmanship. Calls *Thomas l'imposteur* a text without psychology, a remedy against modernism. Defends himself against accusations of treating the war as a joke and against accusations of being obscure.

Poetry

Bessière, Luc. Artifice et art poétique chez Jean Cocteau. AUMLA 33:48–60, 1970.
11828

After criticizing *Opéra* for being studied and artificial, analyzes C.'s orphism or use of magical power of words. Compares C.'s technique to that of Picasso's collages. Praises *Plain-chant* for the authenticity of its personal sentiments and its lyricism.

Chanel, Pierre. Les vocalises de Bachir-Selim. RLM 298–303:9–24, 1972.   **11829**

An introduction to C.'s *Les vocalises de Bachir-Selim,* a previously unpublished collection of poems. Discusses C.'s trip to Algiers with Lucien Daudet in 1912 as source of inspiration for the poems. Regards *Les vocalises* as transitional work between C.'s early poetry and his poetic novel *Le Potomak.*

Ghéon, Henri. La danse de Sophocle. NRF 45:507–11, 1912.   **11830**

Sees C. as charming young genius, modern incarnation of Musset, but warns against excessive facility. Calls for some modesty on C.'s part.

Jones, E. Some aspects of the image in the poetry of Jean Cocteau. ArL 15:43–86, 174–215, 1963.   **11831**

Analysis of four categories of source material for C.'s images: nature, contemporary civilization, arts and sciences, and everyday life. Extensive examples of various types of images are given from C.'s poems. In the second part of the article, the form of the images is discussed. The nature and function of the image are also analyzed: sensory images, intellectual images, and the symbol. Remarks on C.'s need to guard against obscurity and superficiality.

Legros, Georges. Un poème de Jean Cocteau: Rien ne m'effraye plus... CahAT 11: 72–82, 1969.   **11832**

Analysis of C.'s poem "Rien ne m'effraye plus..." from *Plain-chant,* II in the form of a detailed *explication de texte,* covering syntax, vocabulary, rhythm, and order of presentation. Emphasizes theme of the separation of lovers in sleep, which causes C. great anxiety. Detailed footnotes quote other poems by C. on same theme.

Magnan, Jean-Marie. Paraprosodies de Jean Cocteau. TR 130:125–32, 1958.   **11833**

A discussion of C.'s conception of mystery as luminous, Greek, and Mediterranean. Analysis of poems in collection *Paraprosodies* with emphasis on the oracle, dreams, and the theme of the mirror which enables the poet to delve into his inner world and meet the Seigneur Inconnu that lives within himself. Regards *Paraprosodies* as a great work in the vein of *L'ange Heurtebise; La crucifixion;* and *Les hommages* from the collection *Clair-obscur.*

Margoni, Ives. Jean Cocteau. Bel 19:306–29, 1964.   **11834**

A discussion of C.'s conception of the nature of poetry as defined in *Le secret professionnel* and as exhibited in C.'s works. Considers C. as a partner to important movements in modernizing the arts, but considers many of C.'s works as charming but empty. Praises *Léone, Plain-chant,* and *Requiem* for their emphasis on true role of the poet, on dreams, and on the unconscious.

Pilon, Jean-Guy. Notes sur le dernier choix de poèmes de Jean Cocteau. RevD 63: 107–10, 1957.   **11835**

A discussion of C.'s poetry with stress on his conception of style as an algebra of words. Discusses C.'s constant struggle with death as revealed in his poems. Regards C. as a true suffering poet who remains hidden by all sorts of masks.

Ringer, Gordon. The angel and the automaton: Jean Cocteau. Spectrum 1:3–12, 1957.   **11836**

An uncritical appraisal of C.'s poetic works, which ranks C. along with Valéry as one of the few great poets of the poet-Symbolist age in France.

Stewart, Desmond. Cocteau: the last imagist poet. Europ 10:37–41, 1957. **11837**

Images with "hard, light, clear edges," as defined by Ezra Pound are found in C.'s poetry. A discussion of C.'s poetry as concentrating on the image rather than the idea or system. Speaks of Pound's admiration for C.'s poetry, especially for the poem *Léone*.

Theater

Auric, Georges. Théâtre des Champs-Elysées—Les ballets russes: à propos de Parade. NRF 89:224–27, 1921. **11838**

Salutes triumph of *Parade* at revival. Discusses scandal at first performance four years earlier. Stresses importance of *Parade* in bringing about new order and clarity and bringing an end to sterile imitation of romanticism.

Bancroft, David. A critical re-assessment of Cocteau's Parade. AUMLA 25:83–92, 1966. **11839**

A discussion of *Parade* as an important date in the history of the theater but as a failure in achieving stage synthesis. The choreography of Massine is analyzed as well as Picasso's backdrop and Satie's music. Criticizes C.'s search for novelty as the prevailing element which prevented *Parade* from having necessary unity. Calls *Parade* an "encyclopedia of modernism."

——. Two early Oedipus works by Jean Cocteau. AUMLA 32:165–76, 1969. **11840**

An analysis of *Œdipe-roi* and the opera-oratoria *Oedipus rex* as important works in preparing the way for *La machine infernale*. Examines the deep personal significance of the Oedipus myth for C. who recognized the necessity to submit to his own destiny. Includes detailed discussion of C.'s collaboration with Stravinsky on oratorio *Oedipus rex*.

Bishop, Thomas. Jean Cocteau revisited. ASLHM 39:139–52, 1968. **11841**

Discussion of C.'s dramatic works with emphasis on C.'s esthetics based on mystery, magic and illusion. Asserts that C.'s stress on visual aspects anticipates the stress on objects by recent avant-garde playwrights such as Ionesco and Adamov. Praises *Parade, Les mariés de la Tour Eiffel, Orphée,* and especially *La machine infernale*. Regards C.'s subsequent works as inferior.

Boorsch, Jean. The use of myths in Cocteau's theatre. YFS 5:75–81, 1950. **11842**

C.'s use of myths is regarded as indicative of his lack of spiritual powers. Criticizes levity with which C. handles the supernatural and C.'s idea that "poetry is pun." Blames over-emphasis on chance and mechanical brand of supernatural.

Canto, Patricio. La humiliación de Cocteau. Sur 12:7–19, 1942. **11843**

A perceptive analysis of C.'s *La voix humaine*, stressing the need for the audience to remain faithful to the spirit of childhood. Compares C. to the heroine of his play since he too humbled himself in trying to please the public by every possible means.

Cutts, John P. They do it with mirrors: Shakespeare and Cocteau. RLC 38:121–27, 1964. **11844**

Analysis of the use of mirrors in Shakespeare's *Richard II* and in C.'s *Orphée* and *Le sang d'un poète* to explore the fragmented depths of the protagonists. Finds many similarities between the character of *Richard II* and that of C.'s poet in film *Le sang d'un poète*.

Dubourg, Pierre. Dramaturgie de Jean Cocteau. Grasset, 1954. 277 p. **11845**

First full-length study of C.'s dramatic works. Lucid analysis of C.'s plays and films. Openly admits own admiration for C.'s works. Argues that C.'s writings should be taken seriously. Defends the play *Bacchus* against attacks by François Mauriac. Contains introduction by Thierry Maulnier who praises Dubourg's study but disagrees with him regarding the quarrel over *Bacchus*.

Farabet, René. Jean Cocteau: une chimie du théâtre. RHT 17:178–81, 1965. **11846**

The theater is regarded as ideal instrument for C.'s natural effervescence. A discussion of C.'s interest in stage decor and mechanisms. Considers C.

most inventive and original in his early theatrical works. Includes letter from C. to Jouvet expressing admiration for Giraudoux's *Intermezzo,* March 1933.

Fergusson, Francis. Edipo según Freud, Sófocles y Cocteau. Asom 21:29–36, 1965. **11847**

A comparison of the character of Oedipus as he appears in Sophocles' tragedy, Freud's theories, and C.'s *La machine infernale,* stressing C.'s debt to Freud in his use of dreams and slips of the tongue. While judging C.'s play somewhat artificial and his protagonists caricatures, the author praises C. for celebrating the mystery of human nature and man's possibilities for good or evil.

———. The infernal machine: the myth behind the modern city. *In his:* The idea of a theatre. Princeton, Princeton univ. press, 1949. p. 197–203. **11848**

This brief essay examines *La machine infernale* for its Pirandellesque use of the stage as an art medium. Fergusson feels that C.'s play is successful in intertwining the common sense aspects of daily life (which occupy the foreground of the drama) with the darkness of the eternal myth (which occupies the background).

Feynman, Alberta E. The infernal machine, Hamlet and Ernest Jones. MD 6:72–83, 1963. **11849**

A discussion of Ernest Jones' interpretation of *Hamlet* as a probable source for C.'s *The infernal machine.* Finds similarities between *Hamlet* and *The infernal machine* in ghost scenes, bedroom scenes, and scene in which hero rejects beautiful young girl. Views C.'s play as masterpiece fusing Sophocles, Shakespeare and Freud.

Fowlie, Wallace. Cocteau. *In his:* Dionysus in Paris. Meridian, 1960. p. 74–88. **11850**

Introductory discussion of C.'s most important plays, with particular emphasis given to *Orphée.* There is nothing very new in this chapter, but the book is valuable for the way it places C. in the context of other major contemporary French dramatists.

———. Cocteau: the theatre. *In his:* Age of surrealism. The swallow press and William Morrow and co., 1950. p. 120–37. **11851**

André Breton and the other surrealists would not approve, but C. has a chapter to himself in this volume as an artist who was "close to surrealism and yet never actively participated in it." C.'s fame will have its surest foundation in his plays. Good discussion of *Orphée* and one of the most sensible essays ever written on *Le sang d'un poète.*

———. Tragedy in the plays of Cocteau. FR 15:463–67, 1942. **11852**

Discussion of C. as one of the few contemporary writers to have understood meaning of tragedy. Praises *Antigone* and *La machine infernale* for showing dual vision of man's grandeur and frailty. Regards *Les chevaliers de la Table Ronde* and *Les parents terribles* as just as oracular as C.'s Greek tragedies. States that public fails to appreciate greatness of C.'s plays because these theatrical works are too simple and luminous to be seen.

Gassner, John. Cocteau and The infernal machine. *In his:* The theatre in our times. Crown, 1954. p. 184–93. **11853**

An ironic attack on C.'s *The infernal machine* as "theatricalism" without humanity. While admitting that C. can be delightful when playfulness is appropriate (as in his films), criticizes *The infernal machine* as a work of clever showmanship, which fails to explore the tragic nature of man.

Gehle, Heinz. Das dramatische Werk von Jean Cocteau. NS n.s. 3:305–11, 1954. **11854**

A survey of C.'s dramatic works with emphasis on the themes of order and disorder, illusion and reality, fate, and the revelation of truth. Regards C. as a serious poet who writes from his own heartfelt experiences.

Grossvogel, David I. Cocteau. *In his:* The self-conscious stage in modern French drama. Columbia univ. press, 1958. p. 47–67. **11855**

Criticizes C. for not creating characters sufficiently real to involve the spectator in their inner drama. Negative analysis of all C.'s plays as superficial poetry of objects where scenic appearances are more important than the dilemma of man.

Guicharnaud, Jacques. The double game: Jean Cocteau. *In his:* Modern French theatre from Giraudoux to Beckett. In collaboration with June Beckelman. New Haven, Yale univ. press, 1961. p. 48–68. *Also in his:* Modern French theatre from Giraudoux to Genet. In collaboration with June Guicharnaud. New Haven, Yale univ. press, 1967. p. 44–64.   **11856**

A good general introduction to C.'s plays. While calling C. an "understudy of genius," this essay also gives serious treatment of C.'s originality: his use of dreams, intimacy, and witchcraft. Concludes with a comparison between C. and Tennessee Williams who both portray a couple, that is actually a divided hermaphrodite who tries in vain to possess himself.

Jones, J. W. Baudelaire's chandelier: poésie de théâtre, Cocteau et Ghelderode. UDR 4:37–50, 1967.   **11857**

Presents C. as forerunner of today's avant-garde theater. Discusses C.'s two precursors, Jarry (*Ubu roi*) and Apollinaire (*Les mamelles de Tirésias*), who paved the way for C.'s *Parade* and *Les mariés de la Tour Eiffel*. C. and Ghelderode are both seen as writing parodies of the *pièce bien-faite*. Examines intrusion of the supernatural in C.'s plays and C.'s pictorial approach to the theater.

Lobet, Marcel. Jean Cocteau chorépoète des Ballets russes. RGB 95:73–84, 1959.   **11858**

A discussion of C.'s work in the field of ballet from *Le dieu bleu* (1912) to the more recent *Phèdre* and *La dame à la licorne*. *Parade* is analyzed as a "fertile failure" which incorporated familiar objects, details of the circus world, and mime, and opened a new era for choreography in the theater. C.'s long association with Diaghilev is examined.

Long, Chester Clayton. Cocteau's Orphée: from myth to drama and film. QJS 51: 311–25, 1965.   **11859**

Three structures: myth, drama, and film are studied for their radical differences. C.'s play is regarded as structurally one long and effective *coup de théâtre*, shattering conventions. Different roles for Death (the Princess), Cégeste, and Heurtebise are discussed in C.'s film. Appreciation is shown for special qualities of both C.'s play and film.

Magnan, Jean-Marie. Lettre à Jean Cocteau. TR 163:25–37, 1961.   **11860**

Discussion of various works by C. including the *Corrida du premier mai*, *Orphée* and *Les mariés de la Tour Eiffel*. Stresses C.'s need for discipline and restraint and his desire to communicate with the common people as expressed in his creation of the Chapel of St. Peter at Villefranche. Concludes with impressions of C.'s film *Le testament d'Orphée* and his death scene in that film.

Mauriac, François. Lettre à Jean Cocteau. FL 1, 5, Dec. 29, 1951.   **11861**

Angry letter in which Mauriac explains the reasons that forced him to walk out before the first curtain call at the premier of C.'s play *Bacchus*. Accuses C. of "tying his Mother the Church to a pillar and whipping Her." This letter provoked a bitter reply from C., entitled *Je t'accuse*, published in *France-Soir*, and led to a break between the two writers. One of the essays in C.'s *Journal d'un inconnu* also deals with this quarrel over *Bacchus*.

Milorad. Le mythe orphique dans l'œuvre de Cocteau. *In:* Jean Cocteau 1. *See* 11783. p. 109–42.   **11862**

A discussion of Orphée as the prototype of the poet. Examines various sources of inspiration for C.'s play *Orphée* and suggests keys to its characters. Describes the reappearance of the characters of the Orpheus myth under different names and sexes in other works by C.

Muir, Lynette R. Cocteau's Les chevaliers de la Table Ronde: a baroque play? ML 40:115–20, 1959.   **11863**

An analysis of *Les chevaliers de la Table Ronde* in which sources such as early 17th-century ballets, pastorals and tragi-comedies are proposed. The role of the enchanter and the use of doubles are discussed in C.'s other theatrical works as well. Asserts that *Les chevaliers* contains the elements of a baroque play as defined by Jean Rousset in his *La littérature de l'âge baroque en France: Circé et le paon* (1953).

Oxenhandler, Neal. Scandal and parade. New Brunswick, N.J., Rutgers univ. press, 1957. 284 p. *Also:* London, Constable, 1958. 294 p.   **11864**

The only full-length study in English of C. as a dramatist. Perceptive thematic analysis of all C.'s plays. Focuses on C.'s persecution complex and on its reflection in C.'s tracked-down heroes. Superior to Dubourg. A fine chapter on C.'s films.

Reviews: C. Christofides in Sym 13: 148–51, 1959; J. O'Brien in TBR 12, Dec. 22, 1957 and in RR 49:313–14, 1958.

Steegmuller, Francis. A propos de l'Antigone de Cocteau. *In:* Jean Cocteau 1. *See* 11783. p. 167–72.   **11865**

A discussion of Gide's negative reaction to C.'s *Antigone,* as stated in Gide's journal entry of Jan. 16, 1923: "Patina is the reward of masterpieces."

Trooz, Charles de. Littérature et impiété. RGB 90:893–906, 1954.   **11866**

A discussion of C.'s *Bacchus,* Mauriac's angry reaction to the play, and Sartre's *Le diable et le bon Dieu.* Regards *Bacchus* as an inferior work that Mauriac should not have even bothered to attack. Discusses similarities between *Bacchus* and Sartre's play, judging both plays cold, artificial, and lacking in nobility. Deplores successes of these two plays and other fashionable works that glorify impiety.

Vial, Fernand. The Mauriac-Cocteau controversy. Ren 5:131–35, 1953.   **11867**

An analysis of the play *Bacchus* and of the ensuing controversy between C. and François Mauriac. Agrees with Mauriac that *Bacchus* is a vicious attack against the Church and adds that C.'s own comments about the play are intentionally confusing and hypocritical.

Wirtz, Otto. Das poetologische Theater Jean Cocteaus. Geneva, Droz; Paris, Minard, 1972. 123 p. (Kölner romanistische Arbeiten, Neue Folge 41)   **11868**

A well-documented study of C.'s theory of poetry and its application to his dramatic works. Focuses on style and structure of C.'s plays and on the problems of C.'s introspective poet-heroes.

Cinema

Bancroft, David. Cocteau-Orphée: filmmaker—poet. Mean 32:73–79, 1973.   **11869**

An analysis of the film *Orphée* as successful fusion of craft and the mysterious beauty of the transcendent experience. Orphée's second visit to the Zone is discussed for the analogy it presents between artistic creation and childbirth and for its vision of the elimination of the normal concepts of time and space. Praises use of camera *trucage* to increase sense of mystery. Agrees with C. that film is ideal medium for having viewer experience the trance ·of poetry.

Bazin, André. Théâtre et cinéma. *In his:* Qu'est-ce que le cinéma? II. Le cinéma et les autres arts. Eds. du cerf, 1959. p. 69–118. *Trans.:* What is cinema? V. I. Berkeley, Univ. of California press, 1967. p. 76–124.   **11870**

A classic essay, arguing that the most successful films made from plays are those that respect the written word and the theatrical nature of the material. One of the examples discussed at length is C.'s film *Les parents terribles,* a great success precisely because C. used cinema not to enlarge the play but to intensify its action. [MP]

Beylie, Claude. Cocteau. *In:* Anthologie du cinéma, 1966. p. 57–112. (Sup. to AvSc-C 56:1966)   **11871**

This booklet, published two years after a study of similar scope by René Gilson, inevitably covers the same ground in somewhat briefer fashion. Nevertheless, Beylie is a fine writer and a perceptive critic who knows how to make firm distinctions (sometimes too firm; he finds *L'éternel retour* "rather insipid"). His viewpoint often differs from that of Gilson, and this study should not be overlooked merely because Gilson's is more readily available. [MP]

Bishop, John Peale. A film of Jean Cocteau. *In his:* The collected essays of John Peale Bishop. Scribner's, 1948. p. 222–26.   **11872**

An important early (1932) American reaction to *Le sang d'un poète.* This essay is mostly plot summary, but Bishop makes many valid points, correctly linking the symbols in the film to C.'s poetry. He calls C. a "dilettante of genius" and compares this film to Buñuel's *Un chien andalou*. [MP]

Boisdeffre, Pierre de. Orphée ou le secret de Jean Cocteau. *In his:* Des vivants et des morts. Témoignages 1948–1953. Eds. universitaires, 1954. p. 279–85.   **11873**
Analysis of film *Orphée* as indicative of C.'s inner nature. Explains how, in *Orphée,* dream has become reality, death has become Orphée's death. Each scene of the film paraphrases a myth. For C. art is seen as a means of communicating with the absolute. [MP]

Cocteau, Jean. La belle et la bête, journal d'un film. J.-B. Janin, 1946. 253 p. 24 photos. *Also:* Monaco, Eds. du rocher, 1958. 269 p. 20 photos. *Trans.:* Diary of a film. London, Dobson, 1950. 216 p. *Also:* New York, Roy, 1950. *Also:* Beauty and the beast: diary of a film. New York, Dover, 1972. 142 p.   **11874**
A day to day account of the making of the film. C. describes his physical and mental states, his anxieties and his triumphs during the filming of *La belle et la bête*. Essential for anyone interested in the finished film, or in any of C.'s films. [MP]

————. Du cinématographe. Pierre Belfond, 1973. 191 p.   **11875**
Shorter writings by C. on the cinema, most of them collected from periodicals dating back as far as 1925. Surprisingly little appears here that adds to the material in previous volumes, but all students of C.'s films will want to read his views on other directors and synopses of the films he was unable to direct. Very few libraries contain more than a fraction of the material reprinted here. [MP]

————. Entretiens autour du cinématographe. André Bonne, 1951. 175 p. *Also in his:* Entretiens sur le cinématographe. Pierre Belfond, 1973. p. 9–91. *Trans.:* Cocteau on the film. New York, Roy, 1954. p. *Also:* London, D. Dobson, 1954. *Also:* with new introduction by George Amberg. New York, Dover, 1972. 141 p.   **11876**
Lively conversations between André Fraigneau and C., interesting and accessible to the layman. C. speaks of cinema as vehicle for promoting thought and excellent medium for communicating with wide audience. Includes discussions on all of C.'s major films. Recommended for all students of cinema. [MP]

————. Entretiens sur le cinématographe. Pierre Belfond, 1973. 188 p.   **11877**
Includes all of *Entretiens autour du cinématographe* (*see* 11876) plus several briefer interviews, including an important one with *Cahiers du cinéma* (1960). The added material is often of great importance, since the interviews with Fraigneau do not include *Le testament d'Orphée*. [MP]

————. Postface. *In his:* Le sang d'un poète. Robert Marin, 1948. p. 95–107. *Also:* Monaco, Eds. du rocher, 1957. p. 103–16. *Trans.:* Postscript. *In his:* The blood of a poet. New York, The Bodley press, 1949. p. 45–53. *Also:* Postscript. *In his:* Two screenplays. New York, The Orion press, 1968. p. 61–67.   **11878**
While refusing to provide his own interpretation of the film, C. actually manages to suggest his own interpretation very clearly. This text of a 1932 talk is the best thing C. wrote about this film. All of these volumes also contain a Preface written in 1948. [MP]

Decock, Jean. Preface. *In:* Cocteau, Jean. La belle et la bête. Scénario et dialogues de Jean Cocteau... Texte inédit présenté par Robert M. Hammond. New York, New York univ. press, 1970. p. v–xiv.   **11879**
A sensitive study of the signs and symbols in C.'s film, comparing the film to the original story. Also in this volume is Robert M. Hammond's account of the fortuitous discovery of the filmscript. Hammond details the differences between the filmscript, reprinted here, and the finished film. [MP]

Gilson, René. Jean Cocteau. Seghers, 1964. 190 p. (Cinéma d'aujourd'hui, 27) *Trans.:* New York, Crown, 1969. 192 p.   **11880**
This volume is invaluable for anyone who is interested in C.'s work as a film-maker. The essay by Gilson is followed by excerpts from C.'s writing on the cinema, from his screenplays, and from critics and C.'s colleagues. The filmography is excellent. *Le sang d'un poète* is treated rather briefly, and

throughout his study Gilson dismisses symbols and explication. He concentrates on the adaptation of plays and other works to the film medium and on major themes, such as "the choice between love and poetry." Gilson has a thorough knowledge of C.'s non-cinematic work and of great films by other directors. [MP]

Review: B. Knapp in JML 1:746–48, 1971 supplement.

Hammond, Robert M. Jensen's Gradiva: a clue to the composition of Cocteau's Orphée. Sym 27:126–36, 1973. **11881**

Gradiva, a surrealist work by the German author Wilhelm Jensen (1902), is examined as an important source that influenced C.'s transformation of his play *Orphée* and his film *Le sang d'un poète* into the film *Orphée.* [MP]

———. The mysteries of Cocteau's Orpheus. CinJ 26–33, spring 1972. **11882**

A summary of other critics' views of C.'s film *Orpheus,* pointing out inadequacies in their interpretations. Some of the mysteries of the film—for example, the enigmatic final line—must remain partly unsolved. The shooting script of the film (discovered by Hammond) is compared in one important respect to the published screenplay: the character played by Maria Casarès was changed from Death to Orpheus' death. [MP]

Oxenhandler, Neal. On Cocteau. FilmQ 18:12–14, 1964. **11883**

An excellent review of *Le testament d'Orphée,* incorporating personal reminiscences. [MP]

Pillaudin, Roger. Jean Cocteau tourne son dernier film. Table ronde, 1960. 173 p., 21 drawings. **11884**

Pillaudin spent six weeks watching the filming of *Le testament d'Orphée,* and while he does not analyze the film at all, he provides every detail imaginable about how it was made. He also interviewed C. at every opportunity, and although most of C.'s remarks about his films repeat material published elsewhere, there is enough new material to make this volume another necessity for every student of C.'s films. [MP]

Simon, Karl Günter. Jean Cocteau oder Die Poesie im Film. Berlin, Rembrandt-Verlag, 1958. 63 p. **11885**

A 29-page study of C.'s career as a film-maker from *Le sang d'un poète* through *Orphée,* followed by 30 pages of photographs from C.'s films. Stresses C.'s uniqueness in being both a Harlequin and a poet. Argues that the fascination of C.'s films stems not from their dramatic plots but from an esthetically perfect form, which is best achieved in *La belle et la bête.*

Wallis, C. G. The blood of the poet. KR 6:24–42, 1944. **11886**

A detailed analysis of the film as an extended allegory. Wallis calls his study "tentative and cursory in scope and presumably incorrect in certain details," but there are few studies that are more impressive. Since Wallis makes scant mention of sexuality and none at all of C.'s other works, this lengthy interpretation is actually a tour de force. [MP]

Weyergans, François, et al. Le chiffre sept. CduC 152:4–18, 1964. **11887**

Seven writers associated with *Cahiers du cinéma* discuss C.'s seven most important films. For CduC during that period C. was one of the most important French directors, and here tribute is paid by Jean-Luc Godard, Jacques Rivette and François Truffaut, among others. Of greatest interest is the discussion of the film *L'aigle à deux têtes* by Jacques Doniol-Valcroze; the play itself has seldom been treated so cogently. [MP]

Rapprochements

Iskander, Fayez. Yeats and Cocteau: two anti-romanticists. CaiSE 4:119–35, 1963–66. **11888**

A discussion of Yeats' anti-romanticism leads to a discussion of C.'s reaction against the romantic cult of Wagnerism. Similarities are found between Yeats' symbolical plays and C.'s theatrical works, which are an amalgamation of various techniques of ballet, acrobatics, pantomime, orchestra and dialog.

Marteau, Robert. De Gongora à Cocteau. Esp 309:333–36, 1962. **11889**

Gongora, Spanish poet of submersion (1561–1627), is compared to C. for whom poetry is also a diving into the mysterious depths. C.'s last book

Requiem, in particular, is considered to show the spiritual lessons of Góngora.

Martin, Claude. Gide, Cocteau, Œdipe: le mythe ou le complexe. *In:* Jean Cocteau 1. *See* 11783. *p.* 143–65.   **11890**

A comparative study of Gide's *Œdipe* and C.'s *La machine infernale,* focusing on their differences. Gide is considered to have sought rational interpretation of human existence in myths while C. leaves the supernatural roots in the myth and gives Freud's Oedipus complex an aura of mystery.

Müller, Bodo. Orpheus und der Schwan vom Betis. Zu Jean Cocteaus Góngora-Rezeption. ZFSL 75:193–227, 1965.   **11891**

A stylistic analysis of C.'s poetic style in comparison with that of the Spanish poet Góngora. Describes C.'s fascination with Spain and Spanish culture.

Neame, Alan. From Léone to Bergotte. FS 13:146–53, 1959.   **11892**

A discussion of C. as disciple of late-Parnassian poets whose works concentrate on images rather than ideas.

Analysis of poem *Léone* stresses theatrical images and importance of Breton legend of Tristan and Isolde. Regards Proust's *Un amour de Swann* as a source of inspiration for *Léone.*

Popo, E. Jean Cocteau en de Franse Six. VlG 49:246–56, 1965.   **11893**

C. and the French Six. In his ballet-scenarios C. emphasizes the dramatic rather than the literary and picturesque; he aims at beauty that is particular to the theater: pantomime, dance, music, sounds, stylized scenery, silence even. His essay *Le coq et l'arlequin* (1918) distinguishes between art based on French sources and traditions and the eclecticism and confusion of late German and Russian romantics. C. wants simple, everyday music. Concludes with a description of works produced by Satie, Durey, Honegger, Milhaud, Tailleferre, Poulenc and Auric in collaboration with C. from 1917 through the fifties in particular the ballet *Les mariés de la Tour Eiffel* (1921) and the films of the 1940's where music, words and image complete each other to form a dramatic whole. [MM]

CHAPTER XXVII

DRAMA: THE *METTEURS EN SCENE*

(Nos. 11894–12185)

Biruta Cap, Laurence W. Cor, Renée Geen, Barbara Gordon, David B. Parsell,
Norman H. Paul, and Alex Szogyi

JEAN-LOUIS BARRAULT
(Nos. 11894–11946)

Alex Szogyi

Biography

Barrault, Jean-Louis. Souvenirs pour demain. Seuil, 1972. 390 p. (Collection Points) *Trans.*: Memories for tomorrow. Trans. by J. Griffin. Dutton, 1974. 335 p. **11894**

B. recounts the story of his career from his early days of theatrical apprenticeship under Charles Dullin. Record of personalities from his mother to Gide, Sartre, Artaud, Claudel. Also the events of 1968 and his production of *Rabelais*. Index and illustrations.

Bourdet, Denise. Images de Paris. RdP 54: 151–55, 1947. **11895**

The history of the couple Renaud-B., how they met and worked together. Basically, the beginnings of B.

————. Pris sur le vif. Préf. de Paul Morand. Avec un portrait de Jean Cocteau. Plon, 1957. 264 p., passim. **11896**

Parisian sketches including Jouvet, Renaud, B., Montherlant, Giraudoux, Salacrou, *et al.* Superficial but vivid treatment of B.

Claudel, Paul. Mémoires improvisés. Quarante et un entretiens avec Jean Amrouche. Texte établi par Louis Fournier. Gallimard, 1969. 380 p. **11897**

Mostly about Claudel himself. Describes the difficulties he had with B. concerning *Partage de midi*. He had several versions submitted to B., who disliked the one Claudel liked best. B. reveals himself as very stubborn and independent.

Le ministère des affaires culturelles licencie Jean-Louis Barrault. Monde 7353:22, Sept. 4, 1968. **11898**

Expresses dismay at B.'s dismissal after the students took over the Odéon theater.

O'Brady, Frédéric. Contributions to the Jean-Louis Barrault story. ASLHM 38: 157–65, 1967. **11899**

A touching memoir of the actor's friendship with B. It begins with B.'s adaptation of Hamsun's *Hunger*, continues with the youthful B. given to imitating Dullin, mentions Etienne Decroux' teaching, *Numancia, Hamlet,* describes meetings with B. during the war and the kindness of B. and Renaud when he was in prison. He chides B.'s critics and shows B.'s Olympian indifference to them.

Barrault on Barrault

Barrault, Jean-Louis. Je suis homme de théâtre. Conquistador, 1955. 146 p. (Mon métier) **11900**

The book is divided into four parts: Generalities; A day in the theater; A production; Everyday life during a *tournée*. B. defines the mission of the theater and its servants, the classical theater, theatrical creativity which is compared to an act of love. The natural environment for him would seem to be the nomadic life.

————. Journal de bord; Japon, Israël, Grèce, Yougoslavie. Julliard, 1961. 218 p. **11901**

The Compagnie Renaud-Barrault visits these countries in 1960, and appears in Tokyo, Osaka, Tel-Aviv, Haifa, Jerusalem, Athens, Belgrade, Zagreb. The actor is fulfilled when on tour. Accurate and detailed accounts.

―――. Nouvelles réflexions sur le théâtre. Préf. d'Armand Salacrou. Flammarion, 1959. 282 p. (Bibliothèque d'esthétique) *Trans.:* The theatre of Jean-Louis Barrault. Trans. by Jòseph Chiari. Hill and Wang, 1961. 244 p. **11902**

B. reviews, ten years after his *Reflections on the theatre,* the accumulated experience of his career, centered especially on his own company and theater. It is a record of thirteen years of work, the dreams, ambitions, theories and drives of a total man of theater at once an actor, a mime, a director, a producer and even a total manager. A rare form of theatrical literary history valuable to scholars as well as to amateurs of the theater; ranging from Giraudoux to Kafka, and from Aeschylus to the *commedia dell'arte.* Reviews: J. Duvignaud in JPNP 58:249–50, 1961; A Szogyi in TBR Nov. 5, 1961.

―――. Paul Claudel. Notizen zu persönlichen Erinnerungen. NRs 1:17–50, 1954. Trans. by W. Reich. **11903**

Narrates B.'s collaboration with Claudel, whom he met at Dullin's theater. Expresses the opinion that the only one who should have exercised the right to criticize Claudel would have been Artaud.

―――. Réflexions sur le théâtre. J. Vautrain, 1949. 212 p. *Trans.:* Reflections on the theatre. Trans. by Barbara Wall. London, Rockliff, 1951. xi, 182 p. *Also:* New York, Macmillan, 1952. **11904**

B. sees the theater not only as the art of the ephemeral, but also of the renewal. The book is subdivided into three parts. From 1931 until 1939, it deals with the young playwrights, their elementary education, Antonin Artaud. Part II, from 1940–1946, deals mostly with the Comédie Française and his work with Claudel. Part III, from 1946–1949: the theater as the art of actuality and justice. Indexed. Drawings by Christian Bérard and others. Review: Anon. in TLS 2559:674, 1951.

―――. The theatrical phenomenon. (Trans. by B. Markus). ETJ 17:89–100, 1956. **11905**

A lecture on the vocation of the actor which is inseparable from the man. After thirty years of experience, the theater appears to be both the grandest and most absurd of professions. B. sees life as a tightrope walk and playing as an essential part of it all. The theater is an independent art, independent from literature and from all other arts. It is also impure because the human being is fragile and inconstant. The actor's art consists of fashioning a disciplined instrument from an undisciplined human being.

Knapp, Bettina L. Interview with Barrault. *In:* Off-stage voices. Interviews with modern French dramatists. Ed. by Alba Amoia. Whitston, 1975. p. 41–46. **11906**

Questions and answers about B.'s career, Stanislavski, Claudel, Vauthier, Blin. Also about his performance of Faulkner's *As I lay dying,* on the actor's profession, on the influence of Stanislavski, on the theater of the absurd, as well as his rehearsal techniques.

Lamont, Rosette C. Entretien avec Jean-Louis Barrault. FR 45:31–36, 1971. **11907**

Interview concerning B.'s dramatization of the *Five books* of Rabelais. B. discusses his affinities with Rabelais and compares him with Villon. Alludes to another "mauvais garçon," Artaud, and speaks of their years together. Mentions the drawings made by Rabelais which he used as panels above the stage and which influenced the costumes worn by the actors.

Pilikian, Houhannes I. Dialogue with Barrault. Dr 89:50–54, 1968. **11908**

Interview during the visit of B. in London. B. remembers his first major appearance in 1935, in a play by Faulkner. His concept of the theater has remained unchanged. He does not feel alone any more since the advent of Grotowski, the Living theater, Béjart, Peter Brook. Yet, total theater is still to come. He views himself and M. Renaud as merely innovators. He favors evolution, not revolution, speaks about his anxieties and the human condition. He feels we are probably going toward a "naked theater."

General Studies: Books

Chancerel, Léon. Jean-Louis Barrault ou L'ange noir du théâtre. Presses littéraires de France, 1953. 83 p. (Les metteurs en scène)   **11909**

Discusses the concept of total theater. Imagines an interview with the reader concerning the influence of Copeau and Jouvet on B. Describes B.'s theatrical methods.

Frank, André. Jean-Louis Barrault. Textes de Jean-Louis Barrault. Points de vue critiques. Témoignages. Chronologie. Bibliographie. Illustrations. Seghers, 1971. 192 p. (Théâtre de tous les temps) **11910**

The only complete work on B. The author was the secretary of the Compagnie Renaud-Barrault. He writes a chronicle encompassing forty years of B.'s activities as a total "homme de théâtre." B. explains himself through his writings and is in turn explained by Artaud, Claudel, Chancerel, etc. Excellent documents on the plays produced.

General Studies: Articles

Bentley, Eric. The actor as a thinker. ThA 34:31–34, 1950.   **11911**

Sees B. as not primarily a writer, but as a thinker from the opposite Brechtian camp. For B., the essence of the theater is in the use of the first person and the present tense; the actor is a child identifying himself with external nature. The language of B. is romantic and grandiloquent, in the manner of Gordon Craig. As a philosopher, he hesitates between estheticism and mysticism. B. is the heir of Copeau. His theater has all the limitations of a certain period, a certain group, a certain class. Even if his writings are bogus, he is a serious thinker.

Brissaud, André. Un mystique du théâtre: Jean-Louis Barrault. SynB 2:40–53, 1947.   **11912**

Considers B.'s meeting with Dullin as crucial. He is a reformist, a revolutionary, but not a rebel. He illustrates brilliantly the concept of total theater.

Lyons, Charles R. La compagnie Madeleine Renaud—Jean-Louis Barrault: the idea

and the aesthetic. ETJ 19:415–25, 1967.   **11913**

Credit is given to B. for maintaining a private theater dedicated to experiments of new playwrights' works which, at the same time, attempted to rediscover the classics in terms of their current vitality. Through his writings, B. notes the artistic advantages of the repertory system. He quotes B. himself as well as Eric Bentley. He praises B.'s unique artistic achievement in self-sustained repertory and explorations of the esthetic.

Mignon, Paul-Louis. La première campagne de Marigny. CRB 5:27–34, 1954. **11914**

From 1946 to 1952, B. created eighteen extraordinary performances, exceptionally diversified. He inherits the experience of the Cartel and completes it.

Briefer Mention

Artaud, Antonin. Œuvres complètes. V. 4. Le théâtre et son double. Le théâtre de Séraphin. Les Cenci. Gallimard, 1964. p. 168.   **11915**

Extremely complimentary regarding B.'s production of *Autour d'une mère.*

———. Œuvres complètes. V. 8. De quelques problèmes d'actualité aux messages révolutionnaires. Lettres du Mexique. Gallimard, 1971. p. 254–55, 362, 366.   **11916**

Deals with B. and asserts that the French theater is looking for a myth.

Billetdoux, François. Lettre à Jean-Louis Barrault. CRB 46:13–17, 1964.   **11917**

The decline of the theater because of the media. He praises B.'s generosity towards the authors and the musicality of his theater. He blames Claudel and Giraudoux. He does not care about the Odéon but about B.

Brunel, Pierre. Claudel et Shakespeare. A. Colin, 1971. p. 237.   **11918**

In Chapter VI the author analyzes B.'s interpretations of *Hamlet.* He also shows that Claudel liked B. only as a mime.

Bugard, Pierre. Jean-Louis Barrault. *In his:* Le comédien et son double. Psychologie

du comédien. Stock, 1970. p. 217–24.
11919

Solitude seen as the main theme of B.'s career. Bugard remembers a dialog with B. who confided in him. For B., theater is love.

Christout, Marie-Françoise. Le merveilleux et le théâtre du silence en France à partir du XVIIᵉ siècle. Paris-The Hague, Mouton, 1965. p. 125, 191, 351, 352, 399, 411. **11920**

Fully indexed and with a 20 p. bibliography. Discusses Bachelard, Claudel, Cocteau, *et al.* B. is considered as a mime and as an interpreter of Claudel.

Corvin, Michel. Le théâtre nouveau en France. Presses univ. de France, 1963. p. 105. (Que sais-je?) *Also:* Deuxième éd. mise à jour. Presses univ. de France, 1967. 126 p. **11921**

B. as a successor of the Cartel. The *mise en scène* becomes with him an act of love, reaching a perfect unity between the audience and the actor and creating something which goes beyond reality. Unfortunately his style is not pure.

Dejean, Jean-Luc. Le théâtre français d'aujourd'hui. F. Nathan, Alliance Française, 1971. p. 145. (Où en est la France?)
11922

Bibliography and illustrations. Subdivided into three parts: *Le théâtre d'inspiration traditionnelle; Le théâtre nouveau; Mise en scène et théâtre public.* B. as a "metteur en scène" together with Vilar. He is considered one of the masters.

Dort, Bernard. Nouveaux théâtres à l'heure du choix. *In his:* Théâtre public. 1953–1966. Essais de critique. Seuil, 1967. p. 334–61. (Pierres vives) **11923**

Analyzes the activity of the Company at the Odéon. He feels that B. is forever young in his passion for the theater.

Flanner, Janet (Genêt). Paris journal, 1944–1965. Edited by W. Shawn. Atheneum, 1965. 615 p., passim. *Also:* London, V. Golancz, 1966. 615 p. **11924**

Fully indexed. B. is often treated, as well as R. Aron, Beckett, Camus, Claudel, Genet, Gide, *et al.* He is considered more as an interpreter of Billetdoux, Kafka, Genet. Very little

on B. specifically and more on M. Renaud.

Fluchère, Henri. Shakespeare in France: 1900–1948. *In:* Shakespearean study and production. 2. Ed. by A. Nicoll. Cambridge univ. press, 1949. p. 115–25. *Also:* 1966. **11925**

Appreciates B.'s productions as having a particular character of their own. The part played by the mask as well as that of tragedy. He requires a luxurious sense of theater to be seen in the costumes, scenery, lighting and the sumptuousness of the *mise en scène.* His production of *Hamlet* is overstylized.

Gouhier, Henri. De l'effort intellectuel au théâtre. TR 179:149–54, 1963. **11926**

The outlook of the philosopher more than of the "amateur de théâtre." Sees B. as a typical intellectual. He falsifies the issues slightly.

Knowles, Dorothy. French drama of the interwar years, 1918–1939. London, Harrap, 1967. 334 p., passim. **11927**

Fully indexed, it treats Copeau, Dullin, Jouvet, Pitoëff, Baty, Artaud, B., *et al.* B. is abundantly mentioned in the context of total theater. Unlike Baty, he defines his position as an actor. B. maintains that there is a visible language, a significant form of body movement which should accompany the spoken language and be consistent with it.

Larthomas, Pierre. Le langage dramatique. Sa nature, ses procédés. A. Colin, 1972. 478 p., passim. **11928**

From Achard to Anouilh and from Sartre to Vilar. B.'s production of the *Oresteia* is disparaged, but his writings on *Phèdre* are commended. He is often quoted *re* gesture. Bibliography.

Sandier, Gilles. Vie et mort des classiques. *In his:* Théâtre et combat. Regards sur le théâtre actuel. Essai. Stock, 1970. p. 151–96 and passim. **11929**

A very important place is accorded B.'s productions of Beaumarchais, Billetdoux, Claudel, Ionesco, Shakespeare. His *Rabelais* is commended. His interpretation of *Bérénice* is praised. Fully indexed.

Surer, Paul. Le théâtre français contemporain. Société d'édition et d'enseignement supérieur, 1964. p. 309–16. **11930**

B. is completely delineated in the chapter entitled "Des nouveaux animateurs." There is first a biographical study of him, then some of his writings. Also included, a thorough analysis of the plays he staged. Total theater is seen as an international theater. B. is a genius with all the shortcomings derived from excess.

Tynan, Kenneth. Tynan on theatre. Harmondsworth, Middlesex, Penguin books, 1964. 364 p., passim. (A pelican book, A657) **11931**

Fully indexed. Covers Anouilh, Beckett, Genet, Giraudoux, Ionesco, Feydeau, et al. B. is given an impressionistic and sympathetic treatment as a man of the theater with an original personality. He is fine with Feydeau and Claudel and not so fine in The Misanthrope. For Tynan, he is a director of high intellectual vigor but he lacks the stature of a great actor. B.'s supreme virtue is that he would attempt anything, Shakespeare as well as Chekhov.

Weber, Warner. Figuren und Fahrten. Aufsätze zur gegenwärtigen Literatur. Zurich, Manesse Verlag, Conzett und Huber, 1956. p. 116–51. **11932**

In the chapter "Pariser Notizen," recalling Jouvet's burial, he writes about B. as Dullin's disciple. He praises B. for having produced Gide's adaptation of Kafka's Trial as well as Claudel's plays. He also emphasizes B.'s interpretation of the French classical theater.

Individual Performances

Barthes, Roland. Comment représenter l'antique. In his: Essais critiques. Seuil, 1964. p. 71–79. (Tel quel) **11933**

B.'s production of the Oresteia was an ambiguous performance breaking with academic style.

Bauër, Gérard. Chroniques 1934–1953. V. 1. Gallimard, 1964. p. 55–58, 78–79, 112–14, 173, 206–07. **11934**

Indexed. Emphasizes B.'s performance of Marivaux in Brussels, 1947,

and his adaptation of the Trial. Also, Les fourberies de Scapin. Personal notes on Madeleine Renaud.

Bentley, Eric. Jean-Louis Barrault. KR 12: 224–42, 1950. **11935**

The complexity of B. as seen through Le procès and Les fourberies de Scapin. Bentley reproaches B. with trying too hard to clarify Kafka and therefore over-interpreting. As he has done with Camus' État de siège, B. carries too much literary ballast. He betrays Artaud but uses Chaplin well. Bentley also feels B.'s relation to Claudel to be a superficial one. But in Scapin he is admirable. The setting combines realism, beauty and utility. He approves of his interpretation of Marivaux. In conclusion, B. creates another Comédie-Française.

———. A one man dialogue on the Barrault repertory. NRep 136, no. 1:20–22, March 18, 1957. **11936**

The American tour, when the Company played in several American universities and at the United Nations. As usual, Bentley's compliments are mixed.

———. What is theatre? Incorporating the dramatic event and other essays, 1944–1967. Atheneum, 1968. p. 38–40, 368–72, passim. Also: London, Methuen, 1969. **11937**

Anouilh...Roussin in alphabetical order. B. as an interpreter of Marivaux and as a mime. His achievement is in being a complete man of the theater. Bentley reviews the Company's visit to New York in 1957. He feels that the choice of plays was an unhappy one. As usual, Bentley gives a tongue-in-cheek review of B.'s merits.

Dominique, Léon. Le théâtre russe et la scène française. Traduit du russe par Nina Nidermiller et Michèle Wiernik. Préf. par P.-L. Mignon. O. Perrin, 1969, 253 p. (Art théâtre métier) **11938**

Entries in alphabetical order. Naturally, B.'s production of The cherry orchard is much discussed.

Gauthier, Jean-Jacques. Théâtre d'aujourd'hui. Dix ans de critique dramatique et des entretiens avec M. Abadi sur le théâtre et sur la critique. Julliard, 1972. p. 291–94, 353–55. **11939**

Congratulates B. on his modernism. He appreciates his production of Giraudoux' *Judith* and Jarry's *Ubu-sur-la-Butte*. He dislikes the adaptation of Kafka.

Magny, Claude-Edmonde. Paul Claudel et Jean-Louis Barrault. TR 15:515–19, 1949.
11940

Against B.'s interpretation of *Partage de midi* which is considered too realistic and therefore unsuitable to Claudel.

Monheim, F. Visages d'aujourd'hui. Jean-Louis Barrault ou la fièvre lucide. RGB 49:126–35, 1958. **11941**

About Claudel's *Christophe Colomb*. The theater as an art of human communion and an art of poetic justice. B. succeeds in both areas.

Monnier, Adrienne. J.-L. Barrault. *In her:* Les gazettes d'Adrienne Monnier, 1925–1945. Julliard, 1953. p. 229–32. **11942**

An enthusiastic portrait of B. and an account of his first successes such as *Numance* or *La faim*. A young B. rich in vitality and poor in material resources.

Savin, Maurice L. Chronique dramatique. Marigny, Les fourberies de Scapin. TM 729–35, April 1949. **11943**

One does not recognize Scapin in B.'s interpretation. It is a Scapin "des délicats," an original concept but not an accurate one. To the author, B. is an actor who is a dancer and a mime.

———. Un spectateur mécontent. TM 340–46, Feb. 1949. **11944**

About *Partage de midi*. He admires B. but dislikes the performance.

Simon, Alfred. Jean-Louis Barrault et le petit coiffeur. Esp 255:569–72, 1957.
11945

About Schehadé's *Histoire de Vasco*. Considers it a genuine success. B. dares and accomplishes.

Simon, John. Theatre chronicles. HudR 17: 233–42, 1964. **11946**

States that the Théâtre de France of B. and Madeleine Renaud came over from Paris and that it is sad to see a company that triumphantly succeeded and seceded from the Comédie-Française end up indistinguishable from

what it rebelled against. Gone are the days of experimentation.

Gaston Baty
(Nos. 11947–11963)

Laurence W. Cor

Collected Articles

Baty, Gaston. Bulletin du studio des Champs-Elysées, 1925. **11947**

A miscellaneous collection of programs, commentaries on current plays, press reviews. This periodical is a continuation of *La chimère, Bulletin d'art dramatique* (1921–1923).

———. La chimère, bulletin d'art dramatique, 1921–1923. 234 p. **11948**

13 fascicules and an inaugural number. Served as program for performances, including articles of doctrine, commentaries on plays in course of production, press reviews.

Gaston Baty 1885–1952. Notes et documents. RHT 5:11–123, 1953. **11949**

A number devoted to B., containing biographical documents; *mises en scène;* letters; works, studies and articles by B.; studies and articles on B.; marionettes. A very important source.

General Studies

Bernard, Jean-Jacques. Gaston Baty. RduC 15:98–102, 1952. **11950**

Brief sketch of B.'s career and clarification of his concept of "Sire le Mot."

———. Gaston Baty devant l'œuvre dramatique. CahGB 1:7–11, 1963. **11951**

Affirms that B. demonstrated profound respect for the text despite his theatrical innovations.

Blanchart, Paul. Gaston Baty. Eds. de la Nouvelle revue critique, 1939. 96 p. (Choses et gens de théâtre) **11952**

A concise, definitive biography of B. treating his personality and cast of mind, apprentice years, stages of his career, descriptions of his theatrical productions, and his associations with actors and playwrights. A thorough consideration of his concept of the theater and the quarrels, controversies and anecdotes about "Sire le Mot." An evaluation of his accomplishments in both contemporary and classic plays. Bibliography and *mises en scène* (p. 90–95). An essential introduction to B.'s contribution to the French theater.

————. Gaston Baty, ses secrets, ses paradoxes et ses rêves. *In his:* Le théâtre en France. Les éditeurs français réunis, 1962. p. 174–83.   **11953**

An authoritative introduction to B.'s theatrical ideals and concepts.

Brasillach, Robert. Gaston Baty. *In his:* Animateurs de théâtre. Corrêa, 1936. p. 129–73.   **11954**

A résumé and critique of B.'s theories and impressions of several plays directed by him.

Brillant, M. Préface. *In:* Baty, Gaston. Le masque et l'encensoir. Bloud et Gay, 1926. 143 p.   **11955**

A response to objections raised against B.'s theories and clarification of certain confusions. Discussion of a few points not treated by B. in this book but developed mostly in *Bulletin de la chimère.* A spirited defense of B., with laudatory comments on his theatrical productions. A definitive study.

Cogniat, Raymond. Gaston Baty. Les presses littéraires de France, 1953. 57 p.   **11956**

A résumé of B.'s career and judicious consideration of his esthetic theory. Photographs of decors from several plays. Chronological list of plays he directed, including marionette productions.

Cor, Laurence W. The supreme art. CMLR 22:28–33, 1966.   **11957**

How B. attempted to create a fusion of the arts in the theatrical experience, and a brief critique of the "drame intégral."

Hort, Jean. Gaston Baty. *In his:* Les théâtres du cartel et leurs animateurs: Pitoëff, Baty, Jouvet, Dullin. Geneva, Skira, 1944. p. 135–52.   **11958**

A critique of B.'s theories, especially his neglect of the actor and a play's inherent quality in favor of the *mise en scène.* Of particular interest: B.'s concept of the theater in relation to St.

Thomas Aquinas and the Church. Highly recommended.

Larkin, Oliver Waterman. Two French directors and their two theatres. ThA 15: 42–48, 1931.   **11959**

A critique of B.'s production, *L'opéra des quat' sous.*

Raymond, Marcel. Gaston Baty. *In his:* Le jeu retrouvé. Montreal, Eds. de l'arbre, 1943. p. 79–93.   **11960**

Highlights of B.'s career and discussion of cardinal points in his esthetic of the theater. Very good as an introductory study.

Tariol, Marcel. Gaston Baty et Racine. AFLT 12:91–112, 1965.   **11961**

Treats B.'s ideas as they were incorporated in his direction of *Phèdre* and *Bérénice.* Especially interesting for the way it evokes the actual *mise en scène* of these two works. A penetrating study of B.'s efforts to establish a rapport between Racine's creations and the modern audience. Excellent article.

Virmaux, Alain. Baty et la fidélité aux classiques. CAIEF 21:87–103, 1969.   **11962**

A thoughtful and evocative essay on B.'s famous interpretations of *Phèdre, Bérénice, Les caprices de Marianne* and *Lorenzaccio.*

————. Baty quinze ans après. Eur 45:218–223, 1967.   **11963**

Treats B.'s influence in the theater today and concludes it is B. the theorist, not the adaptor or director, who will survive. Brings up an interesting relationship between B. and Artaud.

Léon Chancerel
(Nos. 11964–11966)

DAVID B. PARSELL

Cusson, Jean. Un réformateur du théâtre: Léon Chancerel. Montreal, Fides, 1942. 95 p.   **11964**

Brief exposition, aimed at general audience, of C.'s theory and practice in working with companies of young actors, particularly among the Scouts de France. Author situates C. in the tradition of Copeau but stresses C.'s contribution to a distinctly Catholic theater. Final portion of book moves away from C. in the direction of polemics, exhorting Canadians to follow his example.

[Léon Chancerel] RHT 20, no. 2:11–248, 1968. **11965**

A memorial issue devoted to C. by the journal that he himself founded. Includes comprehensive chronology and bibliographies, together with appreciation and reminiscences by various hands. Essential resource material for any further work on C.

Raymond, Marcel. Léon Chancerel. *In his:* Le jeu retrouvé. Montreal, L'arbre, 1943. p. 175–87. **11966**

Cursory but useful discussion of C.'s contribution to dramatic art, citing memorable productions and principal theories. Concludes with observation that C. has returned the theater to its legitimate roots among the people.

Jacques Copeau
(Nos. 11967–12029)

NORMAN H. PAUL

Editions

Copeau, Jacques. Registres I. Appels. Textes recueillis et établis par Marie-Hélène Dasté et Suzanne Maistre Saint-Denis; notes de Claude Sicard. Gallimard, 1974. 360 p. (Pratique du théâtre) **11967**

Unpublished speeches, articles, notes and correspondence, all carefully annotated, which reflect C.'s life-long preoccupation with theoretical and analytic approach to theater. First volume of his complete works. Indispensable source.

Reviews: H. Bianciotti in QL March 16-31, 1975; J.-J. G. in Fig Nov. 2, 1974; N. Paul in ETJ 28:134–35, 1976 and in MD 19:107–08, 1976; R. Speaight in TLS Dec. 6, 1974.

———. Registres II. Molière. Textes rassemblés et présentés par André Cabanis. Gallimard, 1976. 365 p. (Pratique du théâtre) **11968**

Second volume of his complete works contains various articles, letters, program notes and his introductions to the 1930 ed. of Molière's plays.

Reviews: N. Paul in ETJ 28:134–

35, 1976; R. Speaight in TLS 3887:1126, Sept. 10, 1976.

Le journal de bord des Copiaus. 1924–1929. Edition commentée par Denis Gontard. Seghers, 1974. 224 p. **11969**

Daily journal kept principally by Suzanne Bing, with entries by Léon Chancerel and C., all unsigned; records activities and organizational details of group of young actors who followed C. into his "exile" in Burgundy upon closing the Vieux-Colombier. Excellent presentation and commentaries, with careful, accurate notes.

Correspondence

Copeau, Jacques. Correspondance Jacques Copeau-Roger Martin du Gard. Texte établi et annoté par Claude Sicard. Introduction par Jean Delay. Gallimard, 1972. 2 v. **11970**

200 letters from C., 204 from Martin du Gard, between 1913–1949; extensive excerpts from their unpublished journals; complete indices of persons and works. Informative introduction summarizes and supplements correspondence. Carefully annotated letters furnish valuable information on biographies of both men. Indispensable source.

Reviews: Anon. in TLS 1017, Sept. 1, 1972; A. Blanchet in Et 337:143–44, 1972; J. Blot in NRF 237:82–85, 1972; P. de Boisdeffre in NL 2322:4, 5, March 27-April 2, 1972, and in RDM 419–26, April-June 1972; A. Brincourt in FL 1346:13, 16, March 4, 1972; A. Miguel in Marg 146–47:58–59, 1972; A. Romus in RevN 56:292–93, 1972.

———. Lettres à Léon Chancerel. *In:* Yvonne Chancerel et Rose-Marie Mouòuès. Notes biographiques. RHT 2:124–29, 1968. **11971**

Dated 1932–1935, letters express C.'s enthusiasm and support for Chancerel's "Comédiens routiers." Selected from unpublished correspondence in Archives Léon Chancerel at the Société d'histoire du théâtre.

———. Lettres de jeunesse à Léon Bellé (1894–1912). MerF 1095:414–44, 1954; 1096:606–29, 1954. **11972**

42 letters, unannotated, which throw

valuable light on C.'s early philosophic and literary development. *See* Pruner for necessary revision of dates of letters.

————. Quatre lettres de Jacques Copeau à Louis Jouvet. CRB 2:101–18, 1953.
11973

Selections from vast unpublished correspondence in Coll. Jouvet, Bibliothèque de l'Arsenal. Letters, dated 1915–1916, discuss future plans for Vieux-Colombier, architecture, and renewal of commedia dell'arte techniques in actor training. *See* Kurtz for additional excerpts from correspondence.
Reviews: L. Chancerel in RHT 4: 316, 1953 and in RHT 1:83–84, 1955.

————. Quatre lettres inédites de Jacques Copeau. Arts 432:1, Oct. 8–14, 1953.
11974

Dated 1913–1931, letters are addressed to André Suarès and relate C.'s discouragement with public reception of his theater. Selection from unpublished collection of circa 200 letters from C. in Bibliothèque Jacques Doucet. 238 unpublished letters from Suarès are in the Bibliothèque de l'Arsenal.

Claudel, Paul. Claudel homme de théâtre. Correspondances avec Copeau, Dullin, Jouvet. Etablies et annotées par Henri Micciollo et Jacques Petit. Gallimard, 1966. 327 p. (Cahiers Paul Claudel, 6)
11975

129 letters between C. and Claudel from 1903–1938; *Hommage à Jacques Copeau* (Nov. 2, 1949), by Claudel. Letters reveal early admiration of C. for Claudel's theater, personal and artistic differences over staging, their long friendship and identity of religious views.

Lerminier, Georges. Péguy et Copeau: lettres et documents. ACPFM 44:1–11, 1955.
11976

Dated 1910–1914, letters reveal admiration of C. for Péguy's dramatic work and their close identity of religious views.

Pruner, Francis. Notes critiques sur les lettres de Jacques Copeau à Léon Bellé. RHT 1:40–47, 1958.
11977

Revision of dates of composition through careful biographical and historical study.

Iconography

Jacques Copeau et le Vieux-Colombier. Bibliothèque nationale, 1963. xxxi, 58 p., 8 pl.
11978

Catalog of exhibition. Valuable source list of some of the material in the Fonds Copeau at L'Arsenal. *See* Christout for description of contents.
Reviews: Anon. in BBF 9, 1964; M. Goring in ThR 6, 2:73–74, 1964.

Biography

Benjamin, René. Jacques Copeau ou le fanatique hésitant. MoiS 50:43–68, May 1943. *Also in his:* L'homme à la recherche de son âme. Geneva, La Palatine, 1943. p. 151–78.
11979

Biographical account, based on long acquaintance, of C.'s intransigent and difficult personality. Author objectively analyzes C.'s lack of popular acceptance but praises his high standards as inspirational to serious dramatists and theater people.

Bost, Pierre. Un entretien avec Jacques Copeau. RHeb 27:111–18, July 6, 1929.
11980

C. reaffirms necessity for theater reforms in staging, acting and playwriting; interviewer wonders at lack of support by public in recalling C. from retirement to direct Comédie-Française. One of many articles by critics and theater people supporting C.'s candidacy.

Gide, André. Lettre inédite de Gide à Copeau, 20 juin 1922. RHT 3:266–67, 1951.
11981

Concerning production of *Saül* at Vieux-Colombier; advice on interpreting role. From Fonds Copeau in L'Arsenal; unpublished correspondence of C.-Gide in preparation by Gallimard.

Jouvet, Louis. Quatre lettres de Louis Jouvet à Jacques Copeau. CRB 7:93–119, 1954.
11982

From Jouvet collection. See comment on C., *Quatre lettres, supra.*

Lefèvre, Frédéric. Une heure avec... Jacques Copeau. NL 227:1, 4, Feb. 19, 1927. *Also in his:* Une heure avec... Gallimard, 1929. p. 87–98.
11983

Interview in which C. reviews his career, explains reasons for sudden retirement, and denounces current theater which cannot appreciate such playwrights as Claudel.

Martin du Gard, Roger. Ma dette envers Copeau. NRF 34:672–86, 1955. *Also in his:* Souvenirs autobiographiques et littéraires (inédit). ┐Œuvres complètes, I. Gallimard, 1955. p. lxii–lxxiv. (Bibliothèque de la Pléiade) *Also in:* Cahier Jacques Copeau. Connaissance du théâtre, n.d. [1959]. p. 11–12 [unnumbered]. **11984**

Incisive critical approach to personal and informative narration of early years of their friendship. Novelist regrets that C. did not use his analytical talents to write novels.

Saint-Denis, Michel. Jacques Copeau: metteur en scène et comédien. *In:* Copeau, Jacques. Notes sur le métier de comédien. M. Brient, 1955. p. 7–12. (Ecrits sur le théâtre) **11985**

Anecdotal consideration of C. as actor and reader. Preface to unpublished excerpts from C.'s journal and lectures.

Review: L. Chancerel in RHT 2: 208, 1955.

Schlumberger, Jean. Les débuts tenaces et hardis du Vieux- Colombier. FL 173:1, 4, Aug. 13, 1949. *Also in his:* Eveils. Gallimard, 1950. p. 232–45. **11986**

Interesting personal reminiscences of the early years of the NRF.

Sutton, Denys. Jacques Copeau and Duncan Grant. Apollo 86:138–41, 1967. **11987**

Account of collaboration of English scenic designer and C., 1912–1919, with excerpts from their correspondence and illustrations of sets and costumes.

General Studies: Books

Anders, France. Jacques Copeau et le cartel des quatre. Nizet, 1959. 340 p. **11988**

Excellent critical study of C.'s contributions to modern theater, his influence on early development of former students, Dullin and Jouvet. Summary biographical data; list of plays in repertory of Vieux-Colombier; extensive bibliography of original and secondary sources is best to date despite many typographical errors.

Reviews: L. Chancerel in RHT 2: 175, 1961; R. Davril in EA 13:172–75, 1960.

Borgal, Clément. Jacques Copeau. L'arche, 1960. 304 p. (Le théâtre et les jours) **11989**

Objective critical biography and a thorough study of C.'s importance in theater history. Close analytic examination of C.'s writings traces development of his theories in action. Lacks bibliography and index.

Review: L. Chancerel in RHT 2: 173–74, 1961.

Cologni, Franco. Jacques Copeau: il Vieux Colombier: i Copiaus. Bologna, Cappelli, 1962. 165 p. (Documenti di teatro, 23) **11990**

Useful compendium of previous biographies; short bibliography.

Cruciani, Fabrizio. Jacques Copeau o le aporie del teatro moderno. Rome, Bulzoni, 1971. 286 p. (Biblioteca teatrale, Studi 7) **11991**

Essentially a reworking of previous biographies. Extensive bibliography adds many items in Italian and updates Anders' work. Good general study.

Doisy, Marcel. Jacques Copeau ou l'absolu dans l'art. Le cercle du livre, 1954. 256 p., ill. **11992**

Conscientious, almost hagiographic biography, based largely on interviews with C.'s colleagues, family and friends. Contains important excerpts from unpublished correspondence with Isabelle Rivière in chapter on C.'s religious crisis. Uncritical praise for C.'s contributions to theater.

Review: L. Chancerel in RHT 1:84–85, 1955.

Jacques Copeau & le théâtre du Vieux-Colombier from Paris. Paris, Aréthuse, Jan. 11, 1917. 68 p. **11993**

Publicity brochure, in English, for New York tour. Letters from H. Bergson, P. Claudel, C. Debussy, A. Gide, E. Verhaeren; biographical essay on C., short account of first season, 1913–1914, with excerpts from critics; essay by André Suarès, *The spirit of the Vieux-Colombier.* Valuable period document.

Kurtz, Maurice. Jacques Copeau: biographie d'un théâtre. Nagel, 1950. 272 p. (Arts) **11994**

First scholarly study of C.; translated from English by C. Cézan, with letter from C. Methodical, chronological history; weak in critical analysis; accurate and informative notes; complete appendices of plays, dramatists and actors in repertory. Bibliography has been updated by Anders and Cruciani. Still the best reference work on C.
Reviews: C. Mauban in Riv May 24, 1951; J. Nepveu-Degas in RHT 1: 71–72, 1951; P. Scize in NL 1226:8, March 1, 1951.

Lerminier, Georges. Jacques Copeau, le réformateur, 1879–1949. Presses univ. de France, 1953. 86 p., ill. (Les metteurs en scène) **11995**

A short, appreciative study containing many quotes from C.'s works, some unpublished correspondence and list of opening nights at Vieux-Colombier. Useful as introduction to C.
Reviews: L. Chancerel in RHT 4: 311–12, 1953; H. Petit in ParL Oct. 15, 1953.

Mahn, Berthold. Souvenirs du Vieux-Colombier. Aveline, 1926. xxii, 150 p. **11996**

Discursive, laudatory memoir by Jules Romains; 55 original sketches by Mahn of actors and productions.

Special Numbers

Hommage à Jacques Copeau à l'occasion du cinquantième anniversaire de la fondation du théâtre du Vieux-Colombier. RHT 4: 355–404, 1963. **11997**

Three unpublished texts by C.; editorial by L. Chancerel; *A la recherche de Jacques Copeau* by M.-F. Christout; *Itinéraire bourguignon* by P. Blanchart. The significant articles have been analyzed separately under the appropriate headings.

Notes biographiques et bibliographiques pour servir à l'histoire de Jacques Copeau et du théâtre et de l'école du Vieux-Colombier. RHT 1:7–50, 1950. **11998**

Special issue; excellent source of information; photos and sketches of theater; text of C.'s 1913 statement founding a repertory theater. Some errors in bibliography.

General Studies: Articles

Bentley, Eric. Copeau and the chimera. ThAM 34:48–51, Jan. 1950. *Also in his:* In search of theater. Knopf, 1953. p. 256–65. *Also:* Vintage books, 1954. **11999**

Acknowledges C.'s seminal position in the theater while questioning his puristic approach as eventually unworkable.

Borgal, Clément. Jacques Copeau. *In his:* Metteurs en scène. F. Lanore, 1963. p. 7–55. **12000**

Adds nothing to his 1960 study.

Chancerel, Léon. Jacques Copeau, l'œuvre et l'esprit du Vieux-Colombier. RdJ 3: 363–77, 1935; 4:540–53, 1935. **12001**

Superficial account of C.'s career; adds nothing to previous studies.

Christout, Marie-Françoise. A la recherche de Jacques Copeau. *In:* Hommage à Jacques Copeau. *See* 11997. p. 391–96. **12002**

Description of material in Fonds Copeau at the Arsenal.

Coindreau, Maurice Edgar. Martyrologie. *In his:* La farce est jouée. New York, La maison française, 1942. p. 226–44. **12003**

Consists mostly of reviews of productions at Vieux-Colombier, 1920–1924, as collected from contemporary press. Relies heavily on Dubech book, 1928.
Review: E[tiemble] in LetFB 6:69–70, Nov. 1, 1942.

Corbin, John. The Vieux Colombier. NYT iv:4, Dec. 23, 1917. **12004**

Review of opening weeks of first New York season. Praise for C.'s contributions to the raising of the level of Broadway theater, and brief outline of C.'s career.

De Foe, Louis V. Page of the players: two seasons of stage impressionism and their doubtful results. NYW M5, April 13, 1919. **12005**

Criticizes monotony of C.'s staging and dullness of repertory; doubts any lasting influence on theater.

Dhomme, Sylvain. [Jacques Copeau]. *In: his:* La mise en scène d'Antoine à Brecht. Nathan, 1959. p. 109–45. **12006**

Attempts to put C.'s influence in perspective. Acknowledges that his high artistic aims inspired many young theater people but doubts that C.'s puristic approach can have lasting effect.

Dubech, Lucien. Le chirurgien. *In his:* La crise du théâtre. Librairie de France, 1928. p. 151–80. **12007**

Sees C. as only savior in era of corrupt, commercial theater of Paris; urges his return from retirement. Summarizes Vieux-Colombier productions and acclaims C.'s intransigent views of theater.

Duhamel, Georges. Le théâtre du Vieux-Colombier. MerF 105:509–18, 1913. **12008**

First critical commentary on C.'s 1913 manifesto founding the Vieux-Colombier; sees it as significant example for modern theater.

Eliot, Samuel A., Jr. Le théâtre du Vieux-Colombier. ThAM 3:25–30, 1919. **12009**

Review of the two New York seasons. Praises C.'s experiment as "the most artistic theatre in the United States."

Fernandez, Ramon. Molière et Copeau. NRF 191:249–53, 1929. **12010**

Attributes contemporary revival of neglected Molière farces to C.'s efforts.

Frank, Waldo. The art of the Vieux Colombier: a contribution of France to the contemporary stage. Paris-New York, Eds. de la NRF, 1918. 58 p. *Also in his:* Salvos. N.Y., Boni & Liveright, 1924. p. 119–67. **12011**

Examines background of C.'s career on the NRF, as drama critic, founder of the Vieux-Colombier; reviews prewar condition of Paris and New York. Has distinction of being first lengthy study of C. and his company. Review: Anon. in ThAM 3:147, 1919.

Gide, André. [Jacques Copeau]. *In his:* Journal. 1889–1939. Gallimard, 1948. passim. (Bibliothèque de la Pléiade) **12012**

Over 80 mentions of C. between 1905–1934 reveal long friendship and collaboration on the NRF, in the composition of some of Gide's early novels, and in the production of *Saül. See* G. Lerminier for study of Gide and C. (12017).

Gignoux, Régis. Une chartreuse de comédiens. Fig 1, Aug. 25, 1913. **12013**

Description of Vieux-Colombier rehearsals before opening of first season. Expresses admiration for their devotion and group spirit, new to contemporary acting methods. First public recognition of C.'s company.

Granville-Barker, Harley. Lettre ouverte à Jacques Copeau sur la Comédie-Française. RHeb 36:98–108, Sept. 7, 1929. *Trans.:* A letter to Jacques Copeau. ThAM 13:753–59, 1929. **12014**

Urges C. to accept directorship of Comédie-Française as opportunity to infuse new life in the tradition ridden theater.

Harrop, John. A constructive promise: Jacques Copeau in New York, 1917–1919. ThS 12:104–18, 1971. **12015**

Useful survey of this period, based on contemporary press reviews and articles; some typographical errors in bibliographical notes.

Jacquot, Jean. Copeau et Comme il vous plaira: de l'Atelier aux jardins Boboli. RHT 1:119–36, 1965. **12016**

Scholarly study of the two productions directed by C. Objective criticism and analysis of his stage techniques and translation. 7 pl. of illustrations.

Lerminier, Georges. André Gide et Jacques Copeau. RechD n.s. 2:149–55, 1952. **12017**

Sees paradoxical effect on Gide of C.'s puristic approach to theater as reason for Gide's disinterest in that genre as well as for C.'s own ultimate failure.

MacGowan, Kenneth, and Robert Edmond Jones. The theater of the three hundred. *In their:* Continental stagecraft. Harcourt Brace, 1922. p. 171–83. **12018**

A professional description and evaluation of the Vieux-Colombier architecture, C.'s production techniques and praise for his use of the bare stage: "expression and idea, poised in the human body, begin to inform acting directly and openly in the company of the Vieux-Colombier."

Mambrino, Jean, S. J. The solitude of Jacques Copeau. DuR 452:83–112, 1951.
12019
Translated from the French by Robert Speaight. Analysis of C.'s spiritual influence on theater and his emphasis on actor training in the Ecole du Vieux-Colombier. Author stresses C.'s educational and vocational qualities as primary contributions.

Paul, Norman H. L'apport de Jacques Copeau. *In:* Aux sources de la vérité du théâtre moderne (Mallarmé, Zola, Claudel, Antoine, Lugné-Poe, Rouché, Copeau, le Cartel). Actes du Colloque de London (Canada), 1972. Texte établi par James B. Sanders. Lettres modernes, 1974. p. 155–71.
12020
Close study of C.'s 1913 manifesto illustrates his aims by survey of his subsequent accomplishments throughout a long career.

Prénat, Jacques. Visite à Copeau. Lat 10: 377–400, 1930.
12021
Useful account of the daily training schedule followed by Les Copiaus under C.'s direction.
Review: [L. Chancerel] in JTP 5: 172–73, 1931.

Raymond, Antonin. The théâtre du Vieux Colombier in New York. JAIA 5:384–87, 1917.
12022
Description by the architect who remodeled the Garrick Theater to C.'s specifications. Author lauds this innovation in artistic cooperation.

Raymond, Marcel. Le jeu retrouvé. Montreal, L'arbre, 1943. xiii, 242 p.   **12023**
Historical and eulogistic study of French theater figures of 20th century. C. chapters occupy one-third of book, but his name is cited throughout as influence on Dullin, Jouvet, Ghéon, Baty, *et al.*
Review: Etiemble in LetFB 11:74–75, Jan. 1, 1944.

Rouveyre, André. Le Vieux-Colombier, promoteur et type du faux théâtre d'art. MerF 702:653–58, 1927.   **12024**
Rather idiosyncratic attack on NRF and C. as "calvinist" and snobbish

milieu. Claims C. plagiarized his 1913 manifesto from 1907 project by Golberg. Praises Lugné-Poe as true theater reformer.

Slaughter, Helena Robin. Jacques Copeau, metteur en scène de Shakespeare et des élisabéthains. EA 13:176–91, 1960. **12025**
Critical analysis of C.'s productions and interpretations through close study of contemporary press reviews.

Suarès, André. Molière au Vieux-Colombier. EcrN 65–72, June 1920. *Also in his:* Présences. Mornay, 1925. p. 103–21. *Another ed.:* Emile-Paul, 1926. *Excerpt in:* Comœdia 3, July 12, 1926.   **12026**
Extended review of C.'s production of *Les fourberies de Scapin* with C. in title role. Compares C. with Molière, the actor-director.

Veinstein, André. Les cahiers du Vieux-Colombier. *In his:* Du théâtre libre au Théâtre Louis Jouvet. Billaudot, 1955. p. 67–81. (Librairie théâtrale)   **12027**
Scholarly study of the periodical literature of the art theaters, with extensive excerpts, notes, bibliographical history, and analytical indices. An indispensable and intelligently prepared critique of the aims and accomplishments of these little theaters.
Reviews: L. Chancerel in RHT 3–4: 366, 1955; R. Saurel in CRB 13:121, 1955.

Vincent, Vincent. [Jacques Copeau]. *In his:* Rideau. Lausanne, Vaney-Burnier, 1929. p. 79–110.   **12028**
Descriptive and detailed reviews of productions by C. and Les Copiaus in Burgundy and Switzerland. One of the rare accounts of this period in C.'s career.

Volbach, Walther R. Jacques Copeau, Appia's finest disciple. ETJ 17:206–14, 1965. *Also in his:* Adolphe Appia, prophet of the modern theatre: a profile. Middletown, Conn., Wesleyan univ. press, 1968. p. 101–06.   **12029**
Cursory appraisal of C.'s relations with Appia. Generally accurate description of Appia's influence on C., except for date of first meeting — Fall 1915, not Summer 1913.
Review: T. Dènes in RHT 2:171–73, 1970.

Charles Dullin
(Nos. 12030–12091)

BARBARA GORDON

Bibliography and Iconography

Notes et documents pour servir à l'histoire de Charles Dullin, du théâtre et de l'école de l'Atelier. RHT 2:161–83, 1950. **12030**
Includes biographical dates, list of roles and repertory, and bibliography of works by and on D.

Yves-Bonnat. Un homme qui fit école. L'exposition à l'Arsenal. NL 2207:7, Dec. 4, 1969. **12031**
Description of Bibliothèque de l'Arsenal exhibit on the life and work of D.

Dullin's Texts on Directing

Correspondance. Revue de l'Atelier. 1–28: 1928–32. **12032**
Journal published as accompaniment to Atelier productions between 1928 and 1932. Contains letters and articles by D. and others. Important document on D.'s goals, methods, and *mises en scène* of that period. Includes writings later found in D.'s *Souvenirs et notes de travail d'un acteur* and *Ce sont les dieux qu'il nous faut, supra.*

Dullin, Charles. A la recherche de Smerdiakov. CRB 6:99–120, 1954. *Also:* 1960. **12033**
Previously unpublished study, written by D. at age twenty-six, in the form of a dialog between actor and character. Valuable revelation of D.'s "interior" approach as actor.

———. Ce sont les dieux qu'il nous faut. Edit. établie et annotée par Charles Charras. Préf. d'Armand Salacrou. Gallimard, 1966. 319 p. (Pratique du théâtre) **12034**
Critical anthology of articles, lectures, essays, interviews, and letters, arranged in chronological order. Includes previously unpublished texts. Primary source of information on theories, goals, methods, and projects of D. throughout his directorial career. Most valuable document to date on history of Atelier theater under D.

Review: J. Lemarchand in FL 1217: 39, Sept. 15–21, 1969.

———. Corneille—Cinna, mise en scène et commentaires. Seuil, 1948. 176 p. **12035**
D.'s complete *mise en scène,* outlined with integral text, detailed stage directions, and sketches. Includes commentaries on play. Offers important insights to D.'s working methods.

———. Deux inédits: ses derniers messages. Arts 242:7, Dec. 23, 1949. **12036**
D.'s last texts. Contain tribute to Copeau, revealing important aspects of D.-Copeau relationship.

———. Metteur en scène et décorateurs. RevTh 8:3–12, 1948. **12037**
Discusses role of director in theatrical production, with references to his own methods. Essential document for understanding of D.'s esthetic concepts.

———. Mise en scène pour L'archipel Lenoir, 1947, Théâtre Montparnasse, Jamois. Acte I. *In:* Ubersfeld, Annie. Armand Salacrou. Seghers, 1970. p. 148–61. (Théâtre de tous les temps, 13) **12038**
D.'s written *mise en scène* of Salacrou's play. Includes text, stage directions, lighting plan, and sketches of stage positions for Act I.

———. Molière—L'avare, mise en scène et commentaires. Seuil, 1946. 181 p. (Mises en scène) **12039**
Presents D.'s complete *mise en scène,* with integral text, detailed stage directions, and sketches of sets and stage positions. Preceded by commentaries on plot, characters, and atmosphere of play. Essential document on D.'s directorial ideas and procedures.

———. Point de vue du metteur en scène: en marge du Soldat et la sorcière. RevTh 1:5–10, 1946. **12040**
Presents directorial interpretation of Salacrou's play. Offers insight to D.'s goals and methods.

———. Souvenirs et notes de travail d'un acteur. Odette Lieutier, 1946. 155 p. **12041**
Primary source of information on D. as actor, documenting formation, theories, and methods. Presents both autobiographical recollections and critical reflections. Includes discussions on in-

fluence of melodrama, Japanese theater, and Meyerhold on his work, his interpretation of various roles, and his acting techniques.

Reviews: L. Chancerel in RevTh 2: 279–80, 1946; R. Maublanc in Pen n.s. 9:87–92, 1946.

General Studies: Books

Anders, France. Jacques Copeau et le Cartel des quatre. A.G. Nizet, 1959. 341 p. **12042**

Important critical study, comprehensive and extremely well-documented. Covers history of the Cartel: formation, evolution, reforms, esthetic formulas, repertory, and artistic influence. Includes evaluation of D. as director. Emphasizes contribution of Cartel to evolution of *metteur en scène* in contemporary theater.

Review: R. Davril in EA 13:172–75, 1960.

Arnaud, Lucien. Charles Dullin. Préf. de Jean Vilar. L'arche, 1952. 259 p. (Le théâtre et les jours) **12043**

Comprehensive, though subjective, description of D.'s career, principles, methods and personality. Concentrates on period between 1921 and 1949. Includes extracts from writings of D. and observations by his students and colleagues. Informative, but more a personal tribute than a critical analysis.

Reviews: J. Lemarchand in FL 434: 10, Aug. 14, 1954; J.-J. Morvan in LetN 3:363–64, 1953.

Arnoux, Alexandre. Charles Dullin. Portrait brisé. Documents biographiques et iconographiques recueillis par Claude Cézan. Emile-Paul frères, 1951. 103 p. **12044**

Biography of D., written by close friend. Concentrates on D.'s character and personality. Well-documented study.

Sarment, Jean. Charles Dullin. Calmann-Lévy, 1950. 151 p. (Masques et visages) **12045**

Study of D. as actor, preceded by reverential eulogy. Subjective approach to analysis of artist and his surroundings. Focuses on early career. Recommended document on work prior to Atelier period.

Teillon-Dullin, Pauline, and Charles Charras. Charles Dullin ou Les ensorcelés du Châtelard. Préface de Jean-Louis Barrault. Michel Brient, 1955. 237 p. (Publications de la Société d'histoire du théâtre) **12046**

Personal recollections by sister of D. Describes family, childhood surroundings, and early life of D. through anecdotes, reflections and letters. Moving document on forces and people influencing D. prior to his theatrical career.

Review: J. Lemarchand in FL 10, Aug. 27, 1955.

Biography

Arnoux, Alexandre. Charles Dullin, le comédien possédé. RevHM 48:315–31, 1950; 49:519–35, 1950. **12047**

Subjective description of D.'s career, with detailed personal recollections. Focuses on character and temperament.

Barrault, Jean-Louis. Charles Dullin. RDM 2:338–43, 1950. *Also:* Dullin pape et martyr. NL 2202:1, 7, Dec. 4, 1969. **12048**

Tribute to D., with personal anecdotes and reflections.

————. Le lit de Volpone. *In his:* Réflexions sur le théâtre. Jacques Vautrain, 1949. p. 22–25. *Also in:* CRB 9:61–63, 1955; Arts 501:5, Feb. 2–8, 1955. **12049**

Sentimental, personal recollections of the Atelier theater-school under the direction of D.

————. Mon apprentissage du théâtre, souvenirs et explications. FL 5–6, Nov. 12, 1949. **12050**

Personal recollections of Atelier theater and school between 1931 and 1936. Describes personality and teachings of D.

————. Pour Dullin. LetF 1312:16–17, Dec. 10–16, 1969. **12051**

Penetrating tribute to D., based on personal recollections. Descriptive, focusing on his artistic temperament and influence as teacher.

Barsacq, André. Mes débuts à l'Atelier. CRB 9:54–58, 1955. **12052**

Personal recollections and anecdotes, with references to D.'s production of *Volpone*.

Borgal, Clément. Charles Dullin. *In his:* Metteurs en scène. Fernand Lanore, 1963. p. 99–132.   **12053**

Concise biography of D., with well-documented analysis of theatrical career. Emphasizes inventiveness, non-commercialism, austerity, and eclecticism of D. as director. Review: H. Gouhier in TR 192: 135–36, 1964.

Charras, Charles. La première pièce. Esp 338:920–24, 1965.   **12054**

Includes references to D. as discoverer of new playwrights.

Claudel, Paul, and Charles Dullin. Correspondance. *In:* Claudel, homme de théâtre. Correspondances avec Copeau, Dullin, Jouvet. Ed. by Henri Micciollo and Jacques Petit. Gallimard, 1966. p. 193–285. (CahPC 6)   **12055**

Series of letters exchanged between 1938 and 1943. Valuable document on abortive collaboration for *L'annonce faite à Marie* and on later relationship between D. and Claudel.

———, and Edouard Bourdet. Correspondance. *In:* Claudel homme de théâtre. *See* 12055. p. 183–92.   **12056**

Letters exchanged in July 1939. Contain references to abortive project of D. and Claudel to stage *L'annonce faite à Marie.*

Galtier-Boissière, Jean. Les débuts de l'Atelier de Dullin. *In his:* Mémoires d'un parisien. V. 2. La table ronde, 1961. p. 234–40.   **12057**

Anecdotes, personal recollections and commentaries on D.'s early years as director of the Atelier theater.

Laurent, Jeanne. Charles Dullin et la décentralisation. LetF 1312:16, Dec. 10–16, 1969.   **12058**

Important description of D.'s role in decentralization of French theater from 1947 to 1949. Includes portion of letter from D. to Laurent on this subject.

Porché, François. Charles Dullin ou l'inventeur des formes. RPar 39, 5:228–40, 1932.   **12059**

General analysis of D.'s early life, career and esthetic experimentation. Stresses rapport between man and artist. Describes D.'s directorial technique as combination of "féerie et réalité."

Rouché, Jacques. Copeau, Dullin, Jouvet au Théâtre des Arts. RDM 7:505–16, 1952.   **12060**

Recalls D.'s early years as member of the Théâtre des arts. Includes illuminating comments on D.'s acting, specifically as Smerdiakov in *Les frères Karamazov.*

Salacrou, Armand. La mort de Dullin. FL 385:1, 4, Sept. 5, 1953. *Also in his:* Note sur la vie et la mort de Charles Dullin. *In his:* Théâtre. V. 6. Gallimard, 1954. p. 97–122. *Also in his:* L'archipel Lenoir, Suivi de La vie et la mort de Charles Dullin. Gallimard, 1970. p. 165–91. (Le livre de poche, 2842)   **12061**

Personal reflections on D.'s later years, with details on his production of Salacrou's *L'archipel Lenoir.*

Dullin as Director

Arnaud, Lucien. Charles Dullin et la mise en scène. ThP 2:27–33, 1953.   **12062**

Comments on directorial principles and methods of D., giving brief examples from various productions.

Artaud, Antonin. L'atelier de Charles Dullin. Act 2: 1921. *Also in his:* Œuvres complètes. V. 2. Gallimard, 1961. p. 171–72.   **12063**

Emphasizes contribution of D.'s Atelier school to the regeneration of French theater. Discusses D.'s experimental methods and esthetic concepts behind them.

———. Lettres à Génica Athanasiou. Gallimard, 1969. 381 p.   **12064**

Includes critical observations on D. as actor and director around 1923, with personal references to collaboration between Artaud and D. in Atelier productions.

Brasillach, Robert. Les héritiers du Vieux Colombier. *In his:* Animateurs de théâtre. Corrêa, 1936. p. 13–76. *Also:* La table ronde, 1954.   **12065**

Personal reflections on work of Cartel des quatre. Includes description of D. as actor and *metteur en scène.* Examines influence of Copeau on D., esthetic tendencies of D., and selected productions at the Atelier.

Claudel, Paul. Trente et unième entretien. *In his:* Mémoires improvisés. Quarante et un entretiens avec Jean Amrouche. Texte établi par Louis Fournier. Gallimard, 1969. p. 271–78. (Idées) **12066**

Contains brief references to discussions between Claudel and D. on possible revisions of *L'annonce faite à Marie.*

Copfermann, Emile. Une exposition Charles Dullin à l'Arsenal. LetF 1312:15, 17, Dec. 10–16, 1969. **12067**

Descriptive introduction to exhibit, with comments on D.'s influence and contribution to theater.

Crémieux, Benjamin. L'art du metteur en scène et du comédien: Copeau, Jouvet, Dullin, Baty, Pitoëff. Eur 47–48:130–50, 1949. **12068**

Valuable critique on work of Copeau and the Cartel des quatre. Includes discussion on D. as director, emphasizing "théâtralité," lyricism and coherence. Describes some of his *mises en scène* and the principles behind them. From lecture given in March 1941.

Dhomme, Sylvain. Le Cartel. *In his:* La mise en scène contemporaine d'André Antoine à Bertolt Brecht. Fernand Nathan, 1959. p. 153–88. **12069**

Describes formation of "Théâtre-Ecole de l'Atelier," with brief references to D.'s goals, methods and repertory.

Elder, Judith. The cartel of four. ThAn 18: 26–37, 1961. **12070**

Discusses history, principles and significance of the Cartel des quatre: Jouvet, D., Pitoëff and Baty.

Hort, Jean. Charles Dullin. *In his:* Les théâtres du Cartel et leurs animateurs. Geneva, Eds. d'art Albert Skira, 1944. p. 173–93. **12071**

Suggestive critical study on D.'s work as director, actor and teacher. Evaluates both theories and practices. Emphasizes D.'s ideal of complete theatrical *spectacle.*

Knowles, Dorothy. The theatres and producers. *In her:* French drama of the inter-war years, 1918–39. London, Harrap, 1967. p. 13–47. *Also:* New York, Barnes and Noble, 1968. **12072**

Includes brief, intelligent analysis of D.'s methods and concepts, with examples from some of his productions. Focuses on achievements as director of the Atelier theater.

Lebesque, Morvan. Charles Dullin. Eur 396–97: 150–57, 1962. **12073**

Evaluation of D. as director and actor. Relates him to "théâtre total" and theater of his time. Stresses artistic integrity and perfectionism.

————. Révélation d'un texte capital. Charles Dullin: prédisait le théâtre populaire. Arts 381:1, 4, Oct. 17–23, 1952. **12074**

Presentation and discussion of important unpublished text by D. Relates D. to Vilar and the theater of the fifties in France. Offers insights to D.'s theories on scenic architecture, *décor,* dramatic repertory, and relationship between actor and audience.

Mignon, Paul-Louis. Un aventurier du théâtre. AvS 481:49–50, Oct. 15, 1971. **12075**

Traces D.'s career as director and actor. Emphasizes experimentalism. Illustrated by photographs of D. in various productions.

Raymond, Marcel. Charles Dullin. *In his:* Le jeu retrouvé. Montreal, Eds. de l'arbre, 1943. p. 123–36. **12076**

Discusses career, working methods and artistic contribution of D. Stresses poetic quality of his productions.

Romains, Jules. Dullin. *In his:* Amitiés et rencontres. Flammarion, 1970. p. 160–64. **12077**

Personal recollections of D. as actor (Smerdiakov in *Les frères Karamazov*) and director (*Volpone*). Praises scope of D.'s work, but considers his potential as producer of modern playwrights to have been unfulfilled.

Rosenberg, Merrill A. Vichy's theatrical venture. ThS 11:124–50, 1970. **12078**

Includes comments on D.'s activity as director of the Théâtre de la Cité during the Occupation.

Salacrou, Armand. Note sur la vie et la mort de Charles Dullin. *In his:* Théâtre, 6. Gallimard, 1954. p. 97–122. *Also in his:* L'archipel Lenoir. Suivi de La vie et la mort de Charles Dullin. Gallimard, 1970. p. 165–91. (Le livre de poche, 2842) **12079**

Penetrating personal reflections on character of D., his goals and methods as director, and the difficulties he encountered. Includes details on D.'s production of *L'archipel Lenoir*. Essential document for research on relationship between D. and Salacrou toward end of D.'s life.

Salvan, J. L. L'esprit du théâtre nouveau. FR 14:109–17, 1940. **12080**

Discusses styles, methods, and repertory of the Cartel des quatre, focusing on relationship to dramatic literature of their time.

Saurel, Renée. Dullin et l'Atelier. *In:* Encyclopédie du théâtre contemporain, 2. Dirigée par Gilles Quéant avec la collaboration de Frédéric Towarnicki, direction artistique et réalisation de Aline Elmayan. Paris, Olivier Perrin, 1959. p. 47–53. **12081**

Sound evaluation of D.'s career. Illustrated with photographs of Atelier productions. Describes details of some productions, including *Les oiseaux, Volpone* and *Les frères Karamazov.*

Verdot, Guy. Charles Dullin au travail. FL 710:4, Nov. 28, 1959. **12082**

Description of D. in rehearsal.

Individual *Mises en Scène*

Henry, Hélène. Charles Dullin et le théâtre élisabéthain. EA 13:197–204, 1960. **12083**

Describes D.'s *mises en scène* of *Epicène ou La femme silencieuse, Volpone, Richard III,* and *Le roi Lear,* with reference to critical reception of these productions.

Lemarchand, Jacques. Le théâtre. Ar 11:117–22, 1945. **12084**

Favorable commentary on D.'s revival of *Le faiseur* at the Théâtre Sarah-Bernhardt.

Mallarmé, Camille. Comment Luigi Pirandello fut révélé au public parisien le 20 décembre 1922. RHT 7:7–37, 1955. **12085**

Detailed document on adaptation of Pirandello's *La volupté de l'honneur* in 1922. Includes letters from D. and Pirandello to Camille Mallarmé. Provides information on evolution of production, working methods of D., and activity of Atelier company at that time.

Rosenberg, Marvin. King Lear in Germany, France and Italy. ThS 9:1–10, 1968. **12086**

Includes critique of D.'s 1945 production. Stresses weaknesses.

Salacrou, Armand. C'est toujours Charles Dullin qui met en scène L'archipel Lenoir. FL 829:19, March 10, 1962. **12087**

Concerns revival of D.'s production by Marguerite Jamois. Briefly discusses D.'s directorial approach and his original *mise en scène* of Salacrou's play.

Sartre, Jean-Paul. Dullin et Les mouches. NouvO 265:44–45, Dec. 8–14, 1969. **12088**

Sartre's personal recollections of his relationship with D. and the latter's *mise en scène* of *Les mouches* in 1943.

Teisseire, Marcel. Charles Dullin nous confie ses impressions. AmiP 299:9, Feb. 24, 1929. **12089**

Interview with D. after one hundredth performance of *Volpone.* Focuses on evolution of production.

Temkine, Raymonde. Charles (Dullin) le téméraire et le théâtre, vingt ans après. Pen 150:110–14, 1970. **12090**

Relates D.'s enterprise to financial difficulties of contemporary theater production in France.

Werrie, Paul. Charles Dullin: Volpone avec sa troupe de l'Atelier. *In his:* Théâtre de la fuite. Brussels-Paris, Les écrits, 1943. p. 112–17. **12091**

Favorable critique of D.'s 1939 production of *Volpone.* Includes comparative references to Max Reinhardt's 1930 production of *Le serviteur des deux maîtres.*

Sacha Guitry
(Nos. 12092–12115)

RENÉE GEEN

Books

Benjamin, René. Sacha Guitry, roi du théâtre. Plon, 1933. 239 p.   **12092**
A fictitious though not implausible recreation of G. on and off stage, written in pseudo play-form.

Choisel, Fernande. Sacha Guitry intime; souvenirs présentés par Jean Salez. Eds. du scorpion, 1957. 283 p.   **12093**
Memoirs of G.'s private secretary, presented under five headings: G.'s five wives. Since they have no literary pretensions, may well be reliable.

Guitry, Lana. Et Sacha vous est conté. Au livre contemporain, 1960. 256 p.   **12094**
Chapters written alternatively by Lana and Sacha create an impressionistic view of the last fourteen years of G.'s private and public life.

Harding, James. Sacha Guitry; the last boulevardier. London, Methuen & co., 1968. 227 p. *Also:* New York, Scribner's, 1968. 277 p.   **12095**
As its subtitle indicates, this is a recreation of a man and a period. Although Harding summarizes the plots of G.'s major plays, he seldom comments on G.'s talents as author, actor or director. It is an entertaining biography, generously sprinkled with anecdotes, *bons mots* and photographs. Lists of G.'s plays with place and date of first performances, of his films with names of principal players, selected critical bibliography and index of proper names.
Reviews: H. Clurman in Nat 208: 88–89, 1969; D. Knowles in FS 25: 109–10, 1971; J. Raymond in Punch 27:785, 1968.

Herment, Raymond. Charlotte Lysès. Nice, Gardescel, 1958. 163 p.   **12096**
Biography of G.'s first wife based on her unpublished memoirs. Chapters 2–7 cover the fourteen years of her life with G. and add an interesting perspective on the beginning of his career.

Lauwick, Hervé. Le merveilleux humour de Lucien et Sacha Guitry. Fayard, 1959. 187 p.   **12097**
Concentrates on Sacha rather than Lucien, and attempts to define his art in the chapter "Un ton nouveau au théâtre." But, on the whole, this work remains a collection of anecdotes about G. and his entourage.

Lorcey, Jacques. Sacha Guitry. Table ronde, 1971. 363 p.   **12098**
The most detailed biography of G. to date, but no evaluation of his theater or his acting. Author, who out of admiration for G. took Lorcey as his stage- and pen-name, contacted various actors associated with G.'s plays and movies. Abundant quotes from newspaper interviews with G., from reviews, and from the legal proceedings in suits against G. Selected bibliography and index of proper names.

Madis, Alex. Sacha. Eds. de l'élan, 1950. 285 p.   **12099**
Lively but somewhat disorganized biography, interspersed with numerous personal reminiscences. Last chapter deals briefly with G.'s non-dramatic writings. Photographs of G. in his most important roles.

Martin du Gard, Maurice. Mon ami Sacha Guitry. Nouvelle revue critique, 1941. 139 p.   **12100**
Apart from personal reminiscences, gives summaries and evaluation of G.'s major plays up to 1939. Incorporates excerpts from reviews by Léon Blum, Léautaud, etc. Ends with a behind-the-scenes account of G.'s election to the Académie Goncourt.

Prince, Stéphane. Sacha Guitry hors sa légende. Presses de la cité, 1959. 251 p.   **12101**
Life with G. as recorded by his private secretary from 1951 to 1957. Presented as the scenario of a film starring G. but all too often directed by Prince. Despite its title, but perhaps not its intention, this work adds another chapter to G.'s legend.

Séréville, Geneviève de. Sacha Guitry mon mari. Flammarion, 1959. 233 p.   **12102**
Personal diary, up to June 1940, rather than biography. As its title indicates, shows G. more as suitor and

husband than as author or actor, but contains some interesting biographical data.

Articles

Achard, Marcel. Sacha Guitry, roi du théâtre. *In his:* Rions avec eux; les grands auteurs comiques. Fayard, 1957. p. 253–98. **12103**

Short, anecdotal biography, synopses of G.'s plays with particular attention paid to *Faisons un rêve* and *La jalousie*. G. is considered the "greatest comical poet" of his time as well as a sound literary critic and moralist.

Basch, Victor. Le muflisme lyrique, le théâtre de M. Sacha Guitry. *In his:* Etudes d'esthétique dramatique; le théâtre pendant une année de guerre. Vrin, 1929. p. 113–34. **12104**

Discussing five plays of G.'s, and more specifically *L'illusionniste,* Basch concludes that G. has an instinctive rather than reflective sense of his craft, that he can portray only one character, himself, in which he combines lyricism with detachment to create the "sentimental cad."

Breton, Guy. Le vrai Sacha Guitry. *In his:* Antiportraits. Presses de la cité, 1968. p. 229–40. **12105**

G.'s courtesy to his actors and respect for the acting profession as seen at a rehearsal of *Pasteur.*

Doisy, Marcel. Sacha Guitry. *In his:* Esquisses; Paul Géraldy, Jean Sarment, Sacha Guitry. Flament, 1950. p. 171–268. **12106**

Sees G. in the lineage of Beaumarchais. Analyzes in some detail *Le comédien, Frans Hals, Pasteur, Mon père avait raison* and *Je t'aime.* Attempt at synthesis is unsuccessful.

Dubech, Lucien. M. Sacha Guitry. *In his:* Les chefs de file de la jeune génération. Plon, 1925. p. 165–73. **12107**

The "Molière of democracy," G., limits his comical gifts by catering to the taste of his public.

Dubeux, Albert. En écoutant Guitry. RDM 406–24, Dec. 1, 1964; 576–91, April 15, 1966. **12108**

Notes taken by Dubeux during various meetings with G., from 1925 on. In the most interesting section, *Le secret du théâtre,* G. sheds some light on the composition of his plays.

Fayard, Jean. Sacha Guitry. RDM 16:677–88, 1957. **12109**

Fayard considers that G.'s main asset was his gift for improvisation, yet believes that some of his plays will survive. He also credits him with some important technical innovations in his films.

Lauwick, Hervé. Sacha Guitry, allumeur de feux d'artifice. *In his:* D'Alphonse Allais à Sacha Guitry. Plon, 1963. p. 189–248. **12110**

Considers G.'s wit "theatrical" rather than "Parisian" but hardly discusses G. in a theatrical context. This is more a portrayal of the humorist and the man.

Le Grix, François. Le théâtre, les films et les mots de Guitry. EPar 153:108–17. **12111**

G. more exceptional as actor than author. His theater not based on situation or character but on words, a "manière" rather than a style. A certain cynicism under its pervasive charm. Severe but not unfair appraisal, subject to caution on G. as film-maker.

Régis, Léon, and François de Veynes. Sur le théâtre de M. Sacha Guitry. NRF 24:316–26, 1925. **12112**

A commendable attempt to distinguish G.'s theater from the "théâtre de boulevard." Authors underline his ability to combine wit and sensitivity, spontaneity and irony, the natural and the unexpected.

Cinema

Mars, François. Citizen Sacha. CduC 88:21–27, 1958. **12113**

By comparing the endings of *Faisons un rêve* and *Désiré* in their play and film versions, shows that G. knew how to adapt his scenarios for the screen.

Siclier, Jacques. Guitry. *In his:* Anthologie du cinéma. V. 2. L'avant-scène, 1967. p. 113–68. **12114**

Most serious study to date of G. as filmmaker. Detailed commentaries on his movies. Siclier stresses the unity of G.'s film-writing and acting. Explains why he has been underestimated as a cinematographer despite his considerable contributions. Valuable filmography but sketchy bibliography.

Truffaut, François. Sacha Guitry fut un grand réaliste. Arts 630:5, July 31-Aug. 6, 1957.   **12115**

"Sacha Guitry fut un vrai cinéaste plus doué que Duvivier, Grémillon et Feyder, plus drôle et certainement moins solennel que René Clément."

Louis Jouvet
(Nos. 12116–12139)

LAURENCE W. COR

Bibliography

Bibliographie: ouvrages et articles de Louis Jouvet. *In:* Louis Jouvet 1887–1951. *See* 12121. p. 163–69.   **12116**

Ouvrages, études et articles sur Louis Jouvet. *In:* Louis Jouvet 1887–1951. *See* 12121. p. 170–79.   **12117**

Very valuable references.

Books

Cézan, Claude. Louis Jouvet et le théâtre aujourd'hui. Emile-Paul, 1938. 220 p. *Also:* 1948.   **12118**

Detailed portrait of J., actor, director, and teacher, with particular reference to prime influences on his career, Copeau and Giraudoux. A homage to J. and his contributions to the theater of his time. Introduction by Giraudoux (p. 7–41) on distinction between the German and French theater between the wars.

Knapp, Bettina Liebowitz. Louis Jouvet man of the theatre. Columbia univ. press, 1957. 345 p.   **12119**

Valuable information on life of J., his development as an actor and director. Relations with Copeau, Romains, Giraudoux. Problems of staging plays and reactions of critics. Very good on J.'s particular concern: respect for the text. Interesting for the intimate rapport between J. and Giraudoux and for J.'s understanding of Molière. Bibliography of sources and interviews. Reviews: J. McClaren in RR 49:233–34, 1958; R. Robinson in ETJ 10: 276–77, 1958.

Marquetty, Valentin. Mon ami Jouvet. Eds. du conquistador, 1952. 219 p.   **12120**

A remarkable book dealing with J.'s professional career, his times, his associates (especially Copeau and Giraudoux), and the qualities of mind and spirit that were reflected in his work as an actor and director. An intimate portrait of a man of the theater and of an individual striving to realize himself. Reveals an aspect of J.'s inner life that only a friend would know.

Special Number

Louis Jouvet 1887–1951. Notes et documents. RHT 4:5–179, 1952.   **12121**

An invaluable storehouse of materials for the researcher. Articles by Brisson and Jamati have been analyzed separately. In addition to bibliographies, listing of J.'s roles and films, information on the J. company, etc., there are the following additional articles: Paul Abram, *Louis Jouvet professeur au Conservatoire,* p. 134–35; Jacques Jaujard, *La décentralisation dramatique,* p. 149–51; Louis Joxe, *Les tournées mondiales. S. E. Louis Jouvet, ambassadeur du génie français,* p. 119–26; Jean Mayer, *La classe de Louis Jouvet au Conservatoire,* p. 136–39; Henri Sauguet, *Louis Jouvet et la musique,* p. 145–48; P.-A. Touchard, *Louis Jouvet à la Comédie française,* p. 132–33.

Articles

Arnold, Paul. Les 5 styles de Louis Jouvet. RGB 90:459–74, 1954.   **12122**

Excellent, concise essay on the directorial styles adopted by J. in mounting the plays of Romains, Giraudoux, Claudel, and Molière, with interesting comments on J.'s efforts to suggest the supernatural on the stage.

Barrault, Jean-Louis. Louis Jouvet, le chef de la famille. NL 2278:14, May 21, 1971.   **12123**

Two aspects of J.: his fear of death and self-deception. Perceptive remarks on the purity of his *mises en scène.*

Beck, William. Louis Jouvet et le théâtre de Jules Romains et de Jean Giraudoux. RUO 39:337–50, 1969. **12124**

What J. was looking for in plays he chose to direct and why he was so successful with plays by Romains and Giraudoux.

Bertin, Pierre. Jouvet, Giraudoux et le langage. RDM 8:693–98, 1959. **12125**

Evolution and defense of the cult of language, supported by relevant quotations from Giraudoux and J.

Brasillach, Robert. Les héritiers du Vieux Colombier. *In his:* Animateurs de théâtre. Corrêa, 1936. p. 11–49. **12126**

Appreciation of J. as an actor and comments on his productions.

Brisson, Pierre. Les deux Jouvet. *In:* Louis Jouvet 1887–1951. *See* 12121. p. 7–16. **12127**

Portrait of J. and his relationships with Giraudoux and Christian Bérard.

Cézan, Claude. Qui était Louis Jouvet? NL 1772:9, Aug. 17, 1961. **12128**

Facets of J.'s personality and character as viewed by his friends (Romains, Jeanson, Neveux, etc.) on tenth anniversary of his death.

Claudel, Paul, and Louis Jouvet. L'annonce faite à Marie: Correspondance. *In:* Claudel homme de théâtre: Correspondances avec Copeau, Dullin, Jouvet. Ed. by Henri Micciollo and Jacques Petit. Gallimard, 1966. p. 206–22. **12129**

Correspondence regarding the staging of *L'annonce faite à Marie.*

Cor, Laurence W. Jouvet on dialogue and the performance. FR 39:426–32, 1965. **12130**

J.'s concern for establishing the playwright's meaning through correct voicing of the words and breathing in a rhythm suggested by the text.

Guth, Paul. Quand Jouvet répète. RdP 56: 133–40, 1949. **12131**

How J. rehearsed a revival of *Knock* and his thoughts on the matter of the actor's "sincerity."

Hort, J. Louis Jouvet. *In his:* Les théâtres du cartel et leurs animateurs: Pitoëff, Baty, Jouvet, Dullin. Geneva, Skira, 1944. p. 153–72. **12132**

The nature of J.'s *mises en scène* and his concern for the success of a play.

Jamati, Georges. Louis Jouvet, esthéticien. *In:* Louis Jouvet 1887–1951. *See* 12121. p. 140–44. **12133**

An interpretation of J.'s art in the light of *Écoute, mon ami* and *Témoignages sur le théâtre.*

Larkin, Oliver Waterman. Two French directors and their two theatres. ThA 15: 42–48, 1931. **12134**

Of interest for a reaction to J.'s production of *Donogoo.*

Lièvre, Pierre. Conversations sur l'art du comédien. NRF 627–50, 1929. **12135**

Interview with J. on Diderot's *Paradoxe du comédien.* Comments on differences between acting for the stage and for films. Discusses nature of theater audience.

Raymond, Marcel. Louis Jouvet. *In his:* Le jeu retrouvé. Montreal, Eds. de l'arbre, 1943. p. 137–50. **12136**

Brief résumé of J.'s career and discussion of salient features of his approach to acting and theatrical direction.

Romains, Jules. Jouvet. *In his:* Amitiés et rencontres. Flammarion, 1970. p. 143–59. **12137**

Impressions of J., with particular reference to the director's anxiety and uncertainty before a performance. How Romains convinced J. to modify the original conception of the central character in *Knock.*

Touchard, Pierre-Aimé. Louis Jouvet. Esp 186:128–34, 1952. **12138**

Excellent appreciation and criticism of J.'s contribution to the French theater and cinema.

———. Louis Jouvet libère ses secrets. Arts 373:2, 4, Aug. 22, 1952. **12139**

Interesting essay on the "paradox" of J.: the conflict between his intelligence and his sensibility.

Georges and Ludmilla Pitoëff
(Nos. 12140–12173)

BARBARA GORDON

Texts by Pitoëff

Pitoëff, Georges. Notre théâtre. Textes et documents réunis par Jean de Rigault. Messages, 1949. 113 p.   **12140**

Contains portions of essays, lectures, program notes and letters composed by P. Presents directorial concepts and interpretations of Shakespeare, Pirandello, Chekhov, Ibsen, Shaw, Lenormand, Molnar, Block, Ferrero, O'Neill, Bruckner, Claudel, Anouilh, Gide, Supervielle and Dumas.

Review: J. Carat in Paru 57:40–43, 1950.

————. Théâtre et metteur en scène. *In:* Gouhier, Henri. L'essence du théâtre. Plon, 1943. p. iii–iv. (Présences)   **12141**

Important document on P.'s directorial theories. Emphasizes role of décor in theatrical production.

Studies: Books

Frank, André. Georges Pitoëff. L'arche, 1958. 160 p. (Le théâtre et les jours)   **12142**

Traces theatrical career of P. from 1904 until his death in 1939. Contains numerous quotations and portions of P.'s writings. Emphasizes artistic integrity of P. and his respect for dramatic literature. Documentary rather than critical study.

Review: J. Bastuji in MD 3:404–05, 1961.

Hort, Jean. La vie héroïque des Pitoëff. Geneva, Pierre Cailler, 1966. 577 p.   **12143**

Vast biographical study of Georges and Ludmilla P. written by actor who worked with them between 1920 and 1939. Based on personal recollections, but comprehensive and discerning. Presents life, epoch and personal relationships of the P.s through their work, emphasizing artistic courage and integrity. Includes detailed observations on persons and events surrounding them and offers insights to cultural movements of their time.

Lenormand, Henri-René. Les Pitoëff, souvenirs. Odette Lieutier, 1943. 203 p.   **12144**

Analyzes the joint theatrical career of Georges and Ludmilla P. Combines personal recollection with objective description. Comments on dramatic interpretations, methods of work and artistic significance of the P.s, emphasizing their professional struggles. Penetrating, compassionate biographical account.

Pitoëff, Aniouta. Ludmilla, ma mère. Vie de Ludmilla et de Georges Pitoëff. René Julliard, 1955. 296 p.   **12145**

Sensitive biography of the P.s, written by their daughter. Reveals human and artistic moments in their lives and careers. Subjective, passionate analysis of events and relationships.

Reviews: G. Cohen in Flam 39:323–24, 1956; J. Lemarchand in FL 10, Aug. 20, 1955; M. Pons in CRB 14:122–25, 1955.

Other Studies

Anders, France. Jacques Copeau et le Cartel des quatre. Nizet, 1959. 341 p.   **12146**

Includes analysis of work of the P.s. Stresses contribution of Cartel directors to evolution of *metteur en scène* in contemporary theater.

Artaud, Antonin. Lettres à Génica Athanasiou. Gallimard, 1969. 381 p.   **12147**

Includes references to personal-professional relationship between Artaud and the P. family around 1923, with observations on *Liliom* (1923) and other important productions.

Bernard, Jean-Jacques. Georges et Ludmilla Pitoëff. RevTh 27:7–16, 1954.   **12148**

Tribute to the artistry of the P.s. Discusses Georges P.'s work as director and actor, relationship with Ludmilla, and collaboration with Bernard, Pirandello, and Shaw.

Borgal, Clément. Georges Pitoëff. *In his:* Metteurs en scène. Fernand Lanore, 1963. p. 165–97.   **12149**

Concise, well-documented biographical study. Covers entire joint career of Georges and Ludmilla P., focusing on scope and diversity of their repertoire.

Review: H. Gouhier in TR 192: 135–36, 1964.

Brasillach, Robert. Georges et Ludmilla Pitoëff. *In his:* Animateurs de théâtre. Corrêa, 1936. p. 77–128. *Also:* Table ronde, 1954. p. 45–73. **12150**
Personal reflections on work of the P.s. Discusses rapport with youth of their period, innovations of Georges P. in *mise en scène* and scene design, and significance of the P.s. as actors. Descriptive and sentimental in tone. Review: J. Cusson in AmF 3:26–31, 1942.

————. Notre avant-guerre. Plon, 1941. 358 p. **12151**
Includes highly personal recollections of the P. family prior to 1940.

Brisson, Pierre. Le souvenir de Georges Pitoëff. FL 158:1, April 30, 1949. *Also:* Pitoëff le visionnaire. *In his:* Propos de théâtre. Gallimard, 1957. p. 111–19. **12152**
Tribute to Georges P., written on tenth anniversary of his death. Briefly analyzes evolution of his "visionary" style as actor and director, with references to interpretations of *Les six personnages, Hamlet* and *L'ennemi du peuple.*

Chenevière, Jacques. Ludmilla. *In his:* Retours et images. Lausanne, Eds. rencontre, 1966. p. 210–16. **12153**
Personal recollections of the P.s, with tribute to Ludmilla as actress.

Cocteau, Jean; Marguerite Jamois; Georges Pitoëff; Svetlana Pitoëff; Varvara Pitoëff; and Catherine Valogne. Hommages à Ludmilla Pitoëff. LetF 430:5, Sept. 11–18, 1952. **12154**
Eulogies for Ludmilla P., with personal anecdotes and reflections on her work. Penetrating and informative.

Crémieux, Benjamin. L'art du metteur en scène et du comédien: Copeau, Jouvet, Dullin, Baty, Pitoëff. Eur 47–48:130–50, 1949. **12155**
Lecture given in March 1941 on Copeau and the Cartel des Quatre. Includes discussion of Georges P. as director and description of the P.s as actors. Emphasizes absolutism and spiritualism, yet considers P. as most "Cartesian" of Cartel directors.

————. Souvenir de Pitoëff. NRF 54:113–18, 1940. *Also in:* Pitoëff, Georges. Notre théâtre. *See* 12140. p. 86–92. **12156**
Tribute to Georges P., describing some of his basic ideas, interpretations and methods. Emphasizes mysticism of P. as director.

Davril, Robert. Les mises en scène de Pitoëff. EA 13:192–96, 1960. **12157**
Brief but well-documented critical description of Georges P.'s Shakespearean productions: *Hamlet, Macbeth, Mesure pour mesure,* and *Roméo et Juliette.* Emphasizes scenic *dépouillement.*

Dhomme, Sylvain. Le cartel. *In his:* La mise en scène contemporaine d'André Antoine à Bertolt Brecht. Fernand Nathan, 1959. p. 153–88. **12158**
Brief summary of the P. enterprise. Emphasizes Georges P.'s eclecticism and esthetic innovations.

Dormoy, Marie. La mise en scène de quelques spectacles Pitoëff. ChTh 1:465–67, 1922. **12159**
Discusses two productions directed by Georges P.: Wilde's *La tragédie de Salomé* and Shaw's *Androclès et le lion.* Focuses on décor.

Elder, Judith. The cartel of four. ThAn 18:26–37, 1961. **12160**
Discusses history, principles and significance of the Cartel des Quatre: Jouvet, Dullin, P., and Baty.

Frank, André. Georges Pitoëff et H.-R. Lenormand, son témoin ... RevTh 29:20–25, 1954. **12161**
Concerns relationship between Lenormand and the P.s. Includes unpublished notes and sketches by Lenormand for *mise en scène* of *Les ratés.*

Hort, Jean. Pitoëff. *In his:* Les théâtres du Cartel et leurs animateurs. Geneva, Skira, 1944. p. 55–120. **12162**
Sound analysis of P.'s work as director and actor. Personal, yet critical document. Evaluates main stages of P.'s career, most significant productions, and influence on theater of his time. Also considers contribution of Ludmilla.

Knowles, Dorothy. The theatres and producers. *In her:* French drama of the interwar years, 1918–39. London, Harrap,

1967 p. 13–47. *Also:* New York, Barnes and Noble, 1968.   **12163**

Includes brief critical analysis of work of Georges and Ludmilla P. Concentrates on Georges P.'s directorial theories and methods, mentioning influence of Dalcroze on his work.

Lenormand, H.-R. Notes sur Ludmilla Pitoëff. ChTh 2:468–71, 1923.   **12164**

Tribute to Ludmilla P. as actress. Discusses style, technique and effect on audience.

Mallarmé, Camille. Comment Luigi Pirandello fut révélé au public parisien le 20 décembre 1922. RHT 7:7–37, 1955.
12165

Mentions Georges P.'s production of *Six personnages en quête d'auteur* in 1922.

Pitoëff, Aniouta. Liste des pièces du théâtre irlandais créées par les Pitoëff. CRB 37:105–06, 1962.   **12166**

Includes plays by Lady Gregory, Shaw, and Synge, with dates and places of productions by the P.s.

Pitoëff, Sacha. Georges Pitoëff et le décor de théâtre. RevTh 9–10:40–44, 1948.
12167

Discusses Georges P.'s work as scenic designer, with references to productions of *Mangeur de rêves, Mixture, La dame aux camélias, Macbeth, Roméo et Juliette, Le singe velu, Les criminels, Liliom,* and *Sainte Jeanne.*

————. Souvenirs sur mon père. MagS 7:7–18, 1946.   **12168**

Suggestive biographical document on Georges P., with interesting personal reflections and anecdotes by his son. Analyzes P.'s temperament, goals, directorial methods, and acting style. Stresses union of artist and man.

Pitoëff, Svetlana. Georges et Ludmilla. Eur 396–97:162–73, 1962.   **12169**

Recounts careers of Georges and Ludmilla P., with personal notes. Focuses on scope of their repertoire and describes representative productions, including *Henri IV, Sainte Jeanne* and *Hamlet.*

Porché, François. Georges Pitoëff. RdP 47:327–33, 1940.   **12170**

Notes on career and esthetic experimentation of P. Emphasizes austerity, economy, and interior life of the "spectacle Pitoëff."

Raymond, Marcel. L'œuvre des Pitoëff. NRel 2:257–66; 345–55, 1943. *Also in his:* Le jeu retrouvé. Montreal, Eds. de l'arbre, 1943. p. 95–121.   **12171**

Describes career, working methods and artistic contribution of the P.s, emphasizing universality of repertoire.

Towarnicki, Frédéric. Les Pitoëff. *In:* Encyclopédie du théâtre contemporain. V. 2. Dirigée par Gilles Quéant avec la collaboration de Frédéric Towarnicki, direction artistique et réalisation de Aline Elmayan. Olivier Perrin, 1959. p. 59–66.
12172

Enthusiastic commentary on theatrical careers of the P.s. Illustrated with photographs of their productions. Emphasizes Georges P.'s audacity as director, diversity of his repertoire and contribution to the evolution of scenic art.

Weiss, Rudolph. Georges Pitoëff—his Shakespeare productions in France. Trans. by Brien Keith-Smith. ThR 5:72–84, 1963.   **12173**

Suggestive critical discussion of P.'s directorial concepts and methods. Emphasizes poetic interpretation of Shakespearean works and includes details on productions of *Hamlet* and *Romeo and Juliet.*

Jean Vilar
(Nos. 12174–12185)

BIRUTA CAP

Baecque, André de. Une expérience décisive: le T.N.P. *In his:* Le théâtre d'aujourd'hui. Seghers, 1964. p. 52–89. (Clefs du temps présent)   **12174**

Highlights of V.'s career. Baecque stresses Dullin's influence on his disciple V. V.'s relationship with Gérard Philipe, with other actors and with the public. Attendance records.

Beigbeder, Marc. La théâtralité intériorisée et ses chefs-d'œuvre. Jean Vilar. *In his:* Le théâtre en France depuis la Libération. Bordas, 1959. p. 192–216.   **12175**

Stresses V.'s efforts to emphasize the inner emotion in the characters, to the detriment of the external aspects such as costumes, decor, gestures. Places V. in the mainstream of an important movement of this century.

Bermel, Albert. Jean Vilar: unadorned theatre for the greatest number. TDR 5:24–43, 1960. **12176**

Thorough and detailed history of the T.N.P. and of V.'s career. Discusses lighting, acting, critical reaction to individual stagings and gives his own critical appraisal of those witnessed personally. Comparison of the T.N.P. and the Comédie Française. V.'s interpretation of various dramatists. A general evaluation of the Vilar-T.N.P. phenomenon. Indispensable study.

Guicharanaud, Jacques. Jean Vilar and the T.N.P. YFS 14:10–18, 1954–55. **12177**

Highly readable and succinct history of V.'s rise. Sketches a panorama of French theater and situates V. Defines V.'s style. List of plays produced by V.

Leclerc, Guy. Les grandes aventures du théâtre. Préf. de Jean Vilar. Les éditeurs français réunis, 1965. p. 381–86. **12178**

Highlights V.'s innovations, particularly in stage setting. Drawings and diagrams.

––––––. Le T.N.P. de Jean Vilar. Union générale d'éditions, 1971. 242 p. (10/18) **12179**

A capital work on V. and the T.N.P. Leclerc, who had followed the T.N.P.'s activities from the beginning as a reporter for *Humanité,* has finally written a thorough historical analysis and evaluation of the functioning of "the theater for the masses." Discusses T.N.P. as an outgrowth of the Resistance; Copeau's as well as Gémier's legacy; theater as a public service and as a "tool of social adaptation;" the composition of the T.N.P.'s audience; V.'s choice of repertory; Brecht's influence and archetypes.

Serrière, Marie-Thérèse. Le T.N.P. et nous. Corti, 1959. 189 p. **12180**

Brief history of V.'s struggles leading to the T.N.P. Theoretical analysis of the components of spectacle: place, décor, lighting, music, acting; the playwright and the public; as well as subtler aspects of their interplay and how they succeed in T.N.P. productions. V.'s work in the context of his precursors and contemporaries. Excellent photographs. A capital work.

Temkine, Raymonde. Le T.N.P. *In her:* L'entreprise théâtre. Cujas, 1967. p. 147–76, 356–58. **12181**

Brief introductory note by V. The economic and political history of the founding and functioning of the T.N.P. under V. Well documented.

Valogne, Catherine. Jean Vilar. Presses littéraires de France, 1954. 80 p. (Les metteurs en scène) **12182**

Traces V.'s development from Dullin's influence to early stagings, to Avignon and the T.N.P. Stresses creation of settings. Chronology of productions. List of actors. Photos of productions.

Vilar, Jean. De la tradition tréâtrale. Paris, L'arche, 1955. 172 p. *Also:* Gallimard, 1963. 188 p. (Idées, 33) **12183**

V. defines his conception of theater, differentiating it from that of his direct predecessors (Dullin) and contemporaries.

––––––. Un lieu théâtral: Avignon. *In:* Le lieu théâtral dans la société moderne. Textes réunis et présentés par Denis Bablet et Jean Jacquot. Centre national de la recherche scientifique, 1963. p. 153–59 and pl. XXIX. **12184**

Precise details about the adaptation and furnishing of the court of the Papal Palace for V.'s productions. 2 photos.

Vilar mot pour mot. Textes réunis et présentés par Melly Touzoul et Jacques Téphany. Stock, 1972. 283 p. (Théâtre ouvert) **12185**

Chronology of V.'s life and works. His thoughts on theater-related subjects and opinions of certain dramatists. V.'s thoughts on Avignon, the art of acting, the representation of historical plays, the reactions of the audience, the role of the producer. V. on the theater in general and the T.N.P. in particular. Some personal notes. Photographs of V. at work and play. List of plays produced at the T.N.P. and before. V.'s roles. Bibliography, p. 269–74. Index. The most complete book on V. to date.

CHAPTER XXVIII

CRITICISM BEFORE 1940

(Nos. 12186–12504)

Chapter Organizer: GERALD PRINCE
JACQUES BOSSIÈRE, ALVIN EUSTIS, DAVID J. KLEIN, JACK KOLBERT,
MOSES M. NAGY, HELEN T. NAUGHTON, GERALD PRINCE, AND ALLEN WHARTENBY

Criticism in General
(Nos. 12186–12214)

GERALD PRINCE

Abirached, Robert. Panorama de la critique littéraire en France de 1945 à nos jours. Tend 177–99, April 1962. **12186**

Discusses three major brands of criticism: the journalistic, judged with severity; the traditional, renewed and deepened by Marxist, psychoanalytic and existentialist thought; and the new criticism, concerned with the very meaning of literature and shifting the established object of critical inquiry. Sometimes dated already in some of its appreciations, particularly in the case of Sartre and Barthes, but lucid and balanced on the whole.

Baldensperger, Fernand. Critique explicative ou critique génétique. *In his:* La critique et l'histoire littéraires en France au dix-neuvième et au début du vingtième siècle. New York, Brentano's, 1945. p. 203–35. **12187**

Quick portraits of important and not so important critics from Faguet to Thibaudet. Includes short passages representative of their work. Often dated and superficial, but useful and not without insights.

Bersani, Jacques; Michel Autrand; Jacques Lecarme; and Bruno Vercier. Les problèmes de la critique. *In their:* La littérature en France depuis 1945. Bordas, 1970. p. 811–37. **12188**

Excellent essay identifying major brands of criticism, from *critique de goût* to *nouvelle critique,* and some of their eminent representatives. Good account of the quarrel between new and old critics. Good distinctions made among various tendencies in new criticism.

Blanzat, Jean. Le critique dans le monde contemporain. *In:* Situation de la critique. Actes du premier colloque international de la critique littéraire (Paris, 4–8 juin 1962). Syndicat des critiques littéraires, 1964. p. 12–25. **12189**

Interesting panorama of the practice of literary criticism in France in dailies and weeklies and on radio and television. Sketches critics' social and intellectual background and position as well as material and moral pressures to which they are subjected.

Brenner, Jacques. Les critiques dramatiques. Flammarion, 1970. 260 p. **12190**

Last two chapters are devoted to important drama reviewers in the twentieth century. Amusing short portraits of Kemp, G. Marcel, J.-J. Gautier, Lemarchand, Sandier and others. Superficial but entertaining and informative.

Carloni, J.-C., and Jean-C. Filloux. La critique littéraire. Presses univ. de France, 1955. 118 p. (Que sais-je, 664) *Also (rev.):* 1969. 128 p. **12191**

The last third of the revised edition deals with major trends in twentieth-century French criticism. Sketchy but useful.

Clancier, Anne. Psychanalyse et critique littéraire. Toulouse, Privat, 1973. 228 p. **12192**

Study of the relationship between psychoanalysis and literary criticism from Freud to Marthe Robert and Charles Mauron. Some interesting pages on such analysts as Delay, Rosolato and O. Mannoni. Clear but superficial on the whole. The lack of a discussion of Lacan's work is remarkable.

Colesanti, Massimo. Panorama della critica francese. Ul 63–73, Dec. 1962. **12193**
Quick study of criticial directions since Sainte-Beuve. Argues that now fundamental distinction between objective and subjective, historical and esthetic criticism goes back to nineteenth century. Useful passages on academic criticism. Overemphasizes avant-garde role of N.R.F.

Costaz, Gilles. La critique littéraire. Tend 673–96, Dec. 1969. **12194**
Interesting study dealing primarily with contemporary criticism in dailies and weeklies. Helpful indications on the critical orientation of major newspapers and literary magazines and on such critics as Billy, Kanters, Nadeau and Pivot. Good bibliographical notes.

Décaudin, Michel. L'année 1908 et les origines de la N.R.F. RSH 17:347–58, 1952. **12195**
Interesting, well-documented article attempting to show that birth of N.R.F. coincided with fundamental reclassification of values. Thinks N.R.F. represented neither a literary party nor a literary group but rather a literary spirit and argues that this constituted its real originality and would become its trademark.

Diéguez, Manuel de. L'écrivain et son langage. Gallimard, 1960. 338 p. (Les essais, 97) **12196**
After a discussion of criticism up to Sainte-Beuve, author studies with intelligence and verve major twentieth-century critics—Valéry, Paulhan, Barthes, Blanchot, Poulet, Béguin and Sartre—and their relation to language. In the final chapter, an existential psychoanalysis of style is proposed.

Fayolle, Roger. La critique littéraire. Armand Colin, 1964. 430 p. *Also:* New York, McGraw-Hill, 1967. 430 p. **12197**
Sections entitled "Critique érudite et critique créatrice" and "Vers une révolution critique" are the relevant ones and constitute a good introduction to twentieth-century French criticism. Con-

temporary critics are treated with perhaps too much diffidence.
Reviews: R. Molho in RHL 66:541–42, 1966; L. Roudiez in RR 57:77–78, 1966; F. Siccardo in SF 10:195, 1966.

Flasche, Hans. Die französische Literaturkritik von 1900–1950. GRM 33:132–50, 1951–52. **12198**
Presents important critics from Anatole France to Albert Béguin, including short vignettes on Bourget, Claudel, Valéry, Larbaud, Thibaudet and Sartre. Stresses accomplishments of criticism. Puts far too much emphasis on "creative" critics and not enough on "professional" critics.

Fowlie, Wallace. The French critic 1549–1967. Carbondale, Southern Illinois univ. press, 1968. viii, 184 p. **12199**
Most of the book is devoted to major trends in twentieth-century criticism. Argues that essential crisis of modern criticism results from the victory of the anthropologist over the impressionist. Not always quite accurate, sometimes arbitrary and hurried, but generally clear and incisive. Fine perception of literary problems.
Reviews: H. Gershman in BA 43: 226, 1969; A. Glauser in FR 43:199–200, 1969; R. Nelly in EspCr 9:314–15, 1969.

Kopp, Robert. Französische Literaturwissenschaft im 20. Jahrhundert. *In:* Literaturwissenschaft und Literaturkritik im 20. Jahrhundert. Ed. by Felix Philipp Ingold. Bern, Kandelaber Verlag, 1970. p. 85–106. **12200**
After clear and faithful presentation of quarrel between new and traditional critics, attempts to show that it is similar to earlier critical quarrels such as the one between Lanson and Péguy. Discusses new critical trends and argues that many of them have their antecedents in writers like Proust and Valéry. Good bibliography.

Lemaître, Henri; Françoise Baqué; and Marie-Céline Serres. L'homme en question dans la littérature. *In:* La littérature française. Ed. by André Lagarde and Laurent Michard. V. 5: La littérature aujourd'hui. Bordas, 1971. p. 247–91. **12201**
Good panorama of critical activity in France from literary history and Jean

Pommier to new criticism and the *Tel quel* group.

LeSage, Laurent. Some new French literary critics. ASLHM 26:297–309 1955. **12202**

Argues that major mid-century critics in France are philosophers and moralists rather than judges or esthetes. Discusses Albérès, Boisdeffre, Nadeau, Picon and P.-H. Simon and exaggerates their historical and critical importance.

————, **and André Yon.** Dictionnaire des critiques littéraires: guide de la critique française du XXᵉ siècle. University Park and London, Pennsylvania State univ. press, 1969. 281 p. **12203**

Useful though often unrewarding bio-bibliographical sketches and thumbnail appraisals of over 100 modern French literary critics, preceded by account of critical trends in France in this century. Some important critics are omitted and scale of values is not always clear. Informative on minor critics of our time. Good general bibliography.

Reviews: J. Clark in FS 25:498–99, 1971; S. Haig in SFr 14:381, 1970; I. Ivask in BA 43:554, 1969; R. Jones in FR 44:472–73, 1970.

Modern French criticism. From Proust and Valéry to structuralism. Ed. by John K. Simon. Chicago and London, Univ. of Chicago press, 1972. xvi, 405 p. **12204**

John K. Simon, *Prefatory note*, p. vii–xvi; Ralph Freedman, *Valéry: Protean critic*, p. 1–40; John Porter Houston, *Proust, Gourmont, and the symbolist heritage*, p. 41–60; Angelo P. Bertocci, *Charles Du Bos and the critique of genius*, p. 61–83; René Wellek, *Albert Thibaudet*, p. 85–107; Alvin Eustis, *The paradoxes of language: Jean Paulhan*, p. 109–22; Frederick Brown, *Creation versus literature: Breton and the surrealist movement*, p. 123–47; Michel Beaujour, *Eros and nonsense: Georges Bataille*, p. 149–73; Robert Champigny, *Gaston Bachelard*, p. 175–91; Fredric Jameson, *Three methods in Sartre's literary criticism*, p. 193–227; Neal Oxenhandler, *Literature as perception in the work of Merleau-Ponty*, p. 229–53; Paul de Man, *Maurice Blanchot*, p. 255–76; J. Hillis Miller, *The Geneva school: the criticism of Marcel Raymond, Albert Béguin, Georges Poulet, Jean Rousset, Jean-*

Pierre Richard, and Jean Starobinski, p. 277–310; Yves Velan, *Barthes*, p. 311–39; Edward W. Said, *Abecedarium culturae: structuralism, absence, writing*, p. 341–92; *Selected general bibliography*, p. 393–96. The relevant articles have been analyzed separately under the appropriate headings.

Reviews: A. Aldridge in BA 47:325–26, 1973; G. Bauer in FR 46:424–25, 1972.

Moreau, Pierre. Vingtième siècle. *In his:* La critique littéraire en France. Armand Colin, 1960. p. 173–202. **12205**

Historical presentation of main trends in French criticism from 1900 to 1950. Voices reservations about critical tendencies emerging after World War II. Some good characterizations of individual critics but, in general, too hurried.

Reviews: E. Caramaschi in SFr 5: 509–13, 1961; A. Moulis in RHL 62: 460–61, 1962.

Morino, L[ina]. La Nouvelle Revue Française dans l'histoire des lettres (1908–1937). Gallimard, 1939. 228 p. **12206**

Interesting description of main characteristics of N.R.F. Concludes that its major strength was stress on quality, balance, depth and rigor. Thinks it was perhaps too intellectual and sometimes too timid. Though not sufficiently critical, provides good initiation to principal collaborators.

Nadeau, Maurice. Esprit et méthodes de la critique contemporaine. *In:* Situation de la critique. Actes du premier colloque international de la critique littéraire (Paris, 4–8 juin 1962). Syndicat des critiques littéraires, 1964. p. 141–57. **12207**

Author divides literary criticism into three categories: impressionist criticism, academic criticism and new criticism. Sketches their fundamental positions and their limitations. Competent panorama in spite of poor organization and overemphasis on new criticism. Discussion of such critics as Starobinski, Sartre and the early Barthes is not satisfactory.

Picon, Gaëtan. Panorama della critica contemporanea. Conv 23:311–22, 1955. *Trans.:* Sur la critique française contemporaine. CahNo 4–5:257–69, 1955–56. **12208**

Good panorama of French criticism around 1955, characterizing it as philosophical, totalitarian and deficient in the domain of esthetics and esthetic judgment. Notes the lack of good Marxist criticism and comments favorably on such critics as Blanchot and Poulet. Makes incisive remarks on important pre-World War II critics.

Pivot, Bernard. Les critiques littéraires. Flammarion, 1968. 236 p. **12209**

Amusing study of book reviewers for French newspapers and periodicals and of the practical imperatives they face. Informative, interesting and demythifying.

Reviews: F. Livi in TR 245:115–16, 1968; A. Marissel in Esp 35:947–49, 1968.

Romani, Bruno. La critica francese. Da Sainte-Beuve allo strutturalismo. Ravenna, A. Longo, 1968. 203 p. **12210**

The second half of the book is the relevant one and constitutes a fair introduction to twentieth century French criticism. Author tends to give too much importance to N.R.F. critics, "creative" critics and, above all, new critics. Neglects more traditional critics and influential early twentieth-century movements like "classical" criticism.

Stevens, Linton C. Major trends in post-war French criticism. FR 30:218–24, 1957. **12211**

Shows that break in continuity between pre-World War II and post-World War II criticism is not as great as it may appear. Then attempts to fit postwar critics in one of five major categories: semantic or style conscious, philosophical, ideological, belletristic and moralistic. Dated, sometimes superficial, but still useful article.

Thibaudet, Albert. Réflexions. NRF 21: 304–14, 1933. *Also as:* Le maurrasisme et la retraite de la critique universitaire. *In his:* Réflexions sur la critique. Gallimard, 1939. p. 220–30. **12212**

Good essay arguing that first third of twentieth century marked a decline of academic criticism. The importance of little magazines during the period as well as the prominence of men like Souday, abbé Bremond, Vandérem, and especially Maurras and his followers are advanced as proofs of this decline. In-

telligent and entertaining characterizations of these influential critics are drawn.

Van Tieghem, Philippe. Tendances nouvelles en histoire littéraire. EFA 22:1–67, 1930. **12213**

Examines debate surrounding the methods and goals of literary history around 1930 and outlines the positions of such critics as Lanson, Mornet and Baldensperger. Thinks that literary history is important but that it must ultimately lead back to the work itself. Dated but still valuable.

Wellek, René. French classical criticism in the twentieth century. YFS 38:47–71, 1967. **12214**

Examines works of Maurras and of contemporaries and followers who accepted and developed his creed. Shows that there were other critics, like Benda, who violently opposed Maurras' ideology and still shared many of his literary doctrines. Points out that some N.R.F. critics as well as Valéry used the term and concept of classicism. Finds it difficult to judge impact of Maurras' positions on the many recourses to classical tradition and to assess influence of French classical criticism abroad. Very good, informative study. Interesting judgments on individual critics.

Henri Bremond
(Nos. 12215–12243)

MOSES M. NAGY AND ALLEN WHARTENBY

Correspondence

Blanchet, André. Claudel, lecteur de Bremond. Et 323:155–74, 1965. **12215**

The B.-Claudel correspondence, edited and annotated by Blanchet, sheds some light on the genesis of B.'s work and on Claudel's reaction to it. Claudel's remarks are pertinent, scholarly, and orthodox. [MMN]

Bremond, Henri, and Maurice Blondel. Correspondance. Ed. by André Blanchet. Aubier Montaigne, 1970–71. 3 v. **12216**

Blanchet follows B. and Blondel step by step and measures all possible dimensions of their mutual friendship because

it coincides with the most important period of their lives. The abundant notes accompanying the letters help the reader to understand both the authors and their epoch. Blanchet poured into these 3 v. his great erudition on B., and the result is a masterpiece of scholarship. [MMN]
Review: Anon. in BCLF 26:854, 1971. Review article: P. Moreau. En marge des commencements d'une amitié. RHL 70: 463–67, 1971.

Biography

Blanchet, André. L'abbé Henri Bremond. *In:* Entretiens sur Henri Bremond. *See* 12224. p. 19–41.   **12217**
Analyzes the contradictory character and enigmatic inner-life of B. Summarizes in two words the man and writer, "protéisme" and "caméléonisme." Excellent portrait of the Mephisto of mystical literature. [MMN]

————. Bremond et Blondel. *In:* Henri Bremond, 1865–1933. *See* 12225. p. 67–74.   **12218**
The B.-Blondel friendship lasted lasted thirty-six years (1897–1933). Good analysis which measures also the extent of the influence they exercised on each other, with the emphasis on that of Blondel who saved B. from "several precipices." [MMN]

————. Henri Bremond, 1865–1904. Préface par Henri Gouhier. Postface du Père Holstein. Aubier Montaigne, 1975. 286 p. (Etudes bremondiennes) **12219**
Blanchet was fascinated with the work and personality of B. and studied extensively his ex-confrere's career. Blanchet gives a detailed account of the birth of the historian, and of the young Jesuit who suffers because of lack of understanding by his contemporaries. An objective biography, but too incomplete, for it stops where B.'s career began to ascend. [MMN]
Review: X. Tilliette in Et 343:463–66, 1975.

————. Redécouverte de Bremond. *In:* Henri Bremond, 1865–1933. *See* 12225. p. 11–25.   **12220**
Excellent introduction to the life and works of B. The quarrel of "poésie pure" and the suspicion of modernism

which overshadows his life eclipsed his major work, *Histoire du sentiment religieux.* [MMN]

Dagens, Jean. Introduction à Henri Bremond. *In:* Entretiens sur Henri Bremond. *See* 12224. p. 1–18.   **12221**
Summarizes the major events in B.'s life with emphasis on his career in the Society of Jesus and the reasons for his leaving this community. [MMN]

Guiral, Pierre. Bremond et Maurras. *In:* Henri Bremond, 1865–1933. *See* 12225. p. 37–49.   **12222**
Not the most original study, but gives a good insight into the conflict between the political philosophy of the Action française and, on the other hand, of the Christian who tried to keep politics and religion apart. [MMN]

Hermans, Francis. L'humanisme religieux de l'abbé Bremond: 1865–1933; essai d'analyse doctrinale. Alsatia, 1965. 286 p. **12223**
Study of B.'s life and work with particular emphasis on his place as a teacher by example rather than as master. Along with long analyses of doctrine and critical theory, it is a detailed account of the development and inner life of a Christian humanist. Written with strong Catholic bias. [AW]

Collected Articles

Entretiens sur Henri Bremond. Ed. by Maurice Nédoncelle and Jean Dagens. Paris-The Hague, Mouton, 1967. 252 p. (Décades du Centre culturel international de Cerisy-la-Salle. Nouvelle série, 4)   **12224**
Contents analyzed separately. [MMN]

Henri Bremond, 1865–1933. Actes du Colloque d'Aix 19 et 20 mars 1966. Gap, Ophrys, 1968. 170 p. (Publications des Annales de la Faculté des lettres, Aix-en-Provence)   **12225**
Principal articles are analyzed separately. [MMN]

General Studies

Arnold, A. James. La querelle de la poésie pure: une mise au point. RHL 70:417–24, 1970.   **12226**

Attempt to reassess the quarrel over pure poetry by stressing B.'s attachments to the past and by correcting recent attempts to link B. with modern thought and tendencies. [AW]

Bernard-Maître, Henri. Les exercices spirituels de Saint Ignace de Loyola, interprétés par l'abbé Henri Bremond. *In:* Entretiens sur Henri Bremond. *See* 12224. p. 167–85. **12227**

Proposes to explain the interpretation of the *Exercices* of St. Ignatius by B. What we learn from the essay is minimal compared to what one would expect. [MMN]

Certeau, Michel de. La métaphysique des saints. *In:* Entretiens sur Henri Bremond. *See* 12224. p. 113–50. **12228**

Analyzes the above work of B. and states that it is "an interpretation and justification of the modern religious experience." [MMN]

Cognet, Louis. Bremond et Port-Royal. *In:* Entretiens sur Henri Bremond. *See* 12224. p. 99–112. **12229**

Criticizes B. for having given an inaccurate picture of Port-Royal and of staying too much under the influence of Sainte-Beuve. Excellent essay showing the crux of Port-Royal's mystery. [MMN]

Dagens, Jean. De Saint François de Sales à Bossuet. *In:* Entretiens sur Henri Bremond. *See* 12224. p. 151–66. **12230**

Dugens reminds us of the great service B. rendered to the science of history. In his *Histoire* B. is looking for the specificity of the religious sentiment, overflies scholasticism, eliminates the word "mystique;" B. becomes the historian of the religious sentiment in France. [MMN]

Decker, Henry W. Pure poetry, 1925–1930: theory and debate in France. Berkeley, Univ. of California press, 1962. vi, 131 p. (Univ. of California publications in modern philology, 64) **12231**

Still valuable as an analysis of B.'s theory of pure poetry and especially of its relationship to Valéry's. Of greatest interest because it places B.'s theory in its proper context. [AW]

Germain, Gabriel. Prière et poésie. *In:* Entretiens sur Henri Bremond. *See* 12224. p. 187–214. **12232**

Gives a vast panorama of B.'s ideas on poetry. Germain affirms that B. proceeds from the experience of the mystic to illumine that of the poet. There is poetical knowledge, but poetry is not a question of ideas (against rationalism); it is an experience. [MMN]

Goichot, Emile. Henri Bremond et Alfred Loisy. *In:* Entretiens sur Henri Bremond. *See* 12224. p. 227–42. **12233**

Promises to prove that although Loisy in his *George Tyrrell et Henri Bremond* states that B. was never a modernist, Loisy is right to identify their mutual "religious philosophy." The texts he quotes are hardly convincing. The author himself comes to the conclusion that Loisy can be explained on the basis of natural religion, while B. is a Christian poet. [MMN]

Goré, Jeanne-Lydie. Bremond et Fénelon. *In:* Henri Bremond, 1865–1933. *See* 12225. p. 113–28. **12234**

Proves that B. defended Fénelon against Bossuet instead of defending his doctrine, giving thus a portrait which remains incomplete. [MMN]

Mesnard, Jean. Bremond et Port-Royal. *In:* Henri Bremond, 1865–1933. *See* 12225. p. 95–112. **12235**

Points out that B. opened a new way of interpreting the Port-Royal phenomenon, but he also repeated some of the mistakes of the past concerning the conversion, morality, and religion of the Port-Royal writers. Excellent essay which offers something new even to the specialists. [MMN]

Moisan, Clément. Henri Bremond et la poésie pure. Minard, 1967. 237 p. (Bibliothèque des lettres modernes, 11) **12236**

Detailed elaboration of B.'s theory of pure poetry and vigorous defense against all rationalist objections and counter explanation. Highly controversial because it is characterized by total sympathy with B.'s point of view. Extensive bibliography. [AW]

Reviews: Anon. in BCLF 23:382, 1968; A. Blanchet in Et 329:325–26, 1968; J. Demmers in EF 4:435–37, 1968; K. Dutton in BCLF 24:337, 1969; R. Légaré in Cul 30:68–69, 1969; M. Lindsay in ELit 1:438–42, 1968; J.-B. Morvan in PrH 94:43–44, 1970; D. Mossop in FS 24:210–12, 1970.

Mounin, Georges. Une relecture de Poésie pure. *In:* Henri Bremond, 1865–1933. *See* 12225. p. 145–56.　　　**12237**

Asserts that the *La poésie pure,* even after several readings, gives him the same impression: the author is conceited, the book is loquacious, deceitfully superficial, quotes more names of poets than poetry, and, when B. makes known his choices, coincides with the baccalaureate program. Informs us that B. confessed to de Luca that *La poésie pure* was meant to be an answer to: what does it mean to pray? Concludes that B. should have stopped at point where he states that poetry is the expression of the ineffable. [MMN]

Nédoncelle, Maurice. Newman selon Bremond ou le procès d'un procès. *In:* Entretiens sur Henri Bremond. *See* 12224. p. 43–68.　**12238**

Repeats the general consensus of contemporary scholars that the *Essai de biographie psychologique* misinterprets Newman. [MMN]

Onimus, Jean. Bremond et l'enseignement des lettres. *In:* Henri Bremond, 1865–1933. *See* 12225. p. 157–67.　　　**12239**

Onimus finds three major characteristics in B.'s pedagogy: realism (one has to know young people), enthusiasm for one's subject, and humor (intelligence). The ultimate purpose of teaching is to transform the child into a poetical being through poetical emotions, for poetry is the first step to mysticism. [MMN]

Pezeril, Daniel. Bremond et Bernanos. *In:* Henri Bremond, 1865–1933. *See* 12225. p. 51–65.　　　**12240**

Affirms that abbé Cénabre of Bernanos' *Imposture* was inspired by B. Bernanos, however, is a great artist who uses also his "imaginary hallucination." From the moment Cénabre ceases to copy B., he gains an unquestionable artistic existence and independence. [MMN]

Poulat, Emile. Bremond et le modernisme. *In:* Entretiens sur Henri Bremond. *See* 12224. p. 69–98.　　　**12241**

Names some of the ancestors of modernism and a few groups surrounding B. and concludes that he was rather "un homme de lettres" than a modern-ist in a theological sense. Like Loisy, B. reached a "general philosophy" of religion by liberating religion from theology. Some questionable statements, but good essay. [MMN]

Souza, Robert de. Henri Bremond et la poésie. La poésie pure. La genèse d'un livre. Lettres et souvenirs. GraR 150:86–105, 262–84, 1936.　　**12242**

Significant article containing valuable information by B.'s collaborator on the development of his theory. B. admitted his ruse of identifying his *poésie pure* with Valéry's to aid Valéry's election to the Académie. Also includes account of B.'s choice of unsuitable material because he thought it would pass undetected. De Souza observes that B. lost sight of poetic theory because he was more concerned with his *Histoire* at that time. [AW]

Venard, Marc. Histoire littéraire et sociologie historique: deux voies pour l'histoire religieuse. *In:* Henri Bremond, 1865–1933. *See* 12225. p. 75–86.　　**12243**

B., being aware of the complexity of social structures, assumes the task of following individuals whose roads often cross and who thus become the representatives of their epoch. B. found a literary way of speaking of the simplicity and charm even of the door keeper nun and shoemaker during the reign of Louis XIII. These too can express the religious and moral truth of an epoch. [MMN]

Benjamin Crémieux
(Nos. 12244–12250)

ALVIN EUSTIS

Comnène, Marie-Anne. France. Gallimard, 1945. 279 p.　　　**12244**

A barely fictionalized biography by C.'s widow.

Crémieux, Benjamin. Le premier de la classe. Grasset, 1921. 274 p.　　　**12245**

Autobiographical novel of importance in determining C.'s critical values, norms and ideals.

Dupeyron, G. Benjamin Crémieux, romancier et critique. Eur 24, no. 20:25–31, 1947.　　　**12246**

A homage to a liberal. Rapidly summarizes life and characterizes works.

Eustis, Alvin. Benjamin Crémieux ou le critique érudit. *In his:* Trois critiques de la Nouvelle Revue Française. Debresse, 1961. p. 71–120. **12247**
Biography, peculiar position in N.R.F. movement, fields of critical activity, component elements of his method, his literary tastes and their sources.
Reviews: L. Pamplume in RR 53: 311–12, 1962; R. Wiarda in FrB 33: 7–9, 1963.

Oddo, Francesco Luigi. I grandi scrittori meridionali nel pensiero critico di Benjamin Crémieux. NQM 385–400, 1965. **12248**
An examination of the theme of regionalism in C.'s *Panorama de la littérature italienne.* Stresses C.'s importance as a critic of Italian literature.

Raymond, Marcel. Benjamin Crémieux. LetG 3:77–81, 1945. **12249**
Memories of the resistance hero and critic.

Ronzy, P. Un amico dell'Italia: Benjamin Crémieux. Ponte 3:135–39, 1946. **12250**
A summary of C.'s activities as a critic of Italian literature.

Charles Du Bos
(Nos. 12251–12286)

JACQUES BOSSIÈRE

Books and Collected Articles

Bertocci, Angelo P. Charles Du Bos and English literature: A critic and his orientation. King's crown press, 1949. 285 p. **12251**
Contains a thorough analysis of D.'s criticism in general with a particular emphasis on English novelists, poets and critics. Bibliography and index.
Review: J.-B. Barrère in FS 4:171–72, 1950.

Bossière, Jacques. Perception critique et sentiment de vivre chez Charles Du Bos. Nizet, 1969. 240 p. **12252**
Author attempts to give a comprehensive analysis of the structures of D.'s critical thinking and philosophy of life. He analyzes the concept of soul in D.,

the various activities of the mind and particularly the purifications of intelligence which lead to an identification of the inner *Moi:* an essential prerequisite to master literary expression and to examine important questions such as: *l'acte d'écrire* versus *l'art d'écrire;* expression and style; exaltation of the soul and perfection.
Reviews: C. Hill in FR 44:446–47, 1970; P. Jodogne in SFr 586–87, Sept. 1973; R. Pouilliart in LR 25:400–01, 1971.

Cahiers Charles Du Bos. La société des amis de Charles Du Bos, 24 Bd. Victor-Hugo, 92-Neuilly. **12253**
First issue Dec. 1956; published sporadically; 18 issues up to May 1974. A first class source of information for unpublished letters and papers by D., and, in general, for any research on D. and his family of thought.

Charles Du Bos. Etudes, souvenirs, témoignages de Gabriel Marcel, Jacques Madaule, Marie-Anne Gouhier, Louis Bonnerot, etc... suivi de fragments inédits du Journal de Charles Du Bos et d'une bibliographie. Didier, 1945. 156 p. (Cahiers de culture chrétienne: Résurrection. 4e série, no. 13) **12254**
Essential. See main articles listed in separate entries. Bibliography of D.'s works only.

Dédéyan, Charles. Le cosmopolitisme littéraire de Charles Du Bos. I. La jeunesse de Charles Du Bos, 1882–1914. S.E.D.E.S., 1965. 349 p. II. La maturité de Charles Du Bos, 1914–1927. C.D.U. et S.E.D.E.S. réunis, 1966. 2 v. (V. I, 743 p.; V. 2, 541 p.) III. Le critique catholique ou l'humaniste chrétien, 1927–1939. C.D.U. et S.E.D.E.S. réunis, 1967. 267 p. **12255**
Methodical, scholarly introduction to the life and works of D. Emphasizes the many philosophical and literary influences among European writers on the formation and development of D.'s mind. An essential tool for any serious approach to D.'s works.
Reviews: P. Moreau in RHL 66: 742–45, 1966; J. Mouton in RSH 126: 330–31, 1967.

Gouhier, Marie-Anne. Charles Du Bos. Avec une préface par François Mauriac. Vrin, 1951. 190 p. (Essais d'art et de philosophie) **12256**

Of no critical value but containing some insights because of D.'s own reading of text. Indispensable bibliography up to 1946.

Halda, Bernard. Charles Du Bos. Wesmaël-Charlier, 1965. 147 p. (Conversions célèbres) **12257**

Well-informed research through a biographical development, which is one of the rare attempts to size up the many aspects of D.'s genius in an effort of "réduction à l'Unité." Yet the author dismisses too lightly the long years before the conversion, when D. tries to define his own spiritual humanism. Review: Anon. in LR 24:93–94, 1970.

Hommage à Du Bos. *In:* Du Bos, Charles. Qu'est-ce que la littérature? Plon, 1945. p. 111–274. (Présences) **12258**

A collection of articles published six years after D.'s death by eminent writers such as François Mauriac, Charles Morgan, Gabriel Marcel, Camille Mayran, Jacques Madaule, J. Schlumberger, etc. An essential source of information.

Mertens, Cornelis J. Emotion et critique chez Charles Du Bos. Nymegen, Janssen, 1967. 156 p. **12259**

The recent thesis is a phenomenological study of sensation and emotion in D.'s works. Excellent bibliography.

Mouton, Jean. Charles Du Bos, sa relation avec la vie et avec la mort. Suivi d'un écrit de Charles Du Bos Sur le bonheur. Desclée De Brouwer, 1954. 160 p. (Les îles) **12260**

The author was married to Madge, the most important of D.'s secretaries. He comments with accuracy and depth on essential aspects of D.'s attitude toward life and death.

Articles

Béguin, Albert. Charles Du Bos et les textes. Qu'est-ce que la littérature? De la sévérité envers soi-même. Le journal de Charles Du Bos. *In his:* Création et destinée. Seuil, 1973. p. 217–33. **12261**

In these four studies, the author tries to situate D. and particularly his unique approach to texts. He is very cautious in emphasizing the subtle nuances of D.'s mind.

Bertocci, Angelo. Charles Du Bos and the critique of genius. *In:* Modern French criticism from Proust and Valéry to structuralism. Ed. by John K. Simon. Chicago, The University of Chicago press, 1972. p. 61–83. **12262**

More than a study on the concept of genius, it is an effort to situate D. among other writers and critics, particularly Bergson, Proust and Nietzsche.

———. The experience of Charles Du Bos. CL 24:1–31, 1972. **12263**

A definition of what the author calls the "totalisme" of D. which plays the role of a measuring scale by which he sizes up the many writers who belong to his house of thought. Review: J. Bossière in EspCr 14: 149–61, 1974.

———. Tensions in the criticism of Charles Du Bos. YFS 2:79–85, 1949. **12264**

This article deals with the process of criticism in D.'s mind and analyzes such notions as "intellectual sensibility," interpretation and expression. It studies the uneasy relationship between intuition and reason and finally the modernity of D.'s "concept," which turns to a metaphor and becomes the handmaid to intuition, thus appearing much more modern than Gide.

Besse, Henri. Le style dicté dans le journal de Charles Du Bos. CahCD 8:25–40, 1963. **12265**

Establishes the amazing contrast between D.'s mastery of vocabulary and his poor knowledge of syntaxis. It explains his frustrations and also the strong emphasis on the role of the will in written expression. Secondly, it shows D.'s respect for the purity and spontaneity of inspiration, which is, in the last analysis, faithfulness to his spiritual vision but always in reference to a spatial world. The soul is shown here as being one with written word.

Bonnerot, Louis. Charles Du Bos, interprète spirituel de la littérature anglaise. *In:* Charles Du Bos. *See* 12254. p. 32–45. **12266**

Beyond English authors like Keats and Walter Pater, Bonnerot tries to reach a comprehensive definition of D.'s criticism, which is "la critique-organe" or creative criticism by opposition to "la critique-instrument," so typical of the French mind. In that sense, D. is more English than French.

Curtius, Ernst-Robert. Charles Du Bos. CahCD 2:5–41, 1957. **12267**

Two articles previously published under the same title, one in *Die Literatur* (Oct. 1925), reproduced in RevN 29–43, July 15, 1926; the other in NR 63:500–24, 1952. He analyzes in the first the concept of exaltation and underlines its importance in French literature. He warns that its nature is to be esoteric and difficult to accept in a tradition of rationalism. The other article is largely biographical and valuable for the understanding of D.'s personality.

Daniel-Rops, Henri. La compréhension de Charles Du Bos. *In:* Du Bos, Charles. Qu'est-ce que la littérature? Plon, 1945. p. 189–93. **12268**

Comprehension, taken in its etymological sense, which includes both a gift for synthesis and an intellectual humility vis-à-vis the "object." Important to understand D.'s critical mind.

Dieckmann, Herbert. André Gide and the conversion of Charles Du Bos. YFS 12: 62–73, 1953. *Also in:* CahCD 3, June 1958. **12269**

The testimony of a man who spent the whole year before D.'s conversion in close contact with him. Beyond Gide it is a large part of himself that D. is trying to fight and eject.

———. Charles Du Bos. Sym 3:31–45, 1947. **12270**

The best study written after the Second World War by one of those "European minds" who knows D. best. Most original is his treatment of D.'s approach to literature. He discerns "a true blending of esthetical elements," which belongs specifically to D. and makes him so different, for example, from Gide. He fairly indicates D.'s shortcomings and particularly his lack of "spontaneous philosophical thought," which prevents him too often from elucidating his implications.

Gouhier, Marie-Anne. L'amour dans la pensée de Charles Du Bos. *In:* Charles Du Bos. *See* 12254. p. 66–93. **12271**

Basic to understanding D.'s definition of love. The author quotes also from

her personal correspondence with D. on this subject.

Halda, Bernard. Bergson et Du Bos. EtBer 9:159–200, 1970. **12272**

The only lengthy study on D.'s debt to Bergson's philosophy.

Hill, Charles. Walter Pater and the Gide-Charles Du Bos dialogue. RLC 3:367–84, 1967. **12273**

One of the best studies on D. which says much more than the title indicates. The comparison Gide-D. sheds light on D.'s superiority to achieve a fusion rather than an equilibrium between sensual and spiritual values. A comparison with Peter helps to ruin Gide's ethical position. The Gide-D. conflict appears here as a catalytic power which, in turn, reveals the true personality of D.

Klossowski, Pierre. Gide, Du Bos, et le démon. TM 59:564–74, 1950. **12274**

Although written in a painful philosophical jargon, this article sheds new light on the *Dialogue avec André Gide.* It demonstrates convincingly that D. never accepted Gide's viewpoint. He wrongly accuses him of being devious and cynical. Furthermore, D., the Christian neophyte, is more anxious to satisfy his own need to deal with the "diabolical dimension" than to understand Gide's real intentions. Therefore, the dialog is more a "malentendu" than a "dialog."

Leleu, Michèle. Les journaux intimes. Presses univ. de France, 1952. p. 84–85, 103–05, 233–34, 257–58, 285–87. **12275**

Essential to understanding why writing a diary was important for the intellectual and literary development of D.

Madaule, Jacques. Charles Du Bos et la critique élective. *In:* Charles Du Bos. *See* 12254. p. 46–65. **12276**

What determined D. to make a choice? A matter of soul, of affinities. The author analyzes the influence of nature and romanticism, the role of Goethe who was essential in the development of D.'s mind, the influence of Constant, Bérulle, Claudel...

Magny, Claude E. Plaidoyer pour la critique. Esp 9:635–46, 1941. **12277**

Although directed almost exclusively against Thibaudet, this article sets rules for truly creative criticism: "sympathiser avec l'essence particulière d'un auteur," which is "attention à l'unique" rather than an abstract mediation between an author and his public. Even D., so aware of this danger, becomes abstract and impersonal in his *Approximations*, which are opposed here to the *Journal*. Brilliant but not fair enough to D.

Marcel, Gabriel. Charles Du Bos dans ses rapports avec lui-même. *In:* Charles Du Bos. *See* 12254. p. 32–45.   **12278**

Notes the deep dualism which opposes body and spirit in D. Yet the unity comes here from the need to be himself, at any cost, which is a need to *express,* to eject, before any attempt to compose, and to rejoin God and people in the deepest part of the self.

————. Hommage à Charles Du Bos. CahCD 1:3–11, 1956.   **12279**

A penetrating analysis of main trends of D.'s thinking.

————. Préface. *In:* Du Bos, Charles. Commentaires. Bruges, Desclée De Brouwer, 1946. p. vii–xxvii.   **12280**

The very nature of D.'s mind made him very clumsy in politics. The author gives the reasons for this weakness and shows D.'s need for contemplation before he can appraise a situation or object.

Mauriac, François. Charles Du Bos et son créateur. Hommage à Charles Du Bos. *In:* Du Bos, Charles. Qu'est-ce que la littérature? Plon, 1945. p. 113–26 (Présences)   **12281**

A study on the theme: D. *anima naturaliter christiana.* The whole relationship of D., the thinker and artist, with God.

Maurois, André. Charles Du Bos. *In his:* De Gide à Sartre. Perrin, 1965. p. 49–91.   **12282**

In the absence of a biography of D., perhaps the best account of D.'s way of life, inseparably connected, of course, with his ways of thinking. It is written by one of D.'s most intimate friends.

Poulet, Georges. La pensée critique de Charles Du Bos. Cr 21:491–516, 1965.   **12283**

The great merit of this study—in spite of some shortcomings—is to have brought to a large public a profound analysis of D.'s critical thinking.

Richard, Jean-Pierre. La méthode critique de Charles Du Bos. MLR 62:420–29, 1967.   **12284**

It is a D. slightly victimized by Richard's method of thinking and yet beautifully situated and projected into the modern currents of literary criticism.

Rousseaux, André. Charles Du Bos. I. Un bienheureux de la littérature. II. Le journal d'un intellectuel. *In his:* Littérature du vingtième siècle. V. 2. Albin-Michel, 1939. p. 64–76.   **12285**

Not an attempt to comprehend the whole of D.'s work but rather a precise analysis of his mind, with reference to physical suffering, so essential to understanding D.'s spiritual and religious development.

Wellek, René. Poulet, Du Bos and identification. CLS 10:173–93, 1973.   **12286**

An effort to deflate D.'s criticism and, through him, not only Poulet but a whole school. To what extent must he react to understand why it is difficult to categorize D?

Ramon Fernandez
(Nos. 11287–12289)

ALVIN EUSTIS

Eustis, Alvin. Ramon Fernandez ou le critique philosophe. *In his:* Trois critiques de la Nouvelle Revue Française. Debresse, 1961. p. 121–92.   **12287**

Career and relations with Rivière, esthetic investigations, the nature of his philosophical criticism, influence of Anglo-Saxon thought, the place of his method in 20th-century critical currents.

Muir, Edwin. The structure of the novel. London, The Hogarth press, 1928. 151 p.   **12288**

Muir utilizes (p. 119–23) F.'s distinction between *récit* and novel, which will henceforth be quoted by English and American theorists of the novel.

Poulet, Georges. Les critiques de la N.R.F. *In his:* La conscience critique. Corti, 1971. p. 57–70.   **12289**

Subsection (p. 67–70) devoted to F., whom Poulet considers one of the four most important critics of the N.R.F. movement (with Thibaudet, Rivière, and Du Bos) and a precursor of the structuralists.

Edmond Jaloux
(Nos. 12290–12311)

JACK KOLBERT

Texts with Autobiographical Information

Jaloux, Edmond. La dernière amitié de Rainer Maria Rilke. Laffont, 1939. 224 p. **12290**

Filled with reminiscences of J.'s personal relationships with the German poet and with data concerning their mutual influences.

———. Essences. Plon, 1952. 244 p. **12291**

A rich collection of maxims and aphorisms that not only reveal J.'s philosophy of literature and life, but also recount many of his dreams and episodes of intimate life.

———. Marseille. Emile Paul, 1926. 92 p. **12292**

A nostalgic recollection of J.'s early childhood days in Marseille, a city which figures so prominently in his fiction and criticism.

———. Rilke. Emile Paul, 1927. 109 p. **12293**

Despite the diminutive proportions of the volume, it is a significant study on the German poet, one which sheds light on Franco-German literary relations at their best. A combination of literary criticism and personal memoirs.

———. Les saisons littéraires. V. 1. Fribourg, Eds. de l'université, 1942. 342 p. V. 2. Plon-LUF, 1960. 347 p. **12294**

A major 2 v. series of literary and personal memoirs dealing mainly with the "Generation of 1900": Gide, J.-L. Vaudoyer, J. Gasquet, G. de Voisins, Valéry, and a host of other literary friends who formed J.'s circle of close friends in Marseilles and Aix-en-Provence. The intellectual-literary evolution of J. Excels in insightful criticism of the works of these writers.

Review: M. Thiébaudet in RdP 18: 152–54, 1951.

———. Souvenirs sur Henri de Régnier. Lausanne, F. Rouge, 1941. 112 p. **12295**

Not only interesting for the criticism of Régnier but also for the large amount of data concerning J.'s personal and literary relationship with this poet.

Biography

Du, Bos, Charles. Figures étrangères de Jaloux. NRF 151:485–87, 1926. **12296**

An important article which accurately defines J.'s peculiar expertise in foreign literature and his role as a catalyst for English and German authors in France.

Jaloux, Edmond. Avec Marcel Proust. Suivi des lettres inédites de Proust. La Palatine, 1953. 152 p. **12297**

Contains a host of anecdotal references to J.'s literary relationships with Proust. The latter's letters to J. indicate his sincere appreciation for the critic.

Review: P. Kolb in RR 46:67–69, 1955.

Lefèvre, Frédéric. Une heure avec Edmond Jaloux. NL 125:March 7, 1925. **12298**

An important tool for the J. specialist. J. is quoted in responses to a number of important literary questions.

Martin du Gard, Maurice. Edmond Jaloux de l'Académie française. NL 716: July 4, 1936. **12299**

Conceivably the most accurate appraisal of J.'s position in the literary world as seen by a contemporary on the occasion of his election into the Academy.

Mauriac, François. Un homme de lettres: Edmond Jaloux. Fig Aug. 29, 1949. **12300**

One of the most insightful evaluations of J. on the occasion of his death. It should be remembered that J. played a major part in helping Mauriac establish himself as a force in the modern French novel.

Miomandre, Francis de. Avec Edmond Jaloux dans la rue des Tonneliers. NL 741, Dec. 26, 1939. **12301**

The most significant early portrait of J., the young budding writer, by Miomandre, who knew him intimately during the early Provençal days. Miomandre recaptures especially the first stage of J.'s literary formation.

General Studies

Delétang-Tardif, Yanette. Edmond Jaloux. La table ronde, 1947. 235 p.   **12302**

The first major book-length study devoted to J. Excels mainly because Mme Tardif knew the author-critic intimately and shares with her readers her very poetic and subjective views of his person and works.

Duhamel, Georges. Allocution à l'occasion de la mort de M. Edmond Jaloux. Séance du 1er septembre, 1949. Firmin-Didot, 1949. 4 p. (Institut de France. Académie française)   **12303**

Duhamel takes stock of J.'s role as a critic and novelist in the general realm of modern letters.

Hommage à Edmond Jaloux. FrA 44:380–410, 1949.   **12304**

Brief articles by Georges Duhamel, Pierre Géguen, Fernand Lot, Francis de Miomandre, Christian Dédéyan, Yanette Delétang-Tardif and André Lebois.

Hommage à Edmond Jaloux. VAC 6:6–31, 1949.   **12305**

The little-known art magazine is an essential research tool for J. studies. It contains a series of generally laudatory articles on J. by Jacques Chennevière, Emile Henriot, Jacques de Lacretelle, Jean Nicollier, etc.

Jaloux, Edmond, and Georges Lecomte. Le fauteuil de Paul Bourget—Discours de réception de Monsieur Edmond Jaloux à l'Académie française et réponse de Monsieur Georges Lecomte. Plon, 1937. 154 p.   **12306**

If J.'s discourse deals mainly with Bourget, the text of Lecomte is essential for J. scholars since it deals with the high points of J.'s literary career.

Kolbert, Jack. Edmond Jaloux and his contemporaries. FR 31:283–91, 1958.   **12307**

J.'s unquestionably important part in advancing the careers of Gide, Proust, Valéry, Mauriac, the surrealists, etc.

————. Edmond Jaloux as a popularizer of English literature. FR 34:432–39, 1961.   **12308**

Analysis of J.'s important role in establishing in France the reputations of such authors as James Joyce, Katherine Mansfield, Virgina Woodlf, Aldous Huxley and others.

————. Edmond Jaloux et sa critique littéraire. Geneva, Droz, 1962. 224 p.   **12309**

The only full-scale monograph on the principal literary critic of Les nouvelles littéraires from the inception of this paper until World War II. Major chapters deal with J. as a discoverer of foreign and young authors. Also, J.'s biography and philosophy of criticism. Preface on J. by Maurois.

Rosenfeld, Marthe. Edmond Jaloux. The evolution of a novelist. With a forward by Gabriel Marcel. Philosophical library, 1972. 188 p.   **12310**

This is the definitive study of J.'s formation as a novelist. Rosenfeld traces the main stages of this formation from regionalism and realism through periods of poetic and psychological experimentation until his eventual evolution into a novelist of mysticism. Contains most complete bibliography available.

Reviews: J. Kolbert in FR 46:1234–35, 1973; A. McConnell in AQ 28:376–77, 1972.

Vaudoyer, Jean-Louis. Discours prononcés dans la séance publique tenue par l'Académie française pour la réception de M. J.-L. Vaudoyer. Firmin-Didot, 1950. 71 p.   **12311**

Vaudoyer summarizes with eloquence the achievements of the writer who preceded him in the Académie. A mixture of sentimental recollections and critical evaluations.

Henri Massis
(Nos. 12312–12315)

DAVID J. KLEIN

Archambault, Paul. Henri Massis. In his: Jeunes maîtres. Bloud & Gay, 1926. p. 119–46.   **12312**

Perceptive chapter which analyzes the fleeting and inconclusive nature of M.'s views as seen especially in his *Les jeunes gens d'aujourd'hui* and *Jugements*. Points to the changing and complex nature of his intellectual thought in light of his growing and fervent Catholicism. His thought is shown to be weak and imprecise resulting from contradictory and antithetical, yet dogmatic pronouncements.

Christophe, Lucien. Regards sur Henri Massis. RGB 17–41, May 1961.   **12313**
Written at time of M.'s induction into the French Academy. An analysis of three late works, *Visages des idées* (1958), *De l'homme à Dieu* (1959), *Charles Maurras et notre temps* (1960), which provide the means to trace the intellectual and spiritual development of M.

Henri Massis, études, temoignages, textes et documents inédits, biographie et bibliographie. Nouvelles éds. latines, 1961. 256 p.   **12314**
A compilation of six literary studies, brief notes, testimonials, letters, a detailed biography, bibliography, and an unedited text, "Du Pape," to honor M. on his election to the French Academy.

Leitolf, Otto. Die Gedankenwelt von Henri Massis. RSt 53:1–118, 1940.   **12315**
Interesting, though biased, German viewpoint. Underscores the missionary zeal and fanatical beliefs of M.'s French-Catholic heritage. Pictures him as chauvinistic and unable to transcend the rigid and narrow framework of his personal beliefs to be objective as a literary critic.

Eugène Montfort
(Nos. 12316–12318)

DAVID J. KLEIN

Coulon, Marcel. Eugène Montfort, romancier. RdH 5:330–50, 1918.   **12316**
The best study of M. as a novelist, though incomplete and treating only those novels written up to 1918. Studies M.'s novels in light of their classical and romantic tendencies while placing them in the same company with those of Madame de Lafayette, l'abbé Prevost and Balzac.

Klein, David J. The conflict between André Gide and Eugène Montfort. FR 46:730–38, 1973.   **12317**
A critical examination of the correspondence between Gide and M., revealing a relationship that turned from cordial to bitter as a result of M.'s participation in the publication of the first issue of the *Nouvelle revue française* in 1908.

Eugène Montfort. Ed. by Louis Bertrand. Albert Messein, 1937. 192 p. (Les marges)   **12318**
Published as the last issue in the series of *Les marges* (1903–1936), and upon the death of M. A testimonial to his life and works. Invaluable especially for understanding the person M. and what he represented. Lists important dates and provides a complete bibliography of his works and his principal collaborations.

Jean Paulhan
(Nos. 12319–12358)

ALVIN EUSTIS

Bibliography

[Zilberstein, Jean-Claude]. Bibliographie. *In:* Jean Paulhan 1884–1968. *See* 12320. p. 1042–54.   **12319**
Most complete at present.

Special Numbers

Jean Paulhan 1884–1968. NRF 17:649–1055, 1969.   **12320**
This commemorative number is of exceptional richness with contributions by many outstanding writers and critics.

Paulhan o del terrore. Verri 32:47–78, 1970.   **12321**
A commemorative number containing several articles on P.'s ambiguity and dialectics by Luciano Anceschi, Renato Barilli and Alessandro Serra.

Portrait de Jean Paulhan. CahSa 10:263–307, 1957.   **12322**
Brief biographical sketches or critical appreciations by twelve critics. Contrib-

utors: Jacques Brenner, Georges-Emmanuel Clancier, Jean-Louis Curtis, André Dhôtel, Jean Grenier, Bernard Groethuysen, Marcel Jouhandeau, Odette Lutgen, René de Obaldia, Francis Ponge, Armand Robin and Henri Thomas.

Correspondence and Biography

Artaud, Antonin. Œuvres complètes. Supplément au tome I. Gallimard, 1970. 242 p.
12323

Contains numerous letters to P., 1926–32.

———. Œuvres complètes VII. Gallimard, 1967. 496 p.   **12324**

Letters to P., 1934 and 1937.

Aury, Dominique. Trois lettres de Jean Paulhan à Franz Hellens. *In:* Franz Hellens. Recueil d'études. Brussels, André de Rache, 1971. p. 189–94.   **12325**

Unpublished correspondence.

Paulhan, Jean. Correspondance. *In:* Jean Paulhan 1884–1968. *See* 12320. p. 988–1042.   **12326**

Letters to Marcel Arland, Antonin Artaud, Georges Braque, Roger Caillois, René Daumal, Yvonne Desvignes, André Dhôtel, Etiemble, Félix Fénéon, André Gide, Jean Grenier, Franz Hellens, Marcel Jouhandeau, Charles Maurras, Pierre Oster, Jacques Paulhan, André Suarès, Guillaume de Tarde and Edith Thomas.

———. Jean Paulhan à Madame xxx. NRF 228:78–90, 1971.   **12327**

Unpublished correspondence.

Poulet, Robert. Un aspect de Jean Paulhan. EPar 93–98, May 1969.   **12328**

Memoirs of period 1951–65. Reasons for P.'s love of paradox.

Rebay, Luciano. Ungaretti a Paulhan: otto lettere e un autografo inediti. FI 6:277–89, 1972.   **12329**

Unpublished correspondence.

Saint-John Perse (pseud. of Alexis Saint-Leger Leger). Œuvres complètes. Gallimard, 1972. p. 580–82, 1022–33. (Bibliothèque de la Pléiade)   **12330**

Letters to P.

General Studies

Anceschi, Luciano. Paulhan o dell'ambiguità delle lettere. Aut 298–316, July 1952. *Also in:* Paulhan o del terrore. *See* 12321. p. 47–63.   **12331**

A brief, but comprehensive examination of dialectic and critical ideas, especially in *Les fleurs de Tarbes* and *Clef de la poésie.*

Bachelard, Gaston. Une psychologie du langage littéraire. RPFE 151–56, April–June 1942–1943. *Also in his:* Le droit de rêver. Presses univ. de France, 1970. p. 176–85.   **12332**

Sees in *Fleurs de Tarbes* an investigation into critical value judgments and a call for a new rhetoric.

Benda, Julien. Un fossoyeur de la France: Jean Paulhan. Eur 26:21–29, 1948.   **12333**

More revealing of Benda's narrow intellectualism than of P.'s work. In the former's terminology, P. was not only a clerk who betrayed, but a byzantine.

Berne-Jouffroy, André. Destin de la rhétorique: Stendhal, Valéry, Paulhan. CahS 31:272–98, 1950.   **12334**

Detailed comparison of the three authors for conception of rhetoric.

Blanchot, Maurice. Le mystère dans les lettres. *In his:* La part du feu. Gallimard, 1949. p. 49–66.   **12335**

A very good exegesis of P.'s thought and an explanation of his paradoxes by a master of paradox. Illuminating analogies established with Mallarmé's theories on poetic language.

———. Le paradoxe d'Aytré. *In his:* La part du feu. Gallimard, 1949. p. 67–79.   **12336**

P.'s fiction in its relations with contemporary ideas.

Boisdeffre, Pierre de. Jean Paulhan; séductions et limites de l'intelligence. Et 260: 188–99, 1949. *Also in his:* Des vivants et des morts. Eds. universitaires, 1954. p. 263–71.   **12337**

Wittily philistine; superficial.

Bousquet, Joë. Les capitales ou de Jean Duns Scot à Jean Paulhan. Le cercle du livre, 1955. 206 p.   **12338**

P. as representative of a hermetical, anti-Cartesian tradition going back to Duns Scot. Murky.

Carmody, Francis J. Jean Paulhan's imaginative writings. FR 23:269–77, 1950. **12339**

A survey and general, somewhat discursive characterization.

Debû-Bridel, Jacques. Jean Paulhan, citoyen. *In:* Paulhan, Jean. Œuvres complètes V. Cercle du livre précieux, 1970. p. 481–92. **12340**

P.'s politics and political writings.

Dhôtel, André. Vers une science de l'illusion littéraire? La méthode de Jean Paulhan. Cr 4:291–306, 1948. **12341**

In spite of his comprehensive attitude, the author reproaches P. for his estheticism and for being too far removed from real life.

Etiemble, René. Jean Paulhan. LetFB 17–23, July 1943. *Also in his:* Hygiène des lettres. V: C'est le bouquet (1940–1967). Gallimard, 1967. p. 416–25. **12342**

Despite digressions, manages to state at an early date P.'s significance for, and influence on, a generation of writers.

Eustis, Alvin. The paradoxes of language: Jean Paulhan. *In:* Modern French criticism. Ed. by John K. Simon. Chicago and London, Univ. of Chicago press, 1972. p. 109–22. **12343**

Main themes and works, dialectic, esthetic, linguistic theories, place of rhetoric and classicism; the terrorists.

Ferenczi, Thomas. Jean Paulhan et les problèmes du langage. *In:* Au temps de Dada. Lettres modernes, 1972. p. 45–63. (CahDS, 4) **12344**

P.'s dialectics and use of paradox to reach the other face of language.

Garcin, Philippe. Le hasard et le récit chez Jean Paulhan. MNP 100:119–29, 1956. **12345**

Excellent short analysis of meaning of fiction.

Grenier, Jean. Jean Paulhan critique d'art. *In:* Jean Paulhan. Œuvres complètes V. Cercle du livre précieux, 1970. p. 261–66. **12346**

An intelligent short discussion of P.'s art criticism.

Guérin, Raymond. Paulhan, ou d'une nouvelle incarnation des lettres. *In his:* Un romancier dit son mot. Corrêa, 1948. p. 57–82. **12347**

Impressions, rather than an analysis, of fiction and criticism; comparison with F. Fénéon; Guérin's personal relations with P. (anecdotal value).

Hellens, Franz. Aspects de Jean Paulhan. SynB 27:31–37, 1972. **12348**

Seeks to show qualities of creative imagination and verbal fantasy through personal reminiscences and examination of works.

Judrin, Roger. Le poids du sanctuaire. *In:* Paulhan, Jean. Œuvres complètes II. Cercle du livre précieux, 1966. p. 331–41. **12349**

P. as a literary critic, with particular reference to his value judgments.

———. La vocation transparente de Jean Paulhan. Gallimard, 1961. 160 p. (Vocations) **12350**

Somewhat anecdotal and impressionistic, but contains intimate details on the man and his circle, which illuminate the work, as well as unpublished letters.

Review: R. Kanters in FL 2, April 8, 1962.

Lefebve, Maurice-Jean. Jean Paulhan: une philosophie et une pratique de l'expression et de la réflexion. Gallimard, 1949. 284 p. **12351**

The most reflective and thorough study, starting with the central paradox of language (terror-rhetoric), following its ramifications into all the branches of P.'s activity, and then attempting to situate him in contemporary literature.

———. Paulhan qui perd l'habitude. CahS 61:110–22, 1966. **12352**

Isolates, studies, and evaluates the dialectical theme of paradox as treated in P.'s works since 1950.

———. Un possédé du réel. *In:* Jean Paulhan. Œuvres complètes III. Cercle du livre précieux, 1967. p. 427–36. **12353**

P. and the problem (paradoxical) of reality.

Lévy, Yves. Jean Paulhan, du jardin fleuri aux catacombes. Preu 153:3–21, 1963.
12354
A general summary of main works and evolution of ideas.

Roy, Claude. Descriptions critiques: Jean Paulhan. Poé 8:15–27, 1947.   **12355**
General impressions of P.'s work; somewhat superficial.

Toesca, Maurice. Jean Paulhan ou l'écrivain appliqué. Variété, 1948. 152 p.   **12356**
A general introduction to the man and his activity which contains good biographical detail but skirts the problems posed by the work.

Vandromme, Pol. Jean Paulhan, terrorisme et rhétorique. RGB 10:21–27, 1968.
12357
Negative and spiteful, but useful to balance the mandarins' sometimes un-discriminating praise.

Weidlé, Wladimir. Sur la notion de procédé. CahS 32:100–08, 1950.   **12358**
Comparison of P.'s notion of rhetoric with French stylistics.

Jacques Rivière
(Nos. 12359–12479)

HELEN T. NAUGHTON

Correspondence

Artaud, Antonin. Correspondance avec Jacques Rivière. In his: Œuvres complètes. V. 1. Gallimard, 1956. p. 19–46. Also (rev.): 1970. Also in his: L'ombilic des limbes, précédé de Correspondance avec Jacques Rivière et suivi de Le pèse-nerfs... Gallimard, 1968. 255 p.   **12359**
Extraordinary letters in which each writer attempts to lay bare his soul. Best document on R. at end of life. R., although refusing to publish Artaud's poems, published this exchange in the NRF 23:291–312, 1924.
Review: M. Arland in NRF 29:681–82, 1927.

Claudel, Paul; Francis Jammes; and Gabriel Frizeau. Correspondance 1897–1938, avec des lettres de Jacques Rivière. Préface et notes par André Blanchet. Gallimard, 1952. passim.   **12360**

Eleven letters from R. dating from 1907–09, one from Frizeau to R.

Proust, Marcel, and Jacques Rivière. Correspondance (1914–1922), présentée et annotée par Philip Kolb. Plon, 1955. 324 p.   **12361**
Most important document on R. in postwar years. Fascinating psychological portraits of writers different in formation and character but sharing common literary views. They discuss their health, their problems, but letters gravitate around Proust's gigantic work which he was struggling to complete and express R.'s boundless admiration for its psychological penetration, humor and poetry.
Reviews: M. Chavardès in VI 26:124, 1955; J. Selz in LN 3:792–95, 1955.

Rivière, Jacques. Lettres à André Gide. In: Hommage à Jacques Rivière. See 12418. p. 759–80.   **12362**
Six letters to Gide stressing essential difference in their view of life, of desire, of happiness and, particularly, of religion. Full of self-revelation by the very young R. Long, detailed explanation of sentiments expressed in De la foi. Admiration and sincere affection and trust are dominant tone.

————, and Alain Fournier. Correspondance 1905–1914. Gallimard, 1926–28. 4 v. Also (rev.): Gallimard, 1948. 2 v. 900 p.
12363
Letters exchanged between R. and his closest friend whom he met in khâgne of Lycée Lakanal when both were seventeen and continuing to death of Fournier. Invaluable document on period and soul of their generation as well as on their spiritual, esthetic and intellectual development. First volume gives preponderant place to long discussions on art, music, literature, and ambitions. Second reveals religious torment and philosophical unrest. Great mutual influence and enrichment. Indispensable reading, with other correspondences and Carnets, for understanding of R. and fascinating mirror of epoch even for non-specialist.
Reviews: R. Fernandez in NRF 28:118–20, 1927; J. Guéhenno in NRF 30:693–96, 1928; E. Jaloux in his De Pascal à Barrès (Plon, 1927, p. 213–24) and in NL March 10, 1928; G.

Marcel in EN April 21, 1928; A. Rousseaux in RU 27:490–98, 1926.

———, **and Paul Claudel.** Correspondance 1907–1914. Plon-Nourrit, 1926. 264 p. (Le roseau d'or, 6) *Also:* Montreal, Fides, 1944. *Also:* Plon, 1963. 188 p. (Livre de vie, 35) **12364**

Overwhelmed by the impact of *L'arbre* and stunned by the news that Claudel was Catholic, the young R. began an impassioned correspondence begging for an answer to his anguish through faith. 1907–09 are the years of deepest questioning during which R. made sincere efforts, analyzing his advances and retreats with pitiless sincerity. More mature letters are less fervent. Volume ends with R.'s return to Church. Introduction of 1963 ed. (xxi p.) presents Isabelle Rivière's point of view on her husband's religious beliefs throughout his life.

Reviews: J. Schlumberger in NRF 26:481–83, 1926; J. Veto in Ren 17:54–56, 1964–65.

Autobiographical Texts

Rivière, Jacques. Aimée. Gallimard, 1922. 189 p. **12365**

Dedicated to Marcel Proust, this autobiographical novel recounts in minute detail a platonic love affair that R. had renounced immediately preceding the war but that haunted him in prison camp.

———. Alain-Fournier. NRF 19:643–68, 1922; 20:374–94, 1923. *Also:* Introduction. *In:* Alain-Fournier. Miracles. Gallimard, 1924. p. 11–89. **12366**

One of most revealing and deeply personal essays written by R. In an attempt to explain the esthetic evolution of his most intimate friend, he traces his parallel development and his differences as well as his influence on Alain-Fournier.

———. A la trace de Dieu, avec une préface de Paul Claudel. Gallimard, 1925. 293 p. **12367**

Consists of two parts: notes for talks to be given to fellow prisoners of war in very incomplete form and destined to serve as basis for apology of Christianity; pages from R.'s Carnets or private diaries kept during captivity

which seem to support or clarify ideas of first part. Intensely personal in second part, never intended for publication, these notes are exceptionally revealing psychological and religious document. Other passages from *Carnets* published in *De la sincérité envers soi-même, La guérison, Carnet de guerre, août-septembre 1914.* Complete *Carnets* published in 1974.

Reviews: P. Archambault in Et 2:25–46, 1926; F. Defrennes in DFR 3:114–25, 197–205, 1930; F. Mauriac in RHeb 35, no. 1:318–401, 1926.

———. Carnet de guerre, août-septembre 1914. Eds. de la belle page, 1929. 137 p. *Also in his:* Carnets 1914–1917. *See* 12369. **12368**

Notes on first days of R.'s war experience and his capture by the Germans. Interesting as account of what he would always refer to as his "humiliation."

———. Carnets 1914–1917, présentés et annotés par Isabelle Rivière et Alain Rivière, préface de Pierre Emmanuel de l'Académie Française. Fayard, 1974. 493 p. **12369**

Publication in entirety of fifteen private notebooks minutely analyzing spiritual, emotional and religious struggle of R.'s years in German prison camps. Written with pitiless sincerity, this lucid inner dialog is a remarkable psychological document disclosing an intimate R., capable of deep emotion, harsh towards himself, searching always to express with profundity and exactitude the inner self, avid for life.

Review: H. Naughton in EspCr 15:475–76, 1975.

———. Chasse à l'orgueil. *In his:* De la sincérité envers soi-même. Introd. de Isabelle Rivière. Gallimard, 1943. p. 103–74. **12370**

Third part of collection composed also of reprints of "De la sincérité envers soi-même" (NRF Jan. 1912) and "De la foi" (NRF Nov.-Dec. 1912). Made up by Isabelle Rivière of sections of captivity notebooks treating subject of R.'s pride and his persistent struggle to overcome it as dominant factor in his personality. Also published as *De la foi* and *De la sincérité.* Chronique des lettres françaises. Aux horizons de France, 1927.

————. Florence (roman) précédé d'une introduction de Madame Jacques Rivière. Corrêa, 1935. 323 p.   **12371**

Rough drafts of second novel R. was struggling to write at time of his death and about which he was enthusiastic, having always wanted to be a creative writer. The Pierre of the novel is obviously R. and the rough drafts are intensely self-revelatory.

Reviews: M. Arland in NRF 44:616–18, 1935; I. Rivière in NL March 30, 1935.

————. Fragments inédits d'un Eloge d'André Gide par Jacques Rivière. BAAG 27:3–8, 1975.   **12372**

Important unpublished text presented by Kevin O'Neill, part of a first version of the study of 1911 published in GraR. Fascinating as revealing spontaneous and sincere first expression of enthusiasm for Gide and method R. used to correct, modify, and often dry out his style. Followed by definitive published text.

————. La N.R.F., champ de bataille. Interview de Roger Vitrac. JduP April 21, 1923. *Also:* NL 2477:8–9, 17–23, 1975.   **12373**

Expresses R.'s sympathy for dada in that it is definitive liquidation of romantic conception of writer as god or high priest revealing absolute, a sterile concept that leads to despair. Aim of literature is more modest, revealing a fruitful disinterest in final causes.

Biography

Alain-Fournier. Lettres d'Alain-Fournier à sa famille: 1898–1914. Avant-propos d'Isabelle Rivière. Plon, 1930. 318 p. (Le roseau d'or) *Also (rev.):* Emile-Paul, 1940. *Also:* 1942. *Also (rev.):* 1949. 391 p.   **12374**

Affectionate and interesting letters in which Alain-Fournier talks to his family about his intimate friend met at the Lycée Lakanal in Paris and, after R.'s marriage to Isabelle Fournier, some letters to them.

Arland, Marcel. L'évolution de Jacques Rivière. *In his:* Essais et nouveaux essais critiques. Gallimard, 1952. p. 92–99.   **12375**

Arland admires first pages of *Aimée,* captivity notebooks and essays on sincerity and faith. Insists on R.'s extreme flexibility which he considers weakness and on his good will: love of life, quest for a master, joy in self-giving. On the whole not very complimentary article. Some paragraphs identical to article of same title in homage volume of NRF, but articles not the same.

Bars, Henry. La littérature et sa conscience. Grasset, 1963. 380 p.   **12376**

Three brief sections on R. Passages on Claudel's attempts to dissuade R. from becoming a writer in chapter "La vocation d'écrivain." In "La littérature et sa poésie" insists that symbolist, Christian, lyric R. was one many young men of his generation knew first. Deplores R.'s postwar esthetic positivism which impoverishes literature. In "De la fête à l'abdication," analysis of R.'s personality is perceptive and subtle.

Beaulieu, Paul. Une grande amitié: Jacques Rivière et Alain-Fournier. ActU 16:32–46, 1950. *Also:* L'amitié dans l'œuvre de Jacques Rivière. Montreal, La nouvelle équipe, 1950. 16 p.   **12377**

Good article based on the R.-Fournier correspondence with emphasis on R. Stresses the intuition of true values in art of the two friends, their sincerity, their search for an absolute and their passion for their period in all its artistic manifestations.

Cap, Jean-Pierre. Une amitié littéraire: Jacques Rivière-Jean Schlumberger. PFr 5:107–12, 1972.   **12378**

Good account by editor of their correspondence of R.'s entrance into the NRF group and of his warm relationship with Schlumberger.

Chaix, Joseph. L'inquiétude religieuse chez Jacques Rivière et Alain-Fournier. *In his:* De Renan à Jacques Rivière. Dilettantisme et amoralisme. Bloud et Gay, 1930. p. 89–109. (CahNJ, 16)   **12379**

Entire second part of book devoted to influences and experiences undergone by two writers. Opposes seriousness of their quest to dilettantism of Renan although R., in final analysis, retains only what helps him uncover himself. Too dogmatic; conclusion definitely moralizing.

Chauvet, Alice. Essai sur Jacques Rivière et Alain-Fournier. Mont-de-Marsan, Librairie D. Chalas, 1929. 136 p.　　**12380**
Conscientious study; a little naive. Traces relationship between two friends but tendency to overemphasize contrast in their personalities, to oppose them in perfect symmetry—the intuitive poet and the analyst. Differences show up more in correspondence than in works. Review: R. Fernandez in NRF 34: 582–83, 1930.

Claudel, Paul. Claudel homme de théâtre: correspondance avec Copeau, Dullin, Jouvet, établies et annotées par Henri Micciollo et Jacques Petit. Gallimard, 1966. 327 p.　　**12381**
References to R. and his wife in Copeau-Claudel correspondence are full of concern and affection. R.'s death and Claudel's poem in *Feuilles de saints* were instrumental in reconciling Copeau and Claudel. Good résumé of R. "quarrel" in NRF in 1926.

————. Lettres à Jacques Rivière. *In his:* Toi qui es-tu? (Tu quis es?) Gallimard, 1936. p. 23–43.　　**12382**
Selected letters to R. (1907–14) taken from the correspondence published by Plon in 1926. No letters by R.

————. Mémoires improvisés recueillis par Jean Amrouche. Gallimard, 1954. 349 p. *Also:* Mémoires improvisés. Quarante et un entretiens avec Jean Amrouche. Texte établi par Louis Fournier. Gallimard, 1969. 380 p. (Idées)　　**12383**
Brief allusions to relationship with R. and influence of their correspondence. Insists on scientific temperament of R. as well as on his sensitivity and on his Christian death. Rather vague memories and intransigent point of view.

Coquoz, François-Marie. L'évolution religieuse de Jacques Rivière. Fribourg, Eds. universitaires, 1963. 204 p. (Textes et études philosophiques et littéraires publiés par la Faculté des Lettres de l'Univ. de Fribourg)　　**12384**
Attempts to follow the religious evolution of R. in all its details and detours. Conscientious and objective study, one of the best documented on the single question of the faith of R. considered by a theologian but without jargon and with understanding. Excellent quotations. Recommended.

Décaudin, Michel. La crise des valeurs symbolistes. Toulouse, Privat, 1960. 532 p.　　**12385**
More important than the numerous references to R. is the indispensable perspective from which to evaluate R.'s reactions to symbolism, proving him typical of his generation from many points of view.

Dédéyan, Charles. La quête de Dieu. IV. Jacques Rivière ou le traqueur de Dieu. *In his:* Le nouveau mal du siècle de Baudelaire à nos jours. V. 2. Spleen, révolte et idéal (1889–1914). Société d'édition d'enseignement supérieur, 1972. p. 475–92.　　**12386**
Good brief review of the whole question of R.'s religious progress and regression. Very close to sources in other writers on subject, particularly Isabelle Rivière and Mauriac.

Du Bos, Charles. Journal. 1946–1961. V. 1–5. Corrêa, 1946–1954. V. 6. La colombe, 1955. V. 9. La colombe, 1961.　　**12387**
Frequent references to R., especially immediately following his death, showing great affection and a deeper understanding than that of any other writer of period. Good discussion of religious question. Fine passage on Isabelle Rivière (9:81–82). Interesting to compare *Journal* with polished articles on R. treating same subject.

Engel, Marc. Jacques Rivière au Luxembourg. *In:* Colpach, présenté par Robert Stumper, édité par un groupe d'amis de Colpach, sous les auspices de la Croix-Rouge Luxembourgeoise et au profit de la Fondation E. Mayrisch, à Colpach. Luxemburg, Imprimerie Victor Buck, 1957. p. 111–36.　　**12388**
Important article on R. describes his five sojourns at Mayrisch estates in Dudelange and Colpach, his lectures in Luxemburg, and particularly his political articles published in *Die Luxemberger Zeitung* reflecting his effort in postwar years to overcome nationalism, effect understanding between former combattants and assure peace in Europe through Franco-German economic entente.

Fernandez, Ramon. Jacques Rivière et le moralisme. NRF 28:279–82, 1927. *Also in:* Rivière, Jacques. Moralisme et littérature. Corrêa, 1932. p. 9–16.   **12389**

R. was pre-moral; he tried to seize life bursting forth before it is deformed by moral concepts. His intellectual morality was severe and strict. Interested in psychological discoveries, in what enriched his knowledge of life.

From the N.R.F.: an image of the twentieth century from the pages of the Nouvelle revue française. Ed. with introduction by Justin O'Brien. New York, Farrar, Straus and Cudahy, 1958. 383 p. *Also:* The most significant writings from the NRF 1919–1940. Ed. with introd. by Justin O'Brien. London, Eyre and Spotteswood, 1958. 408 p.   **12390**

Two articles by R. under the rubric "Esthetic attitudes" are the initial essay on his assumption of editorship in 1919, his esthetic manifesto, and "Questioning the concept of literature," answering Marcel Arland's "Concerning a new 'mal du siècle,' " which repeats his basic beliefs.

Review: Anon. in SatR 21, June 14, 1958.

Gide, André. Jacques Rivière. *In:* Hommage à Jacques Rivière. *See* 12418. p. 497–502. *Also:* Jacques Rivière. Eds. de la belle page, 1931. 24 p. *Also in his:* Eloges. Neuchâtel, Ides et calendes, 1948. p. 27–37.   **12391**

Gide's contribution to the *Hommage* volume following R.'s death. Sometimes called cold, it is a fine tribute to R. Recounts their first meeting, characterizes R.'s conversation, and denies his "discipleship," insisting on their essential differences and the profit stemming from the fact that they were adversaries, especially on the subject of Christianity, moralism, and psychological "globalism." Praises R. as writer, psychologist, artist and friend.

Guérard, Albert. André Gide. Cambridge, Mass., Harvard univ. press, 1951. 263 p.   **12392**

Contains detailed and intriguing, though debatable, account of Gide's influence as thinker, writer and person on R. He certainly reinforced tendencies or ideas preexisting in R.: sincerity, *disponibilité,* desire, love of inner contradictions, self-delight. May have had religious influence. May have suggested structure of *Aimée* and style of some essays.

LeBreton, Jules. Les traces de Dieu dans la vie de Jacques Rivière. RosO 10:311–81, 1926.   **12393**

Sensitive and solidly documented study on the religious evolution of R. Basing his study on numerous texts, the author situates remarkably well the obstacles met by R. in his search for faith and the fundamental attitude of his mind, avid for comprehension and analysis, which the adoption of a doctrine as complete and final as Christianity would continually fill with fear and hesitation, in spite of the particularly lucid and penetrating insights that R. would express throughout his life on faith. One of the most profound studies on this subject.

Lefèvre, Frédéric. Une heure avec Jacques Rivière. NL Dec. 1, 1923. *Also in his:* Une heure avec..., 2ᵉ série. Eds. de la Nouvelle revue française, 1924. p. 95–109. *Also:* NL March 12–23, 1975.   **12394**

Interview in which R. touches on Freud and Proust, answers attacks of Massis and Manian against the N.R.F., and defines how he differs from Gide in novelistic technique.

Lelong, M.-H. Pour la révélation de Jacques Rivière. VI 1:498–512, 1928.   **12395**

Difficulty of knowing someone as complex and reticent as R. *A la trace de Dieu* and correspondence with Claudel are keys. Article is principally a commentary on the correspondence with Alain-Fournier as revelatory of first step in R.'s religious evolution.

Madaule, Jacques. Alain-Fournier et Jacques Rivière d'après leur correspondance. RdJ 20:532–69, 1928. *Also in his:* Reconnaissances III. Desclée De Brouwer, 1946. p. 257–95.   **12396**

Intelligent reflections on the correspondence stressing the differences between the two friends which resulted in a fecund collaboration. Good quotes often truncated. Religious interpretation.

Massis, Henri. André Gide et son témoin. *And:* Jacques Rivière (1886–1925). In memoriam. *In his:* Jugements II. Plon, 1924. p. 79–108; 285–94. *Also (rev.) in*

his: D'André Gide à Marcel Proust. Lyon, Lardanchet, 1948. p. 131–56; 157–65. *Also (rev.):* Complexité de Jacques Rivière. De la sincérité à la croyance. *In his:* De l'homme à Dieu. Nouvelles éds. latines, 1959. p. 279–90.   **12397**
Second article also published as: *Jacques Rivière.* A la cité des lunes, 1925. 20 p. First article, discussing Gide's immoralism, claims R. is disciple most heavily marked by Gidean influence morally. R. refuses normalcy and equilibrium; his goal is not to be better but to know himself better. Complexity and contradictions of his personality. But R. is fundamentally afraid of immoralism which is against his nature and his religious inclinations. Second article praises R.'s openness to the new, his curiosity, his honesty.

Mauriac, François. Du côté de chez Proust. Table ronde, 1947. 155 p. *Also in his:* Ecrits intimes. Geneva-Paris, La palatine, 1953. p. 191–247.   **12398**
Includes article "De Marcel Proust à Jacques Rivière," blaming Proust's total submission to reality, ignoring any supernatural element, for a postwar "de-conversion" on R.'s part. Reprints *Le tourment de Jacques Rivière* (*see* 12425) on R.'s religious state during captivity and five important letters of R. dating from the last months of his life. Excellent flashes of intuition on R.'s personality. The letters are proof of R.'s state of mind just before his death and also contain critical comments on Mauriac's work.

Morino, L[ina]. La nouvelle revue française dans l'histoire des lettres (1908–1937). Gallimard, 1939. 229 p.   **12399**
Insists on importance of R. in N.R.F. from 1910 on, his new approach to criticism, his moral and philosophical lack of partiality, his need to probe a subject until he fully understood and explained it, the direction he gave to French letters.
Review: J. O'Brien in RR 30:190–94, 1940.

Naughton, Helen T. At home with Madame Isabelle Rivière. Ren 22:87–98, 1969–70.   **12400**
Account of week's visit to Isabelle Rivière, sister of Alain-Fournier and widow of R. Slight literary importance. Contains memories of two writers and attempts to describe the personality of Mme Rivière and the atmosphere in which she lived.

La nouvelle revue française de 1919 à 1925. Lyon, Imprimerie de l'Université de Lyon II pour le Centre d'études gidiennes, 1975. 130 p.   **12401**
First in series of four systematic studies in several parts of NRF, continuing monumental research of Auguste Anglès on the NRF, 1909–1914. Contains excellent summary of editorship and personality of R., unpublished publicity pages probably written mainly by R., contemporary opinions on NRF, chronological volume content summaries, alphabetical index of authors and their contributions, list of principal texts and authors treated, and index of other reviews cited. Important distinction made between R., the theoretician, orienting the review by his major articles and R., the editor, publishing freely authors whose views differed from his. Precise and valuable details given with admirable accuracy. Exemplary scholarly work.

O'Brien, Justin. Portrait of André Gide. Knopf, 1953. 404 p.   **12402**
Laudatory references to R. particularly as Gide's disciple and in reference to the conversion of the former. Good perspective on Gide-R. relationship.

Proust, Marcel. Lettres à la NRF. Gallimard, 1932. 283 p. (Cahiers Marcel Proust, 6)   **12403**
Letters to Gaston Gallimard concerning the publication of *A la recherche du temps perdu* as well as the extracts in the NRF, full of affectionate references to R. Most interesting is protest against Gide's "Billet à Angèle" on R.'s editorship of the review.

Psichari, Henriette. Les convertis de la belle époque. Préf. de Jean Pommier. Eds. rationalistes, 1971. 191 p.   **12404**
Treats temptation of Christianity for Alain-Fournier and R. Full of errors. Disagreeable, sarcastic in tone, especially for Isabelle Rivière, and extremely partial.

Rivière, Alain. Cinquantenaire de la mort de Jacques Rivière, avec une lettre inédite de Jacques Rivière et deux lettres inédites de Charles Du Bos. CahCD 19:41–47, 1975.   **12405**

Sensitive commentary joins a passage from Du Bos's *Journal* eight months after R.'s death expressing the depth of their friendship. The letter from R. appeals for Du Bos's advice after the publication of his provocative lead article for the first issue of the NRF in 1919 of which he was editor. Du Bos's answer is excellent and his letter to Anne Heurgon-Desjardins after R.'s death exceptionally perceptive. The final letter is a moving tribute to the influence of Isabelle R. in Du Bos's religious evolution.

Rivière, Isabelle. A la trace de Dieu: Jacques Rivière (1886–1925). Louvain, Symons, 1951. 16 p. (Convertis du XXᵉ siècle, 14) *Also in:* Convertis du XXᵉ siècle, I. Ed. by F. Lelotté. Tournai, Casterman; Brussels, Foyer Notre Dame, 1953–54. p. 215–30.   **12406**

Contains biographical facts not found elsewhere. Simple and sincere account of R.'s spiritual evolution worth more than lengthy, verbose and literary accounts which say essentially the same thing. Testimony of person who knew R. best.

—————. Le bouquet de roses rouges. Corrêa, 1935. 339 p. *Also:* Livre de poche, 1968. 381 p.   **12407**

Thinly disguised autobiography of R.'s first years of married life, Isabelle's conversion, and the birth of their daughter Jacqueline. Among the obvious characters are Alain-Fournier, Claudel and Gide.

Reviews: M. Arland in NRF 45: 922–25, 1935; R. Pons in his *Procès de l'amour.* Casterman, 1955. p. 143–64.

—————. La guérison. Corrêa, 1937. 304 p.   **12408**

Half fiction, half reality, this pseudo-novel is made up of an imaginary framework composed by Isabelle Rivière and actual entries from R.'s *Carnets* written while a prisoner of war. The book had documentary value before the publication of the complete *Carnets* in 1974.

Review: M. Arland in NRF 48:284–86, 1937.

—————. Vie et passion d'Alain-Fournier. Monaco, Jaspard, Polus et Cie., 1963. 535 p.   **12409**

Essentially the story of the sentimental life of Alain-Fournier, but R. inevitably enters into the account, especially in the anxious period following his disappearance at the beginning of the First World War. Contains valuable unpublished material.

Rivière-Leproust, Jeanne. Sur mon frère. NRF 37:513–20, 1931.   **12410**

Saw R. every day after publication of *Aimée.* Reports child-memories of brother as rough and dictatorial, mercurial, and leader of younger children. Intense desire to live at end of life. Was recovering health. Loss of religious faith. Enthusiasm about novel *Florence.* Picture of R. during this period has been questioned.

Saint-John Perse. Lettre sur Jacques Rivière. NRF 24:455–62, 1925. *Also:* Liège, Eds. Dynamo, 1963. 16 p. *Also:* Sur Jacques Rivière. Lettre à la Nouvelle Revue Française. *In his:* Œuvres complètes. Gallimard, 1972. p. 466–72. (Bibliothèque de la Pléiade)   **12411**

Reveals friend's knowledge of R.'s character. Expresses belief that at end of life R.'s doctrines ran counter to his deepest inclinations.

—————. Lettres à Jacques Rivière. *In his:* Œuvres complètes. Gallimard, 1972. p. 664–710, 893. (Bibliothèque de la Pléiade)   **12412**

Letters from a close friend expressing enthusiastic praise of R.'s writings as they appeared.

Schlumberger, Jean. Eveils. Gallimard, 1950. 250 p.   **12413**

Relates founding of NRF. States unequivocal admiration for R. and minimizes disparity in their literary ideals.

Turnell, Martin. The problem of Jacques Rivière. DuR 100:385–98, 1936.   **12414**

Good article devoted to religious views of R. Representative of his period and "modern" in his approach to God, he has much to offer thoughtful people of differing views. Turnell condemns R.'s method while admiring his insight.

[Van Rysselberghe, Maria]. Les cahiers de la Petite Dame: notes pour l'histoire authentique d'André Gide. 1918–1929. Préf. d'André Malraux. Gallimard, 1973–74. 2 v. (Cahiers André Gide, 4, 5) **12415**

Scattered friendly allusions to R. Gide's reaction to his death and the publication of his posthumous works. Obvious hostility to Isabelle Rivière.

Special Numbers

Clinq rencontres de Jacques Rivière. CahXXs 3:1–111, 1975. **12416**

Issue is work of eminent university professors, each a specialist in the author whose impact on R. he treats. The communications, originally presented during the Journée Jacques Rivière on November 24, 1973 in Paris under the auspices of the Société d'étude du 20ᵉ siècle, are outstanding for quality, scholarship and clarity of presentation. Issue contains definitive bibliography of works by R., a partial bibliography of criticism on him, and a list of studies in progress. Excellent. See separate articles.

Cinquantenaire de la mort de Jacques Rivière. BuAJR 1:1–143, 1975. **12417**

First publication of newly-formed association. Includes important unpublished letters, hitherto unavailable lecture given by R. on Alain-Fournier in Geneva in 1918, sensitive article by André Guyon on R.-Fournier friendship, rare press articles and private condolences at time of death of R., and valuable, extremely detailed account of texts, mss. and *inédits* available in R.-Fournier archives in Viroflay, including names of R.'s correspondents and number of letters to each in collection. Indispensable for scholars.

Hommage à Jacques Rivière. NRF 24:1–832, 1925. **12418**

74 articles of varying importance but, taken together, a moving tribute to R.'s importance in the eyes of his contemporaries. Divided into personal memories; tributes to R. as a person; articles on his role as editor of NRF, on his novels, on his non-literary and political essays; and the testimony of 21 foreign critics and writers. Almost every major contemporary author is represented. Includes 11 photographs and ms. pages, unpublished letters to Alain-Fournier and Gide, and excerpt from the cap-

tivity *Carnets,* and the lecture on Proust given in Monaco and republished in *Quelques progrès dans l'étude du cœur humain.* Extensive bibliography of R.'s work. Indispensable reading for light thrown on R. as man and writer from variety of angles.

Hommage à un ami d'André Gide. BAAG 25:3–52, 1975. **12419**

On occasion of fiftieth anniversary of R.'s death, bulletin of Gide association (Claude Martin, director) makes available unpublished letters from R., Gide, and Isabelle R., clarified by excellent, precise notes. Most interesting is frank, judicious criticism by R. of *Caves du Vatican.* Bulletin also contains text of R.'s lecture on Gide delivered first in Geneva (March 1918). A perceptive but not completely flattering critique of Gide's work.

Jacques Rivière et La Nouvelle revue française. NRF 226:1–49, 1975. **12420**

Homage volume dedicated to R. for fiftieth anniversary of his death. Brief but moving tribute followed by texts, most hitherto unpublished, assembled and commented on by Alain Rivière, written by Alain-Fournier, Arland, Breton, Claudel, Copeau, Ghéon, Gide, Jouhandeau, François Mauriac, Morand, Paulhan and Schlumberger. *Inédits* of R. are psychologically revealing and important for the light they throw on his nomination as director of the N.R.F., his intentions for the review, the opposition he met from his former collaborators, and above all his fascinating critical correspondence with contributors. Must be read by anyone interested in the period and R.

General Studies: Books

Beaulieu, Paul. Jacques Rivière. La colombe, Eds. du Vieux Colombier, 1956. 237 p. **12421**

Sincere study written primarily from point of view of R.'s religious positions by devotee who sees in R.'s example a lesson for contemporaries. Traces friendships and literary discipleships: Alain-Fournier, André Lhote, Symbolism, Barrès, Claudel, Gide, Proust, underplaying role of last two. Studies novels and theory of novel, evolution of critical ideas and practice, and dedication to role as editor of NRF. Flaws: incomplete study of religious writings in book with R.'s religious fluctuations as theme, neglect of major prewar essays, lack of discussion of work on Proust other than lectures. Literary importance subordinated to religious position. Subjective but with arguments to support point of view. Well written. Bibliography.

Cook, Bradford. Jacques Rivière: a life of the spirit. Oxford, Blackwell, 1958. 158 p. **12422**

Fascinating if sometimes debatable interpretation of R.'s spiritual development. Thesis is that although R. wrote penetratingly and prophetically on literature, painting, ballet, music and politics, he was one of the most interesting, moving, and profound of France's religious thinkers. Book traces inner life without a knowledge of which understanding of critical and creative work is impossible. Debatable are love of wounds, religious interpretation of *Aimée*, planned religious regression in postwar years. More acceptable is view of political action as charity and reversal of R.'s energies rather than his thinking after war. Extremely provocative book. Extensive bibliography.

Reviews: V. Mercier in HR 11:454–60, 1958; R. Weiss in Ren 12:86–88, 1960.

Doelker, Christian. Lire et dire: essai de biographie intérieure de Jacques Rivière. Zurich, City-Druck, S.A., 1963. 103 p. (Diss., Zurich) **12423**

Sees in R. a fundamental weakness and insufficiency in search of a plenitude which could not exist within the self. In contrast to the insufficiency of the person, the work of art seems a sufficiency, symbolized by woman, incarnating the plenitude of the ocean and, through love, promising life. His repeated attempts to find fullness in himself, in art, in God resulted in failure but make him profoundly appealing. Short bibliography. Extensive quotes from novels and autobiographical works but without concern for chronology. Study full of valuable insights, but danger of "interior biography."

Jans, Adrien. La pensée de Jacques Rivière. Brussels, Eds. de la cité chrétienne, 1938. 95 p. **12424**

Fairly complete book on R.'s life and work considered above all from the viewpoint of the search for God and the need for sincerity and truth. Justifies the non-conventional aspect of R.'s faith. Well documented on the different aspects of R.'s personality and his works. A good résumé for the reader desiring to cover the essential quickly.

Mauriac, François. Le tourment de Jacques Rivière. Strasbourg, Eds. de la nuée-bleue, 1926. 34 p. **12425**

Reprint of "Anima naturaliter christiana" taken from *Hommage à Jacques Rivière*, NRF 24:465–68 and "Un livre posthume de Jacques Rivière: A la trace de Dieu," RHeb 35:398–401, 1926. Reprinted in turn in his *Du côté de chez Proust* (*see* 12398).

Naughton, Helen Thomas. Jacques Rivière; the development of a man and a creed. The Hauge-Paris, Mouton, 1966. 180 p. (Studies in French literature, 6) **12426**

Attempts to draw a psychological portrait of R. and recount the events of his period and personal life which shaped his esthetic evolution. Book discusses polarities reconciled by polyphonic R. and warns that his positions were far from definitive at time of early death. Question of religious belief in postwar period not treated. Extensive bibliography.

Reviews: Anon. in TLS 3382:1188, 1966; M. Maclean in MLJ 59:396–97, 1975; A. Pénot in FR 41:894–95, 1968.

Raymond, Marcel. Etudes sur Jacques Rivière. Corti, 1972. 220 p. **12427**

By far the most scholarly and perceptive book on R. Will remain touchstone for some time to come. Six separate but coordinated essays passing chronologically through R.'s life. Considers different aspects of his literary and critical activity, traces the evolution of his thought inevitably affected by the artistic currents of the period 1905–1925, and assesses the originality of his critical approach. Certain themes and problems reappear, particularly the tie between esthetics and ethics. Treatment of R.'s view of sincerity, his search in his criticism for the profound central unifying force in an author, his tenacious hold on life and reality. Most of the major articles analyzed except *Rimbaud,* introduction to Alain-Fournier's *Miracles* and religious work. Essential reading.

Reviews: Anon. in TLS 3736:1257, Oct. 12, 1973; A. Anglès in QL 164: 7–8, 1973; R. Kanters in FL 1405:9, April 21, 1973; H. Naughton in EspCr 14:182–87, 1974.

Suffran, Michel. Jacques Rivière ou la conversion à la clarté. Wesmaël-Charlier, 1967. 187 p. (Conversions célèbres)
                                          12428
Well-intentioned but verbose and partial book. Neither biography nor literary criticism; interested only in R.'s spiritual journey. Literary essays misunderstood or twisted to suit purpose of author; incorrect chronology and some errors of fact. Annoying habit of addressing R. directly or making God speak to him. Excellent photographs.

Review: Anon. in BCLF 23:398, 1968.

Turnell, Martin. Jacques Rivière. New Haven, Yale univ. press, 1953. 64 p. (Studies in modern European literature and thought)   **12429**
First study in English devoted to R. Considers that his work must be seen as a whole. Devotes chapters to religious and political thought and to novels but considers his importance greatest as critic. Unjustly severe criticism of prewar *Etudes.* Annoying patronizing tone in discussion of religious views, "man-of-letters" novels, and "precious" early style. Impression Turnell is attempting to be clever at R.'s expense. Errors of fact and interpretation. Turnell's articles in reviews are superior to book.

Reviews: Anon. in List 1300:191, Jan. 28, 1954; B. Cook in Ren 6:159–62, 1954; W. Fowlie in Cweal 59:144–45, Nov. 13, 1953.

General Studies: Articles and Miscellaneous

Anex, Georges. La critique de Jacques Rivière. *In:* Lettres d'occident de l'Iliade à l'Espoir. Etudes et essais offerts à André Bonnard. Neuchâtel, A la Baconnière, 1958. p. 257–76.   **12430**

Extremely perceptive study of R.'s critical development, esthetic point of view, and particular qualities.

Archambault, Paul. Jacques Rivière. Les influences acceptées. Aspirations et oscillations. Et 1:664–80, 1926. *Also:* Jacques Rivière. *In his:* Jeunes maîtres. Bloud et Gay, 1926. p. 149–90.   **12431**
First part of article analyzes work published during R.'s lifetime. Second treats R.'s struggle with Catholicism, indicating his adherence only from 1913 to 1919 and basing statements on texts. Explains postwar apparent religious indifference to passion to understand life in its fullness. Tone of "affectionate veneration."

Carlin, Warren R. Jacques Rivière: the heart's reasons revisited. Cweal 102, no. 16:490–94, 1975.   **12432**
Good article containing account of R.'s captivity years, time of meditation and self-scrutiny. Analyzes *Carnets.*

Catalogne, Gérard de. Jacques Rivière ou la lutte contre l'ange. *In his:* Les essais. Le rouge et le noir, 1930. p. 79–103. *Also in his:* Les compagnons du spirituel. Montreal, Eds. de l'arbre, 1945. p. 125–54.
                                          12433
In vein of Massis but worse. Could not more completely misunderstand and misjudge R. Errors, misquotations. Misjudges R.'s religious position. Insists he could have been great Christian writer.

Du Bos, Charles. Fragments d'un journal. *In his:* Approximations II. Corrêa, 1932. p. 204–12.   **12434**
Moving memories of R. noted by Du Bos in his journal after the death of the former. Deep affection, admiration, and true judgment of R. by critic who perhaps understood him best. Discusses first meeting, reaction to early works. States idea that postwar R. tried to think against his own propensities. Excellent quotes.

———. Jacques Rivière. *In his:* Approximations II. Corrêa, 1932. p. 189–94. *Also:* Approximations. Fayard, 1965. p. 459–63.
                                          12435
Brief appreciation of R.'s work on occasion of his reception of the Blumenthal prize.

————. Jacques Rivière et de la féconde humilité. NRF 26:49–63, 1926. *Also in his:* Approximations II. Corrêa, 1932. p. 222–36. *Also:* Approximations. Fayard, 1965. p. 489–503.　　**12436**

Meditation on *A la trace de Dieu,* full of Du Bos's keen insights and fine quotations. Rather than commenting on richness of text, Du Bos wishes to indicate special quality which underlies its composition — a fruitful humility basic to R.'s personality which permits a patient, slow, groping acquisition of bits of spiritual truth. Ends with discreet and wise comments on R.'s postwar religious state.

————. Jacques Rivière et la perfection abstraite. NRF 24:580–88, 1925. *In his:* Approximations II. Corrêa, 1932. p. 213–21. *Also:* Approximations. Fayard, 1965. p. 480–88.　　**12437**

Tries to define what R. meant by the phrase "an exhaustive knowledge of the self." The living out of his ideas complicated by polarity between his intelligence and his sensitivity. He desired perfection but refused to touch anything in himself.

Garreau, Albert. Jacques Rivière et les nourritures terrestres. *In his:* Inquisitions III. Eds. du cèdre, 1974. p. 103–31.　**12438**

Partial and prejudiced, as the title indicates. The documentation is carefully chosen with the single object of proving R.'s lack of religious faith in the postwar period, accusing Isabelle R.'s testimony as being twisted by a desire for "vengeance" and basing its argument on that of Gide, Mauriac and others. Even the analysis of *A la trace de Dieu* tends to underline its limitations. However, the author grants a deathbed conversion.

Gide, André. Billets à Angèle. NRF 16:462–66, 1921. *Also in his:* Incidences. Gallimard, 1924. p. 49–53. *Trans.:* Notes to Angèle. *In:* Pretexts. Reflections on literature and morality. Ed. by Justin O'Brien. New York, Meridian books, Greenwich eds., 1959. p. 208–12. *Also:* New York, Dell, 1964. *Also:* Freeport, N.Y., Books for libraries press, 1971.　　**12439**

First note criticizes R.'s editorship of the NRF, admitting that some of the founding fathers had "evolved" during the war but requesting more interesting material, the old critical spirit, and an end to the subordination of the intellect to patriotism. Second note briefly mentions R. whose projects Gide seconds especially when they differ from his point of view.

————. Lettres ouvertes. I. A. Jacques Rivière. NRF 12:121–25, 1919. *Also in his:* Incidences. Gallimard, 1924. p. 63–66. *Trans.:* Open letters. I. To Jacques Rivière. *In:* Pretexts. Reflections on literature and morality. Ed. by Justin O'Brien. New York, Meridian books, Greenwich eds., 1959. p. 219–22. *Also:* New York, Dell, 1964. *Also:* Freeport, N.Y., Books for libraries press, 1971.　　**12440**

Criticizes R.'s *L'Allemand,* stating that R. paints reaction of representative Frenchman faced with German characteristics. Book is his own portrait as well as that of German. Points out that traits R. dislikes are found in other peoples and are not typically German.

Greenwood, E. B. Jacques Rivière, 1886–1925. EIC 10:422–33, 1960.　　**12441**

Fine study with excellent insights and comparisons of R. to other writers. Literary critic is cerebral but precision with which R. can define his relationship to his various enthusiasms marks his originality. Constantly refused to surrender to a formula that oversimplifies.

Léonard, Albert. La crise du concept de littérature en France au XXᵉ siècle. Corti, 1975. p. 50–64, 113–21, 186–94.　**12442**

Discusses the Marcel Arland-R. debate (p. 50–64); R.'s theory of an open complex novel following the lead of Dostoevsky (p. 113–21); and R.'s critical method and directorship of the NRF (p. 186–94). Recommended.

Marcel, Gabriel. Jacques Rivière et l'idéalisme. Eur 3:560–62, April 15, 1926.　　**12443**

Question of *A la trace de Dieu* and R.'s later philosophical positions. Subtly makes distinctions on opinions advanced and insists that a philosophical position cannot be depersonalized but is the intellectual transmutation of an intimate experience without which speculative acrobatics are in vain.

Maritain, Jacques. L'apologétique de Jacques Rivière. RU 26:101–08, 1926. **12444**

Expresses fraternal affection for author of correspondence with Claudel and *A la trace de Dieu,* but criticizes the exclusively psychological treatment of religious dogma. R. lacked theological training. Discusses principally R.'s ideas on the social sense of a Christian and his pages on prayer and providence.

Naughton, Helen T. The realism of Jacques Rivière. MLQ 25:171–80, 1964. **12445**

R. strongly influenced by philosophical idealism which caused a profound state of despair. Like many young men of his generation he turned back to reality, rejecting also symbolism and impressionism, but, in so doing, he attempted to include in his concept of the non-self dream, fantasy and emotion.

――――. Temperament and creed: a note on Jacques Rivière. FR 36:474–81, 1963. **12446**

R.'s literary criticism marked by his temperament: dualities within his personality and deep-seated inability to renounce one alternative in order to adopt its opposite. Total acceptance of possibilities was fundamental to his thinking and was chief reason for refusal to adopt Catholicism in crisis of 1907–09, Mind works in terms of conciliations: in politics, morals, religion, esthetics. In art he found the central problem to be the synthesizing of emotion and intelligence. The sensual and affective world must be encircled, defined and generalized by a penetrating effort of man's intellect.

Peyre, Henri. The age of sincerity. *In his:* Literature and sincerity. New Haven and London, Yale univ. press; Paris, Presses univ. de France, 1963. p. 237–75. (Yale Romanic studies, second series, 9) **12447**

R. is one of most complex literary sensibilities of last two hundred years. His novels, typically French, treat fascination of unloving for analyst who sees through delusions of love. In literary criticism he searched for a new facet of himself through others. Sincerity for him led to dispersal, disintegration of the ego and the subordination of the will to the delight of the dissecting intellect.

――――. Jacques Rivière and the pursuit of truth. EspCr 14:110–20, 1974. **12448**

Keen, perceptive, well-written article. Rates R. with Du Bos and Blanchot as only critics of first half of century to be read in 2000. Stresses R.'s work after 1919. R.'s peculiar gifts were discriminating taste which kept him from ever making a marked error of judgment, pliability, polymorphic complexity, and the perception of the tie between literature, the other arts and politics. Relentless probing of self, part of his concept of sincerity, led him never to be satisfied with a superficial explanation. Peyre emphasizes R.'s criticism of Rimbaud, Proust and moralism in literature.

Poulet, Georges. Une critique d'identification. *In:* Les chemins actuels de la critique. Centre culturel international de Cerisy-la-Salle, 2–12 sept. 1966. Sous la direction de Georges Poulet. Ed. by Jean Ricardou. Plon, 1967. p. 9–35. *And:* Les critiques de la N.R.F. *In his:* La conscience critique. Corti, 1971. p. 60–64. **12449**

Paper read by Poulet referring in particular to R. Substantially same text as in his *La conscience critique.* Discussion following insists on distinction between R., critic, and R., editor of NRF. Marcel Raymond comments that R. taught him to avoid preparations and introductions and drive directly to vital center of author studied.

Price, Blanche. Jacques Rivière on moralism and literature. FR 17:214–19, 1944. **12450**

R.'s objection to moralistic point of view is that it permits author to judge his characters before observing their behavior dispassionately. He attempts to judge, teach, or shock, but he should assign values to the product of his research only after examination and analysis.

Proulx, Pierre Marie. Jacques Rivière et sa quête de la vérité. RUL 21:43–62, 1966. **12451**

First of four good articles devoted to R.'s spiritual evolution. Ends with analysis of R.'s literary enthusiasms (Barrès in particular) and temptation to return to faith.

――――. Rivière en lutte avec la vérité. RUL 21:126–48, 1966. **12452**

R.'s moral life disturbed and transformed by his reading of Claudel's *L'arbre*. Article discusses R.'s sincerity and good will but his delight in his own complexity, his pride, his pleasure in the dialog of the dilettante. During captivity, after R.'s return to Church in 1913, he recognized his spiritual debt to Claudel.

————. Rivière en progrès vers la vérité. RUL 21:270–88, 1966.   **12453**
Devoted to R.'s war experience, his desire to exhibit heroism, the "humiliation" of his capture, and the effect of the three years in German prison camps where he was totally cut off from his former loves and occupations.

————. Rivière et la vérité dernière. RUL 21:358–77, 1966.   **12454**
Discussion of R.'s religious stand in postwar years. Testimony that he himself felt eclipse of grace. R. was never a stolid believer; his quest for truth is marked by progress and retrogression. Controversy after his death.

Raymond, Marcel. Jacques Rivière devant l'histoire et les nationalités. EspCr 14: 121–37, 1974.   **12455**
Close and intuitive study of R.'s political views and lengthy writings on political events and problems.

Richard, Lionel. Jacques Rivière et l'Allemagne. Ethp 29:51–80, 1974.   **12456**
Excellent article on R.'s promotion of Franco-German relations. Discusses his knowledge of Germany, the influence of *L'Allemand*, his numerous political articles in the NRF and *Die Luxemberger Zeitung,* the importance of the Emile Mayrisch family and the Cercle de Colpach in Luxemburg.

[Rivière, Jacques] The ideal reader: selected essays by Jacques Rivière. Ed., trans., and introd. by Blanche A. Price. With a pref. by Henri Peyre. Meridian, 1960. 282 p.   **12457**
Preface captures essentials concerning R. Stresses his impeccable taste, openness to the new, sensuous perception of literature and lucidity in analyzing it. Introduction is not only accurate and well-written; it is the most impartial and complete short summary of R.'s life and work to date. Model translations of difficult texts.

Reviews: A. Alvarez in NewS 63, no. 1624: April 27, 1962; and T. Tanner in T&T 43, no. 16:33, April 19, 1962.

Turnell, Martin. The criticism of Jacques Rivière. MLR 35:470–82, 1940.   **12458**
Brief mention of R.'s religious evolution but main emphasis on literary criticism. Distrust of dogma and insistence on intuition or experience are weaknesses in theologian but assets for critic who must be pragmatist.

————. The criticism of Jacques Rivière. PR 20:179–90, 1953.   **12459**
Excellent article. R. is not typical French critic proving a system; he distrusts the neat formula and is sensitively responsive to texts. He used criticism not for purely polemic purposes but to try to influence the writers of his day. Not same text as 1940 article but many similarities.

————. A note on Jacques Rivière. Cweal 54:479–81, Aug. 24, 1951.   **12460**
Unacceptable conclusion on R. as high priest of cult of unrest setting off wave of diarykeepers on religious fluctuations. *Carnets* were never meant for publication.

Novel

Du Bos, Charles. Aimée par Jacques Rivière. NRF 20:560–66, 1923. *Also in his:* Approximations II. Corrêa, 1932. p. 195–203. *Also:* Approximations. Fayard, 1965. p. 464–79.   **12461**
Praise of novel. Stresses François' need for torment and suffering as means to greater self-knowledge, but originality of book is that love and lucid vision of inner self go hand in hand instead of being successive. Du Bos sees underlying religious inclinations and R.'s sense of constant responsibility towards the totality of his inner being.

Jaloux, Edmond. Aimée par Jacques Rivière. RHeb 621–25, Dec. 30, 1922. *Also in his:* De Pascal à Barrès. Plon, 1927. p. 175–81.   **12462**
Perceptive, laudatory article on *Aimée*. Final renunciation is unbelievable and novel is too abstract but psychological portrait of Aimée is masterful and study of secret contradictions of human heart is worth pages of action.

————. Jacques Rivière romancier. *In his:* De Pascal à Barrès. Plon, 1927. p. 203–11. **12463**

Reworking of previous article on *Aimée* but more specifically an attempt to draw a psychological portrait of R. and his hero François.

Magny, Claude-Edmonde. Jacques Rivière le trop caressant. *In her:* Histoire du roman français. Eds. du seuil, 1950. p. 81–86. **12464**

Severe criticism of *Aimée,* a narcissistic novel in which the passive hero sees in his passive heroine a mirror image of himself and the same delight in the subtle exploration of delicate and rare feelings, the same love of one's tormented and unusual soul. Novel lacks weight, reality, plot, and movement. Overuse of imperfect tense creates impression of stagnation. R. is passive observer who notes his strange feelings with conscious delectation.

Naughton, Helen T. The critic's cure: Rivière's Aimée. Ren 17:201–06, 1965. **12465**

His attempts at creative writing were few before the First World War but in German prison camps he composed *Aimée,* a thinly veiled autobiographical novel. It in no way lives up to his prewar prescriptions; it is abstract and intellectual. By writing out his experience R. helped dissociate himself from it permanently.

Contacts and Comparisons

Alden, Douglas W. Marcel Proust and his French critics. Los Angeles, Lymanhouse, 1940. 259 p. *Also:* New York, Russell & Russell, 1973. **12466**

Various references to R. between pages 31 and 85; his critical articles on Proust aptly and succinctly judged in this monumental piece of scholarly research. Of particular interest are comments on R.'s reaction to awarding of Goncourt prize, the *Hommage* volume, and *Quelques progrès dans l'étude du cœur humain.*

Beaulieu, Paul. Jacques Rivière et Paul Claudel: à l'occasion du 25ᵉ anniversaire de la mort de Jacques Rivière (février 1925–février 1950). RevD 56:136–42, 1950. **12467**

Beaulieu deems it necessary to evaluate carefully influence of Claudel on R.'s spiritual development. Two men were different temperamentally and mentally. Tactical errors on part of Claudel, but at a decisive moment of R.'s life, by his charity and his firmness, he made his mark and having fulfilled his role of guide left the rest to grace. Proof is faith of captivity years and R.'s death.

Bersani, Jacques. Rivière et Proust, ou la fascination. *In:* Cinq rencontres de Jacques Rivière. *See* 12416. p. 65–77. **12468**

Sees R.'s relationship to Proust as made up of as many misunderstandings as affinities, an ambivalent fascination coupled with fear. Article carefully restricts what was formerly considered R.'s all-embracing acceptance of Proust's work choosing to point to an increasing vocabulary of anguish as well as one of ecstasy as evidence of the critic's personal choice of life over art.

Cook, Bradford. Jacques Rivière and symbolism. YFS 9:103–11, 1952. **12469**

R.'s life spanned culminating years and decline of symbolism. His connection with the movement was specifically evolutionary, his nature being first passionately drawn to it and later decisively away.

Décaudin, Michel. Rivière et Dada. *In:* Cinq rencontres de Jacques Rivière. *See* 12416. p. 79–88. **12470**

Valuable study situating R.'s reaction to Dada in the context of his period and esthetic formation and referring to contemporary texts by Tzara, Breton and Gide which complement "Reconnaissance à Dada" and without a knowledge of which that key article can be misconstrued.

Eustis, Alvin. Rivière's crew: Crémieux, Fernandez, Arland. EspCr 14:138–45, 1974. **12471**

Describing three authors as "unruly crew," Eustis discusses points on which they took issue with R.'s views, particularly that of morality or an ethical slant in literature as opposed to objective psychological analysis.

Garniez, Bernard. Dostoïevski et l'ambivalence de la critique de La Nouvelle Revue Française. ESl 6:241–45, 1961.　**12472**

R. recognizes richness of Dostoevsky's novels but contrasts their complexity to French need for coherence.

Jaloux, Edmond. Jacques Rivière et Marcel Proust. NRF 24:548–53, 1925. *Also in his:* De Pascal à Barrès. Plon, 1927. p. 193–201.　**12473**

Proust analyzed emotions with suspicion and distance, not at peak of exaltation. Did not reveal R. to himself but helped him progress more rapidly along his own path.

Jans, Adrien. Jacques Rivière et Marcel Proust, raisons et fruits d'une amitié. Communication de M. Adrien Jans à la séance mensuelle du 11 septembre 1971. BARLLF 49:198–214, 1971.　**12474**

Sees R.-Proust friendship as awaited and inevitable because of affinities between two men: observation of feeling before description, desire to explore and understand complex psychological depths. Proust's influence on second version of *Aimée,* and on R.'s conception of friendship, love, the subconscious.

Lefèvre, Roger. Rivière lecteur de Rimbaud. *In:* Cinq rencontres de Jacques Rivière. *See* 12416. p. 49–64.　**12475**

Uncovers four stages in R.'s reaction to Rimbaud. First, Rimbaud's visions are the products of a ferverish mind or a systematic fabrication; later, they are a poetic work capable, like music, of introducing us into the mysterious but real world of dreams—art not religion. Third, in the immediate prewar years R. underwent a mystical experience in which he saw the poet's visions not as esthetically beautiful but as a document on transcendental reality, a step on the path to faith. Following the war he no longer recognized a mystical interpretation but, coupled with a return to esthetic appreciation, saw Rimbaud's subconscious as the object revealed.

LeSage, Laurent. Jacques Rivière. *In his:* Marcel Proust and his literary friends. Urbana, Univ. of Illinois press, 1958. p. 99–103. (Illinois studies in language and literature)　**12476**

Sees Proust-R. friendship, although not without self-interest, as exceedingly fruitful for each writer and for French letters.

Naughton, Helen T. A contemporary views Proust. EspCr 5:48–55, 1965.　**12477**

R.'s relationship with Proust and recognition of his worth date from 1913. R. persistently claimed the honor of revealing Proust to the public. Friendship genuine and fruitful on both sides.

O'Neill, Kevin. Jacques Rivière et André Gide: deux épisodes dans l'histoire de leurs relations (1920–1921). *In:* Cinq rencontres de Jacques Rivière. *See* 12416. p. 23–47.　**12478**

Psychologically fascinating article treats with humor and erudition two periods of discord in an otherwise genuine friendship, controlled in its enthusiasm by the counter influence of Claudel.

Rivière, Isabelle. Jacques Rivière et André Gide. VI 21:280–306; 480–505, 1933.　**12479**

Refutes allegation that R. remained a disciple of Gide after enthusiasm of youth. Insists that after war, in his lecture on Gide, he felt anxiety and fear rather than blind admiration. Opposes two writers in all ways possible, stating particularly that the self was starting point for R., end for Gide. Truth was object of ardent quest for R., a plaything for Gide. R. was self-giving, Gide self-sufficient.

Ernest Seillière
(Nos. 12480–12484)

DAVID J. KLEIN

Bonnecase, Julien. Philosophie de l'impérialisme et science du droit. Bordeaux, Delmas, 1932. 290 p.　**12480**

Book devoted to an understanding of the legal and judicial significance of S.'s work. Finding S.'s doctrine only implicitly conceptualized, Bonnecase proceeds to establish the philosophic base as preparatory material for his legalistic conclusions.

Conem, Francis. Ernest Seillière, père de l'impérialisme radical. RSH 126:307–19, 1967.　**12481**

By citing passages from S.'s works and from his critics, Conem recreates tone of S.'s work and critical reaction to it. Valuable for its critical reference and for updating studies made on S.

Gillouin, René. Une nouvelle philosophie de l'histoire moderne et française. Bernard Grasset, 1921. 278 p. **12482**

Work dedicated to the exposition and criticism of S.'s ideology which Gillouin reduces essentially to "imperialism," "mysticism," "reason," "Christianity and stoicism," and "virility and femininity." These are seen as the historical, moral, and social foundation for a new philosophy of history of the modern era. S.'s "Rousseauism" is explored in depth with Gillouin tracing its genesis and development in conjunction with the above categories.

Rudrauf, Lucien. Le mysticisme esthétique selon la doctrine d'Ernest Seillière. RTASMP 98–105, 2ᵉ semestre, 1960. **12483**

Article which opposes S.'s naturistic concept of mysticism to Catholic mysticism as source for human artistic accomplishment. S.'s thoughts on the role of the subconscious, reason, and the moral implications of the romantic movement are reviewed and analyzed.

Sprietsma, Cargill. We imperialists. Columbia univ. press, 1931. 153 p. **12484**

A basic attempt to summarize and clarify the more than forty to fifty volumes of criticism published by S. between 1897 and 1930. Sprietsma proceeds chronologically, starting with the early essays, and adds helpful comments and brief analysis to his résumé.

Albert Thibaudet
(Nos. 12485–12504)

GERALD PRINCE

Bibliography

Davies, John C. Bibliographie des articles d'Albert Thibaudet. RSH 86:197–229, 1957. **12485**

A useful piece of work. Contains an index of authors commented on by T. in his major articles.

Biography

Bopp, Léon. Portrait d'Albert Thibaudet. DisV 3:51–75, 1953. **12486**

A valuable portrait of T. by his friend and literary testator. Thinks that T.'s tendency to vacillation and his lack of dogmatism as a man is at the root of his conception of the critic as an agent of reconciliation.

Crémieux, Benjamin. Les débuts d'Albert Thibaudet. NRF 47:116–24, 1936. **12487**

A good account of T.'s early academic and literary carrer.

General Studies

Bergson H[enri]. Quelques mots sur Thibaudet critique et philosophe. NRF 47:7–14, 1936. *Trans.:* Remarks on Thibaudet as critic and philosopher. *In:* From the N.R.F. An image of the twentieth century from the pages of the Nouvelle revue française. Ed. by Justin O'Brien. Farrar, Straus and Cudahy, 1958. p. 261–67. *Another ed.:* N.R.F. The most significant writings from the Nouvelle revue française 1919–1940. London, Eyre & Spottiswoode, 1958. p. 279–85. **12488**

A moving tribute to the critic's memory. Speaks of "pre-established harmony" (rather than mutual influence) which existed between them.

Bopp, Léon. Albert Thibaudet (caractéristique générale de sa pensée). NRF 47:15–23, 1936. **12489**

A pleasant presentation of T. as the product of Burgundian good humor, incomparable erudition, Bergsonism and relativism.

Davies, John C. Héraclès — un ouvrage peu connu d'Albert Thibaudet. RSH 94:185–94, 1959. **12490**

Finds that T.'s posthumously published narrative is unsuccessful because the critic knew how to give life to ideas but not to characters. Underlines his Bergsonism, dualism and capacity for fruitful analogies.

———. L'œuvre critique d'Albert Thibaudet. Geneva, Droz; Lille, Giard, 1955. 206 p. **12491**

A clear and well-documented study of T.'s criticism, its evolution and its

method. Thinks, somewhat unjustly, that the critic enters a period of decline after his *Flaubert*. Does not distinguish sufficiently between journalistic criticism and academic or "creative" criticism.
Reviews: J.-A. Bédé in RBPH 35: 417–21, 1957; R. Pouilliart in LR 12: 215–17, 1958.

————. Thibaudet and Bergson. AUMLA 9:48–59, 1958.   **12492**
Argues that the relationship between T.'s critical thought and the ideas of Bergson is the result of a close affinity between the two men as well as of a deliberate attempt by T. to apply in his work the principles of a well-loved master. A good discussion of T.'s Bergsonian qualities.

————. Thibaudet and the problem of literary generations. FS 12:113–24, 1958.
                                        12493
While acknowledging that T. gained certain advantages by using the method of literary generations in his *Histoire de la littérature française,* argues convincingly that he did not always avoid the pitfalls to which this method exposes the critic: excessive simplification, artificiality and arbitrariness.

Devaud, Marcel. Albert Thibaudet critique de la poésie et des poètes. Fribourg, Eds. universitaires, 1967. 304 p.   **12494**
Examination of R. as a critic of poetry in general and such poets as Ronsard, Hugo, Mallarmé and Rimbaud. Too many paraphrases of the critic and too many generalizations. The bibliography is not very helpful.
Review: A. Glauser in FR 41:747–48, 1968.

Duckworth, Colin. Albert Thibaudet and the Berger de Bellone. FS 7:18–34, 1953.
                                        12495
Good presentation of one of the longest of T.'s purely imaginative works. T.'s collection of poems is seen as his Odyssey and as "a sort of *Légende des siècles* of literary history." Appreciative and interesting.

Fernandez, Ramon. La critique d'Albert Thibaudet. NRF 47:47–54, 1936. *Also in his:* Itinéraire français. Eds. du pavois, 1943. p. 43–55.   **12496**
Good characterization of T. as a critic capable of mediating between the

literature of the past and literature in the making. Thinks *Flaubert* is his most exemplary work. Notes his gift for metaphor.

Glauser, Alfred. Albert Thibaudet et la critique littéraire. Boivin, 1952. 296 p.
                                        12497
After a rapid and discreet portrait of T. and a discussion of his failure as a poet, examines the creative nature of his criticism. Interesting but often unconvincing study. Exaggerates the power and subtlety of the critic's style.
Reviews: D. Heiney in Eras 6:146–47, 1963; A. Soreil in RBPH 31:1070–77, 1953.

Kurris, F. Le bergsonisme d'Albert Thibaudet. EtBer 7:137–78, 1966.   **12498**
A detailed study of Bergsonian traits in T.'s work. A useful study.

Sigaux, Gilbert. Notes pour un portrait d'Albert Thibaudet. Nef 28:53–58, 1947.
                                        12499
Excellent discussion of T.'s criticism. Brings out the unity of his thought and its dialectical rhythm.

Spitzer, Leo. Patterns of thought in the style of Albert Thibaudet. MLQ 9:259–72; 478–91, 1948. *Also in his:* Romanische Literaturstudien 1936–1956. Tübingen, Max Niemeyer, 1959. p. 294–328.   **12500**
Very suggestive discussion based on excerpts from two of T.'s posthumously published pieces. Thinks that T. is a conservative historian for whom all existing historical entities are patterned on France. Concludes that T. is not a Bergsonian and that the primordial principle of his work is not Heraclitean flux but Eleatic being.

Tomlinson, Muriel D. Albert Thibaudet, European. MLQ 12:487–91, 1951.   **12501**
Disagrees with Spitzer's view of T. as a conservative historian whose world is strictly modeled after France. Argues that, encompassing T. the Frenchman, was T. the European. Spirited but superficial.

————. Thibaudet in the Dépêche de Toulouse. FR 40:765–73, 1967.   **12502**
Studies T.'s contributions to the *Dépêche de Toulouse* and attempts to show that they are important for an understanding of T. the man and for

an appreciation of his socio-political stance. Depicts T. as, above all, a man of dialog in an age of resurgent nationalism. Interesting but overly enthusiastic.

————. Thibaudet, the universal critic. FR 36:293–300, 1963.   **12503**

Argues that T. was not only the worthy successor of Sainte-Beuve but also a spiritual descendant of Montaigne and a great essayist. Praises his tolerance and universalism. Defends his rejection of the literary and artistic movements of the twenties as a rejection of movements emphasizing only the immediate and the temporary. Not always incisive.

Wellek, René. Albert Thibaudet. *In:* Modern French criticism from Proust and Valéry to structuralism. Ed. by John K. Simon. Chicago and London, Univ. of Chicago press, 1972. p. 85–107.   **12504**

Excellent presentation of T.'s critical work. Underlines T.'s intellectual ideal of criticism. Praises his analyses of style.

CHAPTER XXIX

ESSAYISTS, MEMORIALISTS, BIOGRAPHERS

(Nos. 12505–12803)

GABRIEL V. ASFAR, PIERRE AUBERY, DOMINIQUE BAUDOUIN, SYDNEY D. BRAUN, JEAN-PIERRE CAP, PIETRO FERRUA, RAYMOND GAY-CROSIER, J. THEODORE JOHNSON, JR., JACK KOLBERT, S. KENT MADSEN, ROBERT J. NIESS, ALAIN SILVERA, AND SEYMOUR S. WEINER

Alain
(pseud. of Emile Chartier)
(Nos. 12505–12584)

S. KENT MADSEN

Bibliography

Dewit, Suzanne. Alain: Essai de bibliographie 1893–Juin 1961. Brussels, Commission belge de bibliographie, 1961. xv, 204 p. **12505**

An extremely detailed list of published works by and about A., including a subsection on texts reproduced as part of other works, and a subsection on reviews of the various major works of A. Can be criticized, however, as too detailed and indiscriminate a compilation. No annotation is provided.

Editions

Alain (pseud. of Emile Chartier). Les arts et les dieux. Texte établi et présenté par Georges Bénézé. Préf. d'André Bridoux. [Gallimard, 1958] xlii, 1442 p. (Bibliothèque de la Pléiade) *Also:* 1961. 1446 p. **12506**

A collection of A.'s major works on art and religion. In his preface, Bridoux characterizes A. as the incarnation of Cartesian *générosité,* and argues that the dominant themes in his work viewed as a whole are founded in his reflection upon the fine arts. In the introduction, Bénézé provides a description of the various original mss. relied upon as well as excerpts from inscriptions by A. on gift copies of the various works. The ed. contains an index.

————. Les passions et la sagesse. Texte établi et présenté par Georges Bénézé.

Préf. d'André Bridoux. [Gallimard, 1960] xlvi, 1430 p. (Bibliothèque de la Pléiade) **12507**

A collection of the major philosophical works prepared by Bénézé. In his preface, Bridoux discusses the dual principles of perception and action as bases of A.'s thought, and argues that his experiences during World War I were crucial to the development of the major themes. Bénézé's introduction is primarily a collection of inscriptions by A. on gift copies of the various works. Indexed.

————. Propos. Ed. by Maurice Savin. Gallimard, 1956. xliv, 1366 p. (Bibliothèque de la Pléiade) **12508**

Short preface by André Maurois, chronological table of quotations and bibliographical information, and a necessarily incomplete index. The postwar *propos* have been heavily favored in the selection, and those dealing with specific political issues and events have been systematically excluded. The arrangement is chronological.

————. Propos II. Ed. by Samuel S. de Sacy. Gallimard, 1970. 1326 p. (Bibliothèque de la Pléiade) **12509**

This magnificent collection of *propos* contains an introduction by Sacy, a chronological table of bibliographical and biographical information, excerpts from various pertinent works by A., an annotated list of all the published collections of *propos,* an index and complete notes. The introduction (35 p.) is the best overview of the *Propos* available to date. Sacy's selection is reasonably well balanced including several of the very first *propos d'un*

Normand. The arrangement is chronological.

Special Numbers

Hommage à Alain. MerF 313:583–769, 1951. **12510**

Contains three biographical articles of no value and four major studies which have been analyzed separately.

Hommage à Alain. Nouvelle revue française, 1952. 378 p. **12511**

A collection of generally short articles assembled the year after A.'s death. Published as separate volume, not part of NRF which resumed publication in 1953. An important source. Important individual articles are discussed separately.

Correspondence

Alain (pseud. of Emile Chartier). Correspondance avec Elie et Florence Halévy. Préf. et notes par Jeanne Michel-Alexandre. Gallimard, 1958. 467 p. **12512**

Correspondence with two life-long friends.

[——— **and Romain Rolland].** Salut et fraternité. Alain et Romain Rolland. Correspondance et textes présentés par Henri Petit. Albin Michel, 1969. 182 p. (CahRR, 18) **12513**

Contains correspondence between A. and Romain Rolland as well as texts in which the two spoke of one another.

Biography

Alain (pseud. of Emile Chartier). Histoire de mes pensées. Gallimard, 1936. 310 p. *Also:* 22nd ed., 1950. **12514**

A somewhat enigmatic intellectual autobiography. Provides an excellent introduction to A.'s thought and manner.

———. Portraits de famille. Mercure de France, 1961. 199 p. **12515**

Contains information on the family setting in which A. was raised as well as two short autobiographies.

Alain Emile Chartier au lycée d'Alençon, 1881–1886. [Alençon?] Association des anciens élèves du lycée Alain à Alençon, 1958. 100 p. **12516**

A collection of speeches and memorabilia published as the *lycée d'Alençon* became the *lycée Alain.* The most notable are by Henri Mondor and Maurice Savin. Also included is an unpublished account by A. himself of experiences as a student.

Alexandre, Jeanne. Alain à Sevigné. *In:* Hommage à Alain. *See* 12511. p. 13–22. **12517**

A balanced portrait of A. as a professor, which goes beyond eulogy and reminiscence. Views A. as the exponent of an informed and studied optimism.

Alexandre, Michel. Rencontre d'Alain. *In:* Hommage à Alain. *See* 12511. p. 98–102. **12518**

A description of Alexandre's first encounter with A. Sheds some light on A.'s social personality and on the charisma that made him a successful teacher.

[Bost, Pierre] Alain professeur. Paul Hartmann, 1932. 52 p. **12519**

A description of A.'s methods and manner in the classroom. Published anonymously. Of considerable biographical interest.

Brodin, Pierre. In his: Maîtres et témoins de l'entre-deux-guerres. Montreal, Valiquette, 1943. p. 99–118. **12520**

A portrait of A. as a professor drawn from the testimony of many of his students.

Cottez, Henri. Témoignage. *In:* Hommage à Alain. *See* 12511. p. 636–44. **12521**

A thoughtful analysis of the nature and causes of A.'s impact on his students.

Demont, Eugène. Alain mon maître. MerF 344:447–55, 1962. **12522**

A fine portrait of A. as a teacher.

Escoube, Pierre. Alain dans sa classe. MerF 342:222–36, 1961. **12523**

Describes A.'s teaching methods. Interesting anecdotal material on the evolution of A.'s attitude toward Valéry.

Massis, Henri. Souvenirs sur Alain. *In:* Hommage à Alain. *See* 12511. p. 72–85. **12524**

An interesting reminiscence, providing insights into A.'s teaching methods, his religious views and his debt to Balzac.

Maurois, André. Mémoires. Flammarion, 1970. p. 41–52. **12525**

An intriguing portrait of A. as a teacher. The book also contains fragmentary information on Maurois' contacts with A. later in life.

Mondor, Henri. Alain. RdP 58, no. 11:5–16, 1951. **12526**

A physical and moral portrait of A.

Moyse, Robert. Alain et Dieu. RMM 57: 255–70, 1952. **12527**

Characterizes A. as one who steadfastly refused to believe.

Savin, Maurice. En Bretagne avec Alain. *In:* Hommage à Alain. *See* 12511. p. 231–56. **12528**

A wide-ranging discussion of the composition of *Les dieux*. Provides one of the best descriptions available of A.'s work habits and methods of composition together with a good deal of interesting anecdotal material. Beautifully written.

General Studies: Books

Bénézé, Georges. Généreux Alain. Presses univ. de France, 1962. 238 p. **12529**

Views A. as a philosopher. Emphasizes his technical competence and contributions in the fields of ethics, esthetics, politics and philosophy of science. Fragmentary attempts to relate A.'s idealism to contemporary and historical currents. No pretensions to comprehensive treatment or synthesis, however.

Reviews: M. Barthélémy-Madaule in RPFE 158:494–96, 1968; J. Robinson in RHL 64:326–27, 1964.

Bridoux, André. Alain; sa vie, son œuvre, avec un exposé de sa philosophie. Presses univ. de France, 1964. 112 p. **12530**

A short, rather general and elementary survey of A.'s thought including selections from his works.

Foulquié, Paul. Alain. Eds. de l'école, 1952. 174 p. **12531**

Contains a thumbnail biographical sketch and psychological portrait as well as general comments on A.'s contributions to psychology, political thought, educational philosophy, ethics, philosophy of religion and esthetics. The principal value of this work is as a topical index to numerous quotations from the works of A.

Giraud, Henri. La morale d'Alain. Toulouse, Edouard Privat, 1970. 288 p. **12532**

Discerns three levels of ethical discourse in A.'s works: (1) specific moral counsel; (2) definitions of the basic human virtues; and (3) elaborations upon general moral principles. Contends that his ethic arises out of a unique nature/spirit dualism, the spirit being defined as that which does not exist in nature, but which can be manifest in the "unnatural" moral actions of free men. A very readable book. One of the best introductions to A. available.

Halda, Bernard. Alain. Eds. de l'école, 1965. 127 p. **12533**

Elegant essays on A.'s various roles: educator, citizen, philosopher, writer, esthetician, and sage. Better than anyone else, Halda gives perspective on the social, political and philosophical roots of A.'s thought. Neither a disciple nor a critic, he realizes a judicious blending of both attitudes.

Hess, Gerhard. Alain in der Reihe der französischen Moralisten. Berlin, Emil Ebering, 1932. 303 p. **12534**

Particularly helpful in situating A. in the French literary tradition. Emphasizes his kinship to the moralists rather than the philosophers. Discusses the political and sociological themes (freedom, citizenship, etc.) primarily. A. substantial work.

Maurois, André. Alain. Domat, 1950. 89 p. **12535**

An excellent comprehensive overview, including discussions of A.'s epistemology, his ethics, his political philosophy, his esthetics and his religious thought.

Mondor, Henri. Alain. Gallimard, 1953. 263 p. **12536**

A loosely structured work. Mondor reminisces, recounting personal experiences with A., quoting him profusely, pointing out the poetic and literary merit of his work.
Reviews: R. Balmès in RPFE 157: 96–100, 1957; S. in MerF 318:104–08, 1953.

Pascal, Georges. L'idée de philosophie chez Alain. Bordas, 1970. 416 p. **12537**

Argues that A.'s principal originality is in abandoning originality as a goal and in seeking to define the philosophical attitude through a total familiarity with the great authors.
Review: L. Millet in EP 26:390, 1971.

————. La pensée d'Alain. Bordas, 1946. 108 p. (Pour connaître...) *Also (rev.):* 1957. 221 p. **12538**

An outline of the major themes. Posits the existence of a fundamental unity to A.'s fragmented thought. Argues that his thought is built upon a fundamental intuition, that of the liberty of judgment as the fundamental mark and virtue of man. An important, readable book.

Reboul, Pierre. L'homme et ses passions d'après Alain. Presses univ. de France, 1968. 2 v. **12539**

An attempt at an exhaustive synthesis. Views A. as a "sage," a seeker of wisdom in an age of technology, politics and mysticism. Sees in his work an almost gratuitous phenomenology of the passions. Tends perhaps to neglect the problem of figurative meanings in the texts cited. Excellent bibliography with some annotations.
Review: T. Quoniam in EP 25:106–07, 1970.

Robinson, Judith. Alain lecteur de Balzac et de Stendhal. Corti, 1958. 284 p. **12540**

Sketches the evolution of A.'s ideas on criticism and his application of these ideas to Balzac and Stendhal. Sees embodied in his criticism of these two writers two facets of A.'s own personality.
Review: J. Alexandre in BAAA 7–8:51–53, 1958.

Solmi, Sergio. Il pensiero di Alain. Milan, Muggiani, 1945. 105 p. **12541**

One of the most important studies to date. Gives particular attention to the classical Greek and Cartesian origins of A.'s thought. Discusses his esthetics, his ethics, and his metaphysics. Characterizes him as an essayist, much more concerned with "living" his thought than with developing it logically and systematically. Contains an excellent chapter on the *Propos*.

General Studies: Articles

Alexander, Ian. Le relatif et l'actuel. En marge des pensées d'Alain. RPFE 124: 155–88, 1937. **12542**

An attempt to relate A.'s work to various narrowly defined currents in 20th-century relativism. Views him as one who was able to integrate the concept of value into an essentially relativistic view of the world. Careful treatment.

Alexandre, Jeanne-Michel. Esquisse d'une histoire des Libres propos, journal d'Alain. BAAA 25:1–143, Dec. 1967. **12543**

Contains vignettes from the *Libres propos* of various periods interspersed throughout an ample historical narrative so as to provide more than an abstract picture of the project. Particular attention is given to defining A.'s "pacifism." Characterizes the *Libres propos* as essentially political works. This is debatable.

Alexandre, Michel. Notes concernant les Libres propos. *In:* Hommage à Alain. *See* 12511. p. 168–74. **12544**

A brief history of the publication of the *Libres propos*.

Ansart, Pierre. La rencontre selon Alain. PRFE 160:275–86, 1970. **12545**

Discusses A.'s views on the value and nature of our encounters with others. Describes his application of phenomenological methods to psychology. Some discussion of the relationship between Sartre and A.

Aron, Raymond. Alain et la politique. *In:* Hommage à Alain. *See* 12511. p. 155–67. **12546**

A criticism of the negative character of A.'s political stance, of his refusal to seek power and of his policy of unconditional resistance.

————. Remarques sur la pensée politique d'Alain. RMM 57:187–99, 1952. **12547**

A generally critical view of A.'s political stance. Bemoans the lack of organization and coherence in his writings. Considers war and the "radical republic" as the basic political realities that concerned him. Sees as fundamental to his thought a distinction between temporal power and spiritual power, justifying on the one hand obedience to the powers that be, and on the other a never-ending criticism of them.

Audry, Colette. Alain et le roman. RMM 57:243–54, 1952. **12548**

Sees as fundamental to A.'s definition of the novel: (1) a death struggle between the hero and necessity; (2) an intuition advancing through a thick fog; and (3) a solidification and substantiation of memory. The novel disposes one to meditation upon, and greater understanding of, one's own past and one's own emotions.

Bénézé, Georges. L'homme et le philosophe. *In:* Hommage à Alain. *See* 12510. p. 645–53. **12549**

Describes a blending of the peasant and the philosopher in A. Discusses his definitions of perception and imagination, of empiricism and idealism, and of the proletarian and the bourgeois mind in light of that dichotomy. Defines A.'s position as essentially Kantian.

Berger, René. D'une esthétique en rupture d'esthétique. *In:* Hommage à Alain. *See* 12511. p. 103–10. **12550**

Views A.'s esthetics as not so much an inquiry into the laws of the beautiful as a search, conducted within the realm of art, for a personal ethic. A.'s ethics and his esthetics are based upon a recognition of the need to reconcile the physical and spiritual components of human nature. This reconciliation is accomplished by a physical/spiritual encounter with resistant objects, the result of which is art.

Brelet, Gisèle. Alain et la musique. *In:* Hommage à Alain. *See* 12511. p. 111–24. **12551**

A discussion of *La visite au musicien.*

Canguilhem, G. Réflexions sur la création artistique selon Alain. RMM 57:171–86, 1952. **12552**

An attempt to relate A.'s *Système des beaux-arts* to major currents in traditional and contemporary esthetic thought. Opposes A.'s esthetics to Plato's, likens it to Bergson's and Kant's.

Fernandez, Ramon. Propos sur Alain. NRF 55:91–99, 1941. **12553**

Sees A.'s habit of returning again and again to certain problems as revelatory of his desire (1) to refine, deepen, and extend the solutions already found and (2) to simplify and relate them to all men. Defines his style and manner as a composite of these two tendencies. A lively and stimulating treatment.

Hampton, John. The humanism of Alain. ContR 199:92–97, 1961. **12554**

The best short introduction to A. available in English. Focuses upon A.'s attitudes toward religion and myth as expressed in *Les dieux.*

Herbelin, André. L'esthétique d'Alain. RduC 28:263–71, 1952. **12555**

Points out the classical, anti-Dionysian character of A.'s esthetic. Questions the originality of his concepts, but applauds the artful manner in which they are developed.

Howell, Ronald F. Emile Chartier becomes Alain. EUQ 17:13–23, 1961. **12556**

A summary of the revelations in *Histoire de mes pensées* concerning A.'s early life.

Hyppolite, Jean. Alain et les dieux. *In:* Hommage à Alain. *See* 12510. p. 611–35. **12557**

Considers A.'s work as essentially a quest for the truth of imagination, that is for a logic of error. *Les dieux* is the culmination of this quest. In it, he went beyond the Cartesian view of imagination to one reminiscent of Hegel and Valéry. Insists that to say that A. is a moralist and not a philosopher is to misunderstand his position. His approach is that of a moralist precisely because of his espousal of a philosophy of judgment rather than of concept.

————. Le peintre et le philosophe. MerF 309:259-74, 1950. **12558**

Discusses Hegel's view of painting in relationship to that of A.

————. L'existence, l'imaginaire et la valeur chez Alain. MerF 307:219-37, 1949. **12559**

Describes A.'s existentialism, leading neither to hope based on some conception of an after-life nor to despair, but to hope and joy based on a preliminary *parti pris,* on an intuitive perception of latent good. The world exists; man exists in the world; the relationship between the two is discerned only through work. A.'s theory of imagination is seen as the basis of much of Sartre's thought. Excellent article.

Khodoss, Florence. Le poème de la critique. RMM 57:215-42, 1952. **12560**

A discussion of *Entretiens au bord de la mer,* emphasizing the Kantian inspiration of A.'s ideas on intuition, nature and freedom.

————. Notes sur les Entretiens au bord de la mer. *In:* Hommage à Alain. *See* 12510. p. 654-61. **12561**

Suggests that in the *Entretiens* there is a consubstantiality of the subject matter and the expression. A. attempts to grasp *l'entendement* by means of a reflexive analysis of its actual operations, not through the verbal description of these operations. The form is never an ornament; it is the heart of his method.

Knight, Everett. Thoughts on Valéry and Alain. TC 157:436-46, 1955. **12562**

Discusses the evolution in 19th and 20th century art from representation to pure creation. Characterizes A. and Valéry as destroyers of any concept of immanence and as advocates of pure creation. Laments the resulting isolation of artists and intellectuals from the world as perceived by the senses.

Lamizet, G. Alain et les atomes. RMM 70:442-67, 1965. **12563**

An excellent discussion of A.'s contributions to the philosophy of science as they relate to current conceptions of the atom, the electromagnetic field and relativity. Sees an opposition in physics today between those who would explain reality in terms of particles and those who would do so in terms of fields. Identifies A. with the latter group.

Lasserre, Pierre. Le philosophe Alain. RU 3:347-56, 1920. **12564**

Applauds A. as a stylist, as an observer of society, and as an analyst of human motives and feelings. Deplores the lack of specific, clear, positive, and practical proposals in his political writing. Criticizes his antipathy for the historical method and his penchant for viewing everything in an eternal perspective. An excellent introduction to the major controversies surrounding the work of A.

Lebecque, Charles. Alain et la liberté. RduC 28:247-62, 1952. **12565**

A rather general summary of the theme of liberty in A.'s works.

Maurois, André. Alain. *In his:* De Proust à Camus. Perrin, 1964. p. 93-121. *Trans.:* From Proust to Camus. Profiles of modern French writers. Trans. by Carl Morse and Renaud Bruce. Doubleday, 1966. p. 96-121. *Also:* From Proust to Camus. Essays on contemporary French writers. Doubleday, 1968. p. 89-112. **12566**

A short but penetrating introduction to A., focusing upon the *Propos,* his political thought, his esthetics, and his view of religion.

————. Alain et le romanesque. *In:* Hommage à Alain. *See* 12511. p. 129-37. **12567**

Discusses the roles of novelist, biographer and historian as defined by A.

————. Alain liseur. *In:* Hommage à Alain. *See* 12510. p. 601-10. **12568**

Discusses A.'s literary preferences and tastes and the crucial influence of his reading patterns on his thought.

————. La politique dans l'œuvre d'Alain. RPP 724:16-22, 1962. **12569**

A review of A.'s basic political stance: a personal refusal of power, obedience to the powers that be, and constant criticism of those in power.

Monod, Sylvère. Alain, lecteur de Dickens. MerF 331:108-21, 1957. **12570**

Points out the gaps and misconceptions in A.'s understanding of Dickens, while praising the acuity of many of his insights.

Montagne, Pierre. Alain et la politique. RPP 74, no. 836:42–56, 1972.   **12571**

Argues for the relevance of A.'s political thought without really answering the major objections.

Morot-Sir, Edouard. Quelques aspects de la pensée sociale et politique d'Alain. RduC 28:272–86, 1952.   **12572**

Points out quite correctly that, in A.'s view, liberty is more important than any other political ideal, including that of justice. Emphasizes the mystical elements of his thought.

Pétrement, Simone. Une politique pour tous les temps. *In:* Hommage à Alain. *See* 12511. p. 138–54.   **12573**

A defense of A.'s political views, with some discussion of how they relate to Rousseau's.

———. Remarques sur Lagneau, Alain et la philosophie allemande. RMM 75:292–300, 1970.   **12574**

Argues that the one branch of French philosophy capable of coping with the revelations of Husserl, Kierkegaard, Heidegger, and Jaspers is that of Lagneau and A.

———. Sur la politique d'Alain. RMM 57:200–14, 1952.   **12575**

Defines the moral and religious base of the political thought of A. and Simone Weil.

———. Sur la religion d'Alain (avec quelques remarques concernant celle de Simone Weil). RMM 60:306–30, 1955.   **12576**

Condemns those who maintain that A. was not religious. Discusses his views on the existence of God, the nature of God, world religions, morality, faith, mysticism, and the Bible, comparing them with those of Simone Weil.

Picon, Gaëtan. Sur les propos d'Alain. MerF 328:114–20, 1956. *Also in his:* L'usage de la lecture. Mercure de France, 1961. p. 175–81.   **12577**

Argues that A.'s political and economic thought is peripheral to his esthetics, to his psychology and to his

ethics. Contends that A.'s thought did not evolve appreciably. Defines the epistemological basis of the form of the *propos*. Excellent article.

Prévost, Jean. Introduction à la doctrine d'Alain. Eur 16:129–38, 1928.   **12578**

A particularly penetrating analysis of the *Lettres au docteur Mondor*. Emphasizes A.'s conception of the need for a union of *esprit* and *cœur* in philosophy. Contains an explanation of his much misunderstood definition of prose.

Régis, Georges. La poésie comme charme et comme expérience selon Alain. RPFE 154:291–300, 1964.   **12579**

Discusses A.'s acceptance of Valéry's concept of the *charme*. Suggests that A. saw poetry as the embodiment of an experience, as the fruit of an exploration.

Rimaud, Jean. Constance du rationalisme. Et 237:447–62, 617–33, 1938.   **12580**

Rationalism, defined as an insistence upon total intellectual self-sufficiency, is the focus of this article. A. is viewed as a representative of 20th-century trends. Particular attention is given to his religious views. *Les dieux* is characterized as a decidedly atheistic document.

Sacy, Samuel S. de. Alain et la lecture. Esp 28:661–75, 1960.   **12581**

Describes A.'s evolution from skepticism to belief with regard to the value of books and reading. To read, for A., was to enter into contact with the superhuman in man.

———. Topo, disciple, philosophe. *In:* Hommage à Alain. *See* 12511. p. 45–59.   **12582**

A description of A.'s teaching during 1923–25. Views him as a *philosophe*, i.e., as one who possessed both erudition and wisdom, both knowledge and morality.

Solmi, Sergio. Alain, aujourd'hui et demain. *In:* Hommage à Alain. *See* 12511. p. 268–73.   **12583**

A brief discussion of the relevance of A.'s work in light of problems of current philosophical and political concern.

Thibaudet, Albert. Le propos d'Alain. Eur 16:138–39, 1928. **12584**

Characterizes the *propos* as Socratic, doubting, and yet optimistic. Sees embodied in them the work ethic of early 20th-century dogmatic socialism.

Julien Benda
(Nos. 12585–12603)

ROBERT J. NIESS

Arland, Marcel. Figure de Julien Benda. *In his:* Lettres de France. A. Michel, 1951. p. 177–89. **12585**

Chiefly a portrait of B. the man. Arland agrees with some of his attacks on modern literary tendencies, but believes that he consistently exaggerated: "Benda n'a que trop bien réussi son personnage." Excellently written.

Belvin, Robert W. The problem of the literary artist's detachment as seen by Julien Benda, Jean-Paul Sartre and Thierry Maulnier. RR 47:270–84, 1956. **12586**

Solid and useful article in which B.'s ideas on the "necessary" detachment of the literary artist are chiefly seen in the context of modern "engagement." Well written and soundly documented.

Benot, Yves. Benda est-il actuel? (1867–1956). Pens 145:43–61, 1969. **12587**

Excellent article, stressing the origin of B.'s principal philosophical and critical positions in his desire to oppose other positions. Discusses him chiefly as political thinker; displays much sympathy for him as a leftist.

Bernoville, Gaëtan. Minerve ou Belphégor? Bloud et Gay, 1921. 236 p. **12588**

A courteous and reasoned defense of many of the aspects of society and literature which B. most frequently attacked, especially romanticism and symbolism. Little more than a well argued critique of *Belphégor*, but valuable nonetheless because of the centrality of *Belphégor* in B.'s work.

Bourquin, Constant. Julien Benda, ou le point de vue de Sirius. Introd. de Jules de Gaultier. Eds. du siècle, 1925. 250 p. **12589**

A highly sympathetic treatment of some aspects of B.'s career, including

his criticism of contemporary society, his long attack on Bergsonism and his esthetic position. Analyzes at some length *L'ordination* and *Belphégor* and presents a good defense of B. against the attacks of the political Right, all the while demonstrating his close early resemblance to Jules de Gaultier and even Charles Maurras. Well written and effective, although incomplete.

Doisy, Marcel. Belphégor et le clerc. Paris, Brussels, Dutilleul, n.d. (1960?). 122 p. **12590**

Good short book very favorable to B. Much attention given to B.'s difficult and complex character and to some of the main elements of his work: the *clerc,* the Dreyfus case, literature, politics, Bergsonism, as well as to his philosophical position. Far from complete, but very penetrating. Clearly and effectively written.

Etiemble, René. Délicieux Eleuthère. NRF 181:40–50, 1968. **12591**

Sympathetic and amusing light essay on B.'s isolated position as thinker and critic and as what Etiemble calls "emmerdeur" of all the new schools and all the new poses in French literature. The author demonstrates how completely he has assimilated B.'s doctrines and how good a student he is of B.'s polemical methods.

——. Julien Benda, ou Petit exercice pour un enterré vif. *In his:* Le péché vraiment capital. Gallimard, 1957. p. 169–89. **12592**

Very sympathetic to B., even affectionate, but criticizes his excesses as literary critic. Praise for *Belphégor* and B.'s autobiographical works. Treats B. above all as a Jew in hostile world.

Marion, Denis. La lutte contre Belphégor. Font 44:563–73, 1945. **12593**

Useful summary, in schematic form, of the principal ideas in B.'s campaign against the social and literary forces he first attacked in *Belphégor*. Quite complete and valuable as an index to B.'s chief positions in his later career.

Mauriac, Claude. La trahison d'un clerc. La table ronde, 1945. 79 p. **12594**

Generally more of a defense of authors attacked by B. than a treatment of the idea of the *clerc.* Mauriac demonstrates how often B. relies on incomplete quotations from his opponents for his own ends and then uses B.'s method himself to refute some of the principal points made by Benda in *La France byzantine*. Sharp in tone but not discourteous; an effective defense especially of Proust, Valéry, Gide and Alain.

Niess, Robert J. Evolution of an idea: Julien Benda's La trahison des clercs. FR 20: 383–92, 1947.   **12595**

Traces the history of the doctrine of the *clerc* from *Dialogues à Byzance* (1900) to *La trahison des clercs* (1937), pointing out that though the idea appears many times, it never evolves profoundly.

————. Julien Benda. Ann Arbor, The univ. of Michigan press, 1956. 361 p.   **12596**

The only attempt at a full-length study of B., treating all major aspects of his work. Generally objective in treatment; much use of quotation from B.'s books and articles. Long bibliography of his works and of works on him.

Reviews: B. Bart in Sym 11:316–21, 1957; E. Harvey in MLQ 18:172, 1957.

————. Julien Benda on thought and letters. Sym 3:261–74, 1949.   **12597**

Discussion of B.'s claim that ideas lose some of their precision, and hence validity, when they are presented in literary form. For B., literature is no proper vehicle for ideas; literature panders to public taste and ideas must be watered down to please that taste, since the public resists and hates ideas.

Patri, A. (sic). Problèmes de poétique. Ar 22:105–16, 1947.   **12598**

Good article dealing with B.'s ideas on the nature of poetry and offering some of his own opinions; especially concerned with the problem of obscurity, so often attacked by B. as a typically "modern" aberration. Not hostile in tone.

Paulhan, Jean. Benda, le clerc malgré lui. Cr 24:387–407; 25:499–513, 1948.   **12599**

Skillful and closely-argued attack on B.'s philosophic stance and the rhetoric he employs to defend it. Offers highly

effective replies to some of B.'s chief arguments and shows that he is not infrequently guilty of the same "errors" he criticizes in modern thinkers. Does not impugn B.'s integrity, but shows that he was capable of self-deception in formulating his negative doctrines.

Picon, Gaëtan. Réponse à Julien Benda. Confl n.s. 6:567–85, 1945.   **12600**

A general attack on B.'s fundamental position as critic of modern social and literary tendencies. Argues that the anti-rationalism which B. sees everywhere today is a justifiable reaction to the hyper-rationalism of the nineteenth century and points out that the "anti-rational" elements of literature which B. criticizes as contemporary have always existed. Claims that the modern world rejects B.'s concept of an ordered and certain system in the universe and demonstrates that the modern world likes art precisely because of its "hypothetical" quality. An excellent presentation of many modern positions and an effective critique of B.'s attack on them.

Roy, Claude. Julien Benda. *In his:* Descriptions critiques. Gallimard, 1949. p. 119–26.   **12601**

Stresses B.'s contradictions, but sees him as solid and original, even though he deliberately systematizes his faults and deficiencies. Admires his egoism and independence, his passion for logic but points out his "trickery" in dealing with literature and *littérateurs*. For him, B. is a sound moralist, a good man at heart in spite of his pose, but afraid of falling into sentimentality or humanitarianism in his support of mankind.

Sarocchi, Jean. Julien Benda, portrait d'un intellectuel. Nizet, 1968. 263 p.   **12602**

A devastating attack on B. as representative of modern intellectualism. Brilliantly conceived and sharply written. Expert use of B.'s own methods in polemical writing and a nearly complete destruction of some of his major arguments. Particularly notable for its definition (highly unfavorable) of the contemporary intellectual.

Reviews: O. de Mourgues in FS 4: 488–89, 1971; R. Niess in FR 44:225–26, 1970.

Thérive, André. Julien Benda, ou la haine de la vie. *In his:* Moralistes de ce temps. Amiot-Dumont, n.d. (1948). p. 51–83. **12603**

Concentrates chiefly on B.'s autobiographical works, especially *La jeunesse d'un clerc, Un régulier dans le siècle,* and on *Délice d'Eleuthère,* which he much admires. Provides an interesting and valid analysis of the man and of his ideas, especially as they are expressed in these works.

Jacques-Émile Blanche
(Nos. 12604–12622)

J. THEODORE JOHNSON, JR.

Correspondence

Collet, Georges-Paul. André Gide, épistolier. FR 38:754–65, 1965. **12604**

Contains generous extracts from the unpublished Gide-B. correspondence which, through the perspicacious interpretations and annotations of Collet, reveal much of the musical, literary and artistic tastes of the two men. Establishes the similarities and above all the differences between them.

———. Jacques-Emile Blanche, épistolier. EF 3:74–93, 1967. **12605**

Reviews B.'s considerable literary production and suggests that the vast correspondence is particularly rich and merits publication and study. The present article consists primarily of large extracts from the B.-Gide correspondence that extends from 1892 to 1939 and which numbers almost 200 pieces, over half of which are by B.

Ricaumont, Jacques de. Lettres à André Gide par Jacques-Emile Blanche. MerF 305:57–69, 1949. **12606**

A brief introduction by Ricaumont assesses the difficulties B. had during his life and even posthumously in achieving a place in art and literature; ultimately this place might be assured through B.'s unpublished memoirs and his correspondence. The seven letters to Gide, published without critical comment, date from 1902 to 1917.

Biography

B., A. Jacques-Emile Blanche, artiste peintre, élu académicien titulaire, le 16 février 1935. ABABT 21:90–94, 1935. **12607**

A brief survey of B.'s life with only passing references to his art criticism, specifically *Les Arts plastiques sous la Troisième république,* and to his memoirs and novels.

Collet, Georges-Paul. George Moore et Jacques-Emile Blanche. *In his:* George Moore et la France. Geneva, Droz; Paris, Minard, 1957. p. 22–29. **12608**

Biographical details relevant to B., his friendship with Moore that extended from the early 1880's down to 1932, as well as his other connections with Britain and British letters. Numerous quotations from B.'s writings as well as extracts from Moore's letters to B.

Review: J. Robichez in RSH 100: 527–28, 1960.

———. Jacques-Emile Blanche and Virginia Woolf. CL 27:73–81, Winter, 1965. **12609**

Documents B.'s role in introducing and disseminating Virginia Woolf in France as he had done previously for George Moore, Arthur Symons, Max Beerbohm, and the painters Walter Sickert, Charles Conder and Aubrey Beardsley.

———. Marcel Proust et Jacques-Emile Blanche. BMP 24:1839–64, 1974. **12610**

The most detailed account of the Proust-B. relationship published to date.

Frantz, Henri. Jacques-Emile Blanche: portrait painter. Studio 30:190–99, 1903. **12611**

A general reassessment of B. at this juncture of his career, emphasizing his attempt to seize the biography of the model in his portraits. Numerous reproductions.

Le Grix, Francis. Jacques-Emile Blanche curieux homme. RHeb 3:457–74, March 1924. **12612**

Although a review of the exhibition at the Galerie Charpentier, provides useful biographical materials and an appraisal of B.'s fictional writing.

Pierhal, Armand. Souvenirs sur Jacques-Emile Blanche. Psy 16:233–42, 1948. **12613**

A detailed biographical portrait of B. with some insights into the man garnered from an interview.

Rothenstein, J. Jacques-Emile Blanche. Apollo 12:201–05, 1930. **12614**

Principally of biographical interest. Emphasizes B.'s sense of balance and compromise in his art, and reproduces, in addition to several English portraits, the portraits of Jean Cocteau, the Comtesse de Noailles, Igor Stravinsky, and André Maurois, all in the Musée de Rouen.

Simon, Jean. Jacques-Emile Blanche et l'Angleterre. RLC 26:182–201, 1952. **12615**

A seminal article demonstrating the need to reconsider B.'s role as an important intermediary between France and England from the 1870's until the eve of World War II.

Vaudoyer, Jean-Louis. Artistes contemporains: Jacques-Emile Blanche. RevAAM 45:251–64, 1924. **12616**

Article written on the occasion of B.'s first one-man show at Galerie Jean Charpentier. Major interest of this article is biographical, with emphasis on the various painters whom B. knew or with whom he had contact. Refers to numerous pictures and contains excellent choice of reproductions, including, among many others, Radiguet, Conder, Princesse L. M. in a Goya costume, friends of Gide, Debussy, Degas, Claudel, Morand and Giraudoux.

Waldemar, George. Jacques-Emile Blanche et Helleu. AdA 14, no. 3:58–59, 1933. **12617**

Later reprinted as a volume in *Histoire de l'art contemporain,* this succinct recapitulation of the life and works, with reproductions of the portraits of Gide and his friends, and Beardsley, is followed by a valuable critical notice by Germain Bazin which includes additional facts about B.'s life and work, and a bibliography.

General Studies

Ferrier, André. Jacques-Emile Blanche, peintre et mémoraliste. Œil 89:58–65, 108, 1962. **12618**

A popular attempt to rehabilitate B. with emphasis on his place as a chronicler in his paintings and in his texts.

Flament, Albert. Jacques-Emile Blanche. RenAF 2:441–48, 1919. **12619**

Praises art and writing of B., emphasizing B.'s ability to create a natural atmosphere for his portraits and to capture the flavor of his era. Reproduces a number of portraits (including Princess E. de Polignac, Comtesse de Noailles, Ida Rubenstein, Conder, Beardsley, Gide, Chéret, Bergson, Hardy, Mallarmé, Nijinski, etc.) and discusses the great war memorial paintings done for the church at Offranville.

Hérain, François de. Jacques-Emile Blanche écrivain d'art. RDM 113:311–18, 1943. **12620**

Admires B.'s gift for the portrait in his prose, and provides, through numerous quotations, a good résumé of B.'s ideas on painters and technique. Emphasis on his volume on the *Beaux-Arts de 1870 à nos jours,* but little mention of his fiction.

Le Grix, François. M. Jacques-Emile Blanche et ses feuilles de température. RHeb 29:466–79, 1920. **12621**

Severe reservations about B.'s voluminous production as novelist, essayist and memorialist. Some discussion of his style, notably certain inversions and tenses.

Proust, Marcel. Préface. *In:* Blanche, Jacques-Emile. Propos de peintre. De David à Degas. Première série: David, Manet, Degas, Renoir, Cézanne, Whistler, Fantin-Latour, Ricard, Conder, Beardsley, etc. Emile-Paul frères, 1919. p. i–xxxv. *Also in his:* Contre Sainte-Beuve, précédé de Pastiches et mélanges et suivi de Essais et articles. Ed. by Pierre Clarac et Yves Sandres. Gallimard, 1971. p. 570–86. **12622**

Biographical details and anecdotes relevant to Proust's Auteuil years as a neighbor of B. who painted his portrait at that time. Some references to B.'s painting, but major thrust of the preface is a severe critique of B.'s essays on painters. In explaining the works of the man, B. commits the same critical error as Sainte-Beuve, producing what Proust called *Les causeries du lundi de la peinture*. Remains the most significant piece of critical writing on B. to date.

Émile-Michel Cioran
(Nos. 12623–12638)

PIETRO FERRUA

Amer, Henri. Cioran, le docteur ès décadences. NRF 92:297–307, 1960. **12623**
Examines *Précis de décomposition* and *Histoire et Utopie* both from the point of view of style and thought. Also attempts to psychoanalyze C. on basis of his prose style. A very dense, serious and percutient article.

An elliptical gloom. TLS no. 3762:389, April 12, 1974. **12624**
C.'s main feature in his *De l'inconvénient d'être né* lies in his absence of structure. The essayist's thought is presented as asystematic and leading to a "knowledge broken," a concept that the reviewer extracts from Bacon's *The advancement of learning*.

Bosquet, Alain. Un cynique fervent: E.-M. Cioran. Monde 12, Dec. 12, 1964. **12625**
Analyzing *La chute dans le temps,* Bosquet affirms that C. is not only one of the greatest thinkers of our time but also the most brilliant French stylist.

————. E. M. Cioran, un moraliste impitoyable. *In his:* Injustice. La table ronde, 1969. p. 139–42. **12626**
One of the best insights into the whole range of C.'s work. Beyond C.'s apparent nihilism, the critic sees the construction of an ethic of hope through the admirable esthetics of his style.

Cioran, E.-M. Beginnings of a friendship. *In:* Myths symbols. Studies in honor of Mircea Eliade. Ed. by M. Joesper and Charles H. Long. Chicago, Univ. of Chicago press, 1969. p. 407–14. **12627**
C.'s reminiscences of his first encounters with the illustrious mythologist Mircea Eliade offers not only a unique perspective on both writers' youthful years in Rumania, but also provides us with one of the rare texts

in which C. uses the first person without subterfuge.

Duvignaud, Jean. E. M. Cioran: La chute dans le temps. NRF 146:338–41, 1965. **12628**
Presents C. as a pure defeatist with no dialectic. If there is a quest for ethics in his writings, it can only be a skeptical one. Suspects C. of exaggerating his nihilism to make use of the seductive power of his simultaneously poetical and logical language.

Ferrua, Pietro. Présence de Pascal dans l'œuvre de Cioran. CulFP 23, no. 4:6–16, 1974. **12629**
After emphasizing the disruptive influence of Rumanian writers on modern French letters, attempts to evaluate C.'s contribution to classical prose style in contemporary French. Traces of Pascal in his work are then studied, the conclusion being that C. is basically a Pascal in reverse, who has replaced faith by systematic doubt.

Gass, William H. The evil demiurge. *In his:* Fiction and the figures of life. Knopf, 1970. p. 253–62. **12630**
Points out C.'s debt to Nietzsche and his more substantial one to Spengler, but defines him more as an undecided Platonist. C.'s style is praised, as well as his choice of themes (alienation, absurdity, decay, etc....), but his reasoning is considered very fallacious and decadent.

Guillermou, Alain. Le livre d'or de la culture française. Silhouette: E.-M. Cioran. CulFP 1:3–11, 1962. **12631**
Places C. in the great tradition of French moralists, those who have been able to unite clarity of language with the deepness of thought.

Marcel, Gabriel. Un allié à contrecourant. Monde 7606:iv, 1969. **12632**
A very honest and dramatic testimony of a philosopher who admires C. as a man and as a stylist, but who would be unable to subscribe to C.'s thought. Marcel dares to hope that behind C.'s nihilism there lies a deeply hidden but sincere anxiety for an order that could only be of divine nature.

Marks, Elaine. The limits of ideology and sensibility: J. P. Sartre's Réflexions sur la question juive and E. M. Cioran's Un peuple de solitaires. FR 45:779–88, 1972. **12633**

Both Sartre and C. adopt an anti-scientific bias, are victims of different language games and distinguish themselves for irrelevance. Besides condemning both for their studies on anti-Semitism, Marks accuses C. of polemicizing subtly with Sartre.

Mauriac, Claude. Cioran et la tentation du néant. Preu 70:85–88, 1956. *Also in his:* L'alittérature contemporaine. Albin Michel, 1958. p. 221–31. **12634**

The most accomplished French study on C.'s thought, style and influence. Considers him as one of the best French writers for his beautiful and precise language which Mauriac compares with that of the French classics. Defines him as a metaphysical essayist.

————. Précis de décomposition par E.-M. Cioran. TR 25:125–30, 1950. **12635**

Compares C. to Grimm for his great mastery of the French language, to Pascal for his classicism, to Camus for his apparent pessimism. Finds in him, despite his more violent diatribes against hope, many reasons for joy and for life.

Newman, Charles. On Cioran. TriQ 20:406–23, 1971. *Also: Introduction. In:* Cioran, E.-M. The fall into time. Chicago, Quadrangle books, 1971. p. 9–32. **12636**

Does not find C.'s thought original but sees in his work the transmission of old ideals through an original style. Considers his vocabulary peculiar, his references obscure, his aphoristic syntax coldly elegant. Defines C. as a "redundant hermit."

Sontag, Susan. On Cioran. TriQ 11:5–20, 1968. **12637**

Situates C. in the tradition of Kirkegaard, Nietzsche, and Wittgenstein because of his particular kind of asystematic and aphoristic philosophizing.

Worms, Janine. Des steppes de fin du monde. Monde 7606:v, 1969. **12638**

Primarily a mosaic of excerpts from C.'s essays, skillfully sewn together and commented upon. Establishes a parallel between C. and Master Eckhart. C. is not a fashionable thinker but certainly one of those who will remain influential.

Paul Desjardins
(Nos. 12639–12645)

Jean-Pierre Cap

Dédéyan, Charles. Desjardins [and] Pontigny. *In his:* Le cosmopolitisme littéraire de Charles Du Bos. SEDES, 1966. p. 171–85; 175–212. **12639**

The relationship between D. and Du Bos who took an active part in the literary *décades* at Pontigny after World War I.

Dietz, Jean. M. Paul Desjardins. CahQ cah. 18, ser. 9:1–69, July 1930. **12640**

Sketches D.'s life and recounts his beginnings as teacher and critic. Explains the foundation, the spirit and goals of *L'union pour l'action morale* (1892) which became *L'union pour la vérité* in 1905. Also important for the origins of l'Action française, Franco-German relations after World War I and influence on Alain, Martin du Gard, Schlumberger, Prévost and Hamp. Concisely provides essential information.

Fassbinder, Klara Marie. Paul Desjardins und die Dekaden von Pontigny. *In her:* Der versunkene Garten. Begegnungen mit dem geistigen Frankreich des entre-deux-guerres 1919–1939. Wiederbegegnungen nach dem zweiten Weltkrieg. Heidelberg, F. H. Kerle Verlag, 1968. p. 138–44; 145–77. **12641**

Defines D. as a conscience of the French intellectual elite and as *animateur* of the literary and philosophical movements of the early 20th century. In her recollections of the two *décades* in which she participated, she describes D. as an exemplary host to the international gatherings at which the stars were Gide and Malraux.

Gilbert, Jean. A Pontigny avec Paul Desjardins. Présentation de J. Schlumberger. MerF 1044:591–611, 1950. **12642**

Numerous useful details in this very good article by a former participant of the *décades*.

Heurgon-Desjardins, Anne. Paul Desjardins et les décades de Pontigny. Etudes, témoignages et documents inédits prés. par Anne Heurgon-Desjardins. Préf. d'André Maurois. Presses univ. de France, 1964. 416 p. **12643**

Thorough bio-bibliography, articles on D.'s life and career as educator and critic, his role in *L'union pour la vérité* and in the *Décades de Pontigny* of which he was the founder and organizer (1910–1914 and 1922–1939). Unpublished texts by D. and letters as well as important iconography.

Painter, George D. Proust, Paul Desjardins et Pontigny. *In:* Entretiens sur Marcel Proust. Ed. by G. Cattaui and P. Kolb. Paris-The Hague, Mouton, 1966. p. 279–83.   **12644**

According to Painter, D. had an important influence on Proust.

Schlumberger, Jean. Rencontres. Feuilles d'agenda. Pierres de Rome. Gallimard, 1968. p. 115–24.   **12645**

One of the most penetrating portraits of D.

Jean Grenier
(Nos. 12646–12654)

RAYMOND GAY-CROSIER

Belaval, Yvon. Un écrivain. NRF 221:37–43, 1971.   **12646**

Characterizes G.'s unpretentious style and natural, yet musical tone. Sees his philosophical ancestors as Montaigne, Pascal, Kierkegaard and Schopenhauer.

Campbell, Robert. L'indifférence selon Jean Grenier. NRF 64:691–701; 65:879–90, 1958.   **12647**

Most extensive discussion of one of G.'s key themes seen as a corrective element of the then prevailing existentialist notion of situational freedom. Assesses also the religious implications of G.'s philosophical position characterized as a discourse on the absence of God. The second part deals mainly with the function of the Absolute, which G. calls "le Neutre indifférencié," and the latter's abolition of values as a condition for wisdom. Traces the oriental origins of his philosophy of detachment.

Camus, Albert. Sur les îles de Jean Grenier. Preu 95:13–15, 1959. *Also in his:* Essais. Gallimard, 1965. p. 1157–61. (Pléiade)
12648

Assesses both the originality of *Les îles* and their impact on young Camus.

Dumur, Guy. Le bon usage de la liberté selon Jean Grenier. TR 18:997–1005, 1949.   **12649**

General assessment of G.'s philosophy and its main problems. Opposes the Mediterranean G. to Occidental and Oriental approaches to the question of freedom, choice, indifference and immanence. Extended review of *Les îles* and *Entretiens sur le bon usage de la liberté*.

Etiemble, [René]. Jean Grenier ou l'homme vrai. NRF 221:5–11, 1971.   **12650**

Personal memories of conflicts and friendship. Shows G.'s influence on part of his contemporary intelligentsia to whom he proved the religiously dogmatic character of Marxism, the necessity of a certain detachment and the difficulty of the choice.

Grenier, Jean. Entretiens avec Louis Foucher. Gallimard, 1969. 106 p.   **12651**

Important self-revelations and analyses casting not only some light on G.'s own philosophy and style, but also on numerous characteristics of his student, Camus.

Hell, Henri. Jean Grenier. Les grèves. TR 124:127–29, 1958.   **12652**

Not only a review of *Les grèves* but also a characterization of G.'s speculative philosophy and an identification of its major themes. G.'s interest in premystical states shows his affinity with Rousseau, Maine de Biran and Amiel.

Howlett, James. Une tendre lucidité: La philosophie de Jean Grenier. LetN 36:433–37, 1956.   **12653**

Attempts to characterize G.'s non-systematic and unpathetic philosophy of existence and compares him to Valéry. Sees in him a bridge between Occidental and Oriental (mainly Taoistic) thought, but also between Logos and Pathos. His is a philosophy of lucid resignation.

Picon, Gaëtan. Sur Jean Grenier. MerF 1137:99–103, 1958. *Also in his:* L'usage de la lecture. II. Suite balzacienne — suite contemporaine. Mercure de France, 1961. p. 235–40.   **12654**

Assesses G.'s production, its undiscovered potential, oscillation between art and philosophy, his appearance as a stranger in the midst of a Hegelian age. Reviews some key notions (choice, freedom, reality) of G.'s thought.

René Guénon
(Nos. 12655–12669)

GABRIEL V. ASFAR

Editions

Guénon, René. Aperçus sur l'ésotérisme chrétien. Ed. by Jean Reyor. Eds. traditionnelles, 1969. 113 p.   12655

Collection of articles published in *Regnabit, Voile d'Isis,* and EtTr 1925–1949. Devoted to aspects of Christian esoterism, particularly the Templars, the Fidèles d'amour, and the Knights of the Grail. Extremely important adjunct to G.'s *Saint Bernard* (1929) and *L'ésotérisme de Dante* (1925).

——. Aperçus sur l'ésotérisme islamique et le taoïsme. Ed. by Roger Maridort. Gallimard, 1973. 168 p.   12656

Collection of articles published in *Voile d'Isis* and EtTr, 1929–1950. De-1950. Devoted to the fundamental doctrinal similarities that G. found between Islamic esoterism (Sufism) and Taoism. Includes related book reviews by G. and bibliographical information.

——. Aperçus sur l'initiation. Eds. traditionnelles, 1964. 303 p.   12657

Collection of articles published in *Voile d'Isis* and EtTr, 1929–1950. Devoted exclusively to subjects directly related to initiation. Edited and annotated by G., fully cross referenced with all his major works. Extremely important to G.'s doctrinal writings.

——. Etudes sur la franc-maçonnerie et le compagnonnage. Ed. by A. André Villain. Eds. traditionnelles, 1965. 2 v. 12658

Collection of articles published in *Voile d'Isis* and EtTr, 1929–1950. Devoted to the history of Freemasonry, apprenticeship and initiation therein. Important adjunct to G.'s *Le théosophisme* (1921). Includes G.'s reviews of related books and articles, as well as cross-referenced, chronological listing of all articles and reviews.

——. Etudes sur l'hindouisme. Ed. by A. André Villain. Eds. traditionnelles, 1968. 286 p.   12659

Collection of articles published in *Voile d'Isis* and EtTr, 1929–1950, devoted to Hinduism. Testifies to G.'s long friendship and intellectual exchange with A. K. Coomaraswamy. Important adjunct to *Introduction générale à l'étude des doctrines hindoues* (1921). Includes G.'s reviews of related books and articles and bibliographical information.

——. Formes traditionnelles et cycles cosmiques. Ed. by Roger Maridort. Gallimard, 1970. 178 p.   12660

Collection of articles published in *Voile d'Isis,* EtTr, and *Journal of the Indian Society of Oriental Art,* 1925–1949. Devoted to aspects of the doctrine of cosmic cycles, particularly myths of Hyperborea and Atlantis, numerology in the Cabbala, and the Hermetic tradition. Includes G.'s reviews of related books and bibliographical information.

——. Initiation et réalisation spirituelle. Ed. by Jean Reyor. Eds. traditionnelles, 1952. 236 p.   12661

Collection of articles published in *Voile d'Isis* and EtTr, 1929–1950. Devoted to initiation in Islamic, Hindu, Christian esoterism. Supervised by G. in 1950, this work complements *Aperçus sur l'initiation, supra.* Important adjunct to G.'s *Autorité spirituelle et pouvoir temporel* (1929), *Les états multiples de l'être* (1932) and *La grande triade* (1946).

——. Symboles fondamentaux de la science sacrée. Ed. by Michel Vâlsan. Gallimard, 1962. 468 p.   12662

Scrupulously edited collection of G.'s shorter writings on traditional symbolism published in *Regnabit, Voile d'Isis,* EtTr, and CahS, 1925–1950. Material organized as follows: 1. Traditional symbolism and some of its general applications (27–79). 2. Symbols of the center and of the world (83–141). 3. Symbols of cyclic manifestation (145–83). 4. Symbolic arms (187–206). 5. Symbolism of the cosmic form (209–57). 6. Constructive symbolism (261–316). 7. Axial and passage symbolism (319–403). 8. Symbolism of the heart (407–53). Includes detailed, cross-referenced chronology of all articles. Copiously annotated. Indispensable reference work.

General Studies

Artaud, Antonin. La mise en scène et la métaphysique. NRF 38:219–34, 1932. **12663**

Cites G.'s authority in formulation of Artaud's ideas on modern theater. Notes significant debt to G. Discussed by G. in *Le théosophisme* (1969), p. 449–50.

Asfar, Gabriel. Naissance d'une œuvre: une correspondance inédite de René Guénon. EtTr 427:193–208, 1971. **12664**

Notes discovery and importance of unpublished correspondence between G. and Noële Maurice-Denis, 1915–1924 (see Boulet, *infra*). Outlines projected volume containing these letters and shows that they foreshadow numerous doctrinal works of G., and reveal armature of G.'s thought.

Boulet, Noële Maurice-Denis. L'ésotériste René Guénon, souvenirs et jugements. PenC 77:17–42; 78–79:139–62; 80:63–81, 1962. **12665**

G.'s classmate at the Sorbonne reminisces about her friendship and substantial correspondence with him, 1915–1924, underlining their disagreements, in particular the conflicts between Boulet's interpretation of medieval scholasticism and G.'s early writings on the primordial tradition. Emotionally charged, often personal discussion of G.'s "Christian" years and subsequent espousal of Islam.

Chacornac, Paul. La vie simple de René Guénon. Eds. traditionnelles, 1958. 131 p. **12666**

Sympathetic and insightful biography by G.'s friend, publisher, and precursor as editor of *Voile d'Isis* (renamed *Etudes traditionnelles* in 1936). Contains much reliable information about G.'s early years, youth in Blois, involvement with Hermetic School of Papus (pseud. of Gerard Encausse) in Paris, disenchantment with occultism, introduction to Oriental philosophy, adoption of Islam and move to Egypt. Illustrations include photographs.

Méroz, Lucien. René Guénon ou la sagesse initiatique. Plon, 1962. 245 p. **12667**

Well-documented examination of G.'s metaphysical universe, tracing develop-ment through, and rejection of, occult-ism, discovery and assimilation of Taoist esoterism, and conversion to Islam. Shows why G. considered Socratic Greece as the barrier between "modern mentality" and the Primordial Tradi-tion. Attempts to clarify the realities of initiation and of metaphysical realiza-tion. Contains useful chronological bio-bibliography.

René Guénon: l'homme et son message. Ed. by Louis Pauwels. PlPl 1–148, April 1970. **12668**

Well-intentioned attempt to pop-ularize G. Sketchy and anodine. Ex-cerpts from a large number of G.'s works. Includes short studies by Jean-Claude Frère, Frithjof Schuon and Paul Sérant. Interviews. Reminiscences. Copiously and not always judiciously illustrated.

Sérant, Paul. René Guénon. Eds. du Vieux Colombier, 1953. 189 p. **12669**

Somewhat tendentious introduction to G.'s thought. The orientation here is often literary (author is a novelist). Deals with G.'s symbolic universe and his ideas on analogy. Interesting critical material on G.'s *Symbolisme de la croix* (1931) and *La grande triade* (1946).

Daniel Halévy
(Nos. 12670–12674)

ALAIN SILVERA

Péguy, Charles. Notre jeunesse. CahQ 11e sér., 12e cah.:1–225, 1910. *Also:* Nouvelle revue française, 1916. 515 p. (Œuvres complètes) *Also:* Gallimard, 1933. 217 p. *Also:* 1948. *Also:* Gallimard, 1969. 253 p. (Idées, 176) *And:* Victor-Marie, comte Hugo. CahQ 12e sér., 1er cah.:1–264, 1910. *Also:* Gallimard, 1934. 241 p. **12670**

These two books, refuting H.'s *Apologie pour notre passé,* which ex-pressed reservations on his Dreyfusard past, formulate Péguy's dialectic rela-tionship between *mystique* and *poli-tique;* dwelling on the ambiguities of H.'s efforts to reconcile his patrician origins with a socialist ideology, Péguy succeeds in illuminating the character of his former collaborator.

Silvera, Alain. Daniel Halévy and his times: a gentleman-commoner in the Third Republic. Ithaca, Cornell univ. press, 1966. 251 p.   **12671**

The only biography of the versatile essayist, critic and historian underlines his role as a guide and interpreter, serving as prism to the generation which reached manhood with the Dreyfus Affair. Treats only briefly his literary criticism as illustrated in his *Cahiers verts* which were inspired by Péguy's *Cahiers de la quinzaine,* stressing instead the contribution he made to French social theory by an examination of his biographies of Nietzsche, Proudhon, Barrès, Sorel and Péguy. Reviews: Anon. in TLS 122, Feb. 16, 1967; J. Colton in AHR 72:996, 1967; J. Joll in List 435, March 30, 1967; M. Murratore in SFr 13:587–88, 1969; J. Néré in RH 40:236–37, 1968; J. Ratté in JMH 43:159–60, 1971; D. Thomson in FS 22:86–87, 1968.

———. Introduction. *In:* Halévy, Daniel. The end of the notables. Ed. by Alain Silvera. Trans. by Alain Silvera and June Guicharnaud. Middletown, Wesleyan univ. press, 1974. 225 p.   **12672**

The introduction to this translation of H.'s *La fin des notables* discusses his role in the historiography of the Third Republic and contains a bibliographical essay.

Sorel, Georges. Réflexions sur la violence. Marcel Rivière, 1908. 458 p.   **12673**

In his "Lettre à Daniel Halévy," serving as the introduction to his classic statement of the syndicalist myth, Sorel acknowledges his debt to the moral pessimism underlying H.'s socialist theories.

Thibaudet, Albert. D'Alexis de Tocqueville à Daniel Halévy. NRF 37:317–26, 1931.   **12674**

In this review of H.'s *Décadence de la liberté,* Thibaudet places H.'s diatribes against the shortcomings of the Radical Republic in the French Orleanist tradition; drawing on H.'s autobiographical *Pays parisiens,* he also contrasts his attitude to the liberal bourgeoisie in the thirties with the popular democratic position adopted by

Jean Guéhenno, editor of Bernard Grasset's series, *Les écrits.*

Paul Léautaud
(Nos. 12675–12714)

Seymour S. Weiner

Texts With Autobiographical Data

Léautaud, Paul. Choix de pages de Paul Léautaud, par André Rouveyre. Avec une introduction, des illustrations et des documents bibliographiques. Eds. du bélier, 1946. 364 p.   **12675**

Each section has a presentation by Rouveyre. Intro., p. 7–24. Appendix, *Léautaud vu par ses contemporains,* p. 327–52. A revised version of the first two chapters of *Le petit ami* is given a title originally chosen by L., *Souvenirs légers.*

———. Journal littéraire; choix par Pascal Pia et Maurice Guyot. Mercure de France, 1968. 927 p.   **12676**

Index, by Guyot, modeled on the one by Buthaud for the "complete" edition.

———. Journal littéraire de Paul Léautaud. Mercure de France, 1954–66. 19 v. **12677**

Covers the period 1893–1956. V. 19 contains *Histoire du journal,* by Marie Dormoy (p. 9–38); *Pages retrouvées* (p. 39–162); *Index général,* established by Étienne Buthaud (p. 163–338). The index includes names, certain initials, titles, and some subjects.

———. Journal of a man of letters, 1898–1907. Trans. by Geoffrey Sainsbury. With a pref. by Alan Pryce-Jones. London, Chatto and Windus, 1960. 259 p. **12678**

Abridgement, from v. 1 and about a fourth of v. 2 of the *Journal littéraire.* About half of the original has been left out. The translator feels that his version is somewhat more "written up" than the original.

———. Journal particulier. Préf. de Pierre Michelot. Monte Carlo, Eds. du Cap, 1956. 2 v. (Domaine privé)   **12679**

Material supposedly too erotic or extra-literary to be used in the *Journal littéraire.* V. 1, 1917–1924; v. 2, 1925–1950.

Correspondence

Léautaud, Paul. Lettres à ma mère. Mercure de France, 1956. 233 p. **12680**
Introduction, p. 9–32, by Marie Dormoy. P. 33–54, other documents, such as letters to Blanche, contemporary notes, and the *faire-part* of Fanny Forestier's death. "Le texte de ces lettres [by L. to his mother and hers to him] est intégral."

————. Lettres à Paul Valéry. Rachilde, Marcel Schwob... 1902–1918. Eds. Mornay, 1929. 126 p. (Collection originale) **12681**
Also letters to Adolphe Paupe, Charles-Henry Hirsch, Remy de Gourmont, Marie Laurencin, André Gide, André Billy, Paul Meurisse, André Rouveyre, Guillaume Apollinaire, R. Foulon, Stuart Merrill. Portrait by Marie Laurencin.

————. Correspondance, 1912–1955. Le bélier, 1968. 238 p. **12682**
Correspondence with André Billy. Introduction, p. 9–12, by Marie Dormoy. 108 letters by L., 30 by Billy. Footnotes, some quite long, explain allusions.

————. Letttres à Marie Dormoy. Albin Michel, 1966. 628 p. **12683**
Selected from 1100 letters, written between 1922 and 1956. Occasional footnotes; an index by Etienne Buthaud, p. 617–23, for the names mentioned in these letters.

————. Correspondance générale de Paul Léautaud, recueillie par Marie Dormoy. Flammarion, 1972. 1239 p. **12684**
Covers the period 1878–1956. Includes correspondence with André Billy. Table of correspondents, p. 1231–37. Few notes; users should consult the index by Etienne Buthaud (v. 19) to the *Journal littéraire*.

Iconography

Dubief, Lise. Paul Léautaud. Bibliothèque nationale, 1972. ix, 85 p. **12685**
Catalog of an exhibit at the Bibliothèque de l'Arsenal. The notes are by Dubief and Marie-Laure Prévost.

Dormoy, Marie. Paul Léautaud. Images et textes réunis par Marie Dormoy. Mercure de France, 1969. 125 p. **12686**
Photos, sketches, binding, etc., and excerpts from his writings.

Special Numbers

Paul Léautaud. MerF 1125:56–126, 1957. **12687**
Articles by Jean Agreil, Marie Dormoy, Henri Martineau, Robert Mallet, Maurice Nadeau, Jean Orieux, Pascal Pia, Robert L. Wagner, and Patrick Waldberg, as well as an excerpt from L.'s *Journal littéraire* of 1925.

Paul Léautaud—pages de journal. Point 44: 48, 1953. **12688**
Whole number on L. Illus. with photos. Introduction, p. 4–8, by Pierre Michelot. Excerpts from the *Journal littéraire* of 1925, 1926, 1950.

Pour les quatre-vingts ans de Léautaud. MerFr 1062:193–254, 1952. **12689**
Part of issue devoted to L. Articles by Adrienne Monnier, Pascal Pia, Maurice Nadeau, Maurice Saillet, as well as excerpts from L.'s *Journal littéraire* of 1949.

General

Auriant (pseud.). Une vipère lubrique: Paul Léautaud. Brussels, Ambassade du livre, n.d. [1965] 226 p. **12690**
Regularly refers to L.'s *Journal littéraire* as the "Journal obscène." L. is "mythomane, érotomane, scatologue, il relève de la pathologie."

Baes, Rachel. Trois entretiens avec Paul Léautaud à Fontenay-aux-Roses. Paris [privately printed] 1949. 48 p. **12691**
Visits in winter 1947, autumn 1948, and summer 1949 reported realistically.

Billy, André. Paul Léautaud. *In his:* Ecrit en songe. Société de France, 1920. p. 17–39. **12692**
Contrasts the young L. bearded and dressing in black with the older clean-shaven dresser in grey. L. prefers *In memoriam* to *Le petit ami*. Quotes L. on style, on Flaubert, on tragedy. Be-

lieves L. could have had the Goncourt Prize.

————. Paul Léautaud. *In his:* Intimités littéraires. Flammarion, 1932. p. 7–27.
12693
Personal reminiscences of discussions with L. and anecdotes about him.

————. Rue de Condé. *In his:* Le pont des Saints-Pères. Flammarion, 1947. p. 31–67.
12694
L. at the Mercure de France and also at Fontenay-aux-Roses.

Brenner, Jacques. Paul Léautaud. *In his:* Les critiques dramatiques. Flammarion, 1970. p. 153–58. (Les procès des juges)
12695
One reads L.'s criticisms for himself rather than the play: "un chroniqueur libre et non pas un véritable critique." Sketches chronology of L.'s contributions to newspapers and periodicals. L.'s *Théâtre de Maurice Boissard* "un livre à ranger sous la rubrique 'écrits intimes'." L. preferred Molière to other dramatists.

Dormoy, Marie. Léautaud. Gallimard, 1958. 288 p. (La bibliothèque idéale)   **12696**
Dormoy is the executor of L.'s literary estate. *L'homme, Les jours, L'œuvre* (by Dormoy), p. 9–106; *florilège,* p. 107–237; *jugements* ("reflets"), p. 240–49; bibliography, phonography, iconography, p. 251–78.

————. Paul Léautaud. *In her:* Souvenirs et portraits d'amis. Mercure de France, 1963. p. 256–300.   **12697**
Personal reminiscences of her dealings with L.

————. La vie secrète de Paul Léautaud. Flammarion, 1972. 234 p.   **12698**
Includes *inédits* of 1906, supplemented by excerpts from the *Journal littéraire* and confidences to Dormoy.

Fagus (pseud. of Georges Faillet). Lettres à Paul Léautaud. Avec un avant-propos et des notes du destinataire. La connaissance, 1928. 77 p. (Les textes, 10)
12699
Letters written between 1923 and 1927; some first published in NL in 1924. Their tone is mocking, familiar, learned.

Gallant, Mavis. Paul Léautaud, 1872–1956. TBR, 6, 10, Sept. 9, 1973.   **12700**
First heard L. on radio in his 38 hours of interviews with R. Mallet. "A literary snapping turtle who bit to wound... *The Journal...*one of the most remarkable studies of character ever written in France." Points out L.'s contrarieties.

Green, John A. Marcel Schwob and Paul Léautaud, 1903–1905. MLQ 29:415–22, 1968.   **12701**
Uses five letters (in the Bibliotheque littéraire Jacques Doucet) by Schwob to L., mid-July 1903 to late Nov. 1904 (Schwob died in Feb. 1905). Schwob liked *Le petit ami* and tried to secure the Goncourt Prize for L. Had L. do the index to his *Parnasse satyrique du XVe siècle; anthologie de pièces libres* (Welter, 1905).

Juin, Hubert. Ecrivains de l'avant-siècle. Seghers, 1972. passim.   **12702**
L. with respect to Remy de Gourmont, Jarry, Mirbeau, Rebell, and Tinan.

————. Paul Léautaud en verve; présentation et choix de Hubert Juin. Pierre Horay, 1970. 126 p. (En verve, 2) **12703**
P. 9–11, introduction; p. 123, sources (abbreviations); p. 125, rubrics (established by Juin). "Le théâtre de Maurice Boissard un ouvrage sans illusion... Or, Paul Léautaud est un moraliste."

Kockelkoren, Matthieu. Gide-Léautaud: de omzichtigheid in den ogen van een bijziende. Maat 17:432–43, 1971.   **12704**
Special number on André Gide, 1869–1951. Gide thought L. was talking about him in his Jan. 1, 1922 article for NRF. L. an eighteenth-century writer in the tradition of Voltaire. Gide too Protestant, too concerned with God for L. A writer should ignore the "utilitarian" importance of his work. L. made fun of Gide's "acte gratuit" but enjoyed the play based on *Les caves du Vatican.*

Le Révérend, Gaston. Le petit ami. *In his:* Le haut-parleur. Eds. de la fenêtre ouverte, 1927. p. 121–75.   **12705**
Presented as a discursive, rambling discussion among friends. L. an author with whom one converses comfortably.

He writes as one speaks, going easily between the serious and the ridiculous; one enjoys his cruelty and wit, that he is individually himself. When he writes on animals, he has nothing else to say. L. is "l'homme des parfaites définitions." Text bears mainly on *Théâtre de Maurice Boissard;* all of his work "un vaste journal."

Magny, Claude Edmonde. Le phénomène Léautaud ou L'art d'être grand-père. Preu 14:3–5, 1952. *Also in her:* Littérature et critique. Payot, 1971. p. 333–37.
12706

L. "nous restitue pêle-mêle ... cinquante années d'anecdotes littéraires et la vie privée de ses chats successifs. Mais on écoute moins ce que dit l'aïeul que son ton de voix, son débit ... il confond pureté et préciosité."

Magny, Olivier de. Paul Léautaud ou Le mauvais exemple. MNo 95:111–17, 1955.
12707

L.'s *Journal* "un vaste document sur la faillite de l'égoïsme intégral ... Chez Léautaud, l'égotisme se dégrade en égoïsme."

Mahieu, Raymond. Paul Léautaud: La recherche de l'identité (1872–1914). Lettres modernes; Minard, 1974. 518 p. (Bibliothèque des lettres modernes, 20)
12708

The best study so far on L. Divided into three major sections: "Ambitions," "Epreuves," "Sagesse" — each with subsections. Appendices include L.'s readings and a close discussion of *Le petit ami.* Good bibliography (more extensive one in preparation).

Martineau, Henri. Paul Léautaud. Div 295:165–78, 1955.
12709

On the first two volumes of the *Journal littéraire.* "Ce sensible effronté est un sentimental. D'une sentimentalité de midinette. ...Le saint François des chiens et des chats." Lauds L.'s probity. Astonished by the narrowness of his views. L. has the lubricity of the *voyeur.*

Maugham, William Somerset. Three journalists. *In his:* Points of view. London: Heinemann, 1958. p. 189–255.
12710

Based on the first volumes of the *Journal littéraire.* Maugham discusses the Goncourts and Jules Renard; L.

"the oddest, the most disreputable, the most outrageous, but to my mind the most sympathetic of the three [i.e., the Goncourts, Renard, L.]." L. is a remarkable and individual talent, an egoist but devoid of vanity. Sketches the biography of L.

Perret, Pierre. Adieu, Monsieur Léautaud. Julliard, 1972. 151 p.
12711

Series of chatty, lively chapters recalling more or less verbatim — based on notes — conversations, or rather statements, by L. in 1954 and 1955, when Perrett was 20. Gives primarily L.'s views — sometimes contradictory — on certain authors and editions.

Rousseaux, André. Paul Léautaud et son journal. *In his:* Littérature du vingtième siècle. V. 6. Albin Michel, 1958. p. 67–75.
12712

Written in 1954, with a note added in 1957. "Ecrit avec une sincérité totale. ...le journal d'un homme de lettres qui se regarde vivre comme tel ... Ce cynique est un timide." L. greatly admired by Roger Martin du Gard.

Uribe Arce, Armando. Léautaud y el otro. [Santiago de Chile. Edit. Universitaria, 1966]. 99 p. (El espejo de papel; quadernos del Centro de investigaciones de literatura comparada, Universidad de Chile).
12713

A sort of search for L., who himself is seeking L.: the unretouched process of discovery. Finds L. a "discípulo inacabado" of Remy de Gourmont, "su passado inmediato, el que lo formó eran los naturalistas." His childhood is in *Le petit ami,* his adolescence in *Amours,* his youth in *In memoriam.* Running commentary on each of L.'s major works; some quotations in French, some in French and Spanish, some only in translation. Has too a *florilège* of texts. First part a discussion by Uribe Arce on the nature of the essay.

Weiner, Seymour S. Sincerity and variants: Paul Léautaud's Petit ami. Sym 14:165–87, 1960.
12714

Examines the pre-original of *Le petit ami* (MerF nos. 153–55, Oct.-Nov. 1902), the first ed. (1903), an annotated copy on Holland (the "Simonson" copy; date of revisions undetermined), and the partial revision for the *Choix de pages* selected by Rouveyre (*Souvenirs légers*), together with data from other writings. Collation and comparison lead to the conclusion that L. failed in his ambition to make the work briefer, but its "authenticity" remains intact.

Emile-Joseph Lotte
(Nos. 12715–12726)

JEAN-PIERRE CAP

Bremond, Henri. Joseph Lotte et les Entretiens de Péguy. Cor 455–82, May 10, 1916.   **12715**

Excellent article on L.'s part in the *Entretiens,* his relationship with Péguy and his importance in his own right.

Fraisse, Simone. Péguy et le monde antique. A. Colin, 1973. 561 p.   **12716**

As most books on Péguy, this one contains useful information on L., especially on his formative years (see index).

Grosse, Karl-Bernhard. Emile-Joseph Lotte. Jena, Universitäts-Buchdruckerei G. Newenhahn, 1932. 62 p. (Diss., Jena)   **12717**

A short biography of L. and the study of his commitment to Catholicism. Useful for the numerous facts it contains on L. and Péguy whose friend and confidant L. was. Also some information on L.'s unpublished works.

Guyon, Bernard. Lotte et Péguy. CahUC 9–10:612–29, 1961.   **12718**

Although L. played a significant role on his own through his bold publication of the *Bulletin des professeurs catholiques de l'Université* and in so doing contributed to the "renouveau catholique," he is known mainly for having been a close friend of Péguy. This relationship is best explained in Guyon's article.

Marre, Jeanne. A propos de Joseph Lotte. CahUC 462–72, May 1965.   **12719**

Useful general article.

Maugendre, L.-A. Biographie. In his: La renaissance catholique au début du XXᵉ siècle. V. 2. P. Beauchesne, 1963. p. 11–73.   **12720**

An excellent study of L., followed by an anthology (p. 77–283) of his literary, philosophical and polemical essays. This is the best study on L. to date which synthesizes practically all available information on him, including Maugendre's earlier studies. Good bibliography, p. 74–76.

Review: P. Duployé in ACPFM 125:34–41, 1966.

Pacary, Pierre (pseud. of l'abbé Paris). Un compagnon de Péguy, Joseph Lotte. Pages choisies et notice biographique. Préf. par Mgr. Pierre Battifol. P. J. Gabalda, 1917. 351 p.   **12721**

Pacary's short biography has been the basis for others. Most of L.'s texts published here had appeared in his *Bulletin des professeurs catholiques de l'Université* which he founded in 1910 and in which he published until the War.

————, and Jérôme and Jean Tharaud. Joseph Lotte. *In:* Anthologie des écrivains morts à la guerre 1914–1918 publiée par l'Association des écrivains combattants. V. 3. Amiens, E. Malfère, 1925. p. 464–76.   **12722**

Bibliography (p. 467–71) gives the pseudonyms of L.

Péguy, Charles. Un nouveau théologien. *In his:* Œuvres en prose 1909–1914. Gallimard, 1951. p. 839–1041. (Bibliothèque de la Pléiade)   **12723**

It is partly in response to a criticism of L. by Fernand Laudet, director of the *Revue hebdomadaire,* that Péguy wrote his famous broadside commonly known as Laudet. It contains numerous allusions to L.

Quoniam, Théodore. Le grand ami de Péguy, Joseph Lotte. Ecc 191:39–45, 1965.   **12724**

Useful biographical information.

Riby, Jules. Lettres à Joseph Lotte. Avant-propos et notes par Th. Quoniam. ACPFM 98:11–33; 99:3–38; 101:5–29; 102:3–19; 104:17–36, 1963; 105:5–31; 106:21–39; 108:5–40; 109:7–30, 1964; 112:11–25; 113:4–22, 1965.   **12725**

These letters to one of Péguy's closest friends and collaborators contain information on L.'s *Bulletin* and several literary personalities, for example Bergson. The "avant-propos" is

superficial and the letters are not systematically annotated.
Review: P. Duployé in ACPFM 125: 35–36, 1966.

Tharaud, Jérôme and Jean. Notre cher Péguy. Plon, 1926. p. 108–16, 125–29, 212–17, 223–85, 251–55. **12726**
Useful biographical passages dealing with L.

Marcello-Fabri
(pseud. of Marcel Faivre)
(Nos. 12727–12737)

DOMINQUE BAUDOUIN

Collected Articles

Marcello-Fabri. AgN 95:55–145, 1955.
12727
Special number. Twenty-six contributors in three parts: *L'homme; trois inédits de Marcello-Fabri; la pensée et l'œuvre.*

Marcello-Fabri, humaniste méconnu. SynB 244:139–210, Sept. 1966. **12728**
Issue partly devoted to M.-F. Articles by various hands.

Le poète dans la cité, Marcello-Fabri et les problèmes de notre temps. Le cercle du livre, 1952. 223 p. (Les univers de la littérature) **12729**
Bibliography is particularly valuable. Important articles have been analyzed separately.

General Studies

Chaix-Ruy, Jean. Marcello-Fabri: existentialisme et humanisme. *In:* Le poète dans la cité. *See* 12729. p. 67–94. **12730**
A study focussing on philosophical issues in M.-F., including the doctrines of the unconscious, Nietzscheism, existential anguish and Marxism. A few hints on M.-F.'s poetic esthetics. The most thorough and suggestive study in this volume.

Lebois, André. Jugements, colères, enthousiasmes de Marcello-Fabri. *In:* Le poète dans la cité. *See* 12729. p. 37–62. **12731**

A lively and well informed general sketch, with valuable quotations.

Mallet, Marc-Georges. Quelques souvenirs sur Marcello-Fabri. *In:* Marcello-Fabri. *See* 12727. p. 5–13. **12732**
Under a modest title proposes the best comprehensive overview in this special issue on M.-F.'s intellectual adventure.

Poetry

Amadou, Robert. La théorie du synchronisme selon Marcello-Fabri. *In:* Marcello-Fabri. *See* 12727. p. 91–102. **12733**
Exposition of this theory as formulated about 1921–23. How poetry, as a synthesis of philosophical contradictions becomes the "autosophie," where ethics and esthetics are "synchrones." A useful and already systematic enough general view.

Chaix-Ruy, Jean. Suggestion, incantation, magie et jugement critique dans l'œuvre de Marcello-Fabri. *In:* Marcello-Fabri. *See* 12727. p. 109–20. **12734**
A good complement to his previous studies on M.-F. An esthetic situation of M.-F, comparing his ideas with Croce's, and pertinent views on his general conception of poetry, the function of which is to regulate the dionysiac delirium from the unconscious.

Rousselot, Jean. Le message de Marcello-Fabri. *In:* Marcello-Fabri. *See* 12727. p. 68–78. **12735**
A good general overview of the principal ethical and esthetic positions of M.-F. as poet-philosopher, "autosophe," or lyrical moralist.

Somville, Léon. Marcello-Fabri. SynB 244: 156–75, 1966. *Also (rev. and enlarged):* Le synchronisme, Marcello-Fabri. *In his:* Devanciers du surréalisme, les groupes d'avant-garde et le mouvement poétique, 1912–1925. Geneva, Droz, 1971. p. 147–67. **12736**
The best systematic and objective study to date of M.-F.'s literary role and ideas among poetic currents of the period. Limited to the *Revue de l'époque* and *1925 et notre art.* Includes lengthy excerpts from *1925 et*

notre art and *Notre-Dame de la chair* (1958).

Novel

Kanters, Robert. Marcello-Fabri et l'art du roman. *In:* Le poète dans la cité. *See* 12729. p. 137–55. **12737**

The critical stands of M.-F. on the problems of the novel. He hardly defines himself in his century, but in relation and strong opposition to naturalism. His attempts to elaborate a new form of collective novel, with *L'inconnu-sur-les-villes,* a novel of the crowds, without characters or heroes. A good objective analysis.

André Maurois
(Name originally
Emile-Salomon-Wilhelm Herzog)
(Nos. 12738–12761)

JACK KOLBERT

Editions

Maurois, André. Œuvres complètes. Fayard, 1950–55. 16 v. **12738**

Never really completed, this 16 v. set contains most of the volume-length works M. selected in an almost arbitrary order. Limited to the titles of the 1918–1955 period. Each volume and work preceded by a special preface by M. in which he analyzes the reasons justifying the publication of these titles. The preface to the first volume especially interesting; in it M. describes his awakening as an incipient writer. The whole collection of prefaces forms an important cumulative statement of self-criticism.

Texts with Autobiographical Information

Maurois, André. L'Amérique inattendue. Mornay, 1931. 187 p. **12739**

M.'s journal of his earliest encounter with the American people at Princeton university and elsewhere. The central theme: most of the myths regarding the Americans are contradicted by his face-to-face contacts with them. His experience as a visiting professor on an American college campus receives sympathetic and intelligent attention.

———. Un art de vivre. Plon, 1939. 242 p. **12740**

The most important statement of M. on his philosophy of life, with particular reference to the arts of thinking, loving, working, commanding, and growing old gracefully.

———. Aspects de la biographie. Au sans pareil, 1928. 93 p. *Also:* Grasset, 1930. **12741**

M.'s definitive statement concerning the art of writing biographies. A series of lectures delivered on the subject in Great Britain.

———. Choses nues. Gallimard, 1963. 282 p. **12742**

A potpourri of notes, memoirs, reflections and recollections of conversations M. had with some of the major leaders and writers of the century. An essential work concerning M.'s central place in the public life of his day.

Review: P. de Boisdeffre in NL 2, May 30, 1963.

———. Etats-Unis 39. Journal d'un voyage en Amérique. Eds. de France, 1939. 199 p. **12743**

The title is self-explanatory. A day-by-day account of M.'s reactions to an America recovering from the great depression. His meetings with American celebrities in all walks of life.

———. Mémoires. New York, Eds. de la maison française, 1942. 2 v. *Trans.:* I remember, I remember. Trans. by Denver and Jane Lindley. New York and London, Harper, 1942. 310 p. *Also (2d ed. in one vol.):* Mémoires. Flammarion, 1948. *Also (rev.):* Memoirs 1885–1967. Trans. by Denver Lindley. London-Sydney-Toronto, Bodley Head, 1970. 439 p. *Also:* New York, Harper & Row, 1970. 439 p. **12744**

An essential work. The final edition is unquestionably the most useful for the scholar. The *Mémoires* may well be M.'s masterpiece. Not only does he analyze his personal life with remarkable objectivity, but his descriptions of eight decades of life on both sides of the Atlantic are an example of lucidity and intelligent understanding of a vital era of contemporary history.

————. Portrait d'un ami qui s'appelait moi. Namur, Wesmael-Charlier, 1959. 221 p. **12745**

A particularly valuable volume in that the author manifests in it a rare degree of self-criticism. In addition to his memoirs he delineates objectively the various phases of his literary development (in chapters entitled "Les écrits" and "Elaboration d'une œuvre; recherche des thèmes choisis") and the principal stylistic traits of his prose (in "Caractéristiques du style"). He concludes with some advice on how properly to read his own works, what to look for, and how to understand his message.

General Studies: Books

Droit, Michel. André Maurois. Eds. universitaires, 1953. 153 p. (Classiques du XXᵉ siècle) **12746**

The finest study written on M. up to 1953. The more useful sections deal with M.'s fiction and biographies. Factual data very reliable. Bibliography.

Fillon, Amélie. André Maurois romancier. Société française d'éds. littéraires et techniques, 1937. 262 p. **12747**

The only volume-length monograph on M.'s novels until 1937. Unfortunately useful only for the first five novels. Sensitive treatment of M.'s characterizations, but somewhat weak in tracing the evolutionary development of his art from novel to novel. A bit too eulogistic.

Guéry, Suzanne. La pensée d'André Maurois. Deux rives, 1941. 142 p. **12748**

The best treatment of M.'s intellectual formation as seen through his literary publications. Helpful for the scholar.

Keating, L. Clark. André Maurois. New York, Twayne, 1969. 172 p. (TWAS 53) **12749**

Despite certain minor errors of fact, this volume must be regarded as the most complete study in the English language to this day. Following an incisive series of chapters devoted to M. the biographer, novelist, critic, historian and essayist, Keating concludes with a generally accurate appraisal of M.'s total significance and his flaws.

Review: J. Kolbert in FR 43:333–35, 1969.

Lemaître, Georges. André Maurois. Palo Alto, Stanford univ. press, 1939. 128 p. **12750**

One of the most insightful works of criticism on M.'s relations with the English people and his art of writing "interpretive biographies." Outdated by Suffel, Droit, and Keating, but particularly strong for M.'s literary production during the twenties and thirties.

Suffel, Jacques. André Maurois. Avec des remarques par André Maurois. Flammarion, 1963. 203 p. (Portrait-dialogue) **12751**

Perceptive portraits and analyses of M.'s worlds, the ones he created and the ones in which he lived. The book is enhanced by M.'s own commentaries on Suffel's presentation of his work. Excellent photographs of the people who figured in M.'s career.

Review: M. Chapelain in FL Dec. 5–11, 1963.

Special Numbers

Le Figaro littéraire. Special issue, Oct. 16–22, 1967. 50 p. **12752**

Contains a number of significant essays and articles on M.'s importance as a literary figure written on the occasion of his death. Articles by Jacques de Lacretelle, André Chamson, Jean Dutourd, Maurice Druon, J.-J. Gautier, Robert Kanters, Jacques Suffel, Michel Droit et al.

Hommage à André Maurois. NL 1977:1–14, July 22, 1965. **12753**

Virtually the entire issue of this paper is devoted to the commemoration of M.'s eightieth birthday. An essential issue for M. specialists. Articles by Jacques Rueff, Françoise Mallet-Joris, Albert Delaunay, Jacques-Henry Bornecque, Jack Kolbert, Pierre de Boisdeffre. Critical articles deal with M. in all of his literary genres.

Biography

André-Maurois, Simone. La femme de l'écrivain. An 65:22–35, 1956. **12754**

The entire text of a lecture presented by M.'s second spouse. Especially vital because it sheds light on the intimate literary relationships between the author and his literary wife.

Hanoteau, Guillaume. L'honnête homme ou la vie d'André Maurois. ParM 967:58–73, Oct. 21, 1967.   **12755**
Special commemorative issue on the death of M. Lavishly illustrated text recapitulating in chronological order the major events in M.'s existence. Though writing for the broad, not necessarily scholarly public, Hanoteau manages to convey to his readers an intelligent and high-level comprehension of the literary and personal forces that comprised this man of letters.

General Studies: Articles

Chaigne, Louis. André Maurois. *In his:* Vie et œuvres d'écrivains. Pierre Bossuet, 1933. p. 149–85.   **12756**
Probably the best article on M. in any single book published up to 1933. Useful analyses of M.'s nonfictional works written during the late twenties.

Chevrillon, André. Réponse. *In:* Maurois, André. Discours de réception à l'Académie française. Didot, 1939. 133 p.   **12757**
A major critical statement on M. as he appeared to his contemporaries during 1939.

Jaloux, Edmond. Climats. *In his:* Perspectives et personnages. L'esprit des livres, série III. Plon, 1931. p. 233–40.   **12758**
Undoubtedly the most appreciative article of criticism written by any critic concerning M.'s novelistic masterpiece, *Climats.* Jaloux deals especially well with the poetic aspects of M.'s prose.

Kolbert, Jack. André Maurois à la recherche d'un genre—la biographie. FR 39:671–83, 1966.   **12759**
An overview of M.'s career as a biographer, starting with *Ariel ou la vie de Shelley,* a "biographie romancée," and culminating in *Prométhée ou la vie de Balzac,* a biography of solid scholarly credentials. The several stages in M.'s distinguished career are delineated.

————. André Maurois' esthetics of biography. BRMMLA 31:45–51, 1967.   **12760**
A systematic study of M.'s principles of biography. Stresses his lifelong

search to fuse readability with scholarly documentation.

————. A few notes on the short fiction of André Maurois. SSF 3:104–16, 1966.   **12761**
An evaluative summary of M.'s efforts in the domain of the short story, one of the genres in which he excelled. Highlights his science-fiction, "salon-type" of story, the longer novella-type, the mini-story, the fairy tale, etc.

Georges Navel
(Nos. 12762–12768)

PIERRE AUBERY

Autobiographical Texts

Navel, Georges. Chacun son royaume. Préf. de Jean Giono. Gallimard, 1960. 324 p.   **12762**
More poetic sketches of the search for happiness and harmony with the environment on the part of a "Syndicalist Hesiod" (according to Giono), who attempts to get away from the drudgery of industrial labor.
Reviews: Anon. in TLS Dec. 30, 1960; J. Bloch-Michel in GazL April 23, 1960; A. Dalmas in TrN March 25, 1960; Y. Hecht in ParN April 8, 1960; A. Jans in SoirB March 30, 1960.

————. Parcours. Gallimard, 1950. 259 p.   **12763**
Sequel to *Travaux.* Poetic sketches of the cultural and political education of a young manual laborer.
Reviews: P. Berger in ParP Oct. 25, 1950; J. Blanzat in FL Nov. 11, 1950; M. Nadeau in MerF 310:682–86, 1950; E.-B. Olivier in FrAmL March 1951; J. Pasteau in Fig Dec. 13, 1950.

————. Sable et limon. Gallimard, 1952. 419 p.   **12764**
Letters to Bernard Groethuysen and Alix Guillain from June 1935 through November 1945. A most lively chronicle of literary, philosophical and political interests of a working class intellectual during these years.
Reviews: A. Blanchard in CahS 513–16, 1953; R. Kemp in NL Sept. 11, 1952; A. Palante in FrCa Aug. 29,

1952; F. Weyergans in PrésL Sept. 5, 1952.

————. Travaux. Stock, 1945. 222 p. *Also* (*rev.*): 1969. 256 p. *Trans.:* Man at work. Trans. by George Reavey. London, Dennis Dobson, 1947. 239 p.   **12765**

Poetic sketches inspired by recollections of a manual laborer who tried to preserve his humanity and freshness of perception despite the experience of poverty, war, deprivation and the alienation of work.

Reviews: Y. Audouard in CanE March 26, 1969; L.-G. Gros in Prov April 27, 1969; P. Labracherie in ParL June 17, 1969; J. Lambert in Font 51:666–67, 1946; F. Lefèvre in NL no. 961, 1946; M. Martini in NL June 5, 1969; P. Morelle in Monde May 3, 1969; R. Proix in LibertéP May 1, 1969; N. Saillet in Ar 14:184–86, 1946.

General Studies

Aubery, Pierre. Navel et l'art d'écrire. LetN 165–80, March 1971.   **12766**

Primarily the question of the sources of literary creativity in N. According to Aubery they are to be found in N.'s desire to initiate a dialog with kindred spirits rather than in his rhetorical skills.

————. Regards sur l'œuvre de Georges Navel. PMLA 77:417–21, 1963.   **12767**

Underlines the literary value of N.'s composition and style. There is little invention in N.'s works which aim at reflecting and translating in a discreet prose the life experience of a manual worker who is more a poet than a militant. Here lies the ambiguity of this critic's point of view obviously more interested in politics than in esthetics.

————. Travaux: invention of a language in Navel's works. FR 46:24–34, 1972.
            12768

At first reading, N.'s works seem intent on showing "how to live." A closer look at them reveals that actually they teach "how to write." Although sympathetic to N.'s approach and views, this article suggests indirectly the major difficulty encountered by proletarian authors writing after the fact and being left behind by more recent social developments. In addition a working class author has to use what remains basically a bourgeois language that inevitably twists and edulcorates his writings.

André Suarès
(pseud. of Yves Scantrel)
(Nos. 12769–12803)

SIDNEY D. BRAUN

Correspondence

Gide, André, and André Suarès. Correspondance André Gide—André Suarès (1908–1920). Ed. by Sidney D. Braun. Gallimard, 1963. 111 p.   **12769**

Reveals beginnings, development, and final rupture of their friendship, with references to their writings. Index of authors and works.

Péguy, Charles, and André Suarès. Correspondance Charles Péguy-André Suarès (1905–1914). Présentée par Alfred Saffrey. Minard, 1961. 83 p. (CACP 14)
            12770

Long introduction explaining beginnings of relationship between Péguy and S. is followed by note from Péguy to S. (1899) concerning ms. sent by latter. Several extracts from unpublished correspondence between S. and Rolland, and S.'s essay for which he received first prize in *classe de rhétorique*.

Rouault, Georges, and André Suarès. Correspondance Georges Rouault-André Suarès (1911–1948). Introd. par Marcel Arland. Gallimard, 1960. 357 p.   **12771**

Valuable biographical portrait of both. Also deals with art and literary matters. Index of names.

Suarès, André. Ignorées du destinataire. Lettres inédites (1888–1948) d'André Suarès. Avant-propos d'Armand Roumanet. Gallimard, 1955. 253 p.   **12772**

Includes 100 letters written, but never sent, by S., in moments of anger and admiration, to his imaginary correspondents. Index for latter.

————, **and Antoine Bourdelle.** Correspondance André Suarès et Antoine Bourdelle (1922–1929). Présentée par Michel Dufet. Documents et dessins inédits d'Antoine Bourdelle. Plon, 1961. 179 p. **12773**

Continued until 1944, after Bourdelle's death, half of this correspondence is addressed to his widow. The letters between S. and Bourdelle cover period of height of latter's artistic achievement.

————, and Paul Claudel. Correspondance André Suarès et Paul Claudel (1904–1938). Ed. by Robert Mallet. Gallimard, 1951. 270 p.   12774

Reveals attempts of Claudel to have S. embrace Catholicism, and latter's hesitations and final refusal. Index of authors and works.

————, and Romain Rolland. Cette âme ardente... Choix de lettres de André Suarès à Romain Rolland (1887–1891). Préf. de Maurice Pottecher. Ed. by Pierre Sipriot. Albin Michel, 1954. 401 p. (CahRR 5)   12775

These letters reveal early friendship, begun at Ecole normale supérieure, between S. and Rolland, and period of S.'s pessimism. Index of names.

Iconography

Baylot, Jean. Catalogue de l'exposition André Suarès. Saint-Maur, Impr. de Saint-Maur, 1950. 27 p.   12776

Includes titles of S.'s works published during his lifetime, of those which appeared posthumously, of prefaces to works by others, of plays found only in journals, of some studies on him, of iconographical items and various mss.

Biography

Braun, Sidney D. André Suarès and Antoine Bourdelle: Vates and Pygmalion. FR 37:41–46, 1963.   12777

Analysis of a friendship based on common interests, devotion to Art, and a similar esthetics.

Dietschy, Marcel. Le cas André Suarès. Neuchâtel, A la Baconnière, 1967. 365 p. (Langages-documents)   12778

An almost definitive biographical and critical study of S., using much unpublished material. Invaluable bibliography.

Review: S. Braun in FR 43:176–78, 1969.

Dormoy, Marie. André Suarès. In her: Souvenirs et portraits d'amis. Mercure de France, 1963. p. 28–49.   12779

Personal, intimate biographical sketch of S., and his friends, until his death; references to the musical affinity between S. and herself.

Lefèvre, Frédéric. André Suarès. In his: Une heure avec... Ire série. Gallimard, 1924. p. 249–66.   12780

S. describes himself, in this interview, as *poète tragique,* who has lived his ideas and sought all knowledge, especially that of the Greek myths, the Bible, Shakespeare, Pascal, Goethe, Stendhal, Bergson, and Dostoevsky.

Maurin, Mario. André Suarès: esquisse de biographie. Preu 2:21–32, 1952.   12781

Good general outline of S.'s life, especially until period of World War I, with emphasis on inner psychology.

General Studies

Barjon, Louis. A la recherche des vraies valeurs avec Suarès. Et 226:5–24; 156–76, 1936.   12782

A Christian assessment of S.'s characteristics and thought. Does not question his sincerity, but challenges his disdain of "revealed truths" and moral values. Characterizes him as victim of his own "false" logic which draws its source from his conscience and not from God.

Barnaud, J.-M. Apollon et Dionysos: André Suarès, lecteur de Nietzsche. RHL 71:270–81, 1971.   12783

A convincing presentation of S.'s reaction against Nietzsche, explained by certain elements in S.'s inner conflicts.

Beucken, Jean de. Un portrait d'André Suarès. SynB 7–8:39–52, 1953.   12784

Interesting account of writer's conversations and correspondence with S., with comments on latter's writings from 1927–1939.

Bounoure, Gabriel. André Suarès. In his: Marelles sur le parvis: Essais de critique poétique. Plon, 1958. p. 104–43.   12785

From his personal acquaintance and knowledge of S.'s work, perceives S.'s attempt to mask his inner conflict between his passions and mind; in this attempt, he claims, reality becomes for S. illusion, and illusion reality.

Braun, Sidney D. André Suarès and Villiers de l'Isle-Adam. *In:* Studies in honor of Prof. S. M. Waxman. Boston, Boston univ. press, 1969. p. 28–35. **12786**

Reveals, from unpublished material, S.'s high regard for Villiers and provides notes on an unpublished play of S. on Villiers.

———. André Suarès' unpublished early notebooks. RR 68:254–70, 1967. **12787**

Valuable description of ms. covering 1887–1901, now at Bibliothèque Jacques Doucet, which reveals S.'s early ambitions to be a dramatist. References to correspondence with R. Rolland.

———. André Suarès, moralist. PMLA 70: 285–91, 1955. **12788**

Critical analysis of S.'s view of man's anguish caused by conflicting physical and spiritual forces. Claims that S. finds solution to this dilemma in internal *grandeur* and love of life.

Busi, Frederick. L'esthétique d'André Suarès: étude thématique sur une vision de l'art. Wetteren, Belgium, Eds. Cultura, 1969. 204 p. **12789**

Based on doctoral dissertation, this study stresses S.'s metaphysical views and mysticism, whose ultimate unity is seen in love and in quest for Beauty. Valuable bibliography and index.
Reviews: G. Ireland in MLR 68: 662–63, 1973; W. Starr in FR 44:612–13, 1971.

———. André Suarès on Nietzsche's myth of the eternal return. FR 43:571–79, 1970. **12790**

A competent outline of this theme which also reveals S.'s understanding of, and differences with, Nietzsche's philosophy.

Dommartin, Henry. Suarès. Bibliothèque de l'occident, 1913. 31 p. **12791**

A brief, penetrating analysis of S.'s thought, originality, and literary characteristics up to 1913.

Girard, René. Suarès et les autres. CahS 41:14–18, 1955. **12792**

Contends, in an interesting dialectic, that to maintain his integrity of *self*, S. wished to be hated in order to remove all indifference toward him; what appears as opposition thus becomes, he asserts, a need of the Other who is in search of S.'s disguised self.

Goldberger, Avriel. André Suarès and the hero-artist. *In her:* Visions of a new hero. The heroic life according to André Malraux and earlier advocates of human grandeur. Minard, 1965. p. 25–51. **12793**

Exposition of S.'s basic views of the hero, with accompanying role of total commitment to art.

Helmke, Bruno. André Suarès als Denker und Künstler. Coburg, A. Rossteucher, 1933. 81 p. (Diss., Jena) **12794**

Not very original. Emphasizes the ultimate value S. gives to life through self-fulfillment of mind and spirit.

Lacaze-Duthiers, Gérard de. André Suarès ou le triomphe du lyrisme. AgN 32:69–74, 1948. **12795**

Succinct summary of S.'s literary qualities, which include sincerity, thought and lyricism. Characterizes his essays as prose poems and as the most important part of his work.

Martin du Gard, Maurice. Un poète intellectuel: André Suarès. *In his:* Harmonies critiques. Eds. du sagittaire, 1936. p. 138–48. **12796**

Characterizes S., in perspicacious essay, as extremely sensitive beneath his cloak of misanthropy; emphasizes his subjective criticism which reflects a personal identification with varying elements in Nietzsche, Pascal, Goethe and Montaigne. Also points to S.'s wish to be musician.

Maurel, André. André Suarès. BURS 86: 91–110, 1917. **12797**

Although critical of S.'s apparent doctrinaire and axiomatic approach, praises his portraits and intuitive sense of the good and true. Characterizes him essentially as lyrical essayist.

Maurin, Mario. Suarès and the third kingdom. YFS 12:34–40, 1953. **12798**

Excellent analysis of S.'s attitude towards religion, which is linked to ethical self-fulfillment.

————. Suarès: portrait tournant. CahS 41: 28–33, 1955.   **12799**

Psychological analysis of S. seen in his *portraits*. Perceives S.'s inner Manichean conflict in wish to accept world and himself.

————. Suarès' critical method: the search. YFS 2:71–73, 1949.   **12800**

Characterizes S.'s work as critical essays, in each of which is reflected an aspect of his *self,* the composite of all his contradictions.

Miomandre, Francis de. Un lyrique du nihilisme: Suarès. Occ 8:226–40, 1905. **12801**

Sees constant struggle of mind and heart within S., which reflects itself in his lyricism and pessimism.

Rigassi, Georges. André Suarès. BURS 77: 399–416, 1915.   **12802**

Excellent article revealing S.'s elevated notion of literature and search of man's inner life. His exaltation of values of life and Art expressed in aphoristic form and reflecting a humanistic view are seen as his originality.

Savet, Gabrielle. André Suarès, critique. Didier, 1959. 187 p.   **12803**

Studies S.'s approach as critic in portraits of writers, artists, and musicians, which reflect, it is claimed, his own observations and meditations on life, art and humanistic values. Relevant list of S.'s works and general bibliography.

A CRITICAL BIBLIOGRAPHY OF FRENCH LITERATURE

was composed in 8-on-8 point Linotype Baskerville and Baskerville bold,
with display type handset in Baskerville italic,
by Joe Mann Associates, Inc.;
printed offset on 50-pound Perkins & Squier acid-free Offset paper stock,
Smyth-sewn and bound over 88-pt. binder's boards in Holliston Roxite Record Buckram,
each set slipcased and packed in individual cartons,
by Maple-Vail Book Manufacturing Group, Inc.;
and published by

SYRACUSE UNIVERSITY PRESS
Syracuse, New York 13210